CILIP: the Chartered Institute of Library and Information Professionals

YEARBOOK 2010

Compiled by

Kathryn Beecroft

facet publishing

Published by Facet Publishing
7 Ridgmount Street, London WC1E 7AE

Facet Publishing is wholly owned by CILIP: the Chartered Institute of Library
and Information Professionals. CILIP was formed in April 2002 following the
unification of the Institute of Information Scientists and The Library
Association.

British Library Cataloguing in Publication Data
A cataloguing record for this book is available from the British Library.

ISBN 978-1-85604-678-7
ISSN 1746-9929

First published 2010

Text printed on FSC accredited material.

Mixed Sources
Product group from well-managed
forests and other controlled sources
www.fsc.org Cert no. SA-COC-1565
© 1996 Forest Stewardship Council
FSC

Typeset by Facet Publishing Production in 10/13 pt Nimbus Sans.
Printed and made in Great Britain by MPG Books Group, UK.

Contents

CONTENTS

CILIP's mission and goals

Mission statement – what we stand for

CILIP's mission is to:

- set, maintain, monitor and promote standards of excellence in the creation, management, exploitation and sharing of information and knowledge resources;
- support the principle of equality of access to information, ideas and works of the imagination which it affirms is fundamental to a thriving economy, democracy, culture and civilisation;
- enable its Members to achieve and maintain the highest professional standards in all aspects of delivering an information service, both for the professional and the public good.

Corporate goals – Community, Advocacy, Workforce development

CILIP will do this via:

- good governance
- stable technology
- good staffing practices
- sound finances.

Advocacy, activism, accreditation, enterprise, administration – and enquiry

CILIP's Corporate Plan for 2010

Introduction (2010)

As a context for the 2010 Corporate Plan, it is important to note that in this election year CILIP articulated six priority issues as a 'Manifesto' for those members of political parties competing for places in the Westminster Government to deliberate upon.

- Statutory School Libraries
- Information Rights
- Information Management
- Public Health
- Preserving the UK's Cultural Heritage
- User Entitlements

These represent a broad range of activities in which the membership of the major professional body for the library, knowledge and information domain in the UK are currently engaged. The full spectrum is constantly extending as the demands of members of our communities and society stretch our resources and challenge our services and facilities. In his introduction to the 2009 CILIP Yearbook, Peter Griffiths commented that 'Few of the previous issues that CILIP addressed have receded, while all the while the information society raises increasingly complex new issues of public concern.' This is equally true for practitioners everywhere in our domain: rarely does anything we undertake have a finite end date. Often we introduce new systems and processes to run in tandem with existing ones, thus adding complexity to our professional practice.

CILIP's advocacy is subject to such accretion and this requires considerable energy and continuity of resource investment to maintain. The importance of activists to the CILIP strategy for advocating on behalf of users, services and members can never be overstated. For a member-led organisation it is essential that practitioners are available to inform and enable policy and to contribute to strategic decisions such as dealing with the recession, the effectiveness of CILIP engagement with employers and meeting the needs of users and non-users in a digital age.

CILIP has a role in the provision of professional qualifications, the accreditation of academic courses and the award of a Seal of Recognition to trainers. These activities can often go unrecognised by employers and managers from other disciplines or operational areas. These awards require high standards of achievement and are given as a result of a robust peer-assessment processes. This issue alone is always worth promotion in any workplace, particularly where other professions may be in a majority. All CILIP members should seek to establish equality across the professions, recognising that this takes confidence and the assurance that comes with having a Code of Professional Practice, a code of Ethics and other pre-requisites of a UK Professional Association with Chartered status.

CILIP will undergo change in the near future, just as all organisations in which members work will be faced with reviews of operations at strategic as well as operational levels. Members should be encouraged to identify and articulate what CILIP stands for and how members can make a positive change to our society. The issues identified in the Manifesto have a longevity that will reach beyond the May 2010 election campaign for the major parties to debate. They are statements of CILIP values and philosophy in an age where media clips and sound bites have taken the place of reasoned and informed exchange of views. They cover the areas of activity that illustrate the difference that CILIP Membership can make to the society in which we live and work.

Biddy Fisher MLib FCLIP
CILIP President 2010

Preamble

Our information society challenges the library and information profession – and our professional institute – in fundamental ways:

- To extend the definition of our professional community in order to include everyone, whatever identities they choose and roles they perform, and whatever the level at which they work.
- To extend the definition of our professional knowledge base and competencies in order to include emerging skill sets and those still to be developed, alongside traditional professional activities.
- To give particular recognition, within our increasingly broad library and information community, to those colleagues who achieve and seek to maintain a high degree of professionalism – in terms of skills, experience, education and ethics.
- To extend the definition of our professional agenda to include international issues of information policy as well as national and local issues.
- To advocate for the continuing value of the library and information profession in the changing information environment.
- To provide opportunities for learning and development for library and information practitioners through activism within the library and information profession.
- To develop ways of accrediting proficiency and professional development at all levels of

the workforce in a way which is relevant and authoritative for practitioners and employers.
- To fit CILIP for the future in a changing professional environment and a challenging financial environment.

To make a valued contribution to our information society CILIP, as the professional institute for the library and information sector in the UK, will speak out for the importance of the library and information domain – locally, nationally and internationally and across all sectors. We will engage with all library and information colleagues whether as members, consumers, or networkers.

CILIP will provide services, products, and networking opportunities for members which add value for everyone in the library and information sector, whatever their skill set and however they see their professional identity and their future.

We will advocate the value of information literacy for all citizens and the role of the profession in supporting information literacy development.

We will set the highest standards of professionalism for the library and information sector through regulation, administration, and governance; and in the quality of our products, services and activities.

Priorities

Library and information services have a positive effect on society – strengthening communities, shaping cultures, driving economies, enabling learning, changing lives and increasing opportunities. CILIP supports the people in the library and information sector who make that difference. In 2010 CILIP will do this by working towards the following set of strategic priorities agreed by CILIP Council in September 2009:

Strategic priorities

1. Over-arching themes

In determining our strategic priorities, we will ensure:

1.1 All activities are carried out in accordance with the objectives of CILIP's Royal Charter, demonstrating public benefit and meeting the requirements of the Charity Commission and the Privy Council.

1.2 That CILIP acts prudently with regard to CILIP's resources, ensuring affordability and sustainability.

1.3 That the communications infrastructure and strategy evolves so as to become comprehensive; extending the use of electronic communications, and strengthening communications with Branches, Groups and CILIP in the Devolved Nations.

1.4 Greater employer engagement: developing and delivering a pan-CILIP employer engagement strategy: building on the value of the CILIP FoQA and CILIP CPD Scheme for employers; and utilising local and specialised knowledge and contacts.

1.5 Effective governance of CILIP and its constituent parts.

1.6 The growth of strategic partnerships in pursuit of CILIP's objectives around advocacy, activism, and accreditation.

1.7 The continuance of work at local, regional and national levels across the UK; and internationally at European, Commonwealth, and global levels, recognising the international nature of the modern LIS profession.

2. Advocacy – campaigning on key issues, and promoting our profession

We will:

2.1 Continue to develop, communicate and promote a set of strategic aims for CILIP advocacy.

2.2 Establish and communicate CILIP's strategic position statements on key issues.

2.3 Support CILIP Members in their advocacy activities.

2.4 Progress policy development and advocacy activity in the priority areas identified – the role of information and libraries in society, the role of professionalism, and the impact of the recession on library and information services.

2.5 Establish a set of measures to evaluate the effectiveness of CILIP's advocacy activities.

3. Activism – supporting professional practice

We will:

3.1 Develop and deliver a strategy to enable, encourage and facilitate activism which will include:
— enabling networking and personal professional development;
— supporting Branches and Groups and CILIP in the Devolved Nations by revising Branch and Group Rules and confirming Branch and Group funding arrangements;
— encouraging more CILIP Members to take up opportunities for activism across CILIP;
— helping CILIP Members to champion CILIP with colleagues, employers, educators, and the wider LIS community;
— expanding the CILIP community;
— growing the member-base of activists.

3.2 Continue to support the CPD activities of CILIP Branches and Special Interest Groups – training, events and publishing – which directly support CILIP's charitable purpose.

4. Enterprise – delivering products and services in support of CILIP's charitable purpose

We will:

4.1. Continue to conduct 'primary purpose trading' through CILIP Enterprises in the four business areas of training, events, publishing and recruitment, seeking to be a market leader in each of these fields.

5. Accreditation– setting standards for the LIS profession

We will:

5.1 Maintain the Register by: delivering FoQA through the work of the Chartership Board and the Accreditation Board; developing a more web-enabled approach to the delivery and administration of FoQA; ensuring that FoQA is compliant with European standards (Bologna); and exploring opportunities for international reciprocity of qualifications.

5.2 Develop and deliver the CILIP CPD Scheme.

5.3 Align FoQA with the new qualifications landscape (including vocational qualifications).

5.4 Continue to promote affirmative action in developing and diversifying the LIS workforce.

6. Administration – ensuring effectiveness

We will:

6.1 Maintain financial prudence based on a policy of affordability and sustainability.

6.2 Invest in continued web/ICT development.

6.3 Strive to maintain a skilled and motivated staff, and an effective organisational and governance structure.

6.4 Keep in good order the premises and facilities owned by CILIP at Ridgmount Street.

6.6 Ensure compliance with all relevant legislation and regulation.

7. and enquiry – fitting CILIP for the future

CILIP faces two major challenges – change in the professional environment as we move into an information age; and change in the financial environment as we move into a post-recession economic environment. To help in planning for CILIP's future in these changing environments CILIP Council in November 2009 agreed to conduct a 'Big Conversation' during 2010 about the future for CILIP. The intention is to consult widely and produce outcomes which will enable CILIP to develop a vision for the future, establish a roadmap to achieve that vision, and generate ownership of both the vision and the roadmap.

Defining CILIP – CILIP explained

A definition of CILIP's diverse roles and activities.

As a **chartered body** CILIP is the awarding and accrediting body internationally recognised as providing the authoritative framework of qualifications for the library and information sector in the UK.

As a **registered charity** CILIP works for public benefit, through education and advocacy, to promote the highest possible standards of library and information practice and service in the UK.

As a **community of practice** CILIP adds value through and for the membership community by enhancing employability, fostering personal development, and offering opportunities for personal involvement.

As an **independent body** CILIP is funded through membership subscriptions and income-generating products and services.

As a **campaigning organisation** CILIP speaks out with a powerful, independent and authoritative voice for the importance of library and information services and the value added by library and information professionals.

As a **national association** for the UK CILIP also has a strong international dimension to its membership and activities and works closely with relevant international organisations such as IFLA, the International Federation of Library Associations and Institutions.

As a **value-driven organisation** CILIP seeks to demonstrate:

- respect for colleagues
- teamwork and partnership
- commitment to agreed objectives
- recognition of achievement
- professionalism in all aspects of our work
- and a focus on good customer service in all that we do.

Feedback – Have your say

How to let CILIP know what you think.
CILIP is a learning organisation, listening to the views of members, customers, and other stakeholders. If you have any comments on this Corporate Plan write to the Chief Executive's Office, CILIP, 7 Ridgmount Street, London WC1E 7AE, UK, or email: corporate.plan@cilip.org.uk.

Keep an eye on the CILIP website at www.cilip.org.uk for more information about the 'Big Conversation'. We want to hear your views about the future for CILIP.

And remember that you can contact the CILIP Trustees at any time with your views on CILIP. They form CILIP Council which is the governing body of CILIP and they can be reached c/o governance@cilip.org.uk.

CILIP equal opportunities and diversity statement

Our vision is an informed society in which everyone has ready access to the knowledge, information and works of imagination appropriate to their needs, wants and aspirations. This is the distinctive contribution of library and information professionals to developing a society where:

- All groups are empowered;
- Attitudes and prejudices that hinder the progress of individuals and groups are confronted and tackled;
- Cultural, racial, and societal diversity is respected and celebrated;
- Individuals and communities live together in mutual respect and tolerance;
- Discrimination is challenged and tackled robustly.

In affirming this vision CILIP will seek:

- To achieve recognisable excellence as an organisation that values and puts into practice equal opportunities and diversity
- To work towards establishing an LIS workforce that is representative of the diversity within UK society
- To facilitate an awareness and appreciation of the value and importance of diversity and equal opportunities to LIS work amongst our members and staff
- To collaborate with other interested parties in the encouragement and mainstreaming of best practice in service delivery so that the values of diversity and equal opportunities are embodied in the services provided by our members
- To tackle prejudice wherever it is found in the LIS domain.

Part 1
THE ORGANISATION

CILIP offices

CILIP: the Chartered Institute of Library and Information Professionals

7 Ridgmount Street, London WC1E 7AE
Telephone: 020 7255 0500* Fax: 020 7255 0501
Textphone: 020 7255 0505
E-mail: info@cilip.org.uk.
Website: www.cilip.org.uk
Office hours: Monday–Friday 09.00–17.00.
Switchboard hours: Monday–Friday 08.30–17.00.
An electronic queueing system is in operation:
calls are answered in sequence.

CILIP in Scotland

First floor, Building C, Brandon Gate,
1 Leechlee Road, Hamilton ML3 6AU
Telephone: 01698 458888 Fax: 01698 283170
E-mail: cilips@slainte.org.uk
Website: www.slainte.org.uk/cilips/cilipsindex.htm

CILIP Cymru/Wales

c/o Department of Information Studies,
University of Wales Aberystwyth, Llanbadarn Fawr,
Aberystwyth, Ceredigion SY23 3AS
Telephone: 01970 622174 Fax: 01970 622190
E-mail: cilip-wales@aber.ac.uk;
        cilip-cymru@aber.ac.uk
Website: www.dis.aber.ac.uk/cilip_w/index.htm

CILIP in Ireland

Executive Officer, CILIP in Ireland, 100 Craigbrack
Road, Eglinton BT47 3BD Northern Ireland
Telephone: 07777 691726
E-mail: elga.logue@btinternet.com
Website: www.cilip.org.uk/ireland

Statutory information

Registered Charity Number: 313014
VAT Number: GB 233 1573 87
Solicitors: Bates, Wells and Braithwaite
Bankers: Bank of Scotland
Auditors: Kingston Smith

*Note To call UK numbers from abroad, start with the
international dialling code from your country (for example: 00).
Next, dial the country code for the UK, which is 44. Finally, dial
the UK number, without the first 0.

7 Ridgmount Street

Structure

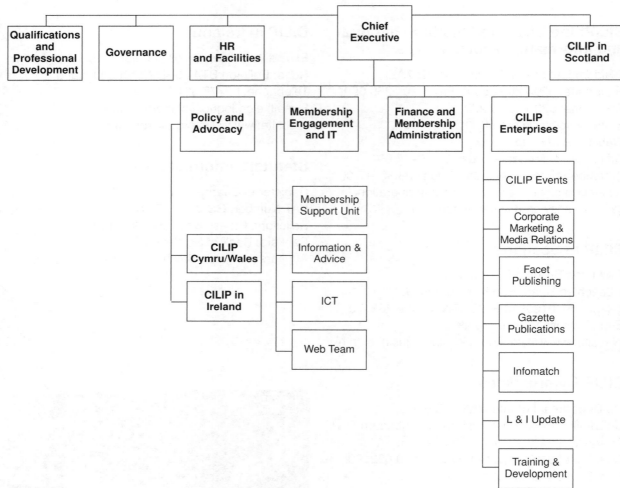

Chief Executive

Qualifications and Professional Development

Governance

HR and Facilities

CILIP in Scotland

Policy and Advocacy

Membership Engagement and IT

Finance and Membership Administration

CILIP Enterprises

CILIP Cymru/Wales

CILIP in Ireland

Membership Support Unit

Information & Advice

ICT

Web Team

CILIP Events

Corporate Marketing & Media Relations

Facet Publishing

Gazette Publications

Infomatch

L & I Update

Training & Development

Bob McKee

Chief Executive

The Chief Executive is responsible for the overall management of the Institute.

Chief Executive:

(until 31 October 2010) **Bob McKee**
bob.mckee@cilip.org.uk
(after 31 October 2010) **Annie Mauger**
annie.mauger@cilip.org.uk

CILIP Cymru/Wales

Development Officer, CILIP Cymru/Wales:
Mandy Powell mdp@aber.ac.uk

CILIP in Ireland

Executive Officer, CILIP in Ireland:
Elga Logue elga.logue@btinternet.com

CILIP in Scotland

Director of CILIP in Scotland and the Scottish Library and Information Council:
Elaine Fulton cilips@slainte.org.uk

[Further Home Nations contact details may be found on page 3.]

Qualifications and Professional Development

Responsible for Certification, Chartership, Fellowship, Revalidation, course accreditation and the Seal of Recognition.

Head of Qualifications and Professional Development:
Marion Huckle marion.huckle@cilip.org.uk

Governance

Responsible for the administration of Committee meetings and the Council, for elections to Council, and for the administration of General Meetings.

Governance Manager:
Daniel Sabel daniel.sabel@cilip.org.uk

HR and Facilities

Responsible for employment matters, staff recruitment and training, buildings management, health and safety, room bookings and catering.

Head of HR and Facilities:
Jill Colbert jill.colbert@cilip.org.uk

Policy and Advocacy

Responsible for developing and sustaining an advocacy strategy across CILIP and supporting its delivery. The Policy and Advocacy Unit also facilitates and supports the development of professional policy in CILIP, supporting Branches and Groups in their new devolved policy development responsibilities, and providing leadership and advice in the policy priority areas identified by Council.

Director of Policy and Advocacy:
Guy Daines guy.daines@cilip.org.uk

Membership Engagement and IT

Responsible for information and advice services, international work, membership engagement, the website and ICT.

Director of Knowledge and Information:
Jill Martin jill.martin@cilip.org.uk

Information and Advice

First point of contact for all enquiries. Offers a range of information and advice services to members. Expert staff are available to deal with simple or complex enquiries. The Information Centre, 2nd Floor, Ridgmount Street is open to Members 9 am–5 pm, Monday–Friday.

Telephone: 020 7255 0620
(10.00–16.00 Monday–Friday)
info@cilip.org.uk

Membership Support Unit

Acts as a focus for member engagement with CILIP. Providing Branch and Group activist support; Supplying professional and career development advice; Facilitating the use of social media particularly CILIP Communities, and the

Network of Expertise and Interests; Supporting members in personal advocacy via the Campaigning Toolkit: Encouraging membership development through campaigns and initiatives; Managing LIBEX the international job exchange scheme; Growing awareness of the CILIP community and the benefits of membership through university visits, New Professionals Awareness Days and competitions.

> Telephone: 020 7255 0616
> msu@cilip.org.uk

ICT

Responsible for: providing the Helpdesk function for CILIP London and homeworkers, maintenance of all equipment, software/hardware upgrades including all databases. Support and maintenance of all telecommunications equipment.
Telephone: 020 7255 0660

ICT Manager:
> **Chris Bacon** ICTDepartment@cilip.org.uk

Web Team

Responsible for: overall management of the CILIP website; development of services to CILIP members and customers over the web; provision of support and advice to CILIP staff, Branches and Groups on website maintenance.

Web Manager:
> **Alan Cooper** web@cilip.org.uk

Finance and Membership Administration

Provides strategic financial advice to trustees, Chief Executive and senior management. Provides an effective financial management service to CILIP and its Branches and Groups. Ensures compliance with statutory and other financial regulations. Also responsible for the accurate processing of all subscriptions sent to CILIP.

Director of Finance and Membership Administration:
> **Rowena Wells** rowena.wells@cilip.org.uk

CILIP Enterprises

A number of income-generating activities comprise CILIP's business portfolio. They focus on four key activities – recruitment, publishing, training and events – and offer a wide range of products and services to Members and the wider information community while contributing professionally and financially to CILIP's mission and objectives.

Managing Director:
> **John Woolley** john.woolley@cilip.org.uk

Gazette Publications

The fortnightly tabloid magazine *Library & Information Gazette* is the UK's leading media for recruitment advertising, together with its associated online services Lisjobnet.com and Lisjobtemps.com. As well as news and features about jobs and career development, it covers suppliers and their products, services and systems Display advertising is included in the magazine and there is also extensive coverage of all CILIP's activities. *The Annual Buyers' Guide* is also published.

Manager, *Gazette* Publications:
> **Gary Allman** gary.allman@cilip.org.uk

Infomatch

CILIP's specialist recruitment agency for library and information staff handles permanent and temporary positions at all levels and across all sectors of the library and information community throughout the UK.

Manager, Infomatch:
> **Francis Muzzu** francis.muzzu@cilip.org.uk

Library & Information Update

Update is published for CILIP members six times a year as a hard-copy magazine with an associated digital issue and six times a year as a web-only publication with video/audio content, web links and access to a digital archive of past articles. Its news and in-depth features cover developments in the public policy arena, the working environment, technology and the profession at large. It is also available on paid subscription.

Editor, *Update*:
Elspeth Hyams elspeth.hyams@cilip.org.uk

Digital edition www.cilip.org.uk/updatedigital

Facet Publishing

The leading publisher of books for library and information professionals worldwide, Facet Publishing has an internationally established list of over 200 specialist titles in print which cover all the major aspects of professional LIS activity. It publishes books for library, museum, archive, records management and publishing communities, as well as students on information, media, business and communications courses. CILIP members receive a 20% discount.

Publishing Director, Facet Publishing:
Helen Carley
helen.carley@facetpublishing.co.uk

Online shop: www.facetpublishing.co.uk
To order Facet Publishing books:
contact Bookpoint Ltd,
Mail Order Department,
130 Milton Park, Abingdon,
Oxon OX14 4SB.
Telephone: 01235 827702
Fax: 01235 827703
E-mail: facet@bookpoint.co.uk
www.facetpublishing.co.uk.

Training & Development

CILIP's Training and Development business provides a major programme of more than 100 professional development courses a year, which are discounted by up to 40% for CILIP members, as well as an expanding on-site training programme and a Summer Training Programme. Each year T&D maintains its impressive 90% Good to Excellent rating from delegates.

Manager, Training and Development:
Penny Simmonds
penny.simmonds@cilip.org.uk

CILIP Events

Organises major commercial conferences and Executive Briefings on specialist topics for the library and information community, and manages CILIP Special Interest Group events on a third-party basis. Also runs LSM Suppliers Showcases and provides support for CILIP Members Day and the AGM.

Manager, CILIP Events:
Jason Russell jason.russell@cilip.org.uk

Corporate Marketing and Media Relations

Responsible for recruiting and retaining CILIP members and handling the institute's corporate marketing, PR, and media relations activity. Manages CILIP's two major Awards – Libraries Change Lives and Carnegie & Greenaway – and supports advocacy and CILIP's commercial operations. Has responsibility for corporate events, branding and design.

Head, Corporate Marketing and Media Relations:
Mark Taylor mark.taylor@cilip.org.uk

Subject directory

accreditation	quals@cilip.org.uk	020 7255 0613
advertising (*Gazette*, *Gazette* Recruitment and *Buyers' Guide*)	advertising@cilip.org.uk	020 7255 0550
advocacy	policy@cilip.org.uk	020 7255 0632
books (purchasing)	info@facetpublishing.co.uk	020 7255 0590
Branch membership	membership@cilip.org.uk	020 7255 0602
Buyers' Guide	advertising@cilip.org.uk	020 7255 0550
careers advice	michael.martin@cilip.org.uk	020 7255 0610
Carnegie/Greenaway (www.carnegiegreenaway.org.uk/)	ckg@cilip.org.uk	020 7255 0650
catering, Ridgmount Street	roombookings@cilip.org.uk	020 7255 0514
Chartering	quals@cilip.org.uk	020 7255 0613
Chief Executive	bob.mckee@cilip.org.uk (until 31 October 2010) annie.mauger@cilip.org.uk (after 31 October 2010)	020 7255 0691
CILIP in Ireland	elga.logue@btinternet.com	028 7181 2680
CILIP in Scotland	cilips@slainte.org.uk	01698 458888
CILIP Wales/CILIP Cymru	cilip-cymru@aber.ac.uk	07837 032536 01970 622174
conferences, exhibitions and special events	events@cilip.org.uk	020 7255 0544
copyright enquiries (members only)		020 7255 0620
corporate marketing	marketing@cilip.org.uk	020 7255 0650
courses	training@cilip.org.uk	020 7255 0560
editorial Facet Publishing *Library & Information Gazette* *Library & Information Update*	sarah.busby@facetpublishing.co.uk debbyraven@btconnect.com update@cilip.org.uk	020 7255 0593 0141 334 6019 020 7255 0580
events	events@cilip.org.uk	020 7255 0544
exhibitions	events@cilip.org.uk	020 7255 0544
Facet Publishing (www.facetpublishing.co.uk)	info@facetpublishing.co.uk	020 7255 0590
Fellowship	quals@cilip.org.uk	020 7255 0613
finance	financedepartment@cilip.org.uk	020 7255 0673
Gazette Advertising (*Gazette*, *Gazette* Recruitment and *Buyers' Guide*)	advertising@cilip.org.uk	020 7255 0550
Gazette Editorial	debbyraven@btconnect.com	0141 334 6019
governance	governance@cilip.org.uk	020 7255 0656
Group membership	membership@cilip.org.uk	020 7255 0602

Infomatch recruitment agency	infomatch@cilip.org.uk	020 7255 0570
information and advice	info@cilip.org.uk	020 7255 0620
international activities	jill.martin@cilip.org.uk	020 7255 0642
LACA: Libraries & Archives Copyright Alliance	info@cilip.org.uk	020 7255 0624
LIBEX job exchange	libex@cilip.org.uk	020 7255 0616
Libraries in the UK and the Republic of Ireland directory and mailing lists	info@facetpublishing.co.uk	020 7255 0590
Library & Information Gazette	advertising@cilip.org.uk	020 7255 0550
Library & Information Update magazine	update@cilip.org.uk	020 7255 0580
mailing lists	membership@cilip.org.uk	020 7255 0603

marketing
  CILIP
  Facet Publishing
  Training & Development
	marketing@cilip.org.uk
	james.williams@facetpublishing.co.uk
	hayley.coulson@cilip.org.uk
	louise.rodriguez-aiken@cilip.org.uk
		020 7255 0650
		020 7255 0597
		020 7255 0563

media	media@cilip.org.uk	020 7255 0650
Membership	membership@cilip.org.uk	020 7255 0602
policy and advocacy	policy@cilip.org.uk	020 7255 0632
press releases and media	marketing@cilip.org.uk	020 7255 0650

publications
  books from Facet Publishing
    purchasing books: www.facetpublishing.co.uk
  Buyer's Guide
  Library & Information Gazette
  Library & Information Update
	info@facetpublishing.co.uk
	facet@bookpoint.co.uk
	advertising@cilip.org.uk
	advertising@cilip.org.uk
	update@cilip.org.uk
		020 7255 0590
		01235 827702
		020 7255 0550
		020 7255 0550
		020 7255 0580

qualifications	quals@cilip.org.uk	020 7255 0610
reception (Ridgmount Street)	reception@cilip.org.uk	020 7255 0500

recruitment
  Infomatch recruitment agency
  lisjobnet.com
	infomatch@cilip.org.uk
	lisjobnet@cilip.org.uk
		020 7255 0570
		020 7255 0550

room bookings (Ridgmount Street)	roombookings@cilip.org.uk	020 7255 0500
switchboard (Ridgmount Street)	reception@cilip.org.uk	020 7255 0500
training and development (CILIP training courses)	training@cilip.org.uk	020 7255 0560
Update magazine	update@cilip.org.uk	020 7255 0580
website	web@cilip.org.uk	020 7255 0623

Books published 2009

 **facet publishing**

Libraries and Information Services in the UK and the Republic of Ireland; 2009–2010. 36th edn
paperback; August;
978-1-85604-679-4; £49.95

Kay Ann Cassell and Uma Hiremath
Reference and Information Services in the 21st Century: An introduction. 2nd edn
paperback; August;
978-1-85604-688-6; £44.95

Barbara Allan
Supporting Research Students
paperback; December;
978-1-85604-685-5; £44.95

Graham P Cornish
Copyright: Interpreting the law for libraries, archives and information services. 5th edn
paperback; November;
978-1-85604-664-0; £44.95

Jeannette A. Bastian and Ben Alexander, editors
Community Archives: the shaping of memory
hardback; November;
978-1-85604-639-8; £49.95

Jane Devine and Francine Egger-Sider
Going Beyond Google: The invisible web in learning and teaching
paperback; March;
978-1-85604-658-9; £44.95

Kathryn Beecroft, editor
CILIP Yearbook;
paperback; March;
978-1-85604-643-5; £49.95

Nancy Dowd, Mary Evangeliste and Jonathan Silberman
Bite-sized Marketing: Realistic solutions for the overworked librarian
paperback; November;
978-1-85604-704-3; £32.95

CILIP Members receive a special 20% discount on all Facet Publishing books

Nicole C. Engard, editor
Library Mashups: Exploring new ways to deliver library data
paperback; September;
978-1-85604-703-6; £29.95

William Saffady
Managing Electronic Records: 4th edn
paperback; May;
978-1-85604-699-2; £52.95

Alan Gilchrist, editor
Information Science in Transition
hardback; April;
978-1-85604-693-0; £49.95

Michael P. Sauers
Searching 2.0
paperback; April;
978-1-85604-629-9; £44.95

Sharon Markless, editor *et al.*
The Innovative School Librarian: Thinking outside the box
hardback; July;
978-1-85604-653-4; £44.95

Hazel Woodward and Lorraine Estelle, editors
Digital Information: Order or anarchy?
hardback; December;
978-1-85604-680-0; £44.95

Martin Palmer
Making the Most of RFID in Libraries
hardback; March;
978-1-85604-634-3; £44.95

Sheila Pantry & Peter Griffiths
How to Give Your Users the LIS Services They Want
paperback; November;
978-1-85604-672-5; £39.95

CILIP Members receive a special 20% discount on all Facet Publishing books

Part 2
GOVERNANCE

Council

CILIP's governing body is its Council, which manages the affairs of the Institute Council is comprised of 12 Councillors elected directly by the Membership in accordance with the Bye-laws and General Regulations. Councillors are also the Trustees of CILIP so the terms may be used interchangeably. There is provision for up to three-co-options on Council.

Judith Broady-Preston (Honorary Treasurer)

(To serve until 31 December 2011)
E-mail: Judy.Broady-Preston@cilip.org.uk

Dr Judith Broady-Preston is Chair of the Management Research Group at DIS, Aberystwyth University, where she has been employed since January 1990, having also been Director of Learning and Teaching, and a member of the Department's Senior Management Team (2000–2007). Prior to 1990, she worked at Leeds Metropolitan and Sheffield Universities. Before becoming a full-time academic, Judith worked originally as a health services librarian and subsequently as an academic librarian.

Her research interests are value, quality, impact, performance measurement and services marketing. She has published extensively in a range of international journals and undertaken national and international consultancy projects. Judith has presented numerous conference papers on all continents bar Australasia and Antarctica, but would be happy to remedy either omission if invited to do so!

Regional Editor of two international journals, *Library Management* and *Journal of Education, Media & Library Sciences*, she is also a member of the editorial boards of *Library and Information Research* and *Performance Measurement and Metrics*. A regular reviewer of journal and conference papers, Judith has been a member of numerous national and international conference planning committees, and assesses new monographs for five commercial publishers.

Secretary of BAILER (1997–2004), she has also been involved actively in professional associations, beginning with election to the IIS Southern Region Committee in 1994, being a member of the final General Council of the IIS. On the inauguration of CILIP, she was firstly Honorary Treasurer CILIP Cymru/Wales, then Vice-Chair and was Chair of CILIP Cymru/Wales (2006–December 2007) until election to Council in December 2007.

John Crawford

(to serve until 31 December 2012)
Email: John.Crawford@cilip.org.uk

John Crawford has worked in public, school and academic libraries. He was formerly the director of the Scottish Information Literacy Project. He became interested in information literacy in 2002 and it has been his main focus of activity since then. He served on the Council of the Chartered Institute of Library and Information Professionals (CILIP) from 2002 to 2007 and during this time served as chair of its Professional Practice Committee and was a member of its Executive Board. He also serves on the CILIP Disciplinary Committee. He is former chair of the Library and Information History Group, is still a committee member and has a strong interest in membership activism. He has written extensively in professional and academic journals and has authored two books. He serves on the editorial board of two scholarly journals and regularly referees journal submissions to a number of refereed journals.

Veronica Fraser

(To serve until 31 December 2010)
E-mail: Veronica.Fraser@cilip.org.uk

The mainstay of her local public library, Veronica was offered a job there as a Saturday assistant and never looked back. Following a degree in Ancient and Mediaeval History, Veronica became a London Borough of Barnet trainee librarian, working as a cataloguer and reference librarian before moving to Hackney where her last post was as Book Bus Librarian (job share). From 1990 to 1996 Veronica was a Professional Adviser at The Library Association, one of CILIP's predecessor organisations leading on employment issues for special and health libraries and equal opportunities, and working closely with several LA special interest groups.

In January 1997 Veronica moved to the Department of Health as their Policy Adviser on library and knowledge services in England, commissioner for the NHS National electronic Library for Health (NeLH) negotiating the first NHS Copyright Licence for NHS England. In her current post in the Department's Customer Service Centre (CSC), she is responsible for CSC's knowledge management and Call Centre and acts as Head of Complaints for the Department.

Veronica has been a Board Member of the Hackney Job Share Project, the Information Services National Training Organisation, the British Library Advisory Committee on Bibliographic Services, LISU, the NHS Regional Libraries Group, LINC Health Panel, a Community Health Council member and chair of Governors for Mill Mead School.

Concern for CILIP's future prompted Veronica to stand as a National Councillor in 2006. As a CILIP Trustee, Veronica's main interests are to keep CILIP solvent and proactive on library issues. She is also interested in training and development and as part of her own CPD hopes to become an Independent Assessor for NVQs.

Isabel Hood (Deputy Leader of Council)

(To serve until 31 December 2012)
E-mail: Isabel.Hood@cilip.org.uk

My career has been a mixture of circumstance, luck and planning – as with many people's!

Beginnings Having spent a lot of my childhood in libraries they seemed the natural place to go career-wise. I did the SCOTVEC National Certificate in Library and Information Science at Telford College in Edinburgh, loved it, and went straight on to do the undergraduate degree level course at RGU in Aberdeen.

Law The fact that I have become a law librarian was initially part-accident, but quickly then a chosen career choice which I have actively followed. I wrote to all the Special Libraries in Glasgow looking for holiday work and ended up at The Royal Faculty of Procurators in Glasgow. And after the initial terror of not knowing anything of specific relevance I really enjoyed it and it started me out on my current path which has involved professional legal society, court and law firm libraries and led to all kinds of time-intensive decisions later on like doing a law degree.

Professional doings Just over a decade ago I had my first and only part-time job for a wee bit. I got bored and allowed myself to be talked onto Career Development Group (Scottish) Committee and somehow I came out of the pub an hour later as three different Officer posts and the learning curve started. Thus my second simultaneous parallel professional life was born, though I didn't know it. Ever since I've done more and more

CILIP-related doings (everything from CDG President to Governance Review to CILIPS Council) and it does take over life, but I've discovered I really believe in progressing things (I'm not good at doing nothing), and I quite like tilting at professional windmills and the unknown, I'm interested to see what will happen and what's on the other side.

Ayub Khan

(To serve until 31 December 2010)
E-mail: Ayub.Khan@cilip.org.uk

Ayub Khan BA(Hons) FCLIP is Head of Libraries (Strategy) for Warwickshire County Council. His role is to provide professional leadership for the library service in relation to library policy and strategy and he is a member of the wider Libraries, Learning and Culture Management team.

He has held a number of posts in public libraries specialising in schools, young people's and community librarianship. Ayub's most recent role was that of Principal Project Officer (Library of Birmingham), working on plans to create a new state of the art city centre library. Ayub is a former member of CILIP's Chartership Board and has served on the joint Chartership/Accreditation regulations working group for the new Framework of Qualifications. Ayub has a strong interest in International Librarianship and is a member of UNESCO's Culture Committee and has recently been elected to the Library Services for Multi Cultural Population standing committee of IFLA. Ayub has also served on the British Council's Knowledge and Information advisory board. He currently chairs CILIP's Equal Opportunities and Diversity panel and is a past President of the Career Development Group.

Ayub was awarded a Centenary Medal from The Library Association in 1998 for services to Librarianship and in 2003 was highly commended in the personal achievement category of the Diversity awards by the Diversity Group. He achieved his Fellowship in 2004.

Ayub is a member of LISU's Advisory board and is an OGC (Office Government Commerce) peer review assessor for Gateway Reviews for project management in the public sector. He has co-written the section on library buildings for the RIBA's *Metric Handbook* and co-authored the trends and policy direction in public libraries during the 1990s chapter in the *British Librarianship and Information Work* publication (2006). Ayub also under took the research and forecasting for the influential report *Fulfilling their Potential* published by the Reading Agency.

Jill Lambert (Deputy Treasurer)

(To serve until 31 December 2011)
E-mail: Jill.Lambert@cilip.org.uk

Jill Lambert began her career as a weekend assistant at Ilkeston Public Library in Derbyshire. After a science degree at Bristol University, she worked for the Paint Research Association, subsequently taking a post graduate diploma in librarianship at Liverpool John Moores University.

Her first professional post was with the University of Westminster, followed by the appointment as Science and Technology Librarian at Northumbria University. During a career break for two children, Jill studied for an MA in Librarianship. For several years, she was a visiting lecturer in the Department of Library and Information Studies at Birmingham City University. On returning to academic libraries, she worked at Birmingham City and Staffordshire Universities, before moving to Aston University. In the Library & Information Services (LIS) at Aston she was responsible for public services and academic liaison for life science and engineering for 10 years until retiring as Assistant Director in Autumn 2007. She is a Fellow and Life Member of CILIP.

Her interests centre around three areas:

- Developing and managing services to users. This has included implementing an access control system, improving services for users with additional needs, and introducing 'walk-in' access for visitors. She was instrumental in achieving Charter Mark, a government award for customer excellence, for LIS at Aston University in 2007.
- Incorporating IT developments into practice. She was involved in the early development of CD-ROM, beta testing databases for OCLC Europe, later publishing a review on the management of CDs in academic libraries. In 2001 she initiated the first e-book service at Aston University, also greatly expanding the provision of e-journals.
- Scientific, technical and medical information. She has sought to develop information literacy in academic libraries, and more widely via the publication of the textbook *Finding Information in Science, Technology and Medicine*, now in its third edition. Her other publications in this area include the books, *Scientific and Technical Journals*, and *Information Resources Selection*.

Acquiring knowledge of practice elsewhere has always been one of her key aims. Jill has made two international study visits, one funded by the British Council to Dutch academic libraries and one by the EU to the James Hardiman Library, part of the National University of Ireland. This Library is a leader in professional practice in Ireland, and the visit enabled her to benchmark her own service in terms of mode of staffing, and IT developments such as federated searching.

Jill has been actively involved in the profession over many years, acting as Secretary of the Midlands Branch of the Institute of Information Scientists for three years, and a member of the Annual Conference Organizing Committee in 1987. She was Treasurer of the JIBS User Group (JISC Assisted Bibliographical Data Services),

covering electronic content of interest to Higher and Further Education institutions, from 2001 to 2006. She also established a local group, under the auspices of the West Midlands Higher Education Association (WMHEA) Information and Learning Group (ILG), for front line library supervisors and managers. Known as the Public Services Sub Group, this was set up to provide a discussion forum for all loan related activities, including issues, fines handling, shelving, staff rotas and IT developments such as RFID.

Dion Lindsay

(To serve until 31 December 2011)
E-mail: Dion.Lindsay@cilip.org.uk

I was born and brought up in the west of Northern Ireland in the 1950s and 1960s, and went to university in glorious Aberystwyth in the mid 1970s. So glorious that I stayed an extra year to study librarianship at College of Librarianship Wales (1977–1978). Then I spent 23 years in Government Departments in London (Agriculture, Cabinet Office and Health), moving towards running high value-added information units for specialists. I spent 1997–2001 as Senior Librarian in various posts in the Department of Health, then made the big move away from the Civil Service and London – to Northampton as Knowledge Manager for the Motor Neurone Disease Association.

I had a great time there introducing formal and informal knowledge management techniques (we invented some of the latter on the fly – that's what a creative, motivated group can do!). In four years we grew from a £6m to a £9m organisation.

I realized that the best bit was internal consultancy – intervening to make a sustainable difference, and decided my skills and experience were robust enough to become a full time consultant. Now I'm consulted mainly by medium sized organisations in London and the Midlands who want knowledge management to help them in their learning and growth aspirations.

I'm delighted to have been elected as a CILIP Trustee to the end of 2011. I'm enjoying playing my part in ensuring that society and the workplace grasp the opportunities we as professionals offer. I believe that a refreshed CILIP and a committed membership provide us with power to create a new and powerful impact.

Nigel Macartney

(To serve until 31 December 2010)
E-mail: Nigel.Macartney@cilip.org.uk

Nigel Macartney is Director of Information Services at the University of Ulster, responsible for the library, archive, computing and reprographic services used by the 23,000 students and 3,500 staff of the University. He served as Director of the British Library Research and Innovation Centre between 1995 and 1999, where he encouraged the development of national research funding strategies and close co-operation between national library organisations. From 1982 to 1995 he was Librarian at the University of Hertfordshire; his roles here included provision of information services to industry and business, academic library co-operation and new technology. He was also Managing Director of Cimtech Ltd during the latter part of this period.

He was born in Manchester and, after taking a degree in History at Cambridge, his early career encompassed experience in public and further education libraries. He has some knowledge of European libraries through his work at the British Library and through an EU TEMPUS project involving collaborative work with Technical Universities in Poland. He has served on several Government advisory committees. His current interests include learning resource centre design and implementation of IT and information strategies. He is also playing a leading role in the business process review programme being

implemented at the University of Ulster. He is a member of the North Eastern Education and Library Board in Northern Ireland and was Chairman of the Board's Library Committee. Nigel chairs NIRAN Ltd, which provides the JANET data network to the province's universities, colleges and research institutions. He served as Honorary Treasurer of CILIP from 2005 to 2007 and was an officer of the former Library Association Audio Visual Group in the 1980s. He is a Fellow of the Royal Society of Arts.

Emma McDonald

(To serve until 31 December 2012)
E-mail: Emma.McDonald@cilip.org.uk

I grew up in Crewe and spent much of my free time at school helping in the school library. This gave me an early taste of many aspects of librarianship and helped ignite a passion for the profession.

While studying English at Cambridge University, I worked in the Peterhouse library as a Library Assistant. After graduating I spent a year working as a law costs draftsman, before getting a job as a Graduate Trainee Librarian at Exeter University.

A fun year at Exeter convinced me that librarianship was what I wanted to do and I applied for a masters' course at Loughborough University.

Since graduating from Loughborough, I've been working in West Sussex as a Trainee Librarian. I served on the South East branch committee as one of the newsletter editors for roughly a year and the positive nature of this experience was what encouraged me to stand for election as a trustee.

Nick Poole

(To serve until 31 December 2012)
E-mail: Nick.Poole@cilip.org.uk

Nick Poole is Chief Executive of the Collections Trust, an independent UK charity working with libraries, archives and museums. He also represents the UK at the Member States Expert Group for Digitisation at the European Commission and is responsible for advising a number of European agencies and Governments on digital priorities in Culture and libraries.

Prior to joining the Collections Trust in 2005, Nick held a number of roles at the Museums, Libraries and Archives Council (MLA), including responsibility for Regional policy development and as a National ICT Adviser. Before this, he worked in the financial services sector. In addition to his role within CILIP, Nick is a Councillor of the Museums Association and a Trustee of the UK part of the International Council of Museums.

Nick is a regular lecturer at several universities and has published on subjects ranging from the economics of cultural services to international copyright and cultural property law. He studied Languages at Cambridge University and holds postgraduate qualifications in Historical Linguistics and Fine Art & Illustration. He also studied the History and Philosophy of Science at Birkbeck College.

In his spare time, Nick enjoys reading, spending time with his family and hosting a successful regular music and poetry event. He also works with a number of HE and FE providers in an advisory capacity on the implementation and use of eLearning systems and Virtual Learning Environments. He was previously compere of a successful comedy club in London's West End.

Bruce Royan

(To serve until 31 December 2011)
E-mail: Bruce.Royan@cilip.org.uk

Bruce Royan has worked in Public, Academic, National, and Government Libraries and is now a Principal Consultant at Concurrent Computing Ltd, whose clients have included Cumbria Libraries, the British Council, Tate Galleries, the Department of Health and the BBC.

He has served as University Librarian and Director of Information Services at the University of Stirling, and Interim Director of Knowledge and Information at Robert Gordon University.

His earlier career in librarianship and information technology has included British Telecom, the London Borough of Camden, The British Library, the National Library of Scotland, the Department of Trade and Industry, and being the founding Director of the Singapore Library Network (SILAS).

Outside Singapore, he may be best known for founding SCRAN, a networked multimedia learning resource base of millions of objects, digitised from libraries, museums, archives and the built heritage, and licensed for educational use.

Bruce has provided library networking consultancy to clients in Japan, Hungary, the Czech Republic and the Philippines, and has lectured on library management issues in 40 countries across six continents.

He has served on the boards of several educational charities, as well as the Councils of the Library Association of Singapore, the Institute of Information Scientists, and The Library Association. He was Chair of the LA IT Group for several years, facilitating its evolution into MmIT.

An Honorary Fellow of CILIP, Bruce is Secretary of the Management and Technology Section of IFLA, IFLA representative on the Coordinating Council of Audiovisual Archives Associations and Visiting Professor in the School of Creative Industries, Napier University.

Edwina Smart

(To serve until 31 December 2010)
E-mail: Edwina.Smart@cilip.org.uk

I graduated from Liverpool Polytechnic in 1978 chartering in 1980. I worked in Public Libraries until 1989 when I became a school librarian in a large inner city comprehensive. I trained as a teacher and taught in primary schools for several years during which time I gained a Master's Degree in Education. Since returning to Librarianship I have been awarded Fellowship of CILIP.

I currently work as a Branch Librarian in a small Welsh valley town. I teach on the Information Communications Diploma Course for Coleg Llandrillo and support their Librarianship Foundation Degree students. I represent Wales on the Jodiawards judging panel which awards annual prizes for excellence in accessible cultural websites and digital media.

I have carried out project work in the United Kingdom and Sri Lanka involving migrant worker websites, using the library as support in post traumatic events and the teaching of Information Technology (ICT). I am particularly interested in supporting Para-professional library workers towards qualification through their use of ICT and also people with disabilities.

I have been the Chartership support Officer for CDG Wales before joining the Chartership Board of CILIP. I am a member of CILIP Cymru Committee, Wales Policy Forum Representative and CDG Wales Chair.

Since the tsunami of 2006 I have supported and regularly visited Andarasgaya School in Sri Lanka with support from CDG Wales and many other people from the Library world. The school continues to thrive and improve. I currently sponsor three of the students to remain in school by giving talks and selling notelets, please contact me if you would like to help or hear me speak.

I am also a tea lady for Pontypridd Cricket Club and am usually found in the summer months watching cricket and making copious amounts of tea. My ambition to have my cakes mentioned on Test Match Special is only hampered by my failure to send in one of my special fruit cakes.

Honorary Officers

Leader of Council

Nigel Macartney (until 31 December 2010)

Honorary Treasurer

Judy Broady-Preston (until 31 December 2010)

2010 President

Biddy Fisher

2010 Vice-President

Brian Hall

CILIP's governance structure

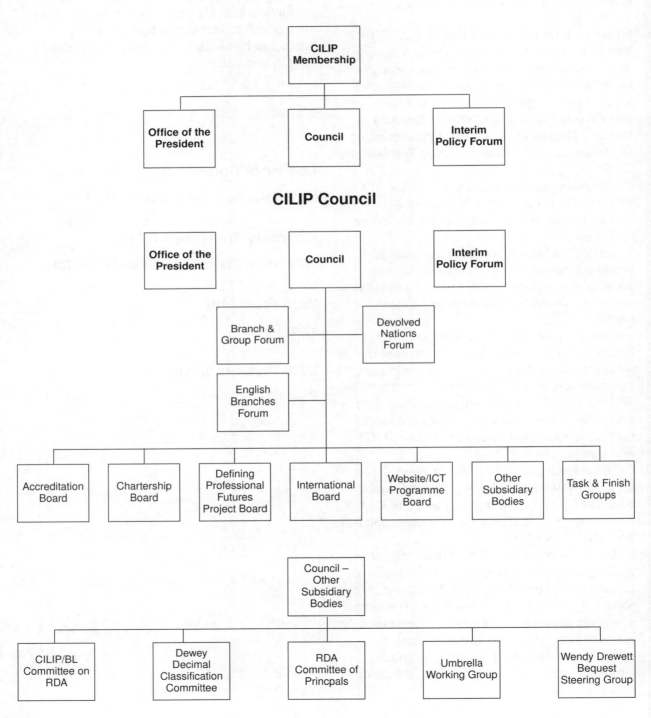

CILIP Council

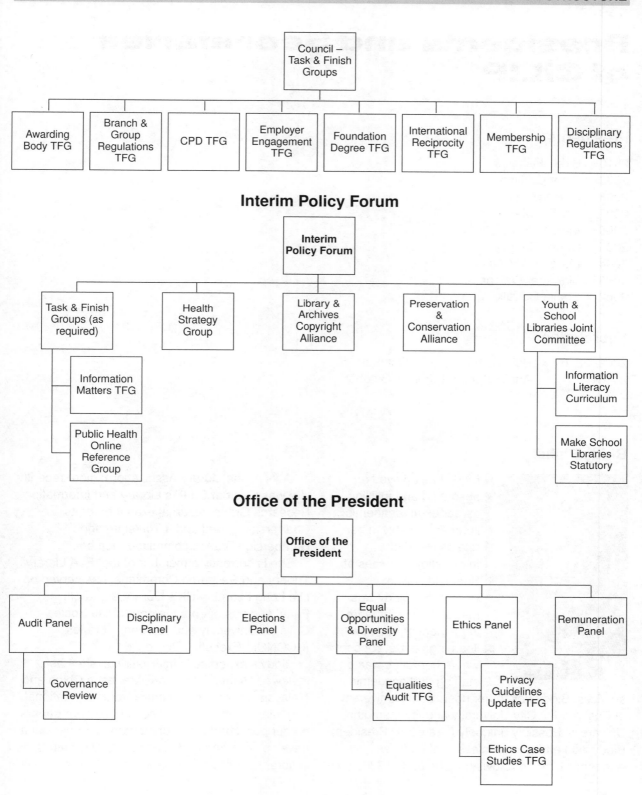

Interim Policy Forum

Office of the President

Presidents and Secretaries of CILIP

Presidents

2010	Biddy Fisher
2009	Peter Griffiths
2008	Bruce Madge
2007	Ian Snowley
2006	Martin Molloy
2005	Debby Shorley
2004	Margaret Haines
2003	Margaret Watson
2002	Sheila Corrall

Secretaries

2002–2010	Bob McKee (until 31 October)
2010–	Annie Mauger (after 31 October)

Biddy Fisher

Biddy has enjoyed an absorbing and fulfilling career as an academic librarian, notably in her role as Head of Information Services at Sheffield Hallam University. Biddy was part of the senior team implementing the new 'learning centre' concept where her focus was on staffing and academic services. Biddy held other posts at the University of East Anglia, City University and Roehampton University. Possibly uniquely for a CILIP President, Biddy worked for the professional body, as Academic Libraries Adviser in the early 1990s (in its days as the Library Association); more recently she was Chair of CILIP's Library and Information Research Group, external examiner for its Chartership Board and a Yorkshire and Humberside Branch committee member.

She is currently a member of the IFLA Library Theory and Research Committee, has served on Life Long Learning UK's Library and Archives Panel and has been a member of the Society of College, University and National Libraries (SCONUL) Executive Board.

Biddy's expertise is international: she has reviewed Higher Education libraries in China and Malaysia as well as presenting regional, national and international conference and seminar papers on her published areas of mentoring, professional development, library design and quality standards in library services.

CILIP Royal Charter

The 1986 Royal Charter on display in the Charter Suite

The text of the Royal Charter was approved by the Privy Council and by the CILIP AGM on 18 October 2007.

ELIZABETH THE SECOND by the Grace of God of the United Kingdom of Great Britain and Northern Ireland and of Our other Realms and Territories Queen, Head of the Commonwealth, Defender of the Faith:

TO ALL TO WHOM THESE PRESENTS SHALL COME, GREETINGS!

WHEREAS Her Majesty Queen Victoria in the year of our Lord One thousand eight hundred and ninety eight by Royal Charter (hereinafter called 'the Original Charter') dated the seventh day of February in the sixty first year of Her Reign constituted a Body Corporate by the name of The Library Association (hereinafter called 'the Association') with perpetual succession and with power to sue and to be sued by this name and to use a Common Seal:

AND WHEREAS the Original Charter was amended by an Order in Council dated the sixteenth day of December One Thousand Nine Hundred and Eighty Six:

AND WHEREAS it has been represented unto Us that the Association seeks with others to unite all persons engaged or interested in library work and information science for the purpose of promoting the development of libraries and information services and the advancement of information science for the public benefit and to that end the Association has resolved to change its name to the Chartered Institute of Library and Information Professionals:

WHEREAS it has been represented unto Us by the Association that it is expedient to revise the objects and powers of the Association and that the provisions of the Original Charter, except in so far as they incorporate the Association, should be replaced:

NOW, THEREFORE, KNOW YE that We, by virtue of Our Prerogative Royal and of all other powers enabling Us so to do, have, of Our especial grace, certain knowledge and mere motion, granted and declared and by these Presents for Us, Our Heirs and Successors, grant and declare as follows:

Interpretation

1. In this Our Charter unless the context otherwise requires:

    (i) 'the Institute' shall mean the Chartered Institute of Library and Information Professionals;

    (ii) 'the Charter' means the Charter of Incorporation of the Institute;

(iii) 'the Byelaws' shall mean the Byelaws set out in the Schedule below as amended from time to time as provided below;

(iv) 'a Member' means a member of the Institute in any category of membership established in accordance with Regulations;

(v) 'Individual Member' means an individual who is admitted as a Member in accordance with Regulations;

(vi) 'Organisation Member' means a corporate body, society or other non-corporate organisation which maintains or is interested in libraries or information services and is admitted as a Member in accordance with the Byelaws;

(vii) 'the Council' means the Council for the time being appointed pursuant to the Charter and the Byelaws;

(viii) 'Councillor' means a member of the Council;

(ix) 'Duly Appointed Body' means any person or body of people to whom or to which powers are reserved or properly delegated under the Charter or Byelaws;

(x) 'Regulations' means regulations made and publicised by the Council in accordance with the Byelaws;

(xi) 'Registered Practitioner' means an Individual Member who is entitled under the Byelaws and Regulations to use after his or her name the letters "MCLIP", "FCLIP", or "ACLIP" and is respectively entitled to describe himself or herself as "Chartered Member of the CILIP", "Chartered Fellow of the CILIP", or "Certified Affiliate of the CILIP".

(xii) Words denoting the singular number include the plural and vice versa;

(xiii) Words importing the masculine gender include the feminine gender; and

(xiv) Words importing persons include corporations.

Objects and powers

2. The objects of the Institute shall be to work for the benefit of the public to promote education and knowledge through the establishment and development of libraries and information services and to advance information science (being the science and practice of the collection, collation, evaluation and organised dissemination of information) and for that purpose the Institute shall have power to do all or any of the following things:

(a) to foster and promote education, training, invention and research in matters connected with information science and libraries and information services and to collect, collate and publish information, ideas, data and research relating thereto;

(b) to unite all persons engaged or interested in information science and libraries and information services by holding conferences and meetings for the discussion of questions and matters affecting information science and libraries and information services or their regulation or management and any other questions or matters relating to the objects of the Institute;

(c) to promote the improvement of the knowledge, skills, position and qualifications of librarians and information personnel;

(d) to promote study and research in librarianship and information science and to disseminate the results;

(e) to promote and encourage the maintenance of adequate and appropriate provision of library and information services of various kinds throughout the United Kingdom, the Channel Islands and the Isle of Man;

(f) to scrutinise any legislation affecting the provision of library and information services and to promote such further legislation as may be considered necessary to that end;

(g) to represent and act as the professional body for persons working in or interested in library and information services;

(h) to maintain a register of Registered Practitioners;

(i) to ensure the effective dissemination of appropriate information of interest to Members;

(j) to work with similar institutes overseas and with appropriate international bodies to promote the widespread provision of adequate and appropriate library and information services;

(k) to provide appropriate services to Members in furtherance of these objectives;

(l) to form and promote the formation of branches, sections or groups of the Institute in any part of the world and to dissolve branches, sections or groups so established;

(m) to print and publish and to sell, lend and distribute any communications, papers or treatises which are relevant to the objects of the Institute;

(n) to raise funds and to invite and receive contributions provided that the Institute shall in raising funds not undertake any substantial trading activities and shall conform to any relevant statutory regulations;

(o) to invest the monies of the Institute not immediately required for the furtherance of its objects in or upon such investments, securities or property as may be thought fit;

(p) to purchase, take on lease or in exchange, hire, or otherwise acquire any real or personal property necessary for or conducive to the objects of the Institute and to maintain and equip the same for use in furtherance thereof;

(q) to borrow or raise money with or without security for the objects of the Institute provided that no money shall be raised by mortgage of any real or leasehold property of the Institute situate in Our United Kingdom without such consent or approval (if any) as may be by law required;

(r) to sell, manage, lease, mortgage or dispose of all or any part of the property of the Institute, provided that no disposition of any real or leasehold property situate in our United Kingdom shall be made without such consent or approval (if any) as may be by law required;

(s) to make and give effect to any arrangements for the joint working or co-operation with any other society or body, whether incorporated or not, carrying on work which is within the objects of the Institute;

(t) to undertake, execute and perform any trusts or conditions affecting any real or personal property of any description acquired by the Institute;

(u) generally to do all other lawful acts whatsoever that are conducive or incidental to the attainment of the objects of the Institute.

Income and property

3. The income and property of the Institute wheresoever derived shall be applied solely towards the promotion of the objects of the Institute as set forth in this Our Charter, and no portion thereof shall be paid or transferred

directly or indirectly by way of dividend, bonus or otherwise howsoever by way of profit to any Member and save as hereinafter provided no Councillor shall be appointed to any office of the Institute paid by salary or fees or receive remuneration from the Institute: provided that nothing herein contained shall prevent the payment in good faith by the Institute:

(a) of fees to any person (not being a Councillor) in return for services actually rendered or reasonable and proper pensions to former employees of the Institute or their dependants;

(b) of fees to any Councillor who possesses specialist skills or knowledge required by the Institute for its proper administration of reasonable fees for work of that nature done by the Councillor when instructed by the Institute to act on its behalf but on condition that:

    (i) at no time may a majority of the Council benefit under this provision; and

    (ii) a Councillor must withdraw from any meeting whilst his or her appointment or remuneration is being discussed and may not vote or count in the quorum in respect of that matter;

(c) of reasonable and proper rent for premises demised or let by any Member or Councillor;

(d) of reasonable and proper interest on money borrowed by the Institute from a Member or Councillor for the objects of the Institute;

(e) of reasonable and proper out of pocket expenses incurred by any Member or Councillor on behalf of the Institute;

(f) of all reasonable and proper premiums in respect of trustees' indemnity

insurance effected in accordance with Article 8 of this Our Charter.

Members

4. The Members shall consist of such persons and shall have such rights and privileges as may be prescribed by or under the Byelaws for the time being to be framed in pursuance of this Our Charter.

5. There shall be such classes of Organisation and Individual Members as may be prescribed pursuant to the Byelaws. The qualifications, method and terms of admission, rights, privileges and obligations of each such class of membership and the disciplinary arrangements to which Members shall be subject shall be as the Byelaws and Regulations prescribe. Members may be designated as belonging to the Institute by such abbreviations as the Byelaws and Regulations shall prescribe. No other abbreviation to indicate a class of membership may be used.

Council

6. The powers of the Institute shall be vested in a Council elected or appointed in accordance with the Byelaws and which may in respect of the affairs of the Institute exercise all such powers and do all such things as may lead to the furtherance of the objects of the Institute including all such powers and things as may be exercised or done by the Institute and are not by this Our Charter or the Byelaws expressly directed or required to be exercised or done by any other person or by the Institute in general meeting.

7. In the execution of their powers under this Our Charter, no Councillor or other office holder shall be liable for any loss to the property of the Institute arising by reason of

any improper investment made in good faith (so long as where appropriate advice shall have been sought before making such investment) or for the negligence or fraud of any other Councillor or other office holder or by reason of any mistake or omission made in good faith by any Councillor or other office holder or by reason of any other matter or thing whatsoever except wilful and individual fraud, wrongdoing or omission on the part of the Councillor or other office holder.

8. The Council may pay out of the funds of the Institute the cost of any premium in respect of insurance or indemnities to cover any liability of the Council (or any Councillor) and any other office holder which by virtue of any rule of law would otherwise attach to them in respect of any negligence, default, breach of duty or breach of trust of which they may be guilty in relation to the Institute; provided that any such insurance or indemnity shall not extend to any claim arising from criminal or wilful or deliberate neglect or default on the part of the Council (or Councillor) or other office holder.

Delegation of the Council's Powers

9. The Council may delegate its powers in such manner as is permitted by the Bye-laws.

Office of the President

10. The Office of the President shall be established under the Byelaws with such powers and functions as are prescribed by the Byelaws.

General meetings

11. Meetings of the Institute shall be convened and the proceedings there regulated in accordance with the Byelaws.

Byelaws

12. The affairs of the Institute shall be managed and regulated in accordance with the Byelaws which shall remain in force until revoked, amended or added to as provided below.

Supplementary provisions

13. The provisions of the Original Charter, except in so far as they incorporate the Institute and confer upon it perpetual succession and a Common Seal, are hereby revoked, but nothing in this revocation shall affect the legality or validity of any act, deed or thing lawfully done or executed under the provisions of the Original Charter.

14. The Byelaws scheduled in the Original Charter as amended from time to time shall be deemed to be and shall continue to be the Byelaws. Any of the Byelaws may from time to time be revoked, amended or added to by a resolution passed by a majority of not less than two thirds of the Individual Members voting in person or by proxy at a duly convened general meeting of the Institute provided that no new Byelaw and no such revocation, amendment or addition as aforesaid shall have any force or effect if it be repugnant to any of the provisions of this Our Charter or the laws of Our Realm, nor until it shall have been approved by Our Privy Council of which approval a certificate under the hand of the Clerk of Our Privy Council shall be conclusive evidence. This provision shall apply to the Byelaws as revoked, altered or added to in manner aforesaid.

15. The Institute may by resolution in that behalf passed by a majority of not less than two-thirds of the Individual Members voting in person or by proxy on the question at a duly convened general meeting of the Institute alter, amend or add to any of the provisions of this Our Charter and such alteration,

amendment or addition shall, when approved by Us, Our Heirs or Successors in Council become effectual so that this Our Charter shall thenceforward continue and operate as though it had been originally granted and made accordingly. This provision shall apply to this Our Charter as altered, amended or added to in manner aforesaid.

16. The Institute may by resolution passed by a majority of not less than two-thirds of the Individual Members voting in person or by proxy on the question at a duly convened general meeting of the Institute surrender this Our Charter subject to the sanction of Us, Our Heirs or Successors in Council and upon such terms as We or They may consider fit and wind up or otherwise deal with the affairs of the Institute in such manner as they shall be directed by the special resolution having due regard to the liabilities of the Institute for the time being and if on the winding up or dissolution of the Institute there shall remain after satisfaction of debts and liabilities any property whatsoever, that property shall not be paid or distributed among the Members or any of them but shall subject to any special trust affecting the same be given and transferred to some other charitable institute or institutes having objects similar to the objects of the Institute to be determined by the Individual Members at or before the time of dissolution.

IN WITNESS whereof We have caused these Our Letters to be made Patent.

WITNESS Ourself at Westminster the Twenty-first day of May in the Fifty-first Year of Our Reign.

Royal Seal of Queen Elizabeth II on the 1986 Royal Charter

CILIP Bye-laws

Made by Council 16 June 1986, as approved by the Annual General Meeting on 10 September 1986 and as allowed by Her Majesty's Privy Council on 15 December 1986. Revised in 1987, 1989, 1997, 2001, 2005, 2007 and 2008.

SECTION 1
Interpretation

1. In the event of any inconsistency between the provisions of the Charter and the provisions of the Bye-laws the provisions of the Charter shall prevail.

2. In these Bye-laws, unless the context otherwise requires: expressions or words used in the Charter shall have the meanings there defined;

2.1 The expressions "Individual Member", "Organisation Member", "President", "Vice-President", "Honorary Treasurer", "Leader of Council", and Chief Executive Officer shall be read and construed as if the words "of the Institute" were inserted thereafter;

2.2 The following expressions have the following meanings:

"**Ballot**" means a Full Ballot or a Written Ballot

"**Board**" means a sub-committee established in accordance with Bye-law 76;

"**Branch**" means a body of Members associated with a geographical area as defined from time to time by the Council;

"**Charter**" means the Charter of Incorporation of the Institute;

"**Chief Executive Officer**" means the person appointed to that post in accordance with Bye-Law 97;

"**Council**" means the Council for the time being appointed pursuant to the Charter and these Bye-laws;

"**Councillor**" means a member of the Council;

"**Duly Appointed Body**" means any person or body of people to whom or to which powers are reserved or properly delegated under the Charter or these Bye-Laws;

"**Full Ballot**" means a ballot of all the Individual Members conducted in accordance with Regulations and not taken at a General Meeting;

"**General Meeting**" means a general meeting in which the Individual Members assemble;

"**Honorary Officers**" means the President, the Vice-President, the Leader of Council, and the Honorary Treasurer;

"**Individual Member**" means an individual who is admitted as a Member in accordance with the Regulations;

"**Member**" means a member of the Institute in any category of membership established in accordance with the Regulations;

"**Organisation Member**" means a corporate body, society or other non-corporate organisation which maintains or is interested in libraries or information services and is admitted as a Member in accordance with the Regulations;

"**Panel**" means a committee established in accordance with Bye-law 82;

"**Registered Practitioner**" means an Individual Member who is entitled under these Bye-laws and the Regulations to use after his or her name the letters "MCLIP", "FCLIP", or "ACLIP" and is respectively entitled to describe himself or herself as "Chartered Member of the CILIP", "Chartered Fellow of the CILIP", or "Certified Affiliate of the CILIP";

"**Regulations**" means regulations made and published by the Council in accordance with Bye-law 42;

"**Special Interest Group**" means a group established with the approval of the Council to further specialist interests within the Institute;

"**Task and Finish Group**" means a committee established in accordance with Bye-law 71;

"**Written Ballot**" means a ballot of the Individual Members present in person or by proxy at a General Meeting and taken at a General Meeting in accordance with Regulations.

3. Where these Bye-laws confer any power to make Regulations that power shall be construed as including power to rescind, revoke, amend or vary any Regulations made in pursuance of that power.

SECTION 2
Categories and Privileges of Membership

4. The categories of Membership and the privileges and obligations applicable to each category shall be established by Regulations provided that Organisation Members shall not be entitled to vote at General Meetings nor on the election of Councillors or the Vice President nor to hold office in the Institute.

5. Membership shall not be transferable and shall cease on death. All the privileges of membership shall be enjoyed by a Member for his or her own benefit and the Member shall not be entitled to transfer such privileges or any of the benefits derived therefrom to any other person, firm, company or body.

Subscriptions

6. The Institute in General Meeting shall have power to determine the amount of all subscriptions, entrance, registration, admission and other fees (except for examination fees) payable by the Members. The Council, however, shall have the power to make Regulations for the payment of subscriptions (including payment by instalment) and for suspension and expulsion from the Institute in the case of a Member failing to pay. The Council may also make Regulations admitting persons to membership or continuing Members in membership at reduced subscriptions. Members paying reduced subscriptions shall enjoy all the privileges of membership applicable to their category of membership, including voting and the receipt of publications usually distributed to Members. The amount of examination fees shall be determined from time to time by the Council.

Admission, Removal and Reinstatement of Members

7. Members shall be admitted by the Council and may be removed in accordance with the procedures prescribed in Regulations.

8. The Council shall have power to reinstate any Member whose membership has been cancelled for any reason, and may cause reinstatement to be subject to previous compliance with such conditions as it may determine, including the payment of subscriptions in arrear.

9. There shall be maintained at the offices of the Institute a Register of Members containing the names of all Members identifying their category of membership and identifying those who are Registered Practitioners.

10. Copies of the Register of Members shall be published in such manner and at such intervals as the Council shall decide.

SECTION 3
Professional Qualifications

11. The Council shall from time to time make Regulations for the purpose of establishing the rights and responsibilities of Registered Practitioners, testing the proficiency of Members desiring to be admitted as Registered Practitioners and testing the continuing proficiency of Members so admitted.

12. The Council shall have power to grant exemption from the provisions contained in the Regulations or parts thereof to Members who are considered by the Council to have satisfied criteria equivalent to those contained in the Regulations.

13. The Council shall issue to each Registered Practitioner a certificate indicating his or her respective Registered Practitioner status. Such certificates shall remain the property of the Institute and shall be returned upon the Registered Practitioner ceasing to be a Member or otherwise upon him or her ceasing to hold the relevant Registered Practitioner status.

14. The Council shall have power to cancel the registration of any Registered Practitioner whose membership is terminated for any reason and to reinstate the registration when such Registered Practitioner has been reinstated to membership under Bye-law 8. The Council may specify the conditions under which reinstatement may be made, including the payment of a further registration fee. Any Registered Practitioner whose registration is so cancelled shall immediately cease to describe himself or herself as a Registered Practitioner and shall return the Institute's certificate indicating his or her Registered Practitioner status.

SECTION 4
Honorary Awards

15. The Council shall have power to nominate as Honorary Fellows individuals who in the opinion of the Council have rendered distinguished service in promoting the objects of the Institute. Honorary Fellows shall be entitled to use after their names the letters "HonFCLIP" and to describe themselves as "Honorary Fellow of the CILIP".

16. The Council may remove any person's Honorary Fellow status, in which case that person shall cease to describe himself or herself as an Honorary Fellow of the CILIP and cease to use the letters "HonFCLIP".

SECTION 5
Conduct of Members

17. The Council shall have power to issue a set of ethical principles and Code of Professional Practice setting out the standards of professional behaviour expected of Members and may from time to time amend the ethical principles and code or any part or parts thereof.

18. Every Member (including every Organisation Member and its representatives) shall observe the provisions of the Charter, the Bye-laws and the Regulations and shall conduct him or herself in such a manner as shall not prejudice his or her professional status or the reputation of the Institute and

without prejudice to the generality of the foregoing shall, in particular, comply at all times with the ethical principles and Code of Professional Practice prescribed and published by the Council under the provisions of the last preceding Bye-law.

19. The Council shall make and publish Regulations for the conduct of the disciplinary proceedings in respect of any complaint made against a Member and such Regulations may establish a range of sanctions including the suspension or expulsion of a Member.

20. Disciplinary proceedings shall be conducted by the Disciplinary Panel and the Office of the President as prescribed by these Bye-laws and Regulations.

SECTION 6
General Meetings

21. The Annual General Meeting of the Institute shall be held once in every year at such place and at such time as the Council may determine, provided that no more than sixteen months shall elapse between such meetings.

22. The Council may whenever it thinks fit convene a General Meeting and the Chief Executive Officer shall convene a General Meeting within one calendar month of receiving a requisition from any one hundred Individual Members, provided that the purpose for which the meeting is to be called is stated in the requisition.

23. The Council may make and publish Regulations for the submission of motions to General Meetings.

24. One month's notice in writing at the least of every Annual General Meeting and twenty-one days' notice in writing at the least of every other General Meeting (exclusive in every case both of the day on which it is served or deemed to be served and of the day for which it is given) specifying the place, the day and the hour of the meeting and in the case of special business the nature of that business, shall be given to the Members and to the auditors of the Institute.

25. The proceedings at any General Meeting or on the conduct of a Ballot shall not be invalidated by reason of any accidental informality or irregularity (including any accidental omission to give or any non-receipt of notice) or any want of qualification in any of the persons present or voting or by reason of any business being considered which is not specified in the notice unless such specification is a requirement of the Bye-laws or Regulations.

26. The business of the Annual General Meeting shall be to receive and consider the annual report of the Institute, the Honorary Treasurer's report and the balance sheet and accounts of the Institute with the auditor's report thereon; to determine the amount of subscriptions and other fees in accordance with Bye-law 6, to appoint auditors in accordance with Bye-law 90; any motions of which notice shall have been given in the notice of the meeting; and to consider any questions submitted to the meeting in accordance with Regulations . The minutes of the preceding Annual General Meeting containing a transcript of all resolutions passed shall be read or submitted to the Annual General Meeting. All other business transacted at any Annual General Meeting and all business transacted at any other General Meeting shall be deemed special business.

27. No business shall be transacted at any General Meeting unless a quorum is present. Save as herein otherwise provided fifty Individual Members present in person shall

constitute a quorum for an Annual General Meeting and twenty Individual Members present in person shall constitute a quorum for any other General Meeting.

28. If within half an hour from the time appointed for the holding of a General Meeting a quorum is not present the meeting, if convened on the requisition of Members, shall be dissolved. In any other case it shall stand adjourned to a date, time and place to be determined by the chair of the meeting and notified to Members, and if at such adjourned meeting a quorum is not present within half an hour from the time appointed for holding a meeting the Individual Members present shall be a quorum.

29. Every General Meeting shall be held at such place as the Council shall appoint. At General Meetings the chair shall be taken by the President. If the President is unable or unwilling to act the chair shall be taken by the Vice-President and failing him or her the Leader of Council. If none of those office holders is able or willing to act, the Individual Members present shall choose one of their number to chair the meeting. The President, though present at a General Meeting, May if he or she sees fit yield the chair to the Vice-President or the Leader of Council or in his or her absence to such other person as the Individual Members present may choose.

30. The chair of any General Meeting may, with the consent of the meeting, adjourn the meeting from time to time, and from place to place as the meeting may determine, but no business shall be transacted at any adjourned meeting other than the business left unfinished at the meeting from which the adjournment took place. No notice need be given of any adjourned meeting unless it is so directed in the resolution for adjournment.

31. At every General Meeting a resolution put to the vote of the meeting shall be decided on a show of hands, unless a Ballot is, before or upon the declaration of the result of the show of hands, demanded by the chair or by at least twenty Individual Members present in person or by proxy, and unless a Ballot be so demanded a declaration by the chair of the meeting that a resolution has been carried or carried by a particular majority, or lost or not carried by a particular majority shall be conclusive, and an entry to that effect in the minutes of the proceedings of the meeting shall be sufficient evidence of the fact so declared, without proof of the number or proportion of the votes given for or against such resolution.

32. If a Ballot is demanded it shall be taken at such time and place and in such a manner as the chair of the meeting shall direct (and may be Written Ballot or a Full Ballot – but see also provisions in Bye-law 40 regarding Full Ballots) provided always that no Ballot shall be taken on the election of the chair, the appointment of scrutineers or the adjournment of the meeting, and that notwithstanding a demand for a Ballot on any resolution, the meeting may continue for the transaction of any other business in respect of which a Ballot has not been demanded. The Individual Members or the chair, as the case may be, demanding a Ballot may nominate up to three persons, who need not be Members, to act as scrutineers. If a Ballot is demanded it shall be taken in such manner as the chair of the meeting directs, and the result of the Ballot shall be deemed the resolution of the General Meeting at which the Ballot was demanded.

33. In the case of an equality of votes, whether on a show of hands or in a Written Ballot, the chair of the meeting shall be entitled to a second or casting vote.

34. The persons entitled to vote at General Meetings are the Individual Members whose subscriptions are not in arrears (as defined in Regulations).

35. Every Individual Member present at a General Meeting in person or by proxy shall have one vote.

36. The instrument appointing a proxy shall be in writing in the form prescribed by Regulations and shall be signed and dated by the Individual Member appointing the proxy. A proxy must be an Individual Member.

37. The instrument appointing a proxy shall be delivered to the Chief Executive Officer not less than forty-eight hours before the time appointed for holding the meeting or adjourned meeting at which the person named in the instrument proposes to vote, and in default the instrument of proxy shall not be valid.

38. A vote given in accordance with the terms of an instrument of proxy shall be valid notwithstanding the previous death or insanity of the principal or revocation of the proxy, provided that no information in writing of the death, insanity or revocation as aforesaid shall have been received by the Chief Executive Officer before the commencement of the meeting or adjourned meeting at which the proxy is used.

39. No objection shall be made to the validity of any vote at a meeting except at the meeting or Ballot at which such vote shall be tendered, and every vote not disallowed at such meeting or Ballot shall be deemed valid. The chair of the meeting shall be the absolute judge of the validity of every vote tendered at any meeting or Ballot.

40. On the demand of one quarter of the Individual Members present in person or by proxy and entitled to vote, the chair shall rule that the motion be referred to a Full Ballot and that the decision of a Full Ballot shall be deemed to be the decision of the meeting. The meeting shall forthwith appoint three persons, who need not be Members, to act as scrutineers. The chair shall reduce the resolutions or amendments into the form of alternative propositions so as best to take the sense of the Individual Members on the substantial question or questions at issue. The wording of the resolution to appear on the Full Ballot paper shall be decided at the meeting by the Individual Members present in person or by proxy and entitled to vote at the meeting. Voting papers setting forth these propositions shall be issued within fourteen days after the meeting and shall be returnable so as to be receivable within twenty one days after the meeting. The scrutineers shall meet not less than twenty one days nor more than twenty eight days after the meeting and shall draw up a report of the result of the voting, stating what voting papers have been rejected for non-observance of the notes and directions thereon or disqualified by reason of the voter being in arrear or otherwise ineligible to vote. The report of the scrutineers shall be conclusive as to the result of the voting and the result shall take effect from the date of that report. In the event of a tie on a Full Ballot conducted under this Bye-law, the resolution shall be declared not carried.

SECTION 7
The Council

41. The management of the affairs of the Institute shall be vested in the Council, which, in addition to the powers and authority expressly conferred on it by these Bye-laws or otherwise, may in respect of the affairs of the Institute exercise all such powers and do all such things as may lead to the furtherance of the objects of the Institute including all such

powers and things as may be exercised or done by the Institute and are not by these Bye-laws expressly directed or required to be exercised or done by any other person or by the Institute in General Meeting.

Regulations

42. Council shall have power from time to time to make, repeal or alter Regulations as to the admission of Members, as to the management of the Institute and its affairs, as to the duties of any officers or employees of the Institute, as to the conduct of business of the Institute, the Council or any other Duly Appointed Body and as to any other matters or things within the powers or under the control of the Council provided that such Regulations shall not be inconsistent with the Charter or these Bye-laws and any Regulations (including any repeal or alteration) affecting or made in accordance with the provisions of the following Bye-laws shall not have effect unless approved by a simple majority vote at a General Meeting or by Ballot:

   - Bye-law 4: categories, privileges and obligations of Members
   - Bye-law 7: admission and removal of Members (but not, for the avoidance of doubt, Bye-law 6)
   - Bye-law 11: rights and responsibilities of Registered Practitioners
   - Bye-law 19: disciplinary proceedings.

Composition of the Council

43. The Council shall consist of the following persons all of whom must be Individual Members:

   a. Twelve Councillors elected by the Individual Members in accordance with Bye-laws 44 to 52

   b. Up to three Co-opted Councillors appointed by the Council with the approval of the Election Panel in accordance with Bye-law 53.

Election of Councillors and Vice-President

44. At the annual election to be held each year for the ensuing year commencing 1 January, the Individual Members shall elect a Vice-President to serve for one year and four Councillors to serve for three years. The election shall be held in accordance with Regulations.

45. The result of the election shall be declared in a list of the candidates in which the names shall be arranged in order of the number of votes received, the candidates with the highest number of votes to be at the head of the list.

46. The Vice-President shall be appointed as the President at the end of his or her year in office as Vice-President with effect from the date of appointment until 31 December in the year of appointment.

47. A retiring Councillor shall be eligible for re-election provided that a Councillor who has held office for six consecutive years will not be eligible for re-election until the annual election in the following year.

48. If the Institute, for any reason, fails to fill a vacant Councillor post then the Election Panel may determine how the vacancy shall be filled and the individual filling the vacancy shall commence his or her appointment on the date of appointment and, notwithstanding Bye-law 44, retire on 31 December in the second full calendar year following his or her appointment.

49. If the Institute, for any reason, fails to elect a Vice-President then the Election Panel may

(with the agreement of the Council) determine how the vacancy shall be filled.

50. Any person who is appointed President, Vice-President or a Councillor may not serve during his or her term in office on any Branch or Special Interest Group.

51. The Council shall make and publish Regulations prescribing the requirements and procedures for the nomination of candidates for election.

52. Voting in annual elections shall be by Full Ballot

Appointment of Co-opted Councillors

53. The Council may appoint up to three Individual Members as co-opted Councillors. Co-opted Councillors shall serve from the date of their appointment until 31 December in the same year and may be re-appointed for one further year ending on 31 December.

54. A co-opted Councillor may stand for election at an annual election and his or her time in office as a co-opted Councillor shall not count towards his or her maximum period in office as an elected Councillor.

Honorary Officers

55. The Councillors shall appoint from among their number the Leader of Council and Honorary Treasurer and may at any time remove them from those offices with the agreement of the Audit Panel. Appointments to those offices shall commence on the date of appointment and end on 31 December in the year of appointment, but may be renewed for subsequent terms of 1 year.

Termination of office and filling of vacancies

56. A Councillor shall vacate office and cease to be a member of the Council if he or she:

   a. ceases to be a Member;
   b. is suspended from membership of the Institute;
   c. is absent from meetings of the Council for three consecutive meetings without the consent of the Council and the Council resolves that his or her office be vacated;
   d. becomes bankrupt or makes any arrangement or composition with his or her creditors;
   e. becomes incapable by reason of mental disorder;
   f. becomes prohibited by law from holding office as a charity trustee;
   g. is removed by a resolution passed by a two thirds majority of the Individual Members present and voting at a General Meeting.

57. A Councillor may at any time give notice in writing of his or her resignation from the Council with effect from such date as the Councillor indicates.

58. When the office of a Councillor becomes vacant other than at the end of a term of office and when a contest took place at a previous election for that office, the unsuccessful candidate who received the highest number of votes in the contest shall, if willing and able to act, automatically fill the vacancy. If no contest for the office took place at the previous election of if there is no unsuccessful candidate able and willing to act, the Council may hold a by-election to fill the vacancy for the remainder of the original term of the vacated office. The term of office served by a Councillor filling a vacancy in this manner shall not be counted for the purpose

of calculating his or her maximum period in office

Proceedings of the Council

59. The Councillors may meet together for the despatch of business and adjourn or otherwise regulate their meetings and proceedings as they think fit

60. The Leader of Council may convene a meeting of the Council. The President on the requisition of any four members of the Council, shall convene a meeting of the Council.

61. The Leader of Council shall preside at meetings of the Council but in his or her absence the chair shall be taken by another Councillor chosen by the Councillors present.

62. The quorum necessary for the transaction of business at Council meetings shall be four[1] Councillors or such higher number as the Council may determine.

63. Every question at meetings of the Council shall be determined by a majority of the votes of the Councillors personally present and voting and if there is an equality of votes the chair of the meeting shall have a second or casting vote.

64. The Councillors may act and exercise all their powers notwithstanding that vacancies for the time being remain unfilled but while there are fewer Councillors than are required for a quorum the Councillors may only act for the purpose of increasing the number of Councillors or of summoning a General Meeting.

65. All acts done by any meeting of the Council or by any Duly Appointed Body shall,

---

[1] On 29 April 2008 the Council resolved that the quorum shall be six.

notwithstanding that it shall afterwards be discovered that there were defects in the appointment of all or any of the members of the Council or of such other duly Appointed Body or that any such person was disqualified from holding office or had vacated office, be as valid as if every such person had been duly appointed and was qualified and had continued in office.

66. A resolution in writing passed in such manner as may be prescribed by Regulations shall be as valid and effectual as if it had been passed at a meeting duly convened and held.

67. A resolution approved by electronic communication in such manner as may be prescribed by Regulations shall be as valid and effectual as if it had been passed at a meeting duly convened and held.

68. Whenever a Councillor has a personal interest in a matter to be discussed at a meeting, and whenever a Councillor has an interest in another organisation whose interests are reasonably likely to conflict with those of the Institute in relation to a matter to be discussed at a meeting, he or she must:

a. declare an interest before discussion begins on the matter;
b. withdraw from that part of the meeting unless expressly invited to remain;
c. in the case of personal interests not be counted in the quorum for that part of the meeting; and
d. in the case of personal interests withdraw during the vote and have no vote on the matter.

Delegation of Council's powers

69. The Council may by power of attorney or otherwise appoint any person to be the agent of the Institute for such purposes and on such conditions as they determine.

70. The Council may delegate any of its powers or functions in accordance with the conditions set out in these Bye-laws, and may delegate day to day management of the affairs of the Institute to the Chief Executive Officer or other staff.

Delegation to Task and Finish Groups

71. In the case of delegation to Task and Finish Groups:

   a. the resolution making that delegation shall specify those who shall serve or be asked to serve on such Task and Finish Group (although the resolution may allow the Task and Finish Group to make co-options up to a specified number);

   b. the composition of any such Task and Finish Group shall be entirely in the discretion of the Council and may comprise such Councillors (if any) as the resolution may specify;

   c. the deliberations of and any resolution passed or decision taken by any such Task and Finish Group shall be reported promptly and regularly to the Council and for that purpose every Task and Finish Group shall appoint a secretary;

   d. all delegations under this Bye-law shall be variable or revocable at any time;

   e. the Council may make such Regulations and impose such terms and conditions and give such mandates to any such Task and Finish Group as it may from time to time think fit;

   f. no Task and Finish Group shall knowingly incur expenditure or liability on behalf of the Institute except where authorised by the Council or in accordance with a budget which has been approved by the Council; and

   g. the meetings and proceedings of any Task and Finish Group shall be governed by the Bye-laws regulating the meetings and proceedings of the Council so far as applicable and not superseded by any Regulations.

Delegation of Investment Management

72. The Council may delegate to one or more investment managers, for such period and upon such terms as it may think fit, power at the discretion of the investment manager to buy and sell investments on behalf of the Institute. Where the Council makes such a delegation it shall ensure that the investment manager is given clear instructions as to investment policy;

73. Except to the extent that the Council has exercised its power of delegation, the Council shall arrange that the investments are kept under review by one or more independent professional advisers, who shall be required to inform the Council promptly about any changes in investments which appear to them to be desirable;

74. Without prejudice to any other of its powers, the Council may if it thinks fit invest in the name of or under the control of any corporation or corporations as nominees of the Council the whole or such part of the investments and income arising from those investments as the Council may determine;

75. The Council may pay reasonable remuneration to the investment managers, independent professional advisers or nominees for services rendered under the above provisions.

Sub-delegation to Boards

76. The Chief Executive Officer may, with the consent of the Council and in accordance

with the following provisions, delegate to Boards such of his or her functions as the Council may approve:

a. the composition of Boards may be prescribed by Regulations and otherwise, shall be agreed between the Chief Executive Officer and the Council;

b. each Board shall report promptly to the Council through the Chief Executive Officer on its activities and recommendations;

c. all delegations under this Bye-law shall be variable or revocable at any time by the Chief Executive Officer and the Council;

d. the Council may make such Regulations and impose such terms and conditions as it may from time to time think fit;

e. no Board shall knowingly incur expenditure or liability on behalf of the Institute except where authorised by the Chief Executive Officer and the Council or in accordance with a budget which has been approved by the Chief Executive Officer and the Council; and;

f. the meetings and proceedings of any Board shall be governed by the Bye-laws regulating the meetings and proceedings of the Council so far as applicable and not superseded by any Regulations.

SECTION 8
Office of the President

77. The Office of the President, shall be controlled by the President, assisted by the Vice-President and any other person (being an Individual Member, but not being a Councillor) as the Council may decide.

78. The Office of the President shall be provided by the Council with such resources as it may reasonably require (but at the discretion of the Council) in order to perform the functions reserved to it in these Bye-laws.

79. The Vice-President shall be elected and a President appointed in accordance with Bye-laws 44 to 52. Neither shall be Councillors.

80. The Vice-President shall:

a. chair the Policy Forum established under Bye-law 84;

b. attend meetings of the Council as an observer with a right to speak but not to vote;

c. assist the President in the running of the Office of the President and in the performance of the President's functions.

81. The President shall:

a. represent the Institute at functions and may delegate this role to any other appropriate Individual Member;

b. co-ordinate the work of each of the Panels reporting to the Office of the President;

c. sit ex-officio on each of the Panels;

d. in consultation with the Vice-President, any other member of the Office of the President and the Leader of Council, appoint the chair of each Panel;

e. oversee the process of appointing all other members of the Panels in accordance with Regulations;

f. be responsible for ensuring that each Panel reports its activities and deliberations promptly to the Council and complies with its terms of reference established by Regulations;

g. perform such functions as may be established by Regulations made by the Council in relation to the hearing of appeals from the decisions of hearing groups established by the Disciplinary Panel.

SECTION 9
Panels

82. The Council shall establish an Election Panel, an Audit Panel, a Disciplinary Panel, an Ethics Panel, an Admissions Panel, a Remuneration Panel, an Equal Opportunities Panel, an Editorial Panel and such other Panels as it may from time to time decide and shall make Regulations prescribing in respect of each Panel:

   a.   its powers and functions (including any powers of delegation);
   b.   its composition (provided that every member of a Panel shall be a Member;
   c.   the appointment and removal processes;
   d.   the requirements for the calling and holding of meetings;
   e.   the requirements for reporting the Panel's deliberations to the Office of the President and the Council;
   f.   such other matters as the Council thinks fit.

83. Each Panel shall be under the supervision and control of the Office of President, subject to the Regulations made in accordance with the preceeding Bye-law.

SECTION 10
Policy Forum

84. The Council shall establish a Policy Forum and shall make Regulations prescribing:

   a.   its powers and functions (including any powers of delegation);
   b.   its composition (provided that every member of the Forum shall be a Member;
   c.   the appointment and removal processes;
   d.   the requirements for the calling of and holding of meetings;

   e.   the requirements for reporting the Forum's deliberations to the Office of the President and the Council;
   f.   such other matters as the Council thinks fit.

85. The Policy Forum shall be chaired by the Vice-President and shall be under the supervision of the Office of President.

SECTION 11
Financial Matters

86. Subject to the authority of the Council the Honorary Treasurer shall supervise the financial affairs of the Institute and in particular the procedures for dealing with receipts, payments, assets and liabilities. The Honorary Treasurer shall submit a report to the Annual General Meeting of the Institute. In the absence of the Honorary Treasurer the report shall be submitted by the Leader of Council. The Council may make such Regulations as it sees fit as regards the payment of accounts and the signature of cheques and other financial documents.

87. The Council may borrow money for the purposes of the Institute and secure the repayment thereof or the fulfilment of any contract or engagement of the Institute in any manner, upon any security, and issue any debentures to secure the same.

88. The Council may, out of the monies of the Institute, by way of reserve fund from time to time reserve or set apart such sums as in its judgement are necessary or expedient to be applied at the discretion of the Council to meet the claims on or liabilities of the Institute, or to be used as a sinking fund to pay off debentures or incumbrances of the Institute, or for any other purpose of the Institute.

Expenses

89. Members of any Duly Appointed Body shall be paid out of the funds of the Institute all reasonable out of pocket expenses properly and necessarily incurred by them on behalf of the Institute.

Audit, Accounts and Reports

90. At each Annual General Meeting an auditor or auditors of the Institute shall be appointed by the members present. No person shall be appointed auditor of the Institute who is employed by or otherwise holds office in the Institute nor unless he or she is qualified for appointment as auditor of a company (other than an exempt private company) under the provisions of the Companies Act 1985 or any statutory re-enactment or modification thereof.

91. The Council shall comply with the requirements of the Charities Act 1993 (or any statutory re-enactment or modification thereof) as to keeping financial records, the audit or examination of accounts and the preparation and submission to the Charity Commission of:

   a. annual reports;
   b. annual returns;
   c. annual statements of accounts.

SECTION 12
Branches

92. The Council may establish Branches and shall prescribe Regulations for their membership, establishment, constitution, functions, financing, dissolution and procedures. The Council may from time to time alter the boundaries of any region served by a Branch.

93. The honorary secretary of a Branch shall deliver a report on the work of the Branch during each year for the scrutiny of the Council.

SECTION 13
Special Interest Groups and Organisations in Liaison

94. The Council may establish Special Interest Groups and shall prescribe Regulations for their membership, establishment, constitution, functions, financing, dissolution and procedures.

95. The honorary secretary of a Special Interest Group shall deliver a report on the work of the Special Interest Group during each year for the scrutiny of the Council.

Organisations in Liaison

96. The Council may from time to time recognise independent organisations which have objects similar to the objects of the Institute and whose membership includes a significant number of Members of the Institute as Organisations in Liaison with the Institute and may determine the rights and obligations of such Organisations in Liaison.

SECTION 14
Chief Executive Officer

97. The Chief Executive Officer shall be appointed by the Council for such term, upon such conditions and by such process as the Council may think fit. The Chief Executive Officer shall keep a record of all proceedings, shall draft reports, issue notices, and conduct correspondence and shall have charge of all books, papers and other property belonging to the Institute and shall have general day to

day conduct of the management of the Institute under the supervision of the Council.

Seal

98. The Seal of the Institute shall only be used by the authority of the Council. Any instrument to which the Seal is affixed may be signed by any two of the following:

    • The President
    • A Councillor
    • The Chief Executive Officer;

    or by such other persons as the Council may authorise.

Notices etc.

99. Unless otherwise provided in these Bye-laws, all notices, voting papers and circulars and other documents required by these Bye-laws to be given or sent may be given personally or by sending the same by post to the registered address of the Member, (or, as appropriate, to the principal office of the Institute) or by email or such other suitable means as the Council may prescribe, provided always that publication of a notice in the official journal of the Institute shall constitute good service of any notice to be served upon all Members.

100. Any such notice, voting paper, circular or other document sent through the post to the registered address of any Member shall have been deemed to have been served on the Member on the third day after the day it is posted if sent by first class post and on the fifth day after posting if sent by second class post, and in proving such service it shall be sufficient to prove that such notice, voting paper or circular was properly addressed and posted. Any such document sent by email shall be deemed served on the day after

transmission and in proving service it shall be sufficient to prove that the document was transmitted by the Institute's email server and was addressed to an email address provided by the Member to the Institute for the receipt of notices.

Indemnity

101. Every Councillor, other officer and every employee of the Institute carrying out the proper business of the Institute shall be indemnified by the Institute against, and it shall be the duty of the Council out of the funds of the Institute to pay, all costs, losses and expenses which any such person may incur or become liable to by reason of any contract entered into, or act or thing done or omitted to be done by him or her as such Councillor, officer or employee or in any other way in the proper discharge of his or her duty, including reasonable travelling expenses.

SECTION 15
Transitional arrangements

102. The Councillors to serve from 1 January 2008 shall be those individuals elected at the annual election in 2007, which shall be conducted in such manner as the Council in 2007 shall have prescribed.

103. Four of the Councillors elected in 2007 shall retire on 31 December 2008 and four of them shall retire on 31 December 2009. Those Councillors retiring shall be eligible for re-election with effect from 1 January 2009 and 1 January 2010 respectively.

104. The President shall be appointed to the role of Past President at the end of his or her year in office with effect from the date of appointment until 31 December in the year of appointment. The Past President shall be an

Honorary Officer and shall be a member of the Office of President for the duration of his or her term as Past President. The role of Past President shall be retained until 31 December 2009, pending review of the post on or before that date by the Council and, until that date (or such earlier date as may be resolved by the Council following its review).

CILIP Regulations 2007

The General Regulations, which sit under the Royal Charter and Bye-laws, were approved by Council in July 2007 and have since undergone minor amendments.

Drawn up under the Provisions of CILIP Bye-law 42.
Adopted by CILIP Council 16 July 2007
Amended by CILIP Council at various meetings up to and including 10 June 2010

Index

Under the provisions of Bye-Law, CILIP Council has the power to make regulations on any matters relevant to CILIP, provided the regulations are not inconsistent with the Charter and Bye-Laws. In addition, certain Bye-laws oblige Council to make regulations to give effect to their provisions. As at 16 July 2007, Council has made regulations on the following matters:

General Regulations

General Regulations

Definitions

1. Words and phrases defined in the Institute's Royal Charter and Bye-laws shall have the same meanings when used in these Regulations.

Categories and Privileges of Members

Bye-law 4

Regulations made under Bye-law 4 require the approval of a simple majority vote at a General Meeting or by Ballot

2. There shall be the following categories of Member:

2.1 Individual members comprising:

2.1.1 Affiliate Members, being individuals who may work in libraries or information services but who are not eligible for admission as Chartered Members or Chartered Fellows;

2.1.2 Certificated Affiliates, being Registered Practitioners admitted to ACLIP status in accordance with these Regulations who are eligible for admission as Chartered Members but have not yet been so admitted;

2.1.3 Associate Members, being individuals who are eligible for admission as Chartered Members or Chartered Fellows but who have not yet been so admitted;

2.1.4 Chartered Members, being Registered Practitioners admitted to MCLIP status in accordance with these Regulations;

2.1.5 Chartered Fellows, being Registered Practitioners admitted to FCLIP status in accordance with these Regulations;

2.1.6 Honorary Fellows, being individuals admitted to Hon FCLIP status in accordance with these Regulations; and

2.1.7 Organisation Members, being corporate bodies, societies and other organisations which maintain, or are interested in, libraries and/or information services.

3. The privileges attached to each category of Member are as follows:

3.1 Certificated Affiliates, Chartered Members, Chartered Fellows and Honorary Fellow have full membership of the Institute with all rights and privileges including the right to vote and the right to use the post-nominals applicable to their status;

3.2 Affiliate Members, Associate Members have full membership of the Institute with all rights and privileges including the right to vote; but excluding the right to use post-nominals;

3.3 Organisation Members have the right to appoint one or more named representatives nominated by the Organisation Member and approved by the Council of the Institute. Such representatives shall enjoy all the privileges of a Member except that they shall not be entitled to be elected onto or to remain on the Register of Registered Practitioners unless they are themselves Certificated Affiliates, Chartered Members or Chartered Fellows. Nor shall they, by virtue only of their appointment as a nominated representative, be entitled to vote, to hold office within the Institute, or to use post-nominals.

Subscriptions

Bye-law 6

4. Date of Payment

4.1 Annual subscriptions shall be due and payable in advance each year on the anniversary of the Member joining.

4.2 If a Member's subscription is not paid within 60 days of the due date for payment then his or her membership shall be deemed to have lapsed and the Member shall not be entitled to vote on any matter in respect of which he or she would otherwise be entitled to vote.

4.3 If a Member whose right to vote has lapsed under Regulation 4.2 pays his or her subscription within a further 60 days then his or her rights to vote shall be restored.

4.4 A Member whose subscription is not paid within 120 days of the due date for payment shall be deemed to have resigned and shall automatically cease to be a Member.

5. Payment by Instalment

5.1 Where any resolution adopted by the annual general meeting of the Institute permits subscriptions, entrance, registration, admission and other fees to be paid by instalments, the provisions of Regulation 4 regarding suspension and termination of membership shall not apply provided each instalment is paid by its due date.

5.2 In the event of an instalment not being paid by the due date, the full subscription or other payment shall fall due immediately and the provisions of Regulation 4 shall apply as if in the case of non-payment.

5.3 The Chief Executive Officer shall have the power to suspend the operation of Regulation 4 if a payment is received after the due date as a result of circumstances outside the Member's control or in cases of hardship.

5.4 Where voting rights are suspended or membership terminated under Regulation 4, no instalment already received shall be refunded to the Member.

Admission and Reinstatement of Members

Bye-laws 7–8

Regulations made under Bye-law 7 require the approval of a simple majority vote at a General Meeting or by Ballot

6. Names of individuals or institutions seeking membership of the Institute will be placed before a meeting of the Council.

7. Admission will be by the majority vote of those Councillors present.

8. The decision on the admission of any candidate may be deferred if agreed by a majority vote of those Councillors present.

9. The Council may also by majority vote reinstate Members whose memberships have been terminated, including reinstatement to the Register of Registered Practitioners.

10. In the event of an application for reinstatement by a person who resigned from his/her former membership of the Institute (or whose membership terminated for any other reason) whilst subject to complaint under consideration under the Institute's disciplinary Procedure, the Council may require such person to co-operate in the completion of the outstanding disciplinary process before considering his/her reinstatement as a Member or as a condition of that re-instatement.

11. The decision of the Council as to the admission or reinstatement of a Member and as to the category of membership to which a person is admitted shall be final and binding.

2. The Council may delegate decisions on the admission and reinstatement of Members on such terms as it thinks fit provided that the decision of any non-admitted person or body shall be subject to appeal to the Council.

Publication of the Registers of Members and Registered Practitioners

Bye-laws 9–10

13. The current Registers of Members and Registered Practitioners will be made available either in print or electronic form or both.

Professional qualifications

Bye-law 11

Regulations made under Bye-law 11 require the approval of a simple majority vote at a General Meeting or by Ballot

14. The Regulations for professional qualifications, by which Members are admitted to the Register of Registered Practitioners, are given at Appendix A.

Exemption from provisions of Bye-law 11

Bye-law 12

15. The Council will ensure that the terms of reference of the Chartership Board include the responsibility of the Board to draw attention to any need for the use of these powers of exemption, and for any subsequent changes to regulations.

Power to Nominate Honorary Fellows

Bye-laws 15-16

16. Nominations for the award of an honorary fellowship may be made by Members, Branches, Special Interest Groups, or the Council.

17. Nominations may be made for individuals who have made a significant contribution to the profession. Nominees need not be Members of the Institute. The criteria for nominations shall be published by the Institute when the call for nominations is made.

18. Nominations for the award of honorary fellowships will be considered in the first instance by an Honorary Awards Panel (established annually by Council as part of the Office of the President), which will propose to Council such of the nominations as it thinks fit.

19. Decisions on the award of honorary fellowships will be made by Council, and Council's decision shall be final.

Ethical Principles and Code of Professional Practice

Bye-laws 17-18

20. The Ethical Principles and Code of Professional Practice are given at Appendix B.

Disciplinary Proceedings

Bye-laws 19-20

Regulations made under Bye-law 20 require the approval of a simple majority vote at a General Meeting or by Ballot

21. These Regulations are given at Appendix B.

Submissions of motions to the AGM

Bye-law 23

22. Notices of motion shall be made in writing and shall be served on the Chief Executive

Officer not less than 60 days before the date of the meeting.

23. Any Member who desires to move an amendment to a notice of motion shall serve on the Chief Executive Officer a notice in writing of such amendment at least one week before the meeting.

Proxy votes

Bye-laws 36-38

24. An Individual Member who is entitled to be present and to vote at a general meeting may appoint a proxy to vote on his or her behalf. A proxy must be an Individual Member.

25. The instrument appointing a proxy shall be delivered in such manner or manners as the Council may require.

26. The instrument appointing a proxy and the power of attorney or other authority (if any) under which it is signed (or a notarially certified or office copy thereof) shall be deposited at the registered office of the Institute not less than forty-eight hours before the time appointed for holding the meeting or

adjourned meeting at which the person named in the instrument proposes to vote and in default the instrument of proxy shall not be treated as valid. No instrument appointing a proxy shall be valid after the expiration of twelve months from the date of its execution.

27. Any instrument appointing a proxy shall be in the following form (see below) or as near thereto as circumstances will admit.

28. The instrument appointing a proxy shall be deemed to confer authority to demand or join in demanding a poll.

Minutes of Meetings of Council, and other Duly Appointed Bodies

Bye-law 42

29. Proper minutes shall be recorded of all resolutions and proceedings of meetings of the Council and other Duly Appointed Bodies, and every minute signed by the chair of the meeting to which it relates or by the chair of a subsequent meeting shall be sufficient evidence of the facts therein stated. Minutes shall be distributed in a timely fashion.

"**Chartered Institute of Library and Information Professionals**

Name of Member appointing the proxy: _____

Address: _____

I hereby appoint [*name of proxy*] of [*address of proxy*] as my proxy to vote in my name and on my behalf at the meeting of the Institute to be held on [*date*], and at any adjournment thereof.

This form is to be used in respect of the resolutions mentioned below as follows:

Resolution 1:	*for	*against	*abstain	*as the	*no vote
Resolution 2:	*for	*against	*abstain	*as the	*no vote
All other resolutions properly put to the meeting	*for	*against	*abstain	*as the	*no vote

*Strike out whichever is not desired. If no indication is given, the proxy may vote as he or she thinks fit.

Signed: _____

Dated: _____ "

Nominations for elections of Vice-President and Councillors and election process

Bye-laws 44-52

30. Candidates for election to the Council and to the post of Vice-President must be nominated by at least 5 Individual Members entitled to vote at the annual election. Every nominator shall provide to the Chief Executive Officer a supporting statement of up to 100 words in favour of the nominee.

31. All nominations together with supporting statements, must be signed by the requisite number of Members qualified to vote and must be received by the Chief Executive Officer by such time as is specified by the Elections Panel.

32. Candidates who are nominated as both Vice-President and Councillor, shall inform the Chief Executive Officer of the post for which they wish to stand but they may not stand for election as both Vice-President and Councillor.

33. Each nominee shall be required to send a signed statement of not more than 300 words about himself / herself for the information of voters (hereafter called a manifesto). The nominee shall take full responsibility for the content of the manifesto but the Chief Executive Officer shall have discretion to refuse to accept a text which he or she reasonably considers to be personally abusive, libellous or otherwise offensive.

34. Not less than 14 days before the issuing of voting papers, the Chief Executive Officer shall cause a notice to be published in the journal of the Institute, or otherwise despatched to Individual Members qualified to vote, stating:

34.1 The date on which voting papers will be issued;

34.2 That any qualified Individual Member failing to receive a voting paper must notify the Chief Executive Officer of that fact within 7 days after the date for the issue of voting papers.

35. Voting papers shall be despatched to Individual Members entitled to vote and shall be printed in such a way, by means of watermarking and numbering, as to make deception by photocopying or reproduction immediately apparent.

36. In issuing voting papers the Chief Executive Officer shall inform Individual Members entitled to vote as to the offices and places on Council for which nominations did not exceed the number of places to be filled and of the names of the persons accordingly to be declared elected without contest.

37. The manifestos of candidates and the supporting statements shall be provided to Individual Members entitled to vote separately from the ballot paper.

38. The Written Ballot papers shall contain no information about candidates except their names. On each ballot paper names shall be printed alphabetically.

39. With each Written Ballot paper there shall be sent an envelope. The envelope shall bear no marking by which voters may be identified.

40. The Chief Executive Officer shall provide instructions on the manner in which the Written Ballot paper is to be completed and general information on the conduct of the election. Such information shall state at least:

40.1 The fact that failure to adhere to the instructions renders the ballot paper liable to be rejected by the scrutineers;

40.2 The latest date for receipt of Written Ballot papers; and

40.3 The right of Members to attend the count.

41. In the event of any dispute on the procedure for the count or on the validity of any Written Ballot paper, the scrutineers shall determine the issue by majority vote of the scrutineers. In the event of a tie, the chair of the meeting shall have a casting vote. For the Elections Panel see Regulations 57-59.

42. It shall be the duty of the Chief Executive Officer to advise the scrutineers on any matter arising at the count.

43. Whenever possible, the counting of the votes shall be completed in a single day. If it is found necessary to continue the count on a second day, the scrutineers and the Chief Executive Officer shall make arrangements to ensure the security of the ballot papers in the intervening period.

44. The scrutineers and the Chief Executive Officer may make use of such staff of the Institute or other persons as they see fit (whether Members or not) to assist in the count and may, with the consent of the Honorary Treasurer, make payments for such work.

45. The scrutineers shall have absolute discretion to admit or not admit Written Ballot papers that they consider not in conformity with the instructions given to voters or which may otherwise be considered spoiled.

46. Written Ballot papers accepted as valid shall be counted in such manner as the scrutineers shall determine and the candidates receiving the most votes shall be declared elected for the number of places to be filled.

47. If there is a tie between any two or more candidates and the addition of one vote would render one or more of the candidates successful, the scrutineers shall exercise their power under these regulations to decide the result forthwith by lot in such manner as to give each such candidate an equal chance of success.

48. If at any election a vacancy requires to be filled under Bye-law 45 for a period of less than a full term (in addition to vacancies for a full term) the candidate or candidates with the highest number of votes shall be declared elected for the full term and the candidate with the next highest number of votes shall be declared elected for the period of less than a full term.

49. The scrutineers shall cause the result of the count to be declared to any Members of the Institute attending the count and shall forthwith approve and sign a report stating:

49.1 Which places were filled without contest and the candidates declared elected;

49.2 The number of votes cast for each candidate for contested places and the candidates declared elected;

49.3 The number of Written Ballot papers issued and returned; and

49.4 The number of returns declared invalid with such analysis of reasons and commentary as the scrutineers think fit.

50. The scrutineers shall declare the result immediately by communicating with the candidates. The report of the scrutineers shall be printed in the journal of the Institute and shall be presented to the next following annual general meeting.

51. The Chief Executive Officer shall inform all existing Councillors of the result of the election.

52. The Chief Executive Officer shall make arrangements for the Written Ballot papers including those declared unacceptable, to be retained in secure conditions for a period of 60 days after the date of the count.

53. If, within 14 days after of the count, a candidate, supported by the persons who nominated that candidate and at least five other Members, declares that he/she has reason to believe that errors were made in the counting of the Written Ballot papers, the scrutineers, in the presence of not more than three persons chosen by the candidate and such other persons as the Council may determine, shall conduct a recount and may make such alteration to the result of the count as previously announced as they see fit. Any such alteration shall be without prejudice to the validity of anything done by a person previously declared elected in the intervening period.

54. When a by-election is held to fill a vacancy on Council, the procedure shall (with necessary changes) follow that prescribed above for annual elections.

Council quorum

Bye-law 62

55. The quorum necessary for the transaction of business at Council meetings shall be six Councillors.[1]

Council written resolutions and electronic communications

Bye-laws 66 and 67

56. A resolution of the Council without holding a meeting may be passed by a majority of not less than six Councillors approving the resolution. Evidence of approval may be the signature of the relevant Councillor on a copy of the resolution returned to the Chief Executive Officer by post or by fax or approval given by email received from any email

address of the Councillor registered with the Institute for the purpose of sending and receiving notices.

Regulations for Task and Finish Groups, Panels and Boards

Bye-laws 71-76 and 82-83

57. The categories of committees and sub-committees shall be as follows:

57.1 **Task and Finish Groups** may be established by Council to advise Council and/or take decisions on behalf of Council, especially when detailed consideration of matters by expert groups is required.

57.2 **Boards** may be established by the Chief Executive Officer with the approval of Council. Boards shall report to Council through the Chief Executive Officer. The remit of each Board shall be determined by the Chief Executive Officer with the approval of the Council. The function of Boards shall be to advise on and perform particular internal and regulatory matters of the Institute and to deal with matters managed in partnership with other bodies. The need for each Board shall be reviewed from time to time by Council. Such reviews shall take place at least every three years. These provisions do not apply to boards of directors of any company owned or controlled by the Institute.

57.3 **Panels** may be established by Council, including the Election Panel, the Audit Panel, the Disciplinary Panel and the Ethics Panel as set out below.

58. **The Elections Panel** shall report to the Office of the President and its functions are to:

58.1 Establish the skill sets required for Councillors and inform Members of the skills most sought;

---

[1] As agreed by Council on 29 April 2008

58.2 Establish the role profile of Councillors;

58.3 Oversee, and advise on, the whole election process to CILIP Council from the call for nominations to the declaration of results;

58.4 Ensure compliance with the Bye-laws and Regulations relating to elections to Council;

58.5 Encourage Members to stand for nomination;

58.6 Provide scrutineers to officiate at counts of ballot papers for elections to Council;

58.7 Develop and promote a Framework of Good Practice for electoral procedures in Branches and Special Interest Groups;

58.8 Advise the President on electoral practice and improvements and developments that could be made;

58.9 Produce reports of concern for consideration by the President when there is reason to suspect poor management or malpractice in an election within the Institute; and

58.10 Produce an annual report to the President on electoral matters in the Institute including scrutineers' reports on elections to Council.

59. On receiving a report from the Elections Panel the President should raise with the Council any matters of concern.

60. The Elections Panel shall comprise the President (ex officio) and at least 8 other individuals appointed from among the Members under the appointments process to be established by the Office of the President under these Regulations. The chair of the Elections Panel shall be appointed by the President from among the members of the Panel and the President may with the approval of the Council also remove the chair of the Panel from that office. In addition, assistant scrutineers may be appointed who will be authorised to officiate at election counts but will not be members of the Panel.

61. Appointments to the Elections Panel shall be for terms of three years (running from 1st January in the year the appointment is made or is to take effect) and members of the Panel may be appointed for one further term after which at least one year must elapse before any further appointment to the Elections Panel.

62. **The Audit Panel** shall report to the Office of the President and its function shall be to provide independent scrutiny and monitoring of financial matters and other areas of governance within the Institute. Its aim is to ensure probity and integrity in such activities. In discharging its duties it shall in particular:

62.1 Monitor the integrity of financial statements of the organisation;

62.2 Review the organisation's internal financial controls and internal audit function;

62.3 Oversee the external audit process;

62.4 Review risk management within the Institute;

62.5 Monitor and review governance, including information governance, matters within the Institute;

62.6 Oversee a whistle-blowing procedure within the Institute;

62.7 Report to Council when necessary but at least annually; and

62.8 Undertake periodic reviews and assessments of the performance of Council and Councillors.

63. The Audit Panel shall comprise the President (ex officio) and five other individuals, appointed from among the Members under the appointments process established by the Office of the President under these Regulations. The chair of the Audit Panel shall be appointed by the President from among the members of the Panel and may,

with the approval of the Council, be removed by him or her.

64. Appointments to the Audit Panel shall be for terms of three years (running from 1st January on the year the appointment is made or is to take effect) and members of the Panel may be appointed for one further term after which at least one year must elapse before any further appointment to the Audit Panel.

65. No Councillor or person who was a Councillor in the previous year may be a member of the Audit Panel.

66. The Audit Panel shall have the power to invite observers to attend their meetings for special purposes, either for a period of up to one year or for particular meetings.

67. **The Disciplinary Panel** shall report to the Office of the President and its function is to consider all complaints relating to the conduct of Members in accordance with the Disciplinary Regulations set out in Appendix B. The Disciplinary Panel shall from time to time report on its activities to the office of the President which will be responsible for overseeing its work. The Disciplinary Panel shall also report to the Council on the outcome of each case considered by it in accordance with the Disciplinary Regulations.

68. The Disciplinary Panel shall comprise the President (ex officio), a maximum of a further 25 individuals, all being Members, of the Institute who shall, if possible, have been Members of the Institute (or a predecessor or analogous organisation) for at least ten years. For the avoidance of doubt, members of the Disciplinary Panel are required to be Members but not necessarily Chartered Members.

69. Members of the Disciplinary Panel shall be appointed under the appointments process established by the Office of the President

under these Regulations. The chair of the Disciplinary Panel shall be appointed by the President from among the members of the Panel and may, with the approval of Council, be removed by him or her.

70. Appointments to the Disciplinary Panel shall be for terms of one year (running from 1st January in the year of appointment or the year in which appointment is to take effect) and members may be re-appointed for further terms.

71. The President shall not take part in hearings of the Disciplinary Panel.

72. **The Ethics Panel** shall report to the Office of the President and its functions are to:

72.1 Provide confidential advice to Members facing ethical problems at work;

72.2 Alert the President and the Institute to more general ethical issues as they emerge and promote a better understanding of professional ethics within the Institute; and

72.3 Keep the Ethical Principles and Code of Professional Conduct (as approved by Council), and the Institute's ethics website, under review and recommend changes when necessary.

73. The Ethics Panel shall comprise the President (ex officio) and up to 15 individuals appointed from among the Members under the appointments process established by the Office of the President under these Regulations. The chair of the Ethics Panel shall be appointed by the President from among the members of the Panel and may, with the approval of Council, be removed by him or her.

74. Appointments to the Ethics panel shall be for terms of one year (running from 1st January in the year of appointment or the year in which appointment is to take effect) and

members may be re-appointed for further terms.

Process of Appointment to Panels

75. The process of making appointments to Panels shall be established by the President and shall be compatible with the standards and processes for making appointments to the boards of non-departmental public bodies.

Composition of Boards and Tenure of Board Members

76. Boards shall comprise such persons as the Chief Executive Officer shall decide with the approval of the Council. The chair of each Board shall be appointed by Council from amongst the Board's members and must be an Individual Member.

77. The tenure of members of the Boards shall be determined by the Chief Executive Officer with the approval of the Council.

Procedures at Meetings of Panels, Boards and Task and Finish Groups

78. The meetings and proceedings of every Panel, Board and Task and Finish Group shall be governed by the Bye-laws regulating the meetings of the Council so far as applicable and not superseded by Regulations.

79. The quorum necessary for the transaction of business at a Panel, Board or Task and Finish Group (except the Accreditation and Chartership Boards and the CILIP Assessment Panel) shall be one third of voting members. Where the voting membership is not divisible by three the lower divisor will be used provided it is three or more.

80. The quorum for the Accreditation Board shall be one-half of its members. If the total voting membership is not divisible by two, then the quorum shall be one half rounded up to the nearest whole number.

81. The quorum for the Chartership Board shall be one-half of its members. If the total voting membership is not divisible by two, then the quorum shall be one half rounded up to the nearest whole number.

82. The quorum for the CILIP Assessment Panel shall be one-half of its members. If the total voting membership is not divisible by two, then the quorum shall be one half rounded up to the nearest whole number.

Policy Forum

Bye-laws 84 and 85

83. The Regulations for the Policy Forum are set out in Appendix E.

Expenses

84. Reasonable expenses incurred by members of Duly Appointed Bodies in attending meetings shall be reimbursed by the Institute. Expenses incurred by Institute representatives on joint and external committees may also be reimbursed. Expenses incurred by observers shall not normally be reimbursed by the Institute, but the Council may authorise reimbursement if it is satisfied that the interests of the Institute make it appropriate to do so.

Open Meetings

85. Individual Members and the nominated representatives of Organisation Members may attend and observe as visitors meetings and other forms of debate (including electronic debates by bulletin board or

otherwise) of Duly Appointed Bodies (other than those of the Disciplinary Panel). Visitors shall be excluded from any part of a meeting at which a Duly Appointed Body is discussing confidential business.

Payment of accounts and signature of cheques

Bye-law 86

86. Payment of accounts

86.1 Heads of a department shall be responsible for managing their department's budget and authorising expenditure.

86.2 Invoices and other requests for payments must be signed by the head of the relevant department, or by another member of the department specifically authorised to do so.

86.3 In exceptional circumstances, payments may be authorised by the Chief Executive Officer, a director or the head of finance.

87. Signature of cheques

87.1 Cheques must be signed by two authorised signatories, at least one of whom must come from the A list.

87.2 The lists of cheque signatories are:

A List (finance staff): director of finance, senior financial accountant and accounts controller

B List (non-finance staff): Chief Executive Officer, directors, and other senior members of staff determined from time to time by the director of finance and notified to the Institute's bankers.

Branches

Bye-law 92

88. A Branch shall appoint a chair, an honorary secretary or honorary secretaries, an honorary treasurer, and such other members as required to form a committee to manage its affairs.

89. A Branch shall not take any action, other than by recommendation to Council, which affects other Branches, the general conduct of the Institute or the external relations of the Institute.

90. The funds and facilities of a Branch shall not be employed to promote the candidature of any candidate for election to office of the Institute; but this shall not prevent the provision of factual information on a non-discriminatory basis.

91. Subject to approval by Council, Branches may create sub-branches to facilitate provision of services to members.

92. Members may pay the Institute an additional fee to be a corresponding member of any Branch of which they are not a member. A corresponding member is entitled to be placed on the mailing list of the Branch and to participate in its meetings and events, but may not vote in Branch proceedings or stand for election within the Branch. [Add opt-in provision subject to decisions at Council on 16 July]

93. A member of a Branch who retires from employment to an address away from that Branch may choose to remain in membership of that Branch.

94. The form of Branch rules, which may be amended for any Branch with the approval of the Council is set out in Appendix F.

Special Interest Groups

Bye-law 94

95. The procedure as set out in Appendix C of the Special Interest Group Rules set out in Appendix F, shall be used by Council when considering the creation or dissolution of Special Interest Groups.

96. Members may join one or more SIGs by notice to the Chief Executive Officer. Council shall determine whether and in what circumstances an additional subscription is to be levied in respect of membership of SIGs and the level of any such additional subscription.

97. A SIG shall appoint a chair, an honorary secretary or honorary secretaries, an honorary treasurer, and such other members as required to form a committee to manage its affairs.

98. A SIG shall not take any action, other than by recommendation to Council, which affects other SIGs, the general conduct of the Institute or the external relations of the Institute.

99. The funds and facilities of a SIG shall not be employed to promote the candidature of any candidate for election to office of the Institute; but this shall not prevent the provision of factual information on a non-discriminatory basis.

100. Subject to approval by Council, SIGs may create sub-groups to facilitate provision of services to members.

Subscribing Members of SIGs

101. The Institute recognises that there are people who are interested in the work of one or more of the Institute's SIGs but who would not wish to become Members of the Institute. The Institute wishes to be hospitable to such people and is therefore willing to allow such people to become subscribing members of a SIG. Subscribing members are entitled to the advantages of membership of the SIG, at whatever annual fee the SIG committee shall decide, but are not members of the Institute.

102. Subscribing members may become members of the SIGs committee, but not in the office of chair, honorary secretary or honorary treasurer, nor may they form the majority of members of the committee.

103. Subscribing members may vote on matters internal to the SIG.

104. Subscribing members cannot comprise more than 25 % of the total membership of a SIG.

Regulations for Affiliated Members

Bye-law 4

Regulations made under Bye-law 4 require the approval of a simple majority vote at a General Meeting or by Ballot

105. The Regulations for Affiliated Members are given at Appendix D.

Regulations for the Retired Members' Guild

Bye-law 42

106. The Regulations are given at Appendix C.

Organisations in Liaison

Bye-law 96

107. The rights and obligations arising from liaison agreements are set out below. Liaison may be terminated at any time by notice from either side.

108. The Institute shall have the right to appoint an observer to the governing body of each

organisation in liaison to effect liaison and to promote partnership activities.

109. An organisation in liaison is entitled to print on its notepaper and reports "An organisation in liaison with the Chartered Institute of Library & Information Professionals".

110. The Institute, if so requested, will offer the following facilities to an organisation in liaison:

110.1 To report news of the organisation's activities in the Institute's journal, at the discretion of the editor; and

110.2 To publish notices of organisation meetings the Institute's journal, subject to space being available.

Appendix A
Regulations for Qualifications and Revalidation

Bye-laws 11, 12 and 15

Bye-law 11

NOTE: These Regulations were approved by CILIP Council in July 2004. They are contained in a set of handbooks for candidates working towards Certification (ACLIP), Chartered Membership (MCLIP) and Fellowship (FCLIP) and in a handbook for Chartered Members who wish to apply for revalidation. All of these are available on the CILIP website. References to appendices etc. are to additional documents that are available as separate documents on the website. The Regulations apply from 1 April 2005.

From January 2009 there is a Single Category for ACLIP Certification. Please refer to previous Yearbooks for information regarding the former Categories 1 and 2. Category 2 continues until the end of July 2009 from which time the Single Category will become the sole means of applying for ACLIP Certification.

Section 1: Gaining CILIP Certification

2005 Regulations drawn up under Bye-law 11

1 Registration

- All applicants must be current members of CILIP (Affiliated Member or Associate Member)
- All applicants must be members currently employed in library and information work for two or more years, who have either:

  taken part in work-based learning activities within their own organisation

  or

  have been involved in relevant out of work self-development activities.

Registration forms are available via the CILIP website at www.cilip.org.uk/ or in the CILIP *Handbook for Certification.*

2 Application

Each applicant will submit a portfolio including:

- Application form
- Curriculum Vitae
- Personal statement, of no more than 4 x A4 sheets, demonstrating experience and/or experiential learning against agreed criteria.
- A Personal Development Plan
- A supporting letter which should evidence achievement and indicate potential for future development, where appropriate. (CILIP will supply a template for this purpose.)

2.1 Notes on submission

- All applications must be in the English or Welsh language

- The CV and supporting letter should be word-processed
- The application form, personal statement, and Personal Development Plan should be on the designated form
- Electronic submission is acceptable, but copies of certificates etc. may be sent by post accompanied by a copy of your application form
- All applications for assessment should be accompanied by the appropriate fee, to be determined annually by CILIP AGM.

2.2 Confidentiality

All applications (electronic and hard copy) will be stored and treated in a confidential manner by CILIP Assessment Panels.

3 Assessment

Each application will normally be assessed by CILIP Assessment Panels in the member's Branch or Home Nation. The submission should be sent to the named Officer of the CILIP Regional Branch or Home Nation. A full list of these officers is available on the website at www.cilip.org.uk/ or from the Qualifications and Professional Development Department.

Overseas members should submit their applications to the Qualifications and Professional Development Department in the first instance.

All applicants will be notified of the outcome in writing within 10 working days of the date of the assessment meeting. All documents will be returned to successful applicants once Certification has been confirmed.

3.1 Criteria for assessment:

All applicants will have gained knowledge and experience of library and information work in a variety of roles and should be able to reflect on that experience, using the templates provided.

All candidates must demonstrate:

1. an ability to evaluate personal performance and service performance.
2. an understanding of the ways in which their personal, technical and professional skills have developed through training and development activities and/or through practice
3. an appreciation of the role of library and information services in the wider community.

3.2 Form of assessment

The CILIP Assessment Panel will determine a method for the additional assessment of any application, if necessary, which may include either of the following:

(a) a request for additional written information or documentary evidence
(b) a request for the candidate to attend an interview

3.3 Admission to the Certification Register

The date of admission to the register will normally be that on which the CILIP Assessment Panel accepts the application.

Once admitted to the Register you must remain in membership of CILIP to retain the use of the post nominal letters ACLIP and to describe yourself as a Certified Member.

4 Appeals

Candidates whose applications are rejected have a right of Appeal, according to procedures approved by Council. A copy of the Appeals Procedures will be sent to unsuccessful candidates. (*See Appendix 1 to these Regulations*).

5 Progression to Chartership

ACLIPs will be eligible to apply for Chartered Membership. Information on applying for

Chartership can be found at www.cilip.org.uk or from the Qualifications and Professional Development Department.

In order to progress to Chartered Membership you must be an Associate Member.

6 Appendices

Appendix 1 Appeals procedure

1) An appeal may be made against a decision of the Assessment Panel not to accept a candidate's Application for Certification.

2) A candidate whose submission is not accepted will be sent the following documents by Recorded Delivery:-
   (a) A letter informing the candidate of the decision and the date of the Assessment Panel meeting at which it was made.
   (b) A summary of the points made at the Assessment Panel meeting and copies of the assessment documents of Panel members, setting out the reasons for rejection.
   (c) A copy of this Appeals Procedure.

3) A candidate who wishes to appeal against the decision of the Assessment Panel must do so within six weeks of the date of receipt of the Recorded Delivery letter referred to in 2. The Appeal must be made in writing to the Chief Executive.

4) The only grounds on which an Appeal may be made are:
   (a) That all or part of the information used by the Assessment Panel was biased or incorrect due to no fault of the candidate and that the Panel did not know this at the time it took its decision.
   (b) That the Assessment Panel failed to follow its own published procedures and that this materially affected its decision.

5) The Chief Executive will decide whether there is a prima facie case for appeal. Where there is not s/he will inform the candidate of the reason for his ruling. In such cases there will be no further appeal.

6) Where there is a prima facie case for appeal the Chief Executive will select an Appeal Panel of three from a panel chosen annually by Council from amongst its membership for this purpose. (These may not be members of a CILIP Assessment Panel, or the Chartership Board).

7) The Chief Executive will set a date for the hearing of the Appeal to take place within six weeks of the date of receipt of the candidate's written Appeal.

8) The Chief Executive will send to each member appointed to the Appeal Panel a copy of the candidate's portfolio submission, the papers sent to the candidate referred to in 2 above, and any papers sent by the candidate in support of his/her Appeal.

9) The candidate will be invited to attend the hearing of the Appeal and may be accompanied by a supporter. A representative of the CILIP Assessment Panel and the Head, Qualifications and Professional Development Department (or the nominee of either) should be present to represent the Assessment Panel and its office based procedures.

10) At an Appeal Panel hearing the matters for consideration will be limited to:
    (a) Evidence from the candidate concerning the grounds for the Appeal, and details of how the information and/or procedures were faulty. The candidate should offer the correct information to the Appeal Panel. Panel members may question both the candidate and the representative of the Assessment Panel. The Assessment

Panel representative should explain the reasons for any failure to comply with published procedures.

(b)   The candidate may ask the supporter to speak on matters concerning the grounds for the Appeal. The supporter may not assist (or speak for) the appellant in answering professional questions put by the Panel.

(c)   The Appeal Panel will be concerned solely to test the candidate's claim that the Assessment Panel used faulty information, biased statements or failed in its own procedures.

11)   Where the Appeal Panel finds that the candidate's claim as set out in 10(c) has not been substantiated the Appeal must fail since the Assessment Panel may not be challenged on other grounds.

12)   Where the Appeal Panel finds that the candidate has made the case they will instruct the Assessment Panel to review the matter. The Appeal Panel will give precise instructions to the Assessment Panel as to the evidence which must be considered, and what must be discounted. The Chair of the Appeal Panel will detail the evidence accepted by the Panel. The evidence and decision cannot be challenged by the Assessment Panel.

13)   The Assessment Panel will review the case at its next meeting after the Appeal Panel hearing. The Panel will give written details of its decision to the Chief Executive and the Chair of the Professional Development Committee.

14)   The Chief Executive will inform the candidate of the final decision of the Assessment Panel.

15)   All candidates are eligible to reapply. No candidate will have to wait longer than one year to reapply for certification from the date of the original Panel decision.

Section 2: Gaining Chartered Membership

Regulations drawn up under Bye-law 11

1 Registration

All applicants for Chartered Membership will be required to complete registration forms and a Personal Professional Development Plan and send them to CILIP in order to register as candidates.

All applicants applying for admission to the Register must:

(i) Have been in membership of CILIP for a minimum of one year *and* be current members at the time that they submit an application for assessment
(ii) Be Associate Members of CILIP
(iii) Provide documentary evidence of meeting the admission requirements (see Regulation 2)
(iv) Register for the CILIP Mentor Scheme or have been participants in another approved mentor programme
(v) Have completed the required period of practical experience (see Regulation 2.1).

2 Admission Requirements

You must have acceptable qualifications to be considered as a candidate for Chartered Membership. You will either have:

Pathway 1:

A Library and Information Studies qualification recognised or accredited by CILIP at Scottish Higher Education Level 10 or England Wales and Northern Ireland Framework Level HE4 (or above) OR you may have:

Pathway 2:

1. CILIP Certification (ACLIP) plus evidence of a minimum period of further personal professional development (see guidance notes)

or

2. A CILIP accredited or approved qualification (an up-to-date list is available on the CILIP website at www.cilip.org.uk)

(Holders of any qualifications listed under 2 will be required to submit copies of certificates etc. to CILIP for verification before registration can be confirmed)

2.1 Practical experience

All candidates must have completed a minimum period of appropriate practical work experience before submitting an application for assessment

Pathway 1: One year full-time equivalent (FTE) work in a library and information service or related environment

Pathway 2: Normally two years FTE work in a library and information service or related environment.

(CILIP may authorise a reduction in the case of individual candidates who can demonstrate substantial previous relevant practical experience, which could have been gained in another discipline)

For advice on the suitability of your work for eventual progression to Chartered status please contact the Qualifications and Professional Development Department

3 Application

3.1

Candidates will normally be expected to make an application for Chartered Membership within one year of completing the required period of practical experience.

3.2 Form of application

Each candidate will submit a portfolio including:

1. Curriculum Vitae (CV)
2. Personal Professional Development Plan (PPDP)
3. Personal statement evaluating progress and achievements against the Personal Professional Development Plan (PPDP); the statement should be no more than 1000 words.
4. Evidence of participation in a mentor scheme.
5. Portfolio of supporting evidence

3.3 Presentation

All applications must be in the English or Welsh language.

The documents should normally be word-processed or in electronic format and be accompanied by the appropriate form.

(Copies of certificates and other original documentary evidence may be sent by post, accompanied by a copy of your application form)

All applications should be accompanied by the appropriate fee, to be determined annually by CILIP AGM.

All documentation should be submitted to the Qualifications and Professional Development Department. All documents (electronic and hard copy) will be stored and treated in a confidential manner by CILIP.

4 Assessment

All applications are assessed by the CILIP Chartership Board that is appointed by CILIP Council.

Assessment will be carried out against clearly identified criteria to ensure transparency and consistency of practice to all candidates.

All applicants will be notified of the outcome in writing within ten working days of the date of the Chartership Board meeting.

4.1 Criteria of assessment

All applications will be assessed against the same criteria. Candidates must demonstrate all of the following:

1. An ability to reflect critically on personal performance and to evaluate service performance
2. Active commitment to continuing professional development
3. An ability to analyse personal and professional development and progression with reference to experiential and developmental activities
4. Breadth of professional knowledge and understanding of the wider professional context

4.2 Forms of assessment

The Chartership Board will determine an appropriate method for the additional assessment of any application, where necessary, which may include one or more of the following:

(a) a request for additional written information and/or documentary evidence
(b) a professional interview of the candidate

4.3 Admission to the Register

The date of admission to the register will normally be that on which the Board accepts the application.

Once admitted to the Register you must remain in membership of CILIP to retain the use of the post nominal letters MCLIP and to describe yourself as a Chartered Member.

5 Appeals

Candidates whose applications are rejected have a right of appeal according to procedures approved by Council. A copy of the Appeals procedures will be sent to unsuccessful candidates. (See Appendix 1 to these Regulations.)

6 Progression to Fellowship

Fellowship is the highest level of professional qualification awarded by CILIP. It is open to all Chartered Members who will normally have completed six years as a Chartered Member.

7 Appendices

Appendix 1 Appeals procedure: Chartered Membership

1) An appeal may be made against a decision of the Chartership Board not to accept a candidate's Application for Chartered Membership submitted for the purpose of gaining admission to the Register.

2) A candidate whose submission is not accepted will be sent the following documents by Recorded Delivery:
   (a) A letter informing the candidate of the decision and the date of the Board meeting at which it was made.
   (b) Copies of the written reports of Board members setting out the reasons for rejection.
   (c) Copies of the reports of Regional Assessors if an interview was held.
   (d) A copy of this Appeals Procedure.

3) A candidate who wishes to appeal against the decision of the Board must do so within six

weeks of the date of receipt of the Recorded Delivery letter referred to in 2. The Appeal must be made in writing to the Chief Executive, or to his/her Deputy.

4) The only grounds on which an Appeal may be made are:
   (a) That all or part of the information used by the Board was biased or incorrect due to no fault of the candidate and that the Board did not know this at the time it took its decision.
   (b) That the Board failed to follow its own published procedures and that this materially affected its decision.

5) The Chief Executive will decide whether there is a prima facie case for appeal. Where there is not he/she will inform the candidate of the reason for his/her ruling. In such cases there will be no further appeal.

6) Where there is a prima facie case for appeal, the Chief Executive will select a panel of three from up to twelve Chartered members, not members of the Chartership Board, chosen annually by Council from among its membership for this purpose.

7) The Chief Executive will set a date for the hearing of the Appeal to take place within six weeks of the date of receipt of the candidate's written Appeal.

8) The Chief Executive will send to each member appointed to the Appeal Panel a copy of the candidate's submission on his/her professional development, the papers sent to the candidate referred to in 2 above, and any papers sent by the candidate in support of his/her Appeal.

9) The candidate will be invited to attend the hearing of the Appeal and may be accompanied by a supporter. The Chair of the Chartership Board and the Head, Qualifications and Professional Development

Department (or the nominee of either) should be present to represent the Board and its office based procedures. The Chief Executive should be present at all times to ensure that the Panel only consider matters appropriate to the Appeal and to offer advice.

10) At an Appeal Panel hearing the matters for consideration will be limited to:
    (a)   Evidence from the candidate concerning the grounds for the Appeal, and details of how the information and/or procedures were faulty. The candidate should offer the correct information to the Panel. Panel members may question both the candidate and the representative of the Chartership Board. The Board representative should explain the reasons for any failure to comply with published procedures.
    (b)   The candidate may ask the supporter to speak on matters concerning the grounds for the Appeal. The supporter may not assist (or speak for) the appellant in answering professional questions put by the Panel.
    (c)   The Panel will be concerned solely to test the candidate's claim that the Board used faulty information, biased statements or failed in its own procedures.

11) Where the Panel finds that the candidate's claim as set out in 10(c) has not been substantiated the Appeal must fail since the Board may not be challenged on other grounds.

12) Where the Panel finds that the candidate has made the case they will instruct the Board to review the matter. The Panel will give precise instructions to the Board as to the evidence which must be considered, and what must be discounted. The Chair of the Panel (with assistance from the Chief Executive) will detail the evidence accepted by the Panel. The evidence and decision cannot be challenged by the Board.

13) The Board will review the case at its next meeting after the Appeal Panel hearing. The Board will give written details of its decision to the Chief Executive and the Chair of the Professional Development Committee.

14) The Chief Executive will inform the candidate of the final decision of the Board.

15) All candidates are eligible to reapply. No candidate will have to wait longer than one year to reapply for Chartered Membership from the date of the original board decision.

Section 3: Chartered Fellow

Regulations drawn up under Bye-law 11

1 Admission requirements

1.1 Normally, applicants for Fellowship will be Chartered Members who have either:

(i) completed a period of not less than 6 years on the Register of Chartered Members of CILIP

or

(ii) completed two successful consecutive cycles of revalidation

1.2 Exceptionally, Associate Members who are not Chartered may apply for Fellowship provided that evidence is produced of having reached a level of professional development commensurate with that required for the award of Chartered Membership, followed by a period of subsequent professional practice and development comparable in duration and quality with the minima required of Chartered Members admitted to Fellowship. This may have been gained in another discipline

2 Membership

All applicants for admission to the Register of Fellows must:

(i) be current members at the time that they submit an application for assessment

and

(ii) have been in membership of CILIP for a minimum of one year at the time that they submit an application for assessment.

3 Applications

3.1 Form of application

Application may be made by submitting documentary or other evidence of any appropriate kind.

Each candidate will submit a portfolio including:

- Curriculum Vitae
- A brief supporting statement setting out the grounds on which the candidate believes Fellowship should be awarded. The statement should be no more than 500 words.
- One copy of each document or other evidence presented in support of the application
- Written support from other Chartered members or senior colleagues who can comment on an applicants suitability for admission to the Register of Fellows

In addition, candidates who are applying on the basis of successful completion of two consecutive cycles of revalidation must also include:

- Evidence of successful participation in the Revalidation Scheme (see Regulation 1.1(ii))

3.2 Presentation

a. Applications may be submitted in the English or Welsh language.

b. Three copies of the Curriculum Vitae, supporting statement and written support together with one copy of each document or other evidence must be provided

c. The documents should normally be word-processed or in electronic format and be accompanied by the appropriate form.

All applications should be accompanied by the appropriate fee, to be determined annually by CILIP AGM.

4 Assessment

All applications are assessed by the CILIP Chartership Board that is appointed by CILIP Council.

Assessment will be carried out against clearly identified criteria to ensure transparency and consistency of practice to all candidates.

All applicants will be notified of the outcome in writing within 10 working days of the date of the Chartership Board meeting. All documents will be returned to successful applicants once election to the Register has been confirmed.

4.1 Criteria for assessment

All applications will be assessed against the same criteria. Candidates must demonstrate the following:

1   Evidence of substantial achievement in professional practice
2   evidence of significant contribution to all or part of the profession*
3   evidence of active commitment to continuing professional development.

The activities that support this criteria may either reflect the candidate's contribution to a broad area of professional work or to work in a very specific and specialised context.

4.2 Forms of Assessment

The Chartership Board will determine an appropriate method for the additional assessment of any application, which may include one or more of the following:

(a)   reference of submitted work to expert referees
(b)   professional interview of the candidate
(c)   visits to inspect buildings or services.

4.3 Admission to the Register

Date of Registration as a Fellow will normally be

that on which the Board accepts the application.

Once admitted to the Register you must remain in membership of CILIP in order to retain your post-nominal letters and to describe yourself as a Chartered Fellow.

5 Appeals

Candidates whose applications are rejected have a right of appeal, following the procedures approved by Council. Any candidate whose submission is rejected by the Board will automatically receive a copy of the Appeals procedure. (See Appendix 1 to these Regulations)

Appendix 1 Appeals Procedure – Fellowship

1)   An Appeal may be made against a decision of the Chartership Board not to accept a candidate's application for the award of Fellowship.

2)   A candidate whose application is not accepted will be sent the following documents by Recorded Delivery:-
(a)   a letter informing the candidate of the decision and the date of the Board meeting at which it was made
(b)   the written reports of Board members, setting out the reasons for rejection
(c)   copies of the reports of Regional Assessors (if applicable)
(d)   a copy of this Appeals Procedure.

3)   A candidate who wishes to appeal against the decision of the Board must do so within six weeks of the date of receipt of the Recorded Delivery letter referred to in 2. The Appeal must be made in writing to the Chief Executive, or to his/her Deputy.

4)   The only grounds on which an Appeal may be made are:
(1)   that all or part of the information used by the Board was biased or incorrect

due to no fault of the candidate and that the Board did not know this at the time it took its decision

(2)   that the Board failed to follow its own published procedures and that this materially affected its decision.

5)   The Chief Executive will decide whether there is a prima facie case for appeal. Where there is not he/she will inform the candidate of the reason for his/her ruling. In such cases there will be no further appeal.

6)   Where there is a prima facie case for appeal, the Chief Executive will select a panel of three from up to 12 Chartered members, not members of the Chartership Board, chosen annually by Council from among its membership for this purpose.

7)   The Chief Executive will set a date for the hearing of the Appeal to take place within six weeks of the date of receipt of the candidate's written Appeal.

8)   The Chief Executive will send to each member appointed to the Appeal Panel a copy of the candidate's application and supporting documents, the papers sent to the candidate referred to in 2 above, and any papers sent by the candidate in support of his/her Appeal.

9)   The candidate will be invited to attend the hearing of the Appeal and may be accompanied by a 'supporter'. The Chair of the Chartership Board and the Head, Qualifications and Professional Development Department (or the nominee of either) should be present to represent the Board and its office based procedures. The Chief Executive should be present at all times to ensure that the Panel only consider matters appropriate to the Appeal, and to offer advice.

10)   At an Appeal Panel hearing the matters for consideration will be limited to:

(i)   evidence from the candidate concerning the grounds for the appeal, and details of how the information and/or procedures were faulty. The candidate should offer the correct information to the Panel. Panel members may question both the candidate and the representative of the Chartership Board. The Board representative should explain the reasons for any failure to comply with published procedures

(ii)   the candidate may ask the 'supporter' to speak on matters concerning the grounds for the Appeal. The 'supporter' may not assist (or speak for) the appellant in answering professional questions put by the Panel

(iii)   the Panel will be concerned solely to test the candidate's claim that the Board used faulty information, biased statements or failed in its own procedures.

11)   Where the Panel finds that the candidate's claim as set out in 10(iii) has not been substantiated the Appeal must fail since the Board may not be challenged on other grounds.

12)   Where the Panel finds that the candidate has made the case they will instruct the Board to review the matter. The Panel will give precise instructions to the Board as to the evidence which must be considered, and what must be discounted. The Chair of the Panel (with assistance from the Chief Executive) will detail the evidence accepted by the Panel. The evidence and decision cannot be challenged by the Board.

13)   The Board will review the case at its next meeting after the Appeal Panel hearing. The Board will give written details of its decision to the Chief Executive and the Chair of the Professional Development Committee.

14) The Chief Executive will inform the candidate of the final decision of the Board.

15) All candidates are eligible to reapply. No candidate will have to wait longer than one year to reapply for Fellowship from the date of the original board decision.

Section 4: CILIP Revalidation Scheme

Regulations drawn up under Bye-law 11

NB *From January 2011 the Revalidation Scheme will be replaced by a mandatory CPD scheme for all Registered Practitioners. Members should consult the Qualifications and Professional Development Department pages of the CILIP website for information on any changes to the Regulations from that date: www.cilip.org.uk/jobs-careers/qualifications/pages/qualifications-.aspx.*

1 Registration

All applicants must:

(i)   be current Chartered Members of CILIP and have worked in library or information work for a minimum of three years full-time equivalent since Chartering

(ii)   must have remained in membership throughout the period covered by the application for revalidation

2 Application

2.1 Form of application

Each applicant will submit a portfolio including:

a.   Application form
b.   Curriculum vitae
c.   Personal statement reflecting outcomes of professional development across the Body of Knowledge achieved since gaining Chartership or the previous successful revalidation. (CILIP will provide the template) The statement should be no more than 1000 words.
d.   Evidence of training or professional activity since gaining Chartership or the previous successful revalidation
e.   A supporting letter which should evidence achievement. Normally this letter should be provided by a Chartered Member or an appropriate senior colleague.

2.2 Submission

All submissions must be in the English or Welsh language.

The CV and personal statement should be word-processed.

The application form should be on the designated form

Electronic submission is welcomed, but copies of certificates and other documentary evidence may be sent by post, accompanied by a copy of your application form.

All applications should be accompanied by the appropriate fee, to be determined annually by CILIP AGM.

The documentation should be submitted to a named Officer of the Member's Branch or Home Nation. A list of Officers is available at the CILIP website at www.cilip.org.uk/ or from the Qualifications and Professional Development Department.

Overseas members should submit their applications to the Qualifications and Professional Development Department in the first instance.

All applications (electronic and hard copy) will be stored and treated in a confidential manner by CILIP Assessment Panels.

3 Assessment

Each submission will normally be assessed by CILIP Assessment Panels in the Member's Branch or Home Nation.

Assessment will be carried out against clearly identified criteria to ensure transparency and consistency of practice to all applicants from all sectors and geographical regions.

All applicants will be notified of the outcome in writing within 10 working days of the date of the assessment meeting. All documents will be returned to successful applicants once Revalidation has been confirmed.

3.1 Criteria of assessment

All applications will be assessed against the same criteria. Candidates must demonstrate the following:

1   Critical evaluation of personal learning outcomes from a range of training and development activities
2   Increased competence in a range of professional skills and, where appropriate, management skills, developed through professional practice
3   Evidence of continuing professional development through reading, participation in professional affairs, and contribution to or attendance at courses/ conferences

The activities that support these criteria may either reflect the candidate's participation in a broad area of professional work or, work in a very specific and specialised context

3.2 Forms of assessment

The CILIP Assessment Panel will determine a method for the additional assessment of any application, where necessary, which may include either of the following:

(a)   a request for additional written information or documentary evidence
(b)   a request for the candidate to attend an interview

4 Appeals

Candidates whose applications are rejected have a right of appeal according to procedures approved by Council. A copy of the Appeals Procedures will be sent to unsuccessful candidates. (See Appendix 1 to these Regulations.)

5 Progression to Fellowship

Chartered Members who have successfully completed two consecutive cycles of revalidation are eligible to apply for Fellowship.

Fellowship is the highest level of professional qualification awarded by CILIP. Information on applying for Fellowship can be found at www.cilip.org.uk/.

6 Appendices

Appendix 1 Appeals Procedure – Revalidation

1)   An appeal may be made against a decision of the Assessment Panel not to accept a candidate's Application for Revalidation.

2)   A candidate whose submission is not accepted will be sent the following documents by Recorded Delivery:
(a)   a letter informing the candidate of the decision and the date of the Assessment Panel meeting at which it was made
(b)   a summary of the points made at the Assessment Panel meeting and copies of the assessment documents of Panel members, setting out the reasons for rejection
(c)   a copy of this Appeals Procedure.

3)   A candidate who wishes to appeal against the decision of the Assessment Panel must do so within six weeks of the date of receipt of the Recorded Delivery letter referred to in 2. The

Appeal must be made in writing to the Chief Executive.

4) The only grounds on which an Appeal may be made are:

    (a) That all or part of the information used by the Assessment Panel was biased or incorrect due to no fault of the candidate and that the Panel did not know this at the time it took its decision.

    (b) That the Assessment Panel failed to follow its own published procedures and that this materially affected its decision.

5) The Chief Executive will decide whether there is a prima facie case for appeal. Where there is not s/he will inform the candidate of the reason for his ruling. In such cases there will be no further appeal.

6) Where there is a prima facie case for appeal the Chief Executive will select an Appeal Panel of three from a panel chosen annually by Council from amongst its membership for this purpose. (These may not be members of a CILIP Assessment Panel, or the Chartership Board).

7) The Chief Executive will set a date for the hearing of the Appeal to take place within six weeks of the date of receipt of the candidate's written Appeal.

8) The Chief Executive will send to each member appointed to the Appeal Panel a copy of the candidate's portfolio submission, the papers sent to the candidate referred to in 2 above, and any papers sent by the candidate in support of his/her Appeal.

9) The candidate will be invited to attend the hearing of the Appeal and may be accompanied by a supporter. A representative of the CILIP Assessment Panel and the Head, Qualifications and Professional Development Department (or the nominee of either) should be present to represent the

Assessment Panel and its office based procedures.

10) At an Appeal Panel hearing the matters for consideration will be limited to:

    (a) Evidence from the candidate concerning the grounds for the Appeal, and details of how the information and/or procedures were faulty. The candidate should offer the correct information to the Appeal Panel. Panel members may question both the candidate and the representative of the Assessment Panel.

    The Assessment Panel representative should explain the reasons for any failure to comply with published procedures.

    (b) The candidate may ask the supporter to speak on matters concerning the grounds for the Appeal. The supporter may not assist (or speak for) the appellant in answering professional questions put by the Panel.

    (c) The Appeal Panel will be concerned solely to test the candidate's claim that the Assessment Panel used faulty information, biased statements or failed in its own procedures.

11) Where the Appeal Panel finds that the candidate's claim as set out in 10(c) has not been substantiated the Appeal must fail since the Assessment Panel may not be challenged on other grounds.

12) Where the Appeal Panel finds that the candidate has made the case they will instruct the Assessment Panel to review the matter. The Appeal Panel will give precise instructions to the Assessment Panel as to the evidence which must be considered, and what must be discounted. The Chair of the Appeal Panel will detail the evidence accepted by the Panel. The evidence and

decision cannot be challenged by the Assessment Panel.

13) The Assessment Panel will review the case at its next meeting after the Appeal Panel hearing. The Panel will give written details of its decision to the Chief Executive and the Chair of the Professional Development Committee.

14) The Chief Executive will inform the candidate of the final decision of the Assessment Panel.

15) All candidates are eligible to reapply. No candidate will have to wait longer than one year to reapply for Revalidation.

Appendix B

Ethical Principles
Code of Professional Practice
CILIP Disciplinary Regulations

Introduction

Library and information professionals are frequently the essential link between information users and the information or piece of literature which they require. They therefore occupy a privileged position which carries corresponding responsibilities. In addition, whether they are self-employed or employed, their position is sometimes a sensitive one, which may impose a need to balance conflicting requirements.

The purpose of the Principles and Code which follow this introduction is to provide a framework to help library and information professionals, who are members of CILIP, to manage the responsibilities and sensitivities which figure prominently in their work. There is a statement of *Ethical Principles* and a more extended *Code of Professional Practice*, which applies these principles to the different groups and professionals to which our members must relate. The *Code* also makes some additional points with regard to professional behaviour. Given the diversity of the information profession, it is inevitable that not every statement in the *Code of Professional Practice* will be equally applicable to every member of CILIP. However, the *Ethical Principles* ought to command more general support, even though some members may not feel the force of each one of them to the same extent in their day-to-day experience. The *Principles* and *Code* assume that respect for duly enacted law is a fundamental responsibility for everybody.

By the terms of its Royal Charter, CILIP has a responsibility to 'the public good'. It is therefore anticipated that our Ethical Principles and our *Code of Professional Practice* may be of interest well beyond the immediate limits of the membership of CILIP, both to those whose work bears close comparison with ours, and also to those who may, from time to time, want a clear statement of our ethical principles and what we consider to be good professional practice.

Associated with these *Principles* and *Code*, there is a growing collection of practical examples, illustrating how information professionals and others can use the *Principles* and *Code* to help them cope with ethical dilemmas they may face. In further support of the *Principles* and *Code*, CILIP has established an Ethics Panel of experienced members of the profession, and they and the professional staff of CILIP are available to members who may need additional help in resolving ethical issues.

CILIP's Disciplinary Regulations provide that a Member will be guilty of professional misconduct if he/she has acted contrary to the aims, objects and interests of CILIP or in a manner unbecoming or prejudicial to the profession. In reaching decisions under the Disciplinary Procedure, regard will be had to the *Statement of Ethical Principles* and the *Code of Professional Practice* and Members should therefore be aware that failure to comply with the *Principles* and *Code* may, depending on the circumstances, be a ground for disciplinary action.

Ethical Principles for Library and Information Professionals

The conduct of members should be characterised by the following general principles, presented here in no particular order of priority:

1. Concern for the public good in all professional matters, including respect for diversity within society, and the promoting of equal opportunities and human rights.

2. Concern for the good reputation of the information profession.

3. Commitment to the defence, and the advancement, of access to information, ideas and works of the imagination.

4. Provision of the best possible service within available resources.

5. Concern for balancing the needs of actual and potential users and the reasonable demands of employers.

6. Equitable treatment of all information users.

7. Impartiality, and avoidance of inappropriate bias, in acquiring and evaluating information and in mediating it to other information users.

8. Respect for confidentiality and privacy in dealing with information users.

9. Concern for the conservation and preservation of our information heritage in all formats.

10. Respect for, and understanding of, the integrity of information items and for the intellectual effort of those who created them.

11. Commitment to maintaining and improving personal professional knowledge, skills and competences.

12. Respect for the skills and competences of all others, whether information professionals or information users, employers or colleagues.

Code of Professional Practice for Library and Information Professionals

This Code applies the ethical principles to the different groups and interests to which CILIP members must relate. The Code also makes some additional points with regard to professional behaviour. The principles and values will differ in their relative importance according to context.

A Personal Responsibilities

People who work in the information profession have personal responsibilities which go beyond those immediately implied by their contract with their employers or clients. Members should therefore:

1. strive to attain the highest personal standard of professional knowledge and competence

2. ensure they are competent in those branches of professional practice in which qualifications and/or experience entitle them to engage by keeping abreast of developments in their areas of expertise

3. claim expertise in areas of library and information work or in other disciplines only where their skills and knowledge are adequate

B Responsibilities to Information and its Users

The behaviour of professionals who work with information should be guided by a regard for the interests and needs of information users. People working in the information profession also need to be conscious that they have responsibility for a growing heritage of information and data, irrespective of format. This includes works of the imagination as well as factual data. Members should therefore:

1. ensure that information users are aware of the scope and remit of the service being provided

2. make the process of providing information, and the standards and procedures governing that process, as clear and open as possible

3. avoid inappropriate bias or value judgements in the provision of services

4. protect the confidentiality of all matters relating to information users, including their enquiries, any services to be provided, and any aspects of the users' personal circumstances or business

5. deal fairly with the competing needs of information users, and resolve conflicting priorities with due regard for the urgency and importance of the matters being considered

6. deal promptly and fairly with any complaints from information users, and keep them informed about progress in the handling of their complaints.

7. ensure that the information systems and services for which they are responsible are the most effective, within the resources available, in meeting the needs of users

8. ensure that the materials to which they provide access are those which are most appropriate to the needs of legitimate users of the service

9. defend the legitimate needs and interests of information users, while upholding the moral and legal rights of the creators and distributors of intellectual property

10. respect the integrity of information sources, and cite sources used, as appropriate

11. show an appropriate concern for the future information needs of society through the long term preservation and conservation of materials as required, as well as an understanding of proper records management.

C Responsibilities to Colleagues and the Information Community

The personal conduct of information professionals at work should promote the profession in the best possible manner at all times. Members should therefore:

1. act in ways that promote the profession positively, both to their colleagues and to the public at large

2. afford respect and understanding to other colleagues and professionals and acknowledge their ideas, contributions and work, wherever and whenever appropriate

3. refer to colleagues in a professional manner and not discredit or criticise their work unreasonably or inappropriately

4. when working in an independent capacity, conduct their business in a professional manner that respects the legitimate rights and interests of others

5. encourage colleagues, especially those for whom they have a line-management responsibility, to maintain and enhance their professional knowledge and competence

6. refrain from ascribing views to, or speaking on behalf of, CILIP, unless specifically authorised to do so

7. report significant breaches of this *Code* to the appropriate authorities[1]

8. refrain from any behaviour in the course of their work which might bring the information profession into disrepute.

D Responsibilities to Society

One of the distinguishing features of professions is that their knowledge and skills are at the service of society at large, and do not simply serve the interests of the immediate customer. Members should therefore:

1. consider the public good, both in general and as it refers to particular vulnerable groups, as well as the immediate claims arising from their employment and their professional duties

2. promote equitable access for all members of society to public domain information of all kinds and in all formats

3. strive to achieve an appropriate balance within the law between demands from information users, the need to respect confidentiality, the terms of their employment, the public good and the responsibilities outlined in this Code

4. encourage and promote wider knowledge and acceptance of, and wider compliance with, this *Code*, both among colleagues in the information professions and more widely among those whom we serve.

E Responsibilities as Employees

Members who are employed have duties that go beyond the immediate terms of their employment contract. On occasion these may conflict with the immediate demands of their employer but be in the broader interest of the public and possibly the employer themselves.[2] Members should therefore:

1. develop a knowledge and understanding of the organisation in which they work and use

their skills and expertise to promote the legitimate aims and objectives of their employer

2. avoid engaging in unethical practices during their work and bring to the attention of their employer any concerns they may have concerning the ethics or legality of specific decisions, actions or behaviour at work.

---

1 The appropriate authority will vary depending on the context of the case. It may be CILIP, the employer, a regulatory body or an officer managing the 'whistle-blowing' procedure or some other body. It is not possible to be prescriptive.

2 It is recognised that sometimes Members, acting as a representative of employers, have to make decisions that may impact adversely on levels of service or the employment of staff. This is not in itself unethical behaviour but there might be circumstances in which it could be - the lawfulness of the action or the way it is managed, for instance.

CILIP Disciplinary Regulations

Introduction

1. These regulations were made by the Council under paragraph 21* of the Bye-laws on 9 February 2005. They came into force on that date, superseding all previous disciplinary regulations.

2. In accordance with Bye-law 21, these regulations set out the procedures to be followed in the investigation and adjudication of any complaint that a Member may have acted in a manner contrary to the aims, objects and interests of CILIP or in a manner unbecoming or prejudicial to the profession. They are intended therefore to cover issues relating to the professional conduct of a Member. It will not normally be within the scope of these regulations to consider grievances against a Member which are of an employment or contractual nature.

3. At all stages of the procedure, regard shall be had to any Statement of Ethical Principles and/or Code of Professional Practice issued by CILIP and in force at the time of the conduct which is the subject of the complaint. Failure to comply with any such Statement or Code may be a ground for disciplinary action as defined at paragraph 10 below.

4. These regulations relate to the conduct of individual (but not institutional) Members of CILIP.

Words and Phrases

5. In these regulations, the following words, phrases and abbreviations shall, except where the contrary intention appears, have the following meaning:

Bye-laws the Bye-laws of CILIP

AHG The Appeal Hearing Group appointed under paragraph 50 below

Council The Council for the time being appointed pursuant to the Charter and Bye-laws

CILIP The Chartered Institute of Library and Information Professionals

The Disciplinary Committee The Disciplinary Committee established by the the Council pursuant to the Bye-laws and described in CILIP General Regulation 62, whose members shall be appointed as set out in CILIP General Regulations 78–80

FHG The Full Hearing Group appointed under paragraph 29 below

Member An individual member of CILIP in any category of membership under paragraph 4.1 or under paragraph 4.2(a), (b) or (c) of the Bye-laws

PHG The Preliminary Hearing Group appointed under paragraph 12 below

PPC The Professional Practice Committee established by Council under the Bye-laws and described in CILIP General Regulation 63

Review Committee The Committee referred to at paragraphs 22 to 25 below, comprising the Immediate Past President, the President and the President-Elect of CILIP, appointed by the Council pursuant to the Bye-laws

Invoking the Disciplinary Procedure

6. A member of CILIP or any other person may make a formal complaint in writing to CILIP concerning the professional conduct of a Member.

---

*The numbering referred to is that of the Bye-laws in force at the time.

7. The Chief Executive (or his/her nominee) shall acknowledge a formal complaint made under paragraph 6 above, if possible, within seven days of receipt.

8. CILIP shall consider and, where the Chief Executive (in consultation with the Chair of the Disciplinary Committee) deems it appropriate, investigate any complaint under paragraph 6 above, provided that it is made within a reasonable period from the time when it arose.

9. CILIP can itself initiate a complaint where the Chief Executive becomes aware of any fact or matter concerning the professional conduct of a Member which in his/her opinion (in consultation with the Chair of the Disciplinary Committee) warrants investigation under these regulations.

Grounds for Disciplinary Action

10. It shall be a ground for disciplinary action if a Member is guilty of professional misconduct. This is defined as a Member having acted:

    (i)   contrary to the aims, objects and interests of CILIP; or
    (ii)   in a manner unbecoming or prejudicial to the profession.

Stage 1 – Disciplinary Investigation

Referral to the Chair of the Disciplinary Committee

11. Where a complaint or matter is to be investigated, the Chief Executive shall refer the matter to the Chair of the Disciplinary Committee.

Appointment of a PHG

12. Upon receipt of a referral under paragraph 11 above, the Chair of the Disciplinary

Committee shall appoint a PHG to consider the matter further.

13. In each case, the PHG shall comprise any three members of the Disciplinary Committee (other than the Chair) who have no interest in the matter. The Chair of the Disciplinary Committee shall appoint one of the members of the PHG to act as its chair.

14. Notwithstanding the requirement for the annual appointment of members to the Disciplinary Committee in accordance with Byelaw 66, a PHG shall continue with its original membership until the matter it was appointed to deal with has been resolved.

Duties and Powers of the PHG

15. The PHG shall consider the matter and decide whether or not there is a case to be answered.

16. In considering the matter, the PHG shall make such inquiries as it considers necessary to establish the facts and circumstances by whatever means it considers appropriate including, at its discretion, raising questions at this stage directly with the Member concerned. The Member shall be informed, upon the raising of any questions with him/her, that such questions are asked in connection with possible disciplinary proceedings.

17. The identity of the complainant shall be made known to the Member unless the PHG determines that there are compelling reasons why the complainant should not be identified taking into account, amongst other things, the need for the Member to fully understand the nature of the complaint against him/her.

18. The PHG shall seek to complete its inquiries within 30 days of the matter being referred to it.

19. Upon completion of its inquiries, the PHG shall decide (by majority vote):

    (i) that there is no case to answer (and proceed as set out at paragraphs 20 and 21 below); or

    (ii) that there is a case to answer (and proceed to offer a consent order as set out at paragraph 26 below); or

    (iii) that there is a case to answer and that the matter should proceed to a full disciplinary hearing as set out at paragraphs 27 and 28 below.

The PHG's decision – No case to answer

20. Upon reaching a decision that there is no case to answer, the PHG shall cause CILIP to inform the complainant (if applicable), giving him/her brief written reasons for the decision and notifying him/her in writing of his/her right to request a review of the decision in accordance with paragraph 22 below.

21. CILIP shall at the same time inform the Member of the decision in writing with brief written reasons, advising him/her that the matter may be reviewed.

Review of decision

22. Provided the complainant makes his/her request for a review in writing and within one month from the date of the decision complained of, it will be considered by the Review Committee.

23. The Review Committee will review the matter (on the basis of the written request for the review together with the papers that were before the PHG when it reached its decision).

24. The Review Committee shall:

    (i) confirm the decision of the PHG that there is no case to answer; or

    (ii) remit the matter to the PHG for reconsideration; or

    (iii) decide that there is a case to answer which shall be remitted to the PHG with a direction to offer the Member the option of accepting a consent Order under paragraph 26 below; or

    (iv) decide that there is a case to answer which shall proceed to a full disciplinary hearing under paragraphs 27 and 28 below.

25. CILIP shall inform both the Member and the complainant of the Review Committee's decision and of the outcome of any reconsideration by the PHG under paragraph 24(ii) above, giving brief written reasons in respect of a decision in either event that there is no case to answer. There shall be no right of appeal by any party against the decision of the Review Committee and the complainant shall have no further right of review of a decision by the PHG that there is no case to answer following a reconsideration under paragraph 24(ii) above.

The PHG's decision – Case to answer

Consent Orders

26.

    (i) If the PHG decides that there is a case to answer but that it is appropriate for it to be dealt with in accordance with this paragraph (or in circumstances where the matter is remitted to the PHG under paragraph 24(iii) above), it may with the agreement of the Member, and instead of referring the matter for a full disciplinary hearing, make a disciplinary order that a written warning or a written reprimand be issued against the Member (but imposing no other sanction).

    (ii) Before making a disciplinary order under paragraph 26(i) above, the PHG shall inform the Member in writing of the course it is considering adopting with the agreement of the Member (and briefly of its reasons for that course of action) giving him/her a fixed period to notify CILIP of his/her written consent.

(iii) If within the period fixed by the PHG, the Member gives his/her written consent, the PHG shall proceed to make the disciplinary order proposed, and agreed to by the Member, by consent.

(iv) If the Member either refuses his/her consent, or does not respond within the period fixed by the PHG, it shall proceed as set out at paragraphs 27 and 28 below.

(v) The complainant shall be informed of actions taken under this paragraph with brief written reason for any disciplinary order made under 26(iii) above.

Full Disciplinary Hearing

27. Upon a decision by the PHG or the Review Committee that there is a case to answer under paragraphs 19(iii) or 24(iv) above, or in the circumstances set out at paragraph 26(iv) above, the PHG shall cause CILIP to inform the Member and the complainant (if applicable) in writing that the matter will proceed to a full disciplinary hearing.

28. The PHG shall also refer the matter to the Chair of the Disciplinary Committee.

Stage 2 – Full Disciplinary Hearing

Referral to Full Disciplinary Hearing

29. Upon receiving a referral from the PHG under paragraph 28 above, the Chair of the Disciplinary Committee shall appoint an FHG to hear the matter.

Composition of the Full Hearing Group (FHG)

30. In each case, the FHG shall comprise any five members of the Disciplinary Committee (other than the Chair), who have not served on the PHG in the same matter and who have no interest in the matter. The members of the FHG shall, where possible, be selected for their relevant experience.

31. The Chair of the Disciplinary Committee shall appoint one of the members of the FHG to act as its chair.

32. The quorum for the hearing of the matter by the FHG shall be 3 members of the FHG. If the Chair of the FHG is absent from the hearing but the hearing remains quorate under this paragraph, the FHG members present may appoint one of their number to be Chair at the hearing.

33. Notwithstanding the requirement for the annual appointment of members to the Disciplinary Committee in accordance with Byelaw 66, an FHG shall continue with its original membership until the matter it was appointed to deal with has been resolved.

The Presenter

34. The Chair of the PHG shall, on behalf of CILIP or a complainant, present the case before the FHG, and for this purpose may instruct a representative (who may be legally qualified).

Procedure of the FHG

35. The hearing of the case shall be conducted in accordance with schedule 1 to these regulations except where to do so would be unjust or inconvenient when the Chair of the FHG may modify the procedure to the extent that he/she deems necessary, provided that

the result is fair to the Member under complaint.

Disciplinary Action

36. Any one or more of the following courses of disciplinary action may be ordered by the FHG as is considered appropriate (and on such terms and conditions and for such period as is considered appropriate) having regard to the nature and seriousness of the professional misconduct, the Member's character and past record and to any other relevant circumstances:

    (a)   a written warning and/or written reprimand; and/or

    (b)   a requirement for the Member to give a written undertaking as to future conduct; and/or

    (c)   a requirement for the Member to undertake specific training and/or to report regularly to or to seek guidance from a senior colleague; and/or

    (d)   a review of the Member's eligibility for office within CILIP, its groups and branches; and/or

    (e)   a review of the CILIP membership grade held by the Member; and/or

    (f)   the withdrawal of CILIP membership benefits and the right to append designatory letters indicating membership grade; and/or

    (g)   a recommendation to the Council that the Member be suspended from membership for a fixed period of time; and/or

    (h)   a recommendation to the Council that the Member be expelled from membership of CILIP.

37. If, notwithstanding its finding that the Member is guilty of professional misconduct, the FHG is of the opinion that in all the circumstances, no such order is appropriate, it may make no order.

38. The FHG may also, wherever it considers appropriate and whether or not it decides to order any disciplinary action, communicate to the Member its advice as to his or her future conduct.

39. Where the FHG determines to recommend to the Council that the Member be suspended or expelled from membership of CILIP, that Member shall be suspended from membership on an interim basis pending the Council's resolution in the matter, and during such interim suspension is entitled to no privileges of membership.

Notification of Decision

40. CILIP shall serve on the Member (and the complainant, if applicable) written notice of the decision of the FHG together with any disciplinary action ordered as promptly as is practicable after the conclusion of the hearing and, whether or not the Member attended the hearing. Where there has been a finding of professional misconduct, the notice shall inform the Member of his/her right of appeal under paragraph 43 below.

Reasons

41. The FHG shall also provide the Member with written reasons for the decision as soon as is practicable.

Recording

42. The proceedings before the FHG shall be recorded and a transcript shall be provided to the Member upon written request by him/her and on payment by him/her of the costs involved.

Stage 3 – Appeal

Right of Appeal

43. A Member may appeal to the Appeal Hearing Group (the AHG) against a finding of the FHG that he/she is guilty of professional misconduct and/or against any disciplinary action ordered by the FHG.

44. There is no right of appeal by a complainant against any aspect of a decision by the FHG.

Notice of Intention to Appeal

45. Notice of intention to appeal shall be lodged with the CILIP Chief Executive in writing within 10 working days of communication of the FHG's decision.

46. If notice of intention to appeal is lodged within the time permitted, the order of the FHG shall not take effect until the determination of the matter on appeal.

Grounds of Appeal

47. The Member shall be permitted a further 20 working days to submit a written statement setting out the grounds upon which the appeal is brought and any facts and matters relied upon by him/her, including, where applicable, a description of any fresh evidence upon which the Member intends to rely and which for good reason was previously unavailable.

48. An appeal may be made on any grounds.

49. CILIP shall inform the complainant (where applicable) where a notice of intention to appeal/grounds of appeal are lodged by the Member.

Composition of the Appeal Hearing Group (AHG)

50. When an appeal is made to the AHG, the Chair of the Disciplinary Committee shall appoint an AHG to consider the matter.

51. In each case, the AHG shall comprise 3 members of the Disciplinary Committee (other than the Chair), who have served on neither the PHG or the FHG in the same matter, and who have no interest in the matter.

52. The Chair of the Disciplinary Committee shall appoint one of the members of the AHG to act as its Chair.

53. The quorum for the hearing of the matter by the AHG shall be 2 members of the AHG. If the Chair of the AHG is absent from the hearing, but the hearing remains quorate under this paragraph, the AHG members present shall decide which one of them shall act as Chair at the hearing.

54. Notwithstanding the requirement for the annual appointment of members to the Disciplinary Committee in accordance with Byelaw 66, an AHG shall continue with its original membership until the matter it was appointed to deal with has been resolved.

The Parties in Proceedings before the AHG

55. The Member shall be the Appellant at this stage and he/she shall be entitled to be represented by any person (who may be legally qualified).

56. The Chair of the PHG shall act on behalf of CILIP as respondent to the Appeal and for this purpose may instruct a representative (who may be legally qualified).

Procedure before the AHG

57. On an appeal, the AHG shall consider the documents, statements and other evidence produced to the FHG and may re-hear any witness called before the FHG and receive any fresh evidence which for good reason was previously unavailable.

58. The hearing of an appeal before the AHG shall be conducted in accordance with Schedule 2 to these regulations except where to do so would be inconvenient or unjust, when the Chair of the AHG may modify the procedure to the extent that he/she deems necessary provided the result is fair to the Member.

Powers of the AHG

59. Having considered the appeal in accordance with these regulations, the AHG may affirm, vary or rescind any finding or order of the FHG and may substitute any other finding or order (on such terms and conditions, if any) as it considers appropriate which the FHG might have made.

Notification of Decision by AHG

60. CILIP shall serve on the Member (and the complainant, if applicable) written notice of the decision of the AHG as promptly as is practicable after the conclusion of the hearing, and whether or not the Member attended the hearing.

Final Decision

61. A decision of the AHG is final save that a recommendation to suspend or expel a Member shall not take effect without being endorsed by the CILIP Council.

Reasons

62. The AHG shall also provide the Member with written reasons for its decision as soon as is practicable.

Recording

63. The proceedings before the AHG shall be recorded and a transcript shall be provided to the Member upon written request by him/her and on payment by him/her of the costs involved.

Stage 4 – Endorsement by Council of Recommendation to Suspend or Expel Member

64. A recommendation that the Member be suspended or expelled from membership of CILIP, shall not take effect without being endorsed by the CILIP Council.

65. The Member shall be advised of the date of the meeting of the Council at which the recommendation will be proposed for endorsement.

66. Council shall meet in private to consider the recommended suspension or expulsion of a Member and shall receive from the Chair of the Disciplinary Committee a paper summarizing the disciplinary proceedings in the matter and the grounds for the recommended suspension or expulsion.

67. Council shall decide either:

   (a) to endorse the recommended suspension or expulsion; or
   (b) to refer the matter back to the FHG or AHG (whichever last considered the matter under these Regulations prior to its consideration by Council), with a brief summary of its reasons for the referral and an instruction that the matter be reconsidered.

68. Council shall reach its decision by a simple majority of those present and entitled to vote. Members of the PPC, the Disciplinary Committee (including those who have served on the PHG, the FHG or AHG in the matter) and the Review Committee who are also members of Council, shall be entitled to vote.

General Provisions

Publication of Findings

69. The Chair of the Disciplinary Committee shall report to the next meeting of CILIP Council on any completed Disciplinary Procedure (save for a case which concluded with Council endorsing a recommendation to suspend or expel a member). Unless otherwise recommended by the FHG or AHG, such report shall be anonymised.

70. Following any report to Council under paragraph 69 above (but not before), the Disciplinary Committee shall

    (i) publish the outcome of the matter in such form and manner as it shall require (taking into account any recommendations made by the FHG or AHG regarding publication of the matter) save that there will be no publication where no action is taken (under paragraph 37) unless the Member so requests (and the Chair of the Disciplinary Committee agrees to publish the matter), and

    (ii) inform the complainant (if applicable, and if not previously informed) in writing of the outcome of the complaint.

71. For the avoidance of doubt, if a Member subject to a complaint resigns his/her membership, or if for any other reason his/her membership terminates whilst the matter remains unresolved under these Disciplinary Regulations, the Disciplinary Committee may,

at its discretion, publish such resignation/termination of membership and inform the complainant in the manner set out at paragraph 70(ii) above.

Time Limits

72. All time limits set out in these regulations shall be doubled when the Member concerned lives outside the UK.

Service of Notices/Documents

73. Any notice or other documents required by these regulations to be sent to or be served on a Member may be delivered either personally or by post (save that any notice required to be sent under paragraphs 21, 26(ii), 27, 40 and 60 and under paragraph 1 of Schedule 1 and paragraph 1 of Schedule 2 shall, if sent by post, be sent by recorded delivery).

74. Where any such notice or any document is served by post or recorded delivery, it shall be sent to the last address of the Member concerned which is recorded by him/her with CILIP and (unless returned to CILIP), it shall be deemed that wherever that address may be, to have been served on the second day following that on which it was posted unless at the place of receipt that latter day is a Sunday or a public holiday in which case service shall be deemed to have occurred on the first day thereafter which is not one of such exceptional days.

UK Law

75. UK law shall apply in resolving any disputes regarding the application of this procedure.

Schedule 1
Procedure before the FHG

(*see paragraph 35 of the Disciplinary Regulations*)

Notification of Hearing and Exchange of Information

1. Following the appointment of the FHG, the Member shall be given at least 21 days' written notice of the date, time and place of the hearing.

2. The notice referred to at paragraph 1 above shall include

   (i) particulars of the conduct or circumstances alleged to amount to professional misconduct;

   (ii) a summary of the facts and matters relied upon, including copies of any written statement and other document that it is proposed to put before the FHG;

   (iii) the names and addresses of any witnesses whom CILIP intends to call in person and an outline of what each witness is expected to say;

   (iv) an invitation to the Member to attend the hearing and/or to submit written representations for consideration by the FHG.

3. At least seven days prior to the date of the hearing, the Member shall:

   (i) confirm whether or not he/she intends to attend the hearing and, if so, the name of any person who will be accompanying or representing him or her (who may be legally qualified).

   (ii) submit:
      (a) brief particulars of any defence intended to be made;
      (b) a summary of the facts and matters that will be relied upon in that defence, including copies of any written statement and other document that he/she intends to refer to;

   (c) the names and addresses of any witnesses whom he/she intends to call in person and an outline of what each witness is expected to say.

4. Neither party shall, without the consent of the other or the permission of the FHG rely on any statement or document or call any witness other than those provided or identified under paragraphs 2 and 3 above.

Adjournment

5. At the request of either party or at his or her own volition, the Chair of the FHG may, at any time, adjourn the hearing if satisfied that it is in the interests of justice so to do. An application for the adjournment of a hearing that has not begun may be agreed between the parties.

6. In the event that any member of the FHG (sitting at the hearing of a case) is unwilling or unable to hear an entire case and the matter cannot be dealt with by adjournment of the hearing, then the Chair of the Disciplinary Committee shall appoint a new FHG and the case shall be re-heard. Members of the FHG who sat previously and were not the member unable or unwilling to continue shall be eligible to be appointed to the new FHG.

The Absence of the Member

7. If at the hearing the Member is not present in person or represented, the FHG may proceed to consider the matter in the Member's absence if it is satisfied that notice was properly served upon him or her in accordance with paragraphs 1 and 2 above.

Joinder of Cases

8. The FHG may hear two or more complaints against a Member at the same time.

Joinder of Members

9. The FHG may also hear complaints against two or more Members at the same time if it considers it convenient and just to do so.

Proof and Evidence

10.

  (i)   The burden of proving the alleged professional misconduct shall lie upon CILIP

  (ii) The professional misconduct shall be proved by CILIP on a balance of probabilities

  (iii) The FHG shall not be bound by strict rules of evidence.

Private Hearing

11. The hearing shall be conducted in private unless the Member requests otherwise save that the complainant (where applicable) shall be permitted to attend unless the Chair of the FGH decides otherwise at his/her sole discretion.

12. For the avoidance of doubt, the Chief Executive of CILIP or his/her nominee and such other persons as are reasonably required by CILIP for secretarial/recording purposes may also be in attendance at the hearing.

Order of Proceedings

13. The order of proceedings for the hearing, unless the Chair of the FHG otherwise directs, will be as follows:

  (i)   Submissions by, on or behalf of, CILIP;

  (ii) Hearing of any witnesses called by CILIP followed by cross-examination of such witnesses by, or on behalf of, the Member;

  (iii) Submissions by, or on behalf of, the Member;

  (iv) Hearing of any witnesses called by the Member followed by cross-examination of such witnesses by, or on behalf of, CILIP;

  (v)   Closing submissions by or on behalf of CILIP;

  (vi) Closing submissions by or on behalf of the Member;

  (vii) After retiring as necessary, the FHG shall advise the Member whether or not it finds any allegation of professional misconduct proven.

14. Members of the FHG may themselves at any stage question witnesses, parties or representatives as they think fit.

15. The decision of the FHG as to whether it finds the Member guilty of professional misconduct shall be reached by a majority of those FHG members present throughout the hearing, save that where their decision is tied, the decision will be that which is most favourable to the Member.

Order of Proceedings Following a Finding of Professional Misconduct

16. CILIP shall, following a finding of professional misconduct, inform the FHG of any further circumstances known to it, whether favourable or adverse to the Member, that might be relevant to any course of action which the FHG might take.

17. The Member shall then be entitled to address the FHG in mitigation, and for this purpose may call witnesses and produce documents.

Decision

18. The FHG may, following a finding of professional misconduct, order any one or more courses of disciplinary action in accordance with paragraphs 36and 37 of the Disciplinary Regulations.

Schedule 2
Procedure before the AHG

(*see paragraph 58 of the Disciplinary Regulations*)

Notification of Hearing and Exchange of Information

1. Following the formation of an AHG under paragraph 50 of the Disciplinary Regulations, the Appellant shall be given at least 21 days' written notice of the date, time and place of the appeal hearing.

2. At least 14 days prior to the date of the hearing, the Appellant shall:

    (i) confirm whether or not he/she intends to attend the hearing and, if so, the name of any person who will be accompanying or representing him or her (who may be legally qualified);

    (ii) if he/she intends to adduce fresh evidence or to call any witness (including a witness previously called before the FHG), submit:

        (a) any such fresh evidence that he/she wishes to rely upon with an explanation as to why it was previously unavailable;

        (b) the names and addresses of any witnesses whom he/she wishes to call in person, and an outline of what each witness is expected to say.

3. At least 7 days prior to the date of the hearing, the Respondent shall provide the Appellant with any further evidence which it wishes to rely upon, together with the names and addresses of any witnesses which it wishes to call in person and an outline of what each witness is expected to say.

4. Neither party shall without the consent of the other or the permission of the AHG rely on any statement or document or call any witness other than those provided or identified under paragraphs 2 and 3 above.

Adjournment

5. At the request of a party or at his or her own volition, the Chair of the AHG may at any time adjourn the Appeal hearing if satisfied that it is in the interests of justice to do so. An application for the adjournment of an Appeal hearing that has not begun may be agreed between the parties.

6. In the event that any one member of the AHG is unwilling or unable to hear an entire case, the matter may proceed to be heard by 2 members of the AHG in accordance with the quorum requirements set out in the Disciplinary Regulations.

7. If the number of the members of the AHG willing or able to hear an entire case falls below 2 at any stage and the matter cannot be dealt with by adjournment of the hearing, a new AHG shall be appointed in accordance with the Disciplinary Regulations and the case shall be re-heard. In this event, a member of the AHG who sat previously and was not either of the members unable or unwilling to attend, shall be eligible to be appointed to the new AHG.

The Absence of the Appellant

8.   If at the Appeal hearing, the Appellant is not present in person or represented, the AHG may proceed to consider the matter in the Appellant's absence if it is satisfied that notice was properly served upon him or her in accordance with paragraph 1 above.

Private Hearing

9.   The hearing shall be conducted in private unless the Appellant requests otherwise save that the complainant (where applicable) shall be permitted to attend unless the Chair of the AHG decides otherwise at his/her sole discretion.

10.   For the avoidance of doubt, the Chief Executive of CILIP or his/her nominee and such other persons as are reasonably required by CILIP for secretarial/recording purposes may also be in attendance at the hearing.

Order of Proceedings

11.   The order of proceedings for the Appeal hearing, unless the Chair otherwise directs, will be as follows:

(i)   The Appellant shall outline the grounds of his/her appeal, adducing (with the agreement of the AHG) any fresh evidence;

(ii)   Hearing of any witnesses called by the Appellant followed by a cross-examination of such witnesses by or on behalf of the Respondent;

(iii)   Response by or on behalf of the Respondent;

(iv)   Hearing of any witnesses called by the Respondent followed by a cross-examination of such witnesses by or on behalf of the Appellant;

(v)   Closing submissions by or on behalf of the Appellant.

12.   If the appeal is against the disciplinary action ordered by the FHG (but not against its finding of professional misconduct), the procedure shall be as follows:

(i)   The Respondent shall outline the facts, informing the AHG of any circumstances known to it, whether favourable or adverse to the Appellant, that might be relevant to any order which the AHG might make;

(ii)   The Appellant shall be entitled to respond.

13.   Members of the AHG may themselves at any stage question witnesses, parties or representatives as they think fit.

14.   The decision of the AHG shall be reached by a majority, save that where the matter is determined by 2 members of the AHG and their decision is tied, the decision will be that which is most favourable to the Member.

Decision

15.   Following a decision by the AHG to affirm the FHG's finding of professional misconduct, the procedure set out at paragraph 12 above shall apply.

16.   The AHG may affirm, vary or rescind any finding or order of the FHG and may substitute any other finding or order (on such terms and conditions, if any) as it considers appropriate which the FHG might have made.

Appendix C

Regulations for the Retired Members Guild

Bye-law 42

Objects

The objects of the Retired Members Guild are to encourage Members of the Chartered Institute of Library and Information Professionals to remain in membership after retirement, to foster their social interaction, and to afford them the opportunity of making a positive contribution to librarianship and information science.

Activities

1. To support the efforts of the Chartered Institute of Library and Information Professionals for the improvement of libraries of all types.

2. To keep Members in touch with one another by arranging meetings and conferences and by the publication of a newsletter.

3. To seek out and make known, further benefits available for retired members.

4. To assist in the work of appropriate voluntary organizations by publicizing their activities and maintaining a register of expertise.

5. To undertake historical research and the conservation of records relating to the history of the Institute and its Branches and Groups.

Membership

Membership of the Guild is open to all personal Members of the Chartered Institute of Library and Information Professionals and to representatives of institutional members appointed in accordance with the bye-laws of the Institute. Persons and institutions shall become members of the Guild on notifying a desire to do so to the Secretary of the Guild and on of payment of the additional subscription.

The Guild shall be able to admit, at the discretion of the National Committee, persons who cannot be Fellows or Members of the Chartered Institute of Library and Information Professionals, as Personal Affiliates. Such members will not have the right to vote and will not be entitled to hold office. They will pay such annual subscriptions as may be determined by the National Committee.

Subordinate Bodies

The Guild Committee shall have authority to establish subordinate bodies on a regional or subject basis. The Committee shall require the Chair or Secretary of any such subordinate body to report regularly on its activities. The National Committee shall lay down such provisions for the conduct of business of subordinate bodies as it sees fit.

Officers

The Officers of the Guild shall be:

Chair
Secretary
Treasurer
Editor

Guild Committee

The affairs of the Guild shall be governed by a committee comprising the officers of the Guild and six elected members of the Guild. In addition the committee may co-opt up to three members of the Guild to the committee.

The Guild Year

The Year for all Guild activities, including terms of office and accounts shall be the calendar year.

Terms of Office

Officers of the Guild shall hold office for two years. Other committee members shall hold office for two years. In both cases terms shall commence on 1 January following election.

Elections

The election of officers and committee members shall be conducted in accordance with the regulations set out in Annex A (available upon application).

Committee Procedure

The Guild Committee shall meet not less frequently than twice a year. Meetings shall be called by the Chair or the Secretary. The Chair or Secretary shall call a meeting whenever required to do so by one third of the members of the committee and at other times at their discretion.

Each member of the committee, including co-opted members, shall exercise one vote. Observers invited to attend committee meetings shall have no vote. In the event of a tie, the chair shall have a casting vote irrespective of whether he/she has exercised his/her initial vote on the same issue. No decisions shall be taken by the committee if fewer than one quarter of the members are present but the committee may continue to sit despite the lack of that quorum.

The committee shall have authority to establish sub-committees and working parties as appropriate to deal with matters within the responsibilities of the Guild.

Accounts and Treasurer

The Treasurer of the Guild shall be responsible for the receipt of all monies due to the Guild and shall make such payments as the committee shall direct and shall maintain accounts of all receipts, payments, assets and liabilities of the Guild. In discharging his/her duties the Treasurer of the Guild shall adhere to the requirements of the bye-laws of the Chartered Institute of Library and Information Professionals and shall abide by such guidance as the Chartered Institute of Library and Information Professionals issues with regard to the keeping of accounts.

Two honorary auditors shall be appointed at the annual general meeting of the Guild. The honorary auditors shall not be members of the Guild committee and need not be members of the Guild. They shall be required to sign a certificate in respect of the adequacy of the accuracy of the accounts as presented to the annual general meeting.

The audited accounts, in addition to being presented to the annual general meeting, shall be communicated to members of the Guild either in the Guild's newsletter or otherwise.

Secretary

The Secretary of the Guild shall maintain a record of all proceedings and shall be responsible for preparing reports, issuing notices, conducting correspondence, giving notice of impending elections, circulating ballot papers in accordance with the election regulations in Annex A, and the safe keeping of ballot papers. She/he shall forward to the Secretary of the Chartered Institute of Library and Information Professionals any reports and records required under the bye-laws of the Institute and shall submit regularly to the Institute copies of the minutes of the Guild Committee meetings and general meetings of the Guild.

Annual General Meeting

A general meeting of the members of the Guild shall be held each year before 30 June.

Preliminary notice of the date of the meeting and the business to be considered shall be given to all members of the Guild not less than five weeks before the date of the meeting. Notice of further business proposed by the members shall be given to all members of the Guild not less than three weeks before the date of the meeting. Notice of the dates of meetings and of the business to be transacted shall be provided to members either by notice in the Chartered Institute of Library and Information Professionals Update or in the Guild newsletter or by other direct postal communication to members of the Guild.

At the annual general meeting there shall be distributed to every member present a copy of the audited accounts and the annual report of the Guild committee for the previous year. The texts of the annual report and accounts shall be communicated to all members of the Guild either in the Guild's newsletter or otherwise.

Special General Meeting

The Secretary of the Guild shall convene a special general meeting of the Guild when required to do so either by the Guild committee or by any 20 members of the Guild. Any demand for a special meeting shall state the business proposed to be conducted at the meeting. A special general meeting shall be held not later than 10 weeks after the receipt of the demand. A notice of the meeting and of the business to be conducted shall be given to all members of the Guild not less than three weeks before the date fixed for the meeting. It shall contain the words of any motion which has been submitted for the meeting. All members of the Guild shall be entitled to vote on any such motion whether present at the special meeting or not and for this purpose ballot papers shall be circulated with the notice of the meeting. The notice shall specify that ballot papers are to be returned not later than the day before the date of the special meeting.

No business shall be conducted at a special meeting unless 30 members of the Guild are present, irrespective of the number of ballot papers which have been returned by post.

Votes at general meetings shall be by show of hands unless the meeting decides otherwise by simple majority. Only those persons entitled to vote in elections of the Guild as detailed above shall be entitled to vote. In the event of a tie the chair of the meeting shall exercise a casting vote irrespective of whether he/she has exercised an initial vote on the issue.

Procedure at General Meetings

The chair of a general meeting shall conduct its business as far as possible in accordance with the rules of procedure adopted by the Chartered Institute of Library and Information Professionals for its general meetings mutatis mutandis.

Accidental omissions

Any accidental omission to give notice to or the non-receipt of notice by any member of the Guild shall not invalidate any resolution passed or proceedings held at any meeting.

Amendment of these rules

These rules may be amended only by decision of a general meeting of the Guild. No amendment shall be adopted unless it has been approved by two-thirds of the members voting in person or by postal ballot as detailed above. No amendment shall take effect until it has been approved by the Council of the Chartered Institute of Library and Information Professionals.

Appendix D

Regulations for Affiliated Members

Bye-law 4

1. Affiliated Membership of the Chartered Institute of Library and Information Professionals is available to all persons working in library and information services other than those entitled to be Chartered, Associate or Supporting Members of the Institute.

2. The purpose of the Affiliated Membership category is to encourage contact between members, to offer opportunity to such members to participate fully in the affairs of the Institute and to contribute to discussion of all matters relevant to the provision of library and information services.

3. There shall be an Affiliated Members' National Committee elected by Affiliated Members.

4. The Committee shall comprise:

   i. Six members elected by Affiliated Members of whom two shall retire each year. Retiring members of the Committee shall be eligible for re-election.

   ii. The two Affiliated Members' Councillors elected under Bye-law 45(e) of the Chartered Institute of Library and Information Professionals.

   iii. Up to three Affiliated Members of the Institute co-opted by the Committee.

5. A postal ballot shall be held annually for the election of the six Members referred to in Regulation 4(i) above. No postal ballot shall be required if the requisite number of nominations shall be made in writing, signed by two Affiliated Members and countersigned by the candidate who must also be an Affiliated Member. Nominations shall be made in writing, signed by two Affiliated Members and countersigned by candidate who must also be an Affiliated Member. Nominations must reach the Secretary of the National Committee by the date specified in the notice of election. All Affiliated Members who have not been suspended under the Institute's Bye-law 18 shall be eligible to vote. Notice of the election shall be published in the Chartered Institute of Information Professionals Update in the month preceding the election and the National Committee shall take such other steps as it deems appropriate to advertise the election to its Members. In the first elections held under this regulation two places shall be for a term of three years. The terms for each elected Member shall be established by lot.

6. The Officers of the Affiliated Membership category shall be:

   A Chair
   An Honorary Secretary
   An Honorary Treasurer

   chosen each year by the members of the Committee from among their own number.

7. Any vacancy occurring in the National Committee (apart from that of the two Affiliated Members' Councillors) shall be filled for the remainder of its term by the unsuccessful candidate at the preceding election who scored the largest number of votes. If there is no such candidate the Committee shall fill the vacancy by co-option.

8. The Committee shall meet at least three times a year. The quorum for a meeting of the National Committee shall be one third of the

members of the Committee subject to a minimum of three.

9. The Committee may authorize the establishment of Affiliated Members' Branches to serve as a vehicle for bringing together Affiliated Members in particular areas and shall make such arrangements for the governance of such Branches as it sees fit, subject to approval by the Council of the Chartered Institute of Library and Information Professionals.

10. The Committee will have the authority to establish special subject sub-committees, when appropriate, to deal with matters which are the concern of Affiliated Members and may nominate to serve upon such sub-committees persons who are not members of the Affiliated Members' Committee.

11. The Honorary Secretary of the Affiliated Membership category shall call all meetings of the National Committee and shall prepare and circulate to other members agendas, minutes and other appropriate papers and shall liaise with Chartered Institute of Library and Information Professionals Headquarters.

12. The Treasurer shall be responsible for all receipts and payments of funds of the Committee.

13. The Committee shall make an annual report to the Chartered Institute of Library and Information Professionals' on the affairs of the Committee and the Treasurer shall provide to Chartered Institute of Library and Information Professionals Headquarters income and expenditure accounts for each calendar year and a balance sheet as at the end of that year before 28 February in the next following year.

14. An Annual General Meeting of the Affiliated Members category shall be called each year on a date between 1 January and 30 April. The Annual General Meeting shall receive the accounts and a report on the activities of the category during the previous year.

15. Notice of the date and place of the Annual General Meeting shall be given to all Affiliated Members at least five weeks before the date of the meeting together with information on the matters to be discussed at the meeting. Any Affiliated Members may submit a motion of consideration at the meeting on giving at least two weeks' notice to the Secretary before the date of the meeting.

16. Any 20 Affiliated Members may require the Honorary Secretary to call a Special General Meeting of Affiliated Members upon serving a written notice requesting the meeting and stating its purpose. Such a meeting shall be held within eight weeks of the notice being served upon the Honorary Secretary of the National Committee. A notice of the meeting and the business to be considered shall be given to all Affiliated Members not less than three weeks before the date fixed for the meeting. Such notification shall contain the words of any motion which the member requiring the meeting intends to introduce.

17. The quorum for a meeting of an Annual or Special General Meeting shall be 20 members.

18. At any Annual or Special General Meeting on the demand of one-quarter of the Members present, rising in their seats after the Members have voted upon a motion but before the next business has been taken the Chairman shall rule that the motion be referred to a postal ballot of the Members and that the decision of the postal ballot shall be deemed to be the decision of the Meeting.

19. In the event of a tie an any vote at an Annual General Meeting, Special General Meeting or at a meeting of the National Committee, the Chair of the meeting shall have a casting vote additional to his/her other original vote.

Appendix E

Regulations for the Interim Policy Forum

Established January 2010
Bye-laws 84 and 85

Definitions

1. Words and phrases defined in the Institute's Royal Charter, Byelaws and General Regulations shall have the same meanings when used in these Regulations.

General

2. These regulations are for an Interim Policy Forum. They may be changed upon recommendation of the Governance Review but, at any rate, if still operational, they will be reviewed by Council at their last meeting in 2011.

Powers and Functions

3. The Interim Policy Forum is the focal point for policy generation on professional matters within CILIP. Its role shall consist of:

3.1. Advising Council and the Office of the President on policy priority areas and developing an annual advocacy Framework for consideration by Council

3.2. Initiating and commissioning policy development activity

3.3. Coordinating policy development activity across CILIP

3.4. Evaluating effectiveness of CILIP policy and advocacy activity

4. The Interim Policy Forum will be under the supervision of the Office of the President. It will formally report to Council which may accept, reject or amend its recommendations as it thinks fit. Council may also refer specific matters for the consideration of the Interim Policy Forum

Composition

5. The Interim Policy Forum shall comprise the following persons, all of whom must be individual members of CILIP:

5.1. The VicePresident who will be chair of the Interim Policy Forum

5.2. The Deputy Chair of the former Policy Forum

5.3. Two members of CILIP Council appointed annually

5.4. A representative from each of the four devolved nations appointed annually

5.5. Three members appointed by the President following an open selection process that shall be compatible with the standards and processes for making appointments to the boards of nondepartmental public bodies.

Meetings and Working Practices

6. Meetings of the Interim Policy Forum shall be called by the Chair:

6.1. At his or her discretion

6.2. By requirement of one third of the members of the Policy Forum

6.3. By requirement of the Council

7. Normally there will be three meetings of the Interim Policy Forum each year

7.1. Reasonable notice shall be given of every meeting to all those entitled to attend;

7.2. The quorum shall be one third of all Members of the Policy Forum;

7.3. Every Member of the Policy Forum shall be entitled to attend and speak at meetings;

7.4. Every Member of the Policy Forum shall be entitled to exercise one vote; and

7.5. In the case of an equality of votes, the Chair shall be entitled to a casting vote in addition to any other vote he or she may have.

8. The Chair shall ensure that a record of the meetings is prepared and delivered promptly to all members. The Chair shall notify Council of the outcomes of all Policy Forum members' meetings.

9. The Policy Forum shall have the power to invite observers (either members of the Institute or others) to attend their meetings for special purposes, either for a period of up to one year or for particular meetings.

10. The Policy Forum will engage all parts of CILIP, especially its Branches and Groups, in policy development as appropriate, through electronic communication and other means.

11. All members of the Institute shall be entitled to attend and observe meetings of the Policy Forum except when confidential matters are being discussed or the nature of the meeting precludes observers. The decision of the Chair shall be final on such matters.

12. Policy Forum may also conduct business electronically. A resolution of the Policy Forum without holding a meeting may be passed by a simple majority of the Policy Forum approving the resolution. Evidence of approval may be the signature of the relevant Member of the Policy Forum on a copy of the resolution returned to the Chief Executive Officer or other nominated officer by post or by fax or approval given by email received from any email address of the Member of the Policy Forum registered with the Institute for the purpose of sending and receiving notices.

Task and Finish Groups and Other Duly Appointed Bodies

13. The Policy Forum may establish Task and Finish Groups, or Joint Committees in cooperation with other bodies.

Appendix F

Part 1 Branch Rules

Established April 2003

Preamble and Interpretation

1. The Branch shall be known as the...
Branch of CILIP: The Chartered Institute of Library & Information Professionals

2. The affairs, procedures and governance of the Branch shall be regulated by the Charter, Bye-laws and Regulations of CILIP which shall apply to the Branch so far as they are applicable, and by these Rules, as approved by the Council of CILIP.

3. These rules may be amended only by decision of a general meeting of the Branch. No amendment shall be adopted unless it has been approved by two-thirds of the members voting in person or by postal ballot. No amendment shall take effect until it has been approved by the Council of CILIP; Council's provisional approval may be sought in advance of the Branch general meeting at which the amendment is to be proposed.

4. The geographical boundaries of the region within the scope of the Branch shall be as determined from time to time by the Council of CILIP. Any question on the definition of boundaries shall be determined by CILIP Council, whose decision shall be final.

Object

5. The object of the Branch is to further the aims of CILIP within its defined region. Aims and objectives are as set out in Appendix A to these Rules.

Activities

6.1 The Branch shall undertake the core roles and activities for branches as prescribed from time to time by CILIP Council set out in Appendix A to these Rules.

6.2 The Branch committee shall use its best endeavours to ensure that Branch activities are accessible to and representative of the interests of as broad a range as possible of the Branch membership.

6.3 The Branch shall not take any action, other than by recommendation to Council, which adversely affects other branches, the general conduct of the Institute or the external relations of the Institute. Any action that the Branch does take must have regard to the public statements made by CILIP and published on its website or by other means.

6.4 The funds and facilities of the Branch shall not be employed to promote the candidature of any candidate for election to office of the Institute or any other professional association; but this shall not prevent the provision of factual information on a non-discriminatory basis.

Members

7.1 All members of CILIP whose residential address (as registered with the Institute) is within the defined region shall be members of the Branch, save where the member has elected to become a member of the Branch serving the region where he or she works and has notified the Institute accordingly; and

7.2 All members of CILIP whose business address is within the region and who have elected to join the Branch, pursuant to clause 7.1; and

7.3 Any member of a branch who retires from employment to an address away from the Branch and who chooses to remain in membership of the Branch.

7.4 No member shall be a member of more than one Branch.

7.5 Supporting and institutional members of CILIP whose address (as registered with the Institute) is within the defined region may appoint a personal representative to be a member of the Branch. A personal representative is entitled to be placed on the mailing list of the Branch and to participate in its meetings and events, but may not vote in Branch proceedings nor stand for election to the Branch committee.

Corresponding Members

8. Any member of the Institute may become a corresponding member of any Branch of which they are not a member upon notification in writing to the Secretary of the Branch and on payment of any additional subscription determined by CILIP. A corresponding member is entitled to be placed on the mailing list of the Branch and to participate in its meetings and events, but may not vote in Branch proceedings nor stand for election to the Branch committee.

General Meetings

9. The annual general meeting of the Branch shall be held each year at such place and such time as the Committee may determine, provided that no more than 16 months shall elapse between such meetings.

10. All general meetings other than the Annual General Meeting shall be called Special General Meetings.

11. No business shall be transacted at any general meeting unless a quorum is present. Unless increased by the Branch in a general meeting, ten members present in person (but excluding the elected officers) shall constitute a quorum for an annual general meeting and 25 members present in person shall constitute a quorum for a special general meeting.

12. If within half an hour from the time appointed for the holding of a general meeting a quorum is not present the meeting, if convened on the requisition of members, shall be dissolved. In any other case it shall stand adjourned to a date, time and place to be determined by the chair of the meeting and notified to members and if, at such adjourned meeting, a quorum is not present with half an hour from the time appointed for holding the meeting the members present shall be a quorum.

13. All business that is transacted at general meetings shall be deemed special business with the exception of the ordinary business of the Annual General Meeting specified in clause 19.

14. The chair of a general meeting shall conduct its business as far as possible in accordance with the rules of procedure set out in Appendix B.

Annual General Meeting

15. Notice of the annual general meeting shall be given to all members of the Branch not less than 35 clear days before the date of the meeting.

16. The notice shall specify the place, the day and the hour of the meeting, the business to be transacted and that attendance at Branch AGMs will be free of charge. General provisions about notices are given in paragraphs 59 and 60.

17. A statement shall appear on the notice that, if a member wishes to put a motion to the meeting, notice of the motion shall be made in writing, signed by the member, and shall be served on the Branch Secretary not less than twenty-one clear days before the date of the meeting.

18. Notice of further business proposed by members shall be given to all members of the Branch not less than fourteen clear days before the meeting. All such further business shall be deemed special business.

19. The ordinary business of the AGM shall be to:

    a) Receive and consider the annual report of the Branch committee which shall include reports from any sub-branches

    b) Receive and consider the Branch accounts and the report thereon by the independent examiners

    c) Appoint independent examiners for the ensuing year

    d) Receive the result of the election of members to the Branch committee

    e) Receive the annual report of the Branch councillor which may be included in the annual report of the Branch Committee. The minutes of the preceding AGM, containing a transcript of all resolutions passed, shall be read at or submitted to the AGM.

20. The accounts and reports shall be distributed to all members of the Branch before the date of the AGM in the Branch newsletter, on the Branch website or otherwise.

Special General Meetings

21. The Branch committee may whenever it thinks fit convene a special general meeting of the Branch.

22. Notice of the place, the day and the hour of a special general meeting and of the business to be transacted shall be given to all members of the Branch not less than 21 clear days before the date fixed for the meeting.

23. The Branch committee shall also convene a special general meeting on the requisition of 25 members of the Branch as at the date of the signing of the requisition. A special general meeting shall be held not later than 10 weeks after receipt of a members' requisition.

24. A requisition must state the objects of the meeting, and must be signed by the members making the requisition and served on the Branch secretary, and may consist of several documents in like form each signed by one or more of the members making the requisition.

25. If the Branch committee does not issue notice of a special general meeting within seven weeks of the receipt of a requisition, the members making the requisition may require the Secretary of CILIP to convene a special general meeting of the Branch.

Votes of Members

26. The persons entitled to vote at general meetings of the Branch are the corporate members of the branch whose subscriptions are not in arrears on 30th April in the year in

which the meeting takes place. Votes may not be given by proxy.

27. At every general meeting a resolution put to the vote of the meeting shall be decided on a show of hands or by secret ballot as appropriate. In the case of an equality of votes, the Chair of the meeting may exercise a second or casting vote.

28. Unless a postal ballot be demanded, a declaration by the Chair of the meeting that a resolution has been carried or carried by a particular majority or lost shall be conclusive, and an entry to that effect in the minutes of the proceedings of the meeting shall be sufficient evidence of the fact so declared.

Postal Ballots

29. On a motion of special business, upon or before the declaration of the result of the show of hands, a postal ballot may be demanded by the Chair or by at least one quarter of the members present and entitled to vote. Notwithstanding a demand for a postal ballot on any motion, the meeting may continue for the transaction of any other business in respect of which a ballot has not been demanded.

30. If a postal ballot is demanded, the meeting shall forthwith appoint three persons, who need not be members, to act as scrutineers. The Chair shall reduce the resolutions or amendments into the form of alternative propositions so as best to take the sense of the members on the substantial question or questions at issue.

    The wording of the resolution to appear on the postal ballot paper shall be decided and agreed by the members present in person and entitled to vote at the meeting. Voting papers setting forth these propositions shall be issued within 14 days after the meeting and shall be returnable so as to be receivable

within 21 days after the meeting. The scrutineers shall meet not less than 21 days nor more than 28 days after the meeting and shall draw up a report of the result of the voting, stating what voting papers have been rejected for non-observance of the notes and directions thereon or disqualified by reason of the voter being in arrears or otherwise ineligible to vote. The report of the scrutineers shall be conclusive as to the result of the voting. In the event of a tie on a postal ballot conducted under this clause, the resolution shall be declared not carried. The result of the postal ballot shall be deemed the resolution of the general meeting at which the ballot was demanded and the result shall take effect from the date of the scrutineers' report.

31. In addition to the right to demand a postal ballot at a general meeting, any member of the Branch eligible to vote is entitled to vote by postal ballot on the election of Branch officers and members of the Branch committee (Appendix C).

32. The Branch committee, at its discretion, may decide to hold a postal ballot on any motion to be put to a special general meeting. In this event, the notice of the meeting shall include a statement of entitlement to vote and ballot papers shall be circulated with the notice of the meeting. The notice shall specify that ballot papers must be returned to the Secretary not later than 48 hours before the time of the meeting.

33. A member whose postal vote has been counted will not be permitted to vote in person at the meeting on the motion for which his/her postal vote has been cast.

34. A postal ballot may be conducted by electronic means in accordance with any guidance on electronic voting as may be issued by CILIP.

Branch Committee

35. The affairs of the Branch shall be governed by a committee comprising:

    a) The elected officers of the Branch

    b) A number of corporate members determined by a general meeting of the Branch but not exceeding 12 and elected in accordance with the procedures set out in Appendix C. Corporate members are defined in the CILIP Bye-laws as Chartered Fellows, Honorary Fellows, Chartered Members and Associates.

    c) One affiliate member elected in accordance with the procedures set out in Appendix C.

    d) The immediate past chair (if any)

36. The committee may co-opt up to four members, who shall hold office until the next following Annual General Meeting. Reasons for co-option should be recorded in committee minutes.

37.1 The committee may invite a representative of each CILIP Special Interest Group active in the region to attend committee meetings from time to time.

37.2 The committee may invite observers from those sub-branches not represented on committee and up to four others to attend its meetings. Observers shall be appointed by the committee for not more than one year, after which their attendance shall be reviewed. Observers shall not be eligible to vote on the business of the Branch committee. Any member of the Branch may attend a meeting of the Branch Committee as a casual observer.

37.3 The CILIP staff liaison officer shall normally attend meetings of the Branch committee as an additional observer and receive all relevant papers.

38. The CILIP Branch Councillor elected in accordance with the CILIP Bye-laws shall be an ex-officio member of the Branch committee and shall make a report to every meeting of the Branch committee.

39. On the death, resignation or termination of office of an elected member, the Branch committee may fill the vacant place for the remainder of the term.

40. A member absent without reason from three consecutive meetings of the committee may have his/her membership of the committee terminated by resolution of the Branch committee. The office of a Branch committee member shall also be terminated in accordance with the CILIP Bye-laws.

Proceedings of the Branch Committee

41. Voting at meetings of the Branch committee shall be by show of hands or by secret ballot as appropriate and, in the case of an equality of votes, the Chair may exercise a second or casting vote. Electronic meetings cannot incorporate voting until any guidance on electronic voting is issued by CILIP.

42. The committee shall meet not less than four times between each Annual General Meeting and at least two of these meetings shall not be conducted by electronic means. The Chair or Secretary shall convene a meeting whenever required to do so by one-third of the members of the committee and at other times at their discretion.

43. The quorum for meetings of the committee shall be six members of the committee including officers present in person or by electronic means for meetings conducted in that manner.

44. The committee may transact business by electronic means and any resolution shall be

deemed to be the resolution of the committee and recorded as such in the minutes of the meeting. The committee will comply with any guidance on electronic meetings and voting as may be issued by CILIP.

45. The committee shall not have power to borrow or raise money, nor to purchase or lease any real property, nor to enter into any operating lease or any other financial commitment in excess of its annual capitation or reserves, whichever is the higher, without the prior approval of CILIP Council.

Officers

46. The elected officers of the Branch shall be:

    - Chair
    - Vice Chair
    - Honorary Secretary
    - Honorary Treasurer

47. From amongst its members, the Branch committee shall appoint the following posts:

    - Editor
    - One representative and deputy representative for each Sub-Branch within the Branch
    - One representative to each working party set up by the committee

48. From amongst its members, the Branch committee may appoint the following posts:

    - Equal Opportunities Officer
    - ICT Development Officer
    - Events Co-ordinator
    - International Relations Officer
    - Membership & Marketing Officer
    - Learning Co-ordinator
    - Web Manager
    - And such other posts as it thinks fit.

Election of Officers and Members of the Branch Committee

49. The election of officers and other members of the branch committee shall be conducted in accordance with the regulations set out at Appendix C.

50.1 A retiring elected officer shall be eligible for re-election to the same post provided that an elected officer who has held elected office for five consecutive years will not be eligible for re-election to the same post until the annual election in the following year.

50.2 A retiring member of the branch committee shall be eligible for re-election provided that a member who has been a member of the branch committee for ten consecutive years will not be eligible for re-election until the annual election in the following year. Any period of office as an elected officer or ex-officio member of the branch committee will count towards the maximum continuous ten year period.

Sub-Branches

51.1 The Branch committee may establish one or more sub-branches to deal with matters within its responsibilities and to facilitate provision of services to members on a geographic basis. The Branch committee shall determine the boundaries of a geographic sub-branch, which shall not necessarily conform to those of any local government boundaries. The Branch committee shall set the terms of reference for all sub-branches.

51.2 The Branch committee may, at its discretion, dissolve a sub-Branch in which case all monies standing to the credit of the sub-Branch after all liabilities have been met shall be returned to the Honorary Treasurer of the Branch. The Branch shall, however, give at least twelve months notice of the intention to dissolve a sub-Branch.

52. The affairs, procedures and governance of any sub-branch shall be regulated by the Branch rules, things being changed that have to be changed and by the Charter, Bye-laws and Regulations of CILIP. The Branch committee may lay down provisions for the conduct of other areas of the business of sub-branches as it sees fit.

53. The Branch committee shall appoint a representative and deputy representative to each sub-branch committee to maintain liaison with the sub-branches. The representative or deputy representative will normally attend sub-branch committee meetings. The Chair of the Branch Committee shall be a member of each subbranch ex officio.

Working Parties

54.1 The Branch committee may establish working parties to deal with a specific task within the responsibilities of the Branch and set their terms of reference. A working party shall not be appointed for a period in excess of 12 months, nor remain in existence for more than 12 without review by the Branch committee and shall report back to the Branch committee.

54.2 The Branch shall appoint a representative to each working party to maintain liaison. The Chair of the Branch Committee shall be a member of each Working Party ex officio.

Accounts

55. The Honorary Treasurer of the Branch shall be responsible for the receipt of all moneys due to the Branch and shall make such payments as the Branch committee shall direct and shall maintain accounts of all receipts, payments, assets and liabilities of the Branch. In discharging his/her duties, the Honorary Treasurer shall adhere to the requirements of the Bye-laws of CILIP and shall abide by such guidance as CILIP issues with regard to the keeping of accounts.

56. The annual accounts shall be prepared on a calendar year basis. Two independent examiners shall inspect the annual accounts of the Branch and, if thought fit, shall sign a certificate in the form specified by CILIP.

57. The independent examiners shall be appointed at the annual general meeting of the Branch. They shall not be members of the Branch committee and need not be members of the Branch.

Secretary

58. The Secretary of the Branch shall maintain a record of all proceedings and shall be responsible for preparing reports, issuing notices, conducting correspondence, giving notices of impending elections, circulating ballot papers in accordance with the election regulations in Appendix C, and the safekeeping of ballot papers. The Secretary shall forward to the Secretary of CILIP any reports and records required under the Byelaws of CILIP and shall submit regularly to CILIP copies of the minutes of the Branch committee meetings and general meetings of the Branch.

Notices

59.1 All notices required by these Rules may be given:

a)   In person; or

b) By an announcement in either CILIP Update/Gazette or in the Branch newsletter; or

c) By an announcement on CILIP's or the Branch's website; or

d) By electronic communication; or

e) By postal communication.

59.2 In the case of postal communication, a notice shall have been deemed to have been served on the member on the third day after the day it is posted if sent by first class post and on the fifth day after posting if sent by second class post.

60. The accidental omission to give notice to or the non-receipt of notice by any member of the Branch shall not invalidate any resolution passed nor the proceedings at any meeting.

Transitional Provisions

61.1 Branch Councillors should propose motions for adoption of these Rules at the next AGM of each Branch, for the Rules to be adopted to take effect from 1 January 2004.

61.2 Any term of office undertaken before the formal introduction of these Rules not later than 1st April 2004 shall not count towards the maximum terms of office set in these Rules.

61.3 At the first meeting of the Branch committee after 1st April 2004, the elected members of the committee shall draw lots to determine which members are to retire after one year's, two years' and three years' service. Members so retiring will be eligible to stand for re-election.

61.4 The Branch committee may apply to Council for agreement to co-opt into membership of the Branch any former member of the Branch whose membership has been terminated as a result of boundary changes. This will apply for

two years from the date of the boundary changes.

61.5 Existing Branches or sub-branches which will be within the boundaries of new Branches will automatically become a sub-branch of the new Branch until at least twelve months after adoption of these Rules by CILIP Council. Committees in office at 31 March 2003 will remain in office until such time as the new Branches have established policies for sub-branch organisation and their Rules. Sub-branch organisations and their Rules will be established by resolution at the Branch AGM or SGM.

Branch Rules – Appendix A

CILIP Branches in England: Roles and Responsibilities

Approved by CILIP Council, April 2006

Background

CILIP Branches in England became co-terminus with Regional Development Agencies (RDAs) by April 2004. This new regional landscape offers fresh challenges and opportunities for the LIS sector generally and CILIP members in particular. It is important that there is a strong LIS focus in each region to promote the sector, its services and its practitioners. And, besides continuing to act as a conduit for matters of national policy and practice, each Branch now has a greater chance to establish its own identity based on regional priorities. CILIP has recognised the implications of the regional structure in its strategic planning. It needs to provide modern, ICT-based, communications and support which will help Branches to play their part in delivering distributed services to members. In many cases it will be appropriate for Branches to enter into partnerships with other key organisations (e.g. LIS education providers or regional training consortia) to provide local services. Sub-Branches should be formed where geographically appropriate, to allow networking and partnerships at sub-regional level. The principle of equity of services to all members should be paramount. One of the purposes of this document is to support the development of a sustainable financial model for CILIP. Budget allocations to English Branches need in future to be based on active business plans which take proper account of varying regional priorities, rather than on the formulaic capitation of the past.

Core Activities

This list of core activities is set in the context of 'what works for the branch'. Each branch will use the mechanisms and methods most appropriate for its local circumstances.

A. Representing CILIP in the Regions

A1. Represent CILIP to Members and Members to CILIP, providing a strong, collective voice to convey Members' views within CILIP

A2. Consult members on local and regional issues, and make representations on their behalf. Taking a view on professional matters that bring together the various sectors of the profession and other related professions where appropriate

A3. Participate in CILIP policy making processes, giving Members a voice in strategic decision-making within CILIP

A4. Implement CILIP policy at Regional level

B. CPD and Training

B1. Support and promote the Framework of Qualifications processes

B2. Establish links with all sections of the community to ensure that all Branch Members have the opportunity to be included and involved in Branch activities

B3. Maintain good relationships with local LIS education providers

B4. Encourage and provide opportunities for CPD

B5. Provide opportunities for Members to participate in and run their professional body

B6. Act as a knowledge management (KM) resource for advice on jobs, careers and personal development

C. Networking, Co-ordination, Support

C1. Co-ordinate opportunities for colleagues to meet to share information and encourage discussion of key issues. Provide a focus for professional activity within the Branch.

C2. Co-ordinate and support professional activity in the Region in liaison with all Special Interest Groups (SIGs) or via Sub-Branches of the Branch

D. Communications

D1. Communicate with members regularly using delivery mechanisms that best meet users' needs and demands. Establish two-way communication channels with the Regions and Home Nations, Ridgmount Street and within the Branch

D2. Establish a pattern of Committee meetings, including virtual ones, varying the location, format and timing of meetings to encourage as wide a range of people as possible to participate

Suggested Activities

1. Promote CPD to employers and monitor progress, e.g. hold a CPD forum to discuss and assess employers' requirements. Arrange courses at low cost to assist development of skills and knowledge. Recognise achievements at the local level, e.g. presentation of Framework of Qualifications Certificates, hold local ceremonies to acknowledge Honorary Awards and Fellowships

2. Collaborate with training organisations, e.g. Ufl, Learndirect, Learning and Skills Council

3. Participate in the marketing of library and information work as a career, e.g. representation at local/regional careers fairs or courses and events, utilising programmes of meetings, conferences, training courses, publications, research and opportunities to learn by experience

4. Promote the interests of the Branch by having or seeking representation on appropriate external bodies

5. Engage at a political level in the wider policies and developments within the region

6. Aim to provide a voice for Members in strategic decision making at RDA levels

7. Participate/be involved in regional LIS planning strategy and development

8. Foster good relationships with local employers, Chambers of Commerce, etc

9. Work with related organisations at local level (e.g. ILAM, SCONUL)

10. Support international relations with Library Associations and other organisations such as VSO

Branch Rules – Appendix B

Rules of Procedure for General and Committee Meetings of the Branch

Chair

1. In the absence of the Chair of the Branch Committee, the Vice Chair or Honorary Treasurer shall take the chair. In the absence of these officers the meeting shall elect a chair from amongst the corporate members present.

Discipline

2. The Chair shall call a member to order for irrelevance, repetition, unbecoming language, imputations of motives or any breach of order, and may direct such member if speaking to discontinue. The Chair may also direct such member to withdraw from the meeting. The ruling of the Chair on points of order, matters arising in debate or the admissibility of a personal explanation shall be final, and shall not be open to discussion.

Moving of Motions

3.1 No motion shall be considered or voted upon unless it has been duly moved and seconded. A motion from the Chair shall require no seconder.

3.2 The Chair or any member present may ask for any motion to be submitted in writing before it is put to the vote.

3.3 Members may seek further information or clarification on any matter under discussion during a meeting but must advise the Honorary Secretary, where possible in advance of the meeting, so that such information can be available.

Withdrawal of Motions

4. A motion may be withdrawn by the mover with the concurrence of the seconder. A member submitting a report may, with the consent of the meeting, withdraw a paragraph or recommendation contained in the report.

Absence of Mover

5. Business under any motion on the agenda paper shall not be proceeded with in the absence of the member in whose name it stands unless he/she has given authority in

writing of his/her consent that it should be taken up by some other member.

Notices of Motion

6. The only motions which will be considered at general meetings are those of which due notice has been given in accordance with the Branch Rules.

Procedural Motions

7. During debate on motions the following procedural motions only shall be admitted:

    i)   To amend the motion
    ii)   That consideration of the question be postponed
    iii) That the meeting does proceed to the next business iv) That the question be now put v) That the meeting does now adjourn

Branch Rules – Appendix C
Regulations for the Conduct of Branch Elections

1. Elections for the elected officers and members of the Branch committee shall take place in the two months preceding the expiry of the existing members' term of office.

2. Subject to CILIP Regulations 12 and 13 concerning payment of subscriptions, corporate members of the branch are entitled to vote in the elections and to be nominated for election.

3. Subject to CILIP Regulations 12 and 13 concerning payment of subscriptions, affiliate members of the branch are entitled to vote for the affiliate member representative in the elections and to be nominated for election as the affiliate member representative.

4. Notice of annual elections and an invitation to submit nominations shall be published in either CILIP Update/Gazette or in the Branch Newsletter at least 14 days before the closing date for nominations. A similar notice shall appear in any bulletin, newsletter, e-lists or circular distributed to all members of the Branch at the appropriate time and on the Branch's website.

5. Nominations of members of the Branch for election as officers or as members of the Branch Committee shall be made in writing, signed by two members of the Branch entitled to vote and counter-signed by the candidate to indicate consent. Nominations must reach the Honorary Secretary not later than 31st January immediately preceding the period for which the election is held. No candidate shall be nominated for more than one category of office and shall specify on the nomination paper the category for which he/she proposes to stand.

6. Election shall be by postal ballot of all members of the Branch who are entitled to vote, namely: a) Corporate members (Chartered Fellows, Honorary Fellows, Chartered Members and Associates) are entitled to vote for the elected officers and Corporate Members of the Branch committee. b) Affiliate Members are entitled to vote for the Affiliate Member of the Branch committee. No other members are entitled to vote.

7. Ballot papers, together with a brief curriculum vitae supplied by the candidate, shall be circulated to all eligible members of the Branch within 14 days of the close of nominations.

8. Two scrutineers shall be appointed by the Committee before each election for the purpose of supervision of the conduct of the election and to record the voting. Such scrutineers shall not be members of the

Committee nor candidates for election, and need not be members of the Branch. The votes shall be counted during the second week in March.

9. The officers of the Branch Committee shall take office from 1st April following the election for a period of one year.

10. The members of the Branch Committee (other than the elected officers) shall take office from 1st April following the election for a period of three years.

11. The names of the members elected to the Branch Committee shall be sent immediately after each election to the Secretary of CILIP together with a copy of the report of the scrutineers.

12. The names of the members elected to the Branch Committee shall be notified to the members of the Branch as soon as practicable after each election, by means of the branch newsletter, website or otherwise.

13. The Scrutineers shall report to the Annual General Meeting on the last election and the results thereof.

Appendix F

Part 2 SIG Rules

Established December 2003

Preamble and Interpretation

1. The Special Interest Group shall be known as the .... Group of CILIP: The Chartered Institute of Library & Information Professionals.

2. The affairs, procedures and governance of the Group shall be regulated by the Charter, Bye-laws and Regulations of CILIP which shall apply to the Group so far as they are applicable, and by these Rules, as approved by the Council of CILIP.

3. These rules may be amended only by decision of a general meeting of the Group. No amendment shall be adopted unless it has been approved by two-thirds of the members, voting in person or by postal ballot. No amendment shall take effect until it has been approved by the Council of CILIP; Council's provisional approval may be sought in advance of the Group general meeting at which the amendment is to be proposed.

4. The Group's sphere of interest shall be as determined from time to time by the Council of CILIP after consultation with the Group Committee, and any question thereon shall be determined by CILIP Council, whose decision shall be final.

Object

5.1 The object of the Group is to further the aims of CILIP within its defined sphere of interest by uniting those members of CILIP and the Group engaged or interested in its issues, fostering communication, facilitating exchange of experience and by promoting relevant work.

5.2 The Group's sphere of interest is
....

Activities

6.1 The Group shall pursue its object by means of meetings, seminars, conferences, publications and by such other means as the Group deems appropriate subject to CILIP's Charter, Bye-laws and Regulations.

6.2 The Group shall not take any action, other than by recommendation to Council, which affects any other Group, the general conduct of the Institute or the external relations of the Institute. Any action that the Group does take must have regard to the public statements made by CILIP and published on its website or by other means.

6.3 The funds and facilities of the Group shall not be employed to promote the candidature of any candidate for election to office of the Institute or any other professional association; but this shall not prevent the provision of factual information on a non-discriminatory basis.

Members

7.1 Any personal member of the Institute may become a member of the Group upon notification in writing to the CILIP Secretariat and on payment of any additional subscription determined by CILIP.

7.2 Supporting and institutional members of CILIP may appoint a personal representative to be a member of the Group upon notification in writing to the CILIP Secretariat and payment of any additional subscription that may be due. Such a personal representative is entitled to be placed on the mailing list of the Group and to participate in its meetings and events, but may not vote in Group proceedings nor stand for election to the Group committee.

Associated Members

8.1 The Group committee may admit persons who are not members of CILIP as associated members of the Group upon application to the Secretary and payment of such subscription as the Group committee may determine.

8.2 Associated members may become members of the Group committee, but not in the office of Chair, Honorary Treasurer or Honorary Secretary, nor may associated members form the majority of members of the committee.

8.3 Associated members may not take part in elections for the Group councillor, but they may vote on the election of officers and members to the Group committee and other matters internal to the Group.

8.4 Unless stated otherwise, all references in these Rules to Group members shall include associated members.

General Meetings

9. The annual general meeting of the Group shall be held each year at such place and such time as the Committee may determine, provided that no more than 16 months shall elapse between such meetings.

10. All general meetings other than the Annual General Meeting shall be called Special General Meetings.

11. No business shall be transacted at any general meeting unless a quorum is present. Ten members present in person (but excluding the elected officers) shall constitute a quorum for an annual general meeting and 25 members present in person shall constitute a quorum for a special general meeting, unless increased by the Group in a general meeting.

12. If within half an hour from the time appointed for the holding of a general meeting a quorum is not present the meeting, if convened on the requisition of members, shall be dissolved. In any other case it shall stand adjourned to a date, time and place to be determined by the chair of the meeting and notified to members and if, at such adjourned meeting, a quorum is not present within half an hour from the time appointed for holding the meeting the members present shall be a quorum.

13. All business that is transacted at general meetings shall be deemed special business with the exception of the ordinary business of the Annual General Meeting specified in clause 19.

14. The chair of a general meeting shall conduct its business as far as possible in accordance with the rules of procedure set out in Appendix A.

Annual General Meeting

15. Notice of the annual general meeting shall be given to all members of the Group not less than 35 clear days before the date of the meeting.

16. The notice shall specify the place, the day and the hour of the meeting and the business to be transacted and that attendance at Group AGMs will be free of charge. General provisions about notices are given in paragraphs 59 and 60.

17. A statement shall appear on the notice that, if a member wishes to put a motion to the meeting, notice of the motion shall be made in writing, signed by the member, and shall be served on the Group Secretary not less than twenty-one clear days before the date of the meeting.

18. Notice of further business proposed by members shall be given to all members of the Group not less than fourteen clear days before the meeting. All such further business shall be deemed special business.

19. The ordinary business of the AGM shall be to:

    a) Receive and consider the annual report of the Group committee which shall include reports from any sub-Groups

    b) Receive and consider the Group accounts and the report thereon by the independent examiners

    c) Appoint independent examiners for the ensuing year

    d) Fix the subscription payable by associated members in the ensuing year

    e) Receive the result of the election of members to the Group committee

    f) Receive the annual report of the Group councillor which may be included in the annual report of the Group Committee. The minutes of the preceding AGM, containing a transcript of all resolutions passed, shall be read at or submitted to the AGM.

20. The draft accounts and reports shall be distributed to all members of the Group before the date of the AGM in the Group newsletter, on the Group website or otherwise.

Special General Meetings

21. The Group committee may whenever it thinks fit convene a special general meeting of the Group.

22. Notice of the place, the day and the hour of a special general meeting and of the business to be transacted shall be given to all members of the Group not less than 21 clear days before the date fixed for the meeting.

23. The Group committee shall also convene a special general meeting on the requisition of 25 members of the Group as at the date of the signing of the requisition. A special general meeting shall be held not later than 10 weeks after receipt of a members' requisition.

24. A requisition must state the objects of the meeting, and must be signed by the members making the requisition and served on the Group secretary, and may consist of several documents in like form each signed by one or more of the members making the requisition.

25. If the Group committee does not issue notice of a special general meeting within seven weeks of the receipt of a requisition, the members making the requisition may require the Secretary of CILIP to convene a special general meeting of the Group.

Votes of Members

26. The persons entitled to vote at general meetings of the Group are the members of the Group whose subscriptions are not in arrears on 30th April in the year in which the meeting takes place. Votes may not be given by proxy.

27. At every general meeting a resolution put to the vote of the meeting shall be decided on a show of hands or by secret ballot as appropriate. In the case of an equality of votes, the Chair of the meeting may exercise a second or casting vote.

28. Unless a postal ballot be demanded, a declaration by the Chair of the meeting that a resolution has been carried or carried by a particular majority or lost shall be conclusive, and an entry to that effect in the minutes of the proceedings of the meeting shall be sufficient evidence of the fact so declared.

Postal Ballots

29. On a motion of special business, upon or before the declaration of the result of the show of hands, a postal ballot may be demanded by the Chair or by at least one quarter of the members present and entitled to vote. Notwithstanding a demand for a postal ballot on any motion, the meeting may continue for the transaction of any other business in respect of which a ballot has not been demanded.

30. If a postal ballot is demanded, the meeting shall forthwith appoint three persons, who need not be members, to act as scrutineers. The Chair shall reduce the resolutions or amendments into the form of alternative propositions so as best to take the sense of the members on the substantial question or questions at issue. The wording of the resolution to appear on the postal ballot paper shall be decided and agreed by the members present in person and entitled to vote at the meeting. Voting papers setting forth these propositions shall be issued within 14 days after the meeting and shall be returnable so as to be receivable within 21 days after the meeting. The scrutineers shall meet not less than 21 days nor more than 28 days after the meeting and shall draw up a report of the result of the voting, stating what voting papers have been rejected for non-observance of the notes and directions thereon or disqualified by reason of the voter being in arrears or otherwise ineligible to vote. The report of the scrutineers shall be conclusive as to the result of the voting. In the event of a tie on a postal ballot conducted under this clause, the resolution shall be declared not carried. The result of the postal ballot shall be deemed the resolution of the general meeting at which the ballot was demanded and the result shall take effect from the date of the scrutineers' report.

31. In addition to the right to demand a postal ballot at a general meeting, any member of the Group eligible to vote is entitled to vote by postal ballot on the election of Group officers and members of the Group committee (Appendix B).

32. The Group committee, at its discretion, may decide to hold a postal ballot on any motion to be put to a special general meeting. In this event, the notice of the meeting shall include a statement of entitlement to vote and ballot papers shall be circulated with the notice of the meeting. The notice shall specify that ballot papers must be returned to the Secretary not later than 48 hours before the time of the meeting.

33. A member whose postal vote has been counted will not be permitted to vote in person at the meeting on the motion for which his/her postal vote has been cast.

34. A postal ballot may be conducted by electronic means in accordance with any guidance on electronic voting as may be issued by CILIP.

Group Committee

35 The affairs of the Group shall be governed by a committee comprising:

   a) The elected officers of the Group
   b) A number of members determined by a general meeting of the Group but not exceeding 12 and elected in accordance with the procedures set out in Appendix B
   c) The immediate past chair (if any)

36. The committee may co-opt up to four members, who shall hold office until the next following Annual General Meeting. Reasons for co-option should be recorded in committee minutes.

37.1 The committee may invite observers from those sub-Groups not represented on committee and up to four others to attend its meetings. Observers shall be appointed by the committee for not more than one year, after which their attendance shall be reviewed. Observers shall not be eligible to vote on the business of the Group committee. Any member of the Group may attend a meeting of the Group committee as a casual observer.

37.2 The CILIP staff liaison officer shall normally attend meetings of the Group committee as an additional observer and receive all relevant papers.

38. The CILIP Group Councillor elected in accordance with the CILIP Bye-laws shall be an ex-officio member of the Group committee and shall make a report to every meeting of the Group committee.

39. On the death, resignation or termination of office of an elected member, the Group committee may fill the vacant place for the remainder of the term.

40. A member absent without reason from three consecutive meetings of the committee may have his/her membership of the committee terminated by resolution of the Group committee. The office of a Group committee member shall also be terminated in accordance with the CILIP Bye-laws.

Proceedings of the Group Committee

41. Voting at meetings of the Group committee shall be by show of hands or by secret ballot as appropriate and, in the case of an equality of votes, the Chair may exercise a second or casting vote. Electronic meetings cannot incorporate voting until any guidance on electronic voting is issued by CILIP.

42. The committee shall meet not less than four times between each Annual General Meeting and at least two of these meetings shall not be conducted by electronic means. The Chair or Secretary shall convene a meeting whenever required to do so by one-third of the members of the committee and at other times at their discretion.

43. The quorum for meetings of the committee shall be six members of the committee including officers present in person or by electronic means for meetings conducted in that manner.

44. The committee may transact business by electronic means and any resolution shall be deemed to be the resolution of the committee and recorded as such in the minutes of the meeting. The committee will comply with any guidance on electronic meetings and voting as may be issued by CILIP.

45. The committee shall not have power to borrow or raise money, nor to purchase or lease any real property, nor to enter into any operating lease or any other financial commitment in excess of its annual capitation or reserves, whichever is the higher, without the prior approval of CILIP Council.

Officers

46. The elected officers of the Group shall be: Chair Vice Chair Honorary Secretary Honorary Treasurer

47. From amongst its members, the Group committee shall appoint the following posts: Editor One representative and deputy representative for each Sub-Group within the Group One representative to each working party set up by the committee

48. From amongst its members, the Group committee may appoint the following posts:

    Equal Opportunities Officer
    ICT Development Officer
    Events Co-ordinator
    International Relations Officer
    Membership & Marketing Officer
    Learning Co-ordinator
    Web Manager and/or Editor

    And such other posts as it thinks fit.

Election of Officers and Members of the Group Committee

49. The election of officers and other members of the Group committee shall be conducted in accordance with the regulations set out at Appendix B.

50.1 A retiring elected officer shall be eligible for re-election to the same post provided that an elected officer who has held elected office for five consecutive years will not be eligible for re-election to the same post until the annual election in the following year.

50.2 A retiring member of the Group committee shall be eligible for re-election provided that a member who has been a member of the Group committee for ten consecutive years will not be eligible for re-election until the annual election in the following year. Any period of office as an elected officer or ex-officio member of the Group committee will count towards the maximum continuous ten year period.

Sub-Groups

51.1 The Group committee may establish one or more sub-Groups to deal with matters within its sphere of interest and/or to facilitate provision of services to members on a geographic basis. The Group committee shall set the terms of reference for all sub-Groups and shall determine the boundaries of a geographic sub-Group, which shall not necessarily conform to those of any local government boundaries. From time to time the Group committee may amend these terms of reference following consultation with the existing sub-Group committee.

51.2 The Group committee may, at its discretion, dissolve a sub-Group in which case all monies standing to the credit of the sub-Group after all liabilities have been met shall be returned to the Honorary Treasurer of the Group. The Group shall, however, give at least twelve months notice of the intention to dissolve a sub-Group.

52. The affairs, procedures and governance of any sub-Group shall be regulated by the Group rules things being changed that have to be changed and by the Charter, Bye-laws and Regulations of CILIP. The Group committee may lay down provisions for the conduct of

other areas of the business of sub-Groups as it sees fit.

53. The Group committee shall appoint a representative and deputy representative to each sub-Group committee to maintain liaison with the sub-Groups. The representative or deputy representative will normally attend sub-Group committee meetings. The Chair of the Group Committee shall be a member of each sub-Group ex officio.

Working Parties

54.1 The Group committee may establish working parties to deal with a specific task within the responsibilities of the Group and set their terms of reference. A working party shall not be appointed for a period in excess of 12 months, nor remain in existence for more than 12 months without review by the Group committee and shall report back to the Group committee.

54.2 The Group committee shall appoint a representative to each working party to maintain liaison. The Chair of the Group Committee shall be a member of each working party ex officio.

Accounts

55. The Honorary Treasurer of the Group shall be responsible for the receipt of all moneys due to the Group and shall make such payments as the Group committee shall direct and shall maintain accounts of all receipts, payments, assets and liabilities of the Group. In discharging his/her duties, the Honorary Treasurer shall adhere to the requirements of the Bye-laws of CILIP and shall abide by such guidance as CILIP issues with regard to the keeping of accounts.

56. The annual accounts shall be prepared on a calendar year basis. Two independent examiners shall inspect the annual accounts of the Group and, if thought fit, shall sign a certificate in the form specified by CILIP.

57. The independent examiners shall be appointed at the annual general meeting of the Group. They shall not be members of the Group committee and need not be members of the Group.

Secretary

58. The Secretary of the Group shall maintain a record of all proceedings and shall be responsible for preparing reports, issuing notices, conducting correspondence, giving notices of impending elections, circulating ballot papers in accordance with the election regulations in Appendix B and the safekeeping of ballot papers. The Secretary shall forward to the Secretary of CILIP any reports and records required under the Byelaws of CILIP and shall submit regularly to CILIP copies of the minutes of the Group committee meetings and general meetings of the Group.

Notices

59.1 All notices required by these Rules may be given: a) In person; or b) By an announcement in either CILIP Update/Gazette or in the Group newsletter; or c) By an announcement on CILIP's or the Group's website; or d) By electronic communication; or e) By postal communication.

59.2 In the case of postal communication, a notice shall have been deemed to have been served on the member on the third day after the day it is posted if sent by first class post and on the fifth day after posting if sent by second class post.

60. The accidental omission to give notice to or the non-receipt of notice by any member of the Group shall not invalidate any resolution passed nor the proceedings at any meeting.

Transitional Provisions

61.1 Any term of office undertaken before the formal introduction of these Rules on 1st April 2004 shall not count towards the maximum terms of office set in these Rules.

61.2 At the first meeting of the Group committee after 1st April 2004, the elected members of the committee shall draw lots to determine which members are to retire after one year's, two years' and three years' service. Members so retiring will be eligible to stand for re-election.

Group Rules – Appendix A

Rules of Procedure for General and Committee Meetings of the Group

Chair

1. In the absence of the Chair of the Group Committee, the Vice Chair or Honorary Treasurer shall take the chair. In the absence of both these officers, the meeting shall elect a chair from amongst the members present (excluding associated members).

Discipline

2. The Chair shall call a member to order for irrelevance, repetition, unbecoming language, imputations of motives or any breach of order, and may direct such member if speaking to

discontinue. The Chair may also direct such member to withdraw from the meeting. The ruling of the Chair on points of order, matters arising in debate or the admissibility of a personal explanation shall be final, and shall not be open to discussion.

Moving of Motions

3.1 No motion shall be considered or voted upon unless it has been duly moved and seconded. A motion from the Chair shall require no seconder.

3.2 The Chair or any member present may ask for any motion to be submitted in writing before it is put to the vote.

3.3 Members may seek further information or clarification on any matter under discussion during a meeting but must advise the Honorary Secretary, where possible in advance of the meeting, so that such information can be available.

Withdrawal of Motions

4. A motion may be withdrawn by the mover with the concurrence of the seconder. A member submitting a report may, with the consent of the meeting, withdraw a paragraph or recommendation contained in the report.

Absence of Mover

5. Business under any motion on the agenda paper shall not be proceeded with in the absence of the member in whose name it stands unless he/she has given authority in writing of his/her consent that it should be taken up by some other member.

Notices of Motion

6. The only motions which will be considered at general meetings are those of which due notice has been given in accordance with the Group Rules.

Procedural Motions

7. During debate on motions the following procedural motions only shall be admitted: i) To amend the motion ii) That consideration of the question be postponed iii) That the meeting does proceed to the next business iv) That the question be now put v) That the meeting does now adjourn.

Group Rules - Appendix B

Regulations for the Conduct of Group Elections

1. Elections for the elected officers and members of the Group committee shall take place in the two months preceding the expiry of the existing members' term of office.

2. Subject to CILIP Regulations 12 and 13 concerning payment of subscriptions, all members of the Group are entitled to vote in the elections and to be nominated for election.

3. Notice of annual elections and an invitation to submit nominations shall be published in either CILIP Update/Gazette or in the Group newsletter at least 14 days before the closing date for nominations. A similar notice shall appear in any bulletin, newsletter, e-lists or circular distributed to all members of the Group at the appropriate time and on the Group's website.

4. Subject to the provisions of paragraph 8 of these Rules, nominations of members of the Group for election as officers or as members of the Group Committee shall be made in writing, signed by two members of the Group entitled to vote and countersigned by the candidate to indicate consent. Nominations must reach the Honorary Secretary not later than 31st January immediately preceding the period for which the election is held. No candidate shall be nominated for more than one category of office and shall specify on the nomination paper the category for which he/she proposes to stand.

5. Election shall be by postal ballot of all members of the Group who are entitled to vote.

6. Ballot papers, together with a brief curriculum vitae supplied by the candidate, shall be circulated to all eligible members of the Group within 14 days of the close of nominations.

7. Two scrutineers shall be appointed by the Committee before each election for the purpose of supervision of the conduct of the election and to record the voting. Such scrutineers shall not be members of the Committee nor candidates for election, and need not be members of the Group. The votes shall be counted during the second week in March.

8. The officers of the Group Committee shall take office from 1st April following the election for a period of one year.

9. The members of the Group Committee (other than the elected officers) shall take office from 1st April following the election for a period of three years.

10. The names of the members elected to the Group Committee shall be sent immediately after each election to the Secretary of CILIP together with a copy of the report of the scrutineers.

11. The names of the members elected to the Group Committee shall be notified to the members of the Group as soon as practicable after each election, by means of the Group newsletter, website or otherwise.

12. The Scrutineers shall report to the Annual General Meeting on the last election and the results thereof.

Creation and Dissolution of Special Interest Groups

This document was agreed by Council at its meeting in June 2006. It is likely to form part of the Group Rules document which is currently being revised.

Creation of Special Interest Groups

1. The Council may, at its discretion, issue a certificate creating a Special Interest Group of the Institute

2. Should a group of CILIP members propose to form a Special Interest Group, a formal application should be made in writing to CILIP Council signed by no fewer than 200 personal members of the Institute

3. The proposed Group must show in their application that:

    a) named members are willing to form a working committee
    b) a clear Plan has been devised for the proposed Group that fulfils CILIP objectives and is financially viable
    c) there is a policy in place for communicating with Group members and promoting the Group to the wider CILIP community
    d) the proposed Group has a unique remit and does not duplicate the work of an existing Group or Panel

4. CILIP Council shall assess each request for the creation of a Special Interest Group on the basis of this application

5. Groups shall be created and authorised by CILIP Council for a probationary period of two years

6. Any Group seeking to continue beyond the probationary period must send notice to Council before the end of that period demonstrating that it has successfully met its objectives and obligations over this designated period and that it wishes to be recognised as a permanent Group

7. In the event of two or more Groups wishing to merge, or one Group wishing to separate into two or more distinct Groups, the arrangements agreed between the Groups must be ratified by Council

Dissolution of Special Interest Groups

CILIP Council may dissolve a Special Interest Group if:

1. The probationary period for the creation of the Group has expired and the Group has not submitted a satisfactory notice for continuation beyond this period; or

2. The Group has repeatedly been unable to fulfil CILIP objectives as agreed by Council; or

3. Membership of the Group has fallen significantly; or

4. The Group applies to CILIP Council to be dissolved

Part 3
GENERAL INFORMATION

Branches

In the developing regional and devolution agenda, CILIP's Branches are an influential voice for the profession, whether in the Home Nations or the English regions.

So CILIP has ensured that the boundaries of its Branches in England match the powerful Regional Development Agencies (RDAs), and allow CILIP's Members to deal with the RDAs, Government regional offices, Regional Cultural Consortia and other important bodies on equal terms.

CILIP in Scotland (CILIPS)

Website: www.slainte.org.uk/cilips/cilipsindex.htm
Contact e-mail: cilips@slainte.org.uk
Geographical coverage: Scotland. Regional sub-branches: Central, Edinburgh and East of Scotland, North East of Scotland, North of Scotland.

Activities and achievements

CILIP in Scotland (CILIPS) is a devolved branch of CILIP with responsibility for policy, advocacy and financial matters on behalf of its membership in Scotland providing professional support and guidance relating to Scottish Government and legislation. A Scottish charity in its own right it acts on CILIP's behalf in all areas apart from membership and qualifications. It has its own governance structure and President. CILIPS delivers a responsive service package tailored to the specific needs and distinctive legislative environment of Scottish CILIP members. This role is carried out by the CILIPS officers in collaboration with four regional sub-branches that help to extend professional participation to all areas of the country. A thriving network of Scottish special interest groups also operates to maximise member engagement. CILIPS also works closely with the Scottish Library and Information Council (SLIC), sharing offices and some members of staff, as well as collaborating on joint initiatives.

CILIPS' core function is to support the library and information profession in Scotland through the combination of a national advocacy strategy and local level events and activities. Advocacy for the profession within a Scottish context is a major priority and CILIPS contributes to key Scottish Government policy documents and consultations concerning libraries and culture.

Support for the profession is delivered nationally on key cross sector issues such as information literacy, readership development, occupational standards and job evaluation. Specific membership services include a programme of CPD activities tailored to Scottish members' needs

and a professional publication, Information Scotland. The Slainte website, a CILIPS and SLIC shared service, offers a comprehensive range of services and professional information for members, including a Slainte 2.0 area aimed at improving communication and collaboration. The CILIPS Annual Conference is a major event in the Scottish library and information calendar, attracting delegates from all over Scotland. This event aims to promote good practice and present networking opportunities across library sectors. The Conference regularly features high-profile speakers from home and abroad, and the popular member-led Branch and Group Day segment of the programme showcases local innovations and achievements.

CILIP Cymru/Wales

Website: www.cilip.org.uk/wales
Contact e-mail: mdp@aber.ac.uk or mandy.powell@cilip.org.uk (Development Officer)
Geographical coverage: Wales.

Activities and achievements

CILIP Cymru/Wales has one full time Development Officer and one part time Assistant Development Officer who both work with the Committee, a team of volunteers. We deliver support to members of CILIP in Wales and represent the views of library and information staff across Wales.

Each year we organise a cross sector conference, the Welsh Libraries, Archives and Museums Conference. Last year the two-day event attracted 300 delegates from across Wales, giving them the opportunity to hear high-calibre speakers from across the UK, take part in networking opportunities and experience the successful Trade Exhibition.

CILIP Cymru/Wales works closely with Special Interest Groups in Wales to support their work within the wider profession in Wales. We support and promote CILIP's Framework of Qualifications and Accreditation.

CILIP Cymru/Wales has also set up a Cross Party Group on libraries – where representatives of CILIP Cymru/Wales have met with Welsh Assembly Members to discuss the future of libraries across Wales.

We are committed to providing a bi-lingual service and produce information in both Welsh and English. Our journal, *Y Ddolen* (*The Link*) published articles in both English and Welsh and the News and People sections are always printed in both languages.

The full committee meets four times a year, a smaller group of Committee Officers meets more often to discuss issues and plan events for the members including a free Members' Day.

We also provide news bulletins to our members; speak to students and staff in the wider profession about the support we can offer them and we work with a wider range of organisations including CyMAL (Museums, Archives and Libraries Wales and SCL Wales (Society of Chief Librarians, Wales).

CILIP in Ireland

Website: www.cilip.org.uk/ireland
Contact e-mail: elga.logue@btinternet.com (Executive Officer)
Geographical coverage: Northern and Southern Ireland.

Activities and achievements

CILIP Ireland had a most successful year, hosting its annual joint conference in the Hilton Hotel, Belfast 29 April–1 May 2009. The conference theme was 'Managing Change in the Information Age' and attracted more than 100 delegates from all sectors and from across the island, as well as representatives from England, Wales and Scotland. Twenty library suppliers displayed their wide range of resources, ensuring a most stimulating exhibition. All speakers and workshop facilitators delivered professional and thought-provoking presentations relevant to the central theme.

A definite highlight was the conference dinner hosted by the Lord Mayor and Belfast City Council. The conference was brought to a most successful conclusion with visits to the new Carnegie Library, Bangor, and Belfast Central Library.

On 7 December 2009, CILIP Ireland ran a course entitled 'Libraries and the Digital Revolution' in the new library, Queen's University Belfast. Four excellent speakers ensured that four sectors were represented: public libraries, academic libraries, government libraries and the Public Record Office Northern Ireland (PRONI). The impact of digitisation in each information sector was widely debated by all present and the course concluded with a tour of the new library, enabling all participants to have a first-hand look at this most impressive building.

The branch also held its successful Members' Day on 25 March 2009 – a joint event with the local Career Development Group – at which the Framework of Qualifications was highlighted and the success of two ACLIP candidates celebrated.

CILIP Ireland continued to produce its newsletter *CILIP Ireland News*, and a special autumn edition was devoted to the annual joint conference, Members' Day and the Framework of Qualifications Mentoring scheme offering Chartered Librarians the opportunity to become Mentors.

CILIP Ireland again welcomed the opportunity in 2009 to be in a healthy financial position to provide financial support, in the form of bursaries, to students accepted on the librarianship courses at the University of Ulster.

East Midlands

Website: www.cilip.org.uk/em
Contact e-mail: emboc@bc-d.co.uk
Geographical coverage: The East Midlands region including Derby, Derbyshire, Leicester, Leicestershire, Lincolnshire, Nottingham, Nottinghamshire, Northamptonshire and Rutland.

Activities and achievements

The branch aims to support and develop our members across all sectors through opportunities for professional and personal development and networking. Our current business plan also highlights our role in promoting the profession, building our library community and ensuring the effective operation of the branch.

Achievements in the past year have included a Members' Day with regional speakers around the theme of 'Selling Yourself Selling Your Service'. Held in conjunction with our 2009 Annual General Meeting, the day was a great opportunity for networking and sharing ideas and expertise. In October we arranged a visit for members to two contrasting libraries in Nottingham: Bromley House and The Meadows Libraries.

The branch continues to work closely with the special interest groups and offer support for those without a regional presence. We are a friendly,

Members of the East Midlands Branch of CILIP enjoying a visit to Bromley House Subscription Library, Nottingham in October 2009

active and motivated branch committee who meet four times a year. We have published three newsletters during the year and communicate regularly with members throughout the region including new CILIP members and colleagues from the Solo Librarians Network.

East of England Branch

Website: www.cilip.org.uk/ee
Contact e-mail: Darren.Smart@essex.gov.uk (Chair)
Geographical coverage: Bedfordshire, Cambridgeshire, Essex, Hertfordshire, Norfolk and Suffolk. The non-metropolitan districts of Luton, Peterborough, Southend-on-Sea and Thurrock.

Activities and achievements

The Branch has been involved in supporting a number of regional events organised by local branches of CILIP groups with which we maintain active links. We held a successful workshop called 'Helping Out' on volunteering, in conjunction with our AGM. We continue to publish our newsletter, *Sunrise*, which is sent to all members of the Branch and made available on our website. We have also begun moving our website over to the CILIP site and the information on it should be growing over the next few months. Finally, we have continued helping to pay for individuals in the region to attend conferences and other professional development activities via our Small Grants Fund.

CILIP in London

Website: www.cilip.org.uk/london
Contact e-mail:
peter.beauchamp1@btinternet.com (President)
Geographical coverage: The Branch is open to members of CILIP living or working in London, and to retired Branch members now living outside London.

Activities and achievements

CILIP in London delivers a range of services to its branch membership. Regular evening meetings, held at the Sekforde Arms, Clerkenwell, are very popular and attract large audiences to witness talks on a variety of subjects linked to the Information Profession given by knowledgeable experts in their field. The annual AGM also features a guest speaker and there is usually a summer outing to a place of mutual cultural interest. Events are open to all (although non-members cannot vote at the AGM). A regular newsletter, the *London CLIP*, advises the membership of news and events across London. Those that are interested in contributing to the committee can join for an 'experience' period on a co-option basis.

North East Branch

Website: www.cilip.org.uk/ne
Contact e-mail: (via website):
www.cilip.org.uk/get-involved/regional-branches/north-east/pages/contact-us.aspx
Geographical coverage: Durham and Northumberland. The metropolitan districts of Gateshead, Newcastle-upon-Tyne, North Tyneside, South Tyneside and Sunderland. The non-metropolitan districts of Darlington, Hartlepool, Middlesborough, Redcar and Cleveland, Stockton-on-Tees.

Activities and achievements

These can be found on the 'Events and conferences' link on the website.

North West Branch

Website: www.cilip.org.uk/nw
Contact e-mail: o.courtney@mmu.ac.uk
Geographical coverage: North West of England (Cheshire, Merseyside, Greater Manchester, Lancashire and Cumbria)

Activities and achievements

- BBC Visit and Pub Quiz, November 2010.
- Career Development Group North West, Chartership Session, February 2010.
- CILIP NW Branch Members Day and AGM, March 2010, Bolton Central Library.
- Pub quiz, Liverpool.

Plans include a Members' Day in Carlisle in 2009.

The branch awards a 'Student Prize' to the two best Library School students in the region, one from Manchester Metropolitan University and one from Liverpool John Moores University.

South East Branch

Website: www.cilip.org.uk/se
Contact e-mail: Hobsonjohn9@aol.com (Honorary Secretary)
Geographical coverage: The CILIP South East Branch runs around the southern side of London from Kent in the south east corner, through Sussex and Surrey to Hampshire and the Isle of Wight then up through Berkshire and Oxfordshire to Buckinghamshire. With over three thousand members, the Branch is the second largest after London. The Branch consists of five active Sub-branches: CILIP in Surrey, CILIP in Sussex, CILIP in Hants and Wight, CILIP in the Thames Valley and the Kent Sub-branch. The Sub-branches each have a Committee that organises a varied and ambitious programme of events and activities and the main aim of the Branch is to encourage, fund and support their work.

Activities and achievements

Local activities include meetings, workshops, visits and other CPD events and networking opportunities. We also aim to build and develop relationships with other bodies and stakeholders that have responsibility for library and information work in the region, and act as a forum for professional communication, working as a key link between CILIP and its members and supporting local activists in the profession. The highlights of the past year, have included in **Hants and Wight**, an AGM with Michael Martin on CILIP qualifications; workshops on 'Running a Website' and 'Reflective Writing', and visits to Winchester College, Treloar College and the National Archives at Kew. **Sussex** held a joint AGM with the Branch at the new Crawley Library, with Peter Daniels from Westminster City Archives. They have also had workshops on 'The Role of Volunteers in Libraries', 'How to Cope With Change', and 'How to Market Yourself', plus visits to the Society of Genealogists and the London College of Fashion. **Surrey's** AGM was addressed by CILIP President Peter Griffiths, and they have held workshops on 'The 2012 Olympics' and a one-day school on 'Personal Development' with Nicola Franklin, plus various visits to major engineering libraries in London and to historic Lingfield and a showing of *The Hollywood Librarian*. **Thames Valley** held a number of meetings including an AGM with Council Chair Caroline Moss-Gibbons, a talk on 'Mash Ups' with Karen Blakeman and a talk on the library of John Dee, plus a tour of Oxford Colleges. **Kent** held its AGM at the new Ramsgate Library and organised a seminar on 'Libraries as Social Spaces'.

South Western Branch

Website: www.cilip.org.uk/sw
Contact e-mail: Lynn.west@devon.gov.uk (Hon. Secretary)
Geographical coverage: The geographical area west of and including Gloucestershire and Wiltshire, and including the Channel Islands.

Activities and achievements

The branch held a course on 'Delivering Proactive Services in Libraries' and sponsored places at the YLG conference and Umbrella . It also awarded the Harry Galloway prize for the best student on

the MSc course at UWE. There were four editions of the Branch newsletter, published both in print and electronically on the Branch website.

West Midland Branch

Website: www.cilip.org.uk/wm
Contact e-mail: mfuller@fireservicecollege.ac.uk
Geographical coverage: We represent library and information professionals living and or working in the counties of Herefordshire, Shropshire, Staffordshire, Warwickshire and Worcestershire. We also serve the metropolitan districts of Birmingham, Coventry, Dudley, Sandwell, Solihull, Walsall and Wolverhampton, as well as the non-metropolitan districts of Stoke-on-Trent and Telford and Wrekin.

Activities and achievements

The role of the West Midland Branch of CILIP is to raise the profile, represent its members and enhance the expertise of library and information workers in the region.

- AGM and Members Afternoon 2010 with a presentation by the President about 'The Big Conversation',
- AGM and Members' Day 2009 with the theme 'Changing Face of Libraries'
- Library Photo Competition 2009
- *Open Access* newsletter published 3 times per year.

Yorkshire and Humberside Branch

Website: www.cilip.org.uk/yh
Contact e-mail (via website): www.cilip.org.uk/get-involved/regional-branches/yorkshire-humberside/pages/contact-us.aspx
Geographic coverage: The districts of Barnsley, Bradford, Calderdale, Doncaster, Kirklees, Leeds,

Rotherham, Sheffield and Wakefield. The East Riding of Yorkshire, Kingston upon Hull, North East Lincolnshire, North Lincolnshire and York. The southern part of the County of North Yorkshire.

Activities and achievements

Please refer to the Branch website.

Special Interest Groups

CILIP's Groups enable Members to share their professional concerns and interests. Membership of two Groups is included in the CILIP subscription but Members may join as many others as they wish on payment of a nominal charge for each. CILIP directly supports its Groups by providing funding for events and activities, as well as helping to cover the costs of production of regular newsletters.

The pages that follow aim to give a flavour of the activities of the Special Interest Groups. More information can be found on each Group's website, the address of which is given in each Group's entry.

Aerospace and Defence Librarians Group (ADLG)

Website: www.adlg.org.uk/
Contact e-mail: cwaters@alibs.detsa.co.uk

Aims and objectives

As laid out in the ADLG Constitution, its objectives as a SIG are:

- to provide a focal point for professional contact
- to promote a dialogue between private industry, the Ministry of Defence and related agencies
- to bring together all persons involved in the provision of library and information services for aerospace and defence.

The high level objectives in ADLG's current Business Plan are:

- to encourage and facilitate the continuing professional development of all members
- to see new members for ADLG and/or CILIP and increase the active involvement of existing members
- to act as an advocate for library and information service professionals working in the aerospace and defence sector
- to ensure the effective running of the SIG.

Activities and achievements

In December 2009 ADLG was confirmed as the newest SIG of CILIP, having successfully passed its probationary two-year period.
Support for members' CPD:

- **May** A visit to King's College Library's War Studies Collection, followed by a historical tour of the Old War Office in Whitehall.
- **July** Members went to RUSI, the Royal United Service Institute, for an overview of their work and library visit. This was followed by attendance at the presentation by the Duke of

Westminster for the RUSI Westminster Medal for Military Literature 2009.

- **July** CILIP's biennial Umbrella conference at Hatfield, where ADLG hosted a session entitled 'Connecting with your customer – outreach and embedding in Government libraries'. The Group also sponsored one of its members to attend Umbrella.
- **September** 2009 was the year for the biennial ADLG seminar. The title of the event was 'Managing Information Security, Data, Social Networking Risks and Knowledge Capability', with speakers from the National Archives, British Standards Institute, Aquila Business Services, University of London, MoD, Rolls Royce and GCHQ. The event received much positive feedback.
- **December** ADLG was awarded the CILIP Seal of Recognition.

Communication with members:

- Two issues of the *ADLG Newsletter* were published, much improved by a new A5 coloured format.
- The ADLG website was successfully migrated over to the new CILIP website.
- Following a competition, the Committee selected a new strapline for the Group: 'Your Knowledge, Our Collaboration'

ADLG committee and members at the 2009 AGM, held at QinetiQ Boscombe Down

Branch and Mobile Libraries Group (BMLG)

Website: www.cilip.org.uk/bmlg
Contact email: via website

Aims and objectives

This group serves staff at all levels working in public libraries, with a special emphasis on frontline staff. This includes librarians and other LIS staff whose duties concern services of all types to branch networks and mobile libraries.

The Group also attracts support and interest from service leaders and senior managers who recognise the importance of the services provided by branch and mobile libraries.

The group's activities focus on strategy, policy and practical development of services within branch and mobile library networks in the UK, with a particular emphasis on attracting and involving frontline staff and junior/middle managers.

The group maintains strong links with public libraries around the world and especially with countries affiliated to IFLA.

Activities and achievements

The Annual National Mobilemeet brings together mobile libraries of varying size and functions and mobile library staff, including drivers and assistants, to hear papers on aspects of mobile library services. In 2009, Mobilemeet was held at Thurston Community College near Bury St Edmunds Suffolk. Peter Maher, an Australian Mobile Librarian from New South Wales was the key speaker. The theme was 'Reaching the People' and 25 vehicles and over 150 delegates attended. Awards are given in various categories and the 2009 award winners were:

- 'State of the Art' – Suffolk Public Libraries
- 'Best Small Van' – Oxfordshire's mini childrens mobile.
- 'Livery' – Cambridgeshire libraries

- 'Concours' – Quaker Homeless Action, a donated home-built Transit-based mini-mobile.
- 'Delegate's Choice' – Buckinghamshire Public Libraries.

The opportunity to look at the most recent examples of mobile library design enables the Group to claim that this annual event has influenced the development and design of mobile libraries in the UK and elsewhere, resulting in stylish, well-fitted and comfortable-to-use vehicles.

BMLG held a wide variety of sessions at Umbrella 2009, ranging from 'Hell's Angels with Shelving' to 'Reading takes the Biscuit'.

The Group journal *ServicePoint* is issued three times per year and has reached a momentous 100 editions.

Career Development Group (CDG)

Website: www.cilip.org.uk/cdg
Contact e-mail: cdgmmo@googlemail.com

Aims and objectives

The Career Development Group (CDG) is CILIP's second largest Special Interest Group. With c.3,500 members in the UK and another 40 countries around the world, employed in all LIS sectors and at all levels of responsibility – from students to senior managers – it represents around 20% of CILIP membership.

CDG's core mission is to support the continuous professional development of its members. CDG delivers CPD events and activities at national and regional level across its 13 Divisions, with national officers and divisional committees working closely together.

CDG has always been committed to provide newer members of the profession and students with access to stimulating and informative events; facilitating their skills, development and professional networking.

CDG has a reputation for consistently attracting committed volunteers over 115 years of distinguished history, and the commitment to continue developing ways to best serve its members and CILIP in ever-changing times and circumstances. CILIP's Seal of Recognition has been awarded in recognition of CDG's high standards.

Furthermore, CDG provides all members with opportunities to find their own professional voice through active involvement in divisional committees, presenting at its national conferences and regional events and by publishing in its quarterly published printed journal, *Impact*.

Activities and achievements

CDG has established a new role: New Professionals Co-ordinator who works in partnership with CILIP Membership Support Unit to support, recruit and engage newer members. This role is replicated at divisional level by a network of New Professionals Support Officers focused on engaging with new professionals at local level by facilitating networking and divisional activities specifically aimed to them, mirroring what CDG is successfully doing for chartership, certification and revalidation candidates, in partnership with CILIP Qualifications Department.

The first New Professionals Conference, held on 6 July in co-operation with CILIP Diversity Group and London Metropolitan University, was attended by about 100 delegates.

CDG National Conference 'Your Wish is my Command': Improving the Customer Experience, held at John Moores University in Liverpool on 20 April, attracted 85 delegates.

CDG also offered an award for a New Professional member to attend Umbrella, including its programme of six successful sessions on positive action, effective horizontal moves, the new CPD scheme, portfolio building, individual career paths and the value of collaborations and partnerships.

CDG Officers contributed to CILIP Political Manifesto with three members on the Task & Finish Group ensuring that the varied and passionate views of CDG members and CILIP new professionals were embodied. Officers also contributed to CILIP Members Day and Training Days for Branches and Groups, and sat on Policy Forum, the Diversity Panel and Task and Finish Groups reviewing the Framework of Qualifications, investigating reciprocal qualifications with the Library & Information Association *New Zealand* Aotearoa, and devising CILIP Equalities Audit.

Cataloguing and Indexing Group (CIG)

Website address: www.cilip.org.uk/cig
Contact email: a.d.chapman@ukoln.ac.uk (Honorary Secretary)

Aims and objectives

The Cataloguing and Indexing Group is a forum for CILIP members interested in the organisation of knowledge to enable resource discovery and collection management. The Group promotes best practice, contributes to the development of metadata, national and international standards and formats and provides opportunities for learning and professional development. CIG members are active in all areas of library and information science and the publishing sector.

The Cataloguing and Indexing Group believes that the storage, organisation and retrieval of information in any form and by any means, is a central and fundamental concern of librarianship and information science. This provides a means of exploiting that information (whether printed or electronic) for the maximum benefit of all users.

The Cataloguing and Indexing Group represents the interests of members of CILIP engaged or interested (in any capacity, technical or managerial, or at any level from student to senior professional) in the following areas: library catalogues, databases, systems or networks; information storage, organisation and retrieval, whether within local or remote databases; the production and use of bibliographic and similar tools and indexes for information recorded in any documentary, audiovisual or electronic form.

Activities and achievements

The group activity plan focuses on relevant and accessible opportunities for Continuing Professional Development, development of standards, publication programme to enable practitioners to demonstrate good practice and a network / community of practitioners to which Group members can contribute and from which they can learn.

The group runs seminars and visits, holding a residential conference every other year and now has CILIP Seal of Recognition status (an indicator of high standards of content and relevance) for its events. In 2009 CIG participated in the Umbrella conference and held its own events – the Standards Forum (held twice) and an authority control seminar – and visits to Chethams Library Manchester, St. Paul's Cathedral Library, the Wellcome Institute Library, Bank of England and the London School of Economics. The 2010 Conference and Annual General Meeting will take place at the University of Exeter 13-15 September.

Group members currently serve on a number of standards and awards bodies: BIC Bibliographic Standards Group, CILIP/BL committee on RDA, CILIP DDC committee, SCOOP and Wheatley Medal.

The CIG Alan Jeffreys Award for 2008 was awarded to John Bowman.

The Group section of the CILIP web site contains a variety of materials, including committee membership, meeting minutes, news, etc. and access to the e-journal *Catalogue and Index* and the CIG blog.

The Scottish branch, CIG Scotland, runs a busy and successful programme of events and visits in Scotland, and hosts the mailing list lis-cigs (https://www.jiscmail.ac.uk/lists/LIS-CIGS.html) and the CIGS website www.slainte.org.uk/CILIPS/sigs/cigs/cigsindex.htm). Contact the CIGS committee via our secretary at: colin.duncan@inverclyde.gov.uk.

Colleges of Further and Higher Education Group (CoFHE)

Website: www.cilip.org.uk/cig
Contact e-mail: www.cilip.org.uk/get-involved/special-interest-groups/c-of-he/Pages/default.aspx or sreed@southdowns.ac.uk (Secretary)

Aims and objectives

CoFHE promotes the role of library and information services, and of the profession, in further education, higher education and sixth form colleges.

Activities and achievements

CoFHE published the *Self Assessment Toolkit* for learning resources services in further education colleges in England. The group are currently working on guidelines on the provision of library and learning resources centre services for 14-16 year olds and Higher Education Students in Further Education. The Circles held a number of successful training events throughout the year. The CoFHE conference for 2010 is the fifth joint conference with UC&R 'Future Proof: Making Libraries Indispensible' University of Exeter 21–3 June 2010.

Commercial, Legal and Scientific Information Group (CSLIG)

Website: www.clsig.org.uk
Contact e-mail: info@clsig.org.uk

Aims and objectives

CLSIG supports and promotes the professional interests of members in all commercial, legal and scientific workplace libraries and information services. This is facilitated by providing professional development training, networking opportunities for members, and representing their interests within CILIP and the wider information community.

Professional development is promoted through an active programme of events and visits. Joint events with other groups have been actively promoted for several years, and since CLSIG has members from all over the UK as well as abroad, efforts are now being made to hold more CLSIG events outside the South East. *CLSIG News* is published six times a year and keeps members up to date on all aspects of the commercial information sector. Personal CLSIG membership is open to all, whether CILIP members or not.

Activities and achievements

We continued with our Seal of Recognition-certified Professional Development Club seminars, with 'Redundancy' in February 2009, 'Be Your Own Boss' in March, 'Preparing a Business Case' seminar in April, followed by an evening on 'Managing Stress in the Workplace' in June. We also ran the highly successful evening discussing Web 2.0, which has recently been repeated in Birmingham. We are keen to expand our offering of seminars to the regions and have Newcastle in our sights for the next rerun. In November we had a 'Marketing Matters' evening, and after the AGM this year we had an excellent seminar on 'Negotiating Contracts'. Online 2009 went very well this year. Interspersed with these seminars we had visits to the Royal Courts of Justice and National Archives. The Group has started collecting feedback from each event using an online survey tool and offering certificates of attendance for delegates at our training events. We have been working through the migration of the CILIP's – and CLSIG's – website to a new server. Our highly successful newsletter *CLSIG News* continues to appear bi-monthly with excellent coverage of events, products and resources in the commercial field.

Community Services Group (CSG)

Website: www.cilip.org.uk/csg
Contact e-mail: Nigel.thomas@leics.gov.uk

Aims and objectives

The Community Services Group works towards creating community cohesion by promoting the use of library and information services to empower people and improve their quality of life

Its objectives are:

- representing and lobbying all sectors of the library and information profession
- developing partnerships and strategic alliances with voluntary and statutory organisations which hold common values
- advocating equal access to and availability of library and information services to all
- providing information and support on relevant issues to library and information staff
- highlighting and promoting services which are examples of good practice.

Activities and achievements

- Co-partner with Cilip of the Libraries Change Lives Award given to innovative library and information projects that celebrate community engagement and good practice. In 2009 the award went to Leeds Library and Information service.

- Commissioning Local-level to produce, on behalf of Cilip, a policy document on Social Justice and Community Engagement.
- Completion of membership survey.
- CSG contributed to another successful UMBRELLA programme in 2009. papers were delivered by Kevin Harris, Debi Boden, John Vincent, Anne Brown, Dr John Crawford, Linda Constable, Sheila Golden, Anna Hannaford, James Radcliffe, and Shelagh Levett, on a wide range of issues that CSG advocates. We have published the conference papers on our website.

Diversity Group

Website: www.cilip.org.uk/dg
Contact e-mail:
rose.johnson@bournemouthlibraries.org.uk

Aims and objectives

The aims of the Diversity Group are:

- to unite those members of CILIP engaged in or interested in issues of diversity as they affect the library and information community
- to foster communication between such members
- to facilitate exchange of experience and the promotion of work relevant to those interests in order to promote and support library and information services to diversity and excluded communities.

'Diversity' covers issues of race, religion, culture, ethnicity, class, gender, sexuality, age, disability – and other factors that result in discrimination and inequality

Activities and achievements

In 2009 the Diversity Group organised a successful conference jointly with Career Development Group for new professionals. It ran five sessions at Umbrella 2009. Margaret Watson was awarded the DG award for her great contribution to Encompass and diversity generally. The group is now on Facebook.

Education Librarians Group (ELG)

Website: www.cilip.org.uk/elg
Contact e-mail: l.gildersleeves·@ucl.ac.uk, or hannah.rose@northampton.ac.uk

Aims and objectives

ELG aims to represent members of the library and information profession involved in supporting education and lifelong learning, within teacher training institutions, schools, educational research and other library services concerned with the learning continuum across educational phases and opportunities.

The Group's objectives are:

- to contribute to national initiatives concerning education and lifelong learning
- to encourage collaboration and exchange of ideas across the education sectors within CILIP and with related organisations
- to develop an international perspective in educational librarianship, building links with relevant organisations overseas
- to provide a forum for discussion of relevant issues and to support the CPD and communication through meetings and events across the UK
- production of publications and discussion list.

Activities and achievements

ELG continued with our programme of Children's Literature events, including sessions on Teachers as Readers: and In The Picture: using picture books to reflect and promote inclusion of images of disability in society. ELG offered four sessions at Umbrella 2009, indipendently and in collaboration with other groups. We visited The National Archives and the Royal Botanical Library at Kew. ELG is involved with the Information Literacy in Schools Taskforce, in partnership with CILIP groups, School Library Association and the former DCSF. We are also part of CILIP development of support for the campaign to make school libraries statutory. An ongoing project is development of pedagogy and teaching skills training for librarians in educational settings.

We are proud to have been able to support students during 2009, through two full-delegate sponsored places to Umbrella 2009 and through an allocation of free attendance for trainee teachers and care workers at Children's Literature sessions. We hope to be able to continue this commitment to new professionals and the closer collaboration of teachers and librarians in future.

Government Libraries and Information Group (GLIG)

Website: www.cilip.org.uk/glig
Contact e-mail: via the website

Aims and objectives

The Government Libraries and Information Group represents the professional interests of librarians and information workers in government departments and agencies, parliamentary and national libraries and welcomes members from any sector of the profession, particularly those with an interest in government information and documentation. As the information profession evolves in breadth and scope, GLIG continues to strive to adequately reflect the range of roles and interests of our members. The Group organises professional training for its members on topical subjects such as freedom of information, mentoring, electronic publishing and information handling. It promotes CILIP's chartership and fellowships in government departments and encourages the use by members and their organisations of the Continuing Professional Development Personal Profile.

Activities and achievements

GLIG continues to work to keep members informed of professional issues. We launched the electronic version of our journal in July 2009; it's available to download from our website. We keep our members updated with news and events of professional interest in a monthly e-mail bulletin.

GLIG has been very active in providing opportunities for professional development; the Group participated in Umbrella 2009, leading sessions covering issues including information assurance, digitising government collections and developing the role of the information professional. The Group continues to arrange visits for members, over the last year these have included trips to the Supreme Court and Inner Temple libraries. In October, GLIG ran a timely training day on electronic resources for parliamentary material at the House of Commons, coinciding with the launch of the Justis Parliament database. The Group also held a very successful conference at the British Library, 'Government Information in the Google Age', chaired by Peter Griffiths.

GLIG has endeavoured to represent the professional interests of our members. The Group has participated in developing plans to fulfil the Government's Information Matters strategy, working with the Knowledge Council, the cross-government body responsible for Knowledge and Information Management. Committee members have worked with CILIP's Policy and Branch and Group forums over the past year, and look forward to playing an active role in this year's Big Conversation initiative.

Finally, we continue to recognise the achievements of our members, this year presenting lifetime achievement awards to acknowledge the significant contributions made to the profession by Anne Bridge and Frank Ryan.

Health Libraries Group (HLG)

Website: www.cilip.org.uk/hlg
Contact e-mail: hlg@cilip.org.uk

Aims and objectives

HLG's mission statement talks of supporting its members to mobilise health information, through advocacy and through continuing professional development.

We regard our diverse and active membership as one of our strengths. Our members come from all health and social sectors and geographical areas in the UK and beyond. Members work for the NHS, the academic sector, the independent sector, government departments, professional associations, charities and public libraries. Students with an interest in health and social care information are also welcome.

In 2009–2010, HLG is working to clarify its identity and aims, ensuring that it understands the needs of its membership and provides services which best meet them. Other key areas are championing health information by developing and strengthening our advocacy role and improving communication with all our stakeholders.

Activities

HLG activities include:

Journal and Newsletter Our journal, *Health Information and Libraries Journal*, published by Wiley Blackwell Scientific Publications, is available to Group members at a reduced subscription rate.

(www.wiley.com/bw/journal.asp?ref=1471-1834).

An electronic Newsletter is published quarterly on www.cilip.org.uk/get-involved/special-interest-groups/health/pages/newsletter.aspx in March, June, September and December. Each subject group has its own newsletter.

Subject Groups There are two subject groups - Information for the Management of Healthcare (IFMH) and Libraries for Nursing (LfN). The Group also has representation on other bodies and maintains links with organisations which have similar interests. HLG Wales offers a range of local events and activities.

Directory *The Health Library and Information Services Directory in the UK and Republic of Ireland*, produced in partnership with the Royal College of Nursing and the National Library for Health, went live in 2005.

CPD Study days and other meetings are held throughout the year. The HLG conference is held biannually and HLG contributes to the CILIP Umbrella conference. We also support our members' CPD by offering bursaries to attend CPD activities.

Information Services Group (ISG)

Website: www.cilip.org.uk/isg
Contact e-mail: ISGHonSecretary@cilip.org.uk

Aims and objectives

The Information Services Group (ISG) seeks to unite members engaged in, or having an interest in, the provision of reference and information services. It will support their interests within CILIP and outside by promoting activities relevant to improving the effectiveness of information provision to all sectors.

The Group:

- champions views and concerns of all sectors of the information profession

- provides advice and training workshops to keep members informed and up to date
- encourages active involvement in professional activities nationally through the regional ISG activities
- provides practical support in the workplace through nationally recognised committees.

Activities and achievements

In 2008/2009:

- ISG published three editions of its prestigious journal *Refer* and launched a Referplus webpage, with expanded articles, links, and a growing set of recommended Reference websites.
- Section committees continued to remain active in East Anglia, South East & London, and Scotland. All these sections ran successful courses during the year.
- Standing committee SCOOP continued to represent the group's interests in official publications and statistics.
- The group continued to administer the highly regarded ISG Reference awards.

International Library And Information Group (ILG)

Website: www.cilip.org.uk/ilig
Contact e-mail: ilig@cilip.org.uk

Aims and objectives

- Raise awareness of international issues concerning the profession.
- Contribute to the development of library and information services internationally.
- Influence and assist CILIP in its formulation of international policy and activities.
- Encourage UK librarians to gain knowledge and practical experience of information and library work overseas.

- Foster networking, linking, and general co-operation among those involved in international library and information work.

Activities and achievements

- The 2009 International Award for making a difference in libraries and information services outside the United Kingdom was awarded to Ruwan Gamage, University of Moratuwa, Sri Lanka, in recognition of his imagination and initiative that conceived and established the Sri Lanka Library Friends e-discussion and communication group.
- We will be making an International Award in 2010 and also the Anthony Thompson Award (see details on our website).
- In 2009 we held successful fund-raising seminars in April (on copyright and services to international students) and October (e-copyright).
- ILIG organised three sessions at Umbrella in July.
- Our ILIG Informals programme goes from strength to strength with meetings held in April, June and October and the annual ILIG quiz in December.
- ILIG also manages ILIGlist , an email forum for all with an interest in international library and information work issues. We also have a Facebook and Twitter presence.
- Our newsletter, *Focus*, is produced three times a year.

Library and Information History Group (LIHG)

Website: www.lihg.org
Contact e-mail: rob@robwestwood.co.uk

Aims and objectives

To act as the historical consciousness of the LIS profession in Britain. To raise awareness of the importance of library and information history both in Britain and abroad. To promote activities – conferences, regional meetings, lectures – in support of all objectives. To communicate research and publication in library and information history.

Activities and achievements

- Annual Library and Information History Conference
- Publication of *Books, Buildings and Social Engineering* by Alistair Black, Simon Pepper and Kaye Bagshaw (Aldershot: Ashgate, 2009)
- Support for a successful monthly 'History of Libraries' seminar series in London
- First issue of *Library and Information History* (edited by Toni Weller) published in March 2009, succeeding our former title, *Library History*
- Continued publication of our group *Newsletter*
- Collaborative initiatives such as mutual promotion of events with The Society for the History of Authorship, Reading and Publishing (SHARP)
- Participation in the CILIP Umbrella Conference
- The year also saw a particularly strong field of submissions for our essay prize.

Library and Information Research Group (LIRG)

Website: www.cilip.org.uk/lirg
Contact e-mail: alan.poulter@cis.strath.ac.uk

Aims and objectives

LIRG aims to:

- raise awareness of, use of, and contributions to research by LIS practitioners
- increase the profile and impact of academic and practitioner LIS research
- influence positively the direction of LIS research
- promote the dissemination of sound research methodologies.

The LIRG Committee contains a representative mix of LIS practitioners from various sectors and academics from different research centres.

LIRG publishes LIS research in its open access journal, *Library and Information Research* (*LIR*), run using the Open Journal System.

LIRG offers the following research annual awards:

- the Student Prize (£300) for the best Post/Under-Graduate dissertation
- the Ex Libris Award (£2500 from the sponsor) for research into library systems
- the Research Award (£2000) for research into any area in LIS.

Activities and achievements

LIRG has been an active partner on behalf of CILIP in the LIS Research Coalition, which is running a conference on research priorities in LIS.

In order to keep in touch with current research, LIRG held peripatetic Committee meetings at Loughborough University and Brighton University.

LIRG is now maintaining two up-to-date online listings of LIS research sources/information/websites and a Researcher Directory listing individual LIS researchers in the UK , using the Web 2.0 database, DabbleDB.

LIRG supported the LIRG Research Award by offering a successful two-part research methods course, which run in London, Birmingham, and Glasgow, giving to help in the writing of research bids.

LIRG has introduced a new, special, research award for 2010, the Scan Award (£500) for a summary of research into a critical area, in this case methods for demonstrating the value of public libraries in the UK.

Local Studies Group (LSG)

Website: www.cilip.org.uk/lsg
Contact e-mail: via website

Aims and objectives

The Local Studies Group (LSG) is a Special Interest Group of CILIP. The object of the Group is to further the aims of CILIP within the Local Studies field by uniting those members of CILIP and the Group engaged or interested in Local Studies, fostering communication, facilitating exchange of experience and continuing professional development, and by promoting relevant work. See website for full details: www.cilip.org.uk/get-involved/special-interest-groups/local-studies/Documents/LSG_Aims_and_Objectives.pdf.

Activities and achievements

The Midlands & Anglia, North-West, and Scottish sub-groups have provided another active programme of events, which have been well attended. A new sub-group for the South of England has been established during the year, and this has also run a successful event.

The Group's website has been kept up-to-date and is increasingly used to publicise events. Committee members have been active in other professional groups, as well as on CILIP's Policy Forum. Several have attended training courses arranged by CILIP's Membership Support Unit.

Regrettably this year there were no nominations for the Group's award, the Dorothy McCulla Memorial Prize. We are working to publicise this better in the future and to encourage nominations from the sub-groups.

The main achievement this year was a conference, Engaging Communities: 'Local Studies in the 21st Century', held on 8 June at The National Archives. This was extremely successful and attended by 50 people from all over the country. The feedback received was positive and encouraging and we plan to organise another conference in 2011.

Multimedia and information Technology Group (MMiT)

Website: www.cilip.org.uk/mmit
Contact e-mail: l.appleton1@ljmu.ac.uk

Aims and objectives

The Multimedia Information and Technology Group aims to unite CILIP members engaged in, or interested in, multimedia information and technology developments in library and information science. It is a means of sharing experience and ideas, and promoting common professional interests. The Group acts as a forum for explaining, and reflecting on, the exploitation of technology in information provision. It deals with the integration and management of all the forms in which information is presented, the use of a range of electronic delivery systems, now including web-based applications, and innovation; all in the interests of communicating information.

Activities and achievements

The *Multimedia Information & Technology Journal* is a central feature of our activities. We have recruited a new journal editor during the 2009–10 year, and are very pleased that Catherine Dhanjal is now a key member of the MmIT team

Our regularly updated newsblog can be used by anyone with a useful contribution to make, whether it is an event, a research report, opinion piece, or anything else relevant to multimedia.

Our autumn conference covers a key topic of the moment, and invariably boasts highly respected speakers. October 2009 saw our first 'Mobile Learning' conference bringing together the very best speakers from around the UK to talk about their experiences of m-learning within a library context. For 2010 we have planned a summer conference about 'Social Networking and Libraries' and our Autumn conference will cover the theme of 'Digital Literacies'.

Patent and Trademark Group (PATMG)

Website: www.cilip.org.uk/patmg
Contact e-mails: achapman@minesoft.com (Secretary); bob.stembridge@thomsonreuters.com

Aims and objectives

PATMG is a special interest group of CILIP. Most members are also CILIP members, but it is not a requirement. Non-library professionals belong such as Trademark and Patent Attorneys and Patent Agents, as well as patent and trademark information searchers and staff working primarily in Industry, located in the UK and abroad. The aim is to provide a lively and stimulating on-going debate and sharing of best practice in this niche area of information retrieval and searching. PATMG runs a website hosted by CILIP at: www.cilip.org.uk/patmg, which helps keep members abreast with PATMG news and activities. The PATMG *Searcher* newsletter is printed four times a year, providing useful information for patent and trademark information searchers.

PATMG participates in the international PIUG (Patent Information Users Group), operating the PIUG-Wiki. Here lively discussions take place and useful advice is shared internationally on a daily basis. A programme of meetings/events is offered during the year, usually free of cost to members. Speakers cover topics suggested by the members.

Activities and achievements

PATMG organised several patent and trademark information lectures and debates, throughout the year. These took place in London and Leeds, as well as meeting at major exhibitions during the year. There were social meetings at the International Patent Information Conference and at the London Online Exhibition and Conference. The events and meetings during the year were well attended by between 20 and 60 people.

PATMG featured speakers from the the public and private sectors, sharing best practice and the latest information from vendors about their products, such as Asian Patent Searching. PATMG paid for a representative to travel to the European Patent Office to participate in the Standing Advisory Committee to the European Patent Office, helping to shape information policies and provision. Stephen Adams was selected to represent the views of PATMG.

The Searcher newsletter was published 4 times, keeping members up to date with news and activities. Bob Stembridge, PATMG Chair, gave a report to the Dutch Patent Information User Group (WON) at their Annual Conference about the UK activities of PATMG.

Bob Stembridge also represented PATMG in the European Group of patent Information User Groups, to dicuss the Certification of Patent Searchers. This represents an attempt by colleagues internationally, seeking to implement a certification scheme that will be recognised internationally. This group is assisted by the European Patent Office.

PATMG members contributed to British Patent & Trade Mark Office consultations, such as the Consultation on Amendments to Trade Mark Rules, which took place this year.

Personnel, Training and Education Group (PTEG)

Website: www.cilip.org.uk/pteg
Contact e-mail: linda.ferguson@nhs.net

Aims and objectives

Our mission is to promote and support excellence in the management and development of the library information services workforce.

We will:

- develop and deliver resources designed to meet identified professional needs within PTEG's area of concern.
- ensure PTEG has an appropriate web presence and publications programme to communicate with members.
- identify groups and networks with which to work proactively and collaboratively to achieve common objectives.
- develop appropriate mechanisms to support succession planning and comply with CILIP regulations.

Activities and achievements

We have:

- delivered training and provided support for new mentors through our Mentor Support Network
- delivered training for CILIP fellowship candidates
- taken an active part in the CILIP CPD Task and Finish Group
- produced a new format (A5) Newsletter that outlines our activities and provides articles of interest to our members
- developed a wiki for the PTEG Committee to carry out some of its business in a virtual manner.
- reviewed out Strategy and started work to update it for 2010-2013
- started to use Twitter as a promotional tool: follow us at http://twitter.com/cilippteg.

Prison Libraries Group (PLG)

Website: www.cilip.org.uk/prlg
Contact e-mail: megan.silver@hmps.gsi.gov.uk

Aims and objectives

The Prison Libraries Group serves the interest of

all members concerned with the provision of library services to prison communities. The Group is committed to improving the quality of the service whilst raising the profile of prison libraries.

The Group aims :

- to share and develop ideas through training and publications
- to be of benefit and support to all members concerned with library services to prisoners, prison and education staff
- to liaise with the Prison Service
- to encourage contracts between local library authorities and Prison Service establishments
- to be an active part of CILIP

Activities and achievements

The Prison Libraries Group runs a training day each year at which we hold our AGM. This is usually attended by around 60 delegates. In 2009 this was on the 13 May and the theme was training opportunities for library staff and orderlies.

Our annual Conference on 6 and 7 October 2009 included a range of speakers offering an insight into international, national and local issues within prison libraries. The **2009 Margaret Watson Award for Best Practice** was presented at the conference by CILIP President Peter Griffiths and Margaret Watson and was won by Alan Smith, Library Supervisor at HMYOI Brinsford (pictured below).

The group produces a training pack for those

new to working in prison libraries which can be downloaded by members from the website.

Public Libraries Group (PLG)

Website: www.cilip.org.uk/plg
Contact e-mail: frances.roberts@library.s-lanark.org.uk

Aims and objectives

The Public Libraries Group aims to share best practice, offer development opportunities and facilitate networking at all levels of the public library sector in the UK.

The Group's objectives are:

- to encourage, publicise and support best practice in public libraries, through events, publications and awards
- to act as a conduit for information on public libraries to the library profession, professional bodies, departments of librarianship, all levels of special interest groups, the book trade and the public at large
- to promote awareness, communication and networking within the public library sector
- to provide services and activities which reflect the views and requirements of all members of the Group and offer opportunities for professional involvement.

Activities and achievements

- Presented the 2009 Public Library Building Awards.
- Managed PLA 2009 in Bristol – 'Impact, Inclusion, Information: the value of libraries in the lives of communities'.
- Contributed to the sucessful 2009 Umbrella programme.
- Awarded the Public Libraries Group Personal Learning Grant.

Publicity and Public Relations Group (PPRG)

Website www.cilip.org.uk/pprg
Contact e-mail: d.omar@kingston.ac.uk

Aims and objectives

- To solicit and distribute best practice on marketing libraries across all library sectors.
- To celebrate marketing successes by running a national award.
- To hold a national conference to share best practice and introduce new techniques/theories.
- To support CILIP in providing CPD opportunities to members and the profession.

Achievements/activities

The past 12 months have been some of the most successful for the group:

- PPRG had a full and strong committee which enabled the group to market our events and awards fully.
- There was an excellent response to the Marketing Excellence Awards in 2009 with a significant increase in entrants and we were able to award a Gold, Silver and Bronze.
- We organised a seminar on 'Marketing Excellence' to present our Marketing Excellence Awards and to hear presentations from the winners. The seminar took place in Leeds and was very successful and well attended.
- Our conference was fully booked and we were able to secure some excellent speakers on a wide variety of topic areas. The conference topic was 'Libraries – A Brand To Be Reckoned With'.
- We arranged three individual sessions at Umbrella 2009 and participated in an additional two.
- The website was maintained and developed throughout the year and *Public Eye* was also published throughout the year.

Rare Books and Special Collections Group (RBSCG)

Website: www.cilip.org.uk/rbscg
Contact e-mail: via website

Aims and objectives

The Rare Books and Special Collections Group unites librarians responsible for collections of rare books, manuscripts and special materials, with other interested individuals.

The group promotes the study and exploitation of rare books, encourages awareness of preservation, conservation and digitisation issues, and fosters training opportunities related to the maintenance, display and use of collections.

Activities and achievements

In 2009 the Rare Books and Special Collections Group continued to support and highlight the work undertaken by a range of professionals in a wide variety of institutions to maintain, and enhance access to, collections of historically significant material. Its flagship event was, as always, its three day annual study conference in September, this year held at Clare College in Cambridge and entitled 'A Special Relationship? Special Collections and the Antiquarian Book and Manuscripts Trade', which offered an opportunity to examine and discuss issues concerning libraries and the antiquarian book trade, including acquisitions, donations, valuations, theft and the sale of library materials, and to visit various historic collections in Cambridge.

As a result of this conference, members of the RBSCG Committee have become involved in liaising regularly with the Antiquarian Booksellers'Association, to co-ordinate efforts on areas of mutual concern and interest.

With regard to describing collections, the Bibliographic Standards Subcommittee arranged two training sessions on DCRM(B) in London and Edinburgh. More generally the Group continued to provide a programme of visits for members, with a summer trip to the John Rylands Library in Manchester, and a 'Great Books' event at the British Library, with curators on hand to explain the significance of each treasure. The *Rare Books Newsletter* continues to be published on-line, and the Committee is in the process of arranging for a second edition of the *Directory of Rare Books and Special Collections* to be published by Facet Publishing.

School Libraries Group (SLG)

Website: www.cilip.org.uk/slg
Contact email: alison.roberts@calderdale.gov.uk (Group Secretary)

Aims and objectives:

The School Libraries Group (SLG) of CILIP affirms that school libraries and school library services are fundamental to the development of a literate population able to participate fully in a thriving democracy, culture, civilization and economy. The SLG is therefore fully committed to enabling its members to achieve and maintain the highest professional standards, and encouraging and supporting them in the delivery and promotion of high quality library and information services responsive to the needs of users.

Activities and achievements

- SLG's national conference was held in April 2009. Entitled 'Seeing the Bigger Picture: school libraries in the learning agenda', it attracted over 150 attendees and was very well received by both delegates and speakers.
- SLG contributed to an Information Skills for Life session with CofHE, ELG and UCR at Umbrella 2009.
- SLG put the proposal to CILIP's Policy Forum

and then Council that CILIP should endorse Alan Gibbon's Campaign for the Book which calls for school libraries to be made statutory. This was ratified by Council so CILIP then signed the e-petition on the Number10.gov.uk website.

- 'Make school libraries statutory' became the first article of CILIP's General Election Manifesto.
- SLG instigated a national survey into the current provision of school libraries (both primary and secondary) in the UK utilising online questionnaires and telephone interviews. This work was supported by the School Library Association and CILIP Scotland, with funds provided by the Wendy Drewett Bequest, and the final report is due to be published in June 2010. The objectives of the survey are to investigate school libraries' funding, staffing and whether activities in and use of library services have changed.
- SLG was instrumental in drafting the CILIP submission to the School Library Commission, chaired by Baroness Estelle Morris. The Commission aims to set a national agenda to ensure school libraries are delivering exceptional services to help young people reach their potential. SLG took part in the Commission's Round Table on 16 March 2010.

The UK eInformation Group (UKeiG)

Website: www.ukeig.org.uk
Contact e-mail: cabaker@ukeig.org.uk

Aims and objectives

UKeiG is a respected and well established forum for all information professionals, users and developers of electronic information resources. The aim of UKeiG is to promote and advance the effective exploitation and management of electronic information. UKeiG offers a wide range of resources including seminars and workshops, the e-journal

eLucidate and a popular series of factsheets. Members of UKeiG come from many sectors including higher education, government bodies, the corporate sector, charities and public libraries.

Activities and achievements

During the past year UKeiG have held around twelve training courses on a variety of topics ranging from advanced searching techniques to legal issues for the information professional, and the training programme has been awarded the CILIP Seal of Recognition. The Intranets Forum meets regularly to discuss and debate various aspects of intranets, and members have the opportunity to see intranets in action at the premises of the hosts who kindly offer their venues.

UKeiG has also given grants and presented awards to those who have contributed significantly to the field of information management and for those who wish to enhance their professional development.

A successful two-day conference was held in June 2009 in Manchester on Innovation in e-Information. Views from key industry experts on how to adapt, change and to improve delivery of e-information services using innovative thought, products and processes were presented, and the feedback from the attendees was very favourable.

University, College and Research Group

Website: www.cilip.org.uk/ucr
Contact e-mail: ucr@cilip.org.uk

Aims and objectives

UC&R Group aims to provide a focus and a forum for the professional concerns and interests of everyone working in national, research or academic libraries, linking those with current and emerging issues and developments and the overall direction of CILIP's corporate plan.

Activities and achievements

The Group continues its programme of regional and national conferences and events, with joint contributions with CoFHE to Umbrella 2009. Regional events have covered topics such as learning technologies, innovations in teaching, behaviour management and Customer Service Excellence.

The Group journal, *Relay* was published twice in 2009 and the editorial team is working on the next issues. There are regular paper newsletters and the JISCmail discussion list, lis-ucr, is an easy and effective way of reaching out to members. In 2009 UC&R started to make use of the CILIP e-mailing service which is sent out to all UC&R members who have registered to receive e-mails via the CILIP website.

The Group continues to promote its two major awards: the Alison Northover Bursary for personal professional development and the UC&R Award for Innovation. In 2009 the Innovation Award was made to Andrew Walsh from the University of Huddersfield. Andrew's project aim is 'to produce and evaluate a small package of information skills and induction materials that incorporate formats suitable for a range of platforms including mobile phones'. The Alison Northover Award was made to Joseph Ripp from the National Portrait Gallery and will enable him to attend a course at the London Rare Books School in July 2010.

Youth Libraries Group (YLG)

Website: www.cilip.org.uk/ylg
Contact e-mail: via website

Aims and objectives

The Youth Libraries Group of CILIP is the organisation of choice for librarians, information professionals and all those working with or interested in children's and young people's books, reading development, the promotion of libraries and reading for pleasure. Our 3000 members come from a wide range of workplaces – public libraries, schools, school library services, colleges, universities and early years settings. We also welcome and have many student, non-working and international members.With twelve groups across the United Kingdom we form one of the largest and liveliest special interest groups in CILIP.

Activities and achievements

In 2009, the Youth Libraries Group contributed to the judging process and administration of the CILIP Carnegie & Kate Greenaway Medals. YLG has also been consulted with about various national projects, including Children's Reading Partners and Book Time. The 2009 conference was entitled 'Read to Succeed' and included keynote presentations from Patience Thomson (co-founder of Barrington Stoke) and Nikki Heath (SLA School Librarian of the Year) as well as a wealth of authors and illustrators including Sir Terry Pratchett and Anthony Browne.

Honorary Membership of the group was awarded to Moira Arthur, outgoing MD of Peter's Book Suppliers, and Wendy Cooling, Children's Literature Consultant.

The *YLG Monthly E-News* disseminated via the CILIP Branch and Groups Mailing System was launched in February 2009 and includes topical professional issues, a what's on guide, sponsorship offers from publishers and a round-up of news.

National committees

Affiliated Members National Committee (AMNC)

Website: www.cilip.org.uk/amnc
Contact e-mail:
karen.newton@sunderland.gov.uk

Aims and objectives

Affiliate Members wish to promote the experienced based professionalism of their membership. We support and promote the Framework of Qualifications and know that our members wish to gain national recognition by working toward the ACLIP award.

Education

- Affiliate Members National Committee (AMNC) will promote the Framework of Qualifications and in particular the ACLIP/MCLIP qualifications .

Advocacy

- AMNC will maintain and encourage the Affiliate role within CILIP and with other CILIP special interest groups
- AMNC will join with other groups to promote CILIP's role in the information and library sector.

Community

- AMNC will provide members with a regular e-newsletter to motivate and encourage our members to see the wider aspects of CILIP membership.
- AMNC will regularly maintain our web pages
- AMNC will investigate the use of web tools to further its aims and objectives.

Activities and achievements

Robinson Award

The CILIP Robinson Award is awarded for excellence and innovation in library administration.

Robinson Award celebrations

Affiliated Members at Umbrella 2009

In 2009, it was awarded to Vikki Thomas who works at Biggart Baillie law firm in Glasgow who devised and implemented an innovative method for improving current awareness services for partners in the Glasgow and Edinburgh offices.

Umbrella conference

The affiliates held five sessions at the 2009 conference along with the AGM where Carole Humphreys of Hertfordshire Libraries told her story of how she went through the ACLIP to MCLIP process. Holders of ACLIP, which was introduced in 2005, are not obliged to obtain MCLIP although 17 people have successfully done so since 2007.

Retired Members Guild (RMG)

Website: www.cilip.org.uk/rmg
E-mail: alison.hall6@btinternet.com

The Guild enables retired librarians to keep in touch with each other, to participate in activities and to assist CILIP in its promotion of libraries of all types.

Activities

Amongst its activities, the Guild arranges meetings and visits to libraries and places of interest to librarians both at home and overseas. Partners are welcome at all of these events.

The Guild also seeks out additional financial and other benefits available for retired and older people and makes these known. It assists CILIP with the organisation of its elections by the provision of scrutineers and the development of guidelines.

It helps the Library Campaign to maintain and improve library services. It also responds to requests from voluntary societies and charities for assistance with their library services where this complies with the CILIP Guidelines for voluntary work.

Suppliers Network

CILIP works across the whole library and information domain and recognises the importance of partnerships with the vendor community. Its Suppliers Network offers companies that sell products and services, systems and software to the library and information sector the opportunity to have a closer association with CILIP, the only chartered body for library and information professionals. This involvement generates better awareness of both sides' needs and expectations for the future and lends a louder voice for our lobbying activities.

Suppliers Network Contact:
Gary Allman
gary.allman@cilip.org.uk
0207 255 0552

Companies in membership

2CQR
3M
ADLIB Information Systems
Applied Network Solutions
Autolib Library & Information Management Systems
Axiell UK
Bailey Solutions
Bertram Library Services
Bowker (UK)
Civica
Conservation by Design
Coutts Information Services
Credo Reference
d_skin UK
D-Tech Direct
EOS International
EX Libris (UK)
FG Library Products
Forster Ecospace
Glen Recruitment
Infor
Innovative Interfaces
Insight Media International
Intrepid Security Systems
IS Oxford
Ken Chad Consulting
Nielsen BookData
OCLC
Plescon Security Products
Point Eight
Primetech (UK)
Radford HMY Group
Reed Business Information
Softlink Europe
Soutron Ltd
Swets Information Services
Talis Information
Total Disc Repair
Waterstone's Booksellers

CILIP Benevolent Fund

The Benevolent Fund was established by The Library Association in the last century and became a registered charity in 1964. With the formation of CILIP in 2002, it changed its name to the CILIP Benevolent Fund and its Trust Deed was amended to enable it to provide help to all Members of CILIP and former members of The Library Association and The Institute of Information Scientists, together with their dependents.

The Fund is able to provide emergency assistance by means of either a grant or an interest free loan, to help in meeting any unusual or unexpected expenses that are causing anxiety and hardship. Its income derives principally from CILIP Members' donations, plus interest on that part of its capital that has been invested. The Fund is a registered charity, separate from CILIP and its finances do not form part of those of CILIP. It is administered by seven Trustees appointed by CILIP Council, who meet at least three times a year. However, between meetings most requests for help can be promptly met as the Chair is authorised to take action provided that is in accordance with agreed policy.

Two leaflets – *What is the CILIP Benevolent Fund?* and *A Will to Help: an opportunity to remember the CILIP Benevolent Fund when making your will* – are readily available from the Secretary of the Fund. All enquiries should be addressed to the Secretary in the first instance.

Trustees

Bernard Naylor (Chair), Mary Auckland, Terence Bell, Graham Cornish, Gillian Pentelow, Jean Plaister, Martin Stone

Secretary

Eric Winter
CILIP Benevolent Fund,
7 Ridgmount Street,
London WC1E 7AE
Telephone: 020 7255 0648
07977 910492 (mobile)
Fax: 020 7255 0501
E-mail: eric.winter@cilip.org.uk

Registered Charity number

237352

Medals and Awards

The CILIP Carnegie and Kate Greenaway Medals

The CILIP Carnegie and Kate Greenaway Medals are the UK's most prestigious children's book awards. The Carnegie Medal is awarded for outstanding writing and The Kate Greenaway Medal is awarded for outstanding illustration, in a book for children and young people.

Nominations are invited from all Members of CILIP via a nomination form, which is published in September in *Library & Information Gazette* and online at www.ckg.org.uk/nomination. Eligible titles must be written in English; be published originally for children and young people and have received their first publication in the United Kingdom between the preceding 1 September–31 August period, or have had co-publication elsewhere within a three month time lapse.

The selection process is organised by CILIP's Youth Libraries Group (YLG), which appoints 12 regional judges who are experienced children's librarians.

A shortlist for each medal is announced in April each year and the winners are announced and presented at a London ceremony in June. The winning author and illustrator receive a golden medal, a certificate and £500 worth of books to donate to a library of their choice. Since 2000 the winner of the Kate Greenaway Medal has also received the Colin Mears Award, which is a cash prize of £5,000.

The accompanying shadowing scheme for children and young people has 3,800 registered reading groups in schools and public libraries. An estimated 90,000 children 'shadowed' the judging process in 2010, reading the shortlisted titles and posting their book reviews on a specially created award website.

For further information on the Carnegie and Kate Greenaway Medals including past winners, criteria and information on the shadowing scheme visit www.ckg.org.uk or contact the CILIP Marketing Team: ckg@cilip.org.uk.

In 2006/7 it was agreed to change the year of the medals from the date of publication to the date of presentation.

Carnegie Medal winners

2010	Neil Gaiman, *The Graveyard Book*, Bloomsbury
2009	Siobhan Dowd, *Bog Child*, David Fickling
2008	Philip Reeve, *Here Lies Arthur*, Scholastic
2007	Meg Rosoff, *Just in Case,* Penguin
2005	Mal Peet, *Tamar*, Walker Books
2004	Frank Cottrell Boyce, *Millions*, Macmillan
2003	Jennifer Donnelly, *A Gathering Light*, Bloomsbury
2002	Sharon Creech, *Ruby Holler*, Bloomsbury
2001	Terry Pratchett, *The Amazing Maurice and His Educated Rodents*, Transworld

Kate Greenaway Medal winners

2010	Freya Blackwood, *Harry and Hopper*, Scholastic
2009	Catherine Rayner, *Harris Finds His Feet*, Little Tiger Press
2008	Emily Gravett, *Little Mouse's Big Book of Fears*, Macmillan
2007	Mini Grey, *The Adventures of the Dish and the Spoon*, Jonathan Cape

2005   Emily Gravett, *Wolves*, Macmillan
2004   Chris Riddell, *Jonathan Swift's Gulliver*,
        Walker Books
2003   Shirley Hughes, *Ella's Big Chance*, The
        Bodley Head
2002   Bob Graham, *Jethro Byrde – Fairy Child*,
        Walker
2001   Chris Riddell, *Pirate Diary*, Walker Books

The CILIP Diversity Awards

These awards aim to recognise outstanding achievement in the promotion of diversity through library and information services. They are awarded biannually by the CILIP Diversity Group.

Winners

2010   Mike Prendergast, Community Library
        Services Manager, and Mike Allport,
        Reader Development Manager, London
        Borough of Southwark, Rotherhithe
        Library, Albion Street, London
2009   Margaret Watson, consultant and trainer
2007   Joanne Harvey, Service Development
        Manager Reader Development, Brighton
        and Hove City Library Service (Personal
        Achievement Award)
        London Borough of Camden
        (Organisational Change Award)
2005   Mrs Jagjit Kohli, Multicultural Librarian,
        Warwickshire County Council (Personal
        Achievement Award)
        Black Country Libraries in Partnership
        (BCLIP) (Organisational Change Award)
2003   Phil Burns, Youth Development Officer,
        Birmingham Library and Information
        Services (Personal Achievement Award)
        Learning Resources at the University of
        Wolverhampton (Organisational Change
        Award)

The CILIP Libraries Change Lives Award

The Libraries Change Lives Award promotes good practice, recognises innovation and celebrates the achievements of grass roots projects and frontline staff, particularly those working with socially excluded groups. The Award is run by CILIP and its Community Services Group (CSG).

A trophy, a certificate and £5,000 are presented to the winning project and two finalists receive £2,000 and a certificate..

The winning project should be a partnership between a library or information service and one or more community agencies. It should be an example of good practice, have started in the past three years and be ongoing. Applications are invited from any type of library or information service throughout the UK. An entry form is sent with *Library & Information Gazette* in November.

Further information and an electronic entry form are available on the CILIP website www.cilip.org.uk/lcla. Entries close early February.

Winners

2010   HMP Edinburgh Library Partnership –
        The City of Edinburgh Council
2009   Across the Board: Autism support for
        families – Leeds Library and Information
        Service
2008   Bradford / Care Trust Libraries
        Partnership Project – Bradford Libraries
        and Archive Information Service
2007   Welcome to Your Library – London
        Libraries Development Agency
2006   Sighthill Library Youth Work – Edinburgh
        City Libraries and Information Service
2005   Northamptonshire Black History Project –
        Northamptonshire Libraries and
        Information Service and the
        Northamptonshire Racial Equality
        Council
2004   The Mobile Library Travellers Project –

Essex County Council Libraries

2003 Eye 2 Eye – Portsmouth City Libraries

2002 The Big Bookshare Nottingham

The CILIP Robinson Award for Innovation in Library Administration by Para-Professional Staff

(formerly the Robinson Medal)

The Robinson Award is one of the ways in which CILIP recognises the contribution of and promotes the value of para-professional staff.

The award is aimed at para-professional library and information staff who have either invented or created a cost-effective solution to an administrative, manual or other procedure. It can be a team effort, or that of an individual, but the original idea must have come from a paraprofessional library worker, who does not have to be a member of CILIP.

The award of Amazon vouchers to the value of £50 and a certificate is made to the submission which, in the judges' opinion, best fulfils the criteria The award is administered by CILIP and the Affiliated Member's National Committee.

Fred Robinson, who left the legacy for this award, invented a permanent fines calculator and the all-in-one book issue label with pocket.

For more information see the Robinson Award page on the CILIP website.

Winners

2009 Vikki Thomas, Biggart Baillie LLP, Glasgow, for devising and implementing an innovative method for improving current awareness services for partners in the Glasgow and Edinburgh offices.

2005 Nathan Owen, Library and Learning Centre, Ysbyty Gwynedd (North West Wales NHS Trust), for JUST AWHiLe,

Joint Union Script Transfer for ALL Wales Health Libraries

2003 Not awarded

2002 Christine Stevenson, University of Sunderland, for a Library Support Service for Distance Learners

The CILIP/ESU Travelling Librarian Award

Each year, the English-Speaking Union (ESU) and CILIP invite applications for the Travelling Librarian Award, from qualified librarians working in UK libraries or information centres. The Travelling Librarian Award is intended to encourage US/UK contacts in the library world and the establishment of permanent links through a professional development study tour. The visit is for two weeks and normally takes place in the autumn.

Applicants must be: (a) qualified librarians and; (b) in membership of CILIP at time of application.

For further information see: www.cilip.org.uk/aboutcilip/medalsandawards/travellinglibrarian.

Winners

2010 David Clover
Jo McCausland

2009 Peter Lund

2008 Sibylla Parkhill

2007 Karen Poole

2006 Kim Sherwin

2005 Heather Lane

2004 Simon Bevan

2003 Anne Peoples

2002 Paula Younger

The ISG Reference Awards

These annual Awards comprise the Besterman/McColvin Medals for an outstanding work of reference (in print and electronic categories) and the Walford Award for an individual who has made a longstanding contribution to bibliography.

The judges represent CILIP's Information Services Group, and Multimedia and Information Technology Group.

Nominations for the Awards are invited from CILIP Members, all information professionals, publishers and other interested individuals. Winners of the Besterman/McColvin Medals receive a certificate and a cash prize of £500. The winner of the Walford Award receives a certificate and £500. The Awards are presented in the following year.

For further information see the CILIP website www.cilip.org.uk/awards.

Besterman/McColvin Medal

Electronic category winners

2007   Not awarded
2006   *Oxford African American Studies Centre*, Oxford University Press
2005   Not awarded
2004   *Oxford Dictionary of National Biography* edited by H. C. G. Matthew and Brian Harrison, Oxford University Press
2003   xreferplus (www.xrefer.com)
2002   *The Visual Culture of Wales: imaging the nation* by Peter Lord. University of Wales Press (CD-ROM)

Printed category winners

2007   *Biographical Dictionary of British Quakers in Commerce and Industry 1775–1920* by Edward H. Milligan. Sessions Book Trust
2006   *Dictionary of Pastellists Before 1800* by Neil Jeffares, Unicorn Press
2005   *Oil Paintings in Public Ownership – West Sussex*, edited by a team led by Andrew Ellis. Public Catalogue Foundation

2004   *The Design Encyclopaedia* by Mel Byars, Laurence King Publishing
2003   *Early Printed Books Catalogue 1478–1840*, compiled for the Royal Institute of British Architects British Architectural Library by Paul W. Nash, Nicholas Savage, Gerald Beasley, John Meriton and Alison Shell
2002   *20th Century Ceramic Designers in Britain* by Andrew Casey. Antique Collectors' Club

Walford Award

Winners

2007   Not yet awarded
2006   Diana Dixon
2005   Alan Day
2004   Ian Maxted
2003   Paul W. Nash
2002   Robin Alston

The PPRG Marketing Excellence Awards

Promoting services is an essential role for librarians and information managers. Across the UK, CILIP Members and others are producing increasingly sophisticated marketing and publicity material and running innovative promotional campaigns, often with limited resources. These Awards aim to recognise and reward this valuable work, which brings library services to new audiences and develops and publicises an extensive range of new activities to existing users.

The Marketing Excellence Awards are organised by CILIP's Publicity and Public Relations Group.

Gold, silver and bronze awards are made for a marketing campaign that includes several promotional elements, which are co-ordinated and presented in an integrated way to increase their impact. Entries should include the following:

printed publicity material, a promotional event/display, media coverage, e-marketing. The judges will be looking for evidence of impact and effectiveness.

Further details are available on the PPRG website: www.cilip.org.uk/pprg.

Winners

2009

Gold Award: The Graphic Novel Festival, Hertfordshire Libraries, Culture and Learning

Silver Award: Friends and Fans of CILT Resource Library, CILT – National Centre for Languages

Bronze Award: Turn a New Page, Newcastle Libraries

2008

Silver Award: Treasures of Central Library, Manchester Library and Information Service

Bronze Award: Ten Outstanding Years of the Learning Resource Centre, University of Teesside Library and Information Services

Bronze Award: E-marketing in Manchester, Manchester Library and Information Service

2007

CATEGORY 1: CREATIVE PRINT CAMPAIGN

Silver Award: Got your Card – Let's Go, Manchester Library and Information Service

CATEGORY 2: NEW MEDIA INNOVATION AWARDS
No awards made.

CATEGORY 3: INTEGRATED MARKETING AWARDS

Gold Award: The 'S' Factor, Solihull Central Library

Silver Award: Off the Page – Stirling Book Festival, Stirling Council Library

Bronze Award: Get your Maisy Card, Surrey County Library

2006

CATEGORY 1: CREATIVE PRINT CAMPAIGN

Silver Award: Concessions Poster Campaign, Leicestershire County Council

Bronze Award: Widening Choice, Essex County Council (Libraries)

CATEGORY 2: NEW MEDIA INNOVATION AWARDS
No awards made.

CATEGORY 3: INTEGRATED MARKETING AWARDS

Gold Award: Welcome Campaign, Manchester Metropolitan University Library

Silver Award: The Library Brand, Gloucestershire County Council Libraries and Information

Bronze Award: Bag for Life, Cheshire County Council Library Service in partnership with Cheshire County Council Waste Management

2005

PROMOTIONAL CAMPAIGN: BUDGET UNDER £500

Gold Award: 'Leeds Reads', Leeds University Library

Bronze Award: Exhibitions in Central Library, Manchester Library and Information Services

PROMOTIONAL CAMPAIGN: BUDGET OVER £500

Gold Award: 'Sorted', Manchester Library and Information Services

Silver Award: Gosport Discovery Centre, Hampshire County Council

Bronze Award: Library Link Volunteer Scheme, Bolton Library

PRINTED PUBLICITY MATERIAL

Gold Award: LIS Induction Guide, University of Teesside

Silver Award: 'Full Volume', Manchester Library and Information Services

Bronze Award: School Library Brochure, Warwickshire County Council

MULTI-MEDIA AND WEB PAGE PUBLICITY MATERIAL

Gold Award: 'Max - the Zone', Devon Libraries

UKeiG Awards

The Jason Farradane Award

The Award is made to an individual or a group of people for outstanding work in the information field. It is an international award, open to all, although nominations must be made by a CILIP

Member. The winner receives a commemorative plaque. The Award is managed by UKeiG

For further information see the UKeiG website www.ukeig.org.uk/awards.

Winners

2009	No award made
2008	No award made
2007	Caroline Williams and the Intute community network
2006	University of Warwick Library, for the development of The Learning Grid
2005	Michael Koenig, Dean of the College of Information and Computer Sciences at Long Island University
2004	Julia Chandler, Department for International Development, for the development of the Intranet Managers' Group
2003	London Metropolitan University and the Trades Union Congress, for The Union Makes Us Strong: TUC History Online (www.unionhistory.info)
2002	William Hann for FreePint

Tony Kent Strix Award

The Award is given in recognition of an outstanding practical innovation or achievement in the field of information retrieval. This could take the form of an application or service, or an overall appreciation of past achievements from which significant advantages have emanated. The Award is open to individuals or groups from anywhere in the world.

The Award is made in memory of Dr Tony Kent, a past Fellow of the Institute of Information Scientists and an innovator in information retrieval software development, who died in 1997. The winner receives a statuette of a Strix owl. The Award is managed by UKeiG in conjunction with a group of experts in the field of information retrieval, many of whom worked with Dr Kent.

For further information see the UKeiG website www.ukeig.org.uk/awards.

Winners

2009	Carol Ann Peters
2008	Kalervo Javelin
2007	Mats Lindquist
2006	Stella Dextre Clarke
2005	Jack Mills
2004	Keith van Rijsbergen
2003	Herbert Van de Sompel
2002	Malcolm Jones

CILIP Honorary Fellows

Every year CILIP invites nominations for Honorary Fellowship (HonFCLIP). This award is made by Council to recognise distinguished service in promoting the purpose and objects of CILIP as laid out in CILIP's Royal Charter.

Nominations may be made by current individual members of CILIP or by any of the Branches and Groups of CILIP or any of the Committees, Boards and Panels of CILIP. Individual members can make only one nomination in each annual round.

Nominees may come either from within the library and information community or from associated professions or disciplines. Fellows of the Institute may be nominated for Honorary Fellowship but it is not necessary to be a Fellow in order to be eligible for Honorary Fellowship. Nominations are made in confidence and are considered in confidence by the Honorary Awards Panel and the Council.

Contact: Chief Executive, CILIP
Tel: 020 7255 0690
Bob.Mckee@cilip.org.uk (Until 31 October 2010)
Annie.Mauger@cilip.org.uk (After 31 October 2010)

2009	Helen Edwards
	Ian Stringer
2008	Saad Eskander
	Carla J Funk
	Bob Janes
	Margaret Oldroyd
2007	Fiona Black
	Carol Campbell-Hayes
	Carol Lefebvre
	Liz MacLachlan
	Keith Manley

	Alli Mcharazo
	Anne Peoples
2006	Karen Blakeman
	Margaret Haines
	John Hobson
	Sharon Markless
	Karen Usher
	Margaret Watson
2005	Peter Adams
	Graham Hedges
	Sandy Norman
	Philip Payne
	Bruce Royan
2004	Lynn Barrett
	Barry Cropper
	Michael Gorman
	Derek Law
	Kay Raseroka
2003	Rosemary Adams
	Suzanne Burge
	Shane Godbolt
	Frank Harris
	Lee Seng Tee
	Neil McClelland
	Jack Mills
	J. A. Muir Gray
	Linda Perham
	Chris Pond
	Anthony Thompson

Ridgmount Street facilities

Ridgmount Street offers Members a range of facilities in London's West End. The building is conveniently located near to several tube stations, and within 10 minutes of King's Cross and Euston main line stations.

Ewart Room

Monday–Friday 9 am–5 pm
Members, and non-members visiting Ridgmount Street for meetings or events, are welcome to use the Ewart Room, situated on the ground floor, as a meeting point. Please check availability in advance. A vending machine is available.

Rooms for hire

All our rooms offer natural light and are fully equipped with air conditioning and audio-visual and presentation equipment. Induction loops are available in Charter East and West. Furniture can be adapted for a range of room layouts. Our friendly staff will ensure that you have an anxiety free meeting or event.

Charter West

The Charter Suite

A double-glazed, air-conditioned room which seats up to 100 people and can be divided into two smaller areas (Charter East and West).

The Lorna Paulin Room

A double-glazed, air-conditioned room which seats up to 40 people. Equipped with full audiovisual facilities and 11 internet-enabled multimedia PCs. Most CILIP Training and Development Events are held in this room.

The Farradane Room

A double-glazed, air-conditioned room which seats up to 32 people. Equipped with audiovisual facilities.

Catering facilities

CILIP provides a wide range of high quality catering services for meetings, courses and seminars held at Ridgmount Street.

Disabled access

There is full disabled access to all public areas of the building.

Further information and bookings

Please contact Room Bookings for further information and bookings. Telephone 0207 255 0500; e-mail: roombookings@cilip.org.uk

The CILIP archive

The CILIP archive incorporates the archives of The Library Association and the Institute of Information Scientists. It consists of such items as:

- FLA theses
- photographs
- slides
- artefacts
- Council and Committee Papers
- publications (own)
- journals (own)
- leaflets
- major project/event files
- the Thorne Papers
- some Group/Branch archives.

Most of the archive is now housed with University College London, who provide a controlled environment in which to store the archive and facilities for researchers to view selected material.

CILIP retains on site at Ridgmount Street a complete set of bound *Library Association*

*Record*s, *Library Association Yearbook*s, Council minutes for the last five years, from 1990 to present, FLA theses and essays and a collection of Library Association Publishing and Facet Publishing books.

In the first instance, all enquiries about the archives should be made to the CILIP Information and Advice team by one of the following methods:

- online enquiry form: www.cilip.org.uk/enquiryform informationadvice/contact/enquiryform.htm
- telephone: 020 7255 0620, Monday to Friday, 10 am–4 pm
- e-mail: info@cilip.org.uk.

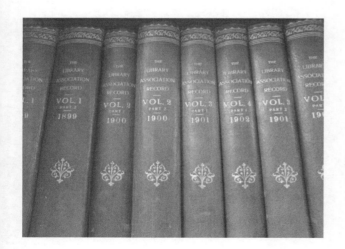

Part 4

CILIP Members

List of Members of CILIP

Professional Register

Personal Members
Organisation Members
Overseas Organisation Members
Note: This list of members reflects the membership of CILIP at 26 July 2010.

Personal Members

The date shown after the square-bracketed Membership number indicates when a member joined the Institute.

Dates of Revalidation are preceded by **RV**.

At the end of each entry, the following abbreviations (in bold) for membership type are given. These are followed by the date of attainment of qualifications (also in bold) where appropriate.

- **CM**: Chartership
- **FE**: Fellowship
- **HFE**: Honorary Fellowship (without other CILIP qualification)
- **ACL**: Certification
- **AF**: Affiliated membership
- **ME**: Associate membership.

Lists of members by country are held at CILIP Ridgmount Street and are available to members on request.

Members' personal addresses are confidential and are in no circumstances sold to outside agencies. However, if members wish to contact one another and the information provided here is insufficient for that purpose, Membership may be able to provide assistance.

Further information

E-mail: membership@cilip. org. uk
Telephone: 020 7255 0600

Abbreviations

The following abbreviations in designations and addresses have been adopted in the Personal Members section.

Admin.	Administration or Administrative	Estab.	Establishment		
		Exec.	Executive	N.	North
Arch.	Archives or Archivist			Nat.	National
Asst.	Assistant	F.E.	Further Education		
Assoc.	Associate or Association	Fed.	Federation	Off.	Office
		Form.	Formerly	Offr.	Officer
Auth.	Authority				
		Grp.	Group	Poly.	Polytechnic
Bibl.	Bibliographer			Postgrad.	Postgraduate
Bor.	Borough	H.E.	Higher Education	P. L.	Public Library(ies)
Br.	Branch	Hist.	Historical or History	Prof.	Professor
Brit.	British	Hon.	Honorary	p./t.	Part time
		Hosp.	Hospital(s)		
Catg.	Cataloguing	H.Q.	Headquarters	Ref.	Reference
Catr.	Cataloguer			Reg.	Region or Regional
C.C.	County Council or City Council	Ind.	Industry or Industries	Rep.	Representative
		Inf.	Information	Res.	Research
Cent.	Central or Centre	Inst.	Inst. or Institution		
Ch.	Chief	Internat.	International	S.	South
Child.	Children('s)			Sch.	School(s)
Circ.	Circulation	L.	Library(ies)	Sci.	Science or Scientific
Co.	Company or County	L.B.	London Borough	Sec.	Secretary
Co. L.	County Library(ies)	Lab.	Laboratory	Sect.	Section
Coll.	College	Lect.	Lecturer	Sen.	Senior
Comm.	Commerce or Commercial	Lend.	Lending	Serv.	Service(s)
		Lib.	Librarian or Librarianship	Soc.	Society
Comp.	Comprehensive			Stud.	Student
				Super.	Supervisor
Dep.	Deputy	M.B.C.	Metropolitan Borough Council		
Dept.	Department			Tech.	Technical, Technology or Technological
Devel.	Development	M.D.C.	Metropolitan District Council		
Dir.	Director			Temp.	Temporary
Dist.	District	Mgmnt.	Management		
Div.	Division or Divisional	Mgr.	Manager	Univ.	University
		Med.	Medical		
E.	East	Met.	Metropolitan	W.	West
Educ.	Education(al)	Min.	Ministry		
Elect.	Electrical	Mob.	Mobile	Yth.	Youth
Eng.	Engineering	Mus.	Museum		

A

Aanonson, Mr A J, BSc MSc MCLIP, BURA/ Res. Mgr., Brunel Univ., Uxbridge. [25199] 15/01/1976   **CM13/02/1978**

Abbay, Miss O J, PhD BA(Hons) FCLIP, Retired. [16487] 20/01/1951   **FE07/04/1980**

Abbey, Miss M R, Dep. Lib., Regent's Coll. L., London. [10004952] 06/06/2007   **ME**

Abbott, Mrs E E, BSc Econ PgDip, Knowledge Resource Offr., NHS Direct, Wales. [64502] 14/04/2005   **AF**

Abbott, Sister E M, SRN BA, Coll. Lib., St. Bonaventure Coll., Lusaka, Zambia. [42541] 09/12/1988   **ME**

Abbott, Ms K J, BSc DipLib MCLIP, Retired. [23406] 06/01/1975   **CM04/03/1977**

Abbott, Mr P A B, BA DipLib MCLIP, Lib., Royal Armouries, Leeds. [9268] 12/01/1986   **CM24/06/1992**

Abbott, Mr R, MA BSc MCLIP, Inst. Serv. Offr., Univ. of Nottingham [60125] 21/04/1975   **CM01/06/1981**

Abbott, Mrs R, MCLIP, Lib., Shropshire Co. L., Shrewsbury. [9667] 13/01/1970   **CM20/08/1973**

Abbott, Miss S J, BA(Hons), Corp. Inf. Serv. Lib., The Nat. Arch. Kew. [38097] 08/01/1985   **ME**

Abbott, Miss S K M, Msc BA PGDipLib MCLIP, Team Leader (Academic Support Consultant), Univ. of Exeter, Exeter [53666] 27/08/1996   **CM07/09/2005**

Abbott, Mr W R, BA DipLib MCLIP, Collections Devel. Lib., Arch. and Heritage, Birmingham Cent. L. [21107] 05/10/1973   **CM30/10/1975**

Abbs, Mr C R, BA(Hons) MA MCLIP, Electronic Res. & Systems Lib., Dept. of Health, Leeds. [55551] 20/10/1997   **CM15/10/2002**

Abdirahman, Mr A M, BA MLIS MA MCLIP, Dir. of L. Resources., American Intercontinental Univ., London [59632] 05/07/2001   **CM21/06/2006**

Abdolhadi, Miss M, Stud. [10016685] 27/04/2010   **ME**

Abel, Mr F Y, BA, Life Member [15] 01/01/1947   **ME**

Abel, Ms Y C, BTech MCLIP, Head of Inf. Resources, Civil Aviation Auth. [60077] 11/01/1977   **CM20/05/1980**

Abell, Mrs A G, BA FCLIP, Consultant, AA Enterprises [17] 01/01/1959   **FE01/04/2002**

Abell, Ms J S T, BA(Hons) FA Dip(Hons) Land. Arc, L. Asst., City Univ. [59484] 09/04/2001   **ME**

Abernethy, Miss S H, BA DipLib MCLIP, Lib., Wansbeck Hosp., Northumbria Healthcare NHS Trust. [37791] 26/10/1984   **CM15/02/1989**

Abhayapala, Ms S, Unknown. [10006736] 17/12/2007   **ME**

Abrahaley-Mebrahtu, Mrs M T, BSc MSc MCLIP, Evening and Weekend L. Mgr. [46079] 01/10/1991   **CM23/06/2004**

Abraham, Miss A C, BA(Hons) MA MCLIP, Unknown [49168] 08/10/1993   **CM18/11/1998**

Abraham, Mr J M, BLib MCLIP, L. Team Mgr., Yate. L., S. Gloucestershire Council [30576] 03/02/1979   **CM05/10/1984**

Abraham, Mr M D, L. Asst. Supply Staff, E. Dunbartonshire Council, Scotland. [63146] 12/02/2004   **ME**

Abrams, Mrs K, BA(Hons), MA, Lib., Croydon High Sch. [10011368] 16/10/2008   **ME**

Abril, Ms M B, MA, Lib. &Media Cent. Mgr., The Brit. Internat. Sch., Vietnam. [10002668] 23/05/2007   **ME**

Aburrow-Jones, Mrs N C, BA(Hons), Suncat Project Offr., EDINA, Edinburgh. [59613] 03/07/2001   **ME**

Acham, Ms K, BSc DipInfSc MCLIP, L. Mgr., Preston Coll. [60701] 24/02/1983   **CM14/07/1988**

Acharya, Miss D, MSc MCLIP, Inf. Lib., E. Sussex Lib. & Inf. Serv. [41994] 14/07/1988   **CM09/11/2005**

Achen-Owor, Ms F, BA(Hons) MA MCLIP, Asst. Campus L. Mgr., Univ. of E. London. [57561] 26/04/1999   **CM17/09/2003**

Ackerman, Miss G S, BA MCLIP, Academic Liaison Lib., Univ. of Westminster. [34255] 09/10/1981 **RV01/10/2008**   **CM24/02/1986**

Ackrill, Dr U, MCLIP, Lib., KBeeston., Notts CC. [64576] 03/03/2005   **CM06/05/2009**

Acreman, Mrs P, MCLIP, Retired. [30] 06/12/1966   **CM01/01/1970**

Acum, Mrs T A, BA(Hons) MCLIP, Comm. Lib., Hull City Council. [42477] 18/11/1988   **CM17/01/2001**

Adair, Ms H W, BA DipLib MCLIP, Child. Serv. Mgr., Aberdeen City C. [32836] 09/10/1980   **CM31/10/1983**

Adair, Miss R K, BSc(Hons) DipIM MCLIP, Faculty Team Lib., Univ. of Nottingham [47516] 22/09/1992   **CM21/05/1997**

Adal, Miss S, Unwaged. [56920] 04/11/1998   **ME**

Adam, Miss J E, MA DipLib MCLIP, Performance Mgr., Sheffield L. Arch. & Inf., Cent. L. [21744] 10/01/1974   **CM03/12/1976**

Adam, Miss J M, BA MSc MCLIP, Serv. Devel. Lib., Curriculum Res. & Inf. Serv., Aberdeen. [30593] 26/02/1979   **CM26/02/1981**

Adam, Mr R, BSc MA MCLIP, Retired. [60127] 22/10/1975   **CM22/10/1975**

Adamiec, Miss B, BA, Asst. Lib. /Corp. Governanace Team/Interim L., Yth. Justice Board for England & Wales. [65996] 11/08/2006   **ME**

Adams, Mr A A, P/T Vol. Lib. Asst., Melbourn L., Royston [10015309] 29/10/2009   **AF**

Adams, Ms A C, BA(Hons), Lib., Brooke Weston, Northhamptonshire. [65811] 10/05/2006   **AF**

Adams, Mrs A F, BA MCLIP, Sch. Lib., E. Renfrewshire Council. [31182] 08/10/1979   **CM20/01/1983**

Adams, Mr A F, MCLIP, Systems Admin., Barnsley Cent. L., S. Yorks. [34] 01/01/1970   **CM18/09/1974**

Adams, Mrs A M, MA DipLib MCLIP, Editor, Bronte Studies [35] 10/10/1967   **CM01/01/1970**

Adams, Mrs A, Stud., Aberystwyth Univ. [10010695] 21/08/2008   **ME**

Adams, Ms B, Unknown. [10010950] 07/09/1995   **ME**

Adams, Mrs C A, BA DipLib MCLIP, Unemployed. [38054] 17/01/1985   **CM15/11/1988**

Adams, Mrs D, BA MCLIP MSc DipM DipMgmt, Learning Resource Mgr., Sydenham Sch., London [32540] 24/04/1980   **CM25/08/1983**

Adams, Mrs E S, BA MCLIP DMS, Serv. Devel. Mgr., Essex C.C. [27865] 15/10/1983   **CM01/01/1980**

Adams, Mrs H, BA(Hons) MA MCLIP, Career Break. [49897] 07/01/1994   **CM16/07/2003**

Adams, Mrs J R, BA MSc MCLIP, Retired. [40697] 01/01/1962   **CM01/01/1966**

Adams, Mrs J, BA MCLIP, Mgr. for Sch. &Young People's L. Serv. Co. Hall, Norwich. [25288] 07/01/1976   **CM01/08/1978**

Adams, Mr K W, BA(Hons) MA MA MCLIP, Res. Team Leader [59509] 18/04/2001   **CM07/09/2005**

Adams, Miss M F, BA MA MCLIP, Retired. [52] 01/01/1964   **CM01/01/1967**

Adams, Mr P K, BLib MCLIP, Sen. Lib. (Systems Support), De Montfort Univ. L., Leicester. [32249] 10/03/1980   **CM12/03/1986**

Adams, Mr P M, MA MCLIP HonFCLIP, Employment not known. [60128] 14/05/1968   **CM26/10/1968**

Adams, Mrs P O M, MA MCLIP, Life Member. [20029] 08/01/1973   **CM23/02/1978**

Adams, Mrs P, BA MCLIP, Dir., Sch. L. Assoc. [18087] 03/10/1972   **CM28/02/1977**

Adams, Mrs R A, MBE BA DipLib MCLIP HonFCLIP, Retired. [11354] 01/01/1968   **CM01/01/1970**

Adams, Mr R E, BA MCLIP, Life Member. [58] 06/10/1960 **CM01/01/1962**

Adams, Mr R S, MCLIP, Vol. Lib., Terence Higgins Trust L. [61] 01/01/1950   **CM01/01/1955**

Adams, Miss R, BA(Hons) MA, Asst. Lib., Barlow Lyde & Gilbert LLP, London [63671] 12/08/2004 **ME**

Adams, Ms S L, BA MA, Sen. Lib. Asst., English Faculty L., Univ. of Oxford [64136] 19/01/2005 **ME**

Adams, Mr S R, BSc MSc CChem MRSC MCLIP, Managing Dir., Magister Ltd., Berks. [60141] 28/02/1982 **CM29/12/1986**

Adams, Mrs S U, BSc MCLIP, Performance Specialist, Audit Commission, Solihull. [27505] 21/02/1977 **CM01/08/1979**

Adams, Mrs S, BA, L. Asst., Norton Radstock Coll., Bath. [57890] 23/09/1999 **AF**

Adams, Mrs S, MA, Unknown. [10016973] 04/10/1972 **CM26/11/1982**

Adams, Ms T L, BA(Hons) MCLIP, Co. Lib., Powys C.C., Llandrindod Wells. [25708] 16/03/1976 **CM11/09/1978**

Adams-Fielding, Mrs K A H, ACLIP, L. & Learning Resources Cent. Asst., Halesowen Coll., W. Mids [10009512] 03/06/2008 **ACL17/06/2009**

Adamson, Mr G W, Res. Lib., Allen & Overy LLP, London. [51023] 09/11/1994 **ME**

Adamson, Mrs J, BA MCLIP, Retired. [5204] 12/01/1965 **CM01/01/1968**

Adamson, Mr T L, MA, Inf. Offr., Trafford Council. [10002899] 10/05/2007 **ME**

Adaran, Mrs O M, BSc(Hons), Unwaged [54703] 07/03/1997 **ME**

Adcock, Miss S J, BA DipLib MCLIP, Sen. Lib., Bromley Cent. L., L.B. of Bromley. [38651] 30/08/1985 **CM14/03/1990**

Adderley, Miss C A, MCLIP, Retired. [70] 01/01/1968 **CM01/01/1971**

Addis, Mrs F E, MCLIP, Retired. [73] 01/01/1956 **CM01/01/1962**

Addison, Ms J F, BA DipLib MCLIP, Retired. [11390] 10/05/1968 **CM01/01/1971**

Addison, Mrs J M, MA(Hons) PgDipInf MCLIP, L. Res. Co-ordinator (Sch.), Hazlehead Academy, Aberdeen City Council. [27414] 01/01/1969 **CM25/03/1988**

Addy, Miss C E, BSc(Hons) PgDipLIM MCLIP, Grp. Leader, L. Serv., BAE Systems, Preston. [58091] 27/10/1999 **CM29/03/2004**

Addy, Mrs M A S, BA MCLIP, Retired. [1907] 01/01/1970 **CM30/09/1973**

Adebajo, Miss O, BA(Hons), MSc, Unwaged. [10008531] 01/04/2008 **ME**

Adekaiyaoja, Mrs L B, LLB(Hons) ICSA MCLIP, Training & Inf. Mgr. - TRL Pharmacy Locum Agency. [62153] 03/03/2003 **CM23/06/2004**

Adelberg, Miss A A C, BA MCLIP, Life Member. [76] 01/01/1949 **CM01/01/1955**

Adeloye, Mr A, MA MPhil MSc MCLIP, Ch. Lib., Nigeria High Commission, London. [45491] 16/01/1991 **CM18/11/1993**

Adeosun, Mrs S, MA(Hons), Stud., MSc Inf. Mgmnt., Univ. of Brighton. [10015451] 19/11/2009 **ME**

Adetoro, Dr A A, DipLib BEd(Hons) MLS PhD, Lect., Tai Solarin Univ. [10008313] 19/03/2008 **ME**

Adey, Mr F C, FCLIP, Life Member [77] 01/01/1929 **FE01/01/1929**

Adey, Mrs H, BA MSc MCLIP, Dep. Univ. Lib., Nottingham Trent Univ., Nottingham. [39602] 17/03/1986 **CM23/03/1993**

Adeyemi, Miss Y, DipLib, L. I. S. Libr(Catg.)., Freshfields Bruckhaus Deringer London. [49342] 26/10/1993 **ME**

Adil, Mr S A, MLiSc, Knowledge Supp. Lib., Basington & N. Hampshire NHS Foundation Trust, Basingtoke. [10008299] 19/03/2008 **ME**

Adiyadorj, Mrs O, Stud. [10017089] 22/06/2010 **ME**

Adlem, Mrs A M, BA DipLib MCLIP MSc, Catr., Coutts Inf. Ser, Ringwood. [36324] 06/10/1983 **CM15/09/1993**

Adnum, Mrs V B, BA MCLIP, Life Member. [16499] 01/01/1941 **CM01/01/1948**

Afghan, Mrs A P, MCLIP, Head Lib., Whitgift Sch., S. Croydon. [65718] 23/02/2006 **CM06/05/2009**

Aga, Mrs W, M Inf. Sc BLIS, Lib., SIAO, Lagos, Nigeria [10013159] 08/04/2009 **ME**

Agar, Mrs S N, MCLIP, L. Serv. Advisor, Keyworth and E. Leake L., Notts CC. [2792] 01/01/1969 **CM11/09/1972**

Agate, Miss C, BA MCLIP, 2nd Fl. Mgr., Norfolk & Norwich Millenium L., Norfolk L. & Info. Servs. [24930] 27/10/1975 **CM02/07/1979**

Ager, Mrs C R, BA(Hons) PGCE MCLIP, Sen. Lib., Taunton Sch., Somerset. [53013] 24/01/1996 **CM22/07/1998**

Ager, Miss N D, BA(Hons), Serv. Dev. Lib., Sandwell and W. Birmingham Hosp. NHS Trust. [64173] 14/01/2005 **ME**

Agheda, Ms R, MSc, Child. Lib., Battersea Park L., London. [10001690] 06/03/2007 **ME**

Agus, Mrs J, BA BMus MCLIP, Lib., Royal Welsh Coll. of Music & Drama, Cardiff. [93] 19/09/1967 **CM01/01/1972**

Ah Fat, Miss P F, B LIB MA MCLIP, Head of Learning Resource Cent., Mauritius Coll. of the Air, Reduit, Mauritius. [28469] 19/01/1978 **CM14/10/1981**

Aherne, Mrs I B, MA MSc, Freelance Knowledge Mgr. [45392] 21/11/1990 **ME**

Ahmad, Dr N, PhD MPhil DipLib MCLIP, Researcher-Freelance. [10687] 01/01/1970 **CM20/06/1974**

Ahmad, Miss S, BA(Hons), Lib. Asst. (Acquisitions), Sackler L., Oxford Univ. [66140] 02/10/2006 **ME**

Ahmed, Mr H S S, BA, Stud. (Res.-PhD), Univ. of London, Inst. of Educ., (Hon. Treasurer-ISG(SE)Sect.). [52341] 30/10/1995 **ME**

Ahmed, Mrs L A, BA(Hons) PG Dip ILM, Knowledge Cent. Mgr., BSI, London. [10015709] 05/10/1995 **ME**

Ahmed, Ms S, BSc PGCE DipLIS MA, Subject. Lib., London Met. Univ., N. Campus. [47577] 02/10/1992 **ME**

Aiken, Mrs J D, BA MCLIP, Asst. Dir. (Collections & Resources) Teeside Univ. L. & Inf. Serv. [33680] 03/02/1981 **CM14/08/1985**

Aikens, Mrs J A, BA, e-Resources Lib., Papworth Hosp. NHS Foundation Trust, Cambridge. [44326] 03/09/1990 **ME**

Ainscough, Mr P J, MA DMS FCLIP, Retired. [104] 01/01/1954 **FE21/07/1989**

Ainsley, Mrs C, BA MA MCLIP, Lib., St. Johns Coll., Nottingham. [26943] 11/01/1976 **CM29/01/1979**

Ainsley, Mrs T A, L. Liason Advisor, L. & Learning Serv., Northumbria Univ., Newcastle. [58064] 22/10/1999 **ME**

Ainslie, Mr P, Child. & Young People Stream Lead, Chertsey L., Chertsey. [10014216] 07/07/2009 **ME**

Ainsworth, Mrs A L, BA Hons MCLIP, Unknown. [10009295] 08/02/1993 **CM24/07/1996**

Ainsworth, Mrs A, BA MCLIP, Operations Mgr: W., Derbys. C.C. [22034] 16/01/1974 **CM01/01/1976**

Ainsworth, Mrs F H S, BA(Hons) DipLib MCLIP, Coll. Mgr., Royal Botanic Gardens Kew, Richmond. [46184] 14/10/1991 **CM06/04/2005**

Ainsworth, Mr M, MA DipLib MCLIP, Unwaged. [60823] 02/08/1989 **CM07/11/1989**

Aird, Mrs C D, MA MCLIP, Life Member. [109] 01/01/1963 **CM01/01/1966**

Aird, Mrs L P, BA DipLib MCLIP, Sch. Lib., St. Christopher Sch. Letchworth, Herts. [36906] 13/01/1984 **CM07/10/1986**

Aird, Mr R C, BSc(Hons), Sen. Offr., ICT and Learning, L. H.Q., W. Dunbartonshire Council, Dumbarton. [10006293] 05/10/2007 **ME**

Airey, Mr J F, MCLIP, Unwaged. [115] 01/01/1969 **CM01/07/1992**

Airey, Ms V E, BBibl MCLIP, Sen. L. Asst., Univ. Nottingham. [58603] 11/04/2000 **CM15/09/2004**

Aitchison, Mrs J, BA FCLIP, Retired. [118] 01/01/1948 **FE01/01/1953**

Aitchison, Miss M J, MPhil MCLIP, Retired [119] 01/01/1963 **CM01/01/1968**

Aitchison, Mr T M, OBE BSc HonFCLIP, Retired. [120] 01/01/1950 **FE01/04/2002**

Aitken, C, BA DipIS MCLIP, Lib., Schlumberger Cambridge Res., Cambs. [59791] 03/10/2001 **RV24/04/2009 CM21/05/2003**

Aitken, Mr D A, BSc PG Dip ACLIP, Systems and Acquisitions Lib., Scottish Government, Edinburgh. [66058] 13/09/2006 **ACL05/10/2007**

Aitken, Miss F, Enquiry Serv. Mgr., Nat. L. Scotland, Edinburgh. [64811] 18/07/2005 **AF**

Aitken, Miss J L, BA(Hons), Lib.,W. Yorkshire Police, Wakefield. [61732] 30/10/2002 **ME**

Aitken, Mrs J, MA(Hons) MCLIP, Principal Lib., Mitchell L., Glasgow. [32706] 04/07/1980 **CM26/07/1982**

Aitken, Miss K A, BSc(Hons), Content Catr., Brit. Council-Scotland, Edinburgh. [59071] 07/11/2000 **ME**

Aitken, Mrs K B, BSc MSc, RDSM Lib., Long Eaton L. [10013436] 24/04/2009 **ME**

Aitken, Miss K V, MA(Hons) DipILS, Principle. L. Asst., Imperial Coll. London, S. Kensington Campus. [58093] 27/10/1999 **ME**

Aitken, Mrs P A, MA DipLib MCLIP, Lib. (Job Share), Hyndland Secondary Sch., Glasgow. [34092] 01/10/1981 **CM26/05/1993**

Aitkins, Ms J U, BA MSc DMS MCLIP, Head of Public Serv., Univ. of Leicester. Leicester [31622] 08/10/1979 **CM25/02/1983**

Aiton, Mrs A, MA DipLib MCLIP, Inf. Mgr., Mental Welfare Commission for Scotland, Edinburgh. [38993] 18/10/1985 **CM06/09/1988**

Aiton, Mr S, Internat. Benefits Researcher, Towers Perrin, London. [63229] 22/03/2004 **ME**

Ajibade, Miss A O A, BSc(Hons) MSc, Prof. Support Lib., Baker & McKenzie, London. [56379] 01/07/1998 **ME**

Ajibade, Miss B A I A, BA(Hons) MSc MCLIP, Inf. Specialist, Dept. for Business, Innovation & Skills (BIS), London. [50843] 21/10/1994 **CM10/07/2002**

Ajigboye, Mr O S, MSc Inf. Sci., Lib. II Center for Learning Resource, Covenant Univ., Ogun State, Nigeria. [10008707] 18/04/2008 **ME**

Akeroyd, Mrs C M, MCLIP, Inf. Offr., Manches Solicitors, London. [19937] 09/01/1973 **CM27/04/1976**

Akeroyd, Mr J, MPhil BSc MCLIP, Freelance Inf. Consultant [31533] 20/10/1979 **CM10/10/1983**

Akers, Ms J M, Asst. Subject Lib., Oxford Brookes Univ., Oxford. [10001554] 23/10/1992 **ME**

Akhtar, Mrs F, Unknown. [10014347] 15/07/2009 **AF**

Akhtar, Mr M, BSc DipIST MCLIP MIET, Inf. Scientist, IET, Stevenage. [60811] 31/10/1989 **CM31/10/1989**

Akinlade, Mrs R O, MA, Learning & Teaching Lib., OU, Milton Keynes [10000581] 14/10/2006 **ME**

Akinwande, Mrs A M, MA BA(Hons), Lib. Asst., Sion Hill L., Bath. (On Maternity leave) [10012672] 02/03/2009 **ME**

Akroyd, Mrs S K, BA(Hons) MA MCLIP, Lib., Nottingham City Council. [51791] 01/07/1995 **CM12/03/2003**

Alabaster, Miss C, BA MCLIP, Retired [128] 01/01/1970 **CM20/12/1974**

Al-Abdulmunem, Mrs S, MA, Ref. &Info. Servs. Specialist., Saudi Arabia. [65662] 08/03/2006 **ME**

Alafiatayo, Mr B O, BSc(Hons) MLS MPhil, Admin. Offr., DWP, Stockport JCP. [56470] 21/07/1998 **ME**

Alayo, Mrs A, BA, Employed. [10001029] 14/12/2006 **ME**

Alberici, Mr S U, L. Mgr., Med. L., Jersey General Hosp., St. Helier. [56312] 01/05/1998 **ME**

Albin, Mrs L E, BA(Hons) DipLib MCLIP, Subject Lib., The Arts Univ. Coll. at Bournemouth, Poole. [47035] 06/04/1992 **CM22/11/1995**

Albrow, Mr A J, BA MCLIP, L. & Inf. Mgr., Med. Protection Soc., Leeds. [10000687] 11/01/1977 **CM31/01/1979**

Albu, Miss K M, BA, Retired. [16517] 01/01/1953 **ME**

Alcock, Miss J E, BSc(Hons), Resource Lib., Walsall Learning Ctr., Univ. of Wolverhampton [65335] 11/01/2006 **ME**

Alcock, Mrs J M D, MA MCLIP, Self-employed. [11343] 01/01/1970 **CM11/09/1972**

Alcock, Ms L, MCLIP, Sen. Lib. :Prison L. Serv., Staffs. L. & Inf. Serv. [135] 01/01/1970 **CM10/09/1973**

Alcock, Ms R J, BA MCLIP, Sch. Lib., Ballakermeen High Sch., Isle of Man. [38080] 08/01/1985 **CM10/05/1988**

Alcock, Mrs S A, BA Dip Lib MSLS MCLIP, Unknown. [10014014] 06/08/1991 **CM01/07/1994**

Alderman, Mrs L A, BA(Hons) DipLIS MCLIP, Unknown. [47959] 28/10/1992 **CM22/05/1996**

Alderson, Ms E M, MCLIP, Lib. Administrator. [26670] 27/10/1976 **CM31/10/1980**

Alderton, Miss S M, BA MCLIP, Life Member. [142] 28/09/1950 **CM01/01/1957**

Aldrich, Mrs E J, BA(Hons) MA MCLIP, Knowledge Mgr., Maidstone & Tunbridge Wells NHS T. [55991] 12/01/1998 **CM21/03/2001**

Aldrich, Mrs E, MLib MCLIP, Retired. [7998] 16/01/1969 **CM19/07/1973**

Aldrich, Mr M J, BA FBCS CIMgt HonFCLIP D. LITT, Hon Fellow. [60718] 01/04/1985 **FE01/04/1985**

Aldrich, Mr S J, BFA MA, L. Asst., Abbey Park L., Leicester Coll. [10006813] 17/12/2007 **AF**

Aldridge, Ms L M, BA(Hons) MA MCLIP, Sen. Lib. -Child. Serv., Cambs. L. [47923] 26/10/1992 **CM17/03/1999**

Aldridge, Mr L, BSc MCLIP, Performance Mgr., Leeds City Council. [20027] 08/01/1973 **CM26/04/1977**

Aldridge, Mrs S, ACLIP, Sunday Lib., Welwyn Garden City P.L. [10010105] 07/07/2008 **ACL04/03/2009**

Aleksandrowicz, Miss F E, Inf. Mgmnt. Consultant, AEGON, Edinburgh. [63122] 11/02/2004 **ME**

Alencar-Brayner, Dr A, BA MA PhD, Graduate Trainee, City Univ., London. [10014552] 02/11/2001 **ME**

Alexander, Mr A, Unknown. [10013983] 15/06/2009 **ME**

Alexander, Mrs D G, BA MCLIP, Head of L. & Arch., King Edward VI Sch., Southampton. [2056] 01/01/1967 **CM01/01/1972**

Alexander, Mrs L M, BA MCLIP, Joint Lib. i/c., Meadowbank L., Falkirk. [26408] 04/10/1976 **CM29/07/1980**

Alexander, Mr M G, BA DipLib, Lib., Redbridge L. [39559] 19/02/1986 **ME**

Alexander, Mr N S, BA MA, Learning Support Lib., Queen's Park L., London [10007702] 21/02/2008 **ME**

Alexander, Mrs R S, BA, Stud. [66099] 25/09/2006 **ME**

Alexander, Mr R, Operations Mgr: Knowledge Devel. Serv., Wokingham Bor. Council [10006635] 11/09/2007 **ME**

Alford, Mrs M, BA(Hons), Asst. Head of Serv. (L. & Inf.)., Hull Cent. L. [61334] 28/05/2002 **ME**

Ali, Miss S, Unknown. [10015391] 12/11/2009 **ME**

Ali, Mrs T J, BA(Hons) MA MCLIP, Retired. [58947] 09/10/2000 **CM29/08/2007**

Al-Kaabi, Mr M, Cultural Attache, Embassy of the State of Quatar, London. [63034] 17/12/2003 **ME**

Allan, Mr A J, BLib MCLIP, Sen. Liaison Lib., Sheffield Univ. L., S. Yorks. [164] 01/01/1968 **CM20/09/1973**

Allan, Dr B C, MSc MA PGCE MEd MCLIP EdD, Sen. Lect., Univ. of Hull. [26671] 11/11/1976 **CM14/12/1978**

Allan, Ms C M, BSc(Hons) MSc MCLIP, Subject Lib. Natural Sci., Univ. of Stirling [49534] 09/11/1993 **CM22/07/1998**

Allan, Mrs G, BA MCLIP, Sen. Lib., Bexley Council. [9363] 25/06/1971 **CM04/04/1975**

Allan, Mr J G, MCLIP, Lib., Falkirk Council. [22273] 21/03/1974 **CM23/08/1976**

Allan, Mrs J M, BA(Hon), Inf. Offr., Univ. of Reading, Berks. [49778] 06/12/1993 **ME**

Allan, Mrs J R, BA Dip Lib MCLIP MBA, H. of Bibl. Servs., Univ. of London, Senate House L. [34578] 15/01/1982 **CM16/02/1988**

Allan, Mrs J, BA(Hons), Sch. L. Adviser, Leeds City Council. [28207] 11/10/1977 **ME**

Allan, Mrs L, MSc, Unknown. [10012368] 29/01/2009 **ME**

Allan, Mrs M E, L. Asst., Canterbury Christ Church Univ. [45095] 10/07/1990 **AF**

173

Allan, Mrs M M, MA MCLIP, Life Member. [12248] 01/01/1950
        CM01/01/1953

Allan, Miss S L, MA(Hons) DipLIS MCLIP, Comm. Lib., Dunblane L., Stirlingshire. [58725] 01/07/2000   **CM15/01/2003**

Allan, Miss V, Community and Inf. Offr., N. Yorks. C.C. [63230] 22/03/2004   **ME**

Allard, Ms M, MA DipLib MCLIP, L. Resource Cent. Mgr., Aberdeen Grammar Sch. [39865] 01/10/1986   **CM15/05/1989**

Allardice, Ms C M, BA HDipLib BA(Hons) MA MBA FCLIP, Ch. Lib., FCO., London. [44598] 02/11/1990   **FE21/05/2003**

Allardice, Mrs E C, BSc (Hons), L. Asst., Woodhall L., Welwyn Garden City. [10009708] 02/06/2008   **AF**

Allardice, Miss J A, MA(Hons), Stud.,PG Dip Inf. &L. Studies, Univ. of Strathclyde. [10015449] 19/11/2009   **ME**

Allaway, Mrs S M, BA MCLIP, Team Lib., L.B. of Camden, Holborn L. [19957] 10/01/1973   **CM31/12/1975**

Allbon, Mrs E, BA(Hons) MSc DipLaw ILTM MCLIP, Law Lib. & Head of Inf. Literacy, City Univ. L., London [62136] 28/02/2003**CM07/09/2005**

Allchin, Mr P W M, BA MSc, Ref. Info. Specialist, Brit. L., London. [10013404] 29/04/2009   **ME**

Allcock, Mrs J V, BA MCLIP, Sen. L. Asst., Knowsley M.B.C., Halewood L. [42750] 16/02/1989   **CM20/03/1996**

Allcock, Mrs K J, BA(Hons) MA MCLIP, p/t Lib., Shropshire Arch. [50621] 01/10/1994   **CM18/03/1998**

Allden, Ms A, BA MSc MCLIP, Dir. or Inf. Serv. & Univ. Lib., Univ. of Bristol. [60778] 31/03/1988   **CM31/03/1988**

Allen, Ms A J, BA MCLIP, Customer Serv. Lib., Wigston Magna L., Leics. [25945] 06/05/1976   **CM28/11/1980**

Allen, Ms A L, Lib., Thorpe St Andrew Sch., Norfolk [10015263] 29/10/2009   **AF**

Allen, Mr A, BSc(Hons), Info. Asst., City Univ., London [10012880] 19/03/2009   **ME**

Allen, Mrs B D, BA MCLIP, Seeking Work. [10013642] 22/10/1990   **CM25/05/1994**

Allen, Mrs B J, MBE MCLIP, Life Member. [192] 01/01/1937   **CM01/01/1940**

Allen, Mr D E, MSc, L. Collections Coordinator, Royal Soc. of Chemistry. [62521] 31/07/2003   **ME**

Allen, Ms D J, BA DipLib MCLIP, Retired. [194] 01/01/1969   **CM01/01/1972**

Allen, Mr D L, BA MCLIP, Life Member. [195] 01/01/1953**CM01/01/1956**

Allen, Mr D W, BScSoc MCLIP, Retired [197] 01/01/1968**CM01/01/1971**

Allen, Ms E R, BA(Hons), Graduate Trainee Lib., Murray Edwards Coll., Cambridge. [10013657] 22/05/2009   **ME**

Allen, Mr G C, MCLIP MILAM, Consultant. Ottimamente Ltd. [25711] 23/02/1976   **CM01/07/1994**

Allen, Mr G R, BA BSc CChem MRSC MCLIP, Retired. [60129] 13/06/1975   **CM13/06/1975**

Allen, Mr I C, BA, Acquisitions Mgr., Slaughter and May, London. [34457] 04/11/1981   **ME**

Allen, Mrs J C, BA MCLIP, Principal Lib., Inf., L. B of Sutton. [34667] 01/02/1982   **CM29/03/1985**

Allen, Mr J D, BA(Hons) MA, Collection Mgmt. Team Leader, Univ. of Salford [64370] 14/03/2005   **ME**

Allen, Mr J E R, BA Dip Lib, Special Projects Asst., City Univ., London. [10013854] 07/05/1988   **ME**

Allen, Mr J N, BA FCLIP, Life Member. [207] 01/01/1952 **FE01/01/1964**

Allen, Mrs J W, MCLIP, Retired. [208] 20/01/1964   **CM01/01/1969**

Allen, Ms K, BA(Hons) MA MCLIP, Knowledge Consultant, Info Hertfordshire, Hatfield, [10013941] 16/09/2009   **CM18/04/2009**

Allen, Mrs K, Outreach Co-ordinator/ Community Lib., Kirkby L., Knowsley [10013665] 15/05/2009   **ME**

Allen, Miss L A, BA(Hons), Knowledge & L. Serv. Mgr., Heart of Birmingham Teaching Primary Care Trust, Birmingham. [37038] 31/01/1984   **ME**

Allen, Miss L E, BA, MA, Inf. Asst., Kingston Univ., London. [10000862] 15/11/2006   **ME**

Allen, Mrs L K, Stud., Aberystwyth Univ. [10010205] 10/07/2008   **ME**

Allen, Mr P N, MCLIP, Retired. [219] 01/01/1961   **CM01/01/1965**

Allen, Ms P, BA, Unwaged. [10011800] 14/11/2008   **ME**

Allen, Mr R, BA(Hons) MCLIP, Child. Lib. Devel. Offr., W. Sussex Lib. Serv. [59107] 16/11/2000   **CM29/11/2006**

Allen, Ms S, Unknown. [10010896] 28/01/2009   **AF**

Allen, Mr T, Job Seeker. [10006110] 05/06/2008   **AF**

Allen, Ms Y, BA(Hons) MA, Academic Liaison Offr., Roehampton Univ., London. [56122] 03/03/1998   **ME**

Allery, Miss J C, BA DipLib, Temp. LIS Worker. [38348] 11/03/1985 **ME**

Alliez, Miss S J, MCLIP, Resource Lib., Bedford B. C. [226] 01/01/1966   **CM01/01/1971**

Allison Bedford, Mrs E R, BSc MA, Sen. L. Asst. - Official Publications, Inst. of Educ., Univ. of London. [65372] 11/01/2006   **ME**

Allison, Miss A G, BA(Hons), Unknown. [56358] 16/06/1998   **ME**

Allison, Mr C, MSc, Unemployed. [48092] 06/11/1992   **ME**

Allison, Miss F I, BA MCLIP, Reader Dev. Offr., Kingston. [34684] 28/01/1982   **CM04/08/1987**

Allison, Mr R D, Inf. Offr., Colliers Internat., Leeds. [57036] 27/11/1998   **ME**

Allister, Mrs S, BA(Hons) MSc, Inf. Offr., Diabetes Res. Unit, Llandough Hosp., Penarth. [57401] 05/03/1999   **ME**

Allott, Ms C, BA MCLIP, Lib., Berks. Hlth. InformaticsShared Serv., Prospect Park Hosp. [236] 01/01/1972   **CM07/01/1975**

Allport, Mr M J, Unknown. [10015011] 06/10/2009   **ME**

Allred, Mr J R, FCLIP MPhil, Retired. [237] 01/01/1953   **FE01/01/1964**

Allsop, Mrs J, BA DipLib MCLIP, P. /t. Night Clerk, Short Loans, Lancaster Univ. L., Lancs. [32799] 10/09/1980   **CM01/09/1987**

Allsop, Mrs P, BA DipLib MCLIP, Corporate Web Mgr., Isle of Anglesey C.C. [33008] 22/10/1980   **CM19/01/1984**

Allsopp, Dr D, BSc PhD CBiol FIBiol MCLIP, Retired. [60130] 21/04/1975   **CM21/06/1979**

Allum, Mr D N, BA MCLIP, Retired. [19462] 01/01/1966 **CM01/01/1970**

Allwood, Mrs C M, MA MCLIP, Asst. Lib., City Business L., London [29236] 08/04/1978   **CM16/12/1982**

Allwood, Mrs L M, L. Mgr., Abingdon L. [10009986] 27/06/2008   **AF**

Alman, Mrs M, BA BCom MCLIP, Life Member [242] 01/01/1937   **CM01/01/1941**

Almeida, Mr D J, MSc MCLIP, Princ. Consultant, PA Consulting Grp., London. [60833] 10/05/1994   **CM10/05/1994**

Almond, Mr C D, MCLIP, Retired. [243] 01/01/1971   **CM25/01/1974**

Almond, Ms M P, BA DipHE DipLib MCLIP, Team Lib., Bracknell Forest Bor. Council. [42304] 17/10/1988   **CM14/08/1991**

Alper, Mrs H A C, MA MHSM MCLIP, Unemployed. [14951] 23/08/1970   **CM17/06/1974**

Al-Shabibi, Mrs A M R, BA DipLib MCLIP, Unwaged Chartered Lib., London. [33970] 01/07/1981   **CM10/05/1985**

Al-Shorbaji, Dr N M A, BA DipDOC MLib PhD, Dir. Knowledge Mgmnt & Sharing, World Heatlh Organisation, Geneva. [34941] 14/05/1982**ME**

Alsmeyer, Mr D H, BA MSc MCLIP, Inf. Serv. Mgr., BT, Ipswich. [60133] 13/04/1976   **CM29/05/1979**

Alston, Prof R C, OBE MA PhD HonFLA, Retired. [39809] 10/09/1986   **HFE10/09/1986**

Al-Talal, Dr G, BSc Mphil PHd, Head of Res. & Inf. Serv., Fed. of Master Builders, London [10008574] 08/12/2000   **ME**

Altaner, Mrs A, BA MLS, Lib., L.B. Harrow. [61022] 01/02/2002   **ME**

Althorpe, Mrs P, BA(Hons) DipLIS MCLIP, Inf. Offr., The Chartered Soc. of Physiotherapy., London [10001182] 03/02/2007
    CM22/01/1997

Alton, Ms C M, BA(Hons) M. Ed. PGCE Cert LIS, Principal Lib., Totnes L., Devon. [10005376] 01/07/2007 **ME**

Alvarez, Mrs N B, BA MCLIP, Retired. [1317] 27/09/1967 **CM01/01/1971**

Alvarez-Araujo, Mr F, BSc, Unwaged. [10016655] 23/04/2010 **ME**

Alves Asensio, Miss M A, Learning Resources Cent. Asst., Newham Sixth Form Coll., London. [66063] 18/09/2006 **ME**

Alvey, Mrs K J, BA(Hons) MCLIP, Stock Mgr., Bath Cent. L., Bath & N. E. Somerset. [39445] 28/01/1986 **CM21/12/1988**

Amador, Dr V, BA MA PhD, Teaching Fellow, Heriot-Watt Univ., Edinburgh. [65075] 24/10/2005 **ME**

Amaeshi, Prof B O, BA MA MCLIP, Retired. [24309] 07/02/1962 **CM01/01/1966**

Amarakoon, Mr L R, FLA(SL) FCLIP, Prgm. Mngr. (RR), Room To Read, Sri Lanka. [60098] 07/12/2001 **FE01/04/2002**

Amatt, Mr L K, FCLIP, Retired. [251] 01/01/1963 **FE05/11/1973**

Ambridge, Mrs A D, BSc(Hons) MSc MCLIP, Unknown. [56482] 22/07/1998 **CM16/07/2003**

Ambrosi, Mrs L A, BA MA, Inf. Adviser., business Link, E. Midlands [59055] 02/11/2000 **ME**

Ames, Mrs D E, BA(Hons), High Sch. Lib., Benjamin Britton High Sch., Suffolk. [61592] 02/10/2002 **ME**

Amies, Mr P S, BA(Hons) DipLIS MCLIP, Catr., Univ. Coll., London. [50659] 05/10/1994 **CM20/09/2000**

Amos, Miss J, BA(Hons) MSc, Sen. Libraian., Denton Wilde Sapte, LLP, London [60871] 18/12/2001 **ME**

Anand, Mrs E, MLIS, Acting Head of L., RCSI, Bahrain. [10016459] 26/03/2010 **ME**

Anderson, Mr A C, BA DMS MCLIP, Ret. [21817] 01/01/1974 **CM24/07/1978**

Anderson, Mrs A M, MCLIP, Community Inf. Lib., Wilts. L. & Heritage, Trowbridge. [5297] 18/05/1970 **CM16/07/1974**

Anderson, Mr B H, BA(Hons) MSc(Econ), Sen. Lib., DWP [54474] 20/12/1996 **ME**

Anderson, Mrs C A, BA MCLIP, Latin American & US Studies. Senate House L., ULRLS [29038] 09/03/1978 **CM06/04/1981**

Anderson, Mr C D, BA, Business Inf. Co-ordinator, Cairn Energy PLC, Edinburgh [10011788] 13/11/2008 **ME**

Anderson, Ms C J, BA(Hons) MCLIP, Inf. Unit Mgr., Linklaters, London. [48073] 04/11/1992 **CM19/07/2000**

Anderson, Mrs D, MA DipLib HonFLA, Dir., I. F. L. A. Off. for U. B. C. [267] 01/01/1953 **CM01/01/1963**

Anderson, Mrs E H, Dep. Lib., Northern Coll., Stainborough. [41786] 06/04/1988 **ME**

Anderson, Mrs F E, BA MCLIP, Retired. [29733] 18/10/1978 **CM28/04/1982**

Anderson, Ms G C, BA MCLIP, Head of L., UHI Millennium Inst., Inverness. [27867] 03/10/1977 **CM18/07/1980**

Anderson, Mr G P J, BA(Hons), Unknown. [10000923] 28/11/2006 **ME**

Anderson, Mr G, BA MCLIP, Serv. Devel. Mgr., The Mitchell L., Culture and Sport Glasgow [37434] 14/09/1984 **CM15/02/1989**

Anderson, Mrs H, BA(Hons) MSc(Econ), Sen. Inf. Asst, Catg. & Metadata/Asst. Lib., Univ. Ulster, Newtownabbey, Co. Antrim. [63745] 01/10/2004 **ME**

Anderson, Mr J E, BA MLib NDipM MCLIP, Enquiry Serv. Mgr., Cambridgeshire C.C., Cambridge Cent. L. [43050] 03/07/1989 **CM24/04/1991**

Anderson, Mrs J E, BA DipLib MCLIP, Ret. [759] 01/01/1970 **CM01/01/1972**

Anderson, Miss J, BA(Hons) MSc, Inf. Adviser, Univ. of Gloucestershire. [10000669] 25/10/2006 **ME**

Anderson, Miss J, MA MCLIP, UWS Univ. of the W. of Scotland, Crichton Libary, Dumfries Campus. [32771] 25/08/1980 **CM03/11/1983**

Anderson, Miss L C, BA MSc, 19th & 20th Century Collections Catr., Eton Coll. L., Eton. [10009526] 02/06/2008 **ME**

Anderson, Ms L E, BA(Hons) MCLIP, Outreach Lib., Bury Primary Care Trust [58431] 11/02/2000 **CM21/08/2009**

Anderson, Ms M E, BA MCLIP, Inf. Serv. Advisor, Napier Univ., Edinburgh. [30082] 06/12/1978 **CM20/10/1981**

Anderson, Ms M L, BSc(Hons), Unknown. [10002004] 20/10/1994 **ME**

Anderson, Mrs P A, MA MCLIP, L. Res. Asst., Carnegie Coll., Dunfermline. [21087] 05/10/1973 **CM24/10/1975**

Anderson, Mrs P K, LLB DipLib MCLIP, Sen. Lib., The Law Soc., London. [38189] 02/02/1985 **CM10/11/1987**

Anderson, Ms R R, BSocSc BA MCLIP, Learning Cent. Mgr., Westminster Kingsway Coll., London. [42397] 27/10/1988 **CM26/05/1993**

Anderson, Mr S C, BA(Hons), Stud., UCL [10015057] 09/10/2009 **ME**

Anderson, Miss S, Stud. [10015334] 11/11/2009 **ME**

Anderson, Mr T J B, BA MCLIP, Retired. [16539] 01/01/1948 **CM01/01/1954**

Anderson, Mrs T, DipILS MCLIP, LRC Co-ord., Aberdeen C.C., Aberdeen [50094] 21/03/1994 **CM15/09/2004**

Anderson, Mr W A, Sch. Lib., Inverness Royal Academy, Highland Council. [57075] 07/12/1998 **ME**

Anderson-Smith, Mrs M, MA DipLib, Retired. [9930] 01/01/1965 **ME**

Anderton, Mrs J F, BA Dip Lib, Lib., Monmouth Sch. [10008445] 12/01/1979 **ME**

Anderton, Miss M F, BSc MSc FCLIP, Inf. Consultant, Self Employed. [60517] 18/01/1978 **FE01/04/1984**

Andrew, Miss E L, BA(Hons) MA, Sen. Inf. Asst., Northubria Univ., Newcastle-Upon-Tyne. [66143] 03/10/2006 **ME**

Andrew, Miss S M, BA PGCE DipLib MCLIP, Sen. L. Asst., Bradmore Green Lib., L.B. of Croydon. [38600] 25/07/1985 **CM12/12/1990**

Andrews, Mr A, BA FCLIP, Life Member. [301] 01/01/1932 **FE01/01/1955**

Andrews, Mr D J, BA MCLIP, Retired. [304] 01/01/1964 **CM01/01/1969**

Andrews, Mr D M, BSc MA, Br. Lib., Wandsworth Town L., L.B. Wandsworth. [62030] 22/01/2003 **ME**

Andrews, Mrs G E, FRSA MCLIP, Life Member. [308] 01/01/1951 **CM01/01/1971**

Andrews, Miss G, BSc PGDip, Knowledge Asst., NHS Western Cheshire. [10001676] 28/11/2000 **ME**

Andrews, Mr J M, BA DipLibInf MCLIP, Acting Subject Advisor for Medicine, Univ. of Birmingham. [42624] 24/01/1989 **CM19/03/2008**

Andrews, Mr J P, DipHE BMus(Hons) MA, Brit. Red Cross [62656] 26/09/2003 **ME**

Andrews, Dr J S, MA PhD MCLIP, Life Member. [16540] 01/01/1951 **CM01/01/1954**

Andrews, Miss J, MA DipLib MCLIP, Dir. of L. & Learning Res., Birmingham City Univ. [32009] 29/01/1980 **CM10/10/1983**

Andrews, Mrs L M, MA, Catr., Environment Agency, Bristol. [35445] 15/10/1982 **ME**

Andrews, Miss L V, BA(Hons), Sen. Super., Chesham L., Bucks. [10007966] 16/09/2003 **ME**

Andrews, Mrs P M, MCLIP, Br. Lib., Penn L., Wolverhampton. [26929] 11/12/1976 **CM07/10/1979**

Andrews, Miss R E, BSc(Hons) MSc MCLIP, Lib., Falkirk Council. [59214] 09/01/2001 **CM08/12/2004**

Andrews, Mrs R M, Unknown. [10013347] 16/04/2009 **AF**

Angell, Miss C, Lib. Asst., St Martin's in the Field Sch., London. [10006081] 24/08/2007 **AF**

Anglim, Mrs A L, BA(Hons) MCLIP, Sen. Offr., Young People's L. Serv., W. Dunbartonshire Council. [37395] 06/08/1984 **CM24/07/1996**

Angrave, Mr N J, BA MCLIP, Mgr., Sch. L. Serv., L.B. of Barnet. [23309] 21/11/1974 **CM14/03/1977**

Angus, Mrs R F, BA(Hons) PGCE, Child. Lib., Earlsfield L., London [10015535] 11/12/2009 **ME**

Angus, Mrs S, MA(Hons) MCLIP, Visual Impairment Resources Offr., Durham Co. Council [21853] 10/02/1974 **CM06/01/1977**

Aning, Mr T K, Arch., Univ. of Ghana, Acera. [49161] 08/10/1993 **ME**

Ankers, Mrs Y M, BA(Hons) MCLIP, Asst. Subject Lib., Univ. Chester. [61667] 16/10/2002 **CM13/06/2007**

Annetts, Mrs E A, BA MCLIP, Brunel Univ., Uxbridge. [23331] 03/12/1974 **CM26/10/1978**

Annis, Mr C H, MA DipLib MCLIP, Lib., Inst. of Classical Studies, London. [24586] 02/10/1975 **CM14/11/1977**

Ansell, Mrs J, MCLIP, Retired. [321] 01/01/1958 **CM25/02/1977**

Ansley, Ms W, BA(Hons) MA, Inf. Offr., Citizens Advice, London [56477] 23/07/1998 **ME**

Anslow, Ms J, BA(Hons) PgDipLIM, Inf. /L. Asst., Bolton L., Bolton. [62295] 17/04/2003 **ME**

Anson, Mrs J M, BA DipLib MCLIP, Lib., Dallam Sch., Cumbria. [33365] 04/11/1980 **CM07/10/1986**

Ansorge, Mrs C A, MA MCLIP, Asst. Under Lib., Cambridge Univ. L. [1760] 01/01/1969 **CM01/01/1971**

Anstey, Mrs K A, MCLIP, career break [22153] 21/02/1974 **CM12/07/1976**

Anstey, Mrs L M, MCLIP, Sch. Lib., All Saints Catholic High Sch., Huddersfield. [6471] 08/10/1971 **CM03/11/1975**

Anstis, Ms P L, Learning Res. Asst., Luther King Hse. L., Partnership for Theological Ed., Manchester. [56924] 06/11/1998 **ME**

Antenbring, Mrs S M, RGN RM BA(Hons) MA MCLIP, Unwaged. [52034] 02/10/1995 **CM22/07/1998**

Anthoney, Mrs F J, MA(Hons) MSc PG Dip, Unknown. [10015605] 17/12/2009 **ME**

Anthony, Ms S G, BSc DipLib, Lib., Cwmbran L., Torfaen C. B. C., Gwent. [39409] 27/01/1986 **ME**

Anthony-Edwards, Mr J, MA MA, Head of L. & Inf., Shropshire Council. [59295] 31/01/2001 **ME**

Antill, Mr J K, FCLIP, Life Member. [16544] 01/01/1953 **FE01/01/1968**

Antill, Mrs M A, MSc MCLIP, Data Analyst, Nat. Trust, Swindon. [57706] 05/07/1999 **CM21/06/2006**

Anuar, Mrs H, BA HonFLA FCLIP, Resident in Singapore. [16545] 01/01/1952 **FE01/01/1958**

Ap Dafydd, Mr I, MLib, N. Reading Room Mgr., Nat. L. of Wales, Aberystwyth. [10001095] 12/01/2007 **ME**

Ap Emlyn, Mr H, BA DipLib MCLIP, Llyfrgellydd Bro. [26673] 09/11/1976 **CM30/10/1979**

Appleby, Mrs F, MA MCLIP, Comm. L. Offr., St. Helens Council. [31754] 11/12/1979 **CM11/12/1981**

Appleby, Mr J M, BA MCLIP, Unwaged. [23231] 12/11/1974 **CM09/01/1978**

Appleby, Mrs S J, BA(Hons), Stud. [10000768] 06/11/2006 **ME**

Appleby, Mrs S, MA(Hons) MCLIP, Sch. Lib., Nairn Academy, Inverness. [61101] 25/02/2002 **CM21/06/2006**

Appleton, Mr C E, MCLIP, Lib., Latymer Upper Sch. [339] 01/01/1970 **CM26/11/1973**

Appleton, Mr L, BA(Hons) MA PGCE MEd, Head of Business & Planning, Liverpool, John Moores Univ. [59163] 04/12/2000 **ME**

Appleton, Mr T J, MA, Stud., Leeds Met. Univ. [10011202] 02/10/2008 **ME**

Appleyard, Sir R, HonFCLIP, Hon. Fellow. [60135] 18/11/1987 **FE18/11/1987**

Appleyard, Miss S C, BA(Hons) ACLIP, Learning & Teaching Lib., Open Univ. L., Milton Keynes [10008128] 20/03/2008 **ACL17/06/2009**

Apted, Mrs L, ACLIP, Learning Ctr. Mgr., Duchy Coll., Rosewarne. [10002971] 10/05/2007 **ACL23/09/2009**

Arai, Mrs R, MCLIP, Lib., Wheldon Sch., Nottinghamshire [10015244] 09/08/1972 **CM12/01/1976**

Arathoon, Mrs P M, BA MCLIP, Retired [22436] 30/04/1974 **CM01/02/1977**

Archdeacon, Mrs J M E, MCLIP, Comm. Lib., Norfolk C.C. [349] 01/01/1967 **CM01/01/1971**

Archer, Mrs A L, L. & Inf. Offr., Newcastle L. [60947] 15/01/2002 **ME**

Archer, Ms B A, BA, Lib., Word & Image Dept., Victoria & Albert Mus., London. [43382] 16/10/1989 **ME**

Archer, Mr D, BA MA, Reader Serv. Lib., London Sch. of Hygiene and Tropical Medicine. [10007990] 18/06/2008 **ME**

Archer, Mr G G, BLib MCLIP, Inf. Serv. Lib., Solihull MBC [29503] 05/09/1978 **CM14/12/1983**

Archer, Mrs J M, MCLIP, Child. Offr. p. /t., Halton Lea L. [7303] 01/01/1965 **CM01/01/1971**

Archer, Mr M K, BSc BA MCLIP, Virtual L. Mgr., AstraZeneca, Loughborough. [60608] 01/01/1983 **CM01/01/1983**

Archer, Mr S, BA, Chief L. Asst. (Reader Serv.), The London L. [10001228] 03/02/2007 **ME**

Archibald, Ms G, Content Mgr., UKBA, Easingwold, York. [38806] 08/10/1985 **ME**

Archibald, Mrs P V, MSc DipEd, L. . Asst., Scotish Police Serv. Auth., Scottish Police Coll. L. [61265] 13/05/2002 **ME**

Archibald, Mrs R, Asst. in Charge, Danderhall L., Midlothian Council. [54147] 07/11/1996 **ME**

Ardener, Mrs M, MCLIP, Retired. [357] 01/01/1949 **CM01/01/1970**

Ardizzone, Ms J T, MA MCLIP, Lib., Deutsch-Franzosisches Inst., Ludwigsburg, Germany. [44083] 25/04/1990 **CM25/09/1996**

Ardley, Mrs A G, BSc(Hons) MCLIP, Lib., The Hazeley Sch., Milton Keynes. [63231] 22/03/2004 **CM21/03/2007**

Arduini, Ms C E, BA PgDip CIM, Asst Lib., Holling's L., Manchester Met. Univ. [66146] 03/10/2006 **ME**

Arens, Mrs E A, Database Lib., Leeds L. & Inf. Serv., LCC [65798] 03/05/2006 **ME**

Arfa, Mrs J A, BA(Hons), Unknown. [51183] 23/11/1994 **ME**

Argent, Mrs L, Team Organiser, Interfleet Tech. Ltd., Derby. [64881] 02/09/2005 **AF**

Arkley, Mrs A D, BA DipLib MCLIP, Sen. Educ. Lib., Sch. L. Serv., Northumberland C.C., Morpeth. [30204] 29/12/1978 **CM11/12/1981**

Armitage, Miss P A M, BA, Unknown. [10011463] 21/10/2008 **ME**

Armitage, Mrs S J, BA(Hons) PGDip, Dir. of L. Sales, Bibliographic Data Serv. Ltd., Dumfries. [62169] 01/04/2003 **ME**

Armitage, Mr T R, BA MCLIP, Researcher, Self-Employed. [29364] 03/07/1978 **CM19/07/1983**

Armour, Ms S P, BLib CertEd MCLIP, Support Lib., Pembrokeshire Co. L., Haverfordwest. [375] 01/01/1971 **CM27/01/1992**

Armsby, Mr A F, BA MCLIP, Retired. [377] 01/01/1962 **CM01/01/1967**

Armsby, Mrs J, MCLIP, Retired. [378] 09/02/1965 **CM01/01/1970**

Armson, Mr P, MCLIP, Life Member. [380] 01/01/1947 **CM01/01/1953**

Armstrong Viner, Mr R F, MA BSc(Hons) MCLIP, Catg. Mgr., Aberdeen Univ., Aberdeen. [56761] 08/10/1998 **CM06/04/2005**

Armstrong, Miss A, BA(Hons) DipILM MCLIP, Audit & Evaluation Offr., Durham Univ., Teeside. [49738] 29/11/1993 **CM22/05/1996**

Armstrong, Mr C J, BLib FIAP FCLIP, Dir., Inf. Automation Ltd., Bronant, Aberystwyth. [48480] 21/01/1993 **FE01/04/2002**

Armstrong, Mrs D M, MCLIP, Retired. [384] 06/03/1963 **CM01/01/1968**

Armstrong, Mrs E J, BA MCLIP, L. Mgr., Hull Coll. [48268] 19/11/1992 **RV27/11/2007** **CM22/05/1996**

Armstrong, Miss E K, Sales Asst., Home Bargains, Leek. [49757] 02/12/1993 **ME**

Armstrong, Ms E, BA(Hons) DipILM MCLIP, Learning Res. Mgr., Cramlington Learning Village, Northumberland [47702] 19/10/1992 **CM23/09/1998**

Armstrong, Ms F A, BA MA DipLIS MScEcon, Asst. Lib., N. Glamorgan NHS Trust L., Prince Charles Hosp. [61306] 20/05/2002 **ME**

Armstrong, Miss H D, MCLIP, Asst. Lib., City Business L., London. [28776] 11/02/1978 **CM17/06/1980**

Armstrong, Ms H, MA(Hons) DipLib MCLIP, Higher L. Exec., House of Commons L. [31742] 25/11/1979 **CM17/12/1982**

Armstrong, Mrs J L, MCLIP, Retired. [16462] 17/03/1967 **CM01/01/1971**

Armstrong, Ms J, BA(Hons) MCLIP, Sen. Lib., L.B. of Enfield, Palmers Green L. [41818] 21/04/1988 **CM18/03/1998**

Armstrong, Mrs K M P, BA MA MCLIP, Young Peoples Serv. Co-ordinator, Cent. L., S. Shields. [33613] 22/01/1981 **CM10/03/1983**

Armstrong, Miss L E, BA(Hons) MCLIP, Acquisitions Lib., S. Ayrshire Council [41575] 25/01/1988 **CM14/09/1994**

Armstrong, Miss L M, Lib., BBC Inf. & Arch., London. [46729] 09/01/1992 **AF**

Armstrong, Miss L, BA MA, Team Lib. for Fiction, Reading L. [64188] 31/01/2005 **ME**

Armstrong, Miss R J, MCLIP, Life Member. [395] 01/01/1951 **CM01/01/1957**

Armstrong, Miss T, BA(Hons) MCLIP, Asst. Inf. Mgr., City of London. [52553] 07/11/1995 **CM17/01/2001**

Armstrong, Ms V, ACLIP, Delivery Super. (Subscriptions), Kings Coll., London. [10001260] 30/01/2007 **ACL04/03/2009**

Arno, Mrs R, BA MCLIP, Lib. Mgr., Bideford L. [10007733] 14/10/1969 **CM01/01/1972**

Arnold, Miss B W, MCLIP, Life Member. [399] 01/01/1950 **CM01/01/1955**

Arnold, Miss C V, PGD BA(Hons), Nursery & Primary Sch. Advisor, Staffordshire CC, Stafford [10015278] 29/10/2009 **ME**

Arnold, Ms E M, BSc(Hons) MA MCLIP, Inf. Scientist, Cochrane Airways Grp., London. [57977] 07/10/1999 **CM28/10/2004**

Arnold, Mr G, Unknown. [10012435] 10/02/2010 **AF**

Arnold, Mrs K J, BA DipLib MCLIP, Dir. . of L. Serv., De Montfort Univ., Leicester. [32872] 12/10/1980 **CM15/11/1982**

Arnold, Ms L, MCLIP, Co. Mgr., L. Servs., Cumbria C.C. [10008545] 07/10/1994 **CM21/05/1997**

Arnold, Mr R J, MA BA MCLIP ALAA, City Lib., Applecross, W. Australia. [16553] 01/01/1948 **CM01/01/1957**

Arnold, Mrs S, Inf. Specialist Nat Collaborating Cent. for Cancer, Cardiff [52999] 14/02/1996 **ME**

Arrand, Mrs C, BSc MCLIP, Site Coordinator., Lincs. Arch., Lincs. C.C. [33443] 08/01/1981 **CM16/04/1984**

Arrowsmith, Mr M R, BA(Hons), Unwaged. [10013782] 29/05/2009 **AF**

Arthur, Miss C, Lib., Sch. L. Serv. Hounslow. [62780] 22/10/2003 **ME**

Arthur, Miss D, MA(Hons) PGDip MSc, Stud., The Robert Gordon Univ., Aberdeen. [10008754] 15/04/2008 **ME**

Arthur, Mrs E M, BA MCLIP DMS, Sen. Mgr. Customer Serv., Dorset L. Serv., Dorset C.C. [40995] 02/10/1987 **CM27/03/1991**

Arthur, Miss J, BA MA MCLIP, Unknown. [36418] 12/10/1983 **CM03/09/1986**

Arthur, Mrs K L, BA(Hons), L. Asst., Wootton Bassett L,Wiltshire. [10014998] 01/10/2009 **ME**

Arthur, Mrs R E, BA FCLIP, Asst. Dir., CILIPS & Scottish Lib. & Inf. Council. Hamilton. [29559] 01/10/1978 **RV31/01/2007 FE21/11/2001**

Arulanantham, Miss S K, BA(Hons) BLS ADISc, Sen. Asst. Lib., Univ. of Jaffna L., Sri Lanka [10001543] 08/07/2004 **ME**

Arunachalam, Mr S, FCLIP HonFCLIP, Hon Fellow. [60105] 07/12/2001 **FE01/04/2002**

Ash, Mr C S, LLB(Hons) PgDip, (F/T) Community L. Mgr., Sandwell L. Serv. [65501] 09/02/2006 **ME**

Ash, Mr T M, BA(Hons), Unknown. [10008636] 16/04/2009 **AF**

Ashbey, Mrs K, MCLIP, Unemployed. [15067] 29/12/1970 **CM07/08/1974**

Ashburner, Mrs S M, BA MCLIP, Stud. [15259] 22/02/1971 **CM08/10/1973**

Ashby, Ms D A, BSc (Hons), Lib., Halton Lea L. . Cheshire. [10016085] 12/11/2002 **ME**

Ashby, Ms K E, BA(Hons), Unemployed. [41331] 02/11/1987 **ME**

Ashby, Miss M M, MA DipEdTech MCLIP, Retired. [431] 01/01/1959 **CM01/01/1963**

Ashcroft, Mrs D, Stud., Aberystwyth Univ. Open Learning [65205] 17/11/2005 **ME**

Ashcroft, Mrs L S, BA DipLib MA MCLIP, Reader, Inf. Mgmt., Liverpool John Moores Univ. [40339] 21/01/1987 **CM22/07/1992**

Ashdown, Mrs L, BSc(Hons) PGCE, Asst. Lib., Univ. Coll. Sch. [65956] 19/07/2006 **ME**

Ashe, Miss J F, BA, p. /t. Stud., City Univ. /Royal Surrey Co. Hosp., Guildford. [10000958] 24/11/2006 **ME**

Ashfield, Mr N D, BA MCLIP, Enquiry Serv. Lib., Birmingham City Univ. L., Birmingham [438] 01/01/1965 **CM01/01/1969**

Ashford, Miss L E, BA, Unknown. [10012019] 10/12/2008 **ME**

Ashill, Mr C G, BA MLib MCLIP, L. Asst., Royal Horticultural Soc., London. [49271] 20/10/1993 **CM20/11/2002**

Ashja-Mahdavi, Ms G, BSc(Hons) MSc, Learning Cent. Co-Cordinator, Harrow Coll. [10002725] 01/05/2007 **ME**

Ashley, Mr B L, BA DipLib MCLIP, Reg. Mgr. (E. Midlands) - Mus.,L. & Arch. Council. [29564] 04/10/1978 **CM11/12/1981**

Ashley, Mrs E, BA MCLIP, L. Asst. [35297] 06/10/1982 **CM19/01/1988**

Ashley, Miss F J, B. Lib MCLIP, Reading & Yth. Mgr., Monmouthshire C.C., Chepstow. [38543] 23/06/1985 **CM14/09/1994**

Ashley, Mrs J, BA(Hons) PGCE MSc MCLIP, Subj. Lib. (Faculty of Arts), Univ. of Liverpool., Sydney Jones Lib., Liverpool [57376] 17/02/1999 **CM15/09/2004**

Ashley, Ms K, ACLIP, L. Asst., Bolsover L., Chesterfield. [10010861] 02/09/2008 **ACL28/01/2009**

Ashley, Mrs K, BA(Hons) MCLIP, Sch. Lib., Post 16 Learning Resource Cent. Mgr. [45390] 23/11/1990 **CM18/03/1998**

Ashley, Ms L, BA MA MCLIP, Sub. Liason Lib., Brunel Univ., Uxbridge [10017178] 12/11/1998 **CM23/06/2004**

Ashman, Mr R A, BA MCLIP DMS, Cent. Lib. Mgr., Southampton Cent. L. [32729] 13/08/1980 **CM24/07/1984**

Ashman, Mrs R, BA(Hons) MCLIP, Asst. Sch. Lib., Southampton Sch. L. Serv. [30577] 27/01/1979 **CM16/04/1984**

Ashmore, Mr W S H, BA FCLIP, Life Member. [444] 01/01/1941 **FE01/01/1954**

Ashraf, Ms F M, BSc MA, Learning Facilitator. Westminster Kingsway Coll. [58782] 20/07/2000 **ME**

Ashraf, Mr S A, MA DipLib MCLIP, Retired. [34207] 12/10/1981 **CM24/03/1987**

Ashton, Mr C A, BA BSc PGCE MBA MCLIP, Prof. Reg., Leicestershire Co. Council [37999] 01/01/1985 **CM18/07/1990**

Ashton, Mrs H C, BSc, Learning Res. Mgr., Bishop Auckland Coll. [40393] 28/01/1987 **ME**

Ashwell, Mr S J, BA(Hons) MCLIP, Inf. Specialist, N. e. L. H., Birmingham. [42269] 13/10/1988 **CM06/04/2005**

Ashwood, Mrs B A, MCLIP, Adult Stock and Promotion Team, Cent. Stock Unit, Cambridge. [457] 01/01/1964 **CM01/01/1972**

Ashworth, Mrs L, BA DipLib MCLIP, Community Child. Lib., City of Salford. [33087] 08/10/1980 **CM08/10/1982**

Ashworth, Prof W, BSc FCLIP ARPS, Life Member. [464] 01/01/1935 **FE01/01/1938**

Asiinwe, Miss G, BLIS, Lib. Offr., African Prisons Project, Uganda [10015550] 14/12/2009 **ME**

Aske, Ms P A, BA(Hons) DipLib MA, Lib., Pembroke Coll., Cambridge. [59933] 06/11/2001 **ME**

Askew, Mrs D V, BA(Hons) MCLIP, Lib., Priory Sch., Lewes, E. Sussex. [43804] 17/01/1990 **CM26/07/1995**

Askey, Mrs J, MCLIP, Stock & Promotion Lib. . Brereton L., Staffs. L. H.Q. [23446] 10/12/1974 **CM11/08/1978**

Askham, Mrs A S, MCLIP, p. /t. Inf. Lib., Univ. of Bath. [62500] 29/07/2003 **CM10/07/2009**

Aslett, Mrs A M, BA MCLIP, Lib., St Paul's Sch., Barnes, London. [2116] 09/05/1972 **CM11/08/1977**

Aspey, Mr R, BSc MA FCMA MCLIP DipClassStud, Programme Mgr., Brit. L., Boston Spa. [60197] 15/11/1982 **CM21/12/1992**

Asquith, Mr P, BA, Coll. Lib., Dearne Valley Coll. [10001981] 07/11/1991 **ME**

Astall, Mr H R, FCLIP, Life Member. [476] 01/01/1953 **FE18/05/1973**

Astbury, Miss F C, Receptionist, Hills Road Sports and Tennis Cen., Cambridge. [37054] 16/01/1984 **ME**

Astbury, Mr R G, FCLIP, Life Member. [477] 01/01/1949 **FE01/01/1958**

Astley, Miss E M, MCLIP, Life Member. [480] 01/01/1968 **CM01/01/1971**

Aston, Mr M, BSc(Hons) MCLIP, Local Hist. Mgr., Finsbury L., L.B. of Islington [46212] 01/10/1991 **CM20/05/1998**

Atanassova, Dr R I, BA(Hons) D. Phil, Curator, Brit. L., London. [10015659] 08/01/2010 **ME**

Atherton, Mrs K, MA, Stud., Liverpool John Moores Univ. [10015225] 27/10/2009 **ME**

Atherton, Mr N E, BSc(Hons), Learning Res. Team Leader, Riverside Coll., Halton. [53179] 01/04/1996 **ME**

Atiogbe, Mrs P K, BSc(Hons) MSc(Dist) MCLIP, Acting Head of L. Serv. & Knowledge Mgmt., Surrey & Sussex Healthcare NHS Trust. [59529] 26/04/2001 **CM23/06/2004**

Atkin, Mrs M S N, BSc MCLIP, Lib., Notts. C.C., Beeston L. [63629] 29/07/2004 **CM21/03/2007**

Atkins, Mr C P, BA(Hons) MCLIP, Lib., Enquires., Windsor & Maidenhead L. [44854] 01/01/1991 **CM31/01/1996**

Atkins, Mr L C, BA(Hons) DipILS MCLIP, Bibliographic Serv. Team Leader, Coutts Inf. Serv., Ringwood. [50958] 03/11/1994 **CM22/01/1997**

Atkins, Mrs N, BA(Hons) MSc MCLIP, Inf. Specialist, HMG. [53537] 15/07/1996 **CM19/03/2008**

Atkins, Mrs P K, BSc DipLib MCLIP, Unknown. [34776] 11/02/1982 **CM16/05/1985**

Atkins, Ms R L, BA, Inf. Asst., Bath Spa Univ., Bath. [10001218] 02/02/2007 **ME**

Atkinson, Mrs A L, BA(Hons) MCLIP, Local Studies Mgr. /Arch. Projects Mgr., Kent C.C. [26767] 23/11/1976 **CM14/10/1980**

Atkinson, Mrs F, BA(Hons) MA MCLIP, Community Serv. Mgr., Bracknell Forest L. [46094] 01/10/1991 **CM23/03/1994**

Atkinson, Ms J C E, BA(Hons) PGDipILS MA MCLIP, Asst. Lib., Univ. of Ulster at Coleraine, Co. Londonderry. [44588] 31/10/1990 **CM21/05/2008**

Atkinson, Ms J D, BA MA DipLib MCLIP, LIS Mgr. IKM, Royal Coll. of Nursing, London [27875] 12/10/1977 **CM29/11/1979**

Atkinson, Mrs J E, Info. Offr., N. Yorks. Co. Council, Northallerton. [63404] 28/04/2004 **ME**

Atkinson, Mrs J, BSc BA MCLIP, Unknown. [8425] 17/01/1967 **CM01/01/1969**

Atkinson, Mrs K A, BA(Hons) MSc MCLIP, Lib., NHS Manchester. [10015807] 15/11/1990 **CM24/07/1996**

Atkinson, Miss K, BA(Hons) MA MCLIP, Asst. Lib., Henry Moore Inst., Leeds. [58928] 05/10/2000 **CM21/06/2006**

Atkinson, Mrs L A, BA MA MCLIP, Catr./Liaison Support Lib., Univ. of Reading. [51909] 04/08/1995 **CM23/06/2004**

Atkinson, Mrs L S, BSc MSc MCLIP, Reader Serv. Mgr., Health Care L., Univ. of Oxford. [26080] 16/07/1976 **CM28/09/1978**

Atkinson, Miss L, MSc BA AKC MCLIP, Lib., Camden PL, London [10016430] 24/01/1973 **CM01/08/1976**

Atkinson, Miss N P, MCLIP, Retired [509] 01/01/1957 **CM01/01/1962**

Atkinson, Mr P J, BSc MPhil MCLIP, Dir. of Learning & Corporate Support Serv., Univ. of Glamorgan. [20485] 01/04/1973 **CM25/09/1975**

Atkinson, Mr R G, BA(Hons) MA MCLIP, Dep. Lib., Birkbeck, Univ. of London. [43670] 22/11/1989 **CM14/09/1994**

Atkinson, Miss R J, MA, Stud., Univ. of the W. of England. [10015223] 27/10/2009 **ME**

Atkinson, Mrs S, BA MCLIP, Lib., Brookfield Comm. Sch., Chesterfield. [28873] 20/01/1978 **CM21/10/1982**

Atkinson, Mr S, BSc DipLib MCLIP, Tech. Serv. Lib., Univ. Coll. Falmouth. [39973] 07/10/1986 **CM15/03/1989**

Atlass, Mrs H J, MCLIP, Resource Delivery Inf. Mgr., Royal Coll. of Nursing, London [7698] 01/11/1970 **CM16/12/1974**

Atlee, Mr I H N, MCLIP, Life Member. [512] 01/01/1962 **CM01/01/1969**

Attar, Dr K, BA PhD MA, Rare Books Lib., Senate House L., Univ. of London. [56653] 01/10/1998 **ME**

Attenborrow, Mr R, MCLIP, Stock Lib., Co. L., Ipswich. [515] 01/01/1970 **CM01/01/1972**

Attwood, Mr C R, BA, Serv. Devel. Lib.,Dudley L. [10007034] 31/07/1990 **ME**

Au, Mr P K K, BSc PGDipIS MCLIP, Lib. (Retired), Greenwich Council. [48889] 12/07/1993 **CM19/11/2003**

Aubertin-Potter, Miss N A R, BA PhD MCLIP, Lib. i. /c., Codrington L., All Souls Coll., Oxford. [43664] 21/11/1989 **CM24/09/1997**

Auchinvole, Miss R, BA MCLIP, Res. Lib., Turnbull High Sch., Bishopbriggs. [38988] 22/10/1985 **CM22/05/1991**

Auckland, Ms M J, OBE BSc MSc MCLIP HonFCLIP, Independent Consultant & Trainer. [522] 01/01/1969 **CM02/01/1973**

Aucock, Miss J, MA DipLib, Bibl. Data Serv. Mgr., LIS, Univ. of St. Andrews, Fife. [36265] 12/09/1983 **ME**

Audsley, Miss E, MCLIP, Inf. Lib., Surrey Co. L. [523] 01/01/1971 **CM22/04/1975**

Auger, Mr C P, FCLIP, Life Member. [525] 01/01/1949 **FE01/01/1965**

Austin, Mrs G M, BA(Hons) MA, Lib., Hulme L., DLSS, Camberley. [47085] 21/04/1992 **ME**

Austin, Mrs J Y, BA MCLIP, Retired. [20347] 12/03/1973 **CM01/12/1975**

Austin, Miss K, BSc, Unknown. [10011805] 14/11/2008 **ME**

Austin, Mr L, Graduate Trainee, Butler L., Corpus Christi Coll., Cambridge. [10005978] 19/10/2007 **ME**

Austin, Mrs M E, BA(Hons) MA, Unknown. [10012469] 10/02/2009 **ME**

Austin, Mrs R M, PG Dip, Lib., Hounslow P. L., [60882] 18/12/2001 **ME**

Austin, Mrs S M, BA(Hons) MAAT DipILM MCLIP, Lib. Knowledge Mgr./Gateshead & S. Tyneside PCTS [47771] 14/10/1992 **CM19/07/2000**

Auty, Miss C C, BA(Hons) MSc MCLIP, Head of Secretariat, Parliamentary ICT Serv. [56267] 23/04/1998 **CM23/01/2002**

Avafia, Mr K E, FCLIP, Retired. [22518] 15/03/1962 **FE29/01/1992**

Avent-Gibson, Ms D J, BScEcon(Hons) MCLIP, Subject Lib. /Asst. Lib., Univ. of Bristol. [48824] 21/06/1993 **CM19/11/2003**

Averill, Miss L J, BA MSc MCLIP, Unknown. [56869] 29/10/1998 **CM08/08/2008**

Avery, Ms A J, BA(Hons), Comm. Lib., Glebe Farm L., Birmingham City Council. [37593] 05/10/1984 **ME**

Avery, Ms N, BA(Hons) MCLIP, Princ. Lib., Inf. Serv., Bedford Cent. L., Beds. C.C. [42129] 04/10/1988 **CM23/03/1993**

Awre, Mr C L, BSc MSc, Head of Inf. Managemnet, Academic Serv., Brynmor Jones L., Univ. of Hull. [60821] 04/12/1989 **ME**

Awwad, Miss N, PGdip, L. Asst., Sydney Jones L., Liverpool. [10006605] 15/11/2007 **ME**

Axelsson, Miss F H, Unknown. [10000627] 18/10/2006 **ME**

Axford, Mr J A, Inf. Mgr., Mailpoint 600, Herrford. [10016565] 14/04/2010 **ME**

Axford, Mrs W, MA MCLIP, Retired. [544] 01/01/1955 **CM01/01/1959**

Axon, Ms C L, BA(Hons) MCLIP, L.,Learning and Print Serv. Mgr., Tameside Coll. [45650] 15/04/1991 **CM14/09/1994**

Ayiku, Ms L T, BA(Hons) MSc MCLIP, Inf. Offr., Univ. of Sheffield. [61143] 08/03/2002 **CM29/11/2006**

Ayling, Ms S M, BA DipLib MA MCLIP, p. /t. Lib., Linslade Lower Sch., Beds. C.C. [30306] 19/01/1979 **CM08/02/1983**

Aynsley, Miss S E, MA, Inf. Skills Trainer, S. London Healthcare NHS Trust. [10012652] 03/03/2009 **ME**

Aynsworth, Mrs J M, BA(Hons), Position unknown, Moulton Coll., Northants. [48785] 24/05/1993 **ME**

Ayoola, Mrs B B E, MSc, Asst. Learing Res. Mgr., Lewisham Coll., London. [10000539] 01/10/1993 **ME**

Ayorinde, Mr J, BLIS (Lib) PGD (Comp. SC), Unwaged. [10006898] 17/12/2007 **ME**

Ayre, Mr A, BA MCLIP, Unemployed. [33260] 12/11/1980 **CM23/02/1986**

Ayre, Mrs C I, BA(Hons) MA MCLIP, Web Programme Admin., Global Care. [58118] 03/11/1999 **CM19/11/2003**

Ayre, Mr S M, BA(Hons) MA(Dist) MCLIP, Clinical Lib., George Eliot Hosp. NHS Trust [57487] 06/04/1999 **CM06/04/2005**

Ayres, Miss C A, BSc DipLib MCLIP, Head of Systems & Serv., Univ. of Reading L. [36003] 11/04/1983 **CM14/04/1987**

Ayres, Mr F H, BA FCLIP, Life Member. [551] 01/01/1947 **FE01/01/1958**

Ayres, Mr J E, MA DipLib MCLIP, Tech. Lib., TWI, Cambridge. [552] 01/01/1971 **CM01/01/1973**

Ayres, Miss S L, Unknown. [62362] 09/05/2003 **AF**

Ayris, Mr D A, BA MCLIP, Life Member. [553] 01/01/1956 **CM01/01/1967**

Azmey, Dr H M, BA MA PhD, Head of Inf. Sci. Program, Qatar Univ., Doha. [37824] 02/11/1984 **ME**

Azubike, Mrs M, BA MCLIP, LRC Mgr. /Subject Specialist, Univ. of E. London. [32915] 03/10/1980 **CM29/04/1986**

B

Baalham, Mrs G R, BSc MCLIP, Gen. Asst., Gusford Comm. Prim. Sch., Ipswich. [35478] 25/10/1982 **CM21/01/1986**

Baalham, Mr M C, Asst. Lib., Tyndale House, Cambridge. [10000991] 12/05/2004 **ME**

Babatope, Mrs I S, BLS MSc LIS, Unwaged. [64619] 29/04/2005 **ME**

Babcock, Mr C J, BA DipLib MCLIP, p. /t. Res. Lib., Croydon Coll. L. [50244] 13/05/1994 **CM24/07/1996**

Bacchus, Miss J, BA DipLib MCLIP, Asst. Lib., Westminster Kingsway Coll., London. [46016] 16/08/1991 **CM24/07/1996**

Bache, Miss A, BEd(Hons) MCLIP, Sch. Lib., Elgin High Sch., Moray. [65428] 23/02/2006 **CM09/09/2009**

Bache, Mrs J A, MA BA(Hons) MCLIP, Lib., St. Matthew Academy. [53766] 01/10/1996 **CM10/07/2002**

Back, Miss C L, BSc, Inf. Serv. Lib., Plymouth L. Serv. [64514] 22/04/2005 **ME**

Backham, Mr D, BA MCLIP, Asst. Lib., Univ. of Liverpool L. [21444] 01/11/1973 **CM16/01/1976**

Backhouse, Miss K L, Unwaged [10006562] 15/11/2007 **ME**

Bacon, Ms A R, MCLIP, Unknown. [31555] 18/10/1979 **CM08/04/1986**

Bacon, Mrs D E, MA MCLIP, Reading Devel. Co-ordinator, Bucks. L. & Heritage. [27880] 11/10/1977 **CM29/11/1979**

Bacon, Mrs H A, BA MCLIP, Lib., Univ. Coll. Creative Arts, Farnham. [26650] 30/09/1976 **CM25/09/1981**

Bacon, Miss J V, MSc MCLIP, Retired [561] 27/11/1972 **CM12/06/1975**

Bacon, Mr N, BEd DipLib MCLIP, Ch. Exec., Warrington Concil for Voluntary Serv. [46882] 21/02/1992 **CM18/11/1993**

Badahdah, Mr M A, Stud., Leeds Met. Univ., Leeds. [10015114] 13/10/2009 **ME**

Badcock, Mrs J, Learning Resource Cent. Mgr., Worksop Post [10007710] 20/03/2008 **ME**

Baddock, Mr C, DMS MIPD MCLIP, Training Consultant-Life Member, Yorkstone, Birches Walk, off Margaretting Rd., Galleywood. [563] 16/03/1956 **CM01/01/1966**

Bader, Miss H V, MSc BA(Hons) PGCert MCLIP, Asst. Lib., Royal Welsh Coll. of Music & Drama, Cardiff [63015] 15/12/2003 **CM11/11/2009**

Badger, Mr I E, BA(Hons) PGDipLIM MCLIP, Lib. & Learning Cent. Mngr., Univ. for the Creative Arts, Rochester. [62907] 18/11/2003 **CM29/03/2006**

Baffour-Awuah, Mrs M, BA PGLib MLIS FCLIP, Princ. Lib., Botswana Nat. L. Serv. [34371] 23/10/1981 **FE08/09/2005**

Baggs, Mrs H, Asst. Lib., Off. for Nat. Statisics, S. Wales. [57557] 01/04/1999 **ME**

Bagley, Mr D E, MA FCLIP, Life Member. [571] 25/09/1948 **FE01/01/1966**

Bagley, Mr S P, BA(Hons) MCLIP, Inf. Offr., Highways Agency, Leeds. [48861] 05/07/1993 **CM22/01/1997**

Bagshaw, Mrs A, p. /t. Stud., Univ. of Wales, Aberystwyth, Llanishen High Sch., Cardiff. [65582] 22/02/2006 **ME**

Bagshaw, Mrs J A, BA MCLIP, Advisory Lib., Sch. L. Serv., Essex C.C. [38551] 02/07/1985 **CM09/08/1988**

Baguley, Mrs G, MA MCLIP, Life Member. [576] 26/09/1950 **CM01/01/1953**

Baig, Mrs Q A, BSc MCLIP, Unwaged. [577] 17/10/1971 **CM08/08/1974**

Baildam, Mrs L J, BEd(Hons) MA, Asst. Lib., Newbold Coll. L., Bracknell, Berks. [57234] 14/01/1999 **ME**

Bailes, Mrs L C, Lib., St James Independent Sch. for Sen. Boys [63262] 23/03/2004 **ME**

Bailes, Mr W R, BA(Hons) DipM PgDipILM, Asst. Lib. (Aquisitions), Univ. W. of England. [61747] 01/11/2002 **ME**

Bailes-Collins, Mrs R A, BLib MCLIP, Sch. Lib. [42151] 10/10/1988 **CM18/07/1991**

Bailey, Mr A E J, BA MCLIP, Inf. Offr., Lewisham P. L., London. [23382] 01/01/1975 **CM21/12/1977**

Bailey, Ms A J, BA MA, Curator in Early Printed Collections, Brit. L., London. [35221] 07/10/1982 **ME**

Bailey, Mrs A J, BA(Hons) MA MCLIP, Inf. Offr., Derbys. C.C., Matlock. [53007] 14/02/1996 **CM19/11/2003**

Bailey, Mrs D A, Sch. Lib. Nottingham [61205] 08/04/2002 **ME**

Bailey, Mrs E, BA FCLIP, Life Member. [8508] 04/04/1932 **FE01/01/1939**

Bailey, Mrs F F, BA MCLIP, Relief Work, Pembrokeshire C.C., Haverfordwest. [38345] 28/03/1985 **CM17/01/1990**

Bailey, Mr G J, PGDipLib, Lib., CIOT, King's Coll. London [36172] 01/07/1983 **ME**

Bailey, Miss J, LLB, Stud., Loughborough Univ. [10011895] 26/11/2008 **ME**

Bailey, Ms L, BA(Hons) MLib MCLIP, Lib. -Faculty of Classics, Univ. of Cambridge. [49281] 20/10/1993 **CM24/07/1996**

Bailey, Ms L, BA(Hons) FRGS FB Cart. S, Unknown. [10012781] 26/10/1981 **ME**

Bailey, Ms M B, MCLIP, Retired. [591] 18/01/1946 **CM01/01/1951**

Bailey, Mrs P M, MA FCLIP, Life Member. [594] 28/02/1944 **FE01/01/1956**

Bailey, Mrs P M, BA MCLIP, Serv. Mgr, Northumbria Univ., Newcastle upon Tyne. [18372] 17/10/1972 **CM01/10/1975**

Bailey, Ms P, BA MCLIP, Managing Dir., Bailey Solutions Ltd, Hove. [10011882] 05/10/1983 **CM16/12/1986**

Bailey, Mrs R, BA MCLIP, p. /t. Stock Lib., Southampton City Coll. [26917] 15/12/1976 **CM10/08/1983**

Bailey, Miss V L, BA(Hons), Stud. [10015104] 23/10/2009 **ME**

Baillie, Ms E M, MTh DipTheol MCLIP MSc, Lib., Glasgow [64009] 02/12/2004 **CM10/07/2009**

Baillie, Mr I M, MCLIP, Sen. Offr. – L., W. Dunbartonshire Council. [601] 01/10/1968 **CM01/01/1971**

Bailly, Ms M C, Unwaged [10015144] 15/10/2009 **AF**

Bain, Mr J R, BA MCLIP, Sen. Mgr., Digital L. Serv., Singapore. [28259] 02/11/1977 **CM08/06/1982**

Bain, Mrs L M, BA MCLIP, Network Lib., Turriff Academy, Aberdeenshire. [21875] 05/02/1974 **CM19/11/1979**

Bainbridge, Miss E L, BA(Hons) DipLib, L. Exec., House of Commons, London. [50635] 01/10/1994 **ME**

Bains, Miss A, BA(Hons) MSc, Sure Start Lib., Chesterfield L., Derbys. C.C. [55963] 02/01/1998 **ME**

Bains, Miss J, BA(Hons) PgDip, Inf. Offr., CMS Cameron McKenna, London. [55165] 28/07/1997 **ME**

Bains, Miss N K, BA(Hons), Unknown [10011612] 29/10/2008 **AF**

Bains, Mrs N, ACLIP, Learning Cent. Advisor, Ealing Hammersmith & W. London Coll., London [10001824] 08/03/2007 **ACL24/04/2009**

Bains, Mr S J, MA MCLIP, Head Digital L., Univ. of Edinburgh, Edinburgh. [50584] 01/10/1994 **CM25/09/1996**

Baird, Mrs B I, Unknown. [65307] 19/12/2005 **AF**

Baird, Mr I S, MA DipLib MCLIP, Subject Lib. (Health), Teesside Univ., Middlesbrough. [36259] 04/09/1983 **CM24/03/1987**

Baird, Mrs J S M, MCLIP, Life Member. [16569] 06/02/1959 **CM01/01/1966**

Baird, Mr T H, MA(Hons) MLitt, Stud. (PhD), Univ. Strathclyde, Glasgow. [59492] 09/04/2001 **ME**

Bairstow, Mrs M, BA MCLIP, Lib., Health & Safety Exec., Sheffield, & Inf. Advisor, Sheffield Hallam Univ., S. Yorks. [25498] 25/01/1976 **CM08/07/1980**

Baker, Mr A J, BA(Hons) MCLIP, Subject Specialist-Music & Arts, Staffs. C.C. [26837] 01/01/1976 **CM01/01/1979**

Baker, Mrs A L, BLib MCLIP, Sch. Lib., Stoke High Sch., Ipswich. [36835] 04/01/1984 **CM16/02/1988**

Baker, Mr A S J, BA DipLib MCLIP, Lib., Haddon L. of Arch. & Anthropology, Cambridge Univ. [34411] 05/11/1981 **RV06/02/2008 CM23/06/1986**

Baker, Mrs B, BA(Hons) MCLIP, Subject Lib., Solihull Coll., W. Midlands. [18357] 05/10/1972 **CM16/02/1976**

Baker, Mrs B, Cert Ed, Tutor Lib., Millfield Sch., Street. [10009376] 15/05/2008 **ME**

Baker, Ms C A, HonFCLIP, Hon. Fellow. [61176] 26/03/2002 **FE26/03/2002**

Baker, Mrs C J, BSc (Hons) DipLib, Info. Researcher, CMI [10015088] 08/10/1986 **ME**

Baker, Mr C R, MCLIP, Retired. [627] 11/10/1965 **CM01/01/1970**

Baker, Ms C, BA MA, Learning Support Lib., Durham Univ. L. [65545] 24/02/2006 **ME**

Baker, Mrs D L, MA MCLIP, Unwaged. [38898] 18/10/1985 **CM08/03/1988**

Baker, Prof D M, MA MMus MLS PhD MBA FCMI FCLIP, Retired. [22964] 31/08/1974 **FE15/03/1983**

Baker, Ms G, BSc MSc MCLIP, Ch. Lib., DCSF, London [43839] 29/01/1990 **CM29/03/2006**

Baker, Ms H, DipLib CertEd, Lib., Huish Episcopi Sch., Somerset. [40848] 12/07/1987 **ME**

Baker, Mrs J K, BLib MCLIP, Lib., Telford L. [32410] 01/04/1980 **CM25/11/1985**

Baker, Miss J K, BA MCLIP, Retired. [633] 16/10/1966 **CM01/01/1970**

Baker, Mr J L, BSocSc MSocSc PhD DipLib MCLIP, Unwaged. [46414] 04/11/1991 **CM15/11/2000**

Baker, Mrs J M, MLS MCLIP, Inf. Specialist, BASF Plc., Cheadle. [12366] 08/10/1969 **CM07/01/1974**

Baker, Mr J, MA MCLIP, Lib., E. Kent Hosp. NHS Trust, Margate. [44610] 06/11/1990 **CM15/05/2002**

Baker, Miss J, BSc(Hons) PgDipILS, Sen. Lib., Lend. Servs., Jersey L. [59729] 10/09/2001 **CM01/02/2006**

Baker, Mr K G, BA DipLib MCLIP, Area Lib., Oban L., Oban, Scotland [10001587] 27/10/1986 **CM04/10/1988**

Baker, Mrs K L, BA MA MCLIP, Lib., Nat. Railway Mus., York [59985] 15/11/2001 **CM13/06/2007**

Baker, Mrs K M, BA(Hons), LRC Mgr., Brentford Sch. for Girls, Middx. [46363] 30/10/1991 **ME**

Baker, Mr L W, FCLIP, Life Member. [637] 15/03/1948 **FE01/01/1958**

Baker, Mr N T, BA(Hons) Dip Lib MCLIP, Ref. and Inf. Mgr, Fulham Ref. L., London. [10007740] 10/01/1986 **CM18/07/1990**

Baker, Mr O A, MCLIP, Retired. [641] 01/01/1963 **CM01/01/1969**

Baker, Miss P, MCLIP, Life Member. [642] 01/01/1934 **CM01/01/1937**

Baker, Ms R J, BA DipLib MCLIP, Unknown. [44035] 01/04/1990 **CM01/04/2002**

Baker, Mrs S E, BA MCLIP, Prison Lib., HMP Winchester. [25226] 08/01/1976 **CM04/10/1978**

Baker, Mr S J, BA MCLIP, Inf. and Learning Devel. Mgr, Notts C.C. Ravenshead. [39271] 01/01/1986 **CM21/07/1993**

Baker, Ms T A, BA DipLib MCLIP, Lib., Warwickshire C.C., Leamington Spa. [38622] 12/08/1985 **CM10/05/1988**

Bakewell, Mrs A, BA FCLIP, Life Member. [650] 06/09/1949 **FE01/01/1955**

Bakewell, Miss G M, MEd MCLIP, Retired. [651] 19/08/1964 **CM01/01/1969**

Bakewell, Prof K G B, MA FCLIP MCMI, Life Member. [652] 28/08/1948 **FE01/01/1958**

Bakker, Mrs S, MSc MSLS, Lib. /Inf. Specialist, Cent. Cancer L., The Netherlands Cancer Inst. [47003] 27/03/1992 **ME**

Balaam, Miss A J, BSc(Hons) MCLIP, Sch. Lib., Copleston High Sch., Ipswich. [49432] 27/10/1993 **CM21/01/1998**

Balaam, Miss D J, BSc DipLib MCLIP, Asst. Tech. Serv. Lib., Univ. Coll. Chichester. [29365] 01/07/1978 **CM21/06/1983**

Balabil, Mrs C P, BA MA MCLIP, Grp. Lib., Crewe L., Cheshire. [41089] 09/10/1987 **CM14/08/1991**

Balasubramaniam, Mr S, BSc DipLib, Employment not known. [37649] 15/10/1984 **ME**

Balchin, Ms J M, BA(Hons) MA MCLIP, Learning Res. Cent. Mgr., The Sixth Form Coll., Farnborough. [50956] 31/10/1994 **CM17/03/1999**

Baldeosingh, Mr S, MA, Asst. Dir., CPA Secretariat, London. [10001301] 26/01/2007 **ME**

Baldwin, Ms A K, Sch. Libr., The Denes High Sch., Lowestoft. [64090] 14/01/2005 **AF**

Baldwin, Mrs B W, BA MCLIP, Retired. [656] 02/10/1960 **CM01/01/1964**

Baldwin, Mr D R, MCLIP, Lib. Arts & Heritage Mgr., Civic Cent., Southampton. [23504] 02/01/1975 **CM03/09/1979**

Baldwin, Mrs J, MCLIP, Retired. [660] 20/01/1969 **CM01/01/1971**

Baldwin, Mrs R J, BA DipHE MCLIP DipLib, Casual p. /t. Arch. Asst., Hants. Record Off., Winchester. [37472] 01/10/1984 **CM06/10/1987**

Baldwin, Mrs S H, BA(Hons) MA, Team Lib., Shrewsbury L., Shropshire. [10015435] 18/11/2009 **ME**

Baleia, Mr J, Lib. Asst., Royal Coll. of Physicians, London. [10014767] 10/09/2009 **ME**

Balfour, Miss E M, BA MCLIP, Info. specialist, Northumbria Univ. [34917] 19/04/1982 **CM03/03/1987**

Balke, Mrs M N, BA MCLIP, Unknown. [16577] 01/01/1940 **CM01/01/1942**

Ball, Mr A J, BA(Hons), Res. Offr., Univ. of Bath. [61771] 05/11/2002 **ME**

Ball, Mr A W, BA FCLIP FSA FRHistS FRSA, Life Member [670] 01/01/1954 **FE01/01/1958**

Ball, Miss A, Stud., Aberystwyth Univ. [10015365] 10/11/2009 **ME**

Ball, Mrs C A, MA MCLIP, Researcher, Dept. Archaeology, Univ. Sheffield. [19582] 16/11/1972 **CM15/10/1975**

Ball, C F, Esq BA MCLIP, Life Member. [672] 29/08/1958 **CM01/01/1963**

Ball, Miss C, BA(Hons) MA, L. Asst., Burton L., Burton on Trent, Staffs. [10005547] 26/07/2007 **ME**

Ball, Mr D J T, MA DipLib MLITT FCLIP, Univ. Lib., Bournemouth Univ., Fern Barrow, Poole. [26222] 06/09/1976 **FE01/04/2002**

Ball, Mr G R, BA(Hons) FCLIP, Retired. [675] 01/02/1951 **FE01/01/1965**

Ball, Mrs H C, BA MCLIP, Unwaged. [34690] 26/01/1982 **CM31/10/1984**

Ball, Ms J E, BA(Hons) MA MCLIP, Res. Liaison Mgr., Univ. of Sussex. [51150] 24/11/1994 **RV09/06/2005 CM23/09/1998**

Ball, Ms J, Reader & Learning Devel. Lib. [10011372] 17/04/2003
ME
Ball, Mrs M J, MA DipLib MCLIP, Liaison Lib., Richmond Upon Thames Coll., Middx. [31724] 12/11/1979 **CM10/11/1987**
Ball, Mr P E, B Phil MLIS, Unwaged. [10010697] 24/08/2008 **ME**
Ball, Miss S E, BBibl, Sen. Inf. Asst., Kings Coll. London. [57741] 19/07/1999 **ME**
Ball, Mrs S G, BA MCLIP, Serv. Devel. Offr., Staffs. L. and Inf. Serv., Stafford. [37778] 09/10/1984 **CM05/07/1988**
Ball, Miss S J, BA, Asst. Lib., GCHQ, L., Cheltenham. [35916] 24/01/1983 **ME**
Ball, Ms S, BA, Stud. [10005076] 06/06/2007 **ME**
Ballantyne, Mr J J, BA DipLib MCLIP, Retired. [686] 01/01/1969
CM01/01/1971
Ballantyne, Mr P G, BA MCLIP, Head of KM & Inf. Serv., ILRI, Ethiopia. [30961] 01/07/1979 **CM14/11/1989**
Ballard, Mrs C F T, BA(Hons), Sen. L. Asst., Downend L., S. Glos. [10005353] 05/07/2007 **AF**
Ballard, Ms H, BLib MCLIP, ICT Devel. Lib., Medway Council. Kent. [37641] 10/10/1984 **CM09/08/1988**
Ballard, Mrs J, BLS MCLIP, Lib. Hockerill Anglo-European Coll., Bishops Stortford, Herts. [27983] 03/10/1977 **CM01/07/1982**
Ballesta-Saeta, Mr L, BA(Hons), Unwaged. [10016694] 28/04/2010 **AF**
Ballouz, Mrs M A, MA DipLib BSc AAS, P. /t. Subject Lib., London Met. Univ. [38735] 01/10/1985 **ME**
Balman, Miss L K, BSc(Hons) MSc, Sr. Asst. Lib., Univ. of Huddersfield [63965] 22/11/2004 **ME**
Balmforth, Mr C J, MSc BA(Hons), Coll. Lib., Dearne Valley Coll., Rotherham. [59244] 15/01/2001 **ME**
Balmforth, Mrs L D, BA(Hons) MCLIP, Inf. Offr. & Lib., Nat. Childbirth Trust, London. [3718] 13/01/1971 **CM15/09/1974**
Balnaves, Dr F J, PhD MA MLitt BA FLAA MCLIP, Life Member. [16579] 27/08/1951 **CM01/01/1954**
Balogun, Mrs A, BA, Unwaged – Seeking Work, Croydon, Surrey [10001652] 06/03/2007 **ME**
Bamber, Mr A L, BA FCLIP, Life Member. [694] 22/01/1954
FE11/12/1989
Bamber, Mrs B E, BA LLB MCLIP, Unemployed. [13819] 15/03/1972
CM11/11/1976
Bamber, Ms J M, L. Asst., John Rylands Univ. L., Manchester [62035] 28/01/2003 **ME**
Bamber, Mr P J C, BA DipLib MCLIP, Inf. Offr., ERA Tech. Ltd., Surrey. [41660] 08/02/1988 **CM19/06/1991**
Bamber, Mr R N, MA MCLIP, Life Member. [696] 09/10/1947
CM01/01/1955
Bamborough, Ms S C, BA MCLIP, L. Sales Mgr., GMTV, London. [29921] 01/11/1978 **CM09/06/1983**
Bamford, Mr P, BA MCLIP, Retired. [697] 01/01/1972 **CM19/09/1989**
Bamidele, Mr J A, BSc MSc MPhil, PhD Researcher, Royal Holloway, Univ. of London. [59477] 04/04/2001 **ME**
Bamigbola, Mrs A A, HND MPP BSc MSc, Unknown. [10016737] 28/05/2010 **ME**
Bamigboye, Ms F J, BSc MBA, Learning Cent. Mgr., S. Thames Coll., Putney, London. [10009359] 11/08/1992 **ME**
Bamkin, Ms M R, Stud., Loughborough [64959] 03/10/2005 **ME**
Bampton, Mrs B M, BA FCLIP, Retired. [18482] 16/10/1943
FE01/01/1953
Bampton, Mr J G, BA, Learning Resource Offr., Lakes Coll. [65194] 17/11/2005 **ME**
Band, Mrs B C, BSc(Econ) MCLIP, Lib., Emmbrook Sch., Berks. [54582] 30/01/1997 **CM10/07/2009**
Banerjee, Mrs R, BA(Hons) MA MCLIP, Lib. Trust L., Cent. Manchester Healthcare NHS Trust. [10016552] 06/02/1987
CM06/02/1987

Banfield, Mrs C, BA(Hons) MCMI A. R. C. M, Joint Serv. Lib., Aldergrove. [10015811] 29/01/2010 **ME**
Banham, Miss C R, MCLIP, Unemployed. [22243] 18/03/1974
CM19/09/1978
Banham, Ms S, BA(Hons) ACLIP, Sen. Lib. Mgr., Cent. L., Nottingham [10011451] 21/10/2008 **ACL04/03/2009**
Banister, Mrs K J, BA(Hons) MCLIP, Sen. L. Asst., Lancs. Co. L., Harris Cent. L. [42258] 13/10/1988 **CM20/05/1998**
Bankes, Mrs L, BA MCLIP, Head of L. Serv., HM Customs and Excise, Salford. [43434] 26/10/1989 **CM15/09/1993**
Bankier, Mrs K, BA MCLIP, Asst. Lib., Lancs. Teaching Hosp. NHS Trust, Royal Preston Hosp. [710] 01/01/1968 **CM09/01/1974**
Banks, Mrs J N, BA(Hons) MCLIP PGCE, Unemployed. [36903] 01/02/1984 **CM15/03/1989**
Banks, Mrs M M, BSc MCLIP, Off. Admin., Buchan Agric. Consultants Ltd., Peterhead. [712] 01/01/1970 **CM09/09/1972**
Banks, Mr P R, MA MCLIP, Inf. &L. Mgr., Tribunals Serv., London. [41193] 15/10/1987 **CM15/08/1990**
Banks, Mr P R, MCLIP, Lib., L.B. of Lewisham. [715] 05/10/1971
CM01/07/1990
Bannister, Miss E L, ACLIP, Stock & Reader Dev. Lib., St. Albans/Dacorum Dist. [64249] 22/02/2005 **ACL17/01/2007**
Bannister, Ms N, MA PGDipILS, Ass. Lib., S. Thames Coll., London. [57047] 30/11/1998 **ME**
Bansal, Mrs R, MLIB BLIB, Unwaged. [10014809] 16/09/2009 **AF**
Banting, Miss V A, DipLib MCLIP, Sen. Lib., Milton Keynes Council. [32010] 28/01/1980 **CM05/05/1982**
Bar, Mrs E A L, MA MCLIP, Grp. Leader, Zentralbibliothek, Zurich. [22498] 28/05/1974 **CM03/11/1977**
Barbarino, Mrs P, MA MA MCLIP, Dir. of Devel. & External Relations, Cass Business Sch., London. [48409] 05/01/1993 **CM17/11/1999**
Barber, Mr A C, BSc DipLib MCLIP, Princ. Community Lib., Rhyl L., Denbighshire C.C. [29575] 04/10/1978 **CM03/10/1980**
Barber, Dr B J, PhD MCLIP, Hd. of Heritage Servs., Herts C.C. [13540] 01/01/1971 **CM01/07/1976**
Barber, Mrs B M, MCLIP, Life Member [726] 04/07/1949 **CM01/01/1956**
Barber, Mrs C E, MCLIP, Community Lib., Holywell L. [23121] 05/11/1974 **CM12/12/1978**
Barber, Ms C, BA(Hons) MCLIP, Subject Lib., Teesside Univ., Middlesbrough. [43856] 02/02/1990 **CM14/09/1994**
Barber, Mr G, MSc BA(Hons) DipLib MCLIP, L. Serv. Mgr., Southampton Inst. [27509] 01/05/1977 **CM24/11/1981**
Barber, Ms J C, MA MCLIP, Mgr., Learning Res. Cent., St. Francis Xavier Coll. [41177] 20/10/1987 **CM24/07/1996**
Barber, Miss J M, BA DipLib MCLIP, Co. Dir. (IT Bureau), Self-employed. [32857] 03/10/1980 **CM04/03/1983**
Barber, Ms L D, BA, p. /t. Stud. /Support Asst., Manchester Met. Univ. /Dept. of Inf. & Comm. [10000718] 19/10/2006 **ME**
Barber, Miss L J, BA(Hons) MCLIP, Customer Serv. Lib., Leics. L. Serv., Hinckley. [35299] 11/10/1982 **CM14/09/1994**
Barber, Mrs M C, BA DipLib MCLIP, Dep. Dir., Knowledge Serv. Coll. of Law. [31840] 07/01/1980 **CM18/01/1982**
Barber, Mrs S M, MCLIP, Retired. [735] 27/09/1967 **CM01/01/1972**
Barber, Dr T, B Med Sci BM BS HND, Unknown. [10014005] 17/06/2009
ME
Barbour, Miss D, Unknown. [62460] 01/07/2003 **ME**
Barclay, Mrs C A, MLib MCLIP, Learning Resource Mgr., Elmwood Coll., Cupar,Fife. [25052] 01/11/1975 **CM25/07/1978**
Barclay, Mrs J M, BA MA MCLIP, Admin., Royal Horticultural Soc. at Wisley [60844] 10/03/1993 **CM01/03/1993**
Barclay, Mr J, Graduate Trainee Lib., BSO, London. [10015730] 19/01/2010 **ME**
Barclay, Miss P M, BA MCLIP, e-Learning Advisor, Citylit, London. [738] 07/07/1967 **CM01/01/1970**

Barclay, Mrs P, BSc DipLib MCLIP, E-Serv. Mgr., Univ. of Westminster. [31257] 10/10/1979 **CM15/03/1983**

Barclay, Mr T, BA MCLIP, Inf. /Local Studies . Lib., Carnegie L., S. Ayrshire Council, Ayr. [20430] 15/03/1973 **CM02/09/1976**

Barclay, Mrs Y, Sen. Lib. Asst., Aberdeen City Council, Aberdeen [64482] 31/03/2005 **ME**

Barden, Mrs H P, ACLIP, L. Asst., St. Austell L., Cornwall. [64240] 22/02/2005 **ACL05/10/2007**

Bardill, Ms A, Stud., Aberystwyth. [65302] 15/12/2005 **ME**

Barefoot, Mrs A L, BA MSc CertMgmt MCLIP, Inf. Specialist, Cranfield Univ., Swindon. [57081] 04/12/1998 **CM28/01/2009**

Bareham, Mr R E, BA DipLib MCLIP, Area Mgr. Southwark [34288] 21/10/1981 **CM16/05/1985**

Barengo, Miss M, BA, MA, Unknown. [10012000] 09/12/2008 **ME**

Barette, Mrs H M, BA MCLIP, Sen. Lib. -Catg., States of Jersey L. Serv. [39199] 04/01/1986 **CM12/12/1990**

Barfield, Mrs P J, BA MCLIP, Lib., Worcs. C.C., Evesham L. [26355] 01/10/1976 **CM03/11/1980**

Barford, Mrs S, MCLIP, Area L. Mgr., L.B. of Enfield. [8552] 07/01/1970 **CM05/01/1973**

Bark, Mr C A, BA(Hons) PgDip, Health Sci. Lib., Lanchester L., Coventry Univ. [54361] 25/11/1996 **ME**

Barke, Mrs C, ACLIP, Learning Res. Advisor, W. Notts. Coll., Mansfield. [63233] 22/03/2004 **ACL23/01/2007**

Barker, Mr A C, BA(Hons) DipILM MCLIP, Head of L. Academic Serv. Univ. of E. Anglia [54189] 30/10/1996 **CM15/11/2000**

Barker, Dr A L, BSc MSc PhD MCLIP, Inf. Projects Specialist, Mercy Ships, Aberystwyth. [25152] 08/12/1975 **CM09/06/1981**

Barker, Ms C A, BA(Hons) CertEd MSc MCLIP, Team Leader: ICT and Info., Staffs. Ls., Burton L. [50350] 04/07/1994 **CM21/03/2001**

Barker, Mrs C K, BA(Hons) DipILM MCLIP, Lib., Howes Percival, Norwich. [52007] 07/09/1995 **CM19/01/2000**

Barker, Mrs C M, BA(Hons) MSc(Econ), L. Asst., Jesus Coll., Cambridge. [63014] 12/12/2003 **ME**

Barker, Mr D C, BA MCLIP, Retired [751] 23/10/1967 **CM01/01/1971**

Barker, Mrs E J, BSc(Hons) MSc(Econ) MCLIP, Unwaged. [55708] 06/11/1997 **CM12/03/2003**

Barker, Mrs G D, BA DipLib MCLIP, Policy Dev. Offr., Glos. L. & Info. Serv. [35530] 26/10/1982 **CM23/07/1985**

Barker, Miss H, MSc, Unwaged. [10001629] 15/12/2003 **ME**

Barker, Miss J M, BA DipLib MCLIP, Lib., Kingswood L., S. Glos. [38026] 14/01/1985 **CM14/03/1990**

Barker, Ms J, Learning Cent. Coordinator, Shrewsbury Sixth Form Coll. [10006767] 17/12/2007 **AF**

Barker, Mrs K M, MSc, Lib. (Psychology), Radcliffe Sci. L., Oxford. [10015727] 12/01/1995 **ME**

Barker, Ms K, BA(Hons), Learning Cent. Asst., Citiy & Islington Coll., London. [64834] 02/08/2005 **ME**

Barker, Mr L A, BA PGCE DipLib MCLIP DMS, Casual Arch. Asst., Essex Record Off. [40976] 02/10/1987 **CM22/05/1991**

Barker, Ms L, Inf. Serv. Mgr., Pinset Mansons, London [64472] 31/03/2005 **ME**

Barker, Miss M A, BA(Hons) MCLIP, Learning Res. Offr., Thomas Rotherham Coll., Rotherham. [44570] 29/10/1990 **CM21/01/1998**

Barker, Mr M C, BA(Hons), Community Lib., Wigmore L., Luton. [65882] 16/06/2006 **ME**

Barker, Miss M G H, MA DipLib MCLIP, Freelance Abstractor & Writer/Academic Lib., Salford Univ. [30578] 06/02/1979 **CM01/07/1994**

Barker, Mr P D, BA, L. Asst., Aberystwyth Univ., Ceredigion. [10015489] 14/12/2009 **ME**

Barker, Mr P H, MA MCLIP, Retired. [764] 16/02/1964 **CM01/01/1967**

Barker, Mrs S G, BSc NVQ3 ILS, Sen. Lib., Yale Coll., Wrexham. [10016952] 10/06/2010 **ME**

Barker, Mrs S, BA DipLib MCLIP, Mgmnt. Inf. Systems Mgr., Leicestershire C.C. [28491] 02/01/1978 **CM18/06/1980**

Barker, Miss V K, BA(Hons) MLib, Index Clerk, Willis, Ipswich. [47857] 21/10/1992 **ME**

Barker-Ottley, Mrs K, MA, Prison Lib., HMP Bure, Norfolk C.C. [10000737] 13/11/2006 **ME**

Barker-Powell, Mrs C M, MA MCLIP, Child. & Yth. L., Notts. [10005124] 01/10/1987 **CM27/07/1994**

Barkess, Ms J E, MA MCLIP, Asst. Head, Libs. &Adult Learning Branches Cents. & Staff Devel., Bury Libs. & Adult Learning. [10006354] 31/07/1978 **CM01/07/1992**

Barksby, Mr D W, MA, Unknown. [10014280] 13/07/2009 **ME**

Barkway, Mrs J A, BA DipLib MCLIP, Team Lib., Wirral Bor. Council, W. Kirby . [40110] 16/10/1986 **CM18/01/1989**

Barlow, Mrs A M, BSc MSc MA, Inf. Lib., Nottinghamshire C.C. [65607] 28/02/2006 **ME**

Barlow, Mrs B A, BA MCLIP, Child. Lib., Wallasey Cent. L., Wirral Bor. Council. [30587] 10/02/1979 **CM25/08/1983**

Barlow, Mrs H C, BSc MCLIP FSI, Self-employed indexer [44295] 20/08/1990 **CM27/05/1992**

Barlow, Mrs J B, MA DipLib MCLIP, HRNet Mgr., Cranfield Trust., Romsey [44399] 04/10/1990 **CM18/11/1993**

Barlow, Mrs J K, BA(Hons) MLIS, Lib., Peter Symonds Coll., Winchester [10015291] 30/10/2009 **ME**

Barlow, Mrs J, BA(Hons) MSc MCLIP, L. Mgr., Bevan L., Birmingham. [59758] 19/09/2001 **CM13/06/2007**

Barlow, Miss L C, BA(Hons) MA MCLIP, Project Loan & ICT Devel. Lib., Southwark Educ. L. Serv., Camberwell [56667] 01/10/1998 **CM20/11/2002**

Barlow, Mrs M T, BA MCLIP, p. /t. Asst. Inf. Adviser, Univ. of Brighton, Eastbourne, E. Sussex. [775] 28/10/1966 **CM01/01/1969**

Barlow, Ms R, BA DipLib, Inf. Offr., Reynolds Porter Chamberlain LLP, London. [49497] 05/11/1993 **ME**

Barlow, Mr S J B, BA(Hons) MA MSc, Lib. Asst., Haddon L. of Archaeology & Anthropology, Univ. of Cambridge [64711] 01/06/2005 **ME**

Barnabas, Mrs S M, MCLIP, Life Member. [779] 06/03/1961 **CM01/01/1969**

Barnard, Mrs F E K, LLB MCLIP, Sch. Lib., Bishops Hatfield Girls Sch., Herts. [781] 04/02/1972 **CM01/09/1974**

Barnard, Mrs G R, BMus DipLib MCLIP, Employment not known. [34437] 23/10/1981 **CM16/12/1986**

Barnard, Mr M W, BA, Unwaged. [10001200] 03/02/2007 **ME**

Barnard, Ms N E, BA DipLIS MCLIP, Sub-Lib., Oxford Brookes Univ. [46484] 12/11/1991 **CM22/05/1996**

Barnes, Ms A J, BA MA DipEngSt MCLIP, Head of L. Serv. (Land), Min. of Defence, Bulford, Wilts. [787] 09/01/1970 **CM25/03/1980**

Barnes, Mr C I, CEng MCLIP MBCS, Retired. [31035] 01/01/1966 **CM14/03/1980**

Barnes, Mr C J, BA MA MCLIP, Retired. [19579] 26/10/1972 **CM09/02/1976**

Barnes, Mrs D J, BA DipLib MSc, E-Inf. Mgr. DE+s Electronic Lib., MOD, Bristol. [38370] 01/04/1985 **ME**

Barnes, Mrs D L, BSc(Hons) MSc MCLIP, Lib., S. Dartmoor Community Coll., Ashburton. [53362] 20/05/1996 **CM01/04/2002**

Barnes, Mrs D M, BA MCLIP, Child. & Young People's Lib., N. Hampshire. [20193] 01/01/1973 **CM01/02/1976**

Barnes, Miss H M, MSc, Info. Cent. Mgr., King Sturge LLP [57474] 01/04/1999 **ME**

Barnes, Mrs H V, ACLIP, S. Area Super., W. C.C. L. & Heritage, Amesbury. [45075] 05/07/1990 **ACL07/06/2006**

Barnes, Mrs J A M, BA DipLib MCLIP, Retired. [39284] 07/01/1986 **CM21/07/1989**

Barnes, Dr J J, BA(Hons) MSc DipRSA EdD MCLIP, Unknown [61171] 26/03/2002 **CM26/03/2002**

Barnes, Miss J M, BA(Hons) PgDipLIM MCLIP, Reader Serv. Offr., RNIB Nat. L. Serv., Peterborough [47595] 05/10/1992 **CM07/09/2005**

Barnes, Mrs J, BA(Hons) MCLIP, Lib., Sch. L. Serv., Northumberland (Job Share) [54363] 25/11/1996 **CM21/05/2003**

Barnes, Mrs L, Lib., Redmoor High Sch., Leics. [64788] 05/07/2005 **ME**

Barnes, Mr M A, Mob. L. Mgr., Schs. L. Serv., Suffolkcc, Lowestoft. [10011807] 14/11/2008 **AF**

Barnes, Miss M J, BA(Hons) MSc MCLIP, Unemployed [43678] 22/11/1989 **CM21/11/2001**

Barnes, Mr M P K, OBE DMA FIMgt MCLIP, Retired. [805] 01/01/1960 **CM01/01/1965**

Barnes, Ms S M, BA(Hons) DipLIS, Devel. Mgr., Westminster Ref. L., London. [51291] 05/01/1995 **ME**

Barnes, Miss W I L, BA MCLIP, Sen. Lib. (Reading and Lend.), Oxfordshire CC. [38414] 17/04/1985 **CM24/06/1992**

Barnett, Dr C A, BSc(Hons) PhD, Knowledge Mgmt. Serv. Mgr., Capgemini UK PLC., Bristol. [10006369] 19/10/2007 **ME**

Barnett, Mr C, MA MInstAM MCLIP, Retired. [810] 01/01/1966 **CM01/01/1970**

Barnett, Mrs E M, MCLIP, Retired. [10562] 18/01/1963 **CM01/01/1967**

Barnett, Mr G, FCLIP, Urdu Team Mgr., Foreign & Commonwealth Off. [811] 11/12/1963 **FE21/02/1974**

Barnett, Miss K L, BA(Hons) MSc(Econ) MCLIP, Asst. Lib., Educ. L. & Res. Serv., Port Talbot. [53397] 03/06/1996 **CM21/05/2003**

Barnett, Mr S J, L. Asst., Gloucester L., Gloucester. [10013675] 18/05/2009 **AF**

Barney, Miss D J, BA(Hons) MA, Lib. /Inf. Specialist, Foreign & Commonwealth Off., London. [49563] 11/11/1993 **ME**

Barney, Dr T H, MA PhD, Res. Fellow, Dept. of Linguistics, Univ. of Lancaster. [40500] 25/02/1987 **ME**

Baro, Ms K, BA PG Cert, Unknown. [10014100] 25/06/2009 **ME**

Baron, Mrs L M, BA DipLib MCLIP, Sch. Lib., Sutton High Sch., Surrey. [29951] 16/11/1978 **CM27/11/1981**

Baron, Miss L, BA(Hons), Inf. Specialist, FCO, London [55526] 20/10/1997 **ME**

Barontini, Ms C, MA MCLIP, Evening & Weekend Mgr., Birkbeck. [47557] 01/10/1992 **CM20/11/2002**

Barr, Mr C B L, MA FSA MCLIP, Life Member. [826] 02/05/1958 **CM01/01/1962**

Barr, Ms D J, BA MIMgt MCLIP, L. Mgr., S. Lanarkshire Council. [18428] 17/10/1972 **CM30/06/1976**

Barr, Miss P J, Lib., Alloa Academy, Clackmannanshire [65096] 01/11/2005 **ME**

Barr, Mr P, Asst. Lib., N. Warwickshire & Hinckley Coll., Hinckley. [10016442] 23/03/2010 **ME**

Barr, Mrs W, BSc MCLIP, Lib., Denny High Sch., Falkirk. [61263] 13/05/2002 **CM06/04/2005**

Barraclough, Miss C E, BA MCLIP, Dist. Lib., Stevenage Cent. L. Hertfordshire. [38753] 04/10/1985 **CM14/11/1989**

Barranco Garcia, Ms I, MA BA, Unknown. [10012266] 26/01/2009 **ME**

Barratt, Ms M M, BA MCLIP DipLaw, L. Strategy + Performance Mgr., L.B. of Enfield. [28778] 19/01/1978 **CM22/01/1981**

Barratt, Miss P M, MCLIP, Life Member. [839] 02/03/1943 **CM01/01/1946**

Barrett, Mr B J, BTh DipLib MCLIP ALAI, Inf. Sci., Health Serv. Exec., St. Josephs Hosp, Republic of Ireland. [41115] 08/10/1987 **CM12/12/1990**

Barrett, Miss C E, BA DipLib MCLIP, Lib., NHS Scotland Cent. Legal Off., Edinburgh. [10001379] 04/10/1988 **CM14/09/1994**

Barrett, Mr D A, BA, Customer Serv. Offr., Ashford L., Kent C.C. [41048] 05/10/1987 **ME**

Barrett, Miss E A, BA(Hons) MSc, Asst. Lib., Leeds Teaching Hosp. NHS Trust, Leeds. [42589] 13/01/1989 **ME**

Barrett, Mrs H, BA, Health Sciences Lib. [10006754] 10/12/2007 **ME**

Barrett, Miss I M R, BA, Lib. LRA, Thames Valley Univ., Slough. [33265] 27/10/1980 **ME**

Barrett, Mrs L M, BA MLS MCLIP HonFCLIP, Independent Trainer. [44405] 05/10/1990 **HFE21/10/2004**

Barrett, Mrs P A, BA MA(Ed) MCLIP, LRC Mgr., Felpham Coll., Bognor Regis. [62349] 07/05/2003 **CM04/10/2006**

Barrett, Mrs S E, BA(Hons) MSc Econ, Collection Devel. Offr., Knowledge Devel., Wokingham Bor. Council. [57794] 11/08/1999 **ME**

Barrett, Ms S, BA MSc(Econ), Subject Lib. for Anthropology, UCL [10005232] 27/06/2007 **ME**

Barretto, Ms T P, MSc, Researcher. [10016971] 16/06/2010 **ME**

Barrie, Miss L A, Document Controller, Interlink, Glasgow [10012684] 05/03/2009 **ME**

Barriskill, Mrs K R, BSc(Hons) DipLIS MCLIP, Sen. Asst. Lib., City of London/Guidhall L. [37497] 01/10/1984 **CM23/09/1998**

Barron, Mrs F M, BSc(Hons) MCLIP, Sales Negotiator, Freelance. [4428] 20/01/1970 **CM18/12/1972**

Barron, Mrs L E, MA DipLib MCLIP, Lib., Gordonstoun Sch., Elgin. [37868] 01/11/1984 **CM05/07/1988**

Barron, Mr S, BA(Hons), Stud. [10014881] 21/09/2009 **ME**

Barrow, Mrs B M, MCLIP, Life Member [858] 09/01/1951 **CM01/01/1958**

Barrow, Mrs J W, MCLIP, Unspecified. [2157] 19/01/1969 **CM01/01/1971**

Barrow, Mr M N J, BA(Hons) MPhil, L. Exec., House of Commons L., London. [62062] 07/02/2003 **ME**

Barrow, Mr R E D, BA(Hons) MCLIP, Dist. Lib., St. Albans Cent. L. [34505] 19/11/1981 **CM08/03/1988**

Barrow, Mr T, Learning Res. Cent. Mgr., Hornsey Sch. for Girls, London. [65444] 24/02/2006 **AF**

Barry, Mrs A J, Clinical Siences Lib. Mgr., Univ. of Leicester. [63870] 11/10/2004 **AF**

Barry, Mrs E C M, BSc (hons) PGCE, Specialist Lib., Stenhouse L., Kingston Hosp. [10007784] 20/11/2003 **ME**

Barry, Mrs F J, BA DipLib MCLIP, Princ. L. Mgr., Warrington L., Warrington Bor. Council. [31983] 06/01/1980 **CM13/04/1982**

Barry, Mrs G R, BA MSc MCLIP, Head of L. Serv., Manchester Met. Univ. [24964] 24/10/1975 **CM07/11/1978**

Barry, Ms J A, BA(Hons) MCLIP, Sch. Lib., Beardsen Academy, Glasgow. [45301] 04/10/1990 **CM27/11/1996**

Barson, Ms A J, BSc MSc MCLIP, Digital Collections Lib. [61234] 17/04/2002 **CM15/09/2004**

Barson, Mrs J M, BA FCLIP, Retired. [2720] 04/02/1960 **FE01/01/1963**

Barstow, Ms C, BSc(Hons) MA DipLS MCLIP, Lib., Bromley House L., Nottingham. [39684] 21/05/1986 **CM15/10/2002**

Barter, Ms A C, Coll. Lib., Seevic Coll., Essex. [62124] 21/02/2003 **AF**

Barter, Mrs E K, Unemployed. [48169] 11/11/1992 **ME**

Bartholomew, Mrs J M, MA DipLib MCLIP, Sch. Lib. [34914] 19/04/1982 **CM26/11/1997**

Bartholomew, Mr J, BSc BA(Hons) PGDip, Asst. Lib., Sainsburys Res. Unit, U. E. A., Cent. for Visual Arts, Norwich. [58466] 24/02/2000 **ME**

Bartholomew, Mrs M L, ACLIP, Learning Resource Cent. Mgr., Sussex Coast Coll. Hastings. [64397] 14/03/2005 **ACL10/01/2006**

Bartle, Dr D G, BA DipLib Phd MCLIP, Arch., Haberdashers Co. [36302] 01/10/1983 **CM20/01/1987**

Bartle, Mr R, MA B LITT FCLIP, Life Member. [870] 10/03/1953 **FE01/01/1960**

Bartlett, Mr D A, L. Asst., Greenwich Sch. of Mgmt., London. [59498] 11/04/2001 **ME**

Bartlett, Miss F L, BA(Hons) MCLIP, Inf. Sci., Det Norske Veritas, Aberdeen. [48065] 04/11/1992 **CM18/11/1998**

Bartlett, Mrs G M, BEd DipLib MCLIP, Comm. Libr., Risca L. [31634] 12/11/1979 **CM28/01/1983**

Bartlett, Mrs J, BA(Hons), Dep. Campus Mgr., Hertford Reg. Coll. - Ware Cent. [10016067] 12/02/2010   **ME**

Bartlett, Mrs K, BA(Hons) MCLIP, p. /t. Bookstart Project Offr., Ulverston L., Cumbria. [36964] 19/01/1984   **CM27/03/1991**

Bartlett, Mrs L J, Inf. Offr., CMS Cameron McKenna, London. [59359] 14/02/2001   **ME**

Bartlett, Mrs R, BA MCLIP, Life Member. [876] 11/09/1956   **CM01/01/1960**

Bartlett, Miss R, Stud., Northumbria Univ. [10013946] 18/06/2009   **ME**

Bartlett, Mrs S J V, BA DipLib MCLIP, Inf. Specialist, HM Revenue and Customs, Ipswich [26865] 28/12/1976   **CM06/09/1979**

Bartlett, Mrs S M, BA AdvDipEdTech MCLIP, Head of L. & Learning Res., Luton & Dunstable Hosp. [23556] 20/01/1975   **CM01/02/1978**

Bartlett, Mrs S, BA(Hons) MSc, Sen. Analyst, Talis Inf. Ltd., Birmingham. [54514] 15/01/1997   **ME**

Bartlett, Mrs W M, BA(Hons), Lib., Wolverhampton Univ., Walsall Campus. [52315] 25/10/1995   **ME**

Bartley, Mrs V J, BSc DipLib MCLIP, Mgr. of Content Devel., Dialog, London. [31557] 03/11/1979   **CM03/11/1981**

Barton, Ms C, BA MA, Comm. Learning & Info. Lib., Derbyshire C.C. [10002005] 28/03/2007   **ME**

Barton, Mrs C, BSc MA MCLIP, Distributed Learning Serv. Advisor, Univ. of Derby. [59276] 25/01/2001   **CM07/09/2005**

Barton, Mrs E, BSc MCLIP, Retired. [8776] 01/02/1972   **CM01/07/1974**

Barton, Mrs H E B, BSc(Hons) MSc MCLIP, Patent Support [47730] 15/10/1992   **CM26/11/1997**

Barton, Ms L A, BA, Unknown. [10014452] 07/03/2003   **ME**

Barton, Miss S E, BA MCLIP, Head of Inf., McCann Erickson, London. [34773] 09/02/1982   **CM04/04/1985**

Barton, Ms V, MA, Customer Serv. Lib., Coalville L., Coalville. [10001314] 15/01/2007   **ME**

Barua, Mr A, MA MPhil, Unemployed. [60892] 20/12/2001   **ME**

Barwell, Miss E R, BA(Hons) MCLIP, Principal Lib., Rutland L. Serv. [59901] 26/10/2001   **CM21/06/2006**

Basham, Mr P, BA(Hons), Stud., Aberystwyth. [64081] 15/12/2004   **ME**

Bashforth, Mr S F, BA MCLIP, Retired [886] 29/05/1970 **CM18/02/1974**

Basing, Miss H, BA MSc, Lib. Asst. [62847] 17/11/2003   **ME**

Basinger, Mrs D R, MCLIP, Sch. Lib., Cowley Lang Coll., Merseyside. [13322] 01/10/1970   **CM04/08/1975**

Basinger, Mrs E C, MCLIP, Inf. Consultant [20238] 13/02/1973   **CM01/09/1976**

Basker, Mr A J, BSc MA MIMgt MCLIP FRSA, Retired. [33668] 01/01/1968   **CM01/01/1972**

Basran, Mrs B K B, LLB/Hons, Stud., Univ. of Wales. [10013547] 05/05/2009   **ME**

Bass, Miss J, MCLIP, Retired. [891] 02/01/1960   **CM01/01/1969**

Bass, Mrs P, BA MCLIP, Retired. [892] 12/10/1960   **CM01/01/1962**

Bass, Ms R, Stud., UCL, London. [10016984] 16/06/2010   **ME**

Bassant, Mr R, Lib., Carnegie Free L., Trinidad, W. Indies. [58422] 07/02/2000   **ME**

Bassett, Ms L, Know How Offr., Slaughter & May, London [64937] 27/09/2005   **ME**

Bassett, Mr P, FCLIP, Retired. [895] 14/03/1955   **FE01/01/1968**

Bassett, Mr T S, Customer Serv. Asst., Bromley Cent. L., London. [10009110] 30/04/2008   **AF**

Bassington, Miss S J, MLS MCLIP, Unknown [36073] 25/04/1983   **CM24/03/1987**

Bastable, Mrs L M, MCLIP, L. Asst., Casual Relief, Kent C.C., Maidstone. [15400] 06/11/1971   **CM01/09/1974**

Bastiampillai, Miss M A, BA MA MCLIP, Learning Resources Mgr., Uxbridge Coll., Middlesex [39299] 15/01/1986   **CM19/08/1992**

Bastin, Mrs E, MA MSc, Inf. Scientist, Oxford Healthcare L., Oxford. [10010505] 30/07/2008   **ME**

Bastone, Mrs S C, MCLIP, Learning Res. Mgr., Licensed Victuallers Sch., Ascot. [51099] 15/11/1994   **CM21/11/2007**

Basvi, Mrs A, Unknown. [10014338] 10/07/2009   **ME**

Batchelor, Miss E J, BA DipILS MCLIP, Dep. Lib., Faculty of Educ., Univ. of Cambridge. [47024] 02/04/1992   **CM23/07/1997**

Batchelor, Mrs K M, BA DipLib MCLIP, Customer Serv. Mgr., Staffordshire Co. L. [32242] 11/02/1980   **CM05/05/1982**

Batchelor, Mr N S, MA MCLIP, Lect., Cent. Coll., Glasgow. [26277] 20/10/1976   **CM15/12/1978**

Batchelor, Mrs S C, BA DipLib MCLIP, Lib., Cambs. C.C., St Neots, Cambs. [35810] 24/01/1983   **CM01/04/1986**

Batcock, Miss C, MCLIP, Retired. [902] 10/02/1959   **CM07/09/1972**

Bate, Mr J L, MBE MA DipEd FCLIP, Retired. [906] 04/10/1937   **FE01/01/1953**

Bate, Mrs K A, Libr., Crewe L., Cheshire. [63365] 20/04/2004   **ME**

Bateman, Mrs M S, Inf. Exec., Inst. of Practitioners in Advertising, London. [10016183] 23/02/2010   **ME**

Bateman-Wang, Mrs M J, Lib. Asst., Frome Lib., Frome. [52955] 31/01/1996   **ME**

Bater, Mr R, MCLIP, Principal Assoc., InfoPlex Associates Ltd., Bristol, UK. [19858] 01/01/1973   **CM02/11/1984**

Bates, Miss C A, BA(Hons) MA MCLIP, Cent. Lib. Mgr., Northants. C.C. [56657] 01/10/1998   **CM29/03/2004**

Bates, Ms C A, BA(Hons) MCLIP, Lib., Nottingham Univ., Samworth Academy. [52352] 26/10/1995   **CM17/09/2003**

Bates, Mr D J, Self Employed. [10000966] 17/01/1983   **ME**

Bates, Mrs H M, MCLIP, Learning Res. Cent. Mgr., Brockenhurst Coll., Hants. [27449] 01/04/1977   **CM19/06/1984**

Bates, Dr J A, PhD MA MSocSc, Lect., Univ. Coll. of Dublin & Univ. of Ulster. [10014536] 11/10/2001   **ME**

Bates, Mrs J H, MSc, L. Asst., NEELB-Glengormley L., Co. Antrim. [59773] 02/10/2001   **ME**

Bates, Ms J, BA MA MA, Unknown. [10015467] 27/11/2009   **ME**

Bates, Miss K F, BA, Stud [10006708] 21/11/2007   **ME**

Bates, Mr P, MA MSc MRS MCLIP, Res. Offr., Merseyside Disability Fed., Liverpool. [60623] 22/10/1987   **CM22/10/1987**

Bates, Miss S E, BSc MSc MCLIP, Patent Analyst, Shell, London [44211] 09/07/1990   **CM01/04/2002**

Bates-Hird, Mrs S B, FCLIP, Inf. Mgr., Sandwell Lib. & Info. Serv., W. Bromwich. [6828] 27/01/1969   **FE17/11/1999**

Bathgate, Miss W, BA MA MCLIP, Learning Res. Cent. Co-ordinator, Bannockburn High Sch., Stirling. [43302] 17/10/1989 **CM27/01/1993**

Batho, Mrs V A, MA DipLib MCLIP, Lib. Asst., Heriot-Watt Univ Lib., Edinburgh [32113] 16/01/1980   **CM15/03/1983**

Batley, Miss P, MA MCLIP, Life Member. [929] 05/02/1958   **CM01/01/1961**

Batra, Mrs O, BA Dip, Stud. [10006440] 18/10/2007   **ME**

Batt, Ms A, BA DipLib MCLIP, Unknown. [31940] 10/01/1980   **CM18/01/1982**

Batt, Mr C, OBE BA FCLIP HonFLA, Ch. Exec., Museums, L. & Arch. Council, London. [930] 17/03/1966   **FE21/12/1988**

Batten, Mr M K, BSc MCLIP, Stock Team Lib., Westminster City L., Victoria L. [21622] 28/11/1973   **CM09/01/1978**

Batten, Miss M L, MCLIP, Project Mgr., Developing Project, London. [10000908] 27/02/1998   **CM27/02/1998**

Batterbury, Mrs J A, BA(Hons) DipIM MCLIP, Inf. & Lifelong Learning Lib., Hampshire C.C. [56672] 01/10/1998   **CM07/09/2005**

Battersby, Mr D R, Inf. Offr., Coll. of Law, Manchester. [62842] 06/11/2003   **ME**

Battersby, Mrs M, BA MCLIP, Sch. Lib., St Georges Sch. Herts. [37796] 28/10/1984   **CM27/07/1994**

Battersby, Mr R, BA DipLib MCLIP, Inf. Serv., Univ. of Edinburgh. [32630] 30/06/1980   **CM23/11/1982**

Battistini, Miss A, BA MA, Business Lib., Freshfields Bruckhaus
Deringer, London. [58888] 01/10/2000   **ME**
Battley, Miss K C, MA MCLIP, Lib., Herbert Smith LLP, London [61013]
01/02/2002   **CM04/10/2006**
Battye, Ms J E, BA MCLIP, Head of L. & Inf. Serv., Cent. L., R. B.
Kensington & Chelsea. [32392] 31/03/1980   **CM01/07/1984**
Baud, Mrs A, MA DipLib MCLIP, Head of L. and Inf. Serv., Bath Spa
Univ. [36540] 19/10/1983   **CM10/02/1987**
Baugher, Mrs J, BA MLIS, Inf. Mgmnt. Asst., Scottish Parliament
[10015338] 11/11/2009   **ME**
Baum, Mrs B, BA MLIS MCLIP DipLib HDipEd, Inf. Offr., Idox, Glasgow.
[29607] 17/10/1978   **CM20/01/1982**
Baveystock, Mrs G Y, BA DipLib MCLIP, Principal Lib., Slough Bor.
Council, Berks. Slough [41214] 16/10/1987   **CM16/05/1990**
Bawdekar, Mrs N, BSc M. Lib I. SC, Sci. /Tech. Offr., IUCAA, Pune,
India. [10002382] 20/04/2007   **ME**
Bax, Mrs K J, B LIB MCLIP, Sch. Lib., Doon Academy, E. Ayrshire
Council. [22207] 25/01/1974   **CM31/08/1977**
Baxendale, Mrs M, BA MCLIP, Life Member. [941] 14/04/1952
                                                              CM01/01/1956
Baxter, Mr D, MCLIP, Life Member. [943] 20/06/1956   **CM01/01/1960**
Baxter, Mrs D, Sen. Asst. Lend., Lancashire C.C. [64599] 29/04/2005
                                                                      AF
Baxter, Miss G, BA(Hons), Stud., Robert Gordon Univ., Aberdeen.
[10012667] 05/03/2009   **ME**
Baxter, Miss K, MA DipLib MCLIP, Retired. [947] 19/10/1971
                                                              CM01/03/1974
Baxter, Mr N, BA(Hons), Mob. Serv. Mgr., Herts CC, Hatfield.
[10013408] 22/04/1993   **ME**
Baxter, Mr P B, B MUS DipLib MCLIP, Lib., Surrey Performing Arts L.,
Surrey. [33477] 05/01/1981   **CM30/05/1985**
Baxter, Mr P, Stud. [10016574] 14/04/2010   **ME**
Bayir, Miss D, MA, L. Dir., Suna Kirac L., Koc Univ., Istanbul. [47372]
27/07/1992   **ME**
Bayley, Miss A, BA MCLIP, L. Tech., Dawson Coll. L., Montreal Quebec,
Canada. [953] 01/07/1972   **CM01/09/1976**
Bayley, Miss D J, MBE BA DipLib MCLIP, Life Member. [954]
01/01/1949   **CM01/01/1952**
Baylis, Miss A C, BA MA DipLib MCMI MCLIP, Learning Resources
Cent. Mgr., Filton Coll., Bristol. [44114] 18/05/1990
                                                              CM25/09/1996
Baylis, Ms J I, BA DipLib MCLIP, Mgr., Dementia Knowledge Cent.,
Alzheimer's Soc., London [31359] 11/10/1979
                                                              CM06/10/1982
Bayliss, Mrs J A, BLib MCLIP, Asst. Lib., Ipswich Hosp. NHS Trust.
[37922] 22/11/1984   **CM21/12/1989**
Bayliss, Mrs J A, Serv. Devel. /Supporting Families, Dudley L., Dudley.
[10015373] 10/11/2009   **AF**
Bayliss, Miss N, Unknown. [10015190] 23/10/2009   **ME**
Bayliss, Miss T K, BA(Hons), Stud., Loughborough Univ.,
Leicestershire. [10015526] 09/12/2009   **ME**
Baynes, Mr D, MCLIP, Retired. [965] 01/04/1965   **CM01/01/1968**
Baynes, Mrs J, MCLIP, Retired. [38322] 01/01/1964   **CM01/07/1994**
Bayo, Mrs I, Lib., Sheldon Jackson Coll., Sitka, Alaska, USA [10012950]
17/03/2009   **ME**
Bazely, Mrs J H, BA DipLib MCLIP, Access Lib., Cent. L., Southend-on-
Sea. [33594] 24/01/1981   **CM01/07/1984**
Beach, Mrs A E, BSc(Hons) PGDipLib, Knowledge and Inf. Adviser,
Natural England, Peterborough. [35312] 07/10/1982   **ME**
Beach, Mrs C A, BD MA, Asst. Lib., Rose Bruford Coll., Sidcup [57791]
06/08/1999   **ME**
Beach, Miss S, Unknown. [10012165] 08/01/2009   **ME**
Beache, Ms E E, BA(Hons), Stud. Aberystwyth Univ [10016319]
05/03/2010   **ME**

Beadle, Miss R C, BSc, Lib. Assist., Davis Langdon LLP., London
[10015393] 12/11/2009   **ME**
Beadle, Miss R V, MCLIP, Lib., HM Prison, Winchester [10014747]
07/10/1986   **CM14/11/1991**
Beadnell, Mrs G E, BA(Hons) MA MCLIP, Princ. L. Asst., Bodleian L.,
Oxford. [55832] 20/11/1997   **CM20/11/2002**
Beahan, Miss K T, HNC BA, Principal L. Asst., Mary Seacole L.,
Birmingham City Univ. [10006764] 03/12/2007   **ME**
Beale, Mrs H E, BA MCLIP, Lib., Morgan Cole Solicitors, Swansea.
[34548] 06/01/1982   **CM06/11/1985**
Beall, Ms J, BA PhD MLS, Asst. Editor,DDC, Lib. of Congress, USA.
[34921] 21/04/1982   **ME**
Beard, Ms J L, BA(Hons) DipILM MCLIP, Liaison Lib., Keele Univ.
[55843] 21/11/1997   **CM18/09/2002**
Beard, Mrs J L, BA(Hons) MCLIP, Lib & Learning Support Mgr.,
Bournemouth Univ., Poole. [2845] 09/01/1970   **CM30/09/1975**
Beard, Mrs J M, L. Mgr., Stoke By Nayland Middle Sch. [10010877]
02/09/2008   **AF**
Beard, Ms L J, BSc(Hons) DipILS MCLIP, Head of Inf. Systems, The
John Rylands Univ. Lib., Univ. of Manchester [49841] 20/12/1993
                                                              CM21/05/1997
Beard, Mr S L, BA MA MCLIP FHEA MifL, Head of Learning Res., City
Lit, London. [31562] 28/10/1979   **CM08/03/1985**
Beard, Miss S, Bsc PGCE, IT & Learning Cent. Facilitator, Aberystwyth
Univ. [10016120] 17/02/2010   **ME**
Beardow, Mrs R J, ACLIP, Asst.-in-charge, Cultural & Community Serv.,
Derbyshire C.C., Matlock. [10001102] 12/01/2007
                                                             ACL01/10/2008
Beards, Mr S P R, BA MCLIP, Lib. Mgr. (Acton Area), Ealing Council
[29880] 17/10/1978   **CM16/07/1982**
Beardsley, Ms H R, MA(Hons) MLib MCLIP, Sen. Subject Lib. (Arts)
[49287] 20/10/1993   **CM27/11/1996**
Beardsmore, Mrs J M, BLib MCLIP, Head of Serv. - L. Operations,
Dudley L. [10001137] 09/10/1979   **CM01/07/1994**
Bearne, Miss V, MCLIP, Special Serv. and Inclusion Offr., Bath & N. E.
Somerset. Customer Serv. Lib. & Info. [993] 20/08/1969
                                                              CM22/08/1974
Beary, Mrs C D, PGCE DipLib MCLIP, Sch. Lib., Parmiters Sch., N.
Watford. [32393] 11/04/1980   **CM25/01/1983**
Beasley, Mr D A, BA MCLIP, Lib., The Goldsmiths' Co., London. [32253]
17/03/1980   **CM19/03/1984**
Beasley, Miss P A, BA DipTEFL, Subject Advisor, Sci. & Eng. Team,
Univ. of Birmingham. [37343] 02/07/1984   **ME**
Beaton, Mr J J, MA MSc(Econ) MCLIP, Vol. Lib., Nat. Piping Cent.,
Glasgow [40878] 20/07/1987   **CM22/07/1992**
Beaton, Mr L, L. Asst., James Watt Coll. of F.E., Ayrshire. [10013742]
27/05/2009   **AF**
Beaton, Miss M, BA MCLIP, Access Serv. Co-ordinator, Glasgow City
L.,Inf. & Learn., Mitchell L. [995] 03/11/1971   **CM02/07/1976**
Beattie, Mr A G J, BEng(Hons) MSc MCLIP, Academic Support Mgr.,
Univ. Coll., London [55955] 24/12/1997   **CM21/03/2001**
Beattie, Mrs A, BA(Hons), Acting L. Mgr., Fauldhouse L., Fauldhouse.
[10015045] 08/10/2009   **ME**
Beattie, Miss E, Stud., Liverpool John Moores Univ. [10011129]
25/09/2008   **ME**
Beattie, Mr W S, BA MCLIP, Retired. [1001] 04/08/1951   **CM01/01/1955**
Beauchamp, Mr P J, MCLIP, Unwaged. [1004] 15/02/1967
                                                              CM01/01/1969
Beaufoy, Mrs M E, FCLIP, Life Member. [1005] 06/10/1938
                                                              FE01/01/1958
Beaumont, Mrs A J, BA DipLib MCLIP, Client Serv. Inf. Mgr., CB
Richard Ellis, London. [23734] 12/02/1975   **CM02/09/1977**

Beaumont, Mrs A M, BA MScEcon MCLIP, Knowledge & L. Serv. Mgr., Royal Preston Hosp., Lancs. Teaching Hosp. NHS Foundation Trust. [46780] 22/01/1992 **RV16/07/2008**   **CM08/12/2004**

Beaumont, Mrs D, BA(Hons) MA, Mgr;Devel.,Childern&Y. People Serv., Coventry L. & Inf. Serv., Coventry [57511] 14/04/1999   **ME**

Beaumont, Mrs F A, BA DipLib, Reader Serv. Lib., Herefordshire L. [26113] 01/01/1976   **ME**

Beaumont, Mrs H A, BA(Hons) MA MCLIP, Coll. Lib., Swindon Coll., Wilts. [1011] 01/01/1967   **CM01/01/1971**

Beaumont, Mr J, LLB LLM MSc, Lib. Harvey Ingram LLP, Leicester. [62757] 20/10/2003   **ME**

Beaumont, Ms M J, MCLIP, Life Member. [16599] 12/02/1964   **CM01/01/1967**

Beautemps, Ms V, MCLIP, Dep. Lib., Oxford Union Soc., Oxford [65586] 23/02/2006   **CM07/07/2010**

Beautyman, Mrs W, Stud., Northumbria Univ. [62962] 25/11/2003 **ME**

Beavan, Dr I M, BA PhD FCLIP, Emeritus Keeper of Rare Books, Historic Collections, Univ. of Aberdeen. [1018] 01/10/1970   **FE23/03/1994**

Beaven, Mr A R, BSc MCLIP, Marketing Dir., EvaluatePharma Ltd. [60793] 03/01/1989   **CM15/05/1990**

Beaven, Mrs O J, BSc(Hons) MSc, Inf. Specialist, BMJ Publ. Grp., London. [47709] 13/03/1992   **ME**

Beaver, Miss W J, BA MCLIP, Comm. Lib., Devizes L., Wilts. C.C. [41207] 19/10/1987   **CM16/11/1994**

Bebbington, Mr L W, MA(Hons) MSc, Dep. Lib. & Head of L. Serv., Univ. of Aberdeen. [10015773] 01/04/1987   **ME**

Beck, Miss C M, MSc(Econ), Lib., Bexley L. Serv. [63530] 04/06/2004   **ME**

Beck, Miss N, BA(Hons), Asst. Lib., Manchester Met. Univ. [63806] 01/10/2004   **ME**

Beck, Mr T J, MSc MBCS MCLIP, Independent Consultant. [1028] 07/12/1967   **CM31/07/1972**

Becker, Mrs H C, BA MCLIP, Dist. Mgr., S. Ribble, Lancs. C.C. [21269] 03/10/1973   **CM21/10/1992**

Beckett, Ms E S, BSc(Hons) MCLIP, Stock Mgmnt. Lib., N. Bristol NHS Trust, Southmead Hosp., L. & Inf. Serv. [44323] 06/09/1990   **CM26/11/1997**

Beckett, Mrs H L, BA(Hons) MCLIP, Community Serv. Lib., Bracknell L. [38208] 27/01/1985   **CM20/11/2002**

Beckett, Miss I C, BA(Hons) MA MCLIP, Clinical Lib., Asst. Mgr. Health L., Rotherham M.B.C., Rotherham Dist. Gen. Hosp. [55191] 07/08/1997   **CM10/07/2002**

Beckett, Mrs S J, BA(Hons) MCLIP, Comm. Lib., Caerphilly Co. Bor. Council, Blackwood L. [42410] 26/10/1988   **CM22/03/1995**

Beckles, Ms Z, BSc MA, Inf. Scientist, [10010529] 01/08/2008 **ME**

Beckley, Miss S G, BA DAA MCLIP, Highland Council Arch., The Highland Council, Inverness. [1032] 16/02/1970   **CM16/02/1988**

Beckwith, Mrs J A, BA MCLIP MSc, Knowledge Serv. Mgr., Royal Coll. of Physicians, London. [30956] 05/08/1992   **CM04/02/1985**

Beddard, Miss A F M, MCLIP, User Serv. Mgr., Arup, London. [18077] 02/10/1972   **CM11/11/1976**

Beddard, Miss V L, BA(Hons) MSc, Lib. Sandwell Academy, W. Midlands [60865] 13/12/2001   **ME**

Beddows, Mrs E A, BA MCLIP, L. Asst., Burntwood/Lichfield L., Staffordshire C.C. [48190] 16/11/1992   **CM15/01/2003**

Bedford, Mr D D, MA PgDip Lib, Sen. L. Asst., Canterbury Christ Church Univ., Canterbury. [10013694] 22/05/2009   **ME**

Bedford, Ms S C, BSc(Hons), Team Lib., Bournemouth & Poole Coll. [58926] 05/10/2000   **ME**

Bednall, Mr P J, BA MCLIP, Inf. Lib., L.B. of Sutton Pub. L., Surrey. [23320] 19/11/1974   **CM09/09/1977**

Bedri, Ms A, BA, Web Mgr., Home Off., London. [40448] 31/01/1987   **ME**

Beduz, Ms L, BA(Hons), Serials Lib., Royal Coll. of General Practitioners, London. [10001373] 07/10/2004   **ME**

Bee, Miss E A, BEd DipLib MCLIP, Inf. Mgr., Funderfinder, Leeds. [32015] 12/02/1980   **CM16/02/1983**

Beebee, Mr S R, p. /t. Stud., Aberystwyth Univ., Strouden L., Bournemouth. [66160] 04/10/2006   **ME**

Beeby, Miss K, BA(Hons), Unemployed – seeking work [10016428] 24/03/2010   **AF**

Beech, Mrs P M, MCLIP, Mgr. RNIB Nat. Lib. Serv. [1039] 16/01/1969   **CM08/02/1973**

Beecher, Ms D, Trials Search Coordinator, Cochrane Multiple Sclerosis Review Grp. [10013869] 04/06/2009   **ME**

Beedle, Mrs F J, Lib., Univ. of Cambridge, Local Exam. Syndicate, Cambridge. [57273] 29/01/1999   **ME**

Beedle, Mr J A, BA MCLIP, Area Lib., Scottish Borders L. Serv., Hawick. [1042] 04/01/1968   **CM09/01/1973**

Beeftink, Miss J, BA MCLIP, Unknown. [10014975] 08/10/1979   **CM30/12/1981**

Beegan, Mrs J, B LIB MCLIP, Sen. Med. Inf. Exec., Solvay Healthcare Ltd., Southampton. [30653] 09/03/1979   **CM10/08/1984**

Beeley, Mrs C, MCLIP, Inf. Lib., Kingston Univ. [671] 01/04/1967   **CM01/01/1971**

Beeley, Mrs J E, MCLIP, Site Lib. Mgr., Maidstone & Tunbridge Wells NHS, Kent & Sussex Hosp. [11869] 29/08/1969 **CM10/09/1973**

Beer, Mrs D M, MA BA MCLIP, Inf. Systems Unit Mgr., Inst. of Devel. Stud., Brighton. [31360] 05/10/1979   **CM11/02/1982**

Beesley, Mr M H G, MCLIP, Retired. [1048] 01/09/1961 **CM01/01/1969**

Beeson, Mrs H, BA(Hons) MA MCLIP AHEA, Academic Lib. Univ. . Northampton. [59111] 17/11/2000   **CM06/04/2005**

Beeson, Mr M L, BA(Hons) DipIS MCLIP, Sen. Academic Liaison Lib., Queen Mary Univ. of London [50561] 16/09/1994 **CM21/11/2001**

Beever, Mrs P A, MA DipLib MCLIP, Reader Serv. Lib., Oakham L., Rutland. [40717] 05/05/1987   **CM14/02/1990**

Beevers, Mr C J, BSc(Hons) PGDipLIM, Document Delivery Super., Univ. of Huddersfield. [58357] 19/01/2000   **ME**

Begg, Mrs K E, MSc(Econ), Coll. Lib., Queen's Coll., Cambridge. [57309] 08/02/1999   **ME**

Begg, Miss R E, BSc(Hons) MA, Inf. Specialist., GCHQ, Cheltenham [64818] 20/07/2005   **ME**

Begley, Miss R M E, B LIB MCLIP, Team Lib.,Lend., L.B. of Kingston, Surrey. [23566] 01/01/1975   **CM24/01/1979**

Begum, Miss S, BSc MSc MCLIP, Skills for Life Prog. Mgr. (Maternity leave), Bromley by Bow Cent. [61636] 07/10/2002 **CM01/02/2006**

Beighton, Miss S, Learning Resources Mgr., Leek coll of FE & Sch. of Art, Staffs. [63062] 27/01/2004   **ME**

Beisty, Ms B M, BA(Hons) MA PgDipLIS MCLIP, Dep. Lib., Salford Royal Hosp. Foundation Trust. [46225] 16/10/1991 **CM06/04/2005**

Belasse-Williams, Mrs M, Mgr. of Inf. Systems, Gleaner Co. Ltd., Jamaica. [10010970] 10/09/2008   **ME**

Belger, Mrs S J, BA(Hons), Stud., Univ. of W. of England. [10016993] 16/06/2010   **ME**

Bell, Mrs A H, BA DipLib MCLIP, Serv. Devel. Leader, Edinburgh City L. [28851] 26/01/1978   **CM06/04/1981**

Bell, Mrs C L, Sen. Lib. & Inf. Asst., Sennelager L & Inf. Cent., Normandy Barracks [10013663] 15/05/2009   **AF**

Bell, Mrs C S, BA MCLIP, Unemployed. [27511] 26/04/1977   **CM24/05/1979**

Bell, Miss C, MCLIP, Multimedia Lib., Aberdeen City L. s. [10000725] 13/11/2006   **CM21/08/2009**

Bell, Mr D J, MCLIP, Asst. Subject Lib., Oxford Brookes Univ. [19619] 24/10/1972   **CM22/11/1976**

Bell, Ms D L, BA(Hons) MA MCLIP, Academic Liaison Lib., Univ. Westminster, London. [52074] 02/10/1995 **RV19/10/2006**   **CM15/03/2000**

Bell, Mrs E L, BA(Hons) Dip Lib Manag MCLIP, Career Break. [53165] 20/03/1996 **CM17/03/1999**

Bell, Mrs E M, BA(Hons) MA MCLIP, Stud. [55393] 09/10/1997 **CM15/10/2002**

Bell, Mrs H C, BA DipLib MCLIP, Lib., Barrow, Cumbria C.C. [35733] 17/01/1983 **CM01/02/1986**

Bell, Mrs H J, BA(Hons), L. Asst., Sutton L., Surrey. [10015377] 10/11/2009 **AF**

Bell, Ms J C, BEd DipLIS MCLIP MBA, Dep. Dir. of L. Serv., UCE Birmingham. [49372] 29/10/1993 **CM20/05/1998**

Bell, Mrs J H M, MCLIP, Unemployed. [20933] 10/09/1973 **CM01/09/1976**

Bell, Mrs J, MCLIP, Acting Head of L. &Inf. Servs., Lancs CC. [30774] 04/04/1979 **CM25/11/1983**

Bell, Ms J, BA MA, Stud. UCL [65177] 14/11/2005 **ME**

Bell, Mrs K E, BSc(Hons) MA, Head of L. & Learning Res., King Edward VI Coll., Stourbridge. [55977] 07/01/1998 **ME**

Bell, Mr K E, BA M Phil DipLib MCLIP, Retired. [1081] 03/02/1970 **CM22/02/1988**

Bell, Mr K W, MBE MInstE MCLIP, Retired. [60519] 03/04/1966 **CM03/04/1966**

Bell, Mrs M A, BA DipLib MCLIP, Head of Lib. Tech. and Operational Serv., Cardiff Univ., Inf. Serv. [21716] 31/12/1973 **CM01/07/1990**

Bell, Miss M C, MCLIP, Young Peoples Serv. Lib., N. Lanarkshire Council, Coatbridge. [21286] 01/10/1973 **CM07/06/1976**

Bell, Mrs M H, BA MSc, p. /t. Lib., Winsford P. L., Cheshire, W. & Chester. [42327] 20/10/1988 **ME**

Bell, Mrs M S, BLS MCLIP, Business Operational Mgr., Area D, Lib. [40524] 25/02/1987 **CM26/05/1993**

Bell, Mrs M, BA DIP LIB MCLIP, Inf. Mgr., Scottish Enterprise, Glasgow [35236] 04/10/1982 **CM29/11/1986**

Bell, Mr P, BSc(Econ) MLib MCLIP, Inf. Consultant, H. M. Revenue & Customs Salford. [50825] 19/10/1994 **RV11/12/2009 CM29/03/2004**

Bell, Mrs S, BA MCLIP, Inf. Serv. Mgr., Aberdeen Cent. L. [22990] 07/10/1974 **CM01/08/1978**

Bell, Mr T I, FCLIP, Life Member. [1098] 15/08/1949 **FE01/01/1958**

Bell, Mrs V N, BSc(Hons) MLIS MCLIP, Asst. Inf. Mgr., Surgeon Generals Dept., Mod. [48426] 04/01/1993 **CM04/02/2004**

Bell, Miss W J, BA(Hons) DipLib MCLIP, Lib., Oak Hill Coll., London. [31511] 18/10/1979 **CM24/01/1984**

Bell, Mr W N, BA MCLIP, Retired. [1099] 15/09/1964 **CM01/01/1968**

Bellamy, Mrs A E, BA(Hons), Resource Cent. Mgr., Kent Police Coll., Maidstone [10014824] 16/09/2009 **AF**

Bellamy, Miss D, Paralegal/Asst. Co. Sec., Total E&P UK Ltd., Aberdeen. [56654] 01/10/1998 **ME**

Bellamy, Mr P D, BA MCLIP, Lib., Falkirk Council. [30597] 01/03/1979 **CM06/07/1981**

Bellamy, Mr P R, BA DipLib MCLIP, Sen. L. Asst., Univ. of Nottingham. [38044] 10/01/1985 **CM17/10/1990**

Bellfield, Mrs L M, Serv. Devel. Lib., Dudley L. [10010064] 22/07/1975 **ME**

Bellinger, Mr R P, BLib MCLIP, Serv. Mgr., L.,Bridgend Co. Bor. Council. [46314] 28/10/1991 **CM25/05/1994**

Bellingham, Mrs J M, BA DipLib MA MCLIP, Lib., Tonbridge Grammar Sch., Kent. [45360] 26/10/1990 **CM24/05/1995**

Bellingham, Mrs R A, MCLIP, P/t. Lib., Bentleys Stokes & Lowless, Solicitors, London. [24716] 07/10/1975 **CM26/11/1980**

Bellingham, Mrs S T, MA DipLib, Career Break. [46396] 31/10/1991 **ME**

Bellis, Mr G O H P, BA(Hons) MA, Media Res. Lib., MOD. Royal Military Academy Sandhurst. [61815] 11/11/2002 **ME**

Bellis, Mr R, L. Asst., DWP L., London [10007234] 25/01/2008 **AF**

Belsham, Mrs C T, N. W. Kent Coll., Dartford. [47504] 14/09/1992 **ME**

Belsham, Ms J K, BA DipLib MCLIP, Sen. Inf. Advisor., Kingston Univ., Kingston. [37422] 30/08/1984 **CM15/08/1990**

Belsham, Mrs S R, MCLIP, Asst. Lib., Thomas Plume L., Maldon. [1108] 08/11/1967 **CM01/01/1972**

Belshaw, Mrs J, Lib., Wickersley Sch. and Sports Coll., Rotherham. [10005501] 25/07/2007 **ME**

Belsten, Miss C, B Lib (Hons) MCLIP, Unwaged. [10015726] 03/11/1975 **CM11/11/1980**

Belton, Mrs M P, BA MCLIP, Lib., Long Eaton L., Derbys. [34658] 21/01/1982 **CM01/07/1990**

Bendall, Dr A S, MA MCLIP, Fellow & Devel. Dir., Emmanuel Coll., Cambridge. [35661] 23/11/1982 **CM17/09/1986**

Benedict Owen, Mrs S, BSc (Hons), Unknown. [10012313] 27/07/2005 **ME**

Benefield, Mrs P M, BA MCLIP, Principal Res. Lib., Nat. Foundation for Educ. Res., Slough. [14914] 01/10/1971 **CM09/09/1975**

Beney, Mr A, BSc(Hons) MA, Learning Resources Asst., Truro and Penwith Coll. [55486] 15/10/1997 **ME**

Beney, Mr C M, MCLIP, Retired. [29366] 08/07/1978 **CM20/05/1982**

Benfield, Miss J C, BA DipIS MCLIP, Lib. Assit., Bibl. Serv., Norfolk C.C., Norfolk. [45538] 04/03/1991 **CM19/11/2003**

Benfield, Mrs R E, BA(Hons), Blagreaves L., Derby City Co. [59981] 15/11/2001 **ME**

Benge, Mrs M E, BA MCLIP, Unemployed. [1120] 01/01/1965 **CM01/01/1969**

Benham, Mrs J, Learning Resource Cent. Mgr., Harrogate High Sch., Harrogate. [63134] 11/02/2004 **AF**

Benjafield, Miss J A, ACLIP, L. Asst., Worksop L., Notts. [65581] 22/02/2006 **ACL29/03/2007**

Benjamin, Mr M S, MCLIP, unemployed [26279] 12/10/1976 **CM23/08/1979**

Benjamin, Mrs P J, BA MCLIP, Lib., Backwell Sch., Bristol. [6030] 06/05/1971 **CM01/07/1974**

Benjamin, Mr S A, BA(Hons) MSc MCLIP, Inf. Mgr., TRL, Crowthorne, Berks. [54260] 11/11/1996 **CM15/05/2002**

Benjamin-Coker, Mr P, BA(Hons), Comm. Lib., Birmingham C.C. [56542] 13/08/1998 **ME**

Benjamin-Fast, Ms S F, Bsc MCLIP, L. Serv. Mgr., Cornwall L. Serv. [57255] 02/02/1999 **CM19/03/2008**

Bennell, Ms A, BSc(Hons) MSc, Data Adminstrator., Syngenta [57295] 21/08/1996 **ME**

Bennet, Mr M C, BSc, p. /t. Stud. /L. Asst., Univ. of Surrey L., Guildford. [64648] 11/05/2005 **ME**

Bennett, Mrs A C, BA(Hons) MA MCLIP, Inf. Advisor, Cyncoed L., UWIC, Cardiff. [57510] 14/04/1999 **CM02/02/2005**

Bennett, Miss A L C, BA(Hons) MA MCLIP, Ch. Lib., Priaulx L., St. Peter Port, Guernsey. [52312] 23/10/1995 **CM26/11/1997**

Bennett, Mrs C P, BA MCLIP, Lib., St. Helens Coll., Merseyside. [34361] 26/10/1981 **CM12/11/1984**

Bennett, Mrs C, BA(Hons) MA, Asst. Lib., Off. for Nat. Statistics, L. and Inf. Serv., Titchfield. [60875] 18/12/2001 **ME**

Bennett, Mrs D A, BA(Hons) DipLib MCLIP, Unknown. [10011622] 21/10/1976 **CM29/02/1980**

Bennett, Mr D E, BSc MSc MCLIP, Bibl. Resources Offr., Univ. of Portsmouth. [65202] 17/11/2005 **CM21/08/2009**

Bennett, Miss F J, MA DipLib, Unknown. [40715] 06/05/1987 **ME**

Bennett, Mr G M, BSc MA, Res. Serv. Lib., Slaughter and May, London. [10005907] 01/10/2004 **ME**

Bennett, Miss G, BA, Learning Resources Advisor, Colchester Inst. L., Essex [10016427] 24/03/2010 **ME**

Bennett, Mrs H R, BA(Hons) MA, Asst Lib., Guildford Coll. [10001222] 02/02/2007 **ME**

Bennett, Mrs J T, BA(Hons), Info. Servs. Mgr., Lazard. London. [65721] 30/01/2006 **ME**

Bennett, Mrs J, BA MCLIP, P/t Sen. Inf. Serv. Asst., Leeds Met. Univ.
P/t, w/e Customer Serv. Off. Birkby L. [36757] 09/11/1983
CM18/07/1990

Bennett, Miss K, BA(Hons), Liaison Lib., Newman Univ. Coll.,
Birmingham. [10011897] 26/11/2008   **ME**

Bennett, Miss M A, BA MCLIP, Branches Mgr., Hendon L., L.B. of
Barnet. [39816] 24/07/1986   **CM26/07/1995**

Bennett, Mrs M E, BA MCLIP, Life Member. [1139] 17/01/1956
CM01/01/1961

Bennett, Mr M R, MCLIP, Retired. [1141] 25/04/1963 **CM01/01/1967**

Bennett, Mr M S, BA MA MCLIP, Knowledge & Inf. Mgr., HM Gov.
Communications Cent., Milton Keynes. [43234] 10/10/1989
CM23/03/1993

Bennett, Mr N, BSc DMS MCLIP, H. of Inf. & Cultural Serv.,
Pembrokeshire C.C. [21935] 29/01/1974   **CM01/10/1976**

Bennett, Ms R, Researcher, Freshfields, London. [63215] 16/03/2004
ME

Bennett, Mr S E, BA, Customer Serv. Offr., Kirklees Cult. & Leisure
Serv., Huddersfield. [40496] 10/02/1987   **ME**

Bennett, Mrs W, BA MCLIP, Lend. Serv. Mgr., N. Lanarkshire Council.
[29474] 29/07/1978   **CM18/03/1981**

Bennie, Miss G K, Unknown. [10006175] 18/09/2007   **AF**

Benoy, Mrs K, BA MCLIP, LRC Mgr., The Heathcore Sch., Stevenage
[34982] 25/05/1982   **CM06/05/1985**

Benson, Miss J E, B Lib MCLIP, Unknown. [1156] 24/10/1968
CM26/09/1973

Benson, Miss J M, BA MCLIP, Retired. [1157] 28/09/1965
CM01/01/1968

Benson, Mrs P, Prof. Lib., Off. of the Prime Minister L. Div., Trinidad.
[55721] 11/11/1997   **ME**

Benstead, Miss K, BA(Hons) MA, Lib., Min. of Defence [59845]
16/10/2001   **ME**

Bent, Mrs M J, MA BSc PGDip MCLIP ILTM, Faculty Liaison Lib.,
Robinson L., Univ. Newcastle, Newcastle. [29170] 29/03/1978
CM30/06/1981

Ben-Tahir, Mr I, BA MS MCASI MCLIP ARAcS, Resident in Canada.
[60082] 07/12/2001   **CM07/12/2001**

Bentley, Mrs E A, BA MCLIP, Lib., Northbrook C. E. Sch., L.B. of
Lewisham. [29008] 08/03/1978   **CM23/03/1981**

Bentley, Ms H J, BA MA, Asst. Lib., The Guardian, London [10007203]
01/02/2008   **ME**

Bentley, Miss L, BA(Hons) MSc, Stud., City Univ. [65389] 03/02/2006
ME

Bentley, Miss M R, MCLIP, Retired. [1166] 18/02/1959 **CM01/01/1963**

Bentley, Mrs M, MCLIP, L. Asst., Surrey C.C. [25947] 18/05/1976
CM01/01/1979

Bentley, Mr S R, MSc, Sen. Inf. Desk Asst., York St John Univ., York.
[65863] 09/06/2006   **ME**

Benton, Mr E, MA(Hons) MA MCLIP, Libr., Godolphin & Latymer Sch.,
London. [59054] 06/11/2000   **CM02/02/2005**

Berendse, Mrs S, MLIS, Inf. Specialist, Nat. Collaborating Cent. for
Cancer [62948] 21/11/2003   **ME**

Bergen, Ms C L, MA MCLIP DipRSA CertEd FRSA, Freelance [26034]
01/07/1976   **CM09/03/1978**

Bergin, Miss C M, BA MA, Stud. [10017112] 23/06/2010   **ME**

Berkeley, Mrs J, BA(Hons) MCLIP, Unknown. [54009] 16/10/1996
CM29/03/2004

Berkmen, Mrs M, MCLIP, Head Lib., Cent. for Advanced Studies in
Music, Istanbul, Turkey. [17039] 30/01/1960   **CM01/01/1964**

Bernard, Miss F J F, BA(Hons), Stud., Robert Gordon Univ., Aberdeen.
[10016165] 19/02/2010   **ME**

Bernard, Miss M A, BA DipLib MCLIP, Business Devel. Mgr.
Bournemouth Bor. Council [32254] 22/02/1980   **CM11/11/1982**

Bernstein, Mrs A J, MA, Sen. L. Asst., Univ. of Sheffield, Main L.
[58654] 04/05/2000   **ME**

Berridge, Mrs J J, BA MCLIP, p. /t. L. Asst., Nailsea Grp., N. Somerset.
[27154] 03/02/1977   **CM02/11/1979**

Berridge, Mrs V, Sen. L. Asst., Educ. L. Serv., Winsford. [10013812]
29/05/2009   **AF**

Berrington, Mr M, BA(Hons) MA DipLib, Dep. Univ. Lib., Boots L.,
Nottingham Trent Univ., Nottingham [10017249] 04/10/1984   **ME**

Berrisford, Miss A J, BSc(Econ), Sch. Lib., The Derby High Sch., Bury,
Lancs. [10005236] 27/06/2007   **ME**

Berrisford, Miss E R, Grad. Trainee Lib. Asst., Crewe L., Cheshire
[10012820] 19/03/2009   **ME**

Berrisford, Ms J, BA(Hons) MA ACLIP, Asst. Learning Cent. Mgr., The
Learning Cent., City & Islington Coll. [64314] 25/02/2005
ACL01/10/2006

Berry, Ms B L, BA MSc(Econ), Lib., Royal Coll. of G. P. 's., London.
[46311] 28/10/1991   **ME**

Berry, Miss H E, BA DipLib Cert Ed MCLIP MCIT MILT, Learning
Resources Mgr, Richmond-upon-Thames Coll. [39288] 09/01/1986
CM19/01/1988

Berry, Mrs H M, BA PGCE MSc MCLIP, Devel. Lib., Leeds City L.
[42412] 30/10/1988   **CM26/02/1992**

Berry, Mrs I A, MCLIP, Cat. Coordinator, Renfrewshire Ls., Paisley.
[31787] 12/12/1979   **CM11/03/1984**

Berry, Miss J P, BA(Hons) MBA MCLIP, Lib., BMA, London. [22833]
12/10/1974   **CM28/07/1977**

Berry, Mrs J, BA DMS MCLIP, Interim Dir., Info & Learning Serv., Univ.
of Salford. [31171] 25/09/1979   **CM07/09/1982**

Berry, Mrs J, BA MCLIP, L. Mgr., Lancashire C.C. [40192] 04/11/1986
CM14/02/1990

Berry, Ms K, BA DMS MCLIP, Mgr., e-Govt., Coventry L. & Inf. Serv.
[30539] 13/03/1979   **CM27/07/1983**

Berry, Mrs N J, BA, MSc, Unknown. [10012024] 10/12/2008   **ME**

Berry, Miss S, BA DipLib MCLIP, Head of Inf. Serv., Clifford Chance,
London. [34235] 15/10/1981   **CM14/11/1969**

Berry, Mr T J, MCLIP, Special Serv. Lib., Hounslow. [1188] 01/10/1971
CM07/11/1974

Berryman, Ms G M, Asst. Lib., NI Assembly L., Belfast. [10002976]
25/11/2003   **ME**

Bertulis, Ms R B, BA MCLIP, Outreach Inf. Mgr., Royal Coll. of Nursing,
London. [37103] 21/02/1984   **CM07/07/1987**

Berube, Ms L, MLS, Tech. Consultant for DCMS. [57383] 24/02/1999
ME

Berwick, Ms J, BA MCLIP, L. & Inf. Serv. Mgr., CMS Cameron
McKenna, London. [32634] 01/07/1980   **CM08/12/1982**

Berwick-Sayers, Mrs S J, FCLIP, Life Member. [1193] 01/01/1939
FE01/01/1948

Besson, Dr A, PhD DipLib MCLIP, Inf. Skills Lib., Queen Mary, Univ. of
London. [26280] 08/10/1976   **CM17/01/1979**

Best, Mrs A C, MCLIP, Project Offr., BECTA, Coventry. [5088]
28/09/1971   **CM19/08/1976**

Best, Mr A J, MCLIP, Life Member. [1196] 31/01/1949 **CM01/01/1952**

Best, Mrs H, L. Asst., Torbay L. Serv., Torquay. [10001330] 08/03/2007
ME

Best, Mr K W, MBE FCLIP, Life Member. [1198] 17/01/1949
FE01/01/1959

Best, Mr S J, MCLIP, Retired. [1200] 18/03/1957   **CM01/01/1962**

Bethencourt, Miss C, MA MCLIP, Ref. Lib., Kensington & Chelsea,
London [65368] 13/01/2006   **CM07/07/2010**

Bethune, Mr A J, BSc DipLib MCLIP, Asst. Customer Serv. Lib., Anglia
Ruskin Univ., Cambridge. [20583] 12/04/1973   **CM08/10/1975**

Beton, Miss H, BA(Hons) MA MCLIP, L. Computing Offr., Canterbury
Christ Church Univ. [56651] 01/10/1998   **CM15/05/2002**

Bett, Miss N K, BA(Hons) MSc MCLIP, Lib., Dumfermline High Sch. [54066] 22/10/1996 **CM02/02/2005**

Betteridge, Mrs J M, MCLIP, L. & Inf. Asst., Liverpool Cent. L. [25217] 22/12/1975 **CM02/03/1979**

Betteridge, Mr R L, ACLIP, Curator, Nat. L. of Scotland, Edinburgh. [64842] 01/08/2005 **ACL07/11/2008**

Bettles, Mrs A, BA(Hons) MCLIP, Inf. Cent. Leader, Infineum UK Ltd., Oxon. [23148] 06/11/1974 **CM02/08/1978**

Bettley, Dr J, MA PhD FSA MCLIP, Self-employed. [46892] 28/02/1992 **CM21/07/1993**

Betts, Mrs A M, BSc(Hons) MA MCLIP, Inf. Res. Offr., EON UK, Notts. [61229] 18/04/2002 **CM13/06/2007**

Betts, Mr D A, BA FCLIP, Retired [1208] 26/02/1958 **FE01/01/1970**

Betts, Mr N, BA(Hons) MCLIP MA, Richmond House Learning Resource Cent. Super., Univ. Coll. of Birmingham. [43710] 05/12/1989 **CM22/11/1995**

Betts-Gray, Mrs M J F, MA MCLIP, Bus. Inf. Specialist, Cranfield Univ., Beds. [33285] 28/10/1980 **CM10/11/1983**

Bevan, Miss C, ACLIP, Sen. Lib. Asst., Univ. of Sunderland, St. Peter's L., Sunderland. [10008686] 09/04/2008 **ACL04/03/2009**

Bevan, Dr E M, M. A., Dip. Loc. Hist., Sen. Asst. Lib., Lytham L., Lancs. Co. L. [58858] 08/09/2000 **ME**

Bevan, Mr N P, BSc MSc DipLib MCLIP, Dir. of L. Serv., Brunel Univ., Middlesex. [27891] 03/10/1977 **CM15/02/1981**

Bevan, Mr S J, BSc(Econ) MA MCLIP, Head of Inf. Systems., Cranfield Univ. [40294] 14/01/1987 **CM18/04/1989**

Bevan, Mrs S, Publications Supply Asst., Manchester Civil Justice Cent. [10014979] 01/10/2009 **AF**

Beveridge, Ms K, BA(Hons) PG DipLIS, Asst. Lib., Dundee Univ. L. [48327] 26/11/1992 **ME**

Beveridge, Miss L, BA(Hons), Stud. [10000651] 19/10/2006 **ME**

Beveridge, Mr R M, BA(Hons) MCLIP, L. Serv. Dir., Instant L. Ltd., London. [48425] 04/01/1993 **CM31/01/1996**

Beveridge, Miss R, Lib. Mgr., Bathgate L., Bathgate. [10000670] 27/10/2006 **ME**

Beverley, Dr C A, BSc MSc MCLIP, Knowledge Mgr., Adult Social Care, Cumbria C.C. [55662] 04/11/1997 **CM21/11/2001**

Beverley, Mrs E F, BA, Reader Devel. Offr., Young People & Families., Wokingham Bor. Council [58133] 04/11/1999 **ME**

Bevin, Dr D J, MA PhD MCLIP, Sen. L. Asst., Faculty of Divinity L., Univ. of Cambridge [10013519] 01/01/1996 **CM17/05/2000**

Bevin, Mrs P J, MA MCLIP, Retired. [1213] 13/09/1951 **CM01/01/1958**

Bevington, Mr R D G, BA(Hons) DipLib MCLIP, Stud. [37895] 15/11/1984 **CM18/07/1990**

Bevis, Mrs J, BA(Hons) MSc MCLIP, Not Employed. [49582] 19/11/1993 **CM17/03/1999**

Bevis, Mrs S A, Sen. Inf. Offr., Communities Dept., Nottinghamshire C.C. [44359] 01/10/1990 **ME**

Bewick, Miss E N, MCLIP, Life Member. [1215] 22/03/1937 **CM01/01/1941**

Bewick, Mrs L F, Inf. Off., UCLAN. [63789] 06/10/2004 **ME**

Beyer, Mrs F R, BSc(Hons) PgDip MCLIP, Inf. Scientist, Univ. of Newcastle upon Tyne. [51401] 06/02/1995 **CM28/01/2009**

Beyers, Mrs N, BA(Hons), Lib., Newton Prep, London. [10010203] 10/07/2008 **ME**

Bhadhal, Miss I, BA DipLib MCLIP, W. Area Mgr. - JLIS Hounslow Contract. [40074] 25/10/1986 **CM14/02/1990**

Bhamra, Mrs R K, Lib., Guru Nanak Sikh Secondary Sch., Hayes. [10011237] 03/10/2008 **ME**

Bhandari, Mrs D, MFA, L. Asst., Paul Hamlyn L., Brit. Mus.,London. [10011650] 11/11/2008 **AF**

Bharj, Mrs J K, DipMgmt, Sen. L. Asst., Univ. of N. London, London Guildhall. [61070] 12/02/2002 **ME**

Bhattacharjee, Dr A G, PhD BSc(Econ), Dir., Aporia Ltd., London. [65170] 01/10/2005 **ME**

Bhatti, Mrs K, ACLIP, Unknown, Yeading Junior Sch., Hayes,Mddx. [10001281] 14/02/2007 **ACL17/06/2009**

Bhimani, Ms N, MA MLS MCLIP, Sch. Liaison Mgr., Learning Resources Academic Support, Middlesex Univ. [39120] 20/11/1985 **CM21/05/2003**

Bhusaraddi, Mr S, Lib., Govt. Higner Secondary Sch., India [10015086] 12/10/2009 **ME**

Bibb, Mrs A, BA MCLIP, Retired. [567] 06/01/1964 **CM01/01/1968**

Bibby, Mrs C, Inf. Asst., Northumbria Univ., Newcastle [10015075] 12/10/2009 **ME**

Bibby, Mrs J M, MA FCLIP, Life Member. [1218] 23/03/1943 **FE01/01/1966**

Bibi, Ms K, Lib. Asst., PDC Tower Hamlets Sch. Serv., London [10015083] 12/10/2009 **AF**

Bickerton, Mrs D N, BA MCLIP, Life Member. [28204] 27/08/1977 **CM05/05/1982**

Bickley, Miss A L, BA(Hons) MA MCLIP, Lib., Peter Symonds Coll., Winchester. [56794] 16/10/1998 **CM18/09/2002**

Bickley, Ms R, BA, Stud., Univ. of Sheffield [10015085] 12/10/2009 **ME**

Bicknell, Mr D J, BA MCLIP, Retired. [1226] 19/05/1967 **CM01/01/1971**

Bicknell, Mr T A, MCLIP, Life Member. [1227] 01/01/1951 **CM01/01/1955**

Bide, Ms E, BA MA (Cantab) MARCA, Asst. to the Lib., Goldsmiths Co., London. [10009897] 05/03/2010 **ME**

Bide, Mrs R A C, Learning Resources Mgr., Teddington Sch., Middlesex. [54985] 03/06/1997 **AF**

Bienek, Ms J, BA MCLIP, Sen. Lib.,Ref. & Inf., Shropshire C.C. [24878] 25/10/1975 **CM31/07/1981**

Biggins, Mr A, BSc MCLIP, L. & Inf. Serv. Mgr., Canning Hse. [1233] 18/01/1972 **CM05/12/1974**

Biggs, Miss P E, BSc DipLib MCLIP, Dep. Lib., Nat. Inst. Med. Res., London. [36331] 05/10/1983 **CM04/10/1988**

Biggs, Ms S M, BA DipLib MCLIP, Unknown. [26937] 12/01/1977 **CM16/07/1979**

Bignell, Mr A P, BA DipLib MCLIP, Hd. of Info. Serv., Herts. C.C., Hatfield [31564] 20/11/1979 **CM16/06/1982**

Bignold, Mrs H, BLib MCLIP MA, Sch. Lib., Clayesmore Prep. Sch., Blandford. [38331] 08/03/1985 **RV29/08/2008** **CM16/02/1988**

Bilgen, Mr D, MSc, Unknown. [10013510] 30/04/2009 **ME**

Bilkhu, Mrs P K, BA MCLIP, Inf. Offr., ERA Tech., Leatherhead. [29528] 28/07/1978 **CM04/06/1981**

Billing, Mrs C, MCLIP, Prison Lib., H. M. P. Haverigg, Cumbria. [6127] 01/01/1972 **CM01/12/1974**

Billingham, Ms C, BScEcon, Child. L., City & Co. of Swansea. [64069] 15/12/2004 **ME**

Billingham, Miss J A, MCLIP, Retired. [1246] 14/03/1963 **CM01/01/1967**

Billings, Ms K A, BSc MCLIP, Inf. Mgr., Becta, Coventry. [34685] 26/01/1982 **CM12/10/1984**

Billington, Mr A R, MCLIP, Life Member. [1248] 10/03/1948 **CM01/01/1963**

Billot, Miss M M, BA, Retired. [1251] 01/01/1966 **ME**

Billson, Mrs R S, BA MA, Lib. [62206] 17/03/2003 **ME**

Bilson, Mrs J, BA MCLIP, Knowledge & Business Intelligence Consultant, Inf. Hertfordshire, Univ. of Hertfordshire, Hatfield. [35673] 01/01/1983 **CM21/12/1988**

Bilton, Ms R A, BLib MA MCLIP, Dist. Lib., Borehamwood L., Herts. [39422] 24/01/1986 **CM14/11/1989**

Bimpeh-Segu, Mr A, BSc, L. Asst., Univ. Coll. London. [10001687] 06/03/2007 **ME**

Bin Ismail, Mr I, MA FCLIP, Unknown. [17093] 19/10/1970 **FE14/07/1986**

Bingham, Miss H E, BSc MSc MCLIP, L. and E-Learning Head, NHS Educ. S. Cent. [39256] 12/01/1986 **CM14/11/1990**

Bingley, Mr C H, MA HonFLA, Publisher. [31194] 30/09/1971
HFE10/09/1986
Binnie, Mrs J G, MA(Hons) DipLib, Unknown. [35583] 03/11/1982 **ME**
Binns, Miss L V, MSc MCLIP, Resource Lib., Millenium L., Bury Coll.
[62950] 21/11/2003 **CM21/03/2007**
Birbeck, Mr V P, BA(Hons) MPhil MCLIP, Inf. Specialist, European
Monitoring Cent. for Drugs & Drug Addiction. [34645] 21/01/1982
CM24/09/1997
Birch, Mrs A, BSc, Patent Info. Analyst, Port Sunlight Lab., Wirral.
[60195] 09/03/1992 **AF**
Birch, Mr J P A, MA PGDip, Legal Deposit Unit Asst., Nat. L. Scotland.
[57265] 02/02/1999 **ME**
Birch, Mrs P A, MCLIP, Lib., Cambs. C.C., Cambridge. [15968]
10/08/1970 **CM01/01/1973**
Birch, Mrs S M, MCLIP, Life Member. [1270] 17/10/1944 **CM01/01/1968**
Birch, Mrs S, MCLIP, Unwaged. [8608] 10/01/1972 **CM12/01/1976**
Birch, Mrs V H, BLib MCLIP, Lib., Herts. C.C. [34934] 29/04/1982
CM05/05/1987
Birchmore, Ms J, BA MCLIP, Dist. L. Mgr., Notts. C.C. [28261]
18/10/1977 **CM08/10/1979**
Bird, Mrs B, BEd DipLIS MCLIP, Principal L. Asst., Solihull Cent. L.
[49392] 21/10/1993 **CM21/07/1999**
Bird, Mrs E M, BSc(Hons) MCLIP, Inf. Serv. Mngr., Health Promotion
Serv., NHS Lothian, Edinburgh [50069] 21/01/1994 **CM15/05/1997**
Bird, Mrs E M, MCLIP, Life Member. [1282] 27/09/1949 **CM01/01/1953**
Bird, Miss H, Stud. [10016048] 10/02/2010 **ME**
Bird, Ms J J, MA DipLib MCLIP, Sch. L. Serv. Mgr., Sandwell MBC,
Oldbury. [41565] 28/01/1988 **CM19/06/1991**
Bird, Miss J V, BSc DipLib MCLIP, Network Serv. Mgr., NERC-Brit.
Geological Survey, Nottingham. [31728] 05/11/1979
CM19/05/1982
Bird, Ms S M, BA MSc MCLIP, Learning Resources Mgr., Henley Coll.
Coventry. [42681] 09/02/1989 **CM12/12/1991**
Bird, Miss V, MSc MCLIP, Collections Project Coordinator., Univ. of
Reading. [64362] 08/03/2005 **CM28/01/2009**
Birdi, Mrs B K, BA(Hons) MA MCLIP, Lect., Dept. of Inf. Studies, Univ.
of Sheffield. [51811] 06/07/1995 **CM08/12/2004**
Birkby, Mrs A E, BA FCLIP, Life Member. [1292] 03/10/1957
FE01/01/1962
Birkenhead, Mr G, BA(Hons) MCLIP, Patent Inf. Cent. Mgr. [10009994]
03/08/1993 **CM19/01/2000**
Birkinshaw, Miss A D, BA DipLib MCLIP, Team Leader, Piershill L.,
Edinburgh City L. [39147] 12/11/1985 **CM15/11/1988**
Birkwood, Miss K I, BA(Hons) MA(Hons), Hoyle Project Assoc., St
John's Coll., Cambridge [66130] 02/10/2006 **ME**
Birrell, Miss G, BA(Hons), Libr., Dumfries & Galloway Coll. [64359]
07/03/2005 **ME**
Birse, Ms S D, BSc(Hons) MLIM MCLIP, Community Lib., Loch Leven
Community L. [53478] 01/07/1996 **CM15/03/2000**
Birt, Mrs H T, MCLIP, Principal Lib. Child. & Young People, Stourbridge
L., Dudley MBC [10001183] 03/02/2007 **CM11/08/1976**
Birtwhistle, Mrs J M, BA(Hons) MA DipIM MCLIP, Unwaged. [55664]
07/11/1997 **CM16/05/2001**
Birtwistle, Mrs J L, BA MCLIP, L. Asst., Bucks. C.C. [27876]
12/10/1977 **CM30/04/1982**
Bishop, Mr E B S, Sen. Lib. Asst., Wellcome Trust, London. [10011839]
19/11/2008 **AF**
Bishop, Mr G B A, MCLIP, Retired. [1305] 08/11/1966 **CM14/08/1972**
Bishop, Mrs H N, Sch. L. Asst., Teesdale Sch., Barnard Castle. [65722]
06/04/2006 **AF**
Bishop, Mrs J E, Audience Devel. Offr., Darlington Bor. Council. [47134]
06/05/1992 **ME**
Bishop, Mr P J, BSc(Hons) MCLIP, Backlog Reduction Proj. Co-
ordinator, Brit. L. Boston Spa [49429] 27/10/1993 **CM24/09/1997**

Bismillah, Mr A, BA Cert Ed., L. Mgr., Healthcare L., Prospect Park
Hosp., Reading. [10015998] 10/02/2010 **ME**
Bisset, Mr D W, MCLIP FSA, Retired. [1316] 05/02/1957 **CM01/01/1961**
Bisset, Mr J M, MA, Lib.,Academic L. Serv.,UWE. [10001147]
12/01/2007 **ME**
Bithell, Miss C J, BSc MSc(Econ) MCLIP, Principal Lib., Young People's
Servs., Jersey L. [54630] 12/02/1997 **CM16/05/2001**
Bithell, Mrs C M, MCLIP, Team Lib., Leics. L. [7584] 06/01/1972
CM15/09/1975
Bitner, Mrs I K, MA MCLIP, Life Member. [16617] 15/01/1953
CM01/01/1956
Bittles, Mrs I, MA MSc, Bedford L., Royal Holloway, Univ. of London,
Egham, Surrey. [10002953] 15/03/2002 **ME**
Bittner, Miss S, Unknown. [64949] 03/10/2005 **ME**
Black, Mr A D L, LLB DipLib MCLIP, Principal Lib. /Sen. Community
Lib., L.B. of Redbridge. [40398] 22/01/1987 **CM18/11/1992**
Black, Miss A J, BA(Hons) MCLIP, Inf. Mgr., Clifford Chance, London.
[36146] 02/07/1983 **CM25/11/1987**
Black, Prof A M, BA MA DipLib PhD, Prof., Graduate Sch. of LIS, Univ.
of Illinois at Urbana-Champaign, USA. [35918] 25/02/1983 **ME**
Black, Mr D A, BSc(Hons) MSc PgDip, Lib. Asst., Wells-next-the-sea L.
[10014432] 30/07/2009 **ME**
Black, Ms E P, BA MCLIP, Team Lib. [52971] 06/02/1996 **CM17/09/2003**
Black, Dr F A, BEd MLIS PhD HonFCLIP, Dir., Sch. of L. & Inf. Studies,
Dalhousie Univ., Nova Scotia. [61294] 14/05/2002 **HFE12/12/2007**
Black, Mrs F J, BA DipEdTech DipCG(HE) MCLIP AMInstLM, Inf. Mgr.,
Career Serv. Univ. of Glasgow, Glasgow. [32779] 23/08/1980
CM18/06/1985
Black, Miss F M, BA(Hons) MCLIP, Quality Mgr., HP Ltd., Hook, Hants.
[35665] 01/01/1983 **CM01/04/2002**
Black, Mr G H, BA(Hons) MCLIP, Media Mgr., BBC, Glasgow. [58055]
21/10/1999 **CM28/10/2004**
Black, Mrs G I, MCLIP, Head of Knowledge Mgmnt., Biggart Ballie LLP,
Glasgow. [59287] 29/01/2001 **CM29/03/2004**
Black, Miss J, Catg. Asst., Nat. L. of Scotland, Edinburgh [10015239]
29/10/2009 **AF**
Black, Ms J, MCLIP, Lifelong Learning Lib., Carnegie L., Ayr.
[10006257] 26/09/2007 **CM17/09/2008**
Black, Miss K J, BA(Hons) MSc, Lib., Scottish Media Grp., Glasgow.
[59467] 03/04/2001 **ME**
Black, Mrs L C, BSc, Inf. Offr., MND Scotland, Glasgow [10015517]
09/12/2009 **ME**
Black, Ms M A, MLib MCLIP, Faculty Lib., Univ. of the W. of England,
Bristol. [1331] 18/02/1966 **CM01/01/1971**
Black, Ms M P, BLib DipLib MCLIP, Unwaged [10007041] 01/10/1987
CM24/04/1991
Black, Miss V, BA(Hons) PgDip, Stud. [10017184] 11/07/2010 **ME**
Blackbourn, Mrs S E, BLib MCLIP, Lib., Hants. C.C. [39504]
11/02/1986 **CM13/06/1990**
Blackburn, Miss A, MCLIP, Asst. Lib., Barnsley Cent. L., Barnsley Bor.
Council. [1336] 05/01/1970 **CM08/01/1974**
Blackburn, Mrs H M, BA(Hons) MCLIP Msc, L. Mgr., Alder Hey Child.,
NHS Found. Trust, Liverpool. [52755] 06/12/1995
CM18/09/2002
Blackburn, Miss K, BA(Hons), Unknown. [10015610] 17/12/2009 **ME**
Blackburn, Mrs M, BA MCLIP, Self Employed Catr., Semi Retired.
[16467] 01/01/1970 **CM22/03/1974**
Blackett, Mr D J, BA MCLIP, Strategic Mgr. Support, Lancashire Co. Lib.
& Info. Serv. [18507] 28/08/1972 **CM10/07/1975**
Blackett, Mrs S, BA(Hons) MCLIP PGCE, Asst. Lib., Co. Durham &
Tees Valley, Primary Care L., Durham. [48814] 07/06/1993
CM20/03/1996
Blackford, Miss K A, BA(Hons), Grad. Trainee, Sidney Cooper L., Univ.
for the Creative Arts, Canterbury. [10011842] 19/11/2008 **ME**

Blackhall, Mrs K, MA, Trial Search Coordinator/Inf. Specialist, London Sch. of Hygiene & Tropical Medicine, London. [52663] 16/11/1995 **ME**

Blackham, Miss S J, BSc Econs, L. Asst., S. Nottingham Coll., W. Bridgford. [10001548] 09/02/2007 **ME**

Blackhurst, Mrs J K, MA(Hons) MA MCLIP, Asst. Lib., Girton Coll., Univ. of Cambridge. [53983] 15/10/1996 **CM19/07/2000**

Blackledge, Ms P J, BSc, Learning Resource Asst., Curriculum Ctr., Univ. of Brighton [10013200] 16/04/2009 **AF**

Blackley, Mrs I, MCLIP, Inf. Delivery Coordinator, Enquiries Direct, C/O Guildford L., Surrey [22099] 29/01/1974 **CM21/09/1977**

Blackman, Mrs A J, BA(Hons) MCLIP AMICS, Lib. Users Servies Mgr., Univ. of Plymouth Devon. [1345] 16/01/1970 **CM05/01/1973**

Blackman, Mr M J R, BSc CChem MRSC MCLIP, Retired. [60791] 20/12/1988 **CM12/12/2001**

Blackmore, Mr A H, BA(Hons) MSc, Subject Lib., Bute L., Cardiff Univ. [65920] 06/07/2006 **ME**

Blackshaw, Mr L R, Resources Offr., Nottinghamshire Co. Teaching PCT, Rainworth. [43900] 15/02/1990 **ME**

Blackwell, Mrs F, MCLIP, Life Member. [1352] 01/01/1933 **CM01/01/1947**

Blagbrough, Mrs H P, BSc DipLib MCLIP, Grp. Mgr. (Job-Share), Longsight L., Manchester. [30367] 26/01/1979 **CM07/09/1982**

Blagbrough, Miss S, BA(Hons) DipILS MCLIP MSc, Res. Asst., Liverpool Hope Univ. [44535] 23/10/1990 **CM22/11/1995**

Blagden, Mr J F, MA MCLIP, Retired. [1359] 28/02/1955 **CM01/01/1958**

Blagden, Mrs P E, BA MA DipLib CertEd FCLIP, Lib. Serv. Mgr., Portsmouth Hosp. NHS Trust. [26970] 10/01/1977 **FE13/06/2007**

Blair Rains, Mrs H K, MCLIP, Life Member. [1369] 01/01/1942 **CM01/01/1948**

Blair, Mrs C L, BA(Hons) MA MCLIP, Asst. Lib., Univ. of Winchester, Winchester. [44868] 02/01/1991 **CM20/03/1996**

Blair, Ms C M, BA DipLib MCLIP, Exec. Offr., Ref. & Reader Serv., House of Commons L. [38952] 21/10/1985 **CM15/08/1989**

Blair, Miss E H, MA(Hons) MSc MCLIP, Sci. Faculty Lib., Andersonian L., Glasgow. [48083] 03/11/1992 **CM01/04/2002**

Blake, Miss B, BA(Hons) MA MSc, Inf. Offr., Norton Rose, London. [10007757] 13/11/2002 **ME**

Blake, Mr D S, BA MSc DipLib MCLIP, Unwaged [30108] 15/01/1979 **CM17/07/1984**

Blake, Mrs F M, BEd DipLib MCLIP, Housewife. [33348] 11/11/1980 **CM21/01/1983**

Blake, Mr J A, BSc DipLib DipEdTech MCLIP, Team Leader(Comm. L. Serv.), Clackmannanshire L., Alloa. [32870] 06/10/1980 **CM10/01/1983**

Blake, Mrs J E, BA MCLIP, Sen. Lib., Serv. Devel., Somerset. [29144] 20/04/1978 **CM14/05/1981**

Blake, Mr J, BA(Hons), Stud., UCL, London. [10006263] 26/09/2007 **ME**

Blake, Mrs M E, BA MCLIP, Unemployed. [28284] 07/11/1977 **CM26/10/1982**

Blake, Ms M M, BA DipInfSc FCLIP MA, Inf. Consultant, Self-employed. [57480] 06/04/1999 **FE01/04/2002**

Blake, Ms N A, MA, Unwaged [10017182] 11/07/2010 **ME**

Blake, Mrs S A, MCLIP, Lib., Oxfordshire C.C. [18042] 08/10/1972 **CM06/01/1976**

Blake, Miss S, BSc(Hons), Lib. Asst., Wellcome Trust, London. [10011837] 19/11/2008 **AF**

Blakeley, Mrs A E, BA MCLIP DMS, L. Operations Mgr., Northumberland C.C. [26035] 07/06/1976 **CM01/10/1979**

Blakeman, Ms K H, BSc DipInfSc FCLIP HonFCLIP, RBA Inf. Serv., Reading. [60146] 10/12/2001 **FE01/04/2002**

Blakeway, Ms A J, MA DipLib, Arch. & Local Studies Asst., Hampshire Record Off., Winchester. [25221] 05/01/1976 **ME**

Blakeway, Miss J, BA MCLIP, Data Support Offr., S. Lanarkshire Council, Hamilton. [21397] 01/11/1973 **CM16/06/1976**

Blakey, Miss E, BA, Unwaged. [10006479] 24/10/2007 **ME**

Blakey, Mrs N R M, BA MCLIP, Lib., The Magnet, E. Sussex. [1376] 29/09/1971 **CM28/02/1974**

Blakley, Miss F, BA, Stud., Aberystwyth Univ. [10013857] 04/06/2009 **ME**

Blanchett, Mrs H, BA(Hons) MSc MCLIP, Consultant Trainer, Netskills, Univ. of Newcastle. [48135] 11/11/1992 **CM27/11/1996**

Blandford, Miss F M, BA MCLIP, Life Member. [1383] 07/10/1948 **CM01/01/1952**

Blandford, Miss S L, MCLIP, Retired. [1384] 14/09/1949 **CM01/01/1955**

Blankson-Hemans, Ms E, BA(Hons) DipLib MCLIP, Dir., Market Devel., Dialog, London. [42324] 20/10/1988 **CM20/05/1998**

Blann, Mrs S, B. A. ACLIP, Local Studies Mgr., Jubilee L., Brighton. [10005456] 26/07/2007 **ACL03/12/2008**

Blatchford, Miss B R, MA, Stud [10006698] 21/11/2007 **ME**

Blaxter, Mrs E, BA(Hons) MA MCLIP, Acting Dep. Dir., Univ. of Strathclyde [41096] 06/10/1987 **CM16/11/1994**

Bleakley, Mrs C, MCLIP, Asst. Lib., Cheltenham Coll. [20551] 02/04/1973 **CM05/07/1976**

Bleakley, Mr S J, BA(Hons) DipLib MCLIP, Comm. Lib., P. L., Enniskillen. [38365] 01/04/1985 **CM24/04/1991**

Bleasdale, Dr C H, MA AIRT MCLIP, Retired. [1387] 03/09/1950 **CM01/01/1959**

Bleasdale, Mrs F, BA MCLIP, Learning Resources Mgr., Aquinas Sixth Form Coll., Stockport. [39701] 20/05/1986 **CM29/01/1992**

Blee, Miss E, BA, Graduate Trainee Lib., New Books, Nat. L. of Ireland, Dublin. [10016983] 16/06/2010 **ME**

Blench, Ms K L, MA, Mayfair Public Lib., Westminster, London [65176] 09/11/2005 **ME**

Blewett, Mrs C A, DipLib MCLIP, Hook Infant Sch. [32147] 16/01/1980 **CM25/04/1984**

Bley, Mr R S, BA DipLib MCLIP, Managing Dir., Ex Libris Ltd., Harefield. [41447] 01/01/1988 **CM15/09/1993**

Blinko, Mr B B, MA MCLIP, Asst. Lib., Univ. of Westminster. [48387] 17/12/1992 **CM24/07/1996**

Bliss, Miss A M, MA MCLIP, Retired. [16622] 07/10/1963 **CM01/01/1968**

Bliss, Mrs M M, MCLIP, Life Member. [1392] 11/02/1948 **CM01/01/1952**

Blom, Mr T, BA MSc, Account Mgr., SirsiDynix, Chesham. [10010366] 27/11/1990 **ME**

Blondiaux-Ding, Mrs E, MA, Systems & Acquisitioms Lib., New Coll. Nottingham / NCN [10007133] 18/01/2008 **ME**

Blood, Dr S, BSc PhD Dip Inf Sci, Lib., Roedean Sch., Brighton [10013124] 01/06/1987 **ME**

Bloom, Miss A J, BA(Hons), Reader and Inf. Serv. Lib., Wimbledon Coll. of Art, Univ. of the Arts, London [61948] 16/12/2002 **ME**

Bloom, Mrs L R, BA(Hons) MA MCLIP, Unwaged. [57303] 05/02/1999 **CM21/05/2003**

Bloom, Mr N H, BA, Dip Lib, Seeking Work. [10011280] 01/10/1992 **ME**

Bloomer, Mrs W, L. Mgr., Kingsbridge L., Devon. [10009332] 01/06/2008 **AF**

Bloomfield, Mrs G M N, BA, Unknown. [41689] 08/02/1988 **ME**

Bloomfield, Mr M A, BA MCLIP, Life Member. [1400] 03/10/1968 **CM01/01/1971**

Bloomfield, Mrs S A, BSc Dip Lib MCLIP, Info. Lib., St. Albans Cent. L., Herts. C.C. [22272] 01/03/1974 **CM13/02/1978**

Bloomfield, Ms S D, MA Cert. Ed., Learning Inf. Adviser, Sussex Coast Coll., Hastings. [10013816] 04/06/2009 **AF**

Blott, Mrs J S, MCLIP, Unemployed. [30292] 05/12/1978 **CM24/06/1983**

Blow, Miss J A, BA MCLIP, Life Member. [1404] 20/09/1954 **CM01/01/1962**

Blower, Mr A V, BA(Hons) DipHE MCLIP, Key Documents Editor (Web), MOD, London. [39212] 01/01/1986 **CM20/03/1996**

Blows, Ms S, DipIS MCLIP, Lib., Diss L., Norfolk. [46210] 10/10/1991 **CM15/03/2000**

Bloxham, Ms H A, MCLIP, L. Mgr., UKAEA, Fusion L., Oxon. [21861] 04/02/1974 **CM01/01/1978**

Bluhm, Mr R K, FCLIP, Life Member. [1410] 31/03/1955 **FE01/01/1968**

Blundell, Miss C J, BA(Hons), Customer Serv. Team Leader, Shire Hall L., Staffs. [65774] 01/05/2006 **AF**

Blundell, Mrs P M, Stud. [51528] 28/03/1995 **ME**

Blundell, Mr S R A, BA DipLib MCLIP, Lib., The Reform Club, London. [39785] 12/07/1986 **CM19/08/1992**

Blunden, Mr A J, BSc MCLIP, Employment not known. [60144] 03/01/1981 **CM03/01/1981**

Blunden, Mr D, BA(Hons) MA, Local Studies Lib., Rotherham Met. Bor. Council. [61814] 11/11/2002 **ME**

Blunt, Mr P, MSc HonFLA, Dir,-Prison Educ. Serv., Strode Coll., Street. [50581] 22/09/1994 **HFE22/09/1994**

Blysniuk, Mrs J A, BA MCLIP, Sen. Lib., Lancs. C.C. [32195] 25/01/1980 **CM17/05/1985**

Blyth, Mr J M, BA(Hons) MCLIP, Unknown. [10007705] 05/03/1974 **CM01/01/1977**

Blyth, Mrs K A, BA(Hons) MA MCLIP PGDip PSM, Serv. Mgr. Readers and Resources [55685] 04/11/1997 **CM17/01/2001**

Blyth, Ms S J, BA MSc MCLIP, Book Processor, Univ. of Edinburgh. [20222] 06/02/1973 **CM21/01/1976**

Boagey, Mr P W, MSc MCLIP, Retired. [1421] 14/01/1971 **CM25/02/1975**

Boal, Mrs C, BA MCLIP, Res. Cent. Mgr., Leith Academy, City of Edinburgh Council. [34605] 19/01/1982 **CM05/06/1986**

Boal, Miss H M, BSc(Hons) DipLIS MCLIP, Stock and Reading Lib., Bristol Cent. Lib., Bristol C.C. [43375] 16/10/1989 **CM25/01/1995**

Boanas, Mrs A E, BA MCLIP, Lib. (Bibl. Serv.), Carcroft L. H.Q., Doncaster M.B.C. [38475] 26/04/1985 **CM05/07/1988**

Boateng, Miss A K, BA MSc MCLIP, Site L. Serv. Mgr., Univ. of Westminster, London. [61482] 14/08/2002 **CM04/10/2006**

Boateng, Mrs R M, BA FCLIP, Life Member. [16625] 01/01/1961 **FE04/09/1978**

Bobeck, Ms L, LLB MS, Lib., IADT, Nevada, USA. [10015530] 09/12/2009 **ME**

Bocking, Miss M, BSc(Econ) MCLIP, Life Member. [1427] 15/03/1955 **CM01/01/1962**

Boczkowski, Mr M, BA, Stud. [10016922] 10/06/2010 **ME**

Boddington, Miss S K, BA MCLIP, Retired. [1428] 01/01/1968 **CM01/01/1970**

Boden, Mrs C, MCLIP, Welsh Materials Lib., City & Co. of Cardiff. [22803] 09/10/1974 **CM08/12/1978**

Boden, Mrs D J, BA(Hons) DipLIS MA FCLIP ILT, Dep. Dir., Inf. and Learning Serv., Univ. of Worcester. [55272] 11/09/1997 **FE17/09/2008**

Bodey, Mrs G M, BEd AALIA MCLIP, Area Lib., N. Bournemouth L. [56545] 17/08/1998 **CM10/07/2002**

Bodian, Mrs M T, BSc MCLIP, Inf. Specialist, Bre Global, Bre, Watford. [60561] 28/03/1980 **CM04/07/1986**

Bodin, Mrs P D, Enquiry Offr., Clacton L., Essex. [59960] 12/11/2001 **AF**

Boeg, Mr N P, BA MA MCLIP, Unknown. [46581] 20/11/1991 **CM25/01/1995**

Boespflug, Ms K, MA MAS, Academic Lib., Eisenbibliothek, Foundation of Georg Fischer Ltd, Schlatt, Switzerland [10006140] 11/09/2007 **ME**

Boffa, Mr J M, FCLIP, Retired, p. /t., Sch. L. Serv., Malta. [21759] 07/01/1974 **FE15/12/1981**

Bogle, Mrs A R, MA DipLib MCLIP, Lib., NHS Nat. Serv. Scotland, Health Mgmnt. L., Edinburgh. [40112] 18/10/1986 **CM11/12/1989**

Bogle, Dr K R, MA MCLIP PhD, Local Studies Offr., Midlothian Council, Loanhead. [41244] 11/10/1987 **CM15/08/1990**

Bohm, Mr J C, MA, Stud [10007225] 25/01/2008 **ME**

Boland, Ms D, Learning Asst., the Manchester Coll. [10013143] 02/04/2009 **AF**

Boler, Mrs J S, BA(Hons) MA MCLIP, L. Mgr., BPP Educ., Manchester. [46056] 13/09/1991 **CM16/11/1994**

Boles, Mrs H, PGCSLM, Asst. Lib., Bloomfield Collegiate Sch., Belfast. [10011051] 18/09/2008 **ME**

Bolsover, Mrs L, MSc, Sen. Inf. Asst., Brunel Univ., Uxbridge [64366] 14/03/2005 **ME**

Bolt, Mr R, BA, L. Super., Bethnal Green L., London. [10014381] 21/07/2009 **AF**

Bolton, Mr D C, BA(Hons) MA MCLIP, Sen. Inf. Advisor, Electronic Res., Univ. of Gloucestershire. [52331] 30/10/1995 **CM17/01/2001**

Bolton, Mrs R P, BA MCLIP, Unwaged [24417] 18/08/1975 **CM19/10/1977**

Bolton, Mrs R, BA(Hons) MLib MCLIP, Outreach Serv. Lib., Wiltshire Council. [48099] 09/11/1992 **CM24/07/1996**

Bolton, Mr T M E, Unknown. [10017064] 21/06/2010 **AF**

Bomford, Mrs H B, BA MCLIP, Sch. Lib., Westonbirt Sch., Gloucestershire [40184] 01/11/1986 **CM30/01/1991**

Bonansea-Ryan, Mrs S, BA MCLIP, Info. & Database Mgr., London Dev. Agency [21904] 24/01/1974 **CM19/12/1980**

Bond McNally, Mrs A, BA(Hons) PGDip, Reader Devel. Lib. Bury MBC [59124] 21/11/2000 **ME**

Bond, Mr A, BA(Hons) MA, Sen. Lib., Luton Bor. Council. [56537] 12/08/1998 **ME**

Bond, Mr C E, FCLIP, Life Member. [1450] 01/01/1944 **FE01/01/1954**

Bond, Mrs C, BA MCLIP, Sch. Lib., Grange Comp. Sch., Runcorn, Cheshire. [10835] 01/01/1971 **CM07/10/1974**

Bond, Mr D R, MCLIP, Retired. [1452] 29/03/1952 **CM01/01/1964**

Bond, Mr H, BA MCLIP, Sen. Lib. Music Cat., Lancs. Co. L., Preston. [1453] 05/02/1964 **CM01/01/1972**

Bond, Miss J, BA(Hons) MA, Inf. Cent. Mgr.,Mayer Brown Inter. LLP. [57385] 24/02/1999 **ME**

Bond, Mr N J, MCLIP, Retired. [1459] 01/01/1961 **CM01/01/1964**

Bond, Mrs S, MCLIP, Retired. [8104] 22/08/1965 **CM01/01/1969**

Bone, Mr J G, BSc(Econ), Asst. Lib. [58996] 18/10/2000 **ME**

Bonham, Mrs A O, BA MCLIP, Bookstart plus dev. worker, Southend-on-Sea L., Essex. [35593] 15/11/1982 **CM15/09/1993**

Boniface, Miss A C, MSc BSc, Stud., Univ. of Sheffield. [10010885] 04/09/2008 **ME**

Bonnell, Miss J L, Lib., Hadden Park High Sch., Nottingham. [64677] 25/05/2005 **ME**

Bonner, Mr A R, MA MCLIP, Life Member. [1467] 29/10/1951 **CM01/01/1955**

Bonnett, Mrs P, BA FCLIP, Asst. Editor, Health Inf. & L. Journal. [9518] 20/02/1962 **FE17/11/1999**

Bonnici, Mrs M E, BA(Hons) MA, HIVE Inf. Offr. [58410] 10/02/2000 **ME**

Bonsall, Mrs S M, BA DipLIS MCLIP, Asst. Lib., Catg., Oxfordshire C.C. [44603] 05/11/1990 **CM18/09/2002**

Boon, Mr J M, BA(Hons), MA, MSc, MPhil, Stud. / Lib. Asst. Caerphilly Lib.,Wales [10011715] 01/11/2008 **ME**

Boon, Mrs M P, Lib., Tudor Hall Sch., Banbury [10016480] 01/04/2010 **ME**

Booth, Mr A, BA DipLib MSc MCLIP, Dir. of Inf. Res., Sch. of Health & Related Res., Univ. of Sheffield. [35227] 01/10/1982 **CM30/01/1991**

Booth, Dr B K W, MA PLD FBCS FRSA FMA MCLIP, Global Ch. Tech. Offr., IPSOS, London [60805] 06/07/1989 **CM06/07/1989**

Booth, Mrs C M, MA MCLIP, Sci. Curator, Nat. L. of Scotland. [22706] 17/09/1974 **CM28/02/1977**

Booth, Ms C, Unknown. [10006912] 17/12/2007 **AF**

Booth, Mrs E R R, BA(Hons) MCLIP, Lib., Cheshire C.C., Crewe. [49843] 21/12/1993 **CM17/09/2003**

Booth, Miss J A, MCLIP, Unknown. [1482] 25/07/1967 **CM01/01/1971**

Booth, Ms P, MED BA MCLIP, Retired. [1485] 12/09/1955 **CM01/01/1962**

Booth, Miss S J, BA(Hons), Asst. Inf. Serv. Lib., Tameside L. [66110] 25/09/2006 **ME**

Booth, Ms S, LLB MSc, Knowledge & Info. Servs. Mgr., Veale
    Wasbrough Vizards, Bristol. [10001898] 19/11/2001   **ME**

Boothroyd, Mrs A, BA MA, Fundraising Res. Offr., Cambridge Univ.,
    Devel. Off. [58308] 06/01/2000   **ME**

Boothroyd, Mrs H R, BA MCLIP, Child., Young people & SLS Mgr.,
    Suffolk L. [25923] 01/04/1976   **CM21/12/1979**

Boothroyd, Miss M J, MIL MCLIP, Life Member. [1487] 15/03/1948
    CM01/01/1951

Boraston, Ms J A, MA AdvDipEd BA(Hons), Mgr., Walsall Adult &
    Comm. Coll. . Walsall [29588] 24/10/1978   **AF**

Borchgrevink, Mrs H, DipLib MCLIP, Lib., Oslo Internat. Sch., Norway.
    [26066] 20/05/1976   **CM16/02/1979**

Bord, Mrs R I, Homevist Serv. Lib., Sefton, Liverpool. [44713]
    13/11/1990   **ME**

Bordiss, Mr P J, BSc MCLIP, Retired [60149] 27/05/1969   **CM11/01/1977**

Boreham, Mrs G M, BA(Hons) MCLIP, Life Member. [1493] 12/02/1949
    CM01/01/1953

Boreland-Testa, Mrs H, BA(Hons) MA MCLIP, Public Serv. Mgr., St
    Mary's Univ. Coll. [61753] 31/10/2002   **CM07/09/2005**

Borland, Miss M C, MCLIP, Life Member. [1494] 12/01/1943
    CM01/01/1949

Bornet, Mr C P, MA DipLib MCLIP, Dep. Lib., Royal Coll. of Music,
    London. [30738] 23/04/1979   **CM08/04/1982**

Borri, Miss A, Unknown. [10014359] 17/07/2009   **ME**

Borrill, Mrs Y, BA(Hons) MA, Lib., Buckinghamshire New Univ., High
    Wycombe [62700] 09/10/2003   **ME**

Borst-Boyd, Mrs R R, BA DipLib MCLIP, Inf. Asst., Oakville P. L.,
    Oakville. [30818] 08/05/1979   **CM11/05/1981**

Borthwick, Miss A, Lib., St. John's Internat. Sch., Belgium. [10011216]
    02/10/2008   **ME**

Borthwick, Mrs F, BA(Hons) MCLIP, Sen. Support Consultant,
    SirsiDynix, Chesham. [54330] 21/11/1996   **CM20/09/2000**

Borthwick, Mrs H E, BSc MCLIP, Lib., General Register Off. for
    Scotland, Edinburgh. [43257] 13/10/1989   **CM16/07/2003**

Borymchuk, Dr O, BA, MA, DPHIL, Unknown. [10012033] 10/12/2008
    ME

Bos, Ms J, L. Asst., Bavarian Inter. Sch., Haupster, Germany.
    [10016471] 14/04/2010   **ME**

Bosanko, Ms S, BSc DipLib MCLIP, Freelance Consult., Self-employed.
    [38705] 01/10/1985   **CM04/10/1988**

Bosch, Ms A S, BSc PGDipLIS, Inf. Specialist, Ashridge Learning
    Resource Cent., Berkhamsted. [54759] 01/04/1997   **ME**

Bosdet, Mrs C C, BA(Hons) DipLib MCLIP, Position unknown, Mole
    Valley Dist. Council, Dorking. [37379] 22/07/1984   **CM20/05/1998**

Bosher, Mrs C, BA FCLIP, Retired. [20246] 01/01/1940   **FE01/01/1951**

Boskett, Miss V J, BA PgDip, Site Mgr. Lib. (Med.) [65773] 01/05/2006
    ME

Boss, Miss C E, MCLIP, Lib. -Sen. Team Leader, Stock-Reader Devel.,
    Nuneaton L., Warks. Co. L. [1500] 04/02/1971   **CM03/10/1973**

Boss, Ms L C, MA(Hons) DipLIS MCLIP, Admin. Asst.,(p/t), St. Martins
    Residential Care Ltd., Westcliff, Essex. [51344] 24/01/1995
    CM12/03/2003

Bostock, Mr A C, MCLIP, Retired. [60147] 17/12/1975   **CM01/10/1982**

Bostock, Mrs G, BA(Hons) MA MCLIP, Local Government Inf. Lib.,
    Leicester CC. [50189] 27/04/1994   **CM12/03/2003**

Boston, Mrs J, BA(Hons) MSc, Subject lib., Univ. of the W. of Scotland,
    Ayr. [63667] 12/08/2004   **ME**

Boswarthack, Ms C A, BA MCLIP, Support Serv. Mgr, L., Arch. &
    Guildhall Art Gallery, Guildhall L., London [34295] 23/10/1981
    CM26/07/1984

Boswell, Mr R C, BA(Hons), Stock Lib. /Learning Support Lib., St
    James's L., London. [63877] 11/10/2004   **ME**

Bosworth, Mr S J, MA MSc MCLIP LTCL, Lib., Bootham Sch., York.
    [64032] 02/12/2004   **CM29/08/2007**

Botterill, Mrs C A, BA(Hons) MCLIP, Lib., Elstree Sch., Reading.
    [35792] 25/01/1983   **CM10/05/1988**

Bottomley, Miss J A, BA MA, Local Studies Lib., City of Westminster
    Archive Cent., London. [10013700] 22/05/2009   **ME**

Boucher, Mrs C M, BA MPhil MA, Dep. Health Sci. Lib., L. I. C.,
    Swansea Univ. [56758] 09/10/1998   **ME**

Boughton, Mr G G, Asst. Lib., Defence Geospatial Intelligence, Middx.,
    [65915] 04/07/2006   **ME**

Boughton, Mr J E, MCLIP, Life Member. [1520] 07/01/1947
    CM01/01/1962

Boughton, Ms L C W, BA DipLib MCLIP, Freelancer. [30364]
    29/01/1979   **CM13/06/1989**

Bould, Ms C M, DipLIS, Info. Resources Asst., London S. Bank Univ.
    [41430] 04/12/1987   **ME**

Boulding, Mrs A D, Retired. [24249] 02/10/1961   **ME**

Boulton, Mr G H, BA MCLIP, L. Strategy & Performance Mgr.,
    Wandsworth Council, London. [29928] 27/10/1978   **CM31/10/1980**

Boulton, Mr K G, MA MCLIP, Inf. Systems Lib., Univ. York. [19792]
    22/11/1972   **CM22/10/1975**

Boulton, Miss M C, BA DipLib MCLIP, Lib., Royal Coll. of Veteinary
    Surgeons. [45629] 08/04/1991   **CM21/07/1993**

Boundy, Mrs N J, BA(Hons) MSc MCLIP, Custometr Serv. Mgr., Kirklees
    Met. Council, Huddersfield. [55868] 02/12/1997   **CM23/01/2002**

Bourguignon, Mrs G V, MCLIP, L. Offr., Cornish Studies L., Cornwall
    C.C., [5651] 10/09/1966   **CM01/01/1971**

Bourne, Mrs E M, MCLIP, Lib., Redcliffe Coll., Gloucester. [6794]
    15/01/1961   **CM01/01/1966**

Bourne, Mr R M, BA FCLIP, Retired. [1527] 01/08/1961   **FE18/11/1993**

Bourner, Mr B V, MA MA DipEdTech MCLIP, Lib. /Inf. Mgr., Scottish
    Government., Edinburgh. [26209] 24/08/1976   **CM14/01/1980**

Bourton, Mrs C M, MCLIP, Lib., Stock Servs., L.B. Bromley, Kent.
    [32648] 19/07/1980   **CM10/11/1982**

Boutland, Mr M T, Admin. Asst., Hertfordshire Co. Council, Hemel
    Hempstead. [59939] 08/11/2001   **ME**

Bouttell, Mr N E, BA MCLIP, Retired. [1529] 10/02/1966   **CM01/01/1969**

Bowden, Mr J, BA(Hons), L. Asst., Bristol Cent. L. [10010204]
    10/07/2008   **AF**

Bowden, Mrs J, BSc, PgC, Stud. [10006491] 07/09/2005   **ME**

Bowden, Ms K S, LLB MA PgDip, Stud. [10001087] 12/01/2007   **ME**

Bowden, Prof R G, MLS FCLIP HonFLA, Life Member. [16634]
    03/07/1961   **FE15/09/1993**

Bowe, Mrs C B, BA MCLIP, Prison Lib., HMP Gloucester, Glos. Co. L.
    [30321] 10/01/1979 **RV22/06/2007**   **CM06/08/1981**

Bowell, Mrs L M, BA(Hons) PGCE MCLIP, Area Community Mgr.,
    Leicestershire L., Loughborough. [10014081] 18/07/1980   **CM20/04/1983**

Bowen, Mr D K, BA MCLIP, Child. and Sch. Lib., Area L., Carmarthen.
    [26686] 08/11/1976   **CM30/10/1979**

Bowen, Mr D M, BA(Hons) DipInf MCLIP, L. Asst., Carmarthen L.
    [56413] 06/07/1998   **CM19/11/2008**

Bowen, Mr G P, MCLIP, Life Member. [1540] 15/09/1950 **CM01/01/1958**

Bowen, Miss L, BA DipLib MCLIP, Lib., Univ. of Westminster. [26286]
    01/10/1976   **CM12/01/1979**

Bowen, Mrs M A, BA MCLIP, Ref. Lib. (Job Share), Carmarthenshire
    C.C., Carmarthenshire P. L. [30225] 02/01/1979   **CM25/08/1981**

Bowen, Mr M, Catr., The Natural Hist. Mus., London. [10001136]
    15/10/1986   **ME**

Bowen, Ms S V, BA DipLib MCLIP, Inf. Lib., Weston Lib., Weston-super-
    Mare. [35268] 03/10/1982   **CM05/05/1987**

Bowen, Miss S, Admin. Asst. [10014593] 17/08/2009   **ME**

Bower, Mrs C, BA DipLib MCLIP, Community & Inf. Offr., N. Yorks. C.C.
    [30334] 22/01/1979   **CM29/06/1981**

Bower, Mr I A, BA, MLA MCLIP, Asst. Mgr., Res. & Performance, City L.
    & Arts Cent., Sunderland. [10013021] 10/10/1979   **CM09/10/1981**

Bower, Mrs P L, OBE BA(Hons) DipLib MCLIP, Retired. [21523] 18/10/1973 **CM11/11/1976**

Bowers Sharpe, Ms K, BA MA, Ref. Lib., Western Illinois Univ. L., USA. [56009] 16/01/1998 **ME**

Bowers, Ms G E, BA(Hons) MCLIP, Br./Community Lib., Bodden Town L., Cayman Islands L. Serv. [61599] 03/10/2002 **CM09/11/2005**

Bowers, Mrs M, M Theol MCLIP, Stud., Univ. Highlands and Islands, Stornoway. [26872] 01/01/1977 **CM18/12/1978**

Bowers, Mrs Z D, Unwaged. [37539] 03/10/1984 **ME**

Bowie, Miss J E, BA MCLIP, Serv. Devel. Mgr., Bristol [25223] 05/01/1976 **CM09/01/1978**

Bowl, Miss C L, BSc MCLIP, Inf. Off., Travers Smith, London. [39767] 01/07/1986 **CM08/03/1989**

Bowler, Miss H R, BA(Hons), Unknown. [10015604] 17/12/2009 **ME**

Bowles, Mr D H, BA(Hons) MA DipLIS MCLIP, Inf. Serv. Lib., Cent. L., Bexleyheath. [46234] 18/10/1991 **CM22/05/1996**

Bowles, Mrs J M, BA(Hons) DipIM MCLIP, Sch. L. Ser. Adviser, Calmore Sch., Hants. C.C., Southampton. [52661] 16/11/1995 **CM20/09/2000**

Bowley, Mrs M S, MCLIP, Lib. Mgr., London Bor. Bexley [25725] 23/09/1975 **CM08/12/1978**

Bowlt, Ms H, BA(Hons) MCLIP, Principal Lib. (Ref. & Inf.), Milton Keynes L. [41788] 08/04/1988 **CM22/07/1992**

Bowman, Dr J H, MA MCLIP, Retired. [24476] 08/09/1975 **CM28/09/1977**

Bowman, Mrs R C, ACLIP, L. Asst., Woodford Lodge High Sch., Winsford, Cheshire. [65877] 14/06/2006 **ACL05/10/2007**

Bowman, Mr S A, BA MA FCLIP, Dir. of Inf. Serv., Ravensbourne Coll. of Design & Communication, Chislehurst. [42457] 16/11/1988 **FE01/06/2005**

Bowring, Mr J R, BA MCLIP, Retired. [1559] 16/03/1965 **CM01/01/1969**

Bowtell, Mrs F L, MCLIP, Learning & Teaching Lib. - Techn., Open Univ., Milton Keynes [62302] 17/04/2003 **CM19/11/2008**

Bowtell, Ms R M, BA MA, Asst. Lib. [50458] 04/08/1994 **ME**

Bowtell, Ms S M, MCLIP, Retired [1561] 07/09/1964 **CM01/01/1968**

Bowyer, Ms S E, BA(Hons) DipLib MCLIP, Asst. Arch., Nat. L. of Wales, Aberystwyth. [45427] 19/02/1991 **CM20/11/2002**

Boxall, Mr J A, BA MA, Unknown. [10006939] 17/12/2007 **AF**

Boxford, Miss A J, BA(Hons) MA MCLIP, Customer Serv. Mgr., Cambs. C.C. [53942] 11/10/1996 **CM12/03/2003**

Boyce, Miss J M, MCLIP, Lib., Colston's Sch., Bristol. [1565] 19/03/1972 **CM10/11/1975**

Boyce, Mr L E, BA DipLib MCLIP, Learning Cent. Team Leader, E. Devon Coll., Tiverton. [24403] 08/08/1975 **CM31/08/1978**

Boyce, Mrs L M A, L. Asst., St. John's Sch., Leatherhead [10017137] 14/07/2010 **ME**

Boyce, Miss M, MSc, Unwaged, Seeking Work. [10014590] 18/08/2009 **ME**

Boyd, Mr A W, Unknown. [10014291] 14/07/2009 **ME**

Boyd, Mr D F, MA MCLIP, Lib., Culture & Sport, Glasgow [18269] 11/10/1972 **CM21/07/1975**

Boyd, Mr D H, MCLIP, Retired. [1569] 09/10/1965 **CM01/01/1968**

Boyd, Ms D, BA(Hons) PGDip MCLIP, Lib., Cent. L., Manchester. [43715] 06/12/1989 **CM04/10/2006**

Boyd, Miss L A, MA(Hons) DipLib MCLIP, Resource Devel. Offr., Educ. Resource Serv., N. Lanarkshire Council [10001133] 05/10/1990 **CM23/01/1993**

Boyd, Ms M A, MA MCLIP, Devel. Lib., Rothley Crossroads, Leics. [38068] 10/01/1985 **CM15/05/1989**

Boyd, Mrs M B, BA MA MCLIP, Sch. Lib., Cleveden Secondary, Glasgow. [42112] 01/10/1988 **CM18/07/1990**

Boyd, Mr N, BA(Hons) MCLIP, Asst. Lib., Customer Serv., Anglia Ruskin Univ., Chelmsford [49296] 20/10/1993 **CM18/09/2002**

Boyde, Miss S J, MA DipLib MCLIP, Retired. [1577] 14/10/1971 **CM22/12/1982**

Boydell, Ms L, BA(Hons) MA MCLIP, Sen. Knowledge Mgr., DLA Piper UK LLP, London. [49163] 08/10/1993 **CM23/07/1997**

Boyden, Mr E W J, BA(Hons), Stud. Univ of Brighton [10011713] 06/11/2008 **ME**

Boyd-Moss, Miss S A L, BSc(Hons) MA, L. Exec., House of Commons L., London. [59486] 09/04/2001 **ME**

Boyer, Mrs A, Arch., Med. Mission Sisters in Acton, London [10006928] 17/12/2007 **ME**

Boyer, Mrs B, MCLIP, Life Member. [1578] 03/10/1941 **CM01/01/1944**

Boyes, Mrs A, MCLIP, Life Member. [14339] 01/01/1950 **CM01/01/1963**

Boyes, Mrs D, BA DipLib MCLIP, Catgr, Dawson Books [35811] 17/01/1983 **CM18/02/1986**

Boyes, Mrs S M, BA, Lib. Mgr. /Lib. Asst.,Bolton Metro L. [62915] 19/11/2003 **ME**

Boylan, Mr B, MCLIP, Team Leader, Bibliographical Serv., Edinburgh City L. [10012236] 06/01/1970 **CM25/07/1974**

Boylan, Ms S, Lib., Young People's Serv., E. Lothian Council. [64445] 30/03/2005 **ME**

Boyle, Miss A M, BA(Hons) DipLib, Sen. Lib. Assist., Wandsworth. [10009899] 01/07/1989 **ME**

Boyle, Mr D N, BA(Hons) MSc, Inf. Mgr., NHS Educ. for Scotland, Glasgow. [55073] 07/07/1997 **ME**

Boyle, Ms G A, User Serv. Lib., Dudley Grp. of Hosp. NHS Tr., W. Mids. [56900] 02/11/1998 **ME**

Boyle, Mrs J V S, BA(Hons), Team Leader – Learning Res., S. Trafford Coll., Altrincham. [49324] 22/10/1993 **ME**

Boynton, Miss J, BA(Hons), Sen. Info. Specialist., Nat. Inst. for Health & Clinical Excellence., Manchester [48650] 01/04/1993 **ME**

Brabazon, Mr C R, BA DipLib MCLIP, Asst. L. & Inf. Serv. Mgr., N. Lincs. Council, Scunthorpe. [38683] 01/10/1985 **CM15/03/1989**

Bracegirdle, Mrs A A S, MA MSc MCLIP, Exams Admin. Asst., Radyr Comp. Sch., Cardiff C.C. [22718] 29/08/1974 **CM11/07/1977**

Bracher, Mrs D M, BA DipLib MCLIP, Connexions Inf. Lib., Guidance Enterprises Ltd., Wakefield. [30229] 17/12/1978 **CM01/01/1981**

Bracher, Mr T N, BA MSc DipLib MCLIP, Arch. & Loc. Studies Mgr., Wiltshire & Swindon Hist. Ctr. [46167] 07/10/1991 **CM15/09/1993**

Brack, Miss K L, MA(Hons) PgDip, Lib., Monifieth Hight Sch., Dundee. [10011819] 17/11/2008 **ME**

Brackenbury, Mrs H L, BA(Hons), Stud [10006809] 10/12/2007 **ME**

Bradbrook, Ms S L, PgDipILM, Knowledge Mngt. Proj., Knowledge Mgnt. Team, Environment Agency [52994] 13/02/1996 **ME**

Bradburn, Mrs J, MCLIP, Ref. & Inf. Offr., Halton Bor. Council. [20134] 01/01/1967 **CM14/11/1974**

Bradbury, Mr D A G, MA MCLIP, Retired. [21747] 10/01/1974 **CM12/08/1976**

Bradbury, Mrs L, BA MCLIP, Retired. [8043] 22/07/1969 **CM19/02/1974**

Braddick, Ms A C, BA(Hons) MSc, Unwaged [43963] 08/03/1990 **ME**

Braddock, Mrs C H, BLIB MCLIP, Dist. Mgr., Staffs. C.C., Leek L. [37287] 01/06/1984 **CM06/09/1988**

Bradford, Miss C, MA MCLIP, Academic Support Lib., Univ. of Warwick. [42607] 18/01/1989 **CM18/11/1992**

Bradford, Ms S E, DipLib, Inf. & Learning Mgr., Chepstow L., Monmouthshire C.C. [38223] 12/02/1985 **ME**

Bradley, Miss A, BA MCLIP, Life Member. [1594] 21/03/1950 **CM01/01/1956**

Bradley, Mrs A, BA(Hons) MA DipLib MCLIP, Retired Inf. Specialist, Foreign & Commonwealth Off. [35172] 06/12/1982 **CM18/07/1991**

Bradley, Mrs C J, MSc BA(Hons) PGCE, Unwaged [57468] 29/03/1999 **ME**

Bradley, Mr G, FCLIP, Life Member [1600] 17/02/1948 **FE01/01/1963**

Bradley, Mr I G, MCLIP, Life Member. [1602] 09/01/1962 **CM01/01/1966**

Bradley, Mr P G, BA MA MCLIP, Inf. Asst., newton Pk. L., Bath Spa Univ. Coll. [58242] 24/11/1999 **CM29/11/2006**

Bradley, Mr P W H, BA(Hons) MCLIP, Internet Consultant. [10016762] 01/11/1979 **CM01/07/1989**

Bradley, Miss S J, BSc MCLIP, Inf. Offr., Univ. UK, London. [44957] 23/01/1991 **CM01/04/1992**

Bradley, Miss S, BA, Stud., Univ. of The W. of England. [10013856] 04/06/2009 **ME**

Bradly, Mrs J E, BA MCLIP, Unknown. [4160] 02/02/1969**CM30/07/1973**

Bradnock, Mrs A M, BA DipLib MCLIP, Head of Inf. Serv., Dulwich Coll., London. [49886] 07/01/1994 **CM25/09/1996**

Bradshaw, Mrs C, BA MA MCLIP, L. Serv. Mgr., Tameside & Glossop Acute Serv., NHS Trust, Ashton-u-Lyne. [55619] 27/10/1997 **CM15/11/2000**

Bradshaw, Mrs E C, BA DipLib MCLIP, Team Lib., Reading L., Reading. [25786] 02/03/1976 **CM11/05/1979**

Bradshaw, Miss J E, BA(Hons) PGDipIS, I. S. Business Admin. Team Leader, Cancer Res., London. [49065] 01/10/1993 **ME**

Bradshaw, Mrs K, BSc(Hons) DipLIS MCLIP, Inf. Serv. Lib., Univ. of Hull, Brynmor Jones L. [47057] 08/04/1992 **CM21/05/1997**

Bradshaw, Ms W A, BA(Hons) MA, Lib., L.B. of Haringey [61557] 01/10/2002 **ME**

Bradwell, Mr A, BA CertEd DipLib MCLIP, Academic Liaison Lib., Anglia Poly. Univ., Chelmsford, Essex [43606] 09/11/1989 **CM27/07/1994**

Brady, Ms A E, BA(Hons) MCLIP, Asst. Dir., Aston Univ., Birmingham. [30298] 17/01/1979 **CM29/01/1985**

Brady, Mrs A P, BA DipLib MCLIP, Lib., M. O. D., London. [28050] 04/10/1977 **CM18/02/1980**

Brady, Mr A, Info. Offr., Weil Gotshal & Manges, London. [10001932] 22/03/2007 **ME**

Brady, Ms D, MRES BSocSc MCLIP, Lib., St. Christophers Hospice, Sydenham. [28270] 31/10/1977 **CM31/12/1979**

Brady, Mrs F I, BSc(Hons) MCLIP, Lib., Harrogate Ladies Coll. [46067] 23/09/1991 **CM23/09/1991**

Bragg, Mr J H R, MSc MCLIP, Life Member. [16640] 28/01/1965 **CM01/01/1970**

Bragg, Mrs J M, BA(Hons) MCLIP, Lib., Mace & Jones, Liverpool. [59934] 07/11/2001 **CM13/06/2007**

Bragg, Lord M, HonFLA, Hon. Fellow. [50582] 22/09/1994 **HFE22/09/1994**

Brahmbhatt, Mrs S G, BA MA MCLIP, Learning Res. Lib., Leicester Coll. [43677] 22/11/1989 **CM21/10/1992**

Brailey, Mrs H G, Stud. [65888] 27/06/2006 **ME**

Brailsford, Mrs C E A, MA, Unwaged. [39049] 31/10/1985 **ME**

Brailsford, Mrs C J, Head L. Learning Cent. Co-ord., S. Kent. Coll., Ashford. [58063] 21/10/1999 **ME**

Braim, Ms E A, BA(Hons) MA MCLIP, Unwaged. [47640] 09/10/1992 **CM24/05/1995**

Brain, Mrs M E, BA MCLIP, Lib., Dr. J. H. Burgoyne & Ptnrs., Ilkley, W. Yorks. [1622] 19/10/1971 **CM03/12/1976**

Brain, Mrs S H, BA(Hons) MScILM MCLIP, Sen. Asst. Lib., Univ. W. of England, Bristol. [58583] 04/04/2000 **CM12/03/2003**

Brall, Mr R J, BA DipLib MCLIP, Lib., Crown Prosecution Serv., London. [33559] 16/01/1981 **CM07/03/1985**

Bramall, Mrs H D, BEd DipLib BA(Hons) Hum(Open), Comm. Lib., Walsall MBC. [34421] 05/11/1981 **ME**

Bramley, Mrs A W, MCLIP, Retired. [7269] 06/01/1965 **CM01/01/1970**

Bramley, Mrs C L, BA(Hons) MSc MCLIP, Unwaged. [55484] 17/10/1997 **CM20/09/2000**

Bramwell, Mrs J F, BA(Hons) DipLib MCLIP, Community Lib., Liniclate L., Western Isles, Scotland. [12854] 21/01/1972 **CM28/08/1975**

Bramwell, Miss V, BA(Hons) MA MCLIP, Outreach Lib., Cheshire & Wirral Partnership NHS. [58907] 03/10/2000 **CM09/07/2008**

Brand, Ms S J, MA PgDP MCLIP, Sch. Lib., Notre Dame High Sch., Glasgow. [10000705] 26/10/2006 **CM10/07/2009**

Brandon, Mrs S A, ACLIP, L. Asst., Watford Cent. L. [64763] 27/06/2005 **ACL01/10/2008**

Brandreth, Mr E, FCLIP, Life Member. [1640] 27/02/1948**FE01/01/1967**

Branford, Mr M E, BA DipLib PGCE MCLIP, Head of L. & LRC, Bridgend Coll., Mid Glamorgan. [19620] 05/10/1972 **CM05/08/1974**

Branigan, Ms J, BA(Hons DipLib MCLIP, Inf. Serv. Exec., NEPIA [43177] 14/09/1989 **CM18/11/1992**

Branney, Ms C M, BA(Hons) MSc MCLIP, Inf. Specialist, Foreign & Commonwealth Off., London. [35836] 21/01/1983 **CM10/05/1988**

Branston, Mrs E M, MCLIP, Sch. Lib. (p/t.), Copthill Sch., Stamford,Lincs. [1645] 01/01/1968 **CM01/01/1971**

Brasch, Mr S, MA, D. b/ Website Mgr., Help the Hospices, London, W/end L. Mgr.,Chelmsford. [59710] 28/08/2001 **ME**

Brasier, Mrs M E, MA DipLib MCLIP, Partner, Melchior Telematics, Nottingham. [34056] 21/08/1981 **CM29/07/1986**

Brassington, Mrs J C, MCLIP, L. Serv. Mgr., Bath & N. E. Somerset Council. [10013097] 12/09/1974 **CM18/07/1977**

Brassington, Mrs M, BA MCLIP, Catalogueing Lib., Spalding Gentlemen's Soc. [1648] 17/01/1966 **CM01/01/1971**

Brathwaite, Miss T, BA(Lis) PGDip(IR) MA(ECP), Lib., Inst. of Internat. Relations [10013115] 03/04/2009 **ME**

Bratt, Miss C, Unknown. [64945] 03/10/2005 **ME**

Bravin, Mrs K B, BA MCLIP, Teacher, Brit. Sch. of Brussels, Tervuren, Belgium. [26302] 01/10/1976 **CM12/12/1979**

Bray, Miss A M, BA MCLIP, Life Member. [1654] 29/01/1955 **CM01/01/1957**

Bray, Mr C M, BLib MCLIP, Adult Lend. Serv. Mgr., Devon L. & Inf. Serv. [52273] 20/10/1995 **CM12/09/2001**

Bray, Mrs J G, BA FCLIP, Retired [1655] 19/12/1966 **FE09/09/2009**

Bray, Ms R E, BA(Hons) MA MCLIP, Sen. Clerical. Offr., Univ. of Huddersfield. [58084] 25/10/1999 **CM15/09/2004**

Brayshaw, Mrs K, BA(Hons) MA, Stud., Aberystwyth Univ. [10008804] 23/04/2008 **ME**

Brazendale, Mrs E H, MA MCLIP, Lib., Robert Gordons Coll., Aberdeen. [29315] 26/05/1978 **CM05/07/1982**

Brazier, Mrs C, MA DipLib MA, Resource Discovery, Brit. L. [34131] 08/10/1981 **ME**

Brazier, Ms H, MA MCLIP, Head, RNIB Nat. L. Serv. [32881] 06/10/1980 **CM01/12/1982**

Brazier, Ms J M, BA MCLIP, Unknown. [25549] 21/01/1976 **CM24/04/1986**

Brazil, Ms C, MLS, Content Acess Mgr, Sno-Isle L., Washington. [64014] 02/12/2004 **ME**

Breag, Mrs L R, BA(Hons) MA MCLIP, Lib., Oakham Sch. [58280] 07/12/1999 **CM15/01/2003**

Bream, Mrs C A, MA MCLIP, Aleph System Lib. /Reseaubib Mgr., European Commission, Brussels. [18223] 01/10/1972 **CM21/08/1975**

Brear, Miss C A, BA MA, User Serv. Libr., Totton Coll., Southampton. [63120] 11/02/2004 **ME**

Breckon, Mr G J, DipLib, Lib., Wirral Hosp. NHS Trust, Arrowe Park Hosp. [57787] 05/08/1999 **ME**

Breeden, Mr M F, BA(Hons), Team Lead: ICT and Local Studies, Lichfield L. [10013738] 22/05/2009 **AF**

Breeden, Miss S B, MCLIP, Life Member. [1667] 01/10/1953 **CM01/01/1966**

Bremer, Mrs P E, BA(Hons), Child. Lib., Beddow L., Portsmouth. [50281] 02/06/1994 **ME**

Bremer, Mrs R A P, MCLIP, Retired. [11495] 31/08/1963 **CM01/01/1967**

Bremner, Mr I C, BSc MCLIP, Career Break [60150] 13/06/1973 **CM01/04/1984**

Bremner, Ms J M, BA DipLib MCLIP, Serv. Dev. Mgr., Bristol L. [32882] 06/10/1980   **CM11/04/1984**

Brennan, Miss E C, Lib. /Head of Res., Beacon Comm. Coll., Crowborough. [55510] 20/10/1997   **ME**

Breslin, Mrs J, BA(Hons) MA MCLIP, Reg. Inf. Resources Mgr., Morrison & Foerster(UK) LLP. [53633] 19/08/1996   **CM10/07/2002**

Breslin, Mrs T R, MCLIP, Self employed writer. [1675] 13/10/1967   **CM31/03/1981**

Brett, Mrs A J, Unknown. [64951] 03/10/2005   **ME**

Brett, Mr C W, BSc MCLIP, Lib., L. Serv. for Educ., Leics. L. [41562] 21/01/1988   **CM18/07/1991**

Brett, Ms J, BLib MCLIP, Asst. Lib., Robinson L., Newcastle Univ. [37234] 08/05/1984   **CM08/12/1987**

Brett, Miss R, BA(Hons) MSc, Asst. Researcher, Lovells, London. [65541] 21/02/2006   **ME**

Brett, Mrs V J, Sch. Lib., Tadcaster Grammar Sch., Tadcaster. [10000777] 09/11/2006   **AF**

Brettle, Mrs A J, Res. Fellow (Inf.), Univ. of Salford, Inst. Hlth. & Soc. Care Res. [10001620] 12/11/1991   **ME**

Brevitt, Mrs B, BA(Hons) MSc MCLIP, Sen. Researcher, House of Commons L., London. [48658] 02/04/1993   **CM22/03/1995**

Brevitt, Mr J, BA MCLIP, Res. Mgr., House of Commons L., London. [60851] 12/12/2001   **CM12/12/2001**

Brewer, Mrs A, BSc DipInfSci MCLIP, Inf. Serv. Mgr., NIBSC, Herts. [10000181] 28/01/1998   **CM11/12/2001**

Brewer, Mrs H K, Business Inf. Serv. Mgr. [38432] 26/04/1985   **ME**

Brewer, Miss J A, MCLIP, Retired. [2216] 20/07/1962   **CM01/01/1966**

Brewer, Mrs M J, BA DipLib MCLIP, Secondary Sch. Lib., Doha Montessori & Brit. Sch., Doha, Qatar. [31975] 10/01/1980   **CM28/05/1982**

Brewer, Miss P M S J, MBIM MCLIP, Life Member. [1684] 03/09/1946   **CM01/01/1952**

Brewerton, Mr A W, MA DipLib FCLIP DipM ACIM, Head of Academic Serv., Univ. of Warwick. [42415] 21/10/1988   **FE20/05/1998**

Brewin, Mr P, MA MCLIP, Retired. [1689] 12/03/1969   **CM01/01/1972**

Brewis, Dr M M, PhD BA DipEdTech MCLIP, Inf. Adviser & Slide Lib., Faculty of Arts, Univ. of Brighton. [21255] 11/10/1973 **CM01/11/1976**

Brewster, Mrs A, BA MCLIP, Br. Lib., Tameside MBC [2797] 16/01/1972 **CM12/07/1976**

Brewster, Mr B P, BA(Hons) MA, Inf. Specialist, NBS, Newcastle upon Tyne. [63733] 06/09/2004   **ME**

Brewster, Ms E A, BA MA, Unknown. [10001098] 12/01/2007   **ME**

Brewster, Mrs E, MCLIP, Retired. [19888] 01/01/1973   **CM21/09/1977**

Brewty, Miss C A, BA MCLIP, L. Res. Mgr., Greig City Academy, Hornsey [38693] 01/10/1985   **CM23/03/1994**

Briant, Mrs K, Stud. [10000659] 27/10/2006   **ME**

Brice, Mrs A, BA(Hons) DipLib MCLIP, Assoc. Dir., NHS Nat. Knowledge Serv. [35248] 05/10/1982   **CM04/10/1988**

Brice, Mrs R E, BSc MA MCLIP, Unwaged. [10001320] 08/11/1996   **CM17/03/1999**

Brick, Ms C L, BA(Hons) MSc(Econ) MCLIP, Unknown. [51445] 14/02/1995   **CM13/06/2007**

Bricknell, Mrs L F, Sen. L. Asst., Glenside L., UWE, Bristol. [65875] 09/06/2006   **ME**

Briddock, Miss R M, MA MA C TEFLA MCLIP, Head Lib., Uskudar American L, Istanbul, Turkey. [31208] 16/10/1979   **CM10/11/1981**

Briddon, Mr J M, BSc PGCE MA MCLIP, Faculty Lib., Health & Social Care, Univ. of the W. of England. [53190] 25/03/1996 **CM08/12/2004**

Bridge, Mrs E H, PGDip LIS, LRC Mgr., Warblington Sch., Havant [10008412] 21/08/1987   **ME**

Bridge, Mrs L E, MCLIP, Lib. Mgr., Bolton M.B.C. [21773] 10/01/1974   **CM23/02/1977**

Bridge, Mrs M A, OBE MA MCLIP, Retired. [12544] 30/10/1971   **CM13/02/1975**

Bridgen, Mr R G, BLib MCLIP, L. & Knowledge Serv. Mgr., United Lincs. Hosp. NHS Trust. [44264] 31/07/1990   **CM13/06/2007**

Bridges, Mrs B M, MCLIP, L. Inf. Offr., Chartered Inst. of Personnel & Dev., London. [26229] 30/08/1976   **CM13/12/1978**

Bridle, Mr O, BSc MA, L. Asst., Plants Sci. L., Oxford [10006799] 13/12/2007   **ME**

Bridson, Mrs P A, MCLIP, Res. Cent. Mgr., Maricourt High Sch., Sefton M.B.C. [3285] 06/01/1969   **CM01/01/1972**

Brien, Ms A, BA MCLIP, Inf. Specialist, Health & Safety Exec.,Sheffield [10001441] 31/08/1976   **CM18/11/1978**

Brierley, Miss J, DipLib MCLIP, Lib. – Leisure L., Cent. L., Nottingham Cent. L. [37995] 01/01/1985   **CM10/11/1987**

Brierley, Mr R J, BA MA MCLIP, Lib., Derby City Council. [45444] 06/02/1991   **CM04/02/2004**

Briers, Mrs P, Learning Support, Graveney Sch., London. [10002656] 01/05/2007   **AF**

Briers, Mrs S C, BA MCLIP, Inf. and Res. Offr., W. Lancs. Disability Helpline, Skelmersdale. [30516] 29/01/1979   **CM14/09/1982**

Briggs, Mr C A, BA DipLib MCLIP, Curator F, Brit. L., Boston Spa,W. Yorks. [37455] 01/10/1984   **CM14/03/1990**

Briggs, Miss C P, BA MCLIP, Career Break. [26292] 16/10/1976   **CM21/05/1980**

Briggs, Mr J W, BSc MCLIP, Unemployed. [29592] 19/10/1978   **CM31/12/1989**

Briggs, Miss L, p. /t. Stud. /L. Asst., Leeds Metro. Univ. /Town Hall, Grimsby. [61892] 28/11/2002   **ME**

Briggs, Mr N W, BSc MA MCLIP, Managing Dir., ILIAC UK Ltd., Reading Cent. L. [60157] 01/02/1970   **CM19/12/1975**

Briggs, Miss R J, BA PGDip, Unwaged. [10006258] 26/09/2007   **ME**

Briggs, Mrs S A, ACLIP, Sch. Lib. & Inf. Mngr, Wilsthorpe Business & Enterprise Coll., Long Eaton, Derbyshire [10010326] 22/07/2008   **ACL04/03/2009**

Briggs, Miss T J, BA(Hons) MCLIP, Lib. Slough Bor. Council. Slough Cent. L. [49011] 27/08/1993   **CM20/05/1998**

Bright, Mr D J, Life Member. [1724] 10/09/1948   **ME**

Bright, Mrs J A, BA MCLIP, Serv. Devel. Lib., Dudley Ls. [10006242] 13/06/1979   **CM13/09/1984**

Bright, Mrs M, MCLIP, Sch. L. & Community Serv. Mgr., L.B. Enfield. [5111] 05/10/1971   **CM14/07/1975**

Brill, Mrs L, MCLIP, p. /t. Lib., The Pilgrims Sch. + p. /t. Lib., St. Swithin's Junior Sch., Winchester, Hants. [49051] 20/09/1993   **CM22/11/1995**

Brimlow, Miss A E, MA DipLib MCLIP, Social Inclusion Mgr., Essex C.C. L., Chelmsford. [27901] 02/10/1977   **CM28/04/1981**

Brindley, Mr G D, Asst. Coll. Lib., Tresham Inst., Kettering. [59975] 14/11/2001   **ME**

Brindley, Dame L J, MA FCLIP, Ch. Exec., Brit. L. [22909] 03/10/1974   **FE18/04/1990**

Brine, Mr A C, BA MSc MCLIP PhD, Hd. of Tech. Servs., De Montfort Univ., Leicester. [40215] 17/11/1986   **CM30/01/1991**

Brine, Mrs A M, BA DipLib MCLIP, Learning Resources Mgr, English Martyrs Sch., Leicester. [43195] 02/10/1989   **CM22/04/1992**

Brine, Dr J J, BA PhD MCLIP, Subject Lib. Health & Medicine Lancaster Univ. L. [1729] 03/01/1972   **CM04/03/1974**

Briscoe, Mr S, BA MA MSc, Lib. Asst., L. &Inf. Serv., Royal Preston Hosp. [10017281] 22/07/2010   **ME**

Briscoe, Mrs W M, MCLIP, Life Member. [1741] 19/01/1940   **CM01/01/1948**

Brisland, Mrs J E, BLS(Hons) MCLIP, Mgr., Birmingham L. Serv., Birmingham. [34734] 22/01/1982   **CM24/05/1995**

Brisley, Mr A J, BLib MCLIP, L. &. Info. Mgr., N. Somerset Council. [23614] 17/01/1975   **CM04/09/1979**

Briston, Ms H I, MSI(ARM) JD, Univ. Arch., Univ. of Oregon, USA [10013102] 26/03/2009   **ME**

Bristow, Mrs P A, MCLIP, Head of Lib. & Knowledge Serv., Beds. & Herts. Health L., Welwyn Garden City. [1746] 01/02/1961
CM01/01/1966

Britchford, Mrs H C, MCLIP, Retired. [5100] 05/09/1963 **CM12/08/1976**

Britland, Miss I, MCLIP, Life Member. [1749] 17/07/1961 **CM01/01/1967**

Britnell, Mrs L J, Lib., St. Stephens Jnr. Sch., Canterbury. [63506] 15/06/2004 **ME**

Britt, Mrs M E, DipLib DipEd MCLIP, p. /t. Law Lib., Russell Jones & Walker, London. [42130] 04/10/1988 **CM14/03/1990**

Britt, Mr R, BSc MIL MITI MCLIP, Translator, Boehringer Ingelheim Ltd., Bracknell. [60158] 18/12/1974 **CM19/07/1979**

Brittan, Miss S O, DipIM, LIC Mgr., Baker & McKenzie, London. [55203] 13/08/1997 **ME**

Brittin, Mrs M E, BA MCLIP, Life Member. [1752] 02/01/1970
CM21/08/1972

Broad, Mrs E B, MA MCLIP, KM Mgr., (Scotland), DLA Piper, Solicitors. [18132] 03/10/1972 **CM01/01/1974**

Broad, Mrs J M, BEd DipLib MCLIP, Customer Serv. & Site Liaison Mgr., Staffs. Univ., Stoke on Trent. [46530] 18/11/1991 **CM26/05/1993**

Broadbent, Miss A Y, BA MCLIP, L. Systems Offr., Oxon. Support Serv., Oxford. [27903] 17/10/1977 **CM11/02/1980**

Broadbent, Mrs E B, BA FCLIP, Life Member. [1761] 01/01/1931
FE01/01/1966

Broadbent, Miss H A, BA MCLIP, Life Member. [1762] 21/03/1971
CM22/05/1974

Broadbent, Mrs K J, BA(Hons), p. /t. Asst. Lib., The Henley Coll., Henley-on-Thames, Oxon. [44981] 24/01/1991 **ME**

Broadbent, Mrs L R, BA FCLIP, Life Member. [13945] 01/01/1957
FE01/01/1962

Broadbent, Ms R E, BTh MA, Unwaged. [10009301] 13/05/2008 **ME**

Broadbent, Mrs V M, BSc MCLIP, Retired. [16645] 13/10/1964
CM01/01/1967

Broadhead, Mrs J E, BA DipLib, L. Asst., Laban Cent., London. [53130] 01/03/1996 **ME**

Broadley, Ms R F, BA(Hons), Stud. [10011493] 22/10/2008 **ME**

Broady-Preston, Dr J E, BA MA PhD AIMgt MCLIP ILTM, Sen. Lect., Aberystwyth Univ. [35476] 13/10/1982 **CM01/04/2002**

Brock, Miss E J, BLS MCLIP, Community Lib., Norfolk L. & Inf. Serv. [27904] 07/10/1977 **CM30/04/1982**

Brock, Dr J R, BSc PhD MCLIP, Unwaged. [43785] 11/01/1990
CM01/04/2002

Brock, Miss S A, BA DipLib MA MCLIP, ISC Mgr., Kings Coll. London, The Maughan L. & ISC. [46135] 07/10/1991 **CM27/07/1994**

Brockhill, Mr K, BA MCLIP, Lib., Kirklees P. L. W. Yorks. [18308] 13/10/1972 **CM06/12/1975**

Brockhurst, Miss R J, BA(Hons), Res. & Inf. Offr., Crafts Council, London. [10010270] 17/07/2008 **ME**

Brocklebank, Mrs J, BA DipLib MIL MCLIP, Unknown. [37482] 01/10/1984 **RV** 13/12/2006 **CM19/08/1992**

Brocklehurst, Mrs M L, BSc(Hons) MA MCLIP, Unknown. [50047] 21/02/1994 **CM15/09/2004**

Brockley, Mrs J M, BA(Hons) MCLIP, Learning Resource Cent. Mgr., Newport High Sch. [64439] 30/03/2005 **CM21/11/2007**

Brodie, Miss A E, BA DipLib MCLIP, Unemployed. [32481] 23/04/1980
CM06/05/1982

Brodie, Mrs A H, MCLIP, Life Member. [1772] 19/04/1944 **CM01/01/1948**

Brodie, Mr C J, BA PgDip MCLIP, L. Serv. Mgr., N. Manchester Primary Care Trust, Chorlton. [50106] 28/03/1994 **CM07/09/2005**

Brodie, Mrs M C D, BA MCLIP, Asst. Lib., Grangemouth. [28416] 07/12/1977 **CM28/08/1981**

Brodie, Mrs M D, BA ANZLA FCLIP, Resident in New Zealand. [6958] 21/10/1970 **FE24/09/1997**

Brodin, Miss K M, BA(Hons) MSc MCLIP, Principil Lib., Culture & Sport., Glasgow. [62624] 01/10/2003 **CM21/06/2006**

Broekmann, Mrs E P, BA HDipLib MCLIP, Lib. :Child. &Young Peoples Serv., Slough L. [61522] 04/09/2002 **CM29/03/2006**

Brogarth, Ms D J, LLB (Hons) LLM DipInfoSc, Inf. Devel. Lib., Health Improvement L., NHS Stoke on Trent. [61001] 29/01/2002 **ME**

Broggi, Mrs C, BA(Hons) MCLIP, Sen. Asst. Lib., W. Sussex L. Serv. [46774] 22/01/1992 **CM22/05/1996**

Brolly, Mrs A M, BA MCLIP, Reader Devel. Lib., Herts. C.C., Bishops Stortford L. [32104] 28/01/1980 **CM25/02/1985**

Bromage, Miss S, BA(Hons) PGE M. LIT PGDip, Res. Fellow, Sapphire(Scottish Cent. for the Book), Edinburgh [10001770] 22/02/2007 **ME**

Bromley, Mr D W, JP MA FCLIP, Life Member. [1780] 03/03/1953
FE01/01/1960

Brook, Ms A E J, BA DipLib MCLIP, Sch. Lib., Highbury Grove Sch., Islington. [25494] 20/01/1976 **CM13/02/1979**

Brook, Mrs A, BA(Open), Sen. Asst. Lib., Exeter Cent. Ref. L. [10000706] 26/10/2006 **AF**

Brook, Mrs L F C, BA MCLIP, Lib., Highpoint Prison, Newmarket. [11475] 01/01/1972 **CM01/01/1974**

Brook, Mr M J, BA(Hons) DipLib MCLIP, Team Leader, Lifelong Learning, W. Berks. Council. [30369] 13/01/1979 **CM01/07/1984**

Brook, Mrs M, BA MSc, Serials Record Handling Coordinator, Brit. L. [10009463] 20/05/2008 **ME**

Brooke, Mr J D, BA, Lib. /Inf. Offr., Ian Smith Drug Ref. Lib., GMW Mental Health Trust [42408] 21/10/1988 **ME**

Brooke, Miss P E M O, MCLIP, Life Member. [1797] 08/03/1949
CM01/01/1954

Brooke, Mrs V A, BA MCLIP, Business & Collections Mgr., RHS Lindley L. [26626] 14/10/1976 **CM04/10/1978**

Brooker, Miss C, BA(Hons) MCLIP, Customer Serv. Lib., Leicestershire Council [66059] 12/09/2006 **CM07/07/2010**

Brooker, Miss D J, BA MCLIP, Online Serv. Mgr., Devon L. Serv. L. H.Q., Exeter. [32883] 06/10/1980 **CM10/08/1984**

Brooker, Mrs J C, MCLIP, Lib., Maidstone Girls Grammar Sch., Kent. [22933] 01/10/1974 **CM23/01/1978**

Brooker, Mrs J, MA BLS MCLIP, Customer Servs. Lib., Herts L. [30096] 08/12/1978 **CM10/08/1982**

Brooker, Ms M, Lib. Mgr., E. Sussex C.C. [64520] 04/05/2005 **ME**

Brookes, Mr D, BA(Hons) MCLIP, Team Lib., Wellingborough L., Northamptonshire. [62218] 19/03/2003 **CM01/02/2006**

Brookes, Mrs J J A, FCLIP, Life Member. [1803] 13/09/1948
FE01/01/1963

Brookes, Mrs J M, MA MCLIP, Nat. Coll. for Leadership of Sch. & Childrens Serv. [37661] 15/10/1984 **CM01/09/1987**

Brookes, Mrs J, BSc MA MCLIP, Community & Inf. Offr., N. Yorks. C.C. [59935] 07/11/2001 **CM10/07/2009**

Brookes, Miss K, BA(Hons) PGCE MCLIP, Acting Child. Servs. Lib., Chichester L., Chichester W. Sussex. [10001449] 14/02/2007
CM27/01/2010

Brookes, Ms L J, MSc MCLIP, Employment not known. [60159] 17/05/1977 **CM17/05/1977**

Brookes, Mrs Y M, BA(Hons) MCLIP, Electronic Res. Lib., HEFT, W. Mids. [28992] 30/01/1978 **CM01/10/1986**

Brooking, Mrs A J, BA MCLIP, Parish Administrator, Waltham Abbey Parochial Church Council. [37548] 10/10/1984 **CM18/09/1991**

Brooking, Mrs R, AUDIS, Team Lib. (Child. & Young People), Kettering L., Northants [10001795] 27/02/2007 **ME**

Brooks, Mrs C, BA FCLIP HonFCLIP, Operations Mgr., L. & Heritage Div., Derbyshire. [27143] 31/01/1977 **FE02/02/2005**

Brooks, Mr D J, MA MCLIP, Area Mgr. S. (Support), Lancs. Co. L. [24477] 29/08/1975 **CM29/08/1977**

Brooks, Miss D M, Sen. Lib., Bristol Grammar Sch. [65104] 01/11/2005
ME

Brooks, Mrs J M, BA MCLIP, Reader Devel. Mgr., Blackpool Council.
[27619] 21/06/1977 **CM21/06/1979**

Brooks, Mrs J, BA MCLIP, Hampshire SLS Lead Adviser, Waterlooville
L., Hants. C.C. [25404] 06/01/1976 **CM05/07/1978**

Brooks, Mrs L G, BA DipLib MCLIP, Lib., The Linnean Soc. Of London.
[26962] 19/01/1977 **CM21/09/1981**

Brooks, Mrs M, BA MCLIP, Knowledge Lib., Bolton Cent. L. [47068]
21/04/1992 **CM20/09/1995**

Brooks, Mr P C, BA(Hons) PGCE MA MCLIP, Head of L. Serv., Royal
Agricultural Coll., Cirencester. [51873] 21/07/1995 **CM18/09/2002**

Brooks, Ms R, BA(Hons) MA PGDip PGCE(FE), Waged [10001776]
10/02/1995 **ME**

Brooks, Ms S A, MA MCLIP, Lib., Mus. of London. [50681] 10/10/1994
CM17/05/2000

Brooks, Miss S L, BA, Lib., Inst. of Sound & Vibration Res., Univ. of
Southampton. [35231] 07/10/1982 **ME**

Brooks-Belo, Mrs P, Sch. Lib., Charles Edward Brooke Sch., London.
[10007218] 18/05/2009 **ME**

Broome, Miss A M, BA(Hons), Lib., Royal Inst. of Cornwall, Truro.
[46858] 19/02/1992 **ME**

Broome, Mr E M, OBE FCLIP HonFLA, Life Member. [1822] 27/09/1943
FE01/01/1957

Broome, Ms J, BA(Hons) MCLIP, Sales Mgr., [10008149] 09/01/1986
CM18/11/1992

Brophy, Prof P, BSc HonFCLIP FCLIP FRSA, Retired. [24063]
14/04/1975 **FE06/09/2000**

Broster, Mr T A, FCLIP, Life Member. [19469] 08/01/1954 **FE01/01/1966**

Brotchie, Mr N G T, MA DipLib MCLIP, Lib., Scottish Law Commission,
Edinburgh. [23247] 12/11/1974 **CM31/12/1979**

Brothers, Ms J, MA, Unknown. [10012807] 05/03/2009 **ME**

Brotherton, Miss J J, BA(Hons), Unknown. [10014287] 14/07/2009 **ME**

Broughton, Mrs D V, BA DipLib MA MCLIP, Asst. Lib., Gray's Inn L.
[43865] 05/02/1990 **CM25/01/1995**

Broughton, Miss N A, BA(Hons), Unknown. [10001213] 02/02/2007 **ME**

Broughton, Miss S C, BA DipLib PgCert MCLIP, Inf. Offr., W. Berks.
Council, Newbury. [30118] 11/01/1979 **CM06/07/1981**

Broughton, Ms V D, MA DipLib., Lect., Univ. Coll. London. [44471]
11/10/1990 **ME**

Brown Jensen, Dr R P, BA MA PhD, Lib., Allenbourn Middle Sch.,
Wimborne. [10001067] 12/01/2007 **AF**

Brown, Mr A A, MA(Hons) FCLIP, Retired. [1935] 01/01/1958
FE09/11/1973

Brown, Mr A D, BSc(Hons) MA MCLIP, L. Systems Liaison Offr., Bury
M.B.C. [49932] 25/01/1994 **CM18/11/1998**

Brown, Mr A E, FCLIP, Life Member. [1836] 26/02/1934 **FE01/01/1953**

Brown, Mr A G, MA DipEd FCLIP, Life Member. [18527] 19/01/1951
FE01/01/1960

Brown, Miss A J, BA MA MCLIP, Asst. Lib., Irish Mgmnt. Inst., Dublin,
Ireland. [59599] 26/06/2001 **CM15/09/2004**

Brown, Mrs A J, MCLIP, Retired. [16653] 01/01/1960 **CM01/01/1963**

Brown, Mrs A M, BA(Hons), Relief L. Asst., Chichester L. [10007996]
05/03/2003 **ME**

Brown, Mr A S, BA(Hons) MPhil MCLIP, L. Asst., Birmingham. [65160]
03/11/2005 **CM23/01/2008**

Brown, Mr A T, BA(Hons) MSc(Econ) MCLIP, Inf. Systems Lib.,
Swansea Univ., Swansea. [52957] 26/01/1996 **CM17/03/1999**

Brown, Mrs A, BA MCLIP, Dep. Learning Resources. Mgr., Harrow Coll.
[32640] 10/07/1980 **CM15/12/1983**

Brown, Ms A, CertED, L. & Inf. Asst., Min. of Defence, Chepstow.
[10010463] 19/08/2008 **AF**

Brown, Mrs A, ACLIP, p. /t. Sen. L. Asst., HMP Kirkham Prison L.
[10007753] 21/02/2008 **ACL04/03/2009**

Brown, Mrs A, BA(Hons) DipLib MCLIP, Sch. Lib., Benton Park Sch.,
Leeds. [35896] 18/02/1983 **CM02/09/1986**

Brown, Mrs B M, MA MSc MCLIP, Web Communications Offr., City of
Edinburgh Council [39195] 05/01/1986 **CM17/01/1990**

Brown, Miss C A, MA MCLIP, L. & Inf. Mgr., Collyer Bristow., London.
[49656] 23/11/1993 **CM22/09/1999**

Brown, Mrs C B, BA, L. & Learning Cent. Mgr., Abingdon & Witney Coll.
[10009339] 28/05/2008 **ME**

Brown, Ms C E, BA(Hons) MA MCLIP, Staff Devel. Mgr.,
Nottinghamshire L. Serv. [42640] 30/01/1989 **CM04/02/2004**

Brown, Miss C L, BSc, Stud., Northumbria Univ. [10015061] 09/10/2009
ME

Brown, Miss C W, BA MCLIP, Asst. Lib., Rhondda Cynon Taff C. B. C.,
Aberdare. [23503] 01/01/1975 **CM12/07/1978**

Brown, Mrs C, MA MCLIP, Inf. Offr., Intellectual Prop. Serv., Manchester
L. [1843] 14/01/1968 **CM01/01/1971**

Brown, Mrs C, Inf. Specialist, Aston Univ. [10006209] 26/09/2007 **ME**

Brown, Ms C, BA MCLIP MLib, L. Operations Mgr., L.B. of Southwark.
[24196] 19/05/1975 **CM15/11/1977**

Brown, Mr C, MCLIP, L. Serv. Mgr., Portsmouth City Council. [1845]
01/01/1969 **CM20/12/1972**

Brown, Mr D B, BA, Stud., Univ. of Sheffield. [10010660] 19/08/2008 **ME**

Brown, Mr D J, BA MA MCLIP, Retired. [1854] 26/02/1965
CM01/01/1968

Brown, Miss E J, BSc MSc MCLIP, Catr., Univ. of Aberdeen. [63100]
28/01/2004 **CM08/08/2008**

Brown, Miss E J, L. & Arch. Graduate Trainee, Magdalen Coll., Oxford.
[10015934] 28/01/2010 **ME**

Brown, Mrs F J L, BScEcon ILS MA(Hons), Liaison Lib., Veterinary
Med., Veterinary Lib., Univ. of Edinburgh. [49134] 07/10/1993 **ME**

Brown, Mr G T, MA(Hons), Stud., Strathclyde Univ. [10015277]
29/10/2009 **ME**

Brown, Mrs G, BSc DipInfSc, L. & Inf. Serv. Mgr., GE Healthcare LTD.,
Amersham. [33794] 05/03/1981 **ME**

Brown, Mr G, BA(Hons) MCLIP, Lib., Bournemouth Bor. Council.
[59128] 21/11/2000 **CM28/01/2009**

Brown, Mrs H E, BA, Stud. [10006690] 21/11/2007 **ME**

Brown, Mrs H J, Voluntary work at local Sch. [44696] 28/11/1990 **ME**

Brown, Mr I H, LLB, Legal Res. Offr. /Lib., Grampian Police, Devel &
Governance. Dept. [10001413] 18/10/1999 **ME**

Brown, Ms J A, Lib., Friends' Sch., Saffron Walden, Essex [63239]
22/03/2004 **ME**

Brown, Mrs J E, BA MCLIP, Business/Mgmt. Lib., Univ. Chester. [22904]
02/10/1974 **CM04/07/1978**

Brown, Mrs J E, BA MCLIP, Local & Naval Studies Lib., Plymouth City
Council. [25011] 05/11/1975 **CM06/12/1979**

Brown, Mrs J M, ACLIP, Prison Lib., HMP & YOI Gloucester, [10011505]
23/10/2008 **ACL30/04/2009**

Brown, Miss J O, FCLIP, Life Member. [1889] 11/10/1946 **FE01/01/1960**

Brown, Miss J R, BA(Hons), Stud., Robert Gordon Univ. [65092]
25/10/2005 **ME**

Brown, Mrs J T, BA(Hons) MCLIP, p. /t. Inf. Advisor, Univ. of Wales Inst.,
Cardiff, Cyncoed Site. [44580] 30/10/1990 **CM21/05/2003**

Brown, Mr J W, BA DipILM MCLIP, LRC Mgr., Heaton Manor Sch.,
Newcastle upon Tyne. [48906] 15/07/1993 **CM25/01/1995**

Brown, Miss J, BA(Hons) MCLIP, Res. Lib., Herts. C.C., Sch. L. Serv.
[44829] 10/12/1990 **CM23/03/1994**

Brown, Ms K B, MA(Hons) PGDip, Catg. Asst., Nat. of Scotland,
Edinburgh. [10005723] 26/07/2007 **ME**

Brown, Miss K I, BA(Hons) MCLIP, Head of L. Serv., Denton Wilde
Sapte,LLP, London [49833] 16/12/1993 **CM21/05/1997**

Brown, Miss K, ACLIP, L. Asst., Hemel Hampstead L., Herts. [66109]
01/10/2006 **ACL23/09/2009**

Brown, Mrs K, BA(Hons) MCLIP, Unknown. [56187] 01/04/1998
CM20/11/2002

Brown, Mr L S, MRSC FInstPet FRSH GrIMFMgt MI MCLIP, Retired. [60160] 05/06/1975 **CM02/05/1980**

Brown, Ms L, BA(Hons), Literacy Devel. Offr., Cent. L., Blackburn. [62904] 18/11/2003 **ME**

Brown, Mrs L, BA MCLIP, Primary Sch. Lib. [26882] 16/12/1976 **CM29/11/1979**

Brown, Ms L, MCLIP, Sen. Lib., WELB [10000755] 06/10/1973 **CM01/04/1977**

Brown, Miss M A, FCLIP, Life Member. [1906] 28/03/1957 **FE01/01/1963**

Brown, Ms M E, BSc MCLIP, Dist. Mgr., Burnley Cent. L. [23166] 07/10/1974 **CM01/03/1977**

Brown, Mr M L, MA PhD DipLib DipMgmt MCLIP, Univ. Lib., Univ. of Southampton, Hartley L. [25229] 05/01/1976 **CM01/01/1978**

Brown, Mr M P, BA(Hons) MSc, Dep. Inf. Serv. Mgr., Lazard, London. [57082] 04/12/1998 **ME**

Brown, Mr M R, BA(Hons), Document Controller, Network Rail, Birmingham. [10014144] 03/09/2003 **ME**

Brown, Miss M, MCLIP, Retired. [1900] 09/01/1968 **CM01/01/1971**

Brown, Mrs M, BA, Unknown. [10016325] 08/03/2010 **AF**

Brown, Mr N, MA, Graduate Trainee Lib. Asst., Courtauld Inst. of Art, London. [10013920] 17/06/2009 **ME**

Brown, Ms N, BEcon DipLib MCLIP, Lib., State L. of Victoria, Australia. [25010] 01/11/1975 **CM09/08/1978**

Brown, Mrs N, BA DipLib MCLIP, Reading & Learning P/T., Weymouth L., Dorset [41718] 22/02/1988 **CM27/01/1993**

Brown, Mrs N, MA, Sen. L. Asst., Newbold Coll., Binfield. [10011796] 14/11/2008 **ME**

Brown, Mr P J T, BA MCLIP, Info. & Digital Citizenship Mgr., L.B. of Enfield [19555] 21/11/1972 **CM01/07/1975**

Brown, Ms P W K, BA MA MCLIP, Asst. Yth. Serv. Mgr., Durham Learning Res., Cultural Serv. Dept. [36926] 16/01/1984 **CM05/05/1987**

Brown, Miss R J, MA BA(Hons), Dep. Coll. and Tech. Lib., RAF Coll. Cranwell, Lincolnshire [64627] 29/04/2005 **ME**

Brown, Mr R W, BA(Hons) MCLIP, Child. & Young People's Lib. Serv. Mgr., NLC [43658] 16/11/1989 **CM23/03/1994**

Brown, Mr R, FCLIP, Life Member. [1922] 01/01/1938 **FE01/01/1953**

Brown, Mrs S A, BA MCLIP, Sen. Lib., Huntingdon L., Cambridge. [24619] 07/10/1975 **CM05/04/1978**

Brown, Ms S J, BA(Hons) DipLib MCLIP, Learning Resource Cent. Mgr., St. Dunstan's Coll., London. [30308] 17/01/1979 **CM09/03/1981**

Brown, Ms S L, BA(Hons) DipLIS MCLIP, Child. Info. Offr., L.B. of Camden, London. [47641] 09/10/1992 **CM18/11/1998**

Brown, Miss S L, BA, Lib., Trinity Coll., Bristol. [35719] 21/01/1983 **ME**

Brown, Mrs S M E, MCLIP, p. /t Lib., Gray's Inn, London. [4614] 26/03/1970 **CM01/07/1974**

Brown, Miss S M, BA(Hons) DipInfMgt, Inf. Specialist, House of Commons L., London. [46101] 02/10/1991 **CM21/11/2001**

Brown, Ms S M, MCLIP, Self-employed, [22349] 09/04/1974 **CM13/07/1977**

Brown, Miss S, BA(Hons) MA MCLIP, Employment not known. [58156] 09/11/1999 **CM23/01/2002**

Brown, Miss S, MA Hons MSc MCLIP, L. & Res. Cent. Co-ordinator, Liberton High Sch., Edinburgh. [57982] 08/10/1999 **CM04/10/2006**

Brown, Mrs S, BA(Hons), Lib., Lord Wandsworth Coll., Hook. [10016304] 05/03/2010 **ME**

Brown, Miss T M, BLib MCLIP, Unwaged. [29601] 23/10/1978 **CM05/04/1985**

Brown, Mr T W B, BSc DipLib MCLIP, Sub-Lib., Univ. of the W. of Scotland [28265] 24/10/1977 **CM16/09/1980**

Brown, Mr T Y, BA, Unknown. [58170] 09/11/1999 **ME**

Brown, Mr T, Res. Cent. Mgr., N. Chadderton Sch., Oldham. [61033] 01/02/2002 **ME**

Brown, Ms V A, BA(Hons) DipLib MCLIP, Resources Lib., Bolton MBC. [44007] 05/04/1990 **CM18/11/1993**

Brown, Mrs V F G, MCLIP, Lib., Lewis & Hickey, Edinburgh. [6476] 21/03/1963 **CM01/01/1967**

Brown, Mrs V, MCLIP, Local Studies Lib., Worcs. Records Off., Worcester. [8209] 14/10/1963 **CM01/01/1970**

Browne, Mrs J H, BA, Unemployed. [61723] 29/10/2002 **ME**

Browne, Miss M A, MCLIP, Life Member. [1950] 01/01/1937 **CM01/01/1944**

Browne, Mr R K, MA FCLIP, Life Member. [1953] 17/09/1955 **FE01/01/1962**

Browne, Mrs S, LLB(Hons), L. Learning Cent. Off. [10016018] 10/02/2010 **AF**

Brownhill, Mrs H K, BA(Hons) DipIM MCLIP, Sen. Lib., Health L., York Hosp. [52241] 18/10/1995 **RV22/06/2007** **CM17/11/1999**

Browning, Mrs D A, BA DipLib MCLIP, Proj. Offr., Bath & N. E. Somerset Auth., Bath. [38008] 04/01/1985 **CM18/04/1989**

Browning, Mrs J W, SRN RMN DipLib, Volunteer Lib., Pallant House Gallery, Chichester. [45404] 01/04/1990 **ME**

Brownlee, Mrs A C, BA MCLIP, Sch. L. Resource Cent. Coordinator, Wester Hailes Educ. Cent., Edinburgh. [28622] 09/01/1978 **CM22/09/1981**

Brownlee, Mr S C, BA DipLib MCLIP, Partner, Sbworks [24329] 07/07/1975 **CM21/06/1978**

Brownlie, Mr I M, Stud. [10005360] 05/07/2007 **ME**

Browse, Mrs D A, MBA MA MCLIP, Serv. Mgr. L. Museums, Fife Council [32262] 03/03/1980 **CM28/10/1982**

Broxis, Mr P F, FCLIP, Retired/Inf. Consultancy. [1961] 24/08/1958 **FE01/01/1967**

Bruce, Mrs A M, BA(Hons), Inf. Serv. Lib., Aberdeenshire L. & Inf. Serv. [34229] 14/10/1981 **CM12/05/1987**

Bruce, Mr C J, MA DipLib MCLIP, Collections Access Mgr., Imperial War Mus., London. [35118] 19/08/1982 **CM01/09/1987**

Bruce, Mr D J L, BA MLIS, Head of Inf. & Knowledge Mgmnt., Brit. Council, London [61806] 11/11/2002 **ME**

Bruce, Mr J, MA, p. /t. Stud., Robert Gordon Univ., Aberdeen. [65394] 30/01/2006 **ME**

Bruce, Miss J, BA(Hons) MCLIP, Sch. Lib., Oriel High Sch., Crawley. [50147] 12/04/1994 **CM23/09/1998**

Bruce, Mr N M, MA DipLib FCLIP LLM, Serv. Mgr.,Culture & Leisure, Aberdeen. [29370] 26/06/1978 **FE18/09/2003**

Brumby, Mrs M S, BA(Hons), Info. Offr., MIDIRS., Bristol. [63052] 27/01/2004 **AF**

Brumhead, Mrs J M, BA(Hons) MCLIP, Pershore Lib. Mngr., Worcs. C.C., Worcester [18326] 07/10/1972 **CM09/08/1976**

Brummitt, Ms P, BA MCLIP, Lib., Burton L., Staffs. C.C. [40379] 23/01/1987 **CM21/07/1993**

Brumpton, Mrs C, MSc Econ BA(Hons), Res. & Resources Mgr., Old palace of John Whitgift Sch., Croydon [10016484] 30/07/1998 **ME**

Brumwell, Ms A D, BA(Hons) MA, Lib. /Inf. Offr., Booksplus, Kirklees Educ. Serv., Huddersfield. [10013721] 22/05/2009 **ME**

Brumwell, Ms J A, MCLIP, Dep. Dir. :Cult. & Comm. Serv., L. & Heritage, Derbys. C.C., Matlock. [21778] 09/01/1974 **CM02/07/1976**

Brunel Cohen, Mr R S, BA DCC DipLib, Unwaged. [41524] 15/01/1988 **ME**

Brunning, Ms L A, Stud., MMU, Manchester. [64871] 22/08/2005 **ME**

Brunt, Mr D, LLB Dip Lib MCLIP, Knowladge Systems Mgr., Derbyshire Co. PCT [33640] 29/01/1981 **CM01/07/1990**

Bruveris, Miss L A, BA(Hons) MA, L. and Inf. Serv. Mgr., Pictons Solicitors LLP, Luton. [56359] 12/06/1998 **ME**

Bruwer, Mrs G S, BA MCLIP, Catr., Melbourne Bus. Sch., Melbourne, Victoria, Australia. [23414] 28/01/1975 **CM20/03/1978**

Bryan, Mr A J, BA MA MCLIP, Coll. Lib., Mid-Kent Coll., gILLINGHAM [29603] 09/10/1978 **CM22/10/1980**

Bryan, Ms A, p. /t. Lib., Grp. 4 Prison Serv., HMP Altcourse, Liverpool. [46389] 31/10/1991 **ME**

Bryan, Mrs G M, BA MCLIP, Team Lib., Glos. C.C. [24038] 09/03/1975 **CM23/06/1977**

Bryan, Miss M A, MSc BA(Hons), Sen. Asst. Inf. Offr., Wolverhampton Ref. L. [60040] 03/12/2001 **ME**

Bryan, Miss S, Asst. Lib., Foreign & Commonwealth Off., London [10007382] 13/02/2008 **ME**

Bryan, Mr T D B, BA MCLIP, Interim Serv. Mgr., L.B. of Harrow. [40980] 01/10/1987 RV19/11/2008 **CM30/01/1991**

Bryant, Mrs A A, BA DIP LIB MCLIP, Childrens Lib., Dudley L. [10007194] 09/01/1976 **CM17/01/1984**

Bryant, Mrs D, Teaching Asst. /Sch. L., Hayward's Primary Sch., Crediton. [10011560] 27/10/2008 **AF**

Bryant, Mrs H M, BA(Hons) MCLIP, Grp. Mgr., Hampshire L. & Inf. Serv., Waterlooville. [43306] 17/10/1989 **CM21/10/1992**

Bryant, Miss J E, MA(Hons) MA MSc MCLIP, Inf. Specialist (Government). [63784] 06/10/2004 **CM06/05/2009**

Bryant, Mr L C, BA(Hons) MA MCLIP, Learning Res. Cent. Mgr., City of Bristol Coll., Learning Res. Cent. [54274] 12/11/1996 **CM21/03/2001**

Bryant, Miss M C, BA MA MCLIP, Catr., Coutts [43860] 05/02/1990 **CM18/11/1993**

Bryant, Mr M E N, BA DipLib DM MCLIP, Retired. [29316] 10/05/1978 **CM10/05/1980**

Bryant, Mr P, HonFLA, Sen. Res. Fellow, Cent. for Bibl. Mgmnt., Univ. of Bath. [1986] 01/02/1950 **CM01/01/1955**

Bryce, Mr A F, FSA SCOT FCLIP, Life Member. [1988] 16/02/1949 **FE01/01/1969**

Bryce, Mrs K, MCLIP, President, Andornot Consulting Inc., Vancouver, Canada. [2158] 19/01/1970 **CM01/01/1973**

Bryceland, Mrs M, MCLIP, Sen. Resource Asst., S. Leicestershire Coll. [22197] 27/02/1974 **CM25/01/1977**

Bryder, Ms J, BA(Hons) DipLIM MCLIP, LLC Mgr., Univ. of the Creative Arts, Kent. [46646] 02/12/1991 **CM15/01/2003**

Bryer, Mr L A, BA(Hons) MA, Res. & Dev. Mgr., Constructionskills., Norfolk. [63119] 11/02/2004 **ME**

Bryn Jones, Mrs L K, BSc MCLIP, Learning Cent. Asst. [4680] 26/03/1969 **CM15/08/1972**

Bryon, Mrs J, MA MCLIP, Retired [1992] 17/03/1961 **CM01/01/1966**

Bryson, Mrs A V, BA DipLib MCLIP, Head of Lib. Serv., NEELB, Ballymena. [32526] 16/05/1980 **CM27/07/1982**

Bubb, Mr A C, MA FCLIP, Life Member. [1994] 02/04/1951 **FE01/01/1957**

Bubber, Ms G, Sci. Inf. Offr. Diabetes UK [65144] 03/11/2005 **ME**

Buchan, Miss M L T, MA DipLib MCLIP, Assoc. Dir. Client Serv., Robert Gordon Univ., Aberdeen. [38549] 01/07/1985 **CM18/07/1990**

Buchanan, Mr A J, MA, Unwaged. [63793] 06/10/2004 **ME**

Buchanan, Miss A, MA(Hons) MPhil, Asst. Lib., Bath & N. E. Somerset Council, Bath. [55810] 19/11/1997 **ME**

Buchanan, Mrs C A, BA(Hons) PGDip MCLIP, Dep. Head, Lend. Serv., Glasgow Univ. L. [58161] 09/11/1999 **CM09/11/2005**

Buchanan, Mrs C M, MCLIP, Principal L. Offr, Cornwall Co. L., Truro. [21263] 03/10/1973 **CM17/10/1975**

Buchanan, Mr D S, MA MCLIP, Life Member. [1997] 14/10/1955 **CM01/01/1958**

Buchanan, Ms H V, BA, Head of Stock Maintenance, Imperial Coll., Univ. of London. [44666] 21/11/1990 **ME**

Buchanan, Miss K L, Comm. L. Mgr., St Julians Community & Learning L. [10000756] 02/12/1989 **ME**

Buchanan, Mr N T, BA(Hons) PgDip MCLIP, Campus L., Univ. of the W. of Scotland, Ayr. [57538] 21/04/1999 **CM23/01/2008**

Buchanan, Ms S, MCLIP, LRC Mgr., Chessington Community Coll., Surrey. [7212] 30/07/1970 **CM05/06/1974**

Buchholz, Ms A, Inf. Devel. Lib. /Sen. Lib. Ass., Westminster Ref. L., London [62835] 06/11/2003 **AF**

Buck, Mrs E M, BA(Hons) MA MCLIP, User Serv. Lib., Univ. Coll. Falmouth [56135] 05/03/1998 **CM01/06/2005**

Buck, Mr G W R, BSc (Hons) DipLis, Unwaged [10015689] 01/10/1985 **ME**

Buck, Mrs R G, BA(Hons) DipIM, Lib., Chantry L., ICON, Oxford [48885] 12/07/1993 **ME**

Buckerfield, Mrs S, Dep. L. Mgr., The Licensed Victuallers Sch., Ascot. [10013609] 13/05/2009 **AF**

Buckham, Mrs C H, BSc DipLib MCLIP, Inf. Asst. Napier Univ. [36725] 10/11/1983 **CM05/05/1987**

Buckland, Ms J M, BSc MSc, Lib., Dorset Co. Hosp. NHS Foundation Trust, Dorchester. [10013458] 27/04/2009 **ME**

Buckland, Mrs R M, BA(Hons), Lib., Ripley St Thomas Sch. & Inf. Offr., Univ of Cumbria, Lancaster [10015055] 09/10/2009 **ME**

Buckland, Mrs S E, BA(Hons), Website Dev. Offr., Lancaster Grammar Sch., Lancaster [10015053] 09/10/2009 **ME**

Buckle, Mr D G R, BA, Retired. [31116] 17/08/1979 **ME**

Buckle, Mrs E W, BA MCLIP, Retired. [23029] 16/10/1974 **CM09/09/1977**

Buckle, Mrs L K, BA MCLIP AI, Freelance Indexer. [32629] 06/07/1980 **CM11/12/1989**

Buckle, Mrs P, MSc MCLIP, Inf. Consultant, Corporate Memory LTD., Derby. [45601] 01/04/1991 **CM21/07/1999**

Buckley Owen, Mrs B J, CertEd BLS FRSA MCLIP, Retired. [27516] 17/05/1977 **CM22/06/1982**

Buckley Owen, Mr T K, BA DipLib MCLIP, Inf. Ind. commentator & trainer, Self-Employed. [11110] 01/01/1972 **CM26/11/1974**

Buckley, Mrs C E, BA(Hons) MCLIP, Asst. Lib., Leeds L., Leeds. [55065] 03/07/1997 **CM19/03/2008**

Buckley, Mrs C, BA(Hons) MSc(Econ) MCLIP, Lib., Shropshire C.C., Shrewsbury L. [55459] 13/10/1997 **CM10/07/2002**

Buckley, Ms J, BA(Hons) MCLIP, Community Devel. Lib., S. Tyneside P. L., S. Shields. [55677] 04/11/1997 **CM11/03/2009**

Buckley, Ms M, BA HDip DLIS ALAI, Lib., Nat. Coll. of Ireland., Dublin. [65929] 10/07/2006 **ME**

Buckman, Mrs E A, MCLIP, Life Member. [11750] 03/09/1959 **CM01/01/1969**

Bucknall, Mrs J A, BA MCLIP, L. Mgr., Oxon. C.C. [21863] 08/02/1974 **CM28/09/1978**

Budd, Mrs A M, BD DipLib MCLIP, p. /t. Sen. Asst. Lib. /Child. Lib., Harrow Council. [40037] 07/10/1986 **CM22/07/1992**

Budden, Mrs Y C, BA(Hons) MSc, Metadata Lib., Univ. of Warwick. [63292] 07/04/2004 **ME**

Buddle, Mrs J, BA(Hons), MSc, L. Mgr., BPP Coll. [62103] 17/02/2003 **AF**

Buddo, Miss N, MA PgDip, Digital Lib., Glasgow Met. Coll. [10012540] 19/02/2009 **ME**

Budgen, Mrs P M, BA MA MCLIP, Lib. Servs. Asst. Mgr. /Serv. Offr., Univ. of Birmingham. [28329] 15/11/1977 **CM19/11/1979**

Buer, Mr V B, MSc, Sen. Asst. Lib., Univ. of Educ., Kumasi, Ghana [64064] 15/12/2004 **ME**

Bugden, Ms R J, BEd DipLIS MCLIP PGDipEd(SEN), Retired. [43190] 01/10/1989 **CM23/03/1994**

Bugden, Mrs S, Visiting Lect., Univ. of Brighton. [57470] 01/04/1999 **ME**

Buick, Mrs L, BLib MCLIP, Operational Mgr., N. Ireland L. Serv., Cent. L., Ballymena. [30856] 03/05/1979 **CM31/08/1982**

Bukhari, Mrs S, Sen. L. Inf. Offr., Hendon Lib., London [10007147] 18/01/2008 **ME**

Bukumunhe, Ms L P R, BSc MA MCLIP, Sen. Lib., Luton Bor. Council, Leagrave L. [61350] 13/06/2002 **CM31/01/2007**

Bukunola, Mrs C A, MCLIP, Retired. [2031] 01/01/1970 **CM11/12/1981**

Bulay, Ms R, MLS, Electronic Servs. Lib., Gibson, Dunn & Crutcher LLP, Los Angeles, CA, USA [10013190] 27/03/2009 **ME**

Bulbrook, Mrs L, LRC Mgr., Neal Wade Community Coll., Cambridgeshire [10012231] 03/02/2009 **AF**

Buley, Mr C G, Unemployed. [42784] 08/03/1989 **ME**

Bulger, Miss S H, MA, Dep. Lib., Univ. of Winchester. [62411] 10/06/2003 **ME**

Bull, Mr E D J, DipLib, Lib., HMRC Libray, London. [37228] 23/04/1984 **ME**

Bull, Mrs E J, BA(Hons) DipInf MCLIP, Dir. of L. Serv., Queen Mary Univ., London. [48010] 02/11/1992 **CM24/05/1995**

Bull, Miss K R, BSc(Hons) MSc MCLIP, Inf. Sci., KIR Div., Imperial Coll., Hammersmith. [47479] 01/09/1992 **CM27/11/1996**

Bull, Mrs P A, MCLIP, Retired [2037] 28/03/1967 **CM01/01/1971**

Bull, Ms S J, BA DipLib MCLIP, Learning Cent. Mgr., Hammersmith and W. London Coll., L.B. Ealing. [21289] 08/10/1973 **CM11/10/1976**

Bull, Mr S T, LRC Mgr., The Gryphon Sch., Sherborne, Dorset. [10002794] 10/05/2007 **ME**

Bullas, Miss S, MSc, Coordinator: Child. & Young People's Serv., Cent. L., Halifax. [10014169] 07/07/2009 **ME**

Bullen, Mr A S, MCLIP, Life Member. [2038] 27/08/1951 **CM01/01/1960**

Bullen, Mrs J M, MCLIP, Life Member. [2039] 16/03/1942 **CM01/01/1954**

Bullen, Mr S P, MSc, Support Asst. [51211] 23/11/1994 **ME**

Bullimore, Mr A M, BA DipLib MCLIP, Asst. Lib., Univ. of Beds. [41823] 19/04/1988 **CM14/03/1990**

Bullivant, Mrs E M, MCLIP, Life Member. [2044] 10/02/1944 **CM01/01/1951**

Bulloch, Miss J, BSc DipLib MCLIP, Sen. Lib., Hutchesons' Grammar Sch., Glasgow. [48118] 09/11/1992 **CM20/11/2002**

Bulloch, Dr P A, MA PhD MCLIP, Lib., The L., Balliol Coll., Oxford. [33522] 08/01/1981 **CM14/01/1988**

Bullock, Mrs J A, MCLIP, Lib., Wilmslow L., Cheshire C.C. [24896] 20/10/1975 **CM11/09/1979**

Bullock, Miss J P, MA FCLIP, Life Member. [2047] 31/10/1940 **FE01/01/1966**

Bulman, Mrs M J, MA MCLIP, Lib., Med. Res. Council, Harwell, Didcot. [16109] 10/11/1971 **CM01/02/1975**

Bulpitt, Mr G, MA CertEd MCLIP, Dir. of Inf. Serv., Kingston Univ. [2051] 07/10/1967 **CM01/01/1971**

Bunch, Ms A J, OBE MA FCLIP FSA(Scot), Retired. [2053] 01/10/1953 **FE06/06/1973**

Bunch, Mr A J, BA(Hons) DMS MCLIP, Retired. [2054] 25/03/1957 **CM01/01/1964**

Bunch, Miss M R, MA DipLib MCLIP, Unemployed. [28267] 07/11/1977 **CM23/01/1981**

Bundy, Ms C M, BSc(Econ) MSc MCLIP, ICT Consultant. [56614] 18/09/1998 **CM21/03/2001**

Bundy, Mr D E, BA MCLIP, Retired. [2055] 14/09/1970 **CM16/10/1973**

Bunn, Miss R M, ISO, Life Member. [2058] 29/07/1960 **ME**

Bunn, Mrs V, MCLIP, Lib., Loughborough Grammar Sch., Leics. [8108] 30/01/1970 **CM30/11/1973**

Bunning, Mrs J, BA(Hons) MSc, Inf. Specialist, HM Revenue & Customs, Ipswich. [57467] 29/03/1999 **ME**

Bunt, Mrs M A, Retired. [38088] 08/01/1985 **ME**

Bunten, Miss L, MCLIP, Prison Lib., HMP Kilmarnock, Premier Prisons. [61124] 19/02/2002 **CM19/03/2008**

Bunting, Miss C A, BA(Hons) DipLib, Sen. Bibliographic Servs. Lib., Leeds Met. Univ. [39939] 02/10/1986 **ME**

Bunting, Miss K M, BLib MCLIP, Catr., Univ. of Derby. [2059] 26/10/1971 **CM03/05/1977**

Bunting, Mrs P A, MCLIP, Retired. [32378] 01/01/1957 **CM15/09/1983**

Bunton, Ms L, MA MSc, Unknown. [10015468] 15/07/2002 **ME**

Bunyan, Mrs J, BA(Hons) MA MCLIP, Sen. Asst. Lib., Kimberlin L., De Montfort Univ., Leicester. [52356] 26/10/1995 **CM19/05/1999**

Bunyan, Ms S A, MA, Recent LIS graduate. [10006342] 10/10/2007 **ME**

Burbage, Mr B E, MRSC MCLIP, Retired. [19884] 01/01/1973 **CM01/04/1976**

Burbage, Mrs D, BA(Hons), Stud., Aberystwyth Univ. [10009344] 01/06/2008 **ME**

Burbridge, Miss J M, BSc MSc, Sen. Communty Lib., Leics. City Council, [2063] 17/02/1969 **ME**

Burch, Mr B, OBE MA MCLIP, Retired. [2064] 01/01/1959 **CM01/01/1961**

Burch, Mrs G E, BA MCLIP, Lib., W. Sussex Co. Council [32941] 01/10/1980 **CM05/10/1984**

Burchett-Vass, Miss J, BSc, Unknown. [10011194] 30/09/2008 **ME**

Burden, Ms L, BA, Head of Inf. & Advisory Cent., Off. of Fair Trading. [37150] 06/03/1984 **ME**

Burford, Miss P H, ACLIP, Inf. Lib., Sandwell L., W. Bromwich. [64103] 17/01/2005 **ACL29/03/2007**

Burge, Ms S M, BA(Hons) FCLIP HonFCLIP, Employment not known. [21247] 08/10/1973 **FE23/09/1998**

Burgess, Miss A F, BA MLib DipLib MCLIP, Sch. L. Serv. Mgr., Dorset Sch. L. Serv., Blandford. [26944] 19/01/1977 **CM15/03/1979**

Burgess, Miss C, BA(Hons) MCLIP, Unwaged. [10003982] 23/05/2007 **CM27/01/2010**

Burgess, Mrs D H, p. /t. L. Asst., N. Somerset Dist. Council. [2431] 15/04/1970 **ME**

Burgess, Mrs H M, MCLIP, Life Member. [2078] 03/03/1942 **CM01/01/1946**

Burgess, Mrs L, BSc Postgrad DiP, Unwaged. [10011704] 12/11/2008 **ME**

Burgess, Miss R P, BLib MCLIP, Head of L., Arts & Heritage, Bracknell Forest Bor. Council. [27910] 04/10/1977 **CM03/08/1983**

Burgess, Ms R S, BA(Hons) PgDip MA, Asst. Lib, MOD, London. [10008211] 27/10/1992 **ME**

Burgess, Miss S C, BA(Hons) MCLIP, Head Lib., Great Western Hosp. NHS Foundation, Gt. Western Hosp. [52357] 26/10/1995 **CM16/05/2001**

Burgess, Mr S P, BA(Hons) MSc, Knowledge Mgr., W. Yorks. Probation Board, Wakefield. [57364] 17/02/1999 **ME**

Burgess, Ms S, BA MCLIP, Lib., Fed. of Master Builders, London [32400] 23/04/1980 **CM19/11/1982**

Burgess, Miss V J, BA MA MCLIP, Unwaged [39731] 04/06/1986 **CM15/09/1993**

Burgess, Mrs V M, MCLIP, Unwaged [5997] 01/01/1969 **CM01/11/1972**

Burgess, Mr V W, MCLIP, Unemployed. [2088] 06/03/1967 **CM15/12/1972**

Burgum, Miss S J, BA DipLib MCLIP, Sch. Lib., Erith Sch., Kent. [34233] 15/10/1981 **CM18/07/1990**

Buri, Mrs R E, BA MCLIP, Self-employed, Abstracting Journals. [31253] 04/10/1979 **CM30/09/1985**

Burioni, Mr L, Managing Dir.,E. S. Burioni Ricerche Bibliografiche, Genoa, Italy [59990] 16/11/2001 **ME**

Burke, Mrs J M, BEd(Hons) MA, Asst. i/c LLC, E. Area, ESCC, Lewes. [62262] 04/04/2003 **AF**

Burkett, Ms L M, BA(Hons) MA, Lib. GCHQ, Glos. [65736] 13/04/2006 **ME**

Burlton, Mrs V, Life Member. [2102] 01/01/1938 **ME**

Burmajster, Mrs A, MA MCLIP, Head of Inf. & Advisory Serv., Inst. of Dir., London. [51803] 04/07/1995 **CM18/03/1998**

Burman, Mrs J, BSc(Econ) MCLIP, Lib., Kirkby in Ashfield L. [65377] 09/01/2006 **CM21/03/2007**

Burnett, Mr A D, MA FIAP MCLIP, Retired. [2109] 15/08/1959 **CM01/01/1964**

Burnett, Miss A, L. Asst., Robert Gordon Univ., Aberdeen. [64761] 30/06/2005 **AF**

Burnett, Ms C F, BA MPhil MCLIP, Clinical Lib., Queen's Hosp., Romford [37318] 02/07/1984 **CM04/10/1988**

Burnett, Mrs J C, BA MCLIP, Info. & People's Network Lib., Herts. C.C., Bishops Stortford L. [28286] 06/11/1977　　**CM09/01/1980**

Burnett, Mrs S, Unknown. [10013987] 15/06/2009　　**AF**

Burns, Mr D J, BA(Hons) DipILS MCLIP, Info. Dev. Offr., NCPO, Univ. of Strathclyde [53960] 16/10/1996　　**CM06/04/2005**

Burns, Mrs E, Lib., Macmillan Academy [65502] 10/02/2006　　**AF**

Burns, Mr J E, BA(Hons) MSc(Econ) MCLIP, Principal Lib. Operations, Southern Area, W. Sussex CC. [52799] 15/12/1995　**CM19/01/2000**

Burns, Mrs J M, MA DipLib MCLIP, Grp. Lib., Newton Stewart L., Dumfries & Galloway Council. [37466] 01/10/1984　　**CM06/09/1988**

Burns, Mrs M, BA(Hons) MCLIP, Asst. Local Stud. Lib., Tameside Local Stud. & Arch. [62345] 06/05/2003　　**CM19/11/2008**

Burns, Ms M, BA PGDipILS MCLIP, Primary Lib., Falkirk L. Serv., Falkirk [62357] 09/05/2003　　**CM09/11/2005**

Burns, Ms N, LLB MSc(Econ), Sen. Mgr. : L. Serv. & Personnel., The Bar L., Belfast. [57565] 05/05/1999　　**ME**

Burns, Mr P, MCLIP, Area Mgr., L. Learning & Culture, Durham C.C. [2125] 28/01/1967　　**CM01/01/1972**

Burns, Ms R A, BA DipLib MCLIP, Lib., Trinity Grammar Sch. Melbourne. [26909] 10/01/1977　　**CM17/01/1979**

Burns, Mrs R O, CPU Co-ord., Univ. of Wolverhampton. [44216] 11/07/1990　　**ME**

Burnside, Mr D W, MA DipLib MCLIP, Sen. Lib., Inf. Serv., Oxfordshire C.C. [27912] 20/10/1977　　**CM21/01/1980**

Burnside, Mrs E L, BA(Hons) HAAD, Families and Out of Sch. Serv. Lib., Hook and Chessington L., Chessington. [10000766] 14/11/2006　　**ME**

Burns-Price, Mrs S, ACLIP, Sch. Lib., Colyton Grammar Sch., Devon. [64400] 14/03/2005　　**ACL05/10/2007**

Burrell, Mrs J W, BA DipLib MCLIP, Res. & Learner Support Offr., Liverpool John Moores Univ. [40900] 16/08/1987　**CM27/01/1993**

Burrell, Mrs K A, MCLIP, Retired. [23980] 01/01/1958　**CM01/01/1964**

Burrell, Miss P J, ACLIP, L. and Inf. Asst., Huish Episcopi Sch., Langport [10008013] 03/03/2008　　**ACL16/06/2010**

Burridge, Miss E, BA MCLIP, Sen. Lib., Inf Coordinator, L. Support Unit, Highland Council [26300] 18/10/1976　　**CM10/07/1981**

Burrin, Mrs M, BA(Hons), Inf. Adv., EMB Ltd, Lincoln. [10015285] 30/10/2009　　**ME**

Burrington, Dr G A, OBE MA FCLIP, Life Member. [2139] 01/01/1962　　**FE01/01/1965**

Burrough, Mrs P J, MCLIP, Life Member. [6591] 15/08/1949　　**CM01/01/1967**

Burroughs, Miss L H, BSc(Hons) MSc(Econ) MCLIP, Faculty Liaison Lib., Canterbury Christchurch Univ. [54364] 25/11/1996　　**CM21/07/1999**

Burrows, Mrs C, MCLIP, Retired [4897] 09/01/1967　**CM01/01/1970**

Burrows, Mr J B S, L. Asst., Music Dept. L., Cambridge Univ. L. [42878] 06/04/1989　　**ME**

Burrows, Mr K, BA DipLib MCLIP, Sen. Ref. Lib., Lancs. C.C., Accrington. [37967] 01/01/1985　　**CM15/02/1989**

Burry, Mrs K M, BA MCLIP, Inf. Asst., Nat. Union of Teachers, London [38356] 25/03/1985　　**CM27/03/1991**

Burscheidt, Ms L, L. Asst., Univ. of Essex. /MLIS stud., HU Berlin [10010125] 04/07/2008　　**ME**

Burslem, Mrs J K, BA MCLIP, Pennine Acute NHS Trust [24378] 18/07/1975　　**CM16/08/1977**

Burt, Mrs A C, MA DipLib MCLIP, Teaching Asst., Northumberland C.C. [29485] 31/07/1978　　**CM08/04/1981**

Burt, Mr A J, Lib., Grays L., Essex. [57617] 18/05/1999　　**ME**

Burt, Miss J H, Life Member. [2150] 16/12/1946　　**ME**

Burton, Ms A J, Asst. Lib., Rastrick High Sch., W. yorkshire [10012561] 24/02/2009　　**AF**

Burton, Sir C A, Kt OBE BA MSc MCLIP FRSA JP, Life Member. [16672] 18/01/1951　　**CM01/01/1954**

Burton, Mrs J E, BA MCLIP, Clerical Offr., Connexions, Derbyshire [23483] 01/01/1975　　**CM01/09/1978**

Burton, Miss J M, BLib MCLIP, L. Devel. Mgr., Bath & N. E. Somerset, Bath. [34175] 07/10/1981　　**CM10/06/1986**

Burton, Mr J R, BA DipLib MCLIP, Quality & Standards Mgr., Thurrock L. [65044] 30/10/1979　　**CM20/01/1982**

Burton, Mr M E, BA DipLib MCLIP, Lib., Arts & Inf. Mgr., S. Gloucestershire C.C. [34744] 16/02/1982　　**CM18/06/1985**

Burton, Mr M, L. Support Analyst, Serials Solutions, Cambridge. [10016651] 23/04/2010　　**AF**

Burton, Miss S A, BA Hons, Sen. L. Asst., Judge Business Sch., Cambridge. [10016015] 10/02/2010　　**AF**

Burtonshaw, Miss B E, MCLIP, Life Member. [2169] 01/02/1948　　**CM01/01/1963**

Burtrand, Mrs D C, MCLIP, Serv. Devel. Offr., Chelmsforrd Cent. L., Essex C.C. [1851] 12/10/1970　　**CM17/07/1973**

Bury, Mr N J, BA MCLIP, Dist. Mgr., Rossendale L., Lancs. [31795] 02/01/1980　　**CM30/11/1983**

Bury, Mr R S, MA MCLIP, Employment not known. [39098] 05/11/1985　　**CM05/07/1988**

Bury, Dr S J, MA MA PhD DipLib FCLIP, Head of Euro. & American Collections Brit. L., London. [24407] 30/07/1975　**FE18/04/1989**

Busby, Mrs J A, BA DipLib MCLIP, Prison Lib., HMP Usk, Monmouthshire L. [28010] 11/10/1977　　**CM11/08/1980**

Busby, Mr N, Asst. Lib., St. Deiniol's L., Hawarden. [10006111] 17/06/2009　　**AF**

Busby, Mr R J, FCLIP FSA, Retired. [2174] 30/01/1962　**FE29/07/1974**

Busby, Miss S, BA MCLIP, Bibl. Serv. Lib., E. Dunbartonshire Council. [2175] 01/01/1972　　**CM02/07/1974**

Bush, Miss A G, BA, Stud., Univ. of Sheffield [10015586] 17/12/2009　　**ME**

Bushell, Mr J M, BA(Hons) MA, Sen. Info. Exec., Inst. of Chartered Accountants L., London. [50207] 04/05/1994　　**ME**

Bushnell, Mr I W, BA MCLIP, Dep. Ch. Lib., Off. for Nat. Stats., Newport. [2182] 01/01/1971　　**CM01/01/1974**

Bussey, Miss J, BA, Inf. Studies Postgrad. Stud., Univ. of Brighton [10013715] 22/05/2009　　**ME**

Bussey, Mrs S J M, L. Res. Mgr., Derby High Sch. [56317] 13/05/1998　　**ME**

Bussey, Mrs S M, BA MCLIP, Retired. [2183] 07/02/1963　**CM01/01/1967**

Butchart, Mr I C, BA MSc MCLIP PGCE, Retired [2185] 01/01/1969　　**CM01/01/1971**

Butcher, Miss A L, Music Catr., BBC Inf. & Arch., London. [38936] 17/10/1985　　**ME**

Butcher, Mrs D P E, MCLIP, Retired. [2186] 01/01/1936　**CM01/01/1941**

Butcher, Mr D R, BA DipLib MCLIP, Lect., Sch. of Inf. Stud., Univ. of Cent. England in Birmingham. [2187] 15/01/1965　　**CM01/01/1967**

Butcher, Mrs D, MCLIP, Freelance Registered Indexer. [1035] 21/07/1969　　**CM31/08/1973**

Butcher, Miss F D, BA MCLIP, Lib., Renfrew Div. Sch. L. Serv. [29606] 15/10/1978　　**CM16/02/1983**

Butcher, Mr J R, BSc(Hons) MSc(Econ) MCLIP, Res. Lib., (Catg. & Acquisitions), Plymouth Cent. L. [56098] 12/02/1998　**CM18/09/2002**

Butcher, Miss K L, MA, Grad. Lib. Trainee, St. Hilda's Coll., Oxford [10012946] 17/03/2009　　**ME**

Butcher, Ms S, community Lib., Medway L. [10002772] 10/05/2007　**ME**

Butchers, Miss T A M, BA(Hons) MA MCLIP, Div. Lib., Stratford-upon-Avon L., S. Warks. [50588] 26/09/1994　　**CM22/09/1999**

Butler, Ms A, BA(Hons) DipILM MCLIP, Asst. Learning Resource Cent. Mgr., Castle Coll., Sheffield. [52457] 02/11/1995　　**CM20/01/1999**

Butler, Miss A, MA MCLIP, Lib., Manches Solicitors, Oxford. [2194] 14/02/1964　　**CM01/01/1968**

Butler, Mrs C E, MCLIP, Retired. [32233] 01/01/1960　**CM28/08/1981**

Butler, Miss E, BA MA MCLIP, Asst. Subject Adviser, Univ. of Derby. [59194] 13/12/2000   **CM07/09/2005**

Butler, Miss F J, Book Selection Specialist, Holt Jackson, Lancashire. [10001333] 06/02/2007   **ME**

Butler, Mrs H S, BA MCLIP, Lib., Gloucestershire C.C., St. Peter's High Sch. [2198] 11/01/1971   **CM02/03/1973**

Butler, Ms H, BA(Hons), Dep. Counter Serv. Super., KCL, London. [10011538] 30/10/2008   **AF**

Butler, Ms J C, BA DipLib MCLIP, Finance Info. & MRD Mgr., Unilever plc, London. [35197] 01/10/1982   **CM01/09/1987**

Butler, Mrs J, BSc, Resource Cent. Asst., Sch. of the Bult Environment, Edinburgh [10014814] 16/09/2009   **AF**

Butler, Miss J, Stud. [10006299] 10/10/2007   **ME**

Butler, Miss K, BA(Hons), Unknown, S. Kent Coll., Kent. [65778] 27/04/2006   **AF**

Butler, Miss K, BA(Hons), Unwaged. [10006214] 26/09/2007   **ME**

Butler, Mrs L L, BA MBA MCLIP, Hd. of Lib. Serv., Birmingham C.C. [24667] 18/10/1975   **CM16/12/1977**

Butler, Mrs L M, BA MCLIP, Interlibrary Loans Lib., Harold Cohen L., Liverpool. [28234] 26/10/1977   **CM10/08/1982**

Butler, Miss M L, BA FCLIP, Retired. [2206] 08/03/1935   **FE01/01/1946**

Butler, Mr M, BA, Stud., Manchester Met. Univ. [10016084] 16/02/2010   **ME**

Butler, Miss N J, BA, Stud [10007563] 13/02/2008   **ME**

Butler, Miss P J, MCLIP, Bibl. Serv. Mgr., L.B. of Barnet. [2208] 08/10/1969   **CM20/08/1973**

Butler, Mrs P, BA(Hons) Humanities/Lit., Lib., Coopers Co. & Coborn Sch., Upminster Essex [10001633] 20/12/1999   **ME**

Butler, Miss S C, BA(Hons) MA MCLIP, Lib., Royal Pharm. Soc., London. [49188] 11/10/1993   **CM19/03/1997**

Butler, Miss S, Public Info. Asst., Cumbria C.C., Adultand Cultural Servs. [64632] 27/04/2005   **ME**

Butler, Mr T, BA(Hons), L. Operations Mgr., Croydon Coll., Surrey. [56028] 28/01/1998   **ME**

Butler, Miss W F, MA DipLib MCLIP, Lib., Newcastle under Lyme Sch. [27308] 01/03/1977   **CM11/05/1979**

Butt, Mrs H M, BA MCLIP, Unwaged. [4121] 18/01/1971 **CM01/03/1976**

Butt, Mrs L, BA MA MCLIP, Sen. Asst. Lib., De Montfort Univ., Leicester. [51531] 01/04/1995   **CM21/11/2001**

Butterfield, Mr D, BA FCLIP, Retired. [2218] 29/07/1952 **FE01/01/1957**

Butterwick, Mr N B, BSc MSc MLS MCLIP, Assoc. Dean of Stud. Support & Info. Servs., Franklin Coll., Switzerland [28271] 31/10/1977   **CM12/05/1980**

Butterworth, Mrs J M, BA MCLIP, Knowledge TL, Bolton M.B.C., Cent. L. [20508] 14/01/1973   **CM08/07/1977**

Butterworth, Mrs S, BA MCLIP, Freelance Indexer. [15752] 21/01/1969   **CM03/12/1976**

Buttle, Mrs F A, BSc(Hons) MSc MCLIP, Hon. Lib. (Volunteer)., Child. English. L., Stuttgart, Germany. [55649] 31/10/1997 **CM20/11/2002**

Buttolph, Miss M E, MCLIP, Resources Lib., Arnold L. [19634] 25/10/1972   **CM09/01/1976**

Button, Mr A J, BA MCLIP, Virtual Lib. Strategy Offr. Warwickshire Co. L. [40275] 09/12/1986   **CM14/11/1990**

Button, Mrs A, BA(Hons), Outreach & E-Resources Lib., Heart of England NHS Foundation Trust, Heartlands Hosp. [49389] 21/10/1993   **ME**

Button, Miss H J, DipLib MCLIP, Reader Serv. Lib.,City Coll. Plymouth [33556] 19/01/1981   **CM16/05/1985**

Butts, Miss S C, MA DipLib MCLIP, Snr. Lib., Moray Council L., Moray [33836] 24/03/1981   **CM20/01/1986**

Buxton, Dr A B, MA PhD FCLIP, Inf. Systems Mgr., Inst. of Devel. Studies, Univ. of Sussex. [60164] 23/02/1977   **FE09/04/1991**

Buxton, Mrs C N, MCLIP, Sch. Lib., Highland Council, Grantown Grammar Sch. [36437] 12/10/1983   **CM27/01/2010**

Buxton, Mrs E, BA DipLib MCLIP, Unemployed. [35688] 24/01/1983   **CM13/05/1986**

Buxton, Mrs H L, BA, Lib. Asst., Irwin Mitchell, Sheffield [10015713] 15/01/2010   **AF**

Byatt, Ms D R, BSc DipLib MCLIP, Academic Liaison Lib., Univ. of Southampton. [31761] 29/11/1979   **CM10/01/1983**

Byatt, Mrs R, BSc (Hons), Sen. Hist. Cent. Asst., Coventry Heritage & Arts Trust Ltd. [10010884] 01/04/1995   **ME**

Bye, Mr D J, BA(Hons) MCLIP, Inf. Adviser, Sheffield Hallam Univ. [43415] 18/10/1989   **CM23/06/2004**

Bye, Mr G F C, BA MCLIP, Front Off. Tech. Team Leader, L.B. of Newham [24617] 01/10/1975   **CM25/06/1979**

Byers, Mrs F M, Asst. Lib. (Chil. & Y.), Upper Norwood Joint L., L.B. Croydon & L.B. Lambeth. [62824] 05/11/2003   **ME**

Byfield, Mr P A, LLB(Hons) MA, Legal Inf. Specialist, EBRD, London. [56448] 06/07/1998   **ME**

Byford, Mr A J, BA, Retired [10008409] 19/10/1970   **ME**

Byford, Mrs E M, Retired. [16675] 08/02/1958   **ME**

Byford, Miss K J, PgCPSM BA MCLIP, Learn. Lib., Suffolk C.C., Ipswich. [26695] 27/10/1976   **CM11/08/1980**

Byford, Mrs R L, BLS MCLIP, Taxonomy Offr., Essex C.C. L., Chelmsford. [33463] 01/12/1980   **CM13/11/1984**

Byon, Mr J, BA MLS, Team Leader, Korea Inst. of Construction Tech., S. Korea. [10013710] 22/05/2009   **ME**

Byrnand, Ms P M, BA MCLIP, Learning Cent. Super., Stanmore Coll., Mddx. [10002756] 27/04/2007   **CM05/05/2010**

Byrne, Miss A, BA(Hons) PGCE MA, Inf. Offr., Eurydice, NFER. [10000939] 01/12/2006   **ME**

Byrne, Mrs B M, BA DipEd DipLib MCLIP, Principle Consultant, BLIS Byrne Lang. & Info. Serv., [23356] 09/12/1974   **CM31/12/1989**

Byrne, Mr D F, BA MLib MCLIP, Head of Knowledge Mgmnt., BT Legal, London [34202] 10/10/1981   **CM18/02/1986**

Byrne, Mrs H M, BA MCLIP, Develpoment Lib: PN, Hertfordshire [28535] 10/01/1978   **CM04/02/1980**

Byrne, Mr M, BA DipLib MCLIP, Community Lib., Birmingham L. Serv. [27141] 27/01/1977   **CM08/03/1979**

Byron, Mrs A H E, MCLIP, Unemployed. [21541] 29/10/1973   **CM04/08/1977**

C

Cabey, Mr J, BA, L. Offr., Univ. of Brighton [10012512] 23/02/2009 **ME**

Cable, Mr P J, BA MSc, Res., Lovells LLP, London. [61157] 15/03/2002   **ME**

Cabrera Perez, Miss E, BA(Hons) PGDip, Lib. in Charge, Great Moor L., Stockport, Cheshire. [10006597] 11/01/1985   **ME**

Cadby, Mrs S E, MCLIP, Head of Learning Res., Stourbridge Coll., W. Midlands. [2248] 14/03/1967   **CM01/01/1971**

Caddy, Miss E A, MA, Stud. [10013144] 02/04/2009   **ME**

Cadge, Mr N L, BA MCLIP, Unknown [2252] 04/01/1964 **CM01/01/1970**

Cadman, Mrs E A, BA(Hons) MCLIP, Sch. Lib., Blackfen Sch. for Girls, Sidcup. [21624] 22/11/1973   **CM21/12/1976**

Cadney, Mr D L J, BA FCLIP, Retired. [2254] 21/01/1953 **FE01/01/1968**

Cadwallader, Ms J, Stud., Aberystwyth. [64159] 19/01/2005 **ME**

Cadwallader, Mr W M, MSc, Music co-ordinator, Leeds Coll. Music, Leeds. [62822] 05/11/2003   **ME**

Cafferata, Mrs H L, BSc MSc, N. Inf. Serv. Mgr., Berrymans Lace Mawer, London [62298] 17/04/2003   **ME**

Cage, Ms S, MSc MCLIP, Sen. Sci. Inf. Specialist, Nat. Poisons Inf. Serv., City Hosp. NHS Trust, Birmingham. [60165] 10/12/2001   **CM10/12/2001**

Cahill, Ms A T, BSc DipLib MCLIP, Head of L. and Culture, London Bor. of Richmond Upon Thames, London [44045] 17/04/1990 **CM27/05/1992**

Cahill, Mr H, BA MA MA MCLIP, Sen. Inf. Asst., Foyle Special Coll. L., Kings Coll. London. [61969] 23/12/2002 **CM11/03/2009**

Cain, Ms C F, MA MSc Dip Psych, Head Lib., Sabhal Mor Ostaig, Isle of Skye. [41906] 16/05/1988 **ME**

Caine, Mr A J, BA MA PhD, P/T Lib. & Info. Asst., Liverpool Lib. [65542] 13/02/2006 **ME**

Caine, Mrs B M, BA MCLIP, Retired. [38670] 01/01/1963 **CM14/10/1985**

Caine, Mrs S J, BSc MCLIP, Retired. [56609] 14/09/1998 **CM01/04/2002**

Caird, Ms S M, BSc MA, Sen. Lib., Ashurst, London. [55417] 10/10/1997 **ME**

Cairns, Miss A M, BA DipLib MCLIP, Area Mgr., S. Area, Eastbourne L., E. Sussex C.C. [30123] 04/01/1979 **CM11/02/1982**

Cairns, Ms A M, Unknown. [65061] 24/10/2005 **ME**

Cairns, Ms C, BA MCLIP MLib, System Mgr., The Civil Aviation Auth., Gatwick. [38306] 01/03/1985 **RV02/03/2010** **CM06/10/1987**

Cairns, Mr G A, BA DMS DipLib MCLIP, L. Registration & Inf. Serv. Mgr., E. Ayrshire Council. [28521] 25/01/1978 **CM25/01/1980**

Cairns, Mrs J, BA MCLIP, Sch. Lib., Canon Slade Sch., Bolton, Lancs. [39864] 01/10/1986 **CM18/07/1990**

Cairns, Mr R J, Enquiries Asst., The Scottish Parliament Inf. Cent., Edinburgh. [10013712] 22/05/2009 **ME**

Calcraft, Mrs P, BA PGDip MCLIP, p. /t. Enquiry Team lib., Business, Cent. Res. L., Hatfield [34919] 20/04/1982 **CM23/06/2004**

Caldwell, Ms A, BA MCLIP, Lib. & Info. Offr., Dundee C.C. [31218] 05/10/1979 **CM21/09/1983**

Caley, Mrs C M, MCLIP, Life Member [2275] 12/11/1940 **CM01/01/1945**

Caley, Mr R J, BA DipLib, Res. & Learner Support Offr., Liverpool John Moores Univ. [33624] 29/01/1981 **ME**

Calff, Mrs J, MA, Dep. Dir. of Univ. L., Univ. Leiden, The Netherlands. [10010640] 19/08/2008 **ME**

Callaghan, Ms H, BA(Hons), Asst. Lib., Iniva [66095] 25/09/2006 **ME**

Callanan, Mrs E D, BA MCLIP, Retired. [2279] 24/03/1955 **CM01/01/1960**

Callear, Mrs J, Head of Bibliographic Serv., Birmingham L. [10002569] 24/05/1986 **ME**

Callegari, Mr L, BA(Hons) MA MSc MCLIP, Learning Support Lib. [54475] 20/12/1996 **CM07/09/2005**

Callen, Mr A L A, BA DipLIS MCLIP, Inf. Specialist (Mus. & Media/Art&Des), Inf. & Learning Serv., Univ. of Salford [37092] 21/02/1984 **CM24/03/1992**

Caller, Mrs A, BA(Hons) PGCE, Lib. Asst., Walkden L., Salford [10015247] 29/10/2009 **ME**

Callow, Ms E, BA(Hons) PGDip MSc ECON MCLIP, Outreach L., Health Care L. s, Univ. of Oxford. [57998] 07/10/1999 **CM29/03/2006**

Callow, Mr M J, BA MCLIP, Salisbury & S. Wiltshire Mus. [19594] 07/11/1972 **CM30/11/1975**

Calver, Mrs M, MCLIP, Dep. Head of L. Serv. Mgr., Worthing Health L., W. Sussex Hosp., NHS Trust, PG Med. Cent. [23336] 31/10/1974 **CM07/12/1977**

Calvert, Mr A, Subject Lib., Arts Univ. Coll., Bournemouth. [64581] 17/05/2005 **ME**

Cameron, Mr A B, BA MCLIP, Life Member. [29296] 05/01/1970 **CM01/01/1973**

Cameron, Mrs A M, MA(Hons) DipILS MCLIP, Lib., Scottish Screen Arch., Glasgow. [55230] 05/09/1997 **CM18/09/2002**

Cameron, Mrs H M, BA(Hons) MSc MCLIP, Inf. Offr., IDOX [65695] 01/04/2006 **CM22/02/2010**

Cameron, Mrs H M, BA MCLIP, Unwaged. [23236] 16/11/1974 **CM30/04/1980**

Cameron, Miss I M M, MA MCLIP, Lib., St. Ann's Hosp., London [2301] 18/09/1968 **CM18/02/1974**

Cameron, Miss L, MA BA(Hons), Lib., Clifford Chance, London [47823] 14/10/1992 **ME**

Cameron, Ms M, Catr., Mitchell L., Glasgow. [10002121] 24/08/2007 **AF**

Cameron, Miss N, BA(Hons), Sch. L. Resource Cent. Mgr., N. Lanarkshire Council, Coatbridge. [64749] 01/07/2005 **ME**

Cameron, Mr W H M, BA DipLib MCLIP, Lib., Highland Theological Coll., Dingwall. [31220] 02/10/1979 **CM10/11/1981**

Camosso-Stefinovic, Mrs J, BA(Hons) MA MSc MCLIP, information Lib., Univ. of Leicester [59938] 08/11/2001 **CM11/03/2009**

Campbell, Mrs C J, BA MCLIP, Asst. Lib. (Counter Serv.), Oxford Brookes Univ. [33045] 16/10/1980 **CM02/07/1984**

Campbell, Mr G A, MA B COM MCLIP, Lib. & Mus. Mgr., The Moray Council. [25499] 09/02/1976 **CM07/02/1978**

Campbell, Dr I, MA DipLib MCLIP, Asst. Dir., E. Sussex C.C., Lib. and Culture. [30125] 16/01/1979 **CM07/10/1981**

Campbell, Mrs J E, BA MCLIP, Lib. Offr. (Team Leader), Cent. Lend. L., Edinburgh [10001574] 13/03/1980 **CM20/08/1982**

Campbell, Mrs J, BSc(Hons) PgDip, Faculty Liaison Lib., Newcastle Univ., Robinson L. [10016536] 01/04/2010 **ME**

Campbell, Mrs K, ACLIP, Lib., Buro Happold, Bath. [57574] 10/05/1999 **ACL23/01/2007**

Campbell, Ms L G, BA, Stud. [10011282] 07/10/2008 **ME**

Campbell, Ms L, MITG MCLIP, Retired [2326] 28/01/1970 **CM01/08/1972**

Campbell, Mrs M I, Sen. Learning Resource Cent. Asst., Moray Coll., Elgin. [63363] 20/04/2004 **AF**

Campbell, Mr M J, MBE MA MCLIP, Retired. [2332] 01/01/1947 **CM01/01/1965**

Campbell, Ms M, MCLIP, Sch. Lib., Oaklands Sch., Tower Hamlets. [9394] 13/01/1968 **CM03/07/1973**

Campbell, Mr R M, BA MA MCLIP, Knowledge Mgr. S. Derby NHS. [2337] 18/09/1970 **CM01/01/1974**

Campbell, Mr R, MCLIP, Area Co-ordinator, Glasgow City Council. [2336] 07/01/1971 **CM04/07/1973**

Campbell, Mrs S A, MCLIP, Princ. Lib. (Cent. Servs.), Moray Council. [3833] 18/03/1972 **CM01/07/1975**

Campbell, Mrs S C C, MCLIP, Sen. Lib., Falkirk Council. [40246] 18/11/1986 **CM24/05/1995**

Campbell, Mr W A, MA MCLIP MA(LIB), Retired. [20459] 21/03/1973 **CM09/08/1976**

Campillos, Miss M, Unwaged. [10016420] 22/03/2010 **ME**

Camps, Mrs P M, MCLIP, Retired. [1920] 13/02/1960 **CM01/01/1964**

Camroux, Miss J A, MSc MCLIP, Retired. [19613] 26/10/1972 **CM07/01/1976**

Canaway, Mr N S, MBA MCLIP, Retired [21824] 07/02/1974 **CM03/03/1977**

Canessa, Mrs J Y, MCLIP, LRC Mgr., Esher Coll., Surrey. [63531] 17/06/2004 **CM09/07/2008**

Canfield, Miss K, BSc (Hons), Stud., State Univ. of New Jersey, USA [10015111] 15/10/2009 **ME**

Canham, Mr J, PGCE BA(Hons), Unknown. [10000648] 24/10/2006 **ME**

Cann, Mrs A J, BA MA, Subj. Liaison Lib., Brunel Univ. [62823] 05/11/2003 **ME**

Cannell, Ms G C, BA(Hons), Sub Lib., Corpus Christi Coll., Cambridge. [63382] 27/04/2004 **ME**

Cannell, Mrs S E, MA MCLIP, Dir of L. Serv., Univ. of Edinburgh. [23170] 02/11/1974 **CM23/04/1985**

Canning, Mrs A, MSc(Hons), Stud. [64230] 21/02/2005 **ME**

Canning, Ms J S, Nursery Sch. Asst. [41852] 28/04/1988 **ME**

Canning, Miss R, L. Asst., N. Middlesex Univ. Hosp. NHS Trust, London. [10015325] 10/11/2009 **AF**

Cannings, Miss C E, BA(Hons), Princ. L. Asst., Univ. of Essex, Colchester. [62871] 17/11/2003 **ME**

Cannon, Ms C J, BA MPhil MA MCLIP, Asst. Dir., Collections & Resource Description, Univ. of Oxford. [50616] 01/10/1994 **CM23/07/1997**

Cannon, Mrs C S, BA DipLib AKC MCLIP, Teaching Asst., St. Wilfred's Sch., Burgess Hill. [40169] 06/11/1986 **CM27/03/1991**

Cannon, Mr P, BA, Inf. Cent. Asst., Scottish Parliament., Edinburgh. [65458] 23/02/2006 **ME**

Cantrell, Mrs A J, BA MA MCLIP, Inf. Offr., Univ. of Sheffield. [61550] 11/09/2002 **CM03/10/2007**

Cantrell, Ms J, BA(Hons) DipLib MCLIP, Unwaged [40337] 12/01/1987 **CM26/02/1992**

Cantwell, Miss I A, BA MCLIP, L. Mgr., Homerton Univ. NHS Trust, London. [21920] 01/02/1974 **CM01/06/1977**

Cape, Mr B E M, BA(Hons) MA MCLIP, Head of Support Serv., L.B. Southwark. [59475] 04/04/2001 **CM02/02/2005**

Capell, Mrs M J, BSc(Hons) MSc, Unwaged. [58936] 09/10/2000 **ME**

Caporn, Ms S L, BA(Hons) PGCE DipLIS MCLIP, LRC Mgr., Coll. Green Cent., Bristol. [36355] 05/10/1983 **CM19/01/1988**

Card, Mr R M, BA MA, Reader Devel. & Stock Lib., Bracknell Forest, Bor. Council. [58200] 16/11/1999 **ME**

Carden, Mrs K J, Acquisitions Lib., Robert Gordon Univ. [58623] 19/04/2000 **ME**

Carden, Mrs S J, MA MA MCLIP, Collection Devel. Mgr., ICAEW, London. [55462] 13/10/1997 **CM15/03/2000**

Carder, Mrs S J, Lib., Norton Radstock Coll., Radstock [43459] 26/10/1989 **ME**

Cardnell, Mrs J A, BA DipLib MCLIP, Sch. Lib., Colfe's Sch., London. [26623] 26/10/1976 **CM09/12/1979**

Cardy, Mr T S, FCLIP, Life Member. [2365] 08/05/1937 **FE01/01/1945**

Care, Mrs R, Meng, Stud [10006819] 17/12/2007 **ME**

Careless, Mr G C, MA MCLIP, Retired. [32404] 01/04/1980 **CM25/01/1985**

Carey, Mrs A J, BSc MCLIP, L. & Inf. Mgr., Bond Pearce, Plymouth. [60444] 11/12/2001 **CM11/12/2001**

Carey, Mrs A, MLIS MLAI, Sen. Inf. Offr., Arup Consulting Engineers, Dublin. [64898] 09/09/2005 **ME**

Carey, Miss G G, BA MCLIP, Unknown. [34314] 14/10/1981 **CM16/10/1989**

Carey, Mr N, BA(Hons) MSc, Dep. Head of Lend. Serv., Univ. Glasgow [61961] 19/12/2002 **ME**

Carey, Mr P, PgDip, Employment unknown. [10001142] 09/02/1999 **ME**

Carey, Mr R E, ACLIP, Sen. Asst. Lib., NHS Sheffield. [10009952] 28/03/1994 **ACL28/01/2009**

Cargill Thompson, Dr H E C, BSc PhD FSA MCLIP, Retired. [2370] 01/01/1966 **CM01/01/1971**

Carle, Mrs A, BA(Hons) MCLIP, Sch. Lib., St. Columba's High Sch. [48071] 04/11/1992 **CM23/01/2002**

Carle, Miss C A, MCLIP, Life Member. [2371] 09/09/1951 **CM01/01/1957**

Carlisle, Mrs C A, BA MCLIP, Unemployed/Housewife. [32178] 25/01/1980 **CM23/04/1982**

Carlisle, Miss J E, Lib. Mgr., Wootton Fields L., Northampton. [10015641] 07/01/2010 **ME**

Carlton, Mrs J, MCLIP, p/t. Comm. Info. Offr., N. Yorkshire C.C., Filey, N. Yorks. [18377] 18/10/1972 **CM29/08/1975**

Carlyle, Mrs E R, MA(Cantab) MA MSc MResMCLIP, Inf. & Support Policy Lead., Macmillan Cancer Support, London. [42046] 18/08/1988 **CM01/04/2002**

Carman, Ms B, BA PGDipLib MCLIP, Vol. Arch., Cranbrook Mus. [12304] 15/09/1955 **CM01/01/1958**

Carmel, Mr M J, BA MSc FCLIP, Life Member. [18545] 01/01/1966 **FE16/10/1989**

Carmichael, Ms E, BA MCLIP, Retired. [22027] 10/01/1974 **CM01/07/1976**

Carmichael, Mrs H P, BA DipLib, Sen. Archive Asst., Conwy Co. Bor. Council, Llandudno. [36571] 18/10/1983 **ME**

Carmichael, Mrs J G, MA MCLIP, Inf. Offr., Coatbridge L., N. Lanarkshire Council. [24684] 07/10/1975 **CM02/02/1978**

Carnaby, Ms P E, BA DipEd MCLIP, Nat. Lib., Nat. L. of New Zealand, Wellington. [21246] 24/09/1973 **CM02/11/1976**

Carnson, Miss S F, BA DipLib MIIS MCLIP, Retired. [26468] 05/10/1976 **CM30/11/1978**

Carpenter, Mrs C D, MCLIP, Retired [2388] 02/10/1967 **CM01/01/1971**

Carpenter, Mr C, MCLIP, Liaison Lib, Univ. of Reading [10000666] 25/10/2006 **CM07/07/2010**

Carpenter, Miss E, MA, Sen. L. Asst., Insitute of Educ., London. [10016149] 19/02/2010 **AF**

Carpenter, Mrs N M, BLib MCLIP, L. Advisor, Essex Sch. L. Serv. [22652] 26/07/1974 **CM01/09/1976**

Carpenter, Mr S B D, BA MSc MCLIP, Inf. Offr. &Lib., Quality Assurance Agency for HE [32405] 04/04/1980 **CM02/02/1987**

Carr, Mr D G, BA(Hons), Unknown. [10006811] 10/12/2007 **ME**

Carr, Mrs H, BA MCLIP, Casual L. Asst., Hampshire C.C. [9699] 06/10/1965 **CM01/01/1969**

Carr, Mr M G, MBiochem(Hons) MA MCLIP BD, Unknown. [58943] 05/10/2000 **CM29/03/2006**

Carr, Ms N E, BA(Hons) PG Dip, Lib., Accrington & Rossendale Coll., Accrington [10007920] 28/02/2008 **ME**

Carr, Mr S J, BA(Hons) MCLIP, Info. Specialist, Health & Safety Exec., Bootle. [43475] 26/10/1989 **CM26/07/1995**

Carr, Miss S M, BSc(Hons), Asst. Lib., Royal Soc. of Med. Support Serv., London. [47802] 19/10/1992 **ME**

Carr, Miss S, Unwaged [10012972] 17/03/2009 **AF**

Carragher, Mrs S A, BA MCLIP, Dir. of Adult Learning & Lib., Essex C.C. [23280] 12/11/1974 **CM06/08/1979**

Carrette, Mrs S E, BSc MCLIP, Inf. Res., Business Link, York. [60156] 07/12/1988 **CM04/05/1993**

Carrick, Mrs E J, BA MCLIP, Sen. Child. Lib., Milton Keynes Council. Sen. Lib., Newport Pagnell L. [40296] 20/01/1987 **CM18/07/1991**

Carrick, Mr G, MA MCLIP, Learning Support Lib.,Maida Vale Lib., Sutherland Avenue ,London [40190] 03/11/1986 **CM13/06/1989**

Carrington, Mrs A, BSc MCLIP, p. /t. Freelance Law Lib. [8268] 20/04/1971 **CM30/09/1973**

Carritt, Ms A S, MA MCLIP, Electronic Resources Lib., Bodleian Law L., Oxford [10007704] 01/10/1994 **CM17/07/2000**

Carroll, Mrs J, BSc NNEB MA MCLIP, Inf. Lib. & Learing Res. Co-ordinator, Kirkby Coll., Notts CC. [61999] 16/01/2003 **CM21/11/2007**

Carroll, Mrs J, Unknown. [10008748] 21/06/2010 **AF**

Carroll, Mrs L K, BA(Hons) MSc MCLIP, p/t Suject Lib. in Social Sciences, Univ. of the W. of Scotland, Paisley [60023] 26/11/2001 **CM13/06/2007**

Carroll, Mrs M M, BA MCLIP, Lib. & Learning Cent., Univ. for the Creative Arts, Epsom [33015] 12/10/1980 **CM16/03/1984**

Carroll, Mrs M, MCLIP, L. Asst., Cult. Serv., Durham C.C. [10289] 26/04/1972 **CM08/01/1975**

Carroll, Ms M, BA(Hons), Sen. Lect., Dept. of Eng. & Tech., Manchester Met. Univ. [56108] 20/02/1998 **ME**

Carroll, Mr R A, BA FCLIP, Life Member. [16736] 12/02/1948 **FE01/01/1963**

Carroll, Mrs S M, BA(Hons) MCLIP, Lib., St. Francis of Assisi RC Sch., Aldridge. [46379] 30/10/1991 **CM22/01/1997**

Carron, Dr H C, BA MA MPhil PhD MCLIP, Employment not known. [25961] 19/05/1976 **CM11/06/1980**

Carruthers, Mrs C A, MCLIP, Asst. Lib., Harris L., Preston. [65107] 01/11/2005 **CM17/09/2008**

Carruthers, Miss V M, BA FCLIP, Retired. [2421] 01/01/1934 **FE01/01/1934**

Carson, Mrs C M, BSc (Econ) MCLIP, L. Mgr., St. Ives & St. Just L. [61682] 21/10/2002 **CM17/09/2008**

Carson, Mr W R H, FLAI HonFCLIP FCLIP, Life Member [2425] 01/01/1949 **FE01/01/1968**

Carter, Mrs A J, Learning Resources Mgr., John of Gaunt Sch., Trowbridge, Wilts. [63475] 14/05/2004 **ME**

Carter, Ms A M, BA(Hons), Lib., Cent. Sussex 6th Form Haywards Heath [10016434] 24/03/2010 **AF**

Carter, Mr A, MA FCLIP FSAS, Life Member. [2426] 24/03/1949 **FE01/01/1968**

Carter, Miss B, BA(Hons) MSc MCLIP, Clinical Lib., York Hosp. NHS Foundation Trust. [61200] 08/04/2002   **CM29/08/2007**

Carter, Mrs C J, BLS MCLIP, Semi-retired. [33460] 01/01/1980   **CM29/01/1985**

Carter, Mr E R, BSc MCLIP, Inf. Advisor, Shell Projects & Tech., Chester. [60525] 04/05/1978   **CM01/01/1981**

Carter, Mrs E R, MCLIP, Life Member. [2433] 29/01/1932 **CM01/01/1944**

Carter, Miss H F, BA(Hons) MCLIP, Unknown. [54008] 16/10/1996   **CM16/05/2001**

Carter, Mrs H M, BA MCLIP, Res./Inf. Offr., Derbyshire & Nottinghamshire Chamber of Commerce [32871] 07/10/1980   **CM30/07/1985**

Carter, Mrs J, BA MCLIP, Retired. [2441] 29/07/1964   **CM01/01/1967**

Carter, Mrs J, Subject Lib. /Univ. Arch./Lib. Acquisitions Asst. [46867] 13/02/1992   **ME**

Carter, Mrs K E, BA(hons.) PGCE MA, Digital Communications Exec., Grant Thornton, London [64389] 14/03/2005   **ME**

Carter, Mrs K, BA MCLIP, Sch. Lib., W. Park Sch., Derby [10014929] 01/05/1984   **CM09/08/1988**

Carter, Mr L J, BSc MSc PhD MCLIP, Retired. [48288] 24/11/1992   **CM26/01/1994**

Carter, Mrs M E, BA FCLIP, Life Member. [2448] 01/01/1940   **FE01/01/1946**

Carter, Mrs M, BA MCLIP, Acting Lib., Bolton Community Coll. [254] 08/06/1971   **CM01/01/1975**

Carter, Dr M, MA DipLib MCLIP, Sch. Lib., Armdale Academy, W. Lothian. [38691] 01/10/1985   **CM10/11/1987**

Carter, Mrs P R, BSc(Hons) BSc(Econ) MCLIP, Asst. Lib., Barbican Lib., City of London [53225] 04/04/1996   **CM25/07/2001**

Carter, Mr R C, BA(Hons) PG Dip MCLIP, Lib, Dept. of Geography, Univ. of Cambridge. [53926] 11/10/1996   **CM17/09/2008**

Carter, Mr R O, BSc, Inf. Asst., Newcastle Univ., Newcastle Upon Tyne. [10005033] 01/12/1980   **ME**

Carter, Mrs S A, BSc MSc MBA HonFCLIP, Retired. [60527] 10/08/1973   **FE01/07/1981**

Carter, Ms S E, BA(Hons) MA MCLIP, Inf. Mgr. Action for Prisoner's Families. [46893] 28/02/1992   **CM18/03/1998**

Carter, Mrs S L, MCLIP, L. Mgr., Cefas, Lowestoft. [59508] 18/04/2001   **CM09/07/2008**

Carter, Miss S, MSc BSc, Asst. Lib.,Park Lane Coll., Leeds [10012349] 05/02/2009   **ME**

Carter, Mr S, BA(Hons) MA, Unwaged. [38932] 21/10/1985   **ME**

Carter, Ms U P, BEd(Hons) DipLIS MCLIP, Asst. Lib., City Business L., London. [49994] 08/02/1994   **CM20/05/1998**

Carter, Ms V I, BSc(Hons) MCLIP, Asst. Lib., Learn. Cent., S. Thames Coll. [58980] 16/10/2000   **CM07/09/2005**

Cartlidge, Mrs C A, MCLIP, Princ. Lib., Shropshire C.C. [1662] 02/10/1971   **CM21/10/1974**

Carty, Ms C J, BA(Hons) MA MCLIP, Unknown. [56985] 18/11/1998   **CM29/03/2006**

Carvell, Mrs P A, BA MCLIP, Head of Tech. Serv., Bermuda Nat. L., Hamilton. [26772] 26/11/1976   **CM06/10/1980**

Carver, Ms K R A, BA MA PGCHE MCLIP FHEA, Academic Lib., The Civic Quarter L., Leeds Met. Univ. [10013811] 21/01/1998   **CM04/02/2004**

Cascant Ortolano, Ms L, B. Lib. I. Sc BS., Inf. Scientist, CIBER Epidemiología y Salud Pública, Barcelona [10016134] 17/02/2010   **ME**

Case, Miss H R, BA(Hons), Stud., Thames Valley Univ., London. [10015113] 15/10/2009   **ME**

Case, Mrs L K, ACLIP, L. Mgr., Beyton Middle Sch., Suffolk [10011275] 07/10/2008   **ACL23/09/2009**

Case, Mr M L, BSc(Hons) PGDipIM MCLIP, Subject Lib., Anglia Ruskin, Chelmsford. [52243] 18/10/1995   **CM16/07/2003**

Case, Ms V P, Stud., Univ. of Sheffield [10015079] 12/10/2009   **ME**

Caseley, Ms E, MCLIP, Metadata Res. Mgr., BBC Inf. & Arch. [63066] 27/01/2004   **CM19/11/2008**

Casey, Mrs E J, BA(Hons), Stud. [66075] 01/10/2006   **ME**

Casey, Miss M E, BSc(Hons) PgDip MCLIP, Site Operations Co-ordinator, Univ. of Salford, Manchester. [65935] 23/06/2006   **CM20/04/2009**

Cashman, Dr H A, MA PhD DipLib MCLIP, Lib., Stockton L., H. M. Prison, Holme House. [32025] 28/01/1980   **CM17/03/1982**

Cashman, Mr J M, BA DipLib MCLIP, Lib. /Arch., Foreign Exchange Co., Killorglin. [41120] 09/10/1987   **CM18/11/1992**

Cashman, Dr N, MscEcon, Repository Adviser, Aberystwyth Univ., Wales. [10015806] 27/01/2010   **ME**

Casimir, Mrs H S, MCLIP, Life Member. [2478] 02/09/1947   **CM01/01/1952**

Cass, Miss E J, BA(Hons) MSc MCLIP, Business Mgr., Brit. L., Yorkshire [52453] 02/11/1995   **CM20/01/1999**

Cassaro, Miss M, BA, PGDip, MSc, Asst. Lib., Cent. Saint Martin's Coll. Art & Design Lib., London [10008297] 19/03/2008   **ME**

Casselden, Ms B, BA(Hons) PGCE MA FHEA MCLIP, Sen. Lect., Northumbria Univ., Newcastle. [49768] 06/12/1993   **CM20/05/1998**

Casselden, Mrs L, BA(Hons) MA MCLIP, Community Devel. Co-ordinator, S. Tyneside L. and Inf. Serv., S. Shields. [44692] 27/11/1990   **CM26/07/1995**

Cassells, Mrs A T S, MA MCLIP, Sch. Lib., Boclair Academy, Bearsden. [28167] 06/10/1977   **CM27/11/1980**

Cassels, Mrs A F, BA MCLIP, Cultural Offr.: Child., Lib., Wakefield L. [32519] 20/04/1980   **CM30/09/1985**

Cassels, Mr A M, MA MSc MBCS MCLIP, Inf. Cent. Mgr., Fera, York. [38099] 17/01/1985   **CM16/05/1990**

Casserley, Miss L D, BA MCLIP, Retired. [28789] 24/01/1978   **CM19/11/1979**

Cassettari, Ms G, MA MCLIP, Inf. & Knowledge Mgr., Met. Police Serv., London [52975] 07/02/1996   **CM20/01/1999**

Cassidy, Mrs A E, BA MSc DipInfSc MCLIP, Programme Mgr., BSI., London. [60137] 23/04/1981   **CM01/05/1985**

Cassidy, Mrs A M, MCLIP, Learning Res. Facilitator., York Coll. [21145] 04/10/1973   **CM01/07/1977**

Cassidy, Ms J, BA DipLIS, Lib., Dept. of Community, Equality & Gaeltacht Affairs, Dublin, Ireland. [57497] 06/04/1999   **ME**

Cassidy, Mrs J, BA DipLib, Sen. L. Asst., Lancashire C. C [49972] 31/01/1994   **ME**

Cassidy, Ms K J, BSc(Hons), Sen. L. & Inf. Offr., Local Studies & Family Hist. Cent., Newcastle [10011223] 02/10/2008   **ME**

Casteleyn, Mrs M T, FCLIP, Life Member. [2483] 18/10/1963   **FE27/11/1984**

Castell, Mrs H S, BSc, Lib., St Joseph's Sch. Launceston. [36102] 27/05/1983   **ME**

Castens, Mrs L D, LLB(Hons) PGDip MSc, Assoc. Dir. Barrington L., Cranfield Univ. [56278] 20/04/1998   **ME**

Castens, Ms M E, BSc MA DMS MCLIP, Dir. of Inf. & L. Serv., Univ. of Greenwich, london. [2484] 18/06/1969   **CM18/11/1974**

Castle, Ms C M, BA(Hons) MCLIP, Lib. i/c., Dept. of Zoology, Univ. of Cambridge. [52425] 25/10/1995 **RV29/03/2007**   **CM23/09/1998**

Castle, Mrs E M, BA MCLIP, Sch. Lib., Perse Prep. Sch., Cambridge. [23323] 27/11/1974   **CM10/01/1977**

Castle, Mr J D, BA(Hons) MA, Asst. Inf. Mgr., AMEY, Oxford. [56844] 26/10/1998   **ME**

Castle, Mrs J M, MCLIP, Learning Resources Cent. Mgr., Burlington Danes Academy [12150] 19/10/1971   **CM25/10/1974**

Castle, Mrs J, MA(Hons) DipILS MCLIP, L. & Heritage Serv. Mgr., W. Lothian Council. [38902] 14/10/1985   **CM05/07/1988**

Castle, Mrs L, B. Ed BA(Hons), Customer Serv. Super. (L. Asst.), The Open Univ., Milton Keynes. [10009491] 21/05/2008   **AF**

Castle, Ms S, MCLIP, Info. Serv. Lib., Univ. of the Arts, London [60034] 29/11/2001 **CM16/07/2003**

Castle-Smith, Mr D, BA(Hons) MCLIP, Coll. Team Leader, Fife C., Dunfermline. [54377] 29/11/1996 **CM17/05/2000**

Caston, Ms L P, MA(Hons) DipLib MCLIP, External Funding Offr., Angus Council. [30126] 17/01/1979 **CM12/11/1981**

Castree, Miss A, MA, Inf. Specialist: Book Acquisitions, Members' L., Nat. Assembly for Wales [63669] 12/08/2004 **ME**

Catchpole, Mrs A D E, BA MCLIP, Relief. Lib. Asst., Norfolk C.C. [9884] 04/01/1972 **CM07/10/1974**

Cater, Mr M, BA(Hons) MCLIP, Asst. Lib., Birmingham Cent. L. [49400] 21/10/1993 **CM20/11/2002**

Cathcart, Ms H, Unwaged. [10015740] 19/01/2010 **ME**

Cather, Ms C, BA MSc MCLIP, Knowledge Serv. Adv., NHS EDUCATION FOR SCOTLAND. [31225] 05/10/1979 **CM30/06/1983**

Catteau, Mr N, BA MA MCLIP, Lib., Croydon Council. [50311] 15/06/1994 **CM22/01/1997**

Cattermole, Ms J, BA(Hons) MCLIP, Asst. Head Learning Res. Middx. Univ. [8639] 03/01/1972 **CM03/07/1974**

Catto, Mr D B, MA DipEd DipMan MCLIP, Local Studies Lib., Aberdeenshire L. & Inf. Serv., Oldmeldrum. [10001057] 19/10/1976 **CM30/10/1979**

Catton, Ms C M, BA MCLIP, Program Dir. -Inf. Res., Amnesty Internat., London. [37585] 01/10/1984 **CM01/04/2002**

Caulfield, Mrs A T, BA MCLIP, Retired [11910] 16/03/1967 **CM01/01/1970**

Caulton, Miss J A, BA(Hons) MA MCLIP, Lib., Castle Coll. Nottingham. [54259] 11/11/1996 **CM10/07/2002**

Cavanagh, Mr M J, MA, Stud., Aberystwyth Univ. [10013551] 05/05/2009 **ME**

Cavanagh, Mrs M S, MA DipLib MCLIP, Head of Local Studies, W. Lothian Council. [26696] 27/10/1976 **CM29/11/1979**

Cavanagh, Mr P, BA(Hons) MScILM MCLIP, Asst. Lib., Kimberlin L., De Montfort Univ., Leicester. [61927] 05/12/2002 **CM23/01/2008**

Cavaroli, Miss A, MA, Unknown. [10012098] 17/12/2008 **ME**

Cave, Mr R J, MA FCLIP, Freelancer [60168] 12/04/1962 **FE01/12/1976**

Cave, Mrs Z T, MLib BA MCLIP, working outside L. Serv. [26922] 13/12/1976 **CM08/07/1980**

Cavill, Mrs C P, MCLIP, Co. Councillor, Pembrokeshire [2514] 06/02/1962 **CM01/01/1966**

Cavill, Ms M, BA(Hons), PGCert, MA, Unwaged. [56365] 17/06/1998 **ME**

Cawkwell, Miss J A, BA MA, Unknown. [10005602] 25/07/2007 **ME**

Cawley, Mrs P A, L. Asst., Kirkham L., Lancs. [65013] 07/10/2005 **AF**

Cawood, Mrs A L, BA(Hons) DipLIS MCLIP, Sci. Inf. Offr., Agriculture & Devel. Board, Stoneleigh park. [48917] 21/07/1993 **CM25/09/1996**

Cawood, Ms D, BA(Hons), Info. Asst., Portsmouth Cent. L., Portsmouth [10014741] 14/01/1991 **ME**

Caws, Mrs S M, BA DipLib MCLIP, Island Heritage Lib., L. H.Q., Cowes, IOW. [30277] 09/01/1979 **CM16/03/1981**

Cawsey, Mrs P M, Lib., Internat. Sch. of Lausanne, Switzerland. [60905] 09/01/2002 **ME**

Cawthorne, Mr D J, BA MCLIP, P.L. Consultant., L. Multimedia Ltd [2518] 24/09/1970 **CM28/08/1973**

Cawthorne, Ms W A, BSc(Hons) DipLib MCLIP, Asst. Lib., Geological Soc. L., London. [26310] 30/09/1976 **CM29/11/1979**

Cawthra, Miss L A, MA DipLib MCLIP, L. Mgr., Working Class Movement L., Salford. [36863] 09/01/1984 **CM18/09/1991**

Cefai, Mrs J A, MCLIP, Staff Learning & Dev. Mgr., Anglia Ruskin Univ., Cambridge [18069] 21/09/1972 **CM11/12/1989**

Ceiriog-Hughes, Mrs S M T, BA MA MCLIP, Moberly L., Winchester Coll. [10016585] 11/10/1989 **CM27/01/1993**

Celac, Miss V, MSc, Unwaged. [10016916] 08/06/2010 **ME**

Celik, Mrs M A R F, BA MCLIP, L. Mgr. (P/T), The Charter Sch., London. [33293] 12/11/1980 **CM10/06/1986**

Centio, Ms J, Knowledge Advisor, Eversheds. [10016042] 10/02/2010 **AF**

Centrone, Ms M C, PG Dip PhD, Inf. Asst., Univ. of Kent. [10013430] 16/07/2010 **ME**

Ceresa, Mr M A, BA DipLib DMS MCLIP, Retired. [21201] 29/09/1973 **CM11/09/1975**

Ceylan Izhar, Mrs H, MCLIP, Lib., The Islamic Foundation, Leics. [58793] 26/07/2000 **CM21/03/2007**

Chaberska, Miss K B L, Retired [21129] 01/10/1973 **ME**

Chachu, Mrs N, Head Lib., Ashesi Univ. Coll., Accra, Ghana [30581] 12/12/1978 **ME**

Chadder, Miss J E, BA MCLIP, Life Member. [2522] 01/01/1954 **CM01/01/1960**

Chadwick, Mrs C A, BA(Hons) MCLIP, Sch. Lib., Clitheroe Royal Grammar Sch., Lancs. [3764] 01/10/1967 **CM01/01/1971**

Chadwick, Miss I J, Stud. [10016587] 14/04/2010 **ME**

Chadwick, Miss S J, BA(Hons) MSc(Econ) MCLIP, Comm. Child. Lib., Salford Educ. & Leisure Dir. (L.), Salford. [59014] 25/10/2000 **CM15/09/2004**

Chafey, Mr K G, MCLIP, Retired. [2532] 01/01/1959 **CM01/01/1963**

Chakrabarty, Mrs E, BA MCLIP, Unknown. [12187] 17/10/1967 **CM01/01/1970**

Chakraborty, Mrs J, BSc BLS MCLIP, Sen. Asst. Lib., L.B. of Harrow, Civic Cent. L. [2535] 02/07/1972 **CM01/03/1977**

Chalk, Mrs S J, Inf. Advisor and Stud., Univ. of Wales Inst., Cardiff [62542] 11/08/2003 **ME**

Chalk-Birdsall, Mrs D, MCLIP, P/T. Architecture & Spatial Design Subj., N. Campus, Holloway Rd. Lib. [29017] 13/03/1978 **CM21/08/1981**

Challen, Mr M, BSc Econ PG Dip, Acquisitions Mgr., L. Resources Cent., Lewisham CC. [10013997] 24/04/1990 **ME**

Challinor, Miss H L, BA(Hons) MCLIP, Inf. Architecture Lib., Dept. for Child., Sch. and Families, Sheffield [42638] 20/01/1989 **CM19/03/2008**

Challinor, Ms J, BA(Hons) DipLib, Careers Info. Mngr., Careers Serv., Univ. of Edinburgh [10015675] 21/10/1985 **ME**

Chalmers, Mrs I C L, BA MCLIP, L. Serv. Mgr., Kingston Hosp., The Stenhouse L., Surrey. [42162] 12/10/1988 **CM01/04/2002**

Chalmers, Miss J E S, MCLIP, Retired. [2541] 01/01/1958 **CM01/01/1965**

Chalmers, Miss V, MA(Hons), Unknown [64981] 06/10/2005 **ME**

Chamberlain, Ms A, MCLIP, Lib., H. M. P. & Y. O. I.,Onley, Northants. [14590] 22/01/1972 **CM30/07/1975**

Chamberlain, Mr D, BA(Hons) PgDip MCLIP, Lead Lib. (Outreach), ICT Serv., Redditch Health L. [57101] 14/12/1998 **RV29/08/2008 CM10/07/2002**

Chamberlain, Mrs E J, MA MCLIP, IT Systems Support Team Leader, Buckinghamshire New Univ., High Wycombe. [37048] 02/02/1984 **CM14/11/1989**

Chamberlain, Mrs H E, BA MCLIP, Lifelong Learning Offr., Bath & N. E. Somerset Council. Somerset [36133] 14/06/1983 **CM26/11/1997**

Chamberlain, Mr R J, BA MCLIP, Head of Collection & Access Mgmt., Univ. of Nottingham, Notts. [25016] 04/11/1975 **CM07/11/1978**

Chambers, Miss C, BA(Hons) MA MCLIP, L. Offr. /Serv. Devel., Edinburgh City L. and Inf. Serv., Edinburgh. [58599] 11/04/2000 **CM19/11/2003**

Chambers, Mr D, Sen. L. Asst., Musgrove Park Hosp., Taunton [10007090] 18/01/2008 **AF**

Chambers, Mrs J A, BA DipLib MCLIP, Dep. Lib., Faculty of Politics,Univ. of Cambridge. [42656] 31/01/1989 **CM24/03/1992**

Chambers, Mrs L, BA MSc MCLIP, Sch. Lib. Serv., LB Tower Hamlets [31848] 08/01/1980 **CM27/07/1982**

Chambers, Mr M W, MA MA DipLib, Ref. Specialist Humanities Ref. Serv., Brit. L. [36406] 05/10/1983 **ME**

Chambers, Mrs N E, BA MCLIP, Sch. Lib., Evesham High Sch., Evesham, Worcs. [28743] 23/01/1978 **CM30/07/1982**

Chambers, Ms S E, BA MA, Project Medewerker, Koninklijke Bibl., The Hague. [54796] 02/04/1997 **ME**

Chambers, Mrs W M, BA Dip LIS, Duty Lib., Edinburgh Univ., Edinburgh. [57897] 01/10/1999 **ME**

Chamley, Miss J S, BA, Stud. Univ. of Northumbria [10015078] 12/10/2009 **ME**

Champion, Mr K J, BA(Hons) MA MCLIP, Global Advisory Knowledge Leader, KPMG, London. [52826] 01/01/1996 **CM23/07/1997**

Champion, Mrs M M, MCLIP, Life Member. [2566] 04/07/1950 **CM01/01/1962**

Champion, Ms O J, BA(Hons) MSc MCLIP, Career Break, [51312] 11/01/1995 **CM26/11/1997**

Champion, Mrs P M, MCLIP, p. /t. Admin. Asst., Prestwood Jnr. Sch., Great Missenden. [23392] 11/01/1975 **CM09/12/1977**

Champion, Mrs S P, MA, Unwaged. [51045] 09/11/1994 **ME**

Champion, Mrs Y, BA DipLib MCLIP, Employment not known. [31607] 15/11/1979 **CM07/12/1982**

Chan Kam Lon, Mr Y, DipLib MSc MCLIP, Dir., Nat. L., Mauritius. [27922] 01/10/1977 **CM13/01/1981**

Chan, Ms A K Y, Tech. Serv., Univ. of Sydney, NSW Australia. [42840] 16/03/1989 **ME**

Chan, Mr B E, BA MSc FRSA MCLIP, Internet Tech. Editor., M. O. D., London. [55876] 27/11/1997 **CM11/03/2009**

Chan, Mrs G C, MCLIP, p. /t. Lib. Asst., Cardiff Council, Cardiff. [22200] 22/02/1974 **CM11/12/1978**

Chan, Mr G K L, MSc MCLIP, Editorial Operations Mgr., Biomed Cent., Liverpool [2569] 30/08/1969 **CM31/05/1973**

Chan, Mr S F, LLB MCLIP, Partner, Chan & Chuk Solicitors, Hong Kong [16743] 01/01/1969 **CM21/08/1972**

Chan, Ms W S M, Knowledge Consultant, Mallesons Stephen Jaques, Hong Kong. [61484] 19/08/2002 **ME**

Chandler, Mrs J M, Online Content Team, D. F. I. D., London. [42198] 10/10/1988 **ME**

Chandler, Miss L, Know-How Offr., Slaughter & May, London [63243] 22/03/2004 **ME**

Chandler, Mrs M R, MA MCLIP, Retired. [9476] 06/10/1971 **CM29/07/1975**

Chandler, Miss M, BA(Hons) MCLIP, Subject Lib., Univ. of Liverpool. [46390] 31/10/1991 **CM16/07/2003**

Chandler, Mr P J, Asst. Lib., Royal Coll. of Defence Studies, London. [51294] 04/01/1995 **ME**

Chandler, Ms P S, BLS MA PGCE MCLIP, Lib., St. Peter's Sch., York. [30129] 05/12/1978 **CM17/08/1982**

Chandler, Mrs S A, BA(Hons) PGCE Dip, L. Asst., N. Somerset Council, Portishead L. [65546] 27/02/2006 **AF**

Chaney, Ms A E P, BA(Hons) MA MCLIP, Institutional Repository Editor, Newsam L. Inst. of Educ., Univ. of London. [29783] 01/10/1978 **CM28/01/1983**

Chaney, Mrs K V, MCLIP, Lib., Canterbury Christ Church Univ., Southborough, Kent. [2579] 07/02/1972 **CM13/02/1976**

Chanlewis, Ms S, PgDip, Res. Offr., UNICEF, London. [10015601] 19/10/1992 **ME**

Channell, Mr B F, L. Mgr. [10007738] 21/02/2008 **ME**

Chant, Mrs I E, Unknown. [10008606] 02/04/2008 **ME**

Chaplin, Miss T, BA(Hons) MSc, Sen. Inf. Asst., City Univ. [60958] 21/01/2002 **ME**

Chapman, Mrs A D, MA FCLIP, Res. Offr., UKOLN, Univ. of Bath. [2589] 08/09/1967 **FE09/07/1981**

Chapman, Mrs A D, Volunteer, Citizen's Advice Bureau [31560] 01/11/1979 **ME**

Chapman, Mrs A V, BA(Open) MCLIP, Retired. [2590] 04/02/1959 **CM01/01/1964**

Chapman, Miss B J, BA DipLib MCLIP, L. & Inf. Mgr., Archway Healthcare L., Middx. Univ. [29263] 26/04/1978 **CM16/02/1981**

Chapman, Ms E A, BA MA DipLib FCLIP, Dir. of L. Serv., BLPES, London Sch. of Economics [18409] 30/09/1972 **FE18/01/1989**

Chapman, Mr E J, MA MILAM FRSA MCLIP, Retired. [19471] 19/10/1954 **CM01/01/1963**

Chapman, Miss E L, MA, Unknown [65834] 18/05/2006 **ME**

Chapman, Mr J H, MSc MCLIP, Retired. [27311] 28/02/1977 **CM22/09/1980**

Chapman, Miss M E, MA MCLIP, Br. Lib., Egglescliffe Br. L., Stockton Bor. Council. [26312] 30/09/1976 **CM13/03/1980**

Chapman, Mr M M, MA MCLIP, Retired. [2609] 16/10/1970 **CM05/12/1972**

Chapman, Ms M, MA CertEd FCLIP, Freelance Trainer & Consultant [2604] 01/01/1971 RV29/11/2006 **FE21/11/2001**

Chapman, Mrs M, MCLIP, Retired. [8884] 01/01/1956 **CM01/01/1970**

Chapman, Mr N G, BA MCLIP, Book Dealer, Self-Employed. [18553] 30/09/1972 **CM21/07/1975**

Chapman, Ms N J, BA(Hons), Sen. Researcher, Lovells LLP, London. [55398] 09/10/1997 **ME**

Chapman, Mr P A, BSc DipILM MCLIP, Head of Lib. & E-Strategy, Leicester Coll. [47241] 19/06/1992 **CM25/05/1994**

Chapman, Mr P J D, MA MCLIP, Inf. Consultant. [28526] 13/01/1978 **CM16/01/1980**

Chapman, Mr P, Managing Dir., Evolve Business Consultancy, Farnham [10008390] 19/03/2008 **ME**

Chapman, Mr R E, MSc BSc MCLIP, Managing Dir., Alsigns Best Surelite Self Powered LTD, Maidenhead [60171] 23/03/1970 **CM31/07/1980**

Chapman, Mrs S M, MA MLib MCLIP, Unemployed. [22584] 04/07/1974 **CM20/09/1995**

Chapman, Mrs S P, BA MCLIP, Sch. Lib., Boston Spa Sch., W. Yorks. [45514] 26/02/1991 **CM15/10/2002**

Chapman, Mrs S, BA(Hons), L. Mgr., Herts C.C. [60881] 18/12/2001 **ME**

Chapman, Mrs S, MCLIP, Life Member. [2610] 01/01/1957 **CM01/01/1966**

Chapman, Mrs S, BLib(Hons) MLib MCLIP, Unwaged. [43866] 30/01/1990 **CM21/05/1997**

Chapman, Mr V S, BLib(Hons) MCLIP, Cent. Lib. LB of Lewisham [31586] 20/10/1979 **CM15/04/1988**

Chapman, Mrs Y M C, BEd(Hons) DipILS MCLIP, p. /t. Team Lib. Books Reading and Learning Team [62040] 28/01/2003 **CM28/01/2009**

Chapman-Daniel, Mrs A, BA, Dir. /Owner, Minesoft Ltd, London. [10009811] 12/12/2001 **ME**

Chapman-Hall, Mrs J, Educ. Consultant (freelance). [10015768] 20/01/2010 **ME**

Chappell, Mr D L, BA(Hons) MSc MCLIP, Academic Liaison Lib., Glasgow Sch. of Art [56513] 04/08/1998 **CM10/07/2009**

Chappell, Mr G D C, BA, Stud., Liverpool John Moores Univ. [10011133] 26/09/2008 **ME**

Chappelle, Mrs C A, BA MCLIP, Stock Mgmt. Asst., John Rylands Univ. Lib., Univ. of Manchester [2614] 10/09/1970 **CM17/06/1974**

Charczuk, Ms A, Unwaged. [10005952] 11/09/2007 **ME**

Chard, Mr R P, BSc, Stud. [10006117] 04/09/2007 **ME**

Charin, Ms S, Lib. & Info. Serv. Mgr. [63244] 22/03/2004 **ME**

Charles, Mrs B J, BSc DipLib MCLIP, Asst. Lib., Scottish Exec., Edinburgh. [28488] 20/01/1978 **CM27/03/1980**

Charles, Ms E E, BA MSc MCLIP, Lib., Birkbeck, London. [37713] 17/10/1984 **CM15/03/1989**

Charles, Mrs J Y, BA(Hons) MSc MRQA, Quality & Compliance Mgr., Global. Inf. Serv. [51040] 09/11/1994 **ME**

Charles, Mrs S, MA MSc(Econ), Asst. Lib., Univ. L., Univ. of Dundee. [46163] 07/10/1991 **ME**

Charlesworth, Miss A D, BA(Hons) MA, Counter Servs. Super., Kings Coll., London. [56799] 19/10/1998 **ME**

Charlesworth, Mrs F M, MCLIP, Life Member. [8730] 01/01/1941 **CM01/01/1948**

Charlton, Mrs H M, BA MCLIP, Unknown [36883] 13/01/1984 **CM21/12/1988**

Charman, Mr D, MA MCLIP, Records Mgmnt. Consultant, Derek Charman Associates, Holcot. [60843] 12/03/1986 **CM12/12/2001**

Charnley, Ms C, BA MSc MCLIP, L. and Knowledge Serv. Mgr., Telford and Wrekin PCT, Shrewsbury. [46457] 07/11/1991 **CM26/01/1994**

Charnock, Ms R M C, MA(Hons) DipILS MCLIP, Head of Buisness Intelligence Serv., Edwards Angell Palmer & Dodge [49439] 27/10/1993 **CM22/07/1998**

Charwat, Mrs E, MA, Msc, Asst. Lib., Special Collections, Boole L., Univ. Coll. Cork. [64891] 07/09/2005 **ME**

Chase, Mr B J, FCLIP, Retired. [2626] 01/01/1959 **FE01/01/1964**

Chase, Ms B, Aquisitions Lib., Univ. of W. Indies, Barbados [10000177] 05/03/2010 **ME**

Chase, Ms S A, BA(Hons) DipInf, Mgr., Weil, Gotshal & Manges, London. [49506] 08/11/1993 **ME**

Chatten, Mrs J, Knowledge Asst., Nabarro, London [10007182] 25/01/2008 **AF**

Chatten, Mr R M, BA, Postperson, Royal Mail. [40283] 12/01/1987 **ME**

Chatten, Mrs Z, BA(Hons) MA MCLIP, Subject Lib., Univ. of Liverpool. [57975] 07/10/1999 **CM08/12/2004**

Chatterton, Miss C J, ACLIP, Tech. Lib., Cornwall Council. [64823] 20/07/2005 **ACL01/09/2006**

Chau, Miss C W C, MLib MCLIP, Asst. Lib., Hong Kong Poly. Univ. L. [42202] 13/10/1988 **CM16/09/1992**

Chaudhri, Mrs D K, MCLIP, Unemployed. [10000536] 05/10/2006 **CM22/11/1995**

Chaudhry, Ms R Y, BA(Hons) MCLIP, Lib., Rugby High Sch., Warks. C.C. [37656] 13/10/1984 **CM14/03/1990**

Chaudhury, Mr M, MBA MA, Head of Study Support, Barking & Dagenham Coll. [58525] 10/03/2000 **ME**

Chedgzoy, Mr J N, BA(Hons) DipLis MCLIP, Sen. Lib., Shropshire C.C., Bridgnorth L. [46986] 20/03/1992 **CM24/07/1996**

Chedgzoy, Mrs S L, BA(Hons) DipLib MCLIP, Principal Offr. : Young People & Learning, Herefordshire C. [46593] 21/11/1991 **CM18/03/1998**

Cheeseborough, Mrs J, BA(Hons) DipLib MCLIP FCLIP, Learning & Devel. Mgr. for Info. & Knowledge Mgmnt., Royal Coll. of Nursing, London. [33034] 17/10/1980 **FE19/03/2008**

Cheeseman, Mrs N, Unknown. [10011450] 23/10/2009 **ME**

Cheesman, Mr B, MA MCLIP, Life Member. [2643] 01/10/1956 **CM01/01/1959**

Cheesman, Miss D A, BA DipLib MCLIP, System Consultant, Ex Libris UK, Harefield. [43572] 09/11/1989 **CM15/09/1993**

Cheesman, Ms R E, MA, Lib. [10015574] 17/12/2009 **ME**

Cheetham, Mrs L M, BA MCLIP, Sch. Lib., Hitchin Girls Sch., Herts. [30196] 08/01/1979 **CM08/01/1981**

Cheicho Pimenta, Mr C M, BA MA, Asst. Lib., Oxford Univ. [10008769] 18/04/2008 **ME**

Chelin, Ms J A, BA DipLib MCLIP, Dep. Lib., Univ. of the W. of England, Frenchay Campus L., Bristol. [39406] 29/01/1986 **CM25/05/1994**

Chell, Mrs J E, Lib. Asst., Tremough L., Penryn [10008302] 20/03/2008 **AF**

Chen, Dr K C, MBA MSc FInstBA FBSC MCLIP PhD, Retired. [16750] 22/06/1969 **CM01/01/1969**

Cheney, Ms C R, BA MCLIP, Biomedical Team Leader, Univ. Coll. London. [36530] 17/10/1983 **CM09/07/1987**

Cherpeau, Ms C M, BSc(Hons) MCLIP, Sen. Lib:Comm. Serv., Knowsley L. Serv., Huyton L. [45304] 04/10/1990 **CM09/09/2009**

Cherry, Mr M, BSc BA(Hons), Lib., L. & Mus. of Freemasonry, London. [62125] 21/02/2003 **ME**

Cherry, Mrs S A, Sen. Lib. Asst., L. Serv., Medway NHS Foundation Trust, Gillingham. [10016567] 14/04/2010 **AF**

Cheshire, Miss M M, BA MCLIP, Retired. [2658] 18/05/1966 **CM01/01/1969**

Chesney, Mrs A R, BA MCLIP, Principal Lib., Milton Keynes Council. [34617] 19/01/1982 **CM16/12/1983**

Chesney, Mr B J, MA MCLIP, Unemployed. [2659] 06/10/1967 **CM01/01/1969**

Chester, Miss J, BA(Hons) DipLib MCLIP, Dir., Smart Programme, Cancer Res. UK, London. [24182] 01/04/1975 **CM01/07/1978**

Chesters, Mrs H A, BA(Hons) MA MCLIP, Asst. Lib., Inst. of Child Health, UCL. [54423] 09/12/1996 **CM25/07/2001**

Chestney, Mr J A, Stud. [10016705] 28/04/2010 **ME**

Chestnutt, Miss M A, BA DipLib MCLIP, Sch. Lib., Down High Sch., Co. Down. [27145] 25/12/1976 **CM23/05/1979**

Chesworth, Mr S, MCLIP, Professional Learning Resource Cent. Advisor, S. Cheshire Coll., Crewe. [62906] 18/11/2003 **CM29/11/2006**

Chetwood, Ms R L, Sen. Lib. – Special Needs L. [63599] 05/07/2004 **AF**

Cheung, Mrs E Y L, BA MCLIP, Retired [43682] 24/11/1989 **CM18/11/1998**

Cheung, Mrs H M, BA DipLib MCLIP MEd, Retired [41261] 21/10/1987 **CM14/08/1991**

Chevallot, Ms I C, BA(Hons) Dip Inf. Serv., Unknown. [10016887] 01/06/2010 **ME**

Chew, Ms A, MSc, Asst. Lib., Brit. Architectural Lib., Riba [65100] 01/11/2005 **ME**

Chew, Mr J K, FCLIP, Life Member. [2664] 26/03/1950 **FE01/01/1960**

Chew, Mrs P, MCLIP, Lib., HMP Edmunds Hill [19716] 19/07/1968 **CM01/01/1972**

Cheyne, Miss P N, BA(Hons) MA MA, Operations Lib., Davis Langdon LLP, London. [10006128] 11/09/2007 **ME**

Cheyne, Mrs S C, MA(Hons) PgDipILS, Sch. Lib. (Job Share), Craigholme Sch., Glasgow. [65396] 27/01/2006 **ME**

Cheyney, Mr K G, MCLIP, Life Member. [2666] 13/03/1951 **CM01/01/1957**

Chibnall, Miss M I, BA MCLIP, Retired [18422] 21/10/1972 **CM07/11/1975**

Chigara, Mrs C, BA ACLIP, Inf. & Resource Coordinator, Uxbridge Coll. [10010855] 02/09/2008 **ACL23/09/2009**

Chikasha, Mr C, BSc, Unknown. [10012401] 03/02/2009 **ME**

Childs Smith, Ms K E, BA MCLIP, Head of L. & Inf. Serv., NSPCC, London. [30895] 05/05/1979 **CM18/06/1984**

Childs, Mr A D, BA FCLIP, Life Member. [2677] 04/03/1948 **FE01/01/1960**

Childs, Mrs E, BA(Hons) DipILM, Requests Mgr., Mob. L. Off., Alfreton. [64319] 02/03/2005 **ME**

Chilmaid, Mrs D J, MBA DipLib MCLIP, Business Support Mgr., Kent Ls. and Arch., Maidstone. [32148] 21/01/1980 **CM27/09/1982**

Chilton, Mrs S, MCLIP, Inf. Mgr., Northumbria Univ., Newcastle. [10001148] 12/01/2007 **CM22/02/2010**

Chilvers, Dr A H, BA(Hons) DipLib MA PhD MCLIP, Career break [43982] 20/03/1990 **CM16/12/1992**

Chilvers, Mrs I, Dip. Ing, Sen. L. Asst., PPSIS L., Univ. of Cambridge. [10016683] 26/04/2010 **AF**

Chinn, Ms M, MCLIP, Res. Off. Resources (Job-share), Age Concern England, London. [21810] 15/01/1974 **CM21/01/1976**

Chinnery, Miss C, BLib MCLIP, L. Mgr., Peterborough Reg. Coll. [21992] 18/01/1974 **CM19/12/1978**

Chinnock, Mrs S J, Community Lib., Walmley L., Birmingham C.C. (Part-time)+ Wylde Green L. [61093] 27/02/2002 **ME**

Chirgwin, Mr F J, BA MSc FCLIP, Life Member. [2685] 21/05/1959
FE01/01/1965
Chirgwin, Mrs T M D W, MA(Oxon) MMus DipLIM MCLIP, Resources
Lib., Cheshire W. C.C., L. H.Q., Chester. [55321] 01/10/1997
CM17/01/2001
Chisholm, Mrs A I, MCLIP, Retired. [2686] 20/01/1961   **CM01/01/1966**
Chiu, Mrs L W, BA(Hons), LRC Mgr., St. Dominic's Sixth Form Coll.,
Harrow-on-the-Hill [10013131] 31/03/2009   **ME**
Chivas, Mrs G, BSc MCLIP, Lib., Cox Green L., Maidenhead. [23816]
31/01/1975   **CM12/01/1979**
Chohan, Mrs N, Stud. [10013509] 30/04/2009   **ME**
Chong, Ms K, Unknown. [10005248] 21/11/2007   **ME**
Choolhun, Mrs N, BA(Hons) Pg DipLib, Info. Offr., Coll. of Law, London.
[60976] 22/01/2002   **ME**
Choong, Mrs C L, BA(Hons) MCLIP, Asst. Lib. Reader Serv.,
Canterbury Christ Church Univ. [59846] 16/10/2001   **CM09/09/2009**
Chopra, Mr P, BA MCLIP, Campus Lib., Univ. of E. London, Stratford
Campus. [37124] 28/02/1984   **CM10/11/1987**
Chopra, Mr V, Learning Ctre Asst., Southampton City Coll. [10006182]
18/09/2007   **AF**
Choudhury, Mrs S, Bsc Msc Ma, L. Asst., Grimsoyke Frist & Middle
Sch. [10016022] 10/02/2010   **ME**
Chouglay, Mrs L A, BSc(Hons) DipLib MCLIP, Unemployed – Full-time
Mother. [39216] 01/01/1986   **CM24/05/1995**
Choules, Ms J E, BA(Hons) MA MCLIP, Stock Dev. Mgr., Bristol L.,
[49237] 14/10/1993   **CM19/03/1997**
Chow, Ms J, MCLIP, Academic Serv. Lib., St. John's Coll., Univ of
Cambridge [64703] 01/06/2005   **CM11/03/2009**
Chowdhury, Dr G G, BSc(Hons) BLib MLib PhD FCLIP, Prof. of Inf.
Studies, Univ. of Tech. Sydney. [56835] 26/10/1998   **FE22/09/1999**
Chrimes, Mr M M, BA MLS MCLIP, Lib., Inst. of Civil Engineers,
London. [26211] 20/08/1976   **CM20/08/1978**
Chrisp, Mr P S, BA MCLIP, Retired. [2696] 09/10/1965   **CM01/07/1988**
Christensen, Ms E, MA, Unknown. [10014351] 17/07/2009 **ME**
Christian, Mr W D, L. & Inf. Advisor, United Lincolnshire Hosp. NHS
Trust. [42549] 07/12/1988   **ME**
Christie, Miss E V, BA DipLib MCLIP, Child. Servs. Mgr – L. NI. [40905]
17/08/1987   **CM15/02/1989**
Christie, Mr G F, MA MSc, Digital L. Offr., Edinburgh Univ. [55796]
24/11/1997   **ME**
Christie, Miss P M, BA MCLIP, Dir. of Inf. Serv., Univ. of the Arts
London. [25018] 02/11/1975   **CM22/03/1983**
Christine, Miss R, MA MCLIP, Lib., Mary Erskine Sch. [53834]
03/10/1996 **RV29/03/2007**   **CM20/09/2000**
Christison, Mrs A, BSc(Hons) MSc MCLIP, Lib.,Nat. Coal Mining Mus.,
Wakefield. [54523] 14/01/1997   **CM18/09/2002**
Christmas, Miss J A, L. Operations Co-ordinator, Allen & Overy,
London. [51182] 23/11/1994   **ME**
Christophers, Mr R A, MA PhD FCLIP, p. /t. L. Consultant. [2700]
14/02/1958   **FE01/01/1963**
Chryssanthopoulos, Mrs P, BSc DipLib MA, Unemployed. [46082]
01/10/1991   **ME**
Chu, Miss S Y, BA(Hons) MCLIP, PGME Lib., UCLH NHS Trust [34294]
14/10/1981   **CM07/11/1985**
Chuah, Miss M, BA MCLIP, Lib., Univ. of Malaya L., Kuala Lumpur.
[24410] 29/07/1975   **CM14/01/1980**
Church, Miss J, p. /t. Stud., Univ. of Wales, Aberystwyth, Montrose L.,
Angus. [65457] 23/02/2006   **ME**
Churches, Mr K J, MCLIP, Life Member. [2705] 30/09/1947
CM01/01/1952
Chute, Mrs M, BA MCLIP, Community L. Mgr., Frankley L., Birmingham.
[9306] 01/01/1972   **CM01/01/1976**

Cieciura, Mrs E K, BA MLib MCLIP, Res. & Enterprise Support Off.,
Financial & Commercial Serv. Bournemouth Univ. [39291]
07/01/1986   **CM26/05/1993**
Cimals, Mrs A D, BA DipLib, Employment not known. [36429]
13/10/1983   **ME**
Cini, Mr L, Asst. Lib., Nat. L. of Malta. [49896] 07/01/1994   **ME**
Cinnamond, Mrs J, MCLIP, Life Member. [2712] 03/03/1960
CM01/01/1965
Cinquin, Miss L C, Unknown. [10012149] 08/01/2009   **ME**
Cipkin, Mr C B, BA(Hons) MA ARCO MCLIP, Faculty Team Mgr., Univ.
Reading. [51805] 04/07/1995 **RV23/01/2007**   **CM17/03/1999**
Cipollone, Ms M, MA, Subject Lib. London Met. Univ. [62084]
12/02/2003   **ME**
Cirtina, Ms O S, BA MCLIP, Administrator. [32020] 12/02/1980
CM11/02/1982
Clackson, Mrs A M, BMus(Hons) DipLib, Asst. Lib., Univ. of Strathclyde.
[34247] 13/10/1981   **ME**
Clague, Mr P, BA FCLIP, Life Member. [2713] 29/03/1955**FE01/01/1967**
Clanchy, Miss J, B Lib MCLIP, Lib., GCHQ, Cheltenham. [2714]
11/10/1970   **CM23/09/1974**
Clanchy, Dr M T, HonFLA, Hon. Fellow. [59434] 15/03/2001
HFE15/03/2001
Clapham, Ms J, BA(Hons)Hum, L. Asst., Nat. Coal Mining Mus.,
Wakefield. [62743] 14/10/2003   **ME**
Clapham, Ms L, BA MCLIP, Sch. Lib., Sidney Stringer Sch., Coventry.
[36716] 11/11/1983   **CM10/12/1986**
Clapham, Mrs S E, Community Info. Offr., Harrogate L. [64231]
21/02/2004   **AF**
Clapp, Mrs F C, MCLIP, Unwaged. [26516] 13/10/1976   **CM25/01/1980**
Clapton, Ms J E, BSc(Hons) MSc MCLIP, Sen. Inf. Specialist, Social Care
Inst. for Excellence, London. [59428] 13/03/2001   **CM19/03/2008**
Clare, Mrs C, MA, Unwaged. [45263] 28/01/1991   **ME**
Clare, Ms H M, BA MA MCLIP, Resources Advisor, Kingston Coll.
Kingston, Surrey [61743] 31/10/2002   **CM10/07/2009**
Clare, Mrs J B, BA(Hons) MCLIP, E-Learning/Resources Mgr., The
Billericay Sch., Essex. [26807] 07/11/1976   **CM15/02/1980**
Claridge, Mr J, Dip, Sen. L. Asst., Queen Mary Univ. of London L.
[64969] 05/10/2005   **AF**
Clark, Miss A H, BA(Hons) MA MCLIP, Lib., Wirral Univ. Teaching Hosp.
NHS Found. Trust [58786] 20/07/2000   **CM29/03/2006**
Clark, Mr A J, BSocSci MCLIP, Designing L. Project Mgr. [22092]
09/01/1974   **CM17/03/1976**
Clark, Mrs A J, L. Asst., The Hazeley Sch., Milton Keynes. [10011434]
20/10/2008   **AF**
Clark, Mr A, MA(Hons), Stud. [10002514] 01/05/2007   **ME**
Clark, Mr B F, BLib MCLIP, Principal L. Offr., Support Serv., Sandwell L.
& Inf. Serv. [29937] 09/11/1978   **CM09/11/1980**
Clark, Ms B, BA(Hons) MA, L. Res. Mgr., Notre Dame R. C. Girls Sch.,
London. [10016708] 29/04/2010   **AF**
Clark, Ms C J, BEd MLib MCLIP, Upper Sch. Lib., American Internat.
Sch. of Budapest, Hungary. [26089] 21/07/1976   **CM09/10/1979**
Clark, Mrs C M, BA(Hons) MSc, Lib. Mngr., Audit Commission, Bristol
[59771] 01/10/2001   **ME**
Clark, Miss C, MA, Unknown. [10013345] 16/04/2009   **ME**
Clark, Mr D A, BA DipLib MCLIP, Sch. Lib., Tarbert/Argyll, Argyll & Bute
Council. [36722] 10/11/1983   **CM23/03/1994**
Clark, Mr D H, MCLIP, Life Member. [2725] 12/10/1944 **CM01/01/1952**
Clark, Mrs D W, MCLIP, Head Ref. Serv., House of Commons L.
London. [780] 23/09/1968   **CM02/03/1973**
Clark, Mr D, MCLIP, Sci. & Tech. Lib., Univ. of Derby. [29019]
21/03/1977   **CM21/03/1980**
Clark, Mrs E K, BA(Hons) DipIS MCLIP, Sen. L. Exec., House of
Commons L., London. [52132] 05/10/1995   **CM17/01/2001**

Clark, Mrs F H, BA MCLIP, L. & Inf. Serv. Mgr, Cent. L., Aberdeen City L. [30394] 07/02/1979 **CM31/08/1983**

Clark, Mr H G, MCLIP, Retired. [2728] 11/10/1941 **CM01/01/1952**

Clark, Miss H J, BA(Hons) MA, L. Mgr., The Angel Foundation, Sunderland. [61697] 21/10/2002 **AF**

Clark, Mr H M, Academic Liaison Lib., Bradford Coll. [49269] 20/10/1993 **ME**

Clark, Mrs H R, BA DipLib MCLIP, L. & Inf. Mgr., Sligo Gen. Hosp., HSE W., Republic of Ireland. [37979] 01/01/1985 **CM01/09/1987**

Clark, Mrs J A, BA MCLIP, Ch. Lib. /Area Mgr., Kirklees MBC. Culture and Leisure Dept., Huddersfield [27860] 28/09/1977 **CM21/11/1979**

Clark, Miss J E, MSc BA MCLIP, Asst. Lib., Religious Soc. Friends, London. [2737] 13/10/1970 **CM01/10/1972**

Clark, Mrs J M, MCLIP, Local Stud. Asst., Oldham M.B.C. [28988] 20/02/1978 **CM31/08/1983**

Clark, Mr J M, BA(Hons), Local Studies Offr. [10005349] 05/07/2007 **ME**

Clark, Mrs J S, BA(Hons) DipILM, Serials Lib., Univ. of Newcastle. [52474] 02/11/1995 **ME**

Clark, Miss J, BA AIL MCLIP, Life Member. [2733] 09/02/1955 **CM01/01/1958**

Clark, Miss K R, Lib. Asst., Guille-Alles L., Guernsey [10017039] 18/06/2010 **AF**

Clark, Mrs K, B LIB MCLIP, Inf. Literacy Mgr., Royal Coll. of Nursing, London. [22511] 13/05/1974 **CM24/11/1977**

Clark, Mrs L J, BA(Hons) DipLib Dip MCLIP, Sen. L. & Info. Mngr., Health Improvement L., NHS Stoke Directorate of Public Health [34570] 04/01/1982 **CM09/03/1985**

Clark, Mrs L M M, MCLIP, Stourbridge L. [10001139] 21/02/1970 **CM13/07/1972**

Clark, Mrs L M, BA MCLIP, Lib. Mgr., Circ. and Operations, Stockport Coll., Stockport. [40421] 22/01/1987 **CM15/08/1990**

Clark, Mrs L M, BA MCLIP, Stock Serv. Lib., E. Kilbride Cent. L., S. Lanarkshire Council. [31261] 12/10/1979 **CM01/07/1989**

Clark, Ms L, BA(Hons) MA, Lib. Mgr., RICS Scotland, Edinburgh [10014570] 11/11/1996 **ME**

Clark, Mrs M E, MCLIP, Child. Lib., Bristol City Council, Cent. L. [1276] 03/09/1968 **CM12/09/1972**

Clark, Mrs M E, MCLIP, Life Member. [2741] 01/01/1957 **CM01/01/1961**

Clark, Mr M, M. Ed, Learner Zone Co-ordinator, Skelmersdale Coll. [10013621] 13/05/2009 **ME**

Clark, Mrs R E, MA(Hons) DipLIS MCLIP, Unknown. [54353] 26/11/1996 **CM20/09/2000**

Clark, Mr R M, BA DipLib MCLIP, External Res. Database Mgr., Slaughter & May, London. [37702] 19/10/1984 **CM02/06/1987**

Clark, Mr R S C, BA MCLIP, Bibl. Serv. Lib., Motherwell L., N. Lanarkshire Council. [19601] 08/11/1972 **CM09/03/1978**

Clark, Mr R, BA(Hons) MA, Temp. L. Asst., Brunel Univ. L., London [65608] 28/02/2006 **ME**

Clark, Mrs S E, BA(Hons) MCLIP, p/t Res. Asst., Univ. of Brighton, St. Peters House L. [2751] 16/07/1968 **CM26/06/1974**

Clark, Mrs S N, MA(Hons) PgDip MCLIP, Asst. Lib., Univ. of the W. of England, Bristol. [63154] 13/02/2004 **CM10/07/2009**

Clark, Mr S, BA MA, Accreditation Co-ordinator, Middlesex Univ. [10007153] 29/04/2005 **ME**

Clark, Mr T J, MA(Hons) MSc, Unknown [65014] 05/10/2005 **ME**

Clark, Ms V M, MA MCLIP, Teacher, St. James Sch., Stockport [23162] 08/11/1974 **CM28/06/1978**

Clark, Miss W, BA(Hons) MCLIP, Audience Devel. Offr., Essex C.C., Brentwood L. [49119] 06/10/1993 **CM18/11/1998**

Clark, Mrs Z M, BA(Hons) MA MCLIP, Career Break. [53692] 06/09/1996 **CM21/11/2001**

Clarke, Mrs A C, LRC Team Leader, Wiltshire Coll., Trowbridge. [10009980] 01/07/1997 **AF**

Clarke, Mrs A M, BA MCLIP, Knowledge Mgr., N. E. Yorkshire & N. Lincs., Workforce Devel Confederation. [24361] 18/07/1975 **CM07/07/1978**

Clarke, Mr A, BA(Hons), MA(Hons), Grad. Trainee, Boland L., Bristol. [10011203] 02/10/2008 **ME**

Clarke, Ms A, L. Mgr. – Mobiles, Cambridgeshire. [10015135] 14/10/2009 **AF**

Clarke, Mrs A, MCLIP, Retired. [2752] 08/02/1962 **CM01/01/1966**

Clarke, Miss C J, MCLIP, F/T Worker, Manor High Sch., Wednesbury. [63507] 16/06/2004 **CM27/01/2010**

Clarke, Mrs C, Learning Resources Coordinator, Coleg Powys, Llandrindod Wells. [10008860] 08/04/1997 **AF**

Clarke, Ms D A, BA DipLib, Asst. Lib., Oxford Brookes Univ. L., Oxford. [51784] 01/07/1995 **ME**

Clarke, Mr D A, MA FRSA MCLIP, Life Member. [20689] 19/03/1948 **CM01/01/1950**

Clarke, Mr D E, MLS MCLIP, Retired. [2759] 01/01/1956 **CM01/01/1958**

Clarke, Miss E J, BSc MCLIP, Dist. Mgr., NEELB L. Serv., Co. Antrim. [22722] 30/08/1974 **CM26/09/1977**

Clarke, Ms E M, BA(Hons) MSc, Lib., Ashurst. [56053] 20/01/1998 **ME**

Clarke, Rev F A, DMS MCMI PGDipTheol MCLIP, Retired. [2765] 20/01/1964 **CM01/01/1967**

Clarke, Mrs F E, BA PgDip, Libr., Halton Bor. Council. [61731] 29/10/2002 **ME**

Clarke, Mrs G J, BA, Open Learning Cent. Mgr, Gillotts Sch., Henley-on-Thames, Oxon [37056] 12/01/1984 **ME**

Clarke, Mrs G L, Unknown. [10012546] 19/12/2008 **AF**

Clarke, Mr G M, BA(Hons) DipLib MCLIP, Learning Cen. Mgr., The Manchester Coll. [25508] 13/01/1976 **CM31/12/1989**

Clarke, Mrs J L, MCLIP, Head of L. & Inf. Serv., Holman,Fenwick Willan, London. [23042] 23/10/1974 **CM27/10/1977**

Clarke, Mrs J M, Lib., Altrincham Grammar Sch. Boys, Cheshire. [52726] 28/11/1995 **ME**

Clarke, Mrs J M, MBE MCLIP, Life Member. [2774] 11/10/1945 **CM01/01/1952**

Clarke, Miss J, BA DMS MCLIP, Career Break [25021] 01/11/1975 **CM27/06/1980**

Clarke, Mr J, BA MCLIP, Team Lib., Weston Favell L., Northampton [10008437] 08/01/1979 **CM16/04/1981**

Clarke, Mrs L A, BA(Hons) PGCE MCLIP, Asst. Electronic Res. Lib., W. Midlands., Stratg. Health, Birmingham. [42268] 13/10/1988 **CM26/11/1997**

Clarke, Mrs L E, BA(Hons) MCLIP, Employed (Part-time), Cheshire CC Bibliographical Serv., Chester [10001631] 11/10/1984 **CM15/11/1988**

Clarke, Mr M E, BA MCLIP, Head of L., L.B. of Camden, London [39336] 17/01/1986 **CM18/07/1991**

Clarke, Miss M E, BA(Hons) MSc MCLIP, Outreach Inf. Mgr., Royal Coll. Nursing, London. [56916] 04/11/1998 **CM15/05/2002**

Clarke, Ms P M, BA MCLIP, Grp. Child. Lib., Redcar Cent. L., Redcar & Cleveland Bor. Council. [19882] 01/01/1973 **CM18/01/1979**

Clarke, Mr P R, BSc MCLIP, Consultant. [2788] 12/08/1968 **CM20/07/1972**

Clarke, Mr P, MCLIP, Grp. L. Mgr., L.B. Greenwich. [23612] 16/01/1975 **CM19/07/1977**

Clarke, Mrs R M, BA(Hons) MCLIP, L. Asst., St. John's Theological Coll., Nottingham. [38199] 28/01/1985 **CM24/05/1995**

Clarke, Mrs R, LRC Mgr., St. Edwards Coll., Liverpool [64299] 23/02/2005 **ME**

Clarke, Mrs S B, MA DipLib MCLIP, Sch. Lib., Tormead Sch., Guildford. [35411] 03/10/1982 **CM07/07/1987**

Clarke, Mrs S D, BSc(Hons), Business Researcher, Career Mgmnt. Consultants Ltd., Cheshrie [59852] 17/10/2001 **ME**

Clarke, Mr S J, BA MCLIP, Stock Devel. Mgr., L.B. of Tower Hamlets. [34296] 20/10/1981 **CM28/02/1985**

Clarke, Miss S K, BSc(Hons) MA, Sen. L. Asst., Lancaster Univ. [56940] 09/11/1998 **ME**

Clarke, Mrs S P, BA FCLIP, Retired. [2793] 03/10/1949 **FE20/01/1999**

Clarke, Mrs T M, BSc MCLIP, Trust Lib., N. Middlesex Univ. Hosp. NHS Trust, London. [3429] 01/01/1970 **CM13/12/1974**

Clarke, Mr T, Relief Lib. Asst., Ipswich Co. Lib., Ipswich [10017173] 11/07/2010 **AF**

Clarke, Mrs V K, Stud., Robert Gorgon Univ. [10013586] 08/05/2009 **ME**

Clarke, Ms Z A, BA MA MCLIP, Principal Devel. Mgr., Community Cohesion, Sefton. [40320] 10/01/1987 **CM13/06/1990**

Clarke-Holmes, Ms S A, BA(Hons) MA PGCE MCLIP, Asst. Lib., Manchester Met. Univ. [65431] 23/02/2006 **CM23/01/2008**

Clarkson, Mr J A J, BA MCLIP, Sch. Lib., Trinity Academy, Edinburgh. [39761] 01/07/1986 **CM13/06/1990**

Clarkson, Mrs M A, BA MCLIP, Sch. Serv. Mgr., Manchester City Council. [39789] 04/07/1986 **CM23/03/1994**

Clarkson, Miss R, MSc BA MCLIP, Unwaged. [35648] 25/11/1982 **CM21/12/1988**

Clark-Webster, Ms E, MSc BA(Hons), L. Customer Serv. Mgr., Univ. of the W. of England, Bristol. [10010959] 03/07/1997 **ME**

Clasen, Ms C F, MA MA, Inf. Offr., Grounds for Learning, Alloa [43549] 06/11/1989 **ME**

Clausen, Dr H, Dr. Hist. Ecc. PhD MA MLSc FCLIP, Ret. [46818] 05/02/1992 **FE21/07/1993**

Clausen, Mrs J H, MCLIP, Retired. [2800] 09/10/1944 **CM01/01/1956**

Clavel-Merrin, Ms G M, MLib MCLIP, Internat. Relations, Swiss Nat. L., Bern, Switzerland. [27544] 28/04/1977 **CM02/03/1983**

Clay, Mrs A J, BA(Hons) MCLIP, Bibl. Serv. Offr., Warrington Bor. Council Ls., Warrington,Cheshire. [48955] 02/08/1993 **CM27/11/1996**

Clay, Mr J, Lib., Min. of Defence, Feltham. [10010242] 17/07/2008 **AF**

Clayton, Mr C, BA DMS MCLIP, Dir., SINTO, Sheffield. [2812] 01/01/1972 **CM23/10/1975**

Clayton, Dr D J, BA MA PhD FRSHist FSA MCLIP, Editor of Bulletin, John Rylands Univ. L., Manchester [10015656] 02/10/1974 **CM01/07/1993**

Clayton, Ms G M, BA DipLib MCLIP, Lib., Emersons Green, S. Glos. Council. [30310] 16/01/1979 **CM24/03/1981**

Clayton, Miss J E, BA MCLIP, Retired. [18169] 04/10/1972 **CM03/04/1975**

Clayton, Miss J M, BA DLIS MCLIP, Employment not known. [25242] 03/01/1976 **CM17/01/1979**

Clayton, Miss L A, BA(Hons) MA MCLIP, Ref. Lib., Southampton Cent. Ref. L. [55219] 20/08/1997 **CM23/01/2002**

Clayton, Miss L, BA MCLIP, Ref. & Inf. Asst., John Rylands Univ. L. of Manchester. [40637] 01/04/1987 **CM25/07/2001**

Clayton, Mr P A, FSA FRNS FCLIP DipArch, Retired. [2817] 14/03/1955 **FE01/01/1964**

Clayton, Mr R E, BA(Hons) MA MCLIP, Co. Lib., Rutland C.C., Oakham. [48366] 08/12/1992 **CM31/01/1996**

Clayton, Mrs S M, BA MCLIP, Unknown. [34061] 02/09/1981 **CM15/09/1983**

Clayton, Mrs S P, BA(Hons) MCLIP, Clinical Lib. [10006653] 08/01/1979 **CM23/09/1982**

Clayton, Mrs V A, BA(Hons) MCLIP, Resourses & Skills Mgr., Sherborne Sch., Sherborne. [41294] 30/10/1987 **CM14/02/1990**

Clear, Mrs F C, BA DipLib MCLIP, Business Mgr., Family Inf. Link, Stockport. [34575] 12/01/1982 **CM11/04/1985**

Clear, Mrs R L, BA(Hons) MA MCLIP, Lib., Clifton Coll. Preparatory Sch., Clifton Bristol. (On Maternity Leave) [56519] 03/08/1998 **CM10/07/2002**

Cleary, Mrs R L, MA MCLIP, Lib., Language Cent., Univ. of Cambridge. [42032] 27/07/1988 **CM16/10/1991**

Cleaver, Mrs A V, MSc MCLIP, Head of Know-How, Maitland Advisory LLP. [26991] 05/01/1977 **CM30/05/1979**

Cleaves, Ms H, BA(Hons) MA, Sch. Lib., St James Sen. Girls Sch. [10006658] 11/09/2007 **ME**

Cleeve, Mrs M L, BA MCLIP, Inf. Consultant. [2825] 01/01/1965 **CM01/01/1969**

Clegg, Mrs A, MA FCLIP, Retired. [2827] 10/03/1960 **FE01/01/1968**

Clegg, Mr D, BA(Hons), Community L. Mgr., Plymouth [10008256] 15/05/1985 **ME**

Clegg, Ms S J, BA MCLIP, General Serv. Co-ordinator, Glasgow City Council, Mitchell L. [33964] 15/06/1981 **CM22/08/1984**

Clegg, Miss S M, BA MBA MCLIP, Univ. Lib. & Dir. of Learning Serv., Roehampton Univ. [2834] 01/01/1970 **CM04/09/1973**

Cleghorn, Ms F A, MSc, Inf. Resource Consultant, NERA, London. [21971] 17/01/1974 **ME**

Clement, Mr A C, MA MCLIP, Inf. Off., IMECHE, London. [62008] 16/01/2003 **CM04/10/2006**

Clement, Mrs A R, Projects and Knowledge Mgmnt Controller., MedilinkWM, Birmingham. [10013697] 22/05/2009 **AF**

Clement, Ms E, BA MA MCLIP, Academic Lib. Applied Sciences, AA Design & Architecture, Univ. of huddersfield [56935] 06/11/1998 **RV17/10/2006** **CM25/07/2001**

Clement, Mrs G E G, FCLIP, Life Member. [2835] 11/10/1942 **FE01/01/1957**

Clements, Mrs C T, BLib MCLIP, Princ. L. Offr. (Young People), Cornwall C.C. [28275] 01/11/1977 **CM08/02/1982**

Clements, Mrs E R, MCLIP, Retired. [7670] 15/07/1955 **CM01/01/1969**

Clements, Mr F A, FCLIP, Retired. [2838] 15/07/1965 **FE27/10/1975**

Clements, Mrs G F, BA(Hons) MCLIP, Lifelong Learning & Local Studies Lib. [40471] 09/02/1987 **CM29/03/2004**

Clements, Mrs G J, BA Dip Lib MCLIP, Unknown. [39383] 21/01/1986 **CM16/02/1988**

Clements, Mrs M, BA MCLIP, p. /t. L. Asst., Heriot-Watt Univ. L., Edinburgh. [9504] 21/09/1970 **CM26/03/1974**

Clement-Stoneham, Mrs G M, MA MCLIP, Knowledge and Inf. Mgmnt. Consultant [53751] 01/10/1996 **CM15/09/2004**

Clemetson, Miss S, BA MCLIP, L. Asst., Oxford Co. L. [36098] 31/05/1983 **CM24/06/1988**

Clemow, Mrs H L, BA(Hons) DipLib MCLIP, Teaching Asst. [46083] 01/10/1991 **CM14/09/1994**

Clemson, Mrs J A, BSc MCLIP, Sch. Lib., Great Sankey High Sch., Warrington. [57645] 14/06/1999 **CM09/07/2008**

Clemson, Mrs T K, BA MCLIP, Unwaged. [33294] 19/11/1980 **CM27/08/1985**

Cleverley, Mrs P E, MCLIP, Dist. Lib., Birmingham. [5769] 02/10/1970 **CM08/01/1974**

Clews, Ms C, BA, Stud., Univ. of Strathclyde, Glasgow. [10011461] 21/10/2008 **ME**

Clibbens, Mrs A, Lib. User Servs. Asst., Univ. of Plymouth [61562] 02/10/2002 **ME**

Click, Miss A, MLIS, Instruction/Ref. Lib., American Univ. of Cairo. [10015280] 30/10/2009 **ME**

Clifford, Mr B E, BA MA HonFCLIP, Dep. Lib., Univ. of Leeds. [25965] 12/04/1976 **FE01/04/2002**

Clifford, Mrs E J, BHum(Hons) MCLIP, Team. Lib., Chipping Barnet L., Herts. [48788] 27/05/1993 **CM01/06/2005**

Clifford, Mr J N, BA DipLib MCLIP, Br. Lib., Bob Lawrence L., L.B. of Harrow. [35795] 12/01/1983 **CM21/07/1989**

Clifford, Mrs K M L, MSc BSc(Hons) MCLIP, Sr. Info. Advisor Bibliographic & Metadata, Info. Servs., Kingston Univ., London [62714] 03/10/2003 **CM21/03/2007**

Clifford, Miss S K, MCLIP, Retired. [2854] 25/08/1948 **CM01/01/1967**

Clifford-Winters, Mr A M, BSc MCLIP, Retired. [60678] 01/05/1969 **CM01/07/1974**

Clift, Mrs C, BA(Hons) MA MCLIP, Lib., Rutlish Sch., Merton. [2855]
14/02/1964 **CM01/01/1968**
Cliftlands, Mr A D, BA(Hons) DipLib, Sen. Lib., MHRA Info. Cent.,
London. [43241] 13/10/1989 **ME**
Clifton, Ms B A, BA(Hons) MCLIP, Mgr., L. & Records Serv., Off. of the
Controller & Auditor General, New Zealand. [10000898] 23/10/1980
CM13/06/1989
Clifton, Mrs S D, BA(Hons) MCLIP, L. & Learning Res. Mgr., Smith's
Wood Sports Coll., Solihull. [46289] 23/10/1991 **CM21/05/1997**
Climpson, Mr D G, MA MCLIP, Retired. [2857] 01/10/1968
CM01/01/1971
Clipsham, Mrs G, BA MCLIP, Child. Reading Devel. Co-Ordinator,
Bucks C. C, Wendover L. [27488] 25/02/1977 **CM12/06/1979**
Clitheroe, Mr F R, BA MCLIP, Literary Editor, The Lymes Press, Staffs.
[2862] 07/06/1963 **CM01/01/1971**
Clogg, Mrs M J, BSc DipLib MCLIP, Retired. [31587] 01/11/1979
CM13/10/1982
Cloke, Miss J E, MBE FCLIP, Life Member. [2865] 04/03/1940
FE01/01/1945
Close, Ms S, BLib MCLIP, Inf. Specialist, BT Grp., Ipswich. [27929]
01/10/1977 **CM10/08/1988**
Clough, Miss C, MCLIP, Unwaged [10074] 29/09/1965 **CM01/01/1970**
Clough, Miss H, MCLIP, Learning L., The Open Univ., Milton Keynes.
[59843] 16/10/2001 **CM11/03/2009**
Clouston, Mr R W, BSc MCLIP, Retired. [2870] 03/11/1967
CM01/01/1971
Clover, Mr D C, BCom DipLib MA MCLIP, Inf. Res. Mgr. /Lib., Inst. of
Commonwealth Studies, London. [57646] 14/06/1999 **CM17/09/2008**
Clower, Mrs M J, BA DipLib MCLIP, Lib., Royal Russell Sch., Croydon.
[24692] 06/10/1975 **CM26/11/1982**
Clowes, Mrs J H, Unknown. [10012318] 27/01/2009 **ME**
Clucas, Mrs M G, BA DipLib MCLIP, Retired. [2873] 27/02/1970
CM01/11/1972
Cluer, Mrs M, Asst. Lib., P/T. [10001244] 03/02/2007 **ME**
Coady, Miss E, Performing Arts Lib., Dorking, Surrey CC. [65464]
23/02/2006 **ME**
Coane, Dr S, MA DPhil, Lib., Sir John Soane's Mus., London [61615]
03/10/2002 **ME**
Coast-Smith, Ms C T, BA(Hons) MCLIP, Lib., Surrey C.C. [10007010]
19/08/1985 **CM27/02/1991**
Coates, Mr A E, MA DPhil DipLib MCLIP, Asst. Lib. -Rare Bks., Univ. of
Oxford, Bodleian L. [37575] 08/10/1984 **CM25/05/1994**
Coates, Mrs A E, BA, L. Mgr., Darwen L., Lancs. [61665] 16/10/2002**ME**
Coates, Ms A, BA(Hons) MA MCLIP, Serv. Mgr. (Digital Lib. Serv.),
Northumbria Univ. [10005103] 23/12/1997 **CM19/07/2000**
Coates, Ms C M, MA MCLIP, Lib., (TUC Collections), London Metro.
Univ. [2884] 28/01/1969 **CM01/07/1972**
Coates, Mrs C, BA MCLIP, Planning & Quality Mngr., L. & Learning
Resources, Nottingham Trent Univ. [18267] 01/10/1972
CM01/12/1975
Coates, Mr E J, HonFLA FCLIP, Retired. [2885] 14/05/1934
FE01/01/1943
Coates, Dr I, BSc(Hons) PhD, L. Asst., Univ. Bristol. [63766] 04/10/2004
ME
Coates, Mr M J, BSc MA, Inf. Specialist, GCHQ, [10000888] 20/11/2006
ME
Cobb, Miss A J, BA(Hons) MCLIP, Customer Serv. Mgr., Univ. of Leeds
[46828] 15/01/1985 **CM24/07/1996**
Cobb, Mrs A, BA MCLIP, Sch. Lib. E. Barnet Sch., Herts. [39897]
06/10/1986 **CM17/10/1990**
Cobb, Ms J L, BA DipLib MCLIP, Unemployed [31770] 02/01/1980
CM29/04/1983
Cobb, Mrs L V, MCLIP, LRC Mgr., Selby High Sch., Selby. [63247]
22/03/2004 **CM17/09/2008**

Cobb, Ms M, BA DipLIS, Lib., Worcester Sixth Form Coll., Worcester.
[49266] 20/10/1993 **ME**
Cobb, Mr W P C, MCLIP, Life Member. [2899] 29/03/1948 **CM01/01/1960**
Coburn, Mr A, BA MCLIP, Acquisitions & Catg. Mgr., Essex C.C.
[22640] 27/07/1974 **CM24/09/1979**
Cochrane, Mr A C, BA MPhil DipEd FCLIP, Retired. [2901] 20/07/1972
FE14/11/1989
Cochrane, Mr F, ISO DGA FCLIP, Life Member. [2903] 19/02/1948
FE01/01/1956
Cochrane, Mrs S E, Lib., L. & Mus. HQ, Haddington. [10015819]
28/01/2010 **AF**
Cockburn, Dr A L, BSc(Hons) MSc PhD, Snr. L. Asst., Strathclyde
Univ., Scotland. [64837] 02/08/2005 **ME**
Cockburn, Ms S E, BA DipHE DipLib MCLIP, Head of Catg., Oxford
Brookes Univ. L. [42332] 19/10/1988 **CM18/07/1991**
Cockcroft, Mrs M, LRC Mgr., Stanley Park High Sch., Carshalton.
[64874] 22/08/2005 **ME**
Cockcroft, Mr M, BSc MSc PgDip, Stud., Univ. of Strathclyde.
[10010499] 15/08/2008 **ME**
Cocking, Miss M F, Unwaged. [10015235] 28/10/2009 **ME**
Cocking, Mrs Y M, MCLIP, Life Member. [5158] 31/01/1963
CM01/01/1966
Cockram, Mr R D, BA(Hons), Stud. [10017107] 23/06/2010 **ME**
Cockrill, Mr I W, BA(Hons) MCLIP, Asst. Learning Res. Cent. Mgr.,
Swansea Coll., Swansea. [44802] 05/12/1990 **CM24/05/1995**
Cockroft, Mrs S, ACLIP, Team Leader, Brighouse L., W. Yorkshire
[10009522] 03/06/2008 **ACL03/12/2008**
Codd, Mr F M, BA(Hons) MSc(Econ) MCLIP, Higher L. Exec., House of
Commons L. [54387] 02/12/1996 **CM15/01/2003**
Codd, Mrs J E, BA MCLIP, Retired. [7195] 01/10/1971 **CM30/09/1974**
Codd, Mrs L M, BA(Hons), Learning Resource Cent. Mgr., Baysgarth
Sch., Lincs. [10002983] 09/05/2007 **ME**
Codina, Miss A, Asst. Lib., Herbert Smith LLP. [10006404] 17/10/2007
ME
Codlin, Mrs E M, FCLIP, Life Member. [2925] 13/03/1930 **FE01/01/1969**
Codrington, Mrs A J, JP MCLIP, Life Member. [492] 02/08/1951
CM01/01/1960
Coe, Mr N, BA MLS MCLIP, Equal Access Mgr., Hants. Co. L. [34307]
19/10/1981 **CM01/04/1986**
Coe, Ms S L, BA(Hons) MCLIP, e Resource Analyst, Foreign &
Commonwealth Off., London [38800] 09/10/1985 **CM09/11/2005**
Coelho, Ms D, BA MA MSc MBA MCLIP, Sub Lib., BMA. [43824]
17/01/1990 **CM27/01/1993**
Coffer, Mr J P, BSc(Hons) PGDipIS, Inf. Specialist, Tobacco
Documentation Cent., Brentford. [48418] 04/01/1993 **ME**
Cogan, Mrs R J, ACLIP, Sen. Inf. Asst., Kimberlin L., De Montfort Univ.,
Leicester [10006073] 03/09/2007 **ACL29/08/2008**
Cogar, Mrs A V, BA MCLIP, Unwaged. [35387] 20/10/1982
CM22/04/1992
Cogdell, Mrs C R, MCLIP, Retired. [2933] 04/09/1952 **CM01/01/1958**
Coghlan, Ms V E, MSc(Econ) FLAI FCLIP, Lib., Church of Ireland Coll.
of Educ., Dublin 6. [37263] 09/05/1984 **FE17/03/1999**
Coglan, Miss S L, BA(Hons), Acquisitions Lib., Cheshire C.C. [49692]
25/11/1993 **ME**
Cohen, Mrs C J, BA DipLib MCLIP, Lib., Charter Academy, Portsmouth.
[33249] 14/10/1980 **CM08/12/1982**
Cohen, Ms J E, BA(Hons) MSc MCLIP, Head of L. & Inf. Serv., Serv.
Cent. L., Aldershot, Hants. [43884] 08/02/1990 **CM27/07/1994**
Cohen, Mr M J, BA(Hons) MSc MCLIP, Team Leader – Collections,
Queen Mary, Univ. of London. [57018] 25/11/1998 **CM23/06/2004**
Cohen, Miss M R E, Unwaged. [64780] 22/06/2005 **ME**
Cohen, Dr P M, BA PhD DipLib MCLIP, Head L. Serv., Dublin Inst. Tech.
[34668] 21/01/1982 **CM16/02/1988**
Coker, Mrs S M, Unknown. [65977] 09/08/2006 **AF**

Colaianni, Ms L A, HonFLA, Assoc. Dir., L. Ops., Nat. L. of Medicine, Bethesda, U. S. A. [53196] 01/01/1996 **HFE01/01/1996**

Colborne, Ms T, BA(Hons) MA MCLIP, Temp. Asst. Lib., Rutherford Appleton Lab., Rutherford [46131] 07/10/1991 **CM31/01/1996**

Colbourn, Dr P, BSc PhD MSc(Econ) MCLIP, Retired. [51195] 23/11/1994 **CM28/10/2004**

Colbourne, Mrs G M, BA, Business Devel. Offr., Warwickshire L. &Inf., Warwick. [60903] 09/01/2002 **ME**

Coldwell, Mrs J, BA MCLIP, Goldthorpe Lib. Br. Mgr., Barnsley MBC [13804] 21/02/1972 **CM13/07/1976**

Cole, Mrs B J, BA MCLIP, Trust Lib., Sir Thomas Browne L., Norfolk & Norwich Univ. Hosp. NHS. [25001] 20/11/1975 **CM14/02/1980**

Cole, Mrs C A, MA MCLIP, Maternity Leave. [36420] 05/10/1983 **CM20/01/1987**

Cole, Ms C E, BA MCLIP, Serv. Quality Lib., Northants. C.C. [32409] 27/03/1980 **CM19/10/1984**

Cole, Mr G P, BA FHEA MCLIP, Faculty Lib. (Creative Arts), Univ. of the W. of England, Bristol. [28277] 09/11/1977 **CM17/04/1980**

Cole, Miss J L, BSc MSc, Unwaged. [37250] 10/05/1984 **ME**

Cole, Ms K M L, BA MCLIP, Serv. Performance & Imporvement Mgr., Bristol C.C. [33804] 02/03/1981 **CM02/07/1984**

Cole, Mrs L, BA(Hons) MCLIP, Sen. Inf. Advisor, Kingston Univ. [44842] 13/12/1990 **CM22/07/1998**

Cole, Miss P V M, BA DipLib MCLIP, Policy & Res. Offr., Pub. & Comm. Serv. Union, London. [29616] 16/10/1978 **CM21/12/1981**

Cole, Mr R E J, BA DipLib MCLIP, Sen. Lend. Lib., Cent. L., Southampton City Council. [35544] 18/10/1982 **CM08/12/1987**

Cole, Miss W E, BA(Hons) MCLIP, Lib., Sch. & Related Serv., Rhondda-Cynon-Taf Co. Bor. Council. [45456] 11/02/1991 **CM20/09/2000**

Colehan, Mr P, FCLIP, Life Member. [2956] 01/01/1941 **FE01/01/1950**

Coleman, Miss A H, BA(Hons) MCLIP, Sen. Researcher, Lovells, London. [53973] 15/10/1996 **CM18/09/2002**

Coleman, Mr A J, MA, Sen. L. Asst., Surrey City Council, Guildford. [63413] 05/05/2004 **AF**

Coleman, Mrs C R, BSc(Hons) MSc MCLIP, Site Lib. Bucks Hosp. NHS Trust, Wycombe Hosp. [56909] 04/11/1998 **CM21/05/2003**

Coleman, Mrs C, BA MA MCLIP, Asst. Learning Resources Mgr., Andover Coll. [43528] 01/12/1989 **CM20/11/2002**

Coleman, Mrs S E, BA MCLIP, Sch. Lib., Bedford High Sch. for Girls, Bedford. [26743] 04/11/1976 **CM05/09/1980**

Coleman, Mrs S E, BA MA MCLIP, Teaching Asst. in a Primary Sch. [42105] 03/10/1988 **CM17/10/1990**

Coles, Mrs A M, BA(Hons) DipHE MPhil MCLIP, Tech. Lib., Plymouth Coll. Further Educ. [25243] 02/01/1976 **CM27/11/1979**

Coles, Ms A, BA MA, Inf. Off., Lawrence Graham, London. [61983] 07/01/2003 **ME**

Coles, Mrs E J P, BSc MCLIP, Inf. Asst. [34376] 01/10/1981 **CM22/05/1991**

Coles, Mrs I, BA MCLIP, Sch. Lib., Bucks. C.C., Milton Keynes. [18127] 03/10/1972 **CM02/10/1975**

Coles, Mrs O R, MCLIP, Retired. [15497] 23/09/1967 **CM01/01/1971**

Coles, Mrs P E, BSc MA, Res. Support Lib. (UK NSC). [10007267] 03/03/2004 **ME**

Coles, Ms S, BA(Hons) MA MCLIP, Asst. Lib., Castle Coll. Nottingham, Beeston. [10000643] 16/10/2006 **CM21/11/2007**

Coley, Mrs A N M, BA DipLib MCLIP, Lib., Royal S. Hants. Hosp., Hants. Partnership Trust. [40058] 20/10/1986 **CM15/05/2002**

Coley, Mrs C, MLib FCLIP, Gen. Mgr. -L. & Knowledge Serv., Basildon & Thurrock Univ. Hosp. NHS FoundationTrust, Essex. [18435] 16/10/1972 **FE03/10/2007**

Colinese, Mr P E, BSc AKC FCIS FCLIP, Retired. [60175] 01/04/1963 **FE02/08/1966**

Coll, Miss L, BA PGCE, Sch. Lib., Raha Internat. Sch., Abu Dhabi. [59454] 30/03/2001 **ME**

Collacott, Mrs S M, B LIB MCLIP, Part -time Supply Teacher. [30503] 14/02/1979 **CM13/11/1981**

Collas, Mr S A, BSc DipLib MCLIP FRSA, Lib. & Inf. Offr., Guille-Allès L., St. Peter Port,Guernsey. [27267] 15/01/1977 **CM09/01/1981**

Colledge, Mrs D A H, BA MCLIP, CHSS Consultancy Team, Univ. of Edinburgh. [5907] 01/01/1969 **CM05/10/1973**

Collence, Mr C, MSc BA HND, Lect., Harare Poly. [10010550] 05/08/2008 **ME**

Collett, Mrs J, MSc, Stud., Aberystwyth Univ. [10010507] 01/08/2008 **ME**

Collett, Mr P J, BA DipLib MCLIP, Unwaged [38700] 01/10/1985 **CM30/01/1991**

Colley, Mrs A, MLib, Unknown. [10016323] 23/10/1987 **ME**

Colley, Mr R P G, BA(Hons) DipLIS MCLIP, Team Leader, L.B. of Enfield, Enfield Cent. [42559] 04/01/1989 **CM17/11/1999**

Collier, Ms A H, BA MCLIP, Life Member. [2985] 25/03/1954 **CM01/01/1960**

Collier, Ms C J, BA(Hons) MA MCLIP, Managing Dir., Constructive Publications Ltd, Newark-on-Trent. [59123] 21/11/2000 **CM16/07/2003**

Collier, Ms D V, BA(Hons), Inf. & Welfare Offr., Brit. Polio Fellowship, S. Ruislip. [42029] 07/08/1988 **ME**

Collier, Mrs E A, MCLIP, Learning Cent. Mgr., Northenden Campus, City Coll. Manchester. [2405] 13/01/1967 **CM05/07/1972**

Collier, Mrs E, BSc DipLib MCLIP, Dist. Mgr., Beaconsfield L., Bucks. [30392] 25/01/1979 **CM10/04/1981**

Collier, Ms J E, BA(Hons) MSc, Asst. Lib., Irwin Mitchell Solicitors, Sheffield [59130] 21/11/2000 **ME**

Collier, Mrs J L, BA MCLIP, Lib., The William Allitt Sch., Derbyshire Co. Council [33451] 09/01/1981 **CM17/01/1985**

Collier, Mr M C, MCLIP, Unknown. [23133] 01/11/1974 **CM19/08/1977**

Collier, Prof M W, MA DipLib FCLIP, L. Dir., Catholic Univ. of Leuven, Belgium. [30606] 19/03/1979 **FE29/05/1981**

Collier, Mr R N, Learning Res. Super., Oxford & Cherwell Coll., Oxford. [62581] 03/09/2003 **ME**

Collier, Mrs R, BSc(Hons) MA, Inf. Mgr., David Lock Associates, Milton Keynes, Bucks. [53924] 10/10/1996 **ME**

Collier, Mrs S E, BSc MA MCLIP, Inf. Serv. Mgr., Scottish Crop Res. Inst., Dundee [13959] 22/10/1970 **CM22/05/1974**

Collier, Mr T, Area Off. Curator, URS, Moray [10013173] 31/03/2009 **ME**

Collin, Dr M Y C, BA PhD MCLIP, Employment not known. [4970] 04/03/1964 **CM01/01/1968**

Collinge, Mrs F H, MCLIP, Unknown. [23031] 01/10/1974 **CM01/11/1976**

Collingham, Miss B, MBE DipLib FCLIP BA(Open), Life Member. [2988] 22/10/1935 **FE01/01/1941**

Collings, Miss A C, MA BA, Ref. Lib., Redcar Ref. L., Cleveland. [62274] 08/04/2003 **ME**

Collingwood, Ms L, BA DipLib MCLIP, L. /Res. Cent. Mgr., Finham Park Sch., Coventry. [48945] 02/08/1993 **CM20/09/1995**

Collins, Miss A C, BSc (Hons), Stud., Aberystwyth Univ. [10014592] 18/08/2009 **ME**

Collins, Mrs A, MA BA MCLIP, Dep. Lib., Med. Lib., Cambridge Univ. [18272] 18/09/1972 **CM04/11/1975**

Collins, Mr B, BA MCLIP, Retired. [2992] 23/09/1969 **CM05/02/1973**

Collins, Ms D B, MA, Health Lib., Austin Health L., Australia. [55469] 14/10/1997 **ME**

Collins, Miss E A, BSc (Econ) MCLIP, Inf. Specialist, Nat. Collaborating Cent. for Cancer Cardiff. [58981] 16/10/2000 **CM01/06/2005**

Collins, Mrs J, MA(Hons) MSc, Asst. Lib., Veterinary Laboratories Agency [58370] 31/01/2000 **ME**

Collins, Miss K, DipLib MCLIP, Mus. & Drama Lib., Co. L. H.Q., Warwick. [34659] 10/01/1982 **CM01/07/1984**

Collins, Mrs L D, BA(Hons), Sch. Lib., St Mary's & St Peter's Care C of E Primary Sch., Teddington, London. [10016495] 14/04/2010 **AF**

Collins, Miss L, BSc (Hons), Stud. [10007205] 01/02/2008 **ME**

Collins, Mrs M T, BSc MSc MCLIP, Head Lib., Regents Coll. London. [27107] 01/01/1965 **CM15/10/1981**

Collins, Mrs N C, BA(Hons), on sabbatical. [47878] 23/10/1992 **ME**

Collins, Mrs P L, BA MCLIP, Intranet Mgr., MOD., London [42913] 19/04/1989 **CM16/10/1991**

Collins, Mr P, BA(Hons) MA MCLIP, Lib., Notts. C.C., Worksop P. L. [58940] 09/10/2000 **CM01/02/2006**

Collins, Mrs P, NHS Business Mgr., Univ. of Wolverhampton, Wolverhampton. [47120] 08/05/1992 **ME**

Collins, Mr S N, BA(Hons) MA MCLIP, Inf. Specialist, Kingston Univ. [52702] 22/11/1995 **CM21/11/2001**

Collinson, Miss J, BA(Hons) MSc, Learning & Teaching Lib., The Open Univ., Milton Keynes. [58160] 09/11/1999 **ME**

Collinson, Mr T, BA(Hons) FRGS FHEA MCLIP ILTM, Faculty Lib., Univ. of Portsmouth. [39496] 07/02/1986 **CM14/09/1994**

Collis, Miss A E, BA, Unknown. [10007816] 28/02/2008 **ME**

Collis, Mr G P, BA(Hons), Arch. Hub Data Editor, Univ. of Manchester. [52561] 06/11/1995 **ME**

Collis, Mr R J, DL HonFLA, Chairman, Connexions Partnership, Milton Keynes. [3009] 06/03/1963 **CM01/01/1967**

Collison, Mrs A M, DipLib MCLIP, Retired. [35774] 24/01/1983 **CM02/07/1987**

Collman, Mr S P, BSc, Unknown. [10007964] 03/03/2008 **ME**

Collop, Miss J H, BA(Hons) MA MCLIP, Not Currently Working in L. & Inf. Sector. [55508] 16/10/1997 **CM21/03/2001**

Colquhoun, Mr H A, FCLIP, Life Member. [3015] 24/09/1954 **FE01/01/1967**

Colquhoun, Mr J W, LLB MSc, Knowledge Mgmt. Mgr., Brodies LLP, Edinburgh. [60239] 09/04/1990 **ME**

Colquitt, Mr P T, MA(Hons), Stud., Univ. of Strathcylde. [10009297] 13/05/2008 **ME**

Colson, Miss C, BLS DUT MCLIP, Sch. Lib., Monkton Snr. Sch., Bath. [65346] 12/01/2006 **CM19/11/2008**

Coltart, Mrs I C, MCLIP, Life Member. [3016] 01/01/1969 **CM26/01/1973**

Colver, Ms L A, BA(Hons), Lib., Derbyshire Co. Council [56798] 19/10/1998 **ME**

Colver, Ms R, MCLIP, Lib., Cambs. C.C., Cambs. [11679] 01/10/1971 **CM01/10/1975**

Colville, Miss L, Inf. Specialist, GCHQ [65095] 01/11/2005 **ME**

Colvin, Mrs K M, BA MLib MCLIP, Retired. [4931] 28/08/1968 **CM05/09/1973**

Comben, Mrs C A, BSc DipLib MCLIP, Lib., RPS Energy, Goldsworth House, Woking, Surrey. [29155] 17/03/1978 **CM12/05/1981**

Comben, Miss H, BA MA MCLIP, Learning Cent. Super., Univ. Gloucestershire. [58104] 27/10/1999 **CM10/07/2002**

Combes, Mrs A J, Teaching Asst. [38308] 08/03/1985 **ME**

Combley, Mr R, MA, Unknown. [10007027] 16/10/2001 **ME**

Comissiong, Miss B L W, BA DipLib MCLIP, Life Member. [16785] 01/01/1950 **CM01/01/1961**

Comley, Mr W R, BA DipLib MCLIP, Outreach Lib., Mental Health Partnership Trust L., Oxford. [31054] 06/08/1979 **CM22/03/1985**

Common, Miss D J, BSc MCLIP, Retired. [3024] 20/03/1964 **CM01/01/1967**

Common, Ms L M, BA(Hons), Res. Lib., ReedSmith, London [10007988] 03/03/2008 **ME**

Compston, Mrs J L, BA(Hons), Lib. -Educ. Serv., S. E. L.B., Armagh. [50410] 19/07/1994 **ME**

Compton, Mrs C M, Sch. Lib., The Rickstones Sch., Essex. [10009310] 15/05/2008 **ME**

Compton, Mrs F D, BA MCLIP, Lib., London Studio Cent., London. [38846] 14/10/1985 **CM05/11/1987**

Compton, Miss P J, BA MCLIP, Retired. [3025] 25/09/1963 **CM01/01/1966**

Compton, Ms R H, Unknown. [10009322] 15/05/2008 **ME**

Compton, Miss S M, BA MSc, Records Offr., The Nat. Trust., Swindon [10005486] 25/07/2007 **ME**

Compton, Mrs S S, BA MCLIP, Sch. Lib., Dame Alice Owen's Sch., Potter's Bar, Herts. [3199] 01/07/1972 **CM12/01/1976**

Conboy, Ms C M, B ED MCLIP, Inf. Serv. Lib., Beds. L. Serv. [40297] 19/01/1987 **CM16/10/1989**

Concannon, Mr J G, BA(Hons) MA, Subject Lib., Tourism, Hospitality & Leisure, Thames Valley Univ., London. [50188] 27/04/1994 **ME**

Condell, Mrs M I, MCLIP, Classroom Asst., Brighton & Hove Council. [12577] 04/10/1971 **CM22/07/1974**

Condon, Mrs J I, BA MCLIP, Retired [3027] 26/09/1969 **CM18/09/1972**

Condon, Mr P, BA MCLIP, L. and Learning Resource Cent. Mgr., Barnfield Coll., Luton. [41792] 08/04/1988 **CM16/10/1991**

Conlon, Mrs C, BA(Hons) DipInf, L. Exec., House of Commons L., London. [47976] 29/10/1992 **ME**

Conlon, Mrs K, BSc GradIPM, Sch. Lib., Palmers Green High Sch., London. [10001328] 06/02/2007 **ME**

Conn, Mrs S, BA(Hons) MSc, Inf. Worker N. and Scotland, Breast Cancer Care, Glasgow. [63984] 22/11/2004 **ME**

Connally, Miss M T, BA(Hons) DipLib, Mgr., Book Supply Unit, Blagreaves L., Derby. [47041] 06/04/1992 **ME**

Connell, Mrs D L, BA(Hons), Inf. Mgr., Health Safety Lab., Buxton. [10016958] 03/03/1987 **ME**

Connell, Ms M A, MA BSc, Inf. Offr., TWI Ltd., Cambridge [59135] 22/11/2000 **ME**

Connell, Rev M G, MA(Hons) MSc MCLIP, Faculty Team Mgr., Univ. of Reading, Berks. [46296] 24/10/1991 **CM22/03/1995**

Connell, Mr P J, Ref. & Inf. Lib., Carmarthenshire C.C., Llanelli. [22788] 16/10/1974 **ME**

Connell, Mr R, BA(Hons) MA PGDip DipILM MCLIP, Academic Supp. Offr., Academic Servs., Univ. of Warwick L. [59006] 20/10/2000 **CM29/08/2007**

Connell, Ms S E, BA DipLib MCLIP, Learning Resources Mngr., City Academy, Hackney [37684] 19/10/1984 **CM05/07/1988**

Connell, Miss S, BA MCLIP, Unknown. [29157] 05/04/1978 **CM21/11/1982**

Connelly, Mr T J, LLB MSc, Lib. Mgr., Almondbank L., Craigshill, Livingston [10012934] 20/03/2009 **ME**

Connery, Ms H, ACLIP, Unknown, L. Serv. at Home, Birmingham [10001478] 26/02/2007 **ACL16/04/2008**

Connew, Ms S J, BA(Hons) MLIS, Lib., Kensington & Chelsea L., London. [64517] 22/04/2005 **ME**

Connolly, Mr T M, BA PGDip, Unknown. [10012580] 19/02/2009 **ME**

Connor, Mrs C A, BA MCLIP, Taxonomies Product Mgr., Lexisnexis, London. [27618] 01/06/1977 **CM22/10/1980**

Connor, Mrs K D, BSc, Sr. Lib. Asst., Lews Castle Coll., Isle of Lewis. [10012893] 19/03/2009 **ME**

Conroy, Mr J P, MCLIP, Lib., Plumstead L., L.B. of Greenwich. [20146] 09/02/1973 **CM20/10/1983**

Considine, Miss J M G, MCLIP, Business Lib., City Business L., London. [8294] 11/10/1972 **CM10/11/1978**

Constable, Mrs C, MA BA(Hons) MCLIP, Online Resources Co-Ordinator., Royal Coll. of Nursing L., London [56815] 20/10/1998 **CM17/09/2008**

Constable, Mrs L, MCLIP, Sen. Mgr., Customer Servs., Dorset L. Serv., Dorset CC. [18116] 02/10/1972 **CM01/07/1975**

Constance, Miss H M, BA MLib MCLIP, Learning Resources Ctr. Offr., Fareham Coll. [43448] 26/10/1989 **CM27/11/1996**

Constance-Hughes, Dr R M, BA(Hons) PhD, Unknown Blackbrook Estate, Monmouthshire [62533] 06/08/2003 **ME**

Constantinou, Ms S, BA, Study Cent. Mgr., Alexandra Park Sch., London [37207] 05/04/1984 **ME**

Conway, Ms A, BA(Hons), Lib., Mount Carmel Secondary Sch., Dublin. [10015707] 20/01/2010 **ME**

Conway, Mr D J J, DipLib MCLIP, Head of Knowledge Res., Nottingham City PCT. [34517] 19/11/1981 **CM13/05/1986**

Conway, Mrs K J, BA MA MCLIP, Inf. & Suppt. Desk Team Leader, Sheffield Hallam Univ. [42963] 10/05/1989 **CM15/09/1993**

Conway, Miss L C, BA(Hons) MA, Stock & Reader Devel. Lib., WGC L., Herts. C.C. [62760] 20/10/2003 **ME**

Conway, Mrs M A, BA MCLIP, Acting YPS Lib., Glasgow City Council, Mitchell L. [35262] 07/10/1982 **CM27/05/1992**

Conway, Mrs M, BA(Hons) CertEd, L. & Inf. Asst., HSE, Knowledge Cent., Bootle. [65355] 01/01/2006 **AF**

Conway, Miss N F M, MCLIP, Learning Support Lib., Durham Univ., Durham. [62800] 22/10/2003 **CM09/07/2008**

Conway, Mr P S, OBE BA MIMgt MILAM FCLIP FRSA, Retired [3048] 02/05/1968 **FE21/11/2001**

Conyers, Dr A D, MA MCLIP, Res. Fellow, Birmingham City Univ. [3049] 11/10/1965 **CM01/01/1969**

Cooban, Mr W A, Ba DipLib, Sen. Lib., Bexley L. Serv., Sidcup [10015642] 29/10/1983 **ME**

Cooch, Mr C, BA MCLIP, Grp. Lib., Halcrow Grp. Ltd, Swindon. [23427] 13/01/1975 **CM05/09/1977**

Cook, Miss A C, BA PGDip, Sen. Lib. Asst., King's Coll. L., Cambridge [10014739] 07/09/2009 **ME**

Cook, Ms A, Grad. Trainee., Glasgow Univ. [10011828] 18/11/2008 **ME**

Cook, Miss B A, BA MCLIP, L. & Inf. Offr., Dundee City Council. [25861] 01/04/1976 **CM15/01/1981**

Cook, Mrs C C, BA MCLIP, Asst. Lib., NERC Lancaster. [18230] 04/10/1972 **CM22/12/1974**

Cook, Ms C, Stud., Aberystwyth Univ. [10013591] 08/05/2009 **ME**

Cook, Mr D G F, MCLIP, Customer Serv. Lib., i/c. Media Team, Cent. Lend. L., L.B. Bromley. [21542] 22/10/1973 **CM10/12/1976**

Cook, Mr D, BA DipLib MCLIP, Global Intranet Content Mgr., Huntsman Tioxide, Billingham [34787] 11/02/1982 **CM11/11/1986**

Cook, Mrs E F, L. Super., Calne L., Wilts. [64852] 25/07/2005 **AF**

Cook, Mrs E, BSc MCLIP, Freelance Indexer. [3056] 15/10/1964 **CM01/01/1968**

Cook, Miss E, BSc, Inf. Offr., Berrymans Lace Mawer, London. [10002790] 10/05/2007 **ME**

Cook, Ms E, BSc MLS MCLIP, Product Mgr. – Knowledge Exploitation (External) [48860] 05/07/1993 **CM16/11/1994**

Cook, Ms F S, MCLIP, Lib., Cheney Sch., Oxford. [30899] 12/06/1979 **CM09/07/1981**

Cook, Mrs H J, BA MCLIP, Lib., Angus Council, Forfar. [29860] 08/10/1978 **CM15/08/1983**

Cook, Mr I N, MCLIP, Inf. Mgr., Communication Workers Union, London. [3058] 01/01/1972 **CM03/04/1975**

Cook, Mrs J A, Relief Asst. Lib., Crawley Pub. Lib., W Sussex. [44758] 15/11/1990 **ME**

Cook, Miss J C, pgDipIS MCLIP, Academic Liaison Lib., Univ. for the Creative Arts, Farnham. [61489] 19/08/2002 **CM09/07/2008**

Cook, Miss J L, BA, Stud., Univ. of Sheffield [10015575] 17/12/2009 **ME**

Cook, Mrs K S M, BSc(Econ) MCLIP, Retired [50152] 01/04/1994 **CM06/04/2005**

Cook, Mrs L J, Employment not known. [45328] 10/10/1990 **AF**

Cook, Mr M, BA(Hons), Lib. Super., NHS Bolton L, Bolton [10013666] 15/05/2009 **ME**

Cook, Mrs N, BA(Hons), Stud. [10015358] 11/11/2009 **ME**

Cook, Mrs R L, BA(Hons) MLib MCLIP, Career Break [49375] 01/11/1993 **CM21/05/1997**

Cook, Mrs S L, MCLIP, Retired. [3071] 01/01/1966 **CM01/01/1972**

Cook, Mr S, BA(Hons) MA, Asst. Lib., Royal Coll. of Obstetricians & Gynaecologists., [57867] 01/10/1999 **ME**

Cook, Mrs S, MCLIP, Customer Serv. Mgr., Cent. L., Sheffield. [18577] 23/09/1968 **CM09/01/1974**

Cook, Miss V C, BA(Hons), Reg. Account Mgr., OCLC PICA, Birmingham. [38156] 24/01/1985 **ME**

Cook, Miss W J, BA MCLIP, Coll. Dev. Mgr., N. Area, Lancs C.C. (Retiring March 2010) [3073] 10/01/1967 **CM01/01/1969**

Cooke, Ms A J, MCLIP, e-learning Mgr., Blackburn Coll. [10002941] 31/01/2007 **CM06/05/2009**

Cooke, Mrs A P L, BA, Stud. [10017095] 23/06/2010 **ME**

Cooke, Miss C D, MCLIP, Retired. [3075] 26/03/1960 **CM16/03/1965**

Cooke, Miss C M, MA ALCM FCLIP, Sen. Business Systems Analyst, Marylebone L., Westminster City Council. [29617] 02/10/1978 **RV09/09/2009** **FE29/03/2006**

Cooke, Mrs C, BA(Hons) DipLib PGCE MCLIP, Electronic Resources Lib., Anglo European Coll. of Chiropractic, Bournemouth. [47749] 16/10/1992 **CM31/01/2007**

Cooke, Mrs G A, MCLIP, Sch. Lib., Carlton Le Willows Sch., Nottingham. [22464] 21/05/1974 **CM09/11/1978**

Cooke, Mr H G, BA MCLIP, Retired. [3080] 10/01/1967 **CM01/01/1969**

Cooke, Mr I C, BA(Hons) MA, Curator, politics & Internat. Studies., The Brit. L. [55515] 16/10/1997 **ME**

Cooke, Mrs J S, BA(Hons), L. and Inf. Co-ordinator, Isle of Wight Council L. Serv., Newport, Isle of Wight. [58535] 24/03/2000 **ME**

Cooke, Ms J, BA(Hons) MCLIP, Trust L. Mgr., Univ. Hosp. Birmingham NHS Trust. [48444] 11/01/1993 **CM22/05/1996**

Cooke, Mrs K M, BA(Hons) MCLIP, Career break. [10016876] 08/01/1979 **CM19/01/1984**

Cooke, Miss L O, MA, Unknown. [10016610] 16/04/2010 **ME**

Cooke, Dr L, PhD MA MCLIP FHEA CLTHE, Lect. in Inf. & Knowledge Mgmt, Loughborough Univ. [28533] 19/01/1978 **CM22/04/1992**

Cooke, Mr P N, BA(Hons) MA, Performance & Devel. Mgr., Rochdale Lib. [51036] 09/11/1994 **ME**

Cooke, Mrs R J, BA MLib MCLIP, Acting NHS E. of England Lead for L. & Knowledge, England Strategic Health Auth. [39151] 07/11/1985 **CM19/08/1992**

Cooke, Mr R, FCLIP FRSA, Retired. [60178] 25/05/1972 **FE27/03/1986**

Cooke, Mrs R, MLI, Unknown. [10007028] 27/04/2001 **ME**

Cookes, Mrs V L, Life Member. [3090] 06/07/1931 **ME**

Cook-Mcanoy, Mrs P M, BA MLib DMS MIMgt MCLIP, Assets/Project Mgmnt Inf. Team GCHQ, Cheltenham. [28280] 01/10/1977 **CM13/02/1980**

Cooksey, Ms J, BA(Hons) DipILS MCLIP, Subject Lib. :Languages, Film Studies, English Studies & Sociology, Oxford Brookes Univ. [48655] 02/04/1993 **CM20/09/2000**

Cookson, Mrs A E, MA, Sen. Lib. Asst., Oxted L., Oxted [10014818] 16/09/2009 **AF**

Coombe, Mrs A R, BScEcon MSc, Inf. Specialist, W. Midlands Deanery, Birmingham Res. Pk. [51259] 12/12/1994 **ME**

Coomber, Miss C, Project Inf. Offi., Social Care Inst. for Excellence (SCIE), London. [49587] 19/11/1993 **ME**

Coomber, Mrs J C, MLib MCLIP, Dep. Head of Knowledge Serv. Devel., KSS L. & Knowledge Serv. [22332] 01/01/1974 **CM25/01/1978**

Coombes, Ms R, BA(Hons) MSc, Liaison Lib., Leeds Trinity & Univ. Coll. [44631] 12/11/1990 **ME**

Coombes, Miss T, BSc MCLIP, Prison Lib., Wormwood Scrubs, L.B. of Hammersmith & Fulham. [32506] 07/05/1980 **CM21/03/1984**

Coombs Tate, Mrs M A, MPhil BA MCLIP, Retired. [3101] 18/02/1941 **CM01/08/1972**

Coombs, Mrs C, BA(Hons) MCLIP, Sch. L. Serv. Mgr., Bedford Bor. Council. [49364] 29/10/1993 **CM25/09/1996**

Coombs, Miss L, BA(Hons), Graduate Trainne Inf. Cent. Assist., George Abbot Sch., Guildford. [10015289] 30/10/2009 **ME**

Cooper, Mr A B, MLS MCLIP, Retired. [3106] 05/02/1962 **CM01/01/1965**

Cooper, Ms A C, BA(Hons), Grad. Trainee, Oxford Union Soc. L.
[10011714] 06/11/2008 **ME**
Cooper, Mrs A L, BA MCLIP, Customer Serv. Super., Braintree Lib.
Essex. [37327] 02/07/1984 **CM23/03/1993**
Cooper, Mr A P, MA BLS MCLIP, Sen. Asst. Lib., De Montfort Univ.,
Leicester. [33452] 01/01/1981 **CM10/08/1985**
Cooper, Mr B, BSc(Econ) GradCertEd AdvDipBFM MCLIP, Life
Member. [3108] 25/08/1964 **CM01/01/1967**
Cooper, Miss C L, MA, Unknown. [10012395] 03/02/2009 **ME**
Cooper, Mrs C M, BA DipLib MCLIP, Community & Sch. Lib., Ullapool
[60698] 03/02/1983 **CM04/04/1986**
Cooper, Miss D, Lib. Super., Frinton L., Essex. [59412] 06/03/2001
AF
Cooper, Mrs E, BA DipLIS MCLIP, Coll. Lib., New Coll., Telford.
[10010643] 01/10/1974 **CM30/04/1994**
Cooper, Mrs E, MCLIP, Life Member. [3113] 07/10/1959 **CM01/01/1964**
Cooper, Mr E, FCLIP, Retired. [18578] 01/01/1954 **FE06/11/1975**
Cooper, Ms G M M, BA(Hons) MLIS, Knowledge & Info. Mngr., Dept. of
Info. Serv., House of Commons, London [10013852] 04/06/2009 **ME**
Cooper, Mrs G S, PGDipLib MCLIP, Catr., Brit. L., Boston Spa. [33600]
22/01/1981 **CM26/01/1984**
Cooper, Mrs H M, BLS MCLIP, Acquistions Lib., Tribal Educ. & Tech.,
Leeds [32179] 08/01/1980 **CM01/07/1993**
Cooper, Mrs H M, MA MCLIP, Life Member. [7164] 08/03/1953
CM01/01/1956
Cooper, Mr J B, MA MCLIP, Retired. [3121] 01/01/1949 **CM01/01/1954**
Cooper, Mrs J C, BA(Hons) PGCE PGDipIS, Dep. Lib., TWI Ltd.,
Cambridge. [47794] 19/10/1992 **ME**
Cooper, Mrs J M, BA MA MCLIP, Lifelong Learning Lib., W. Berks L.,
Newbury L. [31300] 11/10/1979 **CM12/02/1982**
Cooper, Mrs J M, BA MCLIP, Team Lib., Shropshire L., Shrewsbury L.
[33816] 11/03/1981 **CM05/12/1985**
Cooper, Mrs K J, BA PGDipLib MCLIP, Lib., NHS Northamptonshire.
[36362] 03/10/1983 **CM02/06/1987**
Cooper, Mr K R, HonFCLIP, Hon Fellow. [60774] 24/03/1988
HFE24/03/1988
Cooper, Mrs K, BA MCLIP, Lib., Cornish Studies L., Cornwall C.C.
[40276] 29/11/1986 **CM18/07/1991**
Cooper, Miss L A, FCLIP, Retired. [3125] 08/11/1969 **FE09/11/2005**
Cooper, Mrs L D, MPhil MCLIP, Unknown. [3126] 10/01/1968
CM01/01/1971
Cooper, Miss L, BSc (Hons), Sch. Lib., Stocksbridge High Sch.,
Sheffield. [10013548] 05/05/2009 **ME**
Cooper, Miss M I, BA FCLIP MBA, Life Member. [3128] 26/09/1949
FE01/01/1961
Cooper, Mr M P, BA MCLIP, Inspection & Review Offr., Reading B. C.
[40785] 08/06/1987 **CM12/12/1990**
Cooper, Ms N F, BA(Hons) PGDipLib, Inter Lib. Loans Co-ordinator.,
Cambridgeshire C.C. [43945] 28/02/1990 **AF**
Cooper, Mrs N J, L. Asst., House of Lords L., London. [10015928]
12/02/2010 **AF**
Cooper, Miss O F, MCLIP, Life Member. [3129] 29/03/1946
CM01/01/1952
Cooper, Miss P I, MCLIP, Life Member. [3131] 16/02/1949
CM01/01/1955
Cooper, Mrs S J, BA(Hons) DipLib MCLIP, Res. Cent. Lib., Brighouse
High Sch. [32269] 12/01/1980 **CM22/03/1995**
Cooper, Mrs S W, BA(Hons) DipLIM MCLIP, Child. Lib., Wrexham L.
[54156] 07/11/1996 **CM19/05/1999**
Cooper, Miss T, BSc ACIM, Unknown. [10013354] 16/04/2009 **ME**
Cooper, Mr W, Lib., Chorlton High Sch., Manchester. [64856]
01/08/2005 **ME**
Coopey, Miss J R, B. Ed(Hons) M. Ed., Lib. & Info. Prof., Okehampton
L., Devon [10013084] 24/03/2009 **AF**

Coopland, Ms H L, Lib., Elliott Sch. L., London. [10000879] 19/01/1978
ME
Cope, Mr A, BA(Hons), Repository Offr., De Montfort Univ. [61865]
22/11/2002 **ME**
Cope, Mr B E, MCLIP DMS, Retired. [20187] 01/02/1973 **CM18/07/1975**
Cope, Mrs E C, BA, Inf. Lib. - Catg., Univ. of Bath. [64928] 13/09/2005
ME
Cope, Mrs Y M, MCLIP, Retired [18382] 18/10/1972 **CM18/07/1975**
Copeland, Dr S M, MA MPhil PhD DipLib MCLIP, Sen. Inf. Advisor, The
Robert Gordon Univ., Aberdeen. [34167] 08/10/1981 **CM17/11/1985**
Copland, Mrs C, MCLIP, Lib. & Arch., Kirkham Grammar Sch., Kirkham.
[10001566] 01/01/1972 **CM01/01/1976**
Copland, Mr I C, MCLIP, Retired. [3145] 26/09/1963 **CM01/01/1970**
Copleston, Mrs N J, BA MCLIP, Serv. Mgr., Stock & Support Serv.
[13663] 05/10/1971 **CM01/09/1976**
Copling, Mrs J M, BLib MCLIP, Systems Lib., Solihull P. L. [18197]
05/10/1972 **CM22/07/1976**
Coppack, Miss M A, BA DipLib MCLIP, Retired. [22039] 17/01/1974
CM22/04/1976
Coppen, Miss J M, MCLIP, Life Member. [3147] 24/02/1934
CM01/01/1938
Coppendale, Ms L M, BA(Hons) DipIS MCLIP, Lib., Danum Sch. Tech.
Coll., Doncaster. [52131] 05/10/1995 **CM17/03/1999**
Coppins, Mr M, career break [50155] 13/04/1994 **ME**
Copsey, Mr D J, MA DipLib FCLIP, Hd. of L. & Knowledge Servs.,
Maidstone & Tunbridge Wells NHS. [3149] 05/10/1971 **FE07/09/2005**
Copus, Mrs A M, MCLIP, Stock Serv. Mgr., Civic Cent., L.B. of Harrow
L. Serv. [20309] 10/01/1973 **CM28/01/1976**
Corben, Miss L M, BA MCLIP, Team Lib., Nottingham City L. and Inf.
Serv., Nottingham. [24411] 07/08/1975 **CM30/01/1978**
Corbett, Miss H L, BLib MCLIP, Lib., Dept. of Health & Soc. Servs. &
Public Safety, Belfast. [38512] 07/05/1985 **CM20/09/1995**
Corbett, Mrs P C, MLib MCLIP, Community Lib., Buckley L., Flintshire
C.C. [23607] 20/01/1975 **CM24/07/1978**
Corbett, Mr S J, BA DipLib MCLIP, Content Mgmt. Lib., Chartered Inst.
of Personnel & Devel London. [30140] 15/01/1979 **CM14/05/1981**
Corbett, Mrs S, BA(Hons), Sen. Lib., St Osmunds' CE VA Middle Sch.,
Dorchester [65701] 19/10/2005 **AF**
Corby, Mrs R J, BA MCLIP, Br. Lib., Torbay L. Serv., Paignton., Devon
[36199] 04/07/1983 **CM11/12/1989**
Corcoran, Mr G J, MA, Sen. Inf. Asst., Kings Coll. London. [63516]
16/06/2004 **ME**
Corcoran, Mrs J, BSc, L. Asst., L. Support Unit, Inverness [10006782]
13/12/2007 **ME**
Cordell, Miss H, BA MA MSc MCLIP, Retired. [3154] 11/10/1971
CM14/11/1973
Cordes, Mr C, MCLIP, Grp. L. Mgr., Walsall M.B.C. [3156] 01/01/1971
CM29/07/1974
Cordin, Mrs E, 1st Asst.,Exeter Cent. L.,Exeter. [10000478] 05/10/2006
AF
Cordiner, Miss M, BSc MCLIP, Various. [24332] 12/07/1975
CM03/10/1977
Cording, Mr I, MCLIP, Unwaged – Looking for Work [60362] 07/05/1996
CM07/05/1996
Cordwell, Mrs J M, BA DipLib, Inf. Serv. Team Lib., Kent C.C.,
Maidstone. [45812] 10/06/1991 **ME**
Core, Mrs A, Unwaged. [10017168] 11/07/2010 **ME**
Corea, Mrs I, BA MCLIP, Retired. [18925] 12/08/1950 **CM01/01/1963**
Corey, Miss I J, BSc DipLib MCLIP, Lib. :Mobiles, Gwent Co. Bor.
Council. [30386] 07/01/1979 **CM21/12/1988**
Corin, Mrs A M, BA MCLIP, Serv. Mgr., Readers & Resources (Job
Share), Notts. Co. L. [21999] 17/01/1974 **CM14/07/1976**
Corke, Miss T A, BA MA, Unknown. [10012168] 15/12/2003 **ME**

Corkett, Mr I M, MA PG, 6th Form Lib. /IB Extended Essay Co-ordinator, The Royal High Sch., Bath. [10011306] 14/11/2008   **AF**

Cormie, Ms V H, MSc MCLIP, Site Lib., Queen Margaret Univ. Coll., Leith Campus L., Edinburgh. [43578] 09/11/1989   **CM22/01/1997**

Cornelius, Dr I V, BA MLitt PhD MCLIP, Sen. Lect., Dept. of L. & Inf. Studies, Univ. Coll. Dublin. [3167] 18/10/1967   **CM18/10/1975**

Cornell, Ms E, BEd DipLib MCLIP, Inf. Lib. (Humanities), Univ. of Leicester. [38415] 15/04/1985   **CM09/08/1988**

Corner, Mrs C, Local Studies Lib., L.B. of Croydon. [37977] 01/01/1985   **ME**

Cornhill, Mrs J, BA(Hons), Stud. [10006302] 10/10/2007   **ME**

Cornick, Mrs M E, MCLIP, LRC Mgr., Norton Radstock Coll., Bath. [23683] 10/01/1975   **CM17/08/1978**

Cornick, Mrs R, BA(Hons) MCLIP, Grad. Lib., [48246] 17/11/1992   **CM21/05/1997**

Cornish, Mr A L, BA DipLib MCLIP, Sen. Lib., Luton Cent. L. [10001567] 01/06/1979   **CM08/07/1983**

Cornish, Rev G P, BA FCLIP, Life Member. [3174] 24/05/1968   **FE27/07/1994**

Cornish, Mrs S R, BA DipLib MCLIP, Serv. Devel. Mgr. -Social Inclusion, Royal Bor. of Kensington & Chelsea. [36306] 01/10/1983   **CM20/01/1987**

Cornmell, Mrs S, BA(Hons) PGDipLib LLB(Hons), Inf. Specialist, Health & Safety Exec., Bootle. [35444] 11/10/1982   **ME**

Cornwall, Ms J L, BA MA DipLib MCLIP, Business and Euro. Info. Mgr., Essex L., Chelmsford. [50064] 02/03/1994   **CM27/11/1996**

Corp, Miss F A N, BA MCLIP, Life Member. [3176] 14/03/1963   **CM01/01/1968**

Corr, Ms M, BA DipLib MCLIP, Freelance. [27146] 20/01/1977   **CM20/09/1979**

Corradini, Mrs E, Ch. Lib., Comune Di Ala, Ala, Italy. [56668] 29/09/1998   **ME**

Corrales Siodor, Mr F R, DipHE, Lib. Shelver [63798] 04/10/2004   **ME**

Corrall, Prof S M, MA DipLib MBA MSc FCLIP FCMI F, Head of Dept. & Prof. of Lib. & Inf. Mgmnt., Univ. of Sheffield, Dept. of Inf. Studies. [24068] 19/04/1975   **FE16/11/1994**

Correa, Mrs E P, MLS BA, Unwaged, Seeking Work. [10014608] 19/08/2009   **AF**

Correia, Prof A M R, PhD HonFCLIP, Prof., ISEGI/UNL, Lisbon. [53437] 01/07/1996   **HFE09/04/1991**

Corrigan, Dr L M, MCLIP, Freelance [3182] 02/09/1970 **CM13/08/1974**

Corrigan, Mrs M, BA(Hons) MA MCLIP, Asst. Lib, Univ. of Ulster [50687] 10/10/1994   **CM19/05/1999**

Corrigan, Mrs M, LLCM(TD) MCLIP, Retired. [3183] 19/01/1967   **CM01/01/1970**

Corson, Ms J, LRC Mgr., Brayton Coll., Selby. [10011843] 19/11/2008 **AF**

Corticelli, Dr M R, PhD, Stud. [10013707] 22/05/2009   **ME**

Cosens, Mrs S J, BA, Bibl. Offr., Cumbria C.C., Mgmnt. & Inf. Unit. [36014] 07/04/1983   **ME**

Cosgrove, Mrs C M, BSc(Hons) BA MCLIP FEi, L. & Inf. Serv. Mgr., Energy Inst., London. [28471] 09/12/1977   **CM08/12/1982**

Cossins, Mrs L, BSc MSc MCLIP, Inf. Sci., Clinical Sci. Cent., Pain Relief Found., Univ. Hosp. Aintree. [41119] 05/10/1987   **CM01/04/2002**

Costanzo, Ms B, BA(Hons) MSc MCLIP, Br. Lib., L.B. Wandsworth, Earlsfield L. [23073] 01/11/1974   **CM01/01/1977**

Costas, Miss V, BA(Hons) MA MCLIP, Inf. Offr., Macfarlanes, London [59696] 08/08/2001   **CM21/06/2006**

Costello, Mr A S, Resources & Dev. L., Cheshire W. & Chester L., Cheshire. [55368] 06/10/1997   **ME**

Costello, Mrs M, BA(Hons) MCLIP, L. Resource Cent. Mgr., Coatbridge High Sch., N. Lanarkshire. [56986] 18/11/1998   **CM12/09/2001**

Costello, Miss S, ACLIP, L. Asst., Watford Cent. L. [63696] 23/08/2004   **ACL05/10/2007**

Costelloe, Miss L, BA PG Dip MSc, Unknown [10001584] 26/02/2007   **ME**

Coster, Mr J H, MCLIP, Life Member. [3189] 22/02/1937 **CM01/01/1945**

Costigan, Ms A T, BSc(Hons) MSc, Lib., J B Priestley L., Univ. of Bradford. [10005075] 02/09/1982   **ME**

Cotera, Miss M, BA MCLIP, Catr., U. C. L., London. [56698] 05/10/1998   **CM15/05/2002**

Cotes, Mrs A A B, BA MCLIP, Team Lib., Norfolk Co. Council, Norwich. [5731] 01/01/1967   **CM01/01/1970**

Coton, Ms R L, BA(Hons) MA, Primary Care Lib., Western Sussex Hosp. NHS Trust, Chichester. [51960] 21/08/1995   **ME**

Cotsell, Miss A R, BA(Hons) MCLIP, Sen. Lib. Child. & Young People Team, Oxfordshire. C.C. [47772] 14/10/1992   **CM06/04/2005**

Cotterill, Ms A, BSc MA MCLIP, Knowledge Mgmnt. & Inf., Home Off. [27941] 02/10/1977 **RV27/06/2006**   **CM31/07/1984**

Cotterill, Mrs L P, BA MCLIP, Lib., Congleton L., Cheshire C.C. [28155] 12/10/1977   **CM18/01/1982**

Cottle, Mr M E, MSc(Econ), Relief Lib., Crickhowell L., Powys [10008398] 19/03/2008   **AF**

Cotton, Miss Y E, BA(Hons) MSc, Sen. Asst. Subject Lib., Teesside Univ., Middlesbrough. [46659] 03/12/1991   **ME**

Cottrell, Mrs J A S, Inf. Specialist, Integreon Managed Solutions Ltd, London. [57239] 19/01/1999   **AF**

Coulling, Ms K R, BA(Hons) DipLib MCQI CQP MCLIP, Quality Assurance Mgr., Learning & Info. Servs., Univ. of Cent. Lancs., Preston [41915] 18/05/1988   **CM22/07/1998**

Coulshed, Mr N J, BA DipLib, Lib., Gtr. Manchester W. Mental Health, NHS Found. Trust, Prestwich Hosp. [39499] 10/02/1986   **ME**

Coulson, Mr G S, BA, Knowledge Technician, Northumbrian Water Ltd., Durham [10015648] 12/01/2010   **ME**

Coulson, Miss G, MSc, Info. Strategy & Servs., Dept. for Business, Innovation & Skills (BIS). [64499] 01/04/2005   **ME**

Coulson, Mrs R H, BA BSc(Hons), Sen. Inf. Specialist, Chartis Insurance, UK Ltd. [50477] 16/08/1994   **ME**

Coulson, Mrs R, Sen. Lib. Asst., Bournemouth Univ. [10004949] 04/06/2007   **AF**

Coupe, Ms M T, MCLIP, Owner of Child. Day Nursery. [24635] 01/10/1975   **CM28/12/1977**

Coupland, Mr J W, BA MCLIP, Mgr. of L. & Arch. Serv., IET, London. [23039] 17/10/1974   **CM11/11/1983**

Courage, Ms F P, MA, Special Collections Mgr., Univ. of Sussex L., Brighton. [57707] 05/07/1999   **ME**

Court, Mrs J E, BA DipLib, Learning Res. Mgr., Coventry City Council, Sch. L. Serv., Cent. L. [30141] 17/01/1979   **ME**

Court, Mrs R, BA(Hons) MA MCLIP, Inf. Specialist, Univ. of Warwick. [58099] 29/10/1999   **CM15/10/2002**

Courtney Bennett, Mrs H M, BA(Hons), Lib. Asst., Goring L., W. Sussex [10017032] 18/06/2010   **AF**

Courtney, Mrs E M, BA DipLib MCLIP, p. /t. Lib., Richmond American Internat. Univ. in London, Richmond. [32151] 01/02/1980   **CM09/08/1983**

Courtney, Mr O J, BA(Hons) PGDipILS MCLIP, Asst. Lib.,MMU, Manchester. [57826] 26/08/1999   **CM23/01/2008**

Cousens, Ms D A, Overseas [65012] 06/10/2005   **ME**

Cousins, Mrs A, MCLIP, Retired [8839] 12/01/1967 **CM01/01/1970**

Cousins, Miss F, BSc (Hons), Stud., Univ. of Strathclyde, Glasgow [10011279] 07/10/2008   **ME**

Cousins, Miss M F, BA(Hons), Family Lib. i. /c., I. O. M. Govt., Douglas, Isle of Man. [56579] 01/09/1998   **AF**

Cousins, Mr P C, BA MCLIP, Retired. [3224] 10/10/1968 **CM01/01/1971**

Cousins, Dr S A, BSc MLib PhD MCLIP, Copac service coordinator, Mimas, Univ. of Manchester [40003] 14/10/1986   **CM01/04/2002**

Coussement, Mrs K A, ACLIP, Team Coordinator, Hebden Bridge L. [10010978] 10/09/2008   **ACL03/12/2008**

Coussins, Mrs S N, BA(Hons) MA PGDip, Unwaged. [61783]
05/11/2002 **ME**
Coutts, Miss M M, MA MA MCLIP, Univ. Lib., Brotherton L., Univ. of
Leeds. [29941] 24/10/1978 **CM15/01/1981**
Coutts, Mrs S, BSc, L. Asst., Surrey Police, Guildford. [65267]
02/12/2005 **AF**
Cove, Mr M A, BA(Hons) ACLIP, L. Asst., Cambridge Cent. L. [64152]
19/01/2005 **ACL01/04/2008**
Coveney, Mrs B H S, Lib. in Charge, Devon CC, Exeter. [65469]
24/02/2006 **ME**
Coveney, Mrs C A, MA MCLIP MCMI, Customer Serv. Mgr. L., the Open
Univ., Milton Keynes [53271] 12/04/1996
CM16/07/2003
Coveney, Miss J, BSc (Hons) ACLIP, Unknown. [10012604] 19/02/2009
ACL11/12/2009
Coventry, Miss R, Music Asst., Nat. L. of Scotland, Edinburgh
[10009762] 09/06/2008 **AF**
Covington, Mrs C R, BA, Lib., St. Philips Chambers, Birmingham.
[44374] 02/10/1990 **ME**
Cowan, Miss M A, MCLIP, Literacy Devel. Co-ordinator, S. Lanarkshire
Council, Cent. L. [18080] 01/10/1972 **CM14/07/1975**
Cowan, Mr P F, BEd DipLib MCLIP, L. Devel. Mgr., N. Ayrshire Council.
[37685] 19/10/1984 **CM10/05/1988**
Cowan, Mrs R M E, MA MCLIP, Sen. Lib., Cambs. L., Cent. L. [42959]
05/05/1989 **CM16/11/1994**
Cowdrey, Mrs A P, Sch. Lib., Bangor Grammar Sch. [59819]
10/10/2001 **ME**
Cowell, Mrs J F, BSc MA, Sen. Inf. Off., London. [65350] 01/01/2006 **ME**
Cowen, Miss N, BA(Hons) MSc MCLIP, Bank of Tokyo Mitsubishi,
London. [58195] 16/11/1999 **CM09/11/2005**
Cowie, Mr C F, BA MCLIP, Retired [60180] 10/12/2001 **CM01/04/2002**
Cowin, Miss P, BA MA MCLIP, Broadcast Media Co-ord. BBC Info.
Arch. [42243] 17/10/1988 **CM22/07/1992**
Cowley, Mr J, BA FCLIP, Life Member. [3254] 10/10/1947 **FE01/01/1959**
Cowley, Mr R J, MCLIP, Reg. Sales Mgr., Ovid Tech., London. [3257]
10/01/1969 **CM01/01/1972**
Cowling, Mrs A, MCLIP, Area L. Mgr., Cumbria C.C., Whitehaven
[20217] 26/01/1973 **CM14/06/1976**
Cowling, Mrs I L, MCLIP, Life Member. [3258] 16/07/1957
CM01/01/1962
Cowling, Miss J C, BA(Hons), Asst. Lib., N. E. Wales Sch. L. Serv.,
Flintshire. [59651] 12/07/2001 **ME**
Cowling, Miss N, Sch. Lib. Adviser., Devon C.C., Exeter. [39503]
12/02/1986 **ME**
Cowperthwaite-Price, Ms K A, BLib MBA MCLIP, Vice President,
Credit Suisse, London. [41162] 14/10/1987 **CM01/04/2002**
Cowsill, Mrs A C, BA DIP LIB MCLIP, Snr. Lib., Cheshire Educ. L.,
Cheshire. [31743] 01/01/1956 **CM04/10/2004**
Cox, Dr A M, BA(Hons) MA MSc(Econ) MCLIP, Lect., Isch., Univ. of
Sheffield [10000937] 04/02/1994 **CM01/07/2001**
Cox, Miss C M, BA, Unemployed. [39485] 02/02/1986 **ME**
Cox, Mrs C, Lib., St Aloysius Coll., Highgate [57390] 01/03/1999 **ME**
Cox, Mr D, BA MCLIP, Life Member. [3273] 01/01/1937 **CM01/01/1939**
Cox, Miss E, BA(Hons), Stud [10006938] 17/12/2007 **ME**
Cox, Mrs H C, BA DipLib MCLIP, p. /t. Team Lib., Sch. L. Serv., Norfolk.
[33227] 01/10/1980 **CM03/08/1983**
Cox, Miss J C, BA MCLIP, Child. Lib., Bromsgrove L., Worcs. C.C.
[47981] 29/10/1992 **CM06/04/2005**
Cox, Mr J G E, MCLIP, Retired. [3281] 18/01/1959 **CM01/01/1964**
Cox, Mr J J, MA DipLib MCLIP, Univ. Lib., Nat. Univ Ireland. Galway.
[35183] 04/10/1982 **CM20/01/1986**
Cox, Mrs J L, BSc(Econ) MCLIP, Stock Serv. Unit Mgr., Cent. L.,
Bromley. [45357] 25/10/1990 **CM25/07/2001**

Cox, Miss J M, BA MCLIP, Team Lib., Brighton L., Brighton & Hove
Council. [40360] 12/01/1987 **CM27/05/1992**
Cox, Miss J, BLib MCLIP, Asst. Dir. - Culture & L. Serv., Staffs. C.C.
[34953] 14/05/1982 **CM07/02/1986**
Cox, Mrs K A, BA(Hons) MSc MCLIP, Career Break [55729] 10/11/1997
CM29/03/2004
Cox, Mrs K L, BA(Hons) DipMS MCLIP, Sch. Lib., Kings Monkton Sch.,
Cardiff. [46589] 20/11/1991 **CM17/11/1999**
Cox, Ms K L, BA(Hons) MA, Sen. Inf. Offr. Res., Greater London Auth.
[59369] 06/02/2001 **ME**
Cox, Ms L A, BA DipLib MCLIP, Head of Internal Communications & Inf.
Mgmnt, Becta. [40941] 08/09/1987 **CM18/07/1990**
Cox, Mrs L A, MSc MCLIP, Lib., ARRB Grp. Ltd., Australia. [23190]
05/11/1974 **CM12/06/1979**
Cox, Mrs L A, B Ed(Hons), Stud. [65785] 21/04/2006 **ME**
Cox, Ms L, Asst. Lib., Slaughter and May. [65135] 03/11/2005 **ME**
Cox, Miss M, BA(Hons) PGCE, Learning Serv. Co-ordinator,
Shakespeare Cent. L. & Arch., Stratford-Upon-Avon. [10015731]
19/01/2010 **AF**
Cox, Mr R D J, MCLIP, Head of Lib & Arch., Laban, London. [31810]
02/01/1980 **CM28/04/1982**
Cox, Mrs R, BSc DipLib MCLIP, Knowledge Serv. Mgr., E. Kent Hosp.
Trust L., Kent & Canterbury Hosp. [20011] 06/01/1973**CM31/12/1989**
Cox, Mrs S E, MA MCLIP, Journals Lib., St. George's L., St. George's
Univ. of London. [65874] 07/06/2006 **CM09/09/2009**
Cox, Miss S J, BA(Hons) DipILS MCLIP, Sen. Inf. Offr., Mayer Brown,
London. [49438] 27/10/1993 **CM26/11/1997**
Cox, Mrs T L, BLS MCLIP, Cent. Area Mgr., Solihull Metro. Bor.
Council., Warks. [34733] 22/01/1982 **CM10/05/1988**
Coxall, Mr O, BA(Hons) MA, Outreach Lib., Univ. of Oxford, Bodleian
Health Care L. s. [66013] 21/08/2006 **ME**
Coyle, Ms J, BSc(Hons) MSc, Lib. [10001974] 28/03/2007 **ME**
Coyle, Mrs M E M, MCLIP, Sen. Lib., W. Educ. & L. Board, Strabane.
[3470] 01/01/1971 **CM30/09/1985**
Coyle, Mrs R J, MCLIP, Retired [7157] 07/10/1967 **CM01/01/1971**
Coyne, Miss A M, BA(Hons) MCLIP, Asst. Lib., Manchester Met. Univ.,
Manchester. [48233] 16/11/1992 **CM23/06/2004**
Coyne, Mr P, Unknown. [63419] 07/05/2004 **ME**
Coysh, Miss C A, Reader development & Stock Mgmnt/CCI Lib. [62186]
10/03/2003 **ME**
Coyte, Miss J, BA MCLIP, L. Serv. Mgr., Lewisham Hosp., Lewisham
Hosp. NHS Trust. [25740] 03/03/1976 **CM21/02/1978**
Cozens, Ms T A, MCLIP, Area Lib. Mgr.,Wiltshire C.C., Trowbridge
[22878] 01/10/1974 **CM26/08/1977**
Crabb, Mrs J M, FCLIP, Life Member. [29118] 23/01/1950**FE01/01/1958**
Crabb, Mrs S M, MLS MCLIP, Reader Dev., Stock Mgmnt. Lib., Derby
C.C., W. Area. [3296] 22/01/1969 **CM16/08/1972**
Crabtree, Mrs S A, BSc(Hons) CPhys MCLIP, Knowledge Mgr. -
Australia, Egon Zehnder Internat., Melbourne. [18324] 10/10/1972
CM07/05/1975
Crabtree, Mrs S M J, BA, Teacher. [64059] 15/12/2004 **AF**
Cracklen, Mrs C M, BA(Hons) MA MCLIP, LRC Mgr., Bournemouth &
Poole Coll., Poole, Dorset. [62001] 08/01/2003 **CM08/12/2004**
Cracknell, Mrs L S, Principal Lib. Asst., Bodleian Law L., Univ. of
Oxford. [64225] 21/02/2005 **ME**
Craddock, Ms C E, BA MA MCLIP, Inf. Specialist, Unilever, Sharnbrook.
[55592] 22/10/1997 **CM06/04/2005**
Craddock, Mr P R, FCLIP HonFLA, Retired. [3301] 09/07/1950
FE01/01/1968
Craddock, Mr S M, BA Lib MCLIP, Devel. Lib., Kirklees M. C. [39222]
01/01/1986 **CM20/03/1996**
Cradock, Mrs E W, BA DipLib MCLIP, Lib. Mgr., Poynton L. Cheshire.
[33492] 13/01/1981 **CM09/09/2009**
Craft, Mr J, BA, Stud. [10013654] 18/05/2009 **ME**

Cragg, Miss C E, MA, Stud. [10011716] 06/11/2008 **ME**

Cragg, Miss E K, BA(Hons), Academic Support Lib., Univ. of Warwick. [65573] 21/02/2006 **ME**

Craig, Mrs A, BLib MSc MCLIP, Res. & Partnerships Mgr., Univ. of Worcester [23673] 23/01/1975 **CM08/08/1980**

Craig, Mrs E I I B, BA MCLIP, Staff Mgr., Knowsley M.B.C., Kirkby. [13896] 21/10/1971 **CM07/10/1974**

Craig, Miss I S H, MA DipLib MCLIP, Retired. [28537] 13/01/1978 **CM06/03/1980**

Craig, Mr J S, Stud., Univ. of Strathclyde, Glasgow [10011960] 19/03/2009 **ME**

Craig, Ms L M, BSc MCLIP, Self Employed Author. [60619] 17/08/1998 **CM17/08/1998**

Craig, Miss M R, BA DipLib, Inf. & Projects Mgr., Chartered Inst. of Personnel & Devel., London. [38778] 08/10/1985 **ME**

Craig, Mr R, OBE BA MA MCLIP HonFCLIP, Dir., CILIP Scotland. [18587] 06/05/1966 **CM01/01/1969**

Craig, Mrs S E, BA(Hons) PGCE MSc, Asst. Lib., Marie Curie Cancer Care, Newcastle Upon Tyne [66024] 24/08/2006 **ME**

Craig, Miss S, MCLIP, Dept. Lib., Computing Sci., Newcastle Univ. [3307] 29/01/1968 **CM01/01/1972**

Craigs, Mrs L, MCLIP, Retired. [25443] 07/01/1976 **CM26/03/1979**

Craine, Mrs A M, BA Cert Ed MCLIP DMS, Retired. [22998] 08/10/1974 **CM02/03/1978**

Crampton, Mr J M, BSc DipLib MCLIP, Retired. [3315] 14/10/1969 **CM05/02/1973**

Crane, Mrs E, BA(Hons) MCLIP, Asst. Lib., Barnsley Cent. L. [50429] 28/07/1994 **CM20/01/1999**

Crane, Mrs L D, BA(Hons) MCLIP, Subject Lib., Univ. of Liverpool [45604] 02/04/1991 **CM22/09/1999**

Crane, Miss R, BA, Unknown. [10009221] 06/05/2008 **ME**

Crane, Mrs S P, ACLIP, Principal L. Asst., Telford L. [45352] 22/10/1990 **ACL04/04/2006**

Crane, Miss V D, MBA MCLIP, Dir. of Academic Servs., Univ. for the Creative Arts, Maidstone [24639] 01/10/1975 **CM01/02/1978**

Cranfield, Miss F S, BVMS, MA Stud., UCL. [10012531] 19/02/2009 **ME**

Cranfield, Mrs R E G, MA FCLIP, Life Member. [3318] 09/10/1946 **FE01/01/1951**

Crang, Mr L T, BA, p. /t. Stud., City Univ. [54099] 28/10/1996 **ME**

Cranmer, Mr C I A, MCLIP, Lib. and Inf. Offr., City Chambers, Dundee. [3320] 17/02/1968 **CM01/01/1972**

Cranmer, Mrs J S J, BSc MLS MCLIP, Unknown. [28205] 12/10/1977 **CM05/11/1979**

Cranmer, Miss S, BSc MCLIP, Unknown. [31591] 26/10/1979 **CM21/11/1988**

Craven, Mrs E A, BA MA MCLIP, Catr., Literary & Philosophical Soc., Newcastle upon Tyne. [20755] 26/06/1973 **CM28/07/1975**

Craven, Miss G, MCLIP, Reader Devel. Offr., Barnsley Cultural L., Barnsley Metro. Bor. Council [19894] 14/12/1972 **CM08/09/1975**

Craven, Mrs J E, BA(Hons) MA MCLIP, Res. Assoc., Manchester Met. Univ. [48521] 02/02/1993 **CM17/11/1999**

Craven, Mr N, MA FSA(SCOT) FCLIP, Retired. [3331] 30/06/1950 **FE01/01/1972**

Crawford, Mrs A, MA(Hons), Lib., W. Dunbartonshire Council, Clydebank High Sch. [61179] 03/04/2002 **ME**

Crawford, Dr A, PhD MA MCLIP, Sen. Academic Liaison Lib., Univ. of St Andrews. [34178] 07/10/1981 **CM18/01/1985**

Crawford, Mr D S, BA DipLib FCLIP, Emeritus Lib., McGill Univ., Montreal, Canada. [16802] 23/10/1966 **FE26/11/1997**

Crawford, Mr D, MA DipLib MCLIP, Sch. Lib., Notre Dame H. Sch., Greenock. [29159] 13/03/1978 **CM22/03/1984**

Crawford, Dr J C, BA MA PhD FCLIP FRSA, Retired [3337] 02/10/1963 **FE21/12/1988**

Crawford, Mrs S, Asst. Lib., Norwich Sch., Norwich [10013094] 26/03/2009 **AF**

Crawforth, Mrs T M, MscEcon, Stud., Aberystwyth. [65006] 06/10/2005 **ME**

Crawley, Ms J A, BH MMus MSc MCLIP, Asst. Lib., Univ. of W. of England. [40323] 05/01/1987 **CM15/09/2004**

Crawshaw, Mr K, BA DLIS MCLIP, Consultant. [19644] 30/10/1972 **CM05/09/1975**

Crawshaw, Ms L A, BA DipLib MCLIP, Knowledge Business & Intelligence Con., Inf. Hertfordshire, Univ. of Hertfordshire. [37899] 12/11/1984 **CM10/05/1988**

Creamer, Mrs L R, MA DipLib MCLIP, Data Mgr., BDS Ltd., Dumfries. [24642] 01/10/1975 **CM07/10/1977**

Creamer, Ms R M E, MSSC MCLIP, Head of Documentation Cent., UNESCO – Internat. Bureau of Educ., Geneva, Switzerland. [29942] 13/11/1978 **CM30/03/1987**

Creaser, Mrs C, BSc, Dir., LISU, Loughborough Univ. [10000462] 10/10/2006 **ME**

Creasey, Mr J C, MA DipLib MCLIP, Life Member. [3351] 06/10/1961 **CM01/01/1964**

Creasey, Mr J O, MA MCLIP, Retired. [3352] 03/10/1956 **CM01/01/1962**

Creaven, Ms T, Unwaged. [52342] 30/10/1995 **ME**

Creber, Mr J K, BA MCLIP, Retired [3354] 28/10/1970 **CM02/08/1973**

Cregg, Ms C L, BA(Hons) MCIPD MCLIP, HR Mgr., Brit. Nuclear Grp., Romney Marsh. [45589] 02/04/1991 **CM16/11/1994**

Crellin, Ms C J, BA MA MCLIP, Legal L., Foreign & Commonwealth Off., London. [43430] 26/10/1989 **CM29/01/1992**

Crennell, Miss C J, BA(Hons) MRES, Lib. & Archive Asst., Univ. Liaison, The Sci. Mus., Swindon. [10000740] 01/11/2006 **ME**

Cresswell, Ms L A, BA DipLib MCLIP, Child. & Sch. Lib., CLLANELLI (Jobshare) [36363] 01/10/1983 **CM19/01/1988**

Creswick, Miss H M, MCLIP, Unemployed. [28797] 07/02/1978 **CM06/07/1981**

Crew, Mr J R, BSc(Hons) MSc MA, Asst. Lib., Inst. of Civil Engineen [66042] 12/09/2006 **ME**

Cribb, Mr P B, BA(Hons) MA MCLIP, Planning, Performance & Projects Mgr., L., Arch. & Info., Notts C.C. [62085] 12/02/2003 **CM20/04/2009**

Crilley, Ms K, MCLIP, Inf. Scientist, Min. of Defence, London. [10006208] 26/09/2007 **CM11/03/1977**

Crilly, Ms J F, BA(Hons) MSc MCLIP, Learning Resources Mgr., The Univ. of the Arts, London. [32473] 21/04/1980 **CM28/04/1982**

Crimp, Miss J K, MCLIP, Sch. Lib., Shrewsbury Internat. Sch., Bangkok. [62805] 24/10/2003 **CM23/01/2008**

Crinnion, Mrs K A, MCLIP, TTRB E-Lib., Inst. of Educ., London. [64730] 08/06/2005 **CM11/03/2009**

Cripps, Mrs A E, MA DipLib MCLIP, Sch. Lib., Charleston Academy, Kinmylies, Inverness. [27864] 30/09/1977 **CM01/01/1980**

Crisp, Mrs J M, MCLIP, Life Member. [3379] 01/01/1933 **CM01/01/1937**

Critchley, Mr D A, BA MCLIP, Programme Delivery Mgr., Inf. Assurance Prog., Home Off. [39035] 29/10/1985 **CM24/03/1992**

Critchley, Mr S M, BA(Hons) MA MCLIP, Prince Mohammad Univ., KSA. [46439] 06/11/1991 **CM01/07/1993**

Croall, Mrs S M, BSc DipLib MCLIP, Team Lib., City of Glasgow Ls. & Arch. [30202] 09/10/1978 **CM09/10/1980**

Crocetti, Ms C, Stud. [10016501] 13/04/2010 **ME**

Crocker, Miss T, BSc (Hons), Knowledge Asst., Nabarro, London [10007179] 25/01/2008 **AF**

Crockford, Mr G N, BA DipTrans FCII FIRM MCLIP, Retired. [60183] 03/09/1981 **CM01/06/1983**

Croft, Mr D, BA MA MSc Econ, Unknown. [10014658] 25/08/2009 **ME**

Crofts, Ms E J, Coll., Lib., Strode's Coll. [10009218] 07/05/2008 **ME**

Crofts, Miss S J, BA DipLib MA MCLIP, Sen. Academic Serv. Lib., Univ. of Greenwich, London. [44185] 02/07/1990 **CM26/01/1994**

Crofts, Mrs S M Q, BA(Hons) PGCE MCLIP, Lib. -Sen. L., Pates
Grammar Sch., Cheltenham. [20875] 27/08/1973 **CM01/10/1975**

Croghan, Mr A, MA FCLIP, Life Member [3392] 01/01/1951
FE01/01/1966

Croll, Mr H, MA MCLIP, Retired. [3396] 19/09/1966 **CM01/01/1969**

Croll, Miss K J, BA(Hons) MSc MCLIP, Child. Stock Lib., Westminster
C.C., London [51292] 06/01/1995 **CM20/05/1998**

Crombie, Ms S, BA(Hons), Business Res. Exex., Business Gateway,
Scottish Enterprise, Clydebank. [10006002] 24/08/2007 **ME**

Cromey, Miss S, MA MA DipLib MCLIP, Oxford Brokes Univ.,
Headington L. [31238] 02/10/1979 **CM02/10/1981**

Crompton, Miss J H, BA MCLIP, Self-employed. [32509] 28/04/1980
CM02/11/1984

Cronin, Prof B, PhD DSSc FCLIP FCMI FRSA, Dean & Prof., Indiana
Univ., Sch. of L. & Inf. Sci., U. S. A. [24487] 15/09/1974
FE19/12/1984

Cronin, Mrs H, BA DipLIS MCLIP, L. Mgr., Molesey L., Surrey. C.C.
[44531] 22/10/1990 **CM24/09/1997**

Crook, Miss C M, BA MCLIP, User Serv. Lib., Univ. of Brighton [33549]
20/01/1981 **CM04/07/1986**

Crook, Rev C, JP BSc DMS FCLIP, Retired. [3400] 03/09/1964
FE18/11/1993

Crook, Mr D A, BA MA MCLIP, Account Mgr. CLA London. [31240]
08/10/1979 **CM17/02/1982**

Crook, Mr D M, MCLIP, Retired. [3402] 07/03/1955 **CM01/01/1961**

Crook, Mrs K E, BA MCLIP, Unwaged [39662] 03/03/1986
CM12/12/1991

Crook, Miss K, BA(Hons) MA MCLIP, Lib., Cheshire CC., Cheshire.
[57642] 09/06/1999 **CM23/06/2004**

Crook, Miss L H, BA(Hons) MA, L. Asst., John Rylands Univ. L. of
Manchester. [58879] 29/09/2000 **ME**

Crook, Miss R J, Y Bont Support Lib., Welsh Assembly Gov.,
Aberystwyth [10012465] 10/02/2009 **ME**

Crook, Ms S A, BA MCLIP, L. & Inf. Mgr., Shetland L., Lerwick. [18418]
21/10/1972 **CM14/05/1984**

Crookall, Miss D M, MA BA, Asst. Subject Lib., Univ. of Chester,
Chester [10017063] 21/06/2010 **AF**

Crookes, Mr R K, BA(Hons) MA MCLIP, Resource Cent. Mgr.,
Knowledge Resources, NHS Nottingham City [52382] 26/10/1995
CM18/11/1998

Crooks, Miss C, MA(Hons) MA, Asst. Lib., MOD [61571] 02/10/2002 **ME**

Crooks-Freeman, Miss H, BSc(Hons), Unknown. [10015611]
17/12/2009 **ME**

Cropley, Mrs J G, BA(Hons) DipLib MCLIP, Managing Consultant,
Mouchel Managment Cosulting, London [18100] 30/09/1972
CM08/12/1975

Cropley, Mr J M A, Chairman, Askews L. Serv., Preston. [58673]
16/05/2000 **ME**

Cropp, Mrs V Y, MA BA MCLIP, Learning Resources Co-ordinator, The
Woodroffe Sch., Lyme Regis. [29270] 03/05/1978 **CM18/07/1980**

Cropper, Mr B, MA DipLib MCLIP MCMI HonFCLIP, Asst. Dir., Libs.,
City of London. [18442] 19/10/1972 **CM22/01/1974**

Cropper, Miss J L, MCLIP, Lib., Worthing L., W. Sussex Co. L. [3410]
01/01/1971 **CM31/08/1977**

Crosbie, Ms H A, BA(Hons) MCLIP, Dir., RMIT Publishing, Victoria,
Australia. [31241] 09/10/1979 **CM21/09/1982**

Crosier, Miss P A, BSc(Hons) DipIS MCLIP, Sen. Inf. Offr., Univ. of
Teesside. [48333] 27/11/1992 **CM21/03/2001**

Cross, Mrs A, BLib PGCE ILTM MCLIP, Asst. Head (Inf. Serv.),
Learning & Corperate Support Serv., Univ. of Glamorgan [33689]
04/02/1981 **CM28/10/1985**

Cross, Mrs C A, BA(Hons), Asst. Lib., Warminster Sch., Wiltshire.
[10016735] 07/06/2002 **ME**

Cross, Miss E O, BA(Hons) MA, Asst. Lib. [10000521] 10/10/2006 **ME**

Cross, Ms E, BA(Hons) MA MCLIP, Sen. Asst. Lib., Univ. of W. England.
[54143] 31/10/1996 **CM17/09/2003**

Cross, Mrs F J, BA, Lib., Arch., Harper Collins, Glasgow, UK [65566]
28/02/2006 **ME**

Cross, Miss J A, Documentalist, Amnesty Internat., London. [56960]
13/11/1998 **ME**

Cross, Mrs J V, MCLIP, Unemployed. [13621] 29/06/1970 **CM24/07/1973**

Cross, Mrs L A, BLIB MCLIP, Prin. Lib.,Inf. Serv. & E-Delivery, Luton L.,
Luton. [30787] 18/04/1979 **CM02/07/1984**

Cross, Miss L B, MA, Unknown. [10011901] 26/11/2008 **ME**

Cross, Miss S A, BA(Hons) MCLIP, Lib., Info. & Lifelong Learning,
Northumberland Co. L. Serv. [34116] 01/10/1981 **CM16/10/1989**

Cross, Miss S L, L. Asst., 5 Boroughs Partnership NHS Trust,
Warrington. [10006121] 11/09/2007 **ME**

Cross, Mrs S, PgDip MCLIP, Sch. Lib., St. Mungo's High, Falkirk.
[10010713] 29/08/2008 **CM10/03/2010**

Crossan, Miss S, Unknown [65231] 25/11/2005 **ME**

Crossingham, Mr A, BSc (Hons) PGCE, Unknown. [10016321]
08/03/2010 **ME**

Crossland, Miss S L, BA(Hons), Site Lib., Doncaster Coll., Learning
Res. Cent. [59921] 02/11/2001 **ME**

Crossland, Mrs T, BA(Hons) DipILM MCLIP, Sch. Lib., Woodcroft Coll.,
Adelaine, S-Australia [46617] 25/11/1991 **CM16/11/1994**

Crossley, Miss C H, Admin., ADECCO, Crewe. [62056] 07/02/2003 **ME**

Crossley, Mrs R, ACLIP, Team Leader, Todmorden L., Lancs
[10009537] 03/06/2008 **ACL03/12/2008**

Crossman, Mrs J A, MCLIP BA(Hons), Sen. Lib., Stock & Reader
Devel., Knowsley M.B.C., Huyton, Merseyside. [20066] 22/01/1973
CM12/01/1976

Crosthwaite, Mrs J E, BScEcon MCLIP, Lib., St Margarets ACAD,
Livingston [59654] 13/07/2001 **CM09/11/2005**

Crouch, Miss A L, Learning Supp. Lib., Westminster Ls. [10006649]
30/10/2007 **ME**

Crouch, Miss A L, BA(Hons) MCLIP, Sen. Special Collections Catr.,
Lancs. Co. L. Serv., Preston. [49752] 01/12/1993 **CM21/03/2001**

Crouch, Ms K E, BA(Hons) MSc MCLIP, Inf. Offr., Coll. of Law, London.
[10002549] 17/08/1993 **CM19/01/2000**

Crouch, Mr S E, BA(Hons) DipIM, Unwaged. [52278] 23/10/1995 **ME**

Crouchen, Mrs L J, BSc (Hons), Lib. Asst. & Study Supp. Offr.,
Callington L., Cornwall [10017019] 18/06/2010 **AF**

Croucher, Dr B C, BA(Hons) DipIS, Inf. Serv. Helpdesk Mgr., Univ.
Edinburgh. [50650] 06/10/1994 **ME**

Croucher, Miss M M, BA DipEd MCLIP, Unknown. [3423] 17/02/1972
CM29/10/1974

Crow, Mrs E, BA(Hons) DipILS MCLIP, Info. Specialist, Wood
Mackenzie, Addlestone [53980] 15/10/1996 **CM20/01/1999**

Crowe, Mrs N J, BA MCLIP, p. /t. Local Stud. Lib., Medway Arch. &
Local Studies Cent., Medway Council. [34402] 29/10/1981
CM07/10/1986

Crowe, Mrs P M, MA DipLib MCLIP, Teaching Asst., Richmond Coll.,
London. [10006017] 24/08/2007 **CM26/09/1979**

Crowe, Mr T R, MCLIP, Retired. [27108] 26/06/1967 **CM01/01/1970**

Crowley, Miss C, BA(Hons) Dip MA MCLIP, Interloans/Training Support,
St. Georges L., London. [62224] 24/03/2003 **CM10/07/2009**

Crowley, Ms E, BSc (Hons) MSc, Sen. Academic Serv. Lib, Univ. of
Greenwich Dreadnought L., London. [10006327] 02/12/2004 **ME**

Crowley, Mrs S A, B LIB MCLIP, Sen. Lib.: Operations, The L., Binford
Place, Somerset CC [29562] 01/01/1978
CM28/09/1984

Crown, Miss S, BSc(Hons) MCLIP, Proj. Assoc., Learning Solutions,
Chartered Insurance Inst., London [60355] 10/02/1995
CM29/03/2006

Crowther, Mrs C A, MCLIP, Sen. Asst. Lib., Wealdstone L., L.B. of
Harrow. [27878] 01/10/1977 **CM14/01/1980**

Crowther, Mrs F F, ACLIP, Sch. Lib., The Romsey Sch., Hants. [65340] 17/01/2006   **ACL04/12/2006**

Crowther, Ms H M, Learning Resources Mgr., Blackpool VI Form Coll., Blackpool. [42683] 06/02/1989   **ME**

Crowther, Mrs R, BA(Hons) MCLIP, Unknown. [30373] 09/01/1979   **CM23/09/1982**

Croxford, Mrs D, BSc(Hons) MSc DipLIS, L. & Inf. Asst., Outer W. L., Newcastle C.C. [58759] 10/07/2000   **ME**

Crozier, Mr D J, BA MSc(Econ) MCLIP, L. & Inf. Serv. Mgr., Cyprus Internat. Inst. of Mgmt., Nicosia. [54322] 20/11/1996 **CM15/10/2002**

Cruddace, Mrs J, BA(Hons), Prison Serv. Lib., Durham C.C. [49860] 12/01/1994   **ME**

Crudge, Mr R J, MCLIP, Retired. [3439] 25/01/1949   **CM01/01/1956**

Crudge, Dr S E, BSc(Hons) MSc MCLIP, Lib., New Coll. Stamford, Lincolnshire [57862] 14/09/1999   **CM08/08/2008**

Cruickshank, Mrs M, Sch. Lib., Sen. L., George Heriot's Sch., Edinburgh. [58122] 02/11/1999   **ME**

Crumplin, Mr J D, MA MLitt, Retrospective Conversion Project Asst., RIBA [59299] 31/01/2001   **ME**

Cruse, Ms J E, BA Dip Lib MCLIP, Bookshop Mgr., Guildford Cathedral, Dean & Chapter of Guildford Cathed. [37581] 09/10/1984   **CM10/05/1988**

Crute, Mr D, MCLIP, Local Studies Lib., Mansfield L., Notts. [10011009] 15/03/1967   **CM20/08/1975**

Cruz, Miss M E, BA MA, Lib., Sotheby's London [10012912] 20/03/2009   **ME**

Cryer, Miss N C, BA(Hons), Lib., English Heritage, Swindon [64017] 02/12/2004   **ME**

Cudden, Mr N A, BA(Hons) PGCE, Sch. Lib., Colegio Canada, Durnago, Mexico. [10015710] 19/01/2010   **ME**

Cuff, Mr R H, Brit. Aerospace(Dynamics)Ltd., Filton, Bristol. [3450] 05/05/1966   **ME**

Culbertson, Mrs K B, MA DipLib MCLIP, NRC Ballymena & Larne L. Co-Ordinator, Co. Antrim. [36356] 03/10/1983   **CM04/08/1987**

Cull, Ms S E, BA MA, Acquisitions Lib.,Serials, Royal Coll. of Nursing, London. [37753] 13/10/1984   **ME**

Cullen, Mrs J R, ACLIP, Sch. Lib., Ludgrove Sch., Wokingham. [61843] 18/11/2002   **ACL06/02/2008**

Cullen, Mrs N, BA(Hons) PgDipLIS, Sen. L. Asst., Home L. Serv., N. Ayrshire L. H.Q. [65336] 11/01/2006   **ME**

Cullen, Prof P B, MEd FCLIP, Emeritus Prof. of Learning Innovation (Retired). [7545] 01/01/1971   **FE14/03/1990**

Cullen, Mrs S, BA MSc MCLIP, Sr. Info. Asst., Arts Faculty Team, Univ. of Nottingham. [64722] 03/06/2005   **CM29/11/2006**

Cullingford, Ms A, BA MA MCLIP, Special Collections Lib., Univ. of Bradford, J. B. Priestley L. [46475] 11/11/1991   **CM27/07/1994**

Cullis, Mr T P, BA MA DipLib MCLIP, Sen. Liaison Lib., Middlesex Univ. [44203] 05/07/1990   **CM26/01/1994**

Culliss, Mr N D, BA(Hons) MA, Asst. Lib., Solicitor's Off. L., Business Support, HM Revenue & Customs, London. [63869] 11/10/2004 **ME**

Cumming, Dr D A, BSc MLib PhD MCLIP, Retired. [20714] 27/04/1973   **CM14/11/1980**

Cumming, Mrs L J, BA MCLIP, Asst. Lib., Tonbridge Sch., Kent. [23544] 03/01/1975   **CM22/05/1978**

Cumming, Ms M L, BA(Hons), Knowledge Mgmnt. & Innovation, DCLG, London [48540] 30/04/1990   **ME**

Cummings, Miss A J, MA, Learning Res. Cent. Asst., Derwentside Coll., Co. Durham. [55709] 10/11/1997   **ME**

Cummings, Mr G K, MLS MSc MCLIP, Reader Serv. Lib., Co. of Los Angeles. [30609] 27/02/1979   **CM27/02/1981**

Cummings, Ms H K, BSc(Hon), L. & Inf. Mgr., Middx. Univ., London. [49772] 06/12/1993   **ME**

Cummins, Ms S, BEd MCLIP, Lib. /L. Advisor, Sch. L. Serv., L.B. Tower Hamlets. [35982] 03/03/1983   **CM23/06/1986**

Cuninghame, Mrs J L, BA MA MCLIP, Retired. [37457] 03/10/1984   **CM14/03/1990**

Cunnea, Mr P A, MA(Hons) PGDipLis, Digital Collections Mgr., Nat. L. of Scotland, Edinburgh [44929] 18/01/1991   **ME**

Cunningham, Mrs A F, BA, Lib. Asst., Berkhamsted L., Herts [10014447] 31/07/2009   **AF**

Cunningham, Mrs A, BA(Hons) MCLIP, Sen. L. Asst., Cheshire CC. [42074] 03/10/1988   **CM06/04/2005**

Cunningham, Dr B, BA MA DipLib PhD, Dep. Lib., Royal Irish Academy, Dublin. [39549] 21/02/1986   **ME**

Cunningham, Mr G, BA BSc(Econ) FCLIP, Hon. Fellow. [47152] 01/01/1992   **FE01/01/1992**

Cunningham, Miss H A, BSc(Hons) DipILM MCLIP, L. Mgr., Xaverian Coll., Manchester. [48857] 02/07/1993   **CM19/03/1997**

Cunningham, Mrs I J, MCLIP, Life Member. [3474] 17/10/1947   **CM01/01/1955**

Cunningham, Mrs J C, BA(Hons), Unwaged. [10015355] 10/11/2009 **AF**

Cunningham, Mr J P, BA MCLIP, Lib. Systems Admin., N. Lanarkshire Council, Motherwell. [29626] 05/10/1978   **CM09/08/1982**

Cunningham, Mrs K A A, MA DipLib, Head of Bibl. Control, Univ. of Strathclyde L. [41589] 25/01/1988   **ME**

Cunningham, Ms M K, MSc MA BA(Hons) PGCE, FOI Act Adviser., Business, Enterprise & Regulatory Reform [59756] 08/11/2001   **ME**

Cunningham, Mr P, BA MCLIP, Advisory Lib., Sch. L. Serv., Suffolk C.C. [37491] 01/10/1984   **CM18/07/1991**

Cunningham, Mrs V, B. Soc. Sc. MA MCLIP, Doctoral stud. (Inf. Sci.), Robert Gordon Business Sch., Aberdeen. [10001645] 06/03/2007   **CM11/11/2009**

Curbbun, Mrs C M B, BA MCLIP, Teching Asst. /Sch. Lib., Thorley Hill Sch. Hertfordshire [36142] 01/07/1983   **CM10/05/1988**

Curphey, Miss H M, MA(Hons), Stud., Univ. of Strathclyde, Glasgow [10012704] 05/03/2009   **ME**

Curran, Mrs E R M, BA DipLib MCLIP, Sen. Lib., S. Hampstead High Sch., London. [37342] 06/07/1984   **CM15/05/1989**

Currie, E, BA MCLIP, e-government Lib., LAI, Suffolk C.C., Ipswich. [44062] 23/04/1990   **CM21/10/1992**

Currie, Mrs J S, BA(Hons), Sen. Community Lib., Plymouth City Council. [57566] 05/05/1999   **ME**

Currie, Mrs K R, MA DipLib MCLIP, Asst. Learning Cent. Mgr., City & Islington Coll., Cent. for Lifelong Learning. [31299] 11/10/1979   **CM10/02/1982**

Currie, Miss L A, Sch. Lib., Stonelaw High Sch., Rutherglen. [10000503] 16/10/2006   **ME**

Currington, Mrs H M, BA MCLIP, Sch. Lib., Tanbridge House Sch., Horsham. [7216] 02/09/1970   **CM22/08/1973**

Curry, Miss D, FCLIP, Retired. [3499] 19/03/1942   **FE01/01/1966**

Curry, Mr R J, BA(Hons) MA MCLIP, Inf. & Learning Resource Mgr., Uxbridge Coll. [62666] 01/10/2003   **CM29/11/2006**

Curry, Mr S T, BA MCLIP, Sr. Team Offr., Surrey C.C., Surrey Co. L. [3504] 19/08/1969   **CM07/10/1974**

Curry, Ms S, Lib. Collaboration Prog. Mgr., Res. Inf. Network [3503] 03/07/1969   **ME**

Curtis, Mr C, BA MCLIP, Retired. [3506] 01/01/1967   **CM01/01/1970**

Curtis, Mrs D J, BA MCLIP DipRSA, L. Serv. Mgr., Glos. Hosp. NHS Trust. [22588] 05/07/1974   **CM22/08/1977**

Curtis, Mrs H, BA MCLIP, L. Mgr., Calderdale Royal Hosp., Halifax [10012515] 08/11/1989   **CM16/12/1992**

Curtis, Ms J A, BA(Hons) DipILS MCLIP, Sub. Lib., Doncaster Coll. [41507] 11/01/1988   **CM21/05/2003**

Curtis, Mr J P, BSc(Hons) DipIM MCLIP, Site Lib., Shrewsbury and Telford Hospt., NHS Trust, Shrewsbury [50389] 13/07/1994   **CM06/04/2005**

Curtis, Mr J S, MA MCLIP, Lib., Davenport Lyons, London. [3512] 01/01/1971   **CM01/03/1973**

Curtis, Mrs L, BA(Hons) MCLIP, Lib. Servs. Mgr., Hereford Hosp. NHS Trust. [54615] 04/02/1997 **CM19/01/2000**

Curtis, Mr R, BA MA, Asst. Lib., Min. of Justice, London. [59807] 04/10/2001 **ME**

Curtis, Mrs R, MA MCLIP, Catg. Co-ordinator, Renfrewshire L., Paisley. [26281] 13/10/1976 **CM01/06/1979**

Curtis, Mrs R, BA(Hons) MCLIP, Sen. L. Asst., Univ. of Nottingham, Med. Lib. [41386] 17/11/1987 **CM22/09/1999**

Curtis, Mrs V H, MCLIP, L. Mgr., Sch. L. [63461] 14/05/2004 **CM17/09/2008**

Curtis-Brown, Miss L A, BA(Hons) MA, Sen. Liaison Lib. . (Soc. Sci.), Middx. Univ. [52201] 12/10/1995 **ME**

Curwen, Mr A G, MA FCLIP, Retired. [3517] 09/02/1951 **FE01/01/1959**

Cusack, Mrs K J, DipLIS MCLIP, Unwaged. [53047] 19/02/1996 **CM24/09/1997**

Cushion, Miss J, BA MA, Asst. Lib., Tameside Coll., Manchester. [10006936] 17/12/2007 **ME**

Cushworth, Mrs E M, MCLIP, L. Asst., St. Peters Lutheran Coll., Queensland, Australia. [3522] 24/08/1967 **CM01/01/1972**

Cusworth, Mrs M R, FCLIP, Trainer/Consultant, Tyrrell Wood Consultants Ltd [3525] 02/08/1967 **FE26/01/1994**

Cuthbertson, Miss J C, MCLIP, Life Member. [3530] 20/09/1948 **CM01/01/1956**

Cuthell, Miss H, MCLIP, Retired. [3531] 23/01/1946 **CM01/01/1951**

Cutler, Miss E J, BA(Hons) MSc(Econ), Sen. Asst. Lib., Dudley Coll. of Tech. [58288] 14/12/1999 **ME**

Cutler, Mr N, BSc(Hons) MA MCLIP, Dept. Lib. Computer Lab., Univ. of Cambridge. [53434] 25/06/1996 **CM10/07/2002**

Cutler, Mrs S S T, BSc(Hons) MSc, Freelance Copy-Editor, Trainer, Proofreader [10015536] 01/12/2009 **AF**

Cutmore, Mrs R A, MCLIP, Life Member. [3534] 27/09/1951 **CM01/01/1957**

Cutts, Ms A L, BA DipLib MCLIP, Lib., Univ. of Cambridge, Faculty of Educ. [37991] 01/01/1985 **CM23/03/1993**

Cutts, Mrs E A, MCLIP, Sen. Lib. -Bibl. Serv. (Job-share), Hounslow Community Trust [23357] 10/12/1974 **CM10/03/1978**

Czajkowskyj, Mrs J, BA(Hons) Dip Lib MCLIP, Ref. and Inf. Offr., Oldham L. [10012467] 06/01/1981 **CM18/07/1985**

D

Da Costa, Mrs H, BA(Hons), Comm. Lib., Kent C.C., Broadstairs L. [47487] 02/09/1992 **ME**

Da Silva, Mr L R, BSc DipLIS MCLIP, Tech. Serv. Lib., Univ. of Chichester. [47692] 15/10/1992 **CM16/05/2001**

Dabbs, Ms R A, LLB (Hons), Dep. Info. Cent. Mgr., Bristows, London [10001638] 06/03/2007 **ME**

Dabiri, Miss K O, BA(Hons), L. Serv. Mgr., Reading & Inf., L.B. of Sutton L. Serv. [51111] 16/11/1994 **ME**

Dace, Mr J M, MCLIP, Retired. [18602] 30/09/1948 **CM01/01/1956**

Dade, Mrs P, BA DipLib MCLIP, Ind. Info. Specialist. [21430] 29/10/1973 **CM10/10/1977**

Dafydd, Mrs M A, BA(Hons) MSc(Econ) MCLIP, Grp. lib., Montgomeryshire. [54621] 04/02/1997 **CM16/07/2003**

Dagger, Mr J R, BA(Hons) MA, Unknown. [60862] 13/12/2001 **ME**

Dagpunar, Miss A S, BA DipLib MCLIP, Asst. Lib., Sch. of Oriental & African Studies, London. [30610] 05/03/1979 **CM06/04/1981**

Dahlke, Miss H, BA(Hons) MA MCLIP, Reader Devel. Lib., W. Berkshire Dist. Council. [63770] 06/10/2004 **CM08/08/2008**

Dai, Mrs L, BA MCLIP, Lib., Newland Sch. for Girls, Hull. [58096] 29/10/1999 **CM12/03/2003**

Daines, Mr G F, BA DipLib MCLIP FRSA, Dir., Policy & Advocacy, CILIP, London. [23173] 05/11/1974 **CM22/08/1977**

Dainton, Mr M, BSc MSc, Lib. Univ. of Wolverhampton [61552] 18/09/2002 **ME**

Dakers, Ms F J G, BA DipIM MCLIP, Lib., Forfar L., Angus. [61074] 01/03/2002 **CM23/06/2004**

Dakers, Mrs H P, MA MSc FCLIP, Freelance Project Mgr. & Consultant. hazel. dakers@blueyonder. co. uk. [24645] 12/10/1975 **FE27/11/1996**

Dakin, Miss A E, MCLIP, Retired. [3548] 09/10/1968 **CM01/01/1972**

Dale, Mr A R, MA FCLIP, Managing Partner, Creatifica Assoc. Ltd., Wellingborough. [60485] 12/10/2000 **FE12/10/2000**

Dale, Mrs K K, MCLIP, Grp. Serv. Mgr (S.), Bristol L. Serv., Bristol. [57415] 03/03/1999 **CM29/08/2007**

Dale, Mrs P G, BA MCLIP FHEA, Retired [3553] 07/10/1968 **CM02/01/1973**

Dale, Mrs R, MCLIP, Resource Acquisitions Lib., Univ. of Nottingham. [41283] 25/10/1987 **CM14/11/1990**

Dale, Dr S M, DipTransIoL ACIL MCLIP, Retired. [3557] 06/04/1963 **CM01/01/1966**

Daley, Mrs M R, BSc DipLib MCLIP, Asst. Lib., Liverpool City L. [40762] 02/06/1987 **CM18/11/1992**

Dalgleish, Dr A J, MA DipLib MCLIP, L. Serv. Mgr., Univ. of Glamorgan, Pontypridd. [42827] 09/03/1989 **CM16/09/1992**

Dalkarl, Ms L B M, MA MSc, Translator & Res., Netherlands. [62102] 17/02/2003 **ME**

Dalley, Mr N M, BA(Hons) DipInfSc, Application Support Mgr., Sirsi Dynix [51817] 06/07/1995 **ME**

Dalley, Mrs P M, BA DipLib MCLIP, Retired. [32533] 30/04/1980 **CM20/01/1986**

Dalling, Miss G M, MSc, Lib., Univ. of Tech., Jamaica. [10016853] 27/05/2010 **ME**

Dallman, Mrs S J, MA DipLib MCLIP, Asst. Lib., Nat. Mus. of Scotland, Edinburgh. [34151] 10/10/1981 **CM23/06/1986**

Dalrymple, Mr I R, Asst. Lib., Network Monitor, The Highland Council, Inverness. [56378] 01/07/1998 **ME**

Dalton, Dr A J, BA DipLib MCLIP MA D. Phil, Univ. Admin. [26338] 04/10/1976 **CM24/04/1979**

Dalton, Mr A M, MA HDipEd MCLIP, Life Member. [16692] 29/03/1962 **CM01/01/1968**

Dalton, Miss H E, BSc MCLIP, Learning Res. Mgr., London Met. Univ., Calcutta House L. [21019] 17/09/1973 **CM13/04/1977**

Daly, Mrs A C, Clinical Lib., NHS [59268] 23/01/2001 **ME**

Daly, Mrs A, MA MCLIP, Asst. Lib., Manchester Met. Univ. [65947] 20/07/2006 **CM19/03/2006**

Daly, Mrs C, BA MCLIP, Administrator, The Voluntary Network, Newmarket. [18313] 12/10/1972 **CM01/11/1975**

Daly, Mr S A, BA(Hons), Bibl. Serv. Lib., Univ. of Liverpool, Sydney Jones L. [48232] 16/11/1992 **ME**

Daly, Mr S, Sen. Lib., European Cent. Bank, Germany [10007214] 09/04/2008 **ME**

Dalziel, Mr A F, MA MCLIP, Acquisitions Mgr., Hants. L. & Inf. Serv., Winchester. [25970] 03/05/1976 **CM23/07/1979**

Dalziel, Mrs K, BA(Hons) MCLIP, Dept. Subject Lib., Swansea Univ. [46081] 01/10/1991 **CM17/03/1999**

Dance, Mr J, BA(Hons) GCGI AMRS, Sen. CLAHRC Health Info. Offr., Bradford & Airedale, Teaching PCT [10006137] 11/09/2007 **ME**

Dandikar-Patel, Ms S, PCE, Unknown. [10016870] 27/05/2010 **AF**

Dane, Mrs K E, BA(Hons) MCLIP, Sys. Lib., Royal Nat. Inst. of the Blind, Peterborough. [37367] 27/07/1984 **CM19/06/1991**

Danels, Miss J L, BD DipLib, Unwaged. [40127] 17/10/1986 **ME**

Danes, Mrs C E, BA MSc, Inf. Unit Mgr., Linklaters, London. [61692] 21/10/2002 **ME**

Danes, Mrs N E, BLIB MCLIP, Advisory Lib., Essex Sch. L. Serv., Chelmsford. [28637] 11/01/1978 **CM21/01/1983**

D'Angeles, Miss A J, BSc Econ, Stud., Aberystwyth Univ. [10009326] 15/05/2008 **ME**

Daniel, Ms C, BA MA MCLIP, Lib., Cumbria Coll. of Art & Design, Carlisle. [43763] 01/01/1990 **CM18/11/1993**

Daniel, Mrs J H M, BLIB MCLIP, Sch. Lib., St. Laurance Sch., Wilts. [29780] 04/10/1978 **CM05/09/1986**

Daniel, Miss L R, BA(Hons) MSc(Econ) MCLIP, Competition Researcher, Freshfields, London. [58305] 04/01/2000 **CM16/07/2003**

Daniels, Mr F, BA(Hons) DipLib MCLIP, Retired. [23440] 01/01/1975 **CM10/11/1978**

Daniels, Mr K, BA MCLIP PGCTHE FHEA, Academic Liaison Lib., Media & Biological Sciences, Univ. of Beds. [40863] 20/07/1987 **CM30/01/1991**

Daniels, Miss R J, MCLIP, Team Leader, L. Customer Serv., Barrington L., Coll. of Mgmnt. & Tech., Wilts. [63364] 20/04/2004 **CM16/04/2010**

Daniels, Mrs T J, BLib MCLIP, Supp. Serv. -Devel. Offr., Torfaen Co. Bor. Council, Inf. Advisor-Catg., UWIC. [34315] 20/10/1981 **CM21/11/1985**

Dann, Mr M J, BA(Hons), Learning Resources Mgr., New Coll., Durham [52584] 09/11/1995 **ME**

Danquah, Miss M A, BSc(Hons) MA, Careers Adviser, Thames Valley Univ. [52117] 05/10/1995 **ME**

Dansey, Mr P, BSc MCLIP, Retired. [60185] 14/10/1971 **CM01/07/1976**

Danskin, Mr A R, MA(Hons) DipLib, Metadata & Bibliographic Standards Coordinator The Brit. L., Boston Spa. [39355] 19/01/1986 **ME**

Dar, Mrs A V, BA(Hons) MA, Asst. Lib., Dept. of Health, Leeds. [57103] 14/12/1998 **ME**

Darbyshire, Mr J B, FCLIP, Retired. [3598] 06/02/1952 **FE01/01/1967**

Darbyshire, Ms V F J, BA(Hons) MCLIP, Community & Inf. Offr., Sch. L. Serv., E. Riding of Yorks. [22056] 07/01/1974 **CM26/01/1976**

D'Arcy-Brown, Mrs R, MA(Hons), Asst. Public Serv. Mgr., City Univ., London [63967] 22/11/2004 **ME**

Dardenne, Ms L, BA, Sch. Lib., Summer Fields, Oxford [10000514] 16/10/2006 **ME**

D'Ardenne, Miss S, BMus MA, Asst. Lib., RNCM, Manchester. [10009361] 15/05/2008 **ME**

Dare, Mrs J E, BA(Hons) MA MCLIP, p. /t. Asst. Lib. [56124] 03/03/1998 **CM29/11/2006**

Darling, Mrs A, MCLIP, Clinical Lib., Pilgrim Hosp., Boston. [5858] 02/10/1968 **CM09/01/1973**

Darling, Miss H O, BA(Hons) MCLIP, p/t Local Studies Lib., Scottish Borders Council, Selkirk. [35854] 31/01/1983 **CM22/05/1996**

Darling, Ms S L, BA MA MCLIP, Self Employed. [45436] 04/02/1991 **CM26/05/1993**

Darlington, Mrs N J, BA(Hons) MCLIP, Faculty Team Lib., Univ. of Nottingham [51173] 23/11/1994 **CM19/01/2000**

Darlington, Mr P M, MCLIP, Opengalaxy Devl., Axiell, Nottingham. [52578] 08/11/1995 **CM01/04/2002**

Darroch, Miss J, MA(Hons) MSc MCLIP, Res. Lib., Berwin Leighton Paisner., London [61989] 06/01/2003 **CM01/02/2006**

Darter, Ms P E, BA MCLIP, Retired. [3610] 03/10/1963 **CM01/01/1968**

Dase, Ms A, MA, Sch. Lib., Trent Coll., Long Eaton, Notts [59138] 23/11/2000 **ME**

Dash, Mr G P, MCLIP, IT Bus. Systems Mgr., Cent. L., L.B. of Sutton. [3614] 03/05/1971 **CM10/07/1974**

Dashfield, Mrs D, BSc (Hons) MLIS, Internet Consultant, Self Employed, Essex. [10006487] 24/10/2007 **ME**

Date, Mrs C L E, MIPD MCLIP, Serv. & Strategy Mgr. (L. & Arts), Bournemouth L. [10299] 09/08/1967 **CM30/05/1973**

Date, Miss R J, BEd, Sch. Lib., Bryntirion Comp. Sch., Bridgend. [64666] 13/05/2005 **ME**

Dattili, Ms M, BA DipLib MCLIP, L. Resource Cent. Mgr., N. Lanarkshire C.C. [37463] 01/10/1984 **CM05/07/1988**

Daudi, Mrs S, MA, Unwaged. [10001754] 01/10/1998 **ME**

Davenhill, Mrs P M, Support Serv. Lib., Stornoway. [59507] 18/04/2001 **ME**

Davenport, Ms K P, MA MCLIP, Head of L., Bristol City Council. [32909] 30/09/1980 **CM19/04/1983**

Davey, Mr A J, BSc MCLIP, L. Mgr., Devon C.C., Exeter. [33283] 27/10/1980 **CM13/12/1983**

Davey, Mr A T, FCLIP, Retired. [3626] 02/01/1933 **FE01/01/1936**

Davey, Mrs A, BA, Subject Lib., Bournemouth Univ., Poole, Dorset [10001728] 28/03/1983 **ME**

Davey, Ms E M, BA, User Serv. Lib., Univ. of Brighton, Aldrich L. [46298] 24/10/1991 **ME**

Davey, Mrs H J, BTH(Hons) PGCE Dip Lib, Lib., Bournemouth Sch. for Girls [10007721] 21/02/2008 **ME**

Davey, Mr R L, BA DipLib, Sen. L. Asst., Univ. of London L. [43150] 23/08/1989 **ME**

David, Baroness Hon. Vice President. [46049] 11/09/1991 **ME**

David, Mrs S J, BA MA MCLIP, Liason Co-ordinator, St Georges Hosp., Univ. of London. [47964] 28/10/1992 **RV27/09/2005 CM24/05/1995**

Davidson, Mr A J, BA DipLIS MCLIP, Sen. Intranet Editor, Foreign & Commonwealth Off., London. [49512] 09/11/1993 **CM23/09/1998**

Davidson, Mrs A, BA MCLIP, Sales & Marketing Asst., Boydell & Brewer, Suffolk. [39604] 19/03/1986 **CM26/05/1993**

Davidson, Ms B T, BSc DipLib MCLIP, Asst. Lib., Capel Manor Coll. Enfield, Middx. [41653] 05/02/1988 **CM12/12/1990**

Davidson, Miss J K, BA(Hons), Stud. [10017252] 15/07/2010 **ME**

Davidson, Mrs J, BSc MCLIP, Res. Catr., Univ. of Worcester [32358] 03/03/1980 **CM21/07/1993**

Davidson, Mrs J, Sen. dmin. /Inf. Offr., L. & Inf. Serv., Glasgow CC. [10009801] 12/06/2008 **AF**

Davidson, Miss K B, MCLIP, Retired. [3643] 15/09/1952 **CM01/01/1963**

Davidson, Mr M J, BA(Hons), Inf. Asst., Nottingham Trent Univ. Notts. [10017154] 12/07/2010 **ME**

Davidson, Mrs M W, BA DipLib MCLIP, Employment not known. [28592] 11/01/1978 **CM28/01/1980**

Davidson, Mrs M, Ma MSc, Sch. Lib., Nairn Academy, Nairn. [10011869] 22/11/2004 **ME**

Davidson, Mrs P B, MA MCLIP, Network Lib., Banchory Acad., Banchory, Kincardineshire. [26368] 11/10/1976 **CM19/01/1979**

Davidson, Mrs P, MCLIP, Sch. Lib. (Job Share), Renfrewshire Council, Renfrewshire. [18106] 01/10/1972 **CM15/07/1975**

Davidson, Mrs S A, BA(Hons) MA, Academic Res. Lib., Univ. of Wolverhampton, Walsall. [47676] 14/10/1992 **ME**

Davie, Mrs D E, BA DipLib MCLIP, Community/Coll. Lib., Notts. C.C. [41256] 26/10/1987 **CM18/07/1991**

Davies Terry, Ms H M, BA DipLib MCLIP, Princ. Lib. -Child. Serv., W. Sussex L. Serv. [35175] 01/10/1982 **CM03/03/1987**

Davies, Ms A E, BA(Hons) MCLIP, Learning Support Lib., Nottinghamshire Co. Council [62392] 22/05/2003 **CM21/03/2007**

Davies, Ms A L, BA PGDip MA MCLIP, Strategic Mgr., Partnerships [46951] 10/03/1994 **CM15/09/1993**

Davies, Miss A M, BA(Hons) PGDipILS MCLIP, Unwaged. [55187] 05/08/1997 **CM08/12/2004**

Davies, Mr A N, BSc MCLIP, Inf. & User Educ. Lib., Tameside Coll., Ashton-under-Lyne. [26340] 01/10/1976 **CM12/09/1979**

Davies, Mrs A, MCLIP, Asst. Lib., Cent. L., Bury Metro. Bor. [19268] 15/08/1972 **CM29/03/1976**

Davies, Mrs A, BA(Hons), Lib., Univ. Coll. Sch. (J. B.), London. [47010] 01/04/1992 **ME**

Davies, Ms A, MCLIP, Unknown. [22690] 15/08/1974 **CM02/08/1978**

Davies, Mr C B, BA MCLIP, Sen. Lib., L.B. of Camden, Swiss Cottage L., London. [31127] 30/08/1979 **CM27/10/1981**

Davies, Mrs C C, ACLIP, Info. Unit Mgr., CBI, Cent. Point, London. [62843] 06/11/2003 **ACL04/07/2006**

Davies, Miss C E, MA(Hons) MSc MCLIP, Learning & Res. Support Co-Ordinator, City Univ. of London [62697] 09/10/2003   CM13/06/2007

Davies, Mrs C, MCLIP, Acqusitions Lib. Dudley Coll. of Tehc., Dudley, W. Mids. [4643] 12/01/1972   CM16/10/1975

Davies, Miss C, Asst. Curator, Official Publications Unit, Nat. L. of Scotland. [10015770] 25/01/2010   ME

Davies, Miss C, Unknown. [10013980] 18/06/2009   ME

Davies, Miss D M W, L. Asst., Victoria Univ. of Wellington, New Zealand. [3671] 02/10/1970   ME

Davies, Mr D T, MA BA MCLIP, Unwaged. [21690] 09/01/1974
                                                     CM27/02/1978

Davies, Mrs D V, BA MCLIP, Unknown. [3673] 01/10/1971
                                                     CM01/02/1977

Davies, Mrs E A, BEd DipLib MCLIP, Br. Lib., L.B. Wandsworth. [42142] 03/10/1988   CM27/07/1994

Davies, Miss E C, MA FCLIP, Life Member [3676] 13/10/1949
                                                      FE01/01/1968

Davies, Mrs E I, MCLIP, Housewife & Mother. [21306] 10/10/1973
                                                     CM19/11/1976

Davies, Mr E J, BA MA DipLib MCLIP, Consultant. [60850] 16/11/1990
                                                     CM16/11/1990

Davies, Miss E W, BA(Hons) MSc (Econ) MCLIP, Learning Resources Advisor, Trinity Univ. Coll., Carmarthen [65439] 23/02/2006
                                                     CM07/07/2010

Davies, Mrs E, BA(Hons), Lib., Veale Wasborough Uzards, Bristol. [63199] 03/03/2004   AF

Davies, Mrs F, MCLIP, Ref. Lib., Newbury L., Berks. [9937] 04/01/1970
                                                     CM21/08/1974

Davies, Mrs F, MCLIP, Sunday Lib., Barnet P. L. and Harrow P. L. [9025] 25/09/1957   CM01/01/1963

Davies, Mrs G C, BA MCLIP, Unwaged. [38992] 22/10/1985
                                                     CM17/01/1990

Davies, Mr G E, MCLIP, Retired. [3687] 31/10/1966   CM01/01/1970

Davies, Miss G M, BA Dip. Lib., Asst. Lib., Nat. Oceanographic L., Southampton. [10017134] 21/10/1981   ME

Davies, Mr G R, BA, MA, LRC Mgr., SCG, Stroud, Gloucestershire. [10008957] 23/04/2008   AF

Davies, Mr G R, BA, Unknown. [10013340] 16/04/2009   ME

Davies, Miss G, MCLIP, Retired. [3682] 18/10/1945   CM01/01/1967

Davies, Ms H J, BA MSc MCLIP, Lib., Enfield Bor. Council. [43427] 26/10/1989   CM29/01/1992

Davies, Mrs H J, BA(Hons) MCLIP, Lib., Wimbledon Coll. . of Art, Surrey. [42668] 06/02/1989   CM27/11/1996

Davies, Mrs H J, MCLIP, Retired. [10740] 21/07/1969   CM05/02/1974

Davies, Miss H, BA, Unknown. [10006901] 17/12/2007   ME

Davies, Ms I J, BA DipLib, Lib., Essex Sch. L. Serv., Chelmsford. [36990] 27/01/1984   ME

Davies, Ms J E, BSc MCLIP, Community Specialist, The Royal Soc. of Chemistry, Cambridge. [60196] 29/06/1992   CM29/06/1992

Davies, Dr J E, MA PhD FCLIP FRSA, Hon. Visiting Res. Fellow, Loughborough Univ., Dept. Info. Sci. [3705] 25/01/1961 FE21/10/1974

Davies, Ms J E, BA MA, Sen. Asst. Lib., Ref. Srvcs., House of Lords L., London. [59831] 15/10/2001   ME

Davies, Mr J I, FCLIP, Life Member. [3709] 27/02/1958   FE29/01/1976

Davies, Miss J M, BSc DipLib MCLIP, Readers Devel. Lib., W. Area, Northants. C.C. [26341] 12/10/1976   CM23/02/1979

Davies, Mr J R M, MA MCLIP, Retired. [18608] 10/04/1965
                                                     CM01/01/1967

Davies, Mrs J, BA MCLIP, H. Learning Res. Cent., Worcester 6th Form Coll., Worcester. [6011] 01/01/1972   CM06/10/1975

Davies, Miss J, LRC Mgr., St. Nicholas Catholic High Sch., Hartford. [64641] 03/05/2005   ME

Davies, Ms J, Unknown. [10015073] 10/05/2010   AF

Davies, Miss K L, BSc(Hons) MA MCLIP, Faculty Liaison Lib., Health & Social Care, Canterbury Christ Church Univ. [59050] 06/11/2000
                                                     CM15/09/2004

Davies, Ms K L, MCLIP, Legal Sec., Ealing, London. [3666] 01/01/1970
                                                     CM16/07/1973

Davies, Miss K, MA, Unknown [64983] 06/10/2005   ME

Davies, Mrs L A, BA MCLIP, Sci. & Biomedical Sci. Lib., Cardiff Univ. [35019] 22/06/1982   CM30/07/1985

Davies, Miss L C, BA FCLIP, Life Member. [3717] 01/01/1956
                                                      FE01/01/1961

Davies, Mrs L I, ACLIP, Inf. Asst., St. Georges Univ. L., London. [65048] 21/10/2005   ACL29/03/2007

Davies, Mrs L J, SDM Child. & Young People., Crowby, Liverpool. [65467] 24/02/2006   AF

Davies, Mrs L Y, BLib MPhil, Resource Cent. Mgr., Sturminster Newton High Sch., Dorset. [43902] 15/02/1990   ME

Davies, Mrs L, BA DipLib MCLIP, Community Lib., Denbighshire C.C., Ruthin L. [43446] 26/10/1989   CM18/11/1992

Davies, Miss L, MA MCLIP, Inf. Offr., Norton Rose LLP, London [62776] 22/10/2003   CM29/11/2006

Davies, Mr M O, BSc MA MCLIP, Enquiries Mgr., House of Commons Inf. Off., London. [54795] 02/04/1997   CM19/07/2000

Davies, Mrs M, MCLIP, Area Mgr., Risca L., Caerphilly Co. Bor. Council. [2470] 16/02/1971   CM01/09/1975

Davies, Mrs M, BA(Hons), Asst. Lib., Brighton and Sussex Univ. Hosp. Trust. [65465] 23/02/2006   ME

Davies, Dr M, BA MSc DipLib MCLIP MBCS, Dep. CIO & Dir. of Res. & Learning Supp., King's Coll., London. [21317] 04/10/1973
                                                     CM11/11/1976

Davies, Mrs M, MA BLib MCLIP, Head of L. & Inf. Serv., Norton Rose LLP, London. [35176] 04/10/1982   CM14/11/1989

Davies, Mrs M, MCLIP, Life Member. [3722] 23/06/1954 CM01/01/1958

Davies, Miss M, BA MCLIP, Life Member. [3720] 19/02/1959
                                                     CM01/01/1961

Davies, Mrs M, MCLIP, Retired [3723] 16/02/1969   CM05/12/1972

Davies, Mr M, Subject Lib. - Law, Cardiff Univ., Cardiff [10001534] 27/10/1993   ME

Davies, Miss N H, BSc(Hons) MA MCLIP, Temping. [61045] 05/02/2002
                                                     CM15/09/2004

Davies, Miss N J, Stud. [10016732] 30/04/2010   ME

Davies, Mrs P H, BA MCLIP, Unwaged. [10033] 06/11/1971
                                                     CM12/07/1978

Davies, Mrs P M, BSc MSc MCLIP, Retired. [22793] 08/10/1974
                                                     CM05/02/1981

Davies, Mrs R E, BA(Hons) Dip ILM, LRC Mngr., Framwellgate Sch., Durham [59424] 12/03/2001   ME

Davies, Mr R N, BA DipLib MCLIP, Dep. Hd. of Lib., Arts & Heritage, London B. of Brent [40477] 16/02/1987   CM14/11/1991

Davies, Mr R R, BA(Hons), Unemployed [59809] 04/10/2001   ME

Davies, Ms R, BLib(Hons), Dir. of Inf. Serv., Hugh Owen L., Aberystwyth Univ. [49016] 06/09/1993   ME

Davies, Miss R, BA(Hons) QTS, Unknown. [10014972] 01/10/2009 ME

Davies, Mrs S A, BA MCLIP, p/t Lib., Stockport M.B.C. [24611] 01/10/1975   CM20/08/1978

Davies, Mrs S I, MCLIP, Retired. [3751] 28/09/1950   CM01/01/1956

Davies, Miss S M, BA MCLIP DMS, Br. Lib., Wealdstone L., L.B. of Harrow. [20179] 01/02/1973   CM10/01/1977

Davies, Mrs S, ACLIP, Snr. L. Asst., Welsh Assembly Gov. [65059] 24/10/2005   ACL05/10/2007

Davies, Mrs W M, BA MCLIP, Loughborough Univ. [18398] 02/10/1972
                                                     CM09/09/1974

Davies, Ms W, BA MCLIP MRTPI, Cultural Mgr. Fishguard L. [8114] 16/01/1968   CM01/01/1972

Davies, Mr W, Knowledge Resource Administrator [10016488]
26/03/2010   **AF**
Davies, Mr W, FCLIP, Retired. [3758] 06/01/1948   **FE01/01/1970**
Davies, Mrs Y V, Knowledge Servs. Asst. Lib., Beds & Herts Health L.
[64646] 05/05/2005   **AF**
Davis, Ms A K, BA(Hons) DipILM MCLIP, Sen. Inf. Advisor, Oxstalls
Campus, Univ. of Glos. [57203] 14/01/1999   **CM17/09/2003**
Davis, Miss A M, BA MCLIP, Life Member [3763] 01/03/1952
CM01/01/1959
Davis, Ms C A, BSc MSc MCLIP, Inf. Serv. Lib., Oxfordshire C.C.
[50265] 25/05/1994   **CM24/07/1996**
Davis, Miss E A, BSc MCLIP, Asst. Dir. -Faculty Support Serv., Imperial
Coll. London, S. Kensington Campus. [28542] 21/01/1978
CM25/01/1980
Davis, Mrs E A, Sch. & Comm. Lib., Clyst Vale Comm. Coll. L.,
Broadclyst. [64930] 16/09/2005   **ME**
Davis, Ms E, Asst. Lib. (Full Time), Off. of Gas & Electricity Markets
[63874] 11/10/2004   **ME**
Davis, Mr H J, BSc FBIS MCLIP, Unemployed. [60272] 20/09/1977
CM31/07/1980
Davis, Mrs H R, BA MA ACLIP, Res. Asst., The Pharmacy Guild of
Australia [10001329] 06/02/2007   **ACL29/08/2008**
Davis, Miss J E, B LIB MCLIP, Head of Customer Serv., Wilts. Co. L. &
Heritage, Trowbridge [26180] 02/08/1976   **CM01/01/1980**
Davis, Mr J G, MA FCLIP, Inventory Catr., Mitchell L., Glasgow. [3777]
01/10/1970   **FE13/12/1979**
Davis, Ms J G, BA(Hons), Unknown. [10002306] 09/07/1991   **ME**
Davis, Mrs J I, Subject Lib. Maths & Physics, Betty & Gordon Moore L.,
Cambridge. [57917] 01/10/1999   **ME**
Davis, Mrs J M, BA DipLib, Asst. Lib., Nat. Police L., Hook, Hants.
[33598] 21/01/1981   **ME**
Davis, Mr J M, FRSA AMRI, Operations Mgr., Mob. & Home Serv. L.,
Kirklees Council., Huddersfield. [10013571] 07/05/2009   **AF**
Davis, Mrs J, MCLIP, Retired. [3776] 01/01/1940   **CM01/01/1961**
Davis, Mrs K A, BSc MCLIP, Sch. Lib., Sheringham High Sch., Norfolk.
[3778] 02/07/1969   **CM01/01/1971**
Davis, Ms K L, MLS, MA, BA, Collection Mgr., Mander & Mitchenson
Theatre Collection, London. [10015390] 10/11/2009   **ME**
Davis, Ms M V, Unwaged [47110] 21/04/1992   **ME**
Davis, Mrs P E, MCLIP, Ch. Lib., States of Jersey [11028] 01/01/1972
CM16/12/1975
Davis, Mr P, MCLIP, Life Member. [3788] 14/03/1951   **CM01/01/1963**
Davis, Mrs S J, Lunchtime Asst. [38087] 14/01/1985   **ME**
Davis, Mr S, Brit. Med. Assoc., London [65249] 01/12/2005   **ME**
Davis, Mrs S, BA(Hons) MA MCLIP, Inf. Res. Offr., EON, Nottingham
[63937] 18/11/2004   **CM29/08/2007**
Davis, Miss S, BA, L. Admin. Asst., Sci. Mus. L., Imperial Coll., London
[10008288] 26/03/2008   **ME**
Davis, Mrs V M, BSc MCLIP, Quality Admin., Rhodia UK Ltd., Oldbury.
[60680] 12/12/2001   **CM01/04/2002**
Davison, Miss A M, BA(Hons) MCLIP, Strategic Mgr. L., Durham C.C.
[45180] 02/08/1990   **CM23/09/1998**
Davison, Mr R A, BA(Hons) Dip Lib, Lib., Med. L., Univ. Hosp. of
Hartlepool [10008006] 26/01/1984   **ME**
Davison, Mrs R, AMRSC, Unknown. [10012161] 08/01/2009   **AF**
Davy, Miss A F, MCLIP, Retired [3801] 20/09/1969   **CM04/08/1972**
Davy, Miss J, BA(Hons), Inf. Asst., Univ. of Westminster, Harrow
Learning Res. Cent. [59991] 16/11/2001   **ME**
Davy, Mr M R, Collection Offr., Inland Revenue, Newcastle upon Tyne.
[38581] 01/07/1985   **ME**
Dawe, Mr R N E, MCLIP, Life Member. [3809] 01/01/1939**CM01/01/1945**
Dawes, Ms L J, BA MCLIP, Head of Inf. Serv., Manchester L. & Info
Serv., Manchester City Council [34979] 24/05/1982   **CM02/06/1987**

Dawes, Mrs L, BA(Hons) M. Phil, Lib. King's Sch. lincolnshire
[10011670] 11/11/2008   **ME**
Dawes, Mrs M I, MCLIP, Strategic Mgr., Child. & Young People's Serv.,
Swindon Bor., Wilts. [3386] 24/03/1971   **CM21/04/1975**
Dawes, Miss P J, BA MCLIP, Systems Lib., Univ. of Bradford. [33998]
08/07/1981   **CM31/10/1984**
Dawes, Mrs S, BA MA DipLib MCLIP, Inf. Mgr., PRPArchitects, Thames
Ditton. [35410] 18/10/1982   **CM01/04/2002**
Dawes, Mrs S, BLib MCLIP, Sen. Lib., City of London Freemen's Sch.,
Surrey. [33725] 09/02/1981   **CM28/09/1984**
Dawkins, Mrs J, BLib MCLIP, Inf. Specialist, Qinetiq, Farnborough,
Hants. [26836] 01/01/1976   **CM27/01/1982**
Daws, Mr A L, BA MCLIP, Media Lib., Inst. of Educ. L., Univ. of London.
[3813] 01/04/1967   **CM01/01/1970**
Dawson, Mr A D, BA MCLIP, MSc Programme Dir., Sch. of L. Arch. &
Inf. Studies, Univ. Coll. London. [32647] 01/07/1980 **CM16/08/1982**
Dawson, Miss A H, BA DipLib, Admin. Asst., Dept. of the Environment.,
Belfast. [35533] 29/10/1982   **ME**
Dawson, Ms A J, BA CertEd MCLIP, Inf. Mgr., Watts Grp. PLC, London.
[32385] 01/01/1972   **CM18/06/1984**
Dawson, Mrs D M, BA MA MCLIP, Arts Lib., Univ. of Nottingham.
[39034] 29/10/1985   **CM19/06/1991**
Dawson, Miss H S, BA MA DipLib MCLIP, Asst. Lib., L. S. E., London.
[46102] 02/10/1991   **CM26/01/1994**
Dawson, Miss J A, BA(Hons) MCLIP, Child. & Young People's, Educ.
Res. Serv., Coatbridge, N. Lanarks. [39923] 02/10/1986
CM27/05/1992
Dawson, Mr J A, BA MA MCLIP, Head of Staff Support & Devel., Univ.
of Sheffield, Sheffield. [39911] 01/10/1986 **RV17/06/2009**
CM18/04/1990
Dawson, Mr J D, BLIB MCLIP, Sen. Lib., Arup, London. [39426]
24/01/1986   **CM15/05/1989**
Dawson, Mrs J E, BA MCLIP, Lib., Warwicks. C.C., Stratford upon Avon
L. [11900] 01/01/1970   **CM25/09/1972**
Dawson, Ms J, MA(Hons), Sch. L. Resource Cent. Co-Ordinator.,
Aberdeen City Council [63176] 03/03/2004   **ME**
Dawson, Ms K A, BA PGDip, L. Res. Cent. Coordinator, Moray Council,
Milnes High Sch. [62563] 20/08/2003   **ME**
Dawson, Mrs L, BA(Hons) MSc MCLIP, Retired. [43960] 05/03/1990
CM25/01/1995
Dawson, Ms M M, BA(Hons) MSc MCLIP, Asst. Lib., NHS Leeds
[58271] 01/12/1999   **CM03/10/2007**
Dawson, Miss N J, BA MCLIP, Early years Lib., Shropshire C.C. [42295]
18/10/1988   **CM25/05/1994**
Dawson, Ms S, Unwaged [10000249] 01/07/2008   **ME**
Day, Mrs A A, BA(Hons) MA MCLIP, Lib., Royal Bournemouth Hosp.
[47482] 01/09/1992   **CM27/11/1996**
Day, Dr A E, MA PhD FRGS FCLIP, Retired. [3837] 30/01/1958
FE01/01/1961
Day, Mrs A M, BA(Hons) MCLIP, Neighbourhood Renewal Mgr., Leeds
L. & Inf. Serv. [47005] 01/04/1992   **CM24/07/1996**
Day, Mrs A, BA MCLIP, Lib., Archway Sch., Stroud. [21454] 18/10/1973
CM01/07/1977
Day, Mrs B E, MCLIP, Bibl. Serv. Lib., Solihull M.B.C. [6398] 05/09/1967
CM01/01/1972
Day, Miss E A, BA(Hons) MA MCLIP, Career break [51761] 01/07/1995
CM17/03/1999
Day, Mrs E V, MCLIP, Maths & Physics Lib., Univ. of Nottingham.
[11726] 26/04/1971   **CM02/08/1974**
Day, Mrs H J, BSc MCLIP, Managing Dir., Intranet Benchmarking
Forum. [60425] 19/06/1997   **CM19/06/1997**
Day, Miss J I C A, MA, Freelance Catr., Royal Irish Academy, Dublin
[32912] 02/10/1980   **ME**

Day, Miss J, Serv. Co-ordinator, Reader Serv. . Nat. L. of Wales. [10000895] 23/11/2006   **AF**
Day, Mr M A T, Stud., Manchester Met. Univ. [10013185] 03/04/2009 **ME**
Day, Mr N J, MCLIP, Life Member. [3842] 27/09/1951   **CM01/01/1955**
Day, Mr S R, BA MLib MCLIP, Product Mgr., OCLC, Birmingham [41393] 20/11/1987   **CM01/04/2002**
Day, Mrs S, BA, Unknown. [32043] 05/02/1980   **ME**
Day, Mr T G, BA(Hons) PGDip MCLIP, Sen. Asst. Lib. (Media), L.B. Wandsworth, Putney L. [48243] 17/11/1992   **CM09/11/2005**
Dayasena, Mr P J U, BSc MIEE MCLIP, Sen. Res. Adviser, Business Link E., Hatfield. [60721] 10/01/1985   **CM10/01/1985**
Day-Stirrat, Miss E, BA, Postgrad. Stud., Dept. of Inf. Studies, The Univ. of Sheffield. [10015975] 29/01/2010   **ME**
De Abaitua, Mrs C A, MSc, Stud. [10015563] 07/10/1997   **ME**
De Brún, Mrs C A, MA DipLIS MCLIP, Lib. – NHS Inst. for Innovation and Improvement [52166] 11/10/1995   **CM18/11/1998**
De Courcy Bower, Mrs J, ICT Support Offr., ESCC L., Lewes. [62820] 05/11/2003   **ME**
de Klerk, Mr M E, BSc(Econ), Res. Cent. Co-ordinator, Dundee City Council. [57590] 13/05/1999   **ME**
De Kock, Ms S A M, BLS, Asst. Lib., NHS Leeds. (Leeds DCT) [61178] 03/04/2002   **ME**
De Pretto, Mrs A, Lib. Asst., Nat. L. of Scotland [10016000] 10/02/2010   **ME**
De Saulles, Dr M R, DPhil MSc BA(Hons) PGCertHE, Head of Div. of Inf. Mgmnt., Univ. of Brighton, Watts. Building. [44909] 15/01/1991   **ME**
de Silva, Mr D P, BSc MSc, Inf. Mgr., Inf. Mgmnt., Foreign & Commonwealth Off., London. [46777] 22/01/1992   **ME**
de Souza, Mrs Y, BA DipLib MCLIP, Lib., Bedford Hosp. [42629] 23/01/1989   **CM24/06/1992**
De Weirdt, Miss N A, BA DipInf MCLIP, Lib., Essex C.C., Rayleigh Pub. L. [46378] 30/10/1991   **CM22/05/1996**
Deacon, Miss A J, BA Msc ECONILS, Inf. Specialist, Civil Serv. [63752] 29/09/2004   **ME**
Deacon, Miss A, BA(Hons) MCLIP, LRC. Co-ordinator, The Brit Sch., Croydon. [62060] 07/02/2003   **CM29/11/2006**
Deacon, Mrs D A, MCLIP, Reader Devel. Lib., Newbury L., W. Berkshire. [22384] 01/04/1974   **CM21/09/1983**
Deacon, Ms H, BScEcon(Hons) MCLIP, Inf. Serv. Mngr., Portsmouth City Council. [45019] 04/06/1990   **CM19/05/1999**
Deacon, Mrs J, BA, L. Asst., Portishead L. [10011227] 03/10/2008 **ME**
Deacon, Ms P A, MA DipLib, Lib., Sherborne Sch. for Girls. [32412] 26/03/1980   **AF**
Deadman, Mrs S, BA, Unknown. [35599] 26/10/1982   **ME**
Deakin, Mrs P J, BA DipLib MCLIP, p. /t. Principal L. Mgr. (Community L.) [38246] 12/02/1985   **CM14/03/1990**
Deakin, Mr P, Knowledge Mgr, Indigo Planning, London [10007666] 19/02/2008   **AF**
Deakin, Mrs S W, MCLIP, Life Member. [3850] 03/02/1949
                                                    CM01/01/1956
Dean, Prof A J E, MA ALAA MCLIP, Prof. of L. & Inf. Studies, Univ. Coll. Dublin, Eire. [16707] 21/01/1952   **CM01/01/1954**
Dean, Mrs E C, BA(Hons), Community & Inf. Offr., Beverley L., Beverley. [65924] 06/07/2006   **AF**
Dean, Mrs E J, BA MCLIP, Employment not known. [33352] 15/10/1980
                                                    CM26/05/1993
Dean, Mrs E J, BA(Hons) MA MCLIP, Lib., Wyke Manor Sch., Bradford. [51743] 12/06/1995   **CM17/05/2000**
Dean, Ms J E, BA MCLIP, Audio Visual Admin., St. Helen's Sch., Middlesex. [22778] 17/10/1974   **CM21/09/1978**
Dean, Ms L A, MA, Lib., Brighton&Hove High Sch., Brighton. [47131] 05/05/1992   **ME**

Dean, Mrs L, MCLIP, Learning Res. Cent. Mgr., Ashton-on-Mersey Sch., Sale. [19847] 02/01/1973   **CM01/09/1975**
Dean, Miss S, BA(Hons), Community Lib., Luton Cent. L. [10006611] 11/09/2007   **ME**
Deans, Miss I M, FSA Scot MCLIP, Life Member. [3863] 24/07/1957
                                                    CM01/01/1969
Dearden, Mr P M, BA(Hons), Stud. [66114] 22/09/2006   **ME**
Dearden, Mr S, BA DipLib MCLIP, Team Leader-Stock Control, Liverpool City L. [32914] 12/10/1980   **CM01/12/1982**
Dearie, Ms S J, BA(Hons) DipLib MCLIP, Lib. / LRC Mngr., Prendergast Ladywell Fields Coll. [34664] 08/01/1982   **CM18/02/1986**
De'Ath, Miss A F, BA DipLib MCLIP, Lib., Eastwood High Sch., Glasgow. [43164] 04/09/1989   **CM21/07/1993**
Deaville, Mrs A M, BA PGDipLib MCLIP, Sen. Sch. Servs. Offr., Sch. L. Serv., Cumbria [38455] 03/05/1985   **CM07/09/2005**
Debnam, Ms A, MCLIP, Retired. [15687] 30/08/1964   **CM07/02/1975**
Deegan-Spragg, Ms C M, BA MA, Child. Co-ordinator, Knowsley M.B.C. [38780] 09/10/1985   **ME**
Deen, Ms F, Lib., OPEC L., Vienna Austria [10001537] 03/10/1984 **ME**
Deering-Punshon, Ms S E, BLib MCLIP, Child. Lib., Newbury P. L., W. Berks. Dist. Council. [21506] 27/10/1973   **CM27/02/1980**
Defriez, Mr P E, MA MCLIP, Database Lib., Dept. of Health L., London. [26713] 19/10/1976   **CM21/12/1978**
Degnan, Mrs A J, BA(Hons) MCLIP, Unwaged. [42644] 30/01/1989
                                                    CM18/11/1993
Del Corno, Mr A, MA MCLIP, Catr./Acquistions Support Lib., The London L. [62214] 18/03/2003   **CM29/03/2006**
Delahunty, Miss S, BA(Hons) MCLIP, L. Customer Asst., Monmouthshire [49740] 29/11/1993   **CM15/03/2000**
Delamore, Miss C, BA MA, Metadata Lib., Newcastle Univ. L., Music Lib., Literary & Philosophical Soc. [10006001] 24/08/2007 **ME**
Delaney, Mrs E A, MCLIP, L. Asst., BSRIA Ltd., Bracknell. [21296] 16/10/1973   **CM02/08/1977**
Delaney, Miss E L, BA(Hons) MCLIP, Unknown. [10001723] 31/10/1994
                                                    CM21/01/1998
Delbridge, Dr R, BA(Hons) PhD, Sen. Lect., Dept. Inf. & Communications, Manchester Met. Univ. [10016123] 16/02/2010 **ME**
Delderfield, Miss J, BA(Hons) MA MCLIP, Lib., Royal Coll. of Physicians, London. [64609] 03/05/2005   **CM31/01/2007**
Delgal, Miss C, Asst. Libr., Inst. Civil Engineers, London. [63541] 17/06/2004   **ME**
Dell, Ms C, BA(Hons) MA PGCE, Subj. Info. Servs., Univ. of Teeside [10013157] 07/01/1986   **ME**
Dellar, Mr G, MCLIP, Retired. [16715] 28/09/1948   **CM01/01/1951**
Dellar, Mr M G, MA MCLIP, Learning Resources Mgr., Coll. of N. W. London., London. [39669] 30/04/1986   **CM15/08/1990**
Deller, Ms C S, BA(Hons), stud. /Asst. Lib., Aberystwyth Univ. /The Skinner's Sch., Tunbridge Wells. [10013470] 28/04/2009 **ME**
Delobel, Mrs H L, BA(Hons), Lib. Asst., Leeds Trinity Univ. Coll. [10015947] 29/01/2010   **ME**
Delve, Mr B, MCLIP, Retired. [3881] 12/09/1961   **CM01/01/1970**
Dempsey, Mr L, BA DLIS ALAI MCLIP, Vice President, Res., OCLC. [41053] 06/10/1987   **CM01/04/2002**
Dempsie, Mrs R E J, MA(Hons), Enq. Offr.,Cent. Lib., Swindon [61567] 02/10/2002   **ME**
Dempster, Dr J A H, MA PhD MCLIP, Sen. Lib. Systems Co-ordinator, Highland Council-Educ., Culture & Sport [20774] 01/07/1973
                                                    CM08/06/1976
Denham, Mrs M E, MA DipLib MCLIP, Primary Sch. Lib., Hutchesons Grammar Sch., Glasgow. [35161] 23/09/1982   **CM23/11/1986**
Denham, Mrs M F, BA MCLIP, p. /t. Early Years Mgr., Manchester City Council. [19081] 01/07/1971   **CM25/03/1975**
Denholm, Mrs V, MA MCLIP, Access Mgr., Rec. Serv., Nat. L. of Scotland [56727] 07/10/1998   **CM13/06/2007**

Dening, Mrs J, BA(Hons), Sch. Lib. Ashville Coll., Harrogate (job share) [57345] 18/02/1999 **ME**

Denmead, Mr J, MA, L. Serv. Mgr.,MoD,London [10001420] 04/10/1988 **ME**

Dennehy, Miss M M, BA DipLib, Unwaged. [33995] 30/06/1981 **ME**

Denning, Mr R T W, BA FCLIP, Retired. [3888] 08/01/1945 **FE01/01/1959**

Dennis, Mrs J M, BA MSc MCLIP, Lib. (Job share)., Nat. Coal Mining Mus. for England., Yorkshire. [25449] 12/01/1976 **CM01/09/1978**

Dennis, Miss N, BSc(Hons) MA MCLIP, Business Inf. Specialist, Aston Univ., Birmingham. [53740] 18/09/1996 **CM15/11/2000**

Dennis, Ms S E, BA DipLib MCLIP, Head of Inf. Serv., Charles Russell, LLP, London. [33720] 02/01/1981 **CM26/05/1983**

Dennison, Ms M, BSocSc MCLIP, Head L. and Res. Serv., Houses of the Oireachtas, Dublin. [60122] 25/01/2001 **CM25/01/2001**

Dennison, Mr P J, BA(Hons) MSc, User Serv. Lib., Inst. Educ., Univ. London. [49467] 03/11/1993 **ME**

Denny, Mr G E, BA(Hons) DipIM MCLIP, Unwaged. [51085] 14/11/1994 **CM08/12/2004**

Denoon, Ms C M, MA DipLib MCLIP, L. Serv. Mgr., NHS Greater Glasgow & Clyde., Maria Henderson L. [43561] 08/11/1989 **CM16/12/1992**

Denovan, Miss C J, BA, Inf. Asst., Aberdeen Coll., Gallowgate L. [57280] 28/01/1999 **ME**

Dent, Mrs K, BEng(Hons) MSc MScIS, Lib., Leeds City Council. [63371] 21/04/2004 **ME**

Denton, Mr D A, Snr. Lib., Key Skills Training Ltd. [63495] 15/06/2004 **AF**

Denton, Mr D, BSc MCLIP, Chartered Inst. of Environmental Health Bus. Dev. Dir. [60456] 06/04/1989 **CM06/04/1989**

Denton, Mrs P E, ACLIP, L. Asst., Watford Cent. L. [64766] 27/06/2005 **ACL28/01/2009**

Denyer, Miss A J C, BA(Hons) MA, Stud., Univ. Coll. London [10013007] 23/03/2009 **ME**

Depledge, Miss A J, BA(Hons) DPS MA MCLIP, Archive Asst., W. Yorkshire Archive Serv. [44670] 22/11/1990 **CM21/07/1999**

Derbyshire, Mrs A J S, Stud [10007560] 13/02/2008 **ME**

Derbyshire, Mrs J D, BA(Hons) PGCE DipLib MCLIP Cer, Learning Devel. Lect., S. Downs Coll., Hampshire. [32954] 01/10/1980 **CM15/08/1989**

DeSilva, Mr M C, BA PGCE, Teacher of Hist. & Politics, Watford Grammar Sch., Watford [10015039] 09/10/2009 **ME**

Deslignères, Ms L, PGDip MCLIP, Lib., Language Cent., Oxford Univ. [63602] 09/07/2004 **CM24/10/2008**

Devalapalli, Mrs U M, MSc BLISc MLISc MCLIP, Lib., W. Middlesex Univ. Hosp. NHS Trust. [60891] 20/12/2001 **CM17/09/2003**

Devaney, Miss K R, BA DipLib, Acquisitions Mgr., Univ. of Reading L. [59890] 29/10/2001 **ME**

Devitt, Ms B, BSc(Hons), Know How Offr., Slaughter and May, London. [55383] 07/10/1997 **ME**

Devitt, Mr T, p. /t. Stud., London Met. Univ., Paddington L. [62686] 17/10/2003 **ME**

Devlin, Mrs L M, DMS MCLIP, Retired. [10625] 16/01/1968 **CM01/01/1972**

Devlin, Mrs N J, MA (LIS), Unknown. [10014156] 19/02/2001 **ME**

Devlin, Ms N M, BA(Hons) MA MCLIP, H. of Inf. Res., Nottingham Trent Univ. [44224] 16/07/1990 **CM29/01/1992**

Devlin, Mr P, BA DLIS MLIS MA MCLIP, Faculty Lib., DIT, Dublin, ROI. [10004709] 01/01/1997 **CM01/04/1999**

Dev-Modak, Mrs R, BA(Hons) MA, Intranet Content Team Leader., Dept of Health., London [55735] 10/11/1997 **ME**

Devnally, Mr D K, BA DipLib HonFLA, Resident Bombay. [39728] 06/07/1956 **HFE13/09/1984**

Devon, Miss J, Lib., Eastbury Comp. Sch., Barking. [63889] 14/10/2004 **AF**

Devonald, Ms J A, BA(Hons) MA, Project Offr, Race Relations Resource Cent., Univ. of Manchester. [56889] 02/11/1998 **ME**

Devoy, Mrs F, MA DipLib MCLIP, Lib., St Mungos High Sch., Falkirk. [36236] 15/08/1983 **CM24/03/1987**

Dew, Miss E E, BA(Hons), Lib. Asst., City Business L., London. [64859] 03/08/2005 **AF**

Dew, Ms H, BA(Hons) MA MCLIP, Customer Devel. Offr., Glos. C.C. [47901] 22/10/1992 **CM21/07/1999**

Dewar, Miss D, BA MCLIP, Unknown. [20594] 03/05/1973 **CM20/02/1981**

Dewar, Mrs H W, MA MCLIP, Cultural Serv. Team Leader, Aberdeenshire Co. [21294] 11/10/1973 **CM01/11/1976**

Dewe, Prof A J, BSc FNZLA AALIA MCLIP, Univ. Lib., La Trobe Univ., Aus. [60070] 07/03/1978 **CM07/03/1978**

Dewhurst, Mrs V B, Lib., Queen Elizabeth's Grammar Sch., Blackburn. [63212] 16/03/2004 **ME**

Dews, Mrs E, BA(Hons) FCLIP, Retired. [3921] 26/02/1951 **FE01/01/1961**

Dexter, Mrs F, MA, Lib., Court Lane Junior Sch., / Lib. Portsmouth C.C. Portsmouth. [62806] 24/10/2003 **ME**

Dexter, Mr S, BSc(Hons), Unknown. [10014336] 10/07/2009 **AF**

Dextre Clarke, Mrs S G, MSc FCLIP, Inf. Consultant, Wantage. [60275] 05/10/1971 **FE22/04/1988**

Dhanjal, Mrs C, BA(Hons) DipCAM(PR) MA, Dir., The Answer Ltd., Woldingham, Surrey. [62634] 01/10/2003 **ME**

Dhawan, Ms K, BA, Part time [10009719] 31/08/1995 **ME**

Dholakia, Mr P, BA, Graduate Trainee Lib. Assit., Gray's inn L., London. [10015680] 13/01/2010 **ME**

Dholiwar, Miss V, MCLIP, Retired. [31814] 15/12/1979 **CM15/09/1983**

Di Tillio, Mr C, Funzionario Biblioteche, Istituzione Biblioteche, Comune Di Roma. [58734] 01/07/2000 **ME**

Diaper, Mrs P H, BLib MCLIP, L. Asst., Fowey L., Cornwall C.C. [19874] 01/01/1973 **CM28/11/1977**

Dibble, Mrs S L, BLib MCLIP, Learning Res. Cent. Mgr., Churchill Comm. Sch., N. Somerset. [44629] 12/11/1990 **CM23/03/1993**

Dick, Miss A M, Inf. Offr., Scottish Envir. Protection Agency, Heriot Watt Res. Park, Edinburgh. [45620] 04/04/1991 **ME**

Dick, Miss B A M, MA DipLib MCLIP, Retired. [27153] 24/01/1977 **CM31/01/1980**

Dick, Miss L, BA MA, Digital Systems Specialist, Australia [53966] 16/10/1996 **ME**

Dick, Miss M H, MCLIP, Retired. [3931] 05/02/1952 **CM01/01/1959**

Dicken, Mrs C M, Inf. Offr., Cent. L., Business Insight, Birmingham. [10006485] 10/09/2001 **ME**

Dickenson, Mrs L J, Lib. Auxillary, Dornoch Academy, Dornoch, Sutherland. [58693] 02/06/2000 **ME**

Dickerson, Ms Y B, BA(Hons) DipM MCLIP, Dep. Mgr. Reader Serv. Lib. SOAS Univ of London [50767] 17/10/1994 **CM20/11/2002**

Dickey, Miss M T, MCLIP, Sen. Asst. Lib., Battersea Ref. L. [30614] 19/02/1979 **CM03/05/1989**

Dickey, Mrs S, MCLIP, Sen. Lib. Catg., Lancashire Co. L. HQ, Preston. [10016202] 04/01/1971 **CM14/01/1974**

Dickinson, Mrs A, MCLIP, Lib., Netherhall Sch., Cambridge. [559] 01/01/1971 **CM01/11/1975**

Dickinson, Miss E, BA MCLIP, Retired. [13246] 01/01/1961 **CM01/01/1963**

Dickinson, Mrs J A, BA MCMI MCLIP, Sen. Lib. Collection Devel. [44509] 16/10/1990 **CM22/04/1992**

Dickinson, Mrs T A, BA MCLIP, Young Peoples Serv. Lib. (Job Share), Torbay L. Serv., Torquay Cent. L. [46877] 20/02/1992 **CM16/11/1994**

Dickinson, Mr T, OBE HonFLA, Hon. Fellow. [46052] 11/09/1991 **HFE11/01/1991**

Dicks, Mrs K L, BA DipLib MCLIP, Part-time Asst., European Collections, Cambridge Univ. L. [42893] 04/04/1989 **CM22/04/1992**

Dicks, Mrs S M, BSc MCLIP, Asst. Lib., Nottingham City PCT., Res. Cent. [41918] 20/05/1988 **CM24/07/1996**

Dickson, Miss D M, FCLIP, Life Member. [3944] 17/02/1951 **FE01/01/1964**

Dickson, Mr E, MA(Hons) DipLib DipGerman, Curator, Nat. L. of Scotland, Edinburgh. [10006176] 11/08/1986 **ME**

Dickson, Mrs E, BA DipLib MCLIP, Sen. Lib., S. E. L.B., Armagh, N. Ireland. [33650] 01/02/1981 **CM21/08/1986**

Dickson, Miss J J, BSc(Hons) MCLIP, Sen. Lib., Herbert Smith, London. [51690] 15/05/1995 **CM19/07/2000**

Dickson, Mr J, MA DipLib MCLIP, Lib., Falkirk Council L. Serv., L. Support, Falkirk. [24651] 30/09/1975 **CM18/09/2002**

Dickson, Mrs K A, MA DipILS, IT Instructor/Lib., Aberdeen Coll. [54620] 04/02/1997 **ME**

Dickson, Mrs M G, MA MCLIP, Learning Resource Cent. Coordinator, Portobello Sch., Edinburgh. [3947] 01/01/1969 **CM10/12/1975**

Dickson, Mrs S M T, BA DipLib MCLIP, L. Resource Cent. Co-Ord., City of Edinburgh Council. [56198] 01/04/1998 **CM20/09/2000**

Dienelt, Mr O, DipLib MCLIP, Lib., Inst. fuer Baustoffe, Tech. Univ. of Braunschweig, Germany. [42897] 18/04/1989 **CM17/01/2001**

Digby, Mrs E J, BA MSc, Collection Risk Advisor, Brit. L., London [58469] 28/02/2000 **ME**

Diggle, Mr A H, BSc MBA MCLIP, Consultant, Self-employed, London. [23176] 02/11/1974 **CM05/01/1978**

Diggle, Mr A W, BA BSc, Stud., Univ. of Brighton [10015549] 14/12/2009 **ME**

Dighe, Mrs S, BA(Hons) LLB BLS, Lib., Park High Sch., Stanmore. [65347] 01/01/2006 **ME**

Dike, Miss K A R, BA(Hons) MSc MCLIP, Lib., London Contemporary Dance Sch., London. [62668] 02/10/2003 **CM05/05/2010**

Dillon, Miss M C, MA, Unknown [10007919] 28/02/2008 **ME**

Dillon, Mrs M, BA DipLib MCLIP, Inf. Cent. Mgr., BNP Paribas., London [35902] 02/02/1983 **CM14/04/1987**

Dimmock, Miss L M, BA(Hons), Inf. Offr., OnePlusOne, London. [10015440] 18/11/2009 **AF**

Dimond, Mrs A M, DipLib MCLIP, Faculty Inf. Consultant, Univ. Herts., Hatfield. [36060] 02/04/1983 **CM16/10/1989**

Dimyan, Mr A J, MCLIP, Community Lib.,Luton [65076] 24/10/2005 **CM28/01/2009**

Dine, Mr D G, MCLIP, Retired. [3962] 24/08/1951 **CM01/01/1956**

Dines, Miss A M, BSc MA, Inf. Serv. Mgr., Med. Toxicology Inf. Serv., Guys & St. Thomas's Foundation Trust. [49758] 02/12/1993 **ME**

Dingley, Mrs P O, BA MCLIP, Retired. [3964] 31/10/1971 **CM04/10/1973**

Diprose, Mrs K A, MSc BSc, Inf. & Support Programme Mngr., Macmillan Cancer Support, London [66044] 08/09/2006 **ME**

Divall, Mrs C M, Info. Cent. Asst., DSTL, Sevenoaks. [63035] 17/12/2003 **AF**

Divall, Mrs P J, BA(Hons) MA MCLIP, Clinical Lib., Univ. Hosp. of Leicester NHS, Leicester Gen. Hosp. [59984] 15/11/2001 **CM08/12/2004**

Dix, Mrs N B, BSc MA MCLIP, Unwaged [62088] 12/02/2003 **CM03/10/2007**

Dix, Ms P E, BA MCLIP, Head, Educ. L. Serv., L.B. Islington. [24338] 01/07/1975 **CM29/09/1978**

Dixon, Mrs A L, BA(Hons) MA MCLIP, Collections Mgr., Brit. Geological Survey, Nottingham. [56642] 01/10/1998 **CM21/11/2001**

Dixon, Mr A T, MA LLM, Res. Enquiries Mgr., Integreon Managed Solutions, Bristol. [43395] 19/10/1989 **ME**

Dixon, Dr D, BA MPhil DipLib PhD MCLIP, Unknown. [18636] 18/10/1969 **CM01/01/1972**

Dixon, Miss E D, Retired. [47216] 08/06/1992 **AF**

Dixon, Mr G J, Blib(Hons) MLib, Br. Mgr., Clarkson L., Ocean Keys, Australia. [10015207] 26/02/1991 **ME**

Dixon, Miss I L, MCLIP, Retired. [3981] 30/03/1944 **CM01/01/1957**

Dixon, Mrs J M, BEd MCLIP, Early Years Lib., Suffolk C.C., Ipswich. [5002] 01/01/1971 **CM01/01/1975**

Dixon, Mr J S, BA(Hons) MA PhD PGCE, Asst. Lib., Food Standards Agency, London. [56136] 05/03/1998 **ME**

Dixon, Miss J, Res. Devel. Mgr., ICAEW L. &Inf. Serv., London. [10016555] 19/11/1993 **ME**

Dixon, Mr K A, MA MA MCLIP, Sci. Inf. Offr., IOM., Edinburgh. [38193] 30/01/1985 **CM01/04/2002**

Dixon, Mrs K, BA(Hons), Unwaged. [10013670] 18/05/2009 **AF**

Dixon, Mrs M L R, MCLIP, Retired. [3987] 01/10/1945 **CM01/01/1957**

Dixon, Mr N, Unwaged. [10011080] 24/09/2008 **ME**

Dixon, Mr R J, BSc MSc, Inf. Offr., Cairn Energy PLC, Edinburgh. [10016932] 10/06/2010 **ME**

Dixon, Miss R P, MCLIP, Retired. [3989] 01/01/1964 **CM01/01/1967**

Dixon, Ms R, MA DipLib MCLIP, Lib. (P/T), Archant Norfolk, Norwich. [39531] 13/02/1986 **CM24/04/1991**

Dixon, Mrs S M, MBE BA Dip Mus BSc(Hons) MCLIP MInstLm, Reader Devel. Co-ordinator, Walsall L. Serv. [47885] 23/10/1992 **CM25/01/1995**

Dlugoszewska, Mrs L J, BA MCLIP, L. Asst., Northants. C.C. [29290] 15/05/1978 **CM16/11/1981**

Dobb, Mr C R, BA MCLIP, L. Serv. Devel. Mgr., Wandsworth Bor. Council. [29636] 05/10/1978 **CM13/01/1984**

Dobbins, Mrs D A, BA(Hons) MCLIP, Indexer/Proofreader. [41645] 03/02/1988 **CM23/07/1997**

Dobbins, Mrs J, BA MSc, Unwaged [56390] 01/07/1998 **ME**

Dobby, Miss P C, BA MCLIP, HR Records Administrator, Univ. Coll. London. [4001] 01/01/1967 **CM01/01/1971**

Dobie, Mrs H D, MA DipLib MCLIP, Unknown. [28116] 04/10/1977 **CM25/03/1980**

Dobreva, Dr M, Sen. Researcher, CDLR, Univ. of Strathclyde. [10014609] 19/08/2009 **ME**

Dobson, Miss E, MA FCLIP, Life Member. [4005] 02/02/1954 **FE01/01/1968**

Dobson, Miss G, BA(Hons) MCLIP, Operations Mgr. -Family Inf. Serv., Salford Council [42050] 19/08/1988 **CM24/05/1995**

Dobson, Mrs K L, BSc(Hons) DipLIS MCLIP, Sen. Asst. Lib. -Lend. Serv., Harris L., Preston, Lancs. [58581] 05/04/2000 **CM13/03/2002**

Dobson, Miss L N, MA(Hons) MCLIP, Tech. Serv. Lib., Queen's Coll., Oxford [59849] 16/10/2001 **CM03/10/2007**

Dobson, Mrs L, BSc(Hons), Online Learn. Coordinator, Durham C.C. [58662] 09/05/2000 **ME**

Dobson, Mr M L, BBibl(Hons), L. Dir., U. S. Embassy L., Pretoria, S. Africa. [63814] 01/10/2004 **ME**

Dobson, Mrs P, BA(Hons) MCLIP, Career Break [39354] 13/01/1986 **RV22/06/2007** **CM17/11/1999**

Dobson, Mrs R, BA(Hons) MA MCLIP, Learning Adv., Univ. L. & Learning Servs., Northumbria Univ. [54327] 15/11/1996 **CM01/06/2005**

Docherty, Mrs J, MA BA MCLIP, Catg. Asst., RNIB, Stockport. [1810] 07/06/1971 **CM31/05/1975**

Docherty, Mrs M T, BA MCLIP, Training Asst., Nat. Probation Serv., Hertford. [2016] 14/01/1970 **CM01/09/1973**

Docherty, Miss T, MCLIP, Br. Co-ordinator Lib., Clacks L., Alloa [64814] 18/07/2005 **CM18/12/2009**

Dodd, Mr D C, BSc(Hons) MCLIP, Unemployed. [4018] 01/01/1967 **CM01/01/1971**

Dodds, Mr I, BSc(Hons) MA MCLIP, Hd. of Cultural Servs., London B. of Richmond upon Thames [51464] 24/02/1995 **CM22/07/1998**

Dodds, Mr J C, FCLIP, Life Member. [4030] 24/09/1951 **FE18/11/1998**

Dodgson, Mrs J, MCLIP, Life Member. [4032] 28/01/1946 **CM01/01/1952**

Dodson, Ms A L, Asst. Lib., Solicitors Legal Inf. Cent., Scottish Gov. Legal Directorate, Edingburgh. [63204] 16/03/2004 **ME**

Dodson, Mrs E R, BA DipLib MCLIP, Head of L. /Resources, Myton Sch., Warwick, Warks. [30152] 17/01/1979 **CM16/01/1981**

Doe, Ms S E, DipLib MCLIP, Dir. of Info. & Res., Sidley Austin, London. [44288] 15/08/1990 **CM26/01/1994**

Doel, Mrs J D, BSc MSc MTOPRA MCLIP, Mgr, Regulatory Intelligence, Glaxosmithkline, Harlow. [60746] 11/05/1986 **CM02/03/1992**

Dogterom, Miss M E, MA PgDip MCLIP, Catr., Brit. L., Boston Spa. [46198] 10/10/1991 **CM08/12/2004**

Doherty, Mr A F, MCLIP, Campus Lib., Univ. Coll. Falmouth (Jobshare) [22740] 02/09/1974 **CM18/08/1977**

Doherty, Ms H J, BA MCLIP, Proj. Offr., Info. Advice & Advocacy, Adult Social Servs., Derbyshire C.C. [4041] 01/01/1972 **CM07/10/1975**

Doherty, Mrs H S, BA, Mus. Galleries Scotland, Edinburgh [43410] 18/10/1989 **ME**

Doherty, Miss S, BA(Hons) MSc MA, Medicines Lib., MHRA, London. [53970] 16/10/1996 **ME**

Doherty-Allan, Ms R, BA MA DipIM, Trust Lib., Altnagelvin Area Hosp., Londonderry. [54702] 06/03/1997 **ME**

Doig, Miss C, MA(Hons) DipILS MCLIP, Lib., Bell Baxter High Sch., Fife. [54391] 02/12/1996 **CM15/10/2002**

Doig, Mr C, BA(Hons) PGDipLIS MCLIP, Postgrad. Stud., Univ. of Paisley [55485] 15/10/1997 **CM15/05/2002**

Doig, Mrs F L, MA DipLib MCLIP, p. /t. Lib. (User Serv.), Univ. of Dundee. [26290] 01/10/1983 **CM19/01/1988**

Dolan, Mr J, OBE BA MCLIP, Independent Consultant [23907] 21/01/1975 **CM21/01/1977**

Dolan, Miss K, BA(Hons) DipILM MCLIP, Reading & Learning Team Leader., L. Inf. Heritage & Arts Serv., Royal Bor. of Windsor & Maidenhead [55487] 15/10/1997 **CM10/07/2002**

Dolan, Rev M J, MA FCLIP, Retired. [4047] 20/01/1956 **FE01/01/1965**

Dolben, Ms L, BA DipLib MCLIP, p. /t. Asst. Lib., Tavistock & Portman NHS Trust [37097] 14/02/1984 **CM06/10/1987**

Doleschal, Miss M, MA PgDip, Unknown. [10013968] 17/06/2009 **ME**

Dolitzscher, Mrs A, MA FCLIP, Retired. [4050] 25/09/1951 **FE01/01/1959**

Dolphin, Ms P M, MA DipLib MCLIP, Retired. [4057] 30/07/1970 **CM04/07/1974**

Donald, Mr P, BLS PGCHE MCLIP, Liaison Lib., Nottingham Trent Univ., L. & Learning Res. [53507] 10/07/1996 **CM17/03/1999**

Donaldson, Miss A, BA MA MCLIP, Liaison Lib., Nottingham Trent Univ. [53228] 09/04/1996 **CM12/03/2003**

Donaldson, Ms E L A, BA(Hons) MA PGCE, Lib. Asst., S. Leics. Coll., Wigston, Leics. [10005041] 06/06/2007 **ME**

Donaldson, Mrs J L, MA DipLib MCLIP, Sch. Lib., Jordanhill Sch., Glasgow. [37694] 16/10/1984 **CM07/06/1988**

Donaldson, Dr R, MA PhD, Life Member [4070] 23/04/1956 **ME**

Donaldson, Mrs S A, BSc PGDipLib MCLIP, Sr. Lib. & Info. Offr., Cent. L., Dundee [35600] 10/11/1982 **CM29/03/2006**

Donegan, Mrs C M, MCLIP, Lib., Sacred Heart Catholic Coll., Crosby. [13550] 22/02/1967 **CM01/01/1970**

Doney, Ms E J, BA(Econ) MSc MCLIP, Nat. Core Content Adminstrator., Nat. L. for Health [54268] 12/11/1996 **CM22/09/1999**

Donkin, Mrs E, MA MCLIP, Learning Cent. Mgr., Biddick Sch. Washington. [59198] 19/12/2000 **CM18/09/2002**

Donlon, Miss R M, BA MA, Lib., Northwick L., Cheshire [10001985] 28/03/2007 **ME**

Donnelly, Mr A A, BSc MA DipLib MCLIP, Ch. Lib., Glasgow Met. Coll. [36378] 05/10/1983 **CM29/01/1985**

Donnelly, Mrs A J, BA(Hons) MCLIP, L. Serv. Mgr., E. Cheshire NHS Trust. [50553] 15/09/1994 **CM06/04/2005**

Donnelly, Ms K, BA, Principal Lib. /Business Inf. Co-ordinator, Mitchell L., Glasgow. [10014143] 07/03/1984 **ME**

Donnelly, Miss M R, BA DipLib MCLIP, Retired. [4080] 06/10/1969 **CM13/02/1973**

Donnithorne, Mrs P J H, PGDip LIS, LRC Mgr., Elthorne Pk High Sch., London [10001711] 18/09/1989 **ME**

Donoghue, Mr S, BA(Hons) PGDipLIS MCLIP, Local Studies Lib., L.B. of Havering, Cent. L. [42834] 14/03/1989 **CM07/09/2005**

Donoghue, Mrs V R, BA MSc MCLIP, Study Cent. Mgr., Wood Green Sch., Witney [27751] 04/08/1977 **CM18/11/1981**

Donohue, Mr N, BA(Hons) PgDip MCLIP, Inf. Specialist, Univ. of Salford. [10010113] 04/07/2008 **CM11/06/2010**

Donovan, Mrs A, MA MCLIP, P. /t. Stud., Univ. Coll. Ferrier Lib., London. [65276] 25/11/2005 **CM07/07/2010**

Doody, Mrs A L, BLS(Hons) MCLIP, L. Adviser, Reading, Berks. [33533] 01/01/1981 **CM25/11/1985**

Doody, Ms M C, BA MCLIP, Family Inf. Off., L.B. of Ealing. [28292] 01/11/1977 **CM15/01/1981**

Doogan, Miss A H, MA(Hons) DipLIS MCLIP, Sch. Lib., St. Andrews High, W. Dunbartonshire Council. [50860] 24/10/1994 **CM23/07/1997**

Dooner, Mrs A M, PgD, Unknown. [10012183] 09/01/2009 **ME**

Dorabjee, Miss S, BSc MCLIP, Inf. Consultant. [60278] 06/06/1980 **CM06/06/1980**

Doran, Ms E, BA MCLIP, Life Member. [24204] 18/04/1975 **CM12/12/1991**

Doran, Ms J D, BA(Hons) MA PgCHE MCLIP, Sen. Inf. Adviser for Law, Univ. of Gloucestershire, Cheltenham. [58214] 18/11/1999 **CM17/09/2003**

Doran, Mrs S, Inf. & Knowledge Mgr., Virgin Media [10000791] 01/11/2006 **ME**

Dorantt, Mrs V T, BSc (Hons) MA, Operations Lib., Cent. Resources L., Hatfield. [10010267] 03/10/1996 **ME**

Dore, Mrs J D, MCLIP, Inf. Lib., Worthing L., W. Sussex C.C. [22783] 15/10/1974 **CM04/08/1977**

Dormer, Ms D, Unwaged. [63417] 06/05/2004 **ME**

Dorney, Mr P A, BA(Hons) MCLIP, Sen. Lib., Sch. L. Serv. [52358] 26/10/1995 **CM18/11/1998**

Doubleday, Miss P A, BA MCLIP, Retired. [4099] 22/09/1956 **CM01/01/1966**

Douce, Mr G O, ICT Technician, Website Mgr., Ashley Sch., Lowestoft. [10006290] 05/10/2007 **AF**

Douch, Mr P, BA MCLIP, IT Learning Coordinator [32922] 25/10/1980 **CM10/05/1988**

Dougan, Mr D J, MA(Hons) PGDipILS MCLIP, Inf. Serv. Mgr., Health Protection Scotland, Glasgow. [46563] 13/11/1991 **CM17/09/2003**

Doughty, Mr K A, FCLIP, Retired. [4103] 27/01/1948 **FE01/01/1957**

Doughty, Miss S J, BA(Hons) PG DipILS MCLIP, Applications Support Offr., Univ. of Aberdeen. [61097] 28/02/2002 **CM11/03/2009**

Douglas, Ms A M, MCLIP, H. of L. Serv., Tavistock & Portman NHS Foundation Trust, London. [18644] 25/09/1972 **CM01/01/1975**

Douglas, Mrs C A M, BA MCLIP, Employment not known. [26631] 04/10/1976 **CM25/06/1979**

Douglas, Miss C E, LLB, BrC, MD CCJ, Grad. Trainee L. Asst., Lambeth Palace L., London [10011283] 07/10/2008 **ME**

Douglas, Mrs E M, BA MSc MCLIP, Stud., Edinburgh Univ. [47993] 30/10/1992 **CM03/10/2007**

Douglas, Miss H R, BA, Stud., Northumbria Univ. [10011576] 29/10/2008 **ME**

Douglas, Mr J D, BA(Hons) DipIS MCLIP, Dir., The Nat. Literacy Trust, London. [51334] 16/01/1995 **CM22/07/1998**

Douie, Mrs M D P, BBIBL(Hons), Acquisitions Lib., City Coll. Plymouth. [62101] 17/02/2003 **ME**

Dourish, Dr E, BA(Hons) MPhil PhD, Unknown [64629] 29/04/2005 **ME**

Douthwaite, Mrs L, BA MCLIP ALAI, Asst. Mgr., Clayton L. for Genealogical Res., Houston P. L., U. S. A. [4115] 23/09/1970 **CM31/10/1973**

Dove, Mr A P, BA(Hons) Msc, Online Resources & Training Lib., Univ. Hosp. of Leicester [65656] 10/03/2006 **ME**

Dover, Miss A, BA(Hons), Learning Resource Cent. Mgr., Wakefield Girl's High Sch., Wakefield. [10014815] 16/09/2009 **ME**

Dovey, Miss A H, BA,MA,PG Cert, MCLIP, Res. Lib., Surrey Police, Guildford. [65266] 02/12/2005 **CM21/11/2007**

Dovey, Mr M J, BA MSc MCLIP, Programme Dir., JISL Exec., Bristol. [60464] 05/07/1999 **CM05/07/1999**

Dovey, Mr S, BA(Hons) MA, Info. Mgr., W. Midlands Reg. Observatory [10012800] 13/03/2009 **ME**

Dowd, Mr J, BA(Hons), Hybrid Serv. Mgr., Univ. of Wolverhampton [42737] 24/02/1989 **ME**

Dowers, Mrs L M, MA DipLib MCLIP, Bibl. Serv. Lib., W. Dunbartonshire Council, Dumbarton. [35340] 08/10/1982 **CM14/04/1987**

Dowey, Mrs E M, BA(Hons) MCLIP, Asst. Subject libraian., Univ. of Chester [47849] 21/10/1992 **CM22/09/1999**

Dowie, Mrs K J, MA(Hons) DipLib MCLIP, Hd. of Cent., Learning Resources, Cent. Coll., Glasgow [10012968] 10/01/1983 **CM10/02/1987**

Dowie, Mrs S J, MA DipLib MCLIP, Inf. Offr., Sandwell MBC, W. Midlands. [40707] 01/05/1987 **CM19/08/1992**

Dowle, Mr T E, BA(Hons) MA, Unemployed [55345] 02/10/1997 **ME**

Dowley, Miss E, BA MCLIP, Sch. Lib., Sch. L. Serv., Sunderland. [22731] 28/08/1974 **CM26/08/1977**

Dowley, Mr M, L. Asst. (Casual), Canterbury Christ Church Univ. [63493] 15/06/2004 **AF**

Dowling, Mr A, BA PhD FCLIP, Life Member. [4124] 07/03/1957 **FE23/03/1976**

Dowling, Mrs C A, MCLIP, Retired. [19695] 19/01/1971 **CM16/08/1973**

Dowling, Mrs E L, BSc Econ LIS, Principle Lib. Asst., Hartley L., Univ. of Southampton [10013653] 01/06/2009 **ME**

Dowling, Mrs H M, BA MCLIP, Customer Serv. Mgr., L.B. of Islington L. Serv., London. [38182] 24/01/1985 **CM16/02/1988**

Dowling, Mr J H, MCLIP, Retired [4126] 18/01/1962 **CM01/01/1966**

Dowling, Ms M E, BA MCLIP, Collections Mgr., Edinburgh Univ. L., [4127] 31/07/1965 **CM01/01/1970**

Dowling, Miss S D, BA MCLIP, Retired. [4129] 14/03/1962 **CM01/01/1966**

Dowling, Ms T L, BA(Hons) DipIM MCLIP, Lib., Swindon Bor. Council, W. Swindon L. [55797] 24/11/1997 **CM17/01/2001**

Downes, Miss D, BA DipLib MCLIP, Learning Cent. Coordinator, Southwark Coll., London. [35936] 14/02/1983 **CM01/04/1986**

Downes, Mrs D, BA, p. /t. Stud. /Sen. L. Asst., Univ. of Wales, Aberystwyth, Univ. of Winchester. [62642] 01/10/2003 **ME**

Downey, Ms J D, MA Dip Lib, Asst. Lib., Sarum Coll., Salisbury. [10014594] 23/10/1986 **ME**

Downey, Mrs L D, MCLIP, Lib., Kent Sch. Lib. Advisory Team, Kent L. [22792] 10/10/1974 **CM28/09/1977**

Downey, Mr W R, BA MCLIP, Inf. Specialist (Engeening) Kingston Univ. [32795] 23/09/1980 **CM11/11/1985**

Downham, Ms G J, BA DipLib MCLIP PGCAP FHEA, Academic Liason Lib., Univ. of Surrey L., Guildford. [34261] 08/10/1981 **CM16/11/1994**

Downham, Mrs K M, Sen. L. Asst. Local & Family Hist., Leeds L., Leeds. [10006902] 17/12/2007 **AF**

Downie, Ms C M, BA, Freelance [44584] 30/10/1990 **ME**

Downie, Miss G M, BA MCLIP, Br. Lib. /Registrar, Lanthorn & E. Calder, W. Lothian Council. [26095] 06/07/1976 **CM06/03/1981**

Downie, Mrs L, BA(Hons) MCLIP, Lib., Angus Council, Brechin High Sch. [50317] 17/06/1994 **CM21/05/2003**

Downie, Miss P M, MA FCLIP, Retired. [4141] 01/01/1929 **FE01/01/1948**

Downie, Mr P, Unemployed. [50509] 26/08/1994 **ME**

Downing, Miss E A J, BA MCLIP, Retired. [16813] 31/08/1945 **CM01/01/1952**

Downing, Miss S, BA(Hons) MA, Knowledge & Inf. Mgr., S. W. RDA. [54089] 25/10/1996 **ME**

Dowson, Miss N, BSc(Hons) DipIS MCLIP, Lib. Team Leader, Open Univ., Milton Keynes. [52539] 06/11/1995 **CM13/03/2002**

Doyle, Mrs A M, BA MCLIP, L. Super., L.B. Bromley. [31788] 14/01/1980 **CM17/11/1983**

Doyle, Mr A, MCLIP, Life Member. [4152] 24/08/1953 **CM01/01/1960**

Doyle, Ms C, BA TEFL, Stud. [65729] 13/04/2006 **ME**

Doyle, Mrs G C A, MCLIP, Lib. /Cheltenham Coll., Cheltenham [21493] 09/10/1973 **CM11/11/1976**

Doyle, Miss H R, BA, Unknown. [10014276] 10/07/2009 **ME**

Doyle, Mrs K M, BA MCLIP, Reader Dev. Lib., L.B. of Havering. [30059] 17/10/1978 **CM18/05/1981**

Doyle, Miss L, PgDip, Inf. Offr., Scottish Enterprise, Glasgow. [10006419] 19/10/2007 **ME**

Doyle, Mrs L, MCLIP, Unemployed. [21353] 17/11/1973 **CM15/11/1976**

Doyle, Ms R A, MBA MCLIP, Head of L. & Heritage Serv., Cent. L., L.B. of Islington. [25730] 11/03/1976 **CM26/07/1978**

Doyle, Ms S M, BA MCLIP, Retired. [4157] 09/10/1969 **CM01/01/1972**

Doyle, Ms S P, MCLIP, Devel. Mgr. Learning & Access., Lambeth L. Arch. & Arts. London [26717] 07/10/1976 **CM29/12/1980**

Dracup, Miss J B, BSc MCLIP, Lib. Teacher [28806] 25/01/1978 **CM13/11/1981**

Draffin, Ms A M, BA DipLib MCLIP, Info. Mgr., Nat. Autistic Soc. London [29638] 03/10/1978 **CM23/01/1981**

Drage, Mrs J M, BSc MCLIP, Retired. [4159] 04/10/1966 **CM01/01/1971**

Drakard, Ms H, BA(Hons), Stud., Loughborough Univ. [10013525] 27/10/2009 **ME**

Drake, Miss C, BA(Hons) MSc(Econ) MCLIP, Inf. Advisor, Univ. of Wales Inst., Llandaff L., Cardiff. (on maternity leave) [54366] 25/11/1996 **CM21/03/2001**

Drake, Mr L S, MA MCLIP, Res. Mgmt. Lib., Univ. of Ulster, Antrim. [4163] 17/10/1966 **CM01/01/1970**

Drake, Mrs P M B, MCLIP MA, Retired [4165] 02/03/1964 **CM01/01/1968**

Draup, Mrs V M, BSc, Lect., Bradford Coll. [10011367] 19/03/1982 **ME**

Drayton, Mrs A C, BA(Hons), Sen. L. Asst., Academy L., Yeovil Dist. Hosp. NHS Foundation Trust [60992] 28/01/2002 **AF**

Drayton, Dr S, BA(Hons) MSc D. Phil, Unknown [10015540] 02/11/1995 **ME**

Drazin, Mrs C A, MCLIP, L. Aide, Tippecanoe Co. P. L., Indiana, U. S. A. [24491] 11/08/1975 **CM13/12/1979**

Dredge, Mrs M R, MA DipLIS MCLIP, Lib., Macicie Academy, Aberdeenshire [36606] 17/10/1983 **CM17/05/2000**

Dreher, Mrs R M, BA MCLIP, Wareham Lib., Wareham L., Dorset Co. L. [27546] 16/05/1977 **CM11/07/1980**

Dresser, Mrs L M, BA DipLib MCLIP, Lib., N. Tyneside MBC., N. Shields L. [35435] 01/10/1982 **CM14/04/1987**

Drever, Ms R M, MA DipLib MCLIP, Assist. Head of Lib. & Info. Serv., E. Sussex C.C., E. Sussex. [37531] 01/10/1984 **CM18/01/1989**

Drew, Mrs H P, BSc MCLIP MA, Unemployed [25080] 11/11/1975 **CM03/10/1978**

Drew, Mrs P A, MCLIP, Retired [4180] 15/12/1965 **CM01/01/1970**

Drew, Mrs S G, BLib MCLIP, Comm. L. Mgr., Langley L., Sandwell M.B.C. [19783] 30/10/1972 **CM12/06/1980**

Drewett, Mrs A J, FCLIP, Inf. Specialist, NDPB. [21912] 04/02/1974 **FE07/09/2005**

Drewett, Mr F P H, MCLIP, Off. Mgr., Staywarm Heating, Exeter. [18046] 11/10/1972 **CM27/10/1975**

Drewett, Mrs H, Unknown [62555] 01/10/2003 **ME**

Driels, Ms J, BA MCLIP, Retired. [4187] 01/01/1967 **CM01/01/1971**

Dring, Mrs S, MA(Hons), LRC Mgr., The Hayfield Sch., Doncaster. [64176] 31/01/2005 **ME**

Drinkwater, Miss C E, MA MCLIP, Special Coll. Lib., Inst. of Educ. L., London. [25521] 10/02/1976 **CM11/12/1978**

Driscoll, Ms M C, BA DipLib MCLIP, Child. Inf. Exchange, Conwy Co. Bor. Council. [34188] 15/10/1981 **CM16/05/1985**

Driver, Miss K A, BA, Dept. Super. Counter Serv., Kings Coll. London, Univ. of London. [40464] 03/02/1987 **ME**

Driver, Ms T, BA DipLib MCLIP, Asst. Lib., Religious Soc. of Friends, London. [34263] 20/10/1981 **CM08/12/1987**

Drumm, Mr P S, BA(Hons) MSc(Econ) MCLIP, Grp. Mgr., L.B. Waltham Forest [54378] 25/11/1996 **CM15/11/2000**

Drummond, Mr G N, MBE MCLIP, Retired. [4199] 01/01/1957 **CM01/01/1964**

Drummond, Miss L H, BA, Stud. Uni of Manchester. [10015172] 21/10/2009 **ME**

Drummond, Mrs M, BA(Hons) MCLIP, Lib.,Fife Council, Glenrothes. [22467] 20/05/1974 **CM01/07/1991**

Drury, Mrs K E, BA(Hons) MA MCLIP, Liaison Lib., Reading Univ. L. [56868] 29/10/1998 **CM10/07/2002**

Drury, Mrs M H, MCLIP, L. :Resources, Basildon Univ. Hosp., NHS Foundation Trust [4206] 01/01/1969 **CM21/09/1983**

Drury, Mr R A, BA MCLIP, Team Leader, City of Edinburgh Council. [32927] 24/10/1980 **CM25/01/1985**

Drury, Ms S M, BA MPhil MCLIP, Business Researcher & Analyst, Self-Employed. [11163] 19/07/1972 **CM09/01/1976**

Drury, Ms S, MEd BA MCLIP, Life Member. [4211] 30/01/1961 **CM01/01/1965**

Drust, Mrs W V, BA MCLIP, Princ. Lib. -Collections Mgmnt., Bibl. Serv., Co. L., W. Sussex. [32633] 04/06/1980 **CM21/12/1984**

Dryburgh, Mrs R F, MA DipLib MCLIP, Asst. Lib., L. H.Q., Midlothian Council. [30550] 05/02/1979 **CM12/02/1981**

Dryden, Mrs R M, BEd MA DipLib MCLIP, Asst. Subject Lib., Oxford Brookes Univ., Oxon. [44424] 08/10/1990 **CM08/12/2004**

Du, Miss M, BSc MA MCLIP, Asst. Lib., Royal Coll. of Veterinary Surgeons Trust L., London [10001701] 15/03/2001 **CM09/07/2008**

Dua, Mr E D, MCLIP, Life Member. [4215] 25/02/1958 **CM01/01/1963**

Dubber, Mrs E H S, BA MCLIP, Freelance. [4216] 18/11/1971 **CM09/12/1974**

Dubber, Dr M J, BA MLS PhD MCLIP, Freelance Writer [31501] 01/10/1979 **CM07/10/1981**

Duce, Mrs M P, MA MCLIP, Retired. [12545] 15/09/1967 **CM30/11/1972**

Ducker, Mrs A J, BSc(Hons), Learning Res. Co-ordinator., Knowsley Comm. Coll. [56706] 01/10/1998 **ME**

Ducker, Mr J M, MA MBCS FCLIP, Retired. [60767] 24/06/1987 **FE24/06/1987**

Duckett, Mrs P N, BSc MA MSc MCLIP, Retired. [4223] 13/10/1966 **CM01/01/1969**

Duckett, Mr R J, PhD FCLIP, Retired. [4224] 03/10/1963 **FE27/05/1992**

Duckworth, Mrs A, BA MCLIP, Acad. Serv. Mgr., Liverpool Hope Univ. Coll. [35829] 17/01/1983 **CM15/08/1989**

Duckworth, Mrs C I, BA DipLib MCLIP, Grp. Mgr. Bexley council [43938] 27/02/1990 **CM18/09/1991**

Duckworth, Mrs C, BA MCLIP, Community Hist. Mgr., Accrington L, Lancs. [19325] 01/10/1972 **CM17/09/1976**

Duckworth, Mrs S J, BA(Hons) MCLIP, Prison Lib., Kent C.C. [49189] 12/10/1993 **CM17/03/1999**

Dudek, Mrs J L, BLib MCLIP, P. /t. Bookseller, Waterstones, Kendal, Cumbria. [11585] 06/03/1969 **CM16/08/1973**

Dudley, Mr E P, HonFLA FCLIP, Editorial Consultant. [4228] 16/02/1937 **FE01/01/1953**

Dudley, Mr P E, BEd(Hons) MA MCLIP, Classroom Teacher, Sybourn Primary Sch., London. [10015043] 06/11/1998 **CM21/11/2001**

Dudman, Miss J A, BSc MSc, L. Researcher, Self-emp., London. [46159] 03/10/1991 **ME**

Dudman, Mr P V, BA(Hons) MSc(Econ) MCLIP, Arch., Univ. of E. London, London. [55112] 15/07/1997 **CM18/09/2002**

Duerden, Miss M G, MCLIP, Retired. [4231] 27/09/1955 **CM01/01/1961**

Duff, Mrs D J, BA(Hons), Lib., E. Lothian Council, L. [10010590] 01/11/1994 **ME**

Duff, Mr H A M, MA M LITT MCLIP, Lib., Gleniffer High Sch., Paisley. [28426] 01/12/1977 **CM21/07/1981**

Duffin, Ms J K, MCLIP, Team Leader Inf. & Advice, CILIP, London [26874] 20/12/1976 **CM22/12/1980**

Duffus, Miss J, BA(Hons), Trust Lib., Learning Cent. L., Manor Hosp., Walsall. [10002805] 27/04/2007 **ME**

Duffy, Mrs A J, BA MCLIP, Retired. [4236] 03/01/1965 **CM01/01/1969**

Duffy, Mr D A, BA MCLIP, Collections & Serv. Devel. Mgr., Calderdale MBC, Halifax. [34514] 02/10/1981 **CM22/07/1985**

Duffy, Mrs D G, BA MCLIP, Electronic Resource Dev. Lib., Bradford Coll. [31639] 18/10/1979 **CM31/10/1984**

Duffy, Mr J O, BA MSc MCLIP ALAI, Sub- Lib. Bar Council Law L. Dublin. [58081] 25/10/1999 **CM16/07/2003**

Duffy, Miss K, DipILS MCLIP, L. & Inf. Offr., Dundee City Council. [61260] 10/05/2002 **CM08/12/2004**

Duffy, Mr R A, BA FCLIP, Retired. [4242] 24/10/1938 **FE01/01/1953**

Duffy, Ms S M, BA MCLIP, Self Employed Inf. Specialist. [22114] 11/03/1974 **CM07/03/1977**

Dufty, Ms E, BA(Hons) DipLIS MCLIP, Knowledge Mngr. [48114] 09/11/1992 **CM23/07/1997**

Dugdale, Mr C E, BA MA, Inf. Specialist, Inf. Serv. and Systems, King's Coll., London. [61423] 08/07/2002 **ME**

Duggan, Mr A, Unknown. [10012440] 17/05/2005 **ME**

Duggan, Ms K A, BA MCLIP, Inf. Mgr., Northumbria Univ. >, Newcastle [40753] 29/05/1987 **CM23/03/1994**

Duguid, Mrs A M, BA DipLib MCLIP, Lib., Mott MacDonald, Croydon. [29387] 29/06/1978 **CM10/11/1980**

Dukes, Ms A J, BA(Hons) MCLIP, Comm. Lib., Caerphilly C. B. C., Bargoed L. [56418] 07/07/1998 **CM04/02/2004**

Duley, Mrs M C, BA(Hons), Unknown. [10016669] 10/01/1994 **ME**

Dumenil, Ms K, BA, Outreach Lib., St. Helens PCT. [62782] 22/10/2003 **ME**

Dumper, Miss L J, BA DipLib MCLIP, Mgr., Inf. Serv., TWI Ltd., Cambridge. [26955] 19/01/1977 **CM19/01/1979**

Dunbar, Mr J A, BA(Hons), Lib., John Laing Integrated Serv., Hounslow, London. [41658] 08/02/1988 **ME**

Dunbar, Mrs J, BA(Hons) PgDip MCLIP, Maternity Leave [64178] 31/01/2005 **CM06/05/2009**

Duncan, Mrs C L, BA MCLIP, Asst. Principal, Learner Serv., N. E. Worcs. Coll. Bromsgrove, Worcs. [27713] 06/07/1977 **CM22/09/1978**

Duncan, Ms C L, BA(Hons) DipLIS MCLIP, Learning Resource Cent. Co-ordinator, Stirling C., Stirling [48084] 03/11/1992 **CM23/07/1997**

Duncan, Mr C M, MA(Hons) DipLib MCLIP, Electronic Serv. Lib., Inverclyde L., Greenock. [40106] 21/10/1986 **CM29/03/2006**

Duncan, Miss H M, BA MCLIP, Br. Serv. Lib., Aberdeen City Council. [33905] 03/05/1981 **CM05/12/1985**

Duncan, Mrs J M, BA MCLIP, Clinical Lib. Royal Berks. Hosp., Reading. [11407] 27/01/1972 **CM13/02/1976**

Duncan, Mr J, MA MCLIP, Retired. [4260] 04/02/1960 **CM01/01/1963**

Duncan, Mrs P H, BSc DipLib MCLIP, Bibl. Serv. Mgr., Anglia Ruskin Univ., Chelmsford. [33185] 01/10/1980 **CM31/01/1996**

Duncan, Mrs P S, BA DipLib MCLIP, L. Offr., Rushmoor, Hampshire C.C. [29379] 27/06/1978 **CM28/11/1980**

Duncan, Mr P, BA, Self-Employed/Stud., Austria. [10003093] 23/05/2007 **ME**

Duncan, Mrs S F, BA MCLIP, Lib. -SIHV, Gaskell House Psychotherapy Cent., Manchester. [25286] 13/01/1976 **CM18/09/1979**

Duncan, Ms S J, BA DipLib MCLIP, Researcher, The Brit. L., London. [36397] 04/10/1983 **CM18/07/1991**

Duncan, Mrs S, BA(Hons) MCLIP, Asst. Dir., Sch. L. Assoc., Swindon, Wiltshire [10001867] 13/03/2007 **CM19/03/1980**

Duncanson, Mrs E A, BA(Hons) MCLIP, Child. & Yth. Lib., Kirkby L. [28975] 07/02/1978 **CM15/09/1980**

Duncombe, Mrs C, BA MA MCLIP, Sales Mngr., Peters Bookselling Serv., Birmingham. [42282] 05/10/1988 **CM26/05/1993**

Dundas, Mrs K M, MA MCLIP, Life Member. [20509] 14/03/1973 **CM01/04/1976**

Dundas, Mrs P J, BA MCLIP, L. Asst., Sefton Park L., Liverpool. [28820] 09/02/1978 **CM16/03/1984**

Dungworth, Mrs N M, BA(Hons) MA MCLIP, Inf. Offr. /p. t., Loughborough Univ., Leics. [48450] 12/01/1993 **CM22/01/1997**

Dunk, Mrs J, BSc(Pend), Lib. Asst., Aberystwyth Univ., Aberystwyth [10008396] 19/03/2008 **ME**

Dunkerley, Mrs H L R D, BA(Hons) MCLIP, Coll. Lib., Notre Dame 6th Form Coll., Leeds [63595] 05/07/2004 **CM08/08/2008**

Dunkerley, Mrs L M, BA MCLIP, Retired. [4267] 27/06/1964 **CM01/01/1968**

Dunkley, Mr M, BA MA, Prin. Inf. Asst., De Montfort Univ., Leicester. [10009844] 25/06/2008 **AF**

Dunlop, Miss J A, BLib MSc (Econ), Unknown. [10012331] 21/10/1980 **ME**

Dunmall, Mrs J E, BA ACLIP, Operations Asst., Camrs Sch. L. Serv., Peterborough. [65429] 24/02/2006 **ACL22/06/2007**

Dunmore, Mrs M C, BA MS, LRC Mgr., Preston Manor High Sch., Wembly, Middlesex. [10001325] 07/02/2007 **ME**

Dunmore, Mr T G, BA(Hons) DipLib, Lib., Royal Automobile Club, London [53958] 16/10/1996 **ME**

Dunn, Miss A, BA, Asst. Lib., Sussex Educ. Cent., Hove. [10003284] 23/05/2007 **ME**

Dunn, Mr A, MA MCLIP, Inf. Lib., David Wilson Lib., Univ. of Leicester. [59118] 20/11/2000 **CM29/08/2007**

Dunn, Miss C I, DIP LOC HIST MCLIP, Retired. [4275] 09/02/1961 **CM01/01/1969**

Dunn, Mrs C, Mgr., Nielsen Media Res. Ltd., Bracknell. [65419] 24/02/2006 **ME**

Dunn, Miss D, BSc(Hons) ACLIP, Prinicpal L. Asst., Learning Cent. Birmingham City Univ., Birmingham. [10001900] 10/09/2001 **ACL06/02/2008**

Dunn, Mrs E B, BA(Hons) MA MCLIP, Libr., Cheshire E. CC., Cheshire [55533] 20/10/1997 **CM02/02/2005**

Dunn, Ms H M, BA DipLib MCLIP, Lib., Higgs & Sons, Brierley Hill. [31605] 25/10/1979 **CM24/01/1986**

Dunn, Miss J M, BA(Hons) DipIM, Stock Lib., L.B. of Barnet, London. [56563] 25/08/1998 **ME**

Dunn, Ms K, MA MCLIP, Resident overseas. [61408] 10/07/2002 **CM04/10/2006**

Dunn, Mr L P, Young People and Child. Serv. Lib., Grimsby Cent. Lib. [63514] 16/06/2004 **ME**

Dunn, Mrs P J, MCLIP, Unwaged. [4281] 15/10/1957 **CM31/10/1974**

Dunn, Mrs R J, BA(Hons) MCLIP, L. Asst., Robinson L., Newcastle Univ. [47696] 16/10/1992 **CM13/06/2007**

Dunn, Mrs S J, BSc, Learning Resource Cent. Mgr., Ludlow Coll., Shropshire [10015419] 19/11/2009 **AF**

Dunn, Miss T, MCLIP, Head Lib., Cent. Leeds Learning Fed. [55855] 02/12/1997 **CM23/01/2008**

Dunne, Mr A, HDipLIS BBS, Lib., Blanchardstown L., Dublin. [10008765] 18/04/2008 **ME**

Dunne, Mr M B, BA MCLIP, Unemployed [41153] 16/10/1987 **CM30/01/1991**

Dunne, Ms M, Stud., Univ. of Aberystwyth. [10009292] 15/05/2008 **ME**

Dunne, Ms P, MA Inf. Serv. Man., Lib. L.B. of Lambeth, Streatham [61594] 02/10/2002 **ME**

Dunnelly, Mr J F, Unknown. [10016936] 10/06/2010 **ME**

Dunnicliff, Ms J, LRC Mgr., Stratford Upon Avon High Sch. [59612] 28/06/2001 **ME**

Dunning, Miss P, BTECH MLib MCLIP ILTM, Sen. Subject Lib., Staffs. Univ. [27962] 05/10/1977 **CM17/01/1980**

Dunsford, Mrs J B I, MCLIP, Life Member. [4291] 04/03/1944 **CM01/01/1947**

Dunsford, Mr S F, FCLIP, Life Member. [4292] 19/01/1950 **FE01/01/1957**

Dunsire, Mr G J, BSc MCLIP, Dep. Dir., Cent. for Digital L. Res., Univ. of Strathclyde. [29551] 26/09/1978 **CM29/09/1980**

Dunstan, Mrs R M, BA MCLIP, L. Mgr., Oxfordshire C.C. [25525] 20/01/1976 **CM27/11/1979**

Dunster, Mrs J M, BA DMS MCLIP, Stock Res. Mgr. (E.), Dorset C.C., Ferndown. [25676] 14/01/1976 **CM19/09/1978**

Durber, Mr D M, BA, Unwaged, [49902] 10/01/1994 **ME**

Durbidge, Mrs D M, MCLIP, Retired. [4297] 01/01/1947 **CM01/01/1950**

Durcan, Mr A J, BA MCLIP, Head of Culture, L. & Lifel. Learn., Newcastle City L. [26956] 14/01/1977 **CM07/12/1981**

Durcan, Mrs J, MCLIP, Sch. Lib., Durham High Sch. [26690] 25/10/1976 **CM28/11/1980**

Durgan, Miss A L, L. Mgr., Tibshelf Community Sch. [10011445] 21/10/2008 **AF**

Durham, Mrs F P R, BA DipLib MCLIP, Learning and Teaching Lib., Open Univ. L., Milton Keynes. [33504] 13/01/1981 **CM23/06/1986**

Durham, Mrs S R, BA DipLib MCLIP, Inf. & Peoples Network Lib., Watford L., Herts C.C. [39408] 24/01/1986 **CM19/09/1989**

Durkan, Mrs S K, BA MCLIP, Resources Cent. Mgr., John Port Sch., Etwall, Derby [30607] 16/02/1979 **CM28/10/1981**

Durndell, Ms H M, MA DipLib, Univ. Lib., Glasgow Univ. L. [27344] 08/03/1977 **ME**

Durrani, Mrs C, BA MCLIP, Lib., Our Lady & St. Patricks High Sch., Dumbarton. [8220] 21/08/1964 **CM01/01/1969**

Durrani, Mr S, MBE BA DipLib FCLIP LTHE, Sen. Lect., London Met. Univ., London. [39636] 14/04/1986 **FE19/03/1997**

Durrans, Miss K, BA DipLib MCLIP, Lib., Hants. Co. L., Winchester. [34392] 28/10/1981 **CM16/11/1994**

Durrant, Miss C L, BA(Hons) MSc MCLIP, Prison L. Mgr., Cambridge. [59017] 26/10/2000 **CM11/03/2009**

Dussin, Mr L, Unknown. [10013018] 23/06/2009 **ME**

Duthie, Mrs T, BSc, Lib. & Inf. Worker, Cent. L., Dundee. [10016793] 18/05/2010 **ME**

Dutt, Mr K K, MA MCLIP, Retired. [4311] 23/01/1967 **CM19/04/1973**

Dutton, Dr B G, BSc PhD CChem FRSC FCLIP, Retired. [60581] 01/01/1965 **FE01/04/2002**

Dutton, Mrs C M, A INST AM MCLIP, Retired. [4313] 03/02/1958 **CM01/01/1968**

Dutton, Mrs M T A, BA(Hons) DPS MCLIP, Lib., Cent. Manchester Child. NHS Trust. [55506] 16/10/1997 **CM07/09/2005**

Dutton, Ms S H, MA, Knowledge Mgr., NHS Norfolk [43089] 21/07/1989 **ME**

Duxbury, Mr A, MA FCLIP, Life Member. [4318] 25/02/1949 **FE01/01/1965**

Duxbury, Mrs P J, BSc(Hons) DipAppSS PGCE MCLIP, Business Inf. Lib., Univ. of Glamorgan, Pontypridd. [61285] 08/05/2002 **CM21/11/2007**

Duxbury, Mrs R, MCLIP, Lib., Walford & N Shropshire Coll., Baschurch, Shrewsbury. [11739] 01/10/1969 **CM05/07/1973**

Dwiar, Miss E, MA PGCE DipIS, Full Time Carer. [43218] 02/10/1989 **ME**

Dwiar, Miss P, BA MSc CertEd DipLib MCLIP, p/t L. Asst., LB of Redbridge [32931] 07/10/1980 **CM06/12/1983**

Dwyer, Mr B A, BA DPA MCLIP, Retired [18652] 03/02/1953 **CM01/01/1964**

Dwyer, Mrs J M, BA DipLib MCLIP, Sen. L. Asst., Sheffield Univ. L. [33141] 05/10/1980 **CM18/06/1985**

Dybkowska, Ms M, P/T Lib. Asst., UCL, London. [10001403] 14/02/2007 **ME**

Dyce, Mrs S E, MA DipLib MCLIP, L. Systems Offr., Aberdeen C.C., Aberdeen. [31384] 01/10/1979 **CM30/04/1982**

Dye, Ms C M, BA LIS, Unknown. [10015667] 09/11/1993 **ME**

Dye, Mrs M A, BSc, Database Engineer, Nat. Grid, Wokingham. [44349] 01/10/1990 **ME**

Dyer, Miss A, BA MCLIP, Inf. Serv. Web Mgr., Univ. of E. Anglia. [42598] 20/01/1989 **CM24/05/1995**

Dyer, Mrs B S, BA MCLIP, Unwaged. [25529] 14/01/1976 **CM18/02/1980**

Dyer, Mrs C H, BA MCLIP, Head of Serv., Nottingham City Council. [31445] 15/10/1979 **CM28/07/1983**

Dyer, Miss C M L, BA MCLIP, Bibliographic Servs. Team Mgr, De Montfort Univ. [30399] 29/01/1979 **CM05/10/1984**

Dyer, Mr G E, MCLIP, Inf. Analyst, Pera Innovation Ltd, Melton Mowbray. [60730] 25/07/1985 **CM25/07/1985**

Dyer, Miss S, BA(Hons) MA, L. Mgr., Black & Veatch Ltd., Redhill. [52828] 17/10/1997 **ME**

Dyke, Mrs L M, BA MCLIP, ICT/Knowledge Team Leader, Staffs. C.C., Cannock L. [43655] 20/11/1989 **CM22/07/1992**

Dykes, Mrs A R, BA, Lib. Asst., E. Lothian L. Serv. [10010657] 19/08/2008 **ME**

Dykes, Mrs E, BA MCLIP, Child. Serv. Lib. (Job Share), Nottingham City Council. [22063] 22/01/1974 **CM26/07/1977**

Dymond, Mr G R, LLB MSc MCLIP, Res. Serv. & Legal Inf. Lib., House of Lords, London. [36375] 01/10/1983 **CM07/10/1986**

Dymott, Mr E A E, BSc MA MSc MRTPI MCLIP, Unknown. [38595] 01/08/1985 **CM18/09/1991**

Dyos, Mrs G, MCLIP, Sch. Lib., Putney High Sch., London. [20381] 22/02/1973 **CM03/11/1976**

Dyson, Ms C J, BA(Hons) MSc MCLIP, Career Break. [39007] 21/10/1985 **CM29/10/1985**

Dyson, Mrs H M, BA MCLIP, Reader Dev. Offr., Wokingham Bo. C. [33587] 21/01/1981 **CM01/07/1984**

Dyson, Mrs P, BA MSc PGCE MCLIP ILTM, Sen. Academic Lib., Univ. Lincoln, Lincoln. [22663] 01/08/1974 **CM31/03/1977**

E

Eacott, Ms C M, BA(Hons), L. Asst., Martial Rose L., Univ. Winchester. [64612] 20/04/2005 **ME**

Eades, Miss V, Stud., UCL. [10015222] 27/10/2009 **ME**

Eadon, Mrs J M, BA(Hons) MSc, Unwaged. [53565] 24/07/1996 **ME**

Eagle, Mr P A C, MChem, Quick Inf. Offr., Brit. L. [61847] 18/11/2002 **ME**

Eagle, Mr R S, MA DPA FCLIP, Life Member. [4339] 04/02/1950 **FE01/01/1959**

Eagles, Mrs J, MSc MCLIP, Retired. [25121] 04/11/1975 **CM30/10/1978**

Eales, Mrs S M, Co. Dir. [53696] 11/09/1996 **ME**

Eames, Miss L L, Li. Asst., Gray's Inn L., London [10015516] 09/12/2009 **ME**

Eardley, Mr D M, MA FCLIP, Retired. [4342] 11/10/1951 **FE01/01/1965**

Earl, Miss A T, BA(Hons), Unknown. [61821] 12/11/2002 **ME**

Earl, Mr C, BSc HonFLA, Inf. Consultant. [4343] 11/01/1960 **CM01/01/1965**

Earl, Mrs G, BA(Hons) MCLIP, L. Serv. Mgr., Health Mgmnt. L., Edinburgh. [47522] 25/09/1992 **CM17/03/1999**

Earl, Mrs J A, BA Pg Dip MCLIP, Liaison Offr., ILS, Univ of Salford [66043] 11/08/2006 **CM19/12/2008**

Early, Mrs F, BA(Hons), L. Asst., St. James Catholic Primary, London. [10001121] 12/01/2007 **ME**

Earney, Miss S L, BA(Hons) MA MCLIP, Mgr., Aberconway L. Serv., Cardiff Univ. [50694] 12/10/1994 **CM21/07/1999**

Earnshaw, Mrs D, BA MCLIP, Resident in USA. [40819] 01/07/1987 **CM27/02/1991**

Earnshaw, Mrs L C, Customer Serv. Offr., Kirklees C.C., Huddersfield. [60036] 30/11/2001 **ME**

Easson, Ms K, MA DipLib MCLIP, Lib., Literary & Philosophical Soc., Newcastle. [43278] 01/01/1947 **CM27/05/1992**

East, Miss J, MCLIP, Life Member. [4353] 12/02/1952 **CM01/01/1959**

East, Mrs S E, BA MCLIP, Unemployed. [21806] 16/01/1974 **CM04/08/1976**

Eastell, Ms C, BA(Hons) MA MCLIP, Sen. Advisor, The Reading Agency, St. Albans. [49267] 20/10/1993 **CM20/03/1996**

Eastoe, Mrs J I, Snr. L. Asst., [64873] 22/08/2005 **AF**

Easton, Mr F M J, FCLIP, Retired. [4362] 16/02/1955 **FE01/01/1965**

Easton, Mr G, BA(Hons) MSc, Lib., St. Stephens High Sch., Glasgow [10017052] 21/06/2010 **ME**

Easton, Ms L, MA(Hons) DipLIS MCLIP, L. Mgr., NHS Greater Glasgow Clyde. [48348] 01/12/1992 **RV06/02/2008 CM18/11/1998**

Eastwood, Ms E J, BA(Hons) MLIS MCLIP, Ref. Lib., Los Alamos P. L., USA. [45721] 07/05/1991 **CM22/11/1995**

Eato, Mrs K A, BA(Hons) DipLib MCLIP, Retired [38201] 09/01/1985 **CM01/09/1987**

Eaton, Mrs C L, BA(Hons) MA MCLIP, Unknown. [40055] 20/10/1986 **CM15/11/1988**

Eaton, Miss C, BA(Hons) PGDip PGCE MCLIP, Performance & Improvment Offr., Policy Partnership & Performance, Doncaster. [47014] 01/04/1992 **CM18/11/1993**

Eaton, Miss J E, BA(Hons), Learning & Inf. Offr., Islington L. [65448] 23/02/2006 **ME**

Eaton, Mr J J, MA, Electronic Res. Mgr., London Business Sch. L. [40228] 07/11/1986 **ME**

Eaton, Ms M M, BA(Hons), Mgr. Sch. Lib. Ser. and YPS, E. Sussex C.C. E. Sussex [39593] 10/03/1986 **ME**

Eaton, Mrs S D, Stud., Aberystwyth. [64128] 18/01/2005 **ME**

Eaton, Mrs S M, MCLIP, Retired. [4372] 11/01/1964 **CM01/01/1968**

Eatwell, Mr R F, MA FCLIP, Retired. [4374] 17/01/1947 **FE01/01/1962**

Eaves, Miss K E, MA(Oxon) DipILS MCLIP, Lib., Southampton City L. [54132] 30/10/1996 **CM20/09/2000**

Ebden, Mr E A M, MA MLib, Unwaged. [38703] 01/10/1985 **AF**

Ebenezer, Ms C M, MSc MA STM AKC MCLIP, Lib. & Info. Serv. Mgr., Tees, Esk & Wear Valleys, NHS Found. Trust [47544] 01/10/1992 **CM13/06/2000**

Eccleston, Mrs H, BA(Hons) LLB(Hons) MCLIP, Reg. Lib., Newcastle Law Courts. [41348] 06/11/1987 **CM22/01/1997**

Ecclestone, Ms B M, MCLIP, Retired. [32417] 24/03/1980 **CM17/04/1986**

Ecclestone, Ms K F, MLib, Learning Cent. Mgr., Cornwall Coll. St. Austell. [41757] 10/03/1988 **ME**

Ecclestone, Mrs M J, BA DipLib MCLIP, Retired. [31129] 04/09/1979 **CM19/06/1984**

Eddisford, Miss R, BA(Hons) MA, Asst. Lib., Guildhall L., London [10017055] 21/06/2010 **ME**

Eddison, Mrs S M, MA MCLIP, Inf. & L. Shared Serv. Mgr. [37669] 17/10/1984 **CM14/11/1989**

Eddleston, Miss J E, MA MCLIP, Unwaged. [47173] 21/05/1992 **CM20/09/2000**

Eden, Mr R, MCLIP, Retired. [4390] 01/01/1968 **CM01/01/1971**

Edgar, Mrs A L, Lib., Innerpeffray L., Perthshire. [10011225] 03/10/2008 **ME**

Edgar, Prof J R, MA FCLIP, Retired. [4392] 23/05/1947 **FE01/01/1964**

Edgar, Miss S C, BA MCLIP, Consultant, Sue Hill Recruitment, London [29954] 28/10/1978 **CM26/08/1982**

Edge, Mrs K, Unknown. [10007452] 13/02/2008 **ME**

Edgington, Mrs H, L. Asst., Faringdon L. [10010986] 12/09/2008 **AF**

Edlin, Mrs D E, BA DIP LIB MCLIP, Stock Mgr., Sandwell L. & Inf. Serv. [34561] 11/01/1982 **CM23/08/1985**

Edmans, Mrs M L, MCLIP, Unknown. [65941] 11/07/2006 **CM16/10/2009**

Edmonds, Mrs D J, MBE BA FCLIP, Asst. Dir., Culture, L. and Learning, L.B. of Haringey. [14993] 01/01/1971 **FE01/04/2002**

Edmonds, Mrs J C, BA MCLIP, Sch. Lib., Nab Wood Sch., Bingley, W. Yorks. [25455] 19/12/1975 **CM01/03/1978**

Edmonds, Mrs L, BA MCLIP, L. & Knowledge Serv. Mgr., Papworth Hosp. NHS Trust. [4402] 04/07/1971 **CM01/01/1974**

Edmonds, Miss M J, BA(Hons) DipIS MCLIP, Coll. Lib., Northwood Coll., Middx. [50395] 15/07/1994 **CM19/05/1999**

Edmonds, Mr R E, MCLIP, Retired. [4404] 12/02/1969 **CM06/12/1972**

Edmondston, Miss M E, BA FCLIP, Life Member. [4408] 18/10/1938 **FE01/01/1944**

Edmunds, Ms A, BA CertEd CertTESOL MCLIP, Employment not known. [4409] 03/10/1968 **CM01/01/1971**

Edmunds, Mr G L, BSc(Econ) DipLib MCLIP, Principal Lib. Operations W. Sussex C.C. [40358] 22/01/1987 **CM15/08/1990**

Edney, Miss C P L, FCLIP, Retired. [4411] 01/01/1939 **FE01/01/1964**

Edser, Ms R M, BA(Hons) MCLIP, Principal Lib., Reading & Learning, W. Sussex C.C. [22434] 29/04/1974 **CM31/10/1977**

Edson, Mrs S, Sen. Lib. Asst,. Sutton-on-Trent L [10012362] 03/02/2009 **AF**

Edward, Mrs T, MA(Hons), Stud., Univ. of Strathclyde [10015110] 15/10/2009 **ME**

Edwardes, Miss G E, BA(Hons) MCLIP, Ch. Catg. /Inf. Lib., Caerleon Campus L., Univ. of Wales. Newport [46675] 06/12/1991 **CM08/12/2004**

Edwards, Mrs A E, Lib. Asst., Potland Sch., Worksop [10015232] 29/10/2009 **AF**

Edwards, Mrs A J, BA(Hons) PG Dip ILS, Lib. & Arch., Pocklington Sch., Pocklington, York. [63748] 29/09/2004 **ME**

Edwards, Mr A J, BA MCLIP, Retired. [4415] 09/01/1953 **CM01/01/1956**

Edwards, Mr A S, BLib(Hons) MCLIP, Head Brit. & Early Printed Coll., Brit. L., London. [38488] 17/05/1985 **CM12/12/1990**

Edwards, Mr A, BA PGCE, Sen. Learning Resource Asst., W. Kent Coll., Tonbridge. [10015591] 23/04/2010 **ME**

Edwards, Ms B C, BSc MCLIP, Inf. Specialist, OSFI, Canada. [38436] 25/04/1985 **CM03/10/1989**

Edwards, Miss C A, MA MIL MCLIP DipTrans, Inf. Policy Mgr., Foreign & Commonwealth Off. [39067] 14/10/1985 **CM09/08/1988**

Edwards, Ms C E, DipLib MA(Hons) MCLIP, Prog. Offr., Civil Soc. Dept., Dept. for Internat. Devel., E. Kilbride. [29643] 11/10/1978 **CM16/10/1981**

Edwards, Mrs C L, BA(Hons) MSc(Econ) MCLIP, Learning and Devel. Lead- L., NHS Westwidlands, Workforce Deanery, Bham. [51186] 23/11/1994 **CM18/03/1998**

Edwards, Ms C M, BA DipLib MCLIP, Feedback & Serv. Devel. Mgr. . - Pub. Serv. Dept., Nat. L. of Wales, Aberystwyth. [40006] 15/10/1986 **CM22/05/1991**

Edwards, Mr C, BA(Hons) DipLib MCLIP, Princ. Lib., Vale of Glamorgan L., Barry. [35127] 01/08/1982 **CM06/12/1985**

Edwards, Ms C, B. Lib Hons MCLIP, Programme Offr. (Self-Employed), Nottingham. [10004962] 01/07/1980 **CM14/08/1985**

Edwards, Mrs E A, BA(Hons) MA MCLIP, Area Co-ordinator: Newark Area L., Newark L. [61870] 22/11/2002 **CM09/11/2005**

Edwards, Ms E C, MCLIP, PIBWRLWYD Learning Center Mgr., Coleg Sir Gar., Carmarthen [30156] 17/01/1979 **CM27/02/1981**

Edwards, Mrs E, BA(Hons) DipILM, Outreach Lib., Western Cheshire Primary Care Trust, Chester. [57424] 15/03/1999 **ME**

Edwards, Mr G B, BA(Hons) MSc(Econ) MCLIP, Local & Family Hist. Lib., Haverfordwest, Pembrokeshire [55494] 15/10/1997 **CM18/09/2002**

Edwards, Miss G, BA(Hons) MSc MCLIP, Acquisitions Lib., Greenwich Council. [36040] 20/04/1983 **CM10/05/1988**

Edwards, Mr G, BA(Hons) MCLIP, Lifelong Learning Lib., Flintshire L. & Inf. Serv., Mold. [40242] 11/11/1986 **CM18/09/2002**

Edwards, Dr H A, BA MA PhD FZSL FRSM MCLIP, p. /t. KT Consultant, Oxford. [60775] 16/05/1988 **CM16/05/1988**

Edwards, Ms H E A, B LIB MCLIP, Princ. Lib. (Field Serv.), Powys C.C., Llandrindod Wells. [14229] 14/05/1970 **CM09/10/1974**

Edwards, Mr H J, MCLIP, Life Member. [4429] 15/03/1951 **CM01/01/1960**

Edwards, Ms H, HonFCLIP, L. Project Mngr. SKOLKOVO Moscow Sch. of Mgmnt. [10014188] 03/11/2009 **HFE13/07/2009**

Edwards, Mrs H, L. Systems Mgr., Co. Hall, Aylesbury. [63537] 17/06/2004 **AF**

Edwards, Mrs J A, MA FCLIP CertEd, Learning Resources Mgr., Kidderminster Coll. [5799] 16/01/1969 **FE14/06/1978**

Edwards, Mrs J A, BSc MA MCLIP, Retired [4436] 14/02/1968 **CM01/01/1970**

Edwards, Mr J A, BA MSc MCLIP, Subject Liaison Mgr., Middlesex Univ., London. [36527] 19/10/1983 **CM05/04/1988**

Edwards, Ms J E, BA MCLIP, Lib., Maclay, Murray & Spens, Edinburgh. [26358] 14/10/1976 **CM04/11/1981**

Edwards, Mrs J G, MCLIP, Freelance L. Serv. to Architects. Glasgow. [4439] 01/01/1963 **CM01/01/1967**

Edwards, Mrs J L, MCLIP CTEFLA, Unwaged [21261] 17/10/1973 **CM31/08/1977**

Edwards, Miss J M, MA MLib MCLIP, Stud. at St. Andrews. [39983] 08/10/1986 **CM27/02/1991**

Edwards, Mr J N, BSc MCLIP, Mgr., Guy's & St. Thomas' Hosp., Med. Toxicology Inf. Serv., London. [60315] 10/12/2001 **CM10/12/2001**

Edwards, Mrs J, Knowledge Serv. Asst., Mersey Care Knowledge & L. Serv., Parkbourne. [10015416] 19/11/2009 **AF**

Edwards, Mrs J, BA MCLIP, Retired. [4432] 04/03/1959 **CM01/01/1961**

Edwards, Miss K E, MSc, Faculty Asst. Co-ordinator, Templeman L., Univ. of Kent, Canterbury. [10006329] 10/10/2007 **ME**

Edwards, Miss K L, BA(Hons) MSc(Econ), Distribution & Stock Lib., Carmarthenshire C.C., Llanelli Reg. L. [56901] 02/11/1998 **ME**

Edwards, Miss K, BSc(Hons) MSc, Knowledge Mgr., Dept. of Health, London. [51580] 03/04/1995 **ME**

Edwards, Mrs L A, BA MCLIP, Sch. Lib., N. Somerset Council, St Katherine's Sch. Ham Green, Pill [38831] 14/10/1985 **CM15/08/1989**

Edwards, Miss L M, MA BA(Hons) DipLib MCLIP, General Mgr., The European L. [34837] 15/03/1982 **CM01/04/2002**

Edwards, Mrs L, BA MCLIP, Asst. Lib. (p. /t), Drayton Manor High Sch., London. [30686] 13/03/1979 **CM10/11/1983**

Edwards, Mrs M B, MCLIP, Asst. Lib., The Ravensbourne Sch., Bromley. [12042] 03/10/1970 **CM16/07/1973**

Edwards, Mr M, BA(Hons), Team Leader, The Univ. of Wales, Newport. [62785] 22/10/2003 **ME**

Edwards, Miss N C, BA(Hons) DipIS MA MCLIP, Sr. Academic Serv. E-Lib., Univ. of Greenwich [50593] 27/09/1994 **CM16/07/2003**

Edwards, Mr P C G, BA MCLIP, Comm. Lib., Amersbury L., Wilts. C.C. [23264] 20/11/1974 **CM12/10/1979**

Edwards, Mr R I, BA MIMgt MCLIP FRSA, Retired. [18662] 30/10/1964 **CM01/01/1968**

Edwards, Mrs R J, BA MCLIP, Sen. Lib., Manchester L., Cent. L. [26106] 01/07/1976 **CM10/12/1979**

Edwards, Miss R K, BA MA, Trainee Lib., Bexley L. Serv. [10010320] 18/07/2008 **AF**

Edwards, Ms R S, MA DipLib, Stock Reader Dev. Lib., Herts. C.C. [36492] 14/10/1983 **ME**

Edwards, Mrs S E, BSc(Hons) MSc PMP MCLIP, IT Project Mngr. UNISYS London [54454] 09/12/1996 **CM24/10/2001**

Edwards, Mr S M, BA(Hons) MCLIP, Bus. Mgr., Adults & Child., W. Sussex [49122] 06/10/1993 **CM26/11/1997**

Edwards, Mrs S P, BA MLS DipLib MCLIP, Comm. Lib., W. Wilts, Dist., Wilts. [30806] 18/04/1979 **CM14/06/1982**

Edwards, Mr S P, DipILS, Outreach Lib., NHS Salford. [43743] 15/12/1989 **ME**

Edwards, Mr S W, BA(Hons) MA, Inf. Offr., Royal Inst. of Brit. Architects, London. [54257] 11/11/1996 **ME**

Edwards, Mr S W, BA DipLib MCLIP, Stock Support Serv. Mgr., Hants. Co. L., Winchester. [29510] 11/09/1978 **CM18/11/1981**

Edwards, Ms S, Inf. Serv. Mgr., Smith & Williamson, London. [60418] 11/03/1997 **AF**

Edwards, Miss V A, BA(Hons), Principal Inf. Offr., Berrymans Lace Mawer, Manchester. [53638] 19/08/1996 **ME**

Edwards, Mrs W E, BA(Hons) MA MCLIP, Asst. Lib., W. Sussex C.C., Horsham L. [58997] 18/10/2000 **CM16/07/2003**

Edyvean, Mrs J, BA DipLib MCLIP, Programme Mgr., L. &Inf. Sci., Hants Co. Council. [38245] 06/02/1985 **CM15/08/1989**

Efstathiou, Miss M, BA, Stud., City Univ., London [10016174] 17/02/2010 **ME**

Egan, Mr P, Asst. Lib., Univ. of Portsmouth. [40126] 17/10/1986 **ME**

Egarr, Mrs H E, MCLIP, Lib. i/c., S. Glos. Council. [21039] 01/10/1973 **CM22/09/1976**

Egbuji, Ms A N, MCLIP, Lib., Stratford Coll., Stratford-upon-Avon. [66134] 29/09/2006 **CM28/01/2009**

Egbuson, Mrs T, Stud., The Robert Gordon Univ., Aberdeen [10008383] 19/03/2008 **ME**

Egerton, Mrs J E, BA MCLIP, Inf. Mgr., ISER, Univ. of Essex, [27659] 04/07/1977 **CM25/02/1980**

Eggleston, Miss K J, MA MEd MCLIP, Life Member. [4469] 25/09/1956 **CM01/01/1959**

Egleton, Miss S, BA(Hons) MA MCLIP, Systems Support Lib., Oxford Univ., Oxford. [55158] 24/07/1997 **CM17/01/2001**

Egwim, Mr U G, Unknown. [10015465] 07/01/2009 **ME**

Ehibor, Mr O, BA MSc MCLIP, Lib., Ras Al Khaimah Men's Coll., Higher Coll. of Tech., U. A. E. [48364] 04/12/1992 **CM19/01/2000**

Ehlers, Dr H J, Dr. phil MCLIP, Resident in Germany. [60060] 28/10/1986 **CM28/10/1986**

Eichhorn, Ms R, BA(Hons) DipILM, Learning Resources Tutor, Luther King House L., Partnership for Theological Educ. [58785] 20/07/2000 **ME**

Eidal, Mrs K, MLIS, Unknown. [10012316] 27/01/2009 **ME**

Eimerman, Ms S, MA MA MCLIP, Sen. Lib., L.B. of Bexley [62701] 09/10/2003 **CM01/02/2006**

Eiremiya Yasso, Mrs N, Sen. L. Asst., Cardiff Univ., Cardiff. [10016632] 01/05/2010 **AF**

Eisenschitz, Dr T S, BSc MSc PhD MCLIP, Lect., Dept of Inf. Sci., City Univ., London. [31267] 05/10/1979 **CM11/11/1985**

Ekberg, Mrs M A, MCLIP, Life Member. [4472] 01/01/1949 **CM01/01/1955**

Ekin, Mrs S M, BA DipLIS MCLIP, Lib., NIPEC, Belfast. [58336] 17/01/2000 **CM15/01/2003**

Ekins, Mr A, Sen. L. Systems Offr., Canterbury Christ Church Univ. [10013276] 25/08/2009 **AF**

Ekue, Miss R A, BSc MSc MCLIP, Med. Inf. and Pharma Mgr., Mulliner House, London. [60358] 05/12/1995 **CM05/12/1995**

El Rayah, Mrs S B, BA PGDipLIS MCLIP, Retired. [40564] 19/03/1987 **CM27/03/1991**

Elce, Mr A, HNC, Unknown. [10015607] 17/12/2009 **ME**

Elcock, Miss Y, Inf. Specialist, Barbados Investment & Devel. Corp. [59988] 16/11/2001 **ME**

Elder, Mr D B, BA MLib FCLIP, Dep. Head, Knowledge Mgmt. Serv., GCHQ, Cheltenham. [36547] 10/10/1983 **RV17/09/2008** **FE08/12/2004**

Elder, Mr M A, BA(Hons) DipILS MCLIP, Inf. Specialist, Cranfield Univ., Swindon. [55522] 20/10/1997 **CM03/10/2007**

Elder, Mrs M, BEng(Hons) PGDipLIM, Lis Mgr. – Warrington Univ. of Chester [62596] 05/09/2003 **ME**

Elder, Mrs V, BA(Hons), Lib., Northumberland Care Trust, Morpeth. [41295] 30/10/1987 **ME**

Elderton, Mrs D L, BA DipEd MCLIP, Lib., Ibstock Place Sch., Roehampton, London. [53647] 13/08/1996 **CM19/07/2000**

Eldridge, Mrs K M, BMus(Hons) MA MSc, Career Break [60016] 26/11/2001 **ME**

Elgar, Mr P G, Retired. [4488] 29/10/1946 **ME**

El-Jouzi, Ms A, BA(Hons) MSc MCLIP, Liaison Lib., St Georges' Univ of London. [54998] 19/06/1997 **CM21/03/2007**

Elkes, Mr M H, BA MCLIP, Team Lead, Info. & Local Studies, Staffs. C.C. Child. Dept., Stafford. [4490] 25/07/1968 **CM01/01/1971**

Elkin, Prof J C, BA PhD FCLIP, Dep. Vice Chancellor Emeritus, Univ. of Worcester. [4491] 13/03/1962 **FE27/03/1991**

Ellam, Ms N, Unknown. [10015460] 27/11/2009 **AF**

Ellard, Ms R, Asst. Dir. : Member Serv., ALIA, Australia. [10013616] 13/05/2009 **ME**

Ellery, Ms J, BSc(Hons) MA MCLIP, Dir. of Knowledge, Gov. & Comm., Lewisham Hosp. NHS Trust Univ. Hosp. Lewisham L. [46836] 14/02/1992 **CM15/03/2000**

Elliott, Mr B, BA (Hons.) MA, Unwaged. [10001268] 14/02/2007 **ME**

Elliott, Ms C A, BA DipLIS MCLIP, Job Seeking. [26361] 15/10/1976 **CM11/12/1978**

Elliott, Mrs C A, BA MCLIP, Lib., Cent. Newcastle High Sch., Newcastle Upon Tyne. [22589] 02/07/1974 **CM02/10/1978**

Elliott, Mrs D A, MA(Hons) MCLIP, Area Lib., E. Lothian Council, [47552] 01/10/1992 **CM24/07/1996**

Elliott, Mrs D D E, BEd(Hons) PGDipILM MA, p. /t. L. Asst., Univ. of Durham. [53046] 19/02/1996 **ME**

Elliott, Mr D T, BA MLS FCLIP MIMgt, Retired. [4501] 25/11/1968 **FE16/09/1976**

Elliott, Miss E M, BA MCLIP, Retired. [4507] 05/10/1961 **CM01/01/1963**

Elliott, Prof G D, BA(Hons) MSc PGCHE FBCS CITP MCLIP, Prof., London S. Bank Univ. [60799] 23/02/1989 **CM31/08/1993**

Elliott, Mrs H L, Sen. Asst., Ref. Lib., Exeter Cent. L, Devon [54853] 15/04/1997 **AF**

Elliott, Miss K, BEd(Hons) DipILS MCLIP, Sch. Lib., Angus Council, Arbroath. [55888] 16/12/1997 **CM17/01/2001**

Elliott, Mrs L P, BA MCLIP, L. Serv. Mgr., Portsmouth Cent. L., Portsmouth City Council. [31268] 02/10/1979 **CM21/02/1985**

Elliott, Mrs L, MA FCLIP, Head of Tech. Serv. /Joint Dep., Manchester Metro. Univ. [4513] 20/01/1965 **FE22/05/1991**

Elliott, Mrs M J, BA(Hons) MCLIP, Lib. (Career Break), Stapleford L., Nottingham. [47921] 26/10/1992 **CM17/03/1999**

Elliott, Mrs P E, M Phil BA MCLIP, Inf. Consultant. [4519] 03/01/1972 **CM23/11/1976**

Elliott, Mr P J V, BSc MCLIP, Sen. Keeper, Royal Air Force Mus., London. [60282] 25/05/1979 **CM24/03/1988**

Elliott, Mr P W, Unknown. [10013970] 17/06/2009 **AF**

Elliott, Mr P, Business Lib., ESCP Europe, London. [10013304] 08/10/2009 **ME**

Elliott, Miss P, BA CertEd MCLIP, Lib., Westminster Sch. L. Serv., London. [28948] 07/02/1978 **CM05/06/1986**

Elliott, Mrs S M, MCLIP, Lib., Truro Coll., Cornwall. [405] 01/01/1971 **CM17/01/1974**

Ellis, Dr A C O, MA PhD FCLIP, Life Member. [4525] 19/01/1950 **FE01/01/1964**

Ellis, Mrs A J, BA MCLIP, Head of L., Blackpool Bor. Council. [22973] 02/10/1974 **CM23/06/1978**

Ellis, Mrs A W, MCLIP, Retired. [4527] 22/01/1950 **CM01/01/1954**

Ellis, Mrs A, LRC Mgr., The Brooksbank Sch., Elland [10017084] 22/06/2010 **AF**

Ellis, Ms C M, BA AKC DipLib MCLIP, Knowledge Access Lib., Rutherford Appleton Lab., Didcot. [31262] 15/10/1979 **CM04/12/1981**

Ellis, Mrs D, ACLIP, Hub L. Mgr., Watford L. [58556] 01/04/2000
ACL17/01/2007
Ellis, Mr D, BA(Hons) DipLib MCLIP, Inf. Res. Mgr., Ashton, Leigh &
Wigan PCT., Wigan. [4530] 01/10/1971 **CM01/04/1975**
Ellis, Mrs F A, MSc MCLIP, Retired. [462] 25/10/1966 **CM01/01/1970**
Ellis, Miss F M, BA MCLIP, Lib. & Web Mgr., Marymount Int. Sch of
Paris. [41646] 05/02/1988 **CM16/11/1994**
Ellis, Mr G J, BA MA, L. & Learning Cent. Mgr., Whitley Bay High Sch.
[10006907] 17/12/2007 **ME**
Ellis, Mr J L, BLib MCLIP, Retired. [4536] 01/01/1968 **CM05/09/1973**
Ellis, Miss K E, Unwaged. [47936] 26/10/1992 **ME**
Ellis, Mrs M J, BSc(Hons) DipInfSci MA MCLIP, Sen. Inf. Researcher,
Roffey Park Inst., W. Sussex. [34375] 26/10/1981 **CM10/10/1983**
Ellis, Mrs M, BA DipLib MCLIP, Sch. Lib., Chepstow Comp. Sch.,
Monmouthshire Educ. Dept. [9852] 01/01/1971 **CM23/06/1975**
Ellis, Mrs N H, BA(Hons) ACLIP, Sen. L. Asst, Southwell L., Nottingham.
[10002894] 10/05/2007 **ACL16/07/2008**
Ellis, Mrs P, BA MEd MCLIP, Knowledge & Learning Res. Mgr., Devon &
Cornwall Workforce Devel. Confed. for the Strat. Hlth. Auth. [8399]
12/10/1971 **CM16/10/1974**
Ellis, Mr R J, MCLIP, Asst., Ceredigion C.C. [21326] 17/10/1973
CM01/01/1978
Ellis, Mr T M, Stud., Aberystwyth Univ. [10015218] 27/10/2009 **ME**
Ellis-Barrett, Mrs L G A, BA(Hons) MSc MCLIP, Lib., Downsend Sch.,
Leatherhead. [56262] 17/04/1998 **CM23/06/2004**
Ellison, Mrs A C, BA(Hons) MA MCLIP, H. of Servs. to Child, Sch. L.
Serv., Dialstone Cent., Stockport. [36076] 11/05/1983 **CM14/03/1986**
Ellison, Miss M J, BA(Hons) MSc, Lib., Skadden, Arps, Slate, Meagher
& Flom (UK) LLP [57413] 04/03/1999 **ME**
Ellison, Mr S B, BSc BSc PGDIP LIS, Registration and Keywording Co-
ordinator, Rex Features Ltd., London. [10006350] 16/10/2007 **ME**
Ellison, Miss S J, BSc(Hons) MSc, Healthcare Analyst, Dept. for
Business [10000950] 04/12/2006 **AF**
Ellison, Ms W L, BA(Hons) MA MCLIP, Subject Lib., Univ. of Chichester.
[48699] 01/04/1993 **CM15/05/2002**
Ellwood, Mrs F, BA MCLIP, Bookseller, Waterstone's, Loughborough.
[27489] 26/04/1977 **CM07/12/1984**
Ellwood, Mr M P, BA MCLIP, Project Mgr, Suffolk C.C. Suffolk. [26363]
04/10/1976 **CM30/10/1979**
Ellyard, Mrs J M, BA MCLIP, Sch. Lib., Glossopdale Comm. Coll.
[31490] 18/10/1979 **CM22/08/1984**
Elmer, Miss L, LLB(Hons) Law, Stud. [10006295] 05/10/2007 **ME**
Elmes, Ms T A, BA(Hons) MA, Sen. Lib., Inf. Mgmnt. Strategy Support
Off., Home Off. London [50805] 18/10/1994 **ME**
Else, Ms O J, BMus MA MCLIP, Academic Liaison Asst., Univ. of York
[10009273] 21/05/2008 **CM16/10/2009**
Elsegood, Ms S A, BSc MCLIP FHEA, Humanities Faculty Lib., Univ. of
E. Anglia, Norwich. [43563] 08/11/1989 **RV04/04/2006**
CM24/09/1997
Else-Jack, Mrs J, BLib MCLIP, Unknown [40782] 08/06/1987
CM27/03/1991
Elsmore, Miss B M, MCLIP, Life Member. [4550] 19/10/1942
CM01/01/1951
Elson, Mr D L, BA(Hons), Unknown. [10014282] 13/07/2009 **ME**
Elson, Miss S A, BA MCLIP, Principal Lib. (Projects & Developments),
Milton Keynes Cent. L. [39225] 01/01/1986 **CM15/08/1989**
Elstob, Miss S, BA(Hons) MA PGCe, Learning Resource Advisor,
Sussex Downs Coll. [10005440] 25/11/1999 **ME**
Elston, Mr L H, MCLIP, Retired. [4554] 04/08/1941 **CM05/09/1972**
Eltringham, Mrs S H, BA(Hons), Unknown. [10012074] 15/12/2008 **ME**
Elves, Mr R J, BSc(Hons) MSc MCLIP, Inf. Specialist, Kingston Univ.
[47361] 23/07/1992 **CM23/09/1998**
Elwell, Ms H, BA(Hons) MSc, Asst. Lib., Brit. Med. Assoc., London.
[47353] 21/07/1992 **ME**

Elwen, Miss C L, BA(Hons), Stud., Leeds Met. Univ., [63966]
22/11/2004 **ME**
Elwick, Miss R A, Diary Mgr. to The Sec. of State., Dept. for
Communities & Local Government [63095] 28/01/2004 **ME**
Ely, Mrs H J, MA MCLIP, Virtual Serv Mgr., Surrey CC, Leatherhead.
[21457] 12/10/1973 **CM10/11/1975**
Emberson, Mrs J E, MCLIP, Retired. [4568] 05/02/1959 **CM01/01/1964**
Emberton, Ms F J, MA DipLIS ALIA MCLIP, Consultant. [41263]
24/10/1987 **CM12/12/1990**
Emeniru, Mr C E, HND, Teacher/Lib., St. Raphael's Sec. Sch., Anambra
State, Nigeria. [59548] 10/05/2001 **ME**
Emerson, Mr S D, BA MCLIP, Sen. Asst. Lib., L.B. of Harrow. [4571]
16/01/1972 **CM22/07/1974**
Emerton, Mrs J J, BA(Hons) MA MCLIP, Subject Lib., Cardiff Univ.
[61121] 20/02/2002 **CM31/01/2007**
Emery, Mr C D, BA MPhil MCLIP, Life Member. [16845] 12/03/1958
CM01/01/1961
Emery-Wallis, Cllr F, CBE HonFLA, Hon. Fellow. [53197] 01/01/1996
HFE01/01/1996
Emly, Mr M A, MA MCLIP, CMS Team Leader, Univ. of Leeds L. [28427]
01/12/1977 **CM19/11/1979**
Emmott, Mrs A J, BSc MCLIP, Br. Lib., L.B. of Wandsworth, York Gdn.
L. & Comm. Cent. [4581] 01/01/1968 **CM10/08/1972**
Emmott, Mrs S J, BA MCLIP, Asst. Lib., Dept. of Health, Leeds. [43698]
28/11/1989 **CM23/06/2004**
Endicott, Mrs A J, BA(Hons) PGDip, Unknown. [10012721] 01/04/1998
ME
Engel, Mr C D, BA DipLib MCLIP, Dep. Lib. Mgr., Russells Hall Hosp.,
Dudley [33491] 10/01/1981 **CM29/07/1985**
Engel-Gough, Miss D N, HNC, Stud., Aberystwyth Univ. [10009492]
21/05/2008 **ME**
England, Mrs A J, BA MLS MCLIP, Lib., Cambridgeshire C.C., Wisbech
(Base L.). [33036] 08/10/1980 **CM13/12/1982**
England, Miss K J, MA MSc MCLIP, Sch. Lib., Tiree High Sch., Isle of
Tiree. [55342] 01/10/1997 **CM15/01/2003**
England, Ms P M, MA BA MCLIP, Info. Advisor (Health), London S.
Bank Univ., [29165] 05/04/1978 **CM24/11/1980**
England, Miss R L, ACLIP, L. Facilitator, Kent & Sussex Hosp.,
Tunbridge Wells, Kent. [10002786] 01/05/2007 **ACL16/07/2008**
England, Dr T G, BSc PhD, Unknown. [10012618] 19/02/2009 **ME**
Englefield, Mrs H, BA(Hons), Stud., Aberystwyth Univ. [10008691]
23/04/2008 **ME**
Englert, Ms G, MCLIP, Lib., Wavelengths L., Lewisham. [10000572]
16/10/2006 **CM13/07/1973**
English, Mr D J, BA MCLIP, Retired. [4596] 07/10/1963 **CM01/01/1966**
English, Miss H E, BA(Hons) MA, Unwaged [59462] 03/04/2001 **ME**
English, Mrs L H, BA(Hons) PgDipILM MCLIP, P/t Learning Advisor.,
Univ. of Cumbria [52195] 12/10/1995 **CM20/05/1998**
English, Mrs Z M, BSc, Stud., Brighton Univ. [10015370] 10/11/2009 **ME**
Englund, Miss A M, BSc MA MCLIP, Inf. Advisor (Bus. & Law),
Kingston Univ. [63710] 13/08/2004 **CM06/05/2009**
Ennion, Mrs C, BA DipEdTech MCLIP, Retired. [23560] 20/01/1975
CM20/01/1977
Ennis, Mrs A P, BSc MCLIP, Marketing Exec., Events, Royal Soc. of
Chemistry, Cambridge. [19994] 11/01/1973 **CM13/07/1976**
Ennis, K A, BA(Hons) DipLib MCLIP, Sen. Adviser, CILIP. [35972]
10/03/1983 **CM05/07/1988**
Enright, Ms S, BA DipLib MCLIP, Dir. ISLS, Univ. of Westminster,
London. [30831] 17/05/1979 **CM03/09/1982**
Enser, Prof P G B, BA(Econ) MTech PhD MBCS FCLIP Head of Sch.,
Sch. of Computing, Math. & Inf. Sci., Univ. of Brighton. [60283]
06/01/1981 **FE01/04/2002**
Ensing, Miss R J, FCLIP, Life Member. [4606] 08/03/1940 **FE01/01/1951**

Ensinger, Mrs T E, Lib. Mngr., Horringer Court Middle Sch., Bury St Edmunds [10015552] 14/12/2009 **ME**

Ensor, Mrs T K, BA(Hons) MA MCLIP, User Serv. Lib., Tattlebury, Goudhurst. [55718] 05/11/1997 **CM18/09/2002**

Entwistle, Miss G A, BA PGDipLib MCLIP, Asst. Div. Lib., Lancs. C.C. L., [41073] 06/10/1987 **CM18/04/1990**

Entwistle, Mr N W, MA MCLIP, Ret. [18345] 13/10/1972 **CM31/10/1974**

Enyiorji, Mr C G, OND HND PG Dip, Dep. Inst. Lib. - Principal Lib. Offr., Nat. Inst. for Hosp. & Tourism, Igano. [10015712] 19/01/2010 **ME**

Epps, Mrs A T, BSc MCLIP, Tech., Prospect Coll., Reading. [60151] 01/07/1979 **CM01/06/1983**

Ernestus, Mr H, FCLIP, Life Member. [16853] 30/01/1956 **FE15/09/1993**

Errington, Mr D J, BSc (Hons), Asst. Lib., Robinson L., Newcastle Upon Tyne [10009450] 18/11/2005 **ME**

Erskine, Mr J G W, BA DIP ED MCLIP, Asst. Lib., Stranmillis Univ. Coll., Belfast. [23911] 22/02/1975 **CM12/01/1982**

Erskine, Mrs J, BSc MCLIP, Local Studies & Fammily Hist. Lib., Fife Council, Dunfermline. [63021] 15/12/2003 **CM19/11/2008**

Erskine, Ms K, MCLIP, Lib., Saint Augustine's L., Canterbury [10007093] 09/10/1987 **CM27/01/1993**

Erskine, Mr S C B, MA MCLIP, Database Integrity Lib., Bournemouth L. [23120] 06/11/1974 **CM10/02/1978**

Escott, Ms A, MA MCLIP, Retired. [4613] 28/01/1967 **CM01/01/1969**

Escreet, Mr P K, MA MCLIP, Life Member. [4615] 15/08/1951 **CM01/01/1955**

Esiet, Mrs I, Unwaged. [10008589] 21/04/2008 **ME**

Eskander, Dr S, HonFCLIP, Unknown. [10011429] 20/10/2008 **HFE16/10/2008**

Espitalier-Noel, Mrs C, BA MCLIP, Unwaged. [36693] 03/11/1983 **CM15/03/1989**

Essakhi, Ms R A, BA DipLib, Lib., Nobel Sch., Stevenage. [34343] 26/10/1981 **ME**

Essex, Mrs L, BEd(Hons) DipLIS MCLIP, Sen. Team Leader, Portfolio, Warwickshire C.C., Nuneaton L. [47454] 19/08/1992 **CM20/01/1999**

Essex, Mrs S E, MCLIP, p/t. Asst. Edu. Serv. Lib., Tameside Sch. /Br. Lib., Tameside [26880] 16/12/1976 **CM03/11/1980**

Esslemont, Mr J L, MA MSc MCLIP, Retired. [60284] 07/11/1975 **CM18/01/1978**

Esson, Mrs A C, BA DipLib MCLIP, Freelance Law Lib., Beachcroft LLP, Manchester. [18765] 07/08/1972 **CM07/08/1972**

Estall, Miss C J, BA(Hons) PGCE, Stud. [10016608] 16/04/2010 **ME**

Esteve-Coll, Dame E A L, DBE BA MCLIP, Vice-Chancellor, Univ. of E. Anglia. [32580] 20/09/1969 **CM01/01/1972**

Etheridge, Mr M, BA(Hons) MSc MSc MIIA MA MCLIP, Business Change & Inf. Mgr., Communities & Local Govt. [59783] 02/10/2001 **CM11/03/2009**

Etim, Mrs F E, BSc, MLS, PhD, Univ. Lib., Univ. of Uyo, Nigeria. [10014847] 21/09/2009 **ME**

Etkind, Mrs A, BA DipLib MCLIP, p. /t. Knowledge Consultant, Univ. of Herts., Hatfield. [26876] 28/12/1976 **CM19/01/1979**

Eu Ahara, Mrs S I T, MCLIP, Retired. [4624] 01/01/1965 **CM01/01/1970**

Euesden, Mr M A, MSc MBA MCLIP, ICT Project Mgr., The Brit. L., Boston Spa. [35440] 01/10/1982 **CM01/07/1989**

Eunson, Miss B G, BA FCLIP, Life Member. [4626] 03/01/1947 **FE01/01/1959**

Evans, Miss A A, Info. Specialist [10000869] 17/11/2006 **ME**

Evans, Mr A C, MCLIP, Visiting Res. Fellow, Dept. of Computing, Goldsmiths Coll. Univ. of London [28754] 06/01/1971 **CM12/07/1978**

Evans, Mrs A E, MA BA MCLIP, H. of Acquisitions Serv., Bodleian L., Oxford. [37633] 16/10/1984 **CM14/03/1990**

Evans, Prof A J, BPharm PhD HonFLA FCLIP, Life Member. [4634] 16/04/1958 **FE01/01/1969**

Evans, Ms A M, BSc(Hons) MA, Sen. Comm. Lib. L. C. C [38960] 15/10/1985 **ME**

Evans, Mr A, BA, Account Mgr. -Academic L. -UK, OCLC UK LTD, Birmingham. [39947] 06/10/1986 **ME**

Evans, Ms A, BA MA MCLIP, Asst. Lib., Swansea Met. Univ. [42325] 12/10/1988 **CM20/10/2005**

Evans, Mrs A, BA(Hons) MSc, Sen. L. Asst., Cardiff Univ. [62471] 08/07/2003 **ME**

Evans, Mr B D, BA MCLIP, Retired. [4641] 10/09/1956 **CM01/01/1963**

Evans, Mrs B T, BSc DipLib MCLIP, Sch. Lib. /Res. Mgr., Temple Moor High Sch. Sci. Coll. [25748] 16/02/1976 **CM15/03/1978**

Evans, Mrs C A, BA MALS, Retired. [42116] 03/10/1988 **ME**

Evans, Mr C J, BSc MSc, Inf. Specialist, Cheltenham [10007015] 07/01/2000 **ME**

Evans, Miss D, Publisher, Ashgate Publishing Ltd., Farnham. [64343] 07/03/2005 **ME**

Evans, Miss E A, MCLIP, Retired. [4655] 01/01/1955 **CM01/01/1969**

Evans, Mrs E E, MCLIP, Life Member. [4658] 10/10/1966 **CM30/01/1973**

Evans, Miss E E, BA MCLIP, Retired. [4657] 09/02/1960 **CM01/01/1966**

Evans, Mr E O, Asst. Enquiries Offr., Nat. L. of Wales, Aberystwith. [10000868] 17/11/2006 **AF**

Evans, Mrs E W, MCLIP, Gp. Lib. E., Pembrokeshire L. Serv. [21547] 16/10/1973 **CM01/07/1991**

Evans, Mrs E, BA MA(Dist), Lib., Leics. C.C., Loughborough L. [58686] 30/05/2000 **ME**

Evans, Mrs F M, BLib MCLIP, Lib., Godstowe Prep. Sch., Bucks. [29508] 18/09/1978 **CM25/01/1985**

Evans, Mr G H, BLib MCLIP, Business dev. Mgr., Caerphilly Co. Bor. Council. [43980] 23/03/1990 **CM26/05/1993**

Evans, Ms G M, BA DipLib MCLIP, Head of L. & Museums, Rhondda Cynon Taff Council, Abercynon. [24663] 07/10/1975 **CM16/05/1980**

Evans, Mrs H J, BA MCLIP, Career Break. [39476] 31/01/1986 **CM12/12/1991**

Evans, Mr H L, BSc DipLib MCLIP, Head of Advice & Support/Pennaeth Cyngor a Chefnogaeth, Cymal Mus. Arch. & L., Wales. [32940] 23/10/1980 **CM19/04/1983**

Evans, Miss H M D, BLib DipIllus, Media Tech. /Asst. Lib., Cheshire E. [26719] 03/11/1976 **ME**

Evans, Mr I W H, MA MCLIP, Sys. Lib., Redgrave Ct., Liverpool. [62958] 25/11/2003 **CM27/01/2010**

Evans, Mr I, Head of External Serv., Welsh Assembly Gov., Cardiff. [10007325] 19/06/2008 **ME**

Evans, Mr J A, BSc MSc MCLIP, Inf. Serv. Offr., Nat. Inst. Biological Standards Ctrl., S. Mimms, Herts. [51970] 24/08/1995 **CM01/04/2002**

Evans, Mrs J A, Sch. Lib., London Met. Univ. [63980] 22/11/2004 **ME**

Evans, Mrs J B, BA(Hons) MA MCLIP, Systems and Procedures Mgr., The Coll. of Law, Chester. [53687] 05/09/1996 **CM12/09/2001**

Evans, Mr J C, MA(Oxon) PGCE MSc(Econ) MCLIP, L. & Inf. Serv. Mgr., Kenilworth Sch, Warwickshire C.C. [54187] 06/11/1996 **CM20/11/2002**

Evans, Mrs J E, Bibl., Carmarthenshire C.C. [62685] 12/10/2003 **ME**

Evans, Mrs J E, BA MCLIP, Retired [18450] 15/10/1972 **CM08/06/1976**

Evans, Miss J M, BA, Liaison Lib., Imperial Coll. London., London. [66009] 25/08/2006 **ME**

Evans, Miss J, BA MCLIP, Policy Offr., European Energy Unit, DECC, London [37925] 17/11/1984 **CM16/10/1991**

Evans, Mrs J, Unknown. [10012933] 06/12/2005 **ME**

Evans, Mrs K T, MCLIP, Info. Lib., Bath Univ. [65038] 13/10/2005 **CM07/07/2010**

Evans, Ms K, BA(Hons) MSc(Econ), Catr., Univ. of Nottingham, Kings Meadow Campus. [58584] 04/04/2000 **ME**

Evans, Ms L G, MA, Stud. [10006352] 16/10/2007 **ME**

Evans, Mrs L S, MCLIP, Sharpe Lib., Giggleswick Sch., N. Yorks. [31803] 18/01/1980 **CM02/02/1983**

Evans, Mr L, BA(Hons) PGCE DipLib MCLIP, Sen. Educ. Lib., L. HQ, Flintshire CC, Mold. [10013095] 17/06/1994 **CM02/05/1998**

Evans, Mrs M A, MA MCLIP, Retired. [16862] 07/04/1951 **CM01/01/1955**

Evans, Mr M P, Lib., MOD, Royal Artillery, James Clavell L., Woolwich. [59304] 31/01/2001 **ME**

Evans, Lord M, of Temple Guiting CBE HonFCLIP, Hon. Fellow. [57252] 04/02/1999 **FE01/01/1999**

Evans, Ms M, L. & Resources Cent. Mgr., Vyners Sch., Ickenham. [65217] 18/11/2005 **ME**

Evans, Mrs M, BA MCLIP, Lib., William Hulmes Grammar Sch., Manchester. [9309] 01/01/1970 **CM01/02/1974**

Evans, Prof M, BA MBA PhD PGCE FCLIP, Retired. [10016069] 10/09/1964 **FE23/03/1993**

Evans, Miss N A, BEd(Hons) DipLIS MCLIP, Art & Design Lib., Univ. of Wales, Newport. [47553] 01/10/1992 **CM22/07/1998**

Evans, Mrs N N, BA MSc, Lib., Knights Templar Sch., Baldock. [54437] 09/12/1996 **ME**

Evans, Mrs N R, Lib., Hampton Coll., Peterborough. [10016070] 12/02/2010 **AF**

Evans, Mrs N, Retired. [4691] 01/01/1952 **ME**

Evans, Miss O P, MCLIP, Life Member. [4693] 24/02/1945 **CM01/01/1955**

Evans, Mr P J, BA MCLIP, Lib. Asst., Norbury L., L.B. Croydon [36855] 11/01/1984 **CM15/02/1989**

Evans, Mrs P J, MA DipLIB MCLIP, Local Studies Team Lib., Northamptonshire L. [29646] 03/10/1978 **CM12/03/1981**

Evans, Mrs P M F, MCLIP, L. Super., Weston L., Somerset. [23613] 20/01/1975 **CM02/10/1978**

Evans, Ms R A, BA(Hons) MA MCLIP, Collection Devel. Lib, IOE, Univ. of London. [10005122] 12/10/1999 **CM12/03/2003**

Evans, Miss R A, Inf. Advisor, Univ. Wales Inst., Cardiff. [59389] 27/02/2001 **ME**

Evans, Miss R C, BA MA, Inf. Specialist, Civil Serv. [10001074] 12/01/2007 **ME**

Evans, Miss R M, MCLIP, Retired. [4699] 01/01/1962 **CM01/01/1966**

Evans, Mrs S E, BA(Hons), P/+ Child. & Young Peopl'es Lib., Aberystwyth [62525] 05/08/2003 **ME**

Evans, Mr S J, BA MSc, Inf. Cent. Mgr., Bristows, London. [54520] 14/01/1997 **ME**

Evans, Mrs S M, MCLIP, Sch. Lib., Wells Cathedral Sch., Somerset. [4704] 27/01/1966 **CM01/01/1969**

Evans, Miss S, BA MA, Lib., Neston High Sch., Wirral. [10014989] 01/10/2009 **ME**

Evans, Mrs S, MCLIP, Unknown [62469] 08/07/2003 **CM09/07/2009**

Evans, Mrs T N, BSc(Hons) MA MCLIP, Resident in U. S. A. [52888] 19/01/1996 **CM16/05/2001**

Evans, Mr W E, MCLIP, Resident Germany. [4707] 25/02/1968 **CM01/01/1971**

Evans, Mrs W J, BA(Hons) MCLIP ILTA, Head Lib., Univ. Coll. Plymouth. St Mark & St John [40407] 02/02/1987 **CM20/11/2002**

Evans, Mrs Y E, MCLIP, Life Member. [4709] 05/01/1949 **CM01/01/1955**

Evason, Mrs C, BA(Hons) MA MCLIP, Educ. Events Co-ordinator. [54144] 01/11/1996 **CM17/01/2001**

Evason, Miss M, MA MCLIP, Retired. [4710] 01/01/1939 **CM01/01/1947**

Eve, Ms J, BA(Hons) MA MSc, Principal Lect., Head of Div. of Inf. & Media Studies, Univ. of Brighton [54044] 22/10/1996 **ME**

Evenson, Ms S E, BA, Info. Servs. Mgr., Slaughter and May, London [47798] 19/10/1992 **ME**

Everall, Mrs A M, OBE BA(Hons) MCLIP, Serv. Mgr., Derbyshire L. & Heritage, Young People & Policy Devel. [26365] 12/10/1976 **CM19/06/1987**

Everall, Mr I R, BA(Hons)Lib MCLIP, Consultant [26366] 12/10/1976 **CM16/01/1979**

Everatt, Mrs J, MCLIP, Sen. Asst. Lib., L.B. of Harrow, Middx. [19818] 01/10/1972 **CM20/07/1976**

Everest, Ms K, MA, Head of L. Serv & Operations, Leeds Met. Univ., Leeds [10017106] 26/11/1990 **ME**

Everett, Mrs J E, BA DipLib MCLIP, Primary Sch. Lib., Northants. C.C., Northampton. [36996] 16/01/1984 **CM11/11/1986**

Everett, Mrs J S, MCLIP, Sen. Team Leader, Warwickshire C.C. [14253] 11/03/1971 **CM11/12/1974**

Everett, Mrs L C A, MCLIP, Lib., St. Georges Sch., Windsor. [2624] 23/02/1971 **CM21/11/1973**

Everhard, Ms C J, MA DipLib MCLIP, Foreign Instructor, Aristotle Univ., Thessaloniki, Greece. [18329] 12/10/1972 **CM23/04/1975**

Everist, Mrs J, Sch. Lib., Holmewood House Sch., Tunbridge Wells. [57067] 07/12/1998 **ME**

Everitt, Ms C E, BA(Hons) CertEd DipLIS MCLIP, Reader Serv. Lib., Bishop Grossteste Univ. Coll. [52330] 30/10/1995 **CM18/09/2002**

Everitt, Mrs E A, BSc MSc MCLIP, p. /t. Acquisitions Lib., Royal Coll. of Nursing, London. [28374] 17/11/1977 **CM31/10/1979**

Everitt, Mrs L, L. Asst., Missionary Inst. London. [45383] 20/11/1990 **ME**

Everitt, Mr P, BA(Hons) MCLIP, L. Mgr., Cheshire C.C. [53003] 14/02/1996 **CM25/07/2001**

Everitt, Mrs R, MSc MCLIP, Learning Resources Mgr., Univ. of Arts, London. [59628] 04/07/2001 **CM15/09/2004**

Everitt, Mrs S M, BSc DipLib MCLIP, L. Asst., Special Needs Unit, Wolverhampton P. L. [30024] 13/11/1978 **CM30/03/1981**

Everson, Mr A D, MA Med MA MCLIP, Retired. [44034] 01/04/1990 **CM20/03/1996**

Everson, Mr M E, BA MCLIP, Knowledge Mgr., The Thomas Saunders Partnership, London. [37454] 02/10/1984 **CM07/07/1987**

Evetts, Mrs L, BA(Hons) MA MCLIP, Unwaged – Full Time Mum [54445] 10/12/1996 **CM15/11/2000**

Evuarherhe Jr, Mr N, MA BENG, Stud., Univ. Coll. London. [10015136] 14/10/2009 **ME**

Ewan, Mr A I, MCLIP, Retired [4721] 01/01/1966 **CM08/09/1970**

Ewart, Ms L, BA(Hons), Djanogly City Academy [62991] 04/12/2003 **ME**

Ewing, Mr D K, BA(Hons), Business Researcher, CMC Ltd., Cheshire [46434] 04/11/1991 **ME**

Ewins, Mrs K B, MCLIP, Retired. . [19702] 06/02/1962 **CM01/01/1966**

Ewins, Mrs M S, Sen. Inf. Mgr., HM Revenue & Customs, London. [64642] 11/05/2005 **ME**

Exton, Miss L S, BSc MSc MCLIP, Inf. Sci. /Lib., King's Coll. London, Polani Res. L., Guys Campus. [60756] 05/01/1987 **CM12/04/1989**

Eynon, Dr A D, BA(Hons) DipLIS MCLIP PhD, L. Resource Mgr., Llandrillo Coll., Colwyn Bay. [45745] 15/05/1991 **CM23/09/1998**

Eyre, Mrs G D, BA PhD MCLIP AALIA, Head of Dept., Univ. of Wales. [15702] 28/09/1970 **CM13/08/1974**

Eyre, Mr J P, BA PG Dip MCLIP, Asst. Lib., De Montfort Univ. [10000628] 18/10/2006 **CM17/09/2008**

Eyre, Ms J, L. Administrator, Chapel En Le Frith High Sch. [10016634] 20/04/2010 **ME**

Eyres, Mrs H, BA(Hons) PGCE, Unknown. [10017017] 17/06/2005 **AF**

Eyres, Mrs R J, BA(Hons) DipLIS MCLIP, Asst. Lib., Manchester Met. Univ., Aytoun L. [50864] 24/10/1994 **CM24/09/1997**

F

Fabling, Miss J L, BA MCLIP, Knowledge Support Lib., Hampshire Healthcare L. Serv. [37284] 31/05/1984 **CM07/07/1987**

Facey, Miss M L, MLIS, Unknown. [10007674] 28/02/2008 **ME**

Fadlallah, Mr M, BSc MSc, Sen. Inf. Asst., Kings Coll., Denmark Hill Campus, Univ. of London. [63800] 01/10/2004 **ME**

Fagg, Mrs S V, BSc(Hons) DipTP, ILS Advisor, Univ. of Worcester, Worcester. [63387] 27/04/2004 **ME**

Fairall, Mrs L, MA, Unknown. [59722] 05/09/2001 **ME**

Fairall, Mrs S A C, Retired. [27759] 01/08/1977 **ME**

Fairbrother, Mr J V, MCLIP, Life Member. [4747] 20/01/1961
CM01/01/1963

Fairbrother, Mr P, BA(Hons) MSc MCLIP, Training Fellow, Edinburgh Napier Univ. [50426] 27/07/1994 **CM18/03/1998**

Fairburn, Ms J, BA MCLIP, Lib. Serv. Operational Mgr., L.B. of Hillingdon. [35716] 18/01/1983 **CM07/06/1988**

Fairclough, Mrs J, BA(Hons) MCLIP, Med. Sch. Lib., Brighton & Sussex Med. Sch., Brighton [51930] 09/08/1995 **CM20/11/2002**

Fairfoul, Ms S, MA, Unknown. [10005492] 06/08/1997 **ME**

Fairlamb, Miss C A, BA(Hons), Stud., Northumbria Univ. [10015551] 14/12/2009 **ME**

Fairman, Mr R B, MSc BSc DipLib MCLIP, L. Serv. Devel., Univ. of Worcester. [33288] 07/11/1980 **CM01/04/2002**

Fairweather, Mrs K J, BA(Hons), L. Res. Cent. Co-ordinator, The Moray Council, Speyside High Sch. [57610] 24/05/1999 **ME**

Fairweather, Miss N, DipLib MCLIP, Co. Stock Mgr., Cambs. [32942] 09/10/1980 **CM22/11/1982**

Fairweather, Mrs P J, MCLIP, Unknown. [29111] 27/02/1978
CM20/08/1981

Fairweather, Ms S K, BA PGDip MA, Ref. Serv. Lib., House of Lords L., London. [55326] 01/10/1997 **ME**

Faithfull, Miss A C, BA(Hons) DipInf, Res. Mgr. (Corporate), Freshfields Bruckhaus Deringer, London. [53020] 31/01/1996 **ME**

Falana, Mrs O F, MLS BLIS, Lib. II, Oyo State L. Board, Ibadan, Nigeria. [10006047] 24/08/2007 **ME**

Falconer, Mrs L, MCLIP, Inf. Devel. Mgr., Leeds City Council. [9040] 23/11/1971 **CM11/11/1975**

Falconer, Mr S W, BSc(Hons), Inf. Offr., Inst. of Directors, London. [10012373] 23/07/1988 **ME**

Falla, Mrs J, BA DipLib MCLIP, Head of Serv. to Educ. & Young People Guille-Alles L., Guernsey. [36629] 24/10/1983 **CM25/09/1996**

Falla, Miss M J, BA MA MLib MCLIP, Ch. Lib., Guille-Alles L., Guernsey. [35477] 06/10/1982 **CM08/12/1987**

Fallis, Mr C A, BA(Hons) MA, Sports Lib., B. B. C., Sports L., London. [55270] 11/09/1997 **ME**

Fallon, Mrs S A, MA, Principal Editor, Sweet & Maxwell, W. Yorks. [52770] 11/12/1995 **ME**

Fallone, Mrs E, BA MCLIP, Unknown. [31200] 02/10/1979 **CM30/11/1987**

Faludi, Ms O, JD MSc, Stud. [10015428] 16/11/2009

Fanner, Ms D A, MCLIP, Staff L., Salisbury Dist. Hosp., Salisbury. [10001350] 09/08/2004 **CM16/10/2009**

Farbey, Mr R A, BA DipLib FCLIP, Head of Lib. & knowledge Serv., Brit. Dental Assoc., London. [27965] 13/10/1977 **FE19/03/2008**

Farley, Miss L S, BA MCLIP, Ret. [4763] 01/01/1971 **CM01/01/1974**

Farley, Mr M J, BSc MSc DipILS MCLIP, L. & Inf. Serv. Researcher, Freshfields Bruckhaus Deringer, London. [59170] 05/12/2000
CM19/11/2003

Farley, Ms S, BA(Hons) MCLIP, Study Centres Co-ordinator, Knowsley Comm. Coll., Knowsley. [55671] 07/11/1997 **CM01/02/2006**

Farmer, Mrs H L, BA(Hons) DipLIS MCLIP, Unwaged. [57621] 19/05/1999 **CM15/05/2002**

Farmer, Miss J K, Unwaged [47135] 06/05/1992 **ME**

Farmer, Miss M, MA DipLib MCLIP, Res. Bibliometrics Offr., Univ. of St. Andrews, Fife. [35694] 14/01/1983 **CM26/10/1985**

Farmer, Miss V G, MSc MA MCLIP, Asst. Lib., Robert Gordon Univ., Aberdeen. [59768] 01/10/2001 **CM21/03/2007**

Farncombe, Mrs J C, BA DipLib MCLIP TTAIT, Self employed Contract Lib., Researcher & Website Designer [36843] 11/01/1984
CM18/07/1990

Farndell, Mrs M, BA(Hons) MCLIP, Employment not known. [48933] 26/07/1993 **CM27/11/1996**

Farndon, Mrs A J, MCLIP, Retired [4770] 15/11/1965 **CM01/01/1970**

Farnham, Miss J M, BSc MCLIP, Academic Liaison Lib., Univ. of Bedfordshire [62479] 10/07/2003 **CM05/05/2010**

Farnley, Mrs S, Inf. Mgr., Rouse, London. [57673] 01/07/1999 **ME**

Farnsworth, Miss L A, Grad. Trainee, Trust L., Torbay Hosp., Torquay [10015688] 14/01/2010 **ME**

Farnworth, Mrs R, DBA MCLIP, Customer Serv. Mgr., Salford Mus. & Art Gallery [25526] 25/01/1976 **CM30/03/1979**

Farquhar, Mr J D, MCLIP, Retired. [4777] 21/09/1955 **CM01/01/1963**

Farquhar, Miss S C, MA DipLib, Tech. Serv. Mgr., Univ. of Aberdeen, Queen Mother L. [27966] 20/09/1977 **ME**

Farquharson, Mrs H, BA(Hons), Clinical Lib., Goodhope Hosp., Sutton Coldfield. [57159] 05/01/1999 **ME**

Farquharson, Miss V R, MA DipLib MCLIP, Community Lib., S. Lanarkshire Council. [31062] 01/08/1979 **CM14/10/1981**

Farr, Mr D J, BA(Hons) MCLIP, Asst. Lib., Staffs. C.C., Stafford, Staffs. [48764] 12/05/1993 **CM21/01/1998**

Farr, Miss E M J, BA MCLIP, Community Serv. Lib., Stirling Council. [4779] 08/05/1970 **CM15/01/1975**

Farr, Mrs H E, BA(Hons) MSc(Econ) MCLIP, Serv. Devel. Offr., Staffs C.C. [51179] 23/11/1994 **CM17/03/1999**

Farr, Miss J M, BA MCLIP, Asst. Lib., Aberdeen City. L., Scotland. [32721] 24/07/1980 **CM27/01/1984**

Farr, Mrs M F, BA DipLib, Local Stud. Lib., Surrey Hist. Cent., Woking. [33289] 16/11/1980 **ME**

Farr, Miss N, BA, Music Lib., Cardiff Cent. L. [10013451] 27/04/2009 **ME**

Farragher, Ms L E, Inf. Specialist, Health Res. Board, Ireland. [65589] 23/02/2006 **ME**

Farrall, Mrs L, BSc(Hons), L. Asst., Clinical Studies L., QEQM Hosp., Margate. [10000953] 30/11/2006 **ME**

Farrar, Mrs H M, BLS MCLIP, Principal l. Mgr., L.B. Ealing [27871] 04/10/1977 **CM03/07/1981**

Farrar, Mrs L, BA(Hons) MA MCLIP, L. &Archive Mgr., Nat. Met. L., Exeter. [49165] 08/10/1993 **CM20/11/2002**

Farrell, Ms C, L. & Collections Mgr., The Kennel Club, London. [10001209] 02/02/2007 **ME**

Farrell, Ms C, BA PgDip. LS, Lib., Inst. of Intern. Relations, Univ. of the W. Indies, Trinidad & Tobago. [10013488] 22/05/2009 **ME**

Farrell, Ms D L, Dep. Lib., Green Templeton Coll., Oxford. [64721] 03/06/2005 **ME**

Farrell, Mrs E J, BA(Hons) MCLIP, L. & Resources Mgr., Salford PCT. [27490] 01/04/1977 **CM15/09/1983**

Farrell, Mrs H E, BA MCLIP, Retired. [12024] 04/04/1967 **CM01/01/1972**

Farrell, Miss H P, BA(Hons) DipILS MCLIP, Lib., Oxfordshire C.C. [42786] 01/03/1989 **CM21/11/2001**

Farrell, Mrs P P, BA MCLIP, Ref. &Inf. Serv. Lib., Bury M.B.C., Lancs. [21838] 08/02/1974 **CM30/10/1978**

Farrelly, Ms C A, BA MCLIP, Sen. L. Asst., Chatsworth L., Lancs. C.C. [30833] 28/04/1979 **CM06/10/1982**

Farrelly, Ms J, MLIS, Unknown, Kerry General Hosp., Co Kerry, Ireland. [65833] 18/05/2006 **ME**

Farrimond, Mrs A E, BA(Hons) MCLIP, Operations Super., Worcs. C.C., Bibl. Serv. Unit. [26738] 07/11/1976 **CM28/06/1984**

Farrow, Mrs A E, BA MA MCLIP, Circ. Super., Univ. of Durham, Palace Green L. [28121] 04/10/1977 **CM18/02/1980**

Farrow, Mrs A J, MA BA MCLIP, Princ. Lect., Liverpool John Moores Univ., Business Sch. [741] 13/10/1970 **CM01/12/1974**

Farrow, Miss E C, BA(Hons) MA MCLIP, L. Devel./ICT Programme Offr., INASP, Oxford. [49849] 22/12/1993 **CM27/11/1996**

Farruggia, Ms J A, BA(Hons), Lib., Univ of Birmingham [10008009] 20/03/2008 **AF**

Farthing, Mrs A B, BA(Hons) MCLIP, Acquisitions Mgr., Cheshire C.C., Chester. [10001552] 02/01/1992 **CM25/01/1995**

Farthing, Mrs T, MA, Lib., The Royal Grammar Sch., Guildford. [10012911] 20/03/2009 **AF**

Fathers, Miss N, MA BA, Dep. L. Mgr., Berwin Leighton Paisner, London. [55637] 30/10/1997 **ME**

Faucher, Mrs E S, BA(Hons) BSc, Unknown. [10010979] 10/09/2008**AF**
Faughey, Mrs L C, MCLIP, Retired. [8923] 17/01/1962   **CM01/01/1965**
Faulds, Miss H, MA(Hons), Sen. Collections Supp Offr., St Andrews
  Univ. L. [10006361] 15/10/2007   **ME**
Faulknall-Mills, Ms J S, BLS MCLIP, Div. Lib., Atherstone L.
  Warwickshire. [39227] 01/01/1986   **CM21/07/1999**
Faulkner Gibson, Ms M, Asst. Lib., Univ. W. England. [65109]
  01/11/2005   **ME**
Faulkner, Ms K, BA(Hons) MSc MCLIP, Unknown. [54755] 01/04/1997
    CM17/01/2001
Faulkner, Mrs M, BA(Hons) MCLIP, Employment not known. [31608]
  09/11/1979   **CM10/09/1984**
Faulkner, Mr M, BA(Hons), Inf. Cent. Mgr., Financial Serv. Auth. London
  [51982] 30/08/1995   **ME**
Faulkner, Mrs S F, BA MCLIP, Learning Resources Mgr., London Met.
  Univ., London. [22235] 18/03/1974   **CM29/03/1976**
Faulkner, Ms S, BSc (Econ), Unknown. [10014743] 04/04/2003   **ME**
Faulkner, Mr T W A, MCLIP, Retired. [4799] 29/01/1948 **CM01/01/1950**
Faulks, Ms K M, MCLIP, Devel. Worker, Voluntary Action Leeds. [23515]
  21/11/1975   **CM29/12/1977**
Faux, Mrs J M, BSc(Hons) MSc MCLIP, Liaison Lib., Newman Coll.,
  Birmingham. [59233] 11/01/2001 **RV17/06/2009**   **CM01/06/2005**
Favell, Mrs V A, MA PGCE MCLIP, Res. Lib., Yth. Serv., Herts. C.C.
  [7509] 23/08/1969   **CM03/10/1972**
Fawcett, Mrs A B, BA MCLIP, Retired. [4802] 25/02/1959**CM01/01/1962**
Fawcett, Mrs C E, MA DipLib MCLIP, Sepcial Collections Lib., Univ. of
  Nottingham. [34326] 18/10/1981   **CM07/02/1985**
Fawcett, Mr D J, FInstPet DipTh MCLIP, Life Member. [4804]
  20/08/1948   **CM01/01/1951**
Fawcett, Mrs G M, BA MLS MCLIP, Business Specialist., Talis,
  Birmingham Business Park [29715] 01/10/1978   **CM20/01/1981**
Fawcett, Mrs H, MCLIP, Unemployed. [12047] 01/01/1970
    CM03/03/1977
Fawcett, Miss L A, Inf. Mgr., Entec UK Ltd., Newcastle upon Tyne.
  [56461] 16/07/1998   **ME**
Fazakerley, Miss M E, BA MCLIP, Life Member. [4808] 04/10/1945
    CM01/01/1948
Fazal, Mrs H M, BA PGCE MA MCLIP, Lib., High Sch. for Girls,
  Gloucester. [41537] 16/01/1988   **CM19/07/2000**
Fearn, Mrs S B, BA MCLIP, Sch. Lib., Eltham Coll., London. [20198]
  07/02/1973   **CM18/10/1977**
Feather, Prof J P, MA BLitt PhD FCLIP, Prof., Dept. of Inf. Sci.,
  Loughborough Univ. [22488] 20/04/1974   **FE14/03/1986**
Featherstone, Ms A W, MCLIP, Serv. Dev. Mngr., Young People,
  Families & Learning., Dunstable L, Beds. [4814] 01/10/1971
    CM11/09/1975
Featherstone, Mr J R, BA DipLib MCLIP, Legal Lib., Off. of the Dep.
  Prime Minister, London. [39918] 01/10/1986   **CM21/12/1988**
Featherstone, Mr T M, BA FCLIP, Life Member. [4815] 03/05/1949
    FE01/01/1961
Febry, Miss J H, BA(Hons) DipIS MCLIP, Careers Offr., Univ. of the Arts
  London, London. [51004] 08/11/1994   **CM23/07/1997**
Feeney, Mr A, BA(Hons) MSc, Lib., Airdrie L., Airdrie, Scotland
  [10001766] 22/02/2007   **ME**
Feest, Miss K A, BA (Honours), Lib., Congleton L., Cheshire CC.
  [10006338] 15/10/2007   **ME**
Feetham, Miss M G, BA DipLib MA FHEA MCLIP PGCHE, Digital Lib.
  Devel. Mgr., Southampton Solent Univ. [39072] 28/10/1985
    CM27/07/1994
Feetham, Mrs S E, Sch. Lib., The Duston Sch., Northants. [64464]
  31/03/2005   **ME**
Fei, Mrs M E, BA(Econ), Asst., Lib., Godolphin and Latymer Sch.
  London [10007000] 17/12/2007   **AF**
Feiler, Ms J, MSc, Unwaged. [65299] 14/12/2005   **ME**

Fell, Miss C, BA DipLib, Lib., Prison Serv. Coll., Rugby. [37160]
  16/02/1984   **ME**
Fell, Mrs R, BA(Hons) MCLIP, Asst. Lib., All Saints L., Manchester.
  [61963] 19/12/2002   **CM13/06/2007**
Fella, Mrs S P, Sen. L. Mgr., Epsom L., Surrey. [64650] 12/05/2005   **AF**
Fellerman, Miss J B, BA MCLIP, Principal Offr., L. & Inf. Cent., N. Yorks
  C.C. [28559] 27/12/1977   **CM17/05/1983**
Fellows, Miss C R, MCLIP, Community Lib., Quinton, Birmingham L. s.
  [23444] 01/01/1975   **CM13/07/1977**
Fellows, Miss S C, MCLIP, Unknown. [19930] 01/01/1973**CM01/01/1975**
Felstead, Ms A P, BA PG DipLib MCLIP, Head of Tech. Serv. Liaison,
  Bodleian L., Oxford Univ. [38730] 01/10/1985   **CM19/01/1988**
Feltham, Mrs S, BSc MA, Sch. L. Mngr Priory Sch., Portsmouth.
  [65437] 24/02/2006   **ME**
Feltham, Mrs V, MA MCLIP, Retired. [10010901] 25/01/1989
    CM26/05/1993
Felton, Miss A E, BA MA(Ed) MCLIP, Lib., Harris Academy Bermondsey
  [24943] 22/10/1975   **CM12/03/1980**
Fender-Brown, Ms A J, BA MCLIP FRSA, Mgr., Educ. Business Servi.,
  Middx. [4828] 22/10/1964   **CM01/01/1969**
Fenerty, Mrs V J, BSc(Hons) MA MCLIP, Academic Liason Lib., Univ. of
  Southampton. [43515] 06/11/1989 **RV28/01/2009**   **CM25/09/1996**
Fenn, Miss J M, BA DipLib MCLIP, Dep. Website Mgr., UK Trade &
  Investment, London. [38949] 23/10/1985   **CM15/11/1988**
Fenn, Miss K L, BA MA MCLIP, Libr., Bramley L., Leeds. [59395]
  28/02/2001   **CM21/10/2008**
Fenn, Mrs L E, BA MA, Reader Devel. Lib., Slough L., Berks. [65430]
  24/02/2006   **ME**
Fennell, Mr G R, BA(Hons) MA MCLIP, Unknown Full time Employment.
  [63964] 22/11/2004   **CM24/10/2008**
Fensome, Ms S M, LLB(Hons) MA MCLIP, Academic Liaison Lib, Univ
  of Bedfordshire, Beds [49586] 19/11/1993   **CM20/05/1998**
Fenton, Mrs A M, Unknown. [10000892] 22/11/2006   **AF**
Fenton, Mrs D E, BA MCLIP, Employed – not in L. & information
  environment [33157] 10/10/1980   **CM05/12/1985**
Fenton, Mrs L, BA MCLIP, Sch. L. Serv. Mgr., Lancs. C.C., Sch. L.
  Serv., Preston. [22426] 29/04/1974   **CM01/08/1976**
Fereday, Miss H J, BA MCLIP, Project Offr. LB of Waltham Forest
  [33218] 16/10/1980   **CM23/11/1982**
Ferguson, Miss C M, MA MCLIP, Unit Leader, Reader Serv., Dundee
  City Council. [28429] 29/11/1977   **CM17/11/1980**
Ferguson, Mrs G M, Stud., The Robert Gordon Univ. [10016449]
  24/03/2010   **ME**
Ferguson, Mr J B, MBE MA FCLIP, Retired. [4850] 10/09/1937
    FE01/01/1949
Ferguson, Miss J M, MCLIP, Retired. [4851] 11/10/1966 **CM01/01/1970**
Ferguson, Mrs K M, BA MCLIP, Retired. [7714] 02/10/1969
    CM16/09/1975
Ferguson, Mrs L J, MA DipLib MCLIP, Unemployed. [35901]
  11/02/1983   **CM06/10/1987**
Ferguson, Mrs L S, MA FCLIP, Dep. Dir. of Health L. NW, NW Health
  Care L. Unit, Wigan. [31643] 25/10/1979   **FE09/09/2009**
Ferguson, Mrs M M, MA MCLIP, Team Leader, Adult L. Serv., Western
  Isles L. [9572] 22/10/1969   **CM01/09/1972**
Ferguson, Mrs M, BLib MCLIP, Sen. Lib., Culture Devel., Lisburn City L.
  [46928] 28/02/1992   **CM26/11/1997**
Ferguson, Miss R A, BA(Hons) MCLIP, Aquisitions & Serials TL, Univ.
  of Salford. [52393] 31/10/1995   **CM15/03/2000**
Ferguson, Mrs S R, MA DipLib MCLIP, Media Specialist, U. S. A.
  [38967] 22/10/1985   **CM06/09/1988**
Ferguson, Mrs S, BA MCLIP, L. & Inf. Offr., Dundee Dist. Council.
  [33130] 01/10/1980   **CM18/07/1983**
Ferguson, Mrs V A, BA FCLIP, Retired. [4862] 03/10/1957
    FE20/12/1976

Fergusson, Mrs A D, MA MCLIP, Comm. Lib., E. Dunbartonshire Council, Kirkintilloch. [21327] 15/10/1973　**CM01/08/1976**
Fergusson-Rees, Mrs L, BA(Hons), Stud. [10006241] 26/09/2007　**ME**
Fernandes, Mr D C, MCLIP, Enquiries & E-Delivery Team Leader. [22025] 21/02/1974　**CM01/01/1976**
Fernandez, Mrs J C, BA MA MCLIP, Unknown. [38244] 04/02/1985　**CM18/07/1991**
Fernandez, Mr N, BA, Stud., City Univ. [10011049] 18/09/2008　**ME**
Fernando, Mrs A, BSc(Hons) MCLIP, Lib., Dep. for Work and Pensions, London. [46645] 02/12/1991　**CM09/11/2005**
Ferrabee, Mrs J A G, BA, Lib., Surbiton High Sch., Kingston, Surrey. [37698] 17/10/1984　**ME**
Ferramosca, Miss B, MSc, Lib. Mgr., Lilian Baylis Tech. Sch., London. [10001666] 06/03/2007　**ME**
Ferrand, Ms H C, MA(Hons) MCLIP, Retired. [58494] 01/01/1958　**CM01/01/1961**
Ferrar, Mrs L, DipEdTech MCLIP, Child. & Young peoples Lib., Child. & Young peoples L. Serv., E. Dunbartonshire. [22005] 11/01/1974　**CM01/10/1977**
Ferreira, Miss L, MA, Reading Devel. Lib., Richmond L. [10005489] 26/07/2007　**ME**
Ferri, Miss V L, MSc, Asst. Lib., Stockport NHS Foundation Trust [10007026] 07/01/2008　**ME**
Ferris, Miss J A, MA DipLIS MCLIP, Res. Lib. Allen & Overy, London. [54018] 18/10/1996　**CM10/07/2002**
Ferris, Mrs M, BA MCLIP, Asst. Lib. (Job Share), Halesowen L., Dudley M.B.C. [4869] 13/09/1965　**CM01/01/1968**
Fevyer, Mrs J C, BA(Hons), Info. Co-ordinator, Graduate Employment Serv., Bournemouth Univ. [58927] 05/10/2000　**ME**
Fiander, Mrs W, BSc MA MCLIP, Dep. Dir. of Learning & Inf. Serv., Univ. of Chester [28394] 20/11/1977　**CM24/07/1980**
Ficken, Miss E J, BSc(Hons) DipILS MCLIP, Lib., Astor Coll. for the Arts, Dover. [48211] 16/11/1992　**CM24/05/1995**
Fiddes, Mr A J C, BSc(Hons) PhD, Inf. Asst., Sheffield Health & Socilal Care NHS Foundation Trust. [53444] 01/07/1996　**ME**
Fidegul, Ms J, BA ACLIP, Sen. L. Asst., Tooting L., London. [65229] 16/11/2005　**ACL29/03/2007**
Fidell, Mrs S, BA(Hons) English, Operational Support Asst., Malton Lib., N. Yorkshire [10012989] 23/03/2009　**AF**
Field, Mr B, FCLIP, Life Member. [4878] 21/10/1940　**FE01/01/1956**
Field, Mr C R, FAMS MIMgt FCLIP, Retired. [4881] 12/02/1959　**FE01/01/1965**
Field, Mrs C, BA(Hons) MA MCLIP, Asst. Lib., English Heritage, Swindon. [49332] 22/10/1993　**CM22/07/1998**
Field, Mrs J, BA(Hons) MCLIP, Res. Lib., Univ. of Wolverhampton. [59038] 31/10/2000　**CM21/06/2006**
Field, Mrs K L, BA(Hons) DipIM MCLIP, Learning Lab. Mgr., Nat. Leadership & Innovation Agency for Healthcare, Bridgend. [49260] 19/10/1993　**CM20/01/1999**
Field, Mr P M, BA, Sen. L. Asst., Sch. of Pharmacy, Univ. of London. [10007597] 21/02/2008　**ME**
Field, Mr S A, Sen. L. Asst., Staff L., Milton Keynes Gen. Hosp., Bucks. [10003175] 18/05/2007　**AF**
Field, Mrs S K, BA(Hons) MA MCLIP, Trainer, Sirsidynix, Melbourne, Victoria, Australia. [55861] 04/12/1997　**CM01/06/2005**
Field, Ms S L, BA(Hons) MCLIP, Academic Liason Lib., Westminster Univ. London. [56055] 28/01/1998　**CM29/11/2006**
Field, Mr T J, BSc MCLIP MISTC, Employment not known. [60610] 23/03/1983　**CM15/05/1990**
Field, Ms W E, BA MCLIP, Lib., William Booth Coll., London. [37700] 11/10/1984　**CM18/07/1990**
Field, Mrs W M, BA MCLIP, Life Member. [4884] 02/07/1953　**CM01/01/1960**
Fielder, Mrs E M, MCLIP, Retired. [4888] 12/03/1938　**CM01/01/1940**

Fielding, Mrs C S, BSc(Hons) MA, L. Asst. [63298] 08/04/2004　**ME**
Fielding, Mr D J, BSc(Hons) PGDip, Asst. Lib., Soc. Inclusion, Bury Met. L. Bury. [57469] 29/03/1999　**ME**
Fielding, Mrs M H L, BA(Hons) DipILM MCLIP, Career Break. [47768] 14/10/1992　**CM31/01/1996**
Fielding, Ms V K, BA(Hons) MCLIP, Resident in Germany. [44685] 26/11/1990　**CM19/03/1997**
Fieldsend, Mrs V C, BA MCLIP, Retired. [4893] 11/01/1956　**CM13/04/1962**
Figes, Mrs H M, Lib., St. Leonards-Mayfield Sch., Mayfield, Sussex. [10005234] 02/08/2007　**ME**
Fileman, Mrs J, BA FCLIP, L. Team Mgr., Brit. Geological Survey, Nottingham. [26394] 10/10/1976　**FE09/07/2008**
Filer, Mr R B, BA MCLIP, Lib., Thornbury L., S. Glos. [4896] 14/03/1971　**CM27/03/1973**
Files, Mr R B, MA MCLIP, Retired. [4898] 10/03/1966　**CM01/01/1970**
Finch, Miss A M, BA(Hons) MSc(Econ) MCLIP, Learning Mgr., Brent L. s., L.B. Brent. [52053] 02/10/1995　**CM22/07/1998**
Finch, Mr J R, BA(Hons) MSc(Econ) MCLIP, Unknown. [54537] 20/01/1997　**CM21/03/2001**
Finch, Mrs J, BA Hons PGCE, Open Learning Cent. Mgr., Valley Park Community Sch., Maidstone [10005585] 25/07/2007　**ME**
Finch, Mr R J A, MA DipLib MCLIP, Head of Academic L. Serv. Univ. of Derby [21422] 22/10/1973　**CM18/11/1975**
Finch, Mr S K W, BA MCLIP, Sen. Lib., Local Studies, Bromley Cent. L. [29650] 19/10/1978　**CM30/11/1984**
Finch, Mr T W, MCLIP, Retired. [4905] 23/01/1966　**CM01/01/1970**
Findlater, Mrs K L, BA(Hons), Lib., Brit Sch., Croydon [10007198] 23/01/2008　**ME**
Findlay, Miss D H, BA(Hons) MCLIP, Dep. Head of L. Serv., Univ. Coll., Birmingham. [56219] 07/04/1998　**CM08/12/2004**
Findlay, Miss J, BSc PGDip MCLIP, Asst. Lib., Semple Fraser, Edinburgh. [60944] 14/01/2002　**CM19/03/2008**
Findlay, Mrs J, BA MCLIP, Learning Res. Cent. Mgr., All Saints Academy, Dunstable. [18093] 01/10/1972　**CM18/10/1976**
Findlay, Ms M, CertEd MA MCLIP, H. of Learning Resources, Lambeth Coll., London. [18681] 26/01/1968　**CM01/01/1971**
Findlay, Mr S R P, BA MCLIP, L. Serv. Offr., NHS Forth Valley [29651] 05/10/1978　**CM01/07/1992**
Findlay, Mrs S, BA(Hons) MCLIP, Community Inf. Offr., Harrogate L. & Inf. Cent. [10008003] 14/10/1985　**CM24/04/1991**
Fineberg, Mr J H, BA(Hons) MSc, Info. Offr., Linklaters, London. [62528] 05/08/2003　**ME**
Finlay, Mrs D, L. Super., Glenwood High Sch., Fife. [63811] 01/10/2004　**ME**
Finlay, Mrs E, BA(Hons) DipLib MCLIP, Cent. & Inf. Lib., Renfrewshire Council. [38675] 19/09/1985　**CM14/02/1990**
Finlay, Mr G, BSc Msc FRSC, L. Asst., Hatfield L. [10016009] 10/02/2010　**AF**
Finlayson, Ms D M, MA MCLIP, Lib., Brit. Coll. of Osteopathic Medicine, London. [21324] 13/10/1973　**CM21/07/1976**
Finlayson, Dr G, PhD, Dir. John Mackintosh Hall, Gibraltar [10011552] 01/07/1997　**ME**
Finn, Ms N, BA(Hons) DipIS MCLIP, Head of Info. & Local Studies, E. Sussex Co. Council, E. Sussex [10001514] 19/10/1992　**CM21/01/1998**
Finn, Miss S L, BA, Stud. Univ. of Southampton [10015030] 07/10/2009　**ME**
Finnett, Ms C E A, BLIB MCLIP, Mgr. Mob. and Home L. Serv., L.B. Barnet. [30162] 27/12/1978　**CM14/10/1982**
Finney, Miss P, ACLIP, L. Asst., Anglia Ruskin Univ. [64973] 05/10/2005　**ACL17/06/2009**
Finnis, Miss M L, FCLIP, Retired. [4919] 11/03/1929　**FE01/01/1933**

Firby, Miss N K, BA M Phil FCLIP, Retired. [4920] 12/03/1935
FE01/01/1946

Firebrace, Ms C, Inf. Offr., London. [55401] 09/10/1997   **ME**

Firth, Miss A, BA(Hons) MSc, Internal Communications Offr., Nat. Child. Bureau, London. [59804] 03/10/2001   **ME**

Firth, Mrs F J, MA(Hons), Stud., Aberystwyth. [63355] 20/04/2004 **ME**

Firth, Mr G W, BA MCLIP, Inf. Consultant, Royal Holloway & Bedford New Coll., Egham. [4924] 22/09/1966   **CM01/01/1969**

Firth, Mrs J C, BAEd MSc MCLIP, Community Lib., Abertridwr L., Caerphilly. [63968] 22/11/2004   **CM17/09/2008**

Firth, Mr T C, DipLib MCLIP, Ref. & Inf. Mgr., Hants. L. & Inf. Serv. [34064] 08/09/1981   **CM28/07/1983**

Fishburn, Mrs R K, MCLIP, Database Mgr., Harrow P. L. [14047] 09/11/1970   **CM05/11/1973**

Fisher, Ms B M, MLib FCLIP, Life Member. [4938] 11/07/1971
FE17/11/1999

Fisher, Miss C M, MA(Hons) DipILS, Customer Serv. Mgr., Univ. of Glasgow L. [58812] 07/08/2000   **ME**

Fisher, Ms C R, BA(Hons), Trust Lib., City Hosp. Sunderland, Sunderland Royal Hosp. [38302] 11/03/1985   **ME**

Fisher, Mrs D C, MA DipLib MCLIP, Self-employed. [29633] 10/10/1978
CM12/02/1981

Fisher, Mrs D J G, BA MCLIP, Online Resources Coordinator., Royal Coll. of Nursing, London [24485] 01/10/1975   **CM14/02/1978**

Fisher, Miss E J, Lib., S. Gloucestershire L. [65213] 18/11/2005 **ME**

Fisher, Mrs E R K, DipLib MCLIP, Mgr., L. & Inf. Serv., Rotherham. [31470] 26/09/1979   **CM11/05/1985**

Fisher, Mrs E, MCLIP, Lib. :Learning Res. Mgr., Truro Coll. (Tertiary), Cornwall. [15169] 02/10/1971   **CM01/09/1974**

Fisher, Mrs H L, Info. & Resource Offr. - CRIS, Belfast Health and Social Care Trust. [65692] 30/03/2006   **AF**

Fisher, Mrs H S, MCLIP, Retired [33771] 18/03/1961   **CM01/01/1965**

Fisher, Miss J K, L. Asst., Nottingham Cent. L. [10009950] 24/06/2008
AF

Fisher, Miss J W, BSc MCLIP, Retired. [21250] 08/10/1973
CM08/10/1975

Fisher, Mrs K J, BA MSc, Academic Lib., Leeds Met. Univ., Leeds [10016645] 25/11/1998   **ME**

Fisher, Miss L J, MA MCLIP, Inf. Cent. Mgr., Competition Commission, London. [31277] 08/10/1979   **CM15/12/1981**

Fisher, Mrs M J, MCLIP, Head of L. Serv., Hadlow Coll., Tonbridge. [21097] 02/10/1973   **CM01/09/1976**

Fisher, Mr P D, BA(Hons) MSc, Cent. L., Bexley Heath, Kent [10001827] 08/03/2007   **ME**

Fisher, Mr R K, M LITT MA FCLIP, Retired. [4950] 02/01/1961
FE16/07/1986

Fisher, Miss R M, BA MCLIP, Life Member. [4951] 24/06/1948
CM01/01/1953

Fisher, Ms S G, BA(Hons), Grad. Trainee Lib., Christ's Coll. L., Cambridge [10013086] 24/03/2009   **ME**

Fisher, Mrs S, BA(Hons) MA MCLIP, Info Specialist, Gloucestershire [61627] 04/10/2002   **CM29/03/2006**

Fisher, Mr W E, BA MEd DipLib MCLIP, Lect., Chiba Inst. of Tech., Japan. [29187] 03/04/1978   **CM17/04/1980**

Fishleigh, Miss J F, BA MA MCLIP, Lib., Payne, Hicks, Beach, London. [40966] 01/10/1987   **CM22/03/1995**

Fishwick, Mrs H P, BA(Hons) MCLIP, Learning Cent. Co-ord., The Manchester Coll. [20037] 16/01/1973   **CM01/11/1975**

Fitch, Mr A C, MCLIP, Enquiries Offr., Colchester Cent. L., Essex C.C. [4956] 21/11/1970   **CM20/08/1974**

Fitches, Ms J G, BA(Hons) MA MCLIP, Sen. Inf. Offr., Inf. Serv., Gtr. London Auth. [23913] 20/02/1975   **CM13/04/1977**

Fitt, Mrs C A, BA MCLIP, Freelance consultant [25541] 25/01/1976
CM01/08/1979

Fittall, Miss P S, MA DipLib MCLIP, Records Administrator, Norman Disney & Young, Australia. [27672] 08/07/1977   **CM18/07/1980**

Fitter, Miss M, BSc MA, System Consultant, ExLibris UK Ltd., Harefield. [57168] 07/01/1999   **ME**

Fitzgerald, Ms D L, BA(Hons) MA MCLIP, Serials & resources Lib., Univ. of Kent [62033] 28/01/2003   **CM21/08/2009**

Fitzgerald, Mrs M T, B LIB MCLIP, New Asst., Moberley L., Winchester Coll. [24152] 10/03/1975   **CM23/07/1980**

Fitzgerald, Mr P, BA(Hons) MA MCLIP, Inf. Specialist. [50231] 11/05/1994   **CM16/07/2003**

Fitzgerald, Miss S M D, BA(Hons) FLS MCLIP, Retired. [4963] 12/08/1958   **CM01/01/1962**

Fitzgerald, Mr S, Vice President, LSSI UK Ltd Liverpool [10011263] 14/05/2010   **AF**

Fitzmaurice, Mrs A M, BA MCLIP, Head of L. R. C., St. Marks Sch., Hounslow. [31308] 01/10/1979   **CM21/10/1982**

Fitzpatrick, Mrs G M, BA MCLIP, Retired [2989] 20/01/1972
CM01/01/1976

Fitzsimons, Mr J, MA MSSC MCLIP, Sub-Lib. (Eng.), Univ. of Ulster, Jordanstown. [22410] 30/04/1974   **CM16/08/1977**

Fitzsimons, Miss K M, BA(Hons), Inf. Offr., Univ. of Liverpool. [51353] 25/01/1995   **ME**

Fitzsimons, Miss M, Head of Res., Houses of the Oireachtas, Dublin. [63422] 07/05/2004   **ME**

Flagner, Ms K E, BA, Sen. Lib., Cumbria CC. [45882] 08/07/1991 **ME**

Flain, Mrs R M, p. /t. Consultant Lib. /Inf. Sci., Envirotox-Internat., Stevenage. [51278] 16/12/1994   **ME**

Flanagan, Mr C J, BA(Hons), DIP CG, Univ. Coll. London. [10015983] 01/02/2010   **ME**

Flanagan, Mrs K D, BA(Hons) MA MCLIP, Dep. Coll. Lib., Eton Coll. [60004] 21/11/2001   **CM11/03/2009**

Fleet, Mrs C J, BA(Hons) MCLIP, Career Break. [49187] 11/10/1993
CM24/07/1996

Fleet, Mr C, BA, Stud., [59364] 22/02/2001   **ME**

Fleet, Mrs D, Lib. Mgr., Middlesbrough Bor. Council. [40303] 20/01/1987
ME

Fleetwood, Mr R, BA FCLIP, Retired. [4981] 06/10/1959 **FE01/01/1966**

Fleetwood, Miss S F, BA, Stud. [10008563] 01/04/2008   **ME**

Fleming, Ms C A, BSc(Hons) DipLib FHEA MCLIP, Project Offr.,Edina, Warrington Off. [38159] 15/01/1985   **CM12/03/2003**

Fleming, Mrs J L, BA(Hons) PgDipILS MCLIP, Learning Ctr. Co-ordinator, Exeter Coll. [10000757] 15/11/1996   **CM19/03/2008**

Fleming, Mrs K E L, BA(Hons) MCLIP, Inf. Professional, Self-Employed. [54614] 04/02/1997   **CM15/11/2000**

Fleming, Miss K E, BSc PgDip, Child. & Young People's Lib., Milton Keynes Cent. L., Milton Keynes. [10013747] 27/05/2009   **ME**

Fleming, Miss L C, BSc(Hons) MSc, Resources Adviser, City Coll. Norwich. [57106] 14/12/1998   **ME**

Fleming, Miss L J, DipIM MCLIP, Lib., London Underground [56021] 28/01/1998   **CM21/05/2003**

Fleming, Mrs R, BA MCLIP, Lib., Sch. L. Serv., Herefordshire Council. [4988] 21/09/1964   **CM01/01/1968**

Fleming, Mr W, BA MCLIP, Retired [4995] 29/10/1969   **CM14/01/1974**

Flemming, Miss K, MCLIP, Inf. Lib., Univ. of Bath [10007119] 18/01/2008   **CM07/07/2010**

Flerlage, Miss E, MA, L. Asst., Learning Resources Cent., Kingston Coll., surrey. [10015524] 09/12/2009   **AF**

Fletcher, Mr A, BA, Unwaged. [41999] 13/07/1988   **ME**

Fletcher, Miss B J, BA DipLib MCLIP, Inf. Consultant [34460] 04/11/1981   **CM19/09/1989**

Fletcher, Mrs C, Lib., Patchway & Filton L., S. Glos. Council. [62616] 18/09/2003   **ME**

Fletcher, Mrs E G, MA MSc MCLIP, Retired. [18688] 02/04/1963
CM21/02/1973

Fletcher, Mrs H A, BA AKC DipLib MCLIP, Sch. Lib., Bishop's Stortford High Sch., Herts. [35773] 20/01/1983   **CM05/04/1988**

Fletcher, Mr J W, BA MA MA MA MCLIP, Liaison Lib., Nottingham Trent Univ. [65909] 04/07/2006   **CM06/05/2009**

Fletcher, Miss K M, Graduate L. Trainee, Univ. Cent. Cesar Ritz, Switzerland. [10015759] 22/01/2010   **ME**

Fletcher, Ms M A, MA MIL MCLIP, Br. Lib., N. Harrow L., L.B. Harrow. [5005] 25/10/1964   **CM01/01/1968**

Fletcher, Dr M, PhD, Cambridge Theological Fed., Cambridge. [65731] 06/04/2006   **AF**

Fletcher, Mr P J, BA(Hons) DipILM MCLIP, Wodehouse Lib. Dulwich Coll [47770] 14/10/1992   **CM24/09/1997**

Fletcher, Miss S J, BA, Unknown. [10015016] 06/10/2009   **ME**

Fletcher, Miss S K, BA MA MCLIP, Asst. Lib., Guille-Alles L., Guernsey, C. I. [44875] 04/01/1991   **CM27/05/1992**

Fletcher, Ms S M, MA MCLIP, Processing S. Mgr., Brit. L., London [18692] 07/09/1969   **CM21/09/1972**

Fletcher, Ms S, MA MCLIP, Inf. Off. [10000431] 10/10/2006   **CM06/05/2009**

Fletcher, Mr T H, BA MCLIP, L. Systems Mgr., Birkbeck Coll, Univ. of London. [23484] 01/01/1975   **CM30/10/1978**

Fletcher, Miss V C, BA MCLIP, Retired. [5008] 16/10/1969   **CM15/06/1973**

Flett, Mrs E D, BSc MCLIP, Retired. [5010] 10/03/1966   **CM01/01/1968**

Flett, Mr J R W, BSc, Sen. L. Asst., Bristol Cent. L., Bristol. [10014826] 18/09/2009   **AF**

Flint, Mrs A M, BSc(Hons) MA, Asst. Lib., MOD [63016] 15/12/2003 **ME**

Flint, Mrs L K, BSc(Hons) MCLIP, Asst. Lib., Univ. Coll. London, DMS Watson Sci. L. [51100] 15/11/1994   **CM21/11/2001**

Flintham, Mrs C H G, MCLIP Hon BA, Unknown. [10921] 08/01/1964   **CM01/01/1967**

Flintoff, Mrs H F, MSc MCLIP, Dep. Learning Res. Cent. Mgr., Brockenhurst Coll., Hants. [58706] 09/06/2000   **CM13/06/2007**

Flitney, Mrs C, BSc DipInfSc MCLIP, Customer Serv. Super., Essex C.C., Saffron Walden. [31547] 20/10/1979   **CM03/12/1981**

Flitton, Mrs H J, MA, Partnerships & Project Supp. Offr. [48893] 12/07/1993   **ME**

Floate, Rev R C, BA DipLib DipThSt MCLIP, Priest-in-charge, Wool and E. Stoke, Diocese of Salisbury [34214] 08/10/1981   **CM23/06/1986**

Flood, Mrs D, BA(Hons) DMS MCLIP, Unemployed. [34597] 07/01/1982
CM08/03/1988

Flor, Mrs P A I, MCLIP, Sen. Lib., Telemark Univ. Coll., Skien, Norway. [5023] 20/09/1967   **CM01/01/1970**

Florence, Miss J, BA MCLIP, Network Lib., Aberdeenshire Council, Inverurie Academy. [39433] 26/01/1986   **CM19/06/1991**

Florey, Mr C C, ALAA FCLIP, Life Member. [16888] 30/10/1948 **FE01/01/1957**

Flory, Mrs C C, ACLIP, L. Asst., Loch Leven Community L., Kinross. [10000512] 16/10/2006   **ACL05/10/2007**

Flower, Ms C S, BA(Hons), Lib., Gensler, London. [47805] 19/10/1992 **ME**

Flower, Mr L, DipHE, Lib., Swindon Cent. Lib., Swindon. [10017159] 11/07/2010   **ME**

Flowers, Miss G M, MCLIP, Retired. Lifeline Vol. (Family Reading) [5026] 31/01/1970   **CM19/12/1972**

Floyd, Ms E K, MA MCLIP, Lib., Paul Mellon Cent. for Stud. in Brit. Art, London. [44408] 05/10/1990   **CM17/11/1999**

Floyd, Mrs H A, BA DipLib MCLIP, Asst. L. Cust. Serv. Mgr., Chipping Barnet Lib., L.B. of Barnet. [27673] 04/07/1977   **CM18/02/1980**

Floyd, Mrs S, BA(Hons) DTLLS, Inf. Store Mgr., City Coll. Norwich. [10015922] 25/01/2010   **ME**

Flude, Mrs E M, MCLIP, Retired. [5028] 17/03/1944   **CM01/01/1955**

Flynn, Ms C M, MA DipLib, Broadcast Media Coordinator, B. B. C., Brentford. [34652] 25/01/1982   **ME**

Flynn, Mr J M, BA MCLIP, Head of Access, V&A, London. [28739] 24/01/1978   **CM28/11/1980**

Flynn, Mrs J, Sen. Sch. Lib., Hall Cross Sch., Doncaster [10001688] 22/03/2007   **AF**

Flynn, Miss J, BA MSc MCLIP, Unknown. [44592] 01/11/1990   **CM14/09/1994**

Flynn, Miss L C, BA, Unknown. [10015395] 27/01/2010   **ME**

Flynn, Ms P A, BA MCLIP, Area Lib., Argyl & Bute L. Serv., Dunoon Br. L. [29961] 07/11/1978   **CM30/06/1983**

Foazdar, Mr M S, MLIS BLIS, Unknown. [10014938] 28/09/2009   **ME**

Foden, Mrs H, BA(Hons), Info. Offr., Hammonds, Manchester [10008389] 19/03/2008   **AF**

Foden, Miss S, BA(Hons), Inf. Mgr., Cadbury UK, Birmingham. [40338] 20/01/1987   **ME**

Foden-Lenahan, Ms E L, BA(Hons) MA MCLIP, Book Lib., Courtauld Inst. of Art, London. [55307] 24/09/1997   **CM02/02/2005**

Fodey, Mr W J, MA DipLib MCLIP, Lib., Glasgow Caledonian Univ. [43580] 09/11/1989   **CM26/02/1992**

Foe, Mr L S, BA(Hons) DipLib, Learning Support Lib., Paddington L., Westminster City Council. [46266] 21/10/1991   **ME**

Fogden, Mrs F M, MA DipLib, Nat. Inf. Serv. Mgr., Baker Tilly, Bromley. [49099] 01/10/1993   **ME**

Fogg, Ms H S, BA, MA, Dir. of L. & Inf. Serv., BPP Coll., London. [55333] 01/10/1997   **ME**

Fogg, Mr N J, DRSAM BA, L. Asst., The Soc. of Genealogists, London. [40791] 15/06/1987   **ME**

Foggo, Ms L, BD (Hons) MSc MCLIP, Academic Liaison Lib., Univ. of York. [10009800] 03/12/1999   **CM01/02/2006**

Fojut, Mr L, MA(Hons), PgDIP, Stud. [66141] 02/10/2006   **ME**

Foley, Miss C R, BA, Admin. Asst., IUCN, Cambridge [10014441] 31/07/2009   **AF**

Foley, Ms J, BA Hons DipLib, Lib., Foster Wheeler Energy Ltd., Reading. [10007172] 28/10/2009   **ME**

Foley, Mr M, MA BEd MSc DipLib MCLIP, Catr. [35008] 15/06/1982   **CM20/12/1986**

Foley, Mr R N, MCLIP, Knowledge Serv. Offr., W. Cheshire PCT., Chester. [10001144] 29/10/1993   **CM01/02/2006**

Folkes, Mrs R, BSc(Hons) MSc(Econ) MCLIP, NVQ Assessor/Trainer, The Manchester Coll. [53868] 07/10/1996   **CM25/07/2001**

Follett, Sir B K, HonFLA, Chairman/Chair, Arts & Humanities Res. Board, Strategy Grp. on Res. L's. [54736] 19/03/1997 **HFE19/03/1997**

Folorunso, Ms I, BSc MCLIP, L. Offr., CIty of Edinburgh Council. [57200] 14/01/1999   **CM29/03/2006**

Fomo, Mrs A E G, MCLIP, Life Member. [16893] 20/03/1961   **CM01/01/1964**

Fone, Mrs C H, MA MCLIP, Knowledge&Lib. Serv. Mgr., Bassetlaw Dist. Gen. Hosp., Worksop. [30081] 29/11/1978   **CM23/04/1982**

Fong, Ms R Y Y, BLib MA, Inf. Adv., London S. Bank Univ., London. [10013810] 24/04/1990   **ME**

Font, Mrs J A, BA(Hons) DipILM MCLIP, Wknd Site Mgr., Leeds Univ. L. [50685] 10/10/1994   **CM22/09/1999**

Foo, Mr K W, BA MCLIP, Life Member. [16894] 12/03/1962   **CM01/01/1966**

Foot, Mr J, MCLIP, L. Mgr., Bodmin L., Cornwall. [64338] 07/03/2005   **CM11/06/2010**

Foote, Mrs L, MCLIP, L. Mgr., Yeovil Dist. hosp. NHS Foundation Trust., Yeovil [8707] 21/11/1969   **CM30/03/1973**

Footitt, Mrs A C, BSc MSc MCLIP, Unwaged. [41271] 23/10/1987   **CM24/05/1995**

Foran, Mr J J, BA MA DipLib, Lib., Inst. of Tech., Sligo, Ireland. [36675] 13/10/1983   **ME**

Forbes, Mr G S, BA MA MBA MCLIP, Head of Aquisition & Description, Nat. L. Scotland. [30906] 13/05/1979 **CM20/05/1981**

Forbes, Ms W E, Bsc. Dip LIB, MCLIP, Unemployed. [10015914] 22/10/1984 **CM01/07/1991**

Ford, Ms A M, BLib MCLIP, Inf. Mgr., Careers Advisory Serv., Aberystwyth Univ. [32518] 29/04/1980 **CM27/09/1982**

Ford, Ms A, BA DipLib MCLIP, Lib., Canterbury Christ Church Univ., Kent. [40828] 03/07/1987 **CM21/07/1989**

Ford, Mrs A, Stud. [10006301] 10/10/2007 **ME**

Ford, Mrs C E M, MA Dip Lib MCLIP, Unknown. [40907] 11/08/1987 **CM29/01/1992**

Ford, Ms H E, BA(Hons), Currently not working. [62523] 05/08/2003 **ME**

Ford, Mr J P, BA MCLIP, Learning Support Lib., Westminster City Council. [5045] 07/10/1970 **CM01/12/1972**

Ford, Miss J R, BSc MA, Inf. Exec:LIS Web Serv., ICAEW, London. [65024] 12/10/2005 **ME**

Ford, Mrs K M, MA DipLib MCLIP, Retired. [5047] 16/10/1967 **CM26/01/1984**

Ford, Mr M G, MSc BSc MCLIP, Retired. [5049] 14/01/1965 **CM01/01/1967**

Ford, Mr N, BSc (Econ) MCLIP, Subject Lib., Bournemouth Univ. [62368] 12/05/2003 **CM06/05/2009**

Ford, Miss S M, BA(Hons) MCLIP, Lib., St. Helens & Knowsley Hosp. Trust, Whiston, Merseyside. [46644] 02/12/1991 **CM01/06/2005**

Forde, Mrs J R, BA PGCE MCLIP, Retired. [5060] 01/01/1965 **CM01/01/1968**

Forde, Miss L L, BA DipLib MCLIP, Head Lib., Cardonald Coll., Glasgow. [43478] 27/10/1989 **CM19/08/1992**

Forder Blakeman, Mr K, BA MCLIP, Life Member. [1373] 01/01/1953 **CM01/01/1962**

Ford-Smith, Ms A M, BA(Hons) MA MCLIP, Principal Lib., Dr. William's Lib., London. [56939] 09/11/1998 **CM15/09/2004**

Fordyce, Mr D W, BSc MSc, Head of Membership and Info. Serv., Brewing Res. Internat., Nutfield. [56083] 13/02/1998 **ME**

Foreman, Mr C, Collections Devel. Mgr., Roehampton Univ. L., London. [10001099] 12/01/2007 **AF**

Foreman, Ms J M, MA DipLib, Inf. Literacy Lib., Scottish Gov. Inf. Serv., Edinburgh. [37781] 17/10/1984 **ME**

Foreman, Mrs L R, MA(Hons) MLib MCLIP, Relocated to Switzerland. [49273] 20/10/1993 **CM22/01/1997**

Foreman, Dr R L E, PhD MLib FCLIP HonFTCL, Retired. [5065] 01/01/1961 **FE13/06/1972**

Foreman, Mrs S E, MA MCLIP, Retired. [12902] 09/09/1964 **CM01/01/1968**

Forrai, Mr D, Asst. to Mngr. Business Info., John Lewis Partnership, London [10015650] 12/01/2010 **AF**

Forrest, Mrs A J, BA DipLib MCLIP, Sch. Lib. - Independant [10001722] 26/10/1993 **CM22/05/1996**

Forrest, Mrs A Y, BA MCLIP, Sutherland Area L. Offr., Highland Reg. L. Serv. [30842] 20/05/1979 **CM04/11/1982**

Forrest, Mr A, BA(Hons), Info. Offr., Univ. of Stirling, Stirling. [65708] 28/03/2006 **ME**

Forrest, Ms E L, BA MCLIP, L. Offr., Edinburgh Cent. L., Edinburgh. [41028] 05/10/1987 **CM12/09/1990**

Forrest, Miss L B, p. /t. Sch. L. [10000833] 09/11/2006 **ME**

Forrest, Mrs M E M, MA MCLIP, Inf. Offr., ISSTI, Edinburgh. [5071] 02/10/1971 **CM01/04/1974**

Forrest, Mrs M E S, MA MSc DipLib FCLIP FSA Scot FHEA, Immediate past President of CILIPS; Academic Liaison Lib., Sch. of Hist., Classics & Archaeology, Univ. of Edinburgh. [36541] 19/10/1983 **FE19/05/1999**

Forrest, Mrs M V, MCLIP, Life Member. [5072] 01/01/1955 **CM01/01/1961**

Forrest, Miss R, BSc(Hons) MCLIP, Collection Devel. Asst. . Lib., Min. of Justice., London [46634] 29/11/1991 **CM24/07/1996**

Forrest, Mrs S A, BA DipLib MCLIP, p. /t. Asst. Subject Advisor, Univ. of Derby. [39569] 04/03/1986 **CM13/06/1990**

Forsey, Mrs S, BSc (Hons) MSc MCLIP, Academic Liaison Lib., Health Serv. L., Southampton. [10007069] 05/01/1972 **CM05/01/1972**

Forster, Mrs A E, BA MCLIP, L. &Inf. Mgr., Newcastle City L. [30114] 10/01/1979 **CM09/09/1981**

Forster, Mr G, BA MA MCLIP, Lib., The Leeds L. [32948] 07/10/1980 **CM21/06/1984**

Forster, Miss L E, BA, Grad. Trainee, Nuffield Coll., Oxford [10015274] 29/10/2009 **ME**

Forster, Mr N D, BA, Sales Controller, BBC Audio Books, Bath. [10014149] 01/07/2009 **ME**

Forster, Mrs T D A, MSc, Inf. Scientist, SARI, Uruguay [60084] 12/11/1984 **ME**

Forsyth, Miss E M, BSc MCLIP, Lib., RCN Scotland, Edinburgh. [28951] 10/02/1978 **CM29/02/1980**

Forsyth, Miss J M, BSc MCLIP, Retired. [5082] 17/09/1951 **CM01/01/1956**

Forsyth, Ms L A, MA(Hons), Unknown. [65027] 13/10/2005 **ME**

Forsyth, Miss S, MCLIP, Asst. Inf. Adviser, Univ. of Brighton. [10001563] 20/10/1997 **CM19/11/2008**

Forsythe, Mrs F M, BA MSc(Econ) MCLIP, Self Employed, Fionn Consultancy Serv., Northumberland. [38078] 17/01/1985 **CM15/05/1989**

Forsythe, Mrs J E, BA MCLIP, Lib., Havering Coll. of F. & H. E., Hornchurch,Essex. [7025] 01/10/1970 **CM23/01/1974**

Fortune, Mrs S C, DipLib MCLIP, Area Lib., Campbeltown L., Argyll & Bute L. Serv. [8263] 16/09/1970 **CM30/05/1977**

Foskett, Prof A C, MA FCLIP AALIA, Life Member. [5087] 09/09/1952 **FE01/01/1958**

Foss, Mrs J A, BA(Hons) MSc(Econ) MCLIP, Child. Lib., Guille-Alles L., Guernsey. [62236] 31/03/2003 **CM10/07/2009**

Foster, Mr A J, BA FCLIP, Inf. Ind. Consultant & Writer, Lancashire. [5094] 21/02/1966 **FE01/04/2002**

Foster, Mrs C A, L. Mgr., Marshalswick L. Hertfordshire [10012350] 03/02/2009 **AF**

Foster, Mrs C E, BA MSc MCLIP, Lib., Drumchaper High Sch., Glasgow [10000511] 16/10/2006 **CM11/06/2010**

Foster, Mrs E M, B LIB MCLIP, Lib. /Sen. Arch., Lodders, Stratford-upon-Avon. [21874] 07/02/1974 **CM08/03/1976**

Foster, Mrs F E, DipPhysEd MCLIP, Life Member, Overseas. [16897] 01/01/1963 **CM01/01/1963**

Foster, Mrs F M, DMS MA MCLIP, Ls. and Learning Cents. Mgr., Dundee City Council. [22054] 16/01/1974 **CM15/12/1977**

Foster, Mrs G, BA MSc MCLIP, Lib., NHS Direct, Newcastle upon Tyne. [38171] 23/01/1985 **CM01/04/2002**

Foster, Mrs H C, BA(Hons) Msc(Econ) MCLIP, Bibliographical Serv. Lib., Sydney Jones L., Univ. of Liverpool [51184] 23/11/1994 **CM18/11/1998**

Foster, Mrs H, BA MCLIP, Unwaged. [33681] 03/02/1981 **CM26/04/1983**

Foster, Mrs J C, BSc PhD DipILS MCLIP, Inf. Specialist, GCHQ, Cheltenham. [51108] 16/11/1994 **CM10/07/2002**

Foster, Mrs J, BA(Hons), Unknown. [10007780] 16/10/1987 **ME**

Foster, Mrs K M, BA(Hons) MCLIP, Retired. [5109] 28/09/1960 **CM01/01/1966**

Foster, Mrs L J, BSc, Stud., Aberystwyth. [47806] 19/10/1992 **ME**

Foster, Ms L M, BA DipLib MCLIP, Area Mgr., Peckham L., London. [40348] 21/01/1987 **CM15/08/1990**

Foster, Mrs L, MA(Hons) MSc MCLIP, Inf. Specialist, NICE, Manchester. [57317] 09/02/1999 **CM08/12/2004**

Foster, Mrs L, BA MSc MCLIP MIHM, L. Serv. Mgr., N. Glamorgan NHS Trust, Merthyr Tydfil. [43064] 10/07/1989 **CM01/04/2002**

Foster, Mr M J, FCLIP, Life Member. [5113] 28/03/1952 **FE01/01/1968**

Foster, Mrs M, BSc MCLIP, ESO Learning Resources, Educ. Devel. Serv., Dundee [10008552] 10/01/1998 **CM20/09/2000**

Foster, Mrs R E, BA MCLIP, Area co-ord. S., Worcester L., Worcs. C.C. [41533] 12/01/1988 **CM16/09/1992**

Foster, Mr R L, BA DipIM MCLIP, Dep. Counter Super., Kings Coll. London, Maughan L. [50807] 19/10/1994 **CM09/11/2005**

Foster, Mrs R, BA(Hons) MCLIP, Area Lib., Chester Lib., Chester [51717] 25/05/1995 **CM17/11/1999**

Foster, Mrs S M, BLib MCLIP, H. of Inf. Servs., Limra Europe Ltd., Watford, Herts. [37102] 13/02/1984 **CM02/06/1987**

Foster, Miss V, BA MCLIP, Lib. Access & Inclusion, Sunderland CC. [10015040] 18/08/1981 **CM01/07/1993**

Foster, Ms W F A, BA(Hons) MCLIP, Asst. Lib., Corp. of London, City Business L. [42950] 04/05/1989 **CM15/11/2000**

Foster, Mrs W J, BA MCLIP, Knowledge Servs. Mgr., Hywel DDA Health Board. [28737] 27/01/1978 **CM08/08/1980**

Foster, Mr W T, BSc DipLib MCLIP, Sen. Lect., Univ. of Cent. England, Birmingham. [26960] 10/01/1977 **CM11/04/1979**

Foster-Jones, Mrs J J, BA(Hons) MCLIP MA ODE FHEA, p. t. Teaching Fellow, Dept. of Info. Studies, Univ. of Aberystwyth [52590] 09/11/1995 **CM15/05/2002**

Fothergill, Mrs I L, BA(Hons) MA MCLIP, Self-Employed. [51077] 14/11/1994 **CM22/09/1999**

Foulds, Mrs B J, BSc(Hons) DipLib MCLIP, Unwaged. [21420] 24/10/1973 **CM03/05/1977**

Foulis, Mrs S, BA(Hons), p. /t. Stud., City Univ. /House of Commons L., London. [10000952] 30/11/2006 **ME**

Foulkes, Mr R M, MCLIP, Br. Lib., Welshpool, Powys C.C. [5126] 06/05/1972 **CM09/12/1975**

Foulkes, Miss S J, BM MRCPath, Catr., Brit. L., Boston Spa. [46146] 07/10/1991 **ME**

Fountain, Mrs K M, MSc(Econ) MCLIP, p. /t. Sch. Lib., Gunnersbury Catholic Sch., L.B. of Hounslow. [22777] 09/10/1974 **CM16/08/1977**

Fountain, Miss P D, BSc, MSc. MCLIP, Asst. Lib., Weydon Sch., Farnham. [10011081] 01/10/2008 **CM14/02/1990**

Fourie, Dr I, BBibl MBilb MCLIP, Prof., Dept. of Inf. Sci., Univ. of Pretoria. [60102] 04/10/2000 **CM04/10/2000**

Fovargue, Miss M, BA MCLIP, Retired. [5127] 08/10/1948 **CM01/01/1953**

Fowke, Mrs A S, BA MCLIP, Inf. Lib., Unitec, New Zealand. [45803] 04/06/1991 **CM23/03/1994**

Fowkes, Mr R, MCLIP, Retired. [5129] 15/08/1938 **CM01/01/1948**

Fowler, Mr A J, BSc (Hons), LRC Facilitator, KGV Coll., Southport. [10016008] 29/01/2010 **ME**

Fowler, Miss A M R, BA MCLIP, Child. & Sch. Lib., L.B. Redbridge. [32653] 23/07/1980 **CM19/01/1984**

Fowler, Ms C A, MA BSc MCLIP MBCS, Head of MHLS Lib. Ser. & E-Lib Ser., Med. Health & Life Sciences, Univ. of Southampton. [31228] 08/10/1979 **CM15/09/1983**

Fowler, Ms C B, BSc(Hons) MA MCLIP, Asst. Subject Lib., Oxford Brookes Univ. L. [56739] 12/10/1998 **CM09/11/2005**

Fowler, Mr G, Retired. [5132] 20/10/1947 **ME**

Fowler, Mrs J B, MCLIP, Inf. Cent. Offr., Tennant Serv. Auth., London. [5133] 03/10/1963 **CM01/01/1967**

Fowler, Miss M K, BA(Hons) MLib(Dist) MCLIP, Team Leader, N. Yorks C.C. Inf. Serv., Richmond. [47987] 30/10/1992 **CM18/09/2002**

Fox, Mr A J, FCLIP, Life Member. [5141] 27/02/1952 **FE01/01/1959**

Fox, Miss C R, MA(Hons), Evening Asst., Brighton Univ. [10016138] 16/02/2010 **ME**

Fox, Mr D J, Systems Lib., Victoria Univ., Canada. [62561] 20/08/2003 **ME**

Fox, Mr E S, MSc MPhil FCLIP, Life Member. [5144] 01/01/1943 **FE01/01/1952**

Fox, Ms J A, BSc, Map Lib., Univ. of Reading, Berks. [35409] 08/10/1982 **ME**

Fox, Miss J E, MA, Lib., Notts. C.C. [45892] 01/07/1991 **ME**

Fox, Mrs J M, MRSC MIMMM MCLIP, Inf. Offr., Dyson Ind. Ltd., Sheffield. [60582] 11/12/2001 **CM11/12/2001**

Fox, Mrs J M, ACLIP, Team Lib., Child. & Young People, Nottingham [65468] 24/02/2006 **ACL05/10/2007**

Fox, Mrs J, BA MCLIP, Unwaged. [34622] 19/01/1982 **CM19/01/1988**

Fox, Mrs M, BSc DLIS MCLIP, Press Offr., Duke of Kent Sch., Ewhurst. [27427] 01/04/1977 **CM12/10/1979**

Fox, Mr N J, BA MCLIP, Inf. Offr., Linklaters, London. [27972] 06/10/1977 **CM30/10/1979**

Fox, Mr N R, BA FCLIP FRSA, Retired. [5149] 01/01/1967 **FE27/01/1993**

Fox, Mr R G, BA(Hons), Info. Specialist, Qinetiq, Portsmouth, Hants. [46344] 29/10/1991 **ME**

Fox, Miss S, BA MCLIP, Asst. Lib., Ardingly Coll., Haywards Heath, W. Sussex. [63818] 06/10/2004 **CM21/11/2007**

Fox, Mrs T M, BA(Hons) ACLIP, L. & Resource Cent. Mgr., Frome Community Coll. [10011093] 24/09/2008 **ACL16/06/2010**

Fox, Mrs V J, MCLIP, Retired. [5602] 18/01/1966 **CM01/01/1970**

Fragkos, Mr D, BA MSc, Catr., The London L. [10014146] 02/07/2009 **ME**

Frame, Mr D A, BA(Hons) PGDIP ILS, Unwaged. [65562] 27/02/2006 **ME**

Franca, Mrs A N, BA, Stud. [10006397] 17/10/2007 **ME**

France, Mrs K, BA(Hons) DipILS, Knowledge Mgmnt. Specialist., Rotherham PCT. [59372] 21/02/2001 **ME**

France, Mrs R F, M. Theol DipLib MCLIP, Sch. Lib., Bradford Girl's Grammar Sch., Bradford [10017048] 22/06/1984 **CM15/11/1988**

Frances, Mr E, Unknown. [10011634] 06/11/2008 **ME**

Francis, Ms C J, BA(Hons) MCLIP, Inf. Devel. Asst., ICIS, Littlehampton [56728] 07/10/1998 **CM12/03/2003**

Francis, Miss E C, BA(Hons) MA MCLIP, Inf. Offr., Sayer Vincent, London [61366] 01/07/2002 **CM01/02/2006**

Francis, Mr J P E, BA FCLIP, Life Member. [5175] 16/10/1948 **FE01/01/1961**

Francis, Ms K, BA, Stud., Aberystwyth Univ. [10016855] 27/05/2010 **ME**

Francis, Mr L, BA(Hons), Sen. Lib., L.B. of Haringey, Wood Green Cent. L. [48557] 15/02/1993 **ME**

Francis, Mrs M A, MCLIP, Employment not known. [20776] 09/07/1973 **CM30/01/1976**

Francis, Mrs P, BSc, Clinical Lib., Bolton Hosp. NHS Trust, The Royal Bolton Hosp. [57836] 03/09/1999 **ME**

Francis, Mr R K, BSc(Hons) MA MCLIP, Head of Arch. & L., Nat. Portrait Gallery, London. [34065] 22/08/1981 **CM12/02/1986**

Francis, Ms R, PgDip, Unknown. [10006247] 26/09/2007 **ME**

Francis, Ms S J, BA(Hons) DipLIB, Locality Mgr. Halesowen, Dudley L., Dudley. [43376] 16/10/1989 **ME**

Francis, Mr S, MA FCLIP, Life Member. [5180] 24/03/1958 **FE02/03/1965**

Franck, Ms M E A, Unknown [64448] 30/03/2005 **ME**

Frangeskou, Dr V, BA PhD MA, Asst. Lib., Bristol Univ. [42217] 03/10/1988 **ME**

Frankland, Mr J M, BA MSc, Community & Inf. Offr., Skipton L. ; Skipton [10005863] 16/08/2007 **ME**

Franklin, Mr A G, MA MCLIP, Lib., Manx Nat. Heritage, Douglas, Isle of Man. [21952] 29/01/1974 **CM14/02/1977**

Franklin, Miss A M, BA MCLIP, Sch. Lib., Canons High Sch., Middx. [33596] 21/01/1981 **CM19/01/1984**

Franklin, Mr A P C, BA PgDip, p. /t. Stud., City Univ. /Economist Intelligence Unit, London. [10000957] 24/11/2006 **ME**

Franklin, Miss C E, BA(Hons) MA MCLIP, Unknown. [51441] 14/02/1995 **CM17/09/2003**

Franklin, Mr C W, FCLIP, Life Member. [5186] 15/02/1941 **FE01/01/1950**

Franklin, Mrs F S, BA MCLIP, Child. Lib., Derby City Council. [25597] 27/01/1976 **CM22/10/1979**

Franklin, Mrs G, BA MA MCLIP, Academic Lib., Loughborough Univ. [43332] 20/10/1989 **CM16/11/1994**

Franklin, Ms G, BSc, Comm. Lib., Roayl Shrewsbury Hosp., Shrewsbury. [10010907] 04/09/2008 **ME**

Franklin, Mrs L E, BA(Hons) DipLib DipIM MCLIP, Sen. L. Asst., Uckfield L., E. Sussex C.C. [18256] 02/10/1972 **CM23/09/1975**

Franklin, Mrs M, BA MCLIP, Retired. [10044] 13/12/1968 **CM30/03/1976**

Franklin, Mrs S M, BA(Hons), Sen. L. Asst., Woodrow L., Worcs. [10011210] 02/10/2008 **AF**

Franks, Mrs D, BSc MCLIP, L. Serv. Devel. Mgr., STFC, Daresbury Lab., Warrington. [37756] 23/10/1984 **CM12/12/1991**

Franssen, Mr J, BA(Hons) MA, Inf. Serv. Mgr., Davies Arnold Cooper, London. [57628] 02/06/1999 **ME**

Fraser, Mr A, MCLIP, Retired. [5189] 10/01/1936 **CM01/01/1939**

Fraser, Mr A, BA, Stud., Robert Gordon Univ., Aberdeen. [10013633] 18/05/2009 **ME**

Fraser, Mrs B A, Unemployed. [38918] 21/10/1985 **ME**

Fraser, Mrs B J, DIPL BIBL., Asst. Lib. Catg. & Metadata Serv., Anglia Ruskin Univ., Chelmsford. [10005879] 20/05/2004 **ME**

Fraser, Mrs C L, Collections Offr., Lincolnshire L. Serv., Lincoln [65945] 14/07/2006 **AF**

Fraser, Dr D M, BA(Hons) MCLIP, Sen. Lib. :Young People's Serv. (Pub.) Norfolk C.C. [19893] 19/12/1972 **CM21/07/1975**

Fraser, Ms F, BA MCLIP, Community Lib. (Job Share)., Larbert L., Falkirk Council [30618] 19/02/1979 **CM21/12/1981**

Fraser, Mrs G R, BA MCLIP, Community Lib., Flintshire C.C., Flint. [28652] 07/01/1978 **CM16/06/1982**

Fraser, Mr J, MA, Sen. Learning Advisor, St. Martin's Coll., Lancaster. [58702] 09/06/2000 **ME**

Fraser, Ms K A, MCLIP, Customer Serv. Lib., Shetland L. [64675] 25/05/2005 **CM10/07/2009**

Fraser, Mr K C, MA BSc MCLIP, Retired. [5197] 19/10/1966 **CM01/01/1969**

Fraser, Mr K G, BA DMS MCLIP, Lib., The Robert Gordon Univ., Aberdeen. [33932] 22/05/1981 **CM05/12/1985**

Fraser, Dr K, BA, MSc, MA, PhD, Asst. Lib., De Montfort Univ., Leicester [10001309] 19/01/2007 **ME**

Fraser, Ms M A, MA MCLIP, KIM Programme Mgr., Dept. for Internat. Devel. L., E. Kilbride. [23251] 15/10/1974 **CM31/08/1977**

Fraser, Mrs M S, MA MCLIP, Child. Serv. Mgr., L.B. of Croydon, Cent. L. [31759] 30/11/1979 **CM16/09/1982**

Fraser, Mrs M, HNC, Lib. Sup., William Patrick L., Kirkintilloch. [10017278] 22/07/2010 **AF**

Fraser, Mrs P D, L. Mgr., Mansfield. L. [10012522] 24/02/2009 **AF**

Fraser, Mrs S, BSc, Sen. Lib. Asst/ Stud. MSc., Aberdeenshire Council [65397] 08/02/2006 **ME**

Fraser, Ms V E, BA DipLib MIPD FCLIP, Hd. of Data Protection & Inf. Risk Mgmnt., Dept. of Health, London [5202] 14/04/1972 **FE15/09/2004**

Fraser, Miss V L, BA(Hons) MCLIP, Asst. Lib., Angus Council [51026] 09/11/1994 **CM21/05/2003**

Fratus, Mrs L M, BA(Hons) MSc(Econ) MCLIP, Resident in Australia. [52504] 02/11/1995 **CM17/11/1999**

Fratzke, Mr T, MA MLITT, Stud., Robert Gordon Umiv., Aberdeen [10000435] 10/10/2006 **ME**

Freebury, Mr R, BA DipLib MCLIP, Head of Hansard Printed Indexes, House of Commons L., London. [40817] 01/07/1987 **CM14/11/1990**

Freedman, Miss E, BA(Hons) MSc PGDE MCLIP, Supply Teacher [59420] 07/03/2001 **CM29/03/2004**

Freedman, Ms J D, BA(Hons), LRC, Sir George Monoux Coll., London. [38091] 08/01/1985 **ME**

Freedman, Ms S B, Learning Resource Cent. Mgr. Hainault Forest High Sch. L.B. Redbridge [49898] 07/01/1994 **ME**

Freedman, Ms V R, BA(Hons), Asst. Lib., Hebrew & Jewish Studies Lib., UCL. [63540] 22/06/2004 **ME**

Freeman, Mrs A, Local & Family Hist. Advisor, L. and Heritage, City of York Council. [10008803] 21/04/2008 **AF**

Freeman, Mrs C A, MCLIP, Catg., Baker & McKenzie, London. [22937] 01/10/1974 **CM22/08/1977**

Freeman, Mrs J H, BA MCLIP, Unknown. [28788] 26/01/1978 **CM15/12/1983**

Freeman, Mrs J, ACLIP, Sen. Lib. Asst., Clipstone L., Nottinghamshire [10012523] 24/02/2009 **ACL11/12/2009**

Freeman, Mrs L A, BA MCLIP, L. Asst., Calderdale M. B. C [41511] 11/01/1988 **CM27/03/1991**

Freeman, Mrs L M, BA MCLIP, Surestart Lib., Derbyshire, C.C. [26915] 04/01/1977 **CM01/07/1992**

Freeman, Mr M C E, BA MCLIP, L. Mgr., S. Tyneside Metro. Bor. [31288] 08/10/1979 **CM14/02/1984**

Freeman, Dr M J, BA MEd PhD FCLIP, Retired. [5216] 30/09/1959 **FE18/04/1989**

Freeman, Miss O J, MLS MCLIP, Trainer, Res. & Inf. Specialist. [5217] 27/09/1967 **CM01/01/1970**

Freeman, Mrs S D, MCLIP, Br. Lib., Stockton Bor. Council. [23217] 15/11/1974 **CM09/08/1977**

Freemantle, Mr D J, BA DipLib MCLIP, Inf. Analyst, BG Grp. plc., Reading. [36404] 08/10/1983 **CM15/02/1989**

French, Ms A, BSc (Econ), Unknown. [10015606] 17/12/2009 **ME**

French, Miss C, MA MCLIP, Asst. Lib., Crawley L., . Sussex C.C. [62046] 28/01/2003 **CM29/11/2006**

French, Mr J M, BA MCLIP, Academic Liaison Lib., Univ. of Manchester. [5223] 19/01/1971 **CM24/01/1974**

French, Mrs L M, BSc MCLIP, p. /t. Child. Lib., Bexley Cent. L. [50131] 06/04/1994 **CM07/09/2005**

Fretten, Miss C E, MCLIP MBE, Retired. [5231] 02/10/1968 **CM01/01/1971**

Frew, Mrs L M, BA MCLIP, Sch. Lib., Bolton Sch. (Girls' Div.), Lancs. [24495] 29/08/1975 **CM16/07/1979**

Frew, Mrs M, MCLIP, Resources Asst., Jewel & ESK Coll., Edinburgh [13638] 18/09/1967 **CM01/01/1971**

Frey, Mrs L, BA(Hons) DipLib, Asst. Lib., DFPNI L., Belfast. [10006146] 11/09/2007 **ME**

Fricker, Mr A, BSc MSc MCLIP, Knowledge & L. Serv. Mgr. Newham Univ. Hosp. NHS Trust [55376] 06/10/1997 **CM12/03/2003**

Fricker, Mr D C, BEd (Hons), Stud., Univ. of Brighton [10014828] 16/09/2009 **ME**

Fricker, Mrs R, BA MA MCLIP, Sen. Inf. Offr., Norton Rose, London. [55369] 06/10/1997 **CM20/11/2002**

Friday, Ms K, Res. Stud., RGU. [63180] 03/03/2004 **ME**

Friedlander, Ms J R, BA MCLIP, Inf. Offr., Nat. Union of Teachers. [32654] 15/07/1980 **CM21/07/1982**

Friel, Mrs J D, BA(Hons), Newcaslte City L. [10006497] 24/10/2007 **ME**

Friend, Mrs S J, PGDipIS MCLIP, Inf. Serv. Mgr., Univ. of Brighton, Hastings. [58427] 16/02/2000 **CM17/09/2003**

Friggens, Ms G L, BA(Hons) MSc(Econ) FHEA MCLIP, Faculty Lib., Univ. of Portsmouth. [52529] 06/11/1995 **CM20/01/1999**

Frodin, Mrs A, BA, E-Communications Mgr., Glos. C.C. [45269] 01/10/1990 **ME**

Frodsham, Miss H, BA(Hons) MSc MCLIP, Inf. Res. Mgr., Off. of Fair Trading [62943] 21/11/2003 **CM19/03/2008**

Froggatt, Ms S J, Head of L. &Inf. Serv., Reynolds Porter Chamberlain LLP, London. [39167] 01/10/1985 **ME**

Frontin, Mr H, Learning Cent. Asst., City & Islington Coll., London [10016477] 01/04/2010 **AF**

Frossman-Finney, Mrs M, BSc(Hons) MCLIP, Ch. L. Asst., Univ. of Strathclyde, Glasgow. [53174] 01/04/1996   **CM23/01/2002**

Frost, Miss A J, BLS MCLIP, Adult Reading & Learning Lib., Norfolk L. & Inf. Serv. [29324] 23/05/1978   **CM10/11/1982**

Frost, Miss S M, BA MCLIP, Learning Advisor, Univ. of Cumbria L. [31826] 18/01/1980   **CM24/01/1985**

Froud, Mr R N, OBE BLib DMS MIMgt FCLIP, Head of Cultural Serv., Somerset Co. L., Bridgwater. [21900] 21/01/1974   **FE23/07/1997**

Froy, Mr S G, BA MCLIP, Website Mgr., Wakefield M.D.C. L. & Inf. [26378] 01/10/1976   **CM31/07/1980**

Fry, Mrs E M, BLib(Hons), Unwaged. [43550] 06/11/1989   **ME**

Fry, Ms R, BA HDipLib, Lib., Peebles High Sch. [10006139] 11/09/2007   **ME**

Frydland, Mrs L C, BA(Hons), Asst. Lib., AWE, Aldermaston [50796] 18/10/1994   **ME**

Fryer, Ms F A, BA(Hons) PG DIP, L. Asst., Univ. of Brighton, Sch. of Computing & Inf. Sciences. [10015778] 25/01/2010   **ME**

Fryers, Mrs H R, MA MA MCLIP, Sen. L. Customer Asst., Cheltenham L. [57494] 06/04/1999   **CM16/07/2003**

Fuchs, Dr H, PhD, Sen. Asst. Lib., Univ. of Gottingen, Germany. [39726] 23/05/1986   **ME**

Fudakowska, Miss E, BA MCLIP, Retired. [5257] 01/01/1953   **CM01/01/1968**

Fuegi, Mr D F, MA MCLIP, Partner, Consultant Partners. [5258] 04/12/1967   **CM01/01/1970**

Fuidge, Miss V R, BA MUS, Stud., Univ. of Sheffield, Dept. of Inf. Studies. [10016186] 23/02/2010   **ME**

Fujiwara, Mr Y, MLS, Assoc. Prof. of Lib., Chubu Gakuin Univ., Seki City, Japan. [57740] 20/07/1999   **ME**

Fulbrook, Mrs L G, BA(Hons), Stud., Aberystwyth Univ. [10008425] 19/03/2008   **ME**

Fuller, Miss M A, BA MCMI FCLIP, Inf. & L. Serv. Mgr., Fire Serv. Coll. [5262] 20/07/1970   **FE21/06/2006**

Fuller, Mrs S J, BA(Hons)DipLIS MCLIP, Primary Res. Adv., Northants LRE (Sch. L. Serv.). [53294] 29/04/1996   **CM20/09/2000**

Fullick, Ms L J, BA DipLib MCLIP, Career Break. [28567] 09/01/1978   **CM14/01/1980**

Fulljames, Mr D R, MSc MCLIP, Retired. [5264] 16/10/1970   **CM05/01/1973**

Fulton, Mr A R, MCLIP, Retired. [5265] 26/02/1968   **CM01/01/1970**

Fulton, Mrs E, BA MCLIP, Dir., CILIPS & SLIC, Hamilton. [31430] 12/10/1979   **CM09/09/1982**

Funk, Ms C, HonFCLIP, Unknown. [10011431] 16/10/2008   **HFE16/10/2008**

Funnell, Ms C L, BA(Hons) MA MLIS MCLIP, Sr. Liaison Lib., Law, Middlesex Univ., London [56340] 27/05/1998   **CM27/05/1998**

Funnell, Mrs M, Unwaged. [10013494] 30/04/2009   **ME**

Furderer, Ms E S, MLIS, L. & Special Collections Asst., BFI Nat. L., London. [10008387] 19/03/2008   **ME**

Furlong, Mrs J C, Lib., Ashlyns Sch. [44999] 04/02/1991   **ME**

Furner, Dr J, MA MSc PhD MCLIP, Assoc. Prof. Univ. of California, USA [60094] 23/12/1991   **CM04/01/1993**

Furness, Miss A, Inf. Specialist, NBS, Newcastle upon Tyne [63117] 11/02/2004   **ME**

Furness, Miss E L, Learning Resources Coordinator, Great Yarmouth, Norfolk [59302] 31/01/2001   **ME**

Furness, Ms H J, MA DipILS MCLIP, Reader Serv. Lib., Edinburgh Coll. of Art L. [54287] 15/11/1996   **CM13/06/2007**

Furness, Mr M, Conservator, John Rylands L., Manchester. [61311] 17/05/2002   **ME**

Furness, Ms R J, Stud. [10017020] 21/06/2010   **ME**

Furnival, Ms C, BA MA MSc Phd, Stud. [10007977] 03/03/2008   **ME**

Furphy, Mr D K, BA DipEd GradDipLS AALIA AIMM, Mgr. L. Serv. /City Lib., City of Cockburn P.L. &Inf. Serv., Bibra Lake, Australia. [57092] 07/12/1998   **ME**

Furse, Mrs H, BA, LRC Mgr. / Lib., Sacred Heart H. S., London [10012733] 03/03/2009   **ME**

Fynes-Clinton, Mrs A B, BA DipLib MCLIP, Lib., Haberdashers' Aske's Sch. for Girls, Elstree. [40152] 09/10/1986   **CM14/02/1990**

G

Gabbatt, Miss J M, BLib MCLIP, Principle Lib. Literary Devel. & Stock, Blackburn with Darwen B. C. [25535] 29/01/1976   **CM26/06/1979**

Gabr, Mrs R A, BA, Lib., Land Warfare Cent. (MOD), Warminser, Wilts. [56284] 28/04/1998   **ME**

Gabriel, Mrs J, Stud., Univ. Brighton. [10015528] 09/12/2009   **ME**

Gadd, Ms E A, MSc, BA(Hons) MCLIP, Academic Serv. Mgr., Loughborough Univ. [10013410] 05/09/2004   **CM22/07/1998**

Gadelrab, Miss M, Stud., Liverpool John Moores Univ. [10013145] 02/04/2009   **ME**

Gadhave, Mrs V, Stud. [10017041] 21/06/2010   **ME**

Gadsden, Mr S R, MLS MCLIP, Life Member. [5282] 08/11/1947   **CM01/01/1958**

Gaffar, Mr S, MA, Mgr. of L. Servs., Knowledge Village, Dubai. [10013814] 17/06/2009   **ME**

Gage, Mrs H P, BLib(Hons) MCLIP, Sch. Lib., Attleborough High Sch., Norfolk. [10004535] 08/01/1981   **CM20/09/1984**

Gahan, Mr P N, MA, Lib., N. Swindon L. [50364] 01/07/1994   **ME**

Gahungu, Mr S, MSc, Unknown. [10017165] 14/07/2010   **ME**

Gaine, Mr F, BSc, Stud. [10003059] 02/10/2002   **ME**

Gair, Miss J, BA MCLIP, Sen. L. Inf. Worker, Arthurstone Community L., Dundee. [36019] 04/04/1983   **CM17/04/1985**

Gair, Ms M J, MA DipLib MCLIP, Lib., MOD Info. Serv., Glasgow. [39068] 30/10/1985 RV23/09/2009   **CM14/09/1994**

Gait-Carr, Miss E, BA(Hons), Stud. [10017044] 21/06/2010   **ME**

Galber, Mrs K D, BA DipLib, Sen. Asst. /Child. Lib., L.B. of Harrow. [56949] 13/11/1998   **ME**

Gale, Mrs C A, BA(Hons) MA MCLIP, Team Leader: Academic Support Consultants (Arts & Social Sciences) [56661] 01/10/1998   **CM21/05/2003**

Gale, Mrs C J, MCLIP, Unemployed. [6778] 01/01/1970   **CM29/07/1975**

Gale, Mr M J M, BA(Hons) MLib MCLIP, Lib., Queens Foundation, Birmingham. [44858] 01/01/1991   **CM18/11/1993**

Gale, Mrs M T C, DipLib MCLIP, Inf. Lib. [33917] 14/05/1981   **CM23/08/1985**

Gale, Mrs P, MCLIP, Retired. [5302] 01/01/1958   **CM01/01/1963**

Gall, Ms J A, MA(Hons) DipILS MCLIP, Sch. Lib., Angus Council, Arbroath High Sch. [58030] 19/10/1999   **CM04/02/2004**

Gallacher, Mrs A, BA(Hons) AUDIS, Business Performance Mgr., Maidenhead L. [61114] 21/02/2002   **ME**

Gallagher, Ms C F, BA(Hons) MA MCLIP, Child. & Yth. Lib., Beeston L., Nottinghamshire. [59348] 13/02/2001   **CM08/12/2004**

Gallagher, Miss E, M. St. (Oxon), BA(Hons), Lib. Asst. /Editor, Bodleian L., Oxford. [10011204] 02/10/2008   **ME**

Gallagher, Mr M T, BA MA, LRC Mgr, William Morris Sixth Form, London. [61933] 11/12/2002   **ME**

Gallagher, Mr P, MA(Hons) DipLIS MCLIP, Sch. Lib., Whitehill Secondary, Glasgow. [43488] 30/10/1989   **CM21/05/2003**

Gallagher, Miss T, BA(Hons), Sch. Lib., Boston High Sch., Lincs. [44759] 15/11/1990   **ME**

Gallart Marsillas, Ms N, Lib., Univ. Autonoma de Barcelona, Spain. [37396] 16/08/1984   **ME**

Gallehawk, Miss R K, BA(Hons) MCLIP, Lib. Thurrock Council, Essex [41744] 10/03/1988   **CM27/11/1996**

Galletly, Mrs C A, BA DipLib MCLIP, Sec. and Res., CING Tech. LTD., Banbury. [36981] 17/01/1984 **CM18/11/1993**

Galloway, Mr J S, MCLIP, Bibl. Serv. Lib., Dunbarton. [24081] 18/03/1975 **CM07/03/1979**

Galloway, Mrs S E, BA(Hons) DipILS MCLIP, Career Break [53976] 15/10/1996 **CM13/03/2002**

Galopin-Dimitriadis, Dr L, BA MA Phd, Lib., Biblioteque Des Chiroux, Belgium [10015145] 15/10/2009 **ME**

Galsworthy, Ms J G, FCLIP, Life Member. [5322] 20/09/1956 **FE01/01/1965**

Galt, Ms C O, BA(Hons) DipILM, Young People's Lib., S. Tyneside Cent. L., S. Shields. [54247] 14/11/1996 **ME**

Galt, Ms E, BA MCLIP, Team Lib., Educ. Resource Serv., Glasgow. [35568] 18/10/1982 **CM24/02/1986**

Galvin, Miss C, BA(Hons), Stud., LJMU, Liverpool. [10015017] 07/10/1998 **ME**

Galway, Miss L, BSc MSc DipILM MCLIP, Sch. Lib., S. Lanarkshire Council. [50729] 14/10/1994 **CM21/01/1998**

Gamage, Miss P, MLS, Lib., Inst. of Policy Studies, Colombo, Sri Lanka. [63102] 05/01/2004 **ME**

Gamble, Mrs A, BA(Hons) MSc MCLIP, Lib., Baker & McKenzie, Saudi Arabia. [55449] 13/10/1997 **CM15/09/2004**

Gammon, Mr M, BA MA MLIS, Asst. Lib., Castlerea Prison, Roscommon L. Serv., ROI [10001822] 27/08/1999 **ME**

Gandon, Ms A, BA MCLIP, Coll. Lib., City Coll., Plymouth [20882] 10/08/1973 **CM06/05/1977**

Gandy, Ms F, MA MCLIP, Fellow Lib., Girton Coll., Univ. of Cambridge. [9054] 01/10/1966 **CM01/01/1970**

Gann, Mr P D, FCLIP, Life Member. [5333] 26/02/1949 **FE01/01/1957**

Gann, Mr R, BA, DipLib, FCLIP, Head of Strategy, NHS Choices, London. [10000238] 12/01/1976 **FE22/05/1991**

Gannaway, Mrs K, B. Ed(Hons) MA MCLIP, Unknown. [59879] 29/10/2001 **CM17/09/2008**

Gannaway, Mr N M, MCLIP, Retired. [5334] 07/01/1953 **CM01/01/1961**

Gant, Mrs D M, BA(Hons) MCLIP, Sen. Res. Offr., City Coll., Birmingham. [9002] 09/10/1969 **CM07/12/1973**

Garbacz, Ms S J, BA(Hons) MA MCLIP, Strategic Mgr., City of york Council [52338] 30/10/1995 **CM20/09/2000**

Garbett, Miss R S, BA(Hons), Unknown. [10000979] 04/12/2006 **ME**

Garcia Serrano, Mr D, Inf. Specialist, Brit. Standards Inst. [10012357] 03/02/2009 **ME**

Garcia, Mrs S, Unknown [10006417] 19/10/2007 **ME**

Garcia-Ontiveros, Ms D M, BA(Hons) MA MCLIP, Head of Retrospective Catg., London L. [58112] 01/11/1999 **RV02/03/2010** **CM19/11/2003**

Garcia-Perez, Mr A, MSc, Stud., Cranfield Univ. [10007572] 18/02/2008 **ME**

Garde, Ms Z A F, Clinical Lib. [10001405] 01/07/1994 **ME**

Garden, Mrs E, MA MCLIP, L. Resource Cent. Co-ordinator, Bridge of Don Academy, Aberdeen. [29475] 17/08/1978 **CM18/08/1980**

Gardiner, Mrs C J, BA MCLIP, Asst. Lib., Andover Coll., Andover. [38148] 22/01/1985 **CM17/01/1990**

Gardiner, Miss D, MCLIP, Inf. Offr., IDOX Inf. Serv., Glasgow. [64432] 17/03/2005 **CM09/07/2008**

Gardiner, Mrs E, MCLIP, Retired. [24047] 08/03/1941 **CM17/02/1976**

Gardiner, Ms G, MCLIP, Lib., Rotherham P. L., S. Yorks. [5341] 03/04/1972 **CM20/08/1975**

Gardiner, Miss L C, BA(Hons) MSc MCLIP, Unwaged. [58105] 27/10/1999 **CM06/04/2005**

Gardiner, Miss L J, MA(Hons) MPhil, Unknown [66155] 04/10/2006 **ME**

Gardner, Miss C A, BA(Hons) MSc, Inf. Offr., Bank of England, London. [49201] 12/10/1993 **ME**

Gardner, Miss C L, BA MA MCLIP, Framework For the Future Support Offr., MLA, London. [59421] 22/03/2001 **RV05/10/2007** **CM23/06/2004**

Gardner, Mr D, GCSEs BTEC, Lib. Asst., Hastings Coll., E. Sussex [10013175] 03/04/2009 **AF**

Gardner, Mrs E, ACLIP, L. Systems Mgr., Parsons L., Newcastle Coll. [64793] 04/07/2005 **ACL01/03/2006**

Gardner, Mrs H C, BSc MCLIP, L. Mgr., Sherwood Forest Hosp. NHS Foundation Trust, King's Mill Hosp. [31456] 18/10/1979 **CM10/10/1985**

Gardner, Mr I, BA MA MCLIP, e-Learning Inf. Specialist, BPP Coll. of Professional Studies, London. [65158] 03/11/2005 **CM20/04/2009**

Gardner, Mrs J E, BSc(Hons) DipILM MCLIP, Learning Resources Mgr., Askham Bryan Coll., York. [46521] 15/11/1991 **CM26/07/1995**

Gardner, Miss J R, BA MCLIP, Retired. [5355] 20/01/1970 **CM16/10/1972**

Gardner, Mrs L, BSc(Hons), L. & Inf. Mgr., Thomson Reuters, Legal, London. [53684] 05/09/1996 **ME**

Gardner, Miss M V, Retired. [20727] 20/06/1973 **ME**

Gardner, Mrs S J, MCLIP, Life Member. [5361] 19/01/1946 **CM01/01/1953**

Gardner, Mrs S, BSc DipLib MLib, Unwaged [38920] 16/10/1985 **ME**

Garfield, Mrs D M, MA MCLIP, Faculty Liaison Lib., Anglia Ruskin Univ., Chelmsford. [53391] 05/06/1996 **CM20/01/1999**

Garfield, Dr E, BSc MS PhD MIEEE HonFCLIP, Hon Fellow. [60072] 24/07/1948 **FE02/08/1966**

Gargett, Miss C, MCLIP, Life Member. [5364] 10/01/1944 **CM01/01/1947**

Garland, Mr J R, BA(Hons) MCLIP, Inf. Lib., W. Sussex L. Serv., Bognor Regis L. [49980] 02/02/1994 **CM17/09/2003**

Garland, Mr R N, Lib., N. E. Lincolnshire L., Grimsby. [10002524] 23/05/2007 **ME**

Garman, Mrs E A, BA MA MCLIP, Comm. Inf. Offr., Harrogate L., N. Yorks. C.C. [56979] 17/11/1998 **CM11/03/2009**

Garner, Mr D K, Knowledge Asst., Nabarro, London [10002233] 20/04/2007 **AF**

Garner, Mrs D M, Unknown. [10014372] 21/07/2009 **AF**

Garner, Mrs E J S, MCLIP, Adviser, sch. L. Serv., Hants. C.C. [13567] 04/01/1972 **CM31/10/1974**

Garner, Ms F A, PGDip MA, L. Mgr., Welsh Coll. of Horticulture, Mold, Flintshire. [57354] 17/02/1999 **ME**

Garner, Ms H J, BA(Hons) DipILM MCLIP, Sen. Inf. Adviser Cataloging., Sheffield Hallam university [45851] 03/07/1991 **CM23/09/1998**

Garner, Ms J E, Sen. Inf. Serv. Mgr., Dept. for Business, Innovation & Skills. [39317] 10/01/1986 **ME**

Garnett, Mrs J K, BSc MA MCLIP, Coll. Lib., Barony Coll., Dumfries. [51220] 29/11/1994 **CM26/11/1997**

Garnett, Mrs L K, Sch. Lib. Mgr., Elizabeth Coll., Guernsey [10008311] 26/03/2008 **ME**

Garnsworthy, Mr A C, MA, Community L. Serv. Mgr., Stoke Newington L., London. [10009775] 06/06/2008 **ME**

Garoli, Miss G, BA, Unknown. [64454] 30/03/2005 **ME**

Garrard, Mrs T, BA(Hons) MA MCLIP, Dep. Lib. Serv. Mgr., Camden PCT L., London. [59724] 05/09/2001 **CM28/01/2009**

Garrett, Mrs M E P, MCLIP, Sch. Lib., Bishops Stortford Coll., Herts. [27061] 20/01/1977 **CM28/08/1979**

Garrett, Miss P L, BSc(Hons) MA, E-Devel. Lib., Portsmouth Cent. L. [61132] 07/03/2002 **ME**

Garrigan, Mrs M R C, MCLIP, Planning Offr., Dundee C.C. [60266] 06/04/1999 **CM06/04/1999**

Garriock, Dr J B, MA PhD FCLIP FRSA, Life Member. [16195] 01/01/1951 **FE01/01/1963**

Garrod, Mr N P S, BA MCLIP, Team Lib., Cent. L., Northampton. [10009807] 19/03/1976 **CM31/03/1990**

Garside, Mrs K L, BSc(Econ), Not working. [53797] 01/10/1996 **ME**

Garside-Neville, Ms S D, BA(Hons), Inf. Specialist, Food & Environment Res. Agency, York. [10010487] 07/10/1991 **ME**

Gartland, Ms L M, BA(Hons) MA MA/MSc, Lib., St. Marys Comp., Newcastle upon Tyne. [61444] 29/07/2002 **ME**

Gartside, Ms E J, BA(Hons) MCLIP, Editor, Career Workshop, Manchester. [42354] 25/10/1988 **CM25/05/1994**

Garvey, Miss A M, BA PGDip MSc ILM, Asst. Lib., Joseph Chamberlain Coll., Birmingham. [10001700] 08/04/2004 **ME**

Garvey, Miss M, Unknown. [10016326] 08/03/2010 **ME**

Garvie, Mr D J, MA, Dep. Lib., Union Theological Coll., Belfast. [10001215] 02/02/2007 **ME**

Gas, Mr Z, BA MA MCLIP AIL, Subject Advisor (humanities), Inf. Serv., Univ. of Birmingham L. [37568] 09/10/1984 **CM21/07/1993**

Gascoigne, Miss J E, BA(Hons), Inf. Resources Grp. Mgr. (Financing), Slaughter and May, London. [54278] 13/11/1996 **ME**

Gascoigne, Mrs J, MCLIP, Retired. [18716] 11/09/1967 **CM01/01/1969**

Gascoyne, Ms H M, MLS CertEd MCLIP, Tutor, S. E. Derbyshire Coll. [5391] 09/09/1969 **CM30/07/1972**

Gaskin, Mrs E, BSc, Stud. [66084] 01/10/2006 **ME**

Gaskin, Mrs M, ACLIP, Asst. L. Mgr., Welwyn Hatfield Hertsmere Herts. C.C. [63526] 17/06/2004 **ACL24/04/2009**

Gaston, Mr R S, BA(Hons) MA MCLIP, Unknown. [57874] 22/09/1999 **CM04/02/2004**

Gater, Miss L, BA(Hons), Lib., St. Thomas More Catholic Coll., Stoke on Trent. [46812] 04/02/1992 **ME**

Gates, Mr D, MA LLB, Website Support Mgr., Blue Compass Ltd., London. [10016407] 22/03/2010 **AF**

Gates, Mrs K, LRC Co-Ordinator, Furness Coll., Cumbria. [62413] 16/06/2003 **AF**

Gatrell, Mrs N M, Lib. Casterton Sch., Casterton Carnforth., Lancashire [64732] 08/06/2005 **AF**

Gattens, Ms D, MSc, PG, Stud., Univ. of Strathclyde., Glasgow. [10011356] 14/10/2008 **ME**

Gatti, Dr I M, MA PhD, Lib. Asst., L. -Royal Sch. of Military Survey, Thatcham. [10008745] 15/04/2008 **ME**

Gaukroger, Mr J, BA(Hons), Lib. Hist. and Culture Content Co-ordinator, L. Support Unit, Inverness. [10006220] 28/09/2007 **AF**

Gault, Mrs C R M, BA PGCE DipLib MCLIP, Asst. Lib., Barbican L., London. [36582] 12/10/1983 **CM21/12/1988**

Gaunt, Miss C L, Lib. Mgr., Big Wood Sch., Nottingham [65553] 17/02/2006 **ME**

Gaunt, Mrs F J, BA(Hons) MLib MCLIP, Sch. Lib., Derbyshire Co. Council [58188] 15/11/1999 **CM28/10/2004**

Gauss, Mr J H, BSc DipLib MCLIP AMinstP, Retired. [21183] 01/10/1973 **CM01/09/1976**

Gavaghan, Miss S H, BA(Hons) DMS PGCE, Learning Resource Cent. Mgr., Sir William Turner Learning Resource Cent., Redcar & Cleveland Coll. [49705] 25/11/1993 **ME**

Gavan, Mrs A, BA, Area Lib., Haddington L., E. Lothian [65960] 21/07/2006 **ME**

Gavars, Mrs R C, Law L. Consultant. and Freelance Indexer [41112] 11/10/1987 **ME**

Gavillet, Mrs E L, BA(Hons) DipLib MA, Med. Lib., Walton L., Med. Sch., Univ. of Newcastle upon Tyne. [49073] 01/10/1993 **ME**

Gavin, Mrs J S, BA(Hons) DipIM MCLIP, Unknown. [52715] 24/11/1995 **CM19/01/2000**

Gaw, Mr P W, BA MCLIP, Head of L.(Arch. & Info.), Notts CC, Nottingham. [43645] 15/11/1989 **CM26/01/1994**

Gawali, Mrs K, Unknown. [10008231] 12/03/2008 **ME**

Gaymard, Ms S F S, BLS Dip, Head Lib., Greenwich Sch. of Mgmnt. LTD, London [61194] 08/04/2002 **ME**

Gayton, Mr S, Lib. Asst., W. Bridgeford L., Nottingham. [10013584] 08/05/2009 **AF**

Gaywood, Miss G M, BSc MSc MCLIP, Learning Resource Adviser, Trinity Coll. Carmarthen, [59824] 10/10/2001 **CM29/11/2006**

Gear, Mr S J, MCLIP, Life Member. [5413] 27/01/1950 **CM01/01/1956**

Gear, Mrs S J, MCLIP, Retired. [33788] 01/01/1953 **CM01/01/1957**

Gebbie, Mrs J D, BA(Hons) DipEurHum PG Dip ILS, Inf. &L. Serv., Scottish Natural Heritage, Inverness. [45680] 18/04/1991 **ME**

Geddes, Mrs A, MCLIP, Comm. Lib. (Heritage), E. Ayrshire Council. [18074] 01/10/1972 **CM24/09/1975**

Geddes, Miss E J, BEd, Stud. [10013646] 18/05/2009 **ME**

Geddes, Mr G T, MA DipLib FHEA MCLIP, Retired. [5415] 21/10/1968 **CM01/01/1971**

Geddes, Mrs L, Lend. Serv. Co-ordinator, Elgin L., Moray [10011475] 21/04/1992 **AF**

Geddes, Mrs M, MCLIP, Retired. [5416] 04/03/1930 **CM01/01/1934**

Geddes, Ms S J, BLib MCLIP, Lib., The Crest Girls' Academy, Neasden. [28662] 10/01/1978 **CM02/11/1982**

Gee, Mr A P, BA DipLib MCLIP, Systems Support Offr., N. Yorks. C.C., L. H.Q. [25036] 10/11/1975 **CM21/06/1979**

Gee, Mr D R, BA MA DipLib MCLIP, Dep. Lib., Inst. Advanced Legal Studies, Univ. of London. [40939] 07/09/1987 **CM24/04/1991**

Gee, Mrs J, BA MCLIP, Lib., S. Tees Hosp. NHS Trust, N. Yorks. [23645] 26/01/1975 **CM29/12/1978**

Gee, Mrs M D, MA(Oxon) MSc, Unknown. [51993] 01/09/1995 **ME**

Gee-Finch, Mrs S J, BA Hons, Asst. Lib. mngr., Stevenage Cent. L. [10013661] 15/05/2009 **AF**

Geekie, Mrs J, BA(Hons) MCLIP, Staff Devel. & Mob. Serv. Lib., ALIS, Oldmeldrum. [44706] 30/11/1990 **CM31/01/1996**

Geh, Dr H P, FCLIP, Hon. Vice President. [46050] 11/09/1991 **FE11/09/1991**

Geldard, Mrs D, BA MCLIP, L. Mgr., Tameside & Glossop pct., Oldham [25718] 29/02/1976 **CM12/11/1980**

Geldenhuys, Mrs P R, Stud. [65902] 26/06/2006 **ME**

Gellatly, Mrs C J, BA MLS MCLIP, Elementary Lib., The American Internat. Sch. of Muscat, Sultante of Oman. [34144] 08/10/1981 **CM24/06/1992**

Gelsthorpe, Mr T P, BA(Hons), Unknown. [10001615] 22/02/2007 **ME**

Genet, Mrs E M, MLS, Unknown. [10016886] 01/06/2010 **ME**

Gent, Ms I, BA LLB(Hons), Info. Offr., Linklaters, London. [10016079] 08/02/2010 **ME**

Gent, Mrs S, BSc(Hons) MCLIP, Inf. Servs. Mgr.,Guildford L., Surrey C.C. [12804] 04/10/1971 **CM01/10/1974**

Gentle, Mrs P R, ACLIP, L. Asst., Chesterfield L., Chesterfield. [66001] 15/08/2006 **ACL05/10/2007**

Gentles, Mrs M M, ACLIP, Unknown. [10014155] 01/07/2009 **ACL16/06/2010**

Geoffroy, Ms J A, BA(Hons) MSc, Unwaged. [52574] 08/11/1995 **ME**

George, Mr B S, MCLIP, Head of L., Cent. Bedfordshire Council, Dunstable [5436] 08/12/1961 **CM01/01/1966**

George, Mrs C, BA DipLib MCLIP, Princ. Lib., Torfaen Co. Bor. Council, Cwmbran. [28330] 01/11/1977 **CM11/07/1980**

George, Mrs J, BA DipLib MCLIP, Sen. Asst. Lib., Univ. of Bristol L. [32959] 06/10/1980 **CM08/11/1982**

George, Miss K R, BA, Dep. Head of Inf., OCIO, Home Off., London [43181] 19/09/1989 **ME**

George, Mrs K, BA(Hons) MCLIP, Principal Lib., Shropshire C.C., Shrewsbury. [36946] 18/01/1984 **CM27/07/1994**

George, Ms L J, BA DMS MCLIP, Dir. of Libs, Luton Cultural Servs. Trust [1656] 28/01/1972 **CM19/08/1975**

George, Mrs L K, BA MCLIP, Sch. Lib., Dover Grammar Sch. for Boys, Dover, Kent. [26936] 17/01/1977 **CM22/10/1981**

George, Ms L, Community L. Mgr., Kilburn L., London. [65887] 27/06/2006 **AF**

George, Mr R H, BA(Hons) MCLIP, Community Lib., Caerphilly, Educ. Leisure & L., Blackwood. [10000688] 25/10/2006 **CM20/01/1999**

George, Mrs S L, BA MSc MCLIP, Subject Lib., Univ. Bradford, Bradford. [63944] 18/11/2004 **CM23/01/2008**

George, Miss S M, BA MCLIP, Lib., ABM Univ., Neath Port Talbot Hosp. [40752] 01/06/1987 **CM24/06/1992**

George, Mr W H, BA DipLib FGS MCLIP, Sen. Lib., L.B. of Barking & Dagenham. [27980] 03/10/1977 **CM07/01/1981**

Georgiou, Mr M, BA MA, Unwaged [58917] 03/10/2000 **ME**

Germany, Mr A, MCLIP, Life Member. [5446] 27/02/1940 **CM01/01/1944**

Gerrard, Mr A D, BA(Hons) MSc(Econ) MCLIP, Catr., Univ. of Cumbria [54299] 20/11/1996 **CM21/05/2003**

Gerrard, Mrs A J, BA MCLIP, L. Asst., Francis Costello L. (P/T) [49549] 09/11/1993 **CM26/11/1997**

Gerrard, Mrs K S, BA(Hons) MSc(Econ) MCLIP, Sen. L. Asst., Lancaster Univ. [53471] 01/07/1996 **CM16/07/2003**

Gerrard, Miss S E, BA(Hons) MA, Info. Offr., The Concrete Soc., Camberley [49929] 25/01/1994 **ME**

Gerrish, Ms A, BA CNAA DipLib MCLIP, Aquisitions & Catg. Lib., Health Care L., Univ. of Oxford. [24883] 06/10/1975 **CM29/12/1978**

Gerritsen, Mrs C L, BA(Hons) MCLIP, Document Logistics Mgr., Allen & Overy LLP., London [39818] 05/08/1986 **CM11/12/1989**

Ghansah, Miss C J, BA(Hons) MSc MCLIP, knowledge Mgr. [55965] 02/01/1998 **CM16/07/2003**

Ghiggino, Mrs R, BA MCLIP, Housewife. [35552] 01/11/1982 **CM27/10/1992**

Ghilchik, Mr T C, BA, Unemployed. [54913] 13/05/1997 **ME**

Ghiotto, Miss A, BA PGDipILS, Lib., Univ. of Bologna, Italy. [57600] 19/05/1999 **ME**

Ghosal, Mr N, BA MCLIP, Life Member. [5450] 01/09/1961 **CM01/01/1966**

Ghosh, Mrs M E, MLS MBA, Academic Liaison Lib., Univ. of London, Senate House L. [58421] 09/02/2000 **ME**

Ghoshray, Mrs A, MCLIP, Asst. Lib, Badminton Sch., Bristol [63370] 21/04/2004 **CM28/01/2009**

Ghumra, Ms I, BA(Hons) MCLIP, Healthcare L. Mgr., Q. E. Hosp. NHS Trust, London. [44778] 19/11/1990 **CM17/01/2001**

Giannakopoulos, Mr T, BSc, Ref. Lib., IAEA L., Austria. [10010840] 29/08/2008 **ME**

Giannitrapani, Ms S, Stud., Inst. of Advanced Legal Stud. [10006112] 03/03/2009 **ME**

Giannola, Ms P, BA MS Ed, Stud., Robert Gorgon Univ., Aberdeen. [10015955] 29/01/2010 **ME**

Gibb, Mrs C E, MA DipLib MCLIP, Asst. Lib., Univ. of the W. of England, Hartpury Campus. [33887] 10/04/1981 **CM11/04/1985**

Gibb, Mr I P, BA MCLIP, Life Member. [5453] 05/10/1950 **CM01/01/1954**

Gibb, Mr K, Unwaged. [62810] 24/10/2003 **ME**

Gibb, Mrs T H, MCLIP, Lib., Young Peoples Serv., Hertfordshire C.C., Hoddesdon [23687] 23/01/1975 **CM31/08/1977**

Gibbins, Miss D M, p. /t. Stud. /Lib., Babcock Integrated Tech., Bristol. [62560] 20/08/2003 **ME**

Gibbins, Mrs K J, BA MCLIP, Project and Operations Mgr., L. Serv., Swansea. [41544] 12/01/1988 **CM24/06/1992**

Gibbons, Mr M, PGDipILM, Lib., Halton Lea L., Cheshire. [61451] 31/07/2002 **ME**

Gibbons, Ms S J, BA MCLIP, Asst. Mgr, CYPS Fosse L. Leicester City L. [36842] 01/01/1984 **CM14/02/1990**

Gibbons, Miss S L, BA(Hons) MCLIP, Unemployed- seeking work [49405] 21/10/1993 **CM12/03/2003**

Gibbs, Mr D W, BA MCLIP, Asst. Dir., Derbys. C.C., Matlock. [35764] 17/01/1983 **CM06/10/1987**

Gibbs, Mrs D, BA MCLIP, Retired. [5461] 05/08/1950 **CM01/01/1955**

Gibbs, Mr G, Grad. Trainee, Treasury Solicitor's L., London [10011904] 15/05/2009 **ME**

Gibbs, Mr J C, BA(Hons) MCLIP, IT and Operations Lib., Barbican L., London. [41020] 01/10/1987 **CM27/05/1992**

Gibbs, Miss J M, BA MCLIP, Life Member. [5462] 01/01/1948 **CM01/01/1955**

Gibbs, Dr S E, BA DipLib FCLIP MA DipCounsell, Prog. Mgr., Lifelong Learning Ctr., Univ. of Leeds [18402] 19/10/1972 **FE15/11/2000**

Gibbs, Miss T A, BA MSc MCLIP, Academic Liaison Lib., Univ. of Southampton, Hartley L. [60008] 21/11/2001 **CM21/03/2007**

Gibbs-Monaghan, Mrs Z A, BA(Hons), Subject Lib., Harold Cohen Univ., Liverpool [10008512] 02/04/2008 **ME**

Giblin, Mrs S, Stud., Aberystwyth Univ. [10013921] 17/06/2009 **ME**

Gibson, Ms A R, BA DipLib MCLIP, Co-Mgr. Learning Res. Cent., Churchill Comm. Sch., N. Somerset. [36562] 19/10/1983 **CM16/12/1986**

Gibson, Ms C, BA MA, L. Customer Serv. Mgr., Communities & Local Government, London [38300] 21/02/1985 **ME**

Gibson, Ms C, BA(Hons), p. /t. Stud., Manchester Met. Univ., Univ. of Cent. Lancs. [10001551] 23/02/2007 **ME**

Gibson, Mr D B, FCLIP, Life Member. [5473] 19/03/1945 **FE01/01/1955**

Gibson, Mrs E A, MCLIP, Res. Cent. Mgr., Third Age Trust, London. [2538] 25/09/1969 **CM06/07/1973**

Gibson, Mrs G, MCLIP, Inf. Serv. Lib., Darlington L., Darlington Bor. Council. [22049] 08/01/1974 **CM01/01/1977**

Gibson, Mrs H, ACLIP, Area Mgr., W. Lothian Lib. HQ, W. Lothian. [65257] 08/12/2005 **ACL04/07/2006**

Gibson, Miss H, BSc(Hons) MA, Cent. Lib., Northampton Coll. at Daventry. [64072] 15/12/2004 **ME**

Gibson, Dr J A, MD FLS FSA, Hon. Lib., Scot. Nat. Hist. L., Renfrewshire. [29887] 14/10/1978 **ME**

Gibson, Mrs J, BSc (Hons), Grp. Mgr., Sedgefield L., Durham. [10009990] 27/06/2008 **ME**

Gibson, Ms J, BA MA MCLIP, Head of L. & Museums, L.B. of Enfield. [35720] 01/01/1983 **CM06/10/1987**

Gibson, Mrs J, BA(Hons) MCLIP, Retired [47714] 19/10/1992 **CM22/05/1996**

Gibson, Mr K L, BA DipLib FCLIP, Life Member. [5478] 01/01/1947 **FE01/01/1958**

Gibson, Mrs L J, MCLIP, Lib., Hounslow L. Network/CIP, Hounslow. [62722] 13/10/2003 **CM19/03/2008**

Gibson, Miss M E, MLS MCLIP, Retired. [5483] 11/03/1960 **CM01/01/1963**

Gibson, Ms M M, BA(Hons) MCLIP, L. Inf. Serv. Mgr., Northern Ireland Housing Exec., Belfast. [50273] 25/05/1994 **CM16/07/2003**

Gibson, Mrs M, MCLIP, Lib., Glasgow C.C. [28300] 10/11/1977 **CM29/02/1980**

Gibson, Miss R E, MTheol DipLib MCLIP, Special Collections Lib., Univ. of Birmingham. [32960] 09/10/1980 **CM22/02/1984**

Gibson, Miss R J, MA(Hons), Mob. Coordinator., Action for Blind People, London. [57330] 12/02/1999 **ME**

Gibson, Ms R, MA DipLib, Grp. Inf. Mgr., Dept. Dept. for Business, Enterprise & Regulatory Reform., London. [38892] 18/10/1985 **ME**

Gibson, Mr S P, Tech. Serv. Lib., Univ. Coll. Falmouth, Falmouth. [34942] 14/05/1982 **ME**

Gick, Dr R C, MA(Hons) MusM PhD, Liasion Lib.(Health)., Keele Univ. [62727] 13/10/2003 **ME**

Gidman, Mrs J E, BA(Hons) DipLib, Sch. Lib., Rudheath High Sch., Northwich. [34742] 13/01/1982 **ME**

Giesbrecht, Mrs B M, MCLIP, Life Member. [17387] 30/01/1951 **CM01/01/1957**

Giffen, Miss S A, BA MCLIP, Retired [5491] 01/10/1968 **CM01/01/1972**

Giggey, Ms S E, MLS MCLIP, Adjunct Lect., Vancouver, Canada. [36539] 23/10/1983 **CM11/02/1986**

Gilani-Williams, Ms F, Ref. Lib., Oberlin P.L., USA [10006215] 26/09/2007 **ME**

Gilbert, Dr G H, PhD FRPharmS WS PhC MCLIP, Retired. [60290] 05/06/1975 **CM10/12/2001**

Gilbert, Ms J A M, BA(Hons) PgDip, L. Asst., Monifieth L., Monifieth. [10001187] 02/10/2002 **ME**

Gilbert, Mr J I D, BA, Stud. [10017025] 18/06/2010 **ME**

Gilbert, Mr L A, MSc HonFLA, Retired. [36768] 19/09/1983 **HFE19/09/1983**

Gilbert, Mrs L, MCLIP, Site Lib., Rutherford Appleton Lab. [63256] 23/03/2004 **CM06/05/2009**

Gilbert, Ms S E, MSc MCLIP, Support Serv. Lib. [23577] 13/01/1975 **CM13/06/1989**

Gilbert, Mr T, BA, Stud., Loughborough Univ. [10014736] 07/09/2009 **ME**

Gilberthorpe, Dr E C, BA PhD FCLIP, Life Member. [5502] 01/01/1948 **FE01/01/1967**

Gilchrist, Mr A D B, D. Litt HonFCLIP, Sen. Partner, Alan Gilchrist & Partners, Brighton. [5506] 21/04/1961 **FE01/04/2002**

Gilchrist, Miss C, BA(Hons), Stud., Manchester Met. Univ. [10014829] 16/09/2009 **ME**

Gilchrist, Mrs J R, MA DipLib MCLIP, Outside Serv. Lib., N. Lanarkshire Council, Coatbridge. [31106] 25/07/1979 **CM07/12/1982**

Gilchrist, Mr N M, MA DipLIS MCLIP, L. Offr., Edinburgh City Council. [59044] 07/11/2000 **CM04/02/2004**

Gilchrist, Mrs P M, BA FCLIP, Retired. [1090] 07/09/1960 **FE01/01/1965**

Gildersleeves, Mrs E L P, MA MLib MCLIP, p. /t. Lect., Univ. Coll. London. [37489] 01/10/1984 **CM18/01/1989**

Giles, Ms A S, BA(Hons) MCLIP, L. & Knowledge Serv. Mgr., Taunton & Somerset NHS Foundation Trust, Somerset. [50498] 22/08/1994 **CM22/09/1999**

Giles, Mrs G, MLib BA MCLIP, Learning Resources Mgr., Heart of England NHS Foundation Trust, Good Hope Hosp., Sutton Coldfield. [25349] 05/01/1976 **CM11/04/1980**

Giles, Mrs H, MA BA MCLIP, Childrens Serv. Devel. Offr. [27804] 02/09/1977 **CM08/07/1980**

Giles, Mrs J B, MA DipLib MCLIP, Legal Deposit Curator, Nat. L. of Scotland, Edinburgh. [35463] 15/10/1982 **CM05/05/1987**

Giles-Bather, Mrs J D, BSc(Hons) MBA(Open), L. Asst. S. Glouchestershire Council. [10008695] 18/04/2008 **AF**

Gilham, Miss J L, MA MCLIP, Life Member. [5521] 27/08/1954 **CM01/01/1958**

Gilham-Skinner, Ms W, MA (hons) Lib Dip, Mob. Coordinator, Eastgate Cent., Lincolnshire. [10007760] 04/03/2002 **ME**

Gilkerson, Mrs E A, MCLIP, Life Member. [5524] 07/03/1949 **CM01/01/1959**

Gilkes, Mr A R, BA DipLib, Unemployed/Unwaged. [38769] 01/10/1985 **ME**

Gill, Ms A J, BA MA, Inf. Offr., Gtr. Manchester Co. Record Off., Manchester. [41052] 05/10/1987 **ME**

Gill, Miss A K, BA(Hons) DMS MCLIP MCMI MInstL, Mgr., HCCLIS, Gosport Discovery Cent. [46325] 28/10/1991 **CM23/03/1994**

Gill, Miss C J, MA, Virtual Support & eServices Developer,Univ. of Surrey, Guildford. [59850] 16/10/2001 **ME**

Gill, Mrs D, BA DipLib MCLIP, Showroom Mgr., Peters Bookselling Serv., Birmingham. [39494] 10/02/1986 **CM06/09/1988**

Gill, Mrs F M, Sr. Asst., Catg., Devon Libs. [10000759] 02/09/1996 **ME**

Gill, Mr J B, BSc MCLIP, Princ. Lib., Poole Hosp. NHS Trust. Dorset. [5531] 26/04/1971 **CM03/01/1974**

Gill, Ms J M, BSc DipEH DipIS, L. Exec., House of Commons L., London. [50502] 23/08/1994 **ME**

Gill, Mrs J R, Team Lib., Inf. Serv., Cent. Bedfordshire C.C. [25342] 09/01/1976 **ME**

Gill, Mrs J, Asst. Lib., The Holy Trinity CE Secondary Sch., Crawley. [10013353] 16/04/2009 **AF**

Gill, Mrs J, BA MCLIP, Inf. Asst., Edinburgh Napier Univ., Borders General Hosp., Melrose. [26102] 30/06/1976 **CM28/04/1980**

Gill, Mrs K L, BA MCLIP, Learning Res. Asst., Lymm High Sch., Cheshire. [30520] 08/01/1979 **CM05/07/1982**

Gill, Miss L V, Trainee Lib., Crawley L. [64155] 19/01/2005 **ME**

Gill, Mrs L, BSc(Hons) PGDIP, Lib. Yorkshire Water Serv. Ltd. [63079] 27/01/2004 **ME**

Gill, Mrs M A, BA DipLib MCLIP, Sen. LIS offr., Univ. of Cumbria [25538] 05/01/1976 **CM01/12/1977**

Gill, Mrs M E, BA MCLIP, Campus L. Mgr., Napier Univ., Edinburgh. [5533] 14/01/1970 **CM11/06/1973**

Gill, Miss M E, BA(Hons) MA PhD, Tutor at The Open Univ., Child. Lit. [43964] 09/03/1990 **ME**

Gill, Mr P G, FCLIP, Life Member. [5534] 16/01/1957 **FE21/08/1974**

Gillam, Mr L A, BD DipSocAdmin MCLIP, Retired. [5537] 08/01/1968 **CM01/01/1971**

Gillan, Mrs L E, MCLIP, Principal Lib., Culture and Sport, Glasgow [20635] 18/05/1973 **CM01/07/1976**

Gillen, Ms L, Lib. Trainee, Nottingham Cent. L. [10013515] 30/04/2009 **ME**

Gillespie, Miss G C, BA(Hons), Young People's Leaning Coordinator, N. Ayrshire Council, IRVINE. [10016502] 02/12/1996 **ME**

Gillespie, Ms H, BSc, Freelance Med. Inf. Offr. [41758] 10/03/1988 **ME**

Gillespie, Mrs K J, BLS MCLIP, p. /t. Asst. Lib., Northern Ireland Assembly, Belfast. [33018] 17/10/1980 **CM01/08/1986**

Gillespie, Mrs M A, BA DipLib MCLIP, Area & Campus Lib., Univ. of Stirling, Inverness. [27189] 06/12/1976 **CM25/11/1981**

Gillespie, Mr R A, FCLIP, Life Member. [5547] 27/09/1949 **FE01/01/1968**

Gillespie, Mrs S M, MCLIP, Life Member. [5548] 01/01/1950 **CM01/01/1956**

Gillespie, Mr T S, FCLIP, Retired. [5549] 10/09/1948 **FE01/01/1957**

Gillies, Mr A S, MA(Hons) DipLib(LIS), Unknown, IDOX Inf. Serv., Glasgow. [48078] 03/11/1992 **ME**

Gillies, Mrs F F, BA MCLIP, Young People & Sch. Res. Lib., Aberdeenshire L. & Inf. Serv. [35608] 19/10/1982 **CM08/12/1987**

Gillies, Mrs K, Lib. Super., L. at Goma, Glasgow [10016472] 01/04/2010 **AF**

Gillies, Mr S, MA, Ref. Team Leader, The Brit. L., London. [41770] 25/03/1988 **ME**

Gilliland, Ms G M, BA PGCE DipLIS MCLIP, Lib.-in-charge., Co. L., Haverfordwest [44661] 20/11/1990 **CM28/10/2004**

Gillings-Grant, Ms F L A, BSc(Hons) DipLS MBA, L. Mgr., Birmingham City Council, Sheldon & Kents Moat L. [58855] 07/09/2000 **ME**

Gillis, Ms H R, Learning & Access Mgr., Museums Galleries Scotland. [61469] 12/08/2002 **ME**

Gillis, Mr I R, BSc MCLIP, Records Assoc., Financial Serv. Auth., London. [5557] 05/10/1968 **CM11/11/1974**

Gilman, Ms A H E, BA MCLIP, Lib., Derbyshire C.C., Derbyshire. . [25037] 14/11/1975 **CM09/08/1979**

Gilman, Miss L J, Stud. [10015363] 12/11/2009 **ME**

Gilman, Ms V, Inf. Offr., Pinsent Masons, London. [53119] 11/03/1996 **AF**

Gilmore, Mr J, BA(Hons) PGCE DipLib MCLIP, Retired Teacher. [31067] 17/08/1979 **CM11/09/1981**

Gilmour, Ms A E, BA DipIT MCLIP, Community Inf. Worker, Dundee City Council. [60258] 21/10/1996 **CM11/01/2001**

Gilmour, Miss A, BA MCLIP, Customer Serv. Team Leader., Dunfermline Carnegie L., Fife Council. [35780] 24/01/1983 **CM31/07/1984**

Gilmour, Ms F, MA(Hons) DipLib MCLIP, Sen. Lib. English Heritage (NMR), Wilts. [27982] 01/10/1977 **CM01/12/1980**

Gilmurray, Mrs S M, MA PGCE DipIS MCLIP, Asst. Lib., Anglia Ruskin Univ., Cambridge. [47090] 28/04/1992 **CM10/07/2002**

Gilpin, Mrs B, PgDip, Stud., City Univ. [10005342] 05/07/2007 **ME**

Gilroy, Mr D P, BA(Hons) MA MCLIP, L. Serv. Mgr., Teaching Hosp. NHS Trust, Bradford. [55282] 15/09/1997 **RV16/04/2008** **CM16/07/2003**

Gilwhite, Mrs J, BA(Hons) MA MCLIP, Resources Lib., Notts. C.C. [59028] 24/10/2000 **CM20/04/2009**

Gilzean, Ms V, Stud., City Univ. [10001056] 12/12/2006 **ME**

Ginn, Mr J W, BSc MA MCLIP, Lib., Med. and Healthcare Products Regulatory Agency, London. [59491] 09/04/2001 **CM09/11/2005**

Ginn, Mrs S J, Lib., Holy Cross 6th Form Coll., Bury. [64501] 13/04/2005 **ME**

Ginnings, Mrs S M, MA LLB BL, Stud. UCL, London. [10010527] 01/08/2008 **ME**

Girdwood, Ms P G, DipLib MCLIP, Lib., Blue Gate Fields Junior Sch., London. [31836] 08/01/1980 **CM13/04/1982**

Girma, Rev A H, BA PGEC, Stud. [10015427] 16/11/2009 **ME**

Gittings, Mrs S, Stud., Aberystwyth Univ. [10015262] 30/10/2009 **ME**

Giurlando, Ms L, BA MCLIP, Lib., Oundle Sch., Oundle [53452] 01/07/1996 **CM23/09/1998**

Givan, Mr A M, MA(Hons) MSc MCLIP, Lib., Ferguslie Park Comm. L., Renfrewshire Council. [51084] 14/11/1994 **CM10/07/2002**

Given, Ms L, ACLIP, Records Mgmnt. Offr., Northern Ireland L. Auth., Ballymena. [65037] 13/10/2005 **ACL01/07/2007**

Gkoutsidou, Miss M A, Stud. [10012365] 23/02/2009 **ME**

Gladden, Mr N J, BA(Hons) PgDip MCLIP, Acq. & Documentation Offr., N. W. Film Arch., Manchester. [58906] 03/10/2000 **CM12/03/2003**

Gladstone, Ms C L, BA, Lib., Birmingham L. Serv., Arts Languages & Literature Sect. [39599] 18/03/1986 **ME**

Gladstone, Mr T M, LLB(Hons), Business Inf. Offr., Inst. of Dir., London. [51740] 12/06/1995 **ME**

Gladwell, Miss E, BA, Lib. Asst., Bartlett L., London [10012936] 20/03/2009 **ME**

Gladwin, Ms A R, BA, Unknown. [47078] 15/04/1992 **ME**

Gladwin, Miss R L, BA, Stud., Loughborough Univ. [10015087] 12/10/2009 **ME**

Glancy, Mr A, MA(Hons), Asst. Lib., Min. of Defence., London [59171] 05/12/2000 **ME**

Glancy, Mr M J, BA MCLIP, L. Operations Mgr., Nat. Museums Scotland. [32520] 21/05/1980 **CM10/08/1982**

Glancy, Mr P C, MA(Hons), Sen. Inf. Asst., De Monfort Univ., Leicester. [42375] 18/10/1988 **ME**

Glanfield, Ms M E, BA(Hons), Lib., Cent. of African Studies, Cambridge Univ. [62676] 02/10/2003 **ME**

Glanville, Ms J M, BA PGDipLib MSc MCLIP, Proj. Dir., York Health Economics Consortium Ltd. [35198] 05/10/1982 **CM01/04/2002**

Glasby, Mrs J B, BA MCLIP, L. Mgr., Leeds Coll. of Music. [27817] 28/08/1977 **CM28/08/1979**

Glasgow, Mrs F, ACLIP, Sch. Lib., Reepham High Sch., Norfolk. [64740] 14/06/2005 **ACL04/03/2009**

Glayzer, Ms J A, MCLIP, Retired. [5586] 06/10/1964 **CM01/01/1968**

Gledhill, Mr P F, BA(Hons) DipLIS MCLIP, Faculty Team Leader, Sheffield Hallam Univ. [46510] 15/11/1991 **CM23/07/1997**

Gledhill, Ms S E, BA DipLib MCLIP, Devel. Lib., Herts. C.C. [39264] 15/01/1986 **CM15/03/1989**

Gledhill, Mrs V C, MA DipLib MCLIP, Extend Hours Lib., Oxford Brookes Univ. & Lib., Chandlings Manor Sch., Oxford [38704] 01/10/1985 **CM13/06/1989**

Gleeson, Miss C, BA(Hons) MCLIP, Subject Lib., Univ. of Chester, Warrington. [62724] 13/10/2003 **CM21/03/2007**

Glen, Mrs S M, BA, Dep. Subject Lib., Univ. of Wales, Swansea. [44058] 20/04/1990 **ME**

Glen, Mrs S, FCSD DipLib MCLIP, Retired. [44403] 04/10/1990 **CM21/01/1998**

Glendinning, Mrs H A, BA(Hons), L. Asst., Buckley L., Flintshire. [10004964] 06/06/2007 **ME**

Glenton, Mrs R, BA, Sure Start Lib., Derbyshire C.C. [61924] 04/12/2002 **ME**

Glover, Mrs G A, BA(Hons) MA MCLIP, Unemployed. [43695] 30/11/1989 **CM24/09/1997**

Glover, Mrs S A, BA MCLIP, Lib., Notts. C.C. Educ. L. Serv. [19627] 23/10/1972 **CM24/12/1974**

Glover, Mr S J, BA(Hons) MA MCLIP, Dep. Lib., Univ. Hosp. of Leicester NHS Trust [57698] 01/07/1999 **CM29/08/2007**

Glover, Mrs S L, BA(Hons), L. Serv. Offr., Royal Blackburn Hosp., Blackburn. [54115] 31/10/1996 **ME**

Glowczewska, Ms J A, BA DipLib, Catr., Brit. L., Boston Spa,W. Yorks. [42853] 01/04/1989 **ME**

Glyde, Mrs H M, MCLIP, Comm. Lib., Wilton L., Wilts. [21781] 14/01/1974 **CM18/10/1976**

Goacher, Mrs W C, MCLIP, Unwaged [10014446] 04/10/1965 **CM01/01/1969**

Gobey, Mr P F, BA DipLib MCLIP, Comm. L. Mgr. -Child. Serv., Leicester City L., Fosse L. [32576] 08/05/1980 **CM30/09/1982**

Godber, Miss F M, MSt BA, Graduate Trainee, Codrington L., Oxford. [10015527] 09/12/2009 **ME**

Godbolt, Mrs L S, BA FCLIP HonFCLIP, Retired. [13786] 01/10/1965 **FE23/05/1975**

Goddard, Mr C, B MUS DipLib MCLIP, Res. & Inf. Mgr., Plymouth L. Serv. [31838] 01/01/1980 **CM25/06/1982**

Goddard, Mrs E L, BA(Hons) ACLIP, Enq. Offr. Ipswich Co. L., Suffolk C. C [56637] 01/10/1998 **ACL06/09/2006**

Goddard, Mr M, MSc BSc(Hons), Inf. Sci., Medicines and Healthcare Products Regulatory Agency, London. [46714] 03/01/1992 **ME**

Goddard, Mr N R, MCLIP, Project Mgr., Wiltshire Council. [26729] 24/11/1976 **CM29/11/1979**

Goddard, Ms S, BA MA MCLIP, Asst. Lib., Univ. of Westminster, Marylebone Campus L. [58274] 06/12/1999 **CM23/06/2004**

Godfree, Ms J C J, MA PGCE DipLib MCLIP, Lib., Portsmouth Grammar Sch. [26533] 06/10/1976 **CM30/01/1979**

Godfrey, Mrs A J, MCLIP, Lib. (Sunday), Balham L., London. [26617] 19/10/1976 **CM20/10/1980**

Godfrey, Mrs J V, MCLIP, Princ. L. Asst., Univ. of Oxford, Acquisitions Serv., Bodleian L. [15634] 29/05/1969 **CM26/02/1973**

Godfrey, Ms M A, MA ARMIT AALIA MCLIP, Life Member. [5625] 03/03/1970 **CM01/01/1972**

Godfrey, Miss S A B, MA MCLIP, Inf. Lib., W. Sussex C.C. I. Serv., Chichester [62091] 12/02/2003 **CM21/06/2006**

Godfrey, Mr T, MA, Stud. [10006581] 23/10/2007 **ME**

Godrich, Mrs D A, BA(Hons) DipIM MCLIP, Career Break. [52437] 31/10/1995 **CM19/01/2000**

Godsell, Miss K, BA(Hons) MCLIP, Dep. Br. Mgr., Leyland L. [40847] 14/07/1987 **CM24/07/1996**

Godsell, Mrs S, BSc MCLIP, Sci. Subject Lib., Birkbeck Coll., Univ. of London. [60830] 01/04/1991 **CM23/08/1993**

Godsmark, Mrs R J, BA DipLib MCLIP, Employment not known. [26986] 10/01/1977 **CM29/01/1979**

Godwin, Mrs J, BA(Hons) MCLIP, Knowledge Offr., Hull and E. Yorkshire Hosp. Trust [33944] 04/06/1981 **CM19/09/1988**

Godwin, Mrs K J, BA(Hons), Unknown. [10013349] 16/04/2009 **ME**

Godwin, Mr P, BA MCLIP CLTHE, Academic Liaison Lib., Bedfordshire Univ. [5632] 03/01/1972 **CM25/01/1974**

Godwin, Ms P, BA(Hons) PGCE, Sch. Lib. Mgr., Leiston High Sch., Suffolk. [59920] 29/10/2001 **ME**

Godwin, Mrs S M, BA(Hons) MA MCLIP, Unwaged. [55360] 03/10/1997 **CM20/11/2002**

Going, Miss H, BA(Hons) MA, Inf. Offr., Clyde and Co., London. [63970] 22/11/2004 **ME**

Gokce, Mrs C M, BSc(Hons) MSc MCLIP FLS, Asst. Dir., ICT Strategy, Cabinet Off., London. [35950] 23/03/1983 **CM17/09/2003**

Gold, Miss S E, BA(Hons) DipLib MCLIP, Lib., Doncaster Coll. [40306] 05/01/1987 **CM07/09/2005**

253

Golden, Mrs S M, BSc(Hons) PGCE, Access Serv. Mgr., Kent C.C. [46158] 03/10/1991 **ME**

Goldfarb, Mr M B, Tower Hamlets Local Hist. Lib. & Arch., London [64849] 28/07/2005 **AF**

Goldfinch, Mrs A M, BSc(Hons) MSc MCLIP, Liaison Lib. (Employed/Tech. Abstractor(Self Employed) [10000839] 02/03/1981 **CM20/11/1989**

Goldfinch, Mr J E, BA(Hons) MA MCLIP, Head, Incunabula & Early W Printed Books, Brit. L., London. [27813] 20/09/1977 **CM29/01/1982**

Goldfinch, Mr R G, MSc MCLIP, Snr. Info. Scientist, MHRA., London [33755] 31/01/1981 **CM01/04/2002**

Goldie, Miss J H, BA DipLib MCLIP, Principle Policy Off., Dumfries & Galloway L. Inf. & Arch., Dumfries. [35504] 20/10/1982 **CM31/12/1986**

Goldie, Mrs J, MCLIP, SLS Lead Adviser, Hants. C.C. [23956] 04/02/1975 **CM01/03/1978**

Goldie, Mrs V S, BA DipIS MCLIP, Sen. Lib., Bournemouth Bor. Council. [30908] 08/06/1979 **CM20/11/2002**

Golding, Mrs V, MCLIP, LRC Mgr., Sheppey Coll. [19918] 08/01/1973 **CM15/12/1975**

Golditch-Williams, Ms O R, BSc (Hons) DipLib MCLIP, Sen. Lib., Grangemouth L. [10010568] 14/04/1977 **CM01/12/1979**

Goldrick, Miss M E, FCLIP, Life Member. [5644] 05/03/1942 **FE01/01/1954**

Goldsmith, Mrs R, BA MCLIP, Staff Devel. Mgr., Cambs. L. & Inf. Serv. [29300] 01/01/1973 **CM01/01/1978**

Goldstone, Mr J, BSc DipLib MCLIP, Employment not known. [26967] 11/01/1977 **CM11/04/1979**

Goldstone, Mrs P A, Bibl. & Systems Offr., Bracknell Forest Bor. Council. [5649] 03/10/1962 **AF**

Goldthorp, Ms J D, Unknown [62595] 05/09/2003 **ME**

Goldwater, Mr S J, BA MCLIP, Inf. Offr., Montagu Evans, London. [24492] 21/08/1975 **CM04/08/1978**

Golland, Mr A R L, BA DipLib MCLIP, Keeper, Printed Books, Imperial War Mus., London. [19839] 10/01/1973 **CM01/01/1975**

Gomersall, Mrs R F, BSc(Econ) MCLIP, L. Mgr., Cheshire E. C., Crewe L. [47402] 10/08/1992 **CM21/03/2001**

Gomm, Miss B, MCLIP, Life Member. [5657] 16/09/1956 **CM01/01/1963**

Gomm, Miss S I, MCLIP, Retired. [5658] 06/03/1945 **CM01/01/1953**

Gommersall, Miss K, BA MCLIP, L. Mgr., Dept. for Work and Pensions, Sheffield [41566] 28/01/1988 **CM26/01/1994**

Gonsai, Mrs A M, BA(Hons), Libr., Swanwick Hall Sch., Derbyshire. [48375] 09/12/1992 **ME**

Gonsalves, Ms M, Inf. Exec., Inst. of Practitioners in Advertising, London. [10016184] 23/02/2010 **ME**

Gonzalez, Mrs A L, BSc(Econ), Sch. Lib., Oswestry Sch. [62732] 15/10/2003 **ME**

Gooch, Mr P S L, BSc MCLIP, Retired. [60292] 18/01/1978 **CM18/01/1978**

Good, Mr D, BA MCLIP, Retired. [5662] 14/01/1958 **CM01/01/1961**

Good, Mrs S D, MA, Inf. Co-Ordinator, London. [10000891] 22/11/2006 **ME**

Goodair, Mrs C M, BA MCLIP MAUA, Programme Co-ordinator, Inter. Cent. for Drug Policy., St Georges Med. Sch., London Univ. [26883] 24/11/1976 **CM23/10/1980**

Goodall, Dr D L, MPhil BA PhD MCLIP, Univ. of Huddersfield. [38792] 07/10/1985 **CM18/09/1991**

Goodall, Ms L, BA(Hons) MA, Catr., Univ. of Leicester [54306] 20/11/1996 **ME**

Goodall, Mr N, MA FCLIP, Retired. [5669] 03/08/1948 **FE01/01/1964**

Goodall, Miss W F, MCLIP, Unwaged [56396] 01/07/1998 **CM19/03/2008**

Gooday, Mrs E M M, BA MCLIP, Inf. Serv. Offr., Inst. of Hospitality. [36897] 13/01/1984 **CM25/09/1986**

Goodchild, Miss G, BA DipLib MCLIP, Coll. Lib., Colchester Sixth Form Coll., Essex. [33810] 10/03/1981 **CM24/01/1986**

Goodchild, Miss L R, BA(Hons) MA MCLIP, Asst. Lib., Guardian News & Media [65424] 24/02/2006 **CM11/06/2010**

Gooderham, Ms J G, BA PGCE MCLIP, Sch. Lib., Sir John Leman High Sch., Suffolk. [5676] 17/07/1971 **CM04/12/1974**

Goodey, Mrs L F, BA(Hons) MA, Res. Serv. Lib., Slaughter and May, London. [57023] 26/11/1998 **ME**

Goodfellow, Mrs J A, MA(Hons) MA MCLIP, Career Break. [53934] 11/10/1996 **CM15/11/2000**

Goodfellow, Mr N J, BA MA MCLIP, Knowledge & Tech. Mgr. & Faculty Inf. Con., Univ. of Herts. [42070] 03/10/1988 **CM17/10/1990**

Goodger, Mrs A N, BA(Hons) MA MCLIP, Lib., NHS Lincolnshire, Lincs. Knowledge & Resource Serv. [49967] 31/01/1994 **CM17/03/1999**

Goodger, Mr C F, MA(Hons), Sr. Researcher, CRA Inter., London. [50575] 21/09/1994 **ME**

Goodger, Mrs G R, BA DipLib, Sen. Lib., Herbert Smith, London. [37372] 25/07/1984 **ME**

Goodhand, Miss E A, MA MCLIP, Asst. Lib., N. Warwickshire & Hinckley Coll., Leics. [64654] 11/04/2005 **CM23/01/2008**

Goodhew, Ms L, BA(Hons) MA MCLIP, Asst Subj Libn., Oxford Brookes Univ. [61302] 16/05/2002 **CM04/10/2006**

Goodier, Mr J C, BSc MSc MCLIP, Inf. Scientist, Forensic Sci. Serv., London. [60690] 21/12/1982 **CM01/08/1986**

Goodier, Miss R, BA(Hons) DipLib, Faculty Team. Lib., The John Rylands Univ. L., Univ. of Manchester. [10000810] 26/07/1984 **ME**

Gooding, Mrs H C, Career Break [63223] 16/03/2004 **ME**

Gooding, Mrs L A, BSc MSc MCLIP, Principal. Lib. Asst. . (p. /t.), Univ. of Southampton. [52754] 05/12/1995 **CM01/04/2002**

Gooding, Miss M I E, BA MCLIP, Retired. [5686] 24/09/1964 **CM01/01/1967**

Gooding, Mrs R, BA DipLib MCLIP, Liaison. Lib., Catg. Dept., Univ. of Reading L. [43494] 30/10/1989 **CM16/11/1994**

Goodlet, Mr A H, MCLIP, Retired. [5687] 15/03/1938 **CM01/01/1948**

Goodliffe, Mr E C, BA(Hons) MCLIP, Retired. [5688] 04/10/1963 **CM01/01/1967**

Goodman, Mr A D, BA MCLIP, Marketing & Customer Serv. Mgr., W. Sussex C.C. L. [35924] 28/02/1983 **CM08/12/1987**

Goodman, Mrs A, BMedSci PgDipLIS, Immanuel Coll.,Herts. [57672] 01/07/1999 **ME**

Goodman, Ms E C, BSc MSc MCLIP, Business & Info. Consultant [10015640] 24/03/1984 **CM29/10/1987**

Goodman, Ms H L, BA DipInfSc MCLIP, L. Mgr., W. London Mental Health NHS Trust. [45873] 03/07/1991 **CM24/07/1996**

Goodman, Mrs M, BA MCLIP, Unwaged. [19980] 15/12/1972 **CM08/01/1976**

Goodman, Ms S L, BSc MA DipLib, Dep. Mgr., Somerset L., Bridgwater. [63673] 12/08/2004 **ME**

Goodman, Miss T J, MCLIP, Life Member. [5695] 17/02/1964 **CM01/01/1969**

Goodman, Mrs T S, BA(Hons) MSc MCLIP, Unwaged. [54552] 20/01/1997 **CM18/09/2002**

Goodridge, Mr I M, BSc(Hons) MA, Inf. Analyst, Qinetiq, Wiltshire. [49255] 18/10/1993 **ME**

Goodwill, Miss G M, BA MCLIP, Retired. [5701] 01/01/1969 **CM01/01/1971**

Goodwill, Ms L D, BA MA, Sen. Lib., E. Sussex L. & Inf. Serv. [64082] 15/12/2004 **ME**

Goodwin, Ms A J, MA DipLib, Crichton Lib., Univ. of the W. of Scotland [36485] 18/10/1983 **ME**

Goodwin, Miss C H, p/t. Stud. /Sen. Learning Res. Cent. Asst., Bridgwater Coll., Somerset. [53787] 01/10/1996 **ME**

Goodwin, Mr C J, Lib. [51200] 23/11/1994 **ME**

Goodwin, Mrs K A, BA(Hons) MA MCLIP, Faculty Liaison Lib., Canterbury Christ Church Univ. [50619] 01/10/1994   **CM19/07/2000**

Goody, Mrs M J, DipLib FRSA FCLIP, Self-employed [28217] 03/10/1977   **FE01/04/2002**

Goom, Miss N, FCLIP, Retired. [5706] 30/09/1935   **FE01/01/1946**

Goonatillake, Mrs T P A, MSc, Unwaged. [10010658] 19/08/2008   **ME**

Goose, Mrs M E, BLS MCLIP, Sch. Lib. (JobShare), Hitchin Girl's Sch., Herts. [28141] 07/10/1977   **CM29/09/1982**

Goostrey, Mrs S C, BA(Hons) MSc, Unwaged [56965] 11/11/1998   **ME**

Gopika Jacob, Mr M J, Stud., Thames Valley Univ., London [10013125] 03/04/2009   **ME**

Goram, Mrs R, BA MA MCLIP, Inf. &Database Off., Age Concern, Norfolk. [59925] 10/09/2001   **CM04/10/2006**

Gordon, Mrs A M, MA MCLIP, Sen. Inf. Specialist, Univ. of Abertay Dundee. [20041] 15/01/1973   **CM13/03/1975**

Gordon, Mr A, MA(Hons) DipLib MCLIP, Sch. Lib., W. Dunbartonshire Council. [46787] 23/01/1992   **CM15/09/1993**

Gordon, Mrs C E, BA MCLIP, Asst. Lib., Sch. of Earth Sci., Leeds Univ. [38811] 09/10/1985   **CM27/05/1992**

Gordon, Mrs J T, BA DipLib MCLIP, Team Co-ordinator, Surrey Lib. [43245] 13/10/1989   **CM18/11/1993**

Gordon, Ms J, BA DipLib, Unwaged. [10003914] 23/05/2007   **ME**

Gordon, Mrs L A, BA(Hons) DipLib MCLIP, Lib., Paisley Grammar, Strathclyde Reg. [45780] 28/05/1991   **CM18/11/1993**

Gordon, Miss L C, BSc MA, Programme Leader., Spec. Cent. [62027] 22/01/2003   **ME**

Gordon, Miss L, BA(Hons) MA MCLIP, Asst. Lib. for Business and Tourism, Sunderland Univ. [62774] 20/10/2003   **CM19/11/2008**

Gordon, Ms M D, BA MCLIP, Community Lib., Perth and Kinross Council. [35233] 07/10/1982   **CM10/10/1985**

Gordon, Mrs M J, BA(Hons) MAAD MMAG, Learning Cent. Asst., NCN Clarendon Coll., Nottingham. [10013735] 27/05/2009   **AF**

Gordon, Mrs R A, BA MCLIP, Local Studs. Lib., Derbys. C.C., Matlock, Derbys. [22697] 15/08/1974   **CM22/02/1977**

Gordon, Mrs S E, BA(Hons) DipLis, p. /t. Inf. Serv. Asst., Davies Arnold Cooper, London. [43015] 14/06/1989   **ME**

Gore, Ms J M, MA DipLib MCLIP, Lib., Communities., Local Government., London [28572] 17/01/1978   **CM16/05/1980**

Gore, Miss N, BSc, Stud., Manchester Met. Univ. [10015238] 29/10/2009   **ME**

Goreham, Miss A L, BLib MCLIP, Principal Lib., Royal Bor. of Kensington & Chelsea, London. [35200] 01/10/1982   **CM21/04/1986**

Goreham, Miss H D, BLib MCLIP, Grp. Lib. Mgr., Bucks Co. L. [32068] 24/01/1980   **CM05/03/1984**

Gorman, Prof G E, BA MDivsTB DipLib MA PhD FCLIP, Prof., Sch. of Info. Mgmt., Victoria Univ. of Wellington, NZ. [10001883] 06/11/1974   **FE17/04/1986**

Gorman, Mr M J, FCLIP HonFCLIP, Dean of L. Serv., California State Univ., Fresno, U. S. A. [5725] 28/09/1963   **FE02/03/1978**

Gorman, Mr P J, BA(Hons) PGDipILS MCLIP, Lib., Glasgow Met. Coll. [63037] 17/12/2003   **CM03/10/2007**

Gorman, Ms S J, BA MCLIP, L. Resource Cent. Co-ord., Castlebrae Community High Sch., Edinburgh. [25146] 14/10/1975 **CM31/07/1980**

Gormley, Mr J S, BA(Hons) MA, Inf. Offr., Macfarlanes, London. [62795] 22/10/2003   **ME**

Gorring, Ms H M, BA(Hons) DipLib MSc, L. Serv. Mgr., Coventry P. C. N. H. S. Trust. [58244] 24/11/1999   **ME**

Gorton, Mrs P, BA MCLIP, Inf. Offr., Stephenson Harwood, London. [30192] 10/01/1979   **CM16/12/1982**

Gosby, Mrs E J, BSc MSc MCLIP, Unemployed. [37950] 25/11/1984   **CM19/01/1988**

Gosden, Mrs C, BSc MSc MCLIP, Sch,Lib., L.B. Tower Hamlets Sch. L. Serv., London. [51397] 03/02/1995   **CM16/07/2003**

Gosland, Miss E M, BSc, Life Member. [5730] 07/01/1948   **ME**

Gosling, Mrs C H, MPhys(Hons) MCLIP, Learning and Teaching Lib., The Open Univ., Milton Keynes. [62769] 20/10/2003 **CM23/01/2008**

Gosling, Miss P L, MCLIP, Retired. [5733] 11/09/1953   **CM01/01/1961**

Goss, Miss L J, BSc MCLIP, Inf. Res. Mgr., Univ. of Herts. [5735] 05/05/1969   **CM01/01/1972**

Goss, Miss P, MCLIP, Life Member [5736] 01/01/1942   **CM01/01/1948**

Gossler, Ms A M, Lib., Cirencester Kingshill Sch., Glos. [51479] 27/02/1995   **AF**

Gossling, Miss L M F, LLB, Unknown. [10017167] 15/07/2010   **AF**

Goswami, Mrs L A, BA(Hons) MA MBA MCLIP, Head of Knowledge Serv. Devel., KSS L. and Knowledge Serv. Team [45636] 08/04/1991   **CM07/11/1996**

Gott, Mr S D, BA MA MCLIP, Asst. Dir., BIS London. [41315] 03/11/1987   **CM22/04/1992**

Gotts, Mr S T, BA DipLib MCLIP, Inf. Lib., Flintshire L. & Inf. Serv., Mold. [33530] 01/01/1981   **CM01/07/1984**

Gouffe, Ms C, DipLib MCLIP, Inf. Mgr., Northunbria Univ. [55027] 01/07/1997   **CM15/10/2002**

Gough, Miss A J, BA(Hons), Unwaged. [47716] 06/12/1990   **ME**

Gough, Mrs J E, ACLIP, Sen. L. Mgr., Swadlincote L., Derbyshire. [10005728] 25/07/2007   **ACL30/01/2009**

Gough, Mrs J V, MCLIP, Life Member [5743] 10/03/1942 **CM01/01/1948**

Gould, Mrs A M, BA(Hons) MSc MCLIP, Res. Lib., Standards and Sch. Effectiveness, Herts. [44068] 09/04/1990   **CM21/01/1998**

Gould, Mrs A, BA(Hons) MCLIP, Lib., Keyll Darree L., Isle of Man Civil Serv. [59500] 05/04/2001   **CM13/06/2007**

Gould, Miss I A, BA MCLIP, Retired. [5750] 09/01/1943 **CM01/01/1968**

Gould, Mrs J M L, ACLIP, L. Asst., Broke Hall Comm. Prim. Sch., Ipswich. [65402] 02/02/2006   **ACL23/09/2009**

Gould, Miss K A, PG Dip, Sch. Lib., Dame Elizabeth Cadbury Tech. Coll., Birmingham [10016671] 28/11/2003   **ME**

Gould, Mrs L V, BA MCLIP, p. /t. Med. Practice Teaching Co-ordinator [27594] 26/05/1977   **CM06/06/1980**

Gould, Miss P M, MCLIP, Retired. [5753] 13/02/1967   **CM01/01/1970**

Gould, Miss R M, MA(Hons), Stud., The Robert Gordon Univ., Aberdeen. [10011529] 17/10/2008   **ME**

Gould, Mrs S, BA MCLIP, Retired [8258] 11/03/1962   **CM01/01/1967**

Goulding, Dr A, BA MA, Reader, Loughborough Univ., Leics. [42698] 07/02/1989   **ME**

Goulding, Miss L V, BA DipLib, Inf. Resources Mgr., Simmons & Simmons, London. [35464] 19/10/1982   **ME**

Goulette, Mrs A K, BA MSc, Operations. Lib., Allen & Overy, London. [59227] 09/01/2001   **ME**

Goult, Mr R, MCLIP, Learning Resources Mgr., Welbeck Defence 6th Form Coll. [5757] 21/09/1966   **CM01/01/1971**

Goult, Mrs S C, L. Devel. Worker., Loughborough L., Leics. L. & Inf. Serv. [39230] 01/01/1986   **ME**

Gourdie, Mrs E, BA MCLIP, Retired. [3577] 07/02/1954 **CM01/01/1957**

Gourlay, Mrs G L, BA MCLIP, Network Lib., Westhill Academy, Westhill. [35937] 18/02/1983   **CM01/07/1990**

Gourlay, Mrs J A, BA MCLIP, Team Lib., Renfrew Council, Johnstone L. [26845] 07/12/1976   **CM14/12/1981**

Gover, Ms B C, MA DipLib MCLIP, Lib., Gordonstoun Sch., Elgin. [24584] 01/10/1975   **CM19/11/1979**

Gover, Miss S A, BA MCLIP, Customer Serv. Lib., Herts C.C. [21750] 11/01/1974   **CM19/01/1976**

Gow, Ms H, BA DipLib MCLIP, Early Years Lib., Kinson L., Bournemouth [51145] 23/11/1994   **CM21/05/2008**

Gowans, Mrs M S, MLIS MCLIP, Yth. Serv. Lib., Halifax P.L., Halifax, Canada [57447] 01/04/1999   **CM01/02/2006**

Gower, Mrs F M, MCLIP, Lib., Inst. of Criminology, Univ. of Cambridge. [5763] 01/01/1967   **CM01/01/1971**

Goy, Mr J R, BA MCLIP, Retired. [5766] 01/10/1961   **CM01/01/1963**

Goy, Miss J, BSc PGDip, Inf. Offr., Thomas Eggar LLP, Chichester.
[59403] 05/03/2001 **ME**

Grace, Mr J R, BSc MSc MA, Unknown [10006722] 03/12/2007 **ME**

Graddon, Mrs P H B, BA(Hons) BA(Hons) MCLIP, Retired. [10006401]
17/07/1984 **CM17/07/1984**

Grady, Ms H J, BA MA MSc MCLIP, Advisor, Univ. of Salford,
Manchester. [37477] 01/10/1984 RV07/06/2006 **CM19/08/1992**

Grafton, Mrs P R, MA MCLIP, Unwaged. [29734] 03/10/1978
CM04/03/1983

Graham, Mrs A, BA(Hons) MSc MCLIP, IT & Res. Co-ordinator, Culture
& Sport Glasgow [52189] 12/10/1995 **CM23/09/1998**

Graham, Mrs C D R, BA(Hons) MCLIP, Lib. Serv. Mgr., Northumberland
Tyne & Wear NHS Trust Knowledge Ctr., Walkergate Park. [46567]
12/11/1991 **CM24/09/1997**

Graham, Miss C I, MSc BA MCLIP, Sen. Lib., Isle of Man Coll., Douglas.
[5776] 01/01/1972 **CM04/02/1975**

Graham, Mr D J, BA, L. Asst., Univ. Strathclyde. [63721] 03/09/2004 **AF**

Graham, Miss E, MA, Educ., Training & Res. Team Leader, Wellcome
Trust, London. [42831] 16/03/1989 **ME**

Graham, Mr J H, BA MCLIP, Retired. [5782] 08/02/1972 **CM09/09/1974**

Graham, Miss J M, ACLIP, L. Asst., Watford Cent. L., Herts. [10002968]
10/05/2007 **ACL07/08/2009**

Graham, Mrs K A, BA(Hons) DipIS MCLIP, Dep. Head Corporate Inf.
Serv., GCHQ, Cheltenham. [49001] 24/08/1993 **CM22/01/1997**

Graham, Mrs M E, MA BSc DipLib MCMI MCLIP, Head of Stud.'
Wellbeing, Northumbria Univ. Sch. of CEIS. [3948] 01/01/1972
CM09/12/1975

Graham, Dr M, MA PhD FSA MCLIP, Unknown. [5787] 03/10/1968
CM12/10/1972

Graham, Miss N, BA, Stud. Aberystwyth Univ. [10015029] 07/10/2009
ME

Graham, Mr S I, BA(Hons), Educ. Cen. L., Cumberland Infirmary,
Carlisle. [58705] 09/06/2000 **ME**

Graham, Mr S P, BSc(Hons) DipLib MCLIP, Product Stewardship
Adviser, Infineum UK Ltd., Abingdon, Oxfordshire [34511]
19/11/1981 **CM23/08/1985**

Graham, Mrs S, BA(Hons) MSc(Econ) MCLIP, Inf. Devel., IBM,
Hampshire [59517] 18/04/2001 **CM21/03/2007**

Graham, Mrs S, BA(Hons) MSc, L. Mgr., Sunderland TPCT. [57223]
20/01/1999 **ME**

Graham, Ms S, BA DipLib MCLIP, p. /t. Asst. Lib., Thames Valley Univ.
[31813] 17/12/1979 **CM05/03/1982**

Graham, Mrs T Y, MA(Hons) DipILS MCLIP, Sch. Lib., Montrose Acad.,
Angus. [53221] 04/04/1996 **CM21/05/2003**

Graham, Mrs V, Manchester Coll. of Arts & Tech., Manchester. [39417]
27/01/1986 **ME**

Grainger, Miss H, BA(Hons) MA MCLIP, Unknown [61675] 17/10/2002
CM28/01/2009

Grainger, Ms J D, BA(Hons) PGCE, Lib.,Chawton House L., Cahwton,
Alton [62903] 18/11/2003 **ME**

Grainger, Mrs P J, BA, Stud., Aberystwyth Univ., & Sen. L. Super.,
Pencoed Br. L. [10013585] 08/05/2009 **ME**

Grainger, Mrs S B, MCLIP, Head of Lib. and Heritage Walsll MBC
Walsall Cent. L. [16239] 29/12/1971 **CM16/09/1974**

Grainger, Miss S E, BA, Asst. Inf. Advisor, Univ. of Brighton. Brighton.
[62300] 17/04/2003 **ME**

Grainger-Jarvis, Mrs E, BSc(Hons), L. Mgr. (Child. Serv.), Wallsall
SLSS, W. Mids. [10005127] 13/10/1989 **ME**

Grajcarek, Mrs J L, MCLIP, Teacher's Asst., Gilbert Colvin Primary
Sch., Ilford. [31851] 07/01/1980 **CM25/10/1983**

Grajera Quesada, Mr D, BA, Business Coordinator, Harrods.
[10014795] 18/09/2009 **AF**

Granger, Mrs A M, BLib MCLIP, Sales Asst., St. Paul's Bookshop,
Leeds [27853] 12/09/1977 **CM11/10/1982**

Grant, Mrs A M, ACLIP, RC Mgr., St Michael's RC Sch., Billingham.
[10000884] 16/11/2006 **ACL16/04/2008**

Grant, Mrs A, MA, Retired. [44043] 17/04/1990 **ME**

Grant, Mrs C G, BA DipLib MCLIP, Field Offr. /Lib., City of Edinburgh
Council. [29719] 18/10/1978 **CM18/11/1981**

Grant, Mrs C, PG Lib, Unknown. [10012330] 03/11/1992 **ME**

Grant, Miss D M, MCLIP, Lib., L. Support, Falkirk Council. [21956]
12/01/1974 **CM09/02/1977**

Grant, Mr E A, MA(Hons) MSc, Sen. Inf. Asst., Univ. of Aberdeen, Taylor
L. & Euro. Doc. Cent. [61309] 20/05/2002 **ME**

Grant, Mrs E, MCLIP, Retired. [9110] 01/01/1938 **CM01/01/1942**

Grant, Mrs F G T, BA(Hons) MA MCLIP, Comm. Lib., Medway Council,
Gillingham L. [56455] 13/07/1998 **CM16/07/2003**

Grant, Mr J D, BA(Hons) MCLIP, Lend. Servs. Mgr., Aberdeen City
Council, Aberdeen. [39922] 01/10/1986 **CM18/11/1993**

Grant, Ms J E, BA(Hons) DipIM MCLIP, Lib., Lewisham L., London.
[48505] 27/01/1993 **CM15/03/2000**

Grant, Mrs J M, BA MCLIP, Inf. & Learning Res. Co-ordinator, St.
Robert of Newminster Sch., Tyne & Wear. [46161] 08/10/1991
CM21/07/1993

Grant, Mr J, BSc DipLib MCLIP, Assoc. Dir. Inf. Serv., Quintiles Ltd.,
Livingston, W. Lothian. [28304] 03/11/1977 **CM12/02/1982**

Grant, Ms J, BSc(Hons), Asst. Lib., Law Soc., London. [59406]
05/03/2001 **ME**

Grant, Mrs K A, BA(Hons) MCLIP, Asst. Lib., Health & Safety Exec., Inf.
& Advisory Serv., Sheffield. [40594] 01/04/1987 **CM08/12/2004**

Grant, Ms K A, BA(Hons) MA Med, Unknown. [10014087] 18/11/1982
ME

Grant, Ms M J, BA(Hons) MSc, Res. Fellow, Salford Univ., Manchester
[10007156] 03/01/1991 **ME**

Grant, Ms M P, MA DipLib MCLIP, Principal Lib., The Mitchell L.,
Glasgow [34491] 17/11/1981 **CM26/02/1992**

Grant, Miss M, BA DipLib MCLIP, Community Lib., S. Lanarkshire
Council. [32070] 07/01/1980 **CM30/09/1982**

Grant, Mrs P, MCLIP, Learning Resources Coordinator, City Literary
Inst., London. [5814] 09/09/1964 **CM01/01/1968**

Grant, Mr S J, MA PGCE MCLIP, Coll. Lib., Reid Kerr Coll., Paisley.
[40979] 01/10/1987 **CM18/07/1991**

Granville, Mr T M, BA, Stud. [10014562] 17/08/2009 **ME**

Graph, Ms F, BA DipLib MCLIP, Intranet Mgr., Foreign & Commonwealth
Off., London. [43547] 06/11/1989 **CM21/07/1993**

Gratsea, Mrs A, BA MSc, Unknown. [10014402] 19/02/2002 **ME**

Grattoni, Ms S, Learning Support Lib., Westminster L. and Arch.,
London. [59365] 22/02/2001 **ME**

Graver, Ms J F, BSc DipLib MIIS MCLIP, Unknown. [21055] 19/09/1973
CM01/10/1975

Graves, Mrs J L, BA MCLIP DMS, Devel. Mgr., L.B. of Merton, Surrey.
[5222] 01/07/1970 **CM31/12/1989**

Graves, Mrs L, BA MCLIP, Inf. Lib., Univ. of Glamorgan, Pontypridd.
[14008] 01/03/1972 **CM01/07/1977**

Graves, Mrs R H, Unknown. [10012094] 17/12/2008 **ME**

Gravett, Ms K L, MCLIP, Seni. Inf. Asst., Royal Holloway, Univ. of
London. [64462] 31/03/2005 **CM23/01/2008**

Gray, Mrs A E, BSc DipLib MCLIP, Outreach Lib. Milton Keynes [30142]
11/01/1979 **CM11/11/1985**

Gray, Miss A J, MA MCLIP, Lib., Slough L. [63129] 11/02/2004
CM03/10/2007

Gray, Mr A, BSc MSc, Asst. Lib., Radley Coll., Abingdon. [10001216]
02/02/2007 **ME**

Gray, Mr A, Culture Project Offr., Camberwell Coll. of Arts, London.
[10001034] 13/02/2004 **ME**

Gray, Mrs B E, BA MCLIP, Lib., King Edward VI Grammar Sch.,
Chelmsford. [16017] 14/04/1970 **CM19/03/1973**

Gray, Mrs C A, Customer Serv. Lib., Orpington L. [10006702] 21/11/2007 **ME**

Gray, Miss C M, MA MPhil DipLib MCLIP, Learning Servs. Mgr., Motherwell Coll. [37743] 16/10/1984 **CM08/12/1987**

Gray, Mrs E W M, MA MCLIP, Sen. Lib., E. Ayrshire Council. [21477] 21/10/1973 **CM01/09/1976**

Gray, Mr F J, Stud. [10016544] 16/04/2010 **ME**

Gray, Mrs G E, BSc PGDipLIS MCLIP, Asst. Lib., Brit. Geological Survey, Edinburgh. [62534] 06/08/2003 **CM03/10/2007**

Gray, Mrs G J, BA MCLIP, Ast. L., Bromley House L. [25679] 15/01/1976 **CM27/09/1979**

Gray, Mrs H, MA DLIS MCLIP, Communications Channel Mgr., Shell Int. Ltd., London. [26571] 01/10/1976 **CM31/12/1979**

Gray, Mrs J A, Unknown. [37677] 04/10/1984 **ME**

Gray, Miss J M, MCLIP, Retired. [5834] 17/01/1947 **CM01/01/1954**

Gray, Miss J, MA MCLIP, Life Member. [5830] 15/09/1954 **CM01/01/1963**

Gray, Miss K A, BA MCLIP, Retired. [60295] 10/12/2001 **CM10/12/2001**

Gray, Mrs K A, BSc(Hons), Sen. L. Asst., Sch. of St. Helen & St. Katharine, Oxon. [59478] 05/04/2001 **AF**

Gray, Ms K J, BA DipLib MCLIP, Head of Inf. Resources., Lawrence Graham LLP, London. [44155] 06/06/1990 **CM21/10/1992**

Gray, Mrs L, BA, Unwaged. [10006252] 26/09/2007 **ME**

Gray, Mr P A, BA, Serials Asst., Southampton Solent Univ. [39835] 16/08/1986 **ME**

Gray, Mr P K, Inf. Offr., Scottish Government, Edinburgh. [51853] 13/07/1995 **ME**

Gray, Mrs S A L, BScEcon(Hons) MCLIP, Lib., Kings Sch., Canterbury. [51570] 01/04/1995 **CM23/01/2002**

Gray, Mrs S I, BA(Hons) DipLIS MCLIP, Local Studies Lib., Warwick L. [57589] 13/05/1999 **CM23/01/2008**

Gray, Mrs S, BA CertEd MCLIP, Relief Lib. Asst., E. Riding Council, Skirlaugh, E. Yorks. [26224] 15/09/1976 **CM28/08/1980**

Gray, Mr T M, DPA FCLIP, Life member. [5843] 01/03/1941 **FE01/01/1967**

Gray, Mrs V C, MSc MA BA DipEd MPhil, Wknd. Lib. Super., Univ. of Reading. [45693] 24/04/1991 **ME**

Grayson, Mrs H E, BA(Hons) DipLib MCLIP, Res. Lib., Nat. Foundation for Educ. Res., Slough. [45515] 28/02/1991 **CM12/09/2001**

Grayson, Mr J, BA(Hons) MA MCLIP, Racing Analyst, The Sportsman, London. [55560] 21/10/1997 **CM20/11/2002**

Greasley, Miss C, BA(Hons) MA MCLIP, Inf. Off., Loughborough Univ., P/T. [64374] 14/03/2005 **CM21/05/2008**

Greasley, Mrs S, Sen. L. Asst., Univ. Coll. Falmouth, Tremough L. [10016203] 12/07/1996 **AF**

Greaves, Mrs J S, L. Asst., Hunsbury L., Northampton. [10005490] 26/07/2007 **AF**

Greaves, Miss K R, BLib MCLIP, L. Serv. Mgr., Harper Adams Univ. Coll. [38545] 17/06/1985 **CM21/12/1988**

Greaves, Miss M A, BA MA FCLIP AI, Life Member. [16954] 08/03/1954 **FE01/01/1966**

Greaves, Ms P, BSc MCLIP, L. Devel. Worker, Leicestershire C.C. [60504] 19/05/2001 **CM19/05/2001**

Greaves, Mrs R M, BA DipLib MCLIP, Leraning Res. Cent. Mgr., weald of Kent Grammar Sch. [35254] 04/10/1982 **CM10/10/1986**

Green, Mrs A C, BA MA MCLIP, Unknown. [29799] 10/10/1978 **CM13/11/1980**

Green, Mrs A E, BA DLIS MCLIP, Learning Resource Cent. Mgr., Garth Hill Coll., Bracknell [18744] 07/08/1972 **CM15/09/1975**

Green, Mr A M W, MA MCLIP, Lib., Nat. L. of Wales, Aberystwyth. [23294] 06/11/1974 **CM30/11/1977**

Green, Miss A M, MCLIP, Employment not known. [5864] 13/05/1971 **CM13/02/1975**

Green, Mr A, BA MLS DMS MCLIP, Head of L. and Inf. Serv., Coventry Council Civic Cent., Coventry. [31069] 27/07/1979 **CM28/09/1981**

Green, Mr B S, MCLIP, Retired. [5868] 12/01/1965 **CM01/01/1970**

Green, Mrs C M, BSc MCLIP, p. /t. Sch. Lib., Ellesmere Port Catholic High Sch., Cheshire C.C. [14775] 01/10/1969 **CM12/07/1972**

Green, Mrs C, BA PGCE MScIM MCLIP, Consultant [52261] 19/10/1995 **CM22/09/1999**

Green, Mrs D J, BA DipLib MCLIP, Gardener. [38383] 03/04/1985 **CM10/11/1987**

Green, Ms D R, BA, Stud. [10012358] 03/02/2009 **ME**

Green, Mrs E C, BA(Hons) MCLIP, Asst. Lib., W. Sussex C.C., Horsham P. L. [49727] 25/11/1993 **CM15/05/2002**

Green, Miss E V, BA DipLib MCLIP, Lib., Southampton Ref. L., Southampton City L. [30172] 10/01/1979 **CM08/02/1982**

Green, Miss G E, MCLIP, Life Member. [5876] 17/08/1955 **CM01/01/1968**

Green, Miss G M, BA MCLIP, Unwaged. [24892] 08/10/1975 **CM06/12/1979**

Green, Mrs H C, BA DipLib MCLIP, Career Break-Unwaged [30588] 14/02/1979 **CM13/02/1981**

Green, Mrs J E, BA MCLIP, Inf. Mgr., Covington & Burling, London. [24771] 29/09/1975 **CM24/01/1978**

Green, Ms J S, BA(Hons) Dip MSc LIS, Lib., NHS Health Scotland, Scotland. [63631] 02/08/2004 **ME**

Green, Miss J, MA, Lib., Chelsea L., London. [65332] 06/01/2006 **ME**

Green, Mrs J, BA MCLIP, Stock & Leader Dev. Lib., Hoddesdon Lib., Herts [35640] 23/11/1982 **CM09/08/1988**

Green, Mrs K A, BA(Hons) DMS MCLIP, Ch. Lib. Offr., Barnsley MBC [31895] 17/01/1980 **CM20/03/1985**

Green, Mrs K L, L. Devel. Worker, Leics. C.C. [65609] 28/02/2006 **AF**

Green, Ms K, BA(Hons) MSc(Econ) MCLIP, Lib., W. Sussex C.C., W. Sussex. [55015] 25/06/1997 **CM17/01/2001**

Green, Miss L G, BSc MA, Inf. Asst., Rockefeller Med. L., London. [66092] 21/09/2006 **ME**

Green, Mr M E, MCLIP, Retired. [5891] 07/10/1961 **CM01/01/1965**

Green, Mrs M H, BSc MSc, Inf. Asst., Napier Univ., Edinburgh. [54094] 25/10/1996 **ME**

Green, Ms M I, Unknown. [10006464] 19/10/2007 **ME**

Green, Mrs M J, BA MLS MCLIP MIFL, Retired Head of L. & Arch. Serv., Stoke-On-Trent L. [29443] 08/08/1978 **CM01/09/1981**

Green, Mrs M M, MCLIP, Retired. [5892] 30/09/1964 **CM01/01/1969**

Green, Mrs N A, BA DipLib, Freelance Indexer [44212] 09/07/1990 **ME**

Green, Miss R A M, FCLIP, Life Member. [5896] 20/10/1949 **FE01/01/1971**

Green, Mrs R J, BA MCLIP, Parish Admin., St Andrew's Church Cent., Bournemouth. [34632] 16/01/1982 **CM16/05/1990**

Green, Mr R S, MA MLib MCLIP, Lib., Howes Percival LLP, Northampton. [28305] 15/10/1977 **CM27/01/1984**

Green, Mrs R S, MCLIP, Young Peoples L. Serv. Mgr., L.B. of Richmond. [19954] 15/01/1973 **CM19/08/1975**

Green, Mrs S M, MCLIP, L. Asst., Herts. C.C. [16219] 02/02/1970 **CM25/07/1973**

Green, Miss S V, DipLib MCLIP, Sch. Lib., Camden Sch. for Girls, London. [34756] 17/02/1982 **CM14/09/1985**

Green, Mr S, MA MCLIP, Lib., Cent. Ref. L., Hull City Council. [18258] 03/10/1972 **CM11/11/1975**

Green, Miss T, BA(Hons), Acquisitions Assit. Linklaters, London. [10016080] 08/02/2010 **AF**

Green, Mr W S, FCLIP, Retired. [5906] 17/01/1940 **FE01/01/1948**

Greenall, Mr J, MCLIP, Retired. [19744] 01/01/1966 **CM01/01/1969**

Greene, Mrs M, BA(Hons) MRes, Stud. [10015339] 11/11/2009 **ME**

Greenfield, Mrs F E, MCLIP, Lib., Parsons Brinckerhoff Ltd., Bristol. [5914] 08/01/1965 **CM01/01/1968**

Greenfield, Miss S J, BA MCMI MCLIP, Retired. [24685] 21/10/1975 **CM29/12/1978**

Greenhalgh, Mrs K E, BA(Hons) PGCE PGDipLIS, Comm. Lib., Medway Council, Gillingham L. [39786] 11/07/1986 **ME**

Greenhalgh, Miss L, MCLIP, Inf. Specialist, Foreign & Commonwealth Off. [64356] 07/03/2005 **CM06/05/2009**

Greenhalgh, Mrs M C, BSc MCLIP, Self-employed. [60368] 29/01/1970 **CM29/01/1970**

Greenhead, Mr J D, BA MA, Sen. Asst. Lib., House of Lords, London [62095] 13/02/2003 **ME**

Greenidge, Mrs C, MSc, Functional Analyst, Univ. of W. Indies [10009472] 20/05/2008 **ME**

Greenidge, Mrs H, Learning Centres Mgr., John Ruskin Coll., S. Croydon. [10006533] 30/10/2007 **ME**

Greenidge-Forsyth, Mrs E, ACLIP, Lib., Battersea Tech. Coll., London. [65252] 06/12/2005 **ACL01/11/2007**

Green-Morgan, Mrs N E, BA MSc(Econ) MCLIP, Researcher, Australian Securities Investment Commision, Sydney. [52059] 02/10/1995 **CM09/11/2005**

Greenslade, Mrs S A, BA(Hons), Patent Inf. Offr., Royal Liverpool Child. Hosp., NHS Trust, Liverpool. [58441] 15/02/2000 **ME**

Greenstreet, Mrs J W, BA(Hons) MSc, L. Asst., Royal Agricultural Coll., Glos. [62280] 10/04/2003 **ME**

Greenway, Mrs J, MCLIP, Comm. L. Mgr., Monmouthshire L. & Inf. Serv. [25862] 25/03/1976 **CM20/11/1984**

Greenway, Ms J, BA Hons, L. Techniician, Bemrose Sch., Derby. [10016068] 10/02/2010 **ME**

Greenway, Mrs M, Lib. Super., HMP YOI Swinfen Hall, Lichfield [10017008] 17/06/2010 **AF**

Greenwood, Mr S, BA, Asst. Lib. [10006504] 24/10/2007 **ME**

Greenwood, Mr A, BSc MSc, Asst. Lib., Anglia Ruskin Univ., Cambridge [65779] 24/04/2006 **ME**

Greenwood, Miss C M, BA MA MCLIP, Learning Facilitator, Part-Time., Hopwood Hall Tertiary Coll., Manchester. [5928] 21/10/1969 **CM29/03/1973**

Greenwood, Ms E L, MA, Lib., Trinity Coll. of Music, London. [66125] 29/09/2006 **ME**

Greenwood, Ms E, BA(Hons) MA MCLIP, Business Lib., L.B. of Croydon, Cent. L. [56968] 11/11/1998 **CM20/11/2002**

Greenwood, Mrs M C, MA(Hons) DipLib, L. Asst. (p. /t.), Canterbury Christ Church Univ., Tunbridge Wells. [48537] 08/02/1993 **ME**

Greenwood, Mrs O, BEd MA MCLIP, Jobshare, Dist. Mgr., Notts. C.C. [46832] 14/02/1992 **CM15/01/2003**

Greer, Ms M J, BA MLS MCLIP, Retired. [60369] 03/10/1980 **CM03/10/1980**

Gregg, Mr A R, DipLib, Lib., Clyde & Co., London. [47289] 03/07/1992 **ME**

Gregory, Mrs A M, MA MCLIP, Hennepin Co. Lib. Minnesota, U. S. A. [37737] 23/10/1984 **CM19/09/1989**

Gregory, Ms A S, BA(Hons) MCLIP, Unwaged [62199] 13/03/2003 **CM07/09/2005**

Gregory, Mrs C M B, BA MA, Legal Lib., Thomas Eggar LLP [41326] 02/11/1987 **ME**

Gregory, Miss E, BA(Hons) PgDip, Virtual L. Mgr., Beds. C.C., Beds. [55428] 09/10/1997 **ME**

Gregory, Miss J R, MCLIP, Retired. [5943] 05/10/1965 **CM04/10/1972**

Gregory, Miss M G G, JP LLB FCLIP, Retired. [5946] 30/09/1938 **FE01/01/1949**

Gregory, Miss N, Asst. Lib., Wigam& Leigh Coll., Manchester Met. Univ. [64375] 14/03/2005 **ME**

Gregory, Mr R J, BTech CertEd DipLib MCLIP, Sen. Tutor Lib., Norfolk Sch. L. Serv. [31133] 21/09/1979 **CM01/07/1984**

Gregory, Mrs R S, BA MCLIP, Sch. Lib., Sinfin Comm. Sch., Derby. [29591] 29/09/1978 **CM29/09/1980**

Gregory, Mr S F, BSc MA MCLIP, Asst. Lib., Welsh Assembly Gov. [43628] 14/11/1989 **RV16/06/2010 CM15/09/1993**

Gregson, Miss V H, BA, Grad. Trainee, Christ's Coll. L., Cambridge [10014563] 17/08/2009 **ME**

Greig, Miss E, BSc(Econ), L. Asst.,St. Helen & St. Katherine, Abingdon [10007011] 28/01/2008 **AF**

Greig, Ms F, BA MCLIP, Content & Devel. Mgr., Univ. of Plymouth. [43862] 05/02/1990 **CM23/03/1993**

Greig, Mrs L R, MCLIP, Southmead L. Mgr., N. Bristol NHS Trust, Bristol. [5953] 07/09/1966 **CM01/01/1970**

Grenza Selandji, Ms M, Primary Sch. Lib., Thomas's London Day Sch., London. [10011141] 13/10/2008 **AF**

Gresser, Mr C, MSc MA, Curator, Brit. L., London [65339] 17/01/2006 **ME**

Gresty, Miss H G, BA MCLIP, Knowledge Mgmnt. Mgr., J. P. Morgan Asset Mgmnt., Luxembourg. [30423] 10/01/1979 **CM07/11/1984**

Gresty, Mrs S, Sen. Coll. Offr., W. Cheshire Coll., Ellesmere Port. [65793] 01/05/2006 **AF**

Greville, Mrs S E, MA, Lib. Asst., Marches Sch., Oswestry. [61160] 20/03/2002 **ME**

Grewcock, Mr J A, BA ACLIP, L. Asst., Watford Cent. L., Herts. [10001556] 06/10/2004 **ACL17/06/2009**

Grey, Miss A, Stud. [10000852] 13/11/2006 **ME**

Grey, Dr D, BSc(Hons) PhD, Asst. Lib., Bloomsbury Healthcare L., London. [62706] 03/10/2003 **ME**

Grey, Miss J M, Graduate. [10007548] 13/02/2008 **ME**

Grey, Mr M L, MA, Hon. Affiliate Scholar, Harvard Business Sch. [41487] 12/01/1988 **ME**

Grice, Ms S M, BSc, L. Super., Univ. of Derby, Derby. [63492] 15/06/2004 **ME**

Grier, Mrs V C, BA MCLIP, Cent. Lib. Operations Mgr., Poole Bor. Council, Dorset. [5962] 01/01/1967 **CM01/01/1971**

Grieve, Mr S, MCIBS, Business Mgr., W. J. Grieve, Dumfriesshire. [49040] 13/09/1993 **ME**

Griffin, Mrs A, BA DipLib PGCE, Sunday Lib., L.B. of Lewisham, Lewisham L. [40856] 10/07/1987 **ME**

Griffin, Mr B C, Researcher, Lazard, London. [65634] 22/03/2006 **ME**

Griffin, Miss C A, Unwaged. [45104] 11/07/1990 **AF**

Griffin, Mrs D, MA MCLIP DMS, Lib. Servs. Mgr., L. Univ. Campus Suffolk, Ipswich. [20582] 22/04/1973 **CM07/05/1976**

Griffin, Miss F R, BSc(Hons) MA MCLIP, Unknown. [44867] 02/01/1991 **CM20/11/2002**

Griffin, Ms J C, MA, Researcher, Lovells LLP, London [63734] 06/09/2004 **ME**

Griffin, Ms M A V, BA, Inf. and Knowledge Mgr., FCO Serv.: CIO Off., London. [40834] 22/07/1987 **ME**

Griffin, Ms S E, BA(Hons), Hist. Boots Lib., Royal Coll. of Physicians of London. [10000664] 24/10/2006 **ME**

Griffin, Mrs S M, BA(Hons) DipLIS, Lib., Hertford Coll., Oxford. [51083] 14/11/1994 **ME**

Griffin, Mrs S, BA DipILS, Sen. Team Offr., Surrey L. [50107] 05/04/1994 **ME**

Griffin, Mrs V C, BA(Hons) MSc MCLIP, Programme Co-ordinator, Dep. of Inf. Serv., House of Commons, London. [54034] 18/10/1996 **CM17/11/1999**

Griffin, Mrs W, BA MCLIP, Sen. Team Offr., Safer & Stronger Comm. Team, Surry C.C. [28306] 03/11/1977 **CM07/08/1980**

Griffith, Mrs J F, BSc MCLIP, Retired. [60710] 12/12/2001 **CM12/12/2001**

Griffith, Mr J H, BA(Hons), Head of Inf. Mgmnt. [47175] 22/05/1992 **ME**

Griffith, Mrs S V, BA DipLib MCLIP, Resident Australia. [25574] 02/02/1976 **CM12/01/1979**

Griffiths, Mrs A A, BA(Hons) MCLIP, Reader Serv. Mgr., Liverpool Hope Univ., Liverpool. [56605] 15/09/1998 **CM12/09/2001**

Griffiths, Mrs A D, BSc, Stud. [66086] 01/10/2006 **ME**

Griffiths, Mrs A J, BA(Hons) MSc(Econ) MCLIP, Unwaged – Career break to bring up family [51167] 23/11/1994 **CM15/03/2000**

Griffiths, Mrs A L, BA(Hons) MA MSc(Econ) MCLIP, Exec. Offr., Welsh Assembly Government, Ceredigion. [55857] 02/12/1997 **CM01/04/2002**

Griffiths, Miss A, BA PGCE, Learning Cent. Mngr., Aberystwyth Univ. [10015691] 14/01/2010 **ME**

Griffiths, Mr D J, BA MA MCLIP, Lib., BMT Grp. Ltd., Teddington, Middx. [25878] 01/01/1976 **CM13/06/1989**

Griffiths, Mrs D V M, B SC MCLIP, Self-Employed. [22893] 01/10/1974 **CM01/09/1977**

Griffiths, Miss F R, BA, Unwaged. [10002309] 20/04/2007 **ME**

Griffiths, Mrs G E, BA DipLib MCLIP, Lib., Shropshire C.C., Oswestry. [45451] 11/02/1991 **CM22/11/1995**

Griffiths, Mr G R, BA DipLib MCLIP, Public Access Area Lib. Mngr., Welsh Assembly Gov., Aberystwyth [45861] 01/07/1991 **CM12/09/2001**

Griffiths, Miss H M M, BEd MA, Sir William Stanier Sch., Crewe, Cheshire [63061] 27/01/2004 **ME**

Griffiths, Mrs H, BA(Hons) MLib, Catr. (Part-Time) [47750] 16/10/1992 **ME**

Griffiths, Miss J A, BA(Hons) MA MCLIP, Operational Mgr., Halton L. Serv., Runcorn. [62764] 20/10/2003 **CM10/07/2009**

Griffiths, Mr J M, MCLIP, Life Member. [5985] 05/09/1959 **CM01/01/1967**

Griffiths, Mrs J M, MA MCLIP, p. /t. L. Asst., Denbighshire C.C. [26649] 12/10/1976 **CM29/12/1980**

Griffiths, Miss J P W, JP BA MCLIP, Life Member. [5987] 19/02/1948 **CM01/01/1962**

Griffiths, Mrs J, BSc MCLIP, Area Lib., Community Serv., Workington L. [21508] 23/10/1973 **CM01/01/1977**

Griffiths, Mrs K J, BA MA, Unknown. [10005485] 25/05/2005 **ME**

Griffiths, Miss L M, MLS BA MCLIP, Inf. Offr. /Lib., Chartered Soc. of Physiotherapy, London. [27678] 13/07/1977 **CM20/05/1980**

Griffiths, Mrs M A, BLib MCLIP, Principal Off., L., Bridgend L. & Inf. Serv. [14566] 04/10/1971 **CM10/10/1974**

Griffiths, Miss P E, MCLIP, Life Member. [5991] 01/01/1957 **CM01/01/1963**

Griffiths, Mr P, BA(Hons) FCLIP MCLIP, Independent Inf. Specialist, Dorset. [5990] 01/01/1970 **FE01/04/2002**

Griffiths, Mr R D, BA MCLIP, Lib., Swindon Bor. Council. [25164] 03/12/1975 **CM01/12/1977**

Griffiths, Mrs S N T, BA MA DipLib MCLIP, Lib., St. Catharine's Coll., Cambridge. [30757] 11/04/1979 **CM10/12/1981**

Griffiths, Miss S T, BA(Hons) MLIS CGA, Business Inf. Specialist, Cranfield Univ. [59009] 24/10/2000 **ME**

Griffiths, Mr T E, MA MCLIP, Retired. [5996] 14/10/1948 **CM01/01/1951**

Griffiths, Mrs V M, OBE BA MCLIP, Consultant. [5998] 15/06/1971 **CM26/09/1973**

Griffiths, Dr W R M, MA MLitt DipLib MCLIP, Retired. [24688] 02/10/1975 **CM07/11/1978**

Griffiths, Miss W R, BA MCLIP, Area Mgr., S. Area L. & Inf. serv., Stockport M.B.C. [32074] 01/02/1980 **CM07/02/1986**

Griggs, Mrs L, BA(Hons) MA MCLIP, Inf. Offr., ERA Tech. Ltd., Surrey [57006] 20/11/1998 **CM29/11/2006**

Grigson, Ms A, BA(Hons) MA MCLIP, E-Resources Mgr., Royal Holloway, London. [49022] 01/09/1993 **RV07/06/2006CM18/03/1998**

Grigson, Mrs G, MA MCLIP, Lib. Training Offr., Cheshire E. Bor. Council. [40307] 01/01/1987 **CM18/01/1989**

Grima, Mr J R, BA MCLIP, Retired. [28818] 02/01/1978 **CM02/01/1980**

Grimmond, Mrs M A G, BA(Hons) MCLIP, Sch. Lib., The High Sch. of Glasgow, Anniesland, Glasgow. [24483] 16/09/1975 **CM25/07/2001**

Grimshaw, Miss J M, BA, Curator-Soc. Sci. Collections, Brit. L., London. [18218] 01/10/1972 **ME**

Grimwood, Mr P A, BSc(Hons), Ref. & Inf. Asst., R. B. of Kensington & Chelsea, London [65425] 23/02/2006 **ME**

Grindlay, Dr D J C, BSc MA PhD MCLIP, Dermatology Inf. Specialist, NHS Evidence – skin disorders, Univ. of Nottingham. [59195] 14/12/2000 **CM21/03/2007**

Grindrod, Ms K J, BA MIL MCLIP, Head of Subsurface & Bus. Data & Doc. Mgmt., Total E & P UK Ltd., Aberdeen. [60237] 27/10/1988 **CM27/10/1988**

Grist, Ms A P, BA(Hons) MA MCLIP, Sch. Lib., Henbury Sch., Bristol. [54757] 01/04/1997 **CM12/03/2003**

Gristwood, Mrs H, MCLIP, Retired. [94] 01/01/1970 **CM17/08/1973**

Grocott, Mrs G, Lib. Health & Safety Exec.,Sheffield [10001439] 02/02/1982 **ME**

Grocott, Mrs J L, BA MCLIP, Stock Mgr., Staffs L. & Inf. Serv. [21230] 10/10/1973 **CM31/10/1978**

Grogan, Miss J C, BTEC HND BLib MCLIP, Lib., Goverment L. [41510] 18/01/1988 **RV27/11/2007** **CM19/06/1991**

Groom, Mrs A M, MA MCLIP, Team Lib., E. Sussex C.C. [47466] 24/08/1992 **CM24/05/1995**

Groom, Miss C J, MA(Hons) MSc, Learning Tech., Carnegie Coll., Dunfermline [62789] 22/10/2003 **ME**

Groom, Mr C, BSc(Hons), Records Mgr., Norwich Bioscience Institutes, Norfolk. [62000] 13/12/2002 **ME**

Groom, Mrs J E C, MCLIP, Legal Inf. Consultant & Lib., Self-Employed. [6021] 27/09/1967 **CM01/01/1972**

Groombridge, Mrs S E A, BA DipLib MCLIP, Knowledge and Inf. Agent, DSTL, Salisbury. [31226] 11/10/1979 **CM24/09/1985**

Groome, Mrs C R, Mayor, Bor. of Kettering [34782] 22/01/1982 **ME**

Grose, Mr M W, MA MCLIP, Retired. [6026] 04/10/1962 **CM01/01/1970**

Grosvenor, Mr J R H, DipLib DipMgmt(Open) MCLIP, Local Studies Lib. & Freedom of Info. Offr., Cent. L., Bexleyheath [31304] 01/10/1979 **CM08/11/1982**

Grout, Mr P N, BA DipLib MCLIP, Ref. Lib., Thames Valley Univ., London. [19648] 30/10/1972 **CM24/03/1975**

Grove, Miss C, BA, L. Asst., Literary & Philosophical Soc., Newcastle Upon Tyne. [10010195] 10/07/2008 **AF**

Grove, Mrs H, MA, Lib., London Transport Mus., London. [56780] 14/10/1998 **ME**

Grover, Ms C, BA (Joint Hons) MCLIP, Academic Liaison Lib., Brunel Univ. L., Uxbridge. [49568] 19/11/1993 **CM06/04/2005**

Grover, Ms S M, BA MA DipLib MCLIP, Res. & Info. Mgr., Inst. of Actuaries, Oxford. [27325] 10/03/1977 **CM10/03/1980**

Groves, Mrs J A, BA MCLIP, Unemployed. [31337] 08/10/1979 **CM27/07/1983**

Grove-Smith, Ms P, BA MCLIP, Br. Lib., Stadtbuecherei Frankfurt, Stadtteilbibliothek Schwanheim. [6029] 08/10/1971 **CM31/08/1974**

Gruffydd, Ms N V, BA MLib MCLIP, Mgr. User Serv., Gwynedd Council. [40205] 06/11/1986 **CM12/09/1990**

Grundy, Ms D L, BA(Hons) MCLIP, Subject Lib. Univ. of Bolton. [10006060] 03/09/2007 **CM27/01/2010**

Gryspeerdt, Mr R G P, BA MCLIP, Sen. Grp. Mgr., Swiss Cottage L., L.B. Camden. [20331] 05/03/1973 **CM15/03/1979**

Guard, Mrs O, BSc(Econ) MCLIP, Locality Mgr., W. Norfolk, Norfolk L. and Inf. Serv. [51507] 13/03/1995 **CM19/01/2000**

Gubbels, Miss W, BA(Hons), Inf. Specialist, Qinetiq, Dorset. [50792] 18/10/1994 **ME**

Gudgeon, Mrs N J, BSc(Hons), Sen. Lib., Dept. of Health. [63912] 26/10/2004 **ME**

Guest, Mr D A, BA(Hons) MCLIP, Nursing & Midwifery Lib., Coventry Univ., Lanchester L. [38098] 17/01/1985 **CM19/11/2003**

Guest, Miss K M, BSc, Stud., Aberystwyth Univ. [10009212] 07/05/2008 **ME**

Guest, Mrs R S, ACLIP, Sen. L. Asst., Strouden L. Bournemouth. [61426] 25/07/2002 **ACL16/06/2010**

Guevara, Ms A P, BA(Hons) MA, Lib., W. Area, E. Sussex L. &Inf. Serv. [61921] 02/12/2002 **ME**

Guilbert, Ms R, BA(Hons), Stud. [10006323] 10/10/2007 **ME**

Guile, Ms H, Stud. [10006601] 21/11/2007 **ME**

Guiney, Mrs P, BA MCLIP, Learning Res. Mgr., Capital City Academy, London. [30758] 17/04/1979 **CM16/07/1982**

Guinn, Mrs V, BSc, Stud., UCL. [65348] 13/01/2006 **ME**

Guite, Miss C J E, MA LTCL MCLIP, Sen. Subject Lib. for Law, Univ. of Sterling, Sterling. [30174] 17/01/1979 **CM23/06/1986**

Guiver, Mrs K, BA MA MCLIP, Academic Serv. Lib., Norwich Univ. Coll. of the Arts, Norfolk. [38805] 08/10/1985 **CM15/02/1989**

Gulland, Mrs D, MCLIP, Retired. [6043] 18/01/1957 **CM01/01/1963**

Gumulak, Ms S M, MA, Stud., Sheffield Univ. [10012907] 19/03/2009 **ME**

Gunatilleke, Miss G D, BA MCLIP ALAA, Freelance Lib. & Reviewer [16969] 01/01/1972 **CM27/11/1975**

Gundersen, Mr R, Unknown. [10007047] 07/01/2008 **ME**

Gunderson, Mrs A E, BA DipLib MCLIP, L. Serv. Outreach Offr., Cornwall Council, Penzance L. [26735] 03/11/1976 **CM13/06/1980**

Gunn, Mrs A A, MCLIP, Trials Search Co-ordinator [25881] 10/04/1976 **CM13/08/1980**

Gunn, Mrs C S, BSc DipLib MCLIP, Child. & Young People's Lib., Clacckmannan Council. [34558] 13/01/1982 **CM14/04/1987**

Gunning, Mr S J, BA(Hons) DipLIS MCLIP, Subject Classifier, Nielsen Bookdata, Stevenage. [44205] 06/07/1990 **CM19/05/1999**

Gunther, Ms Y, MCLIP, Lib. Nottingham High Sch. [65131] 03/11/2005 **CM28/01/2009**

Gunton, Mr D H, OBE MA FCLIP, Life Member. [16970] 07/01/1947 **FE05/03/1973**

Guo, Ms X, MA, Unknown. [10007662] 19/02/2008 **ME**

Gupta, Mrs C, BLS(Hons), Learning Resources Facilitator, Sparsholt Coll. [10004831] 01/06/1981 **ME**

Gura, Mrs E, MCLIP, Life Member. [6054] 28/01/1953 **CM01/01/1956**

Gurajena, Miss C R, LLB(Hons) MSc MCLIP, Sen. Lib., HM Land Registry, London [56964] 13/11/1998 **CM21/05/2003**

Gurjar, Mr R, PGCE, Unknown. [66076] 01/10/2006 **ME**

Gurnsey, Mr J, FCLIP, Retired. [6057] 09/07/1966 **FE26/09/1977**

Gustafson, Ms H L, BSc(Econ), Sen. L. Asst., Liverpool City C. [10006131] 01/07/1995 **ME**

Gutridge, Mrs J N, MCLIP, Child. Offr., Portsmouth L. [6308] 15/01/1971 **CM19/09/1974**

Gutteridge, Mr P J, BA MSc MCLIP, Lib., The Stationery Off., London. [34886] 27/03/1982 **CM10/05/1984**

Gutteridge, Mr S R, BA MCLIP, Asst. Lib., Biggleswade L., Beds. C.C. [38602] 18/07/1985 **CM16/02/1988**

Gutwein, Mrs T E, BA MCLIP, Retired [7724] 26/09/1966 **CM01/07/1991**

Guy, Mrs C A, BA MCLIP, Comm. Lib., Connahs Quay L., Deeside. [50347] 04/07/1994 **CM20/03/1996**

Guy, Mrs J E, MCLIP, Retired. [20768] 02/07/1973 **CM22/08/1975**

Guy, Mr J, PgDipILM, LRC Mgr., Stanchester Comm. Sch., Somerset. [49904] 10/01/1994 **ME**

Guy, Miss M M, BA DipLib MCLIP, Coll. Lib. & Arch., RAF Coll., Cranwell. [39877] 01/10/1986 **CM18/04/1989**

Guy, Mr N G, MA MCLIP, Mgr. -Inf. Serv., BHR Grp. Ltd., Cranfield. [60372] 11/12/2001 **CM11/12/2001**

Guy, Mr R F, BA MA MCLIP, Project Mgr. [6070] 01/07/1971 **CM31/01/1974**

Guyatt, Miss E J, BA FCLIP, Life Member. [6071] 04/10/1950 **FE01/01/1954**

Guyon, Ms A A M, MSc MCLIP, Sen. Lib., Young People's Serv., E. Lothian [54622] 04/02/1997 **CM09/07/2008**

Gwenlan, Miss S, Inf. Serv., Aberystwyth Univ. [65150] 03/11/2005 **ME**

Gwilliam, Mr A B, MA MCLIP, Life Member. [6073] 10/09/1955 **CM01/01/1969**

Gwilliam, Mrs S M, BLS MCLIP, Lib., Beau Soleil Coll., Alpin Internat., Switzerland [30209] 05/12/1978 **CM21/06/1983**

Gwilt, Ms R V, BA MA MCLIP, Fcaulty Lib., Univ. for Creative Arts,Canterbury. [42924] 20/04/1989 **CM24/06/1992**

Gwinn, Mrs H E, B LIB MCLIP, Inf. Offr., Blake Lapthorn, Southampton. [40757] 29/05/1987 **CM14/03/1990**

Gwyer, Ms R, BLib MSc FCLIP PGCert FHEA, Assoc. Univ. Lib., Univ. of Portsmouth. [27187] 12/01/1977 **FE09/07/2008**

Gwynn, Ms L, BA(Hons), Project Lib., The Huguenot L., UCL, London [65230] 24/11/2005 **ME**

Gynane, Mrs C D, BA MCLIP, Coll. Lib., Hills Rd. Sixth Form Coll., Cambridge. [21461] 18/10/1973 **CM01/12/1976**

H

Haardt, Ms M, MA MCLIP, Dep. Sen. Lib. & Catr.,Wiener L., Inst. of Contemporary Hist., London. [65837] 23/05/2006 **CM03/10/2007**

Haberer, Miss I J, MA FCLIP, Life Member. [16972] 26/02/1951 **FE01/01/1965**

Habibi, Ms K, BA(Hons) MA MCLIP, L. Mgr., Coulsdon and Bradmore Green L. Croydon. [53781] 01/10/1996 **CM23/01/2002**

Hackett, Ms A J, BA(Hons) MA MCLIP, Res. Stud., Cambridge. [25949] 13/01/1975 **CM13/01/1975**

Hackett, Mrs L, MSc MCLIP, Educ. Sch. & Child. Serv. Mgr., Calderdale L., Mus. & Arts, Cent. L., Halifax [9895] 01/01/1970 **CM14/10/1974**

Hacking, Ms E, BA(Hons) PgDip, Grad. Trainee. [10015417] 16/11/2009 **AF**

Hadaway, Mrs K A, BSc(Econ), Principal L. Asst., Univ. of Southampton. [65879] 16/06/2006 **ME**

Haddock, Mrs S J F, BSc, L. Asst., Anglia Ruskin Univ., Cambridge. [10016526] 01/04/2010 **AF**

Haddow, Dr G C, PhD, Unknown. [10014619] 20/08/2009 **ME**

Hadfield, Ms E J, BA(Hons) MA, Learning Resources Mgr., Thomas Rotherham Coll. [10005089] 06/06/2007 **ME**

Hadley, Mrs J E M, FCLIP BSc, Life Member. [6084] 17/09/1956 **FE01/01/1966**

Hadwick, Mrs K E, BA DipLib, Lib., Surrey Co. L. [34688] 25/01/1982 **ME**

Haerkoenen, Miss S, DipLBibl MCLIP, Subject Lib., Cardiff Univ. [62104] 19/02/2003 **CM23/06/2004**

Hagemann, Mrs H C, BA, Stud. [10017087] 22/06/2010 **ME**

Hager, Ms T, BA(Hons) Msc, Area Child. & Young Persons Lib., Chippenham L. [65247] 25/11/2005 **ME**

Hagger Street, Mrs E M, BA(Hons) CertEd MCLIP, Sen. Learning Res. Advisor, Barnet Coll., London. [26023] 25/09/1967 **CM23/02/1984**

Haggerty, Ms M H, BA MCLIP, LRC Co-ordinator, Kincorth Acad., Aberdeen. [20713] 29/05/1973 **CM31/07/1975**

Hagon, Mrs D J, ACLIP, Lib., Brookfields Hosp., Cambridge. [65142] 03/11/2005 **ACL06/12/2006**

Hague, Mr H R, MA MCLIP, Retired. [16974] 02/10/1969 **CM15/12/1972**

Hague, Miss V L, BA MA, Unknown. [61935] 11/12/2002 **ME**

Haigh, Miss J M, BA, Stud., Leeds Met. Univ. [10011218] 02/10/2008 **ME**

Haigh, Mrs V C, BA MSc MCLIP, L. Mgr., Salford Royal Hosp. NHS Found. Trust. [41451] 01/01/1988 **CM19/06/1991**

Haines, Mrs C M C, MA BA BSc CBiol, Writer/Researcher/Abstractor [33238] 30/10/1980 **ME**

Haines, Mrs J H, BA(Hons) DipMgmnt MCLIP, Learning Resource Cent. Mgr., The Milton Keynes Academy, Milton Keynes. [10011238] 03/10/2008 **CM07/07/2010**

Haines, Mrs J M, MA BLib DipM ACIM MCLIP, Head of Lib. Serv., Learning Resources L., Oxford Brookes Univ. [24143] 24/03/1975 **CM31/08/1979**

Haines, Mr M J, BSc MSc MCLIP, L. Mgr., BPP Law Sch.,London. [52740] 30/11/1995 **CM15/05/2002**

Haines, Ms M P J, BA MLS FCLIP HonFCLIP, Univ. Lib., Carleton Univ., Ottawa, Canada. [43248] 09/10/1989 **FE29/03/2004**

Haines, Mrs P G, MCLIP, Hon. Lib., Sussex Archaeological Soc., Lewes. [6103] 01/01/1950 **CM01/01/1966**

Haining, Mr C, Catr., Bibliographic Data Serv. Ltd, Dumfries. [10016002] 10/02/2010 **ME**

Hair, Ms F M, BA DiplLM MCLIP, Asst. Lib., Sheppard-Worlock L., Liverpool Hope Univ. Coll. [55160] 28/07/1997 **CM12/09/2001**

Hair, Mrs F, BA MA MCLIP, Sen. L. & Inf. Offr., Newcastle Libs. & Inf. Serv. [20292] 26/01/1973 **CM01/01/1976**

Haiselden, Mr G C, MCLIP, Stock Lead, Surrey C.C., Guildford. [23339] 26/10/1974 **CM21/10/1977**

Hajnal, Miss A D, Stud. Lon. Met Univ. [10011699] 06/11/2008 **ME**

Halabura, Miss K J, MA, Sen. L. Asst., Northcote L., London. [64966] 05/10/2005 **ME**

Haldane, Mr G C, BD MSc MCLIP, Unwaged. [10016308] 12/10/1981 **CM31/10/1985**

Hale, Mrs C J, BA MCLIP, Unwaged. [27545] 16/05/1977**CM07/08/1980**

Hale, Ms E M, BA(Hons), Independent Consultant [63911] 26/10/2004 **ME**

Hale, Mrs H R, BA MCLIP, Unemployed [24597] 01/10/1975 **CM14/11/1978**

Hale, Ms J, BEd MA, Young People`s Serv. Mgr. Plymouth City Council [58141] 13/02/2003 **ME**

Hale, Mrs P C, BA DipLib MCLIP, Unemployed. [24343] 05/06/1975 **CM13/03/1978**

Hale, Mrs P S, Unknown. [10015562] 15/12/2009 **AF**

Hale, Mr P, BSc, Stud., Univ. of the W. of England, Bristol. [10009347] 01/06/2008 **ME**

Hale, Mr W A, MA, Asst. Under-Lib., Rare Books Specialist, Cambridge Univ. L. [50339] 01/07/1994 **ME**

Hales, Mrs C A, BA(Hons) MA, Team Lib., Egham L., Surrey C.C. [35558] 04/11/1982 **ME**

Haley, Ms B J, Systems Lib., Dept. of Printed Books, Imperial War Mus. [65317] 23/12/2005 **ME**

Haley, Miss M J, BA MCLIP, L. & Inf. Asst., E. Grp. Sheffield City L. [6117] 01/01/1972 **CM12/08/1977**

Halfhide, Mrs D G, MA DipLib MCLIP, L. Inf. Serv. Mgr., Peterborough & Stamford Hosp. NHS Foundation Trust. [37438] 10/09/1984 **CM14/04/1987**

Halford, Mrs E D, BA(Hons) MCLIP, Sch. Lib., St Mary's Catholic Sch., Bishop's Stortford. [52321] 26/10/1995 **CM06/04/2005**

Halford, Mrs E J, BSc DipLib MCLIP, L. & Inf. Mgr, Charles Taylor & Co. Ltd., London. [27195] 28/01/1977 **CM22/03/1979**

Halford, Ms S L, BA(Hons) MA, Liaison Lib., Middlesex Univ., London [65244] 25/11/2005 **ME**

Halfpenny, Mrs K, BA(Hons) MCLIP, Lib. & Learning Mgr., Southport Coll., Merseyside [40132] 17/10/1986 **CM13/06/2007**

Hall, Mr A C L, MA MCLIP, Life Member. [6118] 21/01/1959 **CM01/01/1963**

Hall, Miss A J B, BA B MUS FCLIP, Retired. [16977] 07/03/1961 **FE26/11/1997**

Hall, Mr A L, BSc Social Sciences, L. Asst., Battersea L., London [10009449] 28/05/2008 **AF**

Hall, Mrs A M, BA(Hons) PGCE DipLib MCLIP, Team Lib., Bolton Cent. L. [38599] 28/07/1985 **CM21/07/1993**

Hall, Mrs A M, BA MCLIP, Unwaged. [31310] 01/10/1979**CM01/10/1981**

Hall, Mr A R, MA MCLIP, Retired. [6120] 01/09/1967 **CM01/01/1969**

Hall, Ms A, BA(Hons), Lib. Mgr., Royal Liverpool & Broadgreen Univ. Hosp. NHS Trust, Liverpool. [46346] 29/10/1991 **ME**

Hall, Mr B M, MLS MCLIP, Retired. [6124] 15/03/1960 **CM01/01/1965**

Hall, Miss B P, MCLIP, Retired. [6125] 16/01/1961 **CM01/01/1970**

Hall, Mr B, BA(Hons) MA, L. Asst., Ashburne L., Univ. of Sunderland. [10014499] 05/08/2009 **AF**

Hall, Mr C A, MA MCLIP, Bibl. Serv. Lib., City of London L., Guildhall L. [26398] 08/10/1976 **CM14/02/1979**

Hall, Mr C J D, BA DipLib MCLIP, Customer Serv. Devel. Lib., Canterbury L., Kent L. & Arch. [36347] 03/10/1983 **CM04/10/1988**

Hall, Ms D M, BA DipLib MCLIP, Bibl. Serv. Lib., Powys L. Serv. H.Q., Llandrindod Wells. [33219] 10/10/1980 **CM02/02/1983**

Hall, Ms D M, BA, Lib. Asst. Map section, Bodleian Lib. Oxford [65169] 01/11/2005 **ME**

Hall, Mrs E A, BA(Hons), Ch. Excutive Offr., ICIS, information for life., W Sussex [58504] 08/03/2000 **AF**

Hall, Ms E, BA, Stud. (DL), Aberystwyth Univ. [10014454] 31/07/2009 **ME**

Hall, Ms G E, MCLIP, UHRA Project Offr., Univ. of Hertfordshire, Hatfield [6133] 01/01/1972 **CM17/01/1975**

Hall, Mr G, BA DipLib MCLIP, Asst. Lib., Eastwood L., Notts. C.C. [37813] 22/10/1984 **CM06/09/1988**

Hall, Dr H E, BSc Phd, Unknown [10006700] 21/11/2007 **ME**

Hall, Dr H J R, BA(Hons) MA PhD FCLIP FHEA, Dir., Cent for Social Informatics., Edinburgh Napier Univ., Edinburgh. / Exec. Sec., L. & Inf. Sci. Res. Coalition. [41231] 19/10/1987 **FE01/04/2002**

Hall, Miss J B, MA MCLIP, Sen. Indexer, House of Commons L., London. [16978] 01/01/1972 **CM16/02/1987**

Hall, Mrs J C, BA DipLib, Acting Acquisitions Mgr., The Coll. of Law. [41667] 11/02/1988 **ME**

Hall, Miss J C, BA, Postgrad. Stud., Manchester, Met. Univ. [10002981] 10/05/2007 **ME**

Hall, Ms J F, BA MCLIP, Asst. Head of Culture & Tourism, Sunderland C.C. [35208] 04/10/1982 **CM16/05/1990**

Hall, Mrs J H, BA(Hons), Lib., Langley Park Girls Sch., Beckenham, Kent. [62645] 01/10/2003 **ME**

Hall, Miss J M, BLib MCLIP, Serv. Delivery & Inclusion Mgr., Tameside M.B.C., Tameside Cent. L. [6141] 01/07/1971 **CM14/10/1975**

Hall, Dr J P, BA(Hons) MA PhD, Asst. Dir. (L. & Res. Support) Univ. of Exeter. [64087] 13/01/2005 **ME**

Hall, Mr J T D, MA PhD, Emeritus Lib., Durham Univ. [42811] 02/03/1989 **ME**

Hall, Mr J, MSc MCLIP, Catr., Hants. Co. L., Winchester. [18347] 12/10/1972 **CM07/10/1975**

Hall, Ms J, BA DipLib MCLIP DMS, Inf. &Heritage Mgr., L.B. Lewisham, Lewisham, London. [31311] 19/10/1979 **CM09/10/1981**

Hall, Mrs J, MCLIP, Priority Serv. Mgr., Byker Br. L., Newcastle upon Tyne. [22409] 06/05/1974 **CM01/02/1977**

Hall, Miss K, BA MCLIP, Serv. Co-ordinator, Northumbria Univ. Lib. [26103] 12/07/1976 **CM26/09/1980**

Hall, Miss L A, L. Asst., Orchard Sch. Bristol. [10016624] 01/05/2010**AF**

Hall, Mrs L A, BSc(Hons) DipILS MCLIP, Unwaged. [53126] 07/03/1996 **CM23/06/2004**

Hall, Dr L, BA PhD, Careers Advisor. [60468] 19/10/1999 **ME**

Hall, Miss M A, BA MCLIP, Mgr., L. Stock Serv., Warks C.C. [25039] 28/10/1975 **CM30/10/1979**

Hall, Mr M D, MSc MLIS, Inf. Specialist, Med. L. Royal Free Hosp., London [10009703] 19/01/2005 **ME**

Hall, Mr M, MA MCLIP, Lib., (Aquistions & Resources), Oxford Brookes Univ. [62670] 02/10/2003 **CM21/06/2006**

Hall, Mr N T A, BEng MSc, Data and Info. Mgmnt. Consultant [58945] 06/10/2000 **ME**

Hall, Mr P F, BA(Hons) PGDipLIS MCLIP, Sch. Lib., St Thomas More Language Coll., London. [53641] 16/08/1996 **CM02/02/2005**

Hall, Mr R A, MCLIP, Inf. Serv. Lib., Sefton MBC, Southport. [6155] 22/10/1970 **CM15/04/1975**

Hall, Mr R E, LLB MA, ICT Devel. Offr. (L.), S. Tyneside M.B.C., Cent. L. [59004] 20/10/2000 **ME**

Hall, Mr R, BLib MCLIP, Vendor Relations Mgr., Lovells LLP, London [30953] 22/06/1979 **CM06/04/1984**

Hall, Mrs S A, BLib BA MA PGCE MCLIP, Lib., Queen Margarets Sch., York. [27579] 18/05/1977 **CM17/11/1980**

Hall, Ms S A, BA, Unemployed. [44365] 01/10/1990 **ME**

Hall, Miss S, BA MCLIP, Employment not known. [26105] 23/06/1976 **CM29/08/1980**

Hall, Mrs S, BA MCLIP, Subject & Learning Support Lib., Staffs. Univ., Beaconside, Stafford. [31125] 09/09/1979 **CM27/11/1996**

Hall, Mr S, CBiol PGDip ILS, Unwaged. [10012727] 20/11/1990 **ME**

Hallam, Miss C M, BA MCLIP, Team Lib., Sound & Vision L., Nottingham. [6161] 01/10/1968 **CM11/09/1972**

Hallam, Ms P A, BSc DipLib MCLIP, Team Leader., L. Resources., Northumberland C. C [35469] 14/10/1982 **CM18/02/1986**

Hallam, Miss R C, Inf. Specialist, GCHQ, Cheltenham. [61134] 07/03/2002 **ME**

Hallam, Ms S M, BA MSc, Internet Marketing Consultant, Hallam Communications Ltd., Nottingham. [60173] 21/03/1989 **ME**

Hallaways, Mrs K, BA MCLIP, Unwaged. [18185] 10/10/1972 **CM05/01/1976**

Hallett, Miss A N E, BA(Hons) MSc, Lib., London. [52213] 10/10/1995 **ME**

Hallett, Miss L A, BSc MSc MCLIP, Career Break [44337] 20/09/1990 **CM20/03/1996**

Hallewell, Prof L, BA PhD FCLIP, Life Member. [6167] 10/01/1950 **FE01/01/1959**

Halliday, Mrs A, BA DipLIS MCLIP, Ch. Lib., Thurrock Council, Essex. [46214] 16/10/1991 **CM25/01/1995**

Halliday, Ms H, BA MCLIP, Serv. Mgr. : Quality & Support, Solihull Cent. L., Birmingham. [10007152] 27/01/1976 **CM24/02/1981**

Halliday, Mr M R, BA MCLIP, Life Member. [6169] 23/08/1957 **CM01/01/1961**

Halliday, Ms S, BA(Hons) DipILM MCLIP, Asst. Knowledge Consultant, Univ. of Hertfordshire. [54120] 30/10/1996 **CM22/09/1999**

Halligan, Mr C F, MA DipLib MCLIP, Lib., St. Lukes H. S., Barrhead. [43489] 30/10/1989 **CM24/03/1992**

Hallinan, Mrs P S, MCLIP, Retired. [23618] 16/01/1975 **CM14/10/1977**

Hallissey, Mr M H, BA(Hons) DipLIS MCLIP, Asst. Lib., Law Comm. L., London. [46623] 28/11/1991 **CM20/05/1998**

Halliwell, Miss M J, BSc, Stud., Manchester Met. Univ. [65193] 17/11/2005 **ME**

Hallman-Lewis, Mrs C, ACLIP, Unknown. [10012420] 05/02/2009 **ACL23/09/2009**

Hallworth, Ms L K, MCLIP, Learning Cent. Asst. (Curriculum), City & Islington Coll., London [63490] 15/06/2004 **CM21/05/2008**

Halper, Mrs S D, BA(Hons) PGDip MCLIP, Lead Content Specialist (Business& Mgmt), Brit. L., London. [58140] 08/11/1999 **CM21/05/2008**

Halsall, Ms J L, MSc MCLIP, Database Mgr., CAB Internat., Wallingford, Oxon. [60373] 28/04/1980 **CM17/07/1984**

Halsey, Ms A G, BA, Customer Serv. Asst., Edward Boyle L., Leeds. [10016201] 05/03/2010 **ME**

Halsey, Mrs M, BA MCLIP, Sch. Lib., The John Lyon Sch. [31372] 15/10/1979 **CM14/08/1985**

Halstead, Mr J C, BA(Hons) MSc MCLIP, Sen. Subject Lib., Health Studies, Middlesex Univ. [57141] 21/12/1998 **CM04/02/2004**

Halstead, Ms S A, BA MCLIP, Area Info. Servs. Mgr., Chorley, Lancs. C.C. [25756] 22/02/1976 **CM22/02/1978**

Halstead, Ms S J, BA DipLib CertEd MCLIP DMS, Corporate Head of Learning Serv., Cornwall Coll. [34662] 22/01/1982 **CM16/05/1985**

Hambelton, Mr P R, MA MCLIP, Nat. L. of Scotland. [59743] 10/09/2001 **CM10/07/2009**

Hambidge, Mrs F A M, BA MCLIP, Business Inf. Specialist, Univ. of Bath in Swindon. [35561] 25/10/1982 **CM21/02/1985**

Hamblett, Miss E, MCLIP, Stock & Systems Mgr., City of York [18251] 04/10/1972 **CM25/07/1975**

Hambrook, Ms K M P, BA DipLib MCLIP, A. V. Lib., Oxford Brookes Univ. [37110] 09/02/1984 **CM15/08/1989**

Hamer, Mrs A F, ACLIP, L. Mgr., St. Lukes Sci. & Sports Coll., Exeter. [65047] 21/10/2005 **ACL06/02/2008**

Hamer, Miss E J, MCLIP, Sch. L. Mgr., Bury P. L. [6190] 07/09/1966 **CM01/01/1971**

Hamer, Mrs L S, MCLIP, Child. Lib., Bath Child. L., Bath & N. E. Somerset. [21300] 16/10/1973 **CM01/11/1976**

Hamill-Stewart, Ms N C, BA DipLib MCLIP, Relief Lib., Cambridgeshire L. [42485] 23/11/1988 **CM26/05/1993**

Hamilton, Miss A E, BA(Hons), St. George Sch. for Girls, Edinburgh. [57726] 08/07/1999 **AF**

Hamilton, Mrs A F, MA MCLIP, Customer Serv. Mgr., City of York Co., Clifton L. [26475] 08/10/1976 **CM12/10/1979**

Hamilton, Mrs C E, MCLIP, Lib., MOD, Ash Vale. [23181] 05/11/1974 **CM11/12/1978**

Hamilton, Mrs C, BA(Hons), Unwaged. [10010491] 30/07/2008 **AF**

Hamilton, Miss D, MTH BA MCLIP, Life Member. [16985] 27/09/1951 **CM01/01/1957**

Hamilton, Mr G E, FCLIP, Life Member. [6200] 14/09/1955 **FE01/04/1960**

Hamilton, Ms G W, BA MCLIP, Systems Lib., Nat. L. of Scotland, Edinburgh. [35235] 05/10/1982 **CM01/09/1987**

Hamilton, Ms G, BA(Hons) MCLIP, Stock Devel. Off. [63258] 23/03/2004 **CM29/11/2006**

Hamilton, Mr J E, FCLIP, Retired. [6203] 05/03/1963 **FE18/06/1976**

Hamilton, Miss J, Stud., Aberystwyth Univ. [10009487] 21/05/2008 **ME**

Hamilton, Miss K M, BA MSc, Asst. Lib., FCO, London. [61337] 30/05/2002 **ME**

Hamilton, Miss M A, Retired. [6208] 04/03/1947 **ME**

Hamilton, Mrs M, LLB (Hons), LIS Training Exec., Freshfields Bruckhaus Deringer, London. [10011675] 21/11/2008 **AF**

Hamilton, Mr P C W, BA(Hons) DipLib MCLIP, Asst. Lib., Food Standards Agency, London. [32076] 11/02/1980 **CM11/05/1984**

Hamlett, Mrs J A, BA(Hons) Msc, Inf. Asst., Bath Spa Univ. [65529] 07/02/2006 **ME**

Hamley, Miss J, BA DipLib MCLIP, Law Lib., Univ. of the W. of England, Bristol. [39582] 07/03/1986 **CM18/07/1991**

Hammond, Mrs D C, BA MCLIP, Lib., Milton Keynes L. [37450] 01/10/1984 **CM30/01/1991**

Hammond, Mrs K M, BSc MSc DipLib MCLIP, Life Member. [6232] 30/01/1964 **CM01/01/1967**

Hammond, Miss S C, BSc(Hons), Catr.,The Brit. L., Boston Spa. [10000812] 16/11/2006 **ME**

Hampshire, Dr M D, BA(Hons) MSc(Econ) PhD MCLIP, Temp. part-time Catr., The Nat. Arch., Kew. [52893] 17/01/1996 **CM11/03/2009**

Hampson, Mrs A M, MCLIP, Unwaged [1611] 21/02/1968 **CM01/01/1970**

Hampson, Mrs E P, MA(Hons) MCLIP, Retired [21283] 12/10/1973 **CM01/11/1976**

Hampson, Mr J P, BSc MSc MRPharmS MCLIP, Public Health Specialist, Western Cheshire Primary Care Trust [60443] 07/08/1998 **CM07/08/1998**

Hampson, Mrs S A, Dev. Offr., Rayleigh L., Essex. [64257] 22/02/2005 **AF**

Han, Ms N, Encompass Trainee Lib., Lewisham L., London [10016416] 22/03/2010 **ME**

Hancock, Mr D C, MCLIP, Unwaged. [16989] 02/02/1970 **CM09/07/1973**

Hancock, Miss K M, MCLIP, Retired. [6249] 01/09/1941 **CM01/01/1948**

Hancock, Mr L J, Unwaged [64207] 02/03/2005 **ME**

Hancox, Miss C, ACLIP, Cummunity Lib., Walsall Council. [10013582] 08/05/2009 **ACL02/03/2010**

Hancox, Mr D G, BA, L. Mgr, Sch. L. Serv., Doncaster M.B.C. [43798] 17/01/1990 **ME**

Hand, Mrs J F, BA(Hons) DipLib MCLIP, Asst. Head of L. and Inf., Gloucester C.C., Gloucester. [39323] 14/01/1986 **CM18/03/1998**

Handfield, Mrs J, BA MCLIP, Community Lib., Luton Cultural Serv. Trust, Luton. [63729] 03/09/2004 **CM23/01/2008**

Handley, Mrs S L, BA MCLIP, Life Member. [6259] 15/02/1950 **CM01/01/1961**

Handy, Mrs J A, MCLIP, L. Asst., Telford & Wrekin Council, Newport. [21092] 03/10/1973 **CM18/08/1976**

Handy, Mrs S D, BA DipLIS MCLIP, Dep. Mgr., Learning Resource Cent., Cent. Sussex Coll. [42771] 23/02/1989 **CM18/11/1993**

Hanes, Mrs J, BA(Hons) MSc MCLIP, Inf. Offr., Coll. of Law, Birmingham. [56829] 20/10/1998 **CM06/04/2005**

Hanes, Mrs S C, BA(Hons) MCLIP, Northumberland Tyne & Wear NHS Trust [54251] 13/11/1996 **CM16/07/2003**

Hanford, Mrs A, MCLIP, Life Member. [6263] 09/09/1954 **CM01/01/1961**

Hanford, Mrs J, MCLIP, Lib., The Athenaeum, Liverpool. [10008995] 25/09/1962 **CM01/01/1970**

Hanks, Miss K L, BA(Hons) MSc, Local Hist. Lib., Poole Mus. [65440] 23/02/2006 **ME**

Hanlon, Mrs C L, BA(Hons) MCLIP, Inf. Offr., Veale Wasbrough Vizards, Bristol. [49853] 07/01/1994 **CM26/11/1997**

Hanlon, Ms C, BA(Hons) MSc(Econ) MCLIP, Sr. Lib., Perse Sch. for Girls & the Stephen Perse Loth Form Coll. [54642] 05/02/1997 **CM21/11/2001**

Hanlon, Miss G, MCLIP, Inf. Offr., CILIPS, Hamilton. [63431] 07/05/2004 **CM13/06/2007**

Hanlon, Mrs S M, BComm PGCE MA, Sen. Lect., Northumbria Univ. [48119] 09/11/1992 **ME**

Hanna, Miss D A, Inf. Offr., Law Soc. of N. Ireland, Belfast. [64228] 21/02/2005 **AF**

Hanna, Mrs E E, BA, Comm. Lib., SELB. [41155] 14/10/1987 **ME**

Hannaford, Mrs L E, BA(Hons) DipLib MCLIP, Unknown. [45785] 28/05/1991 **CM25/01/1995**

Hannah, Miss I, MCLIP, Retired. [6270] 29/03/1950 **CM01/01/1964**

Hannah, Mrs J, BA(Hons) DipILM MCLIP, Unwaged. [50499] 22/08/1994 **CM25/07/2001**

Hannah, Mrs P A, MCLIP, Asst. Area Lib., Highland C. [20993] 25/09/1973 **CM01/10/1976**

Hannah, Mr T, BA(Hons) MCLIP, Learning Cent. Facilitator, Swansea Coll. Learning Cent. [61126] 19/02/2002 **CM23/06/2004**

Hanney, Mrs J B, BSc MSc DIC MCLIP, Employment unknown. [60375] 14/11/1977 **CM04/10/1982**

Hanney, Ms P M G, BA(Hons) MA, L. Res. Mgr., Stafford Coll. [50117] 05/04/1994 **ME**

Hannington, Mrs P E, MCLIP, Law & Legal Inf. Lib. (Freelance). [17098] 28/09/1967 **CM04/09/1972**

Hannon, Mrs E, Head of Main Issue Desk, UCL. [62845] 06/11/2003 **ME**

Hannon, Mr M S M, MA DipLSc FRSA MCLIP, Retired. [6277] 02/10/1969 **CM01/01/1972**

Hanrahan, Miss F M, DipLib MCLIP, Co. Lib., Wexford C.C. [25296] 14/01/1976 **CM02/01/1986**

Hans, Mrs K A, BSc(Hons) MA MCLIP, Sch. Lib., St. Martin-in-the-Fields High Sch., London. [51849] 13/07/1995 **CM21/11/2001**

Hansbury, Ms E, BA MA, Unknown. [10007128] 28/10/1994 **ME**

Hansen, Ms M E, MA MLib MCLIP, Retired. [16993] 13/10/1965 **CM10/02/1969**

Hanson, Mr D T, BA DipLib MCLIP, Lib., Bethnal Green Tech. Cent., London. [22681] 11/08/1974 **CM03/02/1978**

Haran, Mr R A, BSc MPhil, Electronic Resources Mgr., Shire Pharm. [61785] 07/11/2002 **ME**

Harbord, Mrs E A, MA MBA MCLIP, Head of Operations., Univ. York. [26185] 09/08/1976 **CM09/08/1979**

Harbord, Mr P J, MA MCLIP, Retired. [24345] 13/07/1975 **CM05/12/1977**

Harbour, Mrs C L, BA, Subject Lib.: Applied Sci., Writtle Coll. [64820] 20/07/2005 **ME**

Harbour, Mrs C M, MCLIP, Unemployed. [13981] 01/03/1968 **CM01/01/1971**

Harbour, Mrs G P, BA MCLIP, Br. Mgr., Colne L., Lancashire C.C. [26734] 19/11/1976 **CM11/08/1980**

Harbour, Miss J, BSc(Hons), Health Info. Scientist, NHS Quality Improvement, Scotland [62792] 22/10/2003 **ME**

Harcup, Mrs S E, BA MCLIP, Retired. [6290] 20/02/1962 **CM24/07/1964**

Hardarson, Mr H A, FCLIP, Ch. Lib., Kopavogur P. L., Kopavogur. [16996] 05/01/1970 **FE27/07/1994**

Harden, Mr R, BA MCLIP, Retired. [6293] 12/10/1967 **CM01/01/1971**

Harden, Mrs S K, BA MCLIP, Unwaged. [20766] 23/06/1973 **CM17/09/1976**

Hardie, Mrs M C, MA, Unknown. [10006952] 17/12/2007 **ME**

Harding, Mrs A C, MA MSc MCLIP, Asst. Lib., Ornithology & Rothschild L., Nat. Hist. Mus., Tring. [35815] 11/01/1983 **CM11/11/1986**

Harding, Ms A R, BA(Hons) MLib MCLIP, Learning Resources Adviser, Learning Resources Cent., Trinity Univ. Coll., Carmarthen. [48278] 20/11/1992 **CM23/07/1997**

Harding, Ms A, MA DipLib MCLIP, Self-Employed, Trainer & Lect., Supporting Child. & Young Peoples, Reading Devel. & L. [30176] 15/01/1979 **CM15/01/1981**

Harding, Mr G L, MCLIP, Life Member. [6304] 14/02/1947 **CM01/01/1962**

Harding, Miss L, Asst. Lib., LRC, Treloar Coll., Alton. [10016928] 14/10/1997 **ME**

Harding, Mrs M A, BA(Hons) MA MCLIP, Inf. Specialist, Northumbria Univ., Newcastle. [47957] 28/10/1992 **CM20/11/2002**

Harding, Mr O L T, BA(Hons) PG. DipLib MA MA, Sen. Lib., Fourah Bay Coll., Univ. of Sierra Leone. [10005496] 25/07/2007 **ME**

Harding, Mrs R, BA(Hons) MA, Head Lib., The King's Sch., Chester [58616] 13/04/2000 **ME**

Harding, Ms S, BA(Hons), Lib., Huddersfield Local Studies L. [10009761] 09/06/2008 **ME**

Hardisty, Mr J K, BA(Hons) MA DipIM, Sen. Lib., RNIB Nat. L. Serv., Stockport. [56548] 17/08/1998 **ME**

Hardley, Ms E, BA(Hons) MCLIP, Psychology Subject Lib., Univ. L., Univ. of Auckland, NZ [10001847] 08/01/1978 **CM19/02/1981**

Hardman, Mr S J, BSc(Econ), L. Serv. Mgr., Civic Cent. City & Co. Swansea, Swansea [59488] 09/04/2001 **ME**

Hards, Mrs J E, BLib MCLIP, Content Manage. Lib., CIPD, London. [27328] 18/02/1977 **CM30/04/1980**

Hardwick, Mrs S A, Lib. Asst. Aberdeenshire L. & Info. Serv [65908] 30/06/2006 **ME**

Hardwick, Miss S E, BA DipLib MCLIP, Inf. Advisor, Univ. of Brighton, Eastbourne Dist. Gen. Hosp. [34902] 01/04/1982 **CM07/07/1987**

Hardwick, Mrs S J, Inf. Resource Asst., Russells Hall Hosp., Dudley. [10008255] 11/03/2008 **AF**

Hardy, Mrs A D, MCLIP, Retired. [25694] 12/02/1959 **CM24/01/1979**

Hardy, Dr G C, MChem MCLIP, Inf. Specialist, Aston Univ., Birmingham. [62959] 25/11/2003 **CM05/05/2010**

Hardy, Miss J E, MSc MCLIP, Life Member. [6326] 28/09/1959 **CM01/01/1965**

Hardy, Ms N A, BLS MCLIP, Community Lib., Sprowston L., Norfolk [28432] 04/12/1977 **CM27/07/1982**

Hardy, Miss S J, MBE FCLIP, Life Member. [6331] 04/10/1935 **FE01/01/1948**

Hardy-Coulter, Ms W B, BA(Hons) DipLit(open) DipEurHu, Sen. Advisor, Corporate Records, New Zealand Qualifications Auth., Wellington. [63368] 21/04/2004 **ME**

Hare, Mrs C E, BA PGCE MCLIP, Retired [6333] 01/10/1971 **CM03/09/1975**

Hare, Mr G, OBE MCLIP, Retired. [6335] 31/08/1954 **CM01/01/1960**

Hare, Miss K L, BA(Hons) MCLIP, Dual-Use Community Lib., Estover L., Plymouth. [65378] 06/01/2006 **CM11/11/2009**

Haresign, Mrs C, BSc MSc MCLIP, Unknown. [54628] 06/02/1997 **CM21/05/2003**

Hargest, Mrs S, BA(Hons) PGDipILM, Serv. Devel. Co-ordinator Child. and Families, Worcestershire C.C. [61639] 07/10/2002 **ME**

Hargis, Mrs J M, Sen. Policy Mgr., LSC. [43646] 17/11/1989 **ME**

Hargreaves, Ms C W, Systems Supp. Lib., Oxford Univ., Systems & e-Res. Serv. [46737] 16/01/1992 **ME**

Hargreaves, Mr J A, BA FCLIP, Life Member. [6347] 17/05/1941 **FE01/01/1958**

Hargreaves, Mr J B G, BA(Hons), Asst. Lib. Law, Univ. of Bristol. [64241] 22/02/2005 **ME**

Hariff, Miss S, BA(Hons) PgDip MCLIP, Partnership & Access Mgr., Bolton Cent. L. [58273] 06/12/1999 **CM15/10/2002**

Harker, Miss S L, BA(Hons), Unknown. [10010196] 10/07/2008 **AF**

Harket, Mrs E J, Retired. [47079] 15/04/1992 **ME**

Harkins, Ms P C, BA(Hons) DipLis, Asst. Lib., Wellcome L., London. [45395] 26/11/1990 **ME**

Harkison, Mrs J A, BSc DipLib MCLIP, Reg. Communications & Inf. Offr., RNID, Manchester. [26964] 17/01/1977 **CM26/03/1979**

Harkness, Mrs C L, Customer Care Lib. Assit., Newcastle Coll., Newcastle. [10015657] 08/01/2010 **AF**

Harkness, Mrs F, MSc, Lib., L. +Elearning Cent., Glasgow Royal Infirmary, Glasgow. [10008532] 01/02/2002 **ME**

Harland, Miss E A, BA MA DipLib MCLIP, Unwaged – Career Break. [32291] 06/03/1980 **CM05/03/1982**

Harland, Ms H F, DipLib, Stock Lib., Herefordshire Co. [18159] 10/10/1972 **ME**

Harland, Miss J, BSc MSc, Stud., Univ. Sheffield. [61917] 03/12/2002 **ME**

Harley, Mrs C J, MCLIP, Retired. [6359] 29/03/1961 **CM01/01/1969**

Harley, Mrs W B, BA MCLIP, Retired. [24312] 01/01/1952 **CM29/09/1977**

Harling, Mrs A M, LLB(Hons) MSc, L. Super., Calderdale Coll., Halifax. [48481] 21/01/1993 **ME**

Harling, Mr B S C, CertEd MCLIP, Retired. [6362] 05/03/1958 **CM24/09/1974**

Harman, Mr C K, BA DipLib MCLIP, Asst. Lib., St. Annes Cent. L., Lancs. Co. L. [39040] 27/10/1985 **CM15/02/1989**

Harman, Ms C M, BSc MSc, Unknown. [58900] 02/10/2000 **ME**

Harman, Lady E J, MA, Life Member. [6363] 13/10/1959 **ME**

Harmer, Miss N A, BA MA MCLIP, Snr Lib.,L.B. of Barnet. [61790] 07/11/2002 **CM14/06/2007**

Harper, Mr A L S, BA MCLIP, Gulidhall Lib., Guildhall L., London. [24949] 21/10/1975 **CM18/08/1980**

Harper, Miss B E, BA MCLIP, Retired. [6372] 01/01/1971 **CM16/01/1973**

Harper, Mrs J, BA MCLIP, Saturday Super., Univ. Coll. Arts, Farnham. [44352] 01/10/1990 **CM27/07/1994**

Harper, Mrs M, Stud., Univ. of Northumbria, [65644] 09/03/2006 **ME**

Harper, Mr R, BA, Inf. Serv. Offr., Infr. Cent. for Health & Social Care [10005967] 02/07/2009 **ME**

Harper, Mr S, Learning Cent. Mgr., Westminster Coll. L. [47943] 27/10/1992 **ME**

Harpham, Mr B, MA MISt, Ref. Lib., Canada [10016317] 05/03/2010 **ME**

Harridge, Mrs J M, BLib MCLIP, Local Studies Lib., Warwickshire Co. L., Leamington Spa. [33758] 20/02/1981 **CM26/08/1987**

Harries, Mrs C W, MA MEd, Community Lib., Lllangollen L. [59522] 24/04/2001 **ME**

Harrington, Mrs A B, MCLIP, Retired. [6390] 22/11/1940 **CM01/01/1946**

Harrington, Mrs B M, BA MCLIP, Retired [6393] 23/01/1968 **CM01/01/1971**

Harrington, Mrs F A, MCLIP, RLIANZA, Lib., Southland Health Board, N. Z. [10012718] 08/03/1963 **CM01/07/1991**

Harrington, Mrs H L, BSc(Hons) MSc ILTM, Campus L. Mgr., St Marys Campus L., Imperial Coll. London [57632] 04/06/1999 **ME**

Harris, Mrs A G, MA MCLIP, PT Lib., Prior's Field Sch., Godalming. [10016884] 01/01/1965 **CM01/01/1968**

Harris, Mrs A M, BLib, Lerning Cent. Mgr., W. Herts. Coll., Watford [33582] 21/01/1981 **ME**

Harris, Miss A M, MBChB MSc MCLIP, Sen. L. Asst., Univ. of Strathclyde, Ref. & Inf. Div., Andersonian L. [49550] 09/11/1993 **CM16/07/2003**

Harris, Mrs A, BA(Hons) DipISM MCLIP, Retired [50512] 30/08/1994 **CM02/02/2005**

Harris, Miss C L J, BA(Hons) MA, Inf. Offr., Prupim, London [59540] 01/05/2001 **ME**

Harris, Mr C W J, MCLIP, Stock Circ. Mgr., Bromley L. [6400] 24/01/1967 **CM01/01/1971**

Harris, Ms C, MusB MA, Res. Serv. Mgr, Irwin Mitchell. [61798] 13/11/2002 **ME**

Harris, Miss E L, BA MCLIP, ICT Team Leader, Leek L., Staffordshire C.C. [30429] 25/01/1979 **CM17/10/1985**

Harris, Mrs E L, MCLIP, Learning Resources Adviser p. /t., Trinity Coll., Carmarthen. [36925] 18/01/1984 **CM13/06/2007**

Harris, Mrs E V, MSc, Asst. Lib., Law Soc., London. [64285] 23/02/2005 **ME**

Harris, Mrs E, BA LTCL DipILS MCLIP, Local Studies Lib., Argyll & Bute Council, L. H.Q., Dunoon. [36706] 03/11/1983 **CM15/08/1990**

Harris, Mr F A, HonFCLIP, Hon. Fellow. [62815] 23/10/2003 **HFE23/10/2003**

Harris, Mr G A, BSocSci MPhil DipKM FCLIP, Business & Career Coach. [6404] 25/06/1970 **FE26/07/1995**

Harris, Ms G R, MA MCLIP, Head of Sch. L. Serv., L.B. of Tower Hamlets. [26404] 12/10/1976 **CM20/01/1981**

Harris, Ms I M, MA DipLib MCLIP, Not working at present. [33521] 16/01/1981 **CM23/08/1985**

Harris, Mrs J A, BA DipLib MCLIP, User Serv. Mgr., Bournemouth Univ. [30838] 02/05/1979 **CM11/12/1981**

Harris, Mrs J B A, BSc DipLib MCLIP, Inf. Offr., The Moray Council, Elgin. [29197] 29/03/1978 **CM28/03/1980**

Harris, Mr J K, MSc MCLIP, Inf. Specialist. [51418] 10/02/1995 **CM01/04/2002**

Harris, Mrs J N, MA Dip Lib PgCE MCLIP, Inf. Mgr., MS Soc. Scotland [10012649] 05/10/1982 **CM21/01/1998**

Harris, Mrs J, Sch. Lib., Worth Sch., Crawley. [10006492] 20/09/1999 **ME**

Harris, Mrs K J, Asst. Catr., Southampton Inst., Mountbatten L. [56555] 18/08/1998 **ME**

Harris, Mrs L I P, MA DipILS MCLIP, Asst. Lib., Univ. of Strathclyde, Glasgow, Catr., Coutts Inf. [51280] 19/12/1994 **CM21/01/1998**

Harris, Mr L K, MA DipLib ALAA FCLIP, L. Mgr., The Queen Elizabeth Hosp., Adelaide, Australia. [40255] 16/11/1986 **FE18/09/2003**

Harris, Mrs L M, BA(Hons) DipLIS, Sch. Lib.,King Edward VI Handsworth Sch., Birmingham [10001429] 18/10/1994 **ME**

Harris, Miss L M, MA MLib MCLIP, Subject Advisor Univ. Birmingham. Main L. [40291] 15/01/1987 **CM22/04/1992**

Harris, Ms L, MCLIP, Idea Store Mgr. (Job Share), L.B. of Tower Hamlets. [8044] 07/03/1972 **CM15/01/1976**

Harris, Mrs M A, MCLIP, Retired. [31876] 01/01/1980 **CM18/08/1982**

Harris, Mrs M A, MCLIP, Sen. Lib. - Info, Lib. Enquiry Cent., Taunton. [33377] 01/11/1980 **CM27/02/1984**

Harris, Mrs M E, BA MCLIP, Child. Serv. Lib., L.B. of Havering, Romford. [14713] 04/02/1970 **CM13/02/1974**

Harris, Ms M, BA DipLib MCLIP, Dep. Head of L. & Inf. Serv., Dept. of Work and Pensions, London. [33536] 19/01/1981 **CM02/06/1987**

Harris, Mrs N J, ACLIP, L. Super., Warminster L., Wilts. [64530] 09/05/2005 **ACL04/04/2006**

Harris, Mr N, BA MA Dip, Stud., UCL. London. [10010583] 08/08/2008
ME

Harris, Mr P A, BA(Hons) MSc, Lib., Silcoates Sch., Wakefield [52403]
30/10/1995
ME

Harris, Mr P, BSc CChem MRSC FCLIP, Retired. [60380] 27/05/1969
FE03/11/1981

Harris, Miss R M, BA MCLIP, Life Member. [6415] 07/02/1965
CM01/01/1967

Harris, Mr R S, BA(Hons) DipLib DMS MCLIP MA, Coll. Lib., St. Luke's
6th form Coll., Sidcup. [43951] 06/03/1990
CM27/07/1994

Harris, Mrs S E, BLib MCLIP, Sch. Lib. [38909] 15/10/1985
CM22/05/1996

Harris, Miss S L, Info. Specialist, GCHQ [10001334] 06/02/2007
ME

Harris, Ms S, BA MA MCLIP, Asst. Lib., The Grammar sch. at Leeds,
Leeds. [39052] 30/10/1985
CM14/03/1990

Harris, Miss S, MA DipLib MCLIP, InfMgr., Campbell Reith, London.
[28311] 07/11/1977
CM25/06/1981

Harris, Miss S, BSc (Hons), Info. Co-ordinator, City Lib.,Northumbria
Univ., Newcastle. [65274] 28/11/2005
ME

Harris, Mr S, MA(Hons) MSc MCLIP, Sen. Lib., Penicuik L., Midlothian
Council [51281] 19/12/1994
CM23/07/1997

Harris, Miss V, BA(Hons), Metadata Admin., The Charles Seale-Hayne
L., Univ. of Plymouth. [10002051] 14/01/2009
ME

Harris, Mrs Y, MCLIP, Area Mgr., Caerphilly Co. Bor. Council, Caerphilly
L. [9095] 28/09/1967
CM16/09/1974

Harrison, Mrs A A M, MCLIP, Principal Lib. Offr., Aberdeenshire L. &
Inf. Serv., Oldmeldrum. [5505] 06/10/1969
CM01/01/1973

Harrison, Mrs A C, MCLIP, Life Member. [6419] 08/03/1950
CM01/01/1955

Harrison, Mrs A J, BA MCLIP, Ref. Specialist, Brit. L., London. [19576]
16/11/1972
CM14/10/1975

Harrison, Miss A L, BA(Hons), Asst. Lib., Lancashire Teaching Hosp.
NHS Foundation Trust [62704] 07/10/2003
ME

Harrison, Mrs A P, BSc MSc MCLIP, Lib., Retford L., Notts. [37875]
05/11/1984
CM15/08/1989

Harrison, Miss A, BA, Grad. Trainee Lib., Emmanuel Coll.,Cambridge.
[10015058] 08/10/2009
ME

Harrison, Ms C L, Inf. Specialist. [65379] 05/01/2006
ME

Harrison, Prof C T, FRSA MIMgt MCLIP, Life Member. [6424]
01/09/1958
CM01/01/1965

Harrison, Mr D, MA HonFLA FCLIP, Hon. Fellow. [6425] 07/01/1950
FE01/01/1954

Harrison, Mr D, MCLIP, Lib., N. Tyneside L., Cent. L. [6426] 24/01/1972
CM11/10/1976

Harrison, Mrs E J, BA(Hons) MCLIP, Asst. Lib., Univ. of Glamorgan,
Pontypridd. [46988] 20/03/1992
CM18/11/1998

Harrison, Mrs E, MCLIP, Info. Offr., Enterprise Eurpoe Network Wales,
Mold [10015694] 20/02/1974
CM01/11/1977

Harrison, Mrs F A, BA(Hons) MPhil MCLIP, Team Leader Reader
Devel., W. Berks. Council. [38090] 08/01/1985
CM01/04/2002

Harrison, Ms F C, BA MA, Retired. [36176] 03/07/1983
ME

Harrison, Mr G V C, BSc MSc MCLIP, Retired Child. & Family Advisor,
Whitechapel L., London. [32292] 03/03/1980
CM03/03/1982

Harrison, Mrs J A, BA MCLIP, p. /t. Learning Resources Asst.,
Birmingham Met. Coll. [33454] 09/01/1981
CM10/10/1984

Harrison, Mr J A, MA MCLIP, Special Collections Lib., St. Johns Coll.,
Cambridge. [55902] 15/12/1997
CM10/07/2009

Harrison, Ms J K, BA DipLib MCLIP, Retired. [6437] 06/01/1967
CM01/01/1969

Harrison, Mrs J M, L. Asst., Hants. C.C., Stubbington L. [54186]
06/11/1996
AF

Harrison, Mrs J, BA MCLIP, Asst. Knowledge Consultant (Inf. Mgmnt.),
Univ. of Herts., Hatfield. [7294] 01/01/1972
CM23/10/1977

Harrison, Miss K J, BA(Hons) MCLIP, Career Break. [51091]
14/11/1994
CM17/11/1999

Harrison, Mrs K, BA DipLib MCLIP, Lib. and Inf. Cent. Area Mgr.,
Kirklees M.D.C. [39198] 06/01/1986
CM15/05/1989

Harrison, Mrs L E, MCLIP, Lib., Bedford Sch. [64363] 14/03/2005
CM07/07/2010

Harrison, Mrs M M, MA MCLIP, Retired. [10834] 03/04/1965
CM01/01/1970

Harrison, Dr N A, BSc PhD DipLib MCLIP, Inf. Sci., [41657] 09/02/1988
CM18/11/1992

Harrison, Mrs N J, BSc PGDip, Tech. Lib., Harley Haddow, Edinburgh
[10008282] 19/03/2008
ME

Harrison, Mrs P A, LRC Mgr., Driffield Sch., Driffield. [10001083]
12/01/2007
AF

Harrison, Mrs P H, MCLIP, Life Member. [6453] 11/03/1948
CM01/01/1955

Harrison, Ms R E J, BA(Hons), Team Leader, Learning Devel., Imperial
Coll., London [55953] 19/12/1997
ME

Harrison, Mr R P, Lib. Asst., Princes Risborough L. [10016557]
14/04/2010
ME

Harrison, Mrs S J, BA DipLib MCLIP, Advisory Lib., Sch. Lib. Serv.,
Essex C.C., Chelmsford [40077] 17/10/1986
CM14/08/1991

Harrison, Miss S L, Stud. [65907] 30/06/2006
ME

Harrison, Miss S M, BA MCLIP, Sen. L. & Inf. Offr. (E. Cluster),
Newcastle L. & Inf. Serv., Newcastle. [10000574] 16/10/2006
CM27/01/1981

Harrison, Mrs S, BA(Hons), Med. Lib., Tameside & Glossop NHS Trust,
Ashton-U-Lyne. [58450] 15/02/2000
ME

Harrison, Mr S, MA MCLIP, Systems Mgr., Holmesglen Inst. of T. A. F.
E., Australia. [22724] 02/09/1974
CM20/01/1977

Harriss, Mr P D, BA DipLib MCLIP, Asst. Lib., City Business L. [27679]
12/07/1977
CM31/10/1980

Harriss, Ms R, BA DipLib MCLIP, Community Lib., Norfolk L. & Info.
Serv. [36853] 01/01/1984
CM05/05/1987

Harrisson, Ms W J, BMUS(Hons) MA MCLIP, Unwaged. [57393]
03/03/1999
CM16/07/2003

Harrity, Mrs S, MBE BA BPhil, Cert. of Merit. [50583] 22/09/1994
ME

Harrop, Miss D, BA, Stud. [65912] 03/07/2006
ME

Harrop, Mr P, BA DipLib MCLIP, Catr. (Temp), Queen Mary Univ. of
London. [35861] 03/02/1983
CM04/08/1987

Harrow, Mr A J, MA DipLib MCLIP, Retired. [6461] 10/03/1958
CM18/01/1989

Hart, Mrs A M, BA MCLIP, Unwaged. [24922] 07/10/1975**CM10/10/1979**

Hart, Dr B A, BA PhD MA, Lib., V&A Theatre Collections, London.
[54812] 08/04/1997
ME

Hart, Mr B, MCLIP, Life Member. [6463] 21/03/1948　　　**CM01/01/1959**

Hart, Mr C P, BSc, Knowledge & Inf. Agent, DSTL Knowledge & Inf.
Serv., Salisbury. [10009712] 02/06/2008
ME

Hart, Ms C, BA(Hons) DipLIS MCLIP, LRC Mgr., Inverness Coll. [45790]
31/05/1991
CM20/09/1995

Hart, Mr D R, MA MCLIP, Reader Serv. Lib., Main L.,Univ of Dundee.
[28582] 28/12/1977
CM17/07/1981

Hart, Mrs E A, BA DipLib MBCS FCLIP, Consultant, Liz Hart Associates.
[24320] 02/10/1974
FE13/06/1990

Hart, Miss E M, BA MCLIP, Audio Visual Serv. Lib., Enfield P. L. [6465]
26/09/1966
CM01/01/1970

Hart, Ms K, LLB MSc, Head of Res. & L., Lovells, London. [65454]
24/02/2006
ME

Hart, Miss L L, L. Asst., Northumberland Coll. [64345] 07/03/2005　**AF**

Hart, Miss R N, MA(Hons) DipILS MCLIP, Lib., Ashcraig Sch., Glasgow.
[58827] 18/08/2000
CM12/03/2003

Hart, Mrs S M, MCLIP, Lib., Cumbria C.C., Workington L. [6475]
02/04/1965
CM01/07/1969

Hart, Ms S, BA(Hons) MA MCLIP, Lib., Brit. Assoc. of Psychotherapists [50375] 07/07/1994 **CM06/04/2005**

Hart, Mrs S, MCLIP, L. Mgr., Kimbolton Sch., Kimbolton, Huntingdon, Cambs [26916] 17/12/1976 **CM09/08/1979**

Hart, Miss V D, BA MCLIP, Asst. Lib., Guildhall L. London. [23571] 07/01/1975 **CM01/07/1988**

Harte, Mrs K, BA(Hons) MA MCLIP, Devel. Lib. Social Inclusion, Sneinton L., Nottingham. [48149] 11/11/1992 **CM12/03/2003**

Hartley, Mr A, MA MCLIP BA(Econ), Retired. [6483] 16/01/1968 **CM01/01/1971**

Hartley, Mr C M, MA FCLIP, Life Member. [6486] 10/10/1946 **FE01/01/1958**

Hartley, Ms C, BSc(Hons) PGDipLIS MCLIP, Not currently employed. [10005513] 11/11/1992 **CM19/03/1997**

Hartley, Miss H M, Admin. Offr., Dept. for Work & Pensions, Leeds. [44769] 14/11/1990 **ME**

Hartley, Mrs I M, Sen. Lib. Asst., Wootton Fields L., Northampton [10017028] 18/06/2010 **AF**

Hartley, Prof R J, BSc MLib FCLIP, Head, Dept. of Inf. & Communications, Manchester Metro. Univ. [6495] 11/01/1972 **FE01/04/2002**

Hartman, Mr A M N, BA(Hons) DipLIS, Asst. Learning Cent. Mgr., City & Islington Coll., London. [50011] 14/02/1994 **ME**

Hartnup, Mrs C A, Sen. L. Asst., Carlton in Lindrick L., Worksop. [10013570] 07/05/2009 **AF**

Hartnup, Dr K, MA(Hons) MSc PhD, Stud., Univ. of Strathclyde. [66124] 01/10/2006 **ME**

Hartridge, Mrs A J, MCLIP, Ret. [16732] 02/09/1964 **CM01/01/1970**

Hartshorne, Mr D I, BA DipLib MCLIP, Coll. Lib., Harrogate Coll., Harrogate [39055] 31/10/1985 **CM15/03/1989**

Hartshorne, Mr S, BA(Hons) MA MCLIP, Knowledge Team Lib., Bolton Met. Bor. Council, Cent. L. [54464] 18/12/1996 **CM07/09/2005**

Hartwell, Mr A, Stud., Univ. of Wales, Aberystwyth. [63727] 03/09/2004 **ME**

Hartzig, Mrs J E, BA(Hons), Counter Serv. Super., Middlesex Univ., Enfield. [10006283] 10/10/2007 **ME**

Harvell, Ms J L, BA(Hons) PGDipLib, Head of Res. Serv. & Special Collections, Sussex Univ., Brighton. [43729] 11/12/1989 **ME**

Harvey, Mr A P, MCLIP, Retired. [20873] 07/08/1973 **CM26/11/1982**

Harvey, Miss A, LLB, Head of L. & Learning Resources., Swansea Met. Univ. [37634] 14/10/1984 **ME**

Harvey, Mr C, BA PGCE DipCG, L., Bishop Thomas Grant Sch. [64702] 01/06/2005 **ME**

Harvey, Mrs E, BA(Hons) MSc, Career Break [61805] 11/11/2002 **ME**

Harvey, Mrs G, BSc(Hons) MCLIP, Div. Mgr. of Operations, L.B. of Barnet. [26550] 01/10/1976 **CM30/11/1979**

Harvey, Mrs J A, MA DipLib MCLIP, Support Serv. Lib., E. Ayrshire Council. [29897] 10/10/1978 **CM28/10/1981**

Harvey, Mrs J D M, BSc(Hons) MCLIP, Civil Servant, Southampton [22126] 21/02/1974 **CM04/11/1982**

Harvey, Dr J, Chair, Sheffield Inf. Org. (SINTO). [59435] 15/03/2001 **ME**

Harvey, Mrs L A, BA(Hons) MCLIP, L. Site Mgr., Manchester Met. Univ. [46785] 23/01/1992 **CM26/11/1997**

Harvey, Ms M E R, Unknown. [10014288] 14/07/2009 **AF**

Harvey, Mr M N, BA MA, Unknown. [10016196] 23/02/2010 **ME**

Harvey, Mr N, BA(Hons) MCLIP, Community Prog. Off., L.B. Haringey [59408] 05/03/2001 **CM15/05/2002**

Harvey, Mr P M, BA(Hons) MA MCLIP, Inf. Mgr., HMGCC [55271] 11/09/1997 **CM21/11/2001**

Harvey, Ms P M, BA(Hons) MSc MCLIP, Sen. Mgr., N. Tyneside Lib., N. Shields Cent. Lib. [47765] 14/10/1992 **CM15/11/2000**

Harvey, Mr R A M, MA MCLIP, Retired [6518] 10/07/1967 **CM01/01/1970**

Harvey, Mrs S C, BA(Hons), Sen. Lib., E. Sussex Co. Council [62172] 07/03/2003 **ME**

Harvey, Mrs S M, MBE BA MCLIP, Retired. [6521] 22/01/1958 **CM01/01/1962**

Harvey, Mrs T R, BSc MCLIP, ICT Lib., Rutland C.C. [56046] 30/01/1998 **CM20/11/2002**

Harvey-Brown, Mrs J, MA MCLIP, Team Lib., Bracknell Forest. [33349] 07/11/1980 **CM23/06/1986**

Harvey-Woodason, Mrs E, BA(Hons) MSc MCLIP, Inf. Serv. Mgr., Clarke Willmott, Bristol. [54165] 06/11/1996 **CM20/11/2002**

Harwood, Mrs C A, PGDipLib, Team Lib., Oxon. C.C., Cent. L. [33006] 01/10/1980 **ME**

Harwood, Mrs G D I, Sch. Lib. Asst. (Volunteer), Qatar [10014453] 31/07/2009 **ME**

Harwood, Mrs J, BSc(Econ) MCLIP, Learning Res. Cent. Lib., Broughton Bus. & Enterprise Coll., Preston. [59641] 09/07/2001 **CM23/06/2004**

Hasan, Ms B, MA(Hons) MSc(Econ), Asst. Lib., FCO., London. [59254] 18/01/2001 **ME**

Haselton, Ms A E, BA DipLib MCLIP, Dep. Lib., Tavistock & Portman L., London. [36148] 04/07/1983 **CM11/11/1986**

Hashmi, Mr N U H, MA, Unknown. [10013573] 07/05/2009 **ME**

Hasker, Mr N A, LLB MCLIP, Retired. [6529] 17/02/1969 **CM01/01/1971**

Haskins, Mr W T, BSc, Inf. Specialist, CIMA, London. [59384] 27/02/2001 **ME**

Haslam, Mrs J E, Retrospective Catr., The London L. [64105] 17/01/2005 **ME**

Haslam-Dockerty, Mrs S, Stud., Manchester Met. Univ. [65192] 17/11/2005 **ME**

Haslem, Mr J, MCLIP, Life Member. [6535] 02/02/1950 **CM01/01/1961**

Hassall, Mrs S, BA(Hons) DipILS, Lib., Anthony Collins Solicitors LLP, Birmingham. [55426] 13/10/1997 **ME**

Hassan, Mrs M, Trainer / Specialist in Environment & Sustainability [10015559] 14/12/2009 **AF**

Hassan, Miss S, BA, L. Exec. Graduate Trainee, House of Commons, London [10016417] 22/03/2010 **ME**

Hassanali, Ms A, BSc(Hons), MKi Observatory System Admin., MKi Team, Milton Keynes. [10006436] 19/10/2007 **ME**

Hassan-Martin, Miss E A, BA, Unknown. [65447] 23/02/2006 **ME**

Hasson, Mr A R C, MA DipLib MBA MCLIP, Head of Community. Serv., Scottish Borders Council, Newtown St Boswells. [33950] 06/03/1981 **CM01/07/1984**

Hasted, Ms K, BA, Administrator, Emmanuel Parochial Church, Loughborough. [59047] 06/11/2000 **ME**

Hastie, Mrs M E, MCLIP, Head of Learning Res. &Info. Centr., Horndean Tech. Coll., Hants. [5083] 18/01/1971 **CM20/12/1974**

Hastie, Miss S E, BA, Learning Cent. Mgr., Ashmole Sch., Southgate. [10016043] 26/09/2003 **ME**

Hateley, Miss D M, BSc(Econ) MCLIP, Lib. (Generic), Warwickshire C.C. [57732] 13/07/1999 **CM21/05/2003**

Hatfield, Mr I J, BA MCLIP, Unknown. [25832] 23/09/1968 **CM01/07/1988**

Hathaway, Ms H M, MA DipLib ILTM, Faculty Team Mgr., Sci., Univ. of Reading L. [6542] 01/01/1972 **ME**

Hatton, Mrs K P, Stud., Aberystwyth. [65072] 24/10/2005 **ME**

Hatton, Dr P H S, PhD MA DipLib MCLIP, Retired. [24693] 07/10/1975 **CM12/05/1980**

Haugh, Miss J M, GRSM DipLib MCLIP, Retired. [31319] 03/10/1979 **CM02/10/1981**

Haugh, Mr W S, BA DPA HonFLA FCLIP, Retired. [6549] 10/03/1931 **FE01/01/1931**

Haule, Mr L L, MA(Hons) LIS, Principal Lib., Bank of Tanzania, Dar Es Salaam. [10010130] 19/10/1993 **ME**

Hauxwell, Mrs H, BA(Hons) MA MSc MCLIP, L. Asst., LRC. Hartpury Coll. [63652] 09/08/2004 **CM21/05/2008**

Havard, Mrs L, MLS, Sch. of Health Sci. & Sch. of Medicine, Swansea Univ. [59808] 14/05/2001　　　　　　　　　　　　　**ME**

Havergal, Mrs V R, BA(Hons) MSc M. Ed FIFL, Learning Cent. & e-Resources Mgr., PETROC, Barnstaple. [10000750] 01/02/1995　**ME**

Haward, Mrs J, MCLIP, L. Mgr. /Coordinator, Richard Lander Sch., Cornwall [6554] 29/01/1970　　　　　　　　　　**CM15/03/1974**

Hawes, Mrs B M, MCLIP, Life Member. [6555] 12/05/1948　**CM01/01/1953**

Hawes, Mr G A, MA(Hons) MPhil, Stud., Robert Gordon Univ., Aberdeen. [10013338] 16/04/2009　　　　　　　　　　　　**ME**

Hawke, Mrs J C, MCLIP, L. Super., Pettswood L., L.B. of Bromley. [10006676] 06/03/1995　　　　　　　　　　　　**CM06/05/2009**

Hawke, Mrs S M, BEd, LRC Mgr., St. Augustine's C.C., Trowbridge, Wilts. [64376] 14/03/2005　　　　　　　　　　　　　　**ME**

Hawker, Mrs K A, BA, Asst Super., Fareham L., Hants. [63476] 14/05/2004　　　　　　　　　　　　　　　　　　　　**ME**

Hawker, Ms L, Circ. Desk Super., St. George's Univ. of London L. [10011473] 21/10/2008　　　　　　　　　　　　　　**ME**

Hawker, Mrs S, BSc(Hons) MSc MCLIP, Self Employed [55453] 13/10/1997　　　　　　　　　　　　　　　　**CM12/03/2003**

Hawker, Miss Z P, BA(Hons) MSc, Lib., Manchester High Sch. for Girls. [64915] 16/09/2005　　　　　　　　　　　　　　**ME**

Hawkes, Miss C E A, BA MCLIP, Retired. [6563] 02/10/1946　　　　　　　　　　　　　　　　　　　　　　　**CM01/01/1952**

Hawkes, Mrs E A, MA MCLIP, Res. Serv. Mgr. EME, Reed Smith, London [24778] 03/10/1975　　　　　　　　　　**CM01/03/1978**

Hawkey-Edwards, Ms S E M, MSc PgDip, Young People's lib., W. Dunbartonshire. [10001304] 16/09/2003

Hawkins, Mrs A C, MCLIP CertEd, Life Member. [14763] 01/01/1949　　　　　　　　　　　　　　　　　　　**CM01/01/1959**

Hawkins, Mrs A M, BA DipLib MCLIP, Sen. Inf. Asst., Guilford Coll. of F. & H.E. [10006328] 29/10/1980　　　　　　　　**CM28/01/1983**

Hawkins, Miss E J, BA(Hons) MScEcon, KM Resources Offr., DLA Piper UK LLP, London [56571] 01/09/1998　　　　　　　**ME**

Hawkins, Mrs J M, BA DipLib MCLIP, L. Asst., Winstanley Coll., Billinge, Lancs. [35808] 17/01/1983　　　　　　　　　**CM23/01/1986**

Hawkins, Ms J, MSc, Lib. & Arch. Super., Reckitt Benckiser, Hull [10017193] 15/07/2010　　　　　　　　　　　　　**ME**

Hawkins, Mr R, BSc MA, P. /T. Stud., UCL, Civic Cent., Enfield. [65657] 15/03/2006　　　　　　　　　　　　　　　　**ME**

Hawkins, Mrs S K, BLib MCLIP, Clerical Asst., Brynmill Primary Sch., Swansea. [12589] 14/06/1972　　　　　　　　**CM31/03/1980**

Hawkins, Mr T, BSc, HSE., London. [65234] 25/11/2005　　　**ME**

Hawkridge, Mrs S A, BSc MA, Unwaged. [64109] 17/01/2005　**ME**

Hawkyard, Mrs L A, Head Lib., Walker Morris, Leeds. [56126] 03/03/1998　　　　　　　　　　　　　　　　　　　**ME**

Hawley, Mr G J, BA(Hons) MSc MCLIP, Corp. Inf. Offr., Nat. L. of Scotland, Edinburgh. [59448] 30/03/2001　　　**CM01/02/2006**

Hawley, Miss R E, BA, Stud. [10006540] 07/11/2007　　　**ME**

Haworth, Mrs V, ACLIP, Asst. Lib., Great Harwood L., Lancs. [64494] 01/04/2005　　　　　　　　　　　　　　　　**ACL24/04/2009**

Hawthorn, Mr T L, BSc(Econ), L. Asst., Haddon L., Cambridge. [53470] 01/07/1996　　　　　　　　　　　　　　　　**ME**

Hawthorne, Ms N, Exec. Asst., Digby Stuart Coll., Roehampton Univ. [10005971] 03/09/2007　　　　　　　　　　　　　**ME**

Hawton, Miss F M, BA, Lib. Asst., Goldsmiths Coll. L., Univ. of London [10012513] 23/02/2009　　　　　　　　　　　**AF**

Haxell, Mrs G C, MA(Hons), Unknown. [48962] 04/08/1993　**ME**

Hay, Mrs C E, MCLIP, Lib., Birmingham Cent. L. [10001138] 05/01/1976　　　　　　　　　　　　　　　　**CM19/09/1978**

Hay, Ms K J, BA MLIS, Inf. Offr., Linklaters, London. [66151] 04/10/2006　　　　　　　　　　　　　　　　　　**ME**

Hay, Mr L, BA(Hons) DipIM MCLIP, Business Devel. Offr, Glasgow C.C. [60304] 25/05/2000　　　　　　　　　　　　**CM16/07/2003**

Hayball, Miss S R, BA MCLIP, L. & Inf. Advisor, Warwicks. C.C. [20613] 30/04/1973　　　　　　　　　　　　　**CM20/07/1976**

Hayden, Mr D, BA Hons, PG Dip, Acting Team Leader, Moredun L., Edingburgh. [10016161] 19/02/2010　　　　　　　　　**ME**

Haydock, Mr I, MCLIP, L. Systems Mgr., Keele Univ. [40488] 12/02/1987　　　　　　　　　　　　　　　　**CM12/09/1990**

Hayes, Miss B E, BA MCLIP, Sch. Lib. [28827] 03/02/1978　　　　　　　　　　　　　　　　　　　　　**CM26/01/1983**

Hayes, Ms B, BA(Hons) MSc DipILM MCLIP, Programme Lead L. Serv., 5 Bor. Partnership NHS Trust, Warrington. [54004] 17/10/1996　　　　　　　　　　　　　　　　　　　　**CM23/01/2002**

Hayes, Mr C E S, BA MA, Unwaged. [10014883] 15/04/1996　**ME**

Hayes, Mr D C, BA(Hons) DipLib, Asst. Lib., Mayday Healthcare NHS Trust, Thornton Heath. [36143] 01/07/1983　　　　　　　**ME**

Hayes, Miss E, MA MCLIP, Team Leader: Learning Resources, W. Nottinghamshire Coll., Mansfield. [62905] 18/11/2003**CM13/06/2007**

Hayes, Miss J H, BA(Hons) MCLIP, Asst. Subject Lib., Oxford Brookes Univ., L. [62475] 07/07/2003　　　　　　　　**CM13/06/2007**

Hayes, Ms J, MCLIP, Bibl. Serv., Cent. L., Edinburgh. [23514] 01/01/1975　　　　　　　　　　　　　　**CM05/06/1979**

Hayes, Miss K V, BA MA, Res. Lib. Allen & Overy LLP [61786] 07/11/2002　　　　　　　　　　　　　　　　　**ME**

Hayes, Ms L, Stud. Aberystwyth. [65001] 06/10/2005　　　**ME**

Hayes, Mr M A, DipLib MCLIP, Co. Studies Lib., W. Sussex C.C., Worthing. [33299] 27/10/1980　　　　　　　　**CM23/11/1982**

Hayes, Ms M, BA, HDipEd, DLIS, ALAI, Unknown. [10010904] 22/03/2010　　　　　　　　　　　　　　　　　　**ME**

Hayes, Mrs R E, BA MCLIP, Lib., Cent. for Policy on Ageing. [5292] 05/10/1971　　　　　　　　　　　　　　**CM05/09/1975**

Hayes, Mr S R, BEng (Hons), Unknown. [10015189] 23/10/2009　**ME**

Hayes, Miss V J, Unknown. [10015012] 06/10/2009　　　**ME**

Hayet, Ms M, MCLIP, Reg. Account Mgr., RCUK SSC ltd., Swindon. [60148] 15/08/1988　　　　　　　　　　　　**CM20/12/1993**

Hay-Gibson, Miss N V, MA/MSc, Graduate [65627] 14/03/2006　**ME**

Hayhurst, Mr G L, BA FCLIP, Life Member. [6600] 05/01/1954　　　　　　　　　　　　　　　　　　　**FE01/01/1960**

Hayler, Mr W E F, MCLIP, Retired. [6604] 01/01/1950　**CM01/01/1963**

Hayles, Miss J M, BA MCLIP, Asst. Dir., Serv. Delivery. [25302] 13/01/1976　　　　　　　　　　　　　　　**CM07/02/1979**

Haynes, Ms A D, BA DipLib PGDip, Reg. Devel. Off., N. Wales [43731] 11/12/1989　　　　　　　　　　　　　　　　**ME**

Haynes, Miss E M, BSc MCLIP, Ret. [6606] 13/09/1969　**CM11/11/1983**

Haynes, Ms E, BA DipLib, Inf. & Knowledge Mgr., Met. Police Serv., London. [44464] 10/10/1990　　　　　　　　　　　**ME**

Haynes, Mrs H J, BA(Hons), Asst. Area Mgr. Lowestoft Cent. L. [10012360] 05/02/2009　　　　　　　　　　　　　**ME**

Haynes, Mr J D, MSc FCLIP, Independant Consultant [33404] 24/11/1980　　　　　　　　　　　　　　　　**FE01/04/2002**

Haynes, Mrs W H, MA, Resources Lib., Univ. of Wolverhampton. [62998] 26/11/2003　　　　　　　　　　　　　**ME**

Haysman, Miss W F, MSc BH MCLIP, Retired [6607] 26/08/1969　　　　　　　　　　　　　　　　　　**CM16/08/1973**

Haysom, Mrs D, BA MCLIP, Academic Liaison Lib., Univ. of Beds. [33869] 07/04/1981　　　　　　　　　　　**CM17/10/1985**

Hayton, Miss J A, BA MCLIP, L. Mgr., Morecambe L. [23485] 01/01/1975　　　　　　　　　　　　　　**CM07/11/1978**

Hayward, Mrs A E, BA MSc(Econ) MCLIP, Sen. Lib., Slough Cent. L., Berkshire. [55399] 09/10/1997　　　　　　　**CM23/01/2002**

Hayward, Mr D L, BA MCLIP, Team Lib., Coventry City Council. [36203] 16/07/1983　　　　　　　　　　　　**CM06/09/1988**

Hayward, Mr K, BA MCLIP, Lib., Cent. Ref. L., Hants. C.C. [6614] 24/01/1965　　　　　　　　　　　　**CM01/01/1967**

Hayward, Miss L D, BA(Hons), Bibl. Lib., Peters Bookselling Serv., Birmingham. [62254] 02/04/2003　　　　　　　　　**ME**

Haywood, Mr E J, MCLIP, Life Member. [6621] 28/03/1941
CM01/01/1956
Haywood, Mr G C, MCLIP, Lib., Tynwald L., Isle of Man Govt. [21854]
14/02/1974 **CM13/03/1978**
Haywood, Miss G, BA MCLIP, Lib., Thames Water, Reading. [30764]
23/04/1979 **CM06/04/1984**
Haywood, Mrs R J, BA MCLIP, Learning resources Cent. Mgr.,
Kimberley Sch. Nottingham [24596] 08/10/1975 **CM20/09/1979**
Hayworth, Mr R A, MA MPhil DipILS MCLIP, Serials & Electronic
Resources Mgr., Univ. of Aberdeen. [55985] 08/01/1998
CM17/01/2001
Hazelwood, Miss S, Unknown. [10001285] 14/02/2007 **ME**
Hazlehurst, Mrs D J, Sch. Lib. Smestow Sch., Wolverhampton [62504]
29/07/2003 **ME**
Hazlehurst, Mrs J, MCLIP, Retired. [17012] 15/02/1962 **CM01/01/1966**
Hazlewood, Mrs C A, BA(Hons) DipLib MCLIP, Lib., HMP Hewell,
Redditch [29168] 11/03/1978 **CM08/10/1980**
Hazlewood, Mrs M, BA(Hons) MA MCLIP, Team Lib., Bournemouth &
Poole Coll. [51456] 27/02/1995 **CM20/11/2002**
He, Miss C, MSc, Inf. Lib., L. Univ. of Bath, Bath [61535] 16/09/2002 **ME**
Heacock, Dr A, BA(Hons) MSc MCLIP, Assoc. Lib., Ottawa, Canada
[65957] 21/07/2006 **CM03/10/2007**
Head, Mrs A D, DipLib MCLIP, L. Learning Resource Cent. Mgr.,
Highfield Sen: Letchworth, Herts. [32170] 06/01/1980 **CM06/10/1982**
Head, Mrs A L, MSc BA MCLIP, Libnel Mgr., Whipps Cross Univ. Hosp.,
London. [6631] 13/03/1967 **CM05/07/1976**
Head, Mr P A, FRSA MCLIP, Retired. [6634] 01/01/1963 **CM01/01/1968**
Head, Mrs S R, MCLIP, Life Member. [6636] 06/03/1950 **CM01/01/1956**
Headford, Mrs J E, MA BA MCLIP, Life Member. [21048] 30/09/1973
CM13/10/1975
Heads, Mrs L M, BA MCLIP, Asst. Lib., Hull Coll. [31540] 24/10/1979
CM18/10/1982
Heald, Mrs M D, MA DipLib MCLIP, Unemployed. [31702] 01/11/1979
CM29/01/1982
Heale, Mrs S P, BSc MA MCLIP, Knowledge & Business Intelligence
Consultant, Univ. of Herts., Hatfield. [47579] 02/10/1992
CM22/11/1995
Healey, Miss A E, BA MCLIP, Retired. [6641] 07/10/1954 **CM01/01/1958**
Healey, Miss N F L, BA(Hons) MSc MCLIP, E. Resources Co-
ordinator,Western General Hosp., Somerset [59578] 05/06/2001
CM13/06/2007
Healey, Mr T B, BA MA, Unwaged. [10005240] 29/06/2007 **ME**
Healy, Mrs R A, BA(Hons) DipIM, Unknown. [10013477] 16/09/1994 **ME**
Heaney, Mrs A G, BA Hons Dip lib, L. Mgr., Maidenhead L. [10016185]
30/01/1980 **ME**
Heaney, Ms M E, BA DipLib FRSA MCLIP ILTM, Dir. of Serv.,
Manchester Met. Univ. [29174] 17/04/1978 **CM01/04/2002**
Heaney, Mr M, MA FCLIP, Exec. Sec. Bodleian Lib., Univ. of Oxford.
[22383] 08/04/1974 **FE15/03/2000**
Heap, Ms A M, BA MCLIP, Freelance [36380] 03/10/1983 **CM04/10/1988**
Heap, Miss B J, MCLIP, Princ. L. Offr. -Support, City of Bradford
M.D.C. [26407] 01/10/1976 **CM30/11/1979**
Heap, Mrs P A, BA MCLIP, Sen. Mgr., Reading Child. Serv., Birmingham
L. Serv., Cent. L. [20319] 01/03/1973 **CM16/09/1975**
Heard, Mrs P M, BA(Hons) DipLib, Inf. Systems Offr., Bexley L. & Mus.,
Sidcup. [34573] 12/01/1982 **ME**
Heard, Mr S C A, BA(Hons) MLIB, Asst. Libr., DEFRA,. London. [64112]
17/01/2005 **ME**
Heard, Ms S C, BA(Hons), PGCE MCLIP, Team Lib., Bedford Cent. L.
[10011444] 21/10/2008 **CM05/05/2010**
Hearn, Mr S K, BScEcon, Unknown. [65065] 24/10/2005 **ME**
Heaslip, Ms G M, BA, Asst. Lib., Chartered Inst. of Marketing, Berks.
[35831] 24/01/1983 **ME**
Heaslip, Ms M E, BA MLS, Retired. [10016880] 01/06/2010 **ME**

Heaster, Miss S C, MA MCLIP, Asst. Lib., Univ. of Nottingham. [24497]
28/08/1975 **CM02/05/1978**
Heath, Miss A K, Unknown. [10014346] 10/07/2009 **ME**
Heath, Mrs C S, BA MCLIP, Asst. Lib., Croydon Coll. [28678]
16/12/1977 **CM23/11/1982**
Heath, Ms E, MA, Unknown. [10008010] 04/03/2008 **ME**
Heath, Ms G M, BA MCLIP, Adult Literacy Tutor, SCOLA, Sutton.
[29824] 17/10/1978 **CM31/07/1984**
Heath, Ms J P, BA(Hons) DipLib MCLIP, Freelance information
professional [10015738] 26/07/1979 **CM04/01/1983**
Heath, Mrs N L, BA(Hons), Sch. Lib., Werneth Sch., Stockport. [57503]
12/04/1999 **ME**
Heath, Mrs P L, Lib. Asst., Cambridgeshire L. Serv., Cambridge
[10016429] 24/03/2010 **ME**
Heath, Mrs P V, BA(Hons), Trainee Asst. Lib., Anglo European Coll. of
Chiropratic L., Bournemouth. [10011321] 13/10/2008 **AF**
Heath, Ms R B, MCLIP, Life Member. [6664] 20/03/1952 **CM01/01/1956**
Heathcote, Mrs C M, CertEd, Sen. L. Asst., Meldrum L., Aberdeenshire.
[63618] 06/07/2004 **ME**
Heathcote, Ms K, BA DipLIS MCLIP, Inf. Serv. Lib., Tameside M.B.C.
[39691] 20/05/1986 **CM18/11/1998**
Heathcote, Miss S L, BA(Hons) PGCE MCLIP, Clerk, Derbyshire Co.
Council, Derby. [10006704] 29/01/1980 **CM06/04/1993**
Heather, Miss G M, Unknown. [10014051] 01/07/2009 **ME**
Heatley, Miss N L, BA DipLib PGCE MCLIP MIfL, Unemployed. [41497]
12/01/1988 **CM18/07/1990**
Heaton, Mrs B C, BA MCLIP, Sch. Lib., Weaverham High Sch.,
Cheshire. [10001131] 11/01/1978 **CM11/01/1980**
Heaton, Mrs J A, MCLIP, Sen. Child. Lib., Bor. Telford and Wrekin
Council [28002] 05/10/1977 **CM22/09/1981**
Heaton, Mrs J D, BA MCLIP, Unknown. [35342] 14/10/1982
CM05/11/1985
Heaton, Mr J M, BA DipLib MCLIP, Mgr., Serv. Design & Devel.,
Rotherham MBC [28236] 12/10/1977 **CM09/01/1981**
Heaton, Miss W, BA(Hons) MCLIP, Operations Mgr., Wigan Leisure &
Cult. Trust. [28957] 16/01/1978 **CM19/07/1983**
Heaven, Ms S, BA(Hons) MA, Sch. Lib., Verdin High Sch., Cheshire.
[57857] 10/09/1999 **ME**
Heaword, Ms R A, BA MSc MCLIP, Retired/Voluntary Work. [60381]
06/04/1977 **CM13/06/1978**
Hebdon, Mr P R, BA MCLIP, Sen. Co-ordinator, N. Tyneside Libs.,
[34766] 24/01/1982 **CM29/07/1986**
Hebron, Ms P E, BA(Hons) PGDipLIM PGCE, Asst. Lib., Llandrillo Coll.
Cymru, Conwy. [49437] 27/10/1993 **ME**
Hector, Miss E J, MA MCLIP, Head of L. & Arch., The Nat. Gallery,
London. [24695] 01/10/1975 **CM18/05/1979**
Hedgecock, Mrs C M, ACLIP, Lib., Portland Comp. Sch.,Worksop.
[64407] 15/03/2005 **ACL28/01/2009**
Hedges, Mr G, MCLIP HonFCLIP, Sen. Asst. Lib., L.B. Wandsworth,
Battersea Ref. L. [22662] 02/08/1974 **CM16/12/1977**
Hee Houng, Mrs M, MCLIP, Freelance Consultant. [17544] 10/10/1961
CM01/01/1967
Heeks, Dr P E, MA FCLIP, Retired. [6685] 31/01/1941 **FE01/01/1959**
Heffer, Mr C M, BA DipLib MCLIP, Customer Serv. Lib., Beckenham L.,
L.B. Bromley. [31857] 16/01/1980 **CM18/02/1983**
Heffernan, Mr R C, BA MCLIP, Asst. Lib., The Inst. of Civil Eng.,
London. [28586] 16/01/1978 **CM30/09/1987**
Hegenbarth, Mrs J A, BA(Hons) MA MCLIP, Subject Advisor, Univ. of
Birmingham, Main L. [51951] 17/08/1995 **CM17/11/1999**
Heinecke, Mr P M, BA MCLIP, Retired. [24697] 06/10/1975
CM12/10/1977
Heinrich, Mrs M, Stud. [10017050] 21/06/2010 **ME**
Heinze, Mrs R M, Sch. Lib., Ryeish Green Sch., Reading. [10009319]
15/05/2008 **AF**

Heissig, Mr H N, BA FCLIP, Life Member. [18764] 15/03/1955
FE01/01/1965
Helgesen, Ms J C, BA(Hons) MA MCLIP, Inf. Skills Lib., Univ. E. Anglia, Norfolk. [58859] 12/09/2000 **CM13/06/2007**
Hellen, Mrs R, MCLIP, Retired. [8495] 04/04/1972 **CM03/07/1975**
Heller, Ms Z, MITI MCLIP DPSI, Retired. [60382] 18/05/1972
CM17/09/1979
Helliwell, Mrs A P, MA FCLIP, Life Member. [788] 09/10/1946
FE01/01/1952
Helliwell, Miss C S, MCLIP BSc, Retired. [21754] 12/01/1974
CM13/02/1976
Helliwell, Mrs J F, Relief Enquiry Offr., Suffolk C.C. [45903] 01/07/1991
AF
Helliwell, Mrs M R, DMS MCLIP, Team Leader, E. Riding Council. [28395] 19/11/1977 **CM17/11/1981**
Hellon, Mrs C, BLS MCLIP, Career Break. [33458] 01/01/1981
CM10/06/1986
Hellon, Mrs S J, BA DipLib MCLIP, Lib., Ilkeston L. Derbys. C.C. [36323] 01/10/1983 **CM29/01/1992**
Helm, Miss S V, BA MCLIP DipMS, Sen. Training & Devel. Offr., Dudley P. L. [29039] 13/03/1978 **CM30/09/1982**
Helsey, Mr M, L. Exec., BTs Dept., House of Commons L., London. [10006752] 22/11/1984 **ME**
Hemming, Ms G M, BA MCLIP, Comm. & Inf. Offr., N. Yorks. C.C., Richmond L. & Inf. Cent. [24272] 10/06/1975 **CM16/07/2003**
Hemming, Mrs H E, BA(Hons), Sch. Lib., Wellstead Promary Sch., Hedge End, Southampton. [49404] 21/10/1993 **ME**
Hemming, Ms R, BA BMus(Hons) MSc, Head of L., Univ. Coll. Sch., Hampstead. [55544] 17/10/1997 **ME**
Hemmings, Mr P M, BLib MCLIP, Cent. L. Mgr., Birmingham City Council, Cent. L. [28314] 07/10/1977 **CM31/07/1980**
Hemmings, Mr R E, BA(Hons), Inf. Exec. (Catr.), ICAEW, London [65789] 01/05/2006 **ME**
Hempshall, Mrs M C S J, L. Res. Co-ordinator (Vol.), Wycliffe Assoc. UK. [52688] 17/11/1995 **ME**
Hemsley, Mr M K, BA(Hons), Lib. Mgr., Brent Lib. [61873] 25/11/2002
ME
Hemsoll, Mrs D S, BA DipLib MCLIP, Professional Lib., Univ. of Birmingham. [34647] 25/01/1982 **CM24/03/1987**
Hemsworth, Miss C, Stud., Strathclyde Univ. [10015233] 29/10/2009**ME**
Hemus, Ms E, BA(Hons) PGDip MCLIP, Inf. Offr., Linklaters, London. [55559] 21/10/1997 **CM01/06/2005**
Hendel, Dr G, MA (hons) MA LIS PhD, Bibliographic & Academic Liason Lib., Wallace Collection, London. [10007777] 19/07/2001 **ME**
Henderson, Mrs A M, BSc Econ, L. Asst., Kirriemuir L., Angus. [10014366] 20/07/2009 **ME**
Henderson, Miss B, MCLIP, Life Member. [6715] 13/03/1943
CM01/01/1947
Henderson, Miss C, L. Asst., Baltasound Jnr. High Sch., Unst. [64615] 29/03/2005 **AF**
Henderson, Mrs E A, Rare books Lib. St. Andrews Univ. [59947] 09/11/2001 **ME**
Henderson, Ms E F, BA DipLib MCLIP, Locality Mgr., Norfolk L. & Inf. Serv., Dereham L. [27737] 21/07/1977 **CM23/10/1980**
Henderson, Mrs E R, B. Ed DipT M. Ed, Head of Learning Resources, Ibstock Place Sch., London [10008566] 03/04/2008 **ME**
Henderson, Mrs J A F, MA MCLIP, Asst. Lib., Co. Reserve Store, Worthing, W. Sussex C.C. [6720] 01/01/1968 **CM01/01/1971**
Henderson, Ms J A, BSc DipLib MCLIP MSc, Freelance Inf. & Knowledge Mgmnt Specialist, Namibia [40377] 23/01/1987
CM18/07/1990
Henderson, Mr J D, BA(Hons), Stud. [56592] 07/09/1998 **ME**
Henderson, Mrs J P, BA DipLib MCLIP, Lib. Offr., Wimbledon L., L.B. of Merton. [36315] 02/10/1983 **CM16/10/1989**

Henderson, Mr J T, BSc, Customer Serv. Asst., Lambeth L. & Arch. [39089] 01/11/1985 **ME**
Henderson, Ms J, BA(Hons) MCLIP, Community Lib., Birmingham L. Serv., Handsworth L. . [32978] 04/10/1980 **CM24/10/1983**
Henderson, Miss J, BA(Hons) MA, Inf. Mgr.,TUC, London. [44407] 04/10/1990 **ME**
Henderson, Mr J, Stud., L. & Inf. Studies, Aberystwyth. [10012167] 08/01/2009 **ME**
Henderson, Miss L W, MCLIP, Team Lib., Renfrew Council L. [31859] 11/01/1980 **CM18/08/1983**
Henderson, Mrs M E, BA DipLib MCLIP, Stock & Online Resources Lib., Bath & NE Somerset L. [29265] 02/05/1978 **CM23/05/1980**
Henderson, Ms M M M, MA(Hons) MLitt PGDip, Principal Inf. Asst., Queen Mother L., Univ. of Aberdeen. [10006181] 22/05/2005 **ME**
Henderson, Mrs M M, BA FCLIP, Retired [15844] 17/02/1951
FE01/01/1968
Henderson, Mrs S G, MCLIP, P/t. Lib., Dundee City Council, Architectural Serv. [1989] 20/10/1969 **CM08/07/1974**
Henderson, Mrs S G, BA MCLIP, Retired. [7658] 02/11/1967
CM15/01/1973
Henderson, Mrs S J, BA MLib MCLIP, LISS MGR., (Learning Resources), Harold Bridges L., Univ. of Cumbria. [36395] 05/10/1983
CM09/07/1986
Henderson, Mrs S M, MCLIP, Lib. i/c., Mob. L., Dept. of Educ., Isle of Man. [28621] 11/01/1978 **CM15/12/1981**
Henderson, Mrs S R, MCLIP, On career break. [29180] 19/04/1978
CM30/07/1980
Hendey, Ms L K, ACLIP, L. Asst., Bridgewater High Sch., Warrington. [65950] 19/07/2006 **ACL29/08/2008**
Hendley, Ms J C, BA(Hons) MSc MCLIP, Inf. Specialist, Cranfield Univ., Swindon. [59275] 25/01/2001 **CM20/04/2009**
Hendrix, Ms G F, JP BA MBA FCLIP, Retired. [6728] 13/02/1963
FE18/11/1998
Hendry, Prof J D, MA FCLIP FSA, City Councillor/Consultant, Carlisle. [6731] 02/12/1963 **FE17/07/1972**
Hendry, Miss J M, BA(Hons) MCLIP, Childrens Lib., Lb of Croyden Lib. Serv., Sanderstead [51027] 09/11/1994 **CM25/07/2001**
Hendry, Mrs M M, MA MBA DipLib FCLIP, Admin. Mgr., Cartmell Shepherd, Solicitors. [26178] 04/08/1976 **FE21/07/1993**
Hendy, Miss P J, BSc MA MCLIP, Community L., Bracknell. [57430] 01/04/1999 **CM29/08/2007**
Heneghan, Mrs L A, Learning Res. Cent. Mgr., Prudhoe Community High Sch. [62083] 12/02/2003 **ME**
Heneghan, Miss M L, MA(Hons), MSc., Unknown. [66138] 02/10/2006
ME
Henley, Miss C J, BA(Hons) Msc, Unknown. [10015921] 05/11/2002 **ME**
Henley, Ms T M, BA MSc MCLIP, Sen. Asst. Subject lib., Teeside Univ., Tees Valley. [37692] 17/10/1984 **CM15/02/1989**
Hennessy, Miss A M, Stud. [65848] 31/05/2006 **ME**
Hennessy, Ms M R M, BA(Hons) MSc, Unknown. [10001662] 06/03/2007 **ME**
Hennin, Miss G M, FCLIP, Retired. [6739] 11/03/1940 **FE01/01/1949**
Henning, Mrs H M E, BA ACLIP, L. Asst., S. Educ. & L. Board, Rathfriland Br. L. [48036] 26/10/1992 **ACL16/07/2008**
Henry, Ms S A, DipILS MCLIP, Sch. Lib., Forfar Academy, Angus [57956] 05/10/1999 **CM19/03/2008**
Henshaw, Miss D A, BA(Hons), Res. Offr, DLA Piper, Manchester. [59093] 14/11/2000 **ME**
Henshaw, Miss J, BMus(Hons) MA MCLIP, Learning Res. Mgr., Music & Performing Arts, Colchester Inst., Essex. [57021] 25/11/1998
CM12/03/2003
Henshaw, Miss S A, MA DipLib MCLIP, Grants Fundraiser., Hope & Homes for Child., Salisbury [37299] 10/06/1984 **CM14/11/1990**

269

Heppell, Mrs C, BSc MCLIP, Academic Lib., Univ. of Northmapton. [62420] 12/06/2003 **CM19/03/2008**

Hepplewhite, Miss S E, BA(Hons) CELTA, L. and Inf. Serv., ICAEW, London. [10000978] 04/12/2006 **ME**

Hepworth, Miss J S, BA(Hons) DipIS MCLIP, Lib., Leeds City L. [52276] 23/10/1995 **CM19/07/2000**

Hepworth, Mrs J, BA, Comm. &. Inf. Offr., Norton L. Yorks. [57899] 01/10/1999 **ME**

Hepworth, Mr M, MA BSc MCLIP, Retired. [6752] 01/01/1968 **CM01/01/1970**

Herbert, Mrs C, BA MPhil, Stud., UCL, London. [63785] 18/10/2004 **ME**

Herbert, Mr D, BA(Hons) MLS MCLIP, Retired. [29678] 02/10/1978 **CM08/10/1980**

Herbert, Ms E, BA DMS MCLIP AMICS, Devel. & Cent. Serv. Mgr., E. Riding of Yorkshire Council, L. H.Q. [23962] 24/02/1975 **CM29/12/1978**

Herbert, Mrs J S, MCLIP, Life Member. [6758] 26/05/1950 **CM01/01/1956**

Herbert, Mrs K E, BA(Hons) DipILS MCLIP, L. &Inf. Serv. Mgr.,p. /t., Hinchingbrooke NHS Healthcare T., Huntingdon. [49462] 02/11/1993 **CM21/01/1998**

Herbert, Ms K J, BA(Hons) ACLIP, L. Asst., Watford Cent. L. [10001310] 01/10/2004 **ACL16/07/2008**

Herbert, Miss N S, BA(Hons), Stud. St. John's Coll., Cambridge. [65967] 31/07/2006 **ME**

Herbert, Mrs N, BA(Hons) MA MCLIP, Info Off., Transport for London [62372] 14/05/2003 **CM04/10/2006**

Herbert, Mrs O T, FCLIP, Life Member. [6759] 07/10/1942 **FE01/01/1969**

Herbert, Mr P, MA PGDipILS MCLIP, Lib., Monklands Hosp. L., Airdrie. [63069] 27/01/2004 **CM04/10/2006**

Herbst, Mrs M, BA PgDip, Stud. [10006389] 23/10/2007 **ME**

Herbstritt, Ms B C, BA(Hons) PG Dip, Lib. Asst., Noel Baker Community Sch. & Language Coll., Derby. [10014676] 27/08/2009 **ME**

Herdan, Mr N, Consultant., U. S. A. [35498] 19/10/1982 **ME**

Heritage, Mr I D, BA MCLIP, Inf. Mgr., Gerlald Eve LLP, London. [34458] 06/11/1981 **CM10/11/1987**

Herlihy, Ms B, BSc(Hons) DLIS, Mgr., Institutional Repository, UCC, Cork [10001248] 02/12/2004 **ME**

Hermiston, Mrs S, BA MA MSc MCLIP, Unknown. [65388] 03/02/2006 **CM05/05/2010**

Hernandez, Ms M, L. Serv. Mgr, Mid-State Tech. Coll., Wisconsin, U. S. A. [10000874] 15/11/2006 **ME**

Herne, Mr I M, BA MA MSc(Econ) FAETC MCLIP, Ch. Lib., S. Bank Intl. Sch., Westminister, London [21256] 05/10/1973 **CM16/08/1976**

Herniman, Miss J, MCLIP, Unemployed. [24390] 15/02/1964 **CM16/02/1983**

Herraiz Rigou, Mrs A, Lib. Asst., Peckham Lib., London [10009470] 20/05/2008 **ME**

Herriman, Mrs M C, BA DipLib MCLIP, Sen. Child. Lib. /Sure Start Lib., Milton Keynes L. [33757] 25/01/1981 **CM01/07/1984**

Herring, Mrs J, BA DipLib MCLIP, Head, Client Serv., Foreign & Commonwealth Off., London. [26409] 07/10/1976 **CM23/05/1979**

Herring, Mrs P S, BA MLS MCLIP, Lib., Nuneaton Training Cent. [21323] 07/10/1973 **CM12/11/1976**

Herring, Mrs R V, BA DipLIS MA MCLIP, Unemployed. [50519] 31/08/1994 **CM04/02/2004**

Herring, Mrs S E, MA BA(Ed) MCLIP, Inf. Specialist, Career Servs., Univ. of Bristol. [57010] 24/11/1998 **CM10/07/2002**

Herriott, Miss N F, BSc(Hons) MA MCLIP, Inf. & People's Network Lib., Hertfordshire C.C., Welwyn Garden City. [50036] 21/02/1994 **CM19/07/2000**

Herrmann, Mrs T S, ACLIP, Sen. L. Asst., Southbourne L., Bournemouth. [10014384] 21/07/2009 **ACL16/06/2010**

Herron, Miss A, MA DipLib MCLIP, Falkirk Council L. Serv. [36616] 24/10/1983 **RV27/09/2006** **CM03/03/1987**

Hesketh, Miss C, BCombStud(Hons) DipLib MCLIP, Stock & Reader Devel. Lib., Conwy Co. Bor. Council, Colwyn Bay L. [42242] 12/10/1988 **CM15/05/2002**

Hesketh, Mrs J E, BA MCLIP, Foreigh & Commonwealth Off. [27664] 04/07/1977 **CM08/11/1979**

Hesketh, Mrs M, MA DipLib MCLIP, Sen. Asst. Lib. (Requests), Lancs. Co. L. [26568] 08/10/1976 **CM18/07/1979**

Heslan, Ms S, MA, Stud., Manchester Met. Univ. [10009315] 20/05/2008 **ME**

Hester, Mrs P I, MCLIP, Life Member. [6785] 01/01/1951 **CM01/01/1964**

Hetherington, Mrs N C, BLS MCLIP, Sch. Lib., Lady Manners Sch., Bakewell. [33457] 01/01/1981 **CM12/03/1986**

Hettiaratchi, Mrs W, BA MCLIP, Life Member. [6786] 02/01/1968 **CM13/07/1972**

Hevey, Mrs M M, MCLIP, Life Member [18766] 15/03/1947 **CM01/01/1952**

Heward, Mrs K, BSc MA, Inf. Offr., Boyes Turner, Reading, Berks. [10005029] 06/06/2007 **ME**

Hewerdine, Mrs V, BSc(Hons), L. Asst., Hertfordshire C.C. [57799] 02/08/1999 **ME**

Hewett, Miss J K, Asst. Llib., NDA, Oxon [10008117] 20/03/2008 **AF**

Hewett, Miss K E, BA(Hons), Stud. [10017070] 21/06/2010 **ME**

Hewings, Mrs R M, BSc DipLib FCLIP DMS FHEA, H. of Learning Inf. Servs., Writtle Coll., Chelmsford. [30575] 29/01/1979 **FE03/10/2007**

Hewins, Mrs J M, BA MCLIP, p. /t. User Serv. Mgr., Bournemouth Univ., Dorset. [31485] 16/10/1979 **CM23/09/1982**

Hewish, Mr D S, Asst. Lib., Univ. W. England. [63191] 03/03/2004 **ME**

Hewison, Mrs H, BA MCLIP, Inf. Serv. Offr., Clarke Willmott Solicitors., Birmingham. [27286] 14/02/1977 **CM30/10/1979**

Hewitt, Mrs J, BEd(Hons) DipILM DipIT MCLIP, Sen. Info. Mgr., HMRC, Liverpool. [10001943] 04/11/1997 **CM16/07/2003**

Hewitt, Miss M J, DipLib MCLIP, Serv. Mgr. N. W. Film. Arch., Manchester Metro. Univ. [28830] 07/02/1978 **CM01/12/1982**

Hewitt, Mr M, Med. Sciences Lib., Bristol Univ. [45504] 26/02/1991 **AF**

Hewitt, Miss P M, BA DipLib MCLIP, Lib., Univ. of E. Anglia, Robert Sainsbury L., Norwich. [29679] 04/10/1978 **CM16/07/1982**

Hewitt, Ms R, BA, Know. Serv. Mgr., Bradford Health Infomatics Serv., W. Yorks. [61421] 15/07/2002 **ME**

Hewitt, Ms S, MCLIP, Retired, Resident S. Africa. [18943] 27/05/1943 **CM01/01/1954**

Hewitt, Mrs V J, MLS MCLIP, Retired. [6799] 01/01/1956 **CM01/01/1969**

Hewlett, Mr J F, MSc(InfSc) MCLIP, Retired. [6801] 11/03/1967 **CM01/01/1970**

Hewlett, Miss M A, MA MCLIP, Retired. [6802] 07/03/1966 **CM01/01/1970**

Hewlett, Miss S, Unknown. [10006378] 15/10/2007 **ME**

Hewson, Mrs A, BA MCLIP, L. Asst., Guilford High Sch. for Girls. [23055] 16/10/1974 **CM27/01/1982**

Hey, Dr J M N, MA MCLIP, Researcher, ECS, Univ. of Southampton, Southampton, Hants. [23655] 22/01/1975 **CM13/04/1977**

Heyda, Miss B M, BSc DipLib MCLIP, Retired. [60733] 30/08/1985 **CM30/08/1985**

Heyes, Mrs J L, BA(Hons) MCLIP, Business Serv. Offr., Kent C.C., Maidstone. [39739] 10/06/1986 **CM12/09/1990**

Heyes, Mr J T, FCLIP, Team Lib., p. /t., Bolton M.B.C. [6807] 24/03/1965 **FE31/03/1980**

Heyes, Mrs R K, MCLIP, Community Lib (Childrens)., Cent. L., Walsall. [25295] 10/01/1976 **CM27/07/1978**

Heyes, Miss S A, BA(Hons) CertEd MCLIP, Head of Sch. L. Serv., W. Sussex C.C., Chichester. [35400] 15/10/1982 **CM22/09/1986**

Heyes, Mrs V L, BA(Hons), Br. Lib., Tameside MBC., Stalybridge. [10008601] 18/04/2008 **ME**

Heywood, Mrs J M, BA MCLIP, p./t. Work experience co-ordinator, Wootton Upper Sch. [18293] 11/10/1972 **CM19/06/1978**

Heywood, Mrs S, BA MCLIP, Sen. Educ. Lib., Educ. L. Serv., Bracknell Forest Bor. Council. [6815] 16/01/1972 **CM13/02/1975**

Hibbert, Miss L, BA(Hons) DipILM, L. Liasion Advisor, Northumbria Univ. [58985] 18/10/2000 **ME**

Hibbert, Mr O D, MSc CChem MRSC CertEd MCLIP, Night Worker, Shearwater Ltd., Ramsey. [60588] 10/11/1971 **CM28/03/1973**

Hibbert, Mrs S H M, MA MCLIP, Freelance Ed. [32223] 05/02/1980 **CM31/08/1983**

Hibbert, Miss V F, BA(Hons) MCLIP, Sen. Inf. Offr., Clifford Chance, London. [39186] 02/12/1985 **CM17/01/1990**

Hibbs, Miss E J, BA DipLib MCLIP, Asst. Head L. Serv. Devel. Delivery, L.B. Kensington and Chelsea. [34422] 28/10/1981 **CM20/01/1987**

Hick, Miss J M, BA MCLIP, Retired. [6825] 01/01/1965 **CM01/01/1967**

Hicken, Mrs M E, MLS MCLIP, Retired. [6827] 24/01/1951 **CM01/01/1956**

Hickey, Mr J A, L. Inf. Systems Specialist, Brit. Med. Ass., London. [56495] 28/07/1998 **ME**

Hickford, Mrs B, MA DipLib MCLIP, Lib., Our Lady's Abingdon. [29680] 09/10/1978 **CM27/11/1980**

Hicklin, Miss P N, BSc, Online Publications Asst., English Heritage. [37540] 06/10/1984 **ME**

Hickman, Mrs L, MCLIP, Lend. Serv. Help Desk Super., Univ. of Wolverhampton. [23048] 20/10/1974 **CM28/11/1977**

Hickman, Mrs M A, BA(Hons), L. & Inf. Serv. Mgr., Derbyshire Mental Health Serv. NHS, Derby. [47136] 06/05/1992 **ME**

Hickman-Ashby, Mrs G I J, MLib MCLIP, IT Mgr., City of London L. Arch. & Guildhall Art Gallery [6835] 05/10/1970 **CM11/06/1981**

Hicks, Mr A F, BA DipLib MCLIP, Unwaged [40096] 15/10/1986 **CM27/03/1991**

Hicks, Miss A, Overseas. [65201] 17/11/2005 **ME**

Hicks, Mr T J, BA(Hons) MCLIP MA, Academic Res. Lib. -Art & Design, Univ. of Wolverhampton. [51443] 10/02/1995 **CM20/03/1996**

Hickson, Mrs C, MA, Lib., Ellesmere Port L. [10001451] 14/02/2007 **ME**

Hickton, Miss J M, BA(Hons) MCLIP, outreach Lib., Health L., Clinical Cent., Stoke-on-Trent. [10015924] 04/10/1994 **CM23/01/2002**

Hider, Dr P M, BSc(Hons) MLib PhD FCLIP, Head, Sch. of Inf. Studies, Charles Stuart Univ. Australia. [49277] 20/10/1993 **FE15/09/2004**

Hidson, Mr R, DIP ARCH FCLIP, Retired. [6844] 01/01/1961 **FE17/10/1990**

Higgens, Mr G L, FCLIP, Life Member. [6848] 01/01/1947 **FE01/01/1953**

Higgin, Mrs J M, BA DipLib MCLIP, Community L. Mgr., Warrington Bor. Council. [42972] 11/05/1989 **CM22/05/1991**

Higgins, Mr C, BA(Hons) MPhil Msc (econ), Lib., St. Catherines Coll., Univ. of Cambridge. [10000629] 18/10/2006 **ME**

Higgins, Mrs E M, BA DipLib, Lib., Madras Coll., Fife Reg. Council Educ. Dept. [28843] 30/01/1978 **ME**

Higgins, Mrs F H, BA(Hons) MA, Knowledge Mgr., McClure Naismith LLP, Glasgow. [59749] 10/09/2001 **ME**

Higgins, Mrs L M, BA(Hons), E-Info. & Records Mngr., Defra, London [58301] 22/12/1999 **ME**

Higgins, Ms M F, p. /t. Stud., Univ. of Wales, Aberystwyth, Magherafelt P. L. [63695] 23/08/2004 **ME**

Higgins, Miss M M, BA(Hons) MA, Unknown. [59429] 13/03/2001 **ME**

Higgins, Mrs R J B, MLib MCLIP, Nursery Woman [21442] 30/10/1973 **CM18/08/1976**

Higginson, Mrs C E, BA(Hons) MSc MCLIP, Sen. Inf. Offr., Nat. Foundation for Educ. Res., Slough. [58362] 25/01/2000 **CM03/10/2007**

Higgison, Ms M S, BA MCLIP, Lib., Scottish Government., Edinburgh. [43916] 19/02/1990 **CM16/07/2003**

Higgs, Mrs G M, BA MCLIP PGCE(PCE), Lib., Cornwall Coll., Cornwall. [25533] 28/01/1976 **CM06/09/1979**

Higgs, Mr G P, BSc(Hons) DipILS, LRC Mgr. [48519] 02/02/1993 **ME**

Higgs, Mr W J, MSc, Unknown. [10006390] 23/10/2007 **ME**

High, Mr B, BA(Hons) MA MCLIP, Sen. Inf. Asst. -Special Collections, Kings Coll., London. [45781] 28/05/1991 **CM18/09/2002**

Higham, Mrs J K, BA(Hons), Lib. of the Insitute of Hist. Res. & Subject Lib. (Hist.), Univ. London. [61301] 16/05/2002 **ME**

Higham, Miss J W, MCLIP, Retired. [6863] 25/09/1950 **CM01/01/1963**

Highwood, Mr R J, BA MCLIP, Retired [10017085] 23/03/1959 **CM02/11/1984**

Higson, Mrs M D, MA MCLIP, L. Serv. Dev. Mngr. Telford & Wrekin Council [13753] 01/01/1967 **CM01/01/1971**

Hikins, Mr H R, FCLIP, Life Member. [6867] 01/01/1936 **FE01/01/1959**

Hilbourne, Mrs R A, Dir. ILIAC, UK [60486] 15/11/2000 **ME**

Hilditch, Mrs K L, BSc(Hons), Learning Resources Mgr., Redhill Sch. [63109] 10/02/2004 **ME**

Hilditch, Mr P J, PhD BA MA, LRC. Asst., Cambridge Reg. Coll. [54440] 12/12/1996 **ME**

Hiles, Miss L H, BSc, Data Mgmnt. Specialist, Schlumberger, Reading. [10016539] 13/04/2010 **ME**

Hill, Mr A J, MCLIP, Retired. [6871] 20/03/1955 **CM01/01/1962**

Hill, Ms A, MA MCLIP, Dir. of Teaching & Learning Resources, Doncaster Coll. [18231] 03/10/1972 **CM15/01/1976**

Hill, Mrs A, MCLIP, Snr. Asst. L. Bibl. Serv. L CC, Accrington L., Lancs. [9601] 01/10/1971 **CM11/08/1975**

Hill, Mrs C A, MCLIP, Retired [28756] 01/01/1965 **CM15/08/1984**

Hill, Mrs C J, BA MCLIP, Acting Dist. lib., Stevenage L. [36586] 24/10/1983 **CM10/05/1988**

Hill, Mrs C, BA MCLIP, L. Mgr., Kingsmead Sch., Enfield. [32207] 15/02/1980 **CM15/08/1984**

Hill, Mr D, BA(Hons) MCLIP, Unknown. [42942] 28/04/1989 **CM23/09/1998**

Hill, Miss E J, BA(Hons), Lib. Asst., Croxley Green L., [10011197] 02/10/2008 **AF**

Hill, Mr F J, MA FCLIP, Retired. [6877] 20/09/1946 **FE01/01/1953**

Hill, Miss I G, BA, Stud., [10011174] 29/09/2008 **ME**

Hill, Mrs J M A, BA MCLIP, Stock & Reader Devel. Lib. Herts. C.C., Watford L. [25344] 21/01/1976 **CM06/06/1979**

Hill, Mrs J M, BA(Hons) MSc(Econ) MCLIP, Subject. Lib., Univ. of Bath [55057] 02/07/1997 **CM28/01/2009**

Hill, Miss J, BA(Hons) MA, Book Acquisitions Grp Leader, Univ. of Nottingham. [10014744] 23/03/2004 **ME**

Hill, Miss J, MCLIP, Retired. [6882] 30/03/1933 **CM01/01/1935**

Hill, Mr J, BSc LLM MCLIP, Retired. [60226] 01/09/1963 **CM01/04/2002**

Hill, Mrs K A, BA(Hons) MCLIP, Devel. and Project Offr., E. Riding of Yorks Council, Skirlaugh. [23303] 30/10/1974 **CM30/06/1978**

Hill, Mrs M E A, BSc DipLib MCLIP, Unemployed. [28741] 14/01/1978 **CM19/03/1980**

Hill, Mrs M E, BA MCLIP, Sch. Lib., W. Dunbartonshire Council. [23666] 25/01/1975 **CM31/08/1977**

Hill, Miss M E, BA MCLIP, Snr. Lib., Camden, London. [24700] 01/10/1975 **CM13/02/1979**

Hill, Mrs M L, BSc(Hons) MPhil DipIM MCLIP, Lib. Mgr., Stockport NHS Foundation Trust [59297] 31/01/2001 **CM21/05/2003**

Hill, Mrs M M, MCLIP, Retired. [10006251] 26/09/2007 **CM29/09/1975**

Hill, Mr M W, MA MSc MRSC CChem FCLIP, Life Member. [6893] 15/02/1965 **FE01/04/2002**

Hill, Ms M, BA MCLIP AdvDipEd, Med. Lib., Royal Bournemouth Hosp., Dorset. [44025] 02/04/1990 **CM20/03/1996**

Hill, Mrs P M, BSc MCLIP, Lib. /Records Mgr., Historic Scotland, Edinburgh. [24827] 10/10/1975 **CM14/12/1978**

Hill, Ms P M, BA(Hons) DIP LIB MCLIP, Principal Area Mgr., S., Ilkeston L., Derbyshire C.C. [26636] 26/10/1976 **CM01/07/1990**

Hill, Mrs R C, BSc MSc MCLIP, Sch. Lib., Skipton Girls High Sch. [39108] 29/10/1985 **CM22/05/1991**

Hill, Mr R J H, BA MCLIP, Local Studies Lib., Herefordshire L. [6898]
06/06/1968　　　　　　　　　　　　　　　　**CM01/01/1970**

Hill, Mrs R M, MCLIP, Programme Team Co-ordinator., Woking L.,
Surrey. [10004065] 01/01/1971　　　　　　　**CM01/01/1973**

Hill, Mrs S A, BA(Hons) MCLIP, Knowledge & Personel Mgr., CMC.
Cheshire. [48345] 01/12/1992　　　　　　　**CM19/03/1997**

Hill, Mrs S A, BA MCLIP, Lib., Falkirk Council. [30247] 30/12/1978
　　　　　　　　　　　　　　　　　　　　　CM18/03/1981

Hill, Mrs S D, BA(Hons) DipIM MCLIP, Unwaged [51975] 29/08/1995
　　　　　　　　　　　　　　　　　　　　　CM23/01/2002

Hill, Mrs S E, MCLIP BA, Retired. [19536] 26/03/1965　**CM01/01/1968**

Hill, Ms S J, HonFCLIP, Dir., Sue Hill Recruitment, London. [40725]
19/05/1987　　　　　　　　　　　　　　　**HFE17/06/1998**

Hill, Mrs S M, BA(Hons) DipILM MCLIP, L. Mgr., Neston L., Cheshire.
[55513] 16/10/1997　　　　　　　　　　　　**CM23/06/2004**

Hill, Mrs S, BA(Hons) MCLIP, Unknown. [39391] 22/01/1986
　　　　　　　　　　　　　　　　　　　　　CM26/07/1995

Hill, Ms V, BA(Hons) MA DipLIS MCLIP, Reader Devel. Lib., L.B. of
Havering, Romford. [50783] 18/10/1994　　　**CM25/07/2001**

Hille, Ms M E, Unemployed. [43500] 31/10/1989　　　　**ME**

Hilliard, Miss N M, BA MCLIP, Head of L. & Inf., Nat. Child. Bureau,
London. [26410] 08/10/1976　　　　　　　　**CM11/02/1980**

Hilliard, Mr R P, BSc(Econ) FCA HonFLA, Form. L. A. Sec. [31110]
29/06/1979　　　　　　　　　　　　　　　**HFE01/01/1979**

Hillier, Mrs J, BA MCLIP, Learning Resources Mgr., New Coll., Swindon.
[10518] 28/06/1970　　　　　　　　　　　　**CM03/05/1988**

Hillier, Ms J, MSc, L. Serv. Mgr., S. Birmingham Coll. [63465]
14/05/2004　　　　　　　　　　　　　　　　**ME**

Hillier, Mr R W E, BA MCLIP, Lib. (Local Studies), Cent. L.,
Peterborough. [24701] 01/10/1975　　　　　**CM28/08/1981**

Hillier, Miss S L, BA PGCE MCLIP, Co. Child. Lib., Westbury L., Wilts.
[37292] 07/06/1984　　　　　　　　　　　　**CM26/02/1992**

Hills, Miss G P, MCLIP, Life Member. [6911] 25/03/1959 **CM01/01/1964**

Hills, Mr K W, BSc ACLIP, Dep. Counter Serv. Super., KCL, London.
[66052] 06/09/2006　　　　　　　　　　　　**ACL03/12/2008**

Hills, Ms S B, BSc MSc FCLIP, Non-Exec. Dir., Northamptonshire
Teaching Primary Care Trust. [60712] 09/03/1984　**FE25/03/1993**

Hills, Mr S J, MA MCLIP, Head of English Catg., Univ. of Cambridge L.
[6912] 30/10/1971　　　　　　　　　　　　**CM19/11/1973**

Hilton Boon, Ms M L, BA MA MLIS MCLIP, Inf. Offr., Scottish
Intercollegiate Guidelines Network, Edinburgh [63548] 30/06/2004
　　　　　　　　　　　　　　　　　　　　　CM21/03/2007

Hilton, Mrs D M, BSc MCLIP FHEA MA, Customer Serv. Mgr., Anglia
Ruskin Univ., Chelmsford. [41705] 15/02/1988　**CM19/06/1991**

Hilton, Mrs J J, L. Serv. Mgr., Derby Coll. [47261] 29/06/1992　**ME**

Hilton, Mr J J, BA(Hons) MA, Sen. L. Asst., Univ. Liverpool. [59159]
04/12/2000　　　　　　　　　　　　　　　　**ME**

Hilton, Mrs W, MCLIP, Community Lib., Salford, Gtr. Manchester.
[20542] 05/04/1973　　　　　　　　　　　　**CM26/07/1976**

Hinchcliffe, Mr P, MCLIP, Life Member. [6921] 23/02/1951
　　　　　　　　　　　　　　　　　　　　　CM01/01/1958

Hinchliff, Mr J P, L. Asst., Balliol Coll. L., Oxford. [10011618]
15/10/1992　　　　　　　　　　　　　　　　**ME**

Hinchliffe, Mrs A L, BSc MCLIP, Employment not known. [60384]
22/10/1974　　　　　　　　　　　　　　　　**CM25/09/1978**

Hindell, Mrs C M, MCLIP, Retired. [6924] 30/01/1957　**CM01/01/1961**

Hinder, Mrs H P, BA PG DipLib MCLIP, Inf. Offr., Coll. of Law, Guildford
[27931] 11/10/1977　　　　　　　　　　　　**CM12/10/1979**

Hindle, Mrs J L, BA AHEA MCLIP, Admin/L. . Asst., Univ. of Exeter,
Exeter. [59662] 23/07/2001　　　　　　　　**CM10/03/2010**

Hindson, Miss A, BA(Hons) DipIM MCLIP, Asst. Lib., Univ. of
Portsmouth L., Portsmouth. [57743] 15/07/1999　**CM18/09/2002**

Hines, Mr W D, MA M LIB MCLIP, Asst. Dir. -Inf. Serv., Univ. of Wales,
Aberystwyth. [23350] 05/11/1974　　　　　　**CM01/12/1976**

Hingley, Dr S M, MCLIP, Head of Heritage Collections, Durham Univ. L.,
Durham. [14159] 01/10/1971　　　　　　　　**CM01/11/1974**

Hinshalwood, Mr K W, MA MCLIP, Life Member. [6935] 07/03/1961
　　　　　　　　　　　　　　　　　　　　　CM01/01/1965

Hinton, Dr B J C, MBE MA MA(OXON) PhD MCLIP, Hon. Lib., Julia
Margaret Cameron Trust, Freshwater Bay, I. O. W. [28344]
08/11/1977　　　　　　　　　　　　　　　　**CM04/02/1980**

Hinton, Mrs C N, BA MCLIP, Resident in New Zealand. [27979]
06/10/1977　　　　　　　　　　　　　　　　**CM10/08/1982**

Hinton, Mrs G H, BA MCLIP, Learning & Devl. Mgr., Herts. C.C.,
Hatfield. [27600] 01/06/1977　　　　　　　　**CM28/08/1981**

Hinton, Mr J R, BA MCLIP, Inf. Off., Sports Council for Wales, Cardiff.
[21603] 30/11/1973　　　　　　　　　　　　**CM03/12/1975**

Hinton, Mr K H, BA MCLIP, Sen. Lib., Neasden L., London. [34576]
16/01/1982　　　　　　　　　　　　　　　　**CM01/07/1987**

Hinton, Mrs M L, MCLIP, Asst. Lib., Oxford Brookes Univ. L. [11300]
01/01/1966　　　　　　　　　　　　　　　　**CM01/01/1970**

Hinton, Mrs S, BA(Hons) MCLIP, p. /t. Inf. Mgr., Manage5Nines Ltd.,
Cambridge. [43878] 07/02/1990　　　　　　　**CM23/03/1994**

Hipkin, Mrs A L, BA DipLib MCLIP, Freelance Indexer. [26401]
11/10/1976　　　　　　　　　　　　　　　　**CM24/12/1979**

Hipkiss, Miss L M, BSc(Hons) FibMS ACLIP, Learning Cent. Asst.,
Halesowen Coll., Halesowen, W. Midlands. [65987] 09/08/2006
　　　　　　　　　　　　　　　　　　　　　ACL05/10/2007

Hirano, Mr A, Lib., Sainsbury Inst., Jap Arts & Cult., Norwich [58892]
02/10/2000　　　　　　　　　　　　　　　　**ME**

Hird, Mrs J, BA(Hons), Reader Devel. Offr., Maltby L., Maltby.
[10015361] 11/11/2009　　　　　　　　　　　**ME**

Hird, Mr S J, BA MCLIP, Retired. [6949] 12/02/1969　**CM01/01/1971**

Hirons, Mrs C M, BSc MSc, Learning Res. Mgr., Oxford & Cherwell
Valley Coll., Banbury Campus. [47320] 10/07/1992　　**ME**

Hirsch, Ms D, BA MSLS, Unwaged. [10010553] 05/08/2008　**ME**

Hirst, Mrs A J, BA MA MCLIP, Res. Lib., Notts. [36456] 10/10/1983
　　　　　　　　　　　　　　　　　　　　　CM02/06/1987

Hirst, Miss R, BLIM, Unknown. [10014054] 23/06/2009　**ME**

Hirst, Ms Y, BEd DipLib MCLIP, Inf. & Communications Mgr., NILA, N.
Ireland [44075] 30/04/1990　　　　　　　　**CM18/07/1991**

Hiscock, Mrs G, Flexible Learning Cent. Mgr., Derby Moor Community
Sch., Derby City Council. [38658] 19/09/1985　　**ME**

Hitchcock, Mrs A M, BA(Hons) MCLIP, LRC Systems Mgr., Guildford
Coll. [51421] 10/02/1995　　　　　　　　　　**CM08/12/2004**

Hitchcock, Mrs N K, BA(Hons) DipILS MCLIP, Comm. L. Mgr.,
Worcester L., Worcester C.C. [52340] 30/10/1995　**CM21/07/1999**

Hitchen, Miss J, BA(Hons) DipLIS MCLIP, Principal Inf. Offr., Univ. of
Cent. Lancs., Preston. [45634] 08/04/1991　　**CM21/05/1997**

Hitchen, Mrs S E, BA(Hons) MCLIP, L. Resource Cent. Mgr., St.
Margaret's High Sch., Airdrie. [49702] 25/11/1993　**CM20/01/1999**

Hitchman, Ms S, Snr. Asst. Info., Maidenhead L. [63352] 19/04/2004**AF**

Hives, Mrs J P, BA MCLIP, Sen. Lib., Adult Stock & Promotion Team,
Cambs. L. & Inf. Serv. [15837] 25/10/1971　　**CM21/07/1989**

Hixon, Ms B C, BA MA MCLIP, Dep. Lib., Heatherwood&Weyham Park
Hos. NHS T., Slough. [28317] 20/11/1977　　**CM21/01/1980**

Ho, Mr A, MCLIP, Resident in Hong Kong [49219] 14/10/1993
　　　　　　　　　　　　　　　　　　　　　CM01/04/2002

Ho, Miss L Y C, BA(Hons), Sen. Inf. Asst., De Montfort Univ., Leicester.
[54310] 18/11/1996　　　　　　　　　　　　**ME**

Hoang, Mrs H, Sch. Lib., Deptford Green Sch., London [10013114]
02/04/2009　　　　　　　　　　　　　　　　**ME**

Hoare Temple, Miss K B, BA DipLib, Unemployed. [33478] 01/01/1981
　　　　　　　　　　　　　　　　　　　　　ME

Hoare, Mrs G M, B LIB MCLIP, Admin. Offr.,The Russell Sch.,
Richmond. [15933] 20/01/1970　　　　　　　**CM04/02/1976**

Hoare, Mr P A, MA FSA MCLIP HonFLA, Retired. [6979] 01/01/1960
　　　　　　　　　　　　　　　　　　　　　CM01/01/1962

Hoban, Ms R, BA(Hons), Grp. Mgr., Durham C.C. [58238] 24/11/1999
ME

Hobart, Mrs J L, BA MCLIP, Lib., Eltham L., L.B. Greenwich. [31338]
01/10/1979 **CM15/08/1984**

Hobbs, Miss D K, MCLIP, Sen. Asst. Lib., Cent. Lend. L., Birmingham P.
L. [22328] 01/04/1974 **CM11/07/1977**

Hobbs, Mr G P, BA(Hons) MSc, Inf. Mgr., Scottish Parliament.,
Edinburgh [61268] 09/05/2002 **ME**

Hobbs, Miss M E, MCLIP, Lib., Bibl. Serv. Dept., Birmingham L. Serv.
[22295] 01/04/1974 **CM11/07/1977**

Hobbs, Mrs M S, MCLIP, Lib. Mgr., Stourport L., Worcs. C.C. [21061]
01/10/1973 **CM22/07/1976**

Hobby, Mr P A, BA DipLib MCLIP, Music Collections, Brit. L., London.
[37501] 01/10/1984 **CM27/11/1996**

Hobson, Mrs A M R, BA DipLib MCLIP, L. Asst., London Met. Univ.
[5621] 28/04/1972 **CM22/02/1978**

Hobson, Ms C R, BA MA, Subject Lib., London Met. Univ. [59084]
10/11/2000 **ME**

Hobson, Mr J, MBE BA DipLib MCLIP HonFCLIP, Consultant, Self-
Employed, Betchworth. [6994] 01/01/1970 **CM13/11/1972**

Hockey, Mrs J, MCLIP, Sen. Asst. Lib., Lancs. Co. L., Thornton-
Cleveleys. [19981] 10/01/1973 **CM01/01/1977**

Hockey, Miss M A, BA(Hons), Stud. [10010176] 08/07/2008 **ME**

Hockey, Ms R M, BA(Hons) DipLIS MCLIP, L. Res. Mgr., Chorlton High
Sch., Manchester. [42635] 26/01/1989 **CM26/11/1997**

Hocking, Miss K M, MCLIP, Unemployed. [27647] 08/01/1964
CM01/01/1968

Hodder, Ms D K, MA MCLIP, Lib., Newnham Coll., Cambridge. [35182]
06/10/1982 **CM13/05/1986**

Hodds, Mr J, BA(Hons) MCLIP, Subject Lib., Univ. of Bath [56645]
01/10/1998 **CM28/10/2004**

Hodge, Mr G, BLib MCLIP, L. Serv. Mgr., N. E. Surrey Coll. of Tech.,
Ewell. [37425] 15/09/1984 **CM07/06/1988**

Hodge, Mrs H M, MCLIP, Subject Lib., Nescot, Surrey. [22700]
22/08/1974 **CM01/02/1978**

Hodge, Miss M E, BA DipLib, Res. Asst. (short project) [30915]
31/05/1979 **ME**

Hodge, Mrs S L, ACLIP, L. Asst., Copleston High Sch., Ipswich.
[10010555] 05/08/2008 **ACL23/09/2009**

Hodgeon, Mrs A, BA DipLib MCLIP, L. Asst., Hebden Bridge L. [39387]
22/01/1986 **CM09/08/1988**

Hodges, Mrs H A, BLIB MCLIP, Sch. L. Serv. Offr., Bucks C.C. [32026]
07/02/1980 **CM12/09/1984**

Hodges, Mrs J S, BA(Hons) MSc MCLIP, Learning Cent. Mgr., Coleg
Morgannwg, Nantgarw Campus [63924] 03/11/2004 **CM29/08/2007**

Hodges, Mrs S A, BA MA MCLIP, Tech. Serv. Mgr., Liverpool John
Moores Univ. [27740] 19/07/1977 **CM19/11/1979**

Hodges, Mrs S L, BA(Hons), Asst. Lib., Bircham Dyson Bell, London.
[63808] 01/10/2004 **ME**

Hodgetts, Ms S L, BA DipLib MCLIP, Training Lib., Heart of England,
NHS Foundation Trust, Good Hope Hosp. [37847] 16/10/1984
CM10/05/1988

Hodgkins, Mrs L K, BA FCLIP, Reg. Lib., LIEM. [29328] 26/05/1978
FE03/10/2007

Hodgkins, Ms L, MLS MCLIP, Lib., Bucks. Chilterns Univ. Coll., High
Wycombe. [50976] 04/11/1994 **CM21/11/2001**

Hodgkinson, Miss C, MA(Hons), Knowledge Co-ordinator, UK
Commission for Employment and Skills [62890] 18/11/2003 **ME**

Hodgkinson, Mrs H M, BA CertEd MCLIP, LRC Mgr., Redland Green
Sch., Bristol [21479] 20/10/1973 **CM06/09/1977**

Hodgkinson, Mr J D, BA MCLIP, Strategic Mgr., Serv., Lancashire Co.
L. & Inf. Serv. [7015] 01/01/1970 **CM25/06/1973**

Hodgkiss, Ms S J, Stud., Aberystwyth Univ. [10014180] 02/07/2009 **ME**

Hodgson, Mrs A J, Dep. Head of Learning Resources, W. Kent Coll.,
Tonbridge. [65646] 08/03/2006 **ME**

Hodgson, Dr A M, BA(Hons) PhD MA(Dist) MCLIP, Sen. L. Asst., Univ.
of Nottingham. [59955] 09/11/2001 **CM06/04/2005**

Hodgson, Mrs C E, BA MCLIP, Mgr. Reader Devel. Serv., Leicester City
Council. [6291] 14/08/1971 **CM07/10/1975**

Hodgson, Ms C, BSc(Hons) PGCE MCLIP, Res. Mgr.,(Mat. Leave)
Holloway Sch., L.B. of Islington. [50868] 24/10/1994 **CM18/11/1998**

Hodgson, Mr D M, BA DipLib CTEFLA, Bibl. Serv. Dep. Mngr., Kings
Coll. London [10013660] 19/12/1979 **ME**

Hodgson, Ms J A, BA(Hons), L. Mgr., Queens's Campus, Durham Univ.
[43602] 09/11/1989 **ME**

Hodgson, Mrs J D, BA MA MCLIP, Head of Special Collections, Univ. of
Sheffield L. [31138] 31/08/1979 **CM21/10/1981**

Hodgson, Mrs K, Learning Mentor, holloway Sch., London. [10013601]
12/05/2009 **AF**

Hodgson, Mr M, BA(Hons) DipLIS MA MCLIP, Inf. Spec. (Arts &
Humanities), King's Coll., London. [47351] 20/07/1992 **CM26/07/1995**

Hodgson, Mr R, BA MA, Asst., Lib., Gray's Inn L. London [10008423]
29/10/2002 **ME**

Hodkin, Mrs A F, BA MCIPD, Unknown. [10012611] 19/02/2009 **AF**

Hodson, Mrs A A, BA(Hons) MSc MCLIP, Dist. Devel. Offr. – Val.
[37084] 08/02/1984 **CM04/10/1988**

Hodson, Miss L, BSc, Inf. Specialist, Nat. Assembly for Wales, Cardiff.
[65878] 07/06/2006 **ME**

Hodson, Mrs M K, DipLib, UK Inf. Mgr., Help the Hospices, London.
[48129] 11/11/1992 **ME**

Hoenig, Mrs C S, BLib MCLIP, Bibliotheksangestellte, Univ. L. of
Bochum, Germany. [28370] 25/10/1977 **CM25/08/1983**

Hoey, Mr J M, MSc, Knowledge Mgr., Norkom Technologies, Ireland.
[10015703] 14/01/2010 **ME**

Hoey, Mr P O, BSc FCLIP, Retired. [60387] 27/01/1964 **FE28/03/1973**

Hoffman, Ms M, HonFLA, Hon. Fellow, Writer. [56142] 11/03/1998
HFE11/03/1998

Hogan, Mr J D, MIS, Unknown. [10016885] 01/06/2010 **ME**

Hogan, Mrs S D, BA(Hons), Asst. Sen. Lib., Manchester Met. Univ
[10007260] 23/10/1992 **ME**

Hogarth, Ms A J, BA DipLib Cert NatSci (Open) MCLIP, Stock Mgr.,
Cent. L., Middlesbrough L. & Inf. [32087] 25/01/1980 **CM08/03/1988**

Hogben, Mr B M, MA MCLIP, Retired. [20606] 08/05/1973
CM04/09/1975

Hogben, Miss R S, L. Mgr., Plymstock Sch., Plymoth. [65853]
31/05/2006 **ME**

Hogg, Ms C G, BA MCLIP, Retired. [7044] 02/02/1968 **CM01/01/1972**

Hogg, Miss C, BA, Stud., London Met. Univ. [10015488] 14/12/2009 **ME**

Hogg, Mr D, BA MCLIP, Sch. Lib., Glasgow City Council, Glasgow.
[36707] 11/11/1983 **CM10/11/1987**

Hogg, Mrs L, BA MCLIP, Educ. Devel. Lib., Glasgow City Council.
[34370] 27/10/1981 **CM03/03/1987**

Hogg, Mrs M A, BLibSc MCLIP, Primary Care Lib., Poole Hosp. NHS
Trust, Dorset. [7679] 27/04/1970 **CM09/10/1974**

Hogg, Miss M, BA, Lib. Asst., Norton L., York St John Univ. [10016482]
01/04/2010 **AF**

Hogg, Mrs R J, BA MSc MCLIP, Inf. Offr., The Coll. of Law, York.
[54953] 28/05/1997 **CM15/05/2002**

Hogg, Miss S E, BA LL. M, Grad. Lib. Trainee, Dept of Obstetrics &
Gynaecology, Univ. of Oxford [10015537] 11/12/2009 **ME**

Hoggarth, Mr R, MA MCLIP, Retired. [7049] 06/09/1969 **CM01/02/1973**

Hoggarth, Mrs S B, MCLIP, Sen. Inf. Advisor, Univ. of Gloucestershire,
Cheltenham. (Retired) [15257] 02/10/1970 **CM26/11/1973**

Hogston, Mr I A, BA, Stud. [10006508] 24/10/2007 **ME**

Hohmann, Ms T, MCLIP, Subject Lib., Writtle Coll. L., Chelmsford.
[64724] 03/06/2005 **CM09/09/2009**

Holberry, Miss K, BA(Hons), Stud. [10007995] 03/03/2008 **ME**

Holborn, Mr G F, MA LLB MCLIP, Lib., Lincolns Inn L., London. [28590] 13/01/1978 **CM26/08/1982**

Holbourn, Mrs C J, MCLIP, Primary Sch. Lib., Sch. L. Serv., London. [7977] 05/01/1972 **CM18/08/1975**

Holcombe, Mrs S J, BA MCLIP, Unemployed (Career Break). [43709] 07/12/1989 **CM25/05/1994**

Holden, Miss C A, ACLIP, Inf. Offr., Hill Dickinson LLP, Liverpool. [66005] 16/08/2006 **ACL17/06/2009**

Holden, Mrs C N, BA MA, Unwaged [58095] 29/10/1999 **ME**

Holden, Mrs C, Learning Res. Mgr., Loughborough Coll. [10001129] 28/07/1994 **ME**

Holden, Mrs D M, BEd DipILS MCLIP, Sen. Lib., Cumbria C.C., Penrith L. [51872] 20/07/1995 **CM18/03/1998**

Holden, Mr D R, BSc(Hons) MSc MCLIP, Sen. Subject Lib., Queens Univ., Belfast. [52246] 18/10/1995 **CM20/05/1998**

Holden, Mrs G M, BA M PHIL DipLib MCLIP, Comm. Lib., Oldham MBC, Crompton, Royton & Mob. [31865] 11/01/1980 **CM05/04/1989**

Holden, Mrs H V, BA MSc MCLIP, Parliamentary Ref. Specialist, House of Commons L., London. [7059] 02/10/1968 **CM01/01/1971**

Holden, Miss K L, BA, Unwaged. [10011554] 27/10/2008 **ME**

Holden, Miss M R, MCLIP, Life Member. [7061] 01/01/1951 **CM01/01/1960**

Holden, Mr P, BA(Hons) MCLIP, Assoc. Business Inf. Mgr., Astrazeneca, Loughborough. [53917] 10/10/1996 **CM23/06/2004**

Holden, Mrs S J, Unknown. [10014022] 18/06/2009 **AF**

Holder, Ms A J, BA(Hons) PG Dip, Online Serv. Coordinator, Westminster Ls. & Arch., London [10017110] 08/07/1996 **ME**

Holdstock, Miss M E, MCLIP, Retired. [7065] 20/03/1943 **CM01/01/1951**

Holdsworth, Ms J M, BA(Hons) ALA, Seeking Work. [10017268] 07/02/1972 **CM02/08/1976**

Holdsworth, Miss L, BA(Hons) MA, Lib., Academy 360, Sunderland. [10009767] 09/06/2008 **ME**

Holdsworth, Miss M E, MCLIP, Lib., L.B. Bexley, Sidcup, Kent. [7068] 21/08/1966 **CM01/01/1971**

Holgate, Mr A G, BA PGDip MA, Sen. L. Asst., Lancaster Univ. L. [63547] 18/06/2004 **ME**

Holgate, Ms C M, BA DipLib MCLIP, Community & Inf. Offr., N. Yorks. C.C., Ripon L. [43651] 16/11/1989 **CM16/09/1992**

Holgate, Mrs R G, L. and Inf. Mgr., Highfields Sch., Matlock. [10001667] 06/03/2007 **ME**

Holland, Mr C J, BA MCLIP, Lib. & Head of Inf. Serv., The Law Soc., London. [25309] 05/01/1976 **CM03/03/1978**

Holland, Miss J E, BA(Hons) MCLIP, Unwaged. [23198] 01/11/1974 **CM01/12/1976**

Holland, Mrs J, BA MCLIP, Head of L. & Inf. Serv., Norfolk C.C. [30419] 08/01/1979 **CM19/07/1983**

Holland, Mrs K J, BA(Hons) MCLIP, Inf. Serv. Lib., Norfolk C.C. [32243] 15/02/1980 **CM28/09/1984**

Holland, Mr M J, BA DipLib MA MCLIP, Outreach Lib., NW Ambulance Trust (NHS), Bolton [10013111] 14/02/1985 **CM01/04/2002**

Holland, Mr M S, BLib MLib MCLIP, Unwaged. [44481] 03/10/1990 **CM22/11/1995**

Holland, Miss P C, BA DipLib MCLIP, Dir., Inf. & Learning Serv., Univ. of Plymouth. [25310] 06/01/1976 **CM10/08/1979**

Holland, Miss P J S, MCLIP, Retired [7078] 01/08/1967 **CM01/01/1970**

Holland, Mrs S A, MCLIP, Lib. Mgr., Burleigh Community Coll., Loughborough. [53922] 10/10/1996 **CM13/06/2007**

Holland, Miss S, BA, L. Exec., House of Commons L. [36227] 08/08/1983 **ME**

Holland-Bright, Mrs D L, BA, Sch. Lib., Walsall Academy. [37037] 31/01/1984 **ME**

Hollander, Ms S, BA, Archiving & Registry Mgr. [10001315] 15/01/2007 **ME**

Hollands, Mrs A M, BSc MCLIP, Lib., Outreach., Maidenhead L., Royal Bor. of Windsor & Maidenhead L. [38825] 14/10/1985 **CM14/03/1990**

Hollenstein, Miss Y, PG Dip, Unknown. [10012212] 27/01/2009 **ME**

Hollerton, Mr E J, MCLIP, Unwaged. [7081] 19/02/1969 **CM03/09/1973**

Holliday, Mrs E M, BSc, Asst. Lib., Univ. of the W. of England, [63826] 07/10/2004 **ME**

Holliday, Mr G W, MA MCLIP, Inf. Mgr., Clyde & Co., London. [22836] 14/10/1974 **CM18/12/1978**

Hollier, Ms C, MLIS, Unwaged. [10016974] 16/06/2010 **ME**

Hollingdale, Miss E A, MCLIP, Retired. [7090] 07/03/1956 **CM01/01/1961**

Hollingsworth, Mr B P, BA(Hons) MA MCLIP, Faculty Team Asst., (Business Data) Manchester Univ. [52611] 13/11/1995 **CM10/07/2002**

Hollington, Mrs R L, BA(Hons) PG Dip, Unknown. [10012187] 09/01/2009 **ME**

Hollingum, Miss J A, BA, Stud., Aberystwyth Univ. [10014974] 01/10/2009 **ME**

Hollins, Mrs J H, MA DipLib MCLIP, Lib., Erlestoke Prison,Wiltshire. [29984] 25/10/1978 **CM30/04/1982**

Hollins, Mr P, BLib MCLIP, Info. Offr., the Open Univ. [40525] 26/02/1987 **CM11/12/1989**

Hollis, Mrs B M E, MCLIP, Retired. [7093] 21/03/1941 **CM01/01/1953**

Hollis, Mrs M E, MCLIP, Life Member. [7094] 19/02/1951 **CM04/03/1965**

Hollis, Mr N G, BA DipLib BA MCLIP, Circ. Serv. Mgr., Reading Univ. L., [36488] 11/10/1983 **CM15/11/1988**

Holloway, Mr M F, BA MCLIP, Retired. [7100] 11/10/1951 **CM01/01/1955**

Holloway, Mr N D, BA DipLib, Academic Liaison Lib., Queen Mary Univ. of London. [30187] 04/01/1979 **ME**

Hollwey, Mrs O, BA, Sen. L. Asst., Guille-Alles L., St. Peter Port, Guernsey. [48476] 22/01/1993 **ME**

Holly, Mrs C S, BSc(Hons) PGDipInf MA, Hosp. Site Lib., Univ. of Chesterr, Arrowe Park Hosp. [44522] 22/10/1990 **ME**

Holly, Ms C, Publns. Team Mgr., BIS, London. [47529] 01/10/1992 **ME**

Hollyfield-Hesford, Mrs A W, BA, Stud. [10005351] 25/07/2007 **ME**

Hollywood, Mr K, BA MSc DipLib MCLIP, Head of Res. Knowledge Serv., Brit. Geological Survey, Nottingham. [32088] 21/02/1980 **CM10/08/1982**

Hollywood, Miss S C, BA(Hons) PgDipILS, Res. Cent. Lib., Anniesland Coll., Glasgow. [61884] 21/11/2002 **ME**

Holman, Miss A P, MCLIP, Life Member. [7102] 22/05/1950 **CM01/01/1956**

Holman, Miss M R, BA(Hons) MSc, Info. Asst/Asst. Lib., Univ. of Ulster., NI [10001804] 02/08/1999 **ME**

Holman, Ms S M, BA(Hons) ACLIP, Br. Mgr., Livesey Lib., Blackburn, Lancs. [66049] 06/09/2006 **ACL16/04/2008**

Holmes, Dr A J, BSc PhD MRSC, Unwaged, Seeking Work. [10008792] 18/04/2008 **ME**

Holmes, Ms A, BA(Hons), Lib., Nantwich L., Cheshire C.C. [32662] 06/07/1980 **ME**

Holmes, Ms F M, MCLIP, Seeking work. [42556] 16/12/1988 **CM01/04/2002**

Holmes, Mrs F, BA MCLIP, p/t. Sch Lib., Hillview Sch. for Girls, Tonbridge. [43266] 12/10/1989 **CM14/11/1991**

Holmes, Mrs G M, BSc, Site Lib., SAC, Aberdeen. [62883] 18/11/2003 **ME**

Holmes, Mrs J C, MA MCLIP, Retired. [28318] 05/11/1977 **CM29/07/1980**

Holmes, Ms J, BA MCLIP DMS, Hd. of Logistics & Continuity, Herts. Libs., Culture & Learning [21328] 15/10/1973 **CM13/07/1978**

Holmes, Miss J, Stud. [65618] 02/03/2006 **ME**

Holmes, Mrs K, BA MA MCLIP, Subject Liaison Lib. [36295] 01/10/1983 **CM07/10/1986**

Holmes, Ms M M, BA(Hons) DipIS MCLIP, p. /t. Lib., Bournemouth L. [45127] 17/07/1990 **CM19/05/1999**

Holmes, Mr M, MA DipLib, Head of Catalogue Support Serv., Oxford Univ. L. Serv. [37490] 04/10/1984　　　　　　　　　　**ME**

Holmes, Mrs M, Stud., Colleg LLandrillo Cymru, Conwy. [10016110] 12/02/2010　　　　　　　　　　　　　　　　　　　**ME**

Holmes, Ms N M, MA MCLIP, Inf. Lib. Notts C.C. [35356] 13/10/1982 **RV23/01/2007**　　　　　　　　　　　　　　**CM21/07/1989**

Holmes, Dr P L, PhD FCLIP, Retired. [30765] 01/04/1979 **FE14/02/1990**

Holmes, Mr R K, BA MA MCLIP, Lib. Asst., e-Resources Co-ordinator, Durham Univ. [57995] 08/10/1999　　　　　　　**CM19/03/2008**

Holmes, Ms R M, MCLIP, Lib., Kelso L., Scottish Borders. [62811] 24/10/2003　　　　　　　　　　　　　　　　**CM21/03/2007**

Holmes, Ms S E, BA(Hons) MA MCLIP, Serv. Devel. Mgr., Dorset C.C. [51587] 04/04/1995　　　　　　　　　　　　**CM15/03/2000**

Holmes, Mrs S J, BSc(Hons) MCLIP, Business Lib., Southampton City L. [15757] 01/10/1971　　　　　　　　　　　　　**CM19/07/1974**

Holmes, Mr T C, Higher L. Exec., House of Commons L. [38808] 10/10/1985　　　　　　　　　　　　　　　　　　**ME**

Holmes, Miss V A, BA MCLIP, Retired. [7125] 30/06/1969　　　　　　　　　　　　　　　　　　　　　　**CM22/08/1972**

Holroyd, Ms G, BA MSc AcDipEd FCLIP, Life Member. [7127] 04/01/1957　　　　　　　　　　　　　　　**FE01/01/1965**

Holroyd, Ms I M, BA, Ch. Bibl. & Editor, biab, c/o. Brit. Academy, London. [62225] 24/03/2003　　　　　　　　　　　**AF**

Holt, Miss A, MA, Electronic Serv. Lib., NESCOT, Surrey. [58663] 09/05/2000　　　　　　　　　　　　　　　　　**ME**

Holt, Ms G A, DipLib BA MCLIP, Consultant [34433] 30/10/1981　　　　　　　　　　　　　　　　　　　**CM18/07/1985**

Holt, Mrs L, BA MCLIP, Ret. [2655] 04/02/1971　　**CM01/01/1974**

Holt, Mrs M B, MA DipLib MCLIP, Bookstart Co-ordinator., Cardiff L., Dominons Way, Cardiff [36467] 08/10/1983　　**CM05/07/1988**

Holt, Miss M, MCLIP, Life Member. [7136] 16/12/1946　**CM01/01/1951**

Holt, Mrs S K, MCLIP, Locality Mgr, S., Norfolk L. & Inf. Serv., Attleborough L. [13226] 17/01/1972　　　　　　**CM15/04/1975**

Holtam, Mrs E D E, L. Admin. Offr., Capel Manor Coll., Middlesex. [62527] 05/08/2003　　　　　　　　　　　　　**ME**

Holton, Mr G S, BA DipLib MCLIP, Sub-Lib., Bibl. Control Div., Univ. of Strathclyde. [24500] 27/08/1975　　　　　　**CM26/02/1979**

Holvey, Mrs L D, BLib MCLIP, Principal Lib., Child. & Families, Northants CC. [27428] 01/04/1977　　　　　　**CM24/07/1980**

Holyday, Mr J R, BA, Inf. Asst., Linklaters, London. [10006553] 30/10/2007　　　　　　　　　　　　　　　　**ME**

Home, Miss M E, BA DipLib MCLIP, Serv. Mgr., Academic Serv., L & LS. [32986] 02/10/1980　　　　　　　　　　　**CM15/02/1983**

Homer, Mrs E A, BA(Hons) MA MCLIP, Collections Dev. Mgr., UEL, London [61831] 14/11/2002　　　　　　　　**CM21/06/2006**

Homer, Miss M, MCLIP, Life Member. [7141] 29/03/1951 **CM01/01/1954**

Homer, Mr S D, BA(Hons) DipLib MCLIP, Inf. Mgr., Univ. of Cent. England. [35885] 07/02/1983　　　　　　　　**CM10/02/1987**

Homer, Mr S J, BA(Hons) MA, LRC Mgr., Littlehampton Academy. [10001889] 22/03/2007　　　　　　　　　　　**ME**

Homer-Brine, Mrs C L, BA(Hons) MA MCLIP, Unemployed. [47725] 15/10/1992　　　　　　　　　　　　　　**CM31/01/1996**

Hone, Mrs G, MCLIP, Life Member. [20796] 21/10/1947 **CM18/08/1982**

Honeyball, Mrs V M, MCLIP, Sch. Lib., Sacred Heart of Mary Sch., L.B. of Havering. [18342] 29/09/1972　　　　　**CM01/08/1975**

Hood, Mr D T, BA(Hons) Msc, Area Co-ordinator, Stretford L., Trafford MBC. [10016086] 09/05/2003　　　　　　　　**ME**

Hood, Mrs E M, BA MSc MCLIP, Job Seeking, Interested in Pharmaceutical and Health sectors. [36537] 04/10/1983　　　　　　　　　　　　　　　　　　　　**CM16/12/1986**

Hood, Mrs G T, BA MCLIP, Lib., Wheatley Park Sch., Oxford. [23118] 05/11/1974　　　　　　　　　　　　　　**CM05/11/1976**

Hood, Miss I Y, BA(Hons) LLB FCLIP, Legal Lib., Semple Fraser, LLP., Glasgow. [51957] 21/08/1995 **RV10/07/2009**　　**FE07/09/2005**

Hood, Mr J R, BA(Hons) DipIS MCLIP, Unemployed. [47059] 09/04/1992　　　　　　　　　　　　　　**CM23/07/1997**

Hood, Mrs M A, BSc DipLib MCLIP, Educ. Res. Lib., Angus Cultural Serv. [31192] 04/10/1979　　　　　　　　**CM08/02/1982**

Hood, Mrs M, MCLIP, Lib. &Inf. Worker, Cent. L., Wellgate, Dundee [10007092] 24/01/2008　　　　　　　　　**CM06/05/2009**

Hook, Mrs R S, BA DPSE DMS MCLIP, Lib., Cent. Bedfordshire Co., Dunstable [34634] 18/01/1982　　　　　　**CM07/07/1987**

Hooker, Miss D J V, BA DipLib MCLIP, Lib., Harbottle & Lewis LLP (Solicitors), London. [34147] 09/10/1981　　　**CM01/04/1986**

Hookway, Sir H T, LLD FCLIP HonFLA, Retired. [24219] 28/04/1975　　　　　　　　　　　　　　　　　**HFE15/06/1982**

Hoolboom-Kuah, Mrs S P, BA(Hons) DipLib MCLIP, Retired. [29717] 04/10/1978　　　　　　　　　　　　　**CM26/05/1982**

Hoole, Mrs N M, BSc(Hons) MSc MCLIP, L. Asst., Solihull Coll. [55011] 24/06/1997　　　　　　　　　　　　　**CM21/11/2001**

Hooper, Ms A, Stock & Reading Lib., Bristol Cent. Lib. [10013197] 03/04/2009　　　　　　　　　　　　　　　**ME**

Hooper, Mrs B R, MCLIP, Mgr., Child. & Sch., N. Yorks. C.C., L. Arch. & Arts. [2428] 22/04/1971　　　　　　　　**CM27/03/1975**

Hooper, Mrs J H, BA(Hons), L. Asst., UBHT, Learning Resource Serv., Bristol [10008697] 22/04/2008　　　　　　**ME**

Hooper, Mrs J M, BA(Hons) MA MCLIP, Dental Lib., Cardiff Univ. [48870] 07/07/1993　　　　　　　　　　**CM21/05/1997**

Hooper, Mr L H, MCLIP, Retired. [7155] 01/01/1964　**CM01/01/1968**

Hooper, Mrs S B, BSc (Hons), Lib., Sha Tin Coll., Hong Kong. [10009234] 07/05/2008　　　　　　　　　　　**ME**

Hoover, Mrs M R, MCLIP, Unknown [17048] 20/10/1965 **CM01/01/1969**

Hope, Mrs J G, MCLIP, Life Member. [7166] 13/10/1965 **CM01/01/1969**

Hope, Mrs L H, BSc MSc MCLIP, Consultant Inf. Sci. [60389] 05/02/1975　　　　　　　　　　　　　　　**CM04/07/1977**

Hope, Ms P A, BA MA MSc DipLib MCLIP, Inf. Cent. Mgr, Bank of England, London. [25561] 05/02/1976　　　**CM15/03/1978**

Hope, Mrs P N, MCLIP, Dep. Lib., The L., Ambleside Campus, St. Martin Coll. [30992] 22/07/1979　　　　　　**CM21/11/1985**

Hope, Ms S M, BA(Hons) MA, Inf. Lib. London Met., The Womens L., London. [62049] 29/01/2003　　　　　　　**ME**

Hopkins, Mr A, BA(Hons) PGDipIS MCLIP, Hd. of Lib., Image Servs. & IT, Courtauld Inst. of Art [52048] 02/10/1995　**CM01/06/2005**

Hopkins, Miss E J, BA(Hons) MA MCLIP, L. & Knowledge Serv. Mgr., NHS Manchester. [64144] 19/01/2005　　**CM11/11/2009**

Hopkins, Mr M, BA PhD MCLIP, Retired. [7178] 06/02/1968　　　　　　　　　　　　　　　　　　　**CM01/01/1971**

Hopkins, Mr N, BSc, Inf. Analyist, Wyeth L., Taplow [10012556] 23/02/2009　　　　　　　　　　　　　　　**ME**

Hopkinson, Mr A, MA DipLib FBCS FCLIP, Tech. Mgr., L. Serv., Middlesex Univ., London. [18783] 05/09/1972　　**FE14/02/1990**

Hopley, Miss E J, BA(Hons) MCLIP, Lib., Moulton Coll., Northants. [50744] 17/10/1994　　　　　　　　　　**CM15/05/2002**

Hopley, Mrs S M, ACLIP, Sen. Lib., St. Thomas More R. C. High Sch., Crewe. [65420] 24/02/2006　　　　　　**ACL29/03/2007**

Hopson, Mrs I, MCLIP, Head of Inf. Cent., George Abbot Sch., Guildford. [6795] 27/10/1971　　　　　　　**CM01/07/1975**

Hopson, Mrs M A, BA MCLIP, Sch. Libr., Don Valley Sch. & Performing Arts Coll., Doncaster [63196] 03/03/2004　　**CM01/02/2006**

Hopwood, Mrs H, BA PGCE DipLib MCLIP, Asst. Lib., Univ. of the W. of England, Bristol. [43915] 19/02/1990　　**CM16/12/1992**

Hopwood, Mr M, MSci ARCS, Sen. Inf. Asst., Royal Holloway Univ. of London, Egham [65670] 20/03/2006　　　**ME**

Horan, Ms A, BA MA MCLIP, position unknown, Dept. for Educ. & Skills, London. [60477] 22/05/2000　　　　**CM01/04/2002**

Horan, Miss J, Stud. [10017183] 11/07/2010　　　　　**ME**

Horan, Mrs L, BA, Seeking Work. [10011526] 17/10/2008　**ME**

Horbacka, Mrs M P, MCLIP, Lib. Devel., Greenwich Council, London.
[7192] 05/04/1967 **CM01/01/1971**

Horder, Miss B, BA MCLIP, Retired. [7193] 11/10/1960 **CM01/01/1962**

Hordon, Mrs F M, MA DipLib MCLIP, Child. Lib.,Batteresa L.,
Wandsworth Bor. Council. [90] 01/01/1971 **CM01/10/1974**

Hordon, Mrs K, BA(Hons) MA MCLIP, Serv. Mgr., Northumbria Univ.,
Newcastle. [42366] 24/10/1988 **CM20/03/1996**

Hore, Miss M I, MCLIP, Asst. Lib., Glasgow P. L [18785] 20/01/1957
CM15/12/1973

Horler, Mrs J, BSc, Lib., Harlington Upper Sch, Harlington, Beds.
[62734] 15/10/2003 **ME**

Horley, Mr N G B, BA(Hons) MSc(Econ) MCLIP, L. & Learning Cent.
Super., Abingdon & Witney Coll. [51225] 30/11/1994 **CM16/07/2003**

Horn, Mrs F N, BA MCLIP, Retired. [7196] 01/01/1966 **CM01/01/1968**

Horn, Mr V, BA MCLIP, Retired. [7198] 01/01/1965 **CM01/01/1968**

Hornbrook, Mrs H C, BA MCLIP, Employment not known. [26850]
08/12/1976 **CM27/07/1983**

Hornby, Miss P, BA, L. Asst., City Univ. London. [10016041] 10/02/2010
ME

Horne, Miss C I, Unknown. [10012162] 08/01/2009 **ME**

Horne, Mr C, Inf. Controller, Network Rail, London. [10010989]
12/09/2008 **ME**

Horner, Miss A A, Asst. Lib., Met. Police Serv. [65305] 19/12/2005 **ME**

Horner, Mrs H, MCLIP, p. /t. Lib., N. W. Evening Mail, Cumbria. [10127]
13/09/1971 **CM08/02/1977**

Hornung, Ms E, DipBibl MLIS ALAI MCLIP, Lib. /Inf. Mgr., Curriculum
Devel. Unit, Dublin. [61527] 13/09/2002 **RV11/12/2009CM01/02/2006**

Horrell, Mrs J F, BA MCLIP, Strategic Commissioning Project Mgr.,MLA
Council. [37182] 21/03/1984 **CM07/06/1988**

Horrigan, Miss M, BA(Hons), Trust Lib., The Cardiothoracic Cent.
Liverpool. [10001030] 21/06/2001 **ME**

Horrocks, Mrs A C M, BA MSc DipLib MCLIP, Inf. Specialist, Inf. Serv.,
Kingston Univ., Surrey. [22794] 12/10/1974 **CM10/03/1978**

Horrocks, Dr N, OC HonFLA BA MLS PhD ALAA FCLIP, Emeritus Prof.,
Sch. of Inf. Mgt., Dalhousie Univ., Canada. [17055] 20/01/1945
FE01/01/1952

Horsburgh, Mrs A M, B LIB MCLIP, Community Lib., Renfrewshire Libs.
[28246] 11/10/1977 **CM21/12/1981**

Horsey, Mrs M A, BA(Hons) DipILS MCLIP, Unknown. [43893]
13/02/1990 **CM26/11/1997**

Horsfield, Mrs K, BEd MCLIP Msc., Mgr., Resources for Learning
[61710] 23/10/2002 **CM21/05/2008**

Horslen, Ms J C, BA MCLIP, Reader Serv. Mgr., Law Soc. L., London.
[28593] 03/01/1978 **CM07/10/1982**

Horsler, Mr P N, Asst. Lib., LSE, London. [63183] 03/03/2004 **ME**

Horsley, Miss J E, MCLIP, Retired. [7220] 24/09/1968 **CM01/01/1972**

Horsnell, Ms P J, DipEdTech MCLIP, Inf. Adviser, London S. Bank Univ.
[7223] 01/10/1970 **CM23/04/1975**

Horsnell, Ms V, BSc MSc FCLIP, Life Member. [31077] 27/08/1979
FE01/04/2002

Horstmanshof, Ms K L, BA(Hons) MSc, LIS Exec., Chartered Inst. of
Building. [66100] 22/09/2006 **ME**

Horth, Ms G B, BA(Hons) MA, Learning Cent. Coordinator, Moorside
Community Tech. Coll., Consett. [10009983] 30/06/2008 **ME**

Horton, Mrs A D, Unknown. [10013971] 11/01/1973 **ME**

Horton, Mrs E, MCLIP, Freelance Editor [60438] 23/03/1998
CM01/04/2002

Horton, Mr H, MA MCLIP, Life Member. [7224] 18/03/1949
CM01/01/1951

Horton, Dr P B, MA DipLib MCLIP, Dep. Lib., (Ref. and Res)., Royal
Coll. of Music, London. [34321] 21/10/1981 **CM10/11/1983**

Horwood, Miss L K, BA MCLIP, Sen. Devel. Consultant &, Special
Advisor in K. M., Dept. for Business, Innovation & Skills (BIS)
[38803] 11/10/1985 **CM15/08/1990**

Horwood, Mrs M, BA MCLIP, Retired. [8120] 09/10/1947**CM01/01/1962**

Hosie, Mrs J, BA(Hons) PgDip MCLIP, Lib., N. Lanarkshire C., Bellshill.
[59535] 01/05/2001 **CM28/01/2009**

Hoskin, Mrs C E, BA(Hons) DipLIS MCLIP, Sen. Lib., Accrington L.,
Lancs. C.C. [46122] 02/10/1991 **CM17/05/2000**

Hosking, Miss E M, MCLIP, Life Member. [7238] 03/10/1947
CM01/01/1953

Hosking, Mr M G, MCLIP, Dir. Community Learning and Devel., Cambs.
C.C., Cambridge. [7239] 19/09/1968 **CM01/07/1972**

Hoskins, Dr I C, BSc., PhD, Content Editor, CABI, Wallingford, Oxon
[10001664] 06/03/2007 **ME**

Hoskins, Mrs J A, Unknown. [39980] 08/10/1986 **ME**

Hoskins, Mrs J K, ACLIP, L. Mgr., Bruton Sch. for Girls, Somerset.
[63473] 14/05/2004 **ACL10/01/2006**

Hoskins, Ms S L, MA MCLIP, L. &Learning Space Mgr., Univ. of Salford,
Salford. [10013453] 03/08/1990 **CM29/01/1992**

Hou, Mrs S G, BA MCLIP, P/T. Sch. Lib., Park Hill Jr. Sch., Croydon
[37120] 30/01/1984 **CM13/06/1989**

Hough, Miss H, BSc MSc, Head of Academic Serv., St. Martin's Coll.,
Carlisle [62487] 21/07/2003 **ME**

Hough, Mrs L J, BA(Hons) MSc, Mother. [46650] 02/12/1991 **ME**

Houghton, Mrs C M, MA MCLIP, Lib., Darlington Bor. Council,
Cockerton L. [32741] 02/07/1980 **CM04/02/2004**

Houghton, Mr D J, BA MCLIP, Life Member. [7250] 25/09/1955
CM01/01/1963

Houghton, Mrs E A, MCLIP, Teaching Asst. Longdon St. Mary's Sch.,
Glos. [21835] 31/01/1974 **CM09/08/1978**

Houghton, Miss E, BA MSc, Asst. Lib., NFER [10006380] 23/10/2007
ME

Houghton, Mr T, BSc DipLib DPA MCLIP MBA, Unemployed. [21360]
20/11/1973 **CM04/09/1979**

Houlihan, Miss G, Stud. [10016698] 28/04/2010 **ME**

Houlton, Ms L, Unknown. [10012028] 10/12/2008 **ME**

Hounsome, Mrs L M, BA MCLIP, Volunteer Lib. [4926] 18/01/1971
CM01/09/1975

Hounsome, Miss M E, BA(Hons), Outreach Clinical Support Lib., Surrey
& Sussex, Healthcare NHS Trust [64815] 18/07/2005 **ME**

Housden, Mr A, BA MA, Unknown. [10012722] 05/03/2009 **ME**

House, Mr D E, BA MCLIP, Dep. Vice-Chancellor, Univ. of Brighton.
[7266] 20/11/1968 **CM01/01/1971**

House, Mrs F L, BA(Hons) DipLIS MCLIP, Unknown. [50950]
31/10/1994 **CM19/05/1999**

House, Mrs M E A, MA DipLib MCLIP, Prison Lib., HMP
Wellingborough, Northants. [34179] 12/10/1981 **CM13/12/1984**

House, Ms S, BA(Hons) MSc MCLIP, Inf. Lib. for Law, Univ. of
Glamorgan, Pontypridd. [47026] 02/04/1992 **CM01/06/2005**

Housley, Mrs B J, B Lib MCLIP, Inf. & People's Network Lib., Cent. L.,
St Albans [12675] 15/06/1972 **CM01/02/1976**

Housley, Mr L D, TSSF BA(Hons) DipLib MCLIP, Lib., Franciscan In.
Study Cent., Canterbury. [27175] 14/01/1977 **CM30/10/1979**

Houston, Mrs L Y, BLS MBA MCLIP, Dir., LISC Northen Ireland [27148]
03/02/1977 **CM20/09/1979**

Houston, Miss M, BA MCLIP, Acting Young People's Co-ordinator, The
Mitchell L., Glasgow City Council. [32747] 26/08/1980**CM03/08/1983**

Houston, Mrs S J, MA MCLIP, Asst. Lib. (Readers'Serv.), Goldsmiths
Coll. L., London. [32055] 12/02/1980 **CM10/11/1982**

Hovish, Mr J J, BA DipLib MLib MCLIP, Retired. [21338] 17/10/1973
CM01/11/1976

Howard, Mrs A G, BA MCLIP, Local Studies Lib., Co. Council, Exeter
Cent. L. [27951] 04/10/1977 **RV16/07/2008** **CM28/08/1981**

Howard, Mr A G, MA FCLIP, Retired. [7270] 06/10/1960 **FE01/01/1970**

Howard, Miss A S, BA MCLIP, Inf. Exec., Royal Inst. of Chartered
Surveyors, London. [33303] 20/11/1980 **CM10/04/1986**

Howard, Mrs A, BSc, Lib. Counter Asst., Hitchin Lib, Hitchin [63901] 26/10/2004 **ME**

Howard, Mrs B A, BA MA MCLIP, P/t. L. Asst., Trinity & All Saints Coll., Horsforth,Leeds. [22808] 08/10/1974 **CM14/09/1977**

Howard, Miss C J, Lib. Asst., Dartington Coll. of Arts., Totnes. [10015739] 19/01/2010 **AF**

Howard, Mrs C, BA(Hons), LRC Mgr., St. Marys Coll., Liverpool. [59748] 12/09/2001 **ME**

Howard, Ms E C, BA DipLib MCLIP, Lib., St. Helens Sch., Northwood, Middx. [34283] 20/10/1981 **CM16/05/1985**

Howard, Mr E S, Grad. Trainee, Oxford Univ. L. Serv. [10000530] 16/10/2006 **ME**

Howard, Mr G, BA DipIS, Exec. Offr., House of Commons L., London. [47127] 05/05/1992 **ME**

Howard, Miss I C, BA DipLib MCLIP, Employment not known. [32989] 16/10/1980 **CM11/01/1987**

Howard, Ms J E, BA MCLIP, Web Mgr., Samuel Whitbread Community Coll., Shefford, Beds. [25762] 10/03/1976 **CM07/06/1978**

Howard, Mrs J, BA(Hons) MCLIP, L. Mgr., Cherry Knowle Hosp., Sunderland. [52779] 12/12/1995 **CM21/03/2001**

Howard, Mr L, BSc MCLIP, Managing Dir., XIP Pty Ltd., Australia. [60106] 07/12/2001 **CM07/12/2001**

Howard, Mr M, BA MCLIP, Unwaged. [24954] 28/10/1975 **CM21/08/1980**

Howard, Miss P J, BSc MA MCLIP, Lib., Trafford Coll., Manchester [55787] 19/11/1997 **CM17/05/2000**

Howard, Ms S V, BA MSc DipLib MCLIP, Asst. Dir., Imperial Coll. London. [29689] 09/10/1978 **CM31/03/1981**

Howard, Mr T W, FCLIP, Retired. [7281] 04/03/1947 **FE01/01/1960**

Howarth, Ms C A, MA MCLIP, L. & Inf. Offr. (Job-share), Cent. L., Sci. & Bus. Cent., Dundee City Council. [37513] 05/10/1984 **CM10/05/1988**

Howarth, Ms C, BA MLS MBA, Br. Lib., Wednesfield L., Wolverhampton. [32091] 07/02/1980 **ME**

Howarth, Mr C, BA MCLIP, Retired. [7283] 29/01/1965 **CM01/01/1969**

Howarth, Mrs H, BA(Hons), Unknown. [64932] 14/09/2005 **ME**

Howarth, Mr J A, BA MA, Asst. Lib., Internat. Inst. for Strategic Studies London. [61606] 03/10/2002 **ME**

Howarth, Mrs K J, BA(Hons) DipInf MCLIP, p/t Lib., Cheshire C.C., Macclesfield L. [46766] 14/01/1992 **CM20/09/1995**

Howat, Mrs M M, BA MCLIP, Retired. [7289] 11/02/1957 **CM01/01/1961**

Howden, Ms J S, MA DipLib MCLIP MPhil, Assoc. Dir., Learner Support, Glasgow Caledonian Univ. [35541] 04/10/1982 **CM08/03/1988**

Howe, Ms A B, BA(Hons) MA MSc, L. Asst., Harringay Sixth Form. [10011785] 13/11/2008 **ME**

Howe, Miss C E A, BLS MCLIP, Unknown. [28022] 02/10/1977 **CM16/11/1994**

Howe, Mrs C E, Stud., Aberystwyth Univ. [10010586] 07/08/2008 **ME**

Howe, Mrs G, MCLIP, Retired. [7884] 24/09/1964 **CM07/02/1973**

Howe, Mr J A, FCLIP, Life Member. [7295] 06/01/1949 **FE01/01/1957**

Howe, Mrs L C, BA(Hons) MCLIP, Sen. Lib., Milton Keynes City Council. [48672] 07/04/1993 **CM21/03/2001**

Howe, Mr M P, BA, LRC Mgr., Hartlepool Coll. of F.E. [35096] 10/08/1982 **ME**

Howe, Miss P J, BEd, Unemployed. [55752] 12/11/1997 **ME**

Howell, Miss E S, BA MCLIP, Head of Inf., Investec, London. [41005] 01/10/1987 **CM22/07/1992**

Howell, Ms J L M, BA(Hons) FRSA MCLIP MBCS, Dir. of Accessability & PR, Fortune Cookie, London [46025] 22/08/1991 **CM01/04/2002**

Howell, Mrs L M, ACLIP, Community Lib., Child. & Young People, Luton Cent. L., Beds. [10005222] 29/06/2007 **ACL16/07/2008**

Howell, Ms M F, BA(Hons) MA MCLIP, Learning Resoures Cent. Mgr., Sutton Cent. community coll., Ashfield. [55077] 09/07/1997 **CM29/11/2006**

Howell, Mrs M R, BA PGDipLib MCLIP, Local Studies Ref. Lib., Skelmersdale L., Lancs. [45777] 22/05/1991 **CM16/11/1994**

Howell, Mr P A, BA(Hons), Clinical Lib., Archway Healthcare L. [62718] 08/10/2003 **ME**

Howells, Mrs G I, MCLIP MLib, Self Employed. [7305] 12/03/1970 **CM31/10/1974**

Howells, Miss J A, BA DipLib MCLIP, Marketing Mgr. Enfield Lib. [31867] 08/01/1980 **CM11/01/1982**

Howells, Miss M A, MA PGCE MCLIP, English teacher., Sheffield [41983] 01/07/1988 **CM21/07/1993**

Howells, Mr W H, BA MLib MCLIP, Swyddog Llyfrgell y Sir, Ceredigion. [23138] 05/11/1974 **CM18/01/1978**

Howes, Mr M G, FCLIP, Retired. [60388] 08/11/1966 **FE03/11/1981**

Howes, Mr R W, MA PhD MCLIP, Asst. Lib., LSE, London. [25169] 01/12/1975 **CM14/06/1978**

Howey, Miss H, BA(Hons) MCLIP, Principal Lib. Operations Horsham Lib. W. Sussex C.C. [43662] 20/11/1989 **CM14/09/1994**

Howick, Mrs C M, ACLIP, Inf. Mngr., Rodborough Sch., Surrey. [65693] 30/03/2006 **ACL28/01/2009**

Howie, Mrs A S, BBibl, Sr. Lib. Asst., Heatherwood and Wexham Park Hosp., NHS Trust [48886] 12/07/1993 **ME**

Howie, Mrs I B, MCLIP, Lib., Mitchell L., Glasgow. [11912] 01/01/1968 **CM01/07/1972**

Howie, Miss J C, BA(Hons) MSc, Dir. of Knowledge Serv., MISCHON DE REYA, London. [48027] 04/11/1992 **ME**

Howkins, Mr S J, BA MCLIP, Corp. Info. Mgr., Devon Co. Co. [26902] 07/01/1977 **CM30/11/1981**

Howland, Mrs V R, BA DipLib MCLIP, Unwaged. [42294] 19/10/1988 **CM24/03/1992**

Howley, Mr P R, BSc PGCE PGDip MCLIP, LR advisor, Joseph Priestly Coll., Leeds. [47492] 04/09/1992 **CM21/08/2009**

Howley, Mrs S M, BA MA MCLIP, Retired [4703] 01/01/1969 **CM01/01/1971**

Howman, Mr R E J, MA MCLIP, Unwaged. [22502] 28/05/1974 **CM24/02/1982**

Howorth, Miss N, Sen. Asst. Lib., L. and Computing Cent., Oldham. [10015678] 13/01/2010 **ME**

Howsam, Miss D C, BA DipLib MCLIP, Principal Lib. Performance, Northants. C.C. [38004] 01/01/1985 **CM11/12/1989**

Howse, Mrs J, BSc MA, Merchant Taylor's Sch., Northwood [64931] 14/09/2005 **ME**

Hoyle, Mrs B, MCLIP, Retired. [3409] 01/01/1961 **CM01/01/1966**

Hoyle, Mr J N, BA(Hons) DipLib, Stud. Gateway Mgr., Marketing Servs., London. [44395] 04/10/1990 **ME**

Hoyle, Miss S E, MA MCLIP, Retired. [7340] 19/07/1971 **CM31/10/1974**

Huang, Miss S W, MA MCLIP, Knowledge Co-ordinator., Ernst & Young, London [62891] 18/11/2003 **CM29/11/2006**

Huang, Ms Z, MSc MCLIP, Sen. Lib. Asst., Eng. Team, Cent. L. Imperial Coll. London. [54624] 27/01/1997 **CM17/01/2001**

Hubbard, Dr T F, MA DipLib PhD FCLIP, Editor BILC, Nat. Univ. of Ireland, Maynooth [28320] 24/10/1977 **FE04/10/2006**

Hubbard, Mr W J I, BSc MA, Inf. Scientist, Mary Seahole Res. Cent., De Montfort Univ. [61361] 26/06/2002 **ME**

Hubble, Mrs M M, MCLIP, Life Member. [7346] 01/01/1951 **CM01/01/1955**

Hubschmann, Ms K, MA MA MCLIP, Snr.,Lib., Wiener L., London. [53688] 05/09/1996 **CM21/05/2008**

Hucbourg-Muller, Mrs L, MA, Unemployed [56141] 05/03/1998 **ME**

Huckfield, Mrs C J, BA MCLIP, Sen. Stock Lib., Herefordshire C.C. [30402] 06/02/1979 **CM16/09/1982**

Huckle, Mr C S, Lib. Asst., Hackney L. s., Hackney. [62160] 04/03/2003 **ME**

Huckle, Mrs F M, BA MCLIP, Freelance Taxonomist & Inf. Specialist [24616] 29/09/1975 **CM10/05/1978**

Huckle, Ms M J, BSc(Hons) MCLIP, Head, Qualifications & Prof. Devel., CILIP. [21069] 21/10/1973   **CM13/07/1978**

Huckstep, Miss I J, MCLIP, Retired. [7347] 28/09/1961 **CM01/01/1970**

Huddart, Mr D J, MA MSc MCLIP, Competitive Intelligence Offr., Rhodia. France [60390] 30/04/1980   **CM22/10/1985**

Huddart, Miss S, ACLIP, Curriculum Support Advisor, Exeter Coll [63620] 26/07/2004   **ACL22/06/2007**

Huddy, Mr E J, BA DipLib FCLIP, Retired. [7349] 14/07/1954
FE01/01/1964

Hudson, Mr A, BSc MCLIP, Retired. [21226] 10/10/1973 **CM19/01/1977**

Hudson, Miss B P, MA MCLIP, Life Member. [7354] 29/02/1948
CM01/01/1956

Hudson, Miss C M, MChem, L. Asst., Inst. Legal Stud., London. [65224] 18/11/2005   **ME**

Hudson, Mrs C M, ACLIP, Principal Inf. Asst., Nottingham Univ. [10006631] 11/09/2007   **ACL07/08/2009**

Hudson, Ms D R, BA(Hons) PgDip, Subject Lib., Univ. Coll. Birmingham. [59036] 31/10/2000   **ME**

Hudson, Mrs G L, MA MPhil MIL MCLIP FHEA, Head of L. Serv., Univ. of Bradford. [18630] 01/01/1972   **CM10/10/1974**

Hudson, Mrs J A, BA MCLIP, Lib., Faringdon Comm. Coll., Oxon. [22578] 07/07/1974   **CM01/08/1976**

Hudson, Mr J, BA MCLIP, pt. Lib. Asst., Bell L., Wolverhampton Med. Inst. [38011] 01/01/1985   **CM15/08/1989**

Hudson, Mrs K M, BA MA, Reading & Comunity Learning Mgr., Dorset C.C. [58028] 19/10/1999   **ME**

Hudson, Mr K, BSc MSc, Publications Co-ord., CABI, UK. [35834] 24/01/1983   **ME**

Hudson, Mr M G, BA, Stud. [10011954] 09/12/2008   **ME**

Hudson, Mrs M P, BA MCLIP, Inf. Lib., Southampton Solent Univ. [40658] 23/04/1987   **CM23/03/1993**

Hudson, Mr P A, BA(Hons) MSc(Econ) MCLIP, Head of Hist. Cent., Worcester. [54415] 05/12/1996   **CM17/01/2001**

Hudson, Mr R E, BA DipLib MCLIP, Outreach Training Lib. [42343] 21/10/1988   **CM01/04/2002**

Hudson, Miss S E, BA DipLib MCLIP, Sen. Lib., Reader Serv. The Bournemouth L. [42222] 14/10/1988   **CM22/04/1992**

Hudson, Mrs S J, BA DipLib MCLIP, Info. & E-Delivery Mgr., L., Info., Heritage & Arts Sci., Royal Bor. of Windsor & Maidenhead [37014] 27/01/1984   **CM03/03/1987**

Hudson, Mr T J, MCLIP, Naval & Maritme Res. Consultant [7368] 04/10/1971   **CM12/08/1974**

Hudson, Mrs W E, BA MCLIP, Learning & Devel. Offr., Sheffield L. Arch. & Inf. [34138] 07/10/1981   **CM27/07/1983**

Huffer, Mrs J, BA DipLib MCLIP, Principal Lib. (Resources), Educ. L. Serv., Nottingham. [25788] 24/02/1976   **CM14/11/1978**

Huggan, Ms A M, BA(Hons) MA MCLIP, Clinical Lib. Serv. Mgr, Dudley Grp. of Hosp. NHS Foundation Trust. [54249] 14/11/1996
CM19/07/2000

Huggett, Mr J M, BA(Hons) MSc(Econ) MCLIP, Unwaged. [57929] 05/10/1999   **CM07/09/2005**

Huggins, Miss D, BA(Hons) MCLIP, Inf. & L. Serv. Mgr., Dickinson Dees LLP, Newcastle upon Tyne. [45225] 31/07/1990 **CM21/11/2001**

Huggins, Mr P, BA(Hons) MA, Knowledge Cent. Mgr., The Chartered Inst. of Logistics and Transport, Northants [46983] 25/03/1992 **ME**

Hughes, Mrs A C, BA(Hons) MA, Forbes Mellon Lib., Clare Coll., Cambridge. [51644] 25/04/1995   **ME**

Hughes, Miss A C, MA, Learning Resources Cent. Mngr., Mayfield Sch., Portsmouth [64669] 13/05/2005   **ME**

Hughes, Ms A L, MA MCLIP, Community Lib., Wrexham [25054] 14/11/1975   **CM14/11/1975**

Hughes, Mr A P, BA(Hons) MA, Asst. L., Coll. of Occupational Therapists, London. [62286] 17/04/2003   **ME**

Hughes, Mr A V, BSc(Hons), p. /t. Stud., Univ. of Wales, Aberystwyth, Nat. L. of Wales. [10001048] 14/12/2006   **ME**

Hughes, Mrs A, BA MCLIP DMS MBA PGCE, Head of ILT & Learning Resources, Sandwell Coll. of F. & H. E., W. Bromwich. [25067] 28/10/1975   **CM16/06/1978**

Hughes, Miss A, BA(Hons) MLIS, Head, Trade Portal Team, UK Trade & Investment London. [56580] 28/08/1998   **ME**

Hughes, Mrs A, BA(Hons) PGDipLIS MCLIP, Prison Lib., Warrington Bor. Council, [54502] 02/01/1997   **CM12/09/2001**

Hughes, Mrs B J, MCLIP, Retired. [7377] 02/03/1941 **CM01/01/1950**

Hughes, Miss B M, BA DipLib MCLIP, L. Adviser, Child. & Young People & Welsh Serv., Denbighshire C.C. L. & Inf. Serv. [41198] 18/10/1987
CM14/08/1991

Hughes, Miss B S, BA, Head of Acquisitions & Metadata Support, Univ of Exeter [44540] 23/10/1990   **ME**

Hughes, Mrs C A, MCLIP, Housewife. [22732] 27/08/1974
CM21/06/1977

Hughes, Mrs C E, BA(Hons) MCLIP, Asst. Community Lib., Selly OaK L., Birmingham. [65776] 01/05/2006   **CM09/09/2009**

Hughes, Mr C E, Customer Contact Advisor, Mobility Operations, Bristol. [10009291] 15/05/2008   **AF**

Hughes, Ms C E, BA. Ma, MSc, Dir. of Knowledge Mgmnt., KPMG, London. [10011118] 07/07/1995   **ME**

Hughes, Mr C J, BA MCLIP Fln St LM, ILM External Verifier / Assessor [7380] 06/03/1961   **CM01/01/1967**

Hughes, Mrs C L, BA(Hons) MA MCLIP, Sen. Lib., Warwickshire C.C. Atherstone L. [51890] 31/07/1995   **CM15/01/2003**

Hughes, Mrs C, BA(Hons) MCLIP, Tech. Serv. Mgr. Liverpool Hope, The Sheppard-Worlock L. [52297] 23/10/1995   **CM18/11/1998**

Hughes, Mr D M, BA FCLIP, Retired. [7385] 03/01/1950 **FE01/01/1959**

Hughes, Mr D R, BSc DipEd MCLIP, Retired. [7386] 07/02/1972
CM18/07/1974

Hughes, Mrs F C M, BA(Hons) MLib MCLIP, L. Serv. Mgr. (Sci. & Eng.), Sir Kenneth Green L., Manchester Met. Univ. [44594] 01/11/1990
CM26/05/1993

Hughes, Ms F L, Stud., Aberystwyth. [63922] 03/11/2004   **ME**

Hughes, Ms F, MA PgDip, Sen. Inf. Offr., Glasgow CC. [10010828] 29/08/2008   **ME**

Hughes, Mr G H, BA MA DipLib MCLIP, Unknown. [10008958] 21/10/1981   **CM13/12/1984**

Hughes, Ms G M, MCLIP, Sen. Asst. Lib., L.B. Harrow. [11419] 01/01/1969   **CM01/12/1972**

Hughes, Mr G W, BA MCLIP, Retired. [7393] 28/04/1965 **CM01/01/1970**

Hughes, Mr G, Unknown. [10016447] 29/03/2010   **ME**

Hughes, Dr H G A, MA DPhil CSc FCLIP FRAI, Life Member. [7394] 06/09/1954   **FE01/01/1960**

Hughes, Mrs J E, BA DipLib MCLIP, Community Lib. (Acting), Dingwall L., Highland Council. [35425] 01/10/1982   **CM05/04/1988**

Hughes, Mrs J E, BA(Hons) PGDipILM MCLIP, Lib., Ellesmere Port Specialist Sch. of Performing Arts Ellesmere Port. [57312] 08/02/1999   **CM06/04/2005**

Hughes, Mrs J E, BA(Hons) MCLIP, Serv. Devel. Lib., Test Valley Hant. CC [46833] 14/02/1992   **CM27/11/1996**

Hughes, Mrs J L, BSc MCLIP, Employment not known. [41236] 20/10/1987   **CM22/05/1991**

Hughes, Ms L M, BA DipLib MCLIP, L. Advisory Offr., Wilts. & Swindon Learning Res., Trowbridge. [22070] 07/01/1974 **CM30/04/1976**

Hughes, Ms L M, Unknown [65125] 03/11/2005   **ME**

Hughes, Mr M J, BA(Hons), Head of Collections, Swansea Univ. [59615] 03/07/2001   **ME**

Hughes, Mr M, FCLIP DMS, Life Member. [7411] 22/09/1954
FE01/01/1962

Hughes, Miss N J, BA MCLIP, Online Serv. Mgr., Cheshire E. C.C. [43604] 09/11/1989   **CM23/03/1994**

Hughes, Mrs P A, DipIT MCLIP, Life Member. [7418] 16/08/1955
CM01/01/1960
Hughes, Ms P M, BA(Hons) MCLIP, Asst. Lib., Nat. Police L., Hook.
[58119] 03/11/1999 **CM23/06/2004**
Hughes, Mr R D, BA DipLib MCLIP, Ls. Offr., Wrexham L. & Inf. Serv.
[34469] 16/11/1981 **CM27/03/1991**
Hughes, Mr R G, BA MSc MCLIP, Learning Res. Advisor, LRC, Perth
Coll. [10001151] 12/01/2007 **CM16/04/2010**
Hughes, Mr R I, BLib MCLIP, Head, Nat. Screen & Sound Arch. of
Wales. [25565] 30/01/1976 **CM10/12/1981**
Hughes, Miss R, FCLIP, Refernce Lib. (Jobshare) [7420] 05/07/1971
FE01/07/1990
Hughes, Mr R, BA(Hons) MA MCLIP, Ret. [22473] 24/05/1965
CM01/01/1969
Hughes, Miss S E, BA Hons, Stud., Univ. Sheffield. [10016003]
11/02/2010 **ME**
Hughes, Mrs S J, MCLIP, Reg. Mgr., E. of England, MLA [249]
28/05/1968 **CM07/12/1973**
Hughes, Mrs S M, MA, Consultant, Self-Employed. [51372] 01/02/1995
ME
Hughes, Mrs S M, BA(Hons) PGCE MCLIP, Learning Cent. Mgr.,
Pontypool Campus, Coleg Gwent,Pontypool. [63366] 20/04/2004
CM24/10/2008
Hughes, Ms S R, Records & Inf. Offr., Norfolk C.C. [45295] 02/10/1990
AF
Hughes, Miss S S, BA(Hons) MA MCLIP, Inf. Servis. Coordinator,
Durham Univ.,Careers Advisory Serv. [62960] 25/11/2003
CM21/05/2008
Hughes, Ms S, OBE HonFLA, Hon. Fellow. [54737] 01/01/1997
HFE01/01/1997
Hughes, Mrs V E, ACLIP, Unknown. [10012656] 05/03/2009
ACL23/09/2009
Hughesdon, Mrs R F, BA MCLIP, Hon. Lib., Surrey Archaelogical Soc.
[21153] 06/10/1973 **CM01/11/1976**
Hughston, Mr D A, BA(Hons), Lib. Asst., Healthcare L., Whiston Hosp.,
Prescot. [10015228] 29/10/2009 **AF**
Huglin, Mrs C L, BA MPhil MCLIP, Inf. Specialist, Aylesbury Study
Cent., Aylesbury. [10006264] 20/10/1983 **CM19/09/1989**
Huish, Mr A W, BA MA FCLIP, Life Member. [7425] 21/01/1947
FE01/01/1967
Hukins, Mrs C E, BA MCLIP, Retired [17072] 01/10/1967**CM01/01/1970**
Hulance, Mrs W P, BLib MCLIP, Operations Mgr., Bedford Bor. L.,
Bedford Cent. L. [27622] 24/05/1977 **CM11/09/1979**
Hull, Mr R C, MA MCLIP, Res. Offr., Liverpool Record Off. [7429]
17/01/1972 **CM27/01/1975**
Hullin, Mrs P M, MCLIP, Life Member. [2990] 22/09/1948**CM01/01/1961**
Hulme, Mrs J M, Unwaged [32289] 19/03/1980 **CM14/02/1986**
Hulme, Mrs L H, BSc, Lib. /Inf.,Advice & Guidance Worker, Halton Lea
L., Runcorn. [10016684] 19/11/2002 **ME**
Hulse, Mrs H J, Lib. & Records Offr., Veterinary Lab. Agency,
Addlestone, Surrey. [39416] 23/01/1986 **ME**
Humble, Mrs W, Snr. Asst. Libr., Exeter Cent. L. [63914] 26/10/2004**ME**
Hume, Mrs C L, BA MSc FCLIP, Head of L. & Arch., Commonwealth
Secretariat [32469] 22/04/1980 **FE29/03/2006**
Hume, Mrs E M, CertEd DipILM MA MCLIP, Head of Trust L. Serv.,
Wirral Hosp. NHS Trust, Arrowe Park Hosp. [49442] 27/10/1993
CM19/03/1997
Hume, Mr F W, MCLIP, Life Member. [7439] 24/03/1948 **CM01/01/1950**
Humfrey, Mr J R, MA BA(Hons) DipLib DipEdMan MCLIP, LLRS Mgr.,
Myerscough Coll., Bilsborrow, Preston, Lancs. [46420] 05/11/1991
CM18/11/1993
Humm, Mrs J B, MCLIP, Princ. Lib. - Child. & Young People, & S. L. S.,
Luton Serv. Trust [21292] 16/10/1973 **CM01/09/1977**
Humphrey, Mrs L A, MCLIP, Retired. [7447] 15/01/1964 **CM01/01/1967**

Humphrey, Mr M, MCLIP, Life Member. [7448] 10/01/1961
CM01/01/1966
Humphrey, Mr N J, BLib MA MCLIP, Sen. Lib., Stock & Community.,
Lib. Admin Cent., Bridgwater [32300] 24/02/1980 **CM01/04/1986**
Humphrey, Mrs P A, BLIB MCLIP, Team Lib., Somerset L. Serv.,
[32202] 30/01/1980 **CM30/05/1985**
Humphrey, Miss S J, BA DipLib, Documentalist, European Space
Agency, Netherlands. [40839] 18/07/1987 **ME**
Humphreys, Mrs D E, MLib MCLIP, World Book Day/Nat. Year of
Reading., Wales Coordinator [7450] 23/02/1970 **CM21/05/2003**
Humphreys, Mr G P, FRSA MCLIP, Retired. [7454] 29/03/1966
CM01/01/1970
Humphreys, Mr J D Y, MA, Unknown [10006652] 11/09/2007 **ME**
Humphreys, Mr J F, MSc MCLIP, L. System Mgr., Univ. of the Arts
London. [7455] 01/05/1972 **CM11/06/1976**
Humphreys, Mrs J M, BA(Hons) MA PgDip MCLIP, Academic Supp.
Offr., Univ. of Warwick. [65392] 02/02/2006 **CM11/03/2009**
Humphreys, Mrs J P, MCLIP, Sen. Lib., Falkirk Council, Falkirk. [4853]
26/01/1969 **CM31/10/1972**
Humphreys, Miss R, BA DipLib MCLIP, Asst. Lib., Dept. for Child., Sch.
and Families, Sheffield. [34161] 05/10/1981 **CM11/11/1986**
Humphreys, Miss R, Lib., Outreach, Maidenhead L., The Royal Bor. of
Windsor & Maidenhead. [61651] 14/10/2002 **ME**
Humphreys, Ms S J, BA(Hons) PGDip LIS, Sch. Lib., Solihull M.B.C.,
Alderbrook Sch., W. Mids. [49091] 01/10/1993 **ME**
Humphreys, Mrs S, BA MCLIP, Retired, [7459] 14/01/1950
CM01/01/1964
Humphries, Mrs A E, B Lib MCLIP, Educ. Admin., Worcester C.C.
[1801] 18/10/1971 **CM27/10/1977**
Humphries, Miss B A, BA, Asst. Lib., Brit. L. of Pol. & Econ. Sci., L. S.
E., London. [27331] 22/02/1977 **ME**
Humphries, Mrs C M, BA DipLib MCLIP, Liaison Lib., Queen Margaret
Univ., Edinburgh. [44736] 21/11/1990 **CM23/03/1993**
Humphries, Dr C R, BSc MSc PhD, Info. Specialist (Health)., Cranfield
Univ. [61324] 22/05/2002 **ME**
Humphries, Mrs J, Learning Res. Cent. Mgr., Coleg Gwent, Ebbw Vale
Campus. [10001332] 06/02/2007 **ME**
Humphries, Mrs L C, MCLIP, Unemployed. [32222] 07/01/1980
CM18/06/1984
Humphries, Miss M, BA(Hons), Sch. Liaison Offr., Bristol Ls.
[10009488] 21/05/2008 **ME**
Humphries, Mr N D, FCLIP, Life Member. [7463] 08/12/1945
FE01/01/1957
Humphries, Miss P K, BA MCLIP, Life Member. [7464] 04/10/1946
CM01/01/1953
Humphris, Mrs J, BA MSc, Data Clerk, Meanwood Grp. Practice,
Leeds. [37734] 16/10/1984 **ME**
Hung, Miss M Y Y, BSc MA, Lib. /Stud. PhD., Tower Hamlets Sch. L.
Serv., London. [10001353] 20/08/1998 **ME**
Hunjan, Miss G K, BA(Hons), Comm. Lib., Spring Hill L., Birmingham.
[52377] 30/10/1995 **ME**
Hunnings, Ms C, BA, Inf. Res. Mgr., UHY Hacker Young, London
[58347] 19/01/2000 **ME**
Hunt, Ms A, MA DipLib MCLIP, Support Serv. Mgr., W. Lothian Council.
[26419] 18/10/1976 **CM08/12/1979**
Hunt, Mrs C E, ILS Support Unit Mgr., Peirson L., Univ. of Worcester.
[64965] 05/10/2005 **AF**
Hunt, Mr C J, BA MLitt FSA MCLIP, Retired. [18798] 14/09/1959
CM01/01/1963
Hunt, Mrs E A, MCLIP, Unemployed. [13210] 04/02/1968**CM03/08/1972**
Hunt, Mr G L, BA MA MCLIP, Univ. Lib., Univ. of the W. Scotland
[44662] 20/11/1990 **CM10/01/1994**
Hunt, Mr G, BA DipLib MCLIP, Lib., Cent. L., L.B. of Croydon. [34786]
02/02/1982 **CM22/04/1992**

Hunt, Mrs H J, BA(Hons) PGCE, L. Offr. – Bookstart & Early Years, Cornwall C.C., St Austell. [10015308] 30/10/2009 **ME**

Hunt, Ms J M, BA(Hons) DipIM MCLIP, Community Lib. (Job Share), Melkham L., Wiltshire C.C. [55367] 03/10/1997 **CM20/09/2000**

Hunt, Mr K, FCLIP, Retired. [7479] 01/04/1938 **FE01/01/1959**

Hunt, Mrs L, MCLIP, Lib., Sutton P. L. [15768] 01/10/1971 **CM25/07/1974**

Hunt, Mrs M C, BA DipLib MCLIP, Unemployed. [36656] 31/10/1983 **CM15/11/1988**

Hunt, Mrs M M, BA MCLIP, Comm. Lib., Kings Heath L., Birmingham P. L. [32988] 10/10/1980 **CM29/07/1983**

Hunt, Mr M, BSc(Hons) MSc, Knowledge Mgr., Royal Coll. of Nursing., London [48836] 01/07/1993 **ME**

Hunt, Ms N J, BA MA MCLIP, Learning Ctr. Coordinator, Southampton City Coll. [38575] 12/07/1985 **CM16/05/1990**

Hunt, Mrs P A, BA MCLIP, Sen. Res. Exec., 3i PLC., W. Midlands. [4827] 21/01/1972 **CM24/10/1975**

Hunt, Mrs R A H, BA DipLib MCLIP, Inf., Guidance & Supp. Offr., Stroke Assoc., Stockport. [41384] 17/11/1987 **CM12/09/1990**

Hunt, Mr R A, FCLIP, Retired. [7484] 02/09/1954 **FE01/01/1967**

Hunt, Mrs R, BSc(Hons) MSc MCLIP, Full-Time Mother. [50526] 01/09/1994 **CM18/03/1998**

Hunt, Dr S E, BA(Hons) MA PhD MCLIP, Asst. Lib., St Matthias L. Univ. of The W. of Enfield [63750] 29/09/2004 **CM11/03/2009**

Hunt, Mr S W, BA MA DipLib MA MCLIP, Data Serv. Mgr., Univ. of Warwick, Coventry. [45898] 09/07/1991 **CM16/11/1994**

Hunt, Ms S, BA DipLib MCLIP, Child. Lib., Stratford upon Avon L., Warwickshire C.C. [33407] 10/11/1980 **CM10/08/1984**

Hunt, Miss T, BA(Hons), MA, Inf. Asst., King's Coll., London [65198] 17/11/2005 **ME**

Hunter, Mrs A M, BA DipLib MCLIP, Princ. L. Offr., E. Lothian Council, Haddington. [33413] 19/11/1980 **CM27/01/1984**

Hunter, Ms C L, BSc (Hons) MCLIP, Learning Resource Cent. Leader, Titus Salt Sch., Baildon. [10014549] 21/03/1983 **CM01/01/1983**

Hunter, Mrs C M, MLib MA FCLIP, DDRB Secretariat, Off. of Manpower Economics, London [24970] 24/10/1975 **FE15/09/2004**

Hunter, Mrs E G, MCLIP, L. Mgr., Armdale L., W. Lothian. [10005219] 28/04/1970 **CM01/07/1994**

Hunter, Prof E J, MA AMIET FCLIP, Life Member. [7494] 16/12/1948 **FE01/01/1966**

Hunter, Mrs E, BA(Hons) LibDip MCLIP, Lib., Morgan Academy, Dundee. [10002649] 21/02/1995 **CM11/03/2009**

Hunter, Mrs G H, MA(Hons) DipILS MCLIP, Subject Lib., Univ. of Bolton, Lancs. [52487] 02/11/1995 **CM20/11/2002**

Hunter, Mr G, MA MA MCLIP, Lib., Angus Council, Brechin L. [44335] 19/09/1990 **RV17/06/2009** **CM20/09/1995**

Hunter, Mr I J, BA(Hons) MSc MCLIP, Shearman & Sterling(London) LLP, London [46741] 14/01/1992 **CM23/07/1997**

Hunter, Mrs J A, MA(Hons) DipILS MCLIP, Unknown. [53948] 15/10/1996 **CM25/07/2001**

Hunter, Mr J G, MCLIP, Retired. [7496] 17/01/1969 **CM29/08/1973**

Hunter, Mr P S, MSc CChem MRSC MCLIP, Retired. [60392] 01/01/1967 **CM03/06/1970**

Huntington, Mrs S, ACLIP, Customer Serv. Leader, Leicester Coll. [63597] 05/07/2004 **ACL22/06/2007**

Hunton, Mrs J E, Ref. Lib., Redcar Ref. L. [10010654] 19/08/2008 **AF**

Hunwick, Ms E R, BA(Hons) MA PGDipLIS MCLIP, Lib. : Serv., Basildon Healthcare L. . [57042] 30/11/1998 **CM29/03/2006**

Hurcombe, Mrs M, BA MCLIP, Project Mgr., Family Advice & Inf. Resource, Edinburgh. [31465] 15/10/1979 **CM22/10/1981**

Hurford, Mr G, MA MCLIP, Temp Aquisitions Asst., Tate [7506] 04/10/1971 **CM21/07/1975**

Hurn, Mr M D, MA MCLIP, Dept. Lib., Inst. of Astronomy, Univ. of Cambridge. [40975] 28/09/1987 **CM16/05/1990**

Hurren, Ms A C, BA(Hons), Asst. Customer Serv. Mgr., L.B. Richmond. [49125] 06/10/1993 **ME**

Hurry, Miss P, MA MCLIP, Lib. Congregational Hist. Soc. [7512] 25/05/1970 **CM01/01/1974**

Hursey, Mrs R A, Unwaged. [46474] 11/11/1991 **ME**

Hurst, Miss A, BA MCLIP, Life Member. [7513] 29/01/1972 **CM09/07/1974**

Hurst, Mrs J, BA(Hons) MA, Inf. Offr., ASH, Scotland. [61646] 11/10/2002 **ME**

Hurst, Mr J, BA DipLib MCLIP, L. Consultant & Trainer, Freelance. [29691] 01/10/1978 **CM04/12/1981**

Hurst, Mrs M E, BSc(Hons) DipLib, Info. Mgmt. Specialist, HMGCC [45691] 24/04/1991 **ME**

Husband, Ms K R, BSc DipLib MCLIP, Res. Lib., Glasgow Univ. [42232] 13/10/1988 **CM16/09/1992**

Husband, Mrs K, BA, Unknown [10010552] 06/09/1996 **ME**

Husbands, Mrs E S, BA DipLib MCLIP, Subject Classifier, Nielsen Bookdata., Herts. [19776] 26/11/1972 **CM18/08/1975**

Husbands, Ms J L, Lib., Barbados Community Coll., W. Indies. [64162] 19/01/2005 **ME**

Husbands, Mrs S D, MCLIP, Life Member. [6284] 30/09/1952 **CM01/01/1964**

Huse, Mr R J, FCLIP, Life Member. [7524] 01/10/1946 **FE01/01/1959**

Hussain, Mr A, MA, Asst. Lib., N. Harrow L., Pinner [10014564] 17/08/2009 **ME**

Hussey, Mrs N M, MCLIP, Lib., Peacehaven Comm. Sch., E. Sussex. [13665] 04/09/1971 **CM07/03/1975**

Hutchens, Mrs E G, BA(Hons) MA MCLIP, Freelance Gardener Surrey. [26421] 14/10/1976 **CM20/09/1995**

Hutcheon, Mr J R, BA MCLIP, Retired. [7529] 09/02/1968 **CM24/10/1972**

Hutchinson, Mr A J, BA(Hons) MCLIP, Head of Army L. &Inf. Serv., DETS(A), Wiltshire [39465] 31/01/1986 **CM12/03/2003**

Hutchinson, Mrs A M, BLib, Dep. Head of L. Serv., St Mary's Univ. Coll., Twickenham, London. [47926] 26/10/1992 **ME**

Hutchinson, Mrs E, BSc MCLIP, Sch. Lib., Ladies Coll., Guernsey [59191] 12/12/2000 **CM19/03/2008**

Hutchinson, Mrs K, BA MCLIP, Asst. Lib., Canterbury Christ Church Univ., Canterbury. [32324] 12/02/1980 **CM12/03/1984**

Hutchinson, Mrs P, BA MCLIP, Lib., N. Tyneside Ls., Northshields. [43608] 09/11/1989 **CM24/05/1995**

Hutchinson, Mr S L, BA MA, Head of L. Serv. for SC+HS, City Univ., London. [65554] 17/02/2006 **ME**

Hutchison, Ms D M E, BA DipLib MCLIP, Under Lib., Hughes Hall, Cambridge. [41001] 01/10/1987 **CM12/09/1990**

Hutchison, Mrs E M, BSc(Econ)(Hons) MCLIP, Asst. Inf. Offr., N. Lanarkshire Council. [47162] 18/05/1992 **CM20/11/2002**

Hutchison, Miss S A, BA MCLIP, Retired. [7549] 02/10/1967 **CM01/01/1971**

Hutt, Ms J, Unknown. [39343] 15/01/1986 **ME**

Hutton, Mr I, BA MA, Unwaged. [39891] 01/10/1986 **ME**

Hutton, Mrs J I F, MCLIP, Retired. [7553] 01/01/1951 **CM01/01/1963**

Hutton, Miss L A, BA, Inf. & Res. Facilitator, NHS Fife. [10007569] 18/02/2008 **ME**

Huws, Mr D R, BA(Hons) PgDipILM, L. & I. T. Workshop Facilitator, Rhyl Coll. [64813] 12/07/2005 **ME**

Huws, Mr R E, MLib FCLIP, Retired [7555] 01/01/1968 **FE07/01/1982**

Hvass, Miss A, MCLIP, Unknown. [62838] 06/11/2003 **CM21/03/2007**

Hwang, Mrs J R, BA MCLIP, Acquisitions and Metadata Mgr., Univ. of Birmingham. [4279] 02/01/1969 **CM01/01/1971**

Hyams, Ms E, HonFCLIP, Editor, CILIP. [59133] 21/11/2000 **HFE01/04/2002**

Hyams, Mr M, FRSC HonFCLIP, Hon Fellow. [60393] 11/12/2001 **FE01/04/2002**

Hyde, Mrs A M, FCLIP, Retired [12448] 14/01/1970 **FE26/07/1995**

Hyde, Ms D, BA(Hons) DipIM, Unwaged. [51286] 20/12/1994   ME
Hyde, Mr J A, FCLIP, Retired. [7558] 02/03/1962   FE01/04/2002
Hyde, Ms J C, BA DipLib MCLIP, Unemployed. [41285] 28/10/1987
                                                       CM18/11/1993
Hyde, Mrs J, BA(Hns) DipLib MCLIP, Resource Mgr., Slough Lib.
    [32848] 01/09/1980   CM27/09/1982
Hyde, Mrs J, MCLIP, Sch. Lib. Advisor, Devon Sch. L. Serv., Torquay L.
    [23620] 13/01/1975   CM23/01/1978
Hyde, Ms K J, MA(Hons), Stud., UCL, London. [10012889] 19/03/2009
                                                              ME
Hyde, Mrs N L, Sure Start Lib., Swadlincote L., Derbyshire [10006461]
    17/10/1996   ME
Hyde, Miss N, BA MCLIP, Life Member. [7559] 21/03/1952
                                                       CM01/01/1954
Hyde, Ms S F, MA PGCE, Serv. Quality Mgr., Univ. of Nottingham.
    [59461] 03/04/2001   ME
Hyde, Ms S G, BSc(Hons) DipLib MCLIP, Inf. Serv. Mgr., Thales Res. &
    Tech. (UK) Ltd., Reading. [32601] 30/05/1980   CM04/10/1983
Hyde, Mrs V A, BA MEd MCLIP, Lib., Blessed Robert Johnson Catholic,
    Coll., Telford. [7563] 01/01/1963   CM01/01/1967
Hyder, Ms G, MCLIP, Retired. [7564] 13/07/1966   CM01/01/1970
Hyett, Mr D J, BSc DipLib MCLIP, Head of Inf. & Records Mgmnt., Brit.
    Antarctic Survey Cambridge. [37170] 14/03/1984 CM16/02/1988
Hyland, Mrs D, BA MCLIP, Sen. Learning Resources Offr., BIFHE,
    Belfast. [59572] 04/06/2001   CM06/04/2005
Hyland, Miss J A, BA(Hons), Lib. Asst., Letworth L., Herts. [10013133]
    02/04/2009   AF
Hyland, Mrs J J, BBA MBA MA, Unwaged. [57718] 06/07/1999   ME
Hyland, Mrs J W, MCLIP, Sen. Asst., Ellon L., Aberdeenshire. [7565]
    08/10/1965   CM01/01/1971
Hyland, Miss S A, BA MCLIP, Policy & Performance Offr., Bucks. C.C.
    [24707] 09/10/1975   CM11/02/1980
Hyland, Mr T D, BA(Hons), ExploreMusic (Music L.) Mgr., Gateshead L.
    [64001] 01/12/2004   ME
Hynes, Mr A R, BA MCLIP, Coll. Lib., Longsands Coll., St. Neots,
    Cambs. [33813] 18/02/1981   CM17/07/1984

I

Icke, Miss A, BA MSt, Unknown. [10015603] 17/12/2009   ME
Ifie, Mrs Y O, Sen. Inf. Assist., De Monfort Univ. L., Leicester
    [10008703] 09/04/2008   ME
Iggulden, Mr D P, BA(Hons) MA, Electronic Resources Mgr., Royal
    Botanic Gardens., Kew [62679] 02/10/2003   ME
Iglesias-Dinneen, Mrs G J, Sen. L. Asst., Univ. of Southampton.
    [62157] 04/03/2003   ME
Ike, Prof A O, MA DipLib, Life Member. [17084] 14/03/1964   ME
Ikeogu, Mrs C E, BA MSc DMS MCLIP, L. Mgr., Harlesden L., L.B. of
    Brent. [30633] 26/02/1979   CM28/09/1983
Iles, Miss C E, ALCM MCLIP, Retired [7578] 20/04/1966 CM01/01/1970
Iles, Mrs K J, BA(Hons) PGCE, Unknown. [10016584] 14/04/2010 AF
Iles, Miss K, MA(Hons) MSc, Team Lib., [10007308] 09/11/1999 ME
Illes, Mr A J, MA MCLIP, Life Member. [7582] 24/01/1953 CM01/01/1955
Illingworth, Miss E, Asst. Inf. Adviser, Univ. of Brighton. [65240]
    25/11/2005   ME
Illingworth, Mrs J E, BA(Hons) MCLIP, Self employed. [49648]
    18/11/1993   CM20/11/2002
Illingworth, Mr M E T, BSc(Hons) DipLib MCLIP, Academic Lib.,
    Southampton Univ. [45618] 04/04/1991   CM18/11/1993
Ilogho, Mrs J E, BSc MLS, Serials Lib., Covenant Univ., Nigeria
    [10017103] 23/06/2010   ME
Ilyas, Mr M M, MLSc., Unknown. [10016130] 16/02/2010   ME

Imi, Mr N, BA DipLib MCLIP, Inf. & Learning Mgr., Jubilee L., Brighton &
    Hove City Council. [32996] 02/10/1980   CM18/06/1985
Imison, Ms N M, BA(Hons) MA, Unknown. [59257] 22/03/2001   ME
Imlah, Mr G B, BSc MSc MCLIP, Exec. Consultant, ATOS Origin,
    London. [10010976] 25/01/1980   CM01/06/1983
Imrie, Mr M P, Teen Lib., L.B. Enfield [63219] 16/03/2004   ME
Inala, Miss P, MSc MCLIP, Temp. Inf. Serv. Mgr., Manchester. [63128]
    11/02/2004   CM11/03/2009
Ince, Mr G, BA MSc, Info. Lib., Univ. of Bath, Avon [10001826]
    08/03/2007   ME
Indran, Mrs N, BA(Hons) PGDip MA, Lib. Child. and Young People Lib.
    Serv., L.B. of Barnet [54516] 15/01/1997   ME
Ingber, Miss L C, BA(Hons), Researcher, Occstrategy, London. [57026]
    26/11/1998   ME
Ingham, Mrs A N, BA PGCE, Stud., Univ. of Brighton. [10016448]
    24/03/2010   ME
Ingham, Mr J L, FCLIP, Retired. [7601] 12/06/1931   FE01/01/1948
Ingham, Mr R A, BA, E-Prints Content Editor., Lancaster Univ. [50720]
    13/10/1994   ME
Inglehearn, Ms A M, BA(Hons) MSc MCLIP, Lib. Mgr., Leeds Coll. of
    Building, [51627] 19/04/1995   CM18/09/2002
Inglis, Mrs A M, MA DipLib MCLIP, Sch. L. Resource Cent. Co-ord/Field
    Offr., James Gillespies High Sch., Edinburgh. [20558] 18/04/1973
                                                       CM01/10/1975
Ingman, Mrs H, BA(Hons) MCLIP, Lib. [54078] 24/10/1996
                                                       CM13/03/2002
Ingold, Ms M, Lib. Univ. of Applied Sciences Northwestern Switzerland,
    Reutteuz. [64755] 30/06/2005   ME
Ingram, Mrs G A, BA MCLIP, Retired. [7611] 26/08/1964 CM01/01/1968
Ingram, Mrs M M, MA(Hons)Geog. PgDip MCLIP, Aberdeenshire L. &
    Inf. Serv., Aberdeen [10001401] 14/02/2007   CM10/03/2010
Ingram, Ms M, MSc MCLIP, Lib. /Inf. Offr., ARC Epidemiology Unit, Univ.
    of Manchester. [21774] 11/01/1974   CM01/01/1977
Ingrey, Miss H M, BA(Hons) MA, Super. -Teaching & Learning Supp.,
    UCL, London. [59922] 02/11/2001   ME
Inman, Mrs J L, FCLIP, Customers & Communications Mgr.,
    Environment Economy, Warks C.C. [11692] 04/09/1971
                                                       FE29/11/2006
Inman, Miss J, BA(Hons) DipLib MCLIP, Lib., Birmingham Sch. L. Serv.,
    Birmingham. [53054] 14/02/1996   CM21/05/1997
Inness, Mrs J E, MA DipLib MCLIP, Acting L. Mgr. [29444] 31/07/1978
                                                       CM25/11/1980
Innis, Mrs J, MCLIP, LRC Mgr., London. [23210] 08/11/1974
                                                       CM26/07/1979
Inns, Mrs C M R, BA(Hons) MCLIP, Higher L. Exec., House of
    Commons L. [39452] 08/02/1986   CM12/03/2003
Inoue, Ms Y, MLS MS MA, Prof., Dokkyo Univ., Japan. [10010712]
    13/08/1992   ME
Inskip, Mr C, MSc LIS, Stud., City Univ. [65303] 19/12/2005 ME
Introwicz, Ms M L A, BSc, Unknown. [10016956] 02/10/1988   ME
Iona, Mr J, Lib., Oasis Academy, Enfield. [10006097] 26/09/2007 ME
Iqbal, Mrs G A, BA DipLib, Team Leader, Hounslow L., L.B. of
    Hounslow. [36837] 09/01/1984   ME
Iqbal-Gillani, Ms N, BA MCLIP, Ret. [29047] 27/02/1978 CM16/07/1980
Iredale, Miss J, BA Hons Dip Im, Languages Res. Super./L. Asst.,
    Hampton Sch., Middex. [10016006] 03/04/1996   ME
Ireland, Miss C, BA, Inf. Offr., CMS Cameron Mckenna, London.
    [64320] 02/03/2005   ME
Ireland, Mrs E J, BEd(Hons) DipILM MCLIP, L. & Resource Cent. Mgr.,
    Ferndown Middle Sch., Dorset. [48241] 17/11/1992 CM24/05/1995
Ireland, Mrs H M, BSc MSc MCLIP, Site Head, Basel, Eclinso AG,
    Switzerland. [27885] 04/10/1977   CM19/12/1980
Ireland, Mrs H, MA MCLIP, Sci. Lib., Univ. of Warwick L. [2623]
    31/10/1971   CM26/07/1977

Ireland, Mr I B, MCLIP, Dep. Ch. Exec., Voluntary Action Barnsley. [7622] 12/02/1968 **CM01/01/1971**

Ireland, Miss J, BA MCLIP, Unwaged. [36857] 11/01/1984 **CM09/08/1988**

Ireland, Mr P D E, BSc MSc MCLIP, Consultant, Paul Designs Ltd., Hull. [60202] 09/06/1994 **CM09/06/1994**

Ireland, Mrs P, BA MSc, Unknown. [10016303] 05/03/2010 **ME**

Ireland, Mrs S M, MCLIP, Principal Offr., Community L., Rotherham MBC [7625] 24/01/1968 **CM01/01/1971**

Iremonger, Ms L I, BA(Hons), Lib., Nottingham City Council. [49593] 19/11/1993 **ME**

Irobi, Mrs K E, BSc (Lib Inf. Sc.) Msc (I. T), Seeking employment. [10015809] 27/01/2010 **ME**

Ironside, Mrs C, MA MCLIP, Lib., Stratton Upper Sch., Biggleswade. [18350] 01/01/1974 **CM01/03/1976**

Irvine, Ms G, ACLIP, Access to Serv. Sen. Mgr. Lancs. C.C. [65228] 17/11/2005 **ACL06/04/2008**

Irvine, Mrs K Y, BSc(Hons)DipLib MCLIP, Subject Lib., Highland Health Sci. L., Univ. of Stirling. [35944] 16/02/1983 **CM16/12/1986**

Irvine, Mr K, BA BSc CEng MBCS CITP MCLIP, Retired. [60397] 06/04/1977 **CM06/04/1977**

Irvine, Mr N, BA DipLib MCLIP, Lib., Slough L., Berks. [44823] 07/12/1990 **CM21/07/1993**

Irving, Dr A, MLS Dip AdEd PhD MCLIP, Retired, Parish Clerk P/T. [7632] 23/08/1961 **CM01/01/1966**

Irving, Ms C M, BA(Hons) MCLIP, Researcher / Project Offr. [57124] 14/12/1998 **CM21/06/2006**

Irwin Tazzar, Mrs J L, BA(Hons) MCLIP, Sen. Asst. Lib., UCP Marjon, Plymouth. [47205] 03/06/1992 **CM18/03/1998**

Irwin, Miss J M, ALAA MCLIP, Retired. [7637] 01/01/1947 **CM01/01/1965**

Irwin, Miss R, BLib MCLIP, Customer Serv. Mgr., Dorset. [38466] 02/05/1985 **CM16/10/1989**

Isaac, Ms A, BA(Hons) DipLib, H.E. Learning Res. Coordinator, PETROC, Barnstaple, Devon. [49046] 14/09/1993 **ME**

Isaac, Mr D G, BA DipLib MCLIP DMS, Lifelong Learning Mgr., Sheffield City L. [7640] 01/10/1971 **CM26/11/1974**

Isaac, Ms K, MCLIP, Inf. Lib., L.B. of Sutton. [26747] 02/11/1976 **CM07/08/1981**

Isaac, Mrs M O, BA MCLIP, Educ. Servs. Lib., Tamside M.B.C., Ashton-under-Lyne [21159] 09/10/1973 **CM10/02/1977**

Isaacs, Mr J M, MA FCLIP, Life Member. [7642] 21/06/1957 **FE01/01/1966**

Isaksen, Miss K G, BA(Hons) DipLib, Somerfield States Plc., Customer Serv. Asst. [7644] 13/07/1971 **ME**

Isherwood, Mrs G M, MCLIP, L. Serv. Mgr., Nottm. city L. & Inf. Serv. [21772] 10/01/1974 **CM23/12/1976**

Ismail, Mrs N, MCLIP, Child. Serv. Lib., W. Sussex C.C. L. Serv., Horsham. [63893] 26/10/2004 **CM17/09/2008**

Isokpehi, Miss O A, BSc, Unknown. [10014003] 17/06/2009 **ME**

Ison, Mrs S J, BSc(Hons) MA, Asst. Inf. Advisor. [10005859] 14/01/2005 **ME**

Issler, Mr A, BA MCLIP, Community & Devel. Mgr., Brighton & Hove City L, Brighton. [22816] 08/10/1974 **CM19/09/1978**

Itayem, Mr M A, MA FCLIP, Life Member. [17094] 20/09/1963 **FE26/02/1992**

Ivanou, Mr I, MA MCLIP, Coll. Lib., N. Warwickshire & Hinckley Coll. [63821] 08/10/2004 **CM27/01/2010**

Ives, Mrs T M, MCLIP, Unemployed. [26968] 20/01/1977 **CM01/01/1980**

Iwugo, Ms I, BSc PGC PGD, Unwaged. [10009355] 31/07/1990 **ME**

Izatt, Mr R J, BA MCLIP, Customer Serv. Team Leader., Fife Council., Dunfermline [32663] 15/07/1980 **CM21/06/1983**

Izzard, Mr D F, BA(Hons) DipIS MCLIP, L. Mgr., Golders Green L., London. [10008990] 15/01/1992 **CM22/09/1999**

J

Jablkowska, Miss H M, MCLIP, Repository Lib., Middelsex Univ. [21800] 15/01/1974 **CM01/10/1976**

Jack, Miss E R, BA(Hons) MCLIP, L. Inf. Serv. Asst., Royal Academy of Dance, London. [62982] 02/12/2003 **CM19/03/2008**

Jack, Mr M J, MA, Dep. Counter Servs. Super., Maughan Lib., King's Coll. London [65182] 16/11/2005 **AF**

Jackman, Mr N, Stud., London Met. Univ. [10013866] 04/06/2009 **ME**

Jackson, Ms A B, BA MCLIP, Career Break. [29667] 05/10/1978 **CM11/08/1987**

Jackson, Mrs A C, BA MCLIP, Inf. Serv. Lib., Cent. L. Halifax [47023] 02/04/1992 **CM20/09/2000**

Jackson, Miss A J, BA MCLIP, Reader Devel. Lib., Tring L., Herts. [7663] 14/01/1971 **CM06/01/1975**

Jackson, Ms A, L. and Inf. Offr., WWF, Godalming [10007792] 11/03/2008 **ME**

Jackson, Mr A, BA MCLIP, Principal Asst. Lib., Univ. Dundee. [39713] 24/05/1986 **CM14/11/1989**

Jackson, Mrs C M, BA MCLIP, Med. Retired/Unemployed. [18361] 01/01/1972 **CM01/01/1976**

Jackson, Mrs C M, BSc(Econ) MSc PGCE(FE), Sen. Consultant Inf. Literacy, Cardiff Univ. [44722] 29/11/1990 **ME**

Jackson, Mrs C S, BA DipLib MCLIP MSc, L. Mgr., Calderdale & Huddersfield NHS, The Calderdale Royal Hosp. [30169] 01/01/1979 **CM27/01/1982**

Jackson, Mrs C, B LIB MCLIP, Lib. [32859] 13/10/1980 **CM30/07/1985**

Jackson, Mrs E K, BA(Hons) DipLIS MCLIP, Young Peoples Serv. Lib., Young Peoples L. Serv., Newport, I. O. W. [50038] 24/02/1994 **CM18/11/1998**

Jackson, Mrs E, MA DipLib MCLIP, Freelance Adult Tutor. [31429] 01/10/1979 **CM22/10/1986**

Jackson, Miss E, BA(Hons), L. &Inf. Serv. Asst., CIOB, Ascot [10016458] 26/03/2010 **AF**

Jackson, Mr E, LLB MCLIP, Lib., Kingston upon Hull City L. [7669] 03/10/1969 **CM10/01/1975**

Jackson, Mrs H F, BLib MCLIP, Princ. Lib., Staffordshire L., Stafford. [23737] 31/01/1975 **CM18/02/1980**

Jackson, Mr I B, BA MCLIP, Dep. Lib., Univ. of Liverpool, Sydney Jones L. [22543] 01/07/1974 **CM08/07/1976**

Jackson, Mr J G, ACLIP, Sen. Inf. Asst. and Law L. Super., Univ. of Exeter [52778] 12/12/1995 **ACL05/05/2005**

Jackson, Mrs K, ACLIP, Asst. Lib., Danum Tech. Coll., Doncaster [63326] 16/04/2004 **ACL05/10/2007**

Jackson, Mr K, BSc MCLIP, Chf. Lib., DEFRA, London. [32094] 28/02/1980 **CM14/01/1985**

Jackson, Mrs L A, BSc, L. Asst. (Technician), Aberstwyth Univ., Royal Bolton NHS Foundation Trust. [10016153] 16/02/2010 **ME**

Jackson, Ms L, Hd. of Info., The Careers Grp., Univ. of London. [37209] 02/04/1984 **ME**

Jackson, Mr M C, MCLIP, Retired. [7680] 05/10/1969 **CM06/09/1972**

Jackson, Ms M E, Learning Resource Cent. Mgr., St Anthony's Girls' Sch., Sunderland. [10010357] 22/07/2008 **ME**

Jackson, Ms M F, MA, Catg., Scottish Parliament Inf. Cent., Edinburgh. [40056] 10/10/1986 **ME**

Jackson, Mrs M J, Head of Inf. Res., Ashton Comm. Sci. Coll., Preston. [64757] 29/06/2005 **AF**

Jackson, Mr M, BA DipILS, Mob. L. Asst. /Driver, Highland Council. [49635] 16/11/1993 **ME**

Jackson, Mrs M, BPhilEd MEd PhD Dip ILM, Retired [50709] 12/10/1994 **ME**

Jackson, Ms N, MSc BA(Hons), Sen. L. Asst., Univ. of Nottingham Adult Educ. Cent. [10001891] 15/03/2002 **ME**

Jackson, Mrs P A, BA(Hons) MCLIP, Unwaged. [10540] 19/01/1968
CM02/08/1972

Jackson, Mr P L, MA DipLib MCLIP, Dep. Lib., Inst. of Classical Studies L., London. [42690] 06/02/1989 CM14/09/1994

Jackson, Ms P S, BA DipEd BEd Grad DipIfs, Knowledge Devel., Herts C.C., [59196] 14/12/2000 ME

Jackson, Mr R A, MA DipLib MCLIP, Sytems Devel. Lib., Rothley, Leicestershire. [36016] 06/04/1983 CM03/03/1987

Jackson, Miss S L, Lib. Mgr., JR Knowles, Warrington [41424] 09/12/1987 ME

Jacob, Miss C H, BSc, Trainee professional Lib. [66103] 25/09/2006 ME

Jacob, Mr E N, MD, Resident in Netherlands. [65259] 01/12/2005 ME

Jacob, Miss F S, BSc DipInf, Researcher, ABN Amro [55144] 23/07/1997 ME

Jacob, Mr T J, MA MCLIP, Sen. L. Asst., Nottingham Univ. L. [46348] 29/10/1991 CM15/10/2002

Jacobs, Miss J K, BSc, Young People Serv. Lib., Rickmansworth L., Herts. [63949] 18/11/2004 ME

Jacobs, Ms M, Lib. Asst., Faculty of Asian & Middle Eastern Studies, Univ. of Cambridge [10007693] 21/02/2008 ME

Jacobs, Ms W M, BA, Prison Lib., HMP Kingston, Portsmouth. [10014634] 10/09/2009 ME

Jacobsen, Ms S E, MA BA MLIS MCLIP, Unknown. [63824] 08/10/2004 CM10/03/2010

Jaco-Oliveira, Dr F, Internet Lib. (Consultant). [10008661] 18/04/2008 ME

Jacques, Miss E L, BA MA, Unknown. [10012150] 08/01/2009 ME

Jacques, Mr M O, BA DipLib MCLIP, Documentation Tech., DSP Design Ltd., Chesterfield, Derbys. [41041] 06/10/1987 CM25/05/1994

Jacques, Miss S E, Asst. Lib., N. E. Wales Sch. L. Serv., Mold. [51328] 12/01/1995 ME

Jaffray, Mrs K C, BA MCLIP, Sen. Lib., Larbert L., Falkirk Council. [35453] 17/10/1982 CM27/03/1991

Jaiteh, Ms S, BA(Hons), Project Mgr., Soutron LTD., Derby [10007125] 07/01/1981 ME

Jakes, Mr C R, MCLIP, Principal Lib. (Local Studies), Cambs. C.C., Cambridge Cent. L. [21715] 02/01/1974 CM24/01/1977

Jamal, Mr J, Unwaged – Seeking Employment [10002193] 04/04/2007 AF

James, Miss A C, BA, Asst.Lib. - Sion Coll. Catg. Project, Lambeth Palace L., London. [64108] 17/01/2005 ME

James, Mr A C, BA MCLIP, Asst. Lib., Soc. of Antiquaries, London. [32602] 19/06/1980 CM31/12/1989

James, Ms A M, BA(Hons) MA PGCE MCLIP, Asst. Inf. Lib. Univ. of Wales [63998] 01/12/2004 CM10/03/2010

James, Miss A M, BA DipLib MCLIP, Unknown. [49062] 28/09/1993 CM26/07/1995

James, Mrs A, Unknown. [10014098] 25/06/2009 ME

James, Ms B E, MCLIP, Info. Resources Asst., London S. Bank Univ., Perry L. [50448] 03/08/1994 CM13/06/2007

James, Mrs B R, BA MCLIP, Life Member. [3215] 07/09/1955 CM01/01/1961

James, Mrs B S, MCLIP, Asst. Lib., Wellington Sch., Somerset. [55034] 01/07/1997 CM15/11/2000

James, Mrs B, BSc DipInf, Sch. Lib., The Knights Templar Sch. [59239] 15/01/2001 ME

James, Mrs C A L, BA(Hons) PGDipILS, Lib., Guille-Alles L., Guernsey. [44476] 11/10/1990 ME

James, Mrs C V, MCLIP, Sen. Lib., S. Warwickshire L. & Inf. Serv. [7709] 15/03/1971 CM05/08/1974

James, Ms D, BTech, MSc DipLib, Freelance Inf. Specialist. [41997] 14/07/1988 ME

James, Miss E A, BA DipLib, Tech. Lib., Liverpool Victoria, Bournemouth. [10011114] 09/01/1984 ME

James, Ms E, MA DipLib, Lib., Nat. Art L., London. [36318] 01/10/1983 ME

James, Mr G H, BA DipLib MCLIP, Head of L., Merthyr. Cent. L., Mid-Glam. [30191] 28/12/1978 CM06/11/1981

James, Mrs G, B LIB MCLIP, Retired. [19733] 10/01/1972 CM04/04/1977

James, Mrs H R, Asst. Lib., Dame Alice Owen's Sch., Potters Bar [64157] 19/01/2005 ME

James, Mr H, BA DipLib MCLIP, Principal Lib., Cyngor Gwynedd, Caernarfon. [29985] 31/10/1978 CM04/01/1982

James, Miss H, MCLIP, Retired. [7713] 17/07/1972 CM01/08/1976

James, Mrs J M, BA MCLIP, Stud. [26924] 11/12/1976 CM12/02/1981

James, Miss J T, BA(Hons) MSc(Econ) MCLIP, Unknown. [52840] 02/01/1996 CM19/05/1999

James, Miss J, Lib. Asst., Northampton Coll., Northampton [10015643] 14/01/2010 AF

James, Miss K T, BA MCLIP, Dep. Lib. Mgr., Barlow Lyde & Gilbert, LLP. [36769] 03/01/1984 CM18/01/1989

James, Mr M C, MSc BA MCLIP, Knowledge Mgr., Occupational Psychology Div., Employment Serv., Sheffield. [32603] 16/06/1980 CM25/05/1983

James, Mr P M, MSc MIIS CertEd MCLIP, Head of L. &Learning Res., Maryvale Institue, Birmingham. [7719] 01/11/1969 CM01/07/1974

James, Mr R S, MA, Asst. Under Lib., Cambridge Univ. L., Cambridge. [10008948] 23/04/2008 ME

James, Mrs S R M, BSc MCLIP, Employment not known. [60707] 07/11/1973 CM07/11/1973

James, Dr S, DUniv BA FCLIP, Retired [7723] 26/10/1965 FE22/07/1992

Jameson, Mr S M, Unknown. [38317] 28/02/1985 ME

Jamie, Mrs E J, MA MSc, Ch. Lib., Internat. Inst. for Strategic Studies London. [55790] 24/11/1997 ME

Jamieson, Mr D, BSc(Hons) MSc, Co. Arch., Harper Collins, Glasgow. [64133] 19/01/2005 ME

Jamieson, Mr I M, FCLIP CertEdFE, Retired. [19503] 27/09/1955 FE01/01/1961

Jamieson, Mrs J, Asst. Lib., Erith Sch. [40054] 16/10/1986 ME

Jamieson, Mrs J, MA DipLib MCLIP, LRC Coordinator, St. John's High Sch., Dundee. [41606] 20/01/1988 CM13/06/1990

Jamieson, Mrs S L, BA MCLIP, System Support Lib., A. L. I. S. [37663] 15/10/1984 CM21/07/1989

Jamieson, Mrs S V, MCLIP, Life Member. [8613] 23/11/1967 CM14/08/1974

Jamieson, Ms S, BA(Hons) MSc DipLIS MCLIP, L. Serv. Mgr., NHS Health Scotland, Edinburgh. [55447] 13/10/1997 CM20/09/2000

Jamnezhad, Miss B, BA(Hons) MA MCLIP, Head of L. & Info. Serv., Weightmans LLP. [51882] 24/07/1995 CM29/03/2004

Janda, Mrs B K, p. /t. Stud., Univ. of Cent. England, Staffs. C.C., Perton L. [65496] 08/02/2006 ME

Jane, Ms L, MSc, Head of L. and Inf. Serv., Lanscape Inst., London. [10014586] 04/12/1995 ME

Janes, Mr A C, BA DipLib MCLIP, Ref. Lib. L.B. of Havering, Upminster Lib. [38136] 21/01/1985 CM16/09/1992

Janes, Cllr B, HonFCLIP, Unknown. [10008037] 16/10/2008 HFE16/10/2008

Janes, Miss C L, Arch. Researcher, ITN, London. [52501] 02/11/1995 ME

Janes, Ms F E, BA MSc(Econ) MCLIP, Reader Devel. Lib., L. B of Havering. [38847] 14/10/1985 CM18/04/1989

Janta-Lipinski, Mrs P M, MCLIP, Lib., High Sch. for Girls, Glouceseter. [24333] 01/07/1975 CM01/01/1978

Jap, Miss Y S, MCLIP, Sen. Asst. Lib., Harrow Council. [61813] 13/11/2002 CM19/11/2008

Jara De Sumar, Mrs J, Liason Lib., McGill Univ. Montreal, Canada. [22781] 19/10/1974 ME

Jardine, Mrs A L, BA MCLIP, Educ. Support Lib., Dumfries and Galloway L., Dumfries. [39444] 29/01/1986   **CM27/05/1992**

Jardine, Mrs H M, BA MCLIP, Bibl. Access Mgr., Guildhall L., London. [24636] 07/10/1975   **CM09/06/1978**

Jardine, Miss S, BA(Hons), Internal Communications Offr., Halton Bor. Council. [10007695] 21/02/2008   **ME**

Jardine-Willoughby, Miss S, BA(Hons) MCLIP, Lib Mgr. CHIC Middlesex Univ. L., Chase Farm Hosp. [26423] 18/10/1976   **CM25/01/1980**

Jarratt, Mr D, MCLIP, Life Member. [7742] 29/03/1942   **CM01/01/1950**

Jarratt, Ms K M, BSc DipILS MCLIP, Unwaged. [54237] 12/11/1996   **CM15/11/2000**

Jarrett, Ms C E, BA(Hons) DipLib, Sen. Asst. Lib., Health & Life Sci., Bristol [10001444] 27/06/1988   **ME**

Jarvis, Miss A E, BA MCLIP, Lib., Newport City Council. [32095] 25/01/1980   **CM06/09/1985**

Jarvis, Mrs A M, BA(Hons) MA MCLIP, Unknown. [58962] 10/10/2000   **CM27/01/2010**

Jarvis, Miss C L, MA(Hons), Dep. Mgr. of Staff Devel., Bodleian L., Univ. of Oxford. [57512] 14/04/1999   **ME**

Jarvis, Ms E, BA MA DipLib DMS MCLIP, Consultant. Culture,Libs.,Inf., [29986] 09/11/1978   **CM23/01/1981**

Jarvis, Mr K A, MA FCLIP, Retired. [17110] 14/03/1955   **FE29/05/1974**

Jary, Mrs C V, BA(Hons), Collection Dev. Mgr., E. Area, Lancashire. [65998] 11/08/2006   **AF**

Jay, Mr K N, BSc, Sen. Analyst, Thomson Reuters (Healthcare & Sci.), London. [61183] 03/04/2002   **ME**

Jay, Miss M E, MA MCLIP, Enquiry and Inf. Mgr., Derby City Lib. [26749] 11/10/1976   **CM11/10/1982**

Jazosch, Ms K, BA(Hons) Phil MA, L. Asst., Biomedical Sci. L., Southampton. [10010322] 18/07/2008   **AF**

Jeal, Ms S M, BA MA, Team Leader: Public Serv., Univ. of London, London [10014789] 10/11/2009   **ME**

Jeal, Mrs Y A, MA DipInfLib MCLIP, Customer Support Mgr., Univ. of Salford, Inf. Serv. Div. [44388] 03/10/1990   **CM24/07/1996**

Jeans, Mrs S M, BA(Hons) DipLib MCLIP, Lib. and EFL Teacher, Internat. Sch. [33719] 06/01/1981   **CM21/03/2007**

Jebson, Mr S, ACLIP, Info. Offr., Nat. Met. L., Devon. [65219] 18/11/2005   **ACL29/03/2007**

Jeeves, Mr J, BA MCLIP, Sen. Asst. Lib., L.B. of Harrow. [31871] 03/01/1980   **CM28/07/1983**

Jeeves, Mrs S J, BA MCLIP, Child. Lib. L.B. of Harrow. [31627] 29/10/1979   **CM29/07/1983**

Jefcoate, Mr G P, MA FRSA MCLIP, Dir., Radboud Univ. Nijmegen L., Netherlands. [22556] 30/06/1974   **CM20/09/1976**

Jeffcock, Ms C, Sen. L. Asst., Fire Serv. Coll., Moreton in Marsh. [64331] 04/03/2005   **ME**

Jeffcote, Mr D P, L. Asst., Sevenoaks L., Kent. [10001024] 02/12/2004   **ME**

Jefferson, Mrs C E, BA(Hons) MA MCLIP, Sen. Researcher, Lovells LLP, London. [56409] 01/07/1998   **CM21/06/2006**

Jefferson, Dr G, BSc MA PhD FCLIP PGCE, Life Member. [7764] 30/04/1948   **FE01/01/1953**

Jeffery, Mrs C I, BA MCLIP, Unknown. [11922] 01/01/1970   **CM01/11/1972**

Jeffery, Ms C M, BSc MCLIP, Head of Learning Resources, Oxford Brookes Univ. L., Harcourt Hill, Oxford. [22721] 30/08/1974   **RV06/04/2006**   **CM19/08/1977**

Jeffery, Mrs H, BA DipLib MCLIP, Asst. Lib., Surrey Archaeological Soc. [31306] 17/10/1979   **CM10/09/1982**

Jeffery, Mrs L C, BA(Hons) MSc MCLIP, Asst. Faculty Lib., Univ. of Portsmouth. [53878] 07/10/1996   **CM09/07/2008**

Jefford, Ms M J, BA MCLIP, ICT Systems Lib., S. Ayrshire Council, Carnegie L. [39762] 01/07/1986   **CM18/04/1990**

Jeffrey, Mrs L K S, BA(Hons) MSc MCLIP, Researcher Training Lib., Durham Univ. [62963] 25/11/2003   **CM08/08/2008**

Jeffries, Mr J, BA FRSA FCLIP, Retired. [7781] 01/10/1969   **FE21/12/1988**

Jeffries, Mrs R J, BA(Hons) MA MCLIP, Lib., Cent. Lib., Swindon [58473] 03/03/2000   **CM23/06/2004**

Jeffries, Mrs S L, BSc(Hons) MSc MCLIP, Admin. Asst. [51444] 10/02/1995   **CM24/07/1996**

Jefkins, Mrs H J, MCLIP, Unemployed. [28646] 12/01/1978   **CM08/10/1981**

Jelley, Mrs R K, BSc, Sci. Inf. Mgr., Bio Products Lab., Elstree. [10010964] 10/09/2008   **ME**

Jelleyman, Miss S, BA MCLIP PGCE, Waste-Edu. Support Prog. Offr., Shropshire C.C. Shropshire [23419] 13/01/1975   **CM05/07/1978**

Jellis, Miss S, FCLIP, Life Member. [7786] 21/09/1944   **FE01/01/1971**

Jenkin, Ms S M, BA(Hons) MA MCLIP, Comm. Lib., Medway Council., Kent. [62024] 20/01/2003   **CM09/07/2008**

Jenkings, Mrs M E, BA MCLIP, Dev. Lib., Notts City L. [29143] 05/04/1978   **CM08/02/1982**

Jenkins, Miss A C, BA DipLib MA MCLIP, Head of Info. and Communications, Alcohol Concern, London. [29695] 30/09/1978   **CM11/11/1983**

Jenkins, Mr A L, BA MA DipLib MCLIP, Sen. Exec. Planning, Cardiff Univ. Inf. Serv., [7790] 06/10/1971   **CM31/12/1989**

Jenkins, Miss C D, BA PGDip MA MCLIP, SUNCAT Bibliographic Asst., EDINA [62908] 18/11/2003   **CM09/09/2009**

Jenkins, Mr D R, BA(Hons), Asst. Lib., Manchester Met. Univ. [10006991] 17/12/2007   **ME**

Jenkins, Mrs E W, BA(Hons) PGDipLib MCLIP, Asst. Lib., Gwynedd Council, Dolgellau, Gwynedd. [42483] 23/11/1988   **CM17/09/2003**

Jenkins, Mrs K, MCLIP, Princ. L. Adviser, Essex C.C., Chelmsford. [30811] 01/03/1970   **CM16/03/1981**

Jenkins, Dr L C, PhD, Unknown. [65601] 27/02/2006   **ME**

Jenkins, Mr M, BSc MCLIP ILTM MEd, Academic Mgr., Cent. for Active Learning, Univ. of Glos. [38160] 24/01/1985   **CM10/05/1988**

Jenkins, Mrs N G, BA DipLib MCLIP, Lib., Conwy & Denbighshire NHS Trust, Glanclwyd Hosp. [46084] 18/09/1991   **CM19/01/2000**

Jenkins, Miss N, BA FCLIP, Retired. [7800] 01/02/1964   **FE11/04/1973**

Jenkins, Mrs R M, BA MCLIP, L. Asst., Bridgend. [33733] 11/02/1981   **CM11/01/1987**

Jenkins, Ms R, BA(Hons) MCLIP, Retired [31040] 26/09/1962   **CM24/02/1986**

Jenkins, Mrs S E, BA(Hons), Child. & Educ. Serv. Mgr., Wolverhampton L. [47890] 22/10/1992   **ME**

Jenkins, Mrs S L, BA(Hons) MA MCLIP, Unknown. [58747] 03/07/2000   **CM31/01/2007**

Jenkins, Mr S, MA MCLIP, Lib., The Cornwall Cent., Redruth. [37788] 19/10/1984   **CM25/05/1994**

Jenkinson, Miss C M, MCLIP, Catr., Goldsmith Coll., Univ. of London. [7805] 15/09/1970   **CM21/11/1973**

Jenkinson, Mrs E M, MCLIP, Life Member. [7806] 01/01/1956   **CM01/01/1970**

Jenkinson, Ms S, BSc DipLib MCLIP, Local Access Offr., Surrey Hist. Serv., Woking,Surrey. [43074] 11/07/1989   **CM18/09/1991**

Jenkinson, Mr T S, BA DipLib MCLIP, Project Offr., N. Yorks. C.C., Northallerton. [43383] 17/10/1989   **CM16/11/1994**

Jenner, Mr A, BA, Info. Offr., Investment Mgmnt. Grp. Linklaters, London. [10000693] 18/10/2006   **ME**

Jennings, Ms B J, BA DipLib MCLIP, Unemployed. [31872] 13/12/1979   **CM10/09/1982**

Jennings, Ms D M, BA MSc DipLib MCLIP, Collection Devel. Lib., Catawba Co. L., Newton., N. Carolina, U. S. A. [26145] 12/07/1976   **CM01/01/1978**

Jennings, Mrs E, BA(Hons) MCLIP, Stud., Robert Gordon Univ., & Inf. Lib., Univ. of Bath [58027] 19/10/1999 **CM19/03/2008**

Jennings, Miss M, BA DipLIS ALAI, Asst. L., Mater Dei Inst. of Educ., Dublin. [10016602] 16/04/2010 **ME**

Jennings, Miss R, BSc, Unknown. [10014097] 25/06/2009 **ME**

Jennings, Ms S C, B. Th. (CANTAB) PGDip. Th. MCLIP MA, Acting Joint Lib., Faculty of Architecture & Hist. of Art, Univ. of Cambridge. [10001966] 29/03/2007 **CM27/01/2010**

Jennings, Ms S L, Outreach Lib., Lancashire Care NHS Foundation Trust. [49064] 01/10/1993 **ME**

Jennings, Ms S L, BSc MA, Web & Interactive Media Mgr., Specialist Sch. & Academy Trust [10007200] 27/08/1996 **ME**

Jennings-Young, Mrs S, BA(Hons) MA MCLIP, Millfield Sch. [35528] 29/10/1982 **CM10/05/1988**

Jeorrett, Mr P W, BA PGDip MCLIP, User Serv. Mgr., Glyndwr Univ., Wrexham [26825] 19/11/1976 **CM17/07/1981**

Jephson, Mrs H, ACLIP, Unknown. [10012473] 10/02/2009 **ACL12/02/2010**

Jepson, Ms A, MLS MCLIP, Team Leader, Books Reading & Learning, Staffordshire Moorlands. [11734] 20/10/1969 **CM26/07/1973**

Jervis, Mrs B, BSc(Hons) MA MCLIP, Sch.'s L. Serv. Mgr. [55410] 10/10/1997 **CM15/05/2002**

Jervis, Mrs J M, BA MCLIP, p. /t. Asst. Co. Reserve Stock, W. Sussex C.C., Worthing. [22087] 28/01/1974 **CM14/11/1978**

Jeskins, Miss L J, BA(Hons) MSc MCLIP, Mimas Devel. Offr. [58732] 01/07/2000 **CM10/07/2002**

Jesmont, Mrs C J, MA DipLib MCLIP, Lib., Strathclyde Police, Force L., E. Kilbride. [33445] 01/01/1981 **CM01/07/1990**

Jess, Mr D, BA DipLib MLS CDipAF MCLIP, Asst. Ch. Lib., Belfast Ed. & L. Board, NI. [10002011] 22/10/1973 **CM21/09/1977**

Jesson, Rev A F, MA MLS FCLIP, Rector of Outwell; Rector of Upwell. [7830] 26/01/1966 **FE27/03/1991**

Jewell, Mr E E, BA(Hons) MA MCLIP, Customer Serv. Lib., Guille-Alles L., Guernsey. [56510] 30/07/1998 **CM16/05/2001**

Jewell, Mr E M, BSc, Reg. L. Mgr., Llanelli Pub. L., Carmarthenshire. [62322] 29/04/2003 **ME**

Jewell, Miss R E, BSc (Hons) Maths Stats Comp, Stud. IOD. Inf. Cent., London [10001399] 14/02/2007 **ME**

Jewitt, Miss V, L. Yth. Offr., Redcar & Cleveland. [55493] 15/10/1997 **ME**

Jhavary, Mr A C, BA DipLib, L. Asst., Tavistock & Portman NHS Trust, London. [41754] 11/03/1988 **ME**

Jimenez-Milian, Mr A P, BA MA MCLIP, Asst. Lib., York Minster L. [10009947] 24/06/2008 **CM27/01/2010**

Jin, Mrs H, MSc, L. Asst., Mary Seacole L., Univ. of C. England,Birmingham. [65921] 06/07/2006 **ME**

Job, Mr D E V, MCLIP, Life Member. [7841] 01/01/1950 **CM01/01/1953**

Job, Ms D M, MA DipLIS, Dir. of L. Serv., The Univ. of Birmingham. [51905] 03/08/1995 **ME**

Jobbins, Miss L, Stud. [10014569] 17/08/2009 **ME**

Jobey, Ms A, BA MCLIP, Collections & Reader Devel. Mgr., Sheffield City Council. [31078] 01/06/1977 **CM24/09/1980**

Jobling, Mr M W, BA MCLIP, Retired [27582] 06/01/1970 **CM01/01/1974**

Jocys, Mr T, Unknown. [10007718] 21/02/2008 **ME**

Joglekar, Mr P L, BSc DipLib MISTC MCLIP, Retired. [26118] 01/02/1973 **CM15/07/1976**

Johannessen, Miss H, BA, Serv. Asst. (PT). [10016542] 14/04/2010 **AF**

John Watson, Mr R D, MA(Oxon) PgDipILS PGCE, Admin Asst., Scottish Assoc. for Mental Health, Aberdeen [54291] 13/11/1996 **ME**

John, Mr A W, MCLIP, Co. Lib., Neath Port Talbot L. HQ, Port Talbot. [10015728] 10/03/1980 **CM01/07/1987**

John, Ms K A, MCLIP, Community Dev. Mgr., Caerphilly L. [32430] 21/03/1980 **CM29/04/1983**

John, Mr K R, BA MSc MCLIP, Lib., The Ref. L., Huddersfield L. [10006779] 04/04/2000 **CM16/04/2010**

John, Miss L F, MSc Econ, Inf. Offr., Inst. of Directors, London. [10015625] 01/01/2010 **ME**

John, Mrs L J, BLib MCLIP, LRC Mgr., S. Leicestershire Coll. [30917] 28/06/1979 **CM22/10/1982**

Johns, Mrs H C, BSc (Hons) ACLIP, Inf. Serv. Asst., Univ. Plymouth [10007016] 04/01/2008 **ACL17/06/2009**

Johns, Miss J A, BA FCLIP, Sen. Ref. Lib., Cent. L., Romford. [25569] 26/01/1976 **FE09/08/1988**

Johns, Mrs J M, BSc(Econ) MCLIP, Retired. [7859] 26/05/1971 **CM31/12/1973**

Johnsen, Mrs J, MCLIP, Retired. [7860] 19/02/1960 **CM01/01/1965**

Johnson, Mr A R I, BA(Hons) ECDL, L. Asst., Donald Mason L., Liverpool Sch. of Tropical Med. [61493] 22/08/2002 **ME**

Johnson, Ms A, Project Coordinator, Skelly & Couch LLP, London. [10013092] 24/03/2009 **ME**

Johnson, Miss A, BA(Hons) MA PGCE MLitt, Stud., Loughborough Univ. [10015735] 19/01/2010 **ME**

Johnson, Mr B G, DipInf, Unemployed. [53312] 02/05/1996 **ME**

Johnson, Miss B L, Temp. Lib. [54336] 20/11/1996 **ME**

Johnson, Mr B, BA MA, Dep. Catalogue Lib., Inst. of Educ., Univ. of London. [64024] 02/12/2004 **ME**

Johnson, Ms C A, BA MA, Subject Lib., Univ. of E. London, London [10001415] 11/12/2002 **ME**

Johnson, Miss C H, BA, Stud., Aberystwyth. [65082] 01/11/2005 **ME**

Johnson, Mrs D S, Stud. [10013652] 18/05/2009 **ME**

Johnson, Mr D, BA DipLib MCLIP, Catr., Brit. L. Boston Spa, W. Yorks. [37948] 28/11/1984 **CM08/03/1988**

Johnson, Mrs E E, FCLIP, Life Member. [7879] 15/10/1937 **FE01/01/1950**

Johnson, Mr F V, LLB DMS MCLIP, Retired [7883] 05/07/1972 **CM28/10/1974**

Johnson, Mr G J, BSc MSc F. HEA MCLIP, LRA Mgr. & Info. Lib., Univ. Leicester [53304] 25/04/1996 **CM06/04/2005**

Johnson, Mrs G, MA MCLIP, Retired. [7885] 04/02/1964 **CM01/01/1968**

Johnson, Ms H F, BA MA MSc MCLIP PGCAP FHEA, Academic Liaison Lib., Univ. of Bedfordshire, Bedford [53530] 09/07/1996 **CM16/05/2001**

Johnson, Ms H J, BA MA MCLIP, Dir. Inf. Serv., Univ. of Northampton [20614] 05/05/1973 **CM01/01/1979**

Johnson, Miss H, Lib., Tobago House of Assembly, L. Serv. Dept., W. Indies. [61035] 05/02/2002 **ME**

Johnson, Prof I M, BA FCLIP FCMI, Dep. of Inf. Mgmnt., Aberdeen Business Sch., The Robert Gordon Univ. [7889] 06/03/1963 **FE26/01/1994**

Johnson, Ms J M, BA DipLib MCLIP, Due Diligence Researcher, Exec. Profiles Ltd, London. [26426] 23/10/1976 **CM12/06/1980**

Johnson, Mrs J, MCLIP, L. Asst., Cheshire C.C. [3700] 22/01/1970 **CM20/07/1972**

Johnson, Miss K C, BA PgDip, Knowledge Cent. Analyst., J R Knowles Ltd, Warrington. [10009809] 12/06/2008 **ME**

Johnson, Miss K F, BA MSc, Info. Skills Trainer, TavistockTtrust L., London. [58075] 25/10/1999 **ME**

Johnson, Miss K M, Stud. [10017140] 14/07/2010 **ME**

Johnson, Miss L C, MLS MCLIP, Collections Consultant, Coutts Inf. Serv. [25326] 15/01/1976 **CM06/06/1980**

Johnson, Mrs L G, MCLIP, Inf. Lib., L.B. of Sutton. [1649] 01/10/1971 **CM09/08/1974**

Johnson, Miss L J, BA, Unknown. [10006422] 19/10/2007 **ME**

Johnson, Mrs L, BA MA, Inf. Offr., Newcastle Univ. [56772] 12/10/1998 **ME**

Johnson, Mrs M D, Retired [12310] 10/11/1971 **ME**

Johnson, Miss M E, BA(Hons), Performance & Excellence Mgr. Adult & Communities Serv. Directorate Suffolk C.C. Ipswich. [51985] 31/08/1995 **ME**

Johnson, Mrs M E, Msc Info. Sci., Unknown. [10015940] 28/01/2010**ME**

Johnson, Ms M S, MA(Hons) MA MCLIP, Project Mgr., IDOX plc., Glasgow. [62090] 12/02/2003 **CM21/05/2008**

Johnson, Mrs M, BA MCLIP, Comm. Lib. Serv. Mgr., Warrington B. C., Stockton Heath L. [46716] 02/01/1992 **CM21/07/1993**

Johnson, Miss M, MA FCLIP, Life Member [7899] 01/01/1939 **FE16/09/1952**

Johnson, Ms M, BA(Hons) DipLib LLA MCLIP, LRC Mgr., Treloar Coll., Alton. [34089] 06/10/1981 **CM07/09/2005**

Johnson, Ms M, MA, p. /t. Customer Serv. Mgr., Hackney L., London. [51683] 28/04/1995 **ME**

Johnson, Mrs N, MCLIP, Sen. L. Customer Care Asst., Newcastle Coll. L. [63320] 13/04/2004 **CM09/07/2008**

Johnson, Mrs P A, MCLIP, Head of L. & Customer Operations., Univ. of Derby [20298] 29/01/1973 **CM10/08/1976**

Johnson, Mr P B, BA MA MCLIP, Inf. Consultant, Royal Holloway [61839] 15/11/2002 **CM31/01/2007**

Johnson, Mr P J, BA MCLIP, Arch., Herefordshire Records Off., Hereford. [36474] 15/10/1983 **CM04/12/1987**

Johnson, Mr P, BA MCLIP, Retired. [43280] 02/02/1964 **CM01/01/1967**

Johnson, Mrs P, MA, Sen. Inf. Advisor, Sheffield Hallam Univ. [10016450] 24/03/2010 **ME**

Johnson, Miss R A, Sch. Lib., Kings Manor Comm. Coll., Shoreham by Sea. [60979] 22/01/2002 **ME**

Johnson, Mr R A, Unknown [65862] 09/06/2006 **ME**

Johnson, Mrs R D A, BA MCLIP, Sch. Lib., Maidwell Hall Sch., Northants. [26223] 12/08/1976 **CM16/09/1980**

Johnson, Dr R E, MA MCLIP, Res. Lib., Univ. of Worcester [23689] 23/01/1975 **CM25/05/1978**

Johnson, Mrs R L, MCLIP, Community Lib., Norfolk C.C. Cultural Serv., Norwich [7643] 01/01/1971 **CM05/08/1974**

Johnson, Ms R N, BA MA MCLIP, Part -Time (Non-Lis) [43199] 03/10/1989 **CM20/03/1996**

Johnson, Mrs R, BSc(Econ) MCLIP, Area Mgr: N., Bournemouth L. & Arts. [56996] 19/11/1998 **CM23/06/2004**

Johnson, Ms R, BA MSc, Resources & Inf. Worker/Weekend Co-ordinator, Sheffield. [51700] 22/05/1995 **ME**

Johnson, Mrs S E, BA(Hons) MSc, Asst. Subject Lib. Media, Chester Univ., Warrington. [58836] 25/08/2000 **ME**

Johnson, Mr S J, BA DipLib MCLIP, Info. &Learning Servs. Mgr., Blackpool P.L., Blackpool. [36186] 13/07/1983 **CM15/03/1989**

Johnson, Mrs S, ACLIP, L. Asst., Sutton-in-Ashfield L., Notts. [65330] 12/01/2006 **ACL29/03/2007**

Johnson, Miss T J, MA(Hons) MCLIP, Position unknown, Sandwell M.B.C., Oldbury. [43432] 26/10/1989 **CM16/07/2003**

Johnson, Mrs W, MLIS, Inf. Offr., Linklaters, London [10007866] 26/02/2008 **ME**

Johnson, Mrs Y K, BEd MCLIP, Freelance Law Lib. [39632] 07/04/1986 **CM12/12/1990**

Johnson, Mrs Z, BA(Hons) MA MCLIP, Sen. Asst. Lib., Huddersfield Univ. [58929] 06/10/2000 **CM23/06/2004**

Johnston, Miss A G, BA MCLIP, Sch. Lib., Dunbar Grammar Sch., Dunbar. [22631] 03/07/1974 **CM26/08/1980**

Johnston, Miss A M, BA DipLib MCLIP, Career break [43034] 13/07/1989 **CM21/07/1993**

Johnston, Mr A R, BA FSA SCOT MCLIP, Retired. [7922] 01/04/1970 **CM09/07/1974**

Johnston, Miss A, BA(Hons) MCLIP, Resident in S. Africa. [26978] 03/10/1976 **CM17/08/1988**

Johnston, Miss E, MA(Hons) MCLIP, Learning Cent. Coordinator, W. Cheshire Coll. [59867] 18/10/2001 **CM23/01/2008**

Johnston, Mrs F E, BLS MCLIP, Career Break. [39429] 19/01/1986 **CM22/05/1996**

Johnston, Dr J O D, DipMgmt(OU) BSc MSc MCLIP, Int. Nepal Fellowship, Nepal. [60401] 03/10/1972 **CM12/10/1973**

Johnston, Miss K, BA(Hons) MA, Performance Analyst, Southern Water, E. Sussex. [56817] 23/10/1998 **ME**

Johnston, Miss L A, BA(Hons) MA, Aquisition. Lib., London Coll. of Fashion L., London [63407] 05/05/2004 **ME**

Johnston, Mrs M, BA MCLIP, Learning Cent. Coordinator, Forth Valley Coll. of F. & H.E. [28337] 27/10/1977 **CM30/11/1983**

Johnston, Mr N E, BA PGDip, Higher L. Exec., House of Commons L., London. [61036] 01/02/2002 **ME**

Johnston, Mrs R A, BA MA MCLIP, Lib., Manor Lodge Sch., Hertfordshire [37399] 09/08/1984 **CM04/10/1988**

Johnston, Mrs S E, BA MLS, Retired. [29454] 18/08/1978 **ME**

Johnston, Mrs S M, BSc MSc FCLIP, Retired. [60402] 19/12/1972 **FE01/03/1986**

Johnston, Mr W C P, BA, Customer Serv. Bibl., Yankee Book Peddler Ltd [41846] 17/03/1988 **ME**

Johnstone, Mr G T, BA(Hons) MCLIP, Lib., L. Support, Falkirk L. Serv. [61401] 09/07/2002 **CM29/03/2006**

Johnstone, Mrs J A, BA MSc, Lib., Scottish Poetry Lib., Edinburgh. [61144] 11/03/2002 **ME**

Johnstone, Miss J C, MA MCLIP, Sch. & Comm. Lib., Highland Council. Acharacle [31339] 01/10/1979 **CM26/10/1982**

Johnstone, Mrs J M, BA(Hons), Msc, Inf. Off., MOD. [10001300] 26/01/2007 **ME**

Johnstone, Miss L A, BA(Hons) MSc, Business Researcher., Allen & Overy., London [62574] 16/09/2003 **ME**

Joice, Mrs S M, BA MCLIP, Customer Serv. Mgr, Fife Council L. and Museums Serv. [10006122] 11/09/2007 **CM01/11/1977**

Joint, Mr N C, BA MA, Head of Ref. & Inf., Univ. of Strathclyde, Andersonian L., Glasgow. [38275] 15/02/1985 **ME**

Jolley, Miss A, Lib. Asst., Learning Resources for Educ., Northampton C.C. [10005880] 03/08/2007 **AF**

Jolley, Mrs M A, Lib. Asst. [10017280] 22/07/2010 **AF**

Jolly, Miss J, MCLIP, Retired. [7945] 01/01/1961 **CM01/01/1970**

Jolly, Ms L, BA(Hons) DipILS FCLIP FRSA, Dir., L. and Inf. Serv., Teesside Univ., Middlesbrough. [43745] 14/12/1989 **FE03/10/2007**

Jones Court, Ms A J, MSc BA(Hons) PgDipILS MCLIP, Chartered Lib., Caerphilly Co. Bor. Council [61637] 07/10/2002 **CM29/11/2006**

Jones, Mr A C, MCLIP, Retired. [61240] 08/09/1983 **CM01/04/2002**

Jones, Miss A E N, BA(Hons) MSc(Econ) MCLIP, Lib. Arch., Glasgow Mus. Res. Cent. [36683] 07/11/1983 **CM19/06/1991**

Jones, Miss A E, BA(Hons) MCLIP, Lib., Telford & Wrekin Council. [61021] 01/02/2002 **CM31/01/2007**

Jones, Mrs A E, BLIB MCLIP, Unknown [29688] 10/10/1978 **CM01/12/1982**

Jones, Mrs A H, MA(Oxon) MA MPhil, Lib., Wolfson Coll., Cambridge. [54024] 23/10/1996 **ME**

Jones, Mrs A J, BLib MSc MCLIP, Asst. Commissioner, Inf. Commissioners Off., Wilmslow. [21126] 12/10/1973 **CM01/01/1981**

Jones, Mrs A J, BA, Career Break. [43023] 21/06/1989 **ME**

Jones, Mrs A J, Retired. [7953] 14/09/1967 **ME**

Jones, Miss A K, BA(Hons) ACLIP, L. Asst., Leicester Coll. [10015775] 25/01/2010 **ACL16/06/2010**

Jones, Mrs A M A, BA DipLib MCLIP, Asst. Subj. Lib. (Business)/Inf. Mgr. (Careers), Cardiff Univ. [40170] 06/11/1986 **CM27/02/1991**

Jones, Mrs A M, BA MCLIP, P/t. Inf. Lib., Kingston Univ., Kingston upon Thames. [28694] 13/01/1978 **CM07/10/1981**

Jones, Mrs A M, MCLIP, Retired. [7955] 10/10/1967 **CM01/01/1970**

Jones, Mr A R, BA MCLIP, Res. Cent. Co-ordinator, Nat. Stem Cent., York. [43513] 01/11/1989 **CM17/05/2000**

Jones, Ms A R, BA(Hons) DipInf, Strategic Mgr., City of York L., York. [37057] 21/01/1984 **ME**

Jones, Mr A W, BA(Hons), Trainee Lib., Caernarfon L., [10010854] 02/09/2008 **ME**

Jones, Miss A, MCLIP, Cultural Serv. Offr., Port Talbot. [20261] 24/02/1973 **CM01/11/1977**

Jones, Mr A, MCLIP, Life Member. [7947] 26/02/1947 **CM01/01/1956**

Jones, Mrs A, FCLIP, Life Member. [7950] 22/01/1952 **FE05/05/1980**

Jones, Mrs A, MLib MCLIP, Princ. Lib., Monmouthshire C.C. [27315] 03/03/1977 **CM05/02/1981**

Jones, Mrs A, BA DipLib MCLIP, Unemployed. [37100] 21/02/1984 **CM10/05/1988**

Jones, Mrs A, BLib MCLIP, Unemployed. [28123] 23/09/1977 **CM31/08/1982**

Jones, Mr B P, BA DipLib FCLIP, Life Member [7966] 01/01/1960 **FE01/01/1968**

Jones, Mrs B, MCLIP, Dev. Mgr., Cent. L., Birmingham [41264] 21/10/1987 **CM05/05/2010**

Jones, Mr C A S, BLib MCLIP, Sen. Mgr., Stream Lead, Redhill L., Redhill, Surrey. [43855] 30/01/1990 **CM26/05/1993**

Jones, Miss C E, Head of Learning Res. Cent., Burgess Hill Sch. for Girls., W. Sussex. [62794] 22/10/2003 **ME**

Jones, Mr C F, BA(Hons) MA, Unwaged. [10011010] 12/09/2008 **ME**

Jones, Mr C G, Unknown. [10012392] 03/02/2009 **ME**

Jones, Miss C L, MA(Hons) DipILS MCLIP, Mgr., Inf. & Learning Resources, City of Edinburgh Council. [41748] 01/03/1988 **CM15/08/1990**

Jones, Mrs C M, BSc MCLIP, Inf. Skills Traininer., Bromley Hosp. NHS Trust. [61915] 03/12/2002 **CM21/03/2007**

Jones, Mrs C M, BSc DipIM MCLIP, Inf. Systems Project Mgr., Sci. & Tech. Facilities Council [52932] 25/01/1996 **CM12/03/2003**

Jones, Mrs C M, BA MCLIP, Life Member [7979] 07/01/1964 **CM01/01/1967**

Jones, Ms C M, BSc, Stud., Aberystwyth Univ. [10015077] 12/10/2009 **ME**

Jones, Mr C M, BA MCLIP, Unknown. [10000645] 23/10/2006 **CM10/03/2010**

Jones, Dr C V, PhD, Independent Scholar. [10006080] 24/08/2007 **ME**

Jones, Mrs C, DipLib, Lib. Offr., W. Barnes L. New Malden. [42800] 01/03/1989 **ME**

Jones, Mrs C, BA MCLIP, Retired. [7972] 12/04/1970 **CM23/10/1972**

Jones, Ms C, Unknown. [10016948] 10/06/2010 **ME**

Jones, Mrs E A, BSc MSc, Inf. Scientist, AstraZeneca, Loughborough. [61796] 08/11/2002 **ME**

Jones, Mrs E L, BA(Hons) MCLIP, Cent. Mgr. /Lib. Serv. Mgr., Swansea Psychiatric Educ. Cent. Cefn Coed Hosp. [49578] 19/11/1993 **CM22/09/1999**

Jones, Miss E L, BA(Hons) PGDipMSc, Web Portal Devel. Co-ordinator., Nat. Sci. Learning Cent., Univ. of York. [58111] 01/11/1999 **ME**

Jones, Miss E M, MCLIP, Retired. [8010] 01/01/1970 **CM08/09/1976**

Jones, Mr E, MA DipMgmt MCLIP, Customer Serv. Mgr., Knowsley L. Serv., Merseyside. [7987] 01/01/1968 **CM01/01/1971**

Jones, Miss E, BA(Hons) MA MCLIP, Sen. Asst. Lib., Manchester Metro. Univ. [58586] 05/04/2000 **CM19/11/2003**

Jones, Ms F A, BA DipLib, Asst. Lib., St Mary's Univ. Coll., Belfast. [25171] 31/10/1975 **ME**

Jones, Mrs G A, BA(Hons) MCLIP, Collections Team Leader, Calderdale M.B.C., Halifax, W. Yorks. [30743] 04/04/1979 **CM18/10/1983**

Jones, Mrs G D, BA MA MCLIP, Lib.,L. Skills Trainer, E. & N. Herts. NHS Trust. [29762] 05/10/1978 **CM31/10/1980**

Jones, Mr G E, BA(Hons), Lib., Min. of Justice., Reg. Lib., HOVE, Crown Court [49121] 06/10/1993 **ME**

Jones, Mrs G H, BLib MCLIP, Sch. Lib. Asst., Ysgol Glan Clwyd.,Denbighshire C.C. [27088] 19/01/1977 **CM20/08/1981**

Jones, Mr G L, FCLIP, Retired. [8020] 28/04/1955 **FE01/01/1967**

Jones, Mr G T, BA MSc, Unknown, Savills Plc, London. [60403] 02/07/1981 **ME**

Jones, Mr G W, BLIB MCLIP, Asst. Lib., Ammanford L. Dyfed C.C. [40799] 26/06/1987 **CM27/02/1991**

Jones, Mr G W, BA(Hons) DipILS MCLIP, L. & Inf. Center Mgr., Islay High Sch., Isle of Islay. [52450] 02/11/1995 **CM13/03/2002**

Jones, Miss G, Retired. [8018] 04/01/1933 **ME**

Jones, Mrs H C, MCLIP, Learning Resources Serv. Mgr., Bedford Coll. [24092] 19/04/1975 **CM06/12/1979**

Jones, Miss H C, BA, Sr. Catr., Tower Project, Univ. Lib., Cambridge [10000752] 02/11/2006 **ME**

Jones, Miss H E, BA, Classifier, Stevenage, Herts. [56915] 04/11/1998 **ME**

Jones, Mrs H J, BA MCLIP, Mimas Devel. Offr. (Intute Content Editor), Univ. of Manchester. [30767] 04/04/1979 **CM10/10/1983**

Jones, Mrs H L, BA(Hons) MCLIP, LISS Mgr. (Learning Resources), Univ. of Cumbria. [40383] 26/01/1987 **CM22/03/1995**

Jones, Mrs H M, BSc(Hons)MSc DipEd MCLIP, Life Member. [19870] 01/01/1973 **CM21/04/1975**

Jones, Mrs H, Document Supply Lib., The IET L., London. [10006125] 11/09/2007 **AF**

Jones, Mrs J A, BSc(Econ)(Hons), Bookstart Devel. Offr., Herts. C.C. [51196] 23/11/1994 **ME**

Jones, Mr J E, BA, Stud., Northumbria Univ. [10014431] 30/07/2009 **ME**

Jones, Mrs J L, Lib. Asst., Univ. of Chester, Ellesmere Port [10015036] 09/10/2009 **AF**

Jones, Mrs J S H, MCLIP, Team Lib., Bedford Cent. L. [12570] 01/01/1970 **CM16/01/1974**

Jones, Mrs J S, B LIB MCLIP, Learning Res. Cent. Mgr., Hereford 6th Form Coll. [27219] 11/01/1977 **CM08/08/1980**

Jones, Mrs J, BA MCLIP, Inf. Serv. Lib., Oxford, Oxfordshire C.C. [11621] 30/09/1971 **CM25/11/1974**

Jones, Mrs J, BA MCLIP, Sen. Br. Lib., Neath & Port Talbot L. & Inf. Serv., Neath L. [24302] 07/06/1975 **CM02/02/1978**

Jones, Miss J, BA(Hons) MA, Unknown. [10012398] 03/02/2009 **ME**

Jones, Mrs K D, LL B MCLIP, Lib., Cheshire C.C. [2092] 28/06/1965 **CM01/01/1969**

Jones, Miss K E, Stud. [10000472] 09/10/2006 **ME**

Jones, Ms K L, MAppSc MCLIP, Res. Publications Lib., Univ. of Bath L. [64929] 13/09/2005 **CM17/09/2008**

Jones, Mrs K M, BA MA MCLIP, Sen. L. Asst., Univ. of Wales Swansea. [43596] 09/11/1989 **CM26/05/1993**

Jones, Mrs K, BA DipLib MCLIP, Lib., Wimbledon High Sch., London. [24754] 01/10/1975 **CM08/03/1979**

Jones, Mrs L I, BA DipLib MCLIP, Subject Lib. (Law and Criminology), Univ. of Portsmouth. [26935] 10/01/1977 **CM06/03/1979**

Jones, Miss L M, BA MLIS, Sen. Res. Lib., Lewis Silkin, [10001206] 02/02/2007 **ME**

Jones, Mrs L U, MSc MCLIP, Ret. [28838] 30/01/1978 **CM29/09/1980**

Jones, Mr M A, Learning Resource Asst, Coleg Llandrillo [10016112] 12/02/2010 **ME**

Jones, Miss M A, Learning Resource Mgr., Internat. Business Sch., Isle of Man. [48821] 09/06/1993 **ME**

Jones, Mr M A, BA(Hons) DipILS MCLIP, Marketing Intelligence Exec., Scottish Power, Glasgow. [54545] 17/01/1997 **CM26/11/2001**

Jones, Ms M A, BSc, Stud.,The Hon. Soc. of Gray's Inn, London [10001392] 14/02/2007 **ME**

Jones, Mrs M E, BLib MCLIP LMusTCL LTCL, Stock L., L.B. of Hammersmith & Fulham [27628] 24/05/1977 **CM22/10/1980**

Jones, Mrs M F, BA(Hons) MCLIP, Life Member. [30322] 23/01/1979 **CM08/10/1981**

Jones, Mr M G, BA, Unknown. [35057] 15/06/1982 **ME**

Jones, Mrs M H, MA BSc(Hons) PGCE, Asst. Lib., Hadlow Coll.,
Tonbridge. [62652] 01/10/2003   **ME**
Jones, Miss M J, BA(Hons) MLitt ACLIP, L. Asst., Harpenden P. L.
[10009805] 11/06/2008   **ACL04/03/2009**
Jones, Mrs M L, BA(Hons), Stud. [10016692] 28/04/2010   **ME**
Jones, Mr M P, BA(Hons) MA, Community and Inf. Offr., N. Yorkshire
C.C. [64235] 22/02/2005   **ME**
Jones, Mr M P, BA(Hons) DipLib MCLIP, Head of Inf. Serv., Napier
Univ., Edinburgh. [37088] 04/02/1984   **CM08/12/1987**
Jones, Miss M, MCLIP, Asst. Head of L. & Heritage Serv., L.B. of
Wandsworth. [8058] 13/10/1970   **CM27/01/1975**
Jones, Mrs M, Resource Cent. Asst. Nat. Sci. Cent. York [10011697]
11/11/2008   **ME**
Jones, Mrs M, MCLIP, Retired [29545] 01/01/1954   **CM02/04/1982**
Jones, Mr M, MCLIP, Retired. [8051] 01/01/1965   **CM01/01/1969**
Jones, Mr M, B LIB MCLIP, Strategic Mgr., Swindon L. Serv. [29699]
05/10/1978   **CM03/02/1982**
Jones, Mrs M, MA, Unknown. [10010857] 27/01/2009   **AF**
Jones, Mrs N M, BA MCLIP, Complex Mgr. (Job Share), Heswall L.,
Wirral [23206] 04/11/1974   **CM07/11/1978**
Jones, Miss N W, BLib MCLIP, Community Lib., Mold L., Flintshire C.C.
[33943] 04/06/1981   **CM06/07/1987**
Jones, Ms N, BA MA, Inf. Analyst, Cushman & Wakefield, London.
[10002673] 05/03/2001   **ME**
Jones, Mrs P A, BSc DipLib MCLIP, Freelance Inf. Sci. /Journalist.
[28606] 19/01/1978   **CM25/01/1980**
Jones, Mr P E, MCLIP, Retired. [8076] 06/03/1957   **CM01/01/1962**
Jones, Mr P F, BA MCLIP, Serv. Devel. Mgr., Tameside M.B.C., L. Serv.
Unit. [8077] 06/10/1970   **CM16/07/1975**
Jones, Mr P H, MA FCLIP, Retired. [8078] 02/01/1968   **FE16/08/1977**
Jones, Mrs P J, BA PGDip, L. Asst., Merchant Taylors'Sch., Northwood.
[61266] 13/05/2002   **ME**
Jones, Mrs P L, BA(Hons) MA MCLIP, Unknown [57232] 15/01/1999
                                                              CM21/05/2003
Jones, Mr P N, BA(Hons) MA, Lib. [10008600] 02/04/2008   **ME**
Jones, Mr P R J, DipLib, Sen. Inf. Offr., Cent. Ref. L., Richmond.
[46143] 07/10/1991   **ME**
Jones, Miss P, JP MCLIP, Life Member. [8074] 11/06/1952
                                                              CM01/01/1962
Jones, Ms P, BA MCLIP, Reading & Learning Serv. Mgr., Knowsley
M.B.C., Page Moss L. [27688] 01/07/1977   **CM30/06/1980**
Jones, Mr R A, DipLib MCLIP, Head of L. & Arch., Denbighshire C.C.
[33009] 20/10/1980   **CM19/07/1984**
Jones, Miss R A, BA, Stud., Aberystwyth Univ., [10011157] 29/09/2008
                                                                       ME
Jones, Mr R B, BA DipLib MCLIP, Collections Support Unit Mgr., Nat. L.
of / Wales, Aberystwyth. [35436] 01/10/1982   **CM16/02/1988**
Jones, Mr R B, BA MCLIP, Mgmt. Inf. Offr., Cult. & Comm. Serv. Dept.,
Derbys. C.C. [28438] 07/12/1977   **CM05/02/1980**
Jones, Miss R C M, MA DipLib MCLIP, Asst. Lib., Welsh Assembly
Gov., Cardiff [43450] 26/10/1989   **CM31/01/1996**
Jones, Miss R E, BA BSc(Econ) B. Th DipLib MCLIP, Inf. Asst.,
Aberystwyth Univ., Llambadarn Campus [41385] 17/11/1987
                                                              CM19/07/2000
Jones, Mr R F, BA MA, Stud. [10016538] 13/04/2010   **ME**
Jones, Miss R J H, BA(Hons) PgDip, Dep. Lib. Serv. Mgr., Manchester
Met. Univ. [61726] 29/10/2002   **ME**
Jones, Mr R J, BA CertEd MCLIP, L. Offr., L. H.Q., Cowes, Isle of Wight.
[26979] 16/01/1977   **CM20/07/1981**
Jones, Mr R L, GradDipMus DipLib MCLIP, Asst. Lib., The Barbican
Music L., London. [45567] 15/03/1991   **CM27/07/1994**
Jones, Mr R M, BA MLS MCLIP, Brit. Med. Assoc. L., London. [34413]
05/11/1981   **CM02/06/1987**

Jones, Mrs R M, BMus CertEd MA, Sch. Librr., Chetham's Sch. of Music,
Manchester. [44297] 21/08/1990   **ME**
Jones, Miss R S, BA(Hons) MA MCLIP, Child. Lib., York Gardens L.,
London. [59796] 03/10/2001   **CM19/03/2008**
Jones, Mr R S, BA(Hons), Info. & E-Serv. Mngr., Ref. & Info. Serv., L.B.
of Hammersmith & Fulham. [32668] 01/07/1980   **ME**
Jones, Miss R, BA(Hons) DipIM MCLIP, Asst. Lib., Applied Sciences.,
De Montfort Univ. Leics. [54032] 21/10/1996   **CM23/01/2002**
Jones, Mrs R, MCLIP, L. Serv. Promoter, Bangor L., Bangor. [8085]
01/01/1970   **CM19/07/1974**
Jones, Dr R, BA MCLIP, Sch. Lib., Malvern St. James [47525]
01/10/1992   **CM20/09/1995**
Jones, Miss S A, BSc MA, Circ. Lib., Regents Coll. L., London. [64635]
27/04/2005   **ME**
Jones, Miss S A, BSc DipLib MCLIP, Inf. Offr. - Law, Liverpool John
Moores Univ., Aldham Robarts Learning Res. Cent. [37909]
15/11/1984   **CM09/08/1988**
Jones, Miss S A, BA DipLib MCLIP, Unknown [36561] 18/10/1983
RV01/10/2008   **CM15/11/1988**
Jones, Miss S C, MA(Hons) PG DipILS MCLIP, Dep. Head Army L. &
Inf. Serv., Germany. [54658] 12/02/1997   **CM09/11/2005**
Jones, Miss S D, BA DipLib MCLIP, Asst. Lib., City of Sunderland
Community & Cultural Serv. [39221] 01/01/1986   **CM15/02/1989**
Jones, Miss S E, BA MCLIP, Asst. Lib., St Catherine's Coll., Univ. of
Oxford. [63082] 27/01/2004   **CM05/05/2010**
Jones, Mrs S E, BScEcon MScEcon MCLIP, Ch. Lib., Vale of
Glamorgan Council, Barry. [23596] 16/01/1975   **CM01/01/1977**
Jones, Mrs S E, BA MA MCLIP, Retired [41305] 01/01/1962
                                                              CM23/08/1966
Jones, Mrs S E, BA(Hons), Stud., Aberystwyth Univ. [10009716]
03/06/2008   **ME**
Jones, Mrs S J, B SOC SC MCLIP, Lib. Music L., Birmingham L. Serv.,
Birmingham. [18054] 18/10/1972   **CM24/03/1975**
Jones, Mr S J, BA, Unknown. [10014627] 25/08/2009   **ME**
Jones, Ms S L, Business Info. Offr. at the Inst of Dir, Pall Mall, London
[62874] 17/11/2003   **ME**
Jones, Mrs S L, BA(Hons), Lib. Asst., Abingdon Lib. Oxon. [10001959]
22/03/2007   **AF**
Jones, Mr S M, BSc, Unknown. [10016569] 14/04/2010   **AF**
Jones, Mrs S, MCLIP, Inf. Resources Offr., Wirral Met. Coll.,
Birkenhead. [29420] 18/07/1978   **CM18/07/1980**
Jones, Mr S, L. Super., Ross-on-Wye L. [10016456] 26/03/2010   **AF**
Jones, Mrs S, BA DipLib MCLIP, Princ. Lib. -Inf., Serv. & Ref., Jersey L.
[41405] 25/11/1987   **CM12/12/1990**
Jones, Mrs S, MCLIP, Retired. [8103] 01/01/1955   **CM01/01/1963**
Jones, Miss S, LLb MA MSc, Support Lib., Welsh Assembly Gov.,
Wales. [10015901] 03/02/2010   **ME**
Jones, Mrs S, BA DipLib MCLIP, Team Leader, Nat. L. Wales [35328]
08/10/1982   **CM14/11/1991**
Jones, Ms T A, L. Mgr., Blaina L., Learning Action Cent., Gwent.
[10015911] 27/01/2010   **AF**
Jones, Mrs T A, BA DipLib MCLIP, Sch. L., Simon Langton Sch.,
Canterbury. [27069] 11/01/1977   **CM24/04/1979**
Jones, Mrs T H, BSc, Researcher, Brunel Univ., Uxbridge, Middx.
[54295] 15/11/1996   **ME**
Jones, Mrs T M, MCLIP, Sen. Lib., Sch. L. Serv., Shropshire C.C.
[26753] 20/11/1976   **CM19/11/1979**
Jones, Mr T R, BA(Hons) DipIA MCLIP, Sen. Lib., Emanuel Sch. L.,
London. [45560] 06/03/1991   **CM25/09/1996**
Jones, Mrs T, BA MCLIP, Stock Spec., Halton Bor. Council. [42707]
10/02/1989   **CM21/07/1993**
Jones, Ms V L, MSc MCLIP, Sen. Lib., Reading and Lend., Oxfordshire
C.C. L. Serv. [58842] 25/08/2000   **CM09/07/2008**

Jones, Mrs V, BSc(Econ) MCLIP, Site Lib., Bridgend Coll., Mid Glam. [45571] 06/03/1991 **CM12/03/2003**

Jones, Mrs W A, BScEcon(Hons) MCLIP, Asst. Lib. (Catg.), Oxford Brookes Univ. [45229] 21/08/1990 **CM23/01/2002**

Jones, Mr W O, BSc DipLib MCLIP, Faculty Lib., Univ. of E. Anglia, Norwich. [37732] 10/10/1984 **CM15/08/1989**

Jones-Evans, Dr A, BLib(Hons) PGCED PhD MCLIP, Independent L. Consultant, Enlli Associates, Cardiff. [39175] 04/12/1985 **CM14/11/1990**

Jordan, Mrs A A, MSc MCLIP, Self Access Language Cent. Mgr., Univ. of Bath, Somerset. [11767] 01/09/1970 **CM01/07/1975**

Jordan, Mrs A M, BA MCLIP, Head of Swindon Lib., Swindon Bor. Co. [24627] 03/10/1975 **CM14/02/1979**

Jordan, Dr A T, BA MCLIP ARCM MLS DLS(Col.), Life Member, Resident Trinidad. [17134] 01/01/1951 **CM01/01/1955**

Jordan, Ms C, PGDip LIS, Unknown. [10016322] 08/03/2010 **ME**

Jordan, Mr H J, BA(Hons) MA, Lib., Chipping Barnet L., L.B. Barnet. [59380] 23/02/2001 **ME**

Jordan, Ms H, BA(Hons), L. &Info. Asst., Leeds Coll. [62577] 03/09/2003 **AF**

Jordan, Mrs J L, BSc MSc MA, Unknown. [10014986] 14/04/1999 **ME**

Jordan, Mr M, BSc(Hons) MA MCLIP, Healthspace Design & Eval. Lead, NHS Nat. Programme for IT, Leeds. [51094] 15/11/1994 **CM20/01/1999**

Jordan, Mrs N J, BA(Hons) MCLIP, Lib., L. Serv. for Educ., Leics. [52322] 26/10/1995 **CM12/03/2003**

Jordan, Mr P, MPhil BSc FCLIP, Retired. [8122] 16/03/1954 **FE01/01/1961**

Jordan, Mr S, Project Mgr., Univ. of Gloucestershire, Cheltenham. [64967] 05/10/2005 **AF**

Joseph, Mrs J A, BA(Hons), L. Mgr., Brit. Inter. Sch., Riyadh. [10016591] 14/04/2010 **ME**

Josh, Mrs H, BA(Hons) MA MCLIP, Primary Dev. Lib., Learning Resources for Educ., Northants C.C. [61793] 08/11/2002 **CM01/02/2006**

Joshi, Ms C, Sch. Lib., Southbank Internat. Sch., London. [10012073] 24/04/2009 **ME**

Jouhal, Ms A, BSc, Res. Assoc., Value Partners, London [10017046] 21/06/2010 **ME**

Jowett, Mrs C E, Unwaged. [10015015] 06/10/2009 **ME**

Jowett, Mr D, BA MCLIP, Lib., Wycliffe Coll., Stonehouse, Glos. [8125] 12/10/1971 **CM30/01/1974**

Joy, Miss K E, BSc MSc, Unknown. [10016324] 08/03/2010 **ME**

Joyce, Mrs E M, BA DipLib MCLIP, Unemployed. [41376] 16/11/1987 **CM22/05/1991**

Joyce, Mrs L, BEd MSc MCLIP, Academic Lib., Leeds Met. Univ. [49851] 07/01/1994 **CM15/05/2002**

Joyce, Miss L, BA(Hons) MCLIP, Child. Lib., Croydon Co., Shirley L., Croydon. [47825] 14/10/1992 **CM19/11/2003**

Joyce, Mrs P, BA(Hons) MCLIP, Asst. Lib. -Bibl. Serv., Somerset C.C., Bridgwater. [18425] 23/10/1972 **CM01/01/1976**

Joye, Mrs G F, BSc(Econ) MCLIP, Retired [49869] 19/01/1994 **CM22/09/1999**

Judd, Mr P M, MA MCLIP, L. Liason Advisor, Northumbria Univ., Newcastle. [25767] 19/03/1976 **CM09/02/1978**

Judge, Ms A, BAgrSc DipLIS ALAI, Teacher of Adults and Inf. Consultant, Freelance [46979] 16/03/1992 **ME**

Judge, Mr J, LLB PG Dip LIS, Unknown. [64346] 07/03/2005 **ME**

Judge, Mrs Y A, BA(Hons) DipLib MCLIP, Sen. Lib., Jumeirah English Speaking Sch., Dubai, United Arab Emirates. [32995] 04/10/1980 **CM11/01/1984**

Judson, Mrs J E, MCLIP, Inf. Offr., Nottingham Community Health [18103] 01/10/1972 **CM07/07/1975**

Julian, Miss L, BA MA MCLIP DMS, Stud. Support Serv. Mgr., Southgate Coll., Southgate. [36508] 18/10/1983 **CM16/09/1992**

Juliusdottir, Mrs S, MS, Asst. Prof., Univ. of Iceland. [41494] 14/01/1988 **ME**

Jung, Mrs I, DipLIng MSc, Solihull Coll. [59267] 23/01/2001 **ME**

Juskaityte, Miss A, Unwaged. [10016677] 18/05/2010 **AF**

Juskaityte, Miss J, Lib. Asst., Sion-Manning RC Sec. Sch., London. [10016917] 10/06/2010 **ME**

K

Kaba, Mr A, MLIS, Unknown. [10013336] 16/04/2009 **ME**

Kadiri, R, Unwaged. [10010174] 08/07/2008 **ME**

Kafetzaki, Mrs J E, BA certED, Lib. (System Mgr), Scottish Natural Heritage, Inverness. [43261] 13/10/1989 **ME**

Kalanzi, Mrs I, BA, Stud., [10011106] 25/09/2008 **ME**

Kale, Miss A, Asst. Lib., Min. of Defence [62665] 01/10/2003 **ME**

Kale, Ms A, BA(Hons) MCLIP, Community Inf. Offr., N. Yorkshire Co. L. [58315] 10/01/2000 **CM31/01/2007**

Kalinda, Ms L L M, MCLIP, Knowledge, L. Inf. Mgr. & E-learning Lead, CPFT, Cambs. [10015366] 14/11/1994 **CM21/05/1997**

Kalivodova, Mrs Z, MA, Unknown. [65017] 10/10/2005 **ME**

Kalsi, Miss B K, Stud. [21227] 08/10/1973 **ME**

Kamal, Mrs P A, Asst. Lib., Dept. for Work & Pensions, London. [62360] 09/05/2003 **ME**

Kamara, Mr I, Stud., Aberystwyth Univ. [10015512] 09/12/2009 **ME**

Kamen, Mrs R H, MBE FCLIP HonFRIBA FRSA, Retired. [23454] 01/01/1975 **FE15/09/1993**

Kammermann, Ms M F, BSc DipInfMan MBIT, Newsletter Editor, HLA News, ALIA Health L. Australia. [62116] 21/02/2003 **ME**

Kan, Ms M Y, MA, Inf. Exec., ICAEW, London. [65184] 17/11/2005 **ME**

Kane, Mrs A D, DipLib MCLIP, Lib., Denefield Sch., Tilehurst Reading [36452] 02/10/1983 **CM29/08/1986**

Kane, Mrs G A, BA MCLIP, Bibl. Serv. Offr., Halton Bor. Council, Cheshire. [33547] 08/01/1981 **CM15/01/1985**

Kane, Miss S M, MCLIP, Retired. [8161] 28/09/1968 **CM18/12/1972**

Kaplish, Ms L, BEng MSc MCLIP, Asst. Lib., Wellcome L., London. [48875] 08/07/1993 **CM12/09/2001**

Kargbo, Mr P A, Unwaged. [65349] 12/01/2006 **ME**

Kargianioti, Mrs E, BA MA, Sen. Offr., Records and Inf., Black Sea Bank, Thessaloniki, Greece. [53876] 07/10/1996 **ME**

Karina, Ms G, Stud., Robert Gordon Univ., Aberdeen. [10016133] 16/02/2010 **ME**

Karn, Miss J C, BA(Hons) MA (His Open) MCLIP, Lib., Blaenau Gwent Co. Bor., Tredegar. [37617] 15/10/1984 **CM16/10/1989**

Karpicki, Miss H, ACLIP, Team Leader, Sowerby Bridge L., Halifax. [10009953] 24/06/2008 **ACL03/12/2008**

Karwat, Mrs A, BA(Hons) MCLIP, Principle Lib., Customer Serv. [39673] 07/05/1986 **CM15/05/2002**

Kasaey Fard, Mrs H, BA, LRC Counter Asst., Coll. of N. W. London [65596] 24/02/2006 **ME**

Kaserah, Mrs C D, DipLib, Bank of Tanzania, Dar Es Salam. [10010131] 03/07/2008 **ME**

Kassir, Miss L, BA, Info. Lib., London Coll. of Communication, Univ. Arts, London. [61416] 12/07/2002 **ME**

Katny, Mrs M, DipIS MA MCLIP, Archive Consultant, BBC Inf. & Arch., London. [46330] 28/10/1991 **CM01/04/2002**

Katsarou, Ms G, MSc Econ, Lib., Dikemes, Athens, Greece. [10014270] 14/07/2009 **ME**

Kattan, Mrs L B, MCLIP, Unknown [21531] 24/10/1973 **CM01/11/1977**

Katts, Mrs M, PGDipLIS BA, Weekend Dep. Mgr., High Wycombe L., Bucks. [61136] 07/03/2002 **ME**

Kattuman, Mrs M P, BA MA DipLIS, Catr., Cambridge Univ. L. [46313] 28/10/1991 **ME**

Kaune, Ms H, BA(Hons) DipLib, Info. & L. Coordinator, Inst. of Materials, Minerals and Mining, London. [10013171] 17/01/1985 **ME**

Kaung, Mr T, BA(Hons) Dip. Lib Hon. D. Litt HonFLA, Lib., Univ. Cent. L., Rangoon, Burma. [17154] 01/01/1960 **CM01/01/1963**

Kaur Bhoda, Mrs M, BSc LIS, Info. Offr., Inst. of Marketing, Maidenhead, Berks [10001812] 15/03/2007 **ME**

Kaur, Mrs H, ACLIP, Sch. Lib., Aldridge Sch., Aldridge. [65933] 30/06/2006 **ACL28/01/2009**

Kaur, Miss R, MCLIP, Ref. Lib., Milton Keynes Cent. L. [62796] 22/10/2003 **CM07/07/2010**

Kay, Mr C H, BA MCLIP, Retired. [24722] 01/10/1975 **CM02/12/1977**

Kay, Ms C, BA MA DipLib MCLIP, Project Mgr., Univ. of Liverpool. [10002657] 01/01/1974 **CM01/07/1988**

Kay, Ms E A, Coll. Lib., Brasenose Coll., Oxford. [59288] 29/01/2001 **AF**

Kay, Mrs I A, L. Asst., Cent. L., Manchester. [64470] 31/03/2005 **AF**

Kay, Mr J, BA(Hons), Lib., Simcyp Ltd, Sheffield [63670] 12/08/2004 **ME**

Kay, Miss K I, BA DipLib MCLIP, Comm. Lib., N. Lanarkshire Council, Cumbernauld. [27533] 05/05/1977 **CM18/01/1980**

Kay, Miss L E, BA(Hons) MA, L. Asst., Queen Mary, Univ. of London, Whitechapel L., London. [10006173] 16/04/2003 **AF**

Kay, Mrs P M, MCLIP, Retired. [60591] 07/07/1970 **CM01/09/1978**

Kay, Mrs S, BA(Hons) DipIM MCLIP, Managing Dir., The Professionalism Grp. [48469] 18/01/1993 **CM23/09/1998**

Kayani-Hogan, Ms M, BA MA MCLIP, Lib., Westminster Kingsway Coll., London. [65286] 28/11/2005 **CM20/04/2009**

Kaye, Mr D, BA MSc FCLIP, Life Member. [8179] 07/01/1954 **FE01/01/1969**

Kaye, Mrs G M, MCLIP, Snr. L. Asst., Illingworth L., Sheffield. [65045] 14/10/2005 **CM28/01/2009**

Kaye, Miss J, BA(Hons), p. /t. Asst. Lib., Tameside Coll., Ashton-under-Lyne. [49360] 28/10/1993 **ME**

Kaye, Miss R, BA MCLIP, Reader Devel. and Stock Lib., Chesterfield L., Derby C.C. [18374] 22/10/1972 **CM11/08/1976**

Kayumba, Mr F, BA, Stud. [60048] 04/12/2001 **ME**

Kazakeviciute, Ms L, Inf. Off., Olswang, Holborn. [10015907] 10/02/2010 **ME**

Kazmierczak, Mr P, BSc(Hons) PGCE MA MCLIP, Sen. Lib., Bournemouth L. [61437] 19/07/2002 **CM23/01/2008**

Keady, Miss M E, CertEd BPhilEd MSc MCLIP, E-Res. Devel. Mgr., Univ. of Derby, Derby. [51039] 09/11/1994 **CM01/04/2002**

Kean, Ms A, BA(Hons), Health Lib. [10007566] 18/02/2008 **ME**

Kean, Mr G, MSc, Stud., Univ. of Strathclyde. [10015561] 15/12/2009 **ME**

Kean, Mrs K F, MCLIP, Off. Asst., SDS Total Solutions Ltd., New Milton. [20982] 03/09/1973 **CM18/07/1976**

Keane, Ms M P, BA DipLib MCLIP, Communities & Learning Mgr., Bolton L. [35405] 13/10/1982 **CM27/07/1985**

Keane, Mrs P, MCLIP, Retired. [8190] 12/04/1962 **CM01/01/1966**

Keane, Mrs R M, B PHIL MA MCLIP, Academic Serv. Mgr., Liverpool Hope Univ. Coll. [40195] 27/10/1986 **CM16/10/1991**

Kearl, Mr D H, BA MCLIP, Community Devel. Lib., Canterbury L, Kent L. [40000] 14/10/1986 **CM18/04/1990**

Kearley, Miss S, BA(Hons) MSc, Inf. Offr., Hill Dickinson LLP, Manchester [10007953] 20/03/2008 **ME**

Kearney, Mrs A, BSc (Hons) DipIInfSci MCLIP, Unwaged. [10008954] 17/06/2004 **CM17/06/2004**

Kearney, Miss B, Stud. [10000789] 31/10/2006 **ME**

Kearney, Ms C, BA MEd DipLib DipEdTech MCLIP, Asst. Dir., CILIPS/SLIC, Hamilton. [37871] 09/11/1984 **CM10/02/1987**

Kearns, Mrs H R, BA DipLib MCLIP, Teacher, Piano. [39681] 07/05/1986 **CM18/04/1989**

Kearns, Mr T G, BA DipLib MCLIP, Music Lib., Harrow Council, London [43841] 06/02/1990 **CM21/07/1993**

Keary, Mrs M, MPhil FCLIP, ICT Advisor, London. [8195] 12/03/1962 **FE31/07/1974**

Keat, Mrs L P S, BSc MA, Lib., Danes Hill Sch. [64908] 08/09/2005 **ME**

Keates, Mr J, MSc, Unknown. [10014285] 14/07/2009 **ME**

Keating, Mrs C, BA DipLib MCLIP, L. Resource Cent. Mgr., Jack Hunt Sch., Peterborough. [30465] 29/01/1979 **CM02/10/1981**

Keating, Mrs L M, BA(Hons) MCLIP, Asst. Lib., Newcastle Univ. [49044] 13/09/1993 **CM22/05/1996**

Keay, Mrs J M, BA MCLIP, I. T. & Systems Lib., S. Lanarkshire Council. [29665] 13/10/1978 **CM16/03/1984**

Keddie, Mrs A, BA(Hons) MCLIP, Inf. Offr. /Subject Specialist, Univ. of Bolton, Bolton. [39741] 10/06/1986 **CM24/04/1991**

Keddie, Ms C A, BA(Hons) MA MCLIP, Sen. Asst. Lib., De Montfort Univ., Leicester. [54462] 16/12/1996 **CM17/01/2001**

Keddie, Mrs J, BA MCLIP, Resources Mgr. /Sen. L. Exec., House of Commons L., London. [41652] 06/02/1988 **CM16/10/1991**

Keefe, Mrs J H, BA MCLIP, Collections Lib., Calgary P. L., Alberta, Canada. [34716] 30/01/1982 **CM17/07/1985**

Keelan, Mr P J, BSc DipLib MCLIP MSc, Head of Special Collections, Cardiff Univ. [29708] 04/10/1978 **CM07/12/1981**

Keeling, Miss D J, Acting Lib., Skelton L., Cleveland. [10010634] 19/08/2008 **AF**

Keeling, Dr D M, BA(Hons) MA PhD MCLIP, Retired. [8205] 19/03/1957 **CM01/01/1963**

Keeling, Mr D, FCLIP, Retired. [8204] 12/03/1956 **FE01/01/1964**

Keen, Miss C L, BA MSc MCLIP, Inf. Offr., NIHRDS E. Midlands, Leicester. [37980] 01/01/1985 **CM14/11/1991**

Keen, Mrs E, MCLIP, Child. s Lib., L.B. of Harrow, Pinner L. [18396] 08/12/1972 **CM09/07/1976**

Keenan, Ms J, Project Mgr. [10000764] 13/10/1992 **ME**

Keenan, Ms M S, BA(Hons) MSc, Lib. & Res. Mgr., NDA-RWMD, Harwell [56771] 12/10/1998 **ME**

Keenan, Ms S, MPhil FCLIP, Retired. [18956] 12/03/1951 **FE01/04/2002**

Keene, Dr J A, BSc DipLib MCLIP, Asst. Dir., ILS, Univ. of Worcester. [42259] 13/10/1988 **CM19/07/2000**

Keeping, Mrs M M, Inf. Mgr., Nestec York Ltd., York. [53116] 15/03/1996 **ME**

Keevil, Mr D, MCLIP, p/t Consultant, Aluminium Fed. [8213] 09/09/1958 **CM01/01/1964**

Kehoe, Miss A, ALAI MCLIP, Retired. [8215] 01/01/1949 **CM30/08/1984**

Keiller, Mrs H C, BA(Hons) MA, Career Break. [55680] 04/11/1997 **ME**

Keir, Mrs K, BA(Hons) DipLIS MCLIP, Customer Serv., Mgr., Glos. Arch., Gloucester. [10001992] 01/07/1984 **CM15/05/2002**

Keith, Mrs S D, BA DipEd MA DipILS MCLIP, Sch. Lib., Glasgow Academy. [55804] 24/11/1997 **CM15/11/2000**

Kelby, Mrs S E, BA MCLIP, Sch. Lib.,Irthlingborough Junior Sch. [20299] 02/02/1973 **CM23/08/1977**

Kell, Mrs N J, BSc, Health Lib, NHS [65595] 24/02/2006 **ME**

Kelland, Mr N E, BSc(Econ), Inf. Serv. Lib., Treorchy L., Rhondda-Cynon-Taff C. B. C. [58626] 18/04/2000 **ME**

Kellas, Mr S D, MA(Hons), Governance Mgr., The Physiological Soc., London. [54729] 12/03/1997 **ME**

Kelleher, Miss J A, DipLib, Inf. Offr., Clifford Chance LLP, London. [50766] 17/10/1994 **ME**

Kelleher, Mr M D, BA(Hons) MSc MCLIP, Bibl. Serv. Lib., Univ. of Liverpool. [56474] 23/07/1998 **CM29/03/2004**

Kellet, Mrs K J, BSc(Hons) MSc PgDip, Site Operations Co-ordinator (Job Share), Univ. of Salford, Inf. Serv. Div. [10000961] 02/11/2001 **ME**

Kellett, Ms A L, Asst. Lib., Water Serv., Birmingham. [65235] 25/11/2005 **ME**

Kelley, Mrs L, BA(Hons) DipIM MCLIP MSc, Lib., St. Paul's Girls Sch. London [50911] 31/10/1994 **RV05/10/2007** **CM19/01/2000**

Kelly, Mrs A F, BLS MCLIP, Life Member. [30350] 30/01/1958
CM23/09/1980

Kelly, Mrs C, BA(Hons), L. Mgr., Whitley L., Reading. [65984]
07/08/2006 **AF**

Kelly, Mrs C, MCLIP, Retired. [15850] 29/08/1968 **CM08/05/1974**

Kelly, Mr D G, MSc MCLIP, Dir. of Ls., Nat. church Inst. of the Church of
E., London. [36557] 19/10/1983 **CM01/04/2002**

Kelly, Mrs E M, BSc DipLib MCLIP, Employment not known. [37152]
16/02/1984 **CM06/09/1988**

Kelly, Mr G I, BA MCLIP, Hist. Res. Consultant, Norwich. [8233]
01/06/1964 **CM01/01/1970**

Kelly, Mrs I, Life Member. [8235] 07/01/1962 **ME**

Kelly, Ms J A, MCLIP, MA/Asst. Lib., N. of England Inst. of Mining and
Mechanical Engineers [65421] 24/02/2006 **CM20/04/2009**

Kelly, Mrs J E, BA(Hons) DipLIS, English Collections Devel. Lib.,
Cambridge Univ. L. [54175] 08/11/1996 **ME**

Kelly, Ms K, DLIS MHSc AHIP, Lib., Mercer L., RCSI, Dublin. [65597]
27/02/2006 **ME**

Kelly, Ms L C, BA(Hons) PGDip DipLIS MCLIP, Team Leader, L.
Operations, Nortumberland C.C. [36692] 07/11/1983 **CM11/11/1986**

Kelly, Mrs L, BA MCLIP, Sen. Asst. Lib., Newcastle-upon-Tyne Univ. L.,
Tyne & Wear. [15998] 15/01/1972 **CM13/08/1975**

Kelly, Ms M A, DipLib MCLIP, Sen. Lib. -Child. Serv., Perth & Kinross
Dist. Lib. [33014] 03/10/1980 **CM31/01/1983**

Kelly, Mr M J, MCLIP, Life Member. [18846] 01/01/1956 **CM01/01/1962**

Kelly, Miss M, MA MCLIP, Retired. [8241] 10/05/1965 **CM01/01/1970**

Kelly, Miss N, BA(Hons), Stud., Univ. of Strathclyde, Glasgow.
[10015094] 23/10/2009 **ME**

Kelly, Mr P G, DipLib Inf, Sen. Trade Inf. Offr., Internat. Trade Cent.,
Geneva [10015510] 01/04/1990 **ME**

Kelly, Miss S A K, p/t L. Asst., Portsmouth C.C. [65042] 12/10/2005 **ME**

Kelly, Mrs S A, MCLIP, Team Leader Aquisitions, London S. Bank Univ.
[10717] 21/02/1972 **CM15/12/1975**

Kelly, Ms S, Stud. [10016920] 16/06/2010 **ME**

Kelly, Mrs T A, BA MCLIP, Unknown. [10013260] 02/04/2002
CM01/04/2002

Kelly, Mrs U W, DIP INF STUD MCLIP, Unwaged [30846] 09/05/1979
CM07/10/1981

Kelly, Dr W, MA MA PhD FCLIP, Hon. Res. Fellow, Scottish Cent. for the
Book, Napier Univ. [8246] 19/10/1966 **FE15/03/1983**

Kelly, Mrs Z C, BA(Hons) MSc, Info. Serv. Mgr., Burges Salmon, Bristol.
[56010] 28/01/1998 **ME**

Kelly-Keightley, Mrs J Y, MA Lib Sci, Learning Resource Mgr.,
Warwickshire Coll. [10007132] 04/10/1989 **ME**

Kelsall, Mrs M D, BA DipLib MCLIP, Life Member. [27690] 08/07/1977
CM12/01/1982

Kelsey, Mrs A, Unknown. [65329] 22/12/2005 **ME**

Kelt, Mr P R, BA PGDip MCLIP, Sch. Lib., Eastbank Academy, Glasgow.
[36241] 10/08/1983 **CM18/11/1993**

Kelvin, Mr P, BA(Hons), unwaged [10014742] 07/05/2004 **ME**

Kemp, Ms A J, BA(Hons) MSc MCLIP, Asst. Lib., Dept. for Work and
Pensions, Leeds. [44572] 29/10/1990 **CM25/09/1996**

Kemp, Mr D A, MSc MBCS MCLIP, Retired. [60405] 11/12/2001
CM11/12/2001

Kemp, Mrs H J, BA MA MCLIP, Lib., Angmering Sch., W. Sussex.
[38925] 21/10/1985 **CM15/09/1993**

Kemp, Mrs L E, BA(Hons), Unknown. [63724] 03/09/2004 **ME**

Kemp, Mrs L M, MCLIP, Inf. Mgr., CTC Kingshurst Academy,
Birmingham. [21709] 07/01/1974 **CM01/05/1977**

Kemp, Ms L, BA MA MCLIP, Sen. L. Asst. &LIS researcher, Univ. of
Sheffield. [61578] 02/10/2002 **CM09/09/2009**

Kemp, Miss S, BA(Hons), p. /t. Stud., Univ. Coll. London, Sutton L.
[65320] 23/12/2005 **ME**

Kempling, Mr H K, DipLib MCLIP, Retired [30668] 10/03/1979
CM11/05/1981

Kempshall, Mrs J R, BA MCLIP, Retired [6933] 28/09/1970
CM07/11/1972

Kempster, Mrs G D, OBE BA(Hons) MLib MCLIP FRSA, L. Serv. Mgr.,
Northamptonshire C.C., Northampton. [27333] 21/02/1977
CM27/07/1981

Kendall, Mrs A J, BSc(Hons) MSc(Hons), Unwaged. [57854]
10/09/1999 **ME**

Kendall, Miss E M, MA, Asst. Lib., Oundle Sch., Peterborough. [58368]
28/01/2000 **ME**

Kendall, Mrs J H, BLib, Sen. Lib. Asst., Thame L., Thame. [10002304]
26/02/1990 **ME**

Kendall, Ms M A, MA MPhil FHEA MCLIP, Sen. Asst. Lib., Manchester
Metro. Univ. [29993] 02/10/1978 **CM20/11/1980**

Kendall, Mr M, BSc MSc GradCerEd MCLIP, Legislation Mgr., Univ. of
Birmingham. [60533] 24/09/1973 **CM28/04/1980**

Kendall, Miss M, MA MCLIP, Lib., Churchill Coll., Cambridge. [8262]
02/04/1972 **CM28/02/1974**

Kendall, Ms S, BA DipLib MCLIP, Lib/Info Serv. Mgr., Mills & Reeve,
Birmingham. [40901] 14/08/1987 **CM17/10/1990**

Kendrick, Miss L, BA(Hons) PgDip, Knowledge & L. Servs. Mgr.,
Queen Elizabeth Hosp., Norfolk. [61618] 03/10/2002 **ME**

Kenefeck, Ms A J, BA(Hons), Unwaged – Seeking Work [10005098]
06/11/1984 **ME**

Kenna, Miss H, BSc DipILM MCLIP, Metadata Repository Offr., Univ. of
Salford. [59875] 29/10/2001 **CM21/11/2007**

Kenna, Mrs S, MA FCLIP, Strategic Devel. Mgr., The Brit. L., London.
[20786] 02/07/1973 **FE29/03/2006**

Kennard, Ms V R, BSocSci DipInf MCLIP, Dir., N. M. Rothschild & Son
Ltd., London. [60684] 12/12/2001 **CM12/12/2001**

Kennaway, Mrs M, FCLIP FSA Scot, Life Member. [8266] 31/03/1939
FE13/02/1975

Kennedy, Mr A J, BA MPHIL MA MCLIP, Asst. Lib., Proudman
Oceanographic Lab., Liverpool [10001833] 09/08/2004
CM21/08/2009

Kennedy, Mrs C M, BA MCLIP, p. /t. Comm. Lib., Wilts. C.C.,
Malmesbury L. [32689] 16/06/1980 **CM30/07/1982**

Kennedy, Mrs D A, Learning Resource Mgr., Wilmington Enterprise
Coll. [10000745] 28/03/2007 **AF**

Kennedy, Mr D, BA DipLib MCLIP, Unknown. [10009276] 25/07/1979
CM01/07/1989

Kennedy, Mrs J C, Snr. L. Asst., W. Cheshire Coll., Chester. [64408]
15/03/2005 **AF**

Kennedy, Miss J L, MA MCLIP, Gallery Records Mgr., Tate [39018]
28/10/1985 **RV07/06/2006** **CM15/11/1988**

Kennedy, Dr J, BA DIP A PhD DipLib, Ret. [40563] 18/03/1987 **ME**

Kennedy, Mr J, MA FCLIP, Retired. [8273] 01/01/1962 **FE29/04/1975**

Kennedy, Mr J, MA(Hons) MSc, Unknown. [57314] 10/02/1999 **ME**

Kennedy, Mrs L M, BA(Hons) PgDip, Sen. L. Asst., Monifieth L., Angus.
[65859] 05/06/2006 **ME**

Kennedy, Mrs M L, MA BSc PGDip MCLIP, Subject Lib., Heriot Watt
Univ. L., Edinburgh. [48769] 17/05/1993 **CM28/01/2009**

Kennedy, Ms N, Stud. [10006594] 23/10/2007 **ME**

Kennedy, Dr R J, BA PhD MRSC CChem, Position unknown, PRA
Coatings Tech. Cent., Teddington. [64621] 27/04/2005 **ME**

Kennedy, Mrs R L, BA MCLIP, Sen. Comm. Lib., Wanstead L.,
Wanstead [30432] 29/01/1979 **CM01/01/1981**

Kennedy, Mrs S A, BA DipLib MSc MCLIP, Learning Cent. Mgr., Univ. of
Gloucestershire, Cheltenham. [13447] 08/06/1971 **CM09/05/1975**

Kennedy, Mr S, L. & Inf. Admin., RoyalColl. of Psychiatrists, London
[65371] 12/01/2006 **ME**

Kennedy, Mrs S, L. Mgr., Ashford L. [10015979] 29/01/2010 **ME**

Kennedy, Mrs U, BA MA PgDip, Asst. Lib., St. Dominic's Grammar Sch., Belfast. [10015091] 23/10/2009 **ME**

Kennedy, Miss Y M, MCLIP, L. Offr., City of Edinburgh Council. [26430] 05/10/1976 **CM25/08/1983**

Kennell, Mrs J M, MCLIP, Unemployed. [18848] 02/12/1968 **CM21/11/1972**

Kennell, Mr R, MCLIP, Unwaged Member. [8283] 15/03/1969 **CM28/09/1972**

Kennerley, Mr F C, FCLIP, Life Member. [8284] 24/04/1935 **FE01/01/1949**

Kennerley, Mrs S J, BA(Hons) MA MCLIP, Unwaged. [47701] 19/10/1992 **CM20/03/1996**

Kenny, Miss A G M, MCIArb, Admin. Asst., Chartered Inst. of Arbitrators, London. [58615] 13/04/2000 **AF**

Kenny, Ms F, BSc, L. Asst., Trinity Coll., Dublin. [10016001] 10/02/2010 **ME**

Kenny, Mrs L E, BA MA MCLIP, Retired. [44324] 04/09/1990 **CM15/09/1993**

Kenny, Ms N, MA LPC LLB MSc, Trainee Lib., Falkirk Council. [10001201] 03/02/2007 **ME**

Kenny, Ms P, MA, Sen. Lib., Derby Local Studies L. [10000535] 05/10/2006 **ME**

Kensington, Miss A, Sr. Team Offr.,Redhill L., Surrey [65905] 29/06/2006 **AF**

Kensler, Ms E, BA(Hons) DipLib MCLIP, Customer Serv. Mgr., Aberystwyth Univ. [50168] 20/04/1994 **CM27/11/1996**

Kenssous, Mr N, Comm. Health Inf. Offr., Edgware Comm. Hosp. [63451] 12/05/2004 **ME**

Kent, Miss C C, ACLIP, L. Serv. Advisor, Retford L., Notts. [65034] 13/10/2005 **ACL29/03/2007**

Kent, Miss C, BSc(Hons) MA, Asst. Lib., Derby Hosp. NHS Foundation Trust [62900] 18/11/2003 **ME**

Kent, Mrs E C, ACLIP, Asst. Lib., St. Edwards Sch., Oxford. [63791] 06/10/2004 **ACL22/06/2007**

Kent, Ms E J, Unknown. [22915] 07/10/1974 **ME**

Kent, Mrs J M, MCLIP, Unemployed. [12598] 23/09/1968 **CM05/02/1973**

Kent, Ms J, MA MCLIP, Sen. Asst. Lib., Royal Inst. of Brit. Architects, London. [38667] 09/09/1985 **CM25/01/1995**

Kent, Miss J, BA MA Pg Dip, Unknown. [10015816] 28/01/2010 **ME**

Kent, Mrs M E, MA, L. Mgr., Wadebridge L., Cornwall. [63586] 01/07/2004 **ME**

Kent, Ms W, BA(Hons) MCLIP, Comm. & Inf. Offr., N. Yorks. C.C., Knaresborough L. & Inf. Cent. [36415] 11/10/1983 **CM20/05/1998**

Kenton-Barnes, Mrs C A, BA, Lib. /Sunday Offr., Oriel High Sch. /L. & Heritage, Gt. Yarmouth. [64783] 01/07/2005 **ME**

Kenvyn, Mr D B, BA MCLIP, Asst. Mgr. Community L., E. Dunbartonshire, William Patrick L. [30323] 17/01/1979 **CM29/12/1981**

Kenward, Miss H E, MA, Team Lib. Cowley L., Oxford. [64062] 15/12/2004 **ME**

Kenwright, Miss C E, BA(Hons) DipInf MCLIP, Head of Dept., Knowledge, Inf. & Records Mgmnt. Serv. [45411] 09/01/1991 **CM25/01/1995**

Kenyon, Mrs A B, LRC Mgr., Cleveland Coll of Art & Design. [62003] 13/01/2003 **ME**

Kenyon, Mr J R, BA FSA FR HIST MCLIP, Lib., Nat. Mus. of Wales. [8300] 29/09/1970 **CM08/07/1974**

Kenyon, Miss R H, BA(Hons) MCLIP, Learning Serv. Mgr., City of Westminster Coll., London. [42593] 12/01/1989 **CM22/05/1996**

Kenyon, Ms R, BA MCLIP, Retired. [35923] 26/02/1983 **CM21/06/1984**

Keogh, Mr M, BA(Hons) DipIM MCLIP, Asst. Lib. Ealing Hosp. NHS Trust, Southall. [55690] 04/11/1997 **CM12/03/2003**

Kerameos, Ms A, Unknown [41019] 02/10/1987 **ME**

Kerboub, Mr S, MS MA, Unknown. [10015466] 27/11/2009 **ME**

Kerby, Ms S, MCLIP, Servs. Dev. Lib., Petersfield L., Hants. C.C. [14827] 14/01/1972 **CM02/07/1975**

Kermode, Mrs M A, MA MLIS, Unwaged. [10014498] 20/08/2009 **ME**

Kernot, Mr A E, BA(Hons) MA, Sr. Info. Offr., Oxford Univ. [57085] 04/12/1998 **ME**

Kernot, Ms C, BA, L. & Know How Asst., Allen & Overy, London. [61960] 19/12/2002 **ME**

Kerns, Ms E A, Lib. Asst., Plashet Sch., London [10007141] 22/01/2008 **AF**

Kerr, Mr A, BSc, Stud., Aberystwyth Univ. [10011281] 07/10/2008 **ME**

Kerr, Mrs C, BA MCLIP, SLRCC, City of Edinburgh, Council. [32798] 24/09/1980 **CM09/10/1986**

Kerr, Miss D S, MA DipLib MCLIP, Websites Mgr, City of Edinburgh Co. [38209] 28/01/1985 **CM08/03/1988**

Kerr, Mr G D, BA MCLIP, Retired. [18850] 01/01/1962 **CM01/01/1966**

Kerr, Mr I R, MA, L. Serv. Mgr., Wellcome Trust Sanger Inst., Hinxton. [10008497] 11/05/1994 **ME**

Kerr, Mrs J, BA(Hons) MCLIP, Child. Lib., Peters Bookselling Servs. [10009277] 15/01/1973 **CM07/09/1976**

Kerr, Ms J, BSc (Hons), Unknown. [10014049] 23/06/2009 **ME**

Kerr, Ms L, BA DipLib MCLIP, Head of Learning Resources, Regent's Coll., Regent's Park, London. [42097] 01/10/1988 **CM24/06/1992**

Kerr, Ms L, MA, PGDip, Serv. Mgr., Heriot-Watt Univ. L, Edinburgh. [10016516] 23/01/1991 **ME**

Kerr, Mrs M G, BA(Hons) MCLIP, Tech. Support Team Leader, Helix RDS, Aberdeen [22296] 01/04/1974 **CM01/01/1979**

Kerr, Mr M W C, BA(Hons) PgDip, Cent. Mgr., London S. Bank Univ. [50310] 15/06/1994 **ME**

Kerridge, Mrs E J, BA, Housewife [35657] 06/12/1982 **ME**

Kerrison, Mr R J, MLS MCLIP, Man. Dir., Botsalo Books (Pty) Ltd., Botswana. [20136] 06/09/1966 **CM01/01/1970**

Kerry, Mr D A, MA DipInf, Between Jobs. [48700] 07/04/1993 **ME**

Kerry, Mr J A, MCLIP, Lib., Leeds Cent. L., Leeds [62499] 29/07/2003 **CM10/07/2009**

Kerry, Mrs J C, BSc MCLIP, Voluntary Worker [38049] 10/01/1985 **CM21/07/1989**

Kerry, Mrs R M, BA MCLIP, Documn. Contr., Network Rail. [38809] 09/10/1985 **CM14/11/1990**

Kersey, Mrs M, MCLIP, Retired. [8316] 23/09/1955 **CM01/01/1964**

Kersey, Mrs S, MCLIP, Lib., Bournemouth L. [21370] 13/11/1973 **CM03/11/1976**

Kershaw, Mrs H, BA DipLib MCLIP, P/T Sch. Lib. [33769] 16/02/1981 **CM01/07/1984**

Kershaw, Miss N J, BA CERT ED MCLIP, Univ. Lib., Anglia Ruskin Univ., Chelmsford. [24353] 28/06/1975 **CM14/09/1977**

Kerslake, Mrs S E, BA(Hons) MA MCLIP, Lib., Barking Havering & Redbridge NHS Trust., Ilford. [48292] 01/01/1993 **CM22/07/1998**

Kesse, Mr E, MSLIS, PrA, Unwaged. [10015781] 26/01/2010 **ME**

Kesteven, Mrs L A, PGDipIS, Sch. Lib., Reading Sch., Reading [61047] 11/02/2002 **ME**

Kettle, Mr S J, BA DipLib MCLIP GDipMan, Dev. Mgr., Leics. L. Serv. [34531] 02/12/1981 **CM18/07/1985**

Kettlewell, Mrs J D, ACLIP, Sen. Inf. Advicer, Nottingham Univ. [10007658] 18/02/2008 **ACL23/09/2009**

Kettlewell, Mr P, MCLIP, Retired. [8329] 08/03/1961 **CM01/01/1966**

Keup, Mr J, MLIS MA, Inf. Specialist, Dept. of Defense Dependent Sch., USA [10014882] 21/09/2009 **ME**

Kevill, Ms S, BA(Hons) MSc(Econ) MCLIP, Inf. Offr., Stirling Univ., Stirling. [62897] 18/11/2003 **CM19/03/2008**

Key, Mrs A, BA MCLIP, Life Member. [8332] 23/08/1955 **CM01/01/1971**

Key, Mrs J, BA MCLIP, Literature Searcher, Royal Coll. of Nursing, London. [34722] 19/01/1982 **CM14/04/1987**

Key, Mr M, BA MCLIP, Lib. (Camomile St.), City of London. [19791] 23/11/1972 **CM01/01/1974**

Keys, Ms J, BSc DipInfMgt, Consultant, Kickstart Innovation Mgmt. Ltd., Northants. [60432] 06/11/1997   **ME**

Keyte, Miss M E, MCLIP, Retired. [21295] 09/10/1973   **CM23/08/1976**

Kgosiemang, Ms R T, MSc, Coordinator, Humanities, Subject Lib., Univ. Botswana. [51436] 14/02/1995   **ME**

Khan, Mr A, BA(Hons) FCLIP, Head of L., Strategy, Warks. C.C., L. & Inf. Serv. [44888] 08/01/1991   **FE15/09/2004**

Khan, Mr H A, MA, Lib., Winchester and Eastleigh Healthcare NHS Trust, Winchester [10006940] 17/12/2007   **ME**

Khan, Ms M, BA(Hons) MA ACLIP, L. Asst., N. Watford L., Hertfordshire. [63645] 09/08/2004   **ACL06/02/2008**

Khan, Mr S A, ACLIP, Learning Serv. facilitator, S. Notts. Coll., Notts. [64822] 20/07/2005   **ACL02/06/2006**

Khetia, Mr K, MSc, Devel. Mgr. (Inf. & Learning), Cent. L., Coventry. [10009912] 06/06/1990   **ME**

Khoo, Mrs Y L L, BA MCLIP, Sen. Asst. Lib., Harrow. [16169] 02/10/1969   **CM15/12/1972**

Khorshidian, Mrs M, BA DipLIS MCLIP, LRC Mgr., The L., Univ. of Ulster at Belfast. [45066] 03/07/1990   **CM22/07/1998**

Kidd, Mr A J, MA MCLIP, Asst. Dir. Inf & Financial Resources, Glasgow Univ. L. [23153] 08/10/1974   **CM29/11/1976**

Kidd, Mrs C R M, MA, Stud., Robert Gordon Univ. [10015581] 17/12/2009   **ME**

Kidd, Ms E, MA(Hons) DipLIS MCLIP, Sen. Lib., Buckie L., The Moray Council. [46174] 09/10/1991   **CM22/05/1996**

Kidd, Mrs J, BEd(Hons) MSc, Principle L. Asst., Pershore L., Worcs. [62383] 19/05/2003   **ME**

Kidds, Mr M D, BA(Hons) DipILM MCLIP, Sys. Lib., Nat. Met. L., Devon. [51620] 13/04/1995   **CM19/07/2000**

Kiehl, Dr C A, MA MCLIP PhD, Dean of Univ. L., Univ. of Southern Mississsippi. [24559] 19/08/1975   **CM30/10/1978**

Kiely, Mrs C M, BA(Hons) DipILS MCLIP, Unknown. [40822] 01/07/1987   **CM01/04/2002**

Kift, Mrs K L, BA(Hons) MSc MCLIP, Eng. Lib., Coventry Univ. [53877] 07/10/1996   **CM01/02/2006**

Kift, Ms S M L, BA MCLIP, Sen. Lib. Lend. – N. Somerset [37032] 30/01/1984   **CM11/12/1989**

Kikteff-Rak, Mrs M, MSc, Unwaged. [10006477] 24/10/2007   **ME**

Kilbourn, Mrs M I, FCLIP, Life Member. [8353] 25/03/1931   **FE01/01/1936**

Kilbride, Mrs S, MA(Hons) DipILS PGCE MCLIP, Child. and Young People's Lib., N. Lanarkshire Council. [46839] 13/02/1992   **CM20/03/1996**

Kilburn-Easlea, Mr A, Career Break [47966] 28/10/1992   **AF**

Kilcawley, Ms A, BA(Hons), Asst. Lib. -Inf. Systems, Prince Consorts L., Aldershot. [49387] 01/11/1993   **ME**

Kiley, Mr R J, BA MSc MCLIP, H. of Systems Strategy, Wellcome Trust L., London. [41662] 07/02/1988   **CM15/09/1993**

Kilgallon, Mrs I J, MCLIP, Inf. Specialist, Faculty of Tech., Univ. of Portsmouth. [13794] 01/10/1971   **CM11/12/1989**

Kilgour, Miss A E, BA(Hons) DipLib MCLIP, Liaison Lib., Queen Margaret Univ., Edinburgh [46120] 02/10/1991   **CM20/09/1995**

Killah, Mr D, MCLIP, Sen. Lib., Falkirk Council. [8355] 13/01/1970   **CM09/01/1974**

Killala, Ms H F, Hillingdon Schs. L. Serv. [65337] 11/01/2006   **ME**

Killalea, Mrs M A, BA PGCE MCLIP, Subject Leader – ICT, St. Bede's High Sch., Blackburn. [10014587] 04/01/1972   **CM01/07/1993**

Killean, Mrs E J, BA MCLIP, Volunteer Lib., Dairsie Primary Sch. [41092] 07/10/1987   **CM25/05/1994**

Killen, Miss C, BA(Hons) MSc, Inf. Offr., Voice of Young People in Care, N. Ireland [10015105] 13/10/2009   **AF**

Killick, Mr J, BA(Hons) DipLIS MCLIP, Sen. Lib., Team Leader Adult Serv, NLBP LB of Barnet [46066] 18/09/1991   **CM19/05/1999**

Killoran, Mrs P A, Coll. Lib. [61003] 29/01/2002   **ME**

Killoran, Ms S A, BA MA(Oxon) DipLib MCLIP, Fellow Lib., Univ. of Oxford., Harris Manchester Coll. [34965] 18/05/1982   **CM11/04/1985**

Kilmartin, Ms O, Stud. [65804] 12/05/2006   **ME**

Kilminster, Mr G J, BA(Hons) FMA, Health & Wellbeing Mgr., Cheshire E. Council. [59187] 11/12/2000   **ME**

Kilmurray, Miss L, MCLIP, Retired. [8358] 17/03/1960   **CM09/03/1982**

Kilmurry, Miss E M, BA MCLIP, Partnership & Inf. Mgr., City of Edinburgh Co. [37874] 06/11/1984   **CM26/02/1992**

Kilner, Mrs A, BA(Hons) MA MCLIP, Asst. Dir., L. & Inf. Serv., Teesside Univ. [51529] 01/04/1995   **CM10/07/2002**

Kilvington, Mrs L M, BA MCLIP, Housewife. [24335] 08/07/1975   **CM10/08/1977**

Kim, Ms S H, MA MCLIP, Lib. Bournemouth Bor. Council [64220] 21/02/2005   **CM19/03/2008**

Kimber, Mrs C E, MA(Oxon) MA MCLIP, Career break [57580] 12/05/1999   **CM29/03/2004**

Kimber, Mrs G, BA(Hons) MSc MCLIP, Learning Resources Adviser (ILT), Thomas Danby Coll., Leeds. [53448] 01/07/1996   **CM16/05/2001**

Kimber, Mr J M, Inf. Specialist, QinetiQ Ltd., Worcs. [59864] 18/10/2001   **ME**

Kincaid, Mrs I C, BA MCLIP, Ref. Lib. Stirling Councils L., Stirling. [26125] 14/07/1976   **CM05/07/1979**

Kindness, Mrs F, BA MCLIP, Lib., E. Kilbride Cent. L. [40103] 21/10/1986   **CM19/08/1992**

King, Mrs A C, BA MCLIP, Advisory Lib., Sch. L. Serv., Chelmsford. [30164] 15/01/1979   **CM01/07/1991**

King, Dr A D, BA PhD, L. Assist., Newington L., Southwark [10015188] 23/10/2009   **ME**

King, Mr A L B, MCLIP, Business Analyst & Con., Axiell, Dorset. [20932] 19/09/1973   **CM16/09/1976**

King, Miss A, BA MCLIP, Retired [8366] 16/07/1971   **CM07/10/1974**

King, Mr B M A, BA(Hons) BA MCLIP, Stock Team, Adult Care & Community Serv. L., Ipswich. [35056] 21/07/1982   **CM24/01/1986**

King, Mrs C M, BA MSc MCLIP, CMFT L. Serv., MRI, Manchester. [27833] 24/08/1977   **CM24/08/1979**

King, Ms C, MA DipLib FSAS MCLIP, Arch./Catr., Dorset Hist. Ctr., Dorchester [29713] 07/10/1978   **CM26/11/1980**

King, Mrs D L, BA(Hons) MA MCLIP, Hd. of Knowledge Servs., Univ. Hosp. Coventry [49418] 21/10/1993   **CM10/07/2002**

King, Miss D R, BA(Hons) MSc MCLIP, L. & Inf. Mgr., Winckworth Sherwood, London. [47160] 20/05/1992   **CM27/07/1994**

King, Miss E J, BA(Hons) MSc MCLIP, Inf. Mgr., PriceWaterhouseCoopers, London. [56279] 20/04/1998   **CM25/07/2001**

King, Ms E, Unknown. [10010123] 26/06/2008   **ME**

King, Mrs F E, BA MCLIP, Partnership Lib., Banbury Sch. Partnership. [29455] 03/08/1978   **CM30/06/1981**

King, Ms G, BA MCLIP, Access & Inclusion Lib., Calderdale MBC [41976] 05/07/1988   **CM17/01/2001**

King, Miss H L A, MA MSc MCLIP, Inf. Mgr., Gloucestershire. [49471] 05/11/1993   **CM18/11/1998**

King, Mrs J C, BA(Hons) MA MCLIP, Inf. Advisor, Sheffield Hallam Univ. [43834] 25/01/1990   **CM26/05/1993**

King, Mrs J L, BA MCLIP, Team Lib., Clifton L, Nottingham [19862] 01/01/1973   **CM30/10/1975**

King, Ms J M, BA MCLIP, Freelance Law Lib., London [17181] 25/09/1968   **CM01/01/1971**

King, Mrs J, BA MCLIP, Lib., Reaseheath Coll., Cheshire. [40514] 27/02/1987   **CM21/07/1993**

King, Mrs J, p. /t. Lib., Warrington Bor. Council. [39721] 22/05/1986 **ME**

King, Mrs J, MCLIP, Unwaged. [9798] 16/02/1970   **CM22/08/1973**

King, Ms K, BA(Hons) MCLIP, Inf. & Learning Resources Mgr., Oakbank Sch., W. Yorkshire. [46028] 06/09/1991   **CM01/04/2002**

King, Mr L J, BA MCLIP, Lib., Shoe Lane L., City of London. [29995]
23/10/1978 **CM26/04/1983**

King, Mr M B, MCLIP FIMgt, Retired. [8393] 03/02/1961 **CM01/01/1967**

King, Mr M C, BA(Hons) ILTHE MCLIP, Soc. & Health Faculty Lib.,
Buckinghamshire New Univ. [10001130] 20/01/1975 **CM18/08/1986**

King, Mrs M, MCLIP, Sch. Lib., Turnford Sch., Cheshunt. [8391]
24/01/1963 **CM01/01/1971**

King, Miss N C S, BA(Hons) MA(Hons) PGCE MCLIP, Learning Advisor.
& Learning Serv., Northumbria Univ. [57041] 27/11/1998
CM10/07/2009

King, Ms P A, BLS DipHE MCLIP, Lib., Brigidine Sch., Windsor [28040]
13/10/1977 **CM19/10/1982**

King, Mr P M, MA DipLib, Dep. Inf. Serv. Mgr., Holman, Fenwick Willan,
London. [35670] 10/01/1983 **ME**

King, Ms P, BA FCLIP, Customer Serv. Mgr., Anglia Ruskin. Univ.,
Cambridge. [8398] 06/10/1970 **FE21/03/2001**

King, Miss R A, MSc L. & Info. Studies BSc, Info. Offr.,Trowers &
Hamlins, London [10001516] 27/04/2004 **ME**

King, Mrs R H, BSc(Econ) MCLIP, The Lib., The Dragon Sch., Oxford.
[8401] 12/10/1965 **CM01/01/1969**

King, Mrs S A, BSc (Hons) MBA, Lib., Hemel Hempstead L. [10014788]
18/09/2009 **ME**

King, Mr S A, BA(Hons) MA (Lib), Sch. Lib., Kilmarnock Academy,
Kilmarnock, Ayrshire [63866] 11/10/2004 **ME**

King, Miss S D, BA(Hons) MCLIP, Lib., Northern Sch. of Contemporary
Dance, Leeds. [48676] 08/04/1993 **CM01/02/2006**

King, Mrs S E, ACLIP, Inf. Specialist, Public Health Wales Observatory,
Swansea. [10000807] 08/11/2006 **ACL16/07/2008**

King, Mrs S H, BA(Hons) DipILS MCLIP, Archive Mngr., MOD [49034]
07/09/1993 **CM22/07/1998**

King, Mrs S J, DipLib MCLIP, Family Info. Ser. Offr. Coventry C.C.,
Coventry. [33240] 27/10/1980 **CM12/04/1983**

King, Mr S J, BSc MCLIP, Resources Lib., Robert Gordon Univ.,
Aberdeen. [20526] 08/04/1973 **CM03/11/1977**

King, Mrs S, BA(Hons) MCLIP FRSA, Head of Inf. Serv., Health and
Safety Exec., Bootle. [38197] 17/01/1985 **CM04/08/1987**

King, Mrs S, MA MCLIP, Tech. Ser. Lib., House of Lords, London.
[8403] 01/01/1969 **CM02/10/1972**

King, Miss T, MA(Hons) MSc, Sr. Health Improvement Prog. Offr.,
Anticipatory Care (Dissemination) NHS Scotland [62737]
15/10/2003 **ME**

King, Mrs X W, BA MA MCLIP, Academic Liason Lib., Univ. of
Westminster, London. [58714] 01/07/2000 **CM12/03/2003**

Kingma, Miss M A, Lib., the Brit. L., London. [65974] 09/08/2006 **ME**

Kings, Ms P A, BA MCLIP, Freelance Lib. :Project Mgmt., Child. Serv.
[32309] 05/03/1980 **CM09/12/1982**

Kingsbury, Mr A M, BA MA, Stud. [10000798] 03/11/2006 **ME**

Kingsbury-Barker, Mrs T C, BA MCLIP, Child. Lib. (Job Share), Bexley
L. Serv. [41964] 04/07/1988 **CM18/11/1992**

Kingsmill, Mrs P J, ACLIP, Lib., Crawley L. [65471] 24/02/2006
ACL01/11/2007

Kingston, Ms P J, BA DipLib PGCE MCLIP, Retired. [40794]
01/06/1987 **CM22/04/1988**

Kinnear, Miss J M M, MA DipLib MCLIP, L. Teaching Asst., Jumeirah
Primary Sch., Dubai. [34317] 29/09/1981 **CM30/08/1985**

Kinnear, Ms K A, BSc MSc, Sen. Inf. Offr., Davies Arnold Cooper,
London. [10002924] 30/01/1992 **ME**

Kinnear, Miss K E, BA(Hons) MA MCLIP, Team Lib. (L. Enviroment).,
Surrey Co. Council [59382] 23/02/2001 **CM21/06/2006**

Kinrade, Mr D C, Retired [10009474] 20/05/2008 **ME**

Kinsella, Ms S, Unwaged. [63693] 23/08/2004 **ME**

Kirby, Mrs C E, BA PGDipLib MCLIP, Asst L., Bridgwater Coll.,
Somerset. [33016] 01/10/1980 **CM08/02/1983**

Kirby, Mrs H G, BA, Retired [20595] 01/04/1973 **ME**

Kirby, Mrs J M, BSc MSc, Sch. Lib., Bedales Sch. Hampshire [63872]
13/10/2004 **ME**

Kirby, Ms J, PCt/Outreach Lib., Univ. of London, London [10012072]
09/10/2009 **ME**

Kirby, Miss K M, MA DipLib MCLIP, Ret. [30448] 31/01/1979
CM05/02/1982

Kirby, Miss M H, BA MCLIP, Life Member. [8429] 06/01/1958
CM01/01/1961

Kirby, Mrs M L, BA, Comm. & Devel. Mgr., L., Info, Heritage & Arts
Serv., Royal Bor. of Windsor & Maidenhead [28326] 11/11/1977 **ME**

Kirby, Mr R C, Retired. [38428] 02/05/1985 **ME**

Kirby, Mrs S M, MCLIP, Princ. Lib., Community L. & Arts, Flintshire C.C.
[12519] 12/01/1972 **CM01/01/1976**

Kirby, Mrs S, PGDip MCLIP, Unwaged [10015690] 15/11/1994
CM18/03/1998

Kirk, Mrs C G, BA MLib MCLIP, Info. Servs. Mgr., Bucks. C.C.,
Aylesbury. [44956] 23/01/1991 **CM27/11/1996**

Kirk, Prof J, BA DipEd MA MLitt PhD FALIA MCLIP, Pro Vice-
Chancellor, RMIT Univ., Melbourne. [60091] 07/12/2001
CM07/12/2001

Kirk, Miss K J, BA(Hons) MCLIP, Area Devel. Lib., City Area., Leeds L.
& Inf. Serv.,Cent. L. [24283] 09/06/1975 **CM17/05/1979**

Kirk, Mr R W, BA MCLIP HonFCLIP, Educ. Lib., Univ. of Leicester.
[8434] 21/03/1966 **CM01/01/1968**

Kirk, Ms S A M, BA(Hons) MCLIP, Sen. Lib., Halton Lea L., Runcorn.
[43623] 13/11/1989 **CM25/05/1994**

Kirk, Mrs S C, BA Lib, Asst. Lib., Banchory L. [10007785] 12/11/1981
ME

Kirk, Ms T, BA(Hons), Rare Books Ref. Team Leader, The Brit. Lib.
[64140] 19/01/2005 **ME**

Kirk, Miss V J, MA, Clinical Lib., Wirral Univ. Teaching Hosp. NHS
Found. Trust [63266] 23/03/2004 **ME**

Kirkby, Mrs E, BA MCLIP, Retired. [8436] 01/01/1966 **CM01/07/1973**

Kirkby, Mr I, BA(Hons) MCLIP, Lib. Dev. Offr., Direct Serv., Edinburgh
[10007759] 09/01/1974 **CM20/07/1976**

Kirkham, Miss B D, BA(Hons) DipLIS MCLIP, Asst. Lib., Denbighshire
C.C. [46441] 06/11/1991 **CM31/01/1996**

Kirkham, Mr N A, LLB MA, Asst. Lib. (Bibliographic Serv)., Gonville and
Caius Coll., Cambridge [64925] 12/09/2005 **ME**

Kirkham, Mrs V E, BA DipLib MCLIP, Tourism Offr., Laugnham – P/T.
[38106] 15/01/1985 **CM14/02/1990**

Kirkness, Ms M F, MCLIP, Lib. (catg.), Buckinghamshire New Univ.,
High Wycombe [35146] 01/10/1982 **CM01/12/1985**

Kirkpatrick, Mrs A S, BA, ICT Tech., All Saints C of E Junior Sch.,
Peterborough. [37707] 10/10/1984 **ME**

Kirkpatrick, Mrs S D, BLS MCLIP, Sen. Mgr., Reading & Learning,
Dorset C.C., Co. L. [32327] 03/03/1980 **CM21/06/1983**

Kirkpatrick, Mrs W H, MA DipLib, Asst. Lib., Kings Coll. L., Cambridge.
[44458] 10/10/1990 **ME**

Kirkwood, Mrs H, Sch. Lib., Springburn Academy L., Glasgow. [64438]
29/03/2005 **ME**

Kirkwood, Mrs L J, MCLIP, Sr. Local Studies Lib., Warwickshire [3240]
30/01/1972 **CM01/01/1976**

Kirkwood, Miss M L, MA(Hons) MSc, Knowledge Serv. Mgr., NHS
Greater Glasgow and Clyde. [55830] 20/11/1997 **ME**

Kirstein, Mr D J, BA(Hons), Asst. Lib. (Weekends & Evenings).,
American Intercontinental Univ., London [64665] 18/05/2005 **ME**

Kirtley, Mr R B, BA(Hons), Unknown. [10012035] 15/12/2008 **ME**

Kirtley, Mrs S, MA(Hons) MSc, Inf. Specialist, Nuffield Dept. of
Obstetrics & Gynae Univ. of Oxford. [56740] 12/10/1998 **ME**

Kirton, Ms J, Lib., Wollongbar Primary Ind. Inst., Australia. [10000796]
03/11/2006 **ME**

Kirton, Miss M H, BA MA MCLIP, Inf. Serv. Advisor, Napier Univ.,
Edinburgh. [36484] 18/10/1983 **CM05/05/1987**

Kirven, Ms S, MA BA MLS, Ref. Lib., Congressman Frank J Guarini L., New Jersey City Univ., U. S. A. [61076] 04/03/2002 **ME**

Kirwan, Mrs P, MCLIP DipPsych, Retired. [9158] 01/01/1967 **CM01/01/1971**

Kisiedu, Prof C O, Prof., Univ. of Ghana, Legon, Accra. [20906] 28/08/1973 **ME**

Kistell, Mr T J, Stud., Univ of Sheffield [10015676] 13/01/2010 **ME**

Kisz, Miss J, BSc MIHort MSc Econ, Unwaged. [59381] 23/02/2001 **ME**

Kitch, Mrs P W, MLib MCLIP, Retired. [34104] 01/01/1960 **CM07/09/1966**

Kitchen, Miss J A, BA MCLIP, Law L. & Inf. Mgr., Cardiff [28613] 04/01/1978 **CM07/10/1981**

Kitchin, Mrs E, MCLIP, Life Member. [8453] 27/02/1947 **CM01/01/1957**

Kitchin, Miss S, BA(Hons) MSc (Econ) MCLIP, L. Liaison Adviser, Northumbria Univ. L. [62783] 22/10/2003 **CM29/08/2007**

Kitson, Ms M, BLIB MCLIP, Trainee Teacher [36672] 03/11/1983 **CM07/07/1987**

Kjaernested, Mrs R, MSc, Head of Dept., FSA Univ. Hosp., Med. L., Iceland. [49893] 07/01/1994 **ME**

Klein, Mrs A, Unknown. [10011831] 18/11/2008 **ME**

Kleinknecht, Ms D I, MSc Econ, Lib., Oxford Cent. L., Oxford. [10000980] 04/12/2006 **ME**

Klijn-Passant, Mrs S, ACLIP, Asst. Young People's Serv.'s Mgr., N. Lancs L. [64575] 06/05/2005 **ACL05/10/2007**

Kloska, Miss B Z, BSc(Hons) MSc MCLIP, Unknown. [43736] 13/12/1989 **CM22/07/1998**

Klotz, Miss K, Learning Cent. Adv., Westminster Kingsway Coll., London. [10015254] 28/10/2009 **AF**

Kmet, Mrs C M, BED M. ED, Teacher Lib., Thomas's London Day Sch., London [10015059] 15/10/2009 **ME**

Knee, Mrs J D, Dip Lib BA MA MCLIP, Unwaged [10015673] 09/10/1987 **CM30/01/1991**

Kneebone, Mrs C, MCLIP, Retired. [8468] 09/02/1960 **CM01/01/1965**

Kneebone, Mr W J R, BSc MCLIP, Retired. [8469] 23/01/1961 **CM01/01/1964**

Knight, Mrs A H, BSc(Hons) MSc MCLIP, Resources & Facilities Mgr., Cranfield Univ., Kings Norton L. [48139] 11/11/1992 **CM15/10/2002**

Knight, Mr C J, BA(Hons) MA PGCHE, Liaison Lib., Nottingham Trent Univ. [55609] 24/10/1997 **ME**

Knight, Mr D, MCLIP, Head of Operations, Planning and Performance, Hertfordshire C.C. [8475] 01/07/1967 **CM01/01/1970**

Knight, Dr G A, PhD FCIL FIAP MCLIP MBCS, Consultant Patent Analyst. [60535] 29/05/1979 **CM29/05/1979**

Knight, Mrs J E, BA PgDip ACLIP, L. Asst., Oxford Brookes Univ. [10010965] 10/09/2008 **ACL23/09/2009**

Knight, Mr J I, BA(Hons), Lib. & Inf. Asst., Exeter Cent. L., Devon [10005569] 25/07/2007 **AF**

Knight, Miss J L, MSc(Econ) MCLIP, Lib., Inst. of Health Studies & Social Care Studies, Princess Elizabeth Hosp., Guernsey. [56524] 10/08/1998 **CM23/01/2002**

Knight, Mrs J S, BA MCLIP, Coll. Lib., Evesham Coll., Worcs. [26600] 30/09/1976 **CM01/01/1981**

Knight, Mrs J, MCLIP, Area Community Mgr., Leics. C.C., Market Harborough L. [8481] 11/03/1966 **CM01/01/1970**

Knight, Miss K E, BSc, Inf. Serv. Grad. Trainee, Pinsent Masons LLP, London. [10011474] 21/10/2008 **ME**

Knight, Mrs L E, BA DipLib, Mother/Unwaged/Career Break. [42131] 06/10/1988 **ME**

Knight, Mrs M E, MCLIP, Lib., Vaughan L., Harrow Sch., Middx. [13989] 23/12/1964 **CM01/01/1969**

Knight, Mr P J, BAHons, Media Mgr., B. B. C. [55540] 20/10/1997 **ME**

Knight, Mr R F E, MA FRSA FCLIP, Life Member. [8488] 14/03/1952 **FE01/01/1969**

Knight, Mr R G, BA MCLIP, Unknown. [23804] 31/01/1975 **CM12/09/1977**

Knight, Mr R, Retired. [8489] 10/01/1950 **ME**

Knight, Miss R, BA(Hons), Stud. [10013651] 18/05/2009 **ME**

Knight, Mrs T, MA MA MCLIP, Head of L. & Inf. Serv., Royal Coll. of Surgeons of England. [29054] 01/03/1978 **CM17/07/1981**

Knights, Ms I E, BMus MA, Sch. Lib., Handcross Park Sch., Haywards Heath [62161] 04/03/2003 **ME**

Knock, Mr L D, BA(Hons) MSc, Healthcare L. Mgr., Queen Elizabeth, S. London Healthcare NHS Trust. [58830] 22/08/2000 **ME**

Knott, Miss K J, BA MA, Unknown. [10013975] 17/06/2009 **ME**

Knowles, Mrs C P, MA MCLIP, Operations & Customer Serv. Mgr., Calderdale MBC, Halifax. [31144] 29/08/1979 **CM14/10/1981**

Knowles, Mrs G A, BA MA MCLIP, Lib. Asst., Lancashire C.C. [43607] 09/11/1989 **CM21/07/1993**

Knowles, Miss J, BSc MSc(Econ) MCLIP, Unknown. [54263] 14/11/1996 **CM25/07/2001**

Knowles, Mrs R A, BSc(Hons) MSc MCLIP, Inf. Specialist, Cranfield Univ., Swindon. [58230] 22/11/1999 **CM20/04/2009**

Knowlson, Mrs A, BA MCLIP, Coll. Lib., City of Sunderland Coll. [32886] 06/10/1980 **CM30/07/1985**

Knox, Mrs A M, BA MCLIP, Unknown. [57375] 26/02/1999 **CM28/10/2004**

Knox, Mrs J, MA MCLIP, Asst. Lib., Univ. of Ulster at Jordanstown, Newtownabbey. [33421] 23/11/1980 **CM02/01/1988**

Knutson, Mrs B, BA(Hons) MCLIP, L. R. C. Mgr., The Kings of Wessex Sch., Cheddar. [45355] 24/10/1990 **CM20/11/2002**

Kobzeva, Mrs I, MSc, Lib. Leeds City Council [10009771] 05/06/2008 **ME**

Koch, Ms L, BA(Hons) MA MCLIP, Asst. Lib., Manchester Met. Univ. [57293] 03/02/1999 **CM10/07/2009**

Koenig, Miss G R N, BA, Child. Lib., Slough L. [62647] 01/10/2003 **ME**

Koh, Miss P S, BA MA, Unknown. [10013177] 27/03/2009 **ME**

Kohli, Mr G, BA BSc DipLib MCLIP, Retired. [8517] 02/02/1966 **CM01/01/1968**

Kohlwagen, Ms J, DipLib MCLIP, Resident in Germany. [52148] 06/10/1995 **CM19/07/2000**

Kondylis, Mr D, PgDipHRM MBA, Arch. - Lib., Min. of Nat. Educ. and Religious Affairs, General State Arch. of Greece. [64794] 04/07/2005 **ME**

Kong, Mr P Y, MCLIP AALIA, Resident in Australia. [18394] 19/10/1972 **CM29/12/1980**

Konieczny, Mr R J, BA, Indigo Operator, MBA Grp. Ltd., London. [10015917] 29/01/2010 **ME**

Konviser, Mrs L D, BA BSocSci H DipLib, Unwaged. [43887] 07/02/1990 **ME**

Kopecky, Mrs B J, MCLIP, Lib., Northampton Sch. for Girls. [30267] 09/01/1979 **CM28/10/1981**

Koper, Mrs E H, BA MA PGCE MCLIP, Reader Serv. Lib., Royal Horticultural Soc., Lindley L., London. [54604] 27/01/1997 **CM16/07/2003**

Koponen, Ms M, MA, Unwaged -seeking work [63083] 27/01/2004 **ME**

Koppelow, Mr A D, Learning Cent. Mgr., The Learning Cent., Cornwall Coll. [10016032] 10/02/2010 **ME**

Koppelow, Mrs J E, Learning Cent. Asst., Cornwall Coll., St. Austell. [10015257] 30/10/2009 **AF**

Korjonen, Ms H M, BSc(Hons) MA MCLIP, Assoc. Dir., Inf. Serv., Nat. Heart Forum, London. [58950] 10/10/2000 **RV01/10/2008 CM02/02/2005**

Korulczyk, Mr R A, Unwaged. [10016877] 28/05/2010 **ME**

Kosinski, Mrs Z E, BA CNAA Dip MCLIP, Lib., Adams Grammar Sch., Telford & Wrekin C.C. [23762] 10/01/1974 **CM01/03/1977**

Koster, Mr C, BA FRSA MCLIP, Life Member. [8524] 17/02/1959 **CM01/01/1963**

Kothary, Mrs Z C, BSc MSc, Info. Sci., HMR & C, London. [55436]
13/10/1997   **ME**

Koumi, Ms P A, BA MCLIP, Ref. Specialist, Brit. L., London. [23849]
13/02/1975   **CM10/11/1978**

Kousseff, Mrs G E, MA(Oxon) FCLIP, Life Member. [8525] 14/10/1938
     FE01/01/1943

Koutroumpeli, Mrs M, Unknown. [10006993] 17/12/2007   **ME**

Koutsomiha, Miss D, MSc Econ, Lib. Coordinator, Greece [10015645]
12/01/2010   **ME**

Kowalczuk, Mr F, BA(Hons) DipILM MCLIP, Dep. Enquiry/Incident Mngr,
Kings Coll. London, London. [52480] 02/11/1995 **RV01/10/2008**
     CM08/12/2004

Kowalski, Mrs R Z, BA(Hons) MSc MCLIP, Career Break, unwaged.
[57506] 14/04/1999   **CM23/06/2004**

Koyama, Mr N, DipLib MCLIP, Under-Lib., Cambridge Univ. L. [32671]
03/07/1980   **CM25/03/1985**

Kozlowska-Wolodkowicz, Mrs A, MA, Sen. Asst. Lib. /Catr., Harrow C.,
Harrow, Middlesex. [63469] 14/05/2004   **ME**

Krabben, Mrs F, MA, Lib., Inst. of Actuaries, Oxford. [63581] 22/06/2004
     ME

Krabshuis, Dr J, MCLIP, Resident in France. [60238] 28/07/1989
     CM28/07/1989

Krajewski, Mrs E, ACLIP, Stud., Univ. of Wales, Aberystwyth (dist.
learning) [64948] 03/10/2005   **ACL28/01/2009**

Krajewski, Miss H, Lib. Asst., Durham Clayport L. [10012831]
19/03/2009   **ME**

Krasodomska-Jones, Mrs I, MSc, Sub-Libr., Corpus Christi Coll.,
Cambridge [49383] 01/11/1993   **ME**

Krethlow Shaw, Mrs M E T, BA MCLIP, Area Mgr. -S. Area, Essex Co.
L. Serv., Basildon L. [34627] 13/01/1982   **CM18/04/1990**

Kriel, Mrs E, BBibl, Inf. Offr., Linklaters, London. [58604] 11/04/2000**ME**

Krishnan, Ms Y C, Msc, MBA, Lib., United World Coll. of Sea,
Singapore. [10016034] 10/02/2010   **ME**

Kroebel, Ms C, BA MSc MA, Hon. Lib. & Arch.,Vol., Whitby Lit. & Phil.
Soc., Whitby Mus., N. Yorks. [44227] 17/07/1990   **ME**

Krogh, Ms P, BA MA, Stud. [10016307] 05/03/2010   **ME**

Krumbach, Ms M, MA, Lib., RPSGB, London [10001460] 26/02/2007
     ME

Kruse, Mrs H C, BA(Hons) MCLIP, Lib., NIACE, Nat. Inst. of Adult Cont.
Educ. [49890] 12/01/1994   **CM22/07/1998**

Kryemadhi, Mrs K M, MA MCLIP, Inf. Offr. DWF LLP. [56958]
13/11/1998   **CM09/11/2005**

Kuhn, Ms I L, MA(Hons) MSc, Reader Serv. Lib., Univ. of Cambridge.
[10008491] 10/12/1997   **ME**

Kulas, Ms M, BSc MCLIP, Academic Lib., Leeds Met. Univ. [10013815]
09/11/1989   **CM22/07/1998**

Kumiega, Miss L U, BA DipLib MCLIP, Learning & Teaching Lib., Open
Univ. L., Milton Keynes. [28999] 10/02/1978   **CM12/05/1980**

Kumra, Miss A, MA, Sen. L. Asst., Goldsmiths, Univ. of London.
[10015429] 16/11/2009   **ME**

Kumuyi, Ms B O, BA(Hons) MSc LIS (Merit), L. Exec., Dep. of Inf.
Servs., House of Commons, London. [64713] 01/06/2005   **ME**

Kunderan, Mrs M, MA(Hons), Child. Activites Lib., N. Lanarkshire
Council. Motherwell. [10000913] 15/10/2003   **ME**

Kurcewicz, Mrs W A, MA MCLIP, Asst. Lib., Derbyshire C.C. [54433]
06/12/1996   **CM12/03/2003**

Kusiak, Miss A M, MA, Resources Asst., Jewel & Esk Coll., Edinburgh.
[10012025] 27/01/2009   **ME**

Kvebekk, Mrs M D, BA MCLIP, Retired. [17207] 07/02/1956
     CM01/01/1960

Kvrivishvili, Dr G, MA, Stud. [10002345] 01/05/2007   **ME**

Kwabla-Oklikah, Mrs G, BA MCLIP, Retired. [8535] 01/01/1955
     CM01/01/1959

Kwan, Miss C L, DipLib MLib MCLIP, Sen. Academic Liaison Lib., Univ.
of Westminster, London. [44725] 27/11/1990   **CM25/01/1995**

Kybird, Mrs C L, MCLIP, L. Mgr. Khartoum Internat. Community Sch.
[1002] 18/01/1970   **CM01/02/1974**

Kyffin, Ms E, BA(Hons) MA DipIS MCLIP, Sen. Academic Liason Lib.,
Univ. of Westminster, Harrow. [52244] 18/10/1995   **CM19/05/1999**

Kyriakides, Mrs C, BA MCLIP, P. /t. Inf. Offr., Child. Aid to Ukraine,
London. [8539] 01/01/1966   **CM14/08/1967**

L

Lacey Bryant, Mrs S M J, BA DipLib MSc MCLIP, Independent Inf.
Specialist. [28615] 16/01/1978   **CM17/03/1980**

Lacey, Mr B K, BA DipLib MCLIP, Sales Devel. Mgr., 3M U. K.,
Bracknell, Berks. [27341] 20/02/1977   **CM27/02/1979**

Lacey, Mr C S, L., F. C. O. Serv., London. [48259] 18/11/1992   **ME**

Lacey, Mrs F K, BA MCLIP CIPD MCMI, Resources Lib. [31881]
01/01/1980   **CM20/12/1982**

Lacey, Mr R, MCLIP, Retired [8543] 15/09/1967   **CM01/01/1972**

Lacey, Mrs S J, Sen. Lib. Assist., Collingham Lib., Newark. [10013402]
23/04/2009   **AF**

Lack, Mr S J, BA(Hons) DipLib MCLIP, Inf. Serv. Mgr., L.B. of Camden,
London. [37932] 16/11/1984   **CM07/06/1988**

Lackey, Ms A, BA(Hons) DMS PGCE, Assoc. L. Serv. Mgr., Brighton &
Sussex Univ. Hosp., NHS Trust, E. Sussex. [37619] 09/10/1984 **ME**

Lacy, Miss C P, BSc MCLIP, Unwaged. [28047] 05/10/1977
     CM13/11/1979

Lacy, Ms J, BA PGDipLib, Coll. Lib., Herefordshire Coll. of Art & Design,
Hereford. [46440] 06/11/1991   **ME**

Ladd, Miss L D, MCLIP, Life Member. [8548] 13/01/1948**CM10/09/1975**

Ladipo, Miss K G, Vol. Classroom Asst., Kidbrooke Park Prim. Sch.,
London [10017172] 11/07/2010   **ME**

Ladizesky, Mrs K A, BA FCLIP, Retired. [28745] 22/01/1978
     FE22/07/1998

Ladjevardi, Miss A M, Sch. Lib., TASIS The American Sch. in England,
Thorpe, Surrey. [63590] 30/06/2004   **ME**

Lafferty, Mrs S, BA DipILS MCLIP, Comm. Access Lib., L.B. of Enfield,
Ordnance Road L. [43820] 17/01/1990   **CM17/05/2000**

Lagus, Mrs V L, BA(Hons) MA MCLIP, Comm. Dev. Libr., Jarrow L.,
Jarrow. [55774] 18/11/1997 **RV07/06/2006**   **CM10/07/2002**

Lahlou, Ms A, Unknown. [10006088] 19/02/2009   **ME**

Lai Sheung, Ms F, Head of Knowledge Cent., Arup, Hong Kong
[10007193] 25/01/2008   **ME**

Lai, Miss S F, MCIM MSc MCLIP, Asst. Lib., Anglia Ruskin Univ., Essex.
[61689] 21/10/2002   **CM31/01/2007**

Laidlaw-Farmer, Mrs A W, MLS BA MCLIP, Evening & Weekend L. R.
C. Mgr., Univ. of E. London. [16868] 23/05/1966   **CM01/01/1971**

Lain, Mr M I J, MPhil BA MCLIP, Retired. [18864] 27/04/1966
     CM01/01/1969

Lainchbury, Mrs A C, BA MCLIP, Lib., The Leys Sch., Cambridge.
[36696] 31/10/1983   **CM16/05/1990**

Laing, Mr C J, BA(Hons) MCLIP, Sen. Asst. Lib., De Montfort Univ.,
Leicester. [52476] 02/11/1995   **CM01/06/2005**

Laing, Mrs F, ACLIP, Sen. Curator, Nat. L. of Scotland, Edinburgh.
[64785] 04/07/2005   **ACL24/04/2009**

Laird, Mrs A, MA MCLIP, P. /t. L. Asst., Educ. Dept., Dundee City
Council, Dundee. [8563] 22/10/1965   **CM01/01/1969**

Laird, Ms A, BA PGDipLib, Sen. Inf. Exec., ICAEW [44498] 16/10/1990
     ME

Laird, Miss E M C, MA MCLIP, Outside Serv. Mgr., N. Lanarkshire
Council, Coatbridge. [26438] 16/10/1976   **CM16/12/1978**

Lake, Mr F H, FCLIP, Life Member. [18090] 03/10/1972   **FE04/12/1985**

Lake, Mr J B, BA MCLIP, Lib., Barbican L., City of London. [22774] 11/10/1974　　　　**CM01/11/1977**

Lake, Miss N J, BA(Hons) MA MCLIP, Sen. Support Consultant., Sirsidynix [55748] 13/11/1997　　　　**CM21/03/2001**

Lake, Miss S L, BA Msc, Asst. Lib. Oxford. [10015953] 03/02/2010　**ME**

Laker, Mr K, MCLIP, Unknown. [8572] 01/05/1969　　　　**CM23/01/1974**

Laker, Miss S C, BA DipLib MCLIP, Dep. Ch. Lib., Priaulx L., St. Peter Port, Guernsey. [37861] 14/10/1984　　　　**CM30/01/1991**

Lakin, Mrs D E, BA DipLib MCLIP, Family Learning Cent. Mgr., The Clarendon Sch., Trowbridge. [34103] 30/09/1981　　**CM06/12/1985**

Lale, Mrs J M, BLib MCLIP, Sen. Lib., W. Suffolk Coll., Bury St. Edmunds. [21284] 12/10/1973　　　　**CM12/09/1977**

Lalic, Ms M M, BA GradDipLIS, Lib., House of Commons L., London. [64123] 17/01/2005　　　　**ME**

Lally, Mrs P, MCLIP, Lib., HMP Coldingley, Surrey. [8199] 01/04/1971　　　　**CM04/03/1975**

Lam, Miss C H, MA, Stud., Manchester Met. Univ. [10015125] 15/10/2009　　　　**ME**

Lam, Mr K F G, MSc, Sen. Economic Res. Offr., Germany Trade & Invest, German Consulate, Hong Kong [10008594] 02/04/2008　**ME**

Lam, Miss W Y W, Asst. Lib., The Chinese Univ. of Hong Kong. [62558] 20/08/2003　　　　**ME**

Lamb, Mrs B, MCLIP, Life Member. [8575] 09/02/1955　**CM01/01/1966**

Lamb, Mrs J O, BA DipLib MCLIP, Lend. Serv. Mgr., Oldham M.B.C., Educ. & Cultural Serv. [28048] 01/10/1977　　　　**CM31/01/1980**

Lamb, Mr K D I, BA(Hons) DipLib,MA, Head of Lib. Serv., Liverpool PCT. [44406] 05/10/1990　　　　**ME**

Lamb, Mrs M, MCLIP, Customer Serv. Mgr., N. Somerset Council. [23195] 25/10/1974　　　　**CM01/08/1977**

Lamb, Mrs R, MA MCLIP, Retired. [20896] 01/10/1958　**CM01/01/1961**

Lamb, Ms S E, BSc(Hons) DPS, Contract, Herbert Smith., London [10001912] 22/03/2007　　　　**ME**

Lambe, Ms M, BA DLIS DAS MA MSc(Econ), Lib., Marino Inst. of Educ., Dublin. [58596] 07/04/2000　　　　**ME**

Lambermont-Ford, Mr J P, BSc MSc, Internal Consultant, Equisoph Ltd., France. [62253] 02/04/2003　　　　**ME**

Lambert, Mrs A D, Lib., Outwood Academy, Adwick Windmill Balik Lane, Woodlands, Doncaster. [65633] 22/03/2006　　　　**ME**

Lambert, Mrs A, BA(Hons) MCLIP, Unknown. [47782] 14/10/1992　　　　**CM13/03/2002**

Lambert, Mrs C L, BA(Hons) MCLIP, p/t Child. Serv. Lib., E. Area, W. Sussex C.C. [40579] 02/04/1987　　　　**CM24/05/1995**

Lambert, Ms C, BA MA, Sen. L. Asst., Univ. of Leicester L. [44614] 06/11/1990　　　　**ME**

Lambert, Mr D D, BA MCLIP, Team Lib., Bedfordshire CC, Leighton Buzzard [62414] 03/06/2003　　　　**CM21/06/2006**

Lambert, Mrs J J, BA DipLib MCLIP, Lib., L.B. of Sutton, Cent. L. [35794] 20/01/1983　　　　**CM13/05/1986**

Lambert, Mrs J, BSc MA FCLIP, Retired [12665] 01/01/1970　　　　**FE23/01/2008**

Lambie, Miss A, BA(Hons) PGDipILS, Inf. Offr., Univ. of Strathclyde, Law Sch. [61804] 12/11/2002　　　　**ME**

Lambie, Ms L T, MA DipLib MCLIP DipLEDQ, Economic Devel. Offr., Inverclyde Council. [39936] 01/10/1986　　　　**CM15/08/1989**

Lamble, Mr W H, RFD BA ALAA MCLIP, Retired. [17225] 21/02/1949　　　　**CM01/01/1959**

Lambon, Mrs A R, BLib MCLIP MA, Lend. Serv. Lib. (Job-share), Univ. of Cent. England, Birmingham. [36129] 02/06/1983　**CM16/12/1986**

Lamming, Mr J D, BA DipLib MCLIP, Info. Exec., Inst. of Chartered Accountants, London. [31346] 30/09/1979　　　　**CM11/01/1984**

Lampard, Miss E M, BA DipLib MCLIP, Lib., Revenue & Customs Prosecutions Off. [33663] 12/01/1981　　　　**CM18/07/1985**

Lampert, Mrs M, Inf. Expert, The Brit. L., London. [10009351] 20/05/2008　　　　**AF**

Lamusse, Mrs F M, BA DipLib, Clinical Outreach Lib., Portsmouth Hosp. NHS Trust, Queen Alexandra Hosp. [58966] 10/10/2000　**ME**

Lamyman, Miss J E, MCLIP, Life Member. [24959] 28/10/1975　　　　**CM19/02/1979**

Lancaster, Mr A, MCLIP, Sch. Lib., Monk's Walk Sch., Welwyn Garden City. [63787] 18/10/2004　　　　**CM13/06/2007**

Lancaster, Mr F W, FCLIP, Retired, Resident U. S. A. [27649] 13/01/1950　　　　**FE01/01/1969**

Lancaster, Miss K, BA Hons, Stud. [10013612] 13/05/2009　　　　**ME**

Lancaster, Mrs P, BA(Hons) MSc MCLIP, Inf. Serv. Team Leader., Calderdale M.B.C., Halifax Cent. L. [56386] 01/07/1998　　　　**CM02/02/2005**

Lancey, Mrs A K, BNurs DPS(m) MA, L. and Knowledge Serv. Mgr., Isle of Wight NHS PCT, Newport. [49075] 01/10/1993　　　　**ME**

Land, Mr A J, Msc BA PGDipIM MCLIP MBCS, Electronic L. Infrastructure Mgr., Univ. of Manchester. [60493] 07/02/2001　　　　**CM07/02/2001**

Landau, Mrs D M, MCLIP, Self Employed [15134] 05/01/1971　　　　**CM03/04/1974**

Landau, Mr T, MCLIP, Life Member [8614] 17/09/1948　**CM01/01/1951**

Lander, Miss K N, BA MCLIP, L. Mgr., BAE Systems Global Combat Systems – Munitions, Glascoed. [48074] 04/11/1992 **CM24/09/1997**

Lander, Mrs S A I, Retired [17229] 30/09/1968　　　　**ME**

Landes, Ms J, Lib., Shakespeare Globe, London. [63879] 12/10/2004　　　　**ME**

Landry, Mr P, MA MLS, Hd. of Subj. Indexing, Swiss Nat. L. Switzerland [10013166] 26/03/2009　　　　**ME**

Lane, Miss A K E, BA(Hons), Inf. Specialist Mgr., Brit. Med. Journal Pub. Grp. [46619] 26/11/1991　　　　**ME**

Lane, Miss C M, BA, Retired [35054] 09/07/1982　　　　**ME**

Lane, Mrs G, BA DipLib MCLIP, Self Employed [22895] 01/10/1974　　　　**CM31/07/1977**

Lane, Mrs J, ACLIP, Inf. Asst., Mansfield L., Notts. [65624] 15/03/2006　　　　**ACL09/01/2007**

Lane, Mr J, MCLIP, L. Serv. Mgr. (Devel.)., Poole L. [23142] 06/11/1974　　　　**CM01/11/1977**

Lane, Mr P G, MA DipLib MCLIP, Princ. Lib. (Ref. & Inf. Serv.), L.B. of Harrow. [24732] 01/10/1975　　　　**CM01/10/1977**

Lane, Mrs R A, BA(Hons), Sch. Lib., Pangbourne Coll., Berks. [34826] 15/03/1982　　　　**ME**

Lane, Ms T, MSc BSc(Hons) DIC, Unknown. [10015612] 17/12/2009 **AF**

Lane-Gilbert, Mrs P, MCLIP, Head of L. & Inf. Serv., R. I. C. S., London. [8625] 02/05/1969　　　　**CM10/11/1972**

Lanfear, Mrs E J, MRES MA PgDip LIS MCLIP, P. /t. Academic Lib., Leeds Met. Univ. [10008974] 07/10/1991　　　　**CM11/11/2009**

Lang, Mr B A, MA PhD HonFLA, Ch. Exec., The Briish L., London. [53387] 01/01/1996　　　　**HFE01/01/1997**

Lang, Mrs J C, BA DipLib MCLIP, Head Lib., Salisbury NHS Foundation Trust [34159] 01/10/1981　　　　**CM08/11/1984**

Langdon, Ms C A, BA DipLib MCLIP, Sr. Lib., Mobiles and Special Servs., Rhondda Cyon Taf, Aderdare Lib. [39060] 31/10/1985　　　　**CM23/03/1993**

Langdon, Ms K, BSc MA, Lib., Radcliffe Sci. L., Oxford. [59545] 02/05/2001　　　　**ME**

Langdon, Miss L E, BA(Hons) MSc MCLIP, Team Lib., Surrey Co. Council, Ewell. [64701] 01/06/2005　　　　**CM06/05/2009**

Langdown, Mrs C H L, BSc MA MCLIP, Inf. Mgr., Pinsents Leeds. [41216] 19/10/1987　　　　**CM14/11/1990**

Langen, Mr M, DipLib BPhil KM, Unwaged [10017150] 11/07/2010　**ME**

Langford, Ms R C, MA MCLIP, Unwaged. [38170] 25/01/1985　　　　**CM03/10/1991**

Langham, Mr M, BA DipLib MCLIP, Dep. Br. Lib., E. Cheshire Council [27692] 06/07/1977　　　　**CM18/07/1980**

Langley, Mr M, MA MSc MCLIP, Intellectual Property Lib., Queen Mary, Univ. of London. [56903] 02/11/1998 **CM29/03/2004**

Langley, Miss S, BA(Hons) MCLIP, Lib., NHS Direct Anglia, Ipswich. [60037] 03/12/2001 **CM09/11/2005**

Langley-Fogg, Mrs L A, Local Studies Libr., Derbyshire CC. [42507] 22/11/1988 **ME**

Langlois, Ms B, MSc, Mgr., Nat. Autistic Soc., London. [50999] 08/11/1994 **ME**

Langman, Mrs C, BSc MSc, Inf. Specialist, Aston Univ., Birmingham. [63006] 28/11/2003 **ME**

Langridge, Mr G M, MA MLS MCLIP, Head of L. & Inf. Serv., Wiltshire Co. Council, [36885] 01/01/1984 **CM06/10/1987**

Langrish, Miss E, Inf. Specialist, Civil Serv. [63267] 23/03/2004 **ME**

Langrish, Mr T M, BA DipLib AIL MCLIP FETC, Princ. L. Asst., Inst. for Chinese Studies L., Univ. of Oxford. [34045] 01/08/1981 **CM18/08/1983**

Langstaff, Miss H, Stud. [10006622] 11/09/2007 **ME**

Lanney, Mrs S F, BLS(Hons) MCLIP, Lib., Basildon & Thurrock NHS Trust, Basildon Hosp. [58575] 04/04/2000 **CM12/09/2001**

Lannon, Mrs A P, MA DipLib MCLIP, Legal Lib., Legal L., 1-11 John Adam St., London. [42161] 10/10/1988 **CM31/01/1996**

Lannon, Mrs I J, MA MCLIP, Retired. [4288] 16/10/1964 **CM20/01/1975**

Lantry, Ms M, MA HDipEd MA MCLIP, Inf. Consultant, ROI [43675] 22/11/1989 **CM01/04/2002**

Lantz, Ms M A, BA DipLib MCLIP, Sch. Lib., Montsaye Community Coll. [33215] 27/10/1980 **CM07/03/1985**

Lapa, Ms A L S, Asst. Lec., Faculade de Letras., Universidade de Coimbra. [50471] 12/08/1994 **ME**

Lapko, Mrs K A, ACLIP, Lib. Asst., Ladybrook L., Mansfield, Notts. [10012897] 19/03/2009 **ACL16/06/2010**

Lara, Miss E J, BA MA DipLib, Lib., Univ. of the W. Indies. [36373] 07/10/1983 **ME**

Larbey, Mrs M A, BA MCLIP, Tech. Lib., TWI, Granta Pk., Cambridge. [29600] 01/10/1978 **CM19/11/1979**

Larbi, Mr K, BA MA MSc MCLIP, Subject Lib., Univ. of E. London, Stratford [8646] 07/07/1971 **CM01/07/1989**

Larby, Mrs P, MA FCLIP, Life Member. [8647] 08/09/1952 **FE01/01/1962**

Lardent, Mrs S M D, BA MCLIP, Retired. [38514] 20/05/1985 **CM17/10/1990**

Lardner, Miss A E, MA, Inf. Offr., Clyde & Co. LLP [62808] 24/10/2003 **ME**

Lardner, Mrs L R, Res. Cent. Mgr., Blackheath High Sch., London. [39461] 10/01/1986 **ME**

Lardner, Mr M D, BA MCLIP, Head of Inf., Worklife Support Ltd., London. [38005] 01/01/1985 **CM16/02/1988**

Lardner, Mrs M, MCLIP, Lib. Resource Cent. Co-ord., Dundee City Council, Dundee. [5318] 23/09/1969 **CM15/08/1973**

Larkham, Mrs E A, BA(Hons) MA MCLIP, Seni. Resources Exec., 3i plc., W. Midlands. [50797] 18/10/1994 **CM18/03/1998**

Larkin, Mr J R W, BA DipLib MCLIP, Internal Comms. Offr., Lib., Action for Child., London [31539] 16/10/1979 **CM30/04/1982**

Larkin, Mrs V S, BA DipLib MCLIP, Lib.,Bexley L. & Mus. [32441] 17/04/1980 **CM07/02/1985**

Larkins, Miss A, BA PGDipIS MCLIP, Journals Lib., Univ. of Huddersfield. [48506] 01/02/1993 **CM07/09/2005**

Laskey, Miss A E, Sen. Lib. -Inf. Serv., L.B. of Barking & Dagenham, Essex [45162] 31/07/1990 **ME**

Laslett, Mrs C J, BA MCLIP, Bibl. Serv. Co-ordinator (Job Share), Yate L., S. Glos. [25339] 01/01/1976 **CM01/01/1978**

Lass, Mr D M, MA DipLib MCLIP ALAI, Vol. Hon. Sec. UCRG London & Reg. Rep. UCRG Nat. Committee. Seeking employment. [24514] 01/10/1975 **CM27/02/1985**

Lassam, Miss C, MCLIP, Retired. [8663] 04/01/1967 **CM01/01/1971**

Last, Mrs L, ACLIP, Acting Head Of LR, Resource Cent. &L., Edmunds, Suffolk. [65940] 11/07/2006 **ACL04/03/2009**

Last, Mrs R A, MLS MCLIP, Consultant for L. in Sch. & Educ. . Rosemary Last L. Serv. [847] 09/02/1960 **CM01/01/1966**

Last, Miss S R, BA(Hons) MSc, Inf. Offr., Linklaters, London. [10007871] 22/03/2000 **ME**

Latham, Ms C E, MA(Hons) PGCE MSc ILS MCLIP, p. /t. Child. Lib., Luton Cultural Serv. Trust. [63383] 27/04/2004 **CM28/01/2009**

Latham, Mrs E A, BA(Hons), p. /t. Asst. Lib., Dr. Challoner's Gramm. Sch., Amersham. [56671] 01/10/1998 **ME**

Latham, Mrs M, BA, Sch. L. Asst., Rhyl High Sch., Denbighshire. [10010955] 10/09/2008 **ME**

Latham, Mr S J, BA MA MPhil MSc MCLIP, Head of Knowledge and Inf. Mgmnt., Dept. for Internat. Devel., London. [43719] 04/12/1989 **CM29/01/1992**

Latham-Bale, Ms S, BA(Hons), Asst. Lib., Univ. of Giamorgan [10012888] 18/05/2005 **ME**

Lathbury, Mrs M G T, BA MLS MCLIP, L. & Knowledge Serv. Mgr., S. Derbys. Acute Hosp. NHS Trust, Derbys. Royal Infirmary. [29850] 01/10/1978 **CM26/06/1981**

Lathrope, Mr D, BSc MCLIP DMS MBE, Devel. Offr., Derbyshire CC [21996] 15/01/1974 **CM30/03/1976**

Latimer, Miss C, BA MCLIP, Learning Support Lib., Notts. C.C. [30849] 23/04/1979 **CM26/08/1982**

Latimer, Mrs C, BA(Hons), Unknown. [10014021] 23/10/1985 **ME**

Latimer, Mrs K, MA DipLib, Med L., Queens Univ., Belfast. [9482] 01/01/1970 **ME**

Lattimer, Ms B I, BA(Hons) MCLIP, Coll. Lib., St. Charles Catholic 6th Form Coll., London. [19844] 01/01/1973 **CM20/07/1978**

Lattimore, Dr M, MA FCLIP, Retired [8675] 14/07/1958 **FE01/01/1965**

Latto, Ms J, BSc (Econ), Academic Serv. Lib., Carnegie Coll., Halbeath. [57076] 04/12/1998 **ME**

Latulip, Ms L, MCS, Adult Serv. Lib., Barnet. [10006221] 26/09/2007 **ME**

Lau, Mr M K K, PgDip, Cent. Serv. Asst., Univ. for the Creative Arts L. & Learning Cent., Farnham. [10015982] 01/02/2010 **ME**

Lau, Miss W H, Inf. Offr., Linklaters, London. [10007865] 26/02/2008 **ME**

Lauder, Mrs H, BA MCLIP, Info. & Records Mgr., N. Ayrshire Council [34218] 13/10/1981 **CM11/04/1985**

Laughton, Miss C L, BA, Stud., Univ. of Sheffield. [10015729] 19/01/2010 **ME**

Laughton, Mr G E, FCLIP, Retired. [8678] 23/07/1938 **FE01/01/1949**

Launder, Mr C, BA(Hons) MA MCLIP, Sen. L. Asst., Performing Arts Dept., Exeter Cent. L. [56791] 23/10/1998 **CM15/05/2002**

Launder, Mrs J S, BA(Hons) MA MCLIP, Info. & Learning Lib., Exeter Cent. Lib. [53993] 14/10/1996 **CM12/03/2003**

Laundy, Mr P A C, FCLIP, Retired. [17236] 22/03/1948 **FE27/09/1976**

Laurence, Mrs M T, MCLIP, Nursery Teacher [12164] 06/10/1967 **CM03/04/1975**

Laurence, Mrs S, BA(Hons) DipLib MCLIP, Asst. head of L. & Inf., Customer Serv., Glos. C.C. [46387] 31/10/1991 **CM31/01/1996**

Laurenson, Mr J C M, BSc(Hons) DipLib MCLIP MBA, L. Mgr., Renfrewshire L. [30208] 19/01/1979 **CM12/10/1981**

Laurie, Mrs E, MCLIP, p. /t. Lib., Thatcham L., W. Berks. Council. [8682] 06/05/1967 **CM01/01/1970**

Laurins, Miss A, BA(Hons) PGDip, Career Break [57188] 07/01/1999 **ME**

Lauriol, Miss C, MA MSc (Econ) MCLIP, Lib. Mgr. Broxburn & W. Calder L. W. Lothian C.C. [58933] 06/10/2000 **CM07/09/2005**

Lavelle, Mrs M E, DipLib MCLIP, Sen. Lib., B. B. C. News V. T. L., London. [31028] 06/07/1979 **CM20/01/1986**

Lavender, Mrs G A, Support Serv. /Reader Devel., Dudley L. [10009970] 24/06/2008 **AF**

Lavender, Ms S, LRC Mgr., Calderdale Coll., Halifax. [10014519] 27/08/2009 **ME**

Laver, Miss S L, MA, Know How Systems Op. Mgr., Slaughter and May, London [52023] 15/09/1995 **ME**

Laverick, Mr D, FCLIP, Life Member. [8688] 13/03/1948 **FE01/01/1961**

Laverick, Ms S J, BA MCLIP, p. /t. Lib., BDP Ltd. [36681] 04/11/1983 **CM05/07/1988**

Lavery, Mrs S M, MA MCLIP, L. Media Technician., Carlsbad Unified Sch. Dist., Carlsbad, California, USA. [27405] 22/03/1977 **CM26/03/1984**

Lavis, Ms P D, BA(Hons) DipInf, Knowledge & Info. Mgr., Young Minds/Royal Coll. of Nursing, London. [50610] 01/10/1994 **ME**

Law, Prof D, MA FCLIP FKC HonFCLIP, Head, Inf. Resources Directorate, Univ. Strathclyde, Glasgow. [8690] 21/10/1969 **FE18/01/1989**

Law, Mr D, BA(Hons) PG cert, Unknown. [10014147] 02/07/2009 **ME**

Law, Mr G S, Unknown. [10015182] 23/10/2009 **ME**

Law, Mr K A, Unknown. [10012585] 23/02/2009 **ME**

Law, Miss M, BA FCLIP, Life Member. [17237] 05/06/1951 **FE22/09/1975**

Law, Mrs M, MA BMus MCLIP, p. /t. Music Teacher, MA Lowe, Sheffield. [8692] 08/11/1968 **CM01/01/1972**

Law, Ms W A, BA(Hons), Super. -Postal Tapes Serv., Cent. L., Cambs. C.C. [61614] 03/10/2002 **AF**

Lawal, Prof O O, BA MA PhD FCLIP, Univ. Lib., Univ. of Calabar, Nigeria. [17238] 19/09/1971 **FE21/11/2001**

Lawanson, Mrs B I M, BA PGDipLib MSc, Defence Terminology Editor, ICAD. [31407] 27/09/1979 **ME**

Lawler, Ms S, MSc, PG Dip, Stud., Univ. of Strathclyde, Glasgow. [10011499] 22/10/2008 **ME**

Lawler, Ms U R E, MLS MCLIP, Unemployed. [8107] 18/08/1967 **CM01/01/1970**

Lawless, Mr T J, MSc ILS, Unknown. [10012299] 26/01/2009 **ME**

Lawrence, Mrs A R, BA MSc MCLIP, Lib. for Child. & Young People, Fareham L. [59858] 17/10/2001 **CM29/03/2004**

Lawrence, Mr B, BMUS (Hons), Child.& Youngh People's L. Offr.: Early Years, Cent. L., Halifax. [10016911] 08/06/2010 **ME**

Lawrence, Mrs C S, MA MSc MCLIP, Retired. [21665] 24/12/1973 **CM11/11/1976**

Lawrence, Mrs D M, BA PGDipIM MCLIP, Employment not known. [36211] 27/05/1983 **CM25/05/1994**

Lawrence, Ms K E, BA(Hons), Knowledge Serv. Lib., Bedfordshire and Hertfordshire Health L., Welwyn Garden City. [52941] 29/01/1996 **ME**

Lawrence, Miss L L, BA, Child. Lib., Ashburton L., Croydon. [52930] 25/01/1996 **ME**

Lawrence, Mrs L, BA(Hons), Clinical Lib., Derby General Hosp. [64614] 20/04/2005 **ME**

Lawrence, Mrs M F, FCLIP, Life Member. [8710] 11/10/1935 **FE01/01/1950**

Lawrence, Mr M W, BSc MCLIP, Local Studies Mgr., Oxfordshire Studies, Cent. L., Oxon. C.C. [37985] 03/01/1985 **CM18/01/1989**

Lawrence, Mrs P, Sr. Team Offr., Chertsey Lib., Surrey [10012729] 25/02/2009 **AF**

Lawrence, Mr R, BA MCLIP, Retired. [8713] 01/01/1964 **CM01/01/1967**

Lawrence, Mr S, BA BSc MSc MCLIP, Retired. [60537] 22/10/1974 **CM22/10/1974**

Lawrence, Dr V J, BA PhD MA PGCHE MCLIP, Liaison Lib., Nottingham Trent Univ., Nottingham. [44642] 13/11/1990 **CM23/06/2004**

Lawrence, Mrs Y T, MLS MCLIP, Retired., Kingston Jamaica [25194] 23/03/1962 **CM01/01/1970**

Lawrie, Mrs H, Super. (p/t), Business & Learning Cent., Bristol Cent. L. [10005271] 29/06/2007 **AF**

Lawrie, Mrs R F, BA(Hons) MCLIP, Dep. Learning Res. Mgr., Luton Sixth Form Coll. Luton, Beds. [19635] 30/10/1972 **CM01/07/1975**

Laws, Mrs A E, BA, Lib. Asst., Goole F.E. Coll., HCUK [39819] 31/07/1986 **ME**

Laws, Miss A M, BSc MSc, Lib. Learning Cent. Mgr. Ponteland High Sch. [62132] 25/02/2003 **ME**

Laws, Ms E L E, BA(Hons) MSc(Econ) MA MCLIP, Curator, Childrens Literature, V&A Mus. [53419] 20/06/1996 **CM15/11/2000**

Laws, Mrs M M, ACLIP, Unknown. [10012338] 27/01/2009 **ACL11/12/2009**

Lawson, Mrs A M, BA(Hons), Unwaged. [10006396] 19/10/2007 **ME**

Lawson, Mrs C A, BSc MCLIP, Area Lib. (p/t) and Lead Advisor (p/t), Hants. Co. Ls., Winchester. [23467] 07/01/1975 **CM07/01/1977**

Lawson, Mrs D, BA DipLib MCLIP, Learning Resources Asst. (P/T)., Craven Coll. [40850] 08/07/1987 **CM14/03/1990**

Lawson, Miss K, BSc MSc MBA MCLIP, Head, Market Inf. & Promotion, Tun Abdul Razak Res. Cent., Hertford. [60720] 23/10/1984 **CM01/02/1986**

Lawson, Mr M J, BA(Hons) MA MCLIP, Dep. Site Mgr., Kings Coll. London, Inf. Serv. Cent. [56588] 04/09/1998 **CM15/05/2002**

Lawson, Miss M, MA DipLib MCLIP, Resource Cent. Mgr., Hist. of Art Dept., Univ. of Glasgow. [31351] 15/10/1979 **CM23/12/1982**

Lawson, Mr R R, FCLIP, Life Member [8723] 01/01/1935 **FE01/01/1946**

Lawson, Miss S, BSc(Hons) DipILM MCLIP, Sen. Inf. Specialist, Med. L., King's Coll London. [50715] 12/10/1994 **CM19/05/1999**

Lawton, Miss A P, BSc MSc MCLIP, Unemployed. [39678] 06/05/1986 **CM06/05/1986**

Lawton, Ms A, MLIS BA, System Lib., Dr. Steven's Hosp., Dublin [10008271] 11/03/2008 **ME**

Lawton, Ms C, BA Grad Dip LIS, Unemployed – seeking work [10015024] 07/10/2009 **ME**

Lax, Mrs M, ACLIP, Sen. Lib. Asst., Brandon L., Durham. (p/t) [65626] 13/03/2006 **ACL28/01/2009**

Laxton, Miss R, MCLIP, Head of L., Learning & Culture Durham C. C [8726] 16/01/1970 **CM17/12/1973**

Lay, Mrs J, BA, Lib. Mngr., Winton L., Bournemouth [10017176] 26/05/1995 **AF**

Lay, Miss L, BSc(Econ) PGDip MCLIP, Lib., Truro & Penwith Coll., Cornwall. [64593] 20/04/2005 **CM09/09/2009**

Lay, Mr S J, GTCL LTCL DipLib MCLIP, Customer Serv. Mgr., Oxfordshire L. Serv. [45941] 26/07/1991 **CM27/07/1994**

Laycock, Mrs P E H, MCLIP, Lib., Rastrick High Sch., W. Yorks. [8729] 01/01/1966 **CM01/01/1969**

Laycock, Mrs V A, ACLIP, Sch. Lib., Cent. Lancaster High Sch., Lancaster. [10005380] 25/07/2007 **ACL01/10/2008**

Layton, Mrs A R, Sen. Lib., Dept. for Communities & Local Government [22347] 01/04/1974 **ME**

Layton, Ms C, BSc(Econ) MCLIP, Unknown. [57394] 03/03/1999 **CM20/04/2009**

Layzell Ward, Prof P J, MA PhD FCLIP FIM, Life Member. [8732] 01/01/1954 **FE01/01/1963**

Lazaridou, Ms E, Stud., Univ. of Strathclyde., Glasgow. [10011875] 25/11/2008 **ME**

Lazim, Mrs A, BA MA MCLIP, Lib., Cent. for Literacy in Prim. Educ., London. [21862] 08/02/1974 **CM16/04/1981**

Le Bihan, Mrs K J, Beng Bcom, Stud. [10015295] 30/10/2009 **ME**

Le Boutillier, Miss F, MCLIP, Life Member. [17243] 12/09/1959 **CM01/01/1964**

Le Chat, Mrs S A, BA DipLib MCLIP, Learning Res. Cent. Mgr., Daventry William Parker Sch. Northants. [33831] 24/03/1981 **CM15/08/1984**

Le Cheminant, Mrs M, MCLIP, Retired. [12409] 08/09/1971 **CM16/02/1976**

Le Couteur, Mrs E M, MCLIP, Life Member. [17244] 01/01/1943 **CM01/01/1947**

Le Grice, Mrs E, MCLIP, Info. Offr. - Art, Penzance Br. L., Cornwall [10001625] 08/01/1970 **CM10/05/1973**

Le Grice, Miss J B, MA MCLIP, Bibliographic Records Mgr., Kingston Univ., Kingston-upon-Thames. [18416] 19/10/1972 **CM08/03/1976**

Le Sadd, Mr W, Prison Lib., Lincolnshire C.C. [52870] 02/01/1996 **ME**

Lea, Mrs E S, BSc DipLIS MCLIP, Serv. Standards Lib., Reading Bor. Council. [43333] 20/10/1989 **CM14/09/1994**

Lea, Miss E, BA(Hons) MSc(Econ), Asst. Lib., New Coll., Swindon. [52451] 02/11/1995 **ME**

Lea, Mr R A, BSc, Inf. Mgr., Glaxosmithkline plc, Greenford. [37990] 01/01/1985 **ME**

Lea, Mrs V, MCLIP, Retired. [8744] 04/02/1959 **CM01/01/1964**

Lea, Mrs Y A, BA MA MCLIP, Team Lib, Lend. Serv., Scunthorpe Cent. L., N. Lincs. [24736] 07/10/1975 **CM14/02/1979**

Leach, Mr A, BA DPA FCLIP, Life Member. [8745] 08/03/1948 **FE01/01/1959**

Leach, Mr C, BA MA DipLib MCLIP, Academic Subject Lib., Univ. of Lincs. [29722] 05/10/1978 **CM06/11/1980**

Leach, Mrs M D, BA MCLIP MBA, Lend. Serv. Lib., Wolverhampton Bor. Council. [28617] 09/01/1978 **CM06/08/1980**

Leach, Mrs M Y, BA MCLIP, Document Delivery Coordinator, Reading Univ. Lib. [22479] 11/06/1974 **CM12/08/1976**

Leach, Miss P R, Unknown. [38758] 06/10/1985 **ME**

Leach, Mrs P, Asst. Lend. Lib. (Job Share), Accrington L., Lancs. C.C. [42504] 21/11/1988 **ME**

Leach, Mrs S E, BA PGCE MCLIP, Employment not known. [35553] 24/10/1982 **CM28/01/1986**

Leach, Ms S P, BA MCLIP, Child. & Yth. serv. Mgr., Hants. L. Serv. [26444] 30/09/1976 **CM22/09/1980**

Leadbeater, Mrs J G, MCLIP, Unemployed. [22131] 12/02/1974 **CM18/08/1978**

Leadbetter, Miss V E, MA MA, Lib., LRC, London Probation, London [10008662] 24/10/2003 **ME**

Leader, Mrs L M, BA MCLIP, Liaison & Planning Mgr., Univ. of Salford. [31927] 17/12/1979 **CM05/08/1983**

Leahy, Ms A, BA(Hons) DipArch MSc, Hd. of Info. Servs., LDA, London [10012996] 23/03/2009 **ME**

Leak, Miss A R, BA(Hons) MA MCLIP, Dep. Lib., Arts Univ. Coll. Bournemouth, Poole. [46011] 22/08/1991 **CM08/12/2004**

Leak, Mrs A, BA DipLib MCLIP, Sr. Liaison Lib. (HRM), Middx. Univ. [29212] 30/03/1978 **CM30/04/1981**

Leake, Miss A, MA(Hons), MSc, Researcher,Lovells,London [10001423] 12/10/1998 **ME**

Leakey, Mrs D, BPharm MRPharmS MCLIP, Head of Communications, MHRA, London. [60853] 11/03/1991 **CM11/05/1993**

Lean, Mrs L, MCLIP, Retired. [16353] 01/01/1968 **CM01/01/1972**

Lear, Mrs A M, BA DipLib MCLIP, Head of L. & Inf. Serv., Oakham Sch., Rutland. [33595] 12/01/1981 **CM16/05/1985**

Lear, Mrs H F, MCLIP, Retired. [13589] 12/01/1969 **CM01/01/1972**

Leary, Mrs J A, BSc(Hons) DipIS MCLIP, Unknown. [48189] 13/11/1992 **CM23/09/1998**

Leather, Mrs C, Sen. L. Offr., Educ. L. Serv., Reading. [61566] 02/10/2002 **AF**

Leatherdale, Mrs D E, MBA MCLIP, Quality Mgr., Univ. of Wales, Newport. [11559] 14/01/1971 **CM29/08/1974**

Lebeter, Mr I, BA MCLIP, Sch. Lib., Hillpark Secondary Sch., Glasgow. [63981] 22/11/2004 **CM19/11/2008**

Leckie, Mrs A S, BA, Trainee Charter L. Offr., Leith L., Edinburgh C.C. [64729] 08/06/2005 **ME**

Lecky-Thompson, Mrs J E, BA(Hons) MA MCLIP, Lib., Faculty of Philosophy, Univ. of Cambridge [55504] 16/10/1997 **RV17/10/2006 CM15/01/2003**

Ledger, Mrs H, MCLIP, Lib. & Learning Resources Mgr., Kennet Sch., Berkshire [10001492] 02/12/1975 **CM21/05/1979**

Ledsom, Miss J, BA(Hons) MCLIP, Lib., Cheshire C.C., Ellesmere Port L. [58961] 10/10/2000 **CM07/09/2005**

Ledson, Mrs A J, Community & Info. Offr., Selby L., N. Yorkshire [10013100] 26/03/2009 **AF**

Ledson, Mrs J E, BA MCLIP, Retired. [17245] 01/01/1967 **CM01/10/1971**

Lee, Mrs A S, BA(Hons) DipILM MCLIP PGCE, Learning Centres Mgr., Rotherham Coll., Sheffield [58512] 06/03/2000 **CM29/03/2004**

Lee, Mrs B, BA MSc, Cultural Serv. Offr., Neath Port Talbot., Co. Bor. Council., Neath Port Talbot [59399] 05/03/2001 **ME**

Lee, Mrs B, MCLIP, Retired. [8772] 31/01/1947 **CM01/01/1953**

Lee, Mrs D E, BA MCLIP, Serv. Devel. Mgr., Hounslow L. [25346] 13/01/1976 **CM23/11/1979**

Lee, Miss D T, BA(Hons) MMus MA, N/A [60876] 18/12/2001 **ME**

Lee, Mrs E C P, MCLIP, Retired. [30343] 01/01/1953 **CM12/03/1982**

Lee, Dr E C, BSc(Hons) DipILS MCLIP, Lib. Serv. Mgr., Directorate of Public Health, NHS Tayside, Dundee. [57247] 20/01/1999 **CM20/09/2000**

Lee, Miss F M, MA MSc(Econ) MCLIP, Inf. Professional, BIS London. [53591] 29/07/1996 **CM20/09/2000**

Lee, Mrs G M, BA MLS DipLib MCLIP, Health Inf. Specialist, Tribal Tech. LTD, Loughborough. [34199] 12/10/1981 **CM06/12/1985**

Lee, Miss G, MCLIP, Retired. [8777] 01/01/1966 **CM01/01/1968**

Lee, Miss H A, Inf. Specialist, CSL, York. [52628] 14/11/1995 **ME**

Lee, Mr J D, FCLIP, Retired. [8781] 05/09/1955 **FE01/01/1960**

Lee, Miss J E, BA(Hons), Lib. & Info. Asst., Great Barr L., Birmingham [10012852] 19/03/2009 **AF**

Lee, Miss J M, MLS BA DipLib MCLIP, Devel. Team Mgr., I. C. T. Serv., Leicestershire Co. Council [29185] 19/04/1978 **CM02/01/1981**

Lee, Mrs J, BA(Hons) DMS MCLIP, Inf. & Resources Offr., Barnsley M.B.C., Cent. L. [28065] 13/10/1977 **CM11/09/1981**

Lee, Mrs J, MCLIP, Operations Mgr, Caerphilly Co. Bor. Council, Pontllanfraith. [22826] 08/10/1974 **CM10/08/1977**

Lee, Miss K J, Stud., Manchester Met. Univ. [10016166] 16/02/2010**ME**

Lee, Mrs L A, BA(Hons) MCLIP, Lib., Newbury Coll., Berkshire. [33208] 01/01/1973 **CM27/09/1982**

Lee, Miss M N J, MAppSc BSc MCLIP, Asst. Lib., Hong Kong Poly. Univ. [60103] 11/10/2000 **CM11/10/2000**

Lee, Mrs M R, BSc, Lib. Clacton Co. High Sch., Clacton-on-sea [10011703] 06/11/2008 **ME**

Lee, Miss M, MSc, Stud. [10015582] 17/12/2009 **ME**

Lee, Ms P, ACLIP, LRC. Mgr., Devizes Sch. Wilts. [64153] 19/01/2005 **ACL05/10/2007**

Lee, Mrs P, MCLIP, Sen. Lib., Cent. L., Liverpool. [20440] 09/01/1973 **CM02/03/1976**

Lee, Miss R A, MA DipILS MCLIP, Unwaged. [50686] 10/10/1994 **CM17/03/1999**

Lee, Mr S J, BA MCLIP, p. /t. Sen. Inf. Lib., Tower Hamlets, London. [38856] 17/10/1985 **CM24/04/1991**

Lee, Mrs S K, Lib. Asst., Exeter Cent. Child. L., Exeter. [10013955] 15/06/2009 **AF**

Lee, Miss S M Y, BA(Hons), Unknown [65290] 25/11/2005 **ME**

Lee, Mrs S M, BA MCLIP, Br. Lib. (Job Share), Roxeth L., L.B. of Harrow. [31203] 14/10/1979 **CM05/10/1984**

Lee, Mrs S M, L. Asst., Univ. Coll. for the Creative Arts, Epsom. [65567] 28/02/2006 **AF**

Lee, Mr S N S, BA(Hons) MCLIP, H. R. Intranet Mgr., Dept. for BIS. [54007] 16/10/1996 **CM15/05/2002**

Lee, Dr S T, HonFCLIP, Hon. Fellow. [62819] 23/10/2003**HFE23/10/2003**

Lee, Miss T, BSc, Learning Resource Mngr., Newall Green 6th Form Coll., Wythenshawe [10015256] 29/10/2009 **ME**

Lee, Mr W L, MLib MCLIP, Lib., Hong Kong Shue Yan Univ., Hong Kong. [50570] 03/10/1994 **CM01/04/2002**

Leech O'Neale, Ms C A S, BSc MCLIP, Sen. Copy Editor, C. E. R. N., Geneva, Switzerland [17254] 26/02/1968 **CM01/01/1971**

Leedham, Miss A, BA MCLIP, Lib. Offr., Stock Serv. Team, L.B. of Merton L., Surrey [28618] 24/01/1978 **CM21/10/1981**

Leem, Ms D, BSc, Unknown. [10006882] 10/09/2009 **AF**

Leeming, Mrs A, MCLIP, Stock Unit Mgr., Suffolk L. [13924] 01/01/1969
CM26/11/1973

Lees, Miss A J, LLB, Stud., Aberystwyth Univ. [10012877] 17/03/2009
ME

Lees, Ms A, DipLib MCLIP, Inf. Serv. Mgr., Knowledge Serv. Grp., NHS
Educ. for Scotland, Glasgow [31352] 15/10/1979 **CM10/11/1981**

Lees, Miss C H, BA MCLIP, Lib., Malvern L., Worcs. [30462] 06/02/1979
CM10/10/1983

Lees, Mrs F A, DipLib MCLIP, Learning Cent. Mgr., Newbury Coll.,
Berks. [37385] 04/08/1984 **CM02/06/1987**

Lees, Ms J S, MA MCLIP, Community Liaison., OCLC., Birmingham
[10245] 01/01/1971 **CM15/08/1973**

Lees, Ms J, BA(Hons), Stud., Univ. of Birmingham. [10008791]
18/04/2008 **ME**

Lees, Mrs L R, BA, Lib., Boston Univ., London. [10006415] 19/10/2007
ME

Lees, Mr N G, MSc MCLIP, Unemployed. [60540] 21/01/1980
CM06/11/1989

Lees, Mr P C, Asst. Inf. Offr., Clifford Chance, London. [10004956]
06/06/2007 **AF**

Lees, Miss R K, MA(Hons), Learning Res. Cent. Mgr., St Margaret's
Academy, Livingston. [10006546] 30/10/2007 **ME**

Lees, Ms S, Lib., The Abbey Sch., Reading. [10009890] 10/07/2008 **ME**

Leese, Mrs I, PG Dip ILS, Unwaged. [10007795] 21/04/1995 **ME**

Leese, Mr P, BA MCLIP, Retired. [8803] 03/02/1964 **CM01/01/1968**

Lees-Oakes, Miss Y, Unknown. [65932] 06/07/2006 **ME**

Leeson, Mrs B D, MCLIP, Life Member. [8804] 01/09/1967
CM01/01/1970

Leeson, Miss D C, BA MCLIP, Content and Access Team Leader,
Brynmor Jones L., Univ. of Hull. [35598] 11/11/1982 **CM09/08/1988**

Leet, Mrs J H, BA(Hons) MA MCLIP, Dep. Lib., St. Andrews Hosp.,
Northampton. [48177] 11/11/1992 **CM20/01/1999**

Leeves, Miss A, BSc(Hons) MA, Knowledge Mgmnt. Mgr, Watson,
Wyatt Worldwide, Surrey. [58551] 01/04/2000 **ME**

Leeves, Ms J, BA MCLIP, L. Systems Consultant, Farnham, Surrey.
[8807] 22/06/1971 **CM15/12/1974**

Lefebvre, Mrs C J, HonFCLIP, Sen. Inf. Specialist, U. K. Cochrane
Cent., Nat. Inst. for Health Res., Oxford [37226] 01/04/1984
HFE12/12/2007

Lefebvre, Ms M J, MA MLS MA AALIA FCLIP, Ch. Lib., Ryerson Univ.,
Toronto, Canada. [18790] 30/09/1972 **FE16/07/2003**

Leftley, Mr C P, BA BSc MCLIP, Lib., Wycliffe Hall, Univ. of Oxford.
[30463] 29/01/1979 **CM05/02/1981**

Legg, Mrs E A, BA DipLib MCLIP, Sch. Lib., Beaulieu Convent Sch., St.
Helier, Jersey. [33026] 10/10/1980 **CM01/11/1982**

Legg, Mrs J C, BA(Hons) MCLIP, p. /t. Lib., Thales Res. & Tech.
(UK)Ltd., Reading. [41328] 03/11/1987 **CM27/07/1994**

Legg, Mr J R, MA, Humanities Lib., Bodleian L., Oxford [39869]
01/10/1986 **ME**

Legg, Mrs R J, BA(Hons) MCLIP, Electronic Serv. Devel. Lib.,
Blackpool, Fylde & Wyre Hosp., NHS Trust, Victoria Hosp. [25669]
21/01/1976 **CM25/05/1994**

Legg, Mr T J, BSc DipLib MCLIP, Grp. Mgr., Essex. C.C., Basildon L.
[42340] 11/10/1988 **CM27/07/1994**

Legge, Mrs K E, BLib MCLIP, Sch. Lib., Hants. C.C., Oak Farm
Community Sch. [29847] 06/10/1978 **CM14/02/1984**

Leggett, Mrs D, BA(Hons) MCLIP, Lib., Local Studies Cent., N. Tyneside
Council. [49992] 08/02/1994 **CM25/07/2001**

Lehmann, Mrs J, MBE BA MCLIP, Head of L. Serv., Brighton & Sussex
Univ. Hosp. NHS Tst. [8817] 23/04/1967 **CM01/01/1970**

Lehva, Mrs M A, MCLIP, Sch. Lib. Serv. Mgr., LB of Havering Cent. Lib.
[10248] 16/01/1971 **CM23/07/1975**

Leibowitz, Miss Y, BA(Hons), Asst. Lib., American Intercontinental
Univ., London. [59631] 05/07/2001 **ME**

Leifer, Mrs J E, BA DipLib MA MCLIP, Sch. Lib., Immanuel Coll.,
Bushey. [42009] 19/07/1988 **CM27/03/1991**

Leigh, Miss B, Unknown. [10012309] 27/01/2009 **ME**

Leigh, Miss P, BA(Hons) MCLIP, Tech. Inf. Specialist, Welsh Assembly
Government., Cardiff. [53560] 22/07/1996 **CM18/03/1998**

Leighton, Mrs E, Lib. Admin., Cent. Bedfordshire Coll., Dunstable.
[10016987] 16/06/2010 **ME**

Leighton, Mrs S J, MA MCLIP, Principal Lib., L.B. of Barking &
Dagenham. Learning & Devel. [20417] 28/02/1973 **CM19/01/1976**

Leighton-Phelps, Mrs H J, MBA BA DipLib MCLIP, Unknown. [29725]
05/10/1978 **CM11/10/1984**

Leitch, Mr A, MCLIP, Lib. /Arch. Technician, Arch. Serv., Univ. Glasgow.
[8825] 16/01/1966 **CM01/01/1968**

Leitch, Mrs C, MCLIP, p. /t. Relief Staff, Redcar & Cleveland Bor.
Council. [17258] 01/01/1960 **CM01/01/1965**

Leith, Mrs A, BA DipLib MSc MCLIP, Lib. (Legal inf. /Horizon),
Freshfields Bruckhaus Deringer, London. [32108] 06/02/1980
CM25/01/1983

Leivers, Mr P, BA MBA MCLIP, Head of Cult. Serv., Dorset C.C.,
Dorchester. [33410] 02/12/1980 **CM01/08/1985**

Lemaitre, Miss V A, MA, Unwaged. [10006558] 30/10/2007 **ME**

Lemonidou, Ms M, BA MA MCLIP, Unemployed. [49173] 08/10/1993
CM19/05/1999

Lendon, Mr J W, FCLIP FRSA, Life Member [8830] 01/01/1951
FE01/01/1968

Lenihan, Ms D F, BA(Hons) DipLib MCLIP, Asst. Subject Lib., Wheatley
L., Oxford Brookes Univ. [50798] 18/10/1994 **CM01/02/2006**

Lenihan, Mr M A, BSc DipLib MCLIP, Ref. Lib., Lewisham L. Lewisham
[30464] 26/01/1979 **CM09/07/1981**

Lennon, Mrs F, BA(Hons) MA, Sch. Lib., Mostyn House Sch., Parkgate.
[65594] 22/02/2006 **ME**

Lennox, Mrs S, BA MCLIP, Tech. Asst., Lloyd's Register, Aberdeen
[32230] 09/02/1980 **CM07/02/1985**

Leonard, Ms C M, BA PGDip LLB, Asst. Inf. Mgr., The Royal Household,
London [10011711] 30/01/2003 **ME**

Leonard, Mrs K, BA(Hons), Community Lib., Flintshire [52418]
26/10/1995 **ME**

Leonard, Mrs L E, BSc(Econ) MCLIP, Lib., Dept. of Veterinary Med.,
Cambridge. [52231] 16/10/1995 **CM12/03/2003**

Leonard, Miss M B, BA DipLib MCLIP, Compliance Mgr., Slaughter and
May, London. [28328] 24/10/1977 **CM09/12/1980**

Leonard, Mrs M H, BSc (Econ), Asst. Lib., Queens Coll. Cambridge
[65036] 13/10/2005 **ME**

Lepley, Mrs D J, BA(Hons) MCLIP, Electronic Inf. Training Lib., Mid
Essex Hosp. Trust, Chelmsford. [44816] 03/12/1990 **CM17/03/1999**

Leppington, Mr C E, BA(Hons) MA MCLIP, Knowledge & Lib., Serv.
Mgr., Bromley Hosp. NHS Trust, Edu. Cent. L. [53947] 15/10/1996
CM21/07/1999

Leppington, Mrs R L, MA MCLIP, Intranet Content Mgr., NSPCC
[52235] 16/10/1995 **CM01/06/2005**

Leslie, Miss A E, BA(Hons) MCLIP, L. Asst., Nat. L. of Scotland,
Edinburgh. [56902] 02/11/1998 **CM08/08/2008**

Leslie, Mrs A H, MA DipLib MCLIP, Res. Devel. Offr., Educ. Devel.
Serv., Dundee. [31243] 15/10/1979 **CM02/11/1982**

Leslie, Mr R, MCLIP, Retired. [8843] 12/09/1967 **CM01/01/1969**

Lester, Dr R G, BSc PhD FCLIP FLS FRSA, Retired. [33852]
01/04/1981 **FE25/03/1993**

Leszczynska, Miss M A, BA MCLIP, Business Systems Offr., Child.
Sch. & Families Dept., L.B. Merton, Morden. [32672] 15/07/1980
CM05/08/1983

Letellier, Mr P L, Stud. [63678] 12/08/2004 **ME**

Letendrie, Mrs F E, BA(Hons) Dip Inf Sci, Inter. Inf. Offr., Help the Hospice, London. [10005499] 09/07/1990 **ME**

Letterborough, Ms C, Stud., Manchester Met. Univ. [60021] 26/11/2001 **ME**

Letton, Miss C R, MA FSA SCOT MCLIP, Area Lib. -Cent. Area, Galashiels L., Scottish Borders Council. [19623] 10/10/1972 **CM21/01/1975**

Letton, Mr S, MCLIP, Retired. [8852] 12/03/1945 **CM01/01/1949**

Letzgus, Ms M, BSc(Hons) MCLIP, Law. Lib., De Montfort Univ., Leicester. [50323] 22/06/1994 **CM20/03/1996**

Leung, Mr K, MCLIP, Mgr. (Knowledge Serv.), Hosp. Auth., Hong Kong. [21669] 01/01/1974 **CM20/07/1978**

Leung, Ms S Y R, BPhil DipLIS MA, Lib., Marymount Prim. Sch., Hong Kong. [50030] 24/02/1994 **ME**

Levay, Mr P, BA(Hons) MA MCLIP, Inf. Specialist, NICE. [58185] 15/11/1999 **CM21/05/2003**

Levene, Mrs A, BA MCLIP, Clinical Support Lib., Whipps Cross Univ. Hosp. Trust, Leytonstone. [10217] 20/04/1969 **CM01/01/1972**

Levene, Miss S V, BA(Hons), Receptionist / Cust. Serv. Asst., Stafford CC, Stafford [10015048] 09/10/2009 **ME**

Levenson, Mrs J, L. Asst., N. London Collegiate Jnr. Sch., Edgware. [57811] 16/08/1999 **AF**

Leventhall, Mr A M, BA(Hons) DipLib MCLIP, Community Lib., Fakenham L., Norfolk C.C. [35762] 01/11/1982 **CM07/07/1987**

Levett, Miss S E, BA CertED MCLIP, Managing Dir., Culture Counts Consultants Ltd. [29518] 23/09/1978 **CM27/10/1980**

Levey, Miss C, MCLIP, Sen. Asst. Lib., Goldsmiths Coll. L., New Cross, London. [10013469] 20/06/1980 **CM27/08/1982**

Levey, Mrs D, DipLib MCLIP, L. Devel. Mgr., W. Herts. NHS Trust, Hemel Hempstead Hosp. [27615] 25/05/1977 **CM14/08/1981**

Levey, Mrs F A M, BA(Hons) PG Dip, Asst. Lib., Aquinas Coll., Stockport. [10002654] 01/05/2007 **ME**

Levi, Miss R, Unwaged. [50889] 27/10/1994 **ME**

Levick, Mrs J E, BA(LIB) MCLIP, Sch. Lib., Sch. L. Serv., Doncaster. [10402] 24/02/1968 **CM05/06/1974**

Levick, Mrs W, Unknown. [10014195] 21/07/2009 **ME**

Levin, Mrs A J T, FCLIP, Life member. [8859] 11/10/1933 **FE01/01/1948**

Levine, Mrs K M, MSc MCLIP, Asst. Lib., Univ. of the W. of England. [15279] 01/01/1968 **CM01/01/1972**

Levingstone, Mrs C, ACLIP, L. Mgr., Dunstable Lib., Beds [64184] 31/01/2005 **ACL07/12/2005**

Leviston, Ms F V, BA MA, Stud., Univ. of Sheffield. [10016854] 27/05/2010 **ME**

Levitt, Mrs C M, BA(Hons) MCLIP, Accredited Indexer [41880] 09/05/1988 **CM19/11/2003**

Lewandowski, Ms S, BFA, SEn. Info. Asst., Northumbria Univ., Newcastle Upon Tyne [10013152] 11/07/2010 **AF**

Lewent, Mrs J A, BSc DipLib MCLIP, p. /t. Sch. Lib., cranborne Primary Sch., Potters Bar, Herts. [33815] 26/02/1981 **CM04/10/1983**

Lewin, Mrs M, BSc MCLIP, p. /t. Asst. Lib., Leeds City Coll.,Park Lane Campus. [23391] 12/01/1975 **CM19/01/1977**

Lewin, Dr S, PhD, MA(Hons), Graduate Trainee, Univ. of Leeds. [10016924] 10/06/2010 **ME**

Lewington, Miss R E, Unknown. [10013923] 17/06/2009 **ME**

Lewington, Dr R J, BSc PhD MCLIP, Retired [60541] 22/10/1974 **CM06/11/1978**

Lewis, Mr A I, BSc DipLib MCLIP, Lib., Moore Stephens LLP, London. [31887] 14/01/1980 **CM21/01/1982**

Lewis, Miss A J, BSc, Child. Lib., Durning L., L.B. of Lambeth. [56983] 18/11/1998 **ME**

Lewis, Miss A, Lib. Asst., Solihull Coll., Solihull [10017101] 01/05/2000 **ME**

Lewis, Mrs C M, BA MCLIP, Res. Mgr., Budde Comm., Australia. [20650] 01/01/1973 **CM27/01/1982**

Lewis, Mrs C, MCLIP, Asst. Lib., Merton Coll., Oxford. [10015453] 14/07/1993 **CM26/11/1997**

Lewis, Ms C, BSc(Hons) PgDip MCLIP, LLS Customer Serv. Mgr. & LLC Mgr., Univ. for the Creative Arts, Epsom, Surrey. [58771] 17/07/2000 **CM10/07/2002**

Lewis, Mr D, BSc MBA CBiol MSB MCLIP, Writer & Translator [60725] 30/04/1980 **CM26/03/1985**

Lewis, Mrs E M, BSc(Econ) DipLib, Lib., Nevill Hall Hosp., Rowland Isaac L., Abergavenny. [55445] 13/10/1997 **ME**

Lewis, Ms F R, BA PGCE, Unknown. [10015564] 15/12/2009 **ME**

Lewis, Ms G R, MCLIP, Lib., HM Prison, Nottingham. [8874] 29/03/1968 **CM01/01/1971**

Lewis, Mr H M, BA(Hons) PGDipILS MCLIP, Lib., Bracknell Forest Council. [58187] 15/11/1999 **CM01/06/2005**

Lewis, Mrs H M, MCLIP, Prison Lib., HMP The Mount. [12995] 17/11/1969 **CM17/08/1973**

Lewis, Miss I A, MLib BA DipLib MCLIP, Practice/Business Mgr., Swindon [24900] 14/10/1975 **CM18/11/1977**

Lewis, Mrs J A, BA DipLib MCLIP, Lib., Hants. Co. L. [27671] 01/07/1977 **CM31/08/1979**

Lewis, Mrs J A, BA(Hons) MSc, Stud. [10013138] 02/04/2009 **ME**

Lewis, Mrs J B, Unknown, Surrey Hist. Cent., woking, Surrey. [65849] 31/05/2006 **AF**

Lewis, Miss J, MCLIP, Sen. Lib., Cent. L., L.B. of Bromley. [8879] 06/07/1972 **CM09/02/1976**

Lewis, Ms K A, BA(Hons)DipLib, Head of Knowledge Mgmnt., Dept. of Health, London. [35871] 26/01/1983 **ME**

Lewis, Miss L M, BSc(Econ), Career Break. [59204] 08/01/2001 **ME**

Lewis, Ms L, BA(Hons), Business Inf. Coord., Arup, London. [61095] 28/02/2002 **AF**

Lewis, Mr M J, MA DipLib MCLIP, Dir. of L. Serv., The Univ. of Sheffield. [28619] 01/01/1978 **CM10/07/1981**

Lewis, Mrs M P, BSc(Hons) Dip Psych (OU) MCLIP, Learning Resource Facilitator, Yale Coll. of Wrexham, N. Wales. [10002763] 27/04/2007 **CM05/05/2010**

Lewis, Mr M R, MCLIP, Retired. [8892] 20/02/1968 **CM01/01/1972**

Lewis, Mr N, BA(Hons) MA MCLIP, L. Dir., Univ. of E. Anglia, Norwich. [54721] 17/03/1997 **CM19/01/2000**

Lewis, Mr P R, MA HonFLA FCLIP, Life Member. [8894] 23/03/1949 **FE01/01/1955**

Lewis, Mrs R J, MCLIP, Asst. Head, Canterbury Christ Church Univ. Kent. [29059] 14/03/1978 **CM21/09/1983**

Lewis, Mr R W, BA DipLib MLS MBA MCLIP, Head, Ch. Scientist's Unit, Health & Saftey Exec., Bootle [34581] 01/01/1982 **CM16/05/1985**

Lewis, Mrs S E, MCLIP, Sch. Lib., Homewood Sch., Tenterden, Kent. [26482] 16/10/1976 **CM31/07/1979**

Lewis, Ms S J I, MCLIP, P. /t. Lib., Hampstead Sch., London. [8900] 09/07/1969 **CM01/07/1972**

Lewis, Ms S J, BEd MLIS MCLIP, Comm. Lib., Biggar L. [41468] 01/01/1988 **CM06/04/2005**

Lewis, Ms S M, BA(Hons) MA MCLIP, Lib., Hampshire Partnership NHS Trust, Hampshire. [53737] 20/09/1996 **CM21/11/2001**

Lewis, Mr T, BA(Hons) MA, Stud., Leed Met. Univ. [10015080] 12/10/2009 **ME**

Lewis, Mrs Y M, Lib., Freelance. [25473] 02/03/1970 **ME**

Lewis, Ms Y, BA MA, Asst. L. Curator, The Nat. Trust, London. [42181] 05/10/1988 **ME**

Lewsey, Miss S W, MCLIP, Life Member. [17264] 11/06/1950 **CM01/01/1955**

Ley, Mrs A K, Sen. Lib. Asst., Perranporth Lib., Cornwall [64414] 15/03/2005 **AF**

Leyland, Mrs M, MCLIP, Inf. Lib., Hillington L., Uxbridge. [8908] 22/10/1969 **CM30/01/1974**

Leyland, Mr T P, BSc(Hons) PGCE PGDipILM, Learning Cent. / Support Serv. Coordinator. Exeter Coll. [61953] 17/12/2002 **ME**

Liang, Ms M, BA, Head of L. &Inf. Serv., Brit. Sch., Rio De Janeiro. [10001252] 18/11/1988 **ME**

Libbey, Miss J P, BA MSc(Econ), Inf. Asst., Brunel Univ., Uxbridge. [61776] 04/11/2002 **ME**

Licence, Mrs H F, BA(Hons) MA MCLIP, Career break [55380] 06/10/1997 **CM18/09/2002**

Lichfield, Mrs L M, BA MCLIP, Learning Resources Mgr., Luton VI Form Coll. [37896] 15/11/1984 **CM10/05/1988**

Lickley, Mr D, BA(Hons) DipLib MA, HR Support Mgr., Kings Coll. London, Waterloo [44453] 09/10/1990 **ME**

Lidbetter, Mrs C S, BA(Hons) MA MCLIP, Asst. Subject Li., Headington L., Oxford Brookes Univ. [52173] 10/10/1995 **CM21/11/2001**

Liddle, Miss M O, MCLIP, Life Member. [8912] 02/03/1950 **CM07/01/1976**

Lightwood, Miss E G, MCLIP, Life Member. [8922] 09/11/1931 **CM01/01/1940**

Lill, Ms F S, Electronic Serv. Mgr., The Brit. L. [41035] 06/10/1987 **ME**

Lilley, Dr G, MA PhD DipLib FCLIP, Life Member & Sen. Res. Fellow in Bibl., Dept. of English, Univ. of Wales. [8927] 06/10/1961 **FE01/01/1970**

Lilley, Mrs J A, BSc(Hons) DipLib MCLIP, Team Lib., Sch. L. Serv., St. Helens. [27005] 11/01/1977 **CM01/07/1988**

Lilley, Mrs M, BA LTCL MCLIP, Retired. [8930] 03/02/1960 **CM01/01/1962**

Lilliman, Mr R M, BA MCLIP, Br. Lib., Q Learningl L., Wandsworth P. L. [20854] 02/08/1973 **CM05/08/1975**

Lillis, Mr M, BTech MCLIP, Records Mgr., Quintiles LTD., Bracknell. [61239] 06/05/1986 **CM06/05/1986**

Lim, Mrs K L, MCLIP, Unknown. [18914] 27/09/1972 **CM19/02/1976**

Lim, S H, BSocSc MCLIP, Ch. Lib., KDU Coll., Selangor, Malaysia. [22989] 08/10/1974 **CM09/09/1977**

Limper-Herz, Mrs K, MA, Curator, The Brit. L., London. [59481] 09/04/2001 **ME**

Lin, Miss D, Stud. [10013644] 18/05/2009 **ME**

Linacre, Miss C E, BA DipLib MCLIP, Head of L. Serv., RICS, London. [37597] 09/10/1984 **CM08/03/1988**

Linardi, Miss J A, MA(Hons), Unknown. [10015178] 23/10/2009 **ME**

Lincoln, Mrs J M, BA MCLIP, Relief Work(p. /t.), Stirling Council L. Dept. [19685] 30/10/1972 **CM04/08/1976**

Linden, Mr H, MA, L. Asst. The Maughan L. King's Coll., London. [10017135] 14/07/2010 **ME**

Lindfield, Mrs M R, MA BA(Hons), Lib., Crawley Lib., Crawley [54660] 04/02/1997 **ME**

Lindley, Mr D, MCLIP, Unknown. [8938] 19/02/1965 **CM01/01/1969**

Lindley, Mrs J M, BA(Hons) MCLIP, Asst. Lib. [48164] 11/11/1992 **CM22/03/1995**

Lindley, Mrs J, MCLIP, Asst. Catr., Coventry L. [8676] 01/01/1969 **CM20/12/1972**

Lindley, Mr P, MCLIP, Customer Serv. Lib., Hinckley Grp., Leics. C.C. (Retiring March) [8939] 04/05/1967 **CM01/01/1971**

Lindsay, Ms A E, LLB MCLIP, EU & Competition Inf. Offr., Lovells LLP, London. [26452] 04/10/1976 **CM24/01/1979**

Lindsay, Mrs C A, BLib MCLIP DMS, Unknown. [32913] 01/10/1980 **CM02/09/1986**

Lindsay, Mr D, BA DipLib MCLIP, Knowledge Mgmnt. Consultant, Northants. [28442] 28/11/1977 **CM22/06/1981**

Lindsay, Miss D, MA DipLib MCLIP, Sen. Lib., Strathclyde Univ., Glasgow. [28058] 01/10/1977 **CM20/10/1980**

Lindsay, Ms G M, BEd CertLS MCLIP, H. of Learning Resources, Warden Pk. Sch., Haywards Heath, E. Sussex. [57911] 01/10/1999 **CM19/11/2003**

Lindsay, Miss J A, BA DipLib MCLIP, LRC Mgr., Long Road 6th Form Coll., Cambridge. [31655] 07/11/1979 **CM08/06/1983**

Lindsay, Mr J W, BA MCLIP, Bibliographic & Support Mgr., N. Lanarkshire Council, Motherwell. [25589] 02/02/1976 **CM16/07/1980**

Lindsay, Dr M, BA MPhil PhD RGN MCLIP, Inf. Offr., Ctre. for Adv. of Learning & Teaching, UCL [8942] 19/07/1971 **CM03/09/1979**

Lindsey, Mr C, MCLIP, Researcher. [8944] 18/03/1965 **CM01/01/1969**

Lindsey, Mrs P, MCLIP, Life Member. [8945] 25/10/1945 **CM01/01/1969**

Line, Prof M B, MA FCLIP HonFLA CCMI HonDLitt HonDSc, Life Member. [8947] 10/04/1951 **FE01/01/1955**

Linfield, Mr A M, BA DipLib MCLIP, Lib., London Sch. of Theology, Northwood. [29729] 04/10/1978 **CM07/12/1980**

Linford, Ms R, MA(Hons) DipILS MCLIP, Owner, Rebecca Linford Indexing & Website Serv., Blairgowrie [52649] 15/11/1995 **CM19/11/2003**

Lingard, Mrs L, BA DipLib MCLIP, Unknown. [35778] 10/01/1983 **CM06/09/1988**

Linin, Mrs S A, Comm. Lib., Kent C.C., Sevenoaks L. [56401] 01/07/1998 **ME**

Linnane, Mr C, BA, L. Offr., Edinburgh. [65102] 01/11/2005 **ME**

Linton, Ms A M, BA(Hons) Dip IT MSc MCLIP, Bibliographic & User Serv. Lib., CCCU L., Canterbury Christ Church Univ. [42238] 06/10/1988 **CM20/05/1998**

Linton, Mr D H, MCLIP, Asst. Area L. Offr., Highland Council, Ross, Skye & Lochaber [8963] 22/02/1969 **CM04/02/1975**

Linton, Mr W D, BSc BLS CBiol MIBiol ALAI HonFLA, Life Member [8965] 23/09/1965 **HFE21/05/1992**

Lipner, Miss L C, Inf. Offr., Inst. of Mechanical Eng., Westminster. [10006374] 23/10/2007 **ME**

Liptrot, Mrs S M, BLib MCLIP, Prison Lib., Eastwood Park Prison, Glos. [1958] 27/04/1970 **CM23/08/1974**

Lipworth, Mrs E L, BA HDLIS HDE, Med. Res., Sci. & Comm. Inf. [48499] 29/01/1993 **ME**

Liquorice, Miss M E, FCLIP, Retired [8969] 01/01/1942 **FE01/01/1955**

Lisle, Mr P E, BA MSc MCLIP, Lib., Newbold Coll. L., Bracknell. [46718] 08/01/1992 **CM24/09/1997**

Lison, Mrs B, Dir., Bremen Pub. L., Germany. [51911] 07/08/1995 **ME**

List, Mr D, Consultant, Self-employed, London. [39181] 11/12/1985 **ME**

Lister, Mrs C A, Acquisitions Lib., Isle of Wight Coll., Newport. [57530] 14/04/1999 **AF**

Lister, Mrs E, BA FCLIP, Life Member. [8974] 07/10/1958 **FE26/10/1962**

Lister, Ms J, MA PGDipILS MCLIP, Dept. Lib., Architecture & Bldg. Sci., Univ. of Strathclyde. [54335] 21/11/1996 **CM17/09/2003**

Lister, Mrs K, Customer Serv. Lib., Leicestershire Co. Council. [64183] 31/01/2005 **ME**

Lister, Mr M J, BA MCLIP, Area L. Mgr., Cumbria C.C., Carlisle L. [24520] 03/09/1975 **CM29/12/1978**

Lister, Ms M, BA MSc MIMgt MILAM MCLIP, Retired. [8975] 28/03/1966 **CM01/01/1971**

Lister, Ms R A, BA(Hons), PGCE, Sch. Lib., Royds Sch. Specialist Language Coll., Oulton. [42360] 27/10/1988 **ME**

Listwon, Ms A, MA, e-Lib., Newcastle Coll. Lib., Newcastle-Upon-Tyne [10013147] 23/04/2009 **ME**

Litchfield, Mrs M, MCLIP, Retired [8978] 10/01/1966 **CM01/01/1969**

Little, Mr B, MPhil FCLIP, Retired. [8979] 18/02/1963 **FE02/11/1973**

Little, Mr D R T, MCLIP, L. Serv. Mgr., Milton Keynes Hosp. [50718] 13/10/1994 **CM13/10/1994**

Little, Mrs F M, MCLIP, Knowledge Serv. Lib., Hants. Partnership NHS Trust, Moorgreen Hosp., Southampton. [26791] 18/11/1976 **CM07/07/1980**

Little, Miss J H, BA MBA MCLIP, Head of the L. & Inf. Serv., Liverpool City Council. [8984] 30/06/1970 **CM05/07/1973**

Littledale, Mrs F J, MA(Hons) MA MCLIP, Liaison Lib., St. Georges, Univ. of London. [57353] 17/02/1999 **CM29/03/2004**

Littlejohn, Ms S, BA(Hons) DipLib DipTrans, Acting Subject Lib. (Social sciences), Senate House L. [28960] 15/02/1978 **ME**

Littlemore, Mrs K V, BSocSc(Hons) MSc MCLIP, Academic Support Mgr., Univ. of Northampton [57992] 11/10/1999 **CM15/09/2004**

Littler, Ms A R, BA(Hons) MLS MCLIP, Tech. Supp. Offr., Surrey Co. Council [31503] 19/10/1979 **CM18/02/1986**

Littler, Miss J, MCLIP, Retired. [8992] 11/02/1963 **CM01/01/1970**

Littler, Mrs V C, ACLIP, Sr. L. Asst., Helsby L., Cheshire. [65694] 01/04/2006 **ACL17/01/2007**

Littlewood, Miss A, BA(Hons) MA MCLIP, Trials Search Co-ordinator, Cochrane Oral Health Grp, Univ. of Manchester. [57215] 19/01/1999 **CM17/09/2003**

Littlewood, Ms F, BA(Hons) MA, Unknown. [10013595] 14/07/2009 **ME**

Litton, Miss J, BA(Hons), Computing Advisor, Univ. of Wales, Aberystwyth,. [57596] 12/05/1999 **ME**

Litwin-Roberts, Mrs M L, BSc(Econ) MA MCLIP, Lib., Southfields Comm. Coll., London. [53146] 01/04/1996 **CM01/02/2006**

Liu Yew Fai, Miss M, Sen. Lib., Municipality of Port-Louis, Mauritius. [52392] 31/10/1995 **ME**

Liu, Mrs C, MSc MCLIP, Systems Asst., Univ. of Surrey L., Guildford [64797] 04/07/2005 **CM09/09/2009**

Liu, Mrs K, BA(Hons), Recruitment Consultant, Sue Hill Recruitment, London. (Currently on Maternity leave) [61864] 22/11/2002 **ME**

Liu, Miss L M C, BEng(Hons) MSc, Asst. Lib., N. W. London Hosp. Trust, Cent. Middlesex Hosp. [57868] 23/09/1999 **ME**

Liu, Miss M, Employed (unknown) [64083] 15/12/2004 **ME**

Livesey, Rev L J, FCLIP, Life Member. [9000] 19/03/1951 **FE01/01/1957**

Llewellyn, Mrs C M, BA, Lib., Dept. for Business, Innovation & Skills, (BIS) London. [35491] 19/10/1982 **ME**

Llewellyn-Jones, Ms F D W, BA MCLIP, p. /t. Lect. /Tutor, F.E. Suffolk C.C., Lowestoft. [16015] 01/01/1971 **CM10/12/1974**

Lloyd, Mrs A M, BA PGDipIM MCLIP, Early Years Lib., Stoke on Trent C.C. [59820] 10/10/2001 **CM08/12/2004**

Lloyd, Ms A, DPhil, L. Mgr., Mavedu Ltd., Milton Keynes. [10006291] 05/10/2007 **AF**

Lloyd, Miss B, BA(Hons) MA, Unknown. [10002920] 10/05/2007 **ME**

Lloyd, Mrs C E, BA MCLIP, Unwaged [37643] 12/10/1984 **CM15/05/2002**

Lloyd, Ms C S, BA MA MCLIP, Head of L. and Arch. Serv., London Sch. of Hygiene & Tropical Med. [47638] 09/10/1992 **CM31/01/1996**

Lloyd, Mr C T, BA(Hons) MCLIP, Dep. Head of L., LB of Hammersmith & Fulham. [38135] 15/01/1985 **CM14/11/1989**

Lloyd, Mr D R, BA, Mgr:Learning Partnerships, Coventry City Council. [54068] 22/10/1996 **ME**

Lloyd, Ms D, BA DipLib MCLIP, Lib., Countryside Council for Wales, Bangor. [33312] 06/10/1980 **CM21/11/1983**

Lloyd, Ms E V, BLib MCLIP, Unwaged. [41546] 20/01/1988 **CM26/02/1992**

Lloyd, Mrs E, BA MEd MCLIP, Retired. Malta. [31002] 10/07/1979 **CM13/06/1989**

Lloyd, Mr G K, MCLIP MA, Life Member. [18888] 21/10/1968 **CM01/01/1971**

Lloyd, Mr H G, MSc BSc HND MCLIP, Asst. Lib., Nat. L. Wales. Ceredgion. [60901] 21/12/2001 **CM28/01/2009**

Lloyd, Mrs J O, BA DipLib MIM MAppSc, Community Liaison Co-ordinator, Hornsby Shire L. & Info. Serv., Hornsby, NSW, Aus. [61476] 12/08/2002 **ME**

Lloyd, Mr P, MCLIP, Employment not known. [9021] 23/09/1969 **CM04/09/1973**

Lloyd, Mrs S, L. Asst., Motor Neurone Disease Assoc., Northampton. [61108] 22/02/2002 **AF**

Lloyd, Mrs V, BA MCLIP, Unwaged [24509] 01/09/1975 **CM30/10/1979**

Lloyd-Brown, Mr G A D, BA(Hons), Unknown. [10005964] 10/10/2008 **ME**

Lloyd-Evans, Miss B, BA(Hons) DipLIS MCLIP, Asst. Lib. (Catg.), The Wellcome Trust, London. [44889] 09/01/1991 **CM15/03/2000**

Lloyd-Wiggins, Mrs A, BA MCLIP, Junior Sch. Lib., Robert Gordon's Coll., Aberdeen. [30559] 08/01/1979 **CM30/09/1982**

Llywelyn, Mr G, BA DipLib MCLIP, Primary Sch. Lib., Carmarthen C.C., [40046] 12/10/1986 **CM12/09/1990**

Loader, Dr R J, BSc Phd MSc, Inf. Specialist, GCHQ, Cheltenham [10007921] 03/03/2008 **ME**

Loake, Miss C, Unknown. [10012003] 09/12/2008 **ME**

Loarridge, Mrs C, BA MCLIP, Unemployed. [2724] 01/01/1972 **CM21/07/1975**

Loat, Ms S M, BA MA MCLIP, Unknown. [36881] 11/01/1984 **CM16/05/1990**

Lobban, Miss M, MA MSc DipLib MCLIP, Dep. Dir. of LIS, Napier Univ. of Edinburgh. [28060] 08/10/1977 **CM28/11/1980**

Lobban, Miss R, BA MCLIP, Retired. [9030] 03/01/1963 **CM01/01/1966**

Lobo, Mrs A, L. Asst., Aston Univ. [10009226] 07/05/2008 **ME**

Lochhead, Mrs A, BA MCLIP, Bibl. Serv. Asst., Napier Univ., Edinburgh. [22542] 22/06/1974 **CM01/08/1977**

Lochhead, Ms I R, BA DipLib MCLIP, Liaison Lib., Norwich City Coll. [36351] 04/10/1983 **CM13/06/1989**

Lochore, Mr S, BA(Hons) MA MCLIP, Inf. Offr., IDOX Inf. Serv., Glasgow. [62217] 19/03/2003 **CM21/05/2008**

Lock, Ms E L, BSc, Inf. Specialist, GCHQ, Cheltenham. [52123] 05/10/1995 **ME**

Lock, Ms M A, BA MPhil MCLIP, Local Studies Lib., Tameside MBC, Lancashire. [24434] 25/07/1975 **CM26/09/1978**

Lock, Mrs T, BA(Hons) QTS HIFL, L. Asst., St Brendans Coll., Brislington, Bristol. [10011961] 05/12/2008 **AF**

Locke, Mr D W, BA MSc MCLIP, Mgr., BBC, London. [20050] 15/01/1973 **CM26/07/1977**

Lockerbie, Miss C, ACLIP, Slide Collection Asst., Boots L., Nottingham. [65838] 25/05/2006 **ACL22/06/2007**

Lockett, Miss K J, BA(Hons) MA MCLIP, Lib., Wellington L., Wellington City L., New Zealand. [60963] 18/01/2002 **CM29/03/2006**

Lockheart, Mr G A, BA MA, Inf. Specialist., King's Coll. London [64310] 25/02/2005 **ME**

Lockley, Mrs U K, BSc MSc(Econ) MCLIP, Lib. in Charge, Oxford Union Soc., Oxford. [29806] 06/10/1978 **CM17/03/1982**

Lockwood, Miss A T, MA, LRC Lib., Ian Ramsey CE Sch., Stockton-on-Tees. [52318] 26/10/1995 **ME**

Lockwood, Mrs J M, Learning Cent. Mgr., Globe Academy. [59579] 05/06/2001 **ME**

Lockwood, Miss R, Pg Diploma BSc MPH, L. Asst., Continuing Educ. L., Oxford [10009532] 03/06/2008 **ME**

Lockyer, Mrs D, FCLIP, Life Member. [9049] 09/09/1955 **FE30/01/1978**

Loder, Miss E P, FCLIP, Life Member. [9051] 01/01/1948 **FE18/08/1975**

Lodge, Mrs A J, BA(Hons) DipInf MCLIP, Lib. (p/t) Hertfordshire Child., Sch. & Families L. [44371] 02/10/1990 **CM24/05/1995**

Lodge, Miss E E, BLib MCLIP, Lib., Serious Fraud Off., London. [39568] 06/03/1986 **CM17/10/1990**

Lodge, Miss H A, BLib MCLIP MSc, Knowledge & Comminications Mgr., London Health Observatory [35272] 01/10/1982 **CM13/06/1990**

Lodge, Mrs M, Head of L. & Learning Res., St. Olave's Grammar Sch., Orpington. [65487] 10/02/2006 **ME**

Lodge, Mrs V, MA MCLIP, Sen. Res. Offr., Arts Univ. Coll. at Bournemouth, Dorset [38897] 14/10/1985 **CM10/05/1988**

Loewenstein, Mr P, BA MSc FCLIP, Retired [37007] 19/01/1984 **FE23/09/1998**

Lofthouse, Mrs A, BA(Hons) MA DipEd MCLIP, Freelance English Tutor [1554] 23/09/1970 **CM12/09/1973**

Loftus, Mrs C J, BA MCLIP, Unemployed [30775] 08/03/1979 **CM11/05/1981**

Logan, Mr A W, BA(Hons), Stud. [10016306] 05/03/2010 **ME**

Logan, Miss E R, BA MSc MCLIP, Serials Lib., Univ. of Ulster, Cent. L., Serials Mgmnt. Div. [25592] 29/01/1976 **CM01/08/1980**

Logan, Mr H J, BA DipLib MCLIP, Lib., Angus Council, Arbroath L. [35372] 18/10/1982 **CM04/08/1987**

Logan, Ms J, DipLib MCLIP, Child. Lib., Romford L., L.B. Havering. and L. Sup., N. Chingford L [37005] 30/01/1984 **CM01/09/1987**

Logue, Mrs L E T, BLS MCLIP, Exec. Offr., CILIP Ireland. [36207] 20/07/1983 **CM15/11/1988**

Lomas, Mrs A M, ACLIP, Snr. L. Mgr., Swadlincote L., Derbyshire. [65188] 17/11/2005 **ACL29/03/2007**

Lomas, Mr D B, MCLIP, Life Member. [9065] 02/02/1949 **CM01/01/1956**

Lomas, Ms J M, BA DipInfSc MCLIP, Trust Lib., Lister Hosp., E. & N. Herts. NHS Trust. [41151] 12/10/1987 **CM16/10/1989**

Lomas, Mrs R A, BA(Hons) MCLIP, Young Peoples Serv. Co-ord., Tameside M.B.C. [41003] 01/10/1987 **CM23/01/2002**

Lomas, Mrs S C, BA MCLIP, Inf. Resource Mgr., R. N. I. B., London. [27432] 01/04/1977 **CM11/04/1979**

Lomas, Mr T C, BA MSc MCLIP, Lib., Stoke Heath HMYOI, Shropshire. [21516] 01/01/1969 **CM21/10/1975**

Lomas, Miss T, Unknown. [10014349] 17/07/2009 **ME**

Lomax, Ms K, BA Grad Dip IMS MCLIP, e-Learning Coordinator, London Deanery, London. [10005596] 25/07/2007 **CM10/03/2010**

Lomax, Mrs S M, BA MCLIP, Inf. Asst., Bolton Univ. L. [25904] 01/04/1976 **CM11/04/1979**

Londero, Ms S, BA(Hons) MSc, Asst. Lib. (Bibl. Serv.), Gonville & Caius Coll., Univ. of Cambridge. [63148] 12/02/2004 **ME**

London, Mr N, BA(Hons) MA MCLIP, Serv. Mngr., Notts. C.C. [36968] 09/01/1984 **CM14/04/1987**

Lonergan, Mrs G F, BA MCLIP, Hd. of Archive & Learning Resources, Cooperative Coll., Manchester [30401] 15/01/1979 **CM27/04/1984**

Long, Mrs C A, Inf. Specialist, Aston Univ. [64457] 31/03/2005 **ME**

Long, Mrs G M, BA, L. Asst., SSEES L., Univ. Coll. London. [52265] 20/10/1995 **ME**

Long, Mrs H M, Stud. /L. Asst., Univ. of the W. of England, Bristol. [65572] 28/02/2006 **ME**

Long, Mr I, BA, Stud., London Met. Univ. [10011884] 26/11/2008 **ME**

Long, Miss K C, BA(Hons), Stud. [10015241] 29/10/2009 **ME**

Long, Mr M T, MCLIP BA DMS, Retired. [10006900] 17/10/1977 **CM01/07/1991**

Long, Mr N W, BLib MBA MCLIP, Lib. Serv. Consultant OCLC Canada. [29731] 20/10/1978 **CM21/02/1984**

Long, Ms S L, BA(Hons) MSc, Sen. Lib. Resource Devel. Dept. of Health L., Leeds [58094] 29/10/1999 **ME**

Long, Mr T N, BA DipLib MCLIP CertNatSci, Inf. Offr., Clifford Chance LLP, London. [36312] 02/10/1983 **CM01/04/2002**

Long, Mrs T, BA MCLIP, L. Serv. MGR., Dorset CC [37983] 01/01/1985 **CM27/05/1992**

Longbottom, Mr P R, BSc(Hons) MA MCLIP DipLIS, Lib. Mgr., Scottish Natural Heritage. [43251] 11/10/1989 **CM22/09/1999**

Longden, Mr P R, MCLIP, Operations Mgr., Bibl. Serv., Bucks L. and Heritage, Aylesbury. [18242] 05/10/1972 **CM04/10/1976**

Longley, Mr N, BA ACLIP, Campus Lib., Usworth Learning Cent., City of Sunderland Coll. [66104] 25/09/2006 **ACL24/04/2009**

Longman, Mr A, Academic Lib., Kingsley Sch., Bideford, Devon [64955] 03/10/2005 **ME**

Longmuir, Ms S J, BA(Hons) MCLIP, Inf. Specialist, NBS, Newcastle. [54266] 11/11/1996 **CM20/11/2002**

Lonsdale, Miss D J, Community Lib., Brotton L. [10012562] 24/02/2009 **AF**

Lonsdale, Mr D, MA(Hons) MSc MCLIP, Lib., Coatbridge Coll., Lanarkshire. [48079] 03/11/1992 **CM26/11/1997**

Lonsdale, Ms J M, BLib MCLIP, Young People and Sch. Inf. Offr., Skipton Area, N. Yorkshire Co. Council [28331] 01/11/1977 **CM09/10/1981**

Lopez Blanco, Mr J M, Dip, Unknown. [10012779] 03/03/2009 **AF**

Lopez-Boronat, Miss L, Unwaged [10015692] 14/01/2010 **ME**

Loth-Hill, Mrs J M, MA PGDipLIS, Learning Res. Lib., William Howard Sch., Brampton, Cumbria. [38082] 11/01/1985 **ME**

Louden, Mrs J A, MA MSc MCLIP MSc, Head of Inf. Serv., Glasgow Met. Coll., Glasgow. [41745] 01/03/1988 **CM18/04/1990**

Louden, Mr M, BA(Hons), Educ. Lib., S. E. E. L.B., L. H.Q., Ballynahinch. [42034] 08/08/1988 **ME**

Loudon, Ms L, Unknown. [10015356] 11/12/2009 **ME**

Loughbrough, Mrs T J, BSc MCLIP, Inf. Mgmnt. Specialist, Unilever R&D, Colworth, Beds. [60501] 23/04/2001 **CM23/04/2001**

Loughlin, Mrs A L, BA(Hons) MCLIP, Asst Serv. Point Offr/Registrar/Lib. Asst., Broadford Serv. Point, Isle of Skye [46823] 11/02/1992 **CM19/07/2000**

Loughridge, Mrs J I, BA MCLIP, Retired. [6204] 25/10/1966 **CM01/01/1969**

Louison, Miss P, BA MCLIP DMS, Subject Lib., Thames Valley Univ., London. [34703] 11/02/1982 **CM07/06/1988**

Lovatt, Mrs V, BA(Hons) MCLIP, Portal Team Leader, Stock & Promotion, Staffs. C.C. [46566] 12/11/1991 **CM26/07/1995**

Love, Ms C M, BA DipLib MCLIP, Network Lib., Portlethen Academy, Aberdeenshire. [44239] 23/07/1990 **CM19/08/1992**

Love, Mr J G, BA DipLib MCLIP, Unknown [33313] 23/10/1980 **CM10/06/1985**

Love, Mrs J H, MA DipLib MCLIP, Project Offr. (L. & Inf.), N. Lanarkshire Council. [37049] 07/02/1984 **CM13/06/1989**

Love, Miss J I, MCLIP, Life Member. [9102] 16/04/1943 **CM01/01/1952**

Love, Mrs L R, BA DipLib MCLIP, Dev. & Operational Mgr., Child. & Young People, L.B. of Enfield. London. [27043] 10/01/1977 **CM10/01/1979**

Love, Mr W M, BA MCLIP, Comm. Lib., N. Lanarkshire Council. [26766] 26/10/1976 **CM03/09/1979**

Lovecy, Dr I C, MA PhD HonFLA FCLIP, Inf. Consultant. [20617] 01/05/1973 **FE18/11/1993**

Loveland, Mr A, BA(Hons) MA MCLIP, Head of L. Servs., Cent. Sch. of Speech & Drama, Univ. of London. [55837] 21/11/1997 **CM07/09/2005**

Lovell, Mrs J R, BA FCLIP, Life Member. [9106] 04/10/1945 **FE01/01/1965**

Lovelock, Mr W, MCLIP, Retired. [9105] 07/02/1949 **CM01/01/1951**

Lovely, Mrs A E, BA(Hons) MCLIP, Principal Lib. Kettering L. [27008] 13/01/1977 **CM02/11/1984**

Loveridge, Mrs G, MBA BA MCLIP, Area Mgr, N. Leicestershire L., Leics. [13574] 05/11/1971 **CM25/11/1974**

Loveridge, Mrs J, MCLIP, Div. Ref. Lib., Lancs. L., Lancaster. [9112] 19/09/1962 **CM01/01/1968**

Lovern, Mrs L A, ACLIP, Community Lib., Walsall Council. [10013581] 08/05/2009 **ACL02/03/2010**

Love-Rodgers, Mrs C R, MA MA MCLIP FHEA, Liaison Lib., Coll. of Humanities & Soc. Sci., Edinburgh Univ. L. [53151] 01/04/1996 **RV03/12/2008** **CM17/03/1999**

Lovett, Mr J H, FCLIP, Life Member. [9116] 06/02/1951 **FE01/01/1959**

Lovett, Miss N J, BA, Stud., Univ. of Wales, Aberystwyth. [64325] 04/03/2005 **ME**

Low, Mrs H, BA MCLIP, Lib., N. Somerset Council., Nailsea Lib. [28281] 01/11/1977 **CM13/11/1980**

Low, Miss Y M, MSc MCLIP, Employment not known. [50341] 01/07/1994 **CM19/07/2000**

Lowe, Mrs A H, BA MCLIP, Sen. Lib. -Equal Access & Comm., Nottinghamshire Ls., Beeston, Nottinghamshire. [33128] 10/10/1980 **CM14/10/1983**

Lowe, Mrs A L, ACLIP, Sen. L. Asst., Edwinstowe L., Notts. [65497] 08/02/2006 **ACL01/03/2007**

Lowe, Mrs C E, MCLIP, NHS, Leeds [25053] 04/11/1975 **CM28/09/1979**

Lowe, Mrs D J, BA(Hons) MCLIP, LRC Mgr., Bemrose Comm. Sch., Derby. [64839] 03/08/2005   **CM11/11/2009**

Lowe, Mrs I, MCLIP, Retired. [9125] 28/03/1947   **CM01/01/1949**

Lowe, Miss J, Head of Knowledge Mgmt., Ward Hadaway, Newcastle upon Tyne. [36927] 12/01/1984   **ME**

Lowe, Mrs K, BSc MCLIP, Lib., Cheshire C.C. Macclesfield L. [23570] 14/01/1975   **CM17/03/1977**

Lowe, Mr R, BSc MCLIP, Database Administrator, Brit. Standards Inst., London. [9128] 14/01/1972   **CM12/06/1975**

Lowe, Ms R, BA(Hons) MA, L. & Info. Asst., Leeds Coll. of Art, Leeds [10016606] 14/04/2010   **AF**

Lowe-Michael, Mrs J, BSc, Study Supp. Facilitator, Epping Forest Coll., Essex [10017188] 11/07/2010   **AF**

Lower, Ms M, Inf. Systems Devel. Mgr., Kensington Cent. L., London. [10010197] 09/07/2008   **ME**

Lower, Mrs S B, DipLib MCLIP, Learning Resources Mgr., Penwith Coll., Penzance, Cornwall. [34486] 12/11/1981   **CM11/11/1986**

Lowes, Mrs D, Unknown. [10012177] 09/01/2009   **AF**

Lowes, Mrs M, BA(Hons), Learning Res. Cent. Mgr., Kenton Sch., Newcastle-upon-Tyne. [47852] 21/10/1992   **ME**

Lowis, Mr D R, BA MCLIP, Cultural Serv. Adviser, Lincolnshire C.C. [20986] 03/09/1973   **CM08/12/1976**

Lowis, Mrs J, BA MCLIP, Retired. [9136] 16/09/1940   **CM01/01/1943**

Lowry, Mr J, BA MCLIP, Life Member. [9143] 25/03/1958 **CM01/01/1969**

Lowther, Mr S R, BA DipLib, Asst. Lib. -Catg., Wellcome L., London. [38111] 20/01/1985   **ME**

Lowton, Miss C L, BA(Hons) PG Dip, Sen. Lib. Asst., All Saints L., Manchester [10014092] 01/07/2009   **AF**

Loy, Mr J A, BA MA, Learning Res. Mgr., Callington Road Hosp., Bristol. [53918] 10/10/1996   **ME**

Loynes, Mrs F L, BA(Hons), Casual Lib., Cheshire W. & Chester C.C. [62019] 17/01/2003   **ME**

Loyns, Mrs K P, BA(Hons) MCLIP, Teacher. Benhurst Primary Sch., Essex [55413] 08/10/1997   **CM23/01/2002**

Lubarr, Ms K, BA, Coll. Lib., Maitland Robinson L. Downing Coll.,Cambridge. [59328] 07/02/2001   **ME**

Luc, Mrs D L, MSc MCLIP, Lib., Craigholme Sch., Glasgow. [42723] 13/02/1989   **CM24/06/1992**

Lucas, Ms C, BSc MSc MCLIP, Dir., Girton Inf. Serv., Cambridge. [60860] 12/12/2001   **CM12/12/2001**

Lucas, Ms I, BSc DipLib, Learning Resources Mgr., The Henrietta Barnett Sch., London. [61919] 02/12/2002   **ME**

Lucas, Mr J M, BA MSc MCLIP, Portal Servs. Mgr. /Learning Advisor, St. Mary's Univ. Coll. [63972] 22/11/2004   **CM16/10/2009**

Lucas, Mrs N, MCLIP, Life Member. [9157] 30/03/1954 **CM01/01/1963**

Lucas, Mrs R M A, MCLIP, Area Lib., Crawley L., W. Sussex C.C. L. Serv. [20095] 21/01/1973   **CM10/08/1976**

Lucas, Mr S T, MA FRSA FCLIP JP, Life Member [9161] 01/10/1953   **FE01/01/1965**

Luccock, Mr R G, BA MCLIP, Retired. [9163] 05/11/1967 **CM01/01/1970**

Luck, Ms M, Asst. Inf. Offr., Macfarlanes, London. [63150] 12/02/2004   **AF**

Luckett, Mrs P Y, BA(Hons) ACLIP, Sen. L. Asst., Oxford Brookes Univ. [58574] 04/04/2000   **ACL27/09/2005**

Lucy, Mrs C M, BA MCLIP, Keeper of the Arch., Dulwich Coll., London [34579] 01/01/1982   **CM01/04/1986**

Luddington, Ms S C, BA DipLib MCLIP, Career break [34170] 05/10/1981   **CM01/04/2002**

Ludditt, Mrs L, Freelance Writer/Trainer. [10000976] 27/11/2006   **ME**

Ludford, Miss J, MCLIP, Life Member. [9166] 30/01/1958 **CM01/01/1963**

Ludlam, Mr R M, BA(Hons) DipLib, LRC Mgr., Gorseinon Coll., Swansea. [43144] 22/08/1989   **ME**

Lum, Ms M, Res. Project Worker, Leeds City Council [10007263] 01/02/2008   **ME**

Lumbard, Mrs M, BA MCLIP, Retired. [9177] 01/09/1949 **CM01/01/1954**

Lumsden, Mr J, MCLIP, Retired. [9180] 12/10/1967   **CM01/01/1971**

Luna, Mrs C, BA, Sen. L. Asst., Judge Business Sch. L., Cambridge. [10010668] 19/08/2008   **AF**

Lund, Mr O P, BSc MSc DipLib MCLIP, Academic Serv. Mgr. (Sci.), Loughborough Univ., Pilkington L. [36442] 11/10/1983 **CM03/03/1987**

Lundstrom, Mr T E, Stud., Coll. of the Bahamas [10002022] 28/03/2007   **ME**

Lungu, Mr C, Libr., Copperbelt Univ., Zambia. [63394] 28/04/2004   **ME**

Lunt, Mr M W, FCLIP, Life Member. [9191] 04/09/1955   **FE01/01/1962**

Lunt, Mr R, BA MCLIP, Unemployed. [9192] 13/10/1970   **CM24/09/1973**

Lunt, Mrs T L, BA(Hons) MSc, Inf. Cent. Mgr. Building Design Partnership, Sheffield. [49521] 10/11/1993   **ME**

Lupton, Miss M, MCLIP, Retired. [9195] 14/01/1963   **CM01/01/1967**

Luscombe, Ms F J, BA(Hons), L. Asst., St. Ives L., Cornwall. [10015817] 29/01/2010   **AF**

Lusted, Ms C A, BA(Hons) MA MCLIP, Sen. Lib., Child. & Yth., LB of Barnet. [57635] 07/06/1999   **CM10/07/2002**

Lustigman, Ms A I, BA, Info. Asst., Linklaters, London. [10006592] 23/10/2007   **ME**

Lusty, Miss K, BA(Hons), Unknown. [10012302] 12/02/1991   **ME**

Luthmann, Ms A L, MCLIP BA MA, Lib., E. Sussex C. C [63936] 18/11/2004   **CM23/01/2008**

Luxford, Mr I W, BA MCLIP, Dir. Learning Serv., Grass Roots Learning, Tring [60798] 01/06/1988   **CM22/01/1991**

Luximon, Mr M, BA(Hons), Stud [10007551] 13/02/2008   **ME**

Luxmoore-Peake, Ms F, BA(Hons) MA, Lib., Cardinal Newman Cath. Sch., Hove. [58973] 13/10/2000   **ME**

Luxton, Mrs J E, BEd, Snr. Subject Lib., Univ. of Plymouth. [57856] 10/09/1999   **ME**

Luxton, Mr T J, BA MCLIP, Retired [21551] 23/10/1973   **CM28/09/1976**

Lyden, Mrs M, Area Lib., Clydebank L., W. Dunbartonshire. [54909] 13/05/1997   **ME**

Lydiatt, Mrs A E, BEd DipLib MCLIP, Child. and Client Grp. Lib., Sandwell L., W. Bromwich. [35676] 01/01/1983   **CM15/02/1989**

Lyle, Mr R M, MCLIP, Life Member. [9208] 01/01/1945   **CM01/01/1963**

Lynas, Mrs H M, MCLIP, Retired. [9210] 14/08/1954   **CM01/01/1959**

Lynch, Miss C A, BA(Hons) MA MCLIP, Inf. Literacy Specialist, Royal Coll. of Nursing, London. [47296] 06/07/1992   **CM17/01/2001**

Lynch, Mr C J, BA DipILM MCLIP, Unwaged. [49765] 06/12/1993   **CM19/05/1999**

Lynch, Ms G, BHum DipLib MCLIP, Stock Serv. Mgr., Hammersmith L., L.B. of Hammersmith & Fulham. [33038] 03/10/1980 **CM10/05/1986**

Lynch, Mr J, MA DipLib MCLIP, Retired. [24741] 04/10/1975   **CM25/06/1981**

Lynch, Prof M F, BSc PhD CChem HonFCLIP, Hon Fellow. [60593] 11/12/2001   **HFE30/09/2000**

Lynch, Ms R C, BA(Hons) MA MCLIP, Dir. L and Learning Cent., Univ. Coll. Creative Arts, Farnham. [38327] 19/03/1985   **CM15/10/2002**

Lynch, Ms R, BSc (Soc. Sci) Young People's Servs. Mgr., Jubilee L., Brighton [10012818] 21/10/1991   **ME**

Lynch, Mrs S M, BA(Hons) MCLIP, Archive Asst., Staffs C.C. [42953] 08/05/1989   **CM27/11/1996**

Lynch, Mrs S V, BA(Hons) MCLIP, Bibliographic Serv. Mgr., W. Lothian Council [49305] 20/10/1993 **RV27/11/2007**   **CM12/03/2003**

Lyngdoh, Miss A, MLISc MSc IS, L. Asst., BMA, London [10008558] 03/04/2008   **ME**

Lynn, Miss I T P, BA MLitt DipLib MCLIP, Lib., The London L. [42658] 31/01/1989   **CM16/09/1992**

Lynn, Mr M, BA(Hons) DipIM MCLIP, Local Studie Devel. Offr., N. E. E. L. B [57403] 16/03/1999   **CM10/07/2002**

Lynwood, Miss W J, BA(Hons) MA MCLIP, Subject Lib. (Law), Birkbeck Coll. [55249] 09/09/1997 **RV27/06/2006**   **CM13/03/2002**

Lyon, Mrs P G, MA MCLIP, L. Inf. Resources Mgr.,Notting Hill and Ealing High Sch., London [17311] 27/09/1967 **CM02/10/1978**

Lyon, Ms W G, BA MSc(Econ) MCLIP, Sch. Lib., Fettes Coll., Edinburgh. [51544] 01/04/1995 **CM12/09/2001**

Lyons, Miss D, MCLIP, Requests Lib., L.B. of Ealing. [19294] 26/08/1972 **CM04/08/1975**

Lyons, Mr P, BA MCLIP, Ref. Lib., Fulham L. [10007747] 17/02/1972 **CM26/11/1982**

Lyth, Mrs H M, BA(Hons) ACLIP, Requests Mgr., Lancashire CC, Preston [65988] 09/08/2006 **ACL03/12/2008**

Lyth, Miss M, BA MCLIP, Retired. [9221] 22/01/1962 **CM01/01/1968**

Lythgoe, Miss C L, Grad. Trainee, Taylor Inst., Oxford. [10015180] 21/10/2009 **ME**

M

Ma, Ms L K, BA PGCE MLib MCLIP, Hosp. Lib., Caritas Med. Cent., Hong Kong. [42512] 22/11/1988 **CM25/05/1994**

Ma, Ms N, MA, Systems & IT Lib., Hertford Reg. Coll. [10013713] 22/05/2009 **ME**

Ma, Dr Y, PhD MCLIP, Health Care Asst., Cambridge Univ. Hosp. [64021] 02/12/2004 **CM08/08/2008**

Mac, Ms J, MLIS, Unknown. [10014001] 17/06/2009 **ME**

MacAllister, Mr G A, Civil Serv. Pensioner [63923] 03/11/2004 **AF**

MacAri, Mrs A E, BSc MCLIP, Sch. Lib., Fife Council. [59553] 16/05/2001 **CM15/09/2004**

MacArthur, Mrs C E, BA(Hons) DipLib MCLIP, Area L. Offr., Iverness, Nairn, Badenoch & Strathspey & Lochber based at Inverness. [15176] 01/01/1972 **CM01/05/1975**

MacArthur, Mr C M, BA MSc MCLIP, Retired. [19821] 20/11/1972 **CM08/10/1975**

MacArthur, Mrs F M, MA DipLib MCLIP, Young Peoples Res. Coordinator, E. Dunbartonshire Council. [35562] 01/11/1982 **CM05/04/1988**

Macartney, Mrs J E, BA(Hons) MCLIP, Lib., Henry Bloom Noble L., Isle of Man [39161] 26/11/1985 **CM24/07/1996**

Macartney, Mr N S, MA DipLib MCLIP, Retired [9230] 21/08/1968 **CM01/01/1972**

MacAulay, Mr J R, BSc DipLib MCLIP, Area Lib., Saltcoats L., Saltcoats. [10001104] 12/01/2007 **CM21/07/1989**

Macbeth, Miss A L, BA(hons), Unknown. [10007694] 21/02/2008 **ME**

MacCormack, Mr J A D, BSc IEng MIAgrE MCLIP, Retired. [60228] 25/01/1972 **CM21/06/1976**

MacCorquodale, Ms M A, MA(Hons) DipLib MCLIP, IS Mgr., Hnats. [46698] 16/12/1991 **CM24/09/1997**

MacDermott, Mr P D, BA DipLib MCLIP, Resources & content Mgr., Warwickshire Co. L., Leamington Spa. [34090] 08/09/1981 **CM20/01/1986**

MacDiarmaid-Gordon, Mrs J, FCLIP, Life Member. [9311] 28/10/1935 **FE01/01/1943**

MacDonald, Mr A M, MCLIP, Support Serv. Lib., AK Bell L., Perth. [10001311] 01/01/1971 **CM20/07/1973**

MacDonald, Mr A, BSc MSc, Res. Assoc. [10006366] 19/10/2007 **ME**

MacDonald, Miss A, MA, Stud., Rober Gordon Univ. [10015173] 21/10/2009 **ME**

MacDonald, Mr B I, MBE MA MCLIP, Retired. [9317] 12/03/1962 **CM01/01/1966**

Macdonald, Mrs C G, MCLIP, Part-retired [32440] 01/04/1980 **CM09/09/1982**

MacDonald, Mr C N, MA DipLib, Arch. Asst., N. Devon Record Off., Barnstaple. [35537] 28/10/1982 **ME**

MacDonald, Mrs E M T, MA DLIS, Sen. Asst. Lib., Nat. L. of Scotland. [39210] 01/01/1986 **ME**

MacDonald, Ms E M, BA MCLIP, Retired. [21619] 27/11/1973 **CM22/03/1976**

MacDonald, Ms E, MA(Hons) DipILS, Inf. Mgmnt. Team Leader., The Scottish Parliament, Edinburgh. [56114] 23/02/1998 **ME**

MacDonald, Miss F V, MA DipLib MCLIP, Sect. Head, - L., W. Dunbartonshire Council, Dumbarton. [30474] 12/02/1979 **CM07/04/1982**

Macdonald, Miss K, BA(Hons) MFA PgDip, Info. Prof., Napier Univ. [65587] 23/02/2006 **ME**

Macdonald, Mrs K, BA(Hons) DipILS MCLIP, Sr. Devel. Mgr., Sefton B. C. [40258] 11/11/1986 **CM25/07/2001**

MacDonald, Miss L, MA(Hons) MSc MCLIP, Global Portal Content Mgr., Hay Grp. [58087] 26/10/1999 **CM06/04/2005**

MacDonald, Miss M I B, MA MCLIP, Life Member. [9330] 26/09/1950 **CM01/01/1956**

MacDonald, Mr R M, B Cert (O. U), L. Super., Wick L. [10015776] 25/01/2010 **AF**

MacDonnell, Mrs R D M, BA MCLIP, Mgr. 'Home Basics' Charity [31804] 09/01/1980 **CM13/11/1984**

MacDougall, Miss S, MA MCLIP, L. Mgr., Inverclyde Council. [26462] 02/10/1976 **CM28/06/1979**

Mace, Mrs J, MCLIP, Enquiries Mgr., NSPCC L. & Inf. Serv., London. [52843] 04/01/1996 **CM23/01/2008**

Mace, Mrs S J, BA MCLIP DMS MIMgt, Dep. Subject Lib., Swansea Univ. + Devel. Offr., Whelf [23531] 01/01/1975 **CM28/07/1978**

MacEachen, Mr A J, BA MCLIP, Team Lib., Cardonald L. Glasgow City Council [24436] 07/08/1975 **CM15/11/1979**

MacEachern, Mrs R, Lib., MOD, Lympstone. [10014390] 21/07/2009 **AF**

Macey, Mr A P, Curriculum Support Advisor, Exeter Coll. [10012879] 19/03/2009 **AF**

Macey, Mr I R, MCLIP, Lib., Halcrow Grp. Ltd., Swindon, Wilts. [23261] 20/11/1974 **CM26/03/1979**

Macfadyen, Mrs J L, MA(Hons) DipLib, L. Res. Cent. Mgr., Our Lady's High Sch., Motherwell. [48188] 13/11/1992 **ME**

MacFarlane, Miss M A C, FCLIP, Life Member. [9366] 01/01/1931 **FE01/01/1933**

MacFarlane, Ms S J, MSc MCLIP, Info. Offr., Scotish CILT [59949] 09/11/2001 **CM29/03/2006**

MacGlone, Miss E M C M, MSci(Hons) MSc, Asst. Catr. /Web Editor, Scottish Screen, Glasgow. [63986] 22/11/2004 **ME**

MacGregor, Mrs E M, BA MCLIP, Asst. Lib., The Scottish Poetry L., Edinburgh. [11155] 01/05/1971 **CM01/02/1974**

Macgregor, Mr G R W, BA(Hons) MSc PGCert LTHE MCLIP, Lect., Liverpool Business Sch., Liverpool John Moores Univ. [59946] 09/11/2001 **CM29/08/2007**

MacHale, Mrs E, BSc DipLib MCLIP, Head of Learning Res. Cent., The Henley Coll., Oxon. [19562] 08/11/1972 **CM08/03/1989**

Machell, Ms F E, BA(Hons) MA MCLIP, Hybrid Collections Coordinator, Univ. of Wolverhampton [58005] 12/10/1999 **CM29/03/2004**

MacHell, Mrs J, MBE MCLIP, Life Member. [9405] 21/03/1955 **CM01/01/1959**

MacHiraju, Mr A F, BSc BD AKC MCLIP FHEA, Inf. Consultant, Royal Holloway, Univ. of London, Egham, Surrey. [30471] 29/01/1979 **CM31/10/1984**

Macho, Mr J, BSc(Hons) MA, P. /t. Lib., Wandsworth Bor. C. /London Met. Univ. [56942] 09/11/1998 **ME**

MacInnes, Mr A, MA MSc MCLIP, Automated Systems Lib., Cent. L., Aberdeen. [61553] 18/09/2002 **CM20/04/2009**

MacInnes, Mr N C, Head of Serv. Improvement, Manchester City Council, Cent. L. [61494] 19/08/2002 **AF**

MacIntyre, Miss C M, BA MScEcon MCLIP, L. Mgr., Carmondean L. W. Lothian [31892] 08/01/1980 **CM01/08/1984**

MacIver, Mr D, BSc BD DipILM, Lib., Nazarene Theological Coll., Manchester. [56296] 08/05/1998 **ME**

MacIver, Ms K A, L. Asst., Lews Castle Coll., Isle of Lewis. [10014486] 04/08/2009 **AF**

Mack, Ms C S, BA(Hons) DiP, Intranet Editor, Foreign & Commonwealth Off., London. [49966] 01/02/1994 **ME**

MacKay, Ms A J E, BA MA MCLIP, Self-employed, community heritage consultant & part time at Brit. Council [21147] 06/10/1973 **CM01/01/1976**

MacKay, Mr D M, MA(Hons) MA MCLIP, Head of Health Care L., Oxford Univ. L. Serv. [48410] 05/01/1993 **CM23/07/1997**

MacKay, Mrs E E, BA, PGDipILM, Copyright Offr., Sabhal Mor Ostaig, Isle of Skye. [10013407] 19/11/1991 **ME**

MacKay, Miss E, BSc(Hons) Economics, Asst. Lib., Univ of W. of England. [10001452] 14/02/2007 **ME**

MacKay, Mr H, BA(Hons) MCLIP, Retired. [9433] 20/03/1958 **CM01/01/1969**

MacKay, Mrs I A, MA MCLIP, Lib., NHS Lothian, Astley Ainslie Hosp. [23093] 24/10/1974 **CM14/03/1977**

MacKay, Mrs J, Young Peoples Serv. Lib., Chesnut L., Herts. [10015766] 21/01/2010 **AF**

Mackay, Ms M A, DipLib BEd(Hons) MCLIP, Lib., Highgate Literary & Sci. Inst., London. [26463] 01/10/1976 **CM19/07/1979**

MacKay, Mrs R C, MA MCLIP, Sch. Lib., Goffs Sch., Cheshunt. [21036] 06/10/1973 **CM01/06/1977**

MacKechnie, Mr J W, MA MCLIP, Retired. [19523] 16/10/1970 **CM09/01/1973**

MacKenzie, Mrs A M, BA DipLib DipEdTech MCLIP, LRC Offr., Moray Coll., Elgin. [33899] 02/04/1981 **CM26/05/1993**

MacKenzie, Ms C, MA(Hons), Unknown. [63220] 16/03/2004 **ME**

MacKenzie, Mr D, MA(Hons) MA MCLIP, Public Serv. Mgr., City Univ. L., London. [52838] 02/01/1996 **CM01/06/2005**

MacKenzie, Ms F M, BA DipLib DipEdTech MCLIP, L. Dir., Christ's Hosp., Horsham. [39321] 13/01/1986 **CM06/09/1988**

MacKenzie, Mr G, BA, PGCE, Asst. Head of Special Educ. Needs, Carlton Bolling Coll., Bradford. [10016419] 15/08/1977 **ME**

MacKenzie, Mrs J C, BA MCLIP, Lib., Bibl. D. Inst. Am. Engl. Garten., Univ. Munich. [19309] 16/08/1972 **CM28/01/1975**

MacKenzie, Ms J M, BA MA MCLIP, Head of Scrutiny Improvement Team, Scottish Government. [31365] 15/10/1979 **CM16/03/1982**

MacKenzie, Ms K A, BA PGCE, Child. Lib., Devon L. & Inf. Serv., Exeter [10002487] 20/04/2007 **ME**

MacKenzie, Miss M F, DHMSA MCLIP, Freelance Info Scientist., Surrey [21242] 04/10/1973 **CM01/03/1977**

MacKenzie, Miss R, BSc MSc MCLIP, Asst. Lib. Bibl. Collections, Brit. Geological Survey, Nottingham [51695] 19/05/1995 **CM17/01/2001**

Mackey, Ms A, BA GRAD DIP. ED., Unwaged. [10006254] 26/09/2007 **ME**

Mackie, Mr A, MA(Hons) MSc MCLIP, Careers Inf. Mgr., Univ. of Aberdeen [55250] 28/08/1997 **CM04/10/2006**

Mackie, Miss A, BA(Hons), Unknown. [10012096] 17/12/2008 **ME**

Mackie, Ms C, MCLIP MINSTLM, Serv. Devel. Offr. – Reader Devel., Warwickshire L. & Inf. Serv. [9467] 01/01/1971 **CM14/11/1974**

Mackin, Mrs H D, BA DipLib MCLIP, Dep. Lib., Barnardos L., Ilford, Essex. [29415] 01/07/1978 **CM22/09/1981**

MacKinnon, Ms A M, BA(Hons) MCLIP, Inf. Mgr., Scottish Environment Protection Agency, Stirling. [28627] 12/01/1978 **CM24/07/1996**

MacKinnon, Mr N A, MA DipLib MCLIP, Independant Consultant. [21646] 18/12/1973 **CM11/04/1979**

MacKintosh, Mrs A M, ACLIP, Sen. L. Asst., Kirriemuir L., Angus. [64496] 06/04/2005 **ACL04/04/2006**

Mackle, Miss R D, BA(Hons), Asst. Lib., Educ. & Health, Anglia Ruskin Univ., Essex. [50185] 26/04/1994 **ME**

Mackoniene, Mrs D, Unknown. [10011890] 08/12/2008 **AF**

MacKown, Ms S E, BSc MSc MCLIP, Knowledge & Inf. Mgr., Lupton Fawcett LLP, Leeds. [43327] 19/10/1989 **CM14/09/1994**

MacKwell, Miss C, MA B LITT MCLIP, Retired. [9483] 09/10/1970 **CM14/01/1974**

MacLachlan, Ms E A, MAHon FCLIP HonFCLIP, Inf. Mgmnt. Consultant, London. [24749] 08/10/1975 **FE18/06/1996**

MacLachlan, Mr H C, MA FCLIP, Life Member. [9486] 15/02/1956 **FE01/01/1967**

Maclaren, Mrs C, L. Super., Hillhead L. & Learning Cent., Glasgow. [10016199] 23/02/2010 **AF**

Maclean, Mrs A D B, BA MSc DIPeurhum DIPpm MCLIP GRADcipd, L. Admin. & MAP Lib., Andersonian L., Univ. of Strathclyde. [28503] 23/11/1977 **CM13/11/1980**

MacLean, Mr C C, BSc DipLib MCLIP, Faculty Liaison Adviser, Robert Gordon Univ. L., Aberdeen. [38860] 17/10/1985 **CM15/03/1989**

MacLean, Mr D, MA(Hons) DipILS MCLIP, Lib., Perth Coll., Scotland. [55476] 17/10/1997 **CM20/09/2000**

Maclean, Ms G, BA MEd MCLIP, L. Staff Devel. Mgr., NHS Educ. for Scotland. [41894] 27/04/1988 **CM11/12/1989**

MacLean, Mrs H, ACLIP, Clerical Asst., E. Kilbride Cent. L. [10001145] 12/01/2007 **ACL27/11/2007**

MacLean, Mr H, MA DipLib MCLIP, Community Lib., E. Ayrshire L. [44924] 16/01/1991 **CM26/05/1993**

MacLean, Miss L J O, BA, Sch. Lib., Perth & Kinross Council, Perth High Sch. [41164] 07/10/1987 **ME**

MacLean, Mr R, BSc MSc, Sr. Lib. Asst., Univ. of Glasgow, Scotland [10001983] 28/03/2007 **ME**

Maclean, Miss S, BSc(Hons), L. Serv. Mgr., Forensic Sci. Serv., London. [63594] 05/07/2004 **ME**

MacLean, Mrs S, MA MCLIP, Retired. [9507] 17/02/1957 **CM01/01/1962**

MacLellan, Miss F, Academic Lib., Univ. of Northampton. [61799] 13/11/2002 **ME**

MacLennan, Mr A, MA MSc PhD, Lect., Robert Gordon Univ., Aberdeen. [46744] 14/01/1992 **ME**

MacLeod, Miss A A, BA(Hons) MA, Lib., Brora Cultural Cent. & L., Brora. [10011874] 25/11/2008 **AF**

MacLeod, Mr A D, B LIB MCLIP, Sen. Lib., Lancs. Co. L., Preston. [29999] 31/10/1978 **CM15/03/1983**

MacLeod, Ms C M E, BSc MSc MCLIP, Asst. Lib., Queen Mary, Univ. of London. [40465] 02/02/1987 **CM14/03/1990**

MacLeod, Mrs C, MA MCLIP, Knowledge Cent. Mgr., RMJM LTD, Edinburgh. [38434] 25/04/1985 **CM10/05/1988**

MacLeod, Mrs D H, BLib MCLIP, Asst. Lib., Lancs. Co. L., Preston. [29736] 04/10/1978 **CM17/11/1999**

MacLeod, Mrs E K, MCLIP, Retired. [27416] 10/02/1958 **CM01/01/1962**

MacLeod, Mrs J, BA(Hons) MCLIP, Child. Reading & Learning Lib., Dorset L. Serv. [44828] 10/12/1990 **CM26/07/1995**

MacLeod, Mr M, BA MCLIP, Lib., Eng. L., London [61538] 17/09/2002 **CM07/09/2005**

MacLeod, Mr N G, BA DipIT MCLIP, Res. Cent. Coordinator, Dundee City Council. [42546] 06/12/1988 **CM27/11/1996**

MacLeod, Ms P C, BA(Hons), MA, MSc, Unwaged. [10011231] 03/10/2008 **ME**

MacLeod, Mr R A, MA DipLib MCLIP, Retired. [25377] 07/01/1976 **CM05/07/1985**

Macleod, Miss R L, MA(Hons), Asst. Lib. [62866] 17/11/2003 **ME**

MacMahon, Ms B B P, BA(Hons) DipLib, Membership Admin., The London L. [48766] 12/05/1993 **ME**

MacMahon, Mr T M, BA DipLib, Lib., Herbert Smith, London. [45516] 28/02/1991 **ME**

MacMaster, Mr T, MA(Hons) DipILS MCLIP, Hd. of Integrated Learner Support Serv., Carnegie Coll., Dunfermline [44740] 21/11/1990 **CM19/05/1999**

Macmillan, Ms A L, MA(Hons) MSc MCLIP, L. Mgr., Cent. L., Inverclyde C., Greenock. [59937] 08/11/2001 **RV27/11/2007 CM29/03/2004**

MacNaughtan, Mr A, BA DMS MCMI MCLIP, City Lib., Plymouth City Council. [9544] 16/10/1969　　　　　　　**CM17/07/1972**

MacNeill, Ms C, MA(Hons) Dip Inf SCs, Unknown. [10008479] 02/04/2008　　　　　　　　　　　　　　　　　**ME**

MacOustra, Mrs J E, Unwaged. [57609] 26/05/1999　　　**ME**

MacPhail, Mrs J C, MCLIP, Unemployed. [27051] 22/01/1977　　　　　　　　　　　　　　　　　　　　　**CM01/10/1986**

Macpherson, Mrs C, MA MCLIP, Retired [9558] 06/03/1962　　　　　　　　　　　　　　　　　　　　　　　**CM01/01/1966**

MacPherson, Miss F, MA DipLib MCLIP, Sen. L. & Inf. Off., Dundee City Council. [34124] 01/10/1981　　　　　　**CM08/11/1984**

MacPherson, Ms K, BSc(Hons) DipILS MCLIP, Health Inf. Sci., NHS Quality Improvement Scotland, Glasgow. [52620] 13/11/1995　　　　　　　　　　　　　　　　　　　　　**CM15/03/2000**

Macpherson, Mrs L M, BA(Hons) MA MA MCLIP, Asst. Lib., Royal Acad. of Arts L., London. [57931] 04/10/1999　　**CM16/07/2003**

MacPherson, Mr S, BA(Hons), MSc, Young People's Asst., The Mitchell L., Glasgow [10011766] 11/11/2008　　　　　**ME**

MacPherson, Mrs T, BSc MA, Lib., N. Tyneside L. Serv. [58414] 04/02/2000　　　　　　　　　　　　　　　　　**ME**

MacQuarrie, Mr A D, DipLib MCLIP, L. & Inf. Offr., Scottish Inst. for Residential Child Care, Univ. of Strathclyde. [49555] 09/11/1993　　　　　　　　　　　　　　　　　　　　**CM24/07/1996**

MacRae, Mr J B, MA MCLIP, Dist. Lib., libraries, Culture & Learning., Welwyn Garden City L., Herts. C.C. [23347] 22/11/1974　　　　　　　　　　　　　　　　　　　　　　　**CM22/11/1976**

Macrae, Mr J H, MA, Lib., L. Cheadle, Marple Sixth Form Coll. [10012238] 15/01/2009　　　　　　　　　　　　**ME**

MacRae, Miss J, BA DipEdTech MCLIP, Retired. [9570] 17/02/1959　　　　　　　　　　　　　　　　　　　**CM01/01/1969**

MacRae, Mrs L, MA(Hons) MCLIP, Catr., Aberdeen Univ. [59959] 12/11/2001　　　　　　　　　　　　　　**CM09/07/2008**

Macrae-Gibson, Miss R, BA(Hons) MA MCLIP, Asst. Lib., London Sch. of Econ., London. [47062] 09/04/1992　　　　**CM17/05/2000**

MacRitchie, Mr D J, BA MCLIP, Local Studies Lib., Manly P. L., Sydney, Australia. [28333] 04/11/1977　　　　　**CM28/10/1981**

Macrow, Mrs F C, BA(Hons) DipLib MCLIP, Perf. Inf. Mgr., L.B. of Enfield [35864] 31/01/1983　　　　　　　**CM20/01/1999**

MacSween, Mrs M R, MA MCLIP, Lib., Larbert High Sch., Falkirk Council. [4064] 13/01/1970　　　　　　　**CM30/09/1972**

Madden, Miss A R, BA(Hons), Stud., Univ. of Strathclyde. [10015038] 07/10/2009　　　　　　　　　　　　**ME**

Madden, Dr J L, CBE HonFCLIP MA, Hon. Fellow. [9590] 04/10/1962　　　　　　　　　　　　　　　　**FE01/01/1964**

Madden, Mrs M J, MA BMus HDE, p. /t. Catr., Univ. lib. [65585] 23/02/2006　　　　　　　　　　　　　　**ME**

Madden, Mrs P, Lib. Super., Langside L., Glasgow [10017069] 21/06/2010　　　　　　　　　　　　　　　**AF**

Maddison, Ms C M, BSc DipLib MCLIP, Br. Lib., Norton Br. L., Stockton. [27192] 27/01/1977　　　　　　**CM23/07/1979**

Maddock, Mr G, BA MCLIP, Retired. [9599] 28/03/1963　**CM01/01/1969**

Maddock, Miss J R, BA DipLib MCLIP, Lib., The Babraham Inst., Cambridge. [28070] 11/10/1977　　　　　　**CM04/03/1982**

Maddock, Mrs L L, BA MCLIP, Mgr. of Learning Resources, Doncaster Coll. [28522] 05/01/1978　　　　　　　**CM13/08/1981**

Maddock, Mrs S R, BA(Hons) MA, L. Serv. Mgr., Oxfordshire& Bucks. Mental Health Partnership NHS Trust [61109] 22/02/2002　　**ME**

Maddocks, Miss J, BA, Unknown. [10008547] 02/04/2008　**ME**

Maddox, Ms J I, BA MA, Team Leader, European Inf. Cent., Pfizer Ltd., UK [44583] 30/10/1990　　　　　　　　　**ME**

Madeira Da Silva Freire, Mr J A, Learning Zone Asst., City of Westminster Coll. [66065] 18/09/2006　　　　**ME**

Madelin, Miss L, MCLIP, Ref. Lib., Exmouth L., Devon C.C. [9604] 14/01/1965　　　　　　　　　　　　　**CM01/01/1968**

Madge, Mr B E, DHSMA FCLIP PGCERT, Dir. of Maketing., London Upright MRI Cent., London [27193] 27/01/1977　　**FE16/07/2003**

Madgwick, Mrs A C, BA MCLIP, Learning Resource Advisor, Treloar Coll., Alton [33267] 05/11/1980　　　　　**CM24/02/1986**

Madhavan, Mrs D M, MCLIP, Area Mgr., Caerphilly Co. Bor. L., Blackwood L. [20378] 27/02/1973　　　　　**CM10/06/1976**

Madin, Mrs A, BA(Hons) MA LLB(Hons) DipApSS Eur. Hum ACLIP, Sen. L. Mgr., Chesterfield L. [10006687] 21/11/2007**ACL04/03/2009**

Madley, Mrs R C, BA(Hons) MA MCLIP, Bus. Inf. Spec., London Business Sch. [54031] 21/10/1996　　　　　**CM21/05/2003**

Madni, Mr S N, Unwaged. [10013162] 02/01/1997　　　**ME**

Madu, Dr E C, BSc MLS PhD, Snr. Lect., Dept. of L. & Inf. Tech., Nigeria. [63270] 24/03/2004　　　　　　　**ME**

Magba, Dr E A, MA MCLIP, Lib., U. C. C. F., Tyndale Hse., Cambridge. [11230] 30/07/1968　　　　　　　　**CM01/01/1971**

Magee, Mrs B, BA MA MCLIP, Team Leader Reader Devel. and Child. Serv., Newbury L., W. Berks. [41438] 09/12/1987　**CM18/04/1990**

Magee, Mrs M, BSc(Hons) MCLIP, Inf. and Communication Offr. S. Lanarkshire Council, Hamilton. [53729] 18/09/1996　**CM01/02/2006**

Maggs, Miss M, MEd MCLIP, Retired. [9610] 22/10/1962**CM01/01/1964**

Maggs, Mr P, BA(Hons) MA DipLib MBA MCLIP, Faculty Liason Lib., Robinson L., Newcastle Univ. [10015674] 01/10/1992**CM27/01/1999**

Maguire, Miss C B, PSAILIS MCLIP, Life Member. [17345] 29/09/1948　　　　　　　　　　　　　　　　　**CM01/01/1955**

Maguire, Mrs L R, MA DipLib MCLIP, Head of Inf. Mgmnt., Open Univ., Milton Keynes. [34329] 20/10/1981　　　**CM10/05/1988**

Maguire, Mr M J, BA(Hons) MA MSc, Inf. Asst., Berrymans Lace Mawer, London. [64904] 09/09/2005　　　　**AF**

Maguire, Mr M L G, MCLIP, Serv. Devel. Mngr., Devon C.C., Exeter. [9615] 14/01/1969　　　　　　　　　**CM13/07/1972**

Maguire, Ms P, DipLib MCLIP, Serv. Devel. Lib., Hampshire L. & Inf. Serv. [33439] 15/01/1981　　　　　　**CM26/01/1983**

Maguire, Mrs V, MCLIP, E-Res. Lib., Inf. & Learning Serv., Univ. of Plymouth. [3540] 01/01/1970　　　　　**CM01/05/1974**

Mahat, Ms N, Unknown. [10014099] 25/06/2009　　　　**ME**

Maher, Mrs S J, Unknown. [10014443] 31/07/2009　　　**AF**

Mahon, Ms C L, Resources Lib., Univ. of Wolverhampton. [56999] 19/11/1998　　　　　　　　　　　　　**ME**

Mahony, Mrs S I, Site Lib., Learning Resources Ctr., Shrewsbury [10013158] 03/09/2003　　　　　　　　**ME**

Mahurter, Miss S J A, BA(Hons) MA MCLIP, Inf. Serv. Mgr., London Coll. of Communication. [43260] 13/10/1989　　**CM15/09/1993**

Maiden, Mr C I, BA MSc MCMI MCLIP, Dir. of Knowledge Mgmnt., Appleby, Bermuda. [10000550] 02/05/2002　　**CM02/05/2002**

Maidment, Mr M, DipLib MCLIP, Dep. Ch. Lib., DEFRA, London. [31658] 12/11/1979　　　　　　　　　**CM03/03/1987**

Mailer, Mrs E, BA MA DipLib MCLIP, Unknown [28005] 11/10/1977
RV27/06/2006　　　　　　　　　　　　　　**CM19/11/1979**

Main, Mr A, MSc, Stud., Aberystwyth Univ. [10014106] 01/07/2009　**ME**

Main, Mr D, BA(Hons), Stud., Manchester Met. Univ. [10001862] 13/03/2007　　　　　　　　　　　　　　**ME**

Main, Mrs J R, BA DipLib MCLIP, L. Asst., Chipping Ongar L., Essex. [36206] 18/07/1983　　　　　　　　**CM06/10/1987**

Main, Mrs L V, MCLIP, L. Mgr., Twickenham Prep. Sch., Middlesex. [26794] 26/10/1976　　　　　　　　**CM11/08/1980**

Mainds, Mr G R, MA MCLIP, L. Offr., Cent. L., City of Edinburgh Council. [53422] 17/06/1996　　　　　**CM19/01/2000**

Mainwaring, Mrs L M, BEd (Hons), Unknown. [10007235] 25/01/2008　　　　　　　　　　　　　　　**AF**

Mainzer, Mr H C, MA DPhil, Retired. [39830] 20/08/1986　**ME**

Mair, Miss A E, BA MCLIP, Record Mgr., Aberdeen City L. [18129] 02/10/1972　　　　　　　　　　　**CM04/07/1975**

Mair, Mrs K, Stud [10007377] 09/07/2001　　　　　　**ME**

Maisey, Mr A S, BA(Hons) MA, Asst. Lib., DCSF, London. [59465] 03/04/2001 **ME**

Maitland, Mrs C A, MA, Lib., Kirkcudbright Academy, Kirkcudbright. [39352] 17/01/1986 **ME**

Maitland, Mrs K, BA MCLIP, Lib. (Job share)., HMP Manchester., Manchester City Council [1814] 15/01/1970 **CM19/09/1974**

Maitland-Cullen, Mr P S, BD PhD DipLIS MCLIP, Communications Offr., NHS Quality Improvement Scotland, Edinburgh. [45992] 12/08/1991 **CM22/09/1999**

Major, Miss G, Site Coordinator., Lincs C. C [59353] 13/02/2001 **AF**

Major, Miss M A, BA(Hons) DipIS, Web Serv. Mgr., St. Marys Coll., Twickenham. [47796] 19/10/1992 **ME**

Major, Mr R, BA MCLIP, Systems Lib., Birmingham City Univ., Kenrick L., Birmingham [38715] 01/10/1985 **CM01/07/1992**

Makeham, Miss J C, BSc(Hons) MSc(Econ) MCLIP, L. & Ind. Serv. Project Offr., Leeds Teaching Hosp. Trust. [56855] 27/10/1998 **CM16/07/2003**

Makepeace, Mr C, BA FSA MCLIP, Retired [9640] 15/10/1965 **CM01/01/1968**

Makin, Mrs A, MCLIP, Freelance Tech. Lib., Working with Construction Ind. Prof. [9642] 01/01/1956 **CM01/01/1962**

Makin, Miss H, FCLIP, Retired. [9643] 28/10/1943 **FE01/01/1954**

Makin, Mrs J M, MCLIP, Inf. Serv. Training Team, Univ. of Nottingham. [11945] 01/01/1965 **CM01/01/1970**

Makin, Miss L, PG DIP BA(Hons) MCLIP, Learning Resource Cent. I M Marsh Campus, Liverpool John Moores Univ. [10005825] 12/12/1998 **CM10/07/2002**

Malcolm, Mrs C, BA MCLIP, Lib., Sir William Perkins's Sch., Chertsey. [25716] 23/02/1976 **CM26/09/1980**

Malcolm, Miss P A, MCLIP, Inf. Serv. Lib., W. Dunbartonshire Council, Clydebank. [23296] 20/11/1974 **CM01/08/1977**

Malcomson, Mrs V, DIP IT PGC, Lib. Asst., Bangor Academy & Sixth Form Coll., Bangor. [10006755] 10/12/2007 **ME**

Malde, Mrs N, BSc MCLIP, Sen. Inf. Sci., Corp. Intellectual Property, GlaxoSmithKline, Brentford. [48325] 25/11/1992 **CM16/05/1983**

Males, Mrs B, BA MCLIP, Retired [9648] 01/10/1968 **CM01/01/1971**

Malesi-Wattiaux, Mrs C, BA, Unknown. [10000758] 02/11/2006 **ME**

Malin, Mrs J, DMS MCLIP, Unknown. [29505] 21/09/1978 **CM13/07/1981**

Malin, Ms M A, BA, Self-employed Literary Agent. [26235] 25/03/1991 **ME**

Malinova, Dr T, MSc PhD, Stud. [66101] 01/10/2006 **ME**

Malinowski, Ms R J, BA(Hons) PGDipLIS, Lib., Oxfordshire C.C. Oxford. [48030] 04/11/1992 **ME**

Maliphant, Miss M, MCLIP, Retired. [9650] 16/05/1951 **CM01/01/1959**

Mallach, Mr R C, MCLIP, Res. Mgr., Ernst & Young, London. [26984] 10/12/1976 **CM09/09/1980**

Mallen, Miss S L, BSc(Hons) DipILS MCLIP, Inf. Mgr., Careers Serv., Univ. of Manchester. [52484] 02/11/1995 **CM20/05/1998**

Mallett, Mr C J, MA MCLIP, Head of L. Serv., Nat. Sch. of Gov. L., Ascot. [43250] 06/10/1989 **CM15/09/1993**

Mallett, Ms D L, BSc(Hons) MA MCLIP, Unknown. [55502] 16/10/1997 **CM21/11/2001**

Mallett, Mrs S, MCLIP, Retired. [9657] 11/01/1953 **CM01/01/1965**

Mallon, Mrs S M, BA MCLIP, Audio-Visual Lib., N. Ayrshire Council, Ardrossan. [31427] 15/10/1979 **CM14/10/1983**

Mallows, Miss K, BA BMus FinalDipLib MCLIP, Brit. L., Boston Spa, W. Yorks. [29402] 01/07/1978 **CM21/12/1981**

Malloy, Ms A, BA LLB MCMI MCLIP MILAM FSA Sc, Managing Dir., Turnaround Assoc. Ltd. [9660] 06/01/1972 **CM31/07/1974**

Malone, Mrs E A, BA DipLib MCLIP, Head of Content Devel., Kingston Univ. L., Surrey. [39200] 01/01/1986 **CM18/07/1991**

Malone, Mrs E M, LLB DipLIS MCLIP, Area Community Mgr., Hinckley Lib., Leics [49390] 21/10/1993 **CM22/07/1998**

Malone, Ms H M, BSc(Hons) MSc, Mgr., GlaxoSmithKline, Greenford, Middx. [48478] 20/01/1993 **ME**

Malone, Ms K, BA(Hons) MSc, Lib. Asst., Harris Manchester Coll., Oxford [64637] 27/04/2005 **ME**

Maloney, Mrs C A, BLib MCLIP, Sen. Lib., Leamington l., Warks. C.C. [32553] 21/05/1980 **CM20/09/1985**

Maloney, Ms F M, BA(Hons) MA, Childrens Serv. Lib., W. Sussex L. [56812] 23/10/1998 **ME**

Maloney, Miss M J, BA MCLIP, Learning Res. Mgr., Basingstoke Coll. of Tech. [38827] 14/10/1985 **CM27/01/1993**

Maloney, Ms P S T, BA(Hons) DipIM, Seeking work [10011962] 05/12/2008 **ME**

Maloney, Mrs R, BA(Hons) PGDip MSc MCLIP, Unknown. [10000584] 12/10/2006 **CM29/08/2007**

Maloney, Mr T, BA MCLIP, Lib., Doughty Street Chambers. [23694] 07/01/1975 **CM19/01/1978**

Malost, Miss S A, Sch. Lib., Nonsuch High Sch., Cheam. [34701] 01/02/1982 **ME**

Malotaux, Mrs S, Head fo L. & Inf. Serv., Institut Nat. Polytechnique de Toulouse. [10012782] 26/07/2004 **ME**

Malouf, Mrs G, BA(Hons), Stud. Manchester Metro Univ. [10014429] 30/07/2009 **ME**

Maltby, Mrs J P L, BA(Hons) MA MCLIP, Sen. L. Asst., Univ. of Nottingham & Faculty Team Lib, UoN (x2 Job Share Roles) [61368] 01/07/2002 **CM13/06/2007**

Mandelstam, Mr C, BA MCLIP, Retired. [9668] 07/10/1948 **CM01/01/1960**

Mander, Mr S G, BA(Hons) PGDipLib, PCT Lib., Dudley Becon & Castle Primary Care Trust. [48523] 05/02/1993 **ME**

Manecke, Dr U, MA PhD, Clinical Supp. Lib., Milton Keynes NHS Foundation Turst. [10012988] 17/03/2009 **ME**

Manghani, Mr P, BA(Hons) PGDipLIS MCLIP, Asst. Hd. of Lib., Sutton L. Serv., L.B. of Sutton [52012] 11/09/1995 **CM17/09/2003**

Mangold, Miss E M, BLib MLib, Dir. Global Biz. Intelligence Cent., Dow Europe GmbH, Horgen, Switzerland. [33043] 01/10/1980 **ME**

Manley, Mrs D A, BA(Hons) PgDipLib MCLIP, L. Mgr., St. Pauls Catholic Sch., Milton Keynes. [32807] 23/09/1980 **CM31/08/1982**

Manley, Dr K A, DPhil FRSA HFCLIP FSA, Retired [9677] 30/09/1969 **CM02/08/1972**

Manley, Mrs P M, BA MLS DipLib MCLIP MA(Educ), Child. & Young People's Lib. Serv. Mgr., Salford M.B.C. [22869] 09/10/1974 **CM08/12/1983**

Manley, Mr W S, MA ACIB MISM MLIA(dip), T/Asst. in Charge, Derbyshire L. Serv., Ashbourne L. [10006520] 15/11/2007 **ME**

Mann, Miss C L, BA DipLib MCLIP, Freelance Legal Indexer (Consultancy, Law L. & Knowledge Mgmnt.) [42091] 01/10/1988 **CM24/04/1991**

Mann, Mrs C, BA MCLIP, Serv. Devel. Offr., [39430] 22/01/1986 **CM29/01/1992**

Mann, Mrs J M, MSc MCLIP, Retired. [10006071] 31/10/1997 **CM12/01/1998**

Mann, Mrs M K, MCLIP, Inf. Specialist, Cardiff Univ. [60466] 26/08/1999 **CM29/08/2001**

Mann, Ms R Y, BA MPhil DipIS, Acting Customer Serv. Mgr., ICAEW, London. [44188] 25/10/1990 **ME**

Mann, Mrs W, BSc(Hons) MCLIP, Operations Mgr. Cent. L., Barnsley M.B.C. [33425] 17/12/1980 **CM27/03/1985**

Mann, Ms W, Unknown. [10006104] 27/01/2009 **AF**

Manners, Mrs G F, MCLIP, Lib., Royal High Sch., Bath. [62851] 17/11/2003 **CM10/07/2009**

Manners, Mrs J, DipLib MCLIP, Equal Access Lib., W. Sussex C.C. L. Serv. [38113] 18/01/1985 **CM04/08/1987**

Manners, Miss L C, BA MA DipLib MCLIP, Inf. & Database Offr., Cent. for Inf. on Beverage Alcohol, London. [38765] 04/10/1985
CM27/03/1991

Manning, Miss C, Inf. Mgr., Linklaters, London. [64381] 14/03/2005 **ME**

Manning, Mr C, BA MA MCLIP, Systems Lib., London Sch. of Hygiene & Tropical Medicine [64556] 11/05/2005   **CM03/10/2007**

Manning, Miss H M, BA MA MCLIP, L. Serv. Devel. Mgr., Child. & Young People., Wandsworth Town Hall. [34078] 23/09/1981
CM16/12/1986

Manning, Mr R, Stud., Robert Gordon Univ. [10015229] 29/10/2009 **ME**

Manning, Mrs T, MSc ILM, Child. Lib., Sutton Child. L., Sutton Coldfield. [10006506] 24/10/2007   **ME**

Manning, Mrs Y A, BSc(Hons) MSc MCLIP, Sen. L. Asst., Warwickshire Coll., Moreton Morrell Cent. [53919] 10/10/1996   **CM21/05/2008**

Manning, Miss Y, MA DipLib MCLIP, Princ. Lib., L. Support, Falkirk Council. [36463] 11/10/1983   **CM19/01/1988**

Manoli, Miss T, MA MCLIP, L. Asst., The Royal Agricultural Coll., Cirencester. [55001] 19/06/1997   **CM08/12/2004**

Mansell, Mrs F J M, Sen. L. Asst., Colchester Sixth Form Coll. [10009972] 24/06/2008   **AF**

Mansfield, Mr D L A, BA(Hons) MSc MCLIP, Academic Subject Lib., Univ. L., Univ. of Lincoln, Lincoln. [10008698] 09/04/2008
CM10/07/2009

Mansfield, Ms J D, MA BA(Hons) DipLIS MCLIP, Inf. Offr., Manchester Met. Univ. [46747] 09/01/1992   **CM25/01/1995**

Mansfield, Mrs J, BA(Hons) MSc(Econ) MCLIP, Sen. Asst. Lib., De Montfort Universtiy [55109] 15/07/1997   **CM21/05/2003**

Mansfield, Ms S, BA(Hons) MSc, Unknown. [10012400] 20/04/1989**ME**

Mansi, Mr D, L. Mgr., Queens Crescent L., London. [10000962] 26/10/1998   **AF**

Manson, Mrs C E, BA(Hons) DipLib MCLIP, Lib., Pinner L., L.B. Harrow. [25015] 01/10/1975   **CM19/01/1979**

Manson, Mrs H E, BA MCLIP, Career break [38353] 01/04/1985
CM21/07/1989

Manson, Ms H, MA(Hons) DipILS MCLIP, L. Offr., Yth. Serv., City of Edinburgh Council. [56788] 15/10/1998   **CM15/09/2004**

Manson, Miss J, BSc PgDip, Asst. Lib., Forrester Cockburn L., Royah Hosp. for Sick Child., Glasgow. [10014457] 31/07/2009 **ME**

Manson, Miss K A, MA(Hons) MSc, p/t L. Asst., Queen's Univ., Belfast [10000900] 07/10/1999   **ME**

Manson, Mrs S L, BA(Hons) MSc MCLIP, Literary Agent (Child. Books), Sarah Manson Literary Agent, London. [50400] 18/07/1994
CM20/01/1999

Mantle, Mr D K, BSc(Hons) MSc, L. Mgr., Barlow Lyde & Gilbert, London. [59363] 14/02/2001   **ME**

Mantle, Mrs S J, MCLIP, Idea Store Super., Idea Store Bow, Tower Hamlets [21675] 03/01/1974   **CM30/10/1979**

Manuel, Dr A L, LLB MA MSc MEd ACA PhD, Lib+Arch., Somerville Coll., Oxford Univ. [10010592] 08/08/2008   **ME**

Manuell, Mrs E C, BA MA, L. /Inf. Serv. Mgr., Mills &. Reeve, Norwich. [58937] 09/10/2000   **ME**

Mao, Mr C C, Assoc. Prof., Taiwan. [10000579] 05/10/2006   **ME**

Mapasure, Mr S, HND MA MCLIP, Asst. Lib., Nat. Inst. for Med. Res. [60041] 03/12/2001   **CM10/07/2009**

Maplesden, Miss C A, MCLIP, Young People's Specialist, Cheshire C.C., Childer Thornton. [23123] 05/11/1974   **CM21/03/1978**

Mapleson, Mrs D, MCLIP, Retired. [9717] 06/03/1940 **CM01/01/1954**

Marais, Ms D J, BSc(Hons) PGDipLIS, Lib., Countess of Chester Hosp., Chester [48883] 08/07/1993   **ME**

Maranti, Mrs E, BA MA, Stud. [10012698] 25/02/2009   **ME**

Maratheftis, Mr A, MLIS, L. Dir., Cyprus L., Nicosia. [51579] 03/04/1995
ME

Marcella, Prof R C, MA(Hons) DipLib DipEd FCLIP Ph, Dean of Faculty, Robert Gordon Univ., Aberdeen. [35650] 21/11/1982 **FE19/01/2000**

March, Mrs B, Lib., King's Sch., Bruton, Somerset. [63569] 08/07/2004
AF

March, Ms M, BA MA MCLIP, Asst. Dir., Academic Servs., Anglia Ruskin Univ., Chelmsford. [40395] 30/01/1987   **CM19/09/1989**

Marchand, Mrs D, MCLIP, Unwaged [63147] 12/02/2004**CM06/05/2009**

Marchant, Mr A S, BA MCLIP, Web Designer. [38395] 16/04/1985
CM14/02/1990

Marchant, Mr P C, BH(Hons) MA MCLIP, Head of L. Serv., Knowsley M.B.C. [36294] 03/10/1983   **CM21/12/1988**

Marchant, Mrs S D, BA MCLIP, Lib., Lancing Coll., W. Sussex [27131] 01/02/1977   **CM30/11/1981**

Marchant, Mrs S M, MCLIP, Sch. Lib., Tunbridge Wells Grammar Sch. for Boys, Tunbridge Wells, Kent. [12060] 27/09/1966 **CM01/01/1971**

Marchesin, Ms R, L. Asst., Bibliographic Serv. Dept., LSE L., London. [65828] 25/04/2006   **AF**

Marcuccilli, Mrs E C, MSc BA(Hons), Unwaged. [59280] 25/01/2001**ME**

Mardo, Mrs P E, BA(Hons) PGCE DipLS MCLIP, Grp. Mgr., Devon L. & Inf. Serv. [50784] 18/10/1994   **CM17/03/1999**

Marett, Mrs L, B Ed MA, Learning Resources Mgr.,Christ the King RC Maths & Computing Coll., Lancashire. [65917] 04/07/2006   **ME**

Margerison, Mr M A, BA(Hons) PGDipILM, Sch. Lib., Bishop Doglass Sch., London. [61139] 12/03/2002   **ME**

Marillat, Mrs I T, Sch. Lib., Tolworth Girls' Sch., Surbiton. [65963] 26/07/2006   **AF**

Marin, Ms A, MSc(Econ) BA DipLIS CIM MCLIP, Serv. Mgr., Learning & Access, Cent. L., L.B. Bromley. [40755] 01/06/1987 **CM23/03/1994**

Marine, Mrs S, M. Litt, Serials/L. Web Administrator, Architectural Assoc. L. [10015352] 12/11/2009   **ME**

Mariner, Miss L, BA(Hons) MA MCLIP, Catr., Poetry Lib., London [52972] 06/02/1996   **CM21/03/2001**

Mark, Miss R J, BSc MSc, Unknown. [49198] 12/10/1993   **ME**

Marke, Mrs K A, BA(Hons) MA MCLIP, Head of L. Resources, House of Commons L., London. [52232] 16/10/1995   **CM18/11/1998**

Marker, Mrs B C B, BA PGDipLIS, Learning Cent. Mgr., Acton & W. London Coll., London. [46048] 01/01/1963   **ME**

Markham, Mrs J A, MA DipLib MCLIP, Lib., Newbury Weekly News. [32929] 08/10/1980   **CM01/07/1992**

Markham, Mrs R, BA DipLib MCLIP, Team Lib., Inf. & Lifelong Learning, Morpeth L., Northumberland C.C. [28225] 12/10/1977**CM26/09/1980**

Markless, Ms S, HonFCLIP, Unknown. [10000814] 20/11/2006
HFE01/10/2006

Marks, Mr H D, BA MCLIP, Res. Mgr., Northants L. & Inf. Serv., Northampton. [21488] 16/10/1973   **CM17/11/1975**

Markus, Ms A, MCLIP, Retired. [940] 30/07/1959   **CM17/11/1975**

Marland, Mr P D, BA MA MCLIP, Principal L. Mgr., Blackpool Council. [37885] 07/11/1984   **CM18/04/1990**

Marley, Miss E A, BA MCLIP, Head of Child. Yth. & Sch. Serv., Hants. C.C. [9749] 26/05/1972   **CM01/08/1976**

Marley, Ms E A, MA MSc, Thesaurus Editor, House of Commons L., London. [10001988] 11/11/1992   **ME**

Marlowe, Mrs M R, Lib. /ATA, Norton Community Primary Sch., [10008373] 19/03/2008   **AF**

Marney, Miss R M, BA MCLIP, L. Mgr, Inst. Civil Eng., London. [33047] 11/10/1980   **CM20/11/1986**

Marr, Ms C F, BA DipLib MCLIP, Lib. Offr., City of Edinburgh Council, Cent. L. [41054] 06/10/1987   **CM16/05/1990**

Marrable, Dr D M, BSc PhD MCLIP, Career Break. [60820] 02/12/1986
CM02/12/1986

Marriott, Ms A, BA(Hons) DipLib MBCS MCLIP, Corp. Data Mgr., London Devel. Agency [25354] 15/01/1976   **CM16/05/1978**

Marriott, Ms D, Unknown. [10015569] 21/01/2010   **AF**

Marriott, Mrs F E, BA(Hons) MCLIP, Principal Lib., Luton Cent. L., Luton. [10005358] 29/10/1986   **CM16/10/1989**

Marriott, Mrs G, MA DipLib MCLIP, LRC Co. ordinator, Currie Comm. High Sch., Edinburgh. [42147] 10/10/1988 **CM27/02/1991**

Marriott, Miss H, MCLIP, Life Member. [9758] 01/01/1951 **CM01/01/1959**

Marriott, Mr J R, BA(Hons) MA MCLIP, L. &Inf. Coordinator, Univ. of Derby. [57980] 08/10/1999 **CM18/09/2002**

Marriott, Mr R, BA(Hons) MA MCLIP, Learning Resources Mgr., E. Midlands Strategic Health Auth., Nottingham. [46872] 17/02/1992 **CM22/03/1995**

Marron, Ms S, Inf. Mgr., MRC Human Genetics Unit, Edinburgh. [10005080] 06/06/2007 **ME**

Marsden, Ms C J, BA MA PGDipLib MCLIP, Serv. Devel. Lib., Hants L. Serv. [30218] 11/01/1979 **CM21/06/1983**

Marsden, Mr T S, BA(Hons) MA MCLIP, Sr. Learning Resources Advisor, City of Sunderland Coll. [56237] 14/04/1998 **CM21/11/2001**

Marsh, Mrs A C, MA MCLIP, Reader Serv. Lib., Jordanhill L., Univ. of Strathclyde. [29755] 09/10/1978 **CM14/10/1981**

Marsh, Ms A M, MA MCLIP, L. &Resources Mgr., Breast Cancer Care, London. [53571] 26/07/1996 **CM04/02/2004**

Marsh, Mrs A M, BLIB MCLIP, Performance Mgmnt. Offr., Lancs. C.C. [30628] 05/03/1979 **CM24/06/1982**

Marsh, Miss A S, BA FCLIP, Life Member. [9774] 04/10/1951 **FE01/01/1956**

Marsh, Mrs B L, BA DipLib MCLIP, Unemployed. [24854] 21/10/1975 **CM05/12/1977**

Marsh, Miss E A, BA MCLIP, p. /t. Learning Support Lib., City of Westminster, London. [25355] 14/01/1976 **CM11/09/1979**

Marsh, Mrs J L, BA(Hons) MSc MCLIP, Repository Dev. Off., Lanchester L., Coventry Univ. [59598] 26/06/2001 **CM21/06/2006**

Marsh, Miss J, BA(Hons) MCLIP, Ret. [45281] 01/10/1990 **CM12/03/2003**

Marsh, Mrs L M, BA(Hons) MSc(Econ) MCLIP, Sen. Asst. Lib. Institutional Repository, UWE [52495] 02/11/1995 **CM12/09/2001**

Marsh, Mrs S B, BA(Hons) DipIS MCLIP, Career Break [51649] 27/04/1995 **CM18/03/1998**

Marsh, Miss S J A, BA DipLib MCLIP, Unknown. [38387] 10/04/1985 **CM22/11/1995**

Marsh, Ms S L, BA MA MCLIP, Dir. of Learner Support Serv., Univ. of Bradford [41489] 08/01/1988 **CM14/08/1991**

Marsh, Mrs S, BA MSc MCLIP, Hd. of Lib. & Knowledge Servs., N. Cumbria., Informatics Serv., Carlisle [37012] 28/01/1984 **CM20/01/1987**

Marshall, Mrs A F, MCLIP, Sen. Teaching Ass. /Lib., Marlborough Sch., Oxon. [1224] 15/03/1972 **CM14/05/1975**

Marshall, Mr A J, BA DipLib MCLIP, Lib. (Local Studies), Hounslow Community Trust, L.B. of Hounslow. [38230] 07/02/1985 **CM27/03/1991**

Marshall, Ms A L, BA(Hons) PGDip, Info. Ctr. Offr., Brit. Dental Assoc. Info. Ctr., London [10002158] 30/03/2007 **ME**

Marshall, Ms A M, MA DipLib MCLIP, Sen. Lect., Univ. of Brighton. [25476] 05/02/1976 **CM24/10/1978**

Marshall, Mr A P, BA MCLIP, Asst. Head of L., Notts. C.C. [21441] 30/10/1973 **CM12/01/1977**

Marshall, Mr A, BA MCLIP, Asst. Lib., Milton Keynes L. Serv., Milton Keynes L. [21367] 12/11/1973 **CM17/01/1977**

Marshall, Mrs C J, BA DipLib MCLIP, Lib. (Job Share), St. George's Sch., Herts. [40930] 01/09/1987 **CM18/04/1989**

Marshall, Mrs C L, BA MCLIP, Sen. Lib. (job share), L. H.Q., Area L., W. Yorks. [25369] 14/01/1976 **CM01/07/1988**

Marshall, Mrs C M, BA MBA MCLIP, Sch. Lib., Lodge Park Tech. Coll., Corby, Northants. [5622] 01/10/1971 **CM08/11/1973**

Marshall, Miss C, BSc MCLIP, Requests Stock Control Mgr., Hants. C.C., Winchester. [44646] 14/11/1990 **CM23/03/1994**

Marshall, Mr D G, BSc DipLib MCLIP, Subject Team Leader, Built Enviro., Sci. & Health, Oxford Brookes Univ. [30001] 24/10/1978 **CM19/01/1981**

Marshall, Miss D L, MCLIP, Head of LRC., Guildford Coll. of F. & H.E. Surrey [21604] 21/11/1973 **CM13/01/1977**

Marshall, Mr D N, Prof. Emeritus, Univ. of Bombay L., India. [17357] 20/05/1953 **ME**

Marshall, Mrs D, BA MCLIP, Info. Cent. Mgr., Portakabin Ltd., York. [44640] 13/11/1990 **CM15/09/1993**

Marshall, Mr D, BSc MA MCLIP, Sheffield City Council [65494] 08/02/2006 **CM10/07/2009**

Marshall, Ms E J, BA(Hons) DipLib MCLIP, Inf. Offr., Manchester Business Sch. [46545] 19/11/1991 **CM26/07/1995**

Marshall, Miss F L, BA, Lib. Admin., Legal Grp., Norfolk C.C. [60014] 23/11/2001 **ME**

Marshall, Mrs G P, MA DipLib MCLIP, L. Res. Cent. Co-ordinator, Aberdeen City Council, Educ. Dept. [31362] 16/10/1979 **CM30/03/1984**

Marshall, Mr G T C, BA MCLIP, Retired. [9794] 01/04/1967 **CM01/01/1970**

Marshall, Mrs H M, BA MCLIP, Child. L. Serv. Mgr., Derby City L. [23145] 06/11/1974 **CM15/08/1978**

Marshall, Miss H, BA, Inf. Cent. Mgr., Taylor Wessing, London. [10011478] 23/10/1995 **ME**

Marshall, Miss H, BA(Hons), Stud., Loughborough Univ. [10015127] 15/10/2009 **ME**

Marshall, Mrs J A, BA, Unemployed-Career Break. [39486] 04/02/1986 **ME**

Marshall, Dr J D, PhD, Rare Books Lib., Edinburgh Univ. Lib. [59792] 03/10/2001 **ME**

Marshall, Ms J K, BLib MCLIP, Head of Serv., Birmingham City Council. [34324] 10/10/1981 **CM01/07/1986**

Marshall, Mr J, MCLIP, Retired. [9797] 19/03/1957 **CM01/01/1964**

Marshall, Mrs K, BA MSc, L. I. S. Lib. (Serials), Freshfields Bruckhaus Deringer, London. [60974] 21/01/2002 **ME**

Marshall, Mrs K, BA(Hons) MA MSc FHEA MCLIP, Learning Resources Mgr., Grantham Coll. [55421] 06/10/1997 **RV30/10/2009 CM09/11/2005**

Marshall, Mrs L A, BA(Hons) MSc, Unwaged-Career Break, [57508] 14/04/1999 **ME**

Marshall, Mrs L T, BA(Hons) MCLIP, Lib., Staffs. C.C. [53285] 24/04/1996 **CM17/09/2003**

Marshall, Miss M, BA(Hons) MCLIP, Cent. Co-Ordinator., Manchester Coll., Learning Res. Cent. [55678] 04/11/1997 **CM29/08/2007**

Marshall, Mrs P M, MCLIP, Lib., Milton Keynes L. [21115] 09/10/1973 **CM15/09/1976**

Marshall, Mr P, MCLIP, Retired. [9805] 23/01/1963 **CM01/01/1967**

Marshall, Mrs R C, BA MA MCLIP, p. /t. Lib., Chilwell Comp. Sch., Notts. C.C. [38861] 17/10/1985 **CM22/05/1991**

Marshall, Mrs R J, MSc(Econ) BA(Hons), Learning Res. Coordinator, Lipson Comm. Coll., Plymouth. [57895] 01/10/1999 **ME**

Marshall, Mr R L, BA(Hons) MA MCLIP, Inf. Mgr., Imperial Coll., London. [55658] 30/10/1997 **CM19/11/2003**

Marshall, Mr S N, FCLIP, Life Member. [9806] 17/09/1949 **FE01/01/1963**

Marshall, Mrs S, MCLIP, Stud., Aberystwyth [64738] 09/06/2005 **CM21/05/2008**

Marshall, Mrs T M, BA MA MCLIP, Academic Lib., Loughborough Univ., Leics. [52401] 30/10/1995 **CM29/11/2006**

Marshall, Mrs V, BA MA, Unknown. [44817] 03/12/1990 **ME**

Marshman, Mr M, MCLIP, Co. Local Studies Lib., Wiltshire C.C. [9811] 12/03/1967 **CM01/01/1971**

Marsland, Mrs A, Asst. Lib., St. Martin-in-the-Fields High Sch., London. [63271] 24/03/2004 **AF**

Marsland, Mr I K, MA, Sen. Lib. Asst., Sir Michael Cobham Lib.,
Bournemouth Univ. [10012510] 23/02/2009 **AF**
Marsterson, Mrs K M, BSc(Hons) MSc MCLIP, Unspecified [57016]
24/11/1998 **CM21/03/2007**
Marsterson, Mr W, MA MCLIP, Retired. [9812] 23/10/1967
CM01/01/1970
Marta, Miss V, Dep. Sen. Lib. Asst., Wootton Fields L., Northampton
[10017027] 18/06/2010 **ME**
Martell, Miss H, MA BA MCLIP, Author. [9814] 28/09/1967
CM01/01/1971
Martens, Ms M, MA, Acting Lib., Stepney Green Maths, Sci. &
Computing Coll., London [10017186] 11/07/2010 **AF**
Martin, Mr A H, BA MCLIP, Enquiry Asst., Southend on Sea Bor.
Council, Southend Cent. L. [23249] 14/11/1974 **CM30/11/1976**
Martin, Miss A J, MSc(Econ), Inf. Offr., Simmons & Simmons, London.
[52447] 02/11/1995 **ME**
Martin, Mrs A L, MA PGCE MCLIP, Ch. Lib. Asst., Med. L., Cambridge
Univ. [59536] 01/05/2001 **CM04/10/2006**
Martin, Ms A M, BA(Hons) DipLIS MCLIP, Asst. Lib., Corp. of London.
[46294] 24/10/1991 **CM20/01/1999**
Martin, Mr A V, MA MCLIP, Currently Unemployed. [25600] 27/01/1976
CM24/03/1978
Martin, Mr A, MA DipLib, Curator, Modern Scottish Collections, Nat. L.
of Scotland. [34273] 19/10/1981 **ME**
Martin, Miss B M, BA(Hons), MSc., Unwaged. [10000964] 23/11/2006
ME
Martin, Mr B, Dep. Head of Acquisitons, UCL, London. [61727]
29/10/2002 **ME**
Martin, Mr C A, Lib., Hadleigh High Sch., Ipswich. [57373] 01/03/1999
ME
Martin, Mr C J, BA MCLIP, Asst. Lib., Univ. of Portsmouth, Frewen L.
[20214] 01/02/1973 **CM02/08/1978**
Martin, Miss C, Sen. L. Asst., House of Lords L., London. [10015926]
12/02/2010 **AF**
Martin, Mr D, FCLIP, Retired [9823] 28/03/1960 **FE18/03/1985**
Martin, Ms D, BA MCLIP, Unwaged. [60221] 23/04/2001 **CM23/04/2001**
Martin, Mrs E A, BLib MCLIP, Retired [4656] 02/01/1969 **CM31/01/1974**
Martin, Miss E G, BA(Hons) MSc, Unwaged [64119] 10/01/2005 **ME**
Martin, Ms E, MA MCLIP, Lib., Nuffield Coll., Oxford. [28074]
02/10/1977 **CM28/11/1980**
Martin, Ms F C, MA BA DipLib MCLIP, Academic Liaison Lib., Univ. of
Westminster [34755] 17/02/1982 **CM20/01/1986**
Martin, Mrs F S, BA DipLib MCLIP, Lib., Special Projects, Wellcome
Trust, Cambs. [31745] 21/11/1979 **CM04/11/1982**
Martin, Miss G M, BA MCLIP, Head Lib., Johns Hopkins Univ., S. A. I.
S, Bologna, Italy. [31367] 08/10/1979 **CM26/05/1983**
Martin, Dr H, BSc BA MCLIP PhD, Dir., Helen Martin, Denmark. [36724]
03/11/1983 **CM10/11/1987**
Martin, Mrs J F, Unknown. [42672] 07/02/1989 **ME**
Martin, Ms J F, BSc MA MCLIP, Unknown. [10000700] 06/11/2006
CM01/10/1996
Martin, Mr J R, MA BA MCLIP, Reader Dev. Lib., Leics. L. & Inf. Serv.
[35092] 02/08/1982 **CM20/11/1985**
Martin, Mrs J, MCLIP, Dir. Memebrship Engagement & IT, CILIP.,
London. [46606] 01/01/1968 **CM01/01/1971**
Martin, Ms J, BA MSc MCLIP, Inf. Serv. Coordinator, Sch. of Tropical
Medicine, Liverpool [33622] 29/01/1981 **CM07/01/1987**
Martin, Mrs J, MCLIP, Retired. [9836] 24/02/1965 **CM01/01/1970**
Martin, Miss J, Retired. [9844] 01/01/1934 **ME**
Martin, Mrs L G, MA MCLIP, Lib., Culford Sch., Bury St. Edmunds.
[38883] 18/10/1985 **CM08/12/1987**
Martin, Mrs L M, MCLIP, Partnership & Devel. Mgr., Cambs. C.C. [7481]
02/01/1969 **CM01/01/1973**

Martin, Mrs M H, MCLIP, L. Shelver, Univ. of Exeter [10002093]
11/01/1973 **CM01/07/1990**
Martin, Mr M, BA DipLIS MCLIP, Adviser, CILIP, London. [48833]
28/06/1993 **RV22/06/2007** **CM31/01/1996**
Martin, Mrs N, Employed in L. Sector [10001775] 20/12/1996 **ME**
Martin, Mr N, BA(Hons) MSc MCLIP, Inf. Offr., Clifford Chance, London.
[9855] 07/04/1972 **CM28/09/1976**
Martin, Mr P D, BA(Hons) MA, Lib., Eastbourne Coll. [55323]
01/10/1997 **ME**
Martin, Miss P J, BA MCLIP, Sen. Public Serv. Offr., E. Riding of
Yorkshire C., Arch. & Local Stud. Serv., The Treasure House,
Beverley. [9854] 04/11/1963 **CM01/01/1971**
Martin, Mr R A, BSc PGDipLIS, Web Co-ordinator., Dept. for Internat.
Devel., E. Kilbride. [46201] 11/10/1991 **ME**
Martin, Mr R, BA(Hons) MA, Know How Offr., Slaughter & May, London.
[10015570] 01/01/2010 **ME**
Martin, Mrs S E, BA MCLIP, Sen. Asst. Lib., De Montfort Univ.,
Leicester. [28532] 05/01/1978 **CM06/03/1981**
Martin, Mrs S I, BA(Hons) MCLIP, Managing Dir., L. Supp. (Int) Ltd.,
Warwickshire. [21355] 19/11/1973 **CM17/11/1978**
Martin, Mr S, ACLIP, Lib, Brinnington L., Stockport [66010] 24/08/2006
ACL16/04/2008
Martin, Mrs W, BSc MCLIP, Catr., Royal Welsh Coll. of Music & Drama,
Cardiff. [9867] 20/09/1968 **CM01/01/1971**
Martin, Miss W, BA FCLIP, Retired. [9868] 01/04/1943 **FE01/01/1957**
Martin-Bowtell, Mrs A E, BA(Hons) MA MCLIP, Unwaged. [55298]
19/09/1997 **CM15/03/2000**
Martindale, Mr C R, BA DipLIS, Faculty Suport Mgr.,Business,
Computing & Law, Univ. of Derby. [33505] 13/01/1981 **ME**
Martindale, Miss P, BA DipLib MCLIP, Area Mgr. (W.), Redruth L.
[32888] 21/10/1980 **CM12/10/1983**
Martinez Ortiz, Ms M I, MSc, Knowledge, Skills and System Lib., Surrey
and Sussex NHS Trust, Crawley. [10005088] 06/06/2007 **ME**
Martinez, Mrs M D J, Jelic Mgr., L. &Inf. Cent., Rooke, Bfpo. [65850]
05/06/2006 **ME**
Martinez-Roura, Ms S, MSc, Asst. Lib., BMA L., London. [10002519]
20/04/2007 **ME**
Martland, Miss D F, BA(Hons), Capital Markets Inf. Offr., Linklaters,
London. [58060] 21/10/1999 **ME**
Martland, Ms K W, BA MCLIP, Life Member. [9874] 08/03/1955
CM08/09/1976
Martlew, Mrs R E, BA Dip Lib MCLIP, p. /t. Asst. Lend. Lib., Lancs. C.C.
[34426] 26/10/1981 **CM08/12/1987**
Marvin, Miss J H L, BA(Hons), Stud., Univ. of Aberystwyth. [10009210]
07/05/2008 **ME**
Marwick, Miss E, BA(Hons) DipIM MCLIP, Unemployed. [53580]
02/08/1996 **CM25/07/2001**
Maryon, Mr A W, BSc DipLib MCLIP, Sen. L. Mgr., Woolwich L.,
London. [30648] 18/02/1979 **CM18/02/1981**
Mascord, Mrs S J, BA PGCE ACLIP, Learning Resource Co-ordinator,
Coleg Powys [10011674] 06/11/2008 **ACL28/01/2009**
Maseide, Mr K E, BA, Asst. Catr., Guildhall Sch. Music & Drama,
London. [64684] 25/05/2005 **ME**
Masheder, Mrs K L, ACLIP, Sen. L. Asst., York Hosp. Health L., York.
[10013723] 14/04/2005 **ACL02/03/2010**
Mashumba, Mr F, PgDip, Lib., The Beeches Mgmnt. Cent., Belfast.
[10015199] 23/10/2009 **ME**
Maskell, Ms A, Inf. Offr., Guilford L. [10014906] 01/04/2010 **ME**
Maskell, Miss K, MA, Asst. Lib., Univ. of the W. of England. [64125]
12/01/2005 **ME**
Mason, Miss C J, LIS/KBD Training Exec., L., Freshfields Bruckhaus
Doringer, London. [10006219] 26/09/2007 **ME**
Mason, Mr D J, BA(Hons) MSc, L. & Info. Serv. Mngr., Salans, London.
[10002663] 07/03/2003 **ME**

Mason, Miss D, MCLIP, Grp. Lib., Durham Co. L. [9888] 30/05/1968
CM01/01/1972

Mason, Mrs E T, BA MCLIP, Special Sch. Asst., Portsmouth C.C.
[10906] 01/01/1972 **CM27/01/1975**

Mason, Mrs F, BA MCLIP, Child., Young People & Community Learning
Lib., L.B. of Bexley. [27755] 01/08/1977 **CM14/08/1981**

Mason, Miss J E, BA MA, Web Coordinator, E. Sussex C.C. [58681]
18/05/2000 **ME**

Mason, Miss J V, BA(Hons) DipLIS MCLIP, Sen. Lib., Westgate L.,
Oxon. C.C. [47509] 16/09/1992 **CM31/01/1996**

Mason, Miss J, BSc, Lib. Mgr., Fire Serv. Coll., London [64655]
17/05/2005 **ME**

Mason, Mrs J, BA(Hons) MCLIP, Sch. Learning Res. Cent. Mgr., St.
Gregory's Catholic High Sch., Warrington. [30355] 24/01/1979
CM21/09/1982

Mason, Mrs K L, BA(Hons) MA MCLIP, Hd. of Info. Servs., Learning &
Skills C., Coventry. [53718] 19/09/1996 **CM04/02/2004**

Mason, Mrs L A, BA MCLIP, Sch. Lib., Belmont Sch., London. [9849]
07/01/1969 **CM15/12/1972**

Mason, Mr M A, BA MCLIP, Trust L. Serv. Mgr., Southport &Ormskirk
Hosp. NHS Trust. [9896] 18/10/1967 **CM01/01/1971**

Mason, Mr M, MCLIP, Retired. [9897] 20/09/1971 **CM16/07/1975**

Mason, Mr P, Site Co-ordinator., LCC, Ermine [59272] 24/01/2001 **AF**

Mason, Mrs R W, BA MCLIP MLib, Lib., N. Highland Coll., Thurso.
[26597] 18/10/1976 **CM15/04/1981**

Mason, Miss V E, BA(Hons) MCLIP, Res. & Performance Offr. [59627]
04/07/2001 **CM20/11/2002**

Massey, Mrs A E, MA(Hons) DipLIS MCLIP, Map Serv. Mgr.(Jobshare).,
Nat. L. of Scotland., Edinburgh [49633] 16/11/1993 **CM23/07/1997**

Massey, Ms C, Learning Rewsources Asst., LRC Norton Radstock Coll.,
Radstock [10015558] 14/12/2009 **AF**

Massey, Mr G J, Learning Resources Team Leader, Oxford & Cherwell
Valley Coll., Banbury. [10010457] 30/07/2008 **ME**

Massey, Mrs S J E, BLib MCLIP, Lib., Illingworth L., Sheffield Child.
NHS Hosp. Trust. [34245] 10/10/1981 **RV04/03/2009 CM12/12/1984**

Massil, Mr S W, BA DipLib FCLIP FSA FRAS, Retired. [9906]
12/01/1970 **FE13/06/1990**

Masson, Dr A J, BSc(Hons) PhD PGCE, Unknown. [10013179]
03/04/2009 **ME**

Masson, Ms S, BA DipLib MCLIP, Catr., London Met. Univ. [31898]
08/01/1980 **CM18/01/1982**

Master, Mr I, Position unknown, Wigston Magna L. [64549] 28/04/2005
ME

Masterman, Miss C, BA(Hons), Lib., Co. Durham & Darlington
Foundation Trust, Darlington [51130] 23/11/1994 **ME**

Masterman, Mrs T J, BA MA MCLIP, Lib., Teignmouth Community Coll.,
Devon [43758] 01/01/1990 **CM25/07/2001**

Masters, Miss F L, BA(Hons) MA MCLIP, Asst. Lib., Chichester L.
[10006459] 19/10/2007 **CM11/10/2009**

Masters, Ms M A, BSc DipLIB MCLIP, Stock Performance Lib., City of
York Council, York [28498] 19/01/1978 **CM28/05/1980**

Masters, Mrs S C, BA(Hons) MA, Asst. Lib., Army L. Serv., Aldershot.
[59816] 10/10/2001 **ME**

Masters, Ms S L, BSc MCLIP, Multi-Media Res. Mgr., Thomas Deacon
Academy, Peterborough. [44880] 08/01/1991 **CM22/11/1995**

Masters, Mr T, MCLIP, Retired [9913] 17/03/1958 **CM01/01/1961**

Masud, Mrs N, Chemical Inf. Specialist, Royal Soc. of Chemistry,
London [10015513] 09/12/2009 **ME**

Masuda, Mrs K, Unknown. [10000861] 15/11/2006 **ME**

Mateer, Miss H E, BA MA MCLIP, Catalogue Mgr., Birkbeck Coll. L,
London. [54408] 04/12/1996 **CM12/09/2001**

Mather, Mr I M, BA MCLIP, Lib., Southend Hosp. NHS Trust, Westcliff-
on-Sea,Essex. [29907] 26/10/1978 **CM26/11/1986**

Matheson, Ms C M, BSc MCLIP, Lib., Highland Council, Glenurquhart
Comm. [25076] 29/10/1975 **CM09/03/1979**

Matheson, Mrs D M, FCLIP, Life Member. [9918] 06/03/1942
FE01/01/1946

Matheson, Miss F M, MA MCLIP, Area Lib., W. Dunbartonshire Council,
Dumbarton. [44525] 22/10/1990 **CM12/03/2003**

Matheson, Miss J C, BSc(Hons), Admin. Asst., Lorn Med. Cent., Oban,
Argyll. [61984] 10/01/2003 **ME**

Matheson, Ms J, BA MCLIP, Unemployed. [33049] 08/10/1980
CM12/02/1986

Mathew, Mr M V, BA MA DLSC FCLIP, Life Member. [9921] 03/01/1958
FE18/04/1989

Mathews, Mrs S E B, BSc(Hons) MSc MCLIP, Unwaged. [51954]
18/08/1995 **CM17/11/1999**

Mathias, Mrs A, ACLIP, LRC Mgr., Holbrook High Sch., Holbrook.
[10011654] 30/10/2008 **ACL23/09/2009**

Mathias, Ms G M, MCMI MLib DipLib CertEd, Arch. Asst., English Nat.
Ballet, London. [25990] 05/05/1976 **ME**

Mathie, Ms A E, MCLIP MPhil, Head of Learning & Inf. Serv., Univ. of
Gloucestershire. [17364] 15/09/1967 **CM01/01/1970**

Mathieson, Miss A, MCLIP, Life Member. [9927] 22/09/1951
CM01/01/1962

Mathieson, Mrs J E, MA BA MCLIP, Reg. Reader Devel. Coordinator,
Time To Read, Manchester. [21464] 16/10/1973 **CM01/10/1980**

Mathieson, Mrs S E, BA(Hons) MA MCLIP, Unknown. [58814]
07/08/2000 **CM29/03/2004**

Matisova, Miss D, MA, L. Asst., Bibliographic Serv., UCL, London.
[10015042] 08/10/2009 **AF**

Matkin, Mrs C A, BA(Hons) MCLIP, Access & Inclusion Mgr., Derbyshire
C.C. Cultural & Community Serv. Dept. [55582] 21/10/1997
CM29/11/2006

Maton, Mrs R J A, Sch. L., Prendergast Hilly Fields Coll., Lewisham.
[57369] 26/02/1999 **ME**

Matsuki, Ms M, MSc, Lib., The United Nations Univ., Tokyo, Japan.
[42394] 17/10/1988 **ME**

Matsumura, Miss T, MA, Emeritus Prof., Univ. of Lib. & Info. Sci.,
Japan. [27280] 01/02/1977 **ME**

Mattewada, Mr S, MBA, Lib. Asst., The Brit. L., London. [10015115]
13/10/2009 **AF**

Matthews, Mrs B S, MCLIP, Sen. Lib., Tonbridge Sch., Kent. [13503]
13/09/1969 **CM02/10/1972**

Matthews, Mrs D, Local Studies Lib., Dudley Archive & Local Hist.
Serv., W. Midlands. [10002043] 21/10/1993 **ME**

Matthews, Mr D, BA FCLIP, Retired. [9934] 03/03/1952 **FE01/01/1954**

Matthews, Mrs E A, BA MCLIP, Area Sch. Lib., Hants. C.C., Sch. L.
Serv. [26248] 21/09/1976 **CM20/05/1980**

Matthews, Mr G, BA DipLib PhD MCLIP, Prof. of Inf. & L. Mgmt., Sch. of
Business Inf., Liverpool John Moores Univ. [25077] 10/11/1975
CM14/11/1977

Matthews, Mrs J A, BA(Hons), Unknown. [10012181] 09/01/2009 **ME**

Matthews, Mr J S, BA DipLib MCLIP, First Floor Mgr., Univ. L., Univ. of
Portsmouth. [29739] 02/10/1978 **CM11/05/1982**

Matthews, Mrs J, Knowledge Resource Administrator, Welsh
Ambulance Serv. NHS Trust, Cwmbran. [10016460] 26/03/2010 **AF**

Matthews, Miss J, BA(Hons) MCLIP, Unknown [10001589] 27/01/1979
CM01/07/1989

Matthews, Mrs N, MA MCLIP, Lib., Cains Advocates, Douglas, I. O. M.
[40050] 13/10/1986 **CM15/11/1988**

Matthews, Mr P F, DipLIS, Catr., TFPL, London. [54664] 13/02/1997 **ME**

Matthews, Miss S A, BA MCLIP, Tenbury Wells Mgr., Worcs. C.C.,
Tenbury Wells. [27699] 04/07/1977 **CM19/05/1982**

Matthews, Mr S A, BEd MSc MCLIP, Unwaged. [40776] 04/06/1987
CM17/05/2000

Matthews, Mrs S C, BA BSc MCLIP, Team Leader: dev. & Outreach Serv., Co. L. Serv., Crahlington. [19332] 01/10/1972 **CM16/04/1975**

Matthews, Mrs S E, BA(Hons) DipLib, Sch'. Liaison and Child. Lib., & Prison Lib. [42524] 30/11/1988 **ME**

Matthews, Mrs S J, BSc DipLib MCLIP, Sch. Lib., Pinewood Sch., Swindon. [35619] 16/10/1982 **CM18/02/1986**

Mattock, Mrs S, BA(Hons) MA (Inf & Lib. Mgmnt) MCLIP, Sen. Info. Asst., De Montfort Univ., Leicester [64568] 11/05/2005 **CM10/03/2010**

Mauger, Ms A J, BA(Hons) MCLIP MBA, Unknown. [37571] 03/10/1984 **CM01/09/1987**

Maughan, Mr G, MCLIP, Life Member. [9957] 24/04/1947 **CM01/01/1955**

Maule, Miss S E, Grad. Trainee, The London L., London. [10015179] 21/10/2009 **ME**

Maung, Miss J N, BA(Hons), Asst. Lib., Faculty of Health & Social Care, Univ. of Chester [46987] 20/03/1992 **ME**

Maville, Mr A J, BA MA MCLIP, Sen. Res., Proj. N. E., Newcastle Upon Tyne. [60210] 17/05/1999 **CM24/05/1999**

Mavin, Mrs H I, Stud., Aberystwyth. [64939] 03/10/2005 **ME**

Mawe, Ms A, MA MSc BSc, Lib. Nat. L. of Ireland [10000661] 24/10/2006 **ME**

Mawer, Mr K P, MCLIP, Lib., Wyke Coll., Hull [39170] 26/11/1985 **CM10/05/1988**

Mawere, Mr G F A, BSc(Hons), Lect., Bulawayo Ploytechnic, Zimbabwe. [10016559] 14/04/2010 **ME**

Mawhinney, Ms E S, BA(Hons), Unemployed. [43564] 08/11/1989 **ME**

Mawson, Ms M B, BA MA MCLIP, Faculty Lib., Univ. of Sheffield. [35462] 20/10/1982 **RV17/06/2009** **CM18/02/1986**

Maxim, Mrs A J, CertEd MCLIP, Life Member. [9970] 22/03/1950 **CM01/01/1963**

Maxim, Mr G E, MA FCLIP, Life Member. [9971] 01/01/1959 **FE01/01/1965**

Maxted, Mrs S J, Asst. Lib., Berkhamsted Sch., Year 2 of M. A L. & Inf. Studies, UCL. [65714] 04/04/2006 **ME**

Maxwell, Mrs C, BSc MCLIP, Unknown [60670] 11/12/2001 **CM11/12/2001**

Maxwell, Mrs H, PGDipLIS, L. Asst.,IDOX PLC, Glasgow. [48061] 03/11/1992 **ME**

Maxwell, Mrs J C, Bibliographic Catr., Bibliographic Data Serv., Dumfries [10011768] 11/11/2008 **ME**

Maxwell, Mr N, FCLIP, Life Member. [9977] 29/02/1960 **FE01/01/1967**

Maxwell, Mrs P, BSc, Retired. [60846] 01/08/1990 **ME**

May, Mrs C A, BA MCLIP, Acting Head of Ls. Arch. & Inf., Cams CC, Cambridge. [39298] 30/01/1986 **CM25/05/1994**

May, Ms C, Strategic Support Offr., Plymouth Cent. L., Plymouth, Devon [10001844] 12/03/2007 **AF**

May, Mr H M H, MA MCLIP, Retired. [17368] 24/09/1953 **CM01/01/1968**

May, Ms J A, BA(Hons) MA MCLIP, Policy Off., Policy & Advocacy Unit, CILIP. [54405] 03/12/1996 **CM25/07/2001**

May, Mrs L C, BA DipLib MCLIP, Head of L. Serv. Univ. of Wales, Newport. [27377] 28/02/1977 **CM10/05/1979**

May, Miss S E, Asst. Lib., Morgan Cole Solicitors, Cardiff. [10015619] 22/12/2009 **ME**

May, Ms T G, BScEcon(Hons) MSc MCLIP, Asst. Lib., Anglia Ruskin Univ., Cambridge. [47531] 01/10/1992 **CM26/07/1995**

Mayanobe, Miss C A, MA English, MA Inf. Stud., Head Lib., Brighton Coll., Brighton [10001577] 26/02/2007 **ME**

Maycock, Miss N A, BA MA, Unknown. [10012381] 30/01/2009 **ME**

Mayers, Mrs A, BSc(Hons) MA MCLIP, Lib., Liverpool Med. Inst. [55890] 16/12/1997 **CM13/06/2007**

Mayers, Mr R O, MCLIP, Life Member. [19335] 01/01/1955 **CM01/01/1970**

Mayes, Mrs A L, MCLIP, Asst. Lib., Queen Mary's Coll., Basingstoke. [61859] 21/11/2002 **CM23/01/2008**

Mayes, Miss G D, BA(Hons) MSc, Lib., Queen's Sch., Chester. [59316] 02/02/2001 **ME**

Maynard, Ms C, MCLIP, Unemployed. [9999] 03/01/1972 **CM10/01/1975**

Maynard, Ms L H, LLB DipLib MCLIP, Head of Inf., Howrey LLP, London. [10010526] 08/10/1988 **CM22/03/1995**

Maynard, Dr S E, BA MSc PhD, Unknown. [10014985] 01/10/2009 **ME**

Mayne, Ms E, BA MA, Stud. [10007905] 16/04/2008 **ME**

Mayor, Mrs F E, BA MCLIP, Learning Resource Cent., Bridgwater Coll., Somerset. [22403] 07/05/1974 **CM05/03/1979**

Mayor, Miss L A, BA MSc MCLIP, Sen. Asst. Lib., Br. Mgr., Bamber Bridge L., Preston. [65926] 07/07/2006 **CM07/07/2010**

Maythorne, Mrs I, MCLIP, Unemployed. [8141] 06/02/1967 **CM01/01/1971**

Mazurek, Miss A Z, Unknown. [10014053] 23/06/2009 **ME**

Mburu, Miss M W, Unknown. [10014002] 17/06/2009 **ME**

Mbuthia, Mrs R D, M ED, P/T L. Asst., Durham Univ. L. [10012593] 19/02/2009 **ME**

Mc Auley, Miss S, MLIS, Asst. Lib., Lib. Inf. Serv., N. Ireland Housing Exec., Belfast [10013437] 29/04/2009 **ME**

Mc Keown, Mr A T, BA MA PG DIP LIM, L. Br. Mgr., Belfast. [10016162] 17/02/2010 **ME**

McAdams, Mr A C, LLB DipAcc, L. Inf. Offr., MacRoberts, Glasgow. [49989] 10/02/1994 **ME**

McAdams, Mrs P, Sen. Lib. Asst., Cent. L., Derry NI [10015587] 17/12/2009 **ME**

McAinsh, Mrs C M, MA(Hons) DipLib MCLIP, Lib., E. Kilbride Cent. L., Glasgow. [31631] 15/10/1979 **CM20/07/1982**

McAllister, Mrs A M, BA(Hons) MCLIP, Primary Educ. Res. Co-ordinator, Educ. Res. Serv., Greenwood Teachers Cent. [38389] 15/04/1985 **CM14/08/1991**

McAlpin, Mrs A, MA MCLIP, Bibl. Support Offr., Edinburgh Univ. L. [8973] 11/11/1969 **CM27/06/1973**

McAlpine, Mr I K, MA, Unknown. [49641] 16/11/1993 **ME**

McAra, Mrs V E M, Community Lib., Bridge of Allan, Stirling Council L. [64583] 13/04/2005 **ME**

McArdle, Mrs C, BA DipLib MCLIP, Dep. Lib., Lincoln's Inn L., London. [38131] 19/01/1985 **CM09/08/1988**

McArdle, Ms C, MLIS BA, Learning Resource Offr., Belfast Met. Coll., Belfast [10017099] 23/06/2010 **ME**

McArthur, Ms C A, L. Asst., Southend Bor. Council, Leisure, Culture & Amenity Serv., London. [59289] 29/01/2001 **AF**

McArthur, Mrs P, ACLIP, Sen. L. Asst., Rothesay L., Isle of Bute. [10006749] 17/12/2007 **ACL01/10/2008**

McAulay, Miss A M N, BA FCLIP, Life Member. [9237] 24/08/1950 **FE01/01/1957**

McAulay, Dr K E, BA MA LTCL DipLib MCLIP, Music & Academic Serv. Lib., Royal Scottish Academy of Music & Drama, Glasgow. [36433] 11/10/1983 **CM20/01/1987**

McAuley, Mrs D E, BA MA MCLIP, Sen. Lib., Dept. for Child., Sch. and Families, [58026] 14/10/1999 **CM01/02/2006**

McAuley, Mrs G, MCLIP, L. Asst., Tamworth Coll., Staffs. [9238] 01/01/1963 **CM01/01/1968**

McBirnie, Mrs A M, BMus, MMus, Asst. Prof. of L. Sci., Oklahoma City Univ., USA. [10001592] 26/02/2007 **ME**

McBride, Miss F, MA, Dept. Lib. St. Charles Cath. Sixth Form Coll., London [59007] 23/10/2000 **ME**

McBride, Mrs V J, BA MCLIP, Team Leader Customer Support, Northumbria Univ., Newcastle. [35800] 25/01/1983 **CM01/04/1986**

McCabe, Ms F A, BSc, Unwaged. (previously Law L.) [63023] 15/12/2003 **ME**

McCabe, Ms R T, BA DipLib MCLIP, L. Resource Cent. Coordinator, Holy Rood High Sch., Edinburgh. [41030] 07/10/1987 **CM01/07/1992**

McCabe, Mrs T L, BA BFA MLS, Resource Ctr. Mgr., Univ. of Glasgow [63319] 13/04/2004 **ME**

McCafferty, Ms C, BA(Hons), Stud. [10006561] 11/10/1982 **ME**

McCaig, Miss L, BSc(Hons) DipILS MCLIP, Asst Project Mgr., Transport Scotland, Glasgow [52191] 12/10/1995 **CM16/07/2003**

McCall, Mrs M R, MCLIP, Life Member. [17315] 01/01/1951 **CM01/01/1954**

McCalley, Mrs M, BA(Hons) MSc MCLIP, Support Worker, Learning Disabilities, Sense Scotland, Glasgow. [37118] 27/02/1984 **CM21/12/1988**

McCallion, Miss C, Unknown. [10014154] 01/07/2009 **ME**

McCallum, Ms A J, Records & Info. Oficer., Li. Countryside Council for Wales [59290] 29/01/2001 **AF**

McCallum, Mr D, MCLIP, Retired, Cllr., N. Lanarkshire Council. [9250] 19/09/1964 **CM17/02/1975**

McCallum, Mr J, BA(Hons) MSc, Sch. Lib., Dunoon Grammar Sch., Argyll and Bute Council. [61700] 14/10/2002 **ME**

McCann, Miss J E, BA MCLIP, Resources & Performance Mgr., Sunderland City Council. [31660] 05/11/1979 **CM05/10/1984**

McCann, Mr P J, BA MCLIP, Culture & Ls. Mgr., Argyll & Bute Council, L. HQ. [39653] 08/04/1986 **CM12/12/1990**

McCargar, Ms T J, MA MCLIP, Lib., Latymer Upper Sch. [63691] 01/10/2004 **CM22/02/2010**

McCarren, Ms J F, BA PGDip MCLIP ILT, Unknown position, De Montfort Univ. [46880] 20/02/1992 **CM25/05/1994**

McCarron, Ms L, BA(Hons) DipILS, Head of Ref. Serv., Nat. L. of Scotland. [57233] 15/01/1999 **ME**

McCarron, Mrs S M T, BA(Hons) DipLIS MCLIP, P. /t. Lib., High Sch. of Glasgow (Jnr. Sch.), Glasgow. [38359] 25/03/1985 **CM23/06/2004**

McCart, Miss A M, BA DipLS, Communities, Learning & Access Mgr., Armagh. [27620] 13/12/2004 **ME**

McCarthy, Mrs A P, BA DipLib MCLIP, Records Managment & Inf. Compliance Adviser, S. W. Reg. Devel. Agency, Devon [28301] 15/11/1977 **CM28/11/1980**

McCarthy, Ms J I, MA MA PGCE MCLIP, Stud. [57031] 13/11/1998 **CM21/05/2003**

McCarthy, Mr P J, BA MCLIP, Bibl. Serv. Mgr., City of Bradford M.D.C., Cent. L. [34803] 26/01/1982 **CM21/07/1989**

McCaskie, Ms L, BA MA MCLIP, Ino. Specialist, Civil Serv. [61596] 02/10/2002 **CM17/09/2008**

McCaul, Miss L C, BA(Hons) MA, Principal L. Assist. Catg., Univ. of Essex, Colchester. [10001365] 01/07/2000 **ME**

McCausland, Miss J D, BLib MCLIP, Consultant, Self-employed. [37344] 04/07/1984 **CM19/06/1991**

McChrystal, Ms M M, BLib (Hons) MCLIP, Partnership & Inf. Mgr., N. Edinburgh Local Off. [10010528] 31/10/1983 **CM17/10/1990**

McClean, Mrs P M, BA MSc DipLib MCLIP, Access Servs. Co-ordinator, Mitchell L., Glasgow. [35406] 05/10/1982 **CM10/11/1987**

McClean, Mrs S A C, BA DipLib MCLIP, p. /t. Lib., Stockport M.B.C. [26712] 12/10/1976 **CM19/01/1979**

McClellan, Mrs J A, MCLIP, Unemployed. [29062] 13/03/1978 **CM16/02/1982**

McClelland, Mr N, HonFCLIP, Hon. Fellow. [62816] 23/10/2003 **HFE23/10/2003**

McClen, Mrs R, BA(Hons) Dip ILM, Inf. Specialist, Nat. L. for Public health. [10012926] 02/11/1995 **ME**

McClintock, Ms E A, BSc MSc, Info. Offr., Westminster CC., London. [65110] 01/11/2005 **ME**

McCloskey, Mrs K M, BA DipLIS MCLIP, Retired. [19565] 26/10/1972 **CM28/08/1975**

McCloskey, Mr P C M, BA DipLib MCLIP, Lib. Dev. Offr., Edinburgh City L. & Inf. Serv. [34906] 27/03/1982 **CM18/06/1985**

McClure, Mr C J, MA MLib MCLIP, Romford Lib. Mngr., Havering L. Serv., LB of Havering [39814] 28/07/1986 **CM18/07/1990**

McCluskey, Miss C J, BA(Hons) MSc MCLIP, Academic Support Lib., York St John Univ. [61782] 06/11/2002 **CM21/06/2006**

McCluskey, Miss F J, BA MCLIP, Unwaged. [18318] 16/10/1972 **CM14/08/1975**

McCoid, Mrs S L, BA(Hons) MCLIP, Unemployed. [33084] 08/10/1980 **CM15/12/1983**

McColl, Miss F M, BA(Hons), LRC Co-ordinator., Cambs. Reg. Coll., Cambridge. [62200] 13/03/2003 **ME**

McCombe, Miss S A, MA MSc, Asst. Lib., Bar L., Belfast. [54709] 06/03/1997 **ME**

McConnell, Mr M R A, MA MSc PgDip MCLIP, Business Apps. Mgr., Univ. of Aberdeen. [60249] 21/06/1994 **CM14/03/2000**

McConville, Ms J, Unknown. [10012468] 22/02/2005 **ME**

McCormack, Miss B, MA(Hons), Lib. Asst., Fife Council L. & Museums, Dunfermline [10014927] 01/10/2009 **ME**

McCormick, Ms C, BA(Hons), Lib., Wyvern Tech. Coll., Fair Oak. [62643] 01/10/2003 **AF**

McCormick, Mr E A, MA DipLib MCLIP, Team Leader, Edinburgh City Ls., McDonald Road L. [45473] 14/02/1991 **CM23/03/1993**

McCorry, Miss M C I, DipLib MCLIP, Asst. Lib., Dublin P. L. H.Q., Eire. [27498] 26/04/1977 **CM07/06/1984**

McCoskery, Mrs W R, BA MCLIP, Unwaged. [27067] 24/01/1977 **CM20/07/1979**

McCourt, Mrs D, MA RCA MCLIP, Faculty Lib., Univ. for the Creative Arts [64725] 07/06/2005 **CM11/06/2010**

McCracken, Mrs H, BSc MCLIP, Unwaged/Mother. [40062] 16/10/1986 **CM12/12/1990**

McCracken, Mr I G, BA MCLIP, Lib. i/c, Govan High Sch., Glasgow City Council. [26776] 26/10/1976 **CM27/09/1982**

McCrea, Mr R, MA(Hons) MSc MCLIP, Inf. Off., Scottish Health C., Glasgow. [61765] 05/11/2002 **CM01/02/2006**

McCready, Mrs A, BA MCLIP, Lib., Cheshire Co. L. [26420] 01/10/1976 **CM13/12/1978**

McCree, Mr M, BSc(Hons) MA MCLIP, Major Projects Mgr., Stamford L., Stamford, Lincs [55135] 16/07/1997 **CM15/05/2002**

McCrohan, Ms M G, BA(Hons), L. Mgr., Orrick Herrington and Sutcliffe, London. [48463] 15/01/1993 **ME**

McCrudden, Ms B, LLB MLIS, Asst. Lib., Public Record Off. of Northern Ireland. [10014591] 22/02/2005 **ME**

McCrudden, Mrs P A, MCLIP, Inf. Mgr. & Reseracher., Hawkins & Associates., Cambridge [32657] 02/07/1980 **CM27/08/1985**

McCubbin, Mrs K J, BA(Hons) MCLIP, Lib. -Learning Devel., City L. & Arts Cent., Sunderland. [28682] 09/01/1978 **CM23/06/1981**

McCue, Ms J, MSc, Team Lib., Childrens L., Aberdeen Cent. L. [10000711] 25/10/2006 **ME**

McCulloch, Mrs C, B. ED, MA, Stud. [10016914] 10/06/2010 **ME**

McCulloch, Mr D, BA MCLIP, Policy Offr., UNISON, London. [25372] 31/12/1975 **CM16/09/1980**

McCulloch, Mr E, MA(Hons) MSc, p. /t. L. Asst., William Patrick L., E. Dunbartonshire Council. [55820] 26/11/1997 **ME**

McCulloch, Mrs S, BA MCLIP, Head of Young People's Serv., Cornwall C.C. [9308] 01/01/1968 **CM01/01/1971**

McCunn, Miss E K, Stud. Univ. of Brighton. [10014471] 12/08/2009 **ME**

McDaid, Mrs Q, MCLIP, Retired. [29461] 17/08/1978 **CM28/04/1981**

McDonagh, Mr M, BLS(Hons) MCLIP, Learning & Access Devel. Lib., Southern Educ. & L. Board, L. HQ, Armagh, N. Ireland [33055] 01/10/1980 **CM16/07/2003**

McDonald, Prof A C, BSc FCLIP, Dir. of Learning Supp. Serv. & Head of Lifelong Learning Cent., Univ. of E. London, Dagenham. [18403] 18/09/1974 **FE19/07/2000**

McDonald, Mr A H, MA, Unemployed. [58676] 15/05/2000 **ME**

McDonald, Mrs C S, BA DipLib MCLIP, Housewife & Mother. [42326] 24/10/1988 **CM18/11/1992**

McDonald, Miss E L, BA, Trainee Lib., W. Sussex., P.L. [65200] 17/11/2005 **ME**

McDonald, Mrs E, BA(Hons) MSc, Unknown [10006462] 24/10/2007 **ME**

McDonald, Miss F, BA DipLib MCLIP, Lifelong Learning Devel. Lib., Herts Co. Council. [37613] 09/10/1984 **CM05/04/1988**

McDonald, Ms G A, MA MCLIP MBA, Acting Univ. Lib., Heriot-Watt Univ., Edinburgh. [31373] 16/10/1979 **CM05/11/1981**

McDonald, Mrs H E, BA, Learning Resources Asst., LRC, Kingston Coll. [10015568] 15/12/2009 **AF**

McDonald, Ms R, Stud., Univ. of Strathclyde [10015553] 14/12/2009 **ME**

McDonald, Mrs S, BSc MLIS, Unknown. [10015964] 03/02/2010 **ME**

McDonald, Mr V, BA MCLIP MCIPR, Retired [9336] 01/01/1971 **CM24/10/1973**

McDonald, Mrs Y M, BA DMS DipLib MCLIP, Asst. Co. Lib., Oxon. Co. L. [30572] 22/01/1979 **CM27/01/1981**

McDonnell, Miss G, BA BA MCLIP, Catg. Lib., Staffs. Univ., Stoke-on-Trent. [9339] 04/10/1967 **CM21/09/1972**

McDonough, Mrs C M, BSc DipLib MCLIP, Head of L. & Heritage, Cent. L., L.B. of Sutton. [31791] 14/01/1980 **CM08/02/1982**

McDougall, Ms A, Unknown. [10006408] 19/10/2007 **ME**

McDougall, Mr G I, BA(Hons) DipIT MCLIP, A. Systems Mgr., Aberdeen City Council. [44905] 11/01/1991 **CM18/11/1998**

McDougall, Miss S, MCLIP, Lib., Deans Community High Sch., Livingston. [28865] 30/01/1978 **CM31/07/1980**

McDowall, Mrs R A C, BEd PGDipILS MCLIP, L. and Inf. Worker, Whitfield L., Dundee. [62266] 07/04/2003 **CM30/11/2009**

McDowell, Mrs B A, Retired. [56380] 01/07/1998 **ME**

McDowell, Mrs J, BA(Hons) MA MCLIP, Info. Serv Advisor, Napier Univ., Edinburgh. [62329] 29/04/2003 **CM11/03/2009**

McEachern, Miss K L, BA MCLIP, Lib., Mearns Castle High Sch., [42380] 28/10/1988 **CM23/03/1993**

McEachran, Mr M A, BA MCLIP, Retired. [24745] 02/10/1975 **CM31/12/1989**

McElligott, Mrs M E, BA DipLib, Unwaged. [34210] 12/08/1981 **ME**

McElroy, Mrs M H, MBA MRPharmS MCLIP, Life Member. [26120] 01/07/1976 **CM24/09/1979**

McElroy, Prof R, MA MBA DipLib FCLIP, Life Member. [9352] 12/10/1967 **FE18/04/1989**

McElwee, Miss E E, Outreach & Surestart Offr., W. Swindon L. [63390] 28/04/2004 **AF**

McElwee, Ms G, BA(Hons) DipLib MCLIP, Strategic Mgr., L. & Heritage Serv., Royal Bor. of Kingston upon Thames. [34661] 21/01/1982 **CM28/10/1985**

McEnaney, Miss C, BA, Catr., Aberdeenshire L. &Inf. Serv., Oldmeldrum. [10013645] 04/11/1998 **ME**

McEntee, Miss E, BSSC Dip. Lib. PGCE DASE MA MCLIP, Teacher, career braek. [10001428] 09/10/1988 **CM22/04/1992**

McEvoy, Miss E M, BA(Hons) MSc MCLIP, Knowledge Mgr., PricewaterhouseCoopers, Australia. [58829] 17/08/2000 **CM15/09/2004**

McEvoy, Ms H, BA(Hons) DipILM, NHS Liason and Faculty Lib., John Rylands Univ. L., Manchester. [58661] 09/05/2000 **ME**

McEwan, Mr K, MCLIP, Retired [9359] 01/01/1957 **CM01/01/1968**

McFadyen, Mrs M M, Unknown. [10014153] 01/07/2009 **AF**

McFadzien, Mrs B W C, FCLIP, Retired. [12897] 01/01/1932 **FE01/01/1938**

McFarland, Mrs M P, BA MCLIP, L. Asst., S. W. Coll., Dungannon [25084] 29/10/1975 **CM26/04/1982**

McFarlane, Ms C J, DipEd DipLib MCLIP, Sch. Lib., Devon C.C., Exeter. [43871] 02/02/1990 **CM16/09/1992**

McFarlane, Ms E G, MA MCLIP MILTHE, Retired. [22930] 23/09/1974 **CM01/03/1978**

McFarlane, Mrs J A, BA MCLIP, Acting L. Mgr., Renfrewshire Council. [23408] 09/01/1975 **CM26/09/1979**

McFarlane, Ms J, BA MCLIP, Head of Partnerships & Professional Adviser, Nat. L. of Scotland. [30890] 21/05/1979 **CM10/07/1981**

McFarlane, Mr J, MCLIP, Unknown. [63963] 22/11/2004 **CM21/11/2007**

McFarlane, Ms K A, BA MLib FCLIP, Head of Corp. Inf. Knowledge Serv., GCHQ, Cheltenham. [28245] 10/10/1977 **FE23/10/2008**

McFarlane, Ms K, LIS Mgr., Last,Cawthra,Feather Solicitors, Bradford. [56806] 19/10/1998 **ME**

McFetridge, Mrs D, BA(Hons) MSc(Econ), Sen. Inf. Offr., Law Soc. of N. Ireland, Belfast. [52844] 09/01/1996 **ME**

McFie, Ms J E, BA MA MCLIP, Unknown. [10014350] 01/07/2001 **CM12/12/1991**

McGale, Miss D, BA(Hons), Stud., UCL [10015557] 14/12/2009 **ME**

McGarrigle, Mrs H P, MCLIP, Prison Lib., Oakham L., Rutland. [25319] 05/01/1976 **CM05/12/1978**

McGarrity, Mr J, BA MCLIP, Inf. Serv. Co-ordinator, S. Lanarkshire Council, Hamilton Town House L. [26476] 01/10/1976 **CM09/09/1981**

McGarry, Ms D, MLS, Retired. [44630] 12/11/1990 **ME**

McGarry, Dr K, PhD FCLIP, Retired. [9372] 28/01/1956 **FE01/01/1967**

McGarry, Ms M, MA DipLib MCLIP, Local Studies Lib., N. Lanarkshire Council. [35253] 01/10/1982 **CM26/02/1992**

McGeachy, Mrs A M S, MSc BSc DipLib MCLIP, FOI and Records Mgr., Univ. W. of Scotland, Paisley [20125] 21/01/1973 **CM07/11/1975**

McGee, Mrs J E, MA, Unemployed. [10015525] 09/12/2009 **ME**

McGee, Mrs K, BA MSc, Unwaged [10012919] 21/10/2002 **ME**

McGettigan, Mrs A M, Lib., Richard Rose Cent. Academy, Carlisle [57695] 01/07/1999 **AF**

McGettigan, Mrs E, BA MCLIP MBILD ACMI, Head of Ls. &Inf. Servs.,Edinburgh City Council. [9649] 05/11/1970 **CM01/07/1975**

McGhee, Ms S M, MA(Hons), MSc., Inf. Offr., NHS Lothian, Edinburgh. [10000770] 06/11/2006 **ME**

McGhee, Ms W, MA MSc, Arch., N. Lanarkshire C. Arch., Cumbernauld. [57985] 08/10/1999 **ME**

McGhie, Ms J, MSc, Unknown. [65064] 24/10/2005 **ME**

McGill, Miss J C, BA(Hons) DipILS MCLIP, Lib., Auchinleck Acad., Auchinleck, Ayrshire. [52845] 09/01/1996 **CM20/11/2002**

McGinley, Dr K J, The L., Dublin Univ. [64308] 25/02/2005 **ME**

McGivern, Ms G, BA, Unknown. [10016889] 28/05/2010 **ME**

McGlamery, Ms S, BA MLS, Sen. Product Mngr., OCLC, Birmingham [10017062] 21/06/2010 **ME**

McGlashan, Mrs G, BA(Hons), Asst. Mgr., Heatherwood Hosp., Ascot. [65880] 16/06/2006 **ME**

McGlen, Miss H E, BSc MCLIP, Inf. Advisor, Shell U. K. Exploration, Aberdeen. [33058] 20/10/1980 **CM17/07/1985**

McGlew, Ms C K, MA(Hons) MSc, Maternity Leave. [53956] 16/10/1996 **ME**

McGlinn, Miss C, BA(Hons) MSc, Sch. Lib., Springburn Academy, Glasgow. [10008414] 27/11/2003 **ME**

McGlynn, Mrs S P, BA MCLIP, Retired. [17329] 04/12/1962 **CM01/01/1963**

McGough, Mrs K E, BA(Hons) MSc MCLIP, S&PC Mgr., Essex C.C., Chelmsford. [49200] 12/10/1993 **CM21/05/1997**

McGovern, Ms M, MCLIP, Inf. & L. Mgr., FPA, London [10000170] 01/05/1975 **CM11/11/1985**

McGowan, Mr I D, BA, Retired. [44953] 22/01/1991 **ME**

McGowan, Ms S, BA MA, L. Inf. Facilitator, (p/t Perm) [62920] 20/11/2003 **ME**

McGrath, Mrs A J, MSc, Unwaged. [49756] 02/12/1993 **ME**

McGrath, Mrs A M, BSc MSc MCLIP, Sr. Info. Specialist, Res. Support, King's Coll., London [45681] 22/04/1991 **CM26/07/1995**

McGrath, Dr B, BA(Mod), MLitt, PhD, Inf. Consultant, Rathmines, Dublin, Ireland. [10008379] 19/03/2008 **ME**

McGrath, Mrs C M, BA MCLIP, Sch. Lib., Bucksburn Academy, Aberdeen. [46402] 01/11/1991 **CM19/03/1997**

McGrath, Ms F M, BA, Unknown, SPICe, Edinburgh. [38875] 16/10/1985 **ME**

McGrath, Mrs K, Br. Lib., Coleg Llandrillo, Rhos-on-Sea. [10016457] 26/03/2010 **ME**

McGrath, Mr M I, BA(Hons), Journal Editor, Self Employed. [62145] 28/02/2003 **AF**

McGrath, Mrs S A, BA(Hons) PG Dip, KBD/LIS Training Mgr., Freshfields, London. [65726] 12/04/2006 **ME**

McGregor, Mr C, BA MCLIP, Lib., Grangemouth L. [28867] 13/02/1978 **CM10/04/1980**

McGregor, Mr R, BA(Hons) MLITT PGDipILS MCLIP, Lib., James Hamilton Academy, E. Ayrshire Council. [61313] 17/05/2002 **CM07/09/2005**

McGrimmond, Miss J, BA MCLIP, Team Lib. Inf., Aberdeen City L. [28080] 11/10/1977 **CM16/02/1982**

McGuinness, Mrs J A, BLib MCLIP, Sen. Inf. Offr., Univ. of Abertay Dundee., Dundee. [36128] 27/05/1983 **CM05/07/1988**

McGuire, Ms P R, BSc, Unknown. [10000679] 27/10/2006 **ME**

McGurk, Miss G R, MCLIP, F/T Carer to elderly parent, Seasonal volunteer work at Chained L., Hereford Cathederal. [19753] 23/09/1967 **CM01/01/1972**

McHale, Mrs C E, BA(Hons), Stud., Aberystwyth Univ. [10009225] 07/05/2008 **ME**

McHarazo, Dr A A S, BA MA PhD HonFCLIP FCLIP, Lib. /Head of Dept., Univ. Coll. of Lands & Arch. Studies, Dar es Salaam, Tanzania. [47548] 01/10/1992 **FE21/11/2001**

McHugh, Ms E A, MA(Hons) DipILS MCLIP, Elect. Resources Mgr., UHI Millennium Inst., Inverness. [52836] 02/01/1996 **CM23/09/1998**

McHugh, Mr J, Info. Offr., Milbank Tweed, London [10012867] 17/03/2009 **ME**

McHugh, Mrs M, MCLIP, LIRC Mgr., London Fire Brigade [19968] 04/01/1973 **CM25/07/1977**

McHugh, Miss P M, BA(Hons), L. Asst., Culture & Sport Glasgow. [10006537] 30/10/2007 **ME**

McHugh, Miss R, BA, Grad. Trainee, Healthcare L., Woolwich. [10016530] 01/04/2010 **ME**

McIlroy, Miss A J, BSc(Hons) MLIS MCLIP, Subject Lib., Queen's Univ. of Belfast Med. L., Belfast. [58222] 12/11/1999 **CM13/06/2007**

McIlwaine, Prof I C, BA PhD FCLIP FSA, Prof. Emeritus, Dept of Inf Studies., Univ. Coll. London. [9414] 01/01/1958 **FE01/01/1962**

McIlwaine, Prof J, BA MCLIP, Prof. Emeritus of the Bibl. of Asia & Africa, Dep of Inf. Studies., Univ. Coll. London. [9415] 05/10/1961 **CM01/01/1965**

McInnes, Mrs A M, BA DipLib MCLIP, Young Peoples Serv. Lib., E. Ayrshire Council, Kilmarnock,Ayrshire. [34745] 05/02/1982 **CM21/12/1988**

McInnes, Mrs A, BA(Hons), Lib. Offr. Young People 0-18, Cornwall L. Serv., Truro. [10005997] 13/05/2005 **ME**

McIntosh, Mrs A R, MLib MCLIP, Sch. Lib., Angus Council, Webster High Sch,. Kirriemuir. [45342] 15/10/1990 **CM17/05/2000**

McIntosh, Mrs G K, ACLIP, Learning Resource Asst., Sheffield Coll. [10006457] 19/10/2007 **ACL23/09/2009**

McIntosh, Ms K, BA(Hons) MA MCLIP, Law Lib., Edinburgh [65946] 17/07/2006 **CM05/05/2010**

McIntosh, Mrs S, BA MSc MCLIP, Learning Res. Mgr., Heanor Gate Sci. Coll. [57524] 20/04/1999 **CM23/01/2002**

McIntyre, Mr A, BSc DipLib MCLIP, Retired [9423] 30/03/1966 **CM01/01/1972**

McIntyre, Miss F R, MCLIP, Asst. Libr., Colne L., Lancashire. [64410] 15/03/2005 **CM19/12/2008**

McIntyre, Miss J I, DipHE MCLIP, Lifelong Learning Lib., Renfrewshire Council, Paisley. [26477] 14/10/1976 **CM12/12/1980**

McIntyre, Mr J, MA(Hons) PgDipILS, Sch. Lib., Hawick High Sch. LRC, Roxburghshire. [64204] 09/02/2005 **ME**

McIntyre, Ms R, BA(Hons) MA MCLIP, Facilities Coordinator, Child. Mob. L., N. Shields Cent. L. [62932] 20/11/2003 **CM05/05/2010**

McIntyre, Mrs S A, CertEd BA(Hons) CDip MCLIP, Mgr. : Lib. Skills and Learning, Leicester L. [51060] 09/11/1994 **CM18/11/1998**

McIver, Mrs H F, Life Member. [21134] 12/10/1973 **ME**

McIver, Mrs S, BA MCLIP, Asst. Lib., Cent. L., Paisley [10013118] 03/10/1989 **CM17/03/1999**

McIvor, Mrs S M, BA MA, Researcher. [65030] 13/10/2005 **ME**

McKay, Miss A L, BA(Hons), Lib., Corby Business Academy, Northants. [10002933] 10/05/2007 **ME**

McKay, Miss C A, MA MCLIP, Inf. Offr., Scottish Consortium for Learning Disability [62742] 14/10/2003 **CM11/03/2009**

McKay, Mr D J, FCLIP, Knowledge Info. Co-Ord. Conocophillips (UK) Ltd., Aberdeen. [22838] 04/10/1974 **FE01/04/2002**

McKay, Mrs E L, BA Dip. Lib. MCLIP, Stock Mgr., Trafford L., Manchester [10007734] 14/12/1983 **CM22/03/1995**

McKay, Mr I S H, Weekend Learning Resources Asst., Chester Univ [10007233] 01/02/2008 **AF**

McKay, Mr M J, MA, Stud. [65786] 18/04/2006 **ME**

McKay, Mrs S H C, BA MCLIP, Lib., Aberdeenshire L. & Inf. Serv. [33417] 29/09/1980 **CM06/03/1986**

McKay, Miss V S M, BEd DipLib MCLIP, Lib., Strathallan Sch. [36464] 11/10/1983 **CM16/10/1991**

McKeating, Mrs S F, MSc MCLIP, Academic Serv. Mgr(Eng), Loughborough Univ., Pilkington L. [42588] 13/01/1989 **CM13/01/1989**

McKechnie, Miss K E, Stud. [10006514] 30/10/2007 **ME**

McKee, Mrs K J, BA MSc MCLIP, Sub. Lib., St. John's Coll., Cambridge. [42110] 01/10/1988 **RV08/09/2005** **CM16/11/1994**

McKee, Dr R A, PhD MCLIP FRSA, Ch. Exec., CILIP, London. [26870] 18/12/1976 **CM14/02/1979**

McKee, Miss T, MA(Hons) MSc MCLIP, Serv. Lib., NHS Greater Glasgow & Clyde [63940] 18/11/2004 **CM11/06/2010**

McKeeman, Mrs R L, BA(Hons) MLib MCLIP, Sch. L. Asst., Foundry Lane Prim. Sch.,Southampton City Council. [43766] 05/01/1990 **CM22/03/1995**

McKeen, Mr M S, DipEarthSci BSc DMS MCLIP, Sen. HR Admin. / Inf. Mgr., Roscin Inst., Univ. of Edingburgh. [31086] 08/08/1979 **CM05/03/1984**

McKellar, Ms J, Serv. Coordinator, Lib. & Learning, Brimbank C.C., Victoria, Aus. [64577] 17/05/2005 **ME**

McKellar, Miss R, MCLIP, Readers Serv. Lib., Inverclyde L. [10000826] 28/02/2002 **CM09/07/2008**

McKellen, Ms C L, BSc FCLIP, Retired [60543] 06/02/1978 **FE11/12/2001**

McKelvey, Mrs C J, BA ACLIP, L. Asst., Hertford L. [63907] 26/10/2004 **ACL17/01/2007**

McKelvie, Ms J, Stud., Telford Coll., Edinburgh. [10008535] 06/05/2008 **ME**

McKenna, Mr D K, BA MA, L. Asst., Q. U. B Sch. of Educ., Belfast. [65648] 13/03/2006 **ME**

McKenna, Mr G, MA FCLIP, Retired. [9445] 13/09/1966 **FE01/06/2005**

McKenna, Mrs G, BA(Hons), Sch. Lib., Austin Friars St. Monica's, Carlisle. [58490] 25/02/2000 **ME**

McKenzie, Ms A K, LLB(Hons), Inf. Serv. Mgr., Olswang, London. [56449] 06/07/1998 **ME**

McKenzie, Mrs H E M, BSc MLS MCLIP MA, Lib., Cardinal Wiseman High Sch., Greenford. [55278] 12/09/1997 **CM04/02/2004**

McKenzie, Mr J M, LLB(Hons) DipLIS MCLIP, Lib., Royal Faculty of Procurators in Glasgow. [54013] 17/10/1996 **CM23/06/2004**

McKeon, Ms S, BA HDipLIS ALAI, Unknown [50943] 02/11/1994 **ME**

McKeown, Miss S, BA(Hons) MSc, Inf. Specialist, NBS, Newcastle Upon Tyne. [59876] 29/10/2001 **ME**

McKernan, Mr S, MSc MEd BA(Hons) MCLIP, Lib., Northern Coll., Barnsley. [42908] 12/04/1989 **CM24/04/1991**

McKichan, Miss F, MA, Learning Resources Asst., Southampton Solent Univ., Hants. [63757] 29/09/2004 **AF**

McKie, Mrs A, BA(Hons) MA MCLIP, LLS Learning & Res. Serv. Mgr., Univ. for the Creative Arts, Maidstone, Kent. [48120] 09/11/1992
RV17/06/2009   **CM19/03/1997**

McKim, Mr J, MSLS, Dep. Records Mgr., Durham Univ. [10010303] 17/07/2008   **ME**

McKinlay, Miss I M C, MCLIP, Life Member. [9472] 22/09/1942
                                                                 CM01/01/1950

McKinlay, Mrs L, BA(Hons), Area L. Mgr., Gateshead Council. [46574] 12/11/1991   **ME**

McKinney, Miss D, MCLIP, Life Member. [9474] 09/05/1956
                                                                 CM01/01/1964

McKinney, Mrs P A, BA(Hons) MSc, Inf. Adviser, Sheffield Hallam Univ., Sheffield. [59928] 06/11/2001   **ME**

McKnight, Prof S, BBus MPubAdmin AALIA FCLIP, Dir. of L. & Knowledge Res., Nottingham Trent Univ., Boots L. [63813] 01/10/2004   **FE31/01/2007**

McKrell, Dr L, BA MSc PhD MCLIP, Comm. Lib., Cent. L., Stirling. [43521] 01/11/1989   **CM22/04/1992**

McLachlan, Mrs K N, BA(Hons) MA MCLIP, Sen. Inf. Offr., Macfarlanes, London. [55427] 07/10/1997   **CM19/11/2003**

McLachlan, Mrs L M, BA MCLIP, Sch. Lib., Beath High Sch., Cowdenbeath. [10407] 06/01/1969   **CM01/01/1972**

McLaney, Mr J, BA MCLIP, Life Member. [9489] 02/04/1953
                                                                 CM01/01/1959

McLaren, Miss C M, BA(Hons) MCLIP, L. Serv. Mgr., George Elliot Hosp., Nuneaton [61994] 16/01/2003   **CM19/11/2008**

McLaren, Miss L, MA(Hons), Unknown. [64506] 15/04/2005   **ME**

McLaughlin, Mrs A J, BA MCLIP, Lib. Serv. Mgr., Jones Day, London. [33935] 28/05/1981   **CM06/02/1986**

McLaughlin, Mr G L, BA, Lib. Asst., Watford Cent. L. [10015566] 15/12/2009   **ME**

McLaughlin, Mr J F E, MA DLIS, Univ. Arch. & Rare Books Curator, Univ. of Ulster [10001732] 07/03/2007   **ME**

McLaughlin, Miss K, BA(Hons), L. Asst., Cootehill L., Ireland. [10009802] 15/03/2000   **AF**

McLaughlin, Ms M E, BA DipLib MCLIP, Sen. Sch. Lib., W. Educ. & L. Board, Co. Tyrone. [33793] 05/03/1981   **CM17/01/1983**

McLaughlin, Mrs S A, BA, LRC Mgr., Coleraine Campus, Univ. of Ulster. [10003424] 05/02/1982   **ME**

McLaven, Miss T J, BA(Hons) MA, Dep. Lib., Educ. Cent. L., Glenfield Hosp., Univ. Hosp. of Leicester. [47792] 27/02/1997   **ME**

McLean, Ms F, BSc MSc RGN RMN MCLIP, career break [55412] 08/10/1997   **CM21/05/2003**

McLean, Mrs H M, Sch. Lib., Magdalen Coll., Oxford. [57669] 01/07/1999   **ME**

McLean, Mr I D, BA MCLIP, Community Ref. Lib., Stirling Council. [25784] 19/01/1976   **CM19/01/1978**

McLean, Mrs J B B, BA MCLIP, Asst. Lib., Renfrewshire Council. [2378] 18/09/1970   **CM01/07/1973**

McLean, Mrs J D, MA(Hons) MSc, Learner Resource Cent. Asst., Clydebank Coll. [61006] 30/01/2002   **ME**

McLean, Ms M, Unknown,Bevan Brittan LLP,Bristol [10001504] 15/12/1995   **ME**

McLean, Prof N, BA DipEd DipLib MCLIP, Retired. [9505] 03/01/1972
                                                                 CM18/12/1978

McLean, Mr R J, MSc MCLIP MBCI, Info. Governance Mngr., Wellcome Trust, London. [60420] 28/02/1997   **CM28/02/1997**

McLean, Miss R, BA, Inf. Offr., SCVO., Edinburgh. [55674] 07/11/1997
                                                                       ME

McLean, Mr R, BA MCLIP, Retired. [9506] 18/09/1948   **CM01/01/1955**

McLean, Mrs S L, BSc DipLib MCLIP, Career Break. [34287] 23/10/1981   **CM15/08/1989**

McLeary, Miss D, Unwaged [10013617] 13/05/2009   **ME**

McLelland, Dr D H, EdD MA MSc FCLIP, Life Member. [15695] 01/01/1956   **FE01/01/1966**

McLennan, Mrs D A, MA(Hons) MCLIP, Yth. Serv. Lib., L. H.Q., Argyll & Bute Council. [9511] 12/01/1968   **CM01/01/1972**

McLeod, Ms F G, MA DipLib MCLIP, Supp. Worker. [33475] 15/01/1981
                                                                 CM31/08/1983

McLeod, Prof J, PhD MSc BSc PGCutl MCLIP, Prof. in Records Mgmnt, Sch. of Computing, Eng. & Inf. Sci., Northumbria Univ. Newcastle upon Tyne. [60167] 27/01/1982   **CM25/07/1989**

McLeod, Mr M, IT Instructor/Lib., Aberdeen Coll. [40541] 06/03/1987**ME**

McLoughlin, Mrs A M, BA MCLIP, Team Lib., Rock Ferry L., Wirral. [39805] 29/07/1986   **CM14/11/1990**

McLoughlin, Mrs R S, BA(Hons), Sen. Learning Cent. Asst., Exeter Coll. [59330] 08/02/2001   **ME**

McLoughlin, Mrs U M, BA(Hons) PGDip MA, L. Training Offr., Cheshire C.C., Chester. [58963] 10/10/2000   **ME**

McLullich, Mrs J J, BA MCLIP, Career Break. [34507] 19/11/1981
                                                                 CM18/09/1991

McMahon, Mrs S J, MCLIP, Lib., Worthing L., W. Sussex C.C. [22790] 21/10/1974   **CM02/09/1977**

McMahon, Ms S T A, BA DipLib MCLIP, Head of L. & Inf. Serv., Brighton & Hove City Council [31731] 23/11/1979   **CM16/08/1982**

McManus, Miss P A, BA MCLIP, Semi-Retired (Working from Home), Otley, W. Yorkshire. [10001755] 04/10/1988   **CM04/10/1988**

McMaster, Mr A R, BA MA MCLIP, Head of Serv. Delivery, (L. Arch. & Inf.), Suffolk C.C. [26988] 10/01/1977   **CM24/01/1979**

McMaster, Mrs C, BLib MCLIP, Faculty Liaison Lib., Anglia Ruskin Univ., Chelmsford. [23265] 18/11/1974   **CM10/09/1979**

McMeekan, Mr I, MA FCLIP, Life Member. [9526] 07/02/1956
                                                                 FE15/02/1989

McMenemy, Mr D, BA(Hons) MSc MCLIP FHEA, Lect., Dept. of Computer & Inf. Sci., Univ. of Strathclyde. [53830] 03/10/1996
                                                                 CM20/09/2000

McMillan, Mrs B M, BA MCLIP, Sch. Lib., King Edward VI Sch., Suffolk. [18371] 21/10/1972   **CM01/01/1976**

McMillan, Mr D H, BSc(Hons) MSc(Econ), Unwaged. [54610] 31/01/1997   **ME**

McMillan, Miss E, BA MCLIP, Asst. Head of L., Slough L. [10007756] 31/08/1982   **CM15/05/1989**

McMillan, Ms J E, BA(Hons) MCLIP, Sch. Lib. /ICT Mgr., Tain Royal Academy, Highland Council. [52507] 02/11/1995   **CM17/11/1999**

McMillan, Mrs S, BA MCLIP, Asst. Lib., Hampton Sch., Middx. [9534] 14/01/1969   **CM01/01/1972**

McMillan, Mr T, BEd, Vol. Lib., Irish Cent., London. [63047] 26/01/2004
                                                                       ME

McMordie, Mrs L, BA(Hons) MSc MCLIP, Lib., Chartered Accountants, Belfast. [57104] 14/12/1998   **CM11/03/2009**

McMullan, Mrs E A, BA, Unknown. [32317] 22/02/1980   **ME**

McNab, Mrs I, BSc(Econ) MCLIP, Business & Marketing Team Leader, Fife Lib. & Museums HQ. [59432] 14/03/2001   **CM21/06/2006**

McNae, Miss H M, BA(Hons) DipILS MCLIP, Sen. Inf. Specialist, Univ. of Abertay Dundee, Inf. Serv. [57842] 09/09/1999   **CM15/05/2002**

McNally, Mrs A M, MCLIP, Retired. [19754] 18/08/1964 **CM01/01/1967**

McNally, Mrs L E, MA(Hons) DipILS MCLIP, Asst. Lib., Glasgow Caledonian Univ., Glasgow. [55821] 26/11/1997   **CM12/03/2003**

McNally, Mrs R C, BSocSci DipLIS MCLIP, Sen. Inf. Specialist Nat. Inst. for Health & Clinical Excellence. [44060] 20/04/1990 **CM16/11/1994**

McNamara, Mr S, BA MCLIP, Lifelong Learning Lib. [10008816] 21/04/2008   **CM10/03/2010**

McNaughton, Mr M, MA, Lib., Inst. for the Study of Islam & Christianity, Pewsey. [10015705] 14/01/2010   **AF**

McNee, Ms N J, BLS MCLIP, Lib., Kingswood Independent Sch., Bath. [34480] 13/11/1981   **CM21/12/1984**

McNeely, Miss A, MCLIP, Sch. Lib., Cathkin High Sch., Cambuslang. [9549] 28/02/1972 **CM04/02/1976**

McNeil, Miss F J, BA MCLIP, Dep. Lib., Inst. of Actuaries, Oxford. [41586] 21/01/1988 **CM14/11/1990**

McNeill, Mr A J J, BA(Hons) MCLIP FSA SCOT, Unknown. [19312] 07/09/1972 **CM01/07/1975**

McNeill, Miss E, BA DLS ATCL MCLIP, Life Member [9554] 07/03/1957 **CM01/01/1967**

McNeill, Mrs J I, BLib MCLIP, Programme Co-ordinator Lib., Health + Wellbeing Northants C. C [34097] 01/10/1981 **CM12/12/1990**

McNeill, Ms M, BA(Hons), Records & Info. Mgmnt. Offr., SFC., Edinburgh [10002157] 16/06/2004 **ME**

McNeill, Mr R, BA, Stud., Thames Valley Univ., London. [10016438] 23/03/2010 **ME**

McNichol, Mrs K A, MA DipLib MCLIP, Force Records Mgr.,HQ, Merseyside Police. [34183] 09/10/1981 **CM18/11/1992**

McNicol, Miss F E, BA(Hons) DipILS MCLIP, Unwaged. [53021] 31/01/1996 **CM12/03/2003**

McNicol, Mr R A, MA(Hons), Sport Media Mgr., BBC Scotland, Glasgow [63648] 09/08/2004 **ME**

McOwat, Mrs H M, BSc DipInfSc MCLIP, Lib., Eng. Dept., Cambridge Univ. [24538] 27/08/1975 **CM24/01/1979**

McPhail, Mrs R J, BA(Hons) MCLIP, Unwaged [44600] 05/11/1990 **CM21/07/1999**

McPhail-Smith, Miss Z C, MA(Hons) MSc, Sen. Serials Catg. Asst., Nat. L. of Scotland. [10000520] 10/12/2006 **ME**

McPherson, Mrs E A, MA MCLIP, Culture & Sport, Glasgow [25373] 07/01/1976 **CM01/12/1977**

McPherson, Miss M, BA MCLIP, Comm. Lib., S. Lanarkshire Council, Stock Servs., E. Killbride Cent. Lib. [29463] 14/08/1978 **CM14/08/1980**

McQueen, Mr G J, BA(Hons) DipIM MCLIP, Lib., (Child.), Collection Dev. Lib., Young People's Lib. Serv., London Bor. of Richmond [53276] 12/04/1996 **CM13/03/2002**

McQuilkin, Miss J M, BA(Hons) MSc(Econ), Asst. Lib., Univ. of Ulster, Magee Coll., Londonderry. [51402] 06/02/1995 **ME**

McQuillan, Miss D, MA(Hons) PGDip MCLIP, Site Lib., Edinburgh Campus, Scottish Agricultural Coll. [61770] 05/11/2002 **CM21/03/2007**

McQuistan, Miss S E, BSc(Hons) MSc MCLIP, I. Mgr., NHS Greather Glasgow & Clyde [54778] 01/04/1997 **CM17/09/2003**

McRae, Mr J A, BSc MCLIP, L. & Inf. Serv. Coordinator, IMAREST, London. [64862] 09/08/2005 **CM04/10/2006**

McRobbie, Mr J D, MA(Hons), Sch. Lib., Newbattle Community High Sch. [10006709] 21/11/2007 **ME**

McRoy, Mrs C, BA(Hons) MCLIP, Trust Lib., Birmingham Childrens Hosp. [31184] 03/10/1979 **CM11/11/1986**

McSean, Mr T, BA DipLib FCLIP, Retired. [30884] 04/10/1973 **FE15/09/1993**

McShane, Ms N H, BA(Hons) MCLIP, Inf. &Recrod Mgr. (p/t), Proudman Oceanographic Lab., Liverpool. [49338] 25/10/1993 **CM07/09/2005**

McSweeney, Mr D, Asst. Lib., Cent. Bank of Ireland [10015597] 12/01/2010 **ME**

McTaggart, Mr A, BA(Hons), L. Offr., Sighthill L., Edinburgh. [10010871] 02/09/2008 **ME**

McTaggart, Mr W J, MA, Catg. & Accesss Asst., N. W. Film Arch., Manchester Met. Univ. [65765] 05/05/2006 **ME**

McTavish, Miss R, Unknown. [10015193] 23/10/2009 **ME**

McVean, Mrs L, MSc MA(Hons), Asst. Lib., NHS Greater Glasgow & Clyde, Glasgow. [10011354] 14/10/2008 **ME**

McVeigh, Ms G F, BA MCLIP, Retired. [29122] 01/01/1962 **CM17/10/1990**

McVey, Mr D M, BSc(Hons) MSc MCLIP, Unemployed. [51213] 25/11/1994 **CM08/11/1999**

McVicar, Mr N, BA MCLIP, Unknown. [24359] 01/07/1975**CM14/02/1979**

McWalter, Mr I B, ND:LIS NHD:LIP, BTECH:LIS, Admin., The CQI, London. [10011877] 25/11/2008 **ME**

McWatt, Mr C W, BA DipLib MCLIP, Retired. [9582] 23/09/1966 **CM02/07/1974**

McWilliam, Mrs C, BA MLS MCLIP, Retired. [11218] 08/10/1969 **CM31/10/1972**

McWilliam, Mrs R, BA(Hons) MCLIP, Sen. Lib., Lancashire C.C. [52128] 05/10/1995 **CM15/03/2000**

Meachem, Mrs L V M, MCLIP, Unemployed [32079] 28/01/1980 **CM25/02/1986**

Mead, Mr W D, BA(Hons) MCLIP, Inf. & Content Mgr., Home Off., London. [50755] 17/10/1994 **CM17/09/2003**

Meaden, Miss K, BA(Hons) MCLIP, Content Mgr., Marketing & Communications, Cranfield Univ. [56102] 17/02/1998 **CM20/11/2002**

Meades, Mr G J, BA(Hons) DipInfSc, Serv. Mgr., Northamptonshire Teaching Primary Care NHS Trust Hosp. L., Northampton. [53204] 09/04/1996 **ME**

Meadows, Prof A J, MA MSc DPhil FCLIP, Prof. of L. & Inf. Studs., Loughborough Univ. [38903] 18/10/1985 **FE13/06/1989**

Meadows, Mr P, BA MCLIP, Retired. [10018] 01/10/1968 **CM01/01/1971**

Meadows, Mrs S K, BA(Hons) MCLIP, Career Break. [41828] 12/04/1988 **CM25/09/1996**

Mealey, Mr A J, MCLIP, Sr. Lib., Coventry Heritage & Arts Trust [10027] 20/03/1961 **CM26/11/1982**

Mears, Miss A M, BSc, Asst. Lib., Univ. of the W. of England. [10006499] 30/10/1996 **ME**

Mears, Miss M, BSc, Stud. [10015571] 17/12/2009 **ME**

Mears, Miss S J, MA BSc DipLib MCLIP, Child. Serv. Dev. Mgr., Essex C.C. L. [41050] 08/10/1987 **CM14/02/1990**

Mears, Ms W E, BA(Hons) MA MCLIP, Learning and Teaching Lib., Open Univ., Milton Keynes. [44824] 07/12/1990 **CM20/11/2002**

Medcalf, Mr J P, BA(Hons) DipLib MCLIP, Area Mngr.,Calderdale MBC Northgate Halifax. [38035] 15/01/1985 **CM14/03/1990**

Medd, Miss K S, BLib MCLIP, LRC Mgr., Sir George Monoux Coll., Walthamstow. [41132] 07/10/1987 **CM16/10/1991**

Medhurst, Mr A R G, Lib., Stopsley High Sch., Luton. [10009975] 30/06/2008 **AF**

Medley, Mrs H E, BA(Hons), Asst. Lib., Fade L., Liverpool. [10001211] 02/02/2007 **ME**

Medley, Miss L, MCLIP, Lib., Lancashire C. C Home L. Serv., Preston. [10038] 16/01/1968 **CM01/01/1971**

Medlock, Miss J, BSc MSc MCLIP, Pharmaco Vigilance Compliance Mgr PPD Cambridge. [60859] 01/09/1983 **CM09/07/1991**

Medway, Mr A, BLib MCLIP, Portal Lib., Staffordshire C.C. . Tamworth L. [31379] 20/10/1979 **CM31/03/1986**

Mee, Mrs L J, BA MCLIP, Lib., Dick Inst., E. Ayrshire Dist. Council. [33574] 21/01/1981 **CM14/10/1985**

Meechan, Mr T M D, BA, Press Off., Dept. for Business, Innovation & Skills, London. [41773] 22/03/1988 **ME**

Meehan, Mr B W, BA(Hons) MMus MSc(Econ) MCLIP, L. Mgr, S. Ham L., Hampshire C.C. [54776] 01/04/1997 **CM15/11/2000**

Meeson, Mrs P L, BA(Hons), Unknown. [10012370] 08/02/1981 **ME**

Mehew, Mrs E K, BSc(Hons), Inf. Specialist, Health and Safety Exec., Liverpool. [55550] 20/10/1997 **ME**

Meier, Mrs V, BA(Hons) MA MCLIP, Dep. Lib. Serv. Mgr., Univ. Hosp. Lewisham. [63600] 09/07/2004 **CM23/01/2008**

Meinbardt, Prof H, Prof., FH Koeln (Applied Univ. Cologne). [10016604] 20/04/2010 **ME**

Meineck, Mrs J, ACLIP, Inf. Asst., Kingston Univ., Surrey. [61449] 31/07/2002 **ACL01/10/2006**

Meiser, Ms M, BA MCLIP, Acquisitions Lib., Wiener L. Inst. of contemporary Hist., London. [10006451] 19/10/2007 **CM10/03/2010**

Melgosa, Mrs A A D, BSc MA MCLIP, Assoc Lib., Walla Walla Univ., USA. [52220] 16/10/1995 **CM20/11/2002**

Melhuish, Miss F H, BA(Hons) MA, Rare Books Lib., Univ. of Reading. [57773] 02/08/1999 **ME**

Melia, Ms K M, BA(Hons) DipIS MCLIP, Unknown. [47810] 19/10/1992 **CM23/07/1997**

Mellenchip, Mrs S, BA(Hons) DipLIS MCLIP, Dist. Mngr., Staffordshire L. [48313] 25/11/1992 **CM31/01/1996**

Melling, Miss M A, MCLIP, Retired [10052] 21/08/1966 **CM20/02/1973**

Melling, Miss P, BA MCLIP, Asst. Lib., Guildhall L., City of London. [10053] 03/10/1968 **CM01/01/1970**

Melling, Miss R H, BA MCLIP, Life Member. [10054] 08/11/1957 **CM01/01/1961**

Mellody, Miss B, BA(Hons) DipILS MCLIP, Lib. Serv. Mgr., Finance & Acquisitions, Manchester Met. Univ. [52597] 10/11/1995 **CM19/05/1999**

Mellor, Mrs A, MA(Hons), Catg. Mgr., BDS, Dumfries. [61086] 04/03/2002 **ME**

Mellor, Miss C, BSc DipLib MCLIP, General Mgr. - L. N. Yorks C.C. [35403] 01/10/1982 **CM16/12/1986**

Mellor, Mrs E M, BA MCLIP, Lib., Young People, N. Somerset [36486] 18/10/1983 **CM05/07/1988**

Mellor, Mr K A, BA DipLib MCLIP, Assoc. Dir. :ICT and Learning Res., W. Notts. Coll., Mansfield. [27350] 15/02/1977 **CM12/01/1980**

Mellors, Mrs A R, BA MCLIP, Access & Inclusion Lib., Derby's C.C., Chesterfield [2012] 12/10/1970 **CM18/01/1974**

Mellors, Mrs M J, DipLib MCLIP, Lib., Hertfordshire C.C., Bishop's Stortford L. [37605] 10/10/1984 **CM13/06/1989**

Melmoth, Mrs A, BA MCLIP MBA, Knowledge & eServices Mgr. [40015] 09/10/1986 **CM13/06/1989**

Melone, Miss H A, BA(Hons) Dip MCLIP, Res. Devel. Offr., N. Lanarkshire Council, Educ. Res. Serv. [56251] 17/04/1998 **CM16/05/2001**

Melrose, Ms E A, MA DipLib MCLIP, Retired [10065] 12/11/1964 **CM31/10/1978**

Melton, Ms M R, BA(Hons) PgDipIS MLitt, Stud., Leeds Met. Univ. & Lib., Queen Ethelburga's Coll. [57163] 05/01/1999 **ME**

Melville, Mrs A, BA(Hons) MCLIP, Retired [10066] 01/01/1958 **CM01/01/1965**

Melville, Mrs D E F, BA MCLIP, Asst. Lib., Univ. of Dundee [21679] 01/01/1974 **CM20/06/1977**

Memmott, Mrs A L, BA(Hons) DipILM, Inf. Mgr., Foreign & Commonwealth Off., London [54368] 25/11/1996 **ME**

Mendham, Mrs C M, BA DipLib MCLIP, Unwaged. [30284] 04/01/1979 **CM10/08/1981**

Mends, Ms S J, BA(Hons) MSc(Econ) PGDip FHEA, Devel. Offr., Univ. of Wales, Aberystwyth. [54395] 03/12/1996 **ME**

Menendez-Alonso, Dr E, BSc(Hons) PhD, Electronic Res. Devel. Offr., Univ. of Plymouth L. [64922] 12/09/2005 **AF**

Mengu, Mr M D, BSc MSc MGIP MCLIP, Ch. Consultant, Danish Tech. Inst. [60054] 07/12/2001 **CM07/12/2001**

Menhinick, Miss M J, BA MCLIP, Business Mgr., CESO (CTLB) MOD Ensleigh, Bath. [34006] 10/07/1981 **CM06/09/1985**

Mennell, Mrs M M, ACLIP, L. Serv. Advisor, Southwell L., Notts. [10012858] 10/03/2009 **ACL11/12/2009**

Mennie, Mr H J, BA MCLIP DMS, Operations Mgr.,L. Cent. Bedfordshire Council. [19890] 01/01/1973 **CM04/09/1975**

Menniss, Mrs J, BA(Hons) DipIM MCLIP DipSM, Head of L. Serv., Slough Bor. C. [50614] 01/10/1994 **CM20/01/1999**

Menzies, Miss K L, MA MSc, Res. Asst., Strathclyde Univ. [10006420] 17/10/2007 **ME**

Menzies, Miss M D, BA MLib MCLIP, L. & Inf. Serv. Mgr., Scottish Borders Council, L. H.Q., Selkirk. [29749] 09/10/1978 **CM02/10/1981**

Mercer, Miss E K, BSc(Econ) MCLIP, Team Lib., Yeovil L., Somerset C.C. [51304] 16/01/1995 **CM16/05/2001**

Mercer, Mrs L, MSc BSc MA, Asst. Lib., Victoria Univ. of Wellington. [10006511] 24/10/2007 **ME**

Mercer, Mrs P A, MCLIP, Retired. [10077] 30/03/1954 **CM01/01/1960**

Merchant, Mr A J, MA, Sen. Lib., Inst. of Ismaili Stud., London. [57012] 20/11/1998 **ME**

Merchant, Mr N, Unknown. [10014620] 20/08/2009 **ME**

Meredith, Mrs C H, BA(Hons) MSc MCLIP, Head of Indexing and Data Mgmnt. Sect., House of Commons L., Westminster. [57532] 23/04/1999 **CM15/09/2004**

Meredith, Ms C, BA(Hons) MA, Asst. Lib., BMA L., London. [55860] 04/12/1997 **ME**

Merison, Mrs S F, BSc MLib MCLIP, p. /t. Lib., Educ. L. Serv., Winsford Cheshire. [43961] 05/03/1990 **CM14/09/1994**

Meriton, Mr J C, BA(Hons) MA DipLib FCLIP, Dep. Keeper, Word & Image Dept., Victoria & Albert Mus. [55956] 22/12/1997 **FE04/10/2006**

Merner, Miss S, BLib MCLIP, Lib., Poole Hosp., Poole,Dorset. [37094] 02/02/1984 **CM14/11/1990**

Merola, Miss B, BA(Hons) DipLib MCLIP, Lib., Learning Res. Mgr., Mary Immaculate High Sch., Cardiff. [37510] 03/10/1984 **CM27/05/1992**

Merricks, Mrs H J, MCLIP, Business Support Mgr., Northants. C.C. [20370] 13/02/1973 **CM05/09/1975**

Merrifield, Mrs B A, BA DipLib MCLIP, Lib. Willen L. [30897] 23/05/1979 **CM03/03/1982**

Merrill, Miss R C, BA MCLIP, Head. L., Barnsley Hosp. NHS Foundation Trust. [32607] 21/05/1980 **CM21/05/1982**

Merriman, Mrs A M, M Lib MCLIP, Asst. Co. Lib., Chichester, W. Sussex C.C. [3368] 14/01/1971 **CM03/01/1975**

Merriman, Mrs H A, MCLIP, P/t. Lib. N. Grp., Portsmouth City Council. [14404] 17/08/1971 **CM01/11/1976**

Merriman, Mr J B, MCLIP, Life Member. [10086] 23/02/1951 **CM01/01/1953**

Merriott, Miss S, BA(Hons), Sr. Asst., Educ. Lib. Serv., Reading [10012956] 19/03/2009 **AF**

Merritt, Mrs E J G, MCLIP, Info. Team Lib., Norfolk Co. L. & Inf. Serv., Norfolk & Norwich Millennium L. [10302] 09/09/1968 **CM01/08/1972**

Merritt, Mrs M A, BEd MCLIP, Career Break. [48820] 07/06/1993 **CM16/11/1994**

Merry, Mrs S K, Stud., Aberystwyth. [65103] 01/11/2005 **ME**

Merskey, Mrs S J, MA MCLIP, Retired. [10088] 14/09/1963 **CM01/01/1965**

Meshack, Mr G, Florist, High Sch/6th Form Secondary. [57963] 06/10/1999 **ME**

Messenger, Mrs G S, MA MCLIP, Inf. Serv. Lib., Royal Horticultural Soc., London. [35502] 12/10/1982 **CM29/07/1986**

Messenger, Mr M F, OBE FCLIP, Life Member. [10091] 13/09/1954 **FE01/01/1964**

Messenger, Mr S P, BSc, Grad. Trainee, Legal L., Foreign & Commonwealth Off., London [10015019] 07/10/2009 **ME**

Messer, Mr I M, BA(Hons), Stud. [10006403] 23/10/2007 **ME**

Messere, Mrs A P, BA MCLIP, L. Mgr., Hendon L., L.B. Barnet. [43299] 16/10/1989 **CM09/07/2008**

Messum, Mrs A P, BA(Hons) DipLib, Unemployed [44502] 16/10/1990 **ME**

Metcalf, Mr A, BSc DipLib MCLIP, Lib. -Support Servs., Liverpool City Council, Liverpool. [38454] 30/04/1985 **CM07/07/1987**

Metcalf, Ms S M, BA MCLIP, Retired. [23723] 14/01/1975 **CM30/03/1977**

Metcalfe, Mrs P A, MCLIP, Life Member. [15551] 14/02/1961 **CM01/01/1965**

Metcalfe, Ms S J, BA(Hons), Lib. (Loc. Studies & Req.), Cumbria C.C., Penrith L. [55852] 02/12/1997 **AF**

Methold, Mrs D M, MCLIP, Learning Res. Cent. Mgr., Woking Coll. [18166] 01/10/1972 **CM02/07/1976**

Methven, Mrs M, MCLIP, Head of L. Inf. & Cultural Serv., Dundee C.C. [9388] 08/09/1969 **CM11/08/1972**

Metzger, Mr A J B, MLS FCLIP, Unwaged. [24462] 01/10/1964 **FE16/05/2001**

Mews, Miss F, BA MSc(Hons), Asst. Lib., Nord Anglia [10006804] 10/12/2007 **ME**

Mews, Miss J E, MCLIP, Asst. Comm. Lib., Birchfield Community L., Birmingham. [10106] 22/02/1970 **CM08/09/1975**

Meyer, Mrs N R, BSc DipLib, Unwaged [44487] 12/10/1990 **ME**

Meyer, Ms R, BA(Hons) MSc MCLIP, Comm. Libr., Melksham L., Wilts. [48810] 02/06/1993 **CM17/03/1999**

Meyering, Ms M A, Unknown. [10016959] 10/06/2010 **ME**

Mghendi, Mr N R, Inf. Offr., Int. Fed of Red Cross, Philippines. [10015583] 17/12/2009 **ME**

Michael, Ms A, BA(Hons) MA, Unknown. [62401] 30/05/2003 **ME**

Michael, Mr D A, BSc DipLib MCLIP, L. Asst., Islington Council. [32320] 12/02/1980 **CM05/04/1982**

Michaelides, Ms C A, BA(Hons) PGCE (FE) MCLIP, Unknown. [10014380] 01/06/2010 **CM01/09/1977**

Michaud, Mrs F, BA PGCE MSc, Customer Serv. Mgr., Royal Soc. of Medicine, London. [10003041] 25/05/2007 **ME**

Michell, Mr M L, L. Exec., H. of Commons L., London. [62097] 13/02/2003 **ME**

Michon-Bordes, Mrs H J M, GradDip, MA, Researcher/Trainee, Folkhemsstudier, Uppsala, Sweden. [10011128] 25/09/2008 **ME**

Middlemist, Miss F E, BA MCLIP, Coll. Lib., Northumberland Coll., Ashington. [21088] 10/10/1973 **CM16/02/1976**

Middleton, Ms A, BSc(Hons) PGDip MSc MCLIP, L. Liaison Adviser, Northumbria Univ., Newcastle. [54195] 28/10/1996 **CM12/03/2003**

Middleton, Miss C L, BA(Hons), Inf. Specialist, GCHQ, Cheltenham. [61310] 17/05/2002 **ME**

Middleton, Mrs C, BSc(Hons) MSc MIMechE MIEE MCLIP, Head of Academic Serv., Univ. of Nottingham. [49561] 12/11/1993 **CM23/07/1997**

Middleton, Mrs H, BA(Hons), Stud., Aberystwyth Univ. [10011104] 24/09/2008 **ME**

Middleton, Mr I A, BSc MSc PGDip MCLIP, Web Devel. - Career Break [60267] 01/07/1999 **CM01/07/1999**

Middleton, Miss K, BSc(Econ) MCLIP, Asst. Lib., Powys Co. Council, Llandrindod Wells [59779] 02/10/2001 **CM06/04/2005**

Middleton, Miss S L, Learning Resources Mgr., Bristol Brunel Academy, Bristol. [10013607] 12/05/2009 **AF**

Midgley, Ms C M, BA MA MCLIP, Unemployed. [35354] 08/10/1982 **CM03/07/1996**

Midgley, Mrs E A, BA(Hons) DMS MCLIP PGCM MCMI M, Asst. Access to Serv. Mgr., Blackpool Bor. Council. [38701] 01/10/1985 **CM18/04/1989**

Midgley, Mrs L, BSc DipLib MCLIP, Lib., Leicester Grammar Sch. [38852] 14/10/1985 **CM21/12/1988**

Midgley, Mrs S M, SRN, Sen. L. Super., Worthing L. [10006261] 28/09/2007 **AF**

Miehe, Ms D, MA MLib MCLIP, Curator – German Sect., The Brit. L., London. [48332] 27/11/1992 **CM16/11/1994**

Miers, Mrs S M, Sch. Lib., Brentwood Co. High Sch., Essex. [55415] 08/10/1997 **ME**

Milby, Ms C L, BA DipLib MCLIP, Inf. & Learning Mgr., Monmouthshire C.C., Chepstow L. (Sabbatical) [34828] 15/03/1982 **CM16/05/1985**

Mildren, Mr K W, BSc MCLIP, Unknown. [10128] 29/08/1968 **CM01/01/1971**

Miles, Mrs E S, Dip. Ed, Lib., King's Sch., Winchester. [10017143] 11/07/2010 **AF**

Miles, Mr P G, BA MCLIP, Retired. [10131] 25/10/1967 **CM01/01/1970**

Miles, Miss R, BA(Hons), Unknown. [57558] 06/04/1999 **ME**

Miles, Miss S J, BA MCLIP, Bibl. & Metadata Advisor, Kingston Univ., Kingston. [35346] 12/10/1982 **CM18/04/1990**

Miles, Mrs S J, MA MCLIP, Head of Catalogue Mgmt., Bodleian L., Univ. of Oxford. [647] 14/10/1971 **CM06/11/1974**

Miles, Miss S L, BA(Hons) MA, Stud., Univ. of Brighton. [10010700] 21/08/2008 **ME**

Millar, Ms K, MA MSc, Indexer, The Scottish Parliament, Edinburgh. [43346] 24/10/1989 **ME**

Millar, Mrs L M M, BA MCLIP, Housewife. [21382] 13/11/1973 **CM26/09/1978**

Millar, Ms M S, BSc DipLib MCLIP, Sen. Inf. Mgr., Univ. Abertay Dundee. [37144] 01/03/1984 **CM01/09/1987**

Millar, Mrs N, BA(Hons) Dip Lib MCLIP, Front Line Serv. Mgr.,SEELB, Co Down [10014571] 23/10/1978 **CM31/12/1981**

Millar, Ms S M, BA(Hons) MSc MCLIP, Snr. Lib., Local Hist. &. Promotions., E. Lothian L. H.Q. [26739] 01/01/1976 **CM23/12/1983**

Millard, Mrs F J, BA PGCE, Digitisation Mgr., Off. Pub., Nat. L. of Scotland [10000713] 25/10/2006 **AF**

Millard, Mr R E, BA(Hons) DipLib MCLIP, Project Mgr., MOD, Bristol [29752] 04/10/1978 **CM26/02/1981**

Miller, Mrs A, MA MCLIP, Life Member. [10141] 20/10/1953 **CM01/01/1959**

Miller, Mrs B, LDipLib MA MCLIP, Academic Liason Lib., Univ. Westminster, London. [61043] 05/02/2002 **CM21/03/2007**

Miller, Miss C A, BA MCLIP, Retired. [10146] 27/02/1969 **CM01/01/1972**

Miller, Mrs C L, BA DipLib MCLIP, Tax Inf. Offr., Allen & Overy LLP, London. [44538] 23/10/1990 **CM24/05/1995**

Miller, Mrs C M, BA DipLib MCLIP, Inf. & Local Studies Lib., William Patrick L., E. Dunbartonshire L. [35752] 10/01/1983 **CM16/12/1986**

Miller, Miss C, BA(Hons), Graduate L. Trainee, NHS Bradford & Airdale, Learning Cent. [10016122] 16/02/2010 **ME**

Miller, Mrs C, BA DipLib MCLIP, p/t Learning Res. Asst., Liverpool Community Coll. [10001677] 05/07/1977 **CM16/10/1979**

Miller, Mrs C, BA(Hons), Stud., Strathclyde Univ. [10015266] 29/10/2009 **ME**

Miller, Miss D, BA(Hons) MA (DUNELM) MA MCLIP, Sen. Inf. Offr., Lawrence Graham, Solicitors, London. [56088] 02/02/1998 **CM12/03/2003**

Miller, Mr G, BA MCLIP, Sales Mgr., OCLC, Birmingham. [10010516] 06/02/1979 **CM17/07/1981**

Miller, Ms H, Unknown. [10012106] 09/09/2005 **ME**

Miller, Mrs J E, Sch. Lib., Horsenden Primary Sch., Greenford [10015320] 09/11/2009 **ME**

Miller, Mr J P, BA MCLIP, Ch. Lib. Unesco, Paris [20790] 06/07/1973 **CM24/01/1977**

Miller, Miss J, MA(Hons) PGDipILS MCLIP, L. Asst., Andersonian L., Univ. of Strathclyde. [61270] 09/05/2002 **CM15/09/2004**

Miller, Mrs J, Life Member. [26778] 04/11/1976 **ME**

Miller, Mrs K C, BSc(Econ) PGAG MCLIP, Unwaged. [52731] 29/11/1995 **CM17/05/2000**

Miller, Miss L, MA, Unknown. [10006387] 23/10/2007 **ME**

Miller, Mrs M D, MCLIP, Life Member [10162] 28/09/1946 **CM01/01/1949**

Miller, Ms M L, BA MCLIP, Sen. Lib. Res. Mgr., Glasgow Caledonian Univ. [26907] 10/01/1977 **CM31/01/1980**

Miller, Ms M M, BA(Hons) PGDip MCLIP, L. Collections Mgr., Tate L. & Arch., London. [37718] 16/10/1984 **CM09/08/1988**

Miller, Mr M M, BSc (Hons), Unknown. [10016972] 16/06/2010 **ME**

Miller, Mrs N M, BSc(Hons), Lib., Nat. Audit Off. L., London. [59397] 28/03/2001 **ME**

Miller, Mr P, BA(Hons), Stud. [10017035] 18/06/2010 **ME**

Miller, Ms S M, MCLIP, Support Serv. Lib., Stirling Council [22733] 22/08/1974 **CM04/08/1977**

Millerchip, Mr J J G, BLib MA FCLIP MCMI, Clerk to Corporation, Northbrook Coll., Worthing. [18392] 16/10/1972 **FE18/11/1998**

Miller-Williams, Mrs W J, BLS MCLIP, Team Lib., Frome L., Somerset. [32164] 09/01/1980 **CM14/01/1985**

Milligan, Ms D E, MA(Hons) PGDipILS MCLIP, Official Publications Curator, Nat. L. of Scotland., Edinburgh. [61322] 22/05/2002 **CM21/06/2006**

Milligan, Mr E H, BA MCLIP, Life Member. [10171] 08/03/1940 **CM01/01/1950**

Milligan, Ms J, BA MA, Full-time, L. Soc. of Friends, London [10001856] 22/04/1997 **ME**

Milligan, Miss L B, BEd MSc(Econ) DipLib MCLIP, Dep. Ch. Lib., Guille-Alles L., Guernsey. [31904] 16/01/1980 **CM05/05/1982**

Milligan, Ms M A T, MA DipLib MCLIP, Curriculum Adviser., Falkirk Council Educ. Serv. [23221] 08/11/1974 **CM13/10/1977**

Milligan, Ms T J, MA DipLIS MCLIP, Sen. Lib., Larbert L., Stenhousemuir, Larbert. [10002993] 04/10/1996 **CM20/01/1999**

Milliken, Mrs A, Lib. & Inf. Administrator, Macmillan Cancer Support, Glasgow [10001263] 14/02/2007 **AF**

Milliken, Miss R J, Unemployed. [20572] 28/04/1973 **ME**

Millin, Ms K J, BLib MCLIP, Asst. Dir., L., Arch., Adult Learning, Dudley M.B.C. [29516] 18/09/1978 **CM03/08/1983**

Millington, Ms K J, BSc MSc, Evening Lib., Birkbeck Coll., London. [51319] 10/01/1995 **ME**

Million, Miss A R, BA MCLIP, Freelance Law Lib. [44197] 04/07/1990 **CM16/11/1994**

Millis, Mrs A J, BSc Hons, PGCE, DIPHEILS MCLIP, Training & Outreach Mgr., Pembury Hosp. L., Pembury [10008501] 30/01/1998 **CM07/07/2010**

Millership, Miss K A, Unknown. [10012809] 19/03/2009 **AF**

Millman, Mrs S M, MCLIP, Retired. [2029] 04/03/1954 **CM01/01/1960**

Mills, Mrs C E L, BA(Hons) MA MCLIP, Principal Lib., Buxton Lib, Derbys C.C., [59011] 24/10/2000 **CM21/06/2006**

Mills, Mr C, BA MA DipLib MCLIP FLS, Head of L. Art & Arch., The Royal Botanic Gardens, Kew. [31664] 05/11/1979 **CM18/11/1981**

Mills, Mr G J, MSc BA DipLib MCLIP, Head of Cent. L., Birmingham. [20191] 06/02/1973 **CM01/01/1976**

Mills, Miss H E, BA(Hons) DipLib MCLIP, Asst. Lib., Homerton Univ. Hosp. NHS Foundation Trust, London [47129] 05/05/1992 **CM12/03/2003**

Mills, Mrs J A, BA DipLib MCLIP, Academic Liaison Lib., Roehampton Univ., London. [31701] 25/10/1979 **CM17/11/1981**

Mills, Mrs J S, BA MCLIP, Retired. [10179] 12/09/1957 **CM01/01/1960**

Mills, Mr J, FCLIP HonFCLIP, Retired. [18034] 04/03/1937 **FE01/01/1950**

Mills, Miss K M, Innovations Offr., The Open Univ. L., Milton Keynes. [56030] 28/01/1998 **ME**

Mills, Miss K, BA MCLIP, SCL (wales) Devel. & Support Offr. [44964] 28/01/1991 **CM27/01/1993**

Mills, Mrs K, MCLIP, Sen. Acquisitions Asst., Lancashire L. Headquaters, Bowran St., Preston. [23787] 08/01/1975 **CM19/12/1977**

Mills, Mr R A, MA MCLIP, Biosciences & Environ. Sci. Lib., Oxford Univ. L. Serv., Plant Sci. L. [10185] 02/04/1970 **CM05/10/1972**

Mills, Mrs S A, L. Administrator, Ashlawn Sch. L., Rugby. [65506] 13/02/2006 **AF**

Mills, Mrs S J, MA MCLIP, Retired. Hon. Fellow Cent. for Baptist Hist. & Heritage Regen't Park Coll., Oxford [11466] 13/07/1970 **CM25/10/1972**

Mills, Mrs S, MCLIP, LRB Mgr., Middleton Tech. Sch., Greater Manchester. [63104] 30/01/2004 **CM18/12/2009**

Milne, Mrs C J, BA MA DipLIS, Learning Res. Mgr., Christie's Educ., London. [55279] 12/09/1997 **ME**

Milne, Mr C, BA(Hons) DipIA MCLIP, Inf. Mgr., Univ. of Abertay, Dundee. [48063] 04/11/1992 **CM17/05/2000**

Milne, Mr D C, BA(Hons) DipLib PGDip MCLIP, Inf. Sci., Yell Ltd., Reading. [49262] 19/10/1993 **CM19/03/2008**

Milne, Mr I A, MLib MCLIP, Head of L. Info. Serv., Royal Coll. of Physicians, Edinburgh. [32446] 11/04/1980 **CM23/04/1982**

Milne, Miss J R, MA(Hons) DipILS MCLIP, L. Devel. Offr., E. Neighbourhood, Edinburgh. [56878] 29/10/1998 **CM13/03/2002**

Milne, Mr J R, BA MCLIP, Lib., The Robert Gordon Univ., Aberdeen. [44814] 04/12/1990 **CM15/05/1997**

Milne, Mr J, MA FCLIP, Life Member, [10194] 25/08/1947 **FE01/01/1966**

Milne, Miss J, BA MCLIP, Sen. L. & Inf. Worker, Cent. L., Dundee. [33067] 01/10/1980 **CM18/07/1983**

Milne, Ms K, BASocSci PGDipLIS MA MCLIP, Eilean Siar [57723] 09/07/1999 **CM04/10/2006**

Milne, Mrs L A, BA MCLIP, Ref. & local Studies Libraian., Bridgend Co. Bor. Council [10197] 04/10/1971 **CM24/10/1973**

Milne, Mr R R, MA FRSE FCLIP FRSA, Assoc. Ch. Lib. (Res. Collections), Alexander Turnbull L., Nat. L. of New Zealand. [34100] 02/10/1981 **FE21/03/2001**

Milne, Mrs S A, MA DipLib MCLIP, Inf. Serv. Lib., Scottish Borders Council, L. Serv. [44777] 21/11/1990 **CM21/10/1992**

Milne, Mr S D, MSc MCLIP, Head of Res. Serv., Glyndwr Univ., Wrexham. [28085] 12/10/1977 **CM06/11/1980**

Milne, Mrs S, BA MCLIP, Life Member. [10201] 16/09/1960 **CM01/04/1996**

Milner, Mr E J, BA, Administrator, Sigma Asset Managment, Surrey [10015031] 07/10/2009 **ME**

Milner, Mrs J A, BA MCLIP, Metadata Specialist, Univ. of Northampton. [24480] 01/09/1975 **CM23/05/1979**

Milnes, Mrs V J, BA MCLIP, Unknown. [3359] 01/10/1971 **CM04/08/1976**

Milns, Ms A V L, BSc(Hons) MCLIP, Asst. Lib., Home Off., London. [54058] 24/10/1996 **CM23/01/2002**

Milot, Miss V C, BA DipLib MCLIP, Lib., Barton Court Grammar Sch., Canterbury, Kent [36767] 16/12/1983 **CM08/03/1988**

Milroy, Mrs M P, BA DIP LIB MCLIP, LRC. Mgr., The City Sch., Sheffield [33068] 06/10/1980 **CM02/11/1984**

Milton, Mrs A M, BA MCLIP, Res. Mgr., Royal Opera House., Covent Garden [19271] 09/09/1972 **CM28/07/1975**

Milton, Mrs C M, BA MCLIP, Life Member. [10212] 05/09/1953 **CM01/01/1956**

Milton, Mr H R, BA DipLib MCLIP; Retired. [10213] 29/01/1969 **CM01/01/1971**

Milton, Miss K M, Stud., The Robert Gordon Univ. [10015374] 19/11/2009 **ME**

Milton, Mr L E, MA MCLIP, Life Member. [10214] 18/07/1954 **CM01/01/1956**

Milton, Mrs M B, BA(Hons) DipLIS MCLIP, Career break [50631] 01/10/1994 **CM22/09/1999**

Milton-Thompson, Miss L M, Asst. Lib., Box Hill Sch., Surrey. [10015035] 07/10/2009 **AF**

Minde, Mrs D, Sen. Inf. Offr., Doc. Delivery & Copyright, Liverpool John Moores Univ. [43904] 14/02/1990 **ME**

Minett, Ms A E, BA MCLIP, Sch. Lib., St Saviours & St Olaves Sch., L.B. of Southwark. [22798] 16/10/1974 **CM16/10/1976**

Minns, Mrs A E, BA DipLib FCLIP, Inf. Adviser, St. Peter's House L., Univ. of Brighton. [18419] 17/10/1972 **FE20/03/1996**

Minott, Mrs C E, BA(Hons) MSc, Legal Researcher, Gibson, Dunn & Crutcher LLP, London. [54977] 09/06/1997 **ME**

Minter, Mrs E C, BA(Hons) DipIS MCLIP, Admin. Asst., Childrens Serv., Dorset C.C. [54818] 11/04/1997 **CM17/05/2000**

Minter, Mrs N, L. Asst., Anglia Ruskin Univ., Cambridge. [65011] 06/10/2005 **AF**

Minter, Mrs S M, BA(Hons) DipLIS MCLIP, Young Peoples Serv. Devel. Lib., Herts. C.C., Welwyn Garden City L. [48465] 19/01/1993 **CM22/01/1997**

Minton, Mrs C, BA MCLIP, Relief Lib., W Berks. [9029] 16/07/1967
CM01/01/1971

Minty, Mrs W L F, M THEOL MA, Head of Acquisitions Mgmnt.,
Bodleian L., Univ. of Oxford. [42023] 25/07/1988 **ME**

Miranda, Mrs M A, BSc(Hons) MCLIP, L. Mgr., elec. Syst. & Outreach,
Harefield Hosp. [53305] 25/04/1996 **CM17/11/1999**

Mircic, Ms A A, BA DipLib MCLIP, Team Leader, N. Yorks. C.C. [40513]
02/03/1987 **CM11/12/1989**

Mires, Miss E, BA(Hons) MA MCLIP, Academic Liaison Lib., Univ. of
Westminster. [59874] 29/10/2001 **CM01/02/2006**

Miskin, Ms C E, LLB MCLIP, Inf. Consultant/Editor, Self-Employed.
[20807] 01/01/1969 **CM24/10/1973**

Missaggia, Miss L, Unwaged. [10007038] 17/12/2007 **ME**

Misso, Ms K V, MCLIP, Unknown. [10008986] 31/10/1996
CM08/01/2002

Mitchell, Miss A J, BA(Hons), MSc, Learning Resources Mgr., Ashton-
Under-Lyne Sixth Form Coll. [64297] 23/02/2005 **ME**

Mitchell, Ms C M, BA MCLIP, Lib., Epping Forest Coll. [33441]
08/01/1981 **CM16/10/1984**

Mitchell, Mrs C M, BA MCLIP, Teaching Asst., Millbrook Junior Sch.,
Kettering. [29205] 07/04/1978 **CM20/08/1981**

Mitchell, Mr D J D, BA MA PgDipELM FCLIP, Employer Engagement
Dev. Offr., Coleg Morgannwg [32129] 28/01/1980 **RV20/04/2009**
FE26/11/1997

Mitchell, Mrs D M J, BA DipLib MCLIP, Retired. [20184] 05/02/1973
CM05/04/1976

Mitchell, Mrs D M, MCLIP, Life Member. [17388] 01/01/1952
CM01/01/1957

Mitchell, Ms D N, BA DipLib, Asst. Inf. Mgr., Off. Parliamentary
Commissioner, London. [60942] 10/01/2002 **ME**

Mitchell, Miss E, BA(Hons), Stud., City Univ. [65686] 31/03/2006 **ME**

Mitchell, Mrs G A, BA DipLib MCLIP, Lib., Millfield L., Belfast Met. Coll.
[31665] 12/11/1979 **CM01/07/1990**

Mitchell, Mr G D, BA MCLIP, Principal Lib., Bletchley L., Milton Keynes.
[28859] 31/01/1978 **CM17/01/1984**

Mitchell, Mrs G, BSc(Econ) MCLIP, LRC Mgr., St Ivo Sch., Huntingdon.
[54540] 20/01/1997 **CM18/09/2002**

Mitchell, Mrs H F, BA MCLIP, Retired. [3697] 04/10/1967**CM01/01/1971**

Mitchell, Ms I, Inf. Unit Mgr., Linklaters, London. [64382] 14/03/2005**ME**

Mitchell, Mr J B, BA, Patent Watch Specialist, RWS Grp. Inf. Div.,
London. [35143] 19/08/1982 **AF**

Mitchell, Mr J E, BA(Hons) DipTP MSc, Inf. Adviser, S. Lanarkshire
Council. [10009710] 03/06/2008 **ME**

Mitchell, Mr J L, BMus MMus Dip MLIS MCLIP, Rare Books Curator,
Nat. L. of Scotland, Edinburgh. [55728] 10/11/1997 **CM18/12/2009**

Mitchell, Miss J S, BA(Hons), Inf. Lib., MIDIRS, Bristol. [47223]
11/06/1992 **ME**

Mitchell, Ms J, Principal L. Asst., City of London. [45901] 01/07/1991**AF**

Mitchell, Mrs K J, BLib MCLIP, Volunteer Serv. Coordinator, Knowledge
Devel. Serv., Wokingham Bor. Council [26112] 16/07/1976
CM14/09/1979

Mitchell, Mrs K, BA ACLIP, Learning Cent. Coordinator, New Coll.
Nottingham. [10006691] 21/11/2007 **ACL28/01/2009**

Mitchell, Miss L A, MA(Hons) MSc DipLib MCLIP, Sch. Lib., Stewarton
Academy, Stewarton. [35932] 20/02/1983 **CM20/01/1987**

Mitchell, Miss L, BSc(Hons) DipLib MCLIP, Asst. Dir., Academic
Support, Brunel Univ. Lib. [48453] 13/01/1993 **CM31/01/1996**

Mitchell, Mrs M A, BA MCLIP, Learning Resource Cent. Mgr., The Holt
Sch., Wokingham [38785] 08/10/1985 **CM18/01/1989**

Mitchell, Mrs M J, MCLIP, Lend. Lib., L.B. of Enfield. [4618] 03/07/1969
CM09/04/1974

Mitchell, Mrs M M, ACLIP, Retired. [45154] 26/07/1990 **ACL01/08/2005**

Mitchell, Mrs M, MA DipLib MCLIP, Subject Lib., Napier Univ., Melrose.
[37838] 22/10/1984 **CM21/07/1989**

Mitchell, Ms O C, BA(Hons) MSc, Unknown. [49780] 22/12/1993 **ME**

Mitchell, Mrs S A, MCLIP, Ref. & Inf. serv. Mgr., Leics. City Council,
Ref. & Inf. L. [26484] 02/10/1976 **CM27/11/1979**

Mitchell, Mrs T, BA MCLIP, Contractor, TFPL, London [42237]
13/10/1988 **CM18/11/1992**

Mitchelmore, Mrs R, MA, Asst. Lib., Oliveira, St. Mary's Hosp., Isle of
Wight [10012955] 25/01/1995 **ME**

Mitcheson, Mrs E A, BA DipLib MCLIP, Retired. [26131] 30/07/1976
CM02/10/1979

Mitlin, Ms J A, BSc Phd DMS, Head of L., Arts & Arch., Bexley L. Serv.,
London [10007540] 13/02/2008 **ME**

Mitten, Mrs A, Leraning Res. Off., Univ. of Ulster. [10015909]
29/01/2010 **ME**

Mizzi, Mr R, Mgr. Inf. Serv., Nat. Statistics Off., Malta. [62069]
07/02/2003 **ME**

Mjamtu-Sie, Mrs L N, MLib FCLIP, Med. Lib., Univ. of Sierra Leone,
Coll. of Med. & Allied Health Sci. [19343] 01/01/1963 **FE20/01/1999**

Mobbs, Mr E A, MCLIP, Retired. [10264] 20/02/1968 **CM01/01/1971**

Mochrie, Mrs D, MCLIP, Life Member. [10265] 19/03/1955
CM01/01/1960

Mocroft, Mrs S K, MCLIP, Employment & Skills Serv. Mgr., Sandwell
MBC, Oldbury. [30297] 01/01/1979 **CM19/08/1981**

Modranka, Miss D, Cent. Circ. Lib. Co-ordinator, Polish L., London
[10012993] 17/03/2009 **ME**

Moffat, Ms E C, BSc(Econ) MCLIP, Comm. Outreach Lib., Stirling L.
[49315] 18/10/1993 **CM21/03/2001**

Moffat, Ms S H, BSc MSc DMS MCLIP, Faculty Inf. Serv. Advisor,
Edinburgh Napier Univ., Edinburgh. [36551] 21/10/1983
CM24/03/1992

Moffatt, Mrs L K, MCLIP, L. Mgr., Austell L., Cornwall. [64237]
22/02/2005 **CM27/01/2010**

Moger, Mr D, BA DipLib MCLIP, Stock Mgr., Wilstshire L. [38399]
17/04/1985 **CM19/09/1989**

Mogg, Miss R J, BA(Hons) MA MCLIP, Inf. Specialist, Cardiff Univ.,
Cardiff. [58885] 01/10/2000 **CM08/12/2004**

Mohamed, Ms Z, PgDip MA BSocSci(Hons), Lib., Singapore Press
Holdings. [10010207] 14/10/1992 **ME**

Mohan, Mr D J, BA(Hons) MA PGCE, Freelance Web-Editor, [58359]
24/01/2000 **ME**

Mohindra, Ms G K, MCLIP, Unwaged [10013678] 01/01/1981
CM01/01/1982

Mole, Mrs K I M, MA DipInfSc, lib., The Naval & Military Club, London &
Brit. Academy, London. [32351] 21/02/1980 **ME**

Moll, Mr C, Finance & Standards Co-ordinator, Brynmor Jones L., Univ.
of Hull. [30011] 30/10/1978 **ME**

Moll, Mrs E, BLib MCLIP, Lib. Hull Hist. Cent., Kingston-Upon-Hull C.C.
[28063] 04/10/1977 **CM11/05/1982**

Moll, Mr P A, BA MCLIP, Consultant [10280] 17/02/1961 **CM01/01/1964**

Moll, Mrs V E P, MBE MLS MCLIP, Ch. Records Mgmnt. Offr., BVI (Brit.
Virgin Islands) Government [19000] 07/11/1968 **CM01/01/1973**

Mollan, Miss M, Young Persons Lib., Berwick Hills L., Middlesbrough
[10007723] 21/02/2008 **ME**

Mollard, Mr T W, MCLIP, Life Member. [19526] 01/10/1948
CM01/01/1957

Mollins, Mrs L, DipIM MCLIP, Part Time [45258] 14/09/1990
CM19/07/2000

Mollison, Mrs J F, MCLIP, Unemployed. [19669] 04/11/1972
CM23/07/1976

Molloy, Mrs B L, MCLIP, Inf. Mgr., Bath Spa Univ. [24791] 01/10/1975
CM01/01/1977

Molloy, Miss C A L, BA(Hons) DipILS MCLIP, Inf. Consultant., Univ. of
Aberdeen [55687] 04/11/1997 **CM21/05/2003**

Molloy, Mr M J, OBE BA DipLib MCLIP, Strategic Dir. Cult. and Community Serv., Derbyshire C.C., Matlock. [29465] 28/07/1978 **CM25/07/1980**

Molloy, Miss R H, BA MA, Stud., Manchester Met. Univ., Lancs. [10015948] 03/02/2010 **ME**

Molloy, Mrs S J, Inf. Serv. Lib., The Chartered Soc. of Physiotherapy, London. [10001180] 03/02/2007 **ME**

Molloy, Mr S P, BA(Hons) DipILM MCLIP, Lib., Liverpool Womens NHS Foundation Trust. [55606] 24/10/1997 **CM21/01/2009**

Molloy, Mrs S, BA(Hons) MA, Sen. L. Asst., Sch. of Medicine & Dentistry L., London. [62166] 05/03/2003 **ME**

Moloney, Ms A M, BA MSc MCLIP, Retired. [10287] 01/01/1971 **CM01/01/1974**

Monaghan, Miss J T, Lib., King Alfred Sch. [64990] 06/10/2005 **ME**

Monaghan, Miss M A, MA DipLib MCLIP, Liaison Lib., Queen Margaret Univ., Edinburgh. [28465] 20/12/1977 **CM08/05/1981**

Monahan, Mr K, MCLIP, Lib., Strouden L., Bournemouth [10006723] 24/05/1982 **CM01/07/1988**

Monds, Mrs J M, BLib MCLIP, Coll. Lib., Sarum Coll. L., Salisbury, Wilts. [31475] 15/10/1979 **CM08/11/1982**

Monem, Mrs I C, Lib., St. George's Coll., Addlestone. [65288] 28/11/2005 **ME**

Moneta, Ms C, Head of Knowledge & Inf. Mgmnt., Veale Wasbrough Vizards, Bristol [40800] 26/06/1987 **ME**

Monk, Mrs A, MA DipLib MCLIP, Mgr. Learning Res. Cent., Car Hill High Sch., Kirkham. [33042] 03/10/1980 **CM19/07/1983**

Monk, Mr G C, BA(Hons) MCLIP, Head of Inf. Serv., Dept. Work and Pensions, London. [26780] 25/10/1976 **CM08/10/1981**

Monk, Mrs L A, BA(Hons) MCLIP, Mob. L. Mgr., Birmingham City Council. [42248] 13/10/1988 **CM17/09/2003**

Monk, Miss R, BA(Hons) MA, Evidence & Inf. Mgr., Dept of Culture Media & Sport, London [49178] 08/10/1993 **ME**

Monk, Mr S A, Asst. Lib., Quarry House, Leeds. [10015996] 03/02/2010 **ME**

Monkman, Miss L, MA BA(Hons), Community and Inf. Asst., Harrogate L. and Inf. Ctre. [10006213] 26/09/2007 **AF**

Monks, Mrs C C, MCLIP, Resource Lib., Bury Coll., Bury. [5870] 28/01/1969 **CM01/01/1972**

Monks, Mr G F, BSc MCLIP, Lib., Southgate Sch., Cockfosters, Herts. [30072] 27/11/1978 **CM02/03/1981**

Monkton, Mrs R C, MCLIP, Sch. Lib., Wootton Upper Sch. Wootton, Bedford. [48794] 26/05/1993 **CM05/10/1994**

Monro, Mr N, Unwaged. [10016686] 30/04/2010 **ME**

Montacute, Ms K, BA FCLIP, Knowledge Servs. Mgr., NHS Yorkshire and the Humber [35430] 04/10/1982 **FE04/10/2006**

Montague, Miss M B, BEd(Hons) DipLib MSc MCLIP, Asst Dir. Business Support, Queen Mary, Univ. of London. [31385] 03/10/1979 **CM10/05/1983**

Montgomery, Mrs A, BA DipLib MCLIP, Lib., Bury Grammar Sch., Boys, Bury. [32777] 25/08/1980 **CM19/04/1983**

Montgomery, Miss F G, BED DipLib MCLIP, Knowldege Mgr., Business Customer Unit., HM Revenue & Customs, London [31667] 02/11/1979 **CM15/12/1983**

Montgomery, Mrs P D, MSc MCLIP, Lib., Crossways Jun. Sch., S. Glos. [10307] 03/01/1966 **CM01/01/1969**

Moodie, Miss E B, BA(Hons) MCLIP, Retired. [25079] 11/11/1975 **CM19/09/1978**

Moody, Mrs D A, BA, Young People Serv. Mgr., Longsight L., Manchester. [36164] 06/07/1983 **ME**

Moody, Mrs J M, BA(Hons) MSc PGCE DipTrans MILMCLIP, Subject Lib., Univ. Plymouth. [59953] 09/11/2001 **CM21/06/2006**

Moody, Mrs K B, BLib MCLIP, Sch. Lib., Herts. C.C. [20442] 05/12/1972 **CM16/10/1975**

Moody, Mrs P H, MCLIP, Res. Cent. Mgr., John Taylor High Sch., Barton-under-Needwood, Staffs. [24999] 18/11/1975 **CM01/02/1979**

Moohan, Mrs G, Lib. -in-Charge, Goethe Inst., Glasgow. [40602] 02/04/1987 **ME**

Moon, Dr B E, MA PhD MPhil FCLIP FRSE, Retired. [10313] 17/03/1954 **FE01/01/1958**

Moon, Miss C, BScEcon, Learning Resource Mgr., Bognor Regis Community Coll., W. Sussex [64386] 14/03/2005 **ME**

Moon, Mr E E, HonFLA FCLIP, Resident in U. S. A. [17404] 01/01/1939 **FE01/01/1950**

Mooney, Mrs C A, B Soc Sc MA, Learning Resource Offr., The Manchester Coll., Manchester [10016673] 23/04/2010 **AF**

Moorcroft, Mrs C R, BA MCLIP, Access Inclusion lib., Chesterfield L., Derbyshire C.C. [40558] 20/03/1987 **CM25/05/1994**

Moore II, W W, MSLS, Unwaged. [65555] 17/02/2006 **ME**

Moore, Ms A P, MBE BA(Hons) MCLIP, Founder & Dir., Kidslibs Trust, Nairobi [33060] 14/10/1980 **CM11/01/1984**

Moore, Miss A, Lib., Salisbury L. [65143] 03/11/2005 **ME**

Moore, Ms C A, BSc MA MCLIP, Chartered Inst. of Personnel & Devel., London. [30223] 10/01/1979 **CM06/04/1981**

Moore, Mrs C A, BA DipLib MCLIP, Learning Res. Lib., Leicester Coll. [27403] 01/03/1977 **CM20/03/1979**

Moore, Mr C C, BA DipLib MCLIP, Principal Lib., Royal Bor. of Kensington & Chelsea, London. [31906] 20/12/1979 **CM13/10/1982**

Moore, Mr C J K, BA(Hons) MSc MCLIP, Head of Reading & Learning Serv., Wilts C.C. [55501] 16/10/1997 **CM20/09/2000**

Moore, Mr D R, BA, Unwaged [58795] 31/07/2000 **ME**

Moore, Mrs H, BA MA MCLIP, Electronics Serv. Offr., KSS L. & Knowledge Serv., Tunbridge Wells. [10009026] 28/04/2008 **CM09/09/2009**

Moore, Mrs J C, BA MCLIP, Area Lib., Southampton City Co., Shirley L. [2511] 19/01/1966 **CM01/01/1970**

Moore, Miss J E, BSc, Catg., Dawson Books, Northants. [41858] 29/04/1988 **ME**

Moore, Mrs J M, BA MCLIP, Freelance Hist. Researcher/Genealogist, Manchester. [24341] 12/07/1975 **CM05/05/1981**

Moore, Mrs J R, BA MSLS MBA PhD, Retired, Resident USA. [17405] 26/07/1961 **ME**

Moore, Miss L, BA, Unknown. [10000656] 25/10/2006 **ME**

Moore, Mr N F, FCLIP, Retired. [10353] 30/03/1960 **FE01/01/1969**

Moore, Mr N L, BTech MCLIP, Consultant Lib., Freelance Abstractor, Self-Employed. [10351] 01/10/1968 **CM12/03/1987**

Moore, Mrs S E, MCLIP, Neighborhood Lib., Southampton City L. [9289] 29/01/1970 **CM01/09/1974**

Moore, Miss S E, BA, Stud., Sheffield Univ. [65041] 12/10/2005 **ME**

Moore, Ms S P, BA(Hons) MCLIP, H. of L. & Inf. Serv., Inst. of Chartered Accountants, London. [18141] 09/10/1972 **CM02/09/1977**

Moore, Mr S R, BA MCLIP, Head of Records. Mgmnt & Buisness Continuity, London Ambulance Serv. NHS Trust, London. [19527] 07/10/1968 **CM31/07/1972**

Moore, Miss S, Stud. [10006368] 16/10/2007 **ME**

Moore, Ms W, MCLIP, Community Lib. Network Mgr., Glasgow C.C., Cultural & Leisure Serv Lib. [27259] 17/02/1977 **CM14/06/1982**

Moorman, Miss B C, BA MCLIP, Unwaged. [24907] 05/01/1970 **CM31/07/1979**

Moors, Mrs R M, BSc DipLib MCLIP, Coll. Lib., Greenhead Coll., Huddersfield. [30328] 19/01/1979 **CM17/07/1981**

Moran, Ms A M, BA(Hons) PGDip PGCET, Sch. Lib., St. Malachy's High Sch., Castlewellan. [40475] 16/02/1987 **ME**

Moran, Mrs E, Sch. Lib., Our Lady's High Sch., N. Lanark Council. [8196] 13/06/1967 **ME**

Moran, Mrs V J, ACLIP, Asst. Super, St. Neots L., Cambs. [64402] 28/02/2005 **ACL08/06/2005**

Morddel, Ms A, MLIS, Unwaged. [10010972] 17/09/2008 **ME**

Morden, Mrs C E, BA MCLIP, Community Lib., Norfolk & Norwich
Millennium L. [10375] 01/01/1967   **CM01/01/1971**
Moreland, Mrs D A, BA DipLib MCLIP, Br. L. Mgr., L. NI, Portstewart.
[22942] 01/10/1974   **CM27/09/1977**
Moreton, Ms N J, Unknown. [10011394] 16/10/2008   **AF**
Morgan, Miss A M, MCLIP, Life Member. [10385] 01/01/1938
                                                   CM01/01/1950
Morgan, Mr B M, BSc DipLib MCLIP, Reg. L. Mgr., Carmarthenshire
C.C., Ammanford. [10387] 11/07/1972   **CM19/11/1974**
Morgan, Ms C E, BEd(Hons) DipIS MCLIP, Asst. Dir. L. Serv., Univ. of
Brighton, [53474] 01/07/1996   **CM15/05/2002**
Morgan, Miss C, ACLIP, L. Asst., The Cornish Cent., Redruth.
[10001103] 12/01/2007   **ACL27/11/2007**
Morgan, Miss D, Sen. L. Asst., St. Athan L., Vale of Glamorgan.
[10005625] 25/07/2007   **AF**
Morgan, Mr E G, BMus DipLib MCLIP, Inf. Advisor, UWIC, Cardiff.
[35288] 01/10/1982   **CM11/12/1989**
Morgan, Mrs E J, DipLib MCLIP, Trust Lib., 2nd Air Div. USAAF
Memorial L., Norwich. [37978] 01/01/1985   **CM16/02/1988**
Morgan, Ms E R, MCLIP, Prison Lib., HMP Whatton, Notts. [10014455]
22/07/1992   **CM18/11/1993**
Morgan, Miss E, BA Hons, Sen. Photo Lib., ARUP, Cardiff. [10015814]
29/01/2010   **ME**
Morgan, Mr G J A, BSc(Hons) MSc Econ, Subject Lib. for Architecture,
Construction and Real Estate Mgmnt., Oxford Brookes Univ. [59576]
04/06/2001   **ME**
Morgan, Ms G M, BA DipLib MCLIP, Adult Community Educ. Co-
ordinator, Cyngor Sir Ceredigion, Aberysthwyth. [24769] 07/10/1975
                                                   CM06/12/1978
Morgan, Mr G, MCLIP, Managing Dir., Ferret Inf. Systems, Cardiff.
[60753] 04/07/1986   **CM04/07/1986**
Morgan, Mrs G, BA, Stud., Liverpool John Moores Univ (Dist. Learning)
[10002182] 01/05/2007   **ME**
Morgan, Miss H L, Database Devel. Lib., Dept. of Health, Leeds.
[58397] 01/02/2000   **ME**
Morgan, Mr H R, Msc (Econ), Unknown. [10015810] 29/01/2010 **ME**
Morgan, Mrs I, MCLIP, Retired. [22453] 01/01/1939 **CM01/01/1941**
Morgan, Mr J H D, BA MLib(Wales) MCLIP, Asst. Lib., Librry & Learning
Resources., Birnimgham City Univ. [41838] 18/04/1988
                                                   CM23/03/1994
Morgan, Ms J L, BA, Bibliographic Serv. Lib., Leeds Met. Univ. [61579]
02/10/2002   **ME**
Morgan, Mr J L, BA MCLIP, Life Member. [10403] 21/10/1950
                                                   CM01/01/1954
Morgan, Miss J R R, BA MCLIP, Life Member. [10404] 20/09/1948
                                                   CM01/01/1964
Morgan, Mrs K B, BA MCLIP, Head Lib. /Arch., N. London Collegiate
Sch., Edgeware. [18379] 09/10/1972   **CM08/03/1978**
Morgan, Mrs K L, BSc(Hons) MSc MCLIP, Web editor, Medicine &
Hcare Prod. Reg. Agency, London. [49597] 19/11/1993
                                                   CM17/03/1999
Morgan, Mrs K S, MCLIP, Sch. L. Serv. Team Leader, Bolton Metro Bor
[4902] 09/01/1970   **CM01/07/1973**
Morgan, Ms K, BA(Hons) MA MCLIP, Marketing Dir., Sidley Austin LLP,
London. [51044] 09/11/1994   **CM10/07/2002**
Morgan, Miss K, Stud [10006426] 17/12/2007   **ME**
Morgan, Miss L P, BA MCLIP, Stock Specialist, Cheshire L., Crewe.
[24910] 16/10/1975   **CM31/10/1978**
Morgan, Mr M G, BA DipLib MCLIP, Dep. Lib., Heythrop Coll., Univ. of
London [39631] 03/04/1986   **CM12/09/1990**
Morgan, Mr N J, BA(Hons) DipLib MCLIP ILTM, Subject Lib., Cardiff
Univ. [43457] 26/10/1989   **CM17/05/2000**
Morgan, Mrs N, BA MCLIP, Mus. Ed. Policy Adviser, Museums L. &
Arch. Council, London. [27590] 24/05/1977   **CM04/07/1979**

Morgan, Mrs P C, MCLIP, L. Asst. (p/t) [10001112] 12/01/2007
                                                   CM22/03/1988
Morgan, Mrs P M, MCLIP, Retired. [329] 31/10/1955 **CM01/01/1963**
Morgan, Mr R L, BA(Hons), Unknown. [10012577] 25/01/1994   **ME**
Morgan, Mr S E, BA MEd MBA FCLIP, Head of Learning Res., Univ. of
Glamorgan. [24113] 07/03/1975   **FE20/01/1999**
Morgan, Mrs S J, L. Mgr., Ampthill L., Beds. [62375] 16/05/2003 **AF**
Morgan, Mrs S L, BA(Hons) DipLIS MCLIP, Performance & Personel
Lib., Conwy L., Conwy Co. Bor. Council. [49949] 28/01/1994
                                                   CM22/01/1997
Morgan, Mr S S, BA, Digital Serv. Lib., RNIB [65716] 03/04/2006 **ME**
Morgan, Mrs S, B LIB MCLIP, Lend. Lib., Carmarthen P.L., Carmarthen.
[10002099] 17/05/1976   **CM26/11/1982**
Morgan, Mrs U M, MCLIP, Life Member. [2869] 03/09/1948
                                                   CM01/01/1953
Morgan, Ms V E, MLS BA MCLIP, Editor, Hong Kong Fed. of Yth. Grps.
[20032] 19/01/1973   **CM15/09/1975**
Morgan-Bindon, Ms M E, Mngr. Lib. Serv. & Cultural Dev., Gold Coast
C.C., Australia. [63185] 03/03/2004   **ME**
Morgan-James, Miss K A, Sch. Lib., Hagley R. C. High Sch. [39232]
01/01/1986   **ME**
Morgans, Mr S G, MCLIP, Retired. [10422] 16/01/1968 **CM01/01/1971**
Morgan-Tolworthy, Mrs V S, BA(Hons), Asst., Lib., Ardingly Coll.,
Haywards Heath. [10016915] 10/06/2010   **ME**
Morita, Ms Y, BA MA, Barnet Public [66153] 04/10/2006   **ME**
Morje, Mrs M, Unwaged. [10015700] 10/02/2010   **ME**
Morley, Ms A, MA BA(Hons) MCLIP, Sch. Lib. /Arch., Benenden Sch.,
Kent. [45635] 08/04/1991   **CM21/10/1992**
Morley, Miss C, BEd MA, Child. and Young People's Serv., E. Sussex
C.C., Uckfield L. [61968] 23/12/2002   **ME**
Morley, Mr G, L. Serv. Mgr., LB Redbridge central L., Ilford [63570]
17/06/2004   **ME**
Morley, Mrs J E, MA DipLib MCLIP, Lib. (Job Share), Hyndland Sec.
Sch., Glasgow. [40196] 27/10/1986   **CM14/03/1990**
Morley, Mrs P, ACLIP, Lib. Asst., Mansfield L., Notts. [10003063]
23/05/2007   **ACL16/07/2008**
Morley, Mr S A, BSc MA PgDipLIM, Inf. Offr., Yorkshiris Film Archive.,
York [62790] 22/10/2003   **ME**
Morley, Miss S A, Records/Customer Admin., Rehab Works, Bury St.
Edmunds. [61282] 08/05/2002   **ME**
Morley, Miss T L, Asst. Subject Lib., Lanchester Lib., Coventry Univ.
[59931] 06/11/2001   **ME**
Moroney, Ms M S, MA MSc MCLIP, Knowledge Mgr., Herts C.C.,
[41538] 14/01/1988   **CM19/06/1991**
Morrell, Mr N, MA, Stud. [65771] 08/05/2006   **ME**
Morrell, Mrs S, BSc MA MCLIP, Tech. Abstractor, PRA, Hampton,
Middx. [18213] 06/10/1972   **CM21/10/1974**
Morrey, Ms E E, BA(Hons), Stud., Northumbria Univ., Newcastle
[10009316] 13/05/2008   **ME**
Morrill, Mrs L M, ACLIP, Lib. Asst., Roedean Sch., Brighton [10013120]
05/05/2009   **ACL16/06/2010**
Morris, Ms B A, MPhil MSc MCLIP, Hudson Rivers, Mgmt. & Training
Consultants, Norfolk [20151] 16/01/1973   **CM07/10/1975**
Morris, Mrs B G, BA(Hons), Dep. Lib., Southport & Ormskirk NHS Trust.
[58036] 18/10/1999   **ME**
Morris, Miss C, Stud., Univ. of Brighton. [10014217] 07/07/2009 **ME**
Morris, Mr D J, BA MCLIP, Unwaged [38442] 01/05/1985 **CM10/05/1988**
Morris, Ms D, MA BA MLib MCLIP, Academic Liaison Lib.,Hartley Lib.,
Univ. of Southampton. [39026] 28/10/1985   **CM14/11/1991**
Morris, Mrs D, BA MCLIP, Freelance Indexer. [29519] 12/09/1978
                                                   CM16/10/1980
Morris, Mrs E L, BA DipLib MCLIP, Asst. Lib., E. Dunbartonshire
Council, Kirkintilloch. [33083] 03/10/1980   **CM26/01/1984**

Morris, Mrs G L, BA(Hons) DipILS MCLIP, Unknown. [51175]
23/11/1994 **CM15/03/2000**

Morris, Mr G, BA DipLib MCLIP, Retired. [60321] 21/10/1992
CM21/10/1992

Morris, Miss H R, Asst. Lib. /Teaching & Learning Liaison, Cardinal
Newman Coll., Preston. [63324] 16/04/2004 **ME**

Morris, Ms H, BA(Hons) MCLIP, Inf. Serv. Co-ordinator (Job share),
General Teaching Council of England [29198] 17/04/1978
CM29/08/1980

Morris, Ms H, BSc (Hons), Unknown. [10011112] 25/09/2008 **ME**

Morris, Mrs I, BSc, Learning Advisor, Univ. of Cumbria, Carlisle [51270]
14/12/1994 **ME**

Morris, Mrs J C, BA DipLib MCLIP, Book Shop Asst., The Book House,
Oxon. [37027] 30/01/1984 **CM14/04/1987**

Morris, Mr J D, Employment not known. [32755] 06/08/1980 **ME**

Morris, Mrs J M, BA DipLib MCLIP, Asst. Lib., Sibthorp L., Bishop
Grosseteste Univ. Coll. [32437] 07/04/1980 **CM27/09/1982**

Morris, Miss J M, BA DipLib MCLIP, Health Matters Mgr., Manchester L.
& Inf. Serv. [30490] 29/01/1979 **CM27/02/1981**

Morris, Mrs J M, FSALA MCLIP, Life Member. [17408] 03/02/1947
CM01/01/1952

Morris, Mr J T, Unwaged. [57002] 19/11/1998 **ME**

Morris, Miss K A, BA MCLIP, Community Lib., Broughton L., Flintshire
C.C. [23078] 14/10/1974 **CM07/11/1978**

Morris, Ms K J, BA(Hons) MCLIP, Serv. Mgr. (Inf. and Digital),
Newcastle L. and Inf. Serv. [48744] 04/05/1993 **CM26/11/1997**

Morris, Ms L A, DipLib, Sen. Policy Adviser, Reg. Policy Unit, Cheshire
C.C. [31391] 04/10/1979 **ME**

Morris, Mrs L A, BA AKC MCLIP, Unemployed. [18156] 01/01/1972
CM01/01/1974

Morris, Mr L D, BA(Hons), Unknown [10013647] 18/05/2009 **ME**

Morris, Ms L M, BA MCLIP, Area Lib. (S.), Rhondda-Cynon-Taff,
Pontypridd L. [13844] 04/10/1970 **CM16/09/1975**

Morris, Ms M E, BA MCLIP, Sen. Lib. (Mob. & Special Serv.), Rhondda
Cynon Taff Unitary Auth., Aberdare. [20208] 29/01/1973
CM27/07/1977

Morris, Mrs M L, MCLIP, Retired. [10455] 01/01/1941 **CM01/01/1944**

Morris, Mr M, BSc DEAB, Enquiry Team Lib., Cent. Resources L.,
Hertfordshire L. [10000811] 15/11/2006 **ME**

Morris, Ms M, Inf. Cent. Mgr., Bevan Brittan, Bristol. [46982] 25/03/1992
ME

Morris, Mrs P M, MCLIP, Retired. [10459] 20/03/1967 **CM01/01/1971**

Morris, Ms R E, LLB(Hons) LLM, KBD Researcher, Freshfields
Bruckhaus Deringer, London. [62137] 28/02/2003 **ME**

Morris, Mr R J I, Team Lib., Ludlow L., Shropshire. [10016590]
14/04/2010 **AF**

Morris, Mrs S J, BSc(Hons) MSc, Team Lib. [55553] 21/10/1997 **ME**

Morris, Mrs S M, BA DipLib MCLIP, Head of Shakespeare Collections,
Shakespeare Birthplace Trust, Stratford-upon-Avon. [28191]
22/10/1977 **CM19/03/1980**

Morris, Mrs S R, BA MCLIP, Unemployed. [10463] 21/10/1969
CM13/02/1973

Morris, Mr T C, BA(Hons), Infocus Programme Mgr., N. W. Healthcare
L. Unit, Warrington. [59472] 04/04/2001 **ME**

Morris, Miss T M, BSc(Hons), Stud. [66082] 01/10/2006 **ME**

Morris, Mrs W D, BSc MCLIP, Sen. Inf. Advisor, Kingston Univ. [28704]
12/01/1978 **CM26/08/1982**

Morris, Miss Y, MA MCLIP, Dep. Inf. Mgr., CILIP, London. [65484]
24/02/2006 **CM09/09/2009**

Morris-Newton, Ms D L, BA(Hons) MCLIP, Lib. Systems Developer,
Leeds Metro. Univ. [48454] 13/01/1993 **RV28/01/2009CM13/03/2002**

Morrison, Mrs A E, BA DipLib MCLIP, L. Offr., Cent. L., Edinburgh.
[33248] 28/10/1980 **CM07/03/1985**

Morrison, Mr A J, BLib MCLIP, Serv. Devel. Lib., L.B. of Lewisham.
[29405] 01/07/1978 **CM22/10/1981**

Morrison, Mr A J, LLB LLM MA, Unemployed. [51500] 05/03/1995 **ME**

Morrison, Mr D A, MA(Hons) BSc(Hons) DipLib MCLIP, Tech. Tutor,
Glasgow. [38708] 01/10/1985 **CM16/02/1988**

Morrison, Dr D J, BA MA PhD, Lib. /Arch., Worcester Cathedral L.,
Worcester. [61448] 22/07/2002 **AF**

Morrison, Miss D M, Admin. Asst., AK Bell L., Perth. [10014797]
18/09/2009 **AF**

Morrison, Mrs D, MA DipLib MCLIP, Info Researcher, Univ. of
Edinburgh Business Sch., Edinburgh. [26067] 10/06/1976
CM03/10/1979

Morrison, Mrs E A, BA, Lib., Stranmillis Univ. Coll., Belfast. [39892]
01/10/1986 **ME**

Morrison, Mrs F M, MA(Hons) PgDip ILS, Sen. L. Asst. [62055]
07/02/2003 **ME**

Morrison, Miss J C, MCLIP, Retired. [10476] 09/03/1962 **CM01/01/1966**

Morrison, Mr J R, Vault Team Leader, Iron Mountain Records Mngmt.,
Antrim [10015121] 15/10/2009 **ME**

Morrison, Mrs J, MSc MA, Inf. Cent. Team Leader, CNR Internat. (UK)
Ltd, Aberdeen. [61508] 28/08/2002 **ME**

Morrison, Miss K, MA(Hons) Pg Dip, Stud., Liverpool John Moores
Univ. [10015818] 28/01/2010 **ME**

Morrison, Mrs P S, BA(Hons) MCLIP, Mob. Serv. & staff Dev.,
Aberdeenshire L. & Inf. Serv., Oldmeldrum. [52633] 16/11/1995
CM06/04/2005

Morrison, Mrs R A L, MCLIP, Retired. [1778] 08/02/1962 **CM01/01/1966**

Morrison, Mr V R, MCLIP, Retired. [60555] 22/10/1975 **CM14/09/1981**

Morten, Mr M, BA MCLIP, Asst. Lib., Worthing L., W. Sussex C.C.
[42200] 14/10/1988 **CM27/11/1993**

Mortimer, Mrs D M, MA DipLib MCLIP, Retired. [31411] 22/10/1979
CM22/10/1981

Mortimer, Ms J R, BA DMS DipLib MCLIP, Academic Team Mgr:
Resources & Serv., De Montfort Univ., Leicester. [39400] 22/01/1986
CM16/02/1988

Mortimer, Ms M A, MCLIP, Unknown. [10015949] 21/03/1962
CM01/01/1966

Mortimer, Mr W, BA MSc PGCE, Res. Support Lib., Open Univ. L.,
Milton Keynes. [61450] 31/07/2002 **ME**

Mortimer, Mrs Z C, CertEd, Lib. (Sch.), Bryanston Sch., Blandford,
Dorset. [53135] 01/04/1996 **AF**

Morton, Mrs A R, ECDL, Unknown. [10016957] 10/06/2010 **ME**

Morton, Ms E A, BA(Hons) MCLIP, Lib., Falkirk P. L. [39960] 04/10/1986
CM26/07/1995

Morton, Mr G, Stud., John Moores Univ., Liverpool. [10015041]
08/10/2009 **ME**

Morton, Miss H J, BLib MCLIP, Sen. Lib., Ref. & Local Studies, Jersey
L. [10499] 27/10/1971 **CM17/12/1976**

Morton, Mrs J A, BA MCLIP, Unwaged. [34793] 15/02/1982
CM13/05/1986

Morton, Mr J C, BA Dip IM, Aquisitions Mngr., Nat. Art L., V& A Mus.,
London [10017090] 27/10/1982 **ME**

Morton, Mrs J, BA(Hons) MCLIP, Comm. Inf. Offr., N. Yorks. C.C.,
Ripon L. & Inf. Cent. [55607] 24/10/1997 **CM06/04/2005**

Morton, Ms J, MA MCLIP FHEA, Faculty Team Lib., Univ. of Leeds,
Brotherton L. [25485] 27/01/1976 **CM29/09/1983**

Morton, Dr M, BSc MLib MCLIP PhD, Sch. Inf. Mgr., Welsh Assembly
Government, Cardiff. [39958] 06/10/1986 **CM14/11/1990**

Morton, Mr N J, BA PGDipILM, Learning Resource Mgr., Manchester
Enterprise Academy, Manchester. [57446] 01/04/1999 **ME**

Morton, Miss S L, MA(Hons) MCLIP, Sch. Lib., John Paul Academy,
Glasgow. [64156] 19/01/2005 **CM17/09/2008**

Moselle, Ms T, BA(Hons), Info. Offr., NSPCC [63085] 27/01/2004 **ME**

Moses-Allison, Mrs L L, BA(Hons) PgDip, Stud. [10001097] 12/01/2007 **ME**

Moss, Mr A, BA MCLIP, Retired. [17411] 25/09/1961 **CM01/01/1966**

Moss, Mrs E J L, BA MA, Stud., MMU [10005896] 02/08/2007 **ME**

Moss, Mrs J E, MCLIP, Learning Cent. Mgr., St. Joseph's Catholic Comp. Sch., Swindon. [1275] 28/08/1969 **CM01/07/1973**

Moss, Miss J E, MCLIP, Strategic L. Serv. Mgr., Cent. Area [23365] 05/11/1974 **CM19/01/1979**

Moss, Mrs L R, Bsc Econ, Inf. Asst. (Stud.) [10015813] 29/01/2010 **ME**

Moss, Mrs S E, MSc(Econ) MCLIP, Retired. [10515] 27/08/1964 **CM01/01/1968**

Moss, Mrs S G, BA LLB FCLIP, Retired. [17413] 01/01/1958 **FE01/07/1969**

Moss, Miss T C, BA MCLIP, Learning Cent. Mngr., Hertford Reg. Coll. [29199] 01/04/1978 **CM21/08/1980**

Moss, Mr W, BA MCLIP, Retired. [10516] 11/01/1965 **CM01/01/1967**

Moss-Gibbons, Ms C A, BLib(Hons) PGCE, H. of L. & Inf. Serv., Royal Coll. of Physicians, London. [32131] 21/01/1980 **ME**

Moth, Ms S J, BA DipLib MCLIP, Audience Dev. Offr., Essex C. L. [43380] 16/10/1989 **CM15/09/1993**

Mottahedeh, Miss L P, BA(Hons) MA, Inf. Consultant, HM Revenue & Customs, Manchester. [53726] 18/09/1996 **ME**

Moug, Mrs C M, BA(Hons) MCLIP, Resource Cent. Coordinator, St. Saviour's RC High Sch, Dundee [10007131] 27/02/1981 **CM10/10/1985**

Moulden, Miss J, BA FCLIP, Life Member. [10528] 21/01/1950 **FE01/01/1958**

Moule, Mrs P, Facilities Mgr., Bracknell L. [45380] 16/11/1990 **AF**

Moulton, Ms J, BA DipIM MCLIP, Child. & Young Persons Lib., L.B. of Lewisham [53873] 07/10/1996 **CM20/01/1999**

Mount, Ms R J, BA(Hons) PhD DipIS MCLIP, Sch. Lib., Upper Shirley High Sch. [51118] 16/11/1994 **CM18/03/1998**

Mountford, Mrs A, BA(Hons) MA, Lib., Nether Stowe High Sch., Staffs. LEA. [55970] 02/01/1998 **AF**

Mountford, Ms B A, BA DipLib MCLIP, p. /t. Sen. Inf. Advisor, Kingston Univ. [38248] 10/02/1985 **CM14/04/1987**

Mousavi-Zadeh, Mrs M S, MA MCLIP, Serials Lib., Univ. of Brighton [59173] 05/12/2000 **CM19/11/2003**

Mousley-Metcalfe, Mrs N, BA(Hons) MSc PGDip MCLIP, Unknown [62065] 07/02/2003 **CM19/11/2008**

Moutrey, Miss D, BA(Hons) MA, L. Asst., Univ. of Cambridge [10009534] 03/06/2008 **ME**

Mowat, Miss M W, BA MLib MCLIP, Sen. Lib., Rowett Res. Inst., Aberdeen. [29077] 25/03/1978 **CM26/08/1982**

Mower, Miss C, BA(Hons), Graduate Trainee, The London L. [10011125] 25/09/2008 **ME**

Moye, Mrs B F, BSc MSc, LRC Mgr., Thames Valley Univ., Reading. [49632] 15/11/1993 **ME**

Moynagh, Mrs J M, MA DipLib MCLIP, Assoc. Dir. Operational Serv., Robert Gordon Univ., Aberdeen. [36477] 14/10/1983 **CM27/03/1991**

Moyses, Mrs V, BA MCLIP, Lib., Ruskin Coll., Oxford. [17115] 01/01/1967 **CM01/01/1970**

Mudau, Ms N K, Relief Asst. Lib. /Stud., W. Sussex C.C., Chichester. [10001143] 12/07/2005 **ME**

Muddiman, Mr D J, MSc BA DipLib MCLIP, Reviews Editor,., Journal of Librarians & Inf. Sci.(Retired) [33450] 01/01/1981 **CM16/05/1985**

Muddyman, Mrs C E, BA(Hons), p. /t. Stud. /L. Asst., Univ. of Wales/Goethe-Inst. L., Aberystwyth/London [56271] 27/04/1998 **ME**

Mudford, Miss J L, BA DipLib MCLIP, Stock Lib., Cardiff Co., Stock Supp. Unit, Cardiff. [29765] 06/10/1978 **CM06/10/1980**

Muggleton, Mr T H, MA(Hons), Unknown. [10015181] 23/10/2009 **ME**

Muir Gray, Sir J A, KB HonFCLIP, Hon. Fellow. [62817] 23/10/2003 **HFE23/10/2003**

Muir, Dr A, MA MSc PhD FHEA MCLIP, Sr. Lect., Loughborough Univ. [45606] 02/04/1991 **CM05/01/1994**

Muir, Mr D, MCLIP, Consultant [10552] 01/07/1967 **CM01/01/1971**

Muir, Ms E P, MA MCLIP, Site Lib., SAC, Auchincruive, Ayr. [38420] 24/04/1985 **CM18/01/1989**

Muir, Mrs H A, BA(Hons) MCLIP, Asst. Lib., Queen Margaret Univ., Edinburgh. [47950] 27/10/1992 **CM31/01/1996**

Muirhead, Mr A T N, MA MLitt MCLIP, Freelance Indexer/Researcher. [22289] 04/04/1974 **CM12/08/1976**

Mulchrone, Mrs J B, BSc DipLIS MCLIP, Head Lib., Haberdashers'Aske's Boys Sch., Elstree,Herts. [44237] 20/07/1990 **CM22/11/1995**

Mulhern, Mr N P, MA MA DipLIS MCLIP, Lib., ACU, London. [50174] 22/04/1994 **CM20/11/2002**

Mulholland, Ms C N, MRPharms, Stud. [10016218] 05/03/2010 **ME**

Mulholland, Ms E, MCLIP, Learning Res. Servs., S. Eastern Reg. Coll. [64515] 27/04/2005 **CM11/03/2009**

Mulla, Ms Z, Stud. [10006130] 10/10/2007 **ME**

Mullan, Mr C, BSc Econ, Intranet Content Coordinator, Fareham [10008422] 19/03/2008 **ME**

Mullan, Mr J P, BA(Hons) MCLIP, KM Systems Mgr., Field Fisher Waterhouse [49852] 07/01/1994 **CM22/09/1999**

Mullen, Miss J L, BA(Hons), Asst. Lib., Newcastle Hosp. NHS Trust, Newcastle upon Tyne. [57366] 26/02/1999 **ME**

Muller, Mrs C S, BA(Hons) MCLIP, Dir., User Servs., Res. Lib. Servs.,Univ of London [2147] 16/10/1968 **CM01/01/1972**

Muller, Miss C S, Sen. Lib. Asst., Haywards Heath Lib. [10009460] 21/05/2008 **AF**

Mullinger, Mrs J K, BA MCLIP, Lib., W. Sussex Co. L., Horsham L. [25952] 06/05/1976 **CM24/04/1979**

Mullins, Mrs C A, BA MCLIP, Sch. Lib., Bishop Walsh Sch., Sutton Coldfield. [24301] 30/05/1975 **CM03/03/1978**

Mullis, Mr A A, MCLIP, Retired. [28924] 21/01/1953 **CM01/01/1962**

Mumford, Mrs H A, BSc(Hons) PGDipLib MCLIP, Principal Inf. Offr., Cobham Tech. Serv., Leatherhead. [33085] 03/10/1980 **CM19/06/1985**

Mumford, Mrs S M, BSc (Hons), Unknown. [10011888] 26/11/2008 **AF**

Mumford, Ms Z E, MCLIP, Lib. (Inf. Serv.), E. Kilbride Cent. L., E. Kilbride [10005897] 12/05/2005 **CM10/07/2009**

Munasinghe, Mrs A I, BA MCLIP, Retired. [20148] 25/01/1973 **CM30/12/1977**

Mundill, Mrs E, MA DipLib MCLIP, P. /t. Sch. Lib., Glenalmond Coll., Perth. [33775] 23/02/1981 **CM14/02/1984**

Munford, Mrs M, BA BSc(Econ) MCLIP, Info. Team Lib., Cent. Info. Team., Norwich [45242] 29/08/1990 **CM21/11/2001**

Muniz, Mr T, BA MSc MCLIP, Unwaged. [63304] 08/04/2004 **CM31/01/2007**

Munks, Miss E J, BA(Hons) DipLib MCLIP, Academic Support Lib., York St. John Univ., Fountains Learning Cent. [42244] 13/10/1988 **CM23/09/1998**

Munn, Mrs G J, MCLIP, Housewife. [6017] 21/01/1972 **CM29/11/1976**

Munns, Mrs K, BLib MCLIP, Sch. Lib.,The Elvian Sch., Reading. [34975] 24/05/1982 **CM12/02/1985**

Munro, Mrs C H, BA(Hons) MCLIP, Web Content Co-ordinator, Strathclyde Police, Glasgow. [34470] 16/11/1981 **CM16/10/1991**

Munro, Ms G, Pg Dip LIS, Unknown. [10012179] 11/01/1996 **ME**

Munro, Mr J A J, MCLIP, Retired. [10576] 22/05/1950 **CM01/01/1953**

Munro, Mrs J H, MSc MBA ARCS MCLIP, Univ. Lib., Univ. of Reading. [60556] 16/11/1977 **CM19/05/1980**

Munro, Mrs J M, BA MCLIP, Retired. [10577] 17/07/1956 **CM01/01/1963**

Munro, Mrs R J, MCLIP, Life Member. [10581] 12/02/1943 **CM01/01/1945**

Munro, Ms T P, BSc DipLib MCLIP, Lib. Offr., Andover, Hants. Co. L. [48847] 01/07/1993 **CM22/05/1996**

Munslow, Miss A M, MCLIP, Retired. [10586] 20/01/1965 **CM01/01/1969**

Murad, Mrs R, DipLib MCLIP, Sch. Lib., King Fahad Academy, London. [36401] 07/10/1983   **CM10/11/1987**

Murch, Miss K A, BA(Hons), Lib., Transport for London [10008498] 02/04/2008   **ME**

Murden, Mrs J P, MCLIP, Learning Cent. Mgr., New Coll., Nottingham. [10590] 12/01/1967   **CM01/01/1970**

Murdoch, Mrs J A, MA MCLIP, Coll. Lib., Bromley Coll. of F.E. & H. E., Kent. [2961] 01/01/1966   **CM01/01/1971**

Murdoch, Mrs J F, MA DipLib MCLIP, Network Lib., Aberdeenshire Council, Ellon Academy. [36505] 11/10/1983   **CM04/08/1987**

Murdoch, Mrs J M, BA MCLIP, Asst. Lib., Nairn L., Highland Council. [39562] 04/03/1986   **CM19/06/1991**

Murdoch, Miss M A S, BA DipLib MCLIP, Retired. [26487] 13/10/1976   **CM03/12/1981**

Murdoch, Ms S A, B. Ed Lib & Inf. Stud. Dip Arts, Local Liaison Offr., ALIA, Australia [10012927] 17/03/2009   **ME**

Murdoch, Mrs S A, LRC Mgr. Fernhill Sch. & Language Coll., Hants [63561] 14/06/2004   **ME**

Murdoch, Mr S G, BSc(Hons) MCLIP, Community Lib., Bloomsbury L., Birmingham City Council. [25179] 04/12/1975   **CM19/04/1979**

Murgatroyd, Miss D C, BA MCLIP, Inf. Mgr., Foreign & Commonwealth Off., London. [35465] 22/10/1982   **CM22/10/1985**

Murgatroyd, Mrs D M, BSc MCLIP, Community Serv. Lib., Bracknell L. [22023] 07/01/1974   **CM13/01/1976**

Muris, Mr C, MA FCLIP, Retired. [10594] 21/03/1952   **FE01/01/1957**

Murison, Miss K J, Stud. [10012300] 26/01/2009   **AF**

Murison, Ms L J, MA DipLib MCLIP, Chartered SLRCC, Boroughmuir High Sch., Edinburgh. [25082] 13/11/1975   **CM29/02/1980**

Murphy, Miss A M, Team Leader Ctr. for the Child, Birmingham Cent. L. [65403] 24/02/2006   **AF**

Murphy, Ms B A, BA, Inf. Mgr. MIND, London [63883] 12/10/2004   **ME**

Murphy, Mr B P, BA MA MCLIP, Mgr., L. & Inf. Serv., Rotherham MBC [35141] 30/09/1982   **CM10/10/1983**

Murphy, Mr B, BA MCLIP, Ret. [10601] 08/04/1970   **CM26/10/1973**

Murphy, Miss C A, BA MCLIP, Communications Offr., Leicestershire Police. [28863] 16/01/1978   **CM29/04/1986**

Murphy, Miss C J, BA, Unwaged. [10007542] 13/02/2008   **ME**

Murphy, Ms E J, BA DipLIS, Asst. Lib. - Collections, Nat. Univ. of Ireland, Maynooth. [48746] 05/05/1993   **ME**

Murphy, Miss E L, BA MA, Academic Liaison Lib., Univ. of Westminster [65056] 24/10/2005   **ME**

Murphy, Mrs G R, MCLIP DipLib, Lib., King William's Coll., Isle of Man. [26994] 12/01/1977   **CM19/03/1980**

Murphy, Ms H, BA(Hons) MSc, Sen. Asst. Subject Lib., Teesside Univ., Middlesbrough [53479] 01/07/1996   **ME**

Murphy, Mr J J, BA MCLIP, Reg. Lib., Min. of Justice, Liverpool. [19673] 30/10/1972   **CM07/01/1976**

Murphy, Miss K A, BA(Hons), Li. Mngr., Cheshunt L., Hertfordshire [10017097] 23/06/2010   **AF**

Murphy, Mr K, Stud., Aberystwyth Univ., Wales [10016175] 17/02/2010   **ME**

Murphy, Miss L A, BSc(Econ) MCLIP, Res. Editor, Good Practice, Edinburgh. [54504] 02/01/1997   **CM15/05/2002**

Murphy, Miss L, MA, Sch. Lib., Belvedere Academy, Liverpool [10006538] 08/11/2007   **ME**

Murphy, Miss M E, BA(Hons) DipLib MCLIP, Head of Young People – Sch. & Equalities, Herts. C.C. Hatfield. [43313] 18/10/1989   **CM23/03/1993**

Murphy, Mrs M K, MCLIP, Retired. [10604] 19/03/1956   **CM01/01/1962**

Murphy, Mrs M, Lib., Islamic Coll., Willesden, London [10012838] 19/03/2009   **AF**

Murphy, Miss P C, BA(Hons) MA DipLib PGCE MCLIP, Inf. Offr., Nat. Child. Bureau, London. [37920] 17/10/1984   **CM15/11/1988**

Murphy, Mr P J, BA DLIS MLIS, Dep. Lib., RCSI, Mercer Lib., Dublin. [65269] 30/11/2005   **ME**

Murphy, Mr R J, Dept. Lib. Allen & Overy, London [63327] 16/04/2004   **ME**

Murphy, Ms R, MA MSc MCLIP, Disabilty Support, Cork Insititute of Tech. [61623] 04/10/2002   **CM23/01/2008**

Murphy, Ms S M J, MA, Qualified [10000859] 15/11/2006   **ME**

Murphy, Miss S, BA(Hons) MA MCLIP, L. Exec., House of Commons, London. [59964] 12/11/2001   **CM11/03/2009**

Murphy, Ms Y, MSSc BA DipEd, Coll. Lib., Keble Coll., Oxford. [42128] 05/10/1988   **ME**

Murr, Mrs S L, MCLIP, Br. Lib., Churston ., Devon. [25364] 07/01/1976   **CM26/02/1981**

Murray, Miss A M, BLib MCLIP, Asst. Lib., Rochdale Cent. L. [31910] 21/01/1980   **CM16/08/1982**

Murray, Miss E, BA(Hons), Asst. Nat. Lib. of Scotland, Edinburgh [10015234] 29/10/2009   **AF**

Murray, Ms E, BA DipInf MCLIP, Lib., London [47155] 13/05/1992   **CM25/01/1995**

Murray, Mrs H L, BSc(Hons) MA, Unwaged [56734] 12/10/1998   **ME**

Murray, Mr I D, MA DipLib MCLIP DAA, Inf. Lib. & Arch., Clackmannanshire L., Alloa. [31395] 01/10/1979   **CM16/07/1984**

Murray, Mrs I S, MCLIP, Lib., Wards Solicitors, Bristol. [3278] 10/01/1972   **CM13/10/1975**

Murray, Mrs J C, MA MCLIP, Lib., Lews Castle Coll., Stornoway. [9515] 01/01/1969   **CM01/01/1972**

Murray, Dr J R, MCLIP, Dir., Murray Consulting & Training Pty. Ltd, Australia. [5017] 19/09/1969   **CM01/07/1972**

Murray, Mrs K E, LLB, Stud., Robert Gordon Univ., Aberdeen [10012940] 17/03/2009   **ME**

Murray, Mr M F, MA MSc MCLIP, Resident in Ireland. [60114] 27/03/1969   **CM05/10/1971**

Murray, Mr N F, MA(Hons) MCLIP, Inf. Specialist, Lib., European Parliament, Brussels. [50309] 14/06/1994   **CM19/11/2003**

Murray, Ms P, Off. of Fair Trading, London. [10001313] 13/10/1997 **ME**

Murray, Mrs R A, BA MA MCLIP, Retired. [7590] 07/01/1957   **CM01/01/1965**

Murray, Dr S J, Res. Asst., Queen Margaret Univ., Edinburgh [54681] 19/02/1997   **ME**

Murray, Ms S, BSc DipLib MCLIP MA, Dep. Dir. (L.), Liverpool Hope Univ. [42305] 17/10/1988   **CM21/07/1993**

Murray, Miss V L, BA(Hons), Sen. Buisness Intelligence Analyst., Edwards Angell Palmer & Dodge UK LLD [59980] 15/11/2001   **ME**

Murray-Rands, Miss S, BA(Hons) MSc(Econ), Learning Resource Asst., Coleg LLandrillo, N. Wales. [63685] 26/08/2004   **AF**

Murrell, Mrs J L, BA(Hons) DipLib MCLIP, Lib., St Simon Stock Catholic Sch. [37265] 21/05/1984   **CM03/03/1987**

Murtagh, Mr T M, BA DLIS MCLIP, Asst. Lib., Mayo Co. L., Ireland. [39839] 22/08/1986   **CM27/07/1994**

Muscat, Ms R, BA(Hons) DipLIS MA MCLIP, Clinical Inf. Support Lib., Friends of the Child. of Great Ormond Street Lib., UCL [63294] 07/04/2004   **CM19/12/2008**

Mussell, Miss J, BA DipLib MCLIP, Dep. Head of L.,Nat. Police L., Hook. [44433] 08/10/1990   **CM21/07/1993**

Mustafa, Ms E, BA(Hons) PgDipInfSc, Team Lib., Edmonton Green L., London. [46105] 01/10/1991   **ME**

Mustard, Miss C A, BEd PGDip MCLIP, Subject Liaision Lib., Brunel Univ. [59516] 18/04/2001   **CM21/06/2006**

Muszynski, Mrs M C, Lib., NHS Fife, Kirkcaldy. [10000622] 20/10/2006   **ME**

Mutch, Mrs L K, BSc(Econ), Asst. LRC Offr., Moray Coll., Elgin [58220] 16/11/1999   **ME**

Myall, Mrs N J, BA(Hons), Knowledge & Inf. Agent, Sevenoaks, Kent [58377] 26/01/2000   **ME**

Myall, Mr R, BA MA MCLIP, Inf. Lib., W. Sussex C.C., Burgess Hill L. [43233] 10/10/1989 **CM19/06/1991**

Myatt, Mrs E J, BA MCLIP, Vol. Lib. & House Tutor at The Royal Hosp. Sch., Ipswich. [28777] 23/01/1978 **CM18/07/1991**

Myatt, Mrs K F, BA DipLib MCLIP, Learning Resources & Support Mgr., Reaseheath Coll., Cheshire. [32981] 08/10/1980 **CM11/10/1982**

Mydrau, Mr N F, BA MCLIP, Retired. [10641] 29/02/1972 **CM19/09/1977**

Myears, Ms M C, BA MCLIP, Lib., Castle Green L., L.B. of Barking & Dagenham. [25083] 20/10/1975 **CM22/10/1980**

Myer, Mrs S, BA MA PgC MCLIP, Subject Info. Team Leader, Univ. of Teeside [10013013] 03/11/1986 **CM15/11/1988**

Myers, Mrs C E, BA(Hons) MA MCLIP, Early Years Lib., Catford, L.B. Lewisham. [54815] 08/04/1997 **CM15/05/2002**

Myers, Miss S, BA, Learning Resources Asst., Univ. of Chester, Sch. of Health & Social Care, Warrington. [10016121] 18/02/2010 **ME**

Myerscough, Mrs M, ACLIP, L. Asst., Lancs Teaching Hosp., Preston. [10001902] 16/03/2007 **ACL29/08/2008**

Myhill, Mrs J L, BA(Hons) DipLIS MCLIP ILTHE, Hd. of Academic Liaison, Univ. of Beds. [47888] 22/10/1992 **CM13/03/2002**

Myhill, Mrs L F, BA DipLib MCLIP, Sch. Lib., Claredon House Grammar Sch. for Girls, Kent [41910] 17/05/1988 **CM19/06/1991**

Myhill, Mr R P, BA, Marketing Mgr. -Audience Dev., Reed Business Inf., Sutton [10016478] 09/11/1982 **ME**

Mylles, Mr M, MCLIP, Knowledge & Business Intelligence Consultant, Univ. of Herts., Hatfield. [38928] 17/10/1985 **CM15/05/1990**

Mynott, Mrs D A, BLib MCLIP, Mgr.: Stories from the Web, Birmingham L. [33724] 09/02/1981 **CM15/08/1984**

Mynott, Ms G J, BA MSc MCLIP, Lect., Liverpool John Moores Univ., Liverpool. [50239] 12/05/1994 **CM25/09/1996**

N

Nadaj, Ms D M, MA, Self-employed. [10006694] 21/11/2007 **ME**

Nadimi, Mrs Z, PgDipLib MCLIP, Outreach Lib., Camden PCT, St. Pancras Hosp. [26381] 15/10/1976 **CM13/05/1981**

Nagar, Mr M H, BSc MSc MCLIP, Inf. Devel. Lib., Leicestershire L. Serv., Rothley. [42146] 04/10/1988 **CM12/09/1990**

Nagata, Mr H, MA, Prof. Emeritus at Univ. of Tsukuba. [28094] 10/10/1977 **ME**

Nagl, Mrs K L, BSc(Hons) PgDip, E-Serv. Asst., Scottish Parliament, Edinburgh. [10016541] 14/04/2010 **ME**

Naglis, Ms S, BA, PhD, Stud., Univ. of Strathclyde. [10011557] 27/10/2008 **ME**

Nahal, Mrs H C, BLib MCLIP, Sen. Lib., Telford L. [35097] 09/08/1982 **CM03/03/1987**

Nail, Mr M, MA DipLib MCLIP, Unemployed. [19985] 08/01/1973 **CM15/01/1975**

Nair, Dr G H, Bsc MLIS PhD, Assoc. Dir. of L., American Univ. of Antigua. [10016163] 17/02/2010 **ME**

Nair, Mrs R, BA MCLIP, L. Serv. Mgr.(Job Share)., Tameside Hosp., NHS Foundation Trust [12837] 01/01/1966 **CM01/01/1969**

Nairn, Mr W K, MCLIP, Comm. &Operations Lib., Scottish Borders L. & Inf. Servs., Selkirk. [10001331] 22/02/2007 **CM11/03/2009**

Naish, Mr P J, BA MLib MCLIP, Acquisitions Mgr., Univ. of Beds. [39630] 11/04/1986 **CM12/09/1990**

Naismith, Mrs R, BLib MCLIP, P/T. Learning Resource Asst. for Sixth Form Study Ctr. /L. [40601] 05/04/1987 **CM14/11/1991**

Nakane, Mr K, Retired. [51661] 01/01/1995 **ME**

Namekawa, Mr T, Lib., P.L., Tsunohazu L., Tokyo, Japan. [10005902] 02/08/2007 **ME**

Namponya, Mr C, BInf MPhil FCLIP, Dir., Univ. of the Free State L., S. Africa. [10009329] 25/08/1967 **FE01/04/1979**

Nangle, Mrs S, MA(Hons) PgDip, Asst. Lib., Lothian NHS Board L. & Res. Cent., Edinburgh. [64433] 18/03/2005 **ME**

Nankivell, Mr B, BSc(Hons) DipILS MCLIP, Community Lib., Chippenham L., Wiltshire. [53875] 07/10/1996 **CM17/05/2000**

Nannestad, Miss E E, BA MCLIP, Site Coordinator, Lincoln Cent. L., Lincs C.C. [24532] 22/09/1975 **CM19/09/1977**

Nanu, Mrs D, MSc BSc MCLIP, Employment not known. [60841] 23/08/1990 **CM23/08/1990**

Napier, Mrs P E N, BA MCLIP, Retired. [30017] 30/10/1978 **CM29/07/1983**

Napper, Mr C J, BA DipLib MCLIP, Retired [30857] 10/05/1979 **CM07/02/1985**

Napper, Mrs J, BA MCLIP, Team Lib., Adult & Comm. Serv., Beds. Co. L., Biggleswade. [30091] 05/01/1979 **CM07/09/1981**

Nash, Ms P, BA(Hons), LRC Mgr., Waltham Forest Coll. [63662] 09/08/2004 **AF**

Nash, Mrs R, BA FCLIP, Retired. [10666] 20/09/1951 **FE01/01/1964**

Nash, Mrs V R, BA MCLIP, Retired. [17435] 17/01/1966 **CM01/01/1969**

Nashnush, Miss R, Info. Offr., Nat. Audit. Off., London [10001519] 01/06/2005 **ME**

Nashwalder, Mrs K, BA(Hons), Lib. Super., Salisbury L., Wiltshire [10014058] 01/07/2009 **ME**

Nason, Mrs G, BSc MSc MCLIP MRSC, Inf. Scientist Team Leader, Environment Agency, Bristol. [52371] 26/10/1995 **CM15/09/2004**

Nathan, Miss A R, Inf. Cent. Asst., DSTL Portsdown W., Fareham. [63583] 23/06/2004 **AF**

Nathan-Marsh, Ms E, LLB BL DipLib, Asst. Lib., Treasury Solicitors, London [55299] 19/09/1997 **ME**

Natt, Mr A, BA MSc, Res., Lazard, London. [64545] 09/05/2005 **ME**

Nattriss, Mr J B, BA FCLIP, Life Member. [10672] 15/03/1953 **FE01/01/1958**

Naughton-Davidson, Mrs M, BA MCLIP, Unknown. [41444] 06/01/1988 **CM30/01/1991**

Navarrete, Mrs M J, BA(Hons) MA, Learning Cent. Mgr., City of Westminster Coll. [59950] 09/11/2001 **ME**

Nawaz, Mrs S F, MA, Unknown. [10010102] 11/08/1995 **ME**

Naylor, Dr B, MA DipLib FRSA MCLIP, Retired. [10680] 23/10/1963 **CM01/01/1969**

Naylor, Mrs C A, MCLIP, Cent. Lend. Lib., Bor. of S. Tyneside. [23582] 13/01/1975 **CM11/01/1978**

Naylor, Mr G, BA Hons, Local Studies Lib., Plymouth Cent. L. [10013394] 27/11/2002 **ME**

Naylor, Mrs J A, BLib MCLIP, Admin. Mgr., RNA, Porlock [28804] 01/02/1978 **CM29/07/1982**

Naylor, Ms L, BA(Hons) MA, L. Asst. (Business L.), Nottingham Cent. L., Notts. [10005114] 13/06/2007 **ME**

Naylor, Mr M A, MCLIP, Sch. Lib., The Comm. Sci. Coll., Thornhill. [65362] 27/01/2006 **CM11/06/2010**

Naylor, Mrs S J, BA MCLIP, Head of Juicial & Court Serv., Min. of Justice. [27638] 29/04/1977 **CM18/11/1981**

Nazir, Ms A E, ACLIP, L. Mgr., Cornwall L. Serv., Truro. [64217] 21/02/2005 **ACL17/01/2007**

Nazir, Mr A, Inf. Offr., FSTC, Manchester. [10006394] 03/06/2005 **ME**

Nazir, Ms R, BLib(Hons), Outreach & Electronic Servs. Lib., Bradford Teaching Hosp. NHS Foundation Trust. [10008234] 01/05/2010 **ME**

Nazir, Mr S, BSc(Hons) DipIS MCLIP, Inf. Offr.,Bank of England, London. [10000561] 22/09/2006 **CM18/03/1998**

Neal, Mr G P, Employment not known. [38445] 03/05/1985 **ME**

Neale, Mrs H J, MSc, Aissistant to the Lib., Braintree Sixth Form [10013587] 08/05/2009 **ME**

Nealon, Ms L A, DipLib MCLIP, Sch. L. Resource Cent. Coordinator, Edinburgh Council/St. Thomas of Aquins Sch., Edinburgh. [37657] 15/10/1984 **CM15/11/1988**

Neath, Mrs C Y, BA(Hons) MA MCLIP, Customer Serv. Lib., Loughborough L., Leic's C.C. [59967] 13/11/2001　**CM04/10/2006**

Neck, Miss E, BA, Stud., Aberystwyth Univ. [10013511] 08/05/2009 **ME**

Neenan, Mrs J, BA(Hons) MA MCLIP, Inf. Advisor., UWIC, Cardiff. [54397] 03/12/1996　**CM10/07/2002**

Neesam, Mr M G, MPhil FCLIP, Unknown. [10713] 07/09/1964 **FE18/07/1991**

Neeve, Mrs M P, BLib MCLIP, Teaching Asst., Essex C.C. [2507] 17/03/1970　**CM18/12/1974**

Negrine, Dr A, BA(Hons) MA PhD MCLIP, Unknown. [10015198] 04/10/1995　**CM23/01/2002**

Negus, Mr A E, MA MCLIP, Retired. [10714] 20/07/1964 **CM01/01/1968**

Negus, Mrs Y, BA MCLIP, Serv. Mgr:Ops&Community Dev., Cent. L., Solihull [18311] 03/10/1972　**CM17/11/1975**

Neil, Mrs V, BA MLS, Burnaby P. L., Burnaby, B. C . Canada [59919] 23/10/2001　**ME**

Neilson, Mr D T, MA(Hons) DipLib MCLIP, Retired. [10010128] 30/09/1977　**CM10/07/1981**

Neilson, Ms J R, BA MPhil DipLib, Inf. Offr., Clifford Chance, LLP, London. [44806] 05/12/1990　**ME**

Neller, Miss R M, BA DipLib MCLIP, Site Coordinator, Skegness, Lincs. Co. L. [25180] 23/11/1975　**CM07/11/1978**

Nelligan, Mrs R L, BA Ma, Issue Desk Head, UCL Main L., London. [10000871] 17/11/2006　**ME**

Nellis, Mrs A J, MCLIP, T. L. Young People & Sch., N. Yorks. C.C., Malton. [14234] 28/01/1972　**CM10/03/1975**

Nelmes, Mrs M L, BSc MCLIP, Dep. Lib., E. Sussex Hosp. Trust. [61705] 22/10/2002　**CM04/02/2004**

Nelson, Miss A, MA(Hons), Unknown. [10015933] 03/02/2010 **ME**

Nelson, Mr C D, MA PgDip, Newspaper Lib., The Scotsman Publications Ltd., Edinburgh. [66097] 25/09/2006　**ME**

Nelson, Ms D G, BSc MPhil DipLib MSc IT, Retired [39907] 05/10/1986 **ME**

Nelson, Mr G A, BA, Stud., Univ. of Brighton. [10011158] 29/09/2008**ME**

Nelson, Mrs G J, BA DipLib MCLIP, p. /t. Sch. Lib., Dorset Co. [35420] 01/10/1982　**CM17/01/1990**

Nelson, Miss J, BA(Hons) DipLib MCLIP, Lib. Advisor, LB Waltham Forest, London [10017029] 01/04/1989　**CM24/07/1996**

Nelson, Mrs M E, MCLIP, Child. Serv. Dev. Offr., Waterlooville L., Hants [23184] 05/11/1974　**CM22/02/1980**

Nelson, Mrs P E, BA MCLIP, Inf. Mgr., Business Intelligence., Savills plc. [25587] 29/01/1976　**CM10/09/1982**

Nelson, Mr S A, BA DipLib MCLIP, Learning Cent. Asst. Mgr., City & Islington Coll., London. [40808] 22/06/1987　**CM09/09/2009**

Nelson, Mrs S E, MCLIP, Inf. Offr., Sheffield Educ. Dept., S. Yorks. [23420] 07/01/1975　**CM12/08/1977**

Nelson, Mrs S J, BA(Hons) PGDipILM, Bibl. Serv. Lib., Univ. of Liverpool, Sydney Jones L. [57406] 15/03/1999　**ME**

Nelson, Mrs S T, BA MCLIP, Asst. Lib., Trinity Coll., Cambridge. [20658] 01/01/1973　**CM21/11/2001**

Nephin, Ms E L, BA(Hons) MSc MCLIP, Academic Lib., Leeds Met. Univ. [61807] 11/11/2002　**CM19/11/2008**

Nesaratnam, Mrs J A, BA MCLIP, Seni. Reader Serv. Lib., Herefordshire Libs. [35021] 09/06/1982　**CM01/10/1986**

Nesterovic, Mrs G, PGDip, Snr. L. Asst., Strathclyde Univ. [64077] 15/12/2004　**ME**

Nettleship, Mrs K L, ACLIP, L. Asst., Illingworth L. Sheffield NHS Foundation Trust, Sheffield [10001485] 26/02/2007 **ACL24/04/2009**

Nettleton, Mrs S J, BA(Hons), Lib.,- Moreton Morrell Cent., Warwicks. Coll., Warwick. [33653] 19/01/1981　**ME**

Nevard, Ms K, BA MCLIP, Unknown. [34639] 22/01/1982**CM13/06/1989**

Neville, Miss K E, BA DipLib MCLIP, Stock Serv. Mgr., Derbys. C.C. [36374] 04/10/1983　**CM05/05/1987**

Neville, Ms L S C, BA(Hons), Asst. Lib., Royal Coll. of Art, London. [46113] 01/10/1991　**ME**

New, Ms S I, BA(Hons) MA MCLIP, Prep. Sch. Lib., Brighton Coll. Prep. Sch., E. Sussex. [47183] 26/05/1992　**CM24/05/1995**

Newall, Ms E, BA(Hons) MA MCLIP, Faculty Team Lib., Arts, Univ. of Nottingham. [52171] 10/10/1995　**CM20/01/1999**

Newbold, Mrs F M, BLib(Hons) MCLIP, Head of Res. & Inf. Serv., Presdales Sch., Ware. [28373] 01/10/1977　**CM04/12/1982**

Newbold, Mrs G, BA(Hons) MA, Head of Inf. Serv., EADS Astruim UK [63913] 26/10/2004　**ME**

Newborough, Miss E C, BA, Unknown. [10011997] 09/12/2008　**ME**

Newbury, Mrs A, BA MCLIP, Local Studies Lib. Northumberland Co. Lib. Serv. [20266] 27/02/1973　**CM01/01/1978**

Newbury, Mrs J I, MCLIP, Retired [10745] 13/10/1964　**CM01/01/1969**

Newbury, Mr K M G, FCLIP, Life Member [10746] 23/03/1932 **FE01/01/1948**

Newbutt, Miss S, BA(Hons), Asst. Lib., The Grammar Sch. at Leeds, Leeds [10006645] 11/09/2007　**ME**

Newby, Mrs T M, BA MCLIP, Reg. Workforce Devel. Offr. [43342] 24/10/1989　**CM26/02/1992**

Newell, Mrs C E, BScEcon(Hons) MCLIP, Subject Support Lib., Univ. of Exeter, Devon. [58517] 20/07/2000　**CM01/02/2006**

Newell, Mrs E, BA(Hons), Subject Lib., Anglia Poly. Univ., Cambridge. [51510] 13/03/1995　**ME**

Newell, Mr G G, BA, Higher L. Exec., House of Commons Commission L., London. [41158] 09/10/1987　**ME**

Newell, Mrs S J, BA(Hons), Grp. Mgr., Newton Hall Grp. of L., Co. Durham [10009336] 20/05/2008　**ME**

Newgass, Mrs O R, MCLIP, Inf. Consultant, Dartmouth. [40737] 22/05/1987　**CM01/04/2002**

Newham, Ms H, MCLIP, Mgmt. Consultant, HNA., Windrush, The Ridgeway, Enfield. [16036] 25/08/1964　**CM01/01/1970**

Newiss, Miss J, MA MCLIP, Hon. Lib., Thoresby Soc. [10755] 23/01/1960　**CM01/01/1962**

Newland, Mrs B J M, BA(Hons), Lib., Natural England, Peterborough. [46160] 03/10/1991　**ME**

Newlove, Mrs C, BA MCLIP, p. /t. Lib., Taylor Vinters Solicitors, Cambridge. [32999] 01/10/1980　**CM20/03/1987**

Newman, Mr C J, BA DipLib MCLIP, Asst. Lib., Corporation of London L., Bibl. Serv. Sect.-Guildhall L. [37923] 19/11/1984　**CM18/04/1990**

Newman, Ms C, BA MCLIP, Serv. Mngr L. (Child., Yth. and Inclusion), Co. L., Nottingham. [41824] 17/04/1988　**CM26/07/1995**

Newman, Miss E, ACLIP, SIR Assoc.,Welwyngarden City [10006996] 17/12/2007　**ACL03/12/2008**

Newman, Mrs H M, BA PGCE MLib MCLIP, Sen. Lib., Sch. L. Serv., W. Sussex C.C. [42371] 27/10/1988　**CM24/06/1992**

Newman, Dr J, PhD, Head of H.E., Brit. Lib., London. [10014970] 01/10/2009　**ME**

Newman, Mrs L E, FCLIP, Retired. [60564] 11/12/2001　**FE01/04/2002**

Newman, Mrs L M, BA PhD MCLIP, Retired. [10765] 06/01/1964 **CM01/01/1968**

Newman, Miss M K, BA(Hons), Asst. Learning Resource Mgr., Lewisham Coll., London [63899] 26/10/2004　**ME**

Newman, Mrs M, MA MCLIP, Unknown. [10766] 07/01/1971 **CM12/10/1973**

Newman, Ms N B, BA(Hons) DipInf MCLIP, Head Lib., St. Andrews Hosp., Northampton. [47690] 15/10/1992　**CM31/01/1996**

Newman, Miss R M, BA MA, Lib., Chipping Barnet L., London [59747] 12/09/2001　**ME**

Newman, Mr S D, PhD MA, Stud., Aberystwyth Univ. [10015260] 30/10/2009　**ME**

Newman, Mrs S, BA DipLib MCLIP, Unknown. [37786] 26/10/1984 **CM18/04/1990**

Newman, Mr W G, MCLIP, Reader Audience Devel. Offr., Derbyshire C.C., Alfreton L. [10772] 12/05/1971 **CM10/02/1975**

Newman, Mrs Z H, BA(Hons), Sen. Asst. Lib., Torbay Ls. [10002035] 20/04/2007 **ME**

Newsam, Mrs A M, BA(Hons) DipLIS MCLIP, L. Mgr., Abergavenny L., Monmourthshire. (On Maternaity Leave) [46473] 11/11/1991 **CM16/11/1994**

Newsome, Miss J, Subject Lib., Doncaster Coll. [56439] 13/07/1998**ME**

Newson, Mr B A R, MCLIP, Retired. [10775] 17/04/1956 **CM01/01/1969**

Newson, Mrs S M, BA DipLib MCLIP, European Inf. Offr. [10006253] 13/05/1986 **CM18/07/1990**

Newstead, Mrs N S, PG Dip, Inf. Offr., Linklaters, London. [10007154] 26/02/2008 **ME**

Newton, Miss A J, BA(Hons) MA MCLIP, Faculty Team Lib., Univ. of Leeds L. (Maternity Leave) [55772] 18/11/1997 **CM10/07/2002**

Newton, Mr A J, BLib MCLIP, Lib. HQ, Wilts. C.C. [28640] 04/01/1978 **CM06/02/1980**

Newton, Mrs C J, BA MA FRSA, Dir. of Collections & Res., Nat. L. of Scotland, Edinburgh. [21288] 14/10/1973 **ME**

Newton, Mrs C, Sen. L. Mgr., Wallesey Cent. L., Wirral. [38177] 24/01/1985 **ME**

Newton, Mrs J L, MCLIP, Asst. Mgr., Marie Curie Cancer Care. [25347] 14/01/1976 **CM14/12/1978**

Newton, Mrs J M, MCLIP, Head of Community Serv., L.B. of Greenwich. [2325] 22/06/1970 **CM16/07/1973**

Newton, Mrs J R D, BA(Hons) BSc MCLIP, Homework Club Support Lib., Torfaen Co. Bor. Council, Pontypool. [54239] 13/11/1996 **CM21/11/2001**

Newton, Mrs K, ACLIP, Mgr., Customer Serv. Cent. and L., Sunderland. [45188] 06/08/1990 **ACL05/05/2005**

Newton, Ms M, BA MCLIP, Lib. & Arch., Mount St Mary's Coll. [44913] 14/01/1991 **CM18/11/1993**

Newton, Mrs R, BA MCLIP, Staff Resources Co-ordinator, Imperial Coll., London [10012856] 23/10/1987 **CM01/07/1994**

Newton, Miss V B, BSc DipLib MCLIP, L. & Knowledge Serv. Mgr., Royal Devon & Exeter Hlthcare. NHS Found. Trust, Exeter. [26996] 19/01/1977 **CM07/02/1979**

Ng Kee Kwong, Mrs S Y R, MSc MCLIP, Head, L.,Sci. Inf. & Pub. Dept., Mauritius Sugar Ind. Res. Inst. [60081] 07/03/1978 **CM20/05/1980**

NG, Mr K N, BA, Unknown. [10016888] 01/06/2010 **ME**

Ng, Miss L H, MCLIP, Sen. Reg. Program Specialist, Internat. Devel. Res. Cent., Republic of Singapore. [17453] 02/02/1968 **CM01/01/1970**

Ng, Miss L, Computing Content Co-ordinator, Heriot Watt L., Edinburgh. [57061] 02/12/1998 **ME**

Ng, Mrs R E, BA(Hons) MScEcon MCLIP, Writer [55431] 13/10/1997 **CM15/10/2002**

Ngimwa, Ms P, MPhil, Stud. [10017031] 18/06/2010 **ME**

Nguyen, Miss H A, Stud. [10005972] 18/02/2008 **ME**

Nguyen, Mrs M D, BA, Sen. L. Inf. Offr., Coventry L. & Inf. Serv. [61863] 22/11/2002 **ME**

Nibbs, Ms A R, BA(Hons) MSc, Learning Devel. & Res. Assoc., CILASS Univ. of Sheffield [10015584] 17/12/2009 **ME**

Niblett, Mrs B S, MSc BSc(Econ) DipLib MCLIP, Application Consultant, Infor L. & Inf. Solutions, Bristol. [19574] 17/11/1972 **CM22/09/1977**

Nicholas, Mr J R, BA MCLIP, Retired. [10794] 18/09/1963 **CM01/01/1969**

Nicholls, Mr D A, BA(Hons) MSc MCLIP, Lib. & Info. Offr.,Tower Hamlets PCT [62793] 22/10/2003 **CM05/05/2010**

Nicholls, Miss E, MCLIP, Life Member. [10799] 02/10/1940 **CM01/01/1952**

Nicholls, Mrs G, BA MCLIP, Inf. Specialist, Bucks. Co. L., Bucks. [33142] 03/10/1980 **CM02/11/1982**

Nicholls, Mrs H T, BA DipLib MCLIP, Lib. /Copyright Mgr., Assessment & Qualifications Allia., Manchester. [23605] 16/01/1975 **CM02/02/1979**

Nicholls, Miss P J, BA DipLib MCLIP, Dep. Lib., Richmond upon Thames Coll., Twickenham. [37371] 16/07/1984 **CM14/02/1990**

Nicholls, Mrs S, MCLIP, Lib., Calthorpe Park Sch., Fleet. [8330] 22/04/1971 **CM20/11/1974**

Nicholls, Mrs W G, MCLIP, Child. & Young Peoples Lib., S. Glos. Council, Downend L. [5467] 05/02/1972 **CM18/08/1975**

Nichols, Mrs L L, BA DipLib MA, Unknown. [43546] 06/11/1989 **ME**

Nichols, Mrs M E, MCLIP, L. Mgr., Holborn L. & Learning Cent., L.B. of Camden. [3095] 12/01/1970 **CM08/03/1974**

Nichols, Mr N J, BA(Hons), Data Mgr., UK Trade and Investment, London. [57958] 05/10/1999 **ME**

Nichols, Mr P E, BA MCLIP, L. & Inf. Mgr., Somerset Co. L. [19214] 04/09/1972 **CM21/07/1975**

Nichols, Mr R M, MCLIP, Retired. [10812] 12/01/1969 **CM22/07/1975**

Nichols, Ms S E, MCLIP, Lib., Streatham & Clapham High Sch., London. [25345] 10/01/1976 **CM15/12/1978**

Nichols, Mrs S J, LIS Mgr., Bircham Dyson Bell, London. [35042] 05/07/1982 **ME**

Nichols, Ms T, Unknown. [10017105] 04/06/2010 **AF**

Nicholson, Mr A P, BA MSc, Knowledge Mgr., Dept. of Health, Nottingham, Gov. Off for the E. Midlands. [60186] 04/09/1989 **ME**

Nicholson, Ms A, MSc BSc, Graduated [10000534] 18/10/2006 **ME**

Nicholson, Miss A, MA(Hons), Lochaber Lib., The Highland Council [64733] 08/06/2005 **ME**

Nicholson, Ms C M, MA DipLib MCLIP, Head Learning Resources, Glasgow Sch. of Art. [21505] 22/10/1973 **CM01/12/1976**

Nicholson, Ms C T, BA MCLIP, Area Mgr., Glos. Lib. & Info. Serv. Gloucester [29640] 09/10/1978 **CM27/07/1983**

Nicholson, Mr D M, BSc DipLib MCLIP, Former, Dir., Strathclyde Univ., Cent. for Digital L. Res. [24912] 11/10/1975 **CM02/11/1984**

Nicholson, Mr H D, MA MCLIP FRSA, Univ. Lib., Univ. of Bath, Bath. [25379] 05/01/1976 **CM11/04/1979**

Nicholson, Mrs J D, MCLIP, Customer Serv. Mgr., Dorset C.C. [19972] 01/01/1973 **CM30/12/1975**

Nicholson, Miss J E, BSc DipLib MSc MCLIP, Asst. Lib., Surrey Inst. of Art & Design, Univ. Coll. Farnham, Surrey. [21178] 30/09/1973 **CM23/09/1976**

Nicholson, Ms J, BA MA, Surestart Lib., Derbyshire C.C. [40138] 17/10/1986 **ME**

Nicholson, Ms K E, Retired. [10821] 12/10/1946 **ME**

Nicholson, Mrs M C, MA(Hons) MSc, Catr., Mitchell L., Glasgow. [57070] 07/12/1998 **ME**

Nicholson, Miss M S, BA(Hons) MA MCLIP, Academic Subject Lib., Univ. of Lincoln. [51877] 24/07/1995 **CM17/09/2003**

Nicholson, Miss M, BA MCLIP, Retired. [10822] 01/01/1961 **CM01/01/1965**

Nicholson, Mr N T, MA DipLib MCLIP, Joint Team Leader, Monographs & Media, Nat. L. of Scotland [31519] 15/10/1979 **CM12/04/1983**

Nicholson, Mrs S A, ACLIP, Inf. on Prescription Project Coordinator [10006574] 14/11/2007 **ACL16/07/2008**

Nicholson, Mrs V V, BLS MCLIP, Adult Learning Serv. Mngr. Area L. H.Q., Ballymena. [48689] 15/04/1993 **CM20/11/2002**

Nicklen, Mr J E, BA(Hons) DipLib MCLIP, Curator of Modern Brit. Collections, Nat. L. of Scotland, Edinburgh. [28348] 31/10/1977 **CM30/10/1979**

Nicol, Miss A, MA, Stud., Univ. of Strathclyde. [10015205] 23/10/2009 **ME**

Nicol, Miss L C, MSc/Pg Dip, Info. Offr., Idox Info. Serv. [10011173] 29/09/2008 **ME**

Nicolaides, Ms E, BA DipLib MCLIP, Employment not known. [35760] 24/01/1983 **CM02/09/1986**

Nicolas, Mr A, BA(Hons), Asst. Lib. Mgr. / Lib. Asst., Oakmere L., Potters Bar [10016433] 24/03/2010 **AF**

Nicoll, Miss F L, MA DipLIS MCLIP, Sen. Devel. Offr., Glasgow City Council. [41639] 05/02/1988 **CM01/12/1994**

Nicolson, Mrs M A S, BA DipLib MCLIP, YPS Lib., Shetland Islands Council, Lerwick. [27986] 03/10/1977 **CM03/10/1979**

Nicolson, Mr M S, BA MA MCLIP, LRC Mgr. Havant Coll., Hampshire. [54253] 11/11/1996 **CM19/11/2008**

Nief, Ms R, BA PGDip, Asst. Lib., Wellcome Trust L., London. [41702] 22/02/1988 **ME**

Nield, Mrs L, BA DipLib MCLIP, Area Lib. W., Dumfries & Galloway Council, Stranraer LIO. [35910] 12/02/1983 **CM29/07/1986**

Nielsen, Mrs J C, BA(Hons) MA, Administrator [55512] 16/10/1997 **ME**

Nielsen, Ms J, Enquiries and Serv. Team Leader, Welcome L., London. [57860] 13/09/1999 **ME**

Nielsen, Mrs M E, BA MLib MCLIP, Retired [34625] 19/01/1982 **CM12/10/1986**

Niemogha, Mrs A O, BA(Hons) MA, Sch. Lib., Archbishop Tenison's Sch., London [54906] 06/05/1997 **ME**

Nieuwold, Ms L, BA MA MCLIP, Self employed [39003] 28/10/1985 **CM15/02/1989**

Niewiadomska, Ms E, MA MCLIP, Inf. Serv. Mgr., Brit. American Tobacco, Southampton. [62926] 20/11/2003 **CM09/11/2005**

Nik Hussin, Ms N N T, ACLIP, Inf. Servis. Adv., Queen Margaret Univ., Edinburgh. [10012056] 15/12/2008 **ACL12/02/2010**

Nile, Ms N J, MSc, Lib. Asst.,Wills Memorial L., Bristol [10014561] 17/08/2009 **ME**

Nimmo, Mrs E C, MA, Preservation Resources Offr., Humanities Advanced Tech. & Inf. Inst., The Univ. of Glasgow [62949] 21/11/2003 **ME**

Nisbet, Mr P W, MA MCLIP, Inf. Editor, N. Lanarkshire Council, Motherwell. [24118] 01/04/1975 **CM01/08/1977**

Nisco, Mrs S L, BSc(Hons) MCLIP, Inf. Specialist., Towers Perrin, London. [49569] 19/11/1993 **CM20/11/2002**

Nitti, Miss C J, BA MA, Access and Inclusion Lib., Matlock L., Derbyshire. [10015364] 09/11/2009 **ME**

Niven, Ms A S, MA(Hons) DipLib MCLIP, Stock Devel. Co-ord., Mitchell L. Glasgow. [32137] 10/01/1980 **CM08/12/1982**

Niven, Ms E S, MA(Hons) DipLib MCLIP, Sch. Lib., Dingwall Academy, Highland Council. [32811] 29/09/1980 **CM27/01/1984**

Nix, Mrs A, BA MSc DipLib MCLIP, Sr. Lib., Somerset Stud., Somerset C.C. [27495] 27/04/1977 **CM07/01/1980**

Nixon, Mrs A, MCLIP, Sch. Lib., Chepstow Comprehensive, Gwent C.C. [8367] 01/01/1971 **CM30/01/1975**

Nixon, Mrs C M, BA(Hons) MSc MCLIP, Campus L. Mgr., Edinburgh Napier Univ., Edinburgh. [61353] 29/05/2002 **CM23/06/2004**

Nixon, Mrs G, ACLIP, L. Asst., Brit. Geological Survey, Nottingham. [64920] 08/09/2005 **ACL22/06/2007**

Nixon, Mrs L A, BLib MCLIP, Inf. Offr., Child. Cent., City Hosp., Nottingham. [23624] 15/01/1975 **CM25/01/1979**

Nixon, Miss M C, BA MA DipLib MCLIP, Lib., Goldsmiths Coll., London. [21110] 08/10/1973 **CM31/12/1989**

Nixon, Ms M, MA, Asst. Lib., The Kennel Club L., London. [10010266] 16/03/2004 **ME**

Njuguna, Mr A K, BSc Info Sci, Unwaged [10013189] 30/03/2009 **ME**

Nkiko, Mr C, BSc MSc MLS, Cent. for Learning Resource, Covenant Univ., Nigeria [10014887] 28/09/2009 **ME**

Noall, Miss C A F, MCLIP, Br. Lib., Cardiff L. Serv. [10857] 03/03/1972 **CM16/07/1975**

Nobes, Mrs A, BSc, Stud. [10013681] 18/05/2009 **ME**

Noble, Miss A D, MA FCLIP, Retired. [10858] 27/09/1943 **FE01/01/1965**

Noble, Mrs A H, BA MCLIP, Greenwood Cent. Lib., Greenwood Cent., Irvine [32271] 24/01/1980 **CM21/03/1984**

Noble, Ms A, BA DipLib MCLIP, Princ. Lib., Sch. L. Serv., Monmouthshire C.C. [38241] 12/02/1985 **CM22/04/1992**

Noble, Mrs C J, BA(Hons), Sen. Lib., Technip UK Ltd., Westhill, Aberdeenshire. [46063] 10/09/1991 **ME**

Noble, Miss J A, BA(Hons) MCLIP, Child. Serv. Lib., Poole Cent. L., Poole. [56045] 30/01/1998 **CM12/03/2003**

Noble, Ms J P, BA(Hons) MSc, Primary Sch. Lib., Tower Hamlets Sch. L. Serv. [55328] 01/10/1997 **ME**

Noble, Mrs J, BA MCLIP, Network Lib. at Westhill Academy, Aberdeenshire L. & Inf. Serv. [32500] 13/05/1980 **CM18/08/1983**

Noble, Miss L, BSc MCLIP, Head of Nat. Marine Biological L., Nat. Environment Res. Council, Devon. [60752] 04/07/1986 **CM04/07/1986**

Noble, Mrs R J, MCLIP, Campus Lib., Univ. of Chichester, Bognor Regis Site. [10869] 02/01/1968 **CM01/01/1971**

Noble-Harrison, Mrs A, BSc, MSc, Lib., Swindon Cent. L., Swindon. [10016925] 16/06/2010 **ME**

Noblett, Mrs L P, MA MCLIP, Ret. [21610] 19/11/1973 **CM10/03/1978**

Noblett, Mr W A, MA MCLIP, Head Official Publications, Cambridge Univ. L. [21517] 11/10/1973 **CM13/02/1984**

Nockels, Mr K H, MA(Hons) DipLib MCLIP, Info. Lib., Univ. of Leicester [39975] 08/10/1986 **CM21/07/1999**

Nolan, Miss A F, MSoc. Sc, hDLIS ALAI, Lib., Woodfarm High Sch. Glasgow [65928] 10/07/2006 **ME**

Nolan, Mrs C A, BA(Hons) MA MCLIP, Volunteer Lib., St. Marks Primary Sch., Bromley. [56356] 11/06/1998 **CM23/01/2002**

Nolan, Mrs C, BEd, Sch. Lib., Newmarket Coll., Suffolk. [10009338] 01/06/2008 **ME**

Nolan, Miss D, Stud., Aberystwyth Univ. [10016860] 27/05/2010 **ME**

Nolan, Mrs H J, MCLIP, Inf. Mgmt. Lib., Dept. for Work & Pensions, Sheffield. [61156] 15/03/2002 **CM11/03/2009**

Nolan, Miss J, BA(Hons), Sen. Lib. Asst., Peter Street/Eccleston, St. Helens [65671] 07/03/2006 **ME**

Nolan, Miss L, BA, Stud. [10015389] 10/11/2009 **ME**

Nolan, Mrs S R, BA(Hons), L., STV, SMG plc. Pacific Quay, Glasgow. [51437] 14/02/1995 **ME**

Nolan, Miss S, BA(Hons) DipLIS MCLIP, Subject Lib. -Fine Art, Middlesex Univ., Barnet. [55139] 23/07/1997 **CM07/09/2005**

Noon, Mr R A, BA, Lib. Asst., Headington L., Oxford Brooks Univ. [10014406] 23/07/2009 **AF**

Norbury, Mrs L, BSc MPhil MCLIP, Academic Support Consultant, Univ. of Birmingham, Main L. [43001] 02/06/1989 **CM15/12/1997**

Norcott, Miss C V, MA CertEd, Learning Resources Offr., Tiffin Girls Sch., Kingston upon Thames. [44079] 26/04/1990 **ME**

Norman, Mrs G, BA MCLIP, Stock Mgr., Bracknell Forest Bor. Council, Bracknell, Berks. [27573] 18/05/1977 **CM24/11/1980**

Norman, Mr J F, BSc DipLib MCLIP, Lib., Nat. Inst. for Med. Res., London. [32138] 29/01/1980 **CM17/02/1982**

Norman, Mrs J, BLib MCLIP, Learning Res. Mgr., Richard Huish Coll., Taunton. [38140] 11/01/1985 **CM16/09/1992**

Norman, Mr M A, BA(Hons) MCLIP, Dist. L. Mgr., Retford L., Notts Co. Council [52365] 26/10/1995 **CM19/05/1999**

Norman, Mr N, BA MA DipInfSc MCLIP, Retired. [30498] 09/02/1979 **CM20/04/1983**

Norman, Miss S A, Lib., Inst. of Oriental Philosophy, Taplow. [24037] 12/03/1975 **ME**

Norman, Ms S A, BA DipLib FCLIP HonFCLIP, Retired. [32451] 01/04/1980 **FE27/07/1994**

Noronha, Miss A P, B Bus MCLIP, Faculty Lib., Edith Cowan Univ., Western Australia. [17468] 06/01/1969 **CM01/01/1971**

Norquay, Ms S, BSc MSc, Asst. Lib., SIRCC, Univ of Strathclyde, Glasgow. [58073] 25/10/1999 **ME**

Norrey, Ms B, L. Serv. Mgr., Essex. [10012195] 12/02/2010 **ME**

Norrie, Ms S M, BA(Hons) MSc, Relations Mngr., Christianity Explored, London [63416] 06/05/2004 **ME**

Norris, Mr C F, MSc MCLIP, Retired. [10899] 01/01/1961 **CM01/01/1968**

Norris, Mr D J, BA(Hons), IT Offr., Imperial Coll. London. [52266] 20/10/1995 **ME**

Norris, Mrs H E, MA DipLib MCLIP, Lib., QUeen Anne's Sch., Caversham, Reading [32894] 02/10/1980 **CM22/12/1982**

Norris, Ms K, BA, MLIS, Asst. Lib., Dept. of Early Printed Books, Trinity Coll., Dublin. [10001624] 07/10/2003 **ME**

Norry, Miss J, BA MA DipLib FCLIP ILTHEM, Dir. of L & Learning Innovation, Leeds Met. Univ. [39205] 01/01/1986 **FE07/07/2010**

North, Ms A, MCLIP, Managing Dir., The Genuine Grp. Ltd, London. [60729] 25/06/1985 **CM25/06/1985**

North, Ms L P, BA DipLib MCLIP, Employment not known. [27772] 26/07/1977 **CM11/12/1989**

North, Mr P M, BA MCLIP, Head of Learning Resources., S. Kent Coll. [19222] 11/08/1972 **CM21/07/1975**

North, Mrs R, BA, Stud. [10006298] 10/10/2007 **ME**

North, Mrs S L, BA(Hons), Info. Advisor, Careers Bradford Ltd. [56333] 20/05/1998 **ME**

Northall, Miss D M, MSc MCLIP, Sci. Lib., Univ. Nottingham. [27000] 19/01/1977 **CM26/03/1979**

Northam, Miss J, BA(Hons) MA MCLIP, Asst. Lib. / Info. Resource Offr., Child. Serv., Cent. L., Barnsley M.B.C. [56689] 05/10/1998 **CM15/09/2004**

Norton, Mr A S, PgDip, Stock Lib., N. Kensington L., London. [10015037] 07/10/2009 **ME**

Norton, Mrs F, DIP NZLS, Unknown. [10014006] 17/05/1994 **ME**

Norton, Mr I C, BLIB MCLIP, Cent. Support Lib., Univ. of Plymouth. [21585] 29/10/1973 **CM14/02/1977**

Norton, Mr J C W, MA MSc MCLIP, Hon. Res. Assoc., Liverpool Hope Univ. [10914] 26/06/1968 **CM15/10/1972**

Norton, Miss J, BSc Econ, L. Asst., Wilmslow L., Cheshire. [10016919] 10/06/2010 **AF**

Norton, Mr N M, MA BA(Hons), L. & Info. Asst., Leeds Coll. of Art, Leeds [10016609] 14/04/2010 **AF**

Norton, Mr P, BSc MCLIP, Retired. [60773] 16/07/1968 **CM16/07/1968**

Norwood, Miss M R, BA(Hons) MCLIP, Constituency Lib., Birmingham L. Serv. [20264] 23/02/1973 **CM12/12/1975**

Norwood, Miss S K W, BA(Hons), Stud., Univ. of Brighton. [10011556] 27/10/2008 **ME**

Nother, Miss M, BA MCLIP, Sen. Lib. Community Engagement, Dialstone L., Stockport Met. B. C. [42361] 25/10/1988 **RV04/12/2006 CM18/11/1993**

Notman, Ms M, MTh(Hons) DipLIS MCLIP, Health Improvement Support Offr., NHS [42125] 04/10/1988 **CM22/11/1995**

Nott, Mr J, BA(Hons) MCLIP, Sen. Devel. Analyst, npower Retail [46535] 18/11/1991 **CM14/03/2000**

Nott, Miss S A, BA(Hons) MSc MCLIP, Subject Lib., PCFE, Plymouth. [55669] 07/11/1997 **CM10/07/2002**

Nowacki-Chmielowiec, Mrs C M, BA(Hons) DipLib MCLIP, Retired. [33095] 06/10/1980 **CM04/08/1987**

Nowell, Mr G F H, BA FCLIP, Life Member. [10925] 03/10/1950 **FE01/01/1955**

Nowell, Ms T C, MCLIP, Subject L. – Learning Res. Cent., St Mary's Coll., Twickenham. [33494] 15/01/1981 **CM01/07/1984**

Nugent, Mrs D M, Sen. Lib., Omagh L. HQ [61130] 19/02/2002 **ME**

Nugent, Mr G T, BA(Hons) DipILM MCLIP, Collections Team Leader (Devel.), Adult & Cultural Serv., Lincolnshire C.C. [47781] 14/10/1992 **CM22/11/1995**

Nugent, Miss M C R, MCLIP, Retired. [10930] 09/09/1957 **CM01/01/1962**

Nunn, Miss R M J, MA MA MCLIP, Publications Mgr., Dept. for Business, Innovation & Skills (BIS), London [58489] 25/02/2000 **CM01/02/2006**

Nurcombe, Mrs V J, BA MCLIP, Freelance Inf. Consultant, Cheshire. [1591] 18/09/1969 **CM16/03/1973**

Nurse, Mr E B, MA FSA MCLIP, Retired. [10934] 19/01/1970 **CM01/01/1972**

Nurse, Mr R A, BA BA MCLIP, Digital Lib. Programme Mgr., Open Univ. [36443] 14/10/1983 **CM16/12/1986**

Nutsford, Miss S G, BA PGCE DipLib MCLIP, Faculty Support Serv. Team Leader, Imperial Coll., London [31401] 08/10/1979 **CM21/12/1981**

Nutt, Mrs M C, Retired [18648] 01/10/1972 **ME**

Nuttall, Mr B S, BA MCLIP, Life Member. [10937] 01/10/1960 **CM01/01/1963**

Nuttall, Mr C, LRA Asst., Univ. of Edinburgh. [10014987] 14/11/2002 **ME**

Nuttall, Mrs J M, Unemployed. [45776] 23/05/1991 **ME**

Nuttall, Ms P A, BA MLS MCLIP, Catr., The Stationery Off., London. [30783] 04/04/1979 **CM18/05/1982**

Nutting, Mrs D E, BA MCLIP, Ret. [6196] 08/08/1967 **CM01/07/1990**

Nwajei, Mrs E F, BA MCLIP DipComp(Open), Admin. Asst., H. M. Revenue & Customs, St. Austell. [15177] 01/01/1968 **CM01/01/1971**

Nyambi, Miss E, Stud., Loughborough Univ., Leicestershire. [10016007] 11/02/2010 **ME**

Nye, Mr D V, BA MCLIP, Area Lib., Southern Area, W. Sussex C.C. L. Serv. [30499] 27/01/1979 **CM07/04/1982**

Nye, Ms N, BA(Hons) ACLIP, Subject Lib., Exeter Coll., Exeter. [64243] 22/02/2005 **ACL02/03/2010**

Nylinder, Ms A M, BA MA, Devel. Off., Kilburn L., London. [55411] 10/10/1997 **ME**

O

Oakden, Mr S, BA DipHE HND MCLIP, Learning Res. Support Off., Hull York Med. Sch. [21755] 08/01/1974 **RV27/11/2007 CM28/12/1977**

Oakes, Mr A J, Sr. Lib. Asst., Educ. L. Serv., Cheshire [10012670] 02/03/2009 **AF**

Oakes, Miss C, BA(Hons), Stud., Manchester Met. Univ. [10015120] 15/10/2009 **ME**

Oakes, Mr P B, BA MSc, Inf. Asst., CBA, London. [61569] 02/10/2002 **ME**

Oakes, Ms R M, BSc MSc(Econ) MCLIP, Inf. Asst., Univ. of Exeter [55374] 06/10/1997 **CM16/07/2003**

Oakley, Mrs A E, BA DipLib MCLIP, p. /t. Sch. Lib., Dame Allans Sch., Newcastle upon Tyne. [30387] 08/02/1979 **CM09/02/1981**

Oakley, Ms H J, BA(Hons) MA MCLIP, Learning Resources Mgr., Hillcroft Coll., Surrey. [44389] 03/10/1990 **CM20/09/1995**

Oakley, Mrs J E, BA MCLIP, Co. Inf. Lib., Worthing L., W. Sussex. [36278] 01/10/1983 **CM10/05/1988**

Oakley, Mr J N G, MCLIP, Snr. Mgr., The Runnymede Cent., Surrey. [18114] 04/10/1972 **CM01/07/1992**

Oakley, Dr T C, BA MSt MA MCLIP, Trainee Teacher, Univ. of Exeter. [49592] 19/11/1993 **CM21/07/1999**

Oaten, Mr T J, BA(Hons) MCLIP RD, Royal Navy [29774] 01/10/1978 **CM01/07/1994**

Oates, Miss J L, BA(Hons) MA MCLIP, Mgr.,Walter Harrison Law L., Univ. of Queensland. [49233] 14/10/1993 **CM22/07/1998**

Oates, Mrs M, MCLIP, Life Member. [10946] 26/03/1944 **CM01/01/1949**

Obasi, Mr J U, MA MCLIP, Retired. [10000683] 01/01/1962 **CM01/01/1970**

O'Beirne, Mr R, BA(Hons) MEd FCLIP, Dir. Learning Devel. & Res., Bradford Coll. [47150] 12/05/1992 **FE23/01/2008**

Oberhauser, Dr O C, FCLIP, Consortium Offr. /Sen. Lib., The Austrian L. Network, & Serv. Ltd., Vienna. [41161] 15/10/1987 **FE18/11/1998**

O'Boyle, Mr J, BSc MSc MCLIP, Sen. Info. Scientist, Napp Pharmacuticals Cambridge [60618] 06/05/1986 **CM06/05/1986**

Obradovic, Ms C L, BA MA MSc, Inf. Professional [62660] 26/09/2003 **ME**

O'Brien, Miss B M, BSc DipLib MCLIP, Tech. Off., Birmingham City Council. [33735] 09/02/1981 **CM23/08/1985**

O'Brien, Ms C P, BA DipLib MCLIP, Asst. Lib. - Staff Training & Devel., Boole L., Univ. Coll. Cork. [40038] 06/10/1986 **CM14/11/1990**

O'Brien, Miss E C, BA(Hons), Inf. Res. Lib., RCSEng. [10012367] 05/02/2009 **ME**

O'Brien, Mrs E, BA MCLIP, Life Member. [10952] 20/02/1960 **CM01/01/1963**

O'Brien, Ms F G, MA MCLIP, Academic Liason mgr. [36644] 27/10/1983 **CM23/03/1993**

O'Brien, Ms H M, BA(Hons) Dip. Lib MCLIP, Project Mngr. - Community Connection, Cent. L., Birmingham [10012555] 13/01/1984 **CM07/07/1987**

O'Brien, Mrs H, BA(Hons), Unknown Wiltshire Coll., Wiltshire. [45719] 07/05/1991 **ME**

O'Brien, Mrs I, Lic. Phil. Hist MA, Catr. - Early Printed Books, Brit. L. [66056] 11/09/2006 **ME**

O'Brien, Mrs J A, BA MCLIP, Learning Res. Facilitator, Kidderminster Coll., Worcs. [39386] 21/01/1986 **CM14/03/1990**

O'Brien, Miss K, MA DipLib MCLIP, Employment not known. [37722] 09/10/1984 **CM15/02/1989**

O'Brien, Mrs M P G, MCLIP, Inf. Researcher, KBR, Leatherhead. [11789] 07/11/1970 **RV19/10/2006** **CM06/08/1975**

O'Brien, Mrs P, BA(Hons) MCLIP, Lib., Chichester L., W. Sussex. [29905] 24/10/1978 **CM28/01/1983**

O'Brien, Mr R A, Learner Support Inf. Asst., Glasgow Caledonian Univ., Glasgow. [56344] 05/06/1998 **AF**

O'Byrne, Ms S, MCLIP, Inf. Specialist, Ontario Min. of the Environment, Canada. [60093] 04/03/1991 **CM16/12/1999**

O'Callaghan, Miss E M, BA DipLib MCLIP, Vernon Hochuli L., Kent Medway Public Health Observatory. [22944] 01/10/1974 **CM03/03/1978**

O'Callaghan, Mrs M C, BSc PGCE MSc MCLIP, Unknown. [37468] 01/10/1984 **CM17/05/2000**

O'Callaghan, Mrs S P, BA MCLIP, Unemployed. [33022] 13/10/1980 **CM30/07/1985**

O'Carroll, Ms V C, MCLIP, Customer Serv. Lib., Welwyn-Hatfield, Hertsmere [63916] 26/10/2004 **CM06/05/2009**

Ocock, Mr K F, MCLIP, Ref. Lib. -Customer Contact Cent., Christchurch City L., New Zealand. [10960] 05/10/1970 **CM09/07/1973**

O'Connell Edwards, Ms L A, BA MA MCLIP, Lib., Worcestershire C.C. [42336] 12/10/1988 **CM16/05/1990**

O'Connor, Ms A, BA HDipEd HDipLis, Lib., St Patrick Hosp., Cork, Ireland. [10000801] 06/11/2006 **ME**

O'Connor, Mrs C L, BA(Hons) DipIM MCLIP, Dep. L. Serv. Mgr., Gloucester Hosp. NHS Trust., Gloucester. [55782] 17/11/1997 **CM10/07/2002**

O'Connor, Ms C, Asst. Lib., Archway L., London. [10001054] 06/12/2006 **ME**

O'Connor, Miss D, Unknown. [10014274] 10/07/2009 **ME**

O'Connor, Miss E, BA, Inf. Offr., Rouse, London. [65679] 31/03/2006 **ME**

O'Connor, Ms E, DipLIS, Inf. Mgr., Yell Grp. Ltd., Reading. [58815] 07/08/2000 **ME**

O'Connor, Miss E, BA MA, Stud., Aberystwyth Univ. [10016439] 23/03/2010 **ME**

O'Connor, Mrs G, BA MCLIP, Comm. Lib., Marlborough L., Wilts. C.C. [35919] 17/01/1983 **CM27/02/1991**

O'Connor, Ms H, BSc DipLIS, Inf. Excutive., Enterprise Ireland, Dublin. [65415] 23/02/2006 **ME**

O'Connor, Mr K, Lib., NBS, Newcastle upon Tyne. [47784] 14/10/1992 **ME**

O'Connor, Ms L A, BA DipLib MCLIP MA, Inst. Lib. (Acting), Dundalk Inst. of Tech., Ireland. [33761] 12/02/1981 **CM14/10/1983**

O'Connor, Mr N M, BA MCLIP, L. Co-ordinator, St Philip Howard Catholic High Sch., W. Sussex. [10002871] 13/08/1980 **CM01/07/1994**

Oda, Mr M, BEd MA, Prof. & Head of Dept., Aoyama Gakuin Univ., Tokyo. [50501] 22/08/1994 **ME**

Oddy, Ms E, BA(Hons) MSc MCLIP, Head of Serv. and Operations, Newcastle Univ. [42270] 13/10/1988 **CM15/10/2002**

Oddy, Mrs J M, BA MCLIP, Life Member. [11100] 24/03/1954 **CM01/01/1956**

Odeinde, Mrs W A, MCLIP, Ch. Lib., Cent. L., Ebute-Metta, Lagos, Nigeria. [22100] 19/03/1956 **CM01/01/1964**

O'Dell, Mr F J, BSc(Hons), L. Asst., Northamptonshire Primary Care Trust [65766] 03/05/2006 **ME**

O'Dell, Mr T, Reader Dev. Offr., L.B. Lambeth [62692] 17/10/2003 **ME**

O'Deorain, Mr F A, BSc DipLib MCLIP, Asst. Lib., Univ. of Ulster, Derry. [33235] 10/10/1980 **CM21/12/1984**

O'Deorain, Mrs S, BLib MCLIP, p. /t. Asst. Lib., Univ. of Ulster, Magee Campus. [34640] 19/01/1982 **CM20/09/1985**

Odie, Mrs T H T, Sch. L. Asst., Anderson High Sch., Shetland. [64426] 16/03/2005 **AF**

Odintsov, Mr I N, Supermarket Asst., Waitrose [43801] 15/01/1990 **ME**

O'Doherty, Mrs P A, MCLIP, Sen. Lib., Medway Council, Gillingham L. [1088] 10/01/1966 **CM01/01/1970**

O'Donnell, Mrs E M, BA DipLib, Lib., Alleyn's Sch., London. [10001032] 25/11/2003 **ME**

O'Donnell, Mrs K H, BA Lic Ed. MCLIP, Lib., Balfron High Sch., Balfron. [62745] 09/10/2003 **CM02/02/2005**

O'Donnell, Mrs M E, BA DipLib, Lib. EDSU, W. Dunbartonshire Council, Scotland. [10003071] 22/10/1991 **ME**

O'Donnell, Mrs M L, MCLIP, Lib., Thomas Bennett Comm. Coll., Crawley. [19944] 15/01/1973 **CM19/07/1976**

O'Donnell, Mrs W A, BSc (Hons), Lib., Balwearie Jigh Sch., Kirkcaldy, Fife [10010360] 22/07/2008 **ME**

O'Donoghue, Ms K M, BA DipLib MCLIP, p. /t. Sch. Lib., Harrytown Catholic High Sch., Stockport. [26000] 03/04/1976 **CM19/03/1979**

O'Donovan, Mrs A, MA, Sch. Devel. Lib., Bucks C.C. L. Sev. [10009763] 09/06/2008 **ME**

O'Donovan, Mr K, BA MLIS, Unknown. [10015306] 30/10/2009 **ME**

O'Driscoll, Mrs C A, BA MCLIP, Dir. -Res. Europe, Russell Reynolds Assoc., London. [38040] 17/01/1985 **CM04/08/1987**

O'Driscoll, Ms G, BA DipLib, Early Years Lib. /Bookstart Co-ordinator, Brent L. [37156] 15/01/1984 **ME**

Ofei, Miss M E, Unwaged. [10010353] 21/07/2008 **AF**

Offord, Mrs A, Grp. Mgr. L., Maldon L., Essex. [10009343] 01/06/2008 **AF**

Offord, Mrs J A, L. Mgr. /Open Learn. Co-Ordinator., Royal Forest of Dean Coll., Coleford. [59546] 04/05/2001 **AF**

Offord, Mrs J D, BEd(Hons) DipLib MCLIP, Advisory Lib., SLS, Suffolk Co. Council. [36744] 25/11/1983 **CM08/03/1988**

O'Flynn, Miss H Y, BA MCLIP, Records Mgr., BIS, London [41031] 03/10/1987 **CM15/09/1993**

Ogden, Mr D, LLB DipLib MCLIP, Sen Lib, Min. of Justice, London. [36745] 24/11/1983 **CM20/01/1987**

Ogden, Mrs R C, Lib. Admin., St John's Coll., Oxford [10017067] 21/06/2010 **ME**

Ogilvie, Miss H D, MA DipLib MCLIP, Sen. Asst. Lib.,p. /t., Harrow L. [36507] 07/10/1983 **CM04/08/1987**

Ogilvie, Mrs K L, BA MCLIP, Lib. -Sch. L. Serv., Stockport M.B.C. [30569] 15/01/1979 **CM21/01/1983**

Ogleby, Miss J A, P. /t. Home-based Indexer, Transport Res. Lab., Berks. [37894] 23/10/1984 **ME**

O'Gorman, Ms S, BA MPHIL MLIS, Exec. Lib., Wexford CC. [10005868] 02/08/2007 **ME**

O'Grady, Mrs J M K, BSc Hons (Econ) MCLIP, L. & Resources Mgr, De La Salle Coll., Jersey. [53022] 06/02/1996 **CM16/05/2001**

Ogundipe, Mr A, MSc, BSc, Asst. Lib., Princess Alexandra Hosp., Harlow. [62121] 21/02/2003 **ME**

Ogundipe, Mr O O, MA FCLIP, Life Member and Fellow, L. Consultant, Retired, London & Nigeria. [17495] 20/02/1957 **FE01/01/1968**

Ogunleye, Miss O M, BA MSc, City & Islington Coll., London. [10016128] 16/02/2010 **ME**

Oguntomeso, Mrs E O, BSc, Unwaged. [10014884] 21/09/2009 **ME**

O'Hagan, Ms A, MLIS, Lib., Denton Wilde Sapte LLP. [10010573] 07/08/2008 **ME**

O'Hanlon, Miss B, BA(Hons) PGCE, Unknown. [10014184] 02/07/2009 **ME**

O'Hara, Mrs A, MSc MCLIP, Lib., Milton Keynes L. [58040] 20/10/1999 **CM29/11/2006**

O'Hara, Mr R, MBE FCLIP, Retired. [17499] 02/03/1963 **FE19/05/1978**

O'Hare, Mr L J, BA(Hons) DipEd DipLib MCLIP, p. /t. Lib., Southern Reg. Coll., Newry [39920] 02/10/1986 **CM19/01/2000**

O'Hare, Miss R, MA PGDipILS MCLIP, Lib., The Mitchell Lib., Glasgow [56787] 15/10/1998 **CM17/09/2003**

O'Hea, Miss C, Stud., Strathclyde Univ. [10015119] 15/10/2009 **ME**

Ojo, Mr L O, B. LIS, Unknown. [10012549] 19/02/2009 **ME**

O'Kane, Mr Q, MA MCLIP, Head of Learning Resources, Bournemouth & Poole Coll. of F. E., Poole. [29469] 22/08/1978 **CM17/11/1980**

O'Kane-Walls, Mrs M, Stud. [10004961] 06/06/2007 **ME**

Okanu-Igwela, Mrs N J B, Ref. Lib., Rivers State Univ. of Sci. & Tech., Nigeria. [65824] 18/05/2006 **ME**

Okechukwu, Mrs N, Lib., Lagos Business Sch., Nigeria. [10016689] 27/04/2010 **ME**

O'Kelly, Ms J L, BA MCLIP, p. /t Sch. Lib., Aylesbury. [22651] 29/07/1974 **CM01/10/1976**

Oketunji, Dr I, BLS (Hons) MLS Phd, Inf. Serv. Mgr., ROSPA, Birmingham. [10006664] 20/11/2007 **ME**

Okonkwo, Mrs A, Position unknown, S. Norwood L., London. [10000720] 13/11/2006 **ME**

Okpokam, Miss A L, BA(Hons), Lib. & inf. Asst., Northumbria Univ., Newcastle [10014928] 01/10/2009 **ME**

Okure, Miss C, BLS MCLIP, Dep. Lib., City Coll. Coventry. Butts. [49925] 24/01/1994 **CM19/07/2000**

Okwok, Mrs E, BSc, Learning Resources Mgr., Kaplan Holborn Coll., London. [10007775] 30/10/1997 **ME**

Oladapo, Mrs O, L. Asst., Treasury Solicitors Dept., London. [63527] 17/06/2004 **AF**

Oladjins, Ms E, MA DipILS MCLIP, Accessions Lib., Aberdeenshire L. & Inf. Serv., Oldmeldrum [57098] 09/12/1998 **CM18/09/2002**

Olandzobo, Mrs D, Prison Lib., HMP Woodhill, Milton Keynes. [10013333] 12/02/2010 **ME**

Olasina, Mr G, Lect., Univ of Ilorin, Nigeria [10001602] 26/02/2007 **ME**

Olcese, Mrs E, BA(Hons), Stud., Aberystwyth. [62671] 02/10/2003 **ME**

Oldcorn, Mr D J, BA(Hons) DipLib MCLIP, L. Mgr., Helston L. [31679] 11/10/1979 **CM24/01/1984**

Oldcorn, Mr P G, BA(Hons) Dip Lib MCLIP, Pub. Info. Offr., Lancs. Co. Lib., Preston [10012947] 31/01/1982 **CM27/02/1991**

Olden, Dr E A, BA MLS PhD FCLIP, Sen. Lect., Thames Valley Univ. [17512] 23/07/1972 **FE12/09/2001**

Oldfield, Mrs C A, BA(Hons) MCLIP, Teaching Asst. [39190] 06/01/1986 **CM18/01/1989**

Oldfield, Ms C, Site Coordinator/Cultural Servs. Adv., Lincolnshire Ls., Lincolnshire. [65886] 27/06/2006 **AF**

Oldfield, Mrs D M, FCLIP, Life Member. [7358] 08/03/1940 **FE01/01/1954**

Oldfield, Ms J M, BSc MCLIP MA, Dep. Lib., The London L. [30859] 27/04/1979 **CM10/05/1984**

Oldham, Miss C A, BA MA DipLib MCLIP, Lib., Forestry Commission, Forest Res. Station,Farnham,Sy. [33330] 20/11/1980 **CM04/04/1984**

Oldham, Mrs C M, Sen. Researcher, Irwin Mitchell, Sheffield. [62059] 07/02/2003 **ME**

Oldman, Miss C L, BA(Hons), Grad. Trainee, Emmanuel Coll., Cambridge. [63827] 07/10/2004 **ME**

Oldman, Mrs H, MA MA MCLIP, Head of Learning Resources., Grammar Sch., Leeds. [53848] 04/10/1996 **CM19/07/2000**

Oldridge, Mr P, BSc(Hons) AMINSTP ACLIP, Customer Serv. Lib., E. Herts & Broxbourne Dist., Herts. [64306] 25/02/2005 **ACL06/02/2008**

Oldridge, Mrs R V, BA(Hons) MSc, Digital Resource Mgr., Univ. of Bedfordshire. [57633] 03/06/1999 **ME**

Oldrini, Mrs S R, BSc(Hons) DipLib MCLIP, Customer Serv. Mgr. [46728] 02/01/1992 **CM22/03/1995**

Oldroyd, Mrs M E, BA MLib HonFCLIP, Staffing & Quality Mgr., De Montford Univ., Leicester. [13811] 01/10/1970 **FE15/09/2005**

Oldroyd, Mr R E, BA MA DipLib FCLIP, Retired. [30344] 15/02/1968 **FE25/05/1994**

O'Leary, Miss R, BA(Hons) MSc MCLIP, Web Content Mgr., Riba Enterprises, Newcastle Upon Tyne. [48271] 20/11/1992 **CM16/11/1994**

Oliff, Mrs L, Sen. Learning Resources Co-ordinator, Southwark Coll., London. [51608] 10/04/1995 **AF**

Oliff, Ms W J, BA, Team Leader-Serials – London Southbank Univ. [43449] 26/10/1989 **ME**

Olive, Mr J M, MA MCLIP, Retired. [11001] 29/10/1964 **CM01/01/1967**

Olive, Mrs M D B, MCLIP, Lib., Charterhouse, Surrey [56307] 06/05/1998 **CM21/05/2008**

Oliver, Mr A, Buisness Dev. Dir., Ex Libris (UK) LTD, Middlesex [45264] 20/09/1990 **AF**

Oliver, Miss B A, BA, Unknown. [10005378] 25/07/2007 **ME**

Oliver, Mr I C, BA(Hons) DipInf/Lib, Enquiries Lib., Keele Univ. Inf. Serv., Staffs. [42916] 19/04/1989 **ME**

Oliver, Mrs J A, BA(Hons) MA MCLIP, Resource & Proj. Lib., Queen Elizabeth Hosp., Birmingham. [55779] 17/11/1997 **CM15/05/2002**

Oliver, Mrs J M, BSc(Hons) MCLIP, Performance & Off. Serv. Lib., L.B. Bexley, Sidup [49732] 25/11/1993 **CM22/05/1996**

Oliver, Mrs J M, Unknown. [10014060] 23/06/2009 **AF**

Oliver, Miss J S, BA MCLIP, Lib., Reading & Learning L., Bor. of Poole. [11002] 17/03/1971 **CM12/01/1973**

Oliver, Mrs J, BSc MCLIP, Customer Serv. Mgr., Teeside Univ., Middlesbrough. [47344] 17/07/1992 **CM09/11/2005**

Oliver, Miss K M, BA MCLIP, Retired. [19055] 09/12/1963 **CM01/01/1967**

Oliver, Miss L S, MSc MA, L. & Inf. Serv. Mgr., Ashridge [51385] 01/02/1995 **ME**

Oliver, Mrs S N, BSc (Hons), Lib. Asst., Trust L., Queen Elizabeth Hosp., Gateshead. [10015219] 27/10/2009 **AF**

Oliver, Mr T, BA(Hons) MSc MCLIP, Sch. Lib. Bathgate Academy, W. Lothian Council [61029] 07/02/2002 **CM31/01/2007**

Olivier, Mr D, Unknown. [10009170] 01/06/2010 **AF**

Ollerenshaw, Mrs H E, BA(Hons) MSc DMS MCLIP, Med. Faculty Lib., Univ. of Bristol. [56165] 01/04/1998 **CM08/01/2002**

Olliver, Mrs A S, BA MCLIP, Br. Lib., Denton L. [21919] 30/01/1974 **CM20/05/1976**

Olney, Ms S D, MA DipLib MCLIP, H. of Collection Storage, Brit. L., Operations & Serv. [35220] 07/10/1982 **CM06/10/1987**

Olorunkosebi, Mr D O, BA, Unwaged. [10015237] 28/10/2009 **ME**

Olsen, Mr A J, BA MCLIP, Retired. [11009] 01/04/1970 **CM26/01/1973**

Olulode, Ms A S, BA(Hons) MA, Literacy Devel. L., L.B. of Lambeth, London. [59904] 31/10/2001 **ME**

Oluwabiyi, Mrs M O, Lib., Ajayi Crowther Univ., Oyo, Nigeria. [10015638] 07/01/2010 **ME**

O'Mahony, Ms M M, BA MA HDipLIS, Knowledge Mgr., RDASH NHS Foundation Trust, Doncaster. [10009364] 25/04/2002 **ME**

Omar, Mrs D J, BA(Hons) MSc MCLIP, Inf. Specialist, Kingston Univ. L. [59656] 07/11/2001 **CM08/12/2004**

Omissi, Mrs L, BA(Hons) MA MCLIP, Sen. Lib., Young Readers Serv., Jersey L., St. Helier. [55019] 01/07/1997 **CM17/11/1999**

Omokaro, Mr G N, BSc(Hons), Com. Helpdesk Admin. (Vol. Work), London Metro. Univ. [59695] 08/08/2001 **ME**

Omordia, Mrs A N, Dep. Lib., Royal Courts of Justice, London. [66060] 06/09/2006 **ME**

Omotayo, Mrs M, BA(Hons) PGDip PGCert, Cent. Enquiry Point Mgr., MHRA, London [61052] 01/02/2002 **ME**

O'Neil, Miss K J, BA MCLIP, Princ. Lib. – Yth. Serv., Bedford C.C. [41726] 24/02/1988 **CM17/10/1990**

O'Neill, Ms A M, BA MA MCLIP, Lib. Serv. Mgr. [55698] 04/11/1997 **CM04/02/2004**

O'Neill, Ms A M, LLB DipLP, Stud. [10015294] 30/10/2009 **ME**

O'Neill, Miss C J, MCLIP, Life Member. [11016] 18/03/1959 **CM01/01/1970**

O'Neill, Mrs C M, BA PGCE PGC, Stud. [65829] 23/05/2006 **ME**

O'Neill, Mr D J, MCLIP, Head of Learning Res., Anglo European Coll. of Chiropratic, Bournemouth. [27202] 14/01/1977 **CM01/01/1981**

O'Neill, Mrs G C, BA MCLIP, Unemployed. [30116] 14/01/1979 **CM30/06/1982**

O'Neill, Ms H A, BA(Hons) MSc MCLIP, Head of Reader Serv.,London L., London. [46456] 07/11/1991 **CM16/07/2003**

O'Neill, Mrs H G, BA MCLIP, Retired. [6595] 22/01/1969 **CM26/03/1973**

O'Neill, Ms K M, MA, MSc, MPHIL, Asst. Lib., Sotheby's Inst. of Art. [10006548] 17/11/2003 **ME**

O'Neill, Ms K, BA(Hons), Lib., St. George's Internat. Sch., Montreux, Switzerland [10006322] 16/10/2007 **AF**

O'Neill, Mrs L, BA MLib, Community Devel. L., Burngreave L., Sheffield. [62761] 20/10/2003 **ME**

O'Neill, Mr M S, BSc MCLIP, Tech. Editor, ISO, Switzerland. [60567] 11/12/2001 **CM01/04/2002**

O'Neill, Mrs R, ACLIP, Subject Lib., Croydon Coll. [10006199] 18/09/2007 **ACL03/12/2008**

Onuchina, Miss N, Unwaged. [10013427] 04/06/2009 **AF**

Oparinde, Mr S A, BSc(Hons) MSc DipIM DMS, Br. Lib., Battersea Park L., Wandsworth Council. [47518] 22/09/1992 **ME**

Oppenheim, Prof C, BSc PhD FCLIP HonFCLIP, Prof. Inf. Sci., Loughborough Univ., Leics. [46639] 29/11/1991 **FE16/09/1992**

Oppenheimer, Mrs K C, BA(Hons) MCLIP, Lib., Assoc. for Advanced Rabbinical & Talmudical Sch., New York. [46155] 07/10/1991 **CM09/11/2005**

Oram, Mrs M A, MCLIP, Retired. [6191] 31/01/1969 **CM20/07/1972**

Orchard, Mrs C, BA, Lib. Volunteer, Moorland Res. L., Edale [10001961] 22/03/2007 **ME**

Ord, Miss S, BA MCLIP, Unemployed. [42169] 06/10/1988 **CM18/09/1991**

Ordidge, Mrs I, BSc DipLib MCLIP, Asst. Dir. LIS, Univ. of Wolverhampton [33648] 20/01/1981 **CM06/12/1985**

O'Regan, Mr J A, BA MCLIP, Asst. Bibl. Serv. Mgr., City Univ., London. [28353] 03/11/1977 **CM10/11/1982**

O'Reilly, Miss M, Stud., Univ. of Sheffield [10015693] 14/01/2010 **ME**

Orfanou-Raftopoulou, Ms E, BScEcon PgDip, Lib. Researcher, Univ. of Patras, Greece. [10000948] 01/12/2006 **ME**

Orford, Mr J P, BSc Econ PGDip MCLIP, Unwaged. [10013187] 03/04/2009 **CM22/07/1998**

Organ, Mrs C H, MA DipLib MCLIP, PMS Subject Lib., NHS L., Treliske Hosp., Truro. [36753] 21/11/1983 **CM19/08/1992**

Orlandi, Mrs A, MA, Stud., UCL. [10009222] 06/05/2008 **ME**

Orme, Mrs S P, MSc BSc MCLIP, Business Analyst [47288] 20/09/1977 **CM20/05/1980**

Orme, Ms V J D, MCLIP, Asst. Lib., Oxford Univ. [64950] 03/10/2005 **CM20/04/2009**

Ormiston, Ms T M, BA MA MSc MCLIP, Data Serv. Dir., IMS Health, London. [60507] 10/06/2001 **CM10/06/2001**

Orna, Ms E, MA DipLib PhD FCLIP, Self-Employed, Inf. Consultant, Orna Inf. & Editorial Consultancy, Norwich. [20478] 01/04/1973 **FE01/04/2002**

Orna, Ms M M, MA MCLIP, Retired. [1086] 02/10/1971 **CM05/12/1974**

O'Rourke, Mr D T, BSc MCLIP DipHSW, Retired. [11038] 01/01/1953 **CM01/01/1956**

Orpen, Mrs A, MCLIP BSc, Sch. Lib., St Andrew's Sch. for Girls., Johannesburg, S.-Africa [20275] 21/02/1973 **CM02/09/1976**

Orr, Mr A J, BMus PGDip MCLIP, Sen. Lit. Dev. Offr., Blackburn with Darwen Bor. Council. Blackburn. [59970] 14/11/2001 **CM17/09/2008**

Orr, Mr C A, Sch. Lib. [66122] 01/10/2006 **ME**

Orr, Mrs P, BA(Hons) DipILS MCLIP, Knowledge Supp. Lib., N. Cumbria Univ. Hosp. NHSTrust., Carlisle. [46673] 06/12/1991 **CM19/03/2008**

Orr, Mr R, Head of Res./Red Team Leader, Warfare Dev. Grp., Warminster. [10016930] 10/06/2010 **ME**

Orr, Mr S A, BSc MSc, Unknown. [62621] 18/09/2003 **ME**

Orsborn, Ms L E A, MA MCLIP, Chamber's Dir., London. [21657] 05/01/1974 **CM15/09/1976**

Ortega, Miss M S L, BA(Hons) MLib MCLIP, Academic Subject Lib., Univ. of Lincoln. [48093] 06/11/1992 **CM24/07/1996**

Orton, Mr G I J, BA MSc DMA FRSA MILAM MIMgt MCLIP, Dir. of Community Serv., Bor. of Broxbourne. [11046] 25/01/1968 **CM01/01/1973**

Orton, Mr R, MA(Hons) MSc MCLIP, Inf. Researcher., Chartered Mgmnt. Inst., Northants. [57216] 20/01/1999 **CM09/09/2009**

Osafo, Mrs L, BA MA, Sen. Lib., Bristol Grammar Sch. [61563] 02/10/2002 **ME**

Osakwe, Mrs B L, BA(Hons) DipLib MCLIP, Learning Cent. Mgr., Stanmore Coll., Mddx. [10002180] 02/10/1987 **CM21/07/1989**

Osborn, Ms H, MLib MCLIP, Dir. of Serv. Delivery, N. Ireland Lib. Auth. [33497] 13/01/1981 **CM16/05/1984**

Osborn, Ms K, MA BA MCLIP, Mental Health Lib., Berkshire Shared Serv. Prospect Park Hosp., Reading. [61632] 08/10/2002 **CM21/03/2007**

Osborn, Mr R M, BA AKC DipLib, Strategic Lib. Serv. Devel. Mgr., NHS London [37413] 30/08/1984 **ME**

Osborne, Mrs A S, BSc DipLib MCLIP, Learning Advisor, St. Marys Coll., Twickenham. [30203] 11/01/1979 **CM30/01/1981**

Osborne, Mrs A V, MCLIP, Learning Cent. Lib., Dixons Allerton Academy, Allerton, Bradford, W. Yorks. [927] 01/01/1969 **CM01/01/1971**

Osborne, Mr A, Msc BA(Hons) FHEA MCLIP, Head of L. Serv., Dept. of Health, Leeds [10016280] 27/10/1989 **CM18/07/1991**

Osborne, Ms E S, BA(Hons) PGCE MA MCLIP, Info. Servs. Mgr., Greater London Auth. [50803] 18/10/1994 **CM20/11/2002**

Osborne, Mrs J E, MA DipLib MCLIP, Life Member. [30021] 05/11/1978 **CM04/01/1983**

Osborne, Mrs L M, BA MCLIP, Dir., SWRLS [10972] 26/07/1972 **CM31/07/1975**

Osborne, Mr M R, BA(Hons), Community & Inf. Offr., N. Yorkshire C.C., Ripon. [63302] 08/04/2004 **ME**

Osborne, Ms S F, BA MSc MCLIP Dip RSA, Sen. Inf. Adviser, Better Choices Ltd., Manchester. [35309] 06/10/1982 **CM05/04/1988**

Osborne, Mrs S L, BA(Hons) MCLIP, Sen. L. Asst., Univ. of Nottingham. [50882] 26/10/1994 **CM15/03/2000**

Osborne, Mrs S M, RGN, Sch. Lib., Mary Webb Sch. & Sci. Coll., Pontesbury, Salop [10001703] 02/03/2007 **AF**

Osgathorpe, Miss E J, BA MA MCLIP, Unknown. [59175] 05/12/2000 **CM28/10/2004**

O'Shaughnessy, Mr P E, BA(Hons) DipInfLib, Asst. Lib., Univ. of the W. of England, Bristol. [47447] 18/08/1992 **ME**

O'Shea, Miss L H, MA PGDipIM MCLIP, Asst. L., Barbican L., London. [58201] 16/11/1999 **CM23/01/2008**

Osler, Mr G, PG Cert., Lib. Asst., Liverpool L. [10016929] 10/06/2010 **AF**

Osman, Miss E A, BA(Hons) MA, Lib., Henley Bus. Sch. [63767] 06/10/2004 **ME**

Osman, Ms S J, MA MSc MCLIP, Night Team Mgr., Kingston Univ., Kingston Upon Thames [42955] 03/05/1989 **CM12/12/1990**

Osman-Weyers, Miss I, BA, Sch. Lib. [65739] 10/04/2006 **ME**

Osment, Mrs M E, MCLIP, Co. Libr., [60480] 06/07/2000 **CM06/07/2000**

Ostler, Mrs E K, BA(Hons) DipILS MCLIP, Child. Lib., Hants. L. & Inf., Ringwood. [48407] 06/01/1993 **CM19/03/1997**

O'Sullivan, Miss C A, BA MCLIP, Systems & Bibl. Serv. Mgr., St. Mary's Uni Coll., Twickenham. [35507] 14/10/1982 **CM18/11/1993**

O'Sullivan, Miss C, Unknown. [10008275] 23/06/2009 **AF**

O'Sullivan, Mr K M C, BA(Hons) MA MSc(Econ) MCLIP, Sr. Rare Books Lib., Univ. of Aberdeen [52814] 18/12/1995 **CM19/07/2000**

O'Sullivan, Mr M, MA MLIS, Unwaged. [10014851] 18/09/2009 **ME**

O'Sullivan, Mr T J, BSc(Hons) MSc, Inf. Offr., Clifford Chance, LLP, London. [56090] 06/02/1998 **ME**

O'Sullivan, Mrs V M, MCLIP, Child. Lib., Hants. C.C. Ls., Winchester. [21886] 20/01/1974 **CM07/07/1976**

Oswald, Mr N, BA DipLib, Unemployed. [39016] 24/10/1985 **ME**

Otim, Mrs N R, Volunteer Support Offr, Nat. Assoc. for Colitis & Crohns Disease, St Albans [65281] 28/11/2005 **ME**

O'Toole, Miss P M, MCLIP, Lib. Inf. Team, Cambs. L. & Inf., Co. L. H.Q. [11073] 01/01/1970 **CM01/01/1973**

O'Toole, Miss T, ACLIP, Div. Operations Super. and L. Inf Asst. (js), Stratford L., Stratford-upon-Avon, Warks. [10002055] 28/03/2007 **ACL16/07/2008**

Ottaway, Ms J, BA MCLIP, Retired. [36411] 06/10/1983 **CM05/04/1988**

Ott-Bissels, Mrs S P, MA MA MCLIP, Catr., The London L., London. [52723] 27/11/1995 **CM19/07/2000**

Ottley, Mrs H E, BA(Hons) MCLIP, Career Break [50905] 28/10/1994 **CM12/09/2001**

Otty, Miss P, Unemployed. [52159] 09/10/1995 **ME**

Outhwaite, Miss H K, BA(Hons) MSc MCLIP, Knowledge Mgr., Yorkshire and Humber Public Health Observatory, York. [52602] 13/11/1995 **RV22/06/2007 CM25/07/2001**

Ovenden, Mr D, BA DipLib MCLIP, Sen. Inf. Offr. (Acquisitions), Liverpool John Moores Univ. [31410] 28/09/1979 **CM18/12/1981**

Ovenden, Mr R, BA DipLib MA, Keeper of Special Collections, Bodleian L., Oxford. [39917] 02/10/1986 **ME**

Ovens, Mr J P, BA(Hons) MCLIP, Resource & Inf. Coordinator, Bristol Primary Care Trust. [49605] 19/11/1993 **CM24/07/1996**

Overall, Ms L A, BSc(Hons), Asst. Lib., Mid Essex PCT NHS Trust [50517] 31/08/1994 **ME**

Overend, Mrs S A, BA DipLib, Reader Serv. Lib., Oxon. Mental Healthcare NHS Trust, Oxford. [35265] 05/10/1982 **ME**

Overin, Mrs C A, MCLIP, Lib. Mgr., Middlesbrough L. & Inf., Middlesbrough. [13204] 25/01/1968 **CM15/12/1973**

Overington, Mr M A, MA PhD FCLIP, Life Member. [17530] 19/09/1955 **FE01/01/1967**

Owen, Ms A J, BA(Hons) MA, Lib., Mundays LLP [51643] 25/04/1995 **ME**

Owen, Mrs A J, BA, Sch. Devel. Lib., Educ. L. Serv., Wednesfield. [54575] 23/01/1997 **ME**

Owen, Mrs A, BA(Hons), Subject Lib., TVU, Reading [59903] 26/10/2001 **ME**

Owen, Mrs C A, BA MCLIP, L. Serv. Mgr., W. Berks. Council, Newbury. [29112] 31/01/1978 **CM05/07/1982**

Owen, Mrs D E, BA MCLIP, L. Mgr., Chester L., Cheshire C. C [40386] 26/01/1987 **CM27/07/1994**

Owen, Mr D, OBE BA DipLib MCLIP, Consultant. [11089] 10/10/1965 **CM01/01/1968**

Owen, Miss K A, BA(Hons) DipILS MCLIP, Inf. Serv. Lib., Vale of Glamorgan Pub. Ls., Barry. [49302] 20/10/1993 **CM17/11/1999**

Owen, Mrs K, BA FCLIP, Serv. Mgr., Customers Staff & Devel., Notts. C.C. [33332] 03/11/1980 **FE13/06/2007**

Owen, Mrs M O W, MCLIP, Lib., Cent. for Advanced Welsh & Celtic Studies, Aberystwyth. ` [11101] 09/04/1965 **CM01/01/1969**

Owen, Mrs M, Law Lib., Bangor Univ. [45253] 06/09/1990 **ME**

Owen, Mr M, BA MCLIP, Life Member. [19234] 14/09/1956 **CM01/01/1963**

Owen, Mrs S J, BLib MCLIP MBA, Sen. L. Asst., Wrighton Wigan & Leigh NHS Trust. [39469] 05/02/1986 **CM13/06/1990**

Owen, Mrs T J, BSc(Hons) MCLIP, Lib., Liverpool PCT, Liverpool. [55579] 21/10/1997 **CM19/03/2008**

Owen-McGee, Mr D J, BA(Hons) MA MCLIP FHEA, IT Advisor & Dev., LIS Univ. of Derby. [57670] 01/07/1999 **CM07/09/2005**

Owens, Ms A J, BA MCLIP, Child. Lib., Barbican L., London. [32530] 24/04/1980 **CM24/10/1983**

Owens, Miss C J O, MA PGDipLIS MCLIP, Lib., High Sch. of Dundee, Dundee. [62729] 13/10/2003 **CM31/01/2007**

Owens, Miss J, BA, Grad. Lib. Trainee, Univ. of Bath, Bath [10015025] 07/10/2009 **ME**

Owens, Mrs S M, BA(Hons), Div. Mgr. (L., Learning & Culture), Durham CC. [10005255] 02/09/1993 **ME**

Owen-Strong, Mrs M, MA, Stud., Aberystwyth Univ. [10015779] 25/01/2010 **ME**

Owopetu, Mr T, Stud. [10011200] 02/10/2008 **ME**

Owston, Ms F C, BA MCLIP, Market Analyst, BT, Ipswich. [29782] 05/10/1978 **CM11/11/1980**

Owston, Mr J A, BA MCLIP, Retired. [21819] 19/09/1953 **CM23/08/1963**

Owusu, Mrs P A, BA DipLib MCLIP, Unwaged. [30986] 03/07/1979 **CM21/09/1982**

Oxborrow, Miss K M, BA, Unwaged. [10011341] 09/10/2008 **ME**

Oxford, Miss S A, BA(Hons), Academic Liaison Lib., Inst. for Educ., Univ. of Worcester. [63720] 09/09/2004 **ME**

Oyebo, Mrs Y G, BA(Hons) PGDE MLS, Head Document Mgmnt., First Bank Nigeria plc. [57821] 24/08/1999 **ME**

Oyedoh, Mrs M, BSc MSc, Lib., St Edward's Sch., Oxford. [61142] 08/03/2002 **ME**

Oza, Ms H, MA, Post Processing, Royal Mail Grp. Plc. [10010232] 01/02/2010 **AF**

P

Pace, Mr C L, BA DipLib MCLIP, Unwaged. [33666] 18/01/1981 **CM10/10/1985**

Pacelli, Mrs D, Lib. Asst., Kings Langley S. S., Herts. [10012970] 17/03/2009 **AF**

Pacey, Mrs G K, BA DMS MCLIP, Retired [11123] 14/10/1968 **CM01/01/1972**

Pachent, Ms G J, BA DLIS MILAM MIMgt MCLIP, Serv. Dir., Suffolk C.C., Ipswich [24770] 01/10/1975 **CM31/10/1977**

Pacht, Miss D, BA(Hons), Ref. Specialist, Brit. L., London. [10002629] 20/04/2007 **ME**

Pachuca, Ms E J, Customer Account Advisor, MMU, Manchester. [10016126] 18/02/2010 **ME**

Pacitti, Mrs M K, BA(Hons) MCLIP, English Teacher, Japan [55665] 07/11/1997 **CM13/03/2002**

Packard, Mrs S A, BSc(Hons) MCLIP, Digital Resources Coordinator., Anglia Ruskin Univ., Chelmsford. [54740] 01/04/1997 **CM15/09/2004**

Packer, Mrs J, BA(Hons) PgDip, Sen. L. Asst., Aboyne L., Aboyne. [10013720] 22/05/2009 **ME**

Packer, Miss N, BA(Hons) MA MCLIP, Lib., Queens Coll., London [62690] 17/10/2003 **CM21/06/2006**

Packwood, Mrs A, MCLIP, Asst. Lib., Anglia Ruskin Univ., Cambridge. [47018] 01/04/1992 **CM11/03/2009**

Padalino, Ms V, BA(Hons) MSc, L. Mgr., Highgate L., London. [10006534] 01/06/2005 **ME**

Paddock, Miss L J, BSc (Hons), Stud., Robert Gordon Univ. [10014877] 18/09/2009 **ME**

Paddock, Mrs R E, BA DipLib MCLIP, Stock Dev. Lib., Hampshire Lib. & InfoServ., c/o Lymington Lib., [35813] 17/01/1983 **CM11/11/1986**

Paddon, Ms P, BA MCLIP, Lib., Cambs C.C., St Ives. [40116] 15/10/1986 **CM26/02/1992**

Paddon, Ms T C, BSc(Hons) MSc Dip AppSS MCLIP, Young People's Serv. Mgr., Newport Cent. L., S. Wales. [57700] 01/07/1999 **RV30/04/2007** **CM19/11/2003**

Paddy, Mrs L, BA(Hons) DipLib MCLIP, Sr. FOI Mgr., Dept. of Health, London. [37511] 03/10/1984 **CM15/05/1989**

Padgham, Mrs S, BA MCLIP, Lib., Crewe L., Crewe [33203] 13/10/1980 **CM27/07/1983**

Padiwa, Mr T, Asst. Lib., BSIX Sixth Form Brookehouse, London [10012347] 19/02/2009 **AF**

Padley, Miss B, MCLIP, Retired. [20083] 28/03/1955 **CM01/01/1960**

Padley, Ms W A, Inf. Offr., De Montfort Univ., Leicester. [63496] 15/06/2004 **ME**

Page, Ms A C, BA(Hons) MSc MCLIP, Clinical Support Lib., Wrightington, Wigan & Leigh NHS Foundation Trust [47916] 26/10/1992 **CM10/03/2010**

Page, Miss A M, BA DipLib MCLIP, Study Cent. Mgr., Surrey C.C. [29280] 18/05/1978 **CM11/01/1982**

Page, Mr B F, FCLIP, Retired. [11136] 17/01/1950 **FE01/01/1968**

Page, Mrs C L, BA MCLIP, Lib., Ipswich High Sch. [30579] 14/02/1979 **CM03/09/1981**

Page, Mrs H M, MCLIP, Lib., Knutsford High Sch., Cheshire C.C. [25025] 29/10/1975 **CM02/10/1978**

Page, Mrs I, MCLIP, Retired. [11140] 20/02/1961 **CM01/01/1966**

Page, Mrs S, BSc DipLIS MCLIP, Princ. Asst. Lib., L.B. of Redbridge, Cent. L. [44460] 10/10/1990 **CM23/03/1994**

Page, Mr T, BA MA, Stud. [10017086] 22/06/2010 **ME**

Page, Ms T, BA(Hons) MA MCLIP, Unwaged. [53824] 03/10/1996 **CM19/07/2000**

Paget-Woods, Ms J, BA(Hons) DipLib MCLIP, L. Learning Environment and Inf. Serv. Mgr., Univ. Plymouth, Plymouth. [44436] 08/10/1990 **CM26/05/1993**

Pailing, Mrs E M, MA, Sch. L. Liaison Offr., Guille-Alles L., Guernsey. [61988] 07/01/2003 **ME**

Pailing, Mrs K, BA(Hons), Faculty Lib., UCA Farnham L., Farnham. [10007993] 03/03/2008 **ME**

Paine, Miss J E, MCLIP, Sen. L. Asst., Univ. Coll. London. [11157] 12/08/1968 **CM01/01/1972**

Paine, Ms K P, BA(Hons) MA MCLIP, Sen. L. Asst., L. S. E, London. [54663] 12/02/1997 **CM03/10/2007**

Painter, Mrs M J, BLib MCLIP, Darwen L. Mgr. [33982] 30/06/1981 **CM14/10/1985**

Painting, Miss J, MCLIP, Inf. Serv. Mgr., Portsmouth City Council, Portsmouth. [10001027] 15/10/1974 **CM01/01/1977**

Pairman, Mrs C P, BA MCLIP, Childrens Lib., Alloa. [19633] 25/10/1972 **CM31/03/1990**

Pairpoint, Ms K, Asst. Lib., V&A Mus., London. [63330] 16/04/2004 **ME**

Paknadel, Mr S, BA(Hons), Lib., Ashurst LLP, London. [62032] 22/01/2003 **ME**

Palfery, Mr R G, BA MSc PGCE MCLIP, Business Performance Mgr., L. Inf. Heritage & Arts Serv., Royal Bor. of Windsor & Maidenhead [62664] 01/10/2003 **CM09/07/2008**

Palfrey, Ms M, BA(Hons) MA MCLIP, Team Lib., Reading Bor. Council. [59992] 16/11/2001 **CM21/05/2008**

Palka, Mrs J B, BA DipLib MCLIP, Lib. [26587] 12/10/1976 **CM18/03/1980**

Pallister, Mrs S M, BA MCLIP, Unwaged. [20530] 04/04/1973 **CM16/11/1977**

Pallot, Miss S, SRN MCLIP, Head of Knowledge and Inf. Serv., Heatherwood & Wexham Pk. Hosp. NHS Foundation Trust, Slough. [23943] 31/01/1975 **CM10/08/1979**

Palmer, Ms B J, B MUS DipLib MCLIP, Asst. Lib., Royal Academy of Music, London. [29784] 06/10/1978 **CM04/03/1982**

Palmer, Mrs C, BA(Hons) MA MCLIP, Head of Inf. Mgmnt, Charltons, Hong Kong [55750] 13/11/1997 **RV01/10/2008** **CM12/03/2003**

Palmer, Mrs D M, MBE, Freelance Consultant. [11169] 06/02/1969 **HFE16/06/1978**

Palmer, Mrs F A, BA(Hons) MA, Inf. Adv., Business Link Leicestershire, Leicester. [10015281] 09/11/1994 **ME**

Palmer, Dr J M P, BSc DipLib PhD MCLIP FCLIP, Retired. [17540] 23/03/1972 **FE21/05/1997**

Palmer, Mrs J M, B. Lib (Hons) MCLIP, Serv. Devel. Lib., Cirencester Bingham L., Gloucestershire. [10009354] 11/05/1981 **CM04/04/1984**

Palmer, Mrs J S, BA MCLIP, Serv. Mgr., Saffron Walden P. L., Essex. [25709] 29/02/1976 **CM22/08/1980**

Palmer, Mrs J T, BA MA, Intranet Editor, MOD, London. [64134] 19/01/2005 **ME**

Palmer, Dr J, BA(Hons) MA DPhil PgDip MCLIP, Unknown. [10014751] 05/02/1977 **CM01/07/1994**

Palmer, Ms K, BA MCLIP, Sen. Inf. Offr., Simmons & Simmons, London. [41739] 02/03/1988 **CM23/03/1993**

Palmer, Mr M E, MA(Cantab) MSc, Content Editor, CAB Internat., Wallingford. [51450] 15/02/1995 **ME**

Palmer, Mrs M, MCLIP, Dist. Mgr., Ribble Valley, Lancashire C.C., Preston. [26139] 21/06/1976 **CM29/08/1980**

Palmer, Mr M, BA MBA MCMI MCLIP, Principal Offr., Lib., Essex C.C. Ls., Chelmsford. [11181] 18/01/1971 **CM01/06/1976**

Palmer, Mr N D, BA MCLIP, Retired. [11184] 14/10/1966 **CM01/01/1968**

Palmer, Mr R, BA(Hons) MSc, Info. Offr, Scottish L. and Inf. Council, S. Lanarkshire. [10001307] 07/02/2007 **ME**

Palmer, Mr S J, BA(Hons) DipLib, LR & Advice Serv. Co-ordinator, Solihull Cent. L., Solihull. [37831] 28/10/1984 **ME**

Palmer, Miss S L, BA(Hons) MA MCLIP, Media Mgr., News L., BBC. [52257] 18/10/1995 **CM01/06/2005**

Pamma, Miss J, MCLIP, Inf. Specialist, GCHQ, Cheltenham. [10001193] 17/02/1999 **CM19/11/2008**

Panagiotopoulou, Mrs A, Msc MBCS, Admin. /IT Professional, Nat. Tech. Univ. of Athens, Greece. [10015986] 03/02/2010 **ME**

Panayi, Mrs G N A, BA(Hons), Team Lend. Lib. L.B. of Enfield, Cent. Lib. . [62689] 17/10/2003 **ME**

Panayiotakis, Mr I, Catr., Univ. of Stirling, Scotland. [10016152] 17/02/2010 **ME**

Panchbhaya, Mr B, Teacher, Islamic Da'wah Academy, Leics. [10016676] 30/04/2010 **AF**

Pandya, Mr H U, Retired. [17542] 01/01/1961 **ME**

Pang, Miss K Y, BSc(Hons) MSc, Sen. Admin. Offr., Hong Kong Housing Soc., Hong Kong. [10016611] 16/04/2010 **ME**

Pang, Ms M, BA MLib FCLIP, Ref. Lib., Hong Kong P. L. [45642] 11/04/1991 **FE18/11/1998**

Pang, Ms S L, BA(Hons), Stud., City Univ. London. [10015226] 27/10/2009 **ME**

Pang, Miss W, MA L. and Inf. Studies, Asst. Campus Mgr., Univ. of E. London, London [63969] 22/11/2004 **ME**

Pankhurst, Mrs R J, MA FCLIP, Retired. [17543] 03/06/1959
FE15/09/1993
Pankiewicz, Miss A M, Unknown. [65157] 03/11/2005 **ME**
Pankiewicz, Mrs S J, BA(Hons) MSc MCLIP, Asst. Lib., Nat. Met. L.,
Exeter. [39201] 01/01/1986 **CM21/07/1998**
Panomereva, Mrs A, MPhie MA, Unknown. [10007949] 20/03/2008 **ME**
Pantin, Mr A D, BA DipLib MSc, Admin. Asst., Dept. for Work &
Pensions, York [34590] 01/01/1982 **ME**
Pantry, Mrs S, BA OBE FCLIP, Dir., Sheila Pantry Assoc. Ltd. [11204]
23/03/1953 **FE18/01/1989**
Panzetta, Ms S J, DipIM, L. & Health Promotion Resources Mgr.,
Camden PCT, London. [49734] 06/12/1993 **ME**
Pao, Mr G, HonFCLIP, Hon. Fellow. [57253] 04/02/1999 **FE01/01/1999**
Papps, Mr T A, MA MCLIP, Systems Support Lib., Bournemouth Univ.
[22703] 18/09/1974 **CM24/05/1977**
Paramour, Ms S, MA(Hons) PGDipILS, Info. Advisor, Pfizer Ltd., Walton
Oaks, Surrey. [57063] 07/12/1998 **ME**
Parboteeah, Mr P, BSc, Stud. [10016913] 10/06/2010 **ME**
Parcell, Ms E J, MA, Sen. E Learning Advisor, Swansea Univ. [38973]
24/10/1985 **ME**
Pardoe, Mrs A, DipLib MCLIP, Learning Resources Mgr., City of
Wolverhampton Coll. [33315] 23/10/1980 **CM26/08/1983**
Pardoe, Mrs F H, BA DipLib MCLIP, Lunchbreak Super., Golden Valley
Primary Sch., Nailsea. [34243] 17/10/1981 **CM22/10/1985**
Parekh, Ms H, MA MCS, Retired. [34030] 27/07/1981 **ME**
Parfitt, Mrs S T, BSc MCLIP, Asst. Lib.,Tanglin Trust Sch., Singapore.
[46003] 19/08/1991 **CM25/09/1996**
Pargeter, Miss S M, MA MA CERT ED MCLIP, Standards & Customer
Projects Mgr., Devon L. & Inf. Serv. [28113] 12/10/1977
CM31/12/1980
Paris, Mr K R, BA PGDipLib, Sen. Km Procurement Offr., DLA Piper
UK, LLP London [43217] 04/10/1989 **ME**
Pariset, Ms C, Lib., Fulham Cross Girls' sch., London. [10016975]
16/06/2010 **ME**
Parish, Mr D R, BA MCMI MCLIP, Inf. Serv. Lib., Bor. of Poole. [21213]
30/09/1973 **CM27/09/1976**
Parish, Mrs F L, MCLIP, Lib. (Local Studies), Cambs. C.C. [11727]
26/02/1969 **CM18/10/1972**
Parish, Mr R H, MCLIP, Retired. [11216] 06/09/1956 **CM01/01/1966**
Parish, Mr R, BA MA MCLIP, Serv. Devel. Lib., Nottingham City L. & Inf.
Serv. [23557] 21/01/1975 **CM02/02/1977**
Park, Mrs A K, MCLIP BA, Sch. Lib. [21656] 05/01/1974 **CM01/08/1977**
Park, Mrs A, MCLIP, Academic Lib., Leeds Met. Univ. [59338]
09/02/2001 **CM19/03/2008**
Park, Mrs B, Unknown. [10011795] 18/11/2008 **ME**
Park, Mr D S, BA(Hons) MA MCLIP ILTA DipMDS, Inf. & Res. Offr.
(P/T), Bradford Link. [48711] 23/04/1993 **RV17/06/2009**
CM24/09/1997
Park, Ms M A, BA(Hons) MA MSc MCLIP, Inf. Specialist, Leeds N. W.
Primary Care Trust. [60050] 06/12/2001 **CM11/03/2009**
Park, Ms P, BA(Hons), Unwaged. [10015276] 28/10/2009 **ME**
Park, Mr R D M, MA(Hons), Subject Lib., Univ. of The W. of Scotland.
[46551] 14/11/1991 **ME**
Parkar, Mr F A, BSc MCLIP, Inf. Sci., GlaxoSmithKline, Harlow. [60326]
06/01/1993 **CM06/01/1993**
Parke, Mr J T E, BA(Hons) DipIM MCLIP, Intensive Care Admin.,
Aldenbrooke's NHS Trust. [55363] 03/10/1997 **CM28/10/2004**
Parker, Mr A D, MA DipLib MCLIP, Higher L. Exec., House of Commons
L., London. [33473] 07/01/1981 **CM20/01/1986**
Parker, Ms A L, BA(Hons) MA MCLIP, Temp. [62178] 07/03/2003
CM19/03/2008
Parker, Miss A M, MBE HonFLA, Life Member [11222] 26/08/1949
CM01/01/1961

Parker, Miss A S, BA(Hons), Learning Cent. Mgr., Birkenhead Sixth
Form Coll., Wirral. [56225] 07/04/1998 **ME**
Parker, Miss B J, BA(Hons) MCLIP DipEngLit, Life Member [19802]
03/10/1972 **CM25/08/1982**
Parker, Mr C C, BSc MPhil FCLIP, Retired. [10013868] 20/03/1986
FE01/03/1986
Parker, Mrs C M, ACLIP, Y. Serv. Lib., Stevenage L. [63917] 26/10/2004
ACL08/03/2006
Parker, Mrs C, Stud. [10000762] 06/11/2006 **ME**
Parker, Mr D F, MCMI FCLIP, Life Member. [19236] 28/02/1954
FE01/01/1959
Parker, Ms E K, BA MCLIP, Sen. Lib. for Child. & Families, Highland
Council, Inverness. [54284] 15/11/1996 **CM20/11/2002**
Parker, Miss E, MA(Hons), Lib., Dundas & Wilson LLP, Edinburgh.
[10005007] 06/06/2007 **ME**
Parker, Mr F N, FCLIP, Life Member. [11232] 10/09/1952 **FE01/01/1966**
Parker, Mrs G D, BA(Hons) MCLIP, Unwaged. [22747] 06/09/1974
CM29/01/1979
Parker, Mr G R, MCLIP, Communications Offr., Brit. L., Boston Spa.
[45434] 01/02/1991 **CM01/04/2002**
Parker, Mrs J E, MCLIP, Community Lib., Northants C.C.,
Wellingborough. [27517] 14/05/1977 **CM23/02/1983**
Parker, Ms J E, BA(Hons) MA MCLIP, Inf. Literacy Unit Mgr., Open Univ.
[52062] 02/10/1995 **CM21/07/1999**
Parker, Mrs J E, BA(Hons) MCLIP, Project Mgr., Qinetiq, Malvern,
Worcs. [52591] 10/11/1995 **CM24/10/2001**
Parker, Mrs J M, BA MCLIP, Learning Cent. Mgr., New Coll.,
Nottingham. [28683] 13/01/1978 **CM10/11/1981**
Parker, Mr J S, FCLIP, Retired. [19237] 26/09/1952 **FE10/08/1978**
Parker, Mrs J, Inf. Asst., Bolton Council [62898] 18/11/2003 **ME**
Parker, Miss J, BA(Hons)LIS, Lib., Filey Lib. & Inf. Cen. [65479]
24/02/2006 **ME**
Parker, Mr K T, BSc(Hons) MLib, Inf. Consultant. [50401] 18/07/1994 **ME**
Parker, Ms L E, Waged, Cent. L., Nottingham [10001814] 08/03/2007
ME
Parker, Mrs L, BA DipLib MEd MCLIP, Head of Academic Devel. Team,
Univ. of Sheffield. [21249] 04/10/1973 **CM29/12/1975**
Parker, Mrs L, BA(Hons) MCLIP, Inf. Mngr., Health & Safety Lab.,
Buxton [10013362] 23/05/1983 **CM01/07/1991**
Parker, Mrs L, ACLIP, Sen. L. Asst., Workshop L., Notts. [10003418]
23/05/2007 **ACL28/01/2009**
Parker, Mrs M J, ACLIP, Asst. in Charge, Killamarsh. [65622]
07/03/2006 **ACL22/06/2007**
Parker, Ms N J, BA(Hons) MCLIP, Head of L. & Inf. Serv., Manchester
City Council. [36870] 12/01/1984 **CM10/05/1988**
Parker, Mr N M, BSc DipLib MCLIP, Operations Mgr., Chartered Mgmnt.
Inst., Corby. [35702] 17/01/1983 **CM13/05/1986**
Parker, Mrs P C, BA DipLib MCLIP, Unemployed. [32891] 20/10/1980
CM08/04/1983
Parker, Miss P E, MCLIP, Unknown. [11244] 10/10/1968 **CM19/12/1972**
Parker, Mr R J, BSocSc MCLIP, Stud. [55099] 08/07/1997
CM21/05/2008
Parker, Ms S A, BSc MA DipM CertEd MCIM MCLIP, Freelance Indexer
& Proofreader [65669] 10/02/2006 **CM03/06/1990**
Parker, Miss S A, BA FCLIP, L. Sectors Mgr., Surrey C.C. [25386]
12/01/1976 **FE03/10/2007**
Parker, Mrs S E, BA MCLIP, PPI Co-ordinator [10012976] 15/01/1979
CM27/03/1981
Parker, Miss S M, BA DMS FCLIP, Retired. [11251] 01/03/1962
FE25/01/1995
Parker, Dr S, PhD, Lect., Robert Gordon Univ., Aberdeen. [64186]
31/01/2005 **ME**
Parker-Dennison, Mrs D C, DipLib, Lib., Chilton Cantelo Sch.,
Somerset. [58632] 20/04/2000 **ME**

Parker-Munn, Mrs S A, BA(Hons) BScEcon(Hons), L. Super., Hugh Owen L., Univ. of Wales, Aberystwyth. [50198] 04/05/1994 **ME**

Parkes, Mr D J, BA(Hons) DipLib MCLIP, Head of Learning Support, Staffs. Univ., Thompson L., Stoke on Trent. [46795] 28/01/1992 **CM26/07/1995**

Parkes, Dr D, BA(Hons) MSc MA MCLIP, Ret. [52897] 17/01/1996 **CM19/01/2000**

Parkhill, Ms S, BA(Hons), Lib., HMP Bronzefield, Ashford. [63925] 03/11/2004 **ME**

Parkin, Mrs C M, BA(Hons) Msc, Academic Lib., Leeds Met. Univ. [58263] 30/11/1999 **ME**

Parkin, Miss E R, BA(Hons) DipIS MCLIP, Team Lib., Norfolk L., Kings Lynn. [48903] 15/07/1993 **CM22/09/1999**

Parkin, Ms S, BA(Hons), Sen. L. Asst., Serials & Resources, Nottingham Trent Univ. [10015529] 09/12/2009 **AF**

Parkinson, Mrs A L, MCLIP, Lib. Asst., Ramsbottom Lib., Bury [2722] 06/10/1971 **CM13/09/1974**

Parkinson, Mr A, BA, Unemployed. [35868] 05/02/1983 **ME**

Parkinson, Mrs C C, ACLIP, L. & Learning Cent. Mgr., Hamworthy Comm. L., Poole. [65185] 17/11/2005 **ACL27/06/2007**

Parkinson, Mrs C M, BA MA, Unknown. [63208] 16/03/2004 **ME**

Parkinson, Mrs D, BA(Hons) MCLIP, Academic Liaison Lib., Bradford Coll. [59594] 21/06/2001 **CM19/11/2008**

Parkinson, Mrs F, BLS MCLIP, Knowledge Mgmnt. BRM, Pricewaterhouse Coopers. [28197] 13/10/1977 **CM28/02/1983**

Parkinson, Mr J K, BA DipLib MCLIP, Inf. Mgr., Cabinet Off. /Emergency Planning Coll., York. [26502] 20/10/1976 **CM26/06/1979**

Parkinson, Mrs J, BA(Hons) MCLIP, Principal Lib., Reader Devel., Sunderland C.C. [50508] 25/08/1994 **CM29/03/2004**

Parkinson, Mrs S A, MCLIP, Life Member. [11273] 01/01/1957 **CM01/01/1962**

Parkinson, Mrs V A, MCLIP, Lib. Mgr., Stokenchurch Lib. [649] 09/05/1968 **CM01/01/1971**

Parkinson, Miss W H, MCLIP, Retired. [11276] 13/02/1947 **CM01/01/1966**

Parkinson-Hardman, Mrs L A, BA(Hons) MSc, The Hysterectomy Assoc., Dorchester. [53255] 17/04/1996 **ME**

Parks, Mrs J, MCLIP, Retired. [11660] 09/01/1964 **CM01/01/1967**

Parlain, Ms K, BA(Hons) MA MCLIP, Performance & Improvement Mgr., Kent C.C. [42695] 25/01/1989 **RV07/06/2006** **CM22/05/1996**

Parmiter, Mr T M, BA MCLIP, Outreach Serv. Mgr., Vertex Data Serv. Westminster, Westminster. [36918] 14/01/1984 **CM16/10/1989**

Parnaby, Ms B, BA DipILS, Lib., Dept for Child. Sch. & Families, London. [61158] 21/03/2002 **ME**

Parnell, Mrs L, Lib., Plumstead Manor Sch., Plumstead [10012873] 19/03/2009 **ME**

Parnell, Mrs S E, BSc(Econ) MCLIP, Electronic Serv. Lib., Redditch Health L., Alexandra Hosp., Redditch [10005858] 02/08/2007 **CM10/07/2009**

Parr, Mrs N R, BA(Hons) DipILM MCLIP, Unknown. [55584] 21/10/1997 **CM25/07/2001**

Parr, Ms S C, BA DipLib MA MCLIP, Lib., Heathfield Sch., Pinner, Middlesex. [35545] 01/11/1982 **CM18/07/1985**

Parratt, Mrs J P, BA MCLIP, User Serv. Lib., Univ. of Brighton, Queenwood L. [40359] 21/01/1987 **CM22/05/1991**

Parris, Ms H W, Inf. Offr., Gt. Manchester Probation Serv. [10003021] 20/10/1990 **ME**

Parrish, Ms L A, BSc MCLIP, Head of Inf. Serv., Esso UK Ltd., Leatherhead. [34930] 24/05/1982 **CM17/08/1984**

Parrott, Mrs R P L N, BSc, Sen. L. Asst., Welcome L., London. [65592] 23/02/2006 **AF**

Parry, Ms A, BA MSc, Stud., Univ. of W. England [10015060] 09/10/2009 **ME**

Parry, Ms C M, BA MA MCLIP, Res. Support Lib., Queen Mary Univ. of London [42346] 24/10/1988 **CM07/10/1997**

Parry, Mr F P, MCLIP, Academic Lib., Loughborough Univ. [30227] 12/01/1979 **CM20/01/1982**

Parry, Mrs J S, BA PGCL MCLIP, Inf. & Project Liaison Mgr., Hillsborough Memorial Arch. Team, Home Off., London. [42183] 10/10/1988 **CM18/11/1993**

Parry, Miss J, BA(Hons) MLIS, L. Serv. Mgr., Powys Teaching Health Board, Bronllys, Nr. Brecon. [56441] 10/07/1998 **ME**

Parry, Mrs K, BA(Hons), Stud., Aberystwyth Univ. [10014988] 01/10/2009 **ME**

Parry, Mrs S M, MA MCLIP, Educ. Lib., Northumberland Sch. L. Serv., Hexham L. [26602] 01/10/1976 **CM31/12/1979**

Parry, Ms S T, BLib MCLIP, Web Content Mgr., Met. Police Serv., London [41756] 10/03/1988 **CM18/09/1991**

Parry, Mr V T H, MA(Oxon) FCLIP FRSA FRAS, Life Member. [11302] 29/09/1950 **FE01/01/1959**

Parry, Mrs W, BA(Hons) PgDipLIS, Acting Head of Study Centres, Worcester Coll. of Tech. [45211] 13/08/1990 **ME**

Parsley, Ms S, BEng BA, p. /t. Stud., City Univ., LSHTM, London. [10000699] 15/11/2006 **ME**

Parslow, Mr R J, PGDip BSc(Hons), Stock & Reader Dev. Lib., Shropshire Council, Shrewsbury [10015231] 07/01/2003 **ME**

Parsonage, Miss A M G, MCLIP, Life Member. [11304] 10/02/1961 **CM01/01/1968**

Parsonage, Ms H L, BA(Hons) MA MCLIP, Liaison Lib., Barckenhurst Campus L., Southwell. [61844] 18/11/2002 **CM09/09/2009**

Parsons, Mr A J, BA(Hons) MPhil MCLIP, Academic Liaison Lib. [38310] 04/03/1985 **CM10/11/1987**

Parsons, Mrs C, B LIB MCLIP, Princ. Lib., Bracknell Forest Bor. Council, Berks. [33075] 01/10/1980 **CM30/07/1985**

Parsons, Miss G L, MSc, Systems Lib., Brunel Univ. [65084] 01/11/2005 **ME**

Parsons, Miss J E, MCLIP, Advisory Lib., Sch. L. Serv., E. Sussex C.C. [11314] 09/02/1964 **CM01/01/1968**

Parsons, Mrs J H, BA DipLib MCLIP, Inf & Knowledge Systems Off., Wokingham Bor. Council. [43768] 08/01/1990 **CM27/05/1992**

Parsons, Miss L D, BSc MCLIP, Unwaged [60735] 22/10/1985 **CM22/10/1985**

Parsons, Miss S C, BA MCLIP, Sen. Lib., N. Area Ls., E. Sussex C.C. [27127] 09/01/1977 **CM01/12/1981**

Partington, Miss J, BA DipLib MCLIP, Sen. Asst. Lib., Goldsmiths, Univ. of London [33333] 07/11/1980 **CM27/07/1983**

Parton, Mrs G, BA(Hons) MCLIP, Lib., Northbrook Coll. Sussex, Worthing. [49114] 06/10/1993 **CM21/07/1999**

Parton, Mr S, BA MA MCLIP, Subject Lib., Bournemouth Univ., Poole. [61024] 05/02/2002 **CM28/01/2009**

Partouche, Miss C, Stud., Robert Gordon Univ. [10013864] 04/06/2009 **ME**

Partridge, Mr D A, FCLIP, Life Member. [11320] 10/02/1950 **FE01/01/1969**

Partridge, Mr G A, BA(Hons), Res. &Devel. Dir.,Soutron Ltd.,Derbyshire. [49845] 21/12/1993 **ME**

Partridge, Miss H, BA(Hons), Lib. /Progression Coach, Houghton Kepier Sports Coll., Houghton-Le-Spring. [10010489] 30/07/2008 **ME**

Partridge, Mrs J E, BA(Hons), Catr., Lincoln Univ. [63905] 26/10/2004 **ME**

Partridge, Mr K A, MCLIP, Inf. Res., Dept. for BERR, London. [61904] 28/11/2002 **CM13/06/2007**

Partridge, Mr R A, BA(Hons) PgDipLIS, Pub. Serv. Mgr., L. Serv., De Montfort Univ., Leicester. [52669] 20/11/1995 **ME**

Partsi, Miss T, Inf. Specialist, QINETIQ, Farnborough. [41403] 24/11/1987 **ME**

Passmore, Mrs K, Unwaged. [64197] 31/01/2005 **ME**

Passmore, Mrs R B, MA MSc MCLIP, Self-employed. [60571]
30/11/1976 **CM30/11/1976**

Patalong, Mrs S L, BA ILTM MCLIP, L. Teaching Fellow & Subject Lib.,
Coventry Univ. [31034] 02/07/1979 **CM19/08/1981**

Patchett, Mrs G W, MCLIP, Unemployed. [3314] 26/08/1969
CM20/09/1972

Patel, Ms D, BA(Hons) MSc, E L. Mgr., Birmingham City Univ. [58232]
22/11/1999 **ME**

Patel, Mrs G, BA B LIB MCLIP, Teaching Asst. (Reading & English),
Reddiford Sch., Pinner, Middx. [30228] 09/01/1979 **CM04/06/1981**

Patel, Miss J, BSc MA, L. Exec., House of Commons, London. [57581]
12/05/1999 **ME**

Patel, Mrs R, BSc(Hons), Tech. Enquiries Mgr. Forensic Sci. Serv.,
Birmingham. [62373] 16/05/2003 **ME**

Pateman, Mr J P, BA DipLib MBA FCLIP, Head of L., Serv. & Lincs. C.C.
[32146] 01/02/1980 **FE26/11/1997**

Paterson, Miss A, BA DipILS MCLIP, Systems Lib., Shetland Islands
Council. [58011] 12/10/1999 **CM16/07/2003**

Paterson, Miss C L L, BA(Hons) MCLIP, Asst. Lib., Systems,
Goldsmiths, London. [43163] 05/09/1989 **CM16/07/2003**

Paterson, Mrs C, MCLIP, Sch. Lib. Clackmannanshire Council, Educ. &
Comm. Serv. [9355] 12/10/1970 **CM15/01/1975**

Paterson, Mrs D W, MA MCLIP, Housewife & Mother. [42133]
05/10/1988 **CM12/12/1991**

Paterson, Mrs E A, MCLIP, Retired. [11338] 02/03/1962 **CM01/01/1965**

Paterson, Ms E C, BA(Hons) MSc, Faculty Librarian., Social Sciences.,
Univ. of E. Anglia, Norwich [61819] 11/11/2002 **ME**

Paterson, Mrs G S, MA DipLib MCLIP, Head of Child. & Young People's
Serv., E. Sussex L. [26871] 14/12/1976 **CM20/12/1979**

Paterson, Miss L C, MA(Hons) MSc, Inf. Serv. Co-ordinator, Young
Scot, Edinburgh. [65576] 28/02/2006 **ME**

Paterson, Mrs M T, BA MCLIP, Bursar/Lib., W. Sussex C.C., Baldwins
Hill C. P. Sch., [11345] 01/01/1969 **CM10/12/1973**

Paterson, Mr M, Unknown. [10014110] 10/07/2009 **AF**

Paterson, Mrs M, ACLIP, Unknown. [10014151] 01/07/2009
ACL16/06/2010

Paterson, Mr N J, MCLIP, Network Lib., Mearns Academy,
Laurencekirk. [10006914] 17/12/2007 **CM11/02/2010**

Paterson, Mr R, Stud., City Univ., London [10005991] 11/09/2007 **ME**

Paterson, Mrs S E, MA DipLib, Curator F,Lib., Dept. of Printed Books,
Imperial War Mus. [38364] 01/04/1985 **ME**

Paterson, Mrs S M, BA MCLIP, Lib., Fortrose L., [23248] 15/11/1974
CM18/10/1977

Pathak, Mrs P, Ethnic Serv. Lib., Cardiff C.C. [59971] 14/11/2001 **ME**

Pathare, Mrs R, BA, Asst. Lib., S. Thames Coll. [10002174] 04/04/2007
ME

Patmore, Mr M R C, BA PG Dip, Stud., UCL, London. [10015702]
14/01/2010 **ME**

Paton, Mr A K, BSc PgDIP MBM, Unwaged [10007227] 25/01/2008 **ME**

Paton, Mr H C M, BA DipLib MCLIP, Devel. & Support Serv. Mgr., L.B. of
Bexley. [30659] 21/02/1979 **CM20/02/1981**

Paton, Miss J C, BA(Hons), Lib Asst., Plumstead Manor Sch.
[10014374] 21/07/2009 **ME**

Paton, Mr M W, FCLIP, Life Member. [11348] 19/10/1940 **FE01/01/1956**

Paton, Miss M, MA(Hons) MCLIP, Lib. Resource Cent. Coordinator,
Broughton H. S.,Edinburgh. [62449] 03/07/2003 **CM03/10/2007**

Patrick, Mr D, Young People's Offr., Access Serv., Mitchell L., Glasgow
[10017115] 23/06/2010 **AF**

Patrick, Mrs N J, LLB MSc, Lib. Asst., Wood Green Sch., Witney
[10012814] 21/04/1997 **ME**

Patrick, Dr S, Inf. Sci., Roche Palo Alto, Palo Alto, CA, U. S. A. [35977]
11/02/1983 **ME**

Pattanaik, Mrs G, BA MA DipLib MCLIP, Retired. [38888] 14/10/1985
CM14/02/1990

Patten, Mrs J, Br. L. Mgr., Ballyclare L., L. N. I. [56412] 06/07/1998 **ME**

Patten, Mr J, BA MA, L. Asst., N. Sheilds. [58023] 14/10/1999 **ME**

Patterson, Mrs C M, Lib. Asst. (Relief), Moray Council. [61137]
07/03/2002 **ME**

Patterson, Miss H E, BA, Stud. [10014497] 05/08/2009 **ME**

Patterson, Mr K R, BMus DipLib dms MCLIP, Operations Mgr., St.
Helen L. [33104] 21/10/1980 **CM24/03/1987**

Patterson, Ms L C, BA(Hons) MA MCLIP, Lib., NHS Direct. [49595]
19/11/1993 **CM26/11/1997**

Patterson, Mrs M C, BA MCLIP, Young Peoples Serv. Lib., E. Ayrshire
Council, Kilmarnock. [30360] 08/02/1979 **CM11/02/1985**

Patterson, Miss M E, BA DipLib MCLIP, Grade 2 Lib., Queens Univ. L.,
Belfast. [26506] 01/10/1976 **CM07/03/1979**

Patterson, Mrs N J, Career Break. [49596] 19/11/1993 **ME**

Patterson, Mrs R A, Inf. Lib., Southampton Solent Univ. [63894]
26/10/2004 **ME**

Patterson, Mrs R M, BA(Hons), Dep. Curator, Ruskin L., Lancaster
Univ. [53513] 10/07/1996 **ME**

Patterson, Mr S J, LVO MA MA MCLIP, Head of Collections & Inf.,
Mgmnt., Royal Collection, Buckingham Palace. [39374] 17/01/1986
CM27/01/1993

Paul, Miss A E, BSc(Econ) MCLIP, Dep. Mgr., L. & Knowledge Serv.,
Ashford & St Peter's Hosp. NHS Trust [54644] 06/02/1997
CM23/06/2004

Paul, Mrs H E, BA DipLib MCLIP, Systems Mgr., Guilles-Alles L.,
Guernsey. [33226] 23/10/1980 **CM18/09/1991**

Paul, Miss H L, MA, Inf. Specialist, Dept. for Business, Innovation &
Skills (BIS) [10008496] 02/04/2008 **ME**

Paul, Mrs J E, MA MCLIP, Retired. [11368] 01/01/1959 **CM01/01/1962**

Paul, Mr R M, BSc(Hons) DipILS MCLIP, Clinical Sciences Lib., Health
Servs. L., Univ. of Southampton [10001117] 12/01/2007
CM17/03/1999

Paul, Dr S, Sub-Lib., Corpus Christi Coll. [10012702] 03/03/2009 **ME**

Pavey, Mr M J, BLib MCLIP, Cent. Lib., Southampton City Council
[31682] 31/10/1979 **CM24/07/1984**

Pavey, Mrs M, BA PgDip MCLIP, Educ. Consultant – L. [10122]
01/01/1966 **CM16/09/1974**

Pavey, Mrs S J, BSc MSc FCLIP, Sr. Lib., Box Hill Sch. [60802]
12/12/2001 **FE31/01/2007**

Pavlik, Mrs D, FCLIP, Retired. [11376] 28/02/1971 **FE29/10/1976**

Pawlus, Mr M C, Stud. [10015333] 10/11/2009 **ME**

Paxton, Ms G, BA(Hons), Lib., Preston Coll., Preston [10016431]
01/10/2002 **ME**

Payne, Miss C S, PgDip, Stud., Liverpool Business Sch. [10015090]
15/10/2009 **ME**

Payne, Mrs D M, BA DipLib MCLIP, Lib., Min. of Defence, Army L. and
Inf. Serv. [40040] 07/10/1986 **CM12/09/1990**

Payne, Mr D, BA MLS, Br. Mgr., Free L. of Philadelphia, USA. [41475]
01/01/1988 **ME**

Payne, Ms E A, BA DipLib MCLIP, Inf. Sci. /Researcher/Indexer, Self-
employed. [44489] 15/10/1990 **CM18/11/1993**

Payne, Ms G F, BA(Hons) MSc MCLIP, Acad. Lib. (Team Leader),Sch.
of the Arts, Univ. of Northampton. [58718] 01/07/2000 **CM13/03/2002**

Payne, Mr G S, MCLIP, Retired. [11388] 09/10/1958 **CM01/01/1963**

Payne, Miss H C, BA MCLIP, Inf. Specialist, GCHQ. [52296] 23/10/1995
CM21/05/2003

Payne, Mr I C, BA MA CertEd DipLib MCLIP, Unknown. [35732]
04/01/1983 **CM06/09/1988**

Payne, Miss J M, ACLIP, L. Asst., Roxeth L., Middlesex. [64412]
15/03/2005 **ACL10/01/2006**

Payne, Mrs K A, MCLIP, Sen. Lib. (Br. Mgr.), Poulton-le-Fylde L. [63994]
01/12/2004 **CM10/07/2009**

Payne, Mrs L M E, MA MCLIP, Asst. Head of Serv. - Devel., Norfolk L. &
Inf. Serv., Norwich. [33212] 28/10/1980 **CM15/02/1983**

Payne, Miss L, BA, L. Asst., Baker and McKenzie LLP, London [10006762] 17/12/2007 **ME**

Payne, Mrs L, BA MA MCLIP, Learning Resources Cent. Mgr.,The Lady Eleanor Holles Sch. [64553] 10/05/2005 **CM05/05/2010**

Payne, Mr M, BA DipLib MCLIP, Sen. Lib., Penarth L., Vale of Glamorgan. [37794] 26/10/1984 **CM14/04/1987**

Payne, Mr M, BA MCLIP, Unknown. [11393] 21/10/1970 **CM10/01/1975**

Payne, Miss N A, BA(Hons) DipILS MCLIP, Asst. Lib., Law Soc., London. [53091] 01/03/1996 **CM06/04/2005**

Payne, Mr P M, BA MCLIP HonFCLIP, Lib., Birkbeck, Univ. of London. [11394] 20/01/1972 **CM17/06/1977**

Payne, Ms S E, BA MA MCLIP, Records Mgr., Brit. Transport Police, London. [43541] 02/11/1989 **CM18/11/1993**

Payne, Ms S, BA DipLib, Inf. Adviser, Electoral Commission [56803] 19/10/1998 **ME**

Payne, Miss V J, BA MLIS DipLib MCLIP ALAI, Periodicals Lib., Nat. Univ. of Ireland, Maynooth. [30784] 03/04/1979 **CM19/05/1982**

Paynter, Mr D F, MCLIP, Head of L. & Inf., Glos. C.C. [11398] 10/01/1968 **CM01/01/1971**

Pazos Galindo, Ms J I, BA(Hons), Stud., Manchester Met. Univ. [10015946] 29/01/2010 **ME**

Pazos, Mr M, BSc MSc, Stud. Hub Project Worker, Univ. of Salford. [10016772] 10/05/2010 **ME**

Peace, Ms A M, BA(Hons) MA ILS MCLIP, Head of Prof. Policy & Inf., The Chartered Soc. of Physiotherapy [49616] 19/11/1993 **RV07/08/2009 CM06/04/2005**

Peach, Mrs S P, BA MCLIP, Local Studies Lib., Derbys. C.C. [23395] 14/01/1975 **CM14/01/1977**

Peacock, Mr D M, BA(Hons) MSc DipLib MCLIP, Reg. Lib. (IM&T), Northumberland Tyne & Wear SHA. [42652] 31/01/1989 **CM18/09/1991**

Peacock, Mrs J A, MCLIP, Retired [12486] 30/09/1968 **CM15/12/1972**

Peacock, Mrs J, MCLIP, Life Member. [24172] 27/10/1948 **CM01/01/1952**

Peacock, Mr T, BEd(Hons), E-Resources Administrator, Univ. of Derby. [10006250] 28/09/2007 **ME**

Peacocke, Ms R, Serv. Dev. Offr., Homes for Islington, London [10015624] 28/10/1997 **ME**

Peaden, Mrs A M, BA MCLIP, Area Mgr., Culture & Leisure Serv., Kirklees Council., Huddersfield [33167] 07/10/1980 **CM03/02/1986**

Peadon, Miss F, BA MCLIP, Teaching Asst., Warwickshire C.C. [23584] 21/01/1975 **CM10/07/1979**

Peagram, Miss E P, BSc(Hons) MSc, Lib., Dr J H Burgoyne and Partners LLP, London. [62630] 01/10/2003 **ME**

Peake, Mrs H M, BSc(Hons) MCLIP, Knowledge Interchange Info. Exec., Cranfield Sch. of Mgmt., Cranfield Univ. [55737] 10/11/1997 **CM29/03/2004**

Peake, Mr H S, BA MCLIP, Life Member. [11412] 23/09/1954 **CM01/01/1957**

Peake, Miss S T, BA MCLIP, Sen. Lib., Educ. L. Serv., Berks. [39392] 22/01/1986 **CM15/08/1990**

Pearce, Mr J K, BA(Hons) DipLIS, Dep. Lib., Royal Military Academy Sandhurst, Camberley. [46781] 22/01/1992 **ME**

Pearce, Ms J, BA, L. Asst., Hertfordshire C.C. / Freelance Indexer/Copy Editor/Proofreader [36676] 04/11/1983 **ME**

Pearce, Ms J, BA DipLib MCLIP, Learning Resources Mgr. (Resources & Systems) Univ. of the Arts London. [22585] 06/07/1974 **CM08/08/1977**

Pearce, Mrs L A, BEd(Oxon), Resource Ctre. Mgr., Kendrick Sch., Reading, Berks. [57922] 05/10/1999 **ME**

Pearce, Mrs L M, BSc MSc MCLIP, Inf. Offr., Univ. of Birmingham. [60836] 01/06/1990 **CM11/03/2009**

Pearce, Mr M J, BA(Hons) MA MCLIP, Unknwon. [55294] 18/09/1997 **CM07/09/2005**

Pearce, Ms M, P. /t. Stud., MMU, Cumbria C.C., Carlisle. [65264] 08/12/2005 **ME**

Pearce, Mrs P, BA MCLIP, Lib. Gloucester L., Glos. C.C. [32033] 11/02/1980 **CM21/02/1985**

Pearce, Mrs P, BA MSc(Econ) MCLIP, Records Mgr., Univ. of the W. of England, Bristol. [12311] 27/01/1966 **CM01/01/1969**

Pearce, Mr R, BA MCLIP, Stock Mgr., Croydon Lib. [38822] 10/10/1985 **CM14/11/1990**

Pearce, Miss S E, BA MA MCLIP, Asst. Lib. for Adult Fiction, Reading Cent. L. [61588] 02/10/2002 **CM19/03/2008**

Peare, Mr J D T, FCLIP, Keeper (Readers' Serv.), Trinity Coll. L., Dublin. [18999] 02/10/1972 **FE07/09/2005**

Pearl, Mr C J, BA MCLIP, Retired. [11432] 25/05/1970 **CM22/03/1974**

Pearlman, Mrs D P, BA MCLIP, Lib., Freelance. [20003] 12/01/1973 **CM02/10/1978**

Pearse, Mrs E M, MCLIP, Life Member. [11461] 19/09/1947 **CM01/01/1954**

Pearson, Mr A R, BSc BA, Inf. Professional, Voluntary Action, Lewisham [10007197] 09/11/1989 **ME**

Pearson, Miss A, BA(Hons) MA, Stock Mgr., Bertram L. Serv., Leeds. [59152] 28/11/2000 **ME**

Pearson, Mr B, DMA MILAM FCLIP, Retired. [11439] 06/02/1957 **FE13/06/1990**

Pearson, Ms C A, BA DipLib MCLIP, Team Leader/Comm. Inf. Offr., Malton, N. Yorks. Co. L. Serv. [27704] 04/07/1977 **CM31/01/1980**

Pearson, Mr D R S, BA MA DipLib FCLIP, Dir., Univ. of London Res. L. Serv., London. [33163] 01/10/1980 **FE25/07/2001**

Pearson, Mrs G H, MA MCLIP, Community Lib., Oldham Met. Bor. Council. [25357] 11/01/1976 **CM17/11/1978**

Pearson, Ms G J, PGDip MA, Clinical Lib., Wirral Univ. Teaching Hosp. NHS Foundation Trust, Wirral. [10014476] 13/02/1992 **ME**

Pearson, Mrs J V, B TECH DipLib MCLIP, Retired. [11447] 25/04/1968 **CM01/01/1970**

Pearson, Miss K E, BA MSc MCLIP, Knowledge Mgr., Bird and Bird, London. [10001361] 08/12/1998 **CM07/09/2005**

Pearson, Mrs M F, BA DipLib MCLIP, Sch. Lib., St. Edwards C. of E. Comp., Romford. [58641] 25/04/2000 **CM04/02/2004**

Pearson, Mr P J, BSc MA MCLIP, Metadata Mgr.,ISLS. Univ. of Westminster. [43273] 09/10/1989 **CM24/03/1992**

Pearson, Dr P M, BTh MTh PhD MA MCLIP, Dir. & Arch., Thomas Merton Cent., Bellarmine Univ., Louisville. [52093] 03/10/1995 **CM15/03/2000**

Pearson, Mr R F M, MCMI MIMS MCLIP, Retired. [11451] 05/02/1964 **CM01/01/1971**

Pearson, Miss T, Reader Serv. Offr., RNIB, Peterborough [10001669] 02/10/2000 **ME**

Pearson, Mr W D, MCLIP, Retired. [19244] 20/01/1965 **CM01/01/1970**

Pease, Ms C A, BA(Hons) DipIM MCLIP, Lib. Res. Mgr., The Law Soc., London. [49645] 17/11/1993 **CM19/01/2000**

Peasgood, Mr A N, BA MCLIP, Retired. [17550] 07/01/1961 **CM01/01/1964**

Peasley, Mr M E, MA(Oxon) DipLib MCLIP, Info. & Learning Servs. Mgr., Devon Lib. [35633] 19/11/1982 **CM18/02/1986**

Peat, Mrs C L, BA(Hons) PGDip, Stud. [10017179] 11/07/2010 **ME**

Peat, Mrs R A, BA(Hons) MCLIP, Sch. Lib., Wick High Sch., Wick/Caithness. [42613] 18/01/1989 **CM12/09/2001**

Peat, Mrs S A, BSc(Econ) MCLIP, Elect. Inf. Offr., Coll. of Law, York. [57194] 12/01/1999 **CM29/11/2006**

Peattie, Mr P R, MCLIP, Coll. Lib., Northern Ireland Civil Serv., Coll. of Agric. Food & Rural Enterp. [26648] 26/10/1976 **CM08/10/1979**

Peberdy, Mrs R J, BA MSc(Econ) MCLIP, Principal Lib. [24782] 14/10/1975 **CM19/07/1979**

Peck, Mrs J E, BA MCLIP, Lib., Cheshire C.C., Chester. [22026] 01/01/1974 **CM21/10/1976**

Pecout, Mr R, MCLIP, Devel. Lib., Herts. [63460] 12/05/2004
                                      CM07/07/2010

Peddie, Mr C, BA MSc, L. & Inf. Offr., Newcastle L. Serv., NEWCASTLE UPON TYNE. [10000878] 16/11/2006 **ME**

Peddlesden, Ms K K, BA(Hons) MCLIP, Info. Scientist, MOD, London. [39752] 16/06/1986 **CM20/01/1999**

Peden, Miss A M, MCLIP, Project Offr., Lincs. Co. L. [11462] 01/08/1967
         CM01/01/1970

Peden, Mrs J E, BLib BA(Hons) MSc MCLIP, Sub-Lib., Univ. of Ulster, Faculty of Life & Health Sciences [44368] 01/10/1990**CM13/03/2002**

Peden, Mrs R C, BLib MCLIP, LRC Mgr., The Bournemouth & Poole Coll., Bournemouth. [26677] 09/11/1976 **CM17/01/1979**

Pedersen, Mr V B, BA(Hons) MA MCLIP, L. Mgr., Civil Aviation Auth., Gatwick. [55744] 12/11/1997 **CM29/03/2004**

Pedley, Mrs A J M, MA MCLIP, Retired [40402] 05/02/1987
         CM16/02/1988

Pedley, Rev C J, BA(Econ) BA MTh ThM, Lib., Heythrop Coll., Univ. of London [57993] 11/10/1999 **ME**

Pedley, Mr P D, MA MLib FCLIP, Head of Res., Economist Intelligence Unit, London. [36884] 11/01/1984 **RV29/03/2006** **FE18/11/1998**

Peel, Mrs J D, BSc MCLIP, Life Member. [22576] 08/07/1974
         CM11/06/1987

Peel, Miss M, BA(HonS) MCLIP, Implementation Offr., Trafford Council [62406] 02/06/2003 **CM19/03/2008**

Pegg, Miss K A, BA DipLib MCLIP, Inf. Offr., Potter Clarkson LLP, Nottingham. [27004] 06/01/1977 **CM02/11/1984**

Pelegrin, Mrs S, BA, Stud., Aberystwyth Univ. [10011113] 25/09/2008
         ME

Pelekanou, Miss A, BA, MA, PhD(Pend), Sen. Inf. Asst., Business L., Nottingham Univ., Nottingham. [10008623] 04/04/2008 **ME**

Pellett, Mrs G R, BA(Hons), Lib., Willingdon Community Sch. [59298] 31/01/2001 **ME**

Pemberton, Mrs M M, MA BA(Hons) MCLIP, Sch. L. Serv. Lib., Bristol L. [16022] 16/06/1971 **CM22/07/1975**

Pemberton, Mr R, Community Lib., Medway L. [63812] 01/10/2004 **ME**

Pemberton, Miss S J, BA DipLib MCLIP, Lib., Continuing Educ. L., Univ. of Oxford. [30025] 23/11/1978 **CM07/04/1982**

Pembridge, Mrs M C, BA(Hons), IM Serv. Mgr., GCHQ, Glos. [10005357] 02/02/1988 **ME**

Pendered, Mr M, BA(Hons), Cover Super./ Lib. Cover, Wembley high Tech. Coll., London [10017113] 23/06/2010 **AF**

Pendred, Miss P L, BA(Hons) MCLIP, L. Customer Serv. Mgr., Church End Libary, L. B of Barnet. [38511] 20/05/1985 **CM15/05/2002**

Pendreigh, Mrs J, Toy Lib., Lochgilphead. [65035] 13/10/2005 **ME**

Penfold, Dr D W, PhD DIC BSc ARCS MCLIP CEng MB, Sen. Lect. /Consultant/Editor, London Coll. of Comm., Edgerton Publishing Serv. [60572] 30/12/1981 **CM30/12/1981**

Penfold, Mrs K A, BA MCLIP, Catr., Univ. of Edinburgh, Main L. [18144] 07/10/1972 **CM13/01/1975**

Penn, Mrs C S, L. Asst. [10012709] 01/03/2009 **AF**

Penn, Ms E A, BA(Hons) MA MCLIP, Lib., Notts. C.C. [51584] 03/04/1995 **CM23/09/1998**

Penn, Mrs S J, BEd DipLib MCLIP, Lib., Hewitsons, Cambridge. [31441] 27/09/1979 **CM23/03/1982**

Penn, Mr S W, BA(Hons) DipLib MCLIP, QA & Release Mgr., Axiell Ltd, Nottingham. [28355] 14/11/1977 **CM12/11/1980**

Pennells, Mr J E, DMS MCLIP, Head & Serv.-L. & Culture L.B. Harrow [11499] 21/02/1965 **CM01/01/1968**

Pennells, Mrs L M, MCLIP, Retired. [11500] 02/10/1965 **CM01/01/1970**

Penney, Mrs B M, MCLIP, Life Member. [28998] 23/08/1950
         CM01/01/1955

Penney, Miss C L, BA DipLib MCLIP, Retired. [11503] 01/01/1966
         CM01/01/1969

Penney, Miss V R, MCLIP, Life Member. [11505] 10/01/1945
         CM01/01/1964

Pennick, Mrs K P, BA MA MCLIP, Lib., Royal Botanic Gardens, KEW [42205] 05/10/1988 **CM22/11/1995**

Pennie, Mr D A, MA MCLIP, Ret. [11507] 14/10/1970 **CM01/03/1973**

Penny, Mr A, BA MCLIP, Career Break [43454] 26/10/1989
         CM18/09/1991

Penny, Mrs D, Asst. L. Mgr., Cuffley L., Cuffley. [10013640] 18/11/2004
         AF

Penny, Mrs M E, MA(Hons) DipLIS MCLIP, Inf. Mgr., Grampion Fire and Resue Serv. [49647] 18/11/1993 **CM19/01/2000**

Penny, Mrs S, MA DipLib MCLIP, Sch. Lib., Tobermory High Sch., Argyll & Bute [43420] 26/10/1989 **CM18/09/1991**

Penrose, Mrs D, BA MCLIP, Learning Centres Co-Ordinator, Sussex Downs Coll., Eastbourne. [10011296] 13/10/2008 **CM18/12/2009**

Pentelow, Mr D, BLib MCLIP, Vice Chair, Trade Union Side, Natural England, Leeds. [11513] 25/10/1971 **CM11/08/1975**

Pentelow, Miss G M, MCLIP, Life Member. [11514] 13/01/1955
         CM01/01/1958

Pentney, Mrs S J, BSc(Econs) MCLIP, Strategic Support Mgr., Plymouth L. [55153] 24/07/1997 **CM19/11/2003**

Penton, Mr S G J, BA(Hons) MA LGSM(Hons) PGCE, Unknown. [10002238] 02/04/2007 **ME**

Peoples, Miss M A, BA HonFCLIP DMS, Asst. Ch. Lib., Western Educ. & L. Bd., Omagh. [21175] 01/10/1973 **CM01/09/1976**

Pepin, Miss S, BA DipLib MCLIP, Reader's Advisor, House of Commons L., London. [36938] 18/01/1984 **CM15/05/1989**

Percik, Mr D, BA(Hons) MPhil, EU Lib., Law Soc. L., London [59221] 09/01/2001 **ME**

Percival, Mr D, MA, Learning and Engagement Mgr. Portsmouth CC. [61420] 15/07/2002 **ME**

Percival, Dr N, BA, PhD, Unknown. [10012166] 08/01/2009 **ME**

Pereira, Ms M J, BA MCLIP MA CTESL, Consultant, Infoman Inc., Canada. [26509] 21/10/1976 **CM07/02/1980**

Pereira, Mrs P, Unwaged. [10016568] 14/04/2010 **AF**

Perella, Mrs J M, BA(Hons) MA, Child. Lib., Harold Wood L., L.B. of Havering. [61333] 28/05/2002 **ME**

Perfitt, Ms M T, FCLIP, Life Member. [11538] 01/01/1961 **FE29/10/1976**

Perham, Mrs L, JP BA MCLIP HonFCLIP FRSA, Dir., Various Charities and Non-Departmental Public Bodies. [11539] 01/01/1969
         CM01/01/1972

Perkins, Mr A B, B Tech M Inf Sc, Unwaged. [35715] 15/01/1983 **ME**

Perkins, Mr C A E, BA, L. Asst., Jesus Coll., Cambridge. [41299] 01/11/1987 **ME**

Perkins, Ms C, L. Operations Mgr., City Law Sch. L., London. [10009053] 01/07/2003 **AF**

Perkins, Mr D, MA, Lifelong Learning Facilitator, Longsight L., Manchester. [10001318] 31/03/2005 **ME**

Perkins, Mrs L J, BScEcon(Hons) MCLIP, P. A Shropshire Primary Health Trust [54349] 14/11/1996 **CM18/09/2002**

Perkins, Mrs N, MCLIP, Lib. Offr., Hants C.C., S. Ham L. [8068] 22/09/1965 **CM01/01/1970**

Perkins, Mrs S A, Sch. Lib., Beauchamps High Sch., Wickford. [65341] 18/01/2006 **ME**

Perreira, Mr S, BMus, Stud., City Univ. [65688] 31/03/2006 **ME**

Perrett, Mrs C H J, BA DipLib MCLIP, Ch. Catr., Middlesex Univ., London. [36620] 24/10/1983 **CM14/03/1990**

Perrin, Miss P M, FRSA BA MCLIP, Retired. [11556] 17/02/1949
         CM01/01/1956

Perrins, Miss R, BA DIP, Unwaged [10017054] 19/09/1994 **ME**

Perrott, Mrs M, BA HDipEd MA MCLIP, Sch. Lib, Cedars Upper Sch. & Comm. Coll., Leighton. [47575] 02/10/1992 **CM12/09/2001**

Perry, Mrs A, BSc DipLib MCLIP, Inf. Specialist, Unilever Res. [42279] 13/10/1988 **CM27/07/1994**

Perry, Mr D A, BA MCLIP, Lib., Health Protection Agency [22104] 20/02/1974 **CM18/08/1980**
Perry, Ms E J, BA(Hons) MCLIP, Asst. Lib., Plumpton Coll., Lewes. [10001319] 07/01/1986 **CM09/09/2009**
Perry, Mrs G E, BA MCLIP, Unemployed. [25804] 26/02/1976 **CM27/04/1982**
Perry, Mrs H, BEd DipILM MCLIP, Lib. Mgr., Wilmslew L., Cheshire C.C. [54707] 06/03/1997 **CM17/09/2003**
Perry, Miss J C, BA(Hons) MA, Asst. Lib., Univ. of the Arts, London. [64844] 02/08/2005 **ME**
Perry, Mrs L M M B, BA(Hons), Asst. L. Manger, Surrey L. [65187] 17/11/2005 **AF**
Perry, Mr M D, BA(Hons) DMS MCLIP, Retired [11562] 14/01/1969 **CM18/07/1972**
Perry, Miss N E, BA(Hons), Systems Lib.,Bishop Grosseteste Univ. Coll., Lincoln. [63946] 18/11/2004 **ME**
Perry, Mr P, MCLIP, Unwaged. [11563] 07/02/1955 **CM01/01/1960**
Perry, Miss R K, BA MCLIP, L. Serv. & E – Learning Mgr., Royal Berks, NHS FT, Reading. [42596] 18/01/1989 **CM22/07/1992**
Perry, Mrs S A, MA MCLIP, Lib., Epsom Coll., Epsom, Surrey. [63458] 12/05/2004 **CM08/08/2008**
Perry, Miss S M, BA Hons MA PhD, F/T Sch. Lib. Highgate Sch., London [10001267] 14/02/2007 **ME**
Persey, Miss V A, MCLIP, Lib. /Copywright Mgr., AQA, Guildford. [18105] 04/10/1972 **CM09/10/1975**
Pestell, Mr R, BSc MSc ALAA FCLIP JP, Dir., Multilingual L. Books, Queensland, Australia. [19247] 01/01/1965 **FE22/01/1997**
Peters, Mrs A E, MCLIP, Life Member. [11569] 03/03/1960 **CM01/01/1966**
Peters, Mrs C, BSc MCLIP, Team Lib., Surrey C.C. [33366] 26/10/1980 **CM13/05/1986**
Peters, Mrs E J, MCLIP, Lib., Steyning Grammar Sch., W. Sussex. [26418] 01/10/1976 **CM04/09/1980**
Peters, Mrs J L, MCLIP, Asst. Lib., W. Sussex C.C. [28241] 21/10/1977 **CM09/02/1982**
Peters, Mrs J M, BA MLS FHEA MCLIP FRSA, Dir. of L. & Univ. Lib., Cardiff Univ. [34208] 12/10/1981 **CM07/07/1987**
Peters, Mr J, LRC Mgr., City & Islington Coll., London. [10013687] 21/10/2009 **ME**
Peters, Ms K M, BA MCLIP, Subject Lib., London Met. Univ., London [62989] 04/12/2003 **CM11/03/2009**
Peters, Dr L J, BSc(Hons) MSc(Econ) MCLIP, Sub. Lib. for Law, Learning & Inf. Serv., Univ. of Chester. [53495] 04/07/1996 **CM15/09/2004**
Peters, Ms M, BA MA MCLIP, Sen. Asst. Lib., Univ. of the W. of England, Bristol. [59929] 06/11/2001 **CM21/06/2006**
Peters, Mrs N A, BA MA MCLIP, p. /t. Lib., Redditch L., Worcs. C.C. [35301] 01/10/1982 **CM05/05/1987**
Petersen, Miss C L, BA(Joint Hons), Child. Lib., Alfreton Lib., Derbyshire [10001947] 01/04/1995 **ME**
Petersen, Mrs L A, p. /t. Stud. /Asst. Lib., Univ. of Cent. England, Birmingham, Lordswood Boys Sch. & 6th Form Cent. [59021] 27/10/2000 **AF**
Peterson, Ms M F, BA(Hons) DipLib PhD, Dep. L. & Educ. Inf. Serv., Royal Adelaide Hosp., Adelaide. [64094] 14/01/2005 **ME**
Peterson, Ms S, BA(Hons), Stud [10006817] 17/12/2007 **ME**
Pethick, Mrs S M, BA MCLIP, Unemployed. [39307] 08/01/1986 **CM17/10/1990**
Peto, Mrs G W, BA DipLib MCLIP, Prison Lib., HMP Whatton. [26307] 01/10/1976 **CM23/10/1979**
Petocz, Mr L, MCLIP, Retired, Resident Australia. [17558] 12/09/1966 **CM01/01/1969**
Petrie, Miss A, MA MCLIP, Head of Trade & Investment, Brit. Embassy, Damascus [11582] 25/09/1968 **CM20/03/1973**

Petrie, Ms H M, BA(Hons) MSc MCLIP, Child. & Younge People's Lib., N. Lanarkshire Co., Wishaw. [51126] 17/11/1994 **CM16/07/2003**
Petrie, Mr J H, BSc MSc MCLIP, Retired [60056] 07/12/2001 **CM01/01/1998**
Pett, Mrs S C, BA, Stud., City Univ., London. [10011311] 13/10/2008**ME**
Pettit, Mr C P C, MA MCLIP, Asst. Co. Lib., Oxon. C.C. [26790] 27/10/1976 **CM18/12/1978**
Pettitt, Mr A J, L. Asst., Asylum & ImmigrationTribunal, London. [10010522] 01/08/2008 **AF**
Pettitt, Miss J M, MCLIP, Life Member. [11586] 31/03/1938 **CM01/01/1953**
Petty, Mr D, BA FCLIP, Assoc. Dir., Univ. of Georgia L., U. S. A. [11590] 01/10/1937 **FE01/01/1957**
Peyn, Ms O B, MA MA, Head of L. Catg., Soc. of Antiquaries of London, Piccadilly, London. [10015206] 07/10/1982 **ME**
Peyton, Mrs P R, Lib. Mngr., Redruth L., Cornwall [10017100] 23/06/2010 **AF**
Phelps, Mr M, MA MCLIP, Lib., Kirkless Metro. Council, Huddersfield [24786] 01/10/1973 **CM03/11/1977**
Phelps, Mrs S H, MCLIP, Unwaged. [31684] 05/11/1979 **CM27/07/1983**
Phelpstead, Mrs L J, BA(Hons) MCLIP, Unknown. [54122] 31/10/1996 **CM10/07/2002**
Philip, Mrs H R, BA MCLIP, Sch. Lib., Millburn Academy, Inverness. [20945] 11/09/1973 **CM04/08/1976**
Philip, Mr M T, BA(Hons), Lib. Asst. Univ. of Huddersfield [10011672] 11/11/2008 **ME**
Phillipps, Mrs T L, BA MCLIP, Pre-Prep Lib., St Martin's Sch., Northwood [35983] 01/03/1983 **CM10/05/1988**
Phillips, Mrs A J, BA(Hons) MCLIP, Career brake [48661] 02/04/1993 **CM22/05/1996**
Phillips, Miss A, Operations Mgr., Stockport MBC, Stockport. [59814] 10/10/2001 **ME**
Phillips, Ms A, BA MA MCLIP, Training Delivery Team, House of Commons L., London. [60951] 15/01/2002 **CM03/10/2007**
Phillips, Mr C J, BA DipLib MCLIP, Retired [25392] 09/01/1976 **CM08/06/1978**
Phillips, Mr C, BA DipLib MCLIP, Retired. [29791] 08/10/1978 **CM31/03/1981**
Phillips, Mrs D J, BA MCLIP, Unknown. [28118] 01/10/1977 **CM01/10/1979**
Phillips, Mr G A, BA(Hons) DipILM, Inf. Serv. Lib., RIS., Bury Cent. L., Bury. [10002978] 04/05/1995 **ME**
Phillips, Mrs H M, MA MSc MCLIP, Unwaged [52548] 08/11/1995 **CM13/03/2002**
Phillips, Dr H P, BA MA DipLib MCLIP, Res. & Mgmt. Consultant (Freelance) [36145] 01/07/1983 **CM16/12/1986**
Phillips, Mrs J B, BLib MCLIP, Unemployed. [25615] 24/01/1976 **CM03/09/1979**
Phillips, Mrs J C S, BA(Hons) MSc MCLIP, Community Lib., Wootton Bassett, Cricklade & Purton Lubraries, Wiltshire. [64838] 02/08/2005 **CM21/05/2008**
Phillips, Mrs K C, BSc MSc, Dir. /Owner, Kindred UK., Newcastle Upon Tyne. [56291] 28/04/1998 **ME**
Phillips, Ms K E, BA MA MCLIP, Lib, Imperial War Mus. [33743] 16/02/1981 **CM14/10/1983**
Phillips, Miss K L, BA(Hons) MCLIP, Asst. Lib., GCHQ, Cheltenham. [51864] 18/07/1995 **CM19/07/2000**
Phillips, Ms L A, BA(Hons), Unemployed. [50824] 20/10/1994 **ME**
Phillips, Ms L M, BA DipEd, Unwaged. [36243] 19/08/1983 **ME**
Phillips, Mr L, BA MCLIP, Leisure Dept. Lib., Cardiff Cent. L. [20913] 18/08/1973 **CM11/09/1975**
Phillips, Miss L, BA MCLIP, Retired. [11625] 30/01/1968**CM01/01/1972**
Phillips, Mrs M E, MCLIP, Stock & Distribution Lib., Carmarthensire C.C. [21595] 16/10/1973 **CM31/08/1978**

Phillips, Mr M E, MA MA MCLIP, Systems Lib., Univ. of Dundee. [50672] 07/10/1994 **CM16/05/2001**

Phillips, Miss M H, BA MCLIP, Retired. [11626] 08/02/1967 **CM01/01/1971**

Phillips, Mr M J, MCLIP, Retired. [11627] 22/09/1931 **CM01/01/1938**

Phillips, Mr M R, MCLIP, Retired. [11629] 23/09/1966 **CM01/01/1972**

Phillips, Mr R D, BA MCLIP, Lib., Haywards Heath L., W. Sussex. [33111] 02/10/1980 **CM15/07/1985**

Phillips, Mr R, BA(Hons) MPhil, Accessions Lib., The Nat. L. of Wales, Aberystwyth. [10006059] 03/09/2007 **ME**

Phillips, Mr R, DipIM MCLIP, Head of Inf. Serv. Devel., King's Fund, London. [56713] 07/10/1998 **CM21/11/2001**

Phillips, Mr R, MA FCLIP, Life Member. [11631] 05/10/1960 **FE01/01/1967**

Phillips, Miss R, User Serv. Lib, Archway Healthcare L., Highgate. [10015769] 27/09/2000 **ME**

Phillips, Mrs S E, BA(Hons) MCLIP, Sch. Lib., Royal Blind Sch., Edinburgh. [57028] 26/11/1998 **CM17/09/2003**

Phillips, Mr S J, BLib MCLIP, Vice President, Morgan Stanley, London. [40788] 06/06/1987 **CM14/11/1991**

Phillips, Miss S J, BA(Hons), Unknown. [10012070] 05/12/1994 **ME**

Phillips, Ms S L, BA, Unemployed. [35699] 17/01/1983 **ME**

Phillips, Mrs S M, Learning Resource Cent. Co-ordinator, Samuel Ward Arts & Tech. Coll., Suffolk. [10011145] 26/09/2008 **AF**

Phillips, Mr S, BA MLib MCLIP, Head of Learning Resources, Univ. Campus Suffolk [24126] 06/04/1975 **CM18/07/1979**

Phillips, Mrs S, BL FCLIP, Retired. [17564] 22/01/1958 **FE13/06/1990**

Phillips, Mr S, BA DipLib MCLIP, Unknown [11636] 02/03/1965 **CM01/01/1968**

Phillips, Mr W T, BA DipLib MCLIP, Reg. L. Mgr., Carmarthenshire C.C., Carmarthen L. [35191] 04/10/1982 **CM30/01/1991**

Phillips-Bacher, Ms J, MLIS, Seeking Work. [10011284] 07/10/2008 **ME**

Phillips-Morgan, Ms S R, BA DIP CCS MLib MCLIP, Freelance Yoga Teacher [42428] 20/10/1988 **CM23/03/1994**

Phillipson, Mrs E A, BA(Hons) PGCE, Unknown. [65899] 27/06/2006 **ME**

Phillpotts, Ms C E, BA(Hons) MA MCLIP, Learning Resources Mgr., London Met. Univ. [43276] 10/10/1989 **CM25/09/1996**

Philpot, Mrs F L, BA MA MCLIP, Arch., Inst. of Mech. Engineers, London. [60475] 11/12/2001 **CM04/02/2004**

Philpott, Mr S J, BLib MSc MCLIP, Business Sen. Consultant, Fujitsu Serv. [36222] 01/08/1983 **CM06/04/1999**

Phul, Miss A, BSc MSc MCLIP, Lib., Birmingham & Solihull Mental HealthT. [62914] 19/11/2003 **CM16/10/2009**

Physick, Miss H M, BA MCLIP, Sen. Asst. Lib., L.B. of Harrow L. [33956] 17/06/1981 **CM30/07/1985**

Piasecki, Miss R, BA(Hons) MA MCLIP, Sen. Lib. Info. & E-Serv., Richmond Ref. L., London [61161] 20/03/2002 **CM21/05/2008**

Pickard, Dr A J, BA(Hons) MA Phd, Head of Info. & Comm. Mnt, Sch. of Computing, Eng. & Inf. Sciences, Northumbia Univ. [10008126] 24/01/1994 **ME**

Pickard-Brace, Mr A, MA BA(Hons), Libr., Univ. Nottingham. [55908] 12/12/1997 **ME**

Pickaver, Miss C E, BA MSc(Econ) MCLIP, Head of L. Serv., Univ. of Kent. [28878] 22/01/1978 **CM05/04/1983**

Picken, Mr D P, MLib MCLIP, Grp. Leader -Knowledge Consultant, Dstl., Farnborough. [30887] 01/01/1963 **CM01/01/1966**

Picken, Ms J E, Prin. L. Asst., Bor. of Telford, Madeley Br. [45598] 01/04/1991 **AF**

Picken, Miss N, BA(Hons) MCLIP, Document Delivery Coordinator, Univ. of Reading, Reading. [62856] 17/11/2003 **CM21/11/2007**

Pickering, Mrs C B, BA(Hons) MA PGDipls MCLIP DMS, L. Offr., L. H.Q., Wakefield. [59358] 14/02/2001 **CM02/02/2005**

Pickering, Mrs O M, BA MA MPhil MCLIP, Asst. Lib., OBMH NHS Foundation Trust [57876] 20/09/1999 **CM16/07/2003**

Pickering, Miss P L, MCLIP, Life Member. [11662] 31/03/1955 **CM01/01/1961**

Pickersgill, Mrs A, BA MCLIP GradIPD, Lib., Hyde Clarendon Sixth Form L. Cheshire. [23879] 07/02/1975 **CM01/01/1977**

Pickett, Mrs K P, BA(Hons) MCLIP, News Co-ordinator & Mid Day Super. [42445] 09/11/1988 **CM14/09/1994**

Pickstone, Ms M E, BSc DipLib MCLIP, Site L. Mgr.,(Alsager), Manchester Met. Univ., Stoke-on-Trent. [34325] 23/10/1981 **CM10/02/1987**

Pickton, Dr M, PhD MCLIP, Res. Support Specialist., Univ of Northampton [63166] 02/03/2004 **CM21/03/2007**

Pickup, Mr P W H, FCLIP, Life Member. [11672] 23/02/1950 **FE01/01/1959**

Picton, Mr H A, BA MCLIP, Parlimentary Affairs Mgr., Bank of England, London. [22940] 21/09/1974 **CM26/07/1977**

Pierce, Mr J D, MLIS, Unwaged [10014813] 16/09/2009 **ME**

Pierce, Dr K F, PhD MPhil BA(Hons), Catr., Cardiff Univ. [61197] 08/04/2002 **ME**

Pieris, Mr K S, BA MCLIP, Retired. [19947] 15/01/1973 **CM21/10/1975**

Pieroni, Mrs W J, Learning Res. Coordinator, Blairgowrie High Sch., Perth. [65105] 01/11/2005 **ME**

Pietsch, Ms A, Academic Liaison Offr., Roehampton Univ., London. [64858] 03/08/2005 **ME**

Piggott, Mr R L, MCLIP, Corporate Lib., Wokingham Bor. Council. [10016452] 30/07/1974 **CM22/08/1977**

Pigott, Mrs F C, BA(Hons), Unwaged. [43324] 19/10/1989 **ME**

Pigula, Mrs E D, MA, Asst. Lib., The Coll. of Law, Guildford, Surrey. [57379] 22/02/1999 **ME**

Pike, Mrs J A, BA MCLIP, LRC Mgr., Southborough Hi. Sch., Surbiton. [32892] 15/10/1980 **CM10/10/1983**

Pike, Miss L J, BSc(Hons) MSc, Inf. Offr., Norton Rose, London. [61737] 30/10/2002 **ME**

Pike, Mrs R A, BA(Hons) DipLib MCLIP, Sch. Lib., Bishops Stortford Coll., Jnr. Sch. [34418] 05/11/1981 **CM16/05/1985**

Pilcher, Miss S L, BA PG Cert, User Serv. Lib., Robert Gordon Univ., Aberdeen. [10014999] 01/10/2009 **ME**

Pile, Mrs F M, MCLIP, Inf. Lib., Univ. of Bath [65516] 15/02/2006 **CM05/05/2010**

Pile, Mrs K N, BSc. Econ PGDipl, Unknown. [10012790] 04/03/2009 **ME**

Pilfold, Mrs J J, ACLIP, Unknown. [64651] 13/05/2005 **ACL16/04/2008**

Pilkington, Mrs C A, BA(Hons) DIPCeD, Info. Adviser, Inf. Team Careers Solutions, Manchester. [53616] 12/08/1996 **ME**

Pilkington, Mrs G H, BSc, Media Cent. Admin., Brit. Sch. in the Netherlands [46516] 15/11/1991 **ME**

Pilkington, Dr K E, BPharm(Hons) DipInfSci MSc PhD, Snr. Res. Fellow, Univ. Westminster, London [62427] 17/06/2003 **ME**

Pill, Mr T J H, MA MLib MA, Unknown. [47740] 16/10/1992 **ME**

Pillans, Mrs H A, BA MCLIP, Sch. Lib., Barrhead High Sch., E. Renfrewshire. [27604] 15/06/1977 **CM12/06/1979**

Pilling, Mr J C, MA MCLIP, Princ. Lib., Holton, Oxon. C.C. [35556] 27/10/1982 **CM05/05/1986**

Pilling, Miss L J, PgDip, Project Co-ordinator, Breightmet L., Bolton. [10010506] 01/08/2008 **ME**

Pilling, Miss S, MA/MSc, Info. Specialist, Cheltenham. [65697] 30/03/2006 **ME**

Pilling, Mrs S, BA MBA DipMus MCLIP, Unknown. [1350] 22/02/1969 **CM01/01/1971**

Pilmer, Mr A C, BA(Hons) MA MCLIP, Loc. Studies Lib., Slough L. [58869] 14/09/2000 **CM09/11/2005**

Pilmer, Ms S J, BSc MSc MCLIP, L. Mgr., NSPCC, London. [48884] 12/07/1993 **CM19/05/1999**

Pimperton, Mrs L, BA(Hons) MA DipIS MCLIP, Asst. Lib., Lancaster Univ., Lancaster. [44879] 08/01/1991 **CM18/11/1998**

Pinder, Mr C J, BA MLib FCLIP, Dir. of Learning Inf. Serv., Edinburgh Napier Univ. Learning Inf. Serv., Edinburgh. [21050] 24/09/1973 **FE29/03/2004**

Pinder, Mrs E, MCLIP, Retired. [9248] 25/03/1943 **CM01/01/1948**

Pinder, Mr F D, BA MCLIP, Princ. Lib., Cent. L. & Arts Cent., Rotherham. [22829] 09/09/1974 **CM14/09/1977**

Pinder, Ms M J, BA(Hons) MA MCLIP, Faculty Team Lib., Brotherton L., Leeds Univ. [47928] 26/10/1992 **CM21/05/1997**

Pine-Coffin, Miss H, BA MA MCLIP, Civil Servant, GCHQ. [55332] 01/10/1997 **RV29/03/2007** **CM15/05/2002**

Pinfield, Mr S J, MA MCLIP, CIO, Univ. of Nottingham. [44397] 04/10/1990 **CM18/11/1992**

Pinfold, Ms D, BA DipLib MCLIP, Head of L. and Info. Serv., Univ. Coll. Falmouth [31924] 07/01/1980 **CM03/03/1982**

Pinfold, Ms J, BA DipLib, Reader Serv. Lib., Plant Sci. L., Oxford Univ. L. Serv. [38051] 09/01/1985 **ME**

Pinion, Miss C F, BA FRSA HonFLA FCLIP, AV Consultant., Sheffield. [11711] 12/03/1961 **HFE20/09/2000**

Pink, Ms S, BA(Hons) MA MCLIP MCMI, Redunndancy. [55152] 23/07/1997 **CM21/11/2001**

Pinnegar, Ms S V, BA DipLib MCLIP, Sch. Lib., St. Catherine's Brit. Embassy Sch., Athens, Greece. [39322] 12/01/1986 **CM14/11/1991**

Pinnock, Mr A C, MA MCLIP, Retired. [19581] 16/11/1972 **CM30/06/1976**

Piotrowicz, Mrs A M, BA(Hons) ALCM PGDipILS LTCL, Unemployed. [48645] 01/04/1993 **ME**

Pipe, Mr C C, BA DipLib MCLIP, Freelance. Watermark, Norfolk. [11715] 01/07/1969 **CM01/07/1993**

Piper, Mrs P A, BA MCLIP, Lib. Mgr., Robert Mays Sch., Odiham, Hants. [36077] 26/04/1983 **CM07/07/1987**

Pir, Ms S E, LLB(Hons), Sen. Asst. Lib., Wandsworth. [10005494] 25/07/2007 **ME**

Pirie, Ms A, BSc(Hons) DipILS MCLIP, Lend. Lib., Perth & Kinross Council, Perth. [51144] 23/11/1994 **CM06/04/2005**

Pirie, Ms F L, MA MSc DipLib MCLIP, E-Serv. Asst., Scottish Parliament Inf. Cent., Edinburgh [31417] 01/10/1979 **CM17/11/1981**

Pirie, Mrs J B, MA(Hons), Inf. Off., Dept. of Special Lib. & Arch., Kings Coll., Univ. Aberdeen. [10016035] 10/02/2010 **ME**

Pirwitz, Ms H, MA DipLib MCLIP, Retired. [30785] 20/01/1979 **CM18/12/1981**

Pitcher, Miss M, BA MCLIP, Sen. Lib. (Acquisitions), Lancs. Co. L. & Inf. Serv., Preston. [23785] 13/01/1975 **CM24/11/1977**

Pitchford, Mr T R, BA, Sch. Lib., Hitchin Boys' Sch. L., Herts. [10013000] 19/03/2009 **AF**

Pitman, Mrs A J, BA MCLIP, Sch. Administrator, Milton Keynes Council. [29181] 06/04/1978 **CM20/08/1981**

Pitman, Mr A J, Sen. L. & IT Cent., Trafford Coll., Manchester. [10016081] 12/02/2010 **ME**

Pitman, Ms C, MA DipLib MCLIP, L. Devel. Advisor, Idea Stores, L.B. of Tower Hamlets. [10000886] 02/12/1981 **CM24/09/1985**

Pitman, Mrs H, ACLIP, Yourspace Proj. Mgr., Lancs Lib. & Info. Serv. [63312] 08/04/2004 **ACL04/03/2009**

Pitman, Miss N J, BA MCLIP, Asst. Lib., Norton Radstock Coll., Radstock [43688] 28/11/1989 **CM23/03/1994**

Pitt, Mrs C E, BSc (Hons), Knowledge & Inf. Agent, DSTL, Salisbury [10015023] 07/10/2009 **AF**

Pivnenko, Mrs N, MA, Sen. L. Asst., Judge Business Sch. L., Cambridge Univ. [64334] 04/03/2005 **ME**

Plaice, Ms C J, BLib(Hons) M. A. MCLIP, Faculty Lib. for Health & Life Sci., Univ. of the W. of Eng. [34174] 07/10/1981 **CM10/02/1987**

Plain, Mr W A, BA(Hons), Sch. Lib., Knox Academy, E. Lothian. [48314] 25/11/1992 **ME**

Plaister, Miss J M, OBE BSc FCLIP, Life Member. [11732] 01/01/1947 **FE01/01/1955**

Plant, Ms A F, BA(Hons), Ref. Lib., Sutton Coldfield L., [10013635] 22/08/1985 **ME**

Plant, Mrs V J, BA MCLIP, Learning Devel. Lib., Leics. L. Serv. [25492] 12/02/1976 **CM01/10/1981**

Platt, Mrs E J, BA(Hons) PGdip LIM, Document Delivery Team Leader, Univ of Salford [10006759] 10/12/2007 **ME**

Platt, Ms G S, BA DipLib MCLIP, Sch. of Mod. Lang. & Ling. Subject Spec., Univ. of Manchester. [22707] 16/09/1974 **CM28/01/1977**

Platt, Mrs M J, BSc DipLib MCLIP, ITC Lib., Cumbria C.C. Whithaven [35691] 19/01/1983 **CM26/02/1992**

Platt, Mr M R, Sen. Inf. Offr., Simmons & Simmons, London. [41450] 01/01/1988 **ME**

Platt, Miss T L, Inf. Offr., Nat. Audit Off., London. [65675] 31/03/2006 **ME**

Platts, Mrs H J, MA DipLib MCLIP, Health Info. Lib., Suffolk C.C. [31854] 09/01/1980 **CM17/05/1983**

Platts, Mrs J K, MCLIP, Principal L. Asst., Manchester Met. Univ. [64143] 19/01/2005 **CM28/01/2009**

Pledge, Ms D, BA(Hons) MSc, Inf. & Records Mgr., BIS, London [61734] 30/10/2002 **ME**

Pledger, Mrs H, BA(Hons) MA, Lib., Dept. for Child., Sch. and Families, Sheffield [54255] 11/11/1996 **ME**

Plenty, Mrs A S, BA(Hons) PGDip, Unwaged [55092] 10/07/1997 **ME**

Plimmer, Miss N J, BA(Hons), Stud., Child. Literature & Culture MA. [58226] 19/11/1999 **ME**

Plom, Ms H L, BA(Hons) MCLIP, Child. Lib., Hampshire CC., Winchester. [58132] 04/11/1999 **CM07/09/2005**

Plouviez, Mr B, Head of Info. Mgmt., Scottish Government, Edinburgh. [65705] 26/01/2006 **ME**

Plowman, Mrs P A, ACLIP, Learning Res. Mgr., Guilsborough Sch., Northants. [62390] 21/05/2003 **ACL23/09/2009**

Pluess, Mrs S, BA MSc, Grad., City Univ. [65687] 31/03/2006 **ME**

Plum, Mrs S M, BA MCLIP, Asst. Lib., Priory Sch. L., Hitchin. [28630] 03/01/1978 **CM17/08/1982**

Plumb, Mr D W, MA MCLIP, Retired [11754] 30/01/1972 **CM28/08/1975**

Poad, Mrs A E D, BA(Hons) MSc MCLIP, Retired. [46824] 11/02/1992 **CM19/05/1999**

Poad, Mrs J E, BA MCLIP, Head of L., Bedford Bor. C.C. [24127] 13/03/1975 **CM21/09/1978**

Pocock Bell, Mrs D S, BA(Hons) MA, Sch. Lib., St. Helen & St. Katharine [57729] 13/07/1999 **ME**

Pogue, Dr C, PhD MA MSc B Ed, Recently ended post as Inf. Mgt. Post, NHS. [10016170] 28/11/1980 **ME**

Pointer, Ms R J, BA MCLIP, Area Community Mgr., Leics C.C., Melton/Market Harborough [31545] 19/10/1979 **CM31/10/1984**

Pointon, Miss H E, MA, Unwaged. [10015450] 19/11/2009 **ME**

Poku, Miss M, MCLIP, Researcher, Hogan Lovells Internat. LLP, London. [64084] 15/12/2004 **CM11/11/2009**

Polchow, Ms S U, BA MA MCLIP FRSA, SLS Advisor, Northants Schs. Lib. Serv. [44647] 14/11/1990 **CM17/11/1999**

Polding, Mrs G M, MCLIP, Unwaged. [21254] 17/10/1973 **CM12/12/1977**

Pollard, Mrs N J A, Sch. Lib., St. John Fisher Catholic H. S., Harrogate [38439] 26/04/1985 **ME**

Pollard, Mr W, BSc(Econ), System Administrator, Anglia Poly. Univ., Cambridge. [61276] 09/05/2002 **ME**

Pollecutt, Ms N A, BA MA MCLIP, L. Systems Offr., Wellcome L., London. [55853] 02/12/1997 **CM17/01/2001**

Pollinger, Miss S L, BA(Hons), Stud. [10015084] 12/10/2009 **ME**

Pollitt, Mr M J, BA MA, Info. Lib., Nottinghamshire CC [64855] 02/08/2005 **ME**

Pollitt, Miss M L, MCLIP, Unemployed, Essex. [11786] 14/02/1972 **CM20/12/1974**

Polson, Mr R G, MA DipLib MCLIP FSA(Scot) MSc(, Subject Lib., Univ. of Stirling, Highland Health Sci. L., Inverness. [44133] 25/05/1990 **CM23/03/1993**

Polush, Ms K, L. Asst.,The Robert Gordon Univ. /Supply Sch. Lib., Aberdeen C.C. [10008002] 05/10/1990 **ME**

Pomeroy, Miss K M, MCLIP, Retired. [11792] 02/09/1968 **CM01/01/1971**

Pond, Mrs C P, MCLIP, Unwaged. [3144] 12/06/1969 **CM11/08/1972**

Pond, Dr C, HonFCLIP, Head Of Ref. Servs., House of Commons L., London [62818] 23/10/2003 **HFE23/10/2003**

Pond, Miss F M, BA DipLib MCLIP, Dep. Info. Mgr, Birm. City Univ., Birmingham. [32610] 04/05/1980 **CM20/05/1982**

Ponka, Mrs J A, BA MCLIP, Asst. Lib. Mgr., Holy Cross 6th Form Coll., Bury,Lancs. [23147] 31/10/1974 **CM31/08/1977**

Ponniah, Mrs G V, BA MCLIP, Corportate Inf. Government Mgr. [40376] 23/01/1987 **CM24/03/1992**

Pons, Ms P A E, MSc MCLIP, Temp. [55296] 19/09/1997 **CM15/05/1999**

Ponsonby, Miss S E, BA MCLIP, Researcher, ITN, London. [31926] 09/01/1980 **CM07/11/1984**

Pontin, Ms D M, MCLIP, Freelance Lib. /L. Consultant. [11796] 14/10/1964 **CM01/01/1969**

Ponting, Mr M, MA(Hons) DipIM, Retired. [56387] 01/07/1998 **ME**

Pool, Miss E R, Life Member. [11798] 25/09/1948 **ME**

Pool, Mr M, MCLIP, Sen. Asst. Lib., Torquay Ref. L., Torbay L. Serv. [11800] 03/12/1969 **CM02/09/1975**

Poole, Miss B M, BA MCLIP, Mgmnt. Co-ordinator., N. Yorks. Co. L., Co. L. H.Q. [21392] 08/11/1973 **CM12/11/1975**

Poole, Miss J L, MCLIP, Retired. [19253] 03/02/1964 **CM01/01/1969**

Poole, Mr K, BA MCLIP, Retired. [11802] 12/02/1952 **CM01/01/1956**

Poole, Miss K, BA MSc MCLIP, Unknown. [61106] 25/02/2002 **CM03/10/2007**

Poole, Mrs L E, BA MCLIP, Life Member. [11803] 16/01/1950 **CM01/01/1955**

Poole, Mr N, BA MA, Ch. Exec., Collection Trust, London. [10013059] 10/09/2009 **AF**

Pooley, Miss A K, BA(Hons) MA, Inf. Asst., Linklaters [66088] 21/09/2006 **ME**

Poolton, Mrs K E, BA MCLIP, Coll. Lib, St Bede's Coll., Manchester. [33888] 30/04/1981 **CM15/08/1984**

Poore, Mrs H M, BA(Hons) MA MCLIP, Asst. Lib., UWE, Bristol. [57976] 07/10/1999 **CM01/02/2007**

Pope, Mr A G, BA(Hons) MLIS CELTA, Networks Content Mgr., ARUP, London. [10014173] 23/06/2003 **ME**

Pope, Mrs A J, BA LLB DipLib MCLIP FHEA, Sen. Subject & Learning Support Lib. Staffs. Univ., Leek Road L., Stoke on Trent. [35207] 05/10/1982 **CM06/09/1988**

Pope, Mrs A V, BA(Hons) MA MCLIP, Knowledge Serv. Programme Mgr., W. Midlands Deanery, NHSWM, St. Chads Court. [47349] 20/07/1992 **CM27/01/2010**

Pope, Miss S D, BSc, Learning Resources Cent. Mgr, Llantarnam Sch., Cwmbran. [10010615] 19/08/2008 **ME**

Pope, Miss S E, BA DipLib MCLIP, Self Employed [35692] 19/01/1983 **CM15/11/1988**

Popham, Mrs R M, MCLIP, Retired. [15726] 01/01/1959 **CM27/08/1974**

Popp, Ms G, Doc. Mgr., Brit. Film Inst. [44982] 24/01/1991 **ME**

Poppleston, Mr M, MCLIP, Life Member. [11817] 07/02/1961 **CM01/01/1964**

Poppy, Miss P A, MCLIP, Asst. Lib., Bournemouth Univ. [11819] 03/01/1972 **CM07/01/1976**

Porritt, Ms F H, BA(Hons) MSc PGDipLib, Sen. Asst. Subject Lib., L. & Inf. Serv., Teeside Univ., Middlesborough. [10013918] 24/02/1989 **ME**

Porteous, Miss L D, BA MA MCLIP, Sen. Inf. Advisor, Kingston Univ. [39978] 07/10/1986 **CM18/04/1990**

Porter, Mrs A K, BA MCLIP, Relief Lib. [20972] 31/08/1973 **CM01/11/1976**

Porter, Mr A, BA BSc MCLIP, Unknown. [10016532] 01/01/1998 **CM31/01/1996**

Porter, Miss C E, BA MLib MCLIP, Dir. of L. & Learning Servs., Newman Univ. Coll., Birmingham. [10014273] 14/10/1986 **CM14/09/1994**

Porter, Ms D, BA MCLIP, Customer Serv. Lib., Wigston L., Leics. [41977] 04/07/1988 **CM25/09/1996**

Porter, Mrs E B, BA MCLIP OBE, Ret. [23273] 25/11/1974 **CM31/08/1978**

Porter, Mr G J, BA MA MCLIP, Network Mgr., Lincolnshire Co. C., Sleaford. [40300] 18/01/1987 **CM23/03/1993**

Porter, Miss R E, BSc (Hons) MSc, Knowledge & Inf. Agent, DSTL, Salisbury [10015021] 07/10/2009 **AF**

Portman, Mrs J E, MCLIP, p/t. Academic Liason Lib., Univ. of Surrey. [1342] 14/09/1967 **CM01/01/1972**

Poskitt, Ms K, MCLIP, Inf. Team Leader, Leeds City Council, Leeds [10007207] 05/01/1980 **CM01/10/1986**

Posner, Ms K, BA, Unknown. [10012034] 10/12/2008 **ME**

Postlethwaite, Mrs F D, BA MCLIP, Sch. Liaison & Child. Lib., City of York Council. [31802] 06/12/1979 **CM22/10/1985**

Poston, Mrs H, BA(Hons) Dip Inf. Mgm. MCLIP, Unknown. [10014348] 23/08/1993 **CM20/11/2002**

Pote, Ms G F, BA MA MCLIP, Adult Lend. Lib., Barbican L. City of London. [34028] 02/07/1981 **CM20/11/1986**

Potten, Mr E J, BA MSc MA, Asst. Keeper of Printed Books, John Rylands Univ. L., Manchester. [58607] 12/04/2000 **ME**

Potter, Mr D C, MSc BA MCLIP, Head of Inf. & Publications, MS Soc., London. [19811] 01/12/1972 **CM24/07/1980**

Potter, Mrs J H, BSc MCLIP, Inf. Serv. & Events Mgr. Access ERA Cobham Tech. Serv. Surrey. [60577] 02/03/1976 **CM07/03/1980**

Potter, Mr J M, BA MCLIP, Life Member. [19535] 26/02/1959 **CM01/01/1964**

Potter, Miss K S, BA(Hons) MA, Sen. Inf. Offr., The Waste & Res. Action Prog., Banbury. [55435] 13/10/1997 **ME**

Potter, Mrs L M, BA DipLib MCLIP, Primary Care/ e Leraning Lib., Milton Keynes Hosp. L. [31571] 04/11/1979 **CM23/02/1982**

Potter, Mr N, BA MA MSc, Life-share Prospect Offr., Univ. of leeds [10012966] 17/03/2009 **ME**

Potter, Mrs S P, BA DipLib MCLIP, Liaison Lib., Nottingham Trent Univ. [37515] 02/10/1984 **CM05/04/1988**

Potterton, Miss R, BA MCLIP, Asst. Libr., Dublin. [63434] 07/05/2004 **CM10/07/2009**

Potton, Mr D M, MA DipLib MCLIP, Head of L. Serv., Derby City Council. [29795] 22/10/1978 **CM28/10/1981**

Potton, Mrs J K, BA MCLIP, Principal Lib., Derbys C.C. [32880] 09/10/1980 **CM17/12/1985**

Poulter, Mr A J, BA MA MSc MCLIP, Lect., Dept. of Comp. & Inf. Sci., Glasgow. [33117] 20/10/1980 **CM01/07/1990**

Poultney, Mrs A, ACLIP, L. Asst., Mansfield L., Notts. [10004167] 07/08/2007 **ACL16/07/2008**

Poulton, Ms A J, BA MA MCLIP FHEA DMS PGDSM PGC, Academic Team Mgr. – Learning and Skills Devel. - De Montfort Univ. [52236] 17/10/1995 **CM21/07/1999**

Poulton, Mrs M, BA MEd DipLib MCLIP, Health Lib., Univ. of Wales, Bangor, Gwynedd. [25630] 26/01/1976 **CM26/01/1978**

Pover, Mrs A E, BSc MCLIP, Unwaged. [32760] 08/08/1980 **CM15/09/1983**

Powell, Miss A F, BA(Hons), Graduate Trainee Lib., Telford L., Telford. [10007321] 13/02/2008 **ME**

Powell, Miss A M, BA MLS, Programme Offr., INASP, Oxford. [56288] 28/04/1998 **ME**

Powell, Mrs C L, BA(Hons) DipILM MCLIP, I. T. & Learning Cent. Facilitator, Denbigh Comm. Coll. [58146] 08/11/1999 **CM06/04/2005**

Powell, Mrs C O J, BA BSc DipLib MCLIP, Lib. Mgr., London Underground [10920] 02/11/1971 **CM12/02/1975**

Powell, Mr D, BA FCLIP, Life Member. [11857] 01/01/1952 **FE01/01/1955**

Powell, Miss E C, BA(Hons) DipLib MCLIP, Head of Catg., The London L. [35286] 09/10/1982 **CM30/03/1999**

Powell, Miss E, P/T Staff, Bath Spa Univ. [63957] 22/11/2004 **ME**

Powell, Mrs E, BA DipLib MCLIP, Serv. Dev. Co-ordinator, Child. & Families, Worcs. C.C. [61020] 01/02/2002 **CM01/02/2006**

Powell, Miss G M, FCLIP, Life Member. [11862] 12/03/1930 **FE01/01/1934**

Powell, Miss G, BA MCLIP, Self Employed [37553] 05/10/1984 **CM18/04/1989**

Powell, Mrs H D, BA MCLIP, Sch. Lib., Claremont High Sch., Kenton,Harrow. [31298] 05/10/1979 **CM11/12/1989**

Powell, Miss H, BSc MCLIP, Stud. [10016045] 10/02/2010 **ME**

Powell, Ms I F, BSc MSc, Advisory Lib., Coventry Sch. L. & Resources Serv., Coventry. [62151] 03/03/2003 **ME**

Powell, Mr J C, FCLIP, Life member. [11867] 01/01/1941 **FE01/01/1954**

Powell, Mrs J R, BA DipLib MCLIP, IP Formalities & Inf. Offr., Foseco Inter. Ltd., Tamworth. [43518] 31/10/1989 **CM21/07/1993**

Powell, Mrs J, BA MCLIP, Dep. Dist. Lib., High Peak, Derbys. C.C. [28801] 02/02/1978 **CM05/02/1981**

Powell, Miss L A, MCLIP, Lib., Maxwelltown High Sch. [64387] 14/03/2005 **CM16/10/2009**

Powell, Mr L B, BA M DIV MCLIP, Pastor, Covenant Baptist Church, Toronto, Ontario, Canada. [17588] 18/09/1953 **CM01/01/1960**

Powell, Mrs M, MCLIP,MSc,BA(Hons) Dip EngLit, Devel. Offr., CILIP Cymru/Wales. [64894] 09/09/2005 **CM21/11/2007**

Powell, Mr M, BA(Hons) MA MSc MCLIP, Head of Inf. Serv., Careers Serv., Univ. of Bristol [54875] 14/04/1997 **RV05/10/2007** **CM10/07/2002**

Powell, Mrs N, MCLIP, P. /t. L. Asst., S. Glos. Council. [23092] 29/10/1974 **CM13/07/1977**

Powell, Mr P E, MCLIP, Retired. [60497] 09/04/2001 **CM09/04/2001**

Powell, Mr S D, BA(Hons) MCLIP, Child. & Yth. Lib., Denman Public Lib., Nottinghamshire CC. [42943] 28/04/1989 **CM26/01/1994**

Powell, Miss S J, Lib. Asst., Allen & Overy, London. [65441] 23/02/2006 **AF**

Powell, Mrs S, BA MCLIP, Head of Ls. &Halls, Westminster House [28786] 23/01/1978 **CM15/02/1983**

Power, Mr A G, BA MCLIP, Inf. Specialist, Bucks C.C., Aylesbury. [34398] 30/10/1981 **CM07/10/1986**

Power, Mr G N, BA DipLib MCLIP, Access Lib., Inst. of Advanced Legal Studies, London. [43193] 01/10/1989 **CM15/10/2002**

Power, Mrs M B A, MA DipLib MCLIP, Network Lib., Aberdeenshire Council, Aboyne Academy. [23207] 09/11/1974 **CM02/05/1978**

Powis, Mr C M, BA MA MLib FCLIP HEA, Dep. Dir. (Academic Serv.) Univ. of Northampton. [42381] 21/10/1988 **FE03/10/2007**

Powis, Ms E, Project Mgr. [10008799] 12/05/1983 **ME**

Powles, Mrs J C, BA MCLIP, Lib., Spurgeons Coll., London. [22916] 08/10/1974 **CM04/11/1976**

Powles, Mrs S M, MCLIP, Learning Res. Cent. Mgr., Bracknell & Wokingham Coll. [11886] 23/09/1969 **CM01/08/1972**

Powling, Mr T J, BA(Hons) Cert ED PGCE, Flexible Learning Mgr., Northbrook Coll., Worthing. [10005983] 21/08/2007 **ME**

Pownall, Miss R L, BA MA PgDipILS MCLIP, Sen. Inf. Advisor, Kingston Univ. [59370] 19/02/2001 **CM29/03/2006**

Powne, Ms C C A, BMus MA MCLIP, Univ. Lib., Lancaster Univ. [36400] 06/10/1983 **CM20/01/1987**

Poyner, Mrs A E, MCLIP, Retired. [32831] 01/01/1963 **CM10/08/1983**

Prada, Mrs J A, BSc(Hons) MCLIP, Inf. Resources Magr., London S. Bank Univ. [42727] 13/02/1989 **CM26/07/1995**

Prady, Mrs N L, BA(Hons) MCLIP, Subject Lib., Anglia Ruskin Univ., Cambridgeshire [60957] 18/01/2002 **CM30/11/2009**

Prangnell, Mr R D, BSc MCLIP, Retired. [60624] 25/09/1964 **CM21/03/1967**

Pratchett, Ms T L, BA(Hons) MSc, Clinical Lib., Lancaster Infirmary, Lancs. [10005107] 13/06/2007 **ME**

Pratt, Mr A L, BA, Asst. Lib. (Catg.), Dept. for Work & Pensions, London. [40214] 17/11/1986 **ME**

Pratt, Mrs C Q, MA DipLib MCLIP, Sen. Offr., Glasgow City Council, Social Work Serv. [26493] 12/10/1976 **CM31/10/1979**

Pratt, Mr D R, BA(Hons), Inf. Offr., The Coll. Law, Birmingham [10016318] 24/04/1985 **ME**

Pratt, Mrs F H, MA, Stock Serv. Offr., L.B. Southwark. [61572] 02/10/2002 **AF**

Pratt, Mrs J, BSc(Hons) DipIM MCLIP, Sen. Lib. (Sch.), London B. of Richmond upon Thames, Surrey. [48626] 19/03/1993 **CM06/04/2005**

Pratt, Miss L A, BA MCLIP, Lib. - Morning Team Leader, Projects, SERCO, Swindon. [58703] 09/06/2000 **CM23/01/2008**

Pratt, Ms L A, BA DipLib MCLIP, Multi-Skilled Developer [24259] 03/05/1975 **CM19/08/1977**

Pratt, Mr M, MA, LLM, Inf. Specialist, Cranfield Univ. [10016464] 28/11/1994 **ME**

Pratt, Mrs P K, BA MCLIP, Retired. [10030] 09/02/1953 **CM01/01/1963**

Preater, Mr A J, BSc, Web App. Mngr. [10014448] 31/07/2009 **ME**

Precious, Ms A J, BA, L. Enquiries. Mgr., MOD [41627] 05/02/1988 **ME**

Precious, Mrs H, BA(Hons) MSc, Career Break [61736] 30/10/2002 **ME**

Preddle, Mr C C, BA MCLIP, Retired. [11904] 27/07/1968 **CM01/01/1971**

Preddle, Ms C, BSc(Hons) MA MCLIP, L. & Inf. Offr., Cent. L., Manchester. [57965] 05/10/1999 **CM28/01/2009**

Preece, Ms J A, BA DipLib MCLIP, Campus L. Mgr., Univ. of E. London. [28655] 11/01/1978 **CM11/04/1980**

Preece, Miss R, BAHons MCLIP, Resources Advisor, Kingston Coll. [65375] 10/01/2006 **CM11/06/2010**

Preest, Ms K J, BA(Hons) DipILM MCLIP, Acting Lib., Rosemurry L., Murray Edwards Coll. [55049] 01/07/1997 **CM25/07/2001**

Prentice, Mrs K M, BLib MCLIP, Area Mgr. -W., Essex C.C., Harlow L. [39436] 22/01/1986 **CM26/02/1992**

Prentice, Mr L, BA, Dir., Prentice Mgmnt Ltd. Bradford. [10016926] 16/06/2010 **ME**

Prescott, Mr A R, BA(Hons) DipILS, Operations Mgr., Newport City Council. [54761] 01/04/1997 **ME**

Press, Mr S J, BSc (Hons) MSc, Academic Lib., PDC., London [10013569] 07/05/2009 **ME**

Prestage, Mrs L R, MA BA MCLIP, Family & Lifelong Learning Serv. Mgr, Kent C.C. [41070] 01/10/1987 **CM13/06/1990**

Preston, Ms I F, BA MA, Unknown. [10012596] 19/02/2009 **ME**

Preston, Miss J C, BA MA, Coll. Lib., Coll. of St. Hild and St. Bede, Durham Univ. [10013155] 19/04/1994 **ME**

Preston, Miss K A, BA(Hons) MSc MCLIP, Community Lib., Bradford & Avon L. [62735] 15/10/2003 **CM21/03/2007**

Preston, Mr M, BA(Hons) MLib MCLIP, Subject Lib., Goldsmiths Coll., London. [48592] 25/02/1993 **CM06/04/2005**

Preston, Mrs S E, BA(Hons) MCLIP, Asst. Lib. (relief), W. Sussex C.C. [4464] 02/06/1970 **CM05/12/1973**

Preston, Mr S, MA PG/Dip ILS, Local Studies Asst., N. Lanarkshire Council. [63293] 07/04/2004 **ME**

Prestwood, Mrs D A, ACLIP, Lib. Asst., Skegby L., Mansfield, Notts [10012664] 01/03/2009 **ACL11/12/2009**

Preuss, Mrs R J, BA MCLIP, Child. Lib., W. Berks. Council, Newbury L. [36908] 13/01/1984 **CM02/06/1987**

Price, Ms A M, MSc, Inf. Scientist, Wessex Inst. for Health R & D, Univ. of Southampton. [61102] 25/02/2002 **ME**

Price, Mrs C L, BA(Hons) MA MCLIP, E-Strategy & Res. Mgr., Univ. of Surrey, Guildford. [51038] 09/11/1994 **RV30/04/2007 CM26/11/1997**

Price, Mrs D M, BA(Hons) MSc MCLIP, Inf. Specialist, GCHQ, Cheltenham. [51054] 09/11/1994 **RV16/04/2008** **CM21/07/1999**

Price, Mr D, BSc(Econ) MCLIP, Br. Lib., Treorchy, Rhondda Cynon Taff CBC., Treorchy, Mid Glamorgan. [56367] 18/06/1998 **CM15/11/2000**

Price, Mr E V, MCLIP, Unknown. [19261] 11/09/1972   **CM07/08/1975**
Price, Mrs E, MCLIP, Retired [11938] 10/01/1965   **CM01/01/1969**
Price, Miss F E M, BA DipLib, L. Technician/Researcher, ITN, London. [33823] 02/03/1981   **ME**
Price, Mr G D, BA DipLib MCLIP, Tech. Serv. Mgr., B. L. P. E. S., (L. S. E.), London. . [32153] 30/01/1980   **CM09/02/1982**
Price, Miss G, BA MA MCLIP, Stud. Serv. Lib., Inst. of Educ. L., London. [40146] 06/10/1986   **CM27/03/1991**
Price, Mrs H T K, BA(Hons) PGCE, Lib., BIWF, Co Durham [10014737] 07/09/2009   **AF**
Price, Mrs J D, MCLIP B. Th, Aquisitions Lib., City Coll. Plymouth, Devon. [4899] 27/01/1972   **CM01/07/1975**
Price, Mrs K M, MCLIP, Life Member. [11948] 14/02/1953   **CM01/01/1958**
Price, Mrs L, MSc, Stud., Glamorgan Univ. [64541] 09/05/2005   **ME**
Price, Mr P J, BSc DipLib MCLIP, LMS Mgr., Univ. of Plymouth. [11952] 14/01/1972   **CM05/05/1975**
Price, Miss P, BA MSc(Econ) MCLIP, Asst. Lib., Swansea Met. Univ. [62748] 01/10/2003   **CM06/05/2009**
Price, Mr R J R, BA(Hons) DipIS MCLIP, Volunteer Coordinator, Leonard Cheshire Disability [49470] 03/11/1993   **CM17/03/1999**
Price, Miss S D, BA BTEC, Princ. L. Asst., Birmingham Conservatoire. [43373] 09/10/1989   **ME**
Price, Mrs S E, BA(Hons) MA MCLIP, Lib. Serv. Mgr., Francis Costello L., Oswestry. [56313] 29/04/1998   **CM02/02/2005**
Price, Miss S E, BSc MSc, Stud. Univ. of Reading, Main L. [65367] 16/01/2006   **ME**
Price, Dr S H, Curriculum Lib., Exeter Coll. [10011079] 24/09/2008   **AF**
Price, Miss S T, BA(Hons) MCLIP, Asst. Br. Lib., Powys C.C. Newtown L. [57025] 26/11/1998   **CM11/03/2009**
Price, Mrs S, BLS MPhil PGCHE MCLIP FHEA, Academic Liaison Team Mgr., Nottingham Trent Univ. [42008] 17/07/1988   **CM01/04/2002**
Price, Mrs T A, BLS MSc MCLIP, Inf. Specialist, NICE, Manchester. [33459] 01/12/1980   **CM24/02/1986**
Price, Mr W A, BA FCLIP, Ret. [11957] 26/07/1962   **FE01/01/1967**
Prichard, Mr J A, FCLIP, Life Member. [11959] 15/02/1943   **FE01/01/1957**
Priddey, Ms D J, BA(Hons) MSc(Econ) MCLIP, BNI Business Mgr., Bournemouth Univ. [49826] 10/11/1993   **CM19/01/2000**
Priddey, Mrs E J, MCLIP, Unknown. [11367] 04/01/1972   **CM03/09/1975**
Priddle, Miss L J, BA(Hons) MA, Dep. Lib., The Inst. of Structural Eng., London. [56821] 23/10/1998   **ME**
Pridgeon, Ms C A, BA(Hons) MSc MCLIP, Sch. Serv. Mgr., Longsight L., Manchester. [43899] 09/02/1990   **CM20/11/2002**
Pridham, Mrs H, BA DipILS MCLIP, Br. Lib., Bridgend Co. Bor. Council, Maesteg L. [54648] 07/02/1997   **CM15/03/2000**
Pridham, Mrs J P, MCLIP, Life Member. [11966] 01/01/1954   **CM01/01/1969**
Pridmore, Miss J, BA DipLib MCLIP, Lib., GWP Consultants [32154] 24/01/1980   **CM04/03/1983**
Priest, Mr D C, B. SOC. SC RMN, Inf. Specialist, BSI Grp., London. [10016636] 20/04/2010   **AF**
Priest, Mrs R E, BA DipLib MCLIP, Coll. Lib., Shetland Coll. UHI/NAFC Marine Cent. [10002653] 02/12/1981   **CM18/07/1985**
Priestley, Mrs J, BSc DipLib, Higher L. Exec., House of Commons, London. [42846] 22/03/1989   **ME**
Priestley, Mrs J, BA MCLIP, Learner Resources Mgr., The Adam Smith Coll., Fife. [30791] 03/04/1979   **CM23/02/1983**
Priestley, Ms M J, BA MCLIP, Lib., G4S, HMP Altcourse, Liverpool. [28129] 03/10/1977   **CM18/10/1979**
Priestley, Mr P, Unknown. [10017016] 18/06/2010   **ME**
Priestley-Eaton, Mrs H C, BSc MCLIP, Lib. in Charge [61418] 15/07/2002   **CM10/07/2009**
Priestner, Mr A J, BA(Hons) MA MCLIP, Head Lib., Judge Business Sch., Cambridge Univ. [51583] 03/04/1995   **CM21/05/1997**

Prince, Mrs C V, BA(Hons) PGCE, Advisory Lib., Portsmouth SLS, Portsmouth [10001793] 27/02/2007   **ME**
Prince, Ms H K, BA MA, L. Serv. Mgr., Princess Alexandra Hosp. NHS Trust, Harlow, Essex. [57991] 08/10/1999   **ME**
Prince, Mrs I, Stud., Aberystwyth Univ. [10010198] 09/07/2002   **ME**
Prince, Miss R J, MA MCLIP, Bibl. Serv. Co-ordinator, S. Glos. L. Serv., Yate. [41108] 12/10/1987   **CM17/01/1990**
Prince, Mr S J, BSc DipLib MCLIP, Head of Lib. Serv., Cent. for Ecology & Hydrology Midlothian. [39988] 08/10/1986   **CM21/07/1989**
Pringle, Miss L A, BA(Hons) DipInf, Sen. Asst. Lib., Wirral Bor. Co., W. Kirby L. [44447] 09/10/1990   **ME**
Pringle, Mrs M C, BSc MSc MCLIP, Dir., Vital Inf. Ltd., Bucks. [37106] 09/02/1984   **CM22/04/1992**
Prior, Miss D E, MA(Hons), Stud., Strathclyde Univ. [64265] 22/02/2005   **ME**
Prior, Miss H I, BA MCLIP, Child. Serv. Lib., L.B. of Harrow, Middlesex. [32334] 06/03/1980   **CM14/11/1985**
Prior, Mrs M R, BA MA MCLIP, Retired. [11986] 04/03/1954   **CM01/01/1963**
Prior, Ms S D, BA(Hons) MA MCLIP, Lib., Bexley C., Footscray Offices, Sidcup [48823] 09/06/1993   **CM25/07/2001**
Prior-Jones, Ms S M, BA MCLIP, P/T Asst. Lib., Shoreham., W. Sussex C.C. [33119] 23/10/1980   **CM11/03/1985**
Pritchard, Mr A W, BA MCLIP, Area Devel. Lib., Leeds L. & inf. Serv. [38012] 01/01/1985   **CM12/09/1990**
Pritchard, Mr A, BA(Hons) MCLIP, Asst. Lib., Pontypridd L., Rhondda-Cynon-Taff Co. Bor. Council. [44965] 28/01/1991   **CM21/03/2001**
Pritchard, Mr A, MPhil FCLIP, Retired [11988] 17/01/1962   **FE01/02/1978**
Pritchard, Miss C A, MSc (Econ) MCLIP, Lib., Leighton Hosp., Mid. Cheshire Hosp. NHS Foundation Trust. [63067] 27/01/2004   **CM08/08/2008**
Pritchard, Mrs E J, BSc(Hons) DipLib MCLIP, Assist. Lib., Veterinary Laboratories Agency Surrey [28392] 16/11/1977   **CM01/07/1992**
Pritchard, Mrs G E, BLib MCLIP, Lib., Oxford Univ. [31413] 15/10/1979   **CM05/04/1983**
Pritchard, Mr H J, BLib MCLIP, Business Eye Inf. Mgr., Welsh Assembley Goverment [22032] 16/01/1974   **CM15/04/1980**
Pritchard, Miss J, BA MCLIP, Administrator, Work place Unknown [30513] 24/01/1979   **CM17/03/1982**
Pritchard, Mrs L C, MCLIP, L. Asst., L. & Inf. Serv., Univ. of Wales, Swansea. [25060] 22/10/1975   **CM29/05/1979**
Pritchard, Mr O J, BA(Hons) MA MCLIP, Asst. Dir. (Serv.), Stud. and Learning Support, Univ. of Sunderland. [45562] 07/03/1991   **CM26/01/1994**
Pritchard, Mrs S E, BA DipLib MCLIP, Br. Lib., Newtown L., Powys. [43751] 01/01/1990   **CM15/09/1993**
Pritchatt, Ms D J, BLS(Hons) DipLib MCLIP, Sen. Inf. Professional., NHS Blood & Transplant., Birmingham [29797] 15/09/1978   **CM22/06/1984**
Pritchett, Mrs C M, BA MA, Univ. Teacher, Loughborough Univ. [48334] 27/11/1992   **ME**
Pritchett, Mrs E, BA, Mother. [42334] 12/04/1966   **ME**
Privetti, Mrs P A, BA(Hons) DipMus MCLIP, Lib., Royal Sch. Haslemere [231] 07/10/1968   **CM22/02/1993**
Procter, Miss S J, BA MCLIP, Area Mgr. Support, N. Lancs. Co. L. [32550] 09/05/1980   **CM30/12/1983**
Proctor, Ms B L, ACLIP, Health & Safety Exec., Knowledge Cent., Merseyside. [64510] 27/04/2005   **ACL22/06/2007**
Proctor, Mr J M, FCLIP, Retired. [19263] 01/01/1949   **FE01/01/1968**
Proctor, Ms J W, BA MCLIP, Lend. Lib., Torbay L. Serv., Torquay. [34692] 27/01/1982   **CM27/02/1987**
Prosser, Mrs J, MA MCLIP, Team Lib., Hendon L., L.B. of Barnet. [59832] 15/10/2001   **CM29/03/2006**

Prosser, Mr R J, BA(Hons) MCLIP, L. Customer Serv. Mgr., Chipping Barnet L., L.B. of Barnet. [43879] 07/02/1990 **CM21/07/1999**

Prosser, Ms S, BA DILS MCLIP, L. Serv. Mgr., ABM Univ. Health Borad, Singleton Hosp. [40538] 16/02/1987 **CM18/04/1989**

Protheroe, Mrs A E, L. Asst., House of Lords L., London. [10015927] 12/02/2010 **AF**

Proudfoot, Mrs E, MCLIP, Retired. [12015] 01/01/1927 **CM01/01/1962**

Prout, Miss R A, BSc DipLib, Asst. Lib., Bridgend Co. Bor. Council, Porthcawl L. [29798] 24/10/1978 **ME**

Prout, Mr R S, BA DCG DipInfSci MCLIP, Head of Stud. Serv., Univ. of Worcester. [60726] 01/04/1985 **CM01/04/1985**

Proven, Mrs J E, BA(Hons) MSc MCLIP, Inf. Specialist, Univ. of Abertay, Dundee. [61763] 05/11/2002 **CM01/02/2006**

Prowse, Mrs C E, BA, Unknown. [10013602] 12/05/2009 **AF**

Prowse, Mr S W, Retired [10016114] 11/02/2010 **ME**

Pryce-Jones, Mrs E M, MA(Hons) DipLib MCLIP, Dep. Dir. L. Serv., Birmingham City Univ. [31901] 17/01/1980 **CM06/10/1982**

Pryce-Jones, Mrs J E, BSc MCLIP, Ch. Catr., Birmingham City Univ. [20221] 31/10/1973 **CM20/10/1975**

Pryer, Mr P L A, MA MCLIP, Life Member. [12019] 01/01/1957 **CM01/01/1965**

Pryor, Miss H E, MCLIP, Arch./Records Mgr., The Manchester Coll., Northenden. [19993] 11/01/1973 **CM16/02/1976**

Ptolomey, Mrs J, BSc DipLIS, Freelance Inf. Worker. [54080] 24/10/1996 **ME**

Publicover, Mr J R, BEM MCLIP, Life Member. [12022] 25/07/1938 **CM01/01/1949**

Publicover, Mrs N C, MCLIP, Life Member. [12023] 23/09/1941 **CM01/01/1946**

Puchtler, Ms J A, MCLIP, Lib., Stantonbury Campus Milton Keynes [65890] 27/06/2006 **CM21/05/2008**

Pudner, Mr B G, BA(Hons) PgDip, LR Offr., Pembrokeshire Coll., Haverfordwest. [10015418] 16/11/2009 **ME**

Pudner, Mr R J, BA DipLib MCLIP, Freelance Lib. [32335] 05/03/1980 **CM24/03/1982**

Pugh, Miss H J, BA(Hons) BA MCLIP, Sch. Lib., Kings Coll. Sch., London. [28401] 22/11/1977 **CM30/10/1979**

Pugh, Miss K E, BA(Hons) MCLIP, Unknown. [10012075] 14/11/1991 **CM22/07/1998**

Puligari, Mrs P, MLISc MCLIP, Outreach & E-Resources Lib., Heart of England NHS Foundation Trust. [59459] 30/03/2001 **CM21/05/2008**

Pullen, Mrs B, MA MCLIP, Child. Lib., Hants. C.C., Petersfield. [37787] 16/10/1984 **CM15/11/1988**

Pullen, Mrs H, BSc, Dep. Learning Resouces Mgr. Bristol Health Care Trust, Bristol. [55313] 01/10/1997 **ME**

Pullen, Mrs J L, MA, Unknown [10001583] 26/02/2007 **ME**

Pullin, Mrs C M, BA(Hons) DipLib MCLIP, Sch. Lib., James Allen's Girls'Sch., London. [23735] 08/01/1975 **CM05/02/1980**

Pullin, Mrs C, Lib. Super. (youth), Dunstable L., Bedfordshire [10017009] 17/06/2010 **AF**

Pullinger, Mr J J, Libr., House of Commons L., London. [64348] 07/03/2005 **ME**

Pullman, Mr T J O, MA MPhil, Junior Lib. Asst., Squire Law L., Cambridge Univ. [10015538] 11/12/2009 **ME**

Punter, Miss C L, Sch. Lib., Sheldon Sch. Wilts. [61461] 12/08/2002 **ME**

Puplett, Mr D, MCLIP, Data Lib., LSE [63186] 03/03/2004 **CM13/06/2007**

Purcell, Mrs C W, MTheol MA MCLIP, Faculty Support Lib., Durham Univ. [28383] 08/11/1977 **CM19/11/1983**

Purcell, Mr J, BA MBA DipLib DMS MCLIP, Univ. Lib., Durham Univ. [31092] 15/08/1979 **CM15/08/1981**

Purcell, Ms K, BA(Hons) MA MCLIP, Subject Lib., Birkbeck Coll., London. [56400] 01/07/1998 **CM12/09/2001**

Purcell, Mrs L M, BA(Hons) PgDipIS, Asst. L.,P. T., Bradford Grammar Sch., Bradford. [61279] 08/05/2002 **ME**

Purchase, Mr S W F, BN(Hons), Asst. Lib., Child. Hosp. NHS Trust, Birmingham. [56975] 17/11/1998 **AF**

Purchon, Mrs K M, BA MA MCLIP, Sch. Lib., St. Francis Coll., Letchworth. [35779] 24/01/1983 **CM18/02/1986**

Purdey, Mr B G, BA FRSA MCLIP, Retired. [12048] 13/01/1965 **CM01/01/1968**

Purdy, Mrs D J, BA DMS MCLIP, Cirriculm & Inf. Serv. Mgr., Connexions, Notts. [37460] 01/10/1984 **CM08/12/1987**

Purkiss, Ms T L, MA, Learning Advisor, Univ. of Cumbria [58430] 11/02/2000 **ME**

Purvis, Mr B S, BA MSc MCLIP, Retired [12058] 05/02/1969 **CM01/01/1971**

Purvis, Ms K, BSc, Stud., Univ of Northumbria. [10014823] 16/09/2009 **ME**

Puscas, Miss I, BLib MCLIP, Lib., Nat. Pub. Health Serv. for Wales, Cardiff. [22089] 22/01/1974 **CM10/11/1978**

Puskas, Ms S E, Dipl., Lib., Univ. Tuebingen L., Germany. [10013618] 13/05/2009 **ME**

Pusram, Ms A J, BSc (Hons), Unknown. [10006699] 21/11/2007 **ME**

Puxley, Mrs N A, BA DipLib MCLIP, Sec., Amphlett Lissimore, London. [32181] 23/01/1980 **CM17/05/1983**

Puzey, Miss S L, BA, Trainee Liaison Lib., Univ. of Reading [10000773] 07/11/2006 **ME**

Pyant, Mr A F, Dip MA MCMI MCLIP, Retired [42611] 16/01/1989 **CM29/04/1994**

Pycock, Mr L R, BA(Hons) MCLIP, Asst. Mgr., L.B. of Southwark., E. St. L. [50788] 18/10/1994 **CM01/06/2005**

Pye-Smith, Ms H M E, MA MCLIP, Head of L., The Nat. Arch., Kew. [40191] 04/11/1986 **CM19/03/2008**

Pygott, Mr D W, MCLIP, Retired. [23988] 13/03/1960 **CM01/04/1984**

Pyle, Mrs B D, MCLIP, Life Member. [12067] 16/10/1943 **CM01/01/1955**

Pyle, Mr J C, MA MCLIP, Head of Communications, Destination Sheffield Ltd. [25398] 28/12/1975 **CM19/01/1978**

Pyves, Mrs I H, MCLIP, Life Member. [12070] 01/01/1955 **CM01/01/1959**

Q

Qazi, Mrs F, BA, Sch. Lib., IFS Sch., USA. [10014140] 01/07/2009 **ME**

Quare, Miss D C, BA M LITT MCLIP, Retired. [22661] 01/08/1974 **CM12/01/1978**

Quarmby Lawrence, Mrs E A, Self Employed, Elizabeth Quarmby Lawrence L. Serv. [40517] 23/02/1987 **ME**

Quayle, Mr D R, BA MCLIP, Principal Lib., (Lend), Milton Keynes Cent. L. [12074] 14/09/1970 **CM15/08/1973**

Quibell, Mr J R C, BA MCLIP, Lib., HMS Sultan L., Gosport. [19272] 02/10/1972 **CM07/10/1974**

Quick, Mrs A, BA(Hons) MA PGCE MCLIP, P/T Lib., Arbroath High Sch. [55275] 12/09/1997 **RV29/03/2007** **CM21/05/2003**

Quick, Mr F M S, MA(Hons) MCLIP, Learning Advisor, St. Mary's Univ. Coll. [62415] 03/06/2003 **CM21/05/2008**

Quick, Mr G H, BA GDipLib MIMSAALIA, Info. Specialist, CSIRO, Australia [65237] 25/11/2005 **ME**

Quilty, Ms L, MSc, Asst. Child. Lib., Bristol Cent. Lend. L. [59504] 18/04/2001 **ME**

Quinlan, Mrs H E, BA(Hons) MA MCLIP, Neigbourhood L. Mgr., City of Salford [59848] 16/10/2001 **CM08/12/2004**

Quinlan, Mrs J, Admin. Asst., Bristows, London. [10001927] 22/03/2007 **AF**

Quinn, Mr G P, BA DipLib DMS, Business & Ref. Lib., W. E. L.B., Londonderry Cent. L. [35437] 01/10/1982 **ME**

Quinn, Miss H F, BA DipLib MCLIP, Lib., Ramboll Whitbybird Limited [37009] 14/01/1984 **CM07/07/1987**

Quinn, Mrs K E, ACLIP, Learning Resource Advisor, W.
Nottinghamshire Coll. [10006910] 17/12/2007 **ACL04/03/2009**
Quinney, Mrs L, MA(Hons) MA MCLIP, MAP Serv. Mgr., Nat. L. of
Scotland [59800] 03/10/2001 **CM29/03/2004**

R

Rabbitt, Miss K, BA(Hons), Asst. Inf. Offr., Leeds City Council
[10013089] 09/01/2001 **ME**
Rabbitt, Mr P, BA LLB DipLib, Sen. Exec. Lib, Galway Co. L. Galway.
[28132] 06/10/1977 **ME**
Rabe, Mrs R, MCLIP, Retired. [12093] 15/10/1936 **CM01/01/1941**
Raby, Ms A S, BA(Hons) DipIS MCLIP, LRC Mgr., Whitcliffe Mount Sch.,
Cleckheaton. [48239] 17/11/1992 **CM21/05/2003**
Rackley, Mrs A L, MCLIP, Sch. L. Serv. Mgr., Blackburn with Darwen
Bor., Blackburn, Lancs. [13034] 26/01/1972 **CM10/02/1975**
Radanne, Miss C, MA DipLib, L. Catr., Warburg Inst., London. [47503]
09/09/1992 **ME**
Radcliffe, Ms P R, BA MSc, L. & Inf. Mgr., N. I. Court Serv., Belfast.
[63054] 27/01/2004 **ME**
Raddon, Miss D L, BLib MCLIP, Implementations Project Mgr., DS Ltd,
Nottingham [29343] 22/05/1978 **CM30/09/1981**
Radford, Ms K, MA MCLIP, Academic Liason Lib., Univ. of York. [49227]
14/10/1993 **CM15/05/2002**
Radford, Mrs S M, BA(Hons) MA, L. Asst., The Third Age Trust,
Bromley. [65514] 11/02/2006 **ME**
Rae, Miss C T, BA(Hons) MA, L. Super., Walthamstow L., London.
[65803] 15/05/2006 **ME**
Rae, Mrs E, MA(Hons) MSc MCLIP, Sch. Lib. /Asst. Lib., Hunter High
Sch., E. Kilbride, Med. L., Western Inf., Glasgow. [65391] 01/02/2006 **CM09/09/2009**
Rae, Miss M A, BA MCLIP, Lib., Culture & Sport Glasgow. [30034]
20/10/1978 **CM18/09/1981**
Rae, Ms P A, BA MCLIP, Unwaged [10006941] 01/02/1977 **CM05/07/1982**
Rae, Mrs S B, MA MCLIP, Resources Coordinator, Jewel & Esk Coll.,
Edinburgh. [31595] 12/11/1979 **CM01/12/1982**
Raffan, Miss A K, BA MCLIP, Unknown. [35770] 12/01/1983 **CM27/07/1994**
Rafferty, Ms E P F, BA MSc MCLIP, Subject Lib., Queen Mary L., Univ.
of London. [26521] 16/09/1976 **CM01/07/1990**
Rafferty, Dr P M, MA MSc PhD MCLIP, Sen. Lect., Univ. of Wales,
Aberystwyth. [40240] 13/11/1986 **CM01/07/1992**
Rafter, Mr D, Accessioner, Sound Archive, Brit. L., London. [10013466]
13/07/2001 **ME**
Ragab, Mrs L A, BA MCLIP, Lib., CABI Europe – UK, Egham, Surrey.
[30412] 25/01/1979 **CM31/10/1983**
Ragaller, Miss I, Stud., Aberystwyth Univ. [10011095] 24/09/2008 **ME**
Raggett, Mr P J E, BA(Hons) MA MCLIP, Head of Inf. Cent., Org. for
Economic Cooperation and Devel., France. [32157] 30/01/1980 **CM29/01/1982**
Rahulan, Ms E M, BA MCLIP, Liaison Offr., Info. & Learning Servs.,
Univ. of Salford. [50916] 31/10/1994 **CM25/09/1996**
Rainbow, Mrs L, BA MCLIP, Stragic Lib., Strood L., Medway Council.
[38556] 01/07/1985 **CM05/04/1988**
Raine, Miss D, BA MA, Lib., Ampleforth Coll. York. [42333] 24/10/1988 **ME**
Raine, Mrs M, MCLIP, Retired. [12118] 13/01/1956 **CM01/01/1961**
Rainer, Mrs J E, BA DipLib MBA MCLIP, Inf. Offr., Carers' Resource,
Bradford. [36333] 01/10/1983 **CM13/08/1986**
Rainey, Miss E M, BA, Retired. [12119] 01/01/1965 **ME**
Rainey, Ms M M, BSc MSc MCLIP, Employment not known. [60785]
01/12/1988 **CM20/05/1993**

Rainey, Miss M, BA(Hons) MSc MCLIP, Sen. Asst. Lib., Denton Wilde
Sapte, LLP, London [57128] 17/12/1998 **CM21/05/2008**
Rainton, Miss A, BSc MA, Br. Lib., Tameside C.C. [10001014]
07/12/2006 **ME**
Raisin, Mrs A, BA DipLib MLib FCLIP, Grp. Inf. Mgr., Dept. for Business,
London. [25399] 05/01/1976 **FE15/09/2004**
Raistrick, Mr C J, MCLIP, L. Serv. Mgr., Procter & Gamble, Newcastle
upon Tyne. [38807] 10/10/1985 **CM18/04/1994**
Raistrick, Mr D, OBE FCLIP, Retired. [12121] 27/03/1962 **FE08/03/1988**
Rajacic, Ms V, BA(Hons) PGDipILS MCLIP, Team Leader – Access
Serv., Edinburgh. (Employment break) [59385] 27/02/2001 **CM13/06/2007**
Rajendran, Miss M Y, BSc MLib DipEd, Knowledge Mgr., Health
Insurance Commision, Australia. [44492] 15/10/1990 **ME**
Rak, Ms O S, MSc, Trust Lib., Wandsworth Recovery Cent., London.
[10017133] 15/10/1999 **CM07/09/2005**
Ralls, Mrs M C, BD MSc MCLIP, Retired. [12125] 25/04/1972 **CM01/12/1982**
Ralph, Ms J K L, MCLIP, Unknown. [10012466] 04/11/1987 **CM26/02/1992**
Ralph, Mrs L C, MCLIP, Selfemployed. [548] 01/01/1972 **CM05/02/1976**
Ramage, Mr M A, Msc BA(Hons), Unknown. [10016005] 10/02/2010 **ME**
Ramalingam, Ms R, LLB(Hons) MCLIP, Retired. [17609] 14/08/1969 **CM21/09/1976**
Ramanayake, Miss S D, BA, MA, Stud., Loughborough Univ.
[10015939] 27/01/2010 **ME**
Ramburrun, Mr R, BA(Hons) MSc, Res. Lib., Baker & McKenzie,
London. [63377] 27/04/2004 **ME**
Rampersad, Ms S, BSc, Systems and Stock Mgr., Greater London Auth.
[10007931] 20/03/2008 **ME**
Rampling, Ms C, Asst. Lib., Lincoln's Inn Lib., London. [62648]
01/10/2003 **ME**
Ramsay, Mrs A P, BA PGCE DipLib, Team Lib., Wirral Bor. Council.
[41066] 07/10/1987 **ME**
Ramsay, Mrs E A, FCLIP, Retired. [8354] 23/09/1957 **FE07/11/1974**
Ramsbotham, Miss B, FCLIP, Life Member. [12134] 11/10/1937 **FE01/01/1949**
Ramsbottom, Miss S, BA MA, Asst. Lib., Royal Preston Hosp.
[10007743] 21/02/2008 **ME**
Ramsden, Ms A E, Ma Ilm, Reg. Inf. Off., Nat. Autistic Soc.,
Northenden. [10016019] 11/12/1997 **ME**
Ramsden, Mrs A, MSc, Sen. Inf. Asst., Taylor Law L., Univ. of
Aberdeen. [10005993] 21/08/2007 **ME**
Ramsden, Mr M J, BA MSOCSC FALIA FCLIP, Retired. [17618]
10/03/1958 **FE01/01/1971**
Ramsden, Mr P A, BA CertEd MCLIP, Accreditation Offr., Brit. Army
[27210] 01/01/1977 **CM31/07/1981**
Ramstead, Miss E J, BA PGCE, Stud., Manchester Met. Univ.
[10010239] 16/07/2008 **ME**
Rana, Mr D, BSc MSc, Devel. Lib., Dudley L. [10015498] 08/10/2003 **ME**
Rand, Ms C, Lib., Brit. L. Serial Aquisitions, Wetherby [10000106]
20/05/2008 **AF**
Randall, Mrs A S, DipLib, Serials Lib., Slaughter & May, London.
[45280] 01/10/1990 **ME**
Randall, Mrs A, BA(Hons) MA MCLIP, Lib., Lampton Sch., Hounslow,
London. [58924] 04/10/2000 **CM29/03/2004**
Randall, Mrs F L, Customer Serv. Offr., Natwest, Reading. [38594]
17/07/1985 **ME**
Randall, Mrs J B, ACLIP, Learning Cent. Mgr., Valley Sch., Worksop.
[10000714] 25/10/2006 **ACL01/10/2008**
Randall, Ms J H, Stud. [10014810] 21/09/2009 **ME**
Randall, Ms J I, MCLIP, Young Peoples Serv. Mgr., Bristol City Council.
[12140] 17/01/1969 **CM28/08/1974**

Randall, Mrs J M, BA(Hons)DipLib MCLIP, Princ. L. Asst. : Issue Desk, Cent. Lib., Imperial Coll. London [3236] 03/01/1972 **CM28/10/2004**

Randall, Ms L, BA(Hons) MCLIP, Sen. L. Asst., Wandsworth Town L., London. [64841] 29/07/2005 **CM09/09/2009**

Randell, Mrs C M, MCLIP, Bookshop Asst., Norfolk Child. Book Cent. [324] 01/01/1969 **CM27/03/1973**

Randhawa, Mrs P K, ACLIP, Asst. Lib., Lampton Sch., Hounslow. [65268] 07/12/2005 **ACL17/06/2009**

Randle, Ms C L, MCLIP, Lib., L. Servs. for Educ., Leics. C.C. [28927] 25/01/1974 **CM07/09/1979**

Ranger, Miss N M, BA MCLIP, Univ. of W. of England Link Lib. Swindon. [20793] 03/07/1973 **CM01/07/1977**

Rankin, Mrs C E M, MA BSocSc DipLib ILTM MCLIP, Sen. Lect., Sch. of Applied Global Ethics, Sage., Leeds Met Univ. [28661] 01/11/1977 **CM06/07/1981**

Rankin, Miss R C, MA(Hons) DipILS MCLIP, Sch. Lib., Hillhead High Sch., Glasgow. [61027] 11/02/2002 **CM15/09/2004**

Ransley, Mrs N, BA(Hons) MA, Lib., The Mount Sch., London [59882] 29/10/2001 **ME**

Ransom, Mrs N, p. /t. Stud., Univ. of Wales, Aberystwyth. [65434] 23/02/2006 **ME**

Ranson, Mr M C, MCLIP, Retired. [12152] 15/02/1949 **CM01/01/1955**

Raper, Ms D, BSc MA MCLIP, Acad. Liaison Lib. (Law), Univ. of Kent. [10016976] 01/01/1975 **CM01/07/1991**

Rasdall, Mr M, BA(Hons) MSc MCLIP, Managing Dir., Burwell web Communications. [10001356] 11/03/1993 **CM01/04/1987**

Raseroka, Ms H K, BSc MA HonFCLIP, Dir., Univ. of Botswana L., Gaborone. [53168] 01/04/1996 **HFE21/10/2004**

Rashid, Miss T, BSc(Hons), Grad. L. Trainee, Plant Sci. /Zoology L., Oxford Univ. [63851] 01/10/2004 **ME**

Rashidah Begum, Miss F M, BA MCLIP, Ch. Lib., Kolej Disted, Penang, Malaysia. [18908] 11/08/1972 **CM01/01/1975**

Rastall, Mrs D M, MCLIP, Life Member. [12156] 01/01/1951 **CM01/01/1956**

Rastrick, Mrs E F, MCLIP, Advisory Lib., L. Arch. & Inf., Sufffolk [18180] 10/10/1972 **CM23/04/1976**

Raszpla, Mrs A, LLB(Hons) MSc MCLIP, Legal Inf. Offr., TLT Solicitors, Bristol. [57230] 25/01/1999 **CM29/03/2004**

Ratajczak, Mr J, BA, Stud. [10015290] 30/10/2009 **ME**

Ratcliff, Mrs C M, BA(Hons) DipLib, Medicines Mgmt. Project Mgr., NHS Suffolk [39977] 01/10/1986 **ME**

Ratcliffe, Dr F W, CBE JP HonFLA MA PhD, Life Member. [12159] 12/03/1962 **HFE06/01/1987**

Ratcliffe, Mr J, MCLIP, Retired. [12161] 21/09/1960 **CM01/01/1964**

Ratcliffe, Mrs R A M, BA MCLIP, Reader Devel. Lib., Hampshire. C.C. [31030] 09/07/1979 **CM21/10/1981**

Ratcliffe, Miss S A, BA(Hons) PgDip MCLIP, Sen. Info. Asst. - Serials (Electronic), King's Coll., Aberdeen. [54623] 04/02/1997 **CM11/03/2009**

Rathe, Ms Z, MA(Hons) Msc, Bookshop Asst., Till's Bookshop, Edingburgh. [10016037] 10/02/2010 **AF**

Ratliffe, Miss H, BA(Hons) Msc, Inf. Offr., Blake Lapthorn, Eastleigh [10017057] 21/06/2010 **ME**

Ratnasamy, Ms T, BA MCLIP, Sen. Lib., NUS L., Nat. Univ. of Singapore. [34054] 01/08/1981 **CM11/11/1985**

Ratner, Mrs T, Info. Specialist, Bio-Tech. General, Israel [10015646] 12/01/2010 **ME**

Rattigan, Mrs G, ACLIP, Lib. Asst., Invergordon L., Invergordon, Ross-shire. [10001962] 19/03/2007 **ACL16/07/2008**

Rauch, Mrs D, BA MCLIP, P. /t., JFS, Kingsbury. [918] 01/01/1971 **CM16/09/1974**

Raven Conn, Mrs C M, BSc(Econ) MCLIP, p. /t. Lib,Nottingham Cent. L. [48726] 27/04/1993 **CM17/09/2003**

Raven, Ms D M, BA DipLib MCLIP, Knowledge Mgr., Inf. Standards Board for Health and Social Care, Leeds. [10012018] 11/10/1983 **CM10/11/1987**

Ravenwood, Mrs J C F, Stud [10007122] 22/01/2008 **ME**

Raw, Mrs A, MCLIP, Unemployed. [10112] 17/09/1969 **CM03/02/1978**

Rawes, Mrs P M, BA(Hons) MCLIP, Unemployed. [34997] 08/06/1982 **CM11/03/1984**

Rawle, Mr P J, BA(Hons) DipLib MCLIP, Lib., PG L., Princess of Wales Hosp., Bridgend, Mid-Glamorgan. [37388] 02/08/1984 **CM10/07/2002**

Rawling, Mrs D A, LRC Mgr., Raincliffe Sch., Scarborough. [62928] 20/11/2003 **ME**

Rawling, Mrs H, BA, Stud., Univ. of Brighton [10011669] 12/11/2008 **ME**

Rawlings, Mr J F, BA MCLIP, Sen. Inf. Offr., Mobilise Organisation, Norfolk [21706] 01/01/1974 **CM04/08/1977**

Rawlings, Mrs S J, BA MCLIP, Cent. Operations Lib., Norfolk LIS [1593] 10/01/1966 **CM01/01/1970**

Rawlinson, Miss K A, MCLIP, Catr., State L. of W. Australia, Perth. [17624] 17/04/1962 **CM01/01/1966**

Rawson, Miss J L, BA(Hons) MA MCLIP, Lib.-in-charge, Vere Harmsworth L., Univ. of Oxford. [61823] 12/11/2002 **CM21/05/2008**

Rawsthorne, Mr L, MLib FCLIP, Co. Lib., Flintshire C.C., Mold. [25095] 05/11/1975 **FE20/05/1998**

Raxworthy, Mrs P M, BA(Hons) DipILS, Reading Devel. Lib., City of York Council. [62061] 07/02/2003 **ME**

Ray, Mr A K, MA MCLIP, Life Member. [17626] 06/01/1956 **CM01/01/1962**

Ray, Ms A, BA DipLib MA MCLIP, Head of L. & Inf. Serv., Scarborough Hosp. L., N. Yorks. [34365] 25/10/1981 **CM08/03/1988**

Ray, Mr C H, FCLIP, Life Member. [12186] 10/03/1947 **FE01/01/1955**

Ray, Ms C, Unwaged. [10005990] 11/09/2007 **ME**

Ray, Mrs E R, MCLIP, Retired. [12188] 13/09/1966 **CM01/02/1972**

Ray, Mrs S G, BA MPhil HonFLA FCLIP, Life Member. [12191] 21/09/1951 **FE01/01/1959**

Raybould, Ms S J, BA MCLIP, Inf. Cent. Mgr. [24445] 10/08/1975 **CM26/08/1980**

Rayment, Mr I, BA(Hons) MA, Subject Lib., Univ. of Plymouth [58901] 01/10/2000 **ME**

Raymont, Mr D M, BA, Lib., Inst. of Actuaries [41549] 18/01/1988 **ME**

Rayner, Ms H E, BA(Hons) DipILS MCLIP, Campus Lib., (Job-share), Bath Spa Univ. [42187] 10/10/1988 **CM20/09/2000**

Raynor, Mrs J M, MCLIP, Not employed. [21004] 03/10/1973 **CM17/10/1975**

Rayson, Miss K S, Info. Mgr., Univ. of Northumbria at Newcastle. [57294] 03/02/1999 **ME**

Rea, Mrs M E, BA MCLIP, Sch. Lib., Merchant Taylors'Boys'Sch., Liverpool. [27011] 10/01/1977 **CM19/01/1979**

Read, Mrs A J, Lib. Asst. Clacton Co. High Sch., Clacton-on-sea [10011701] 06/11/2008 **AF**

Read, Miss C A, MA MCLIP, Life Member. [12200] 07/10/1971 **CM31/07/1975**

Read, Mrs C R, Retired [47373] 27/07/1992 **ME**

Read, Ms F M A, LLB DlpLP DipInf, Unwaged [10017012] 17/05/2002 **ME**

Read, Mr G, BA DipLib, Print Collections Mgr., LSE, London. [47502] 09/09/1992 **ME**

Read, Ms K J, BA MA MCLIP, Principal L. Asst, IALS, London. [43599] 09/11/1989 **CM22/05/1996**

Read, Miss L A, MA BA MCLIP, Coll. Lib., Robinson Coll., Cambridge. [25401] 18/01/1976 **CM13/09/1979**

Read, Mrs M A, Lib., Morrab L., Penzance, Cornwall. [57105] 14/12/1998 **ME**

Read, Miss M M, BA(Hons), Stud. [10013737] 27/05/2009 **ME**

Read, Ms M, MA, Self-employed. [43562] 08/11/1989 **ME**

Read, Mrs N C, BA(Hons) MCLIP, Life Member. [12208] 11/06/1935
CM01/01/1941

Read, Dr R M, MA(Hons) PhD MCLIP, Sen. Inf. Advisor, Kingston Univ.
[62002] 24/12/2002 **CM23/01/2008**

Read, Miss S F B, FCLIP, Retired. [12209] 21/09/1940 **FE01/01/1953**

Reade, Mrs J G, BA MLS MCLIP, Retired [12210] 01/01/1966
CM01/01/1970

Reader, Mr D K, MCLIP, Retired. [12211] 01/10/1971 **CM01/08/1974**

Reading, Ms J A, BA(Hons) MA MCLIP, Liaison Lib., Univ. of Sydney,
Sydney. [43293] 16/10/1989 **CM25/01/1995**

Ready, Ms K W, B ED DipLib MCLIP, Faculty Liaison Lib., Anglia Ruskin
Univ., Cambridge. [38557] 01/07/1985 **CM10/11/1987**

Ready, Ms S E, BSc, Lib., The Greneway Sch., Royston, Herts. [66025]
24/08/2006 **AF**

Reardon, Dr M, PhD MA, Business Intelligence Asst., EAPD, London.
[10006107] 03/07/2008 **ME**

Reason, Mrs C, DipLS, Floor Mgr., Univ. L., Univ. of Portsmouth.
[36034] 19/04/1983 **ME**

Redfearn, Mrs J, MCLIP, p. /t. Prison Lib., Leyhill Open Prison, S. Glos.
L. [22879] 01/10/1974 **CM20/09/1977**

Redfern, Ms F M M, MA MCLIP, Life Member. [15788] 13/03/1952
CM01/01/1964

Redhead, Miss J V, BA M LITT MCLIP, Retired. [23634] 20/01/1975
CM20/01/1977

Redhead, Mrs J W, MCLIP, Retired. [3124] 17/09/1962 **CM01/01/1967**

Redhead, Mr M K, MA MCLIP, Retired. [20773] 02/07/1973
CM15/12/1975

Redican, Ms H, MA, Unwaged. [42518] 21/11/1988 **ME**

Redlinski, Ms L, MSc, Stud. [10015236] 27/10/2009 **ME**

Redman, Mr G C, MA MCLIP, Inf. Lib., Chichester L. W. Sussex. C.C.
[61037] 11/02/2002 **CM29/11/2006**

Redman, Ms J, BSc(Hons) MSc PGCE MCLIP, Sen. Asst. Lib.,UWE,
Bristol. [57093] 07/12/1998 **CM23/01/2002**

Redman, Miss P, BA(Hons) MCLIP, Res. & Inf. Advisor, Lifetime Devel.
N. E. LTD Barnsley, Doncaster & Rotherham. [48739] 30/04/1993
CM25/01/1995

Redpath, Ms A E, BA MCLIP, Acquisitions Mgr., Napier Univ. Learning
Inf. Serv. [53346] 20/05/1996 **CM11/03/2009**

Redrup, Mrs R M J, BA MLib MCLIP, Marketing Co-ordinator, Univ. of
Reading L. [40997] 02/10/1987 **CM25/05/1994**

Redwood, Mrs H M, B Lib MCLIP, L. Asst. -in-charge, Colyton L.,
Devon. [5172] 29/04/1971 **CM01/02/1975**

Reed, Mrs A J, L. Asst., Birmingham Child. NHS Foundation Trust.
[10015335] 09/11/2009 **AF**

Reed, Miss A, MSc MCLIP, Intute Content Co-ord., Univ. of Manchester
[60770] 12/12/2001 **CM12/12/2001**

Reed, Mrs C, BA MCLIP, Strategic L. Mgr.,Worcs. C.C. [10001495]
01/07/1980 **CM23/12/1983**

Reed, Mrs D J, BA, P. /t. Lib., Hurstpierpoint Coll. Prep Sch. [10008809]
21/04/2008 **ME**

Reed, Mr D M, BA MCLIP, Div. Lib. Mgr., Warwickshire C.C., Nuneaton
& Bedworth. [40484] 12/02/1987 **CM30/01/1991**

Reed, Miss E, BA(Hons), Stud., Aberystwyth Univ. [10011351]
14/10/2008 **ME**

Reed, Mrs J F, BA MCLIP, Inf. Sepecialist, England. [64251] 22/02/2005
CM28/01/2009

Reed, Mrs J M, MCLIP, Electronic Inf. Enviroment Lib., Univ. of
Worcester [6375] 01/01/1970 **CM04/01/1978**

Reed, Mrs J M, BA(Hons) MCLIP, Prison L. Serv., Y01 Staffordshire
LOINE Serv. [25419] 16/12/1975 **CM01/07/1992**

Reed, Miss L C, Unknown. [10012464] 10/02/2009 **ME**

Reed, Mr M W, BA, Constituency Lib. Serv. Mgr, Birmingham C.C.
[46895] 28/02/1992 **ME**

Reed, Mr R A, LLB DipLib MCLIP, Asst. Lib., RIBA, London. [43224]
05/10/1989 **CM24/06/1992**

Reed, Miss S E, BA(Hons) MA, Asst. Lib., Collection Mgmnt. [56730]
07/10/1998 **ME**

Reed, Ms S P, BA MA MBA MCLIP, Resident In Austrailia [38151]
22/01/1985 **CM29/01/1992**

Reed, Mrs S, BA FCLIP, Learning Resources Mgr., S. Downs Coll. of F.
E., Waterlooville. [28965] 06/02/1978 **FE28/01/2009**

Reedie, Mrs S P, BA MA DipLib MCLIP, Casual Relief, Dorset C.C.,
Weymouth L. [29557] 07/10/1978 **CM24/10/1980**

Reedy, Mrs K J, BA MA MCLIP, Inf. Literacy Specialist, Open Univ. L.,
Milton Keynes. [38724] 01/10/1985 **CM24/03/1992**

Reekie, Mrs C S, MSc(Econ) MCLIP, Fed. Lib., Cambridge Theological
Fed. [22560] 01/07/1974 **CM03/07/1978**

Reeks, Mrs J M, MCLIP, Sch. Lib., Aylesbury Grammar Sch. [7175]
01/01/1972 **CM24/12/1974**

Reen, Miss J, MA, Sen. Inf. Offr., Kennedys. [59712] 28/08/2001 **ME**

Rees, Mr A D W, BA MCLIP, Learning Resources Mgr., Coleg Menai,
Bangor. [38022] 16/01/1985 **CM30/01/1991**

Rees, Mr A G, BSc MIBiol MCLIP, Retired. [60627] 27/05/1969
CM18/11/1971

Rees, Mrs A H, BLib MCLIP, Local Studies Lib., Shakespeare Birthplace
Trust, Stratford-Upon-Avon. [19837] 01/01/1973 **CM01/07/1975**

Rees, Mr D H, Asst., Pembs. Co. L. [12239] 22/01/1966 **ME**

Rees, Mr D, BA(Hons) PGCE Pg Dip, Asst. Lib., Welcome L., London.
[61039] 11/02/2002 **ME**

Rees, Mrs F A, BLib(Hons) MCLIP, Lib., S. Staffs. Healthcare NHS
Trust, Stafford. [28864] 23/01/1978 **CM10/07/2002**

Rees, Ms H A, BA MEd MCLIP, Head of Learning Resources, City Coll.,
Plymouth [17632] 29/09/1969 **CM12/04/1973**

Rees-Jones, Mrs E A, BA MCLIP, Principal Lib., Community Devel &
Partnerships., Staffs. C.C. [26702] 29/10/1976 **CM29/02/1980**

Rees-Jones, L, BA MCLIP FRSA, Sen. Advisor., Membership Support
Unit., Cilip, London [26594] 26/10/1976 **CM16/05/1988**

Reeve, Mr C, BA MCLIP MSc, Prof. Lib. Consultant, Self Employed
[23179] 31/10/1974 **CM01/01/1977**

Reeve, Mrs S, Asst. Inf. Advisor., Univ. of Brighton. [64191] 31/01/2005
ME

Reeves, Miss C L, MSc, L. Enquiry Serv. Co-ordinator., Allen & Overy,
London. [53539] 15/07/1996 **ME**

Reeves, Miss K, BA(Hons) MA MCLIP, Unknown. [61140] 08/03/2002
CM28/10/2004

Reeves, Mrs S, BA(Hons) MCLIP, Relief Asst. Lib., W. Sussex L. Serv.
[49790] 08/11/1993 **CM04/02/2004**

Reeves, Mrs T L, BA(Hons) MA, Res. Asst. FCO., London [59978]
15/11/2001 **ME**

Refson, Mrs M M, BA MCLIP, Retired. [12261] 02/10/1948
CM01/01/1951

Regan, Mrs C A E, BLS MCLIP, Asst. Lib., Taunton & Somerset NHS
Trust. [30845] 09/05/1979 **CM28/07/1983**

Regan, Mrs E A, MA DipLib MCLIP, P. /t. Asst. Lib., Pwllheli L.,
Gwynedd. [32926] 04/10/1980 **CM16/05/1984**

Regan, Mrs M E, BA(Hons), L. Asst., New Univ. of Ulster, Jordanstown
Campus. [10015815] 29/01/2010 **ME**

Regan, Mr T, BA(Hons) DipILS, Sen. Lib. -E. Area, Dalkeith L. [51621]
18/04/1995 **ME**

Rehahn, Ms A S, BA MSc MCLIP, Asst. Child. & Young People's Off.,
RNIB, London. [12268] 01/01/1971 **CM18/12/1973**

Reid, Mrs A J, Stud. [10006296] 10/10/2007 **ME**

Reid, Ms A M, MA DipInfSc MCLIP, Serials Mgr. (Job Share), Brit. L. of
Political & Economical Sci., London. [60650] 15/06/1982
CM14/07/1988

Reid, Mr A, MA MCLIP, L. Serv. Mgr., MidLothian Council, Dalkeith.
[22822] 04/10/1974 **CM31/08/1977**

Reid, Mr B J, BA AALIA MCLIP, Retired. [38965] 23/10/1985 **CM13/06/1989**

Reid, Mrs C A, BSc(Hons) MSc MCLIP, Lib., Univ. of Cambridge, Lucy Cavendish Coll. [47377] 28/07/1992 **CM22/05/1996**

Reid, Miss C D, BA MA FCLIP, Learning Res. Mgr., Business Sch., Univ. of Strathclyde. [12270] 01/07/1972 **FE01/04/2002**

Reid, Ms C J, MA(Hons) DipLib MCLIP, Unwaged. [46302] 25/10/1991 **CM20/09/1995**

Reid, Mrs E M, BA MCLIP, Sen. Comm. Lib., Redbridge L., Redbridge. [10006740] 06/07/1979 **CM20/08/1982**

Reid, Mrs E, MA MCLIP, HR Offr., Banff & Buchan Coll. [60318] 28/07/1992 **CM28/07/1992**

Reid, Mrs F S, BSc, Learning Resource Asst. [10006608] 11/09/2007 **ME**

Reid, Miss F, BSc(Hons), Stud., Manchester Met. Univ. [10001950] 22/03/2007 **ME**

Reid, Miss J L H, BA MCLIP, Sch. Lib., Grange Acad., Kilmarnock, E. Ayrshire. [37890] 11/10/1984 **CM22/05/1996**

Reid, Miss J, BA PgDip MCLIP, Bookstart Co-ordinator, Dundee C.C. [64658] 18/05/2005 **CM21/05/2008**

Reid, Mrs J, MCLIP, Clerical Offr., Croydon Primary Care Trust [9837] 01/01/1971 **CM19/12/1974**

Reid, Ms K, BSc (Hons) MSc, Info. Scientist, Royal Coll. of Physicians, London [10001854] 15/07/1999 **ME**

Reid, Ms L C, BA(Hons) MA, Head of Info. Serv., Royal Coll. Obstetricians and Gynaecologists. [53760] 01/10/1996 **ME**

Reid, Ms L C, BA MCLIP, Info. Serv. Mgr., W. Lothian, [33122] 01/10/1980 **CM17/07/1984**

Reid, Mrs L J, BLS MCLIP, Asst. Lib., Univ. of Ulster, Belfast. [41736] 29/02/1988 **CM06/05/2009**

Reid, Mr M A, MCLIP, Clinical Lib., Hosp. NHS Foundation Trust, Blackpool Fylde & Wyre. [52003] 06/09/1995 **CM23/09/1998**

Reid, Mrs M, BA MCLIP, Comm. Lib., Renfrewshire L., Renfrewshire Council. [32445] 16/04/1980 **CM12/08/1985**

Reid, Miss M, BLib MCLIP, Inf. Specialist, Cranfield Univ., Cranfield. [12273] 17/10/1971 **CM03/12/1976**

Reid, Mr P D R, MPhil, Lib. Asst., Sch. of Med. Sciences, Bristol. [10014050] 01/07/2009 **ME**

Reid, Dr P H, BA(Hons) PhD FSA(Scot), Head of Dept., Robert Gordon Univ., Aberdeen. [48679] 13/04/1993 **ME**

Reid, Mrs R J, BA, Sen. Inf. Adviser (Humanities), Univ. of Gloucestershire, Cheltenham. [59497] 11/04/2001 **ME**

Reid, Mr R, BA(Hons) PGdip MSc, Lib. Data Creator, Highland L., Inverness. [10006757] 10/12/2007 **ME**

Reid, Mrs S D, BA(Hons) MA PGCE MCLIP, Academic Lib., Pilkington L., Loughborough Univ. [62312] 23/04/2003 **CM13/06/2007**

Reid, Mrs S M, MA MCLIP, Retired. [5182] 16/10/1968 **CM01/01/1971**

Reid-Smith, Dr E R, BA MEd FCLIP MEdAdmin MBus Dip, Life Member [12283] 01/01/1947 **FE01/01/1967**

Reid-Tome, Mrs L M, L. Admin., Lovells LLP, London. [10000485] 12/10/2006 **AF**

Reilly, Mrs A M, BA MCLIP, Child. & Young People's Lib., N. Lanarkshire Council, Coatbridge. [19545] 20/10/1969 **CM31/07/1973**

Reilly, Ms C, BA(Hons) PGCE PgDipILS, Unemployed. [43027] 26/06/1989 **ME**

Reilly, Miss J A, Lib., Joseph Chamberlain Coll., Birmingham. [57030] 26/11/1998 **ME**

Reilly, Mr L J, BA DipLib MCLIP, Arch. & L. Mgr., L.B. Lambeth. [39084] 29/10/1985 **CM15/02/1989**

Reilly, Mr P M, BSc DipInfSc, Unwaged [35974] 09/02/1983 **ME**

Reilly, Miss R A, BA(Hons) MA, Child. & Yth. Lib., Barnet L. [53867] 07/10/1996 **ME**

Reilly-Cooper, Mrs P, BSc DipLib MCLIP, L. Serv. Mgr., Halton Bor. Council. [34607] 11/01/1982 **CM21/12/1985**

Reiter, Mrs J, Stud. [66115] 22/09/2006 **ME**

Relf, Mrs K, MCLIP, Asst. Lib., Kimberlin L., De Montfort Univ.,Leicester. [8447] 01/09/1968 **CM16/10/1972**

Relph, Mr T R, BA(Hons) MCLIP, Inf. Lib., Cent. L., S. Tyneside M.B.C. [43721] 01/12/1989 **CM24/07/1996**

Relton-Elves, Mrs D, Lib., Severn Trent Water, Coventry [10008400] 19/03/2008 **AF**

Relves, Miss V J, BA(Hons) DipLib MCLIP, Lib., Arup, Solihull. [44449] 09/10/1990 **CM20/05/1998**

Rench, Mr S F, BA, Photographic Collections Offr., Oxfordshire Studies, Oxford. [42879] 04/04/1989 **ME**

Rendell, Mrs F J, BA(Hons) MSc MCLIP, Inf. Specialist. [62765] 20/10/2003 **CM03/10/2007**

Rendle, Miss A E, BSc MCLIP, Retired [26025] 07/10/1974 **CM15/10/1976**

Rendle, Mrs L C, BA(Hons), Stud., Aberystwyth Univ. [10011885] 26/11/2008 **ME**

Renfrew, Ms F, MCLIP, L. Co-ordinator, S. Lanarkshire Council, Hamilton Town House L. [10001565] 10/10/1987 **CM18/07/1990**

Renner, Mrs C A, BA(Hons) Dip Lib, Lib. (PT), Newark L., Notts [10012676] 02/03/2009 **ME**

Renney, Mr D A, BA MA MCLIP, Team Lib., Northants. C.C. [58047] 14/10/1999 **CM23/06/2004**

Rennie, Mr C, MA DipLib, Systems Lib., Sch. of Oriental & African Studies, London [10016475] 26/04/1994 **ME**

Rennison, Mrs S, BA FCLIP, Life Member. [4013] 19/03/1957 **FE29/09/1986**

Renson, Ms H A, BA DipLib MCLIP, Admin. Asst & Operations. Mgr., Sundays Jubiliee L., Brighton. [34424] 30/10/1981 **CM16/05/1985**

Renton, Miss A M, MCLIP, Retired. [12294] 15/03/1968 **CM01/01/1971**

Renwick, Ms F M, BA(Hons) MA MCLIP, Asst. Head of L. Serv., Regeneration & Community, Derby C.C. [36047] 28/04/1983 **CM17/05/2000**

Repp, Miss M C, MA, Unknown. [56348] 03/06/1998 **ME**

Revell, Miss N J, BSc, Unknown. [10014094] 25/06/2009 **ME**

Rex, Mrs C M, BSc MCLIP MAML, Head of L. Serv., Univ. of the W. of England, Bristol. [25532] 02/02/1976 **CM07/02/1978**

Rex, Mr S P, BLib(Hons), Inf. Serv. Mgr., Building Societies Assoc., London. [55184] 04/08/1997 **ME**

Rey, Mrs P B L, BA MCLIP, L. Serv. Mgr., Queen Vic. Hosp. NHS Trust., E. Grinstead, W. Sussex. [29351] 14/06/1978 **CM19/02/1981**

Reyner, Mr R J, Reserche., Deutsche Bank. London [57112] 11/12/1998 **ME**

Reynish, Mr P E, Sen. Lib. Asst., Legal Practice L.,Cardiff [10014091] 01/07/2009 **ME**

Reynolds, Mrs A W, Unknown. [10016310] 08/03/2010 **AF**

Reynolds, Ms J A, MSc, Sen. Br. Super., Univ. of Bristol. [66008] 23/08/2006 **ME**

Reynolds, Miss J E, BA MSc DipLib MCLIP, Training Devel. Lib., W. Herts. Hosp. NHS Trust. [42372] 20/10/1988 **CM24/06/1992**

Reynolds, Mr J G, BA(Hons), Knowledge Offr., Nabarro, London. [10001558] 24/02/1983 **ME**

Reynolds, Mr J, L. Offr., Dept. of Health L., Leeds. [56179] 01/04/1998 **AF**

Reynolds, Ms L, BA(Hons) MCLIP, Inf. Manger, HM Revenue & Customs [52429] 01/11/1995 **CM23/01/2002**

Reynolds, Mr P C, BA DipLib MCLIP, Inf. Offr. Royal Inst. of Chartered Surveyors, London. [35072] 01/07/1982 **CM01/04/1986**

Reynolds, Mr P R, MA MCLIP, Univ. Lib., Keele, Staffs. [41834] 14/04/1988 **CM18/07/1991**

Reynolds, Mrs S J, BA(Hons) PG Dip, Resources Co-ordinator, Language Learning Cent., Univ. of Sussex. [10016969] 29/05/1986 **ME**

Reynolds, Miss T M, Stud. [10007007] 17/12/2007 **ME**

Rhee, Mrs H, BA FCLIP, Retired. [17635] 01/01/1949   FE01/01/1954
Rhodes, Mrs C A, BA MA MCLIP, Sci. & Eng. Faculty Lib., Univ. of
Liverpool. [44917] 14/01/1991   CM18/11/1992
Rhodes, Mr C J, MA, Lib. Exec., House of Commons, London. [65966]
31/07/2006   ME
Rhodes, Ms H J, BSc(Hons) MSc MCLIP, Mgmnt. Subject Lib. [53244]
19/04/1996   CM15/05/2002
Rhodes, Ms J B L, LLB DipLib MCLIP, Stock Serv. Lib., Leeds L. & Inf.
Serv. [25638] 21/01/1976   CM30/01/1978
Rhodes, Miss J, MCLIP, Life Member. [12317] 24/11/1960
CM01/01/1969
Rhodes, Ms L A, BA(Hons) DipLib MCLIP, Local Studies Lib., Valence
House Mus., Dagenham. [33124] 09/10/1980   CM26/05/1983
Rhodes, Miss S A, BSc(Hons) MA MCLIP, Ref. Lib., N. Lincs. Cit. L.,
Lincs. [59681] 31/07/2001 RV04/02/2009   CM15/09/2004
Rhodes, Mrs S, BLib(Hons), Admin. Offr. p. /t. /L. Offr., Bath Co. Court.
[38502] 15/05/1985   ME
Rhys, Mr R C G, L. Asst., Nat. L. of Wales, Aberystwyth. [65959]
21/07/2006   AF
Rhys-Jones, Miss R H, BSc MCLIP, Retired [12327] 07/10/1970
CM06/02/1974
Riccalton, Miss C L, Overseas [40261] 21/11/1986   ME
Rice, Mr A D R, Part-Time Inf. Assitant., Univ. of Nottingham [60915]
10/01/2002   ME
Rice, Mrs B, BA, L. Serv. Delivery Mgr., Leeds City Council, Leeds
Cent. L. [47184] 26/05/1992   ME
Rice, Mrs J J, BA DipLib MCLIP, Lib., E. Barnet Sch., L.B. Barnet.
[39853] 05/09/1986   CM19/09/1989
Rice, Mrs L, BA(Hons), Community Hist. Lib., Knowsley L. Serv.
[10009017] 05/03/1985   ME
Rice, Ms R M, BA(Hons) RSA Dip Lis Dip, Unwaged [10017033]
18/06/2010   ME
Rice, Mr S A, MCLIP MBA, Asst. Head of L. &Inf. Serv., Coventry City
Council, Coventry. [25639] 27/01/1976   CM08/09/1978
Rich, Mrs L, BA MCLIP DMS MCMI, Dist. Mgr.,Tunbridge Wells, Kent
C.C. L. &. Arch. [22832] 09/10/1974   CM11/09/1978
Richards, Mrs A C, MA DipLib MCLIP, Unknown. [31428] 01/10/1979
CM14/10/1981
Richards, Ms A F M, BA(Hons) DipLib MCLIP, Freelance. [18276]
25/09/1972   CM05/08/1975
Richards, Mrs A J, Ethnic Serv. Mgr., Wolverhampton P. L.,
Wolverhampton. [56034] 28/01/1998   ME
Richards, Mr A, BSc FCA MCLIP, Retired. [60687] 12/01/1982
CM12/01/1982
Richards, Ms C L, BA(Hons) MA MCLIP, Sch. Lib., The Venerable Bede
C. of E. Sec. Sch., Sunderland. [56779] 14/10/1998 CM19/11/2003
Richards, Mr D F, FCLIP, Life Member. [12336] 23/09/1949
FE01/01/1964
Richards, Ms D P, MCLIP, p./t. Vol. and Charity, Tenovus [32338]
07/03/1980   CM12/11/1984
Richards, Mr E L, MCLIP, Asst. Lib., Ceredigion Co. L. [12338]
01/01/1970   CM25/01/1974
Richards, Mrs J, Learning Resource Mgr., The Meridian Sch., Royston
[10006942] 17/12/2007   AF
Richards, Miss J, MCLIP, Lib., Tech. Info., Ctr. Royal Engineers, MoD
[64276] 22/02/2005   CM24/10/2008
Richards, Mrs K P, BA MCLIP, Teaching Asst. Coopers Tech. Coll.,
Kent. [35473] 14/10/1982   CM10/11/1987
Richards, Mr L C I, MCLIP, Principal Lib., Serv. Delivery & Training
[12345] 27/02/1969   CM01/01/1971
Richards, Miss M, BA(Hons) MA, Knowledge Mgr., Eversheds LLP,
Manchester. [10014475] 01/02/2002   ME
Richards, Mrs N C, BA(Hons) DipLib MCLIP, Cent. L. Mgr., Cardiff
Cent. L. [47455] 19/08/1992   CM12/09/2001

Richards, Mrs N M, BA MCLIP, Unemployed. [60852] 15/02/2000
CM15/02/2000
Richards, Miss N, BA(Hons) DipL MCLIP, Asst. Lib., Ceredigion Co. L.,
Aberystwyth [10005807] 07/11/1988   CM14/09/1994
Richards, Mrs P D, BSc MSc CPhys MInstP MCLIP, Reg. Dir., EMEA &
Gobal Sales Admin., IET, Stevenage. [60628] 20/04/1979
CM20/04/1979
Richards, Miss S L, Asst. Lib., Sandwell & W. Birmingham Hosp., NHS
Trust [64254] 22/02/2005   ME
Richardson, Mr A G, MCLIP, Health Specialist Lib., Colchester Hosp.
Univ. NHS Foundation Trust, Colchester. [25402] 04/12/1975
CM01/08/1978
Richardson, Mrs C A, BA, Lib., JLIS, Hounslow [62939] 21/11/2003 ME
Richardson, Ms C K, BA DipLibStud MEd AALIA, Unknown. [10013330]
08/04/1991   ME
Richardson, Miss D M E, BA MCLIP, Life Member. [12358] 07/01/1952
CM01/01/1958
Richardson, Ms F B, BA MSc MCLIP, Retired [1866] 14/01/1969
CM01/01/1972
Richardson, Mr G M, MCLIP, Retired. [19282] 24/03/1965
CM01/01/1969
Richardson, Mrs J C, Peak Relief Employee for Essex L. [61442]
18/07/2002   AF
Richardson, Mrs J M, BLIB MCLIP, p. /t. Sen. Child. Lib., Kingston L.
Kingston-On-Thames [22689] 15/08/1974   CM19/11/1979
Richardson, Ms J, MA, Ass. Lib., Northumbria Healthcare NHS Trust.
[61624] 04/10/2002   ME
Richardson, Mr K F, BA(Hons) DipLib MCLIP, Retired. [29496]
12/10/1969   CM01/01/1973
Richardson, Miss K J, BA(Hons), Lib., Home Off., London. [54043]
22/10/1996   ME
Richardson, Mrs M H, MCLIP, Retired. [12370] 26/09/1962
CM01/01/1968
Richardson, Ms M J, BA(Hons) DipIM, Web Mgr., City of London,
Guildhall [51973] 29/08/1995   ME
Richardson, Miss M L, MSc Econ MILS, Researcher, NHS Direct N. E.,
Newcastle-upon-Tyne. [10006351] 01/10/1994   ME
Richardson, Mr P, ACLIP, Lib., Astley Comm. High Sch.
Northumberland. [65919] 05/07/2006   ACL04/03/2009
Richardson, Mrs R E, MCLIP CertHE, Retired. [15595] 18/02/1964
CM01/01/1969
Richardson, Mrs S E, ACLIP, Sch. Lib., Gumley House Convent Sch.,
Middlesex. [10009306] 15/05/2008   ACL01/10/2008
Richardson, Mrs S J, MCLIP, Area Child. & Learning Lib., Solihull
M.B.C. [19852] 01/01/1973   CM05/09/1975
Richardson, Mrs S J, MCLIP, Retired. [3085] 21/01/1959 CM01/01/1963
Richardson, Mrs S, BSc DipLib MCLIP, Unwaged. [27776] 22/07/1977
CM01/07/1984
Richardson, Mrs V M, BA(Hons) MCLIP, Sen. Devel. Offr.,
Cambridgeshire Ls. Inf. Archive. [10009971] 14/05/1982
CM29/07/1986
Richens, Miss A E, BA(Hons), Asst. Lib., [66069] 14/09/2006   ME
Richens, Ms E J, BSc(Hons) MSc, Asst. Lib., Wellcome L., London
[62762] 20/10/2003   ME
Richens, Ms H, BA(Hons) DipILM MCLIP, Princ. Lib. :Child. & Yth., L.B.
of Barnet. [52670] 20/11/1995   CM20/05/1998
Riches, Mr W, BA MA MSc PGCE, Seeking Work. [10016868]
02/08/1999   ME
Richmond, Mrs A G, Asst. Mgr. -Young Peoples Serv., Nelson L.,
Lancs. [65373] 11/01/2006   AF
Richmond, Mrs H J, BSc MSc, Unknown. [10016309] 05/03/2010 ME
Richmond, Miss R L, BA, Stud., Aberystwyth Univ. [10009944]
24/06/2008   ME

Richmond, Mrs S E, BA DipLib MCLIP, Strategic Lib. Mgr., Hull Cent. L. [31817] 02/01/1980 **CM13/12/1984**

Rickard, Mr M D, BA MA MA, Principal Support Offr., Bill Douglas Cent., Special Collections, Univ. of Exeter. [35569] 02/11/1982 **ME**

Rickeard, Ms S M, MSc, Inf. Offr., Lawrence Graham, London. [65813] 11/05/2006 **ME**

Rickers, Mrs C M, MCLIP, Volunteer, Rural Housebound Serv., Warks. Co. L. /Age Concern. [38] 01/01/1961 **CM01/01/1967**

Ricketts, Mr A N, MA MCLIP, Retired. [12390] 08/07/1946 **CM01/01/1949**

Ricketts, Miss E A, BA DipLib MCLIP, Teenage Serv. Mgr., Basingstoke L., Hants. C.C. [26795] 26/10/1976 **CM10/12/1979**

Ricks, Miss A E, BA MCLIP, Retired. [12393] 12/07/1967**CM01/01/1971**

Riddell, Miss A M, LLB DipLP, Unknown. [10015197] 23/10/2009 **ME**

Riddell, Mrs L M, BA(Hons) DipILM MCLIP, Team Lib., Morpeth Lib., Northumberland. [58939] 09/10/2000 **CM29/03/2004**

Riddington, Mrs L, BA(Hons) MA, Asst. Lib., Gloucestershire Hosp. NHS Foundation Trust. [10000463] 10/10/2006 **ME**

Riddle, Miss J S, BSc MA, Inf. Offr., Ward Hadaway, Newcastle [65422] 24/02/2006 **ME**

Rider, Mr P, BA MA PGCE, Teacher/Lib., Strothoff Internat. Sch. Germany. [10016878] 01/06/2010 **ME**

Ridgill, Mrs J, ACLIP, Lib. Asst., Kent Coll., Canterbury, Kent. [10005138] 20/06/2007 **ACL28/01/2009**

Riding, Miss R E, MCLIP, Life Member. [12405] 18/03/1954 **CM01/01/1964**

Ridout, Mrs J M, MA BA(Hons), Inf. Serv. Lib, Altrincham L., Manchester [65806] 16/05/2006 **ME**

Ridsdale, Mr J, BA, PGDip, Asst. Lib., Riba L., London [10008386] 25/03/2008 **ME**

Rieg, Mr F, Researcher, Farrer & Co., London. [64388] 14/03/2005 **ME**

Rigby, Miss A, BA(Hons), Liaison Lib., Sci. & Eng., Univ. of Sheffield [66108] 25/09/2006 **ME**

Rigby, Ms K I, BA(Hons) MSc MCLIP, L. and Inf. Serv. Mgr., Hinchingbrooke Healthcare L., Hinchingbrooke Hosp., Cambs. [60035] 29/11/2001 **CM06/04/2005**

Rigglesford, Mr D N, BA MCLIP, Res. Lib., Employment Relations Ltd., Cambs. [12416] 01/10/1964 **CM01/07/1989**

Riggs, Mrs M, Educ. Resources Ctr., Dorset Sch. Lib. Serv. [62873] 17/11/2003 **AF**

Riggs, Ms S, BSc PgDipILS, Lib., J Rothschild Capital Mgmnt Ltd., London. [61643] 10/10/2002 **ME**

Rikowski, Mrs R L, BA DipLib MSc MA MCLIP CLTHE AHEA, Visiting Lect., S. Bank Univ., London. [28194] 20/10/1977 **CM16/04/1981**

Riley, Miss A E, BA(Hons), Stud., City Univ., London. [10015932] 28/01/2010 **ME**

Riley, Mrs C L, BA(Hons) (MA) MCLIP, Knowledge & L. Mgr., E. Lancs. Hosp. NHS Trust, Blackburn. [50539] 09/09/1994 **CM15/11/2000**

Riley, Miss C, MA MSc, Unknown. [66157] 04/10/2006 **ME**

Riley, Mr D W, FCLIP, Life Member. [12417] 01/09/1952 **FE01/01/1963**

Riley, Mrs E H, MA MCLIP, Law Lib., Univ. of Warwick L., Coventry. [30456] 25/01/1979 **CM12/03/1981**

Riley, Mrs E J, Mgr. Inf., Huntingdon Life Sciences, Huntingdon [56509] 30/07/1998 **ME**

Riley, Mrs H, BA(Hons) MCLIP, Principal Lib., Adult Serv., Dudley L. [10007732] 11/12/1979 **CM14/11/1985**

Riley, Mr J P, BA DIP ED MCLIP, Retired. [26001] 10/05/1976 **CM15/08/1990**

Riley, Mrs L E, BA(Hons) DipEd MA CBA MCLIP, Dist. Mgr., Staffs C.C. [46922] 24/02/1992 **CM19/03/1997**

Riley, Mr R B, MCLIP, Retired. [12424] 15/01/1940 **CM01/01/1963**

Riley, Miss S, BA(Hons) MA MCLIP, Learning Resource Mgr., St. Neots Community Coll., Cambs C.C. [54273] 11/11/1996 **CM15/03/2000**

Riley-Smith, Mrs P A, BA(Hons) MSc, Sch. Lib., Fulneck Sch., Pudsey. [56373] 01/07/1998 **ME**

Rillie, Mrs C M, BLib(Hons) MCLIP, Classroom Asst., Bracknell BFBC. [45728] 02/05/1991 **CM14/09/1994**

Rimmer, Mrs J E, BLib MCLIP, Team Lib., Eccleston L. [32965] 08/10/1980 **CM02/01/1986**

Rimmer, Mrs S E, MA AI, E-Resources Co-ordinator, Univ. of Derby. [10002096] 19/11/1993 **ME**

Ring, Ms V J, BA(Hons) DipIM MCLIP, Lib., Falkirk Council, Denny L. [49894] 07/01/1994 **CM22/09/1999**

Ringrose, Miss J S, MA MCLIP, Under Lib., Univ. of Cambridge L. [12431] 06/10/1967 **CM01/01/1969**

Ripley, Mr S C, BA(Hons), Learning Cent. Asst., City & Islington, London [10008543] 02/04/2008 **AF**

Ripp, Mr J, Lib., Nat. Portrait Gallery, London [63317] 13/04/2004 **ME**

Ripper, Ms A H, BSc, Sr. Lib. Asst., UWE, Bristol [10000799] 03/11/2006 **ME**

Riste, Mr J R, BA(Hons) MCLIP, L. Mgr., Hillingdon Hosp. NHS Trust, Uxbridge. [44049] 10/04/1990 **CM19/01/2000**

Ristic, Mrs L, PgDipILS MCLIP, Physical Sci. Lib. Subject Consultant, Univ. of Oxford [51848] 13/07/1995 **CM23/01/2002**

Ritchie, Mr J S, MCLIP, Inf. Offr., Univ. of Glasgow. [60246] 25/04/1993 **CM10/12/2001**

Ritchie, Ms J, BA DipLib MCLIP, Coll. Lib., Kirklees Coll., Huddersfield. [39679] 07/05/1986 **CM13/06/1989**

Ritchie, Mrs S F C, MA DMS MCLIP, Self Employed, Mgmnt. Skills Trainer, Huntingdon. [12439] 01/01/1967 **CM01/01/1971**

Rivers-Latham, Mrs M J, BA(Hons) DipIS MCLIP, Knowledge & Business Intelligence Consultant. [55474] 17/10/1997**CM21/03/2001**

Rivers-Moore, Miss A R, BA DipLib MCLIP, Chief Lib., Hanover P.L., Canada [35035] 13/07/1982 **CM01/08/1991**

Rix, Mr D W, MCLIP, Sch. Lib., Tideway Sch., Newhaven, E. Sussex. [26240] 17/09/1976 **CM11/11/1980**

Rix, Mrs R S, MCLIP, Retired. [12444] 02/04/1959 **CM01/01/1961**

Rixham, Ms M J, Unknown [10001077] 12/01/2007 **ME**

Rizvi, Mrs I J, BA(Hons) PGDipLib MCLIP, Dev. Co-ordinator, LB of Brent, Wembley [41980] 01/07/1988 **CM12/12/1990**

Rizzo, Mr A T, BA PhD MA, Serv. Mgr., Lewisham L. & Inf. Serv., London. [55627] 28/10/1997 **ME**

Roach, Mrs M F, BA MCLIP, Unknown. [26895] 05/01/1977 **CM09/09/1981**

Roache, Miss A, BA MA, Head of Inf. Serv., Weil, Gotshal & Manges, London. [44475] 11/10/1990 **ME**

Road, Mr J R, Sr. Team Offr., Surrey C.C., Drill Hall [39990] 09/10/1986 **ME**

Robalino, Ms S C, BA(Hons), MSc, Lead Inf. Specialist, Nat. L. for Public Health [64912] 14/09/2005 **ME**

Robb, Mrs A J, MA(Hons) DipILS MCLIP, Local Studies Lib., E. Renfrewshire Council. [51600] 06/04/1995 **CM23/07/1997**

Robb, Mr C I, BA(Hons) DipILS, Unemployed. [58740] 03/07/2000 **ME**

Robb, Mr D E, ACLIP, Performing Arts Lib., Performing Arts L., Hatfield. [64126] 10/01/2005 **ACL04/04/2006**

Robb, Mrs F M, L. Asst., Monifieth High Sch., Scotland. [10016127] 16/02/2010 **AF**

Robb, Mrs H D, BA DipLib MCLIP ILTM, Faculty Support Lib., Durham Univ. L. [38788] 09/10/1985 **CM07/06/1988**

Robbins, Mrs M O, DipIS MCLIP, Lib., Brillantmont Int. Sch., Switzerland [52627] 14/11/1995 **CM18/11/1998**

Robbins, Mrs R M, BA, Lib., Min. of Justice, London. [43289] 16/10/1989 **ME**

Roberts Cuffin, Mrs T L, BA(Hons) MCLIP, L. & Knowledge Serv. Mgr., Morecambe Bay Health Comm., Royal Lancaster Infirmary. [40664] 28/04/1987 **CM04/02/2004**

Roberts, Miss A L, MSc BA(Hons) MCLIP, Liaison Lib., Queen Margaret Univ., Edinburgh. [61131] 07/03/2002 **CM28/01/2009**

Roberts, Mrs A L, BA(Hons) MCLIP, Sen. Asst. Lib., Worthing, W. Sussex. [10002795] 27/04/2007 **CM27/11/1996**

Roberts, Mrs A M, BLib MCLIP, Customer Serv. Mgr., Univ. of Warwick L. [22007] 19/01/1974 **CM01/08/1977**

Roberts, Ms A M, BA(Hons) PGCE, L. Serv. Coordinator, Calderdale Sch., Northgate [10006776] 12/10/1982 **ME**

Roberts, Ms A, BA MA, Asst Lib. Trainee (Health and Social Care), Anglia Ruskin Univ., Essex [10006439] 19/10/2007 **ME**

Roberts, Mr B F, CBE MA PhD HonFLA, Lib., Nat. L. of Wales, Aberystwyth. [39278] 06/01/1986 **HFE01/01/1994**

Roberts, Mrs C A H, BSc DipLib MCLIP, p. /t. Lib., The Kings Sch. /The Queen's Sch. Chester [17126] 04/04/1972 **CM16/09/1975**

Roberts, Miss C I, BA(Hons) MSc Econ, Collections, Standards & Training Off., Cynal Museuems, Arch. & L. Wales. [49087] 01/10/1993 **ME**

Roberts, Mrs C L, MA DipLib MCLIP, Network Lib., Peterhead Academy. [33069] 08/10/1980 **CM27/10/1983**

Roberts, Ms C, MA DipIS MCLIP, Learning Resources Asst., Cent. Coll., Glasgow [55240] 08/09/1997 **CM12/03/2003**

Roberts, Mr C, MA(Hons) MSc MCLIP, Subject Lib., Univ. of Bath. [59818] 10/10/2001 **CM23/06/2004**

Roberts, Mr D A W, BA, Customer Serv. Advisor, Capita CRB, Liverpool. [10007553] 13/02/2008 **ME**

Roberts, Mr D G, BA MCLIP, Life Member. [12468] 15/04/1961 **CM01/01/1971**

Roberts, Miss D S, BA(Hons) MA, Stud. [10017045] 21/06/2010 **ME**

Roberts, Mr D, BA(Hons) MA, Comm. Learning & Inf. Lib., Chesterfield L., Derbyshire C.C. [58006] 12/10/1999 **ME**

Roberts, Mrs D, BA MSc MCLIP, Lib., Burnetts Solicitors. [5472] 29/01/1968 **CM01/01/1971**

Roberts, Mrs D, MCLIP, Retired. [15095] 29/03/1963 **CM01/01/1971**

Roberts, Ms D, BLib MCLIP, Team Lead L. & Knowledge Mgmt., NPHS, Swansea. [27458] 01/04/1977 **CM01/07/1990**

Roberts, Mrs E C, BA(Hons) MA MCLIP, Learning Resources Co-ordinator, St. Frances Assisi Catholic Tech. Coll., Walsall [50952] 31/10/1994 **CM21/05/2003**

Roberts, Ms E H, BSc, Sch. Lib., The Ravensbourne Sch., Bromley. [49489] 05/11/1993 **ME**

Roberts, Miss E K, BA DipLib MCLIP, Serv. Devel. Lib., Cirencester Bingham L., Glos. C.C. [41713] 20/02/1988 **CM22/05/1991**

Roberts, Ms E, BA MA, Lib. Art & Music/Rare Books, Los Angeles P.L., USA. [10014382] 22/10/1997 **ME**

Roberts, Mrs F M, BA MSc, Lib. [10006921] 17/12/2007 **ME**

Roberts, Mrs F W, MA MSc MCLIP, Unwaged. [25323] 05/01/1976 **CM23/01/1978**

Roberts, Miss F, BA MCLIP, Serv. Devel. Co-ord., S. Lanarkshire Council. [35194] 04/10/1982 **CM02/06/1987**

Roberts, Mrs H M, BA(Hons) MSc MCLIP, Lib., Reigate Grammar Sch., Surrey. [62773] 20/10/2003 **CM13/06/2007**

Roberts, Mrs H M, Sch. Libr., Lea Valley High Sch., Herts. [63904] 26/10/2004 **ME**

Roberts, Miss I M B, MCLIP, Retired. [12483] 20/03/1964 **CM01/01/1972**

Roberts, Miss J E, BA(Hons), Stud [10006662] 21/11/2007 **ME**

Roberts, Mrs J F E, MCLIP, Retired [12489] 20/01/1960 **CM01/01/1966**

Roberts, Ms J L, BA(Hons) MscIS, Unknown [55840] 21/11/1997 **ME**

Roberts, Ms J, BA(Hons) MCLIP, Arch., Leonard Cheshire Disability, Netherseal. [45791] 31/05/1991 **CM22/05/1996**

Roberts, Miss K A, BA(Hons), Unknown. [10007177] 24/01/2008 **ME**

Roberts, Miss K L, BA(Hons), Unknown. [10009992] 30/06/2008 **AF**

Roberts, Mrs L M, BA MCLIP, Inf. Offr. (Job Share), Child. Inf. Bureau, Wrexham L. & Arts Cent. [28451] 04/11/1977 **CM06/03/1981**

Roberts, Mrs M A F, MCLIP, Life Member. [12498] 01/01/1957 **CM01/01/1961**

Roberts, Miss M E, MCLIP, Retired. [12500] 07/10/1947 **CM01/01/1971**

Roberts, Mr M J, MCLIP, Dir., Infodoc Serv. Ltd., London. [12502] 09/08/1961 **CM01/01/1965**

Roberts, Mr M V, MA MCLIP, Retired. [12505] 01/01/1964 **CM01/01/1967**

Roberts, Mr M, MA MA MCLIP, Dep. Dir. of Lib. Servs., Andersonian L., Univ. of Strathclyde. [21828] 15/02/1974 **CM03/11/1976**

Roberts, Ms M, ACLIP, Not Known, CEFAS, Suffolk. [10004196] 23/05/2007 **ACL01/10/2008**

Roberts, Miss M, BA(Hons), Res. Consultant, Oxford Innovation [62270] 07/04/2003 **ME**

Roberts, Mr N R, BA(Hons), Asst. Lib., Univ. of Glamorgan. [54125] 30/10/1996 **ME**

Roberts, Miss N W, BA(Hons), Lib., Old Road Campus L., Univ. of Oxford. [56867] 29/10/1998 **ME**

Roberts, Mrs P J, BA MCLIP, Div. Mgr., IPC Grp., St. Ives. [26306] 01/10/1976 **CM07/07/1980**

Roberts, Mrs R E, BSc(Hons) MA Ed MSc MCLIP, Retired. [61255] 29/04/2002 **CM21/11/2007**

Roberts, Mr R J, MA FSA MCLIP, Retired. [12513] 20/10/1953 **CM01/01/1956**

Roberts, Mrs R, BA(Hons) MCLIP, Learning Cent. Coordinator., Wolverhampton Coll. [43082] 25/07/1989 **CM25/05/1994**

Roberts, Dr S A, MA MA PhD MCLIP, Sen. Lect., Cent. for Inf. Mgmt., Thames Valley Univ. [12516] 29/08/1969 **CM01/01/1972**

Roberts, Mrs S M, BA MCLIP MA, Head of L. and Inf. Serv., The Grammar Sch. at Leeds, W. Yorks [1159] 11/01/1972 **CM21/06/2006**

Roberts, Miss S M, BA(Hons) MCLIP, Knowledge Cent. Mgr., HEFCE, Bristol. [51123] 17/11/1994 **CM08/12/2004**

Roberts, Mrs S, BA(Hons) MA MCLIP, Trial Search Co-ordinator, Cochrane Schizophrenia Grp. [59635] 09/07/2001 **CM28/10/2004**

Roberts, Dr T, PhD, Sen. Careers Inf. Offr., Univ. of Reading, Careers Advisory Serv. [49652] 19/11/1993 **ME**

Roberts, Mr W D, MA MCLIP, Principal Advisor – Intl., Nat. L. of NZ, Wellington [10008012] 03/03/2008 **CM11/11/1980**

Roberts, Mrs W J, MCLIP, Lib., Ardingly Coll., Haywards Heath. [14774] 01/10/1968 **CM02/03/1973**

Roberts, Mr W R G, BA MCLIP, L. Mgr., Thornton Heath & Broad Green L., Croydon [20692] 08/06/1973 **CM01/09/1976**

Robertshaw, Miss J, MA DipLib MCLIP, Collections Devel. Mgr., Dept. of Printed Books, Imperial War Mus., London. [39378] 23/01/1986 **CM16/05/1990**

Roberts-Maloney, Mrs L M, Learning Asst., Riverside Coll. Halton, Cheshire [64532] 09/05/2005 **ME**

Robertson, Mrs A C, BA(Hons) DipLib MAppSc(LIM) MCLIP, Academic Liason Lib., Univ. of Bedfordshire [35534] 21/10/1982 **CM21/05/2003**

Robertson, Miss A J, BA(Hons) DipLib, p/t. Med. records Clerk, NHS, Caithness Gen. Hosp. [41777] 08/04/1988 **ME**

Robertson, Miss A K, MA, Quality Control and Documentation Lib., Fife Council. [57785] 14/08/1999 **ME**

Robertson, Mr B, BA DipLib MCLIP, Gallery Attendant, MOMA Wales. [29804] 16/10/1978 **CM26/05/1982**

Robertson, Mrs C A, BA MCLIP, Freelance Proofreader & Res. Worker. [12527] 17/05/1965 **CM01/01/1970**

Robertson, Mr C L, FCLIP, Retired. [26259] 28/10/1943 **FE04/06/1964**

Robertson, Mr C P, MCLIP, Life Member. [12528] 22/03/1938 **CM01/01/1952**

Robertson, Mrs D K, FCLIP, Life Member. [12529] 05/03/1940 **FE01/01/1968**

Robertson, Mr D, MA(Hons), Sr. Lib. Asst., Carnoustie L. [64214] 21/02/2005 **ME**

Robertson, Mrs E M, BSc INF SC MCLIP, Head of Health Serv. L., Univ. of Southampton. [14025] 18/06/1969 **CM27/02/1976**

Robertson, Mrs E, BA MCLIP, Network Lib., Fraserburgh Acad., Fraserburgh. [28517] 01/01/1978 **CM28/08/1981**

Robertson, Mrs F E, MA MCLIP, Team Leader, Comm. Inf. Team, Cent. L., Dundee City Council. [21084] 04/10/1973 **CM01/11/1975**

Robertson, Ms F M, BA MCLIP, Network Lib., Aberdeen Lib. & Info. Serv. [37829] 29/10/1984 **CM11/12/1989**

Robertson, Miss F, BA DipLib, Sub-Lib., Brit. Med. Assoc., London. [42163] 07/10/1988 **ME**

Robertson, Mrs H J, MCLIP, L. Asst., Gloucester L. 's. [31783] 21/01/1980 **CM27/01/1984**

Robertson, Miss I M, MCLIP, Life Member. [12536] 06/09/1955 **CM01/01/1962**

Robertson, Mrs J A, MA(Hons) DipILS MCLIP, Mgr. -L. Serv. (Europe), Booz Allen Hamilton, Strand. [51067] 10/11/1994 **CM21/11/2001**

Robertson, Ms J M, BA MCLIP, L., Royal Courts of Justice. [42560] 03/01/1989 **CM26/05/1993**

Robertson, Mrs K M, MA DipLib MCLIP, Community Lib., S. Lanarkshire Council, Carluke Community L. [13398] 15/10/1970 **CM28/02/1974**

Robertson, Miss L J, BA(Hons) MSc, Sch. Lib., Uddingstom Grammar Sch., Glasgow. [10010638] 29/08/2008 **ME**

Robertson, Mrs L M, MA MSc MCLIP, Liaison Lib., Biological Sciences and Preclinical Medicine Univ. of Southampton. [26141] 01/07/1976 **CM01/07/1989**

Robertson, L, BSc(Hons) MSc MCLIP, Lib., Shepherd and Wedderburn LLP, Edinburgh. [49607] 19/11/1993 **CM20/11/2002**

Robertson, Miss M, BA(Hons) MSc, CINDEX Health Inf. Offr, L.B. of Camden [63391] 28/04/2004 **ME**

Robertson, Mrs P A C, BSc(Hons) DipILS MCLIP, Learning & Teaching Lib. [51747] 14/06/1995 **RV11/12/2009** **CM22/09/1999**

Robertson, Ms P, BA PgDip MCLIP, Inf. Architecture Mgr., Scottish Qualifications Auth. (SQA) [57275] 26/01/1999 **CM02/02/2005**

Robertson, Mrs P, BA(Hons) MCLIP, Lib., Alloa, Clackmannanshire [62713] 09/10/2003 **CM05/05/2010**

Robertson, Mrs R M, MCLIP, Network Lib., Meldrum Academy, Aberdeenshire. [12546] 12/10/1966 **CM01/01/1969**

Robertson, Mrs S E, BLib MCLIP, Lib. & Info. Servs. Mgr., Nuffield Orthopaedic Ctre. [34584] 01/01/1982 **CM02/01/1986**

Robertson, Prof S E, PhD MBCS FCLIP, Researcher, Microsoft Res. Ltd., Cambridge. [60632] 16/07/1968 **FE25/01/1979**

Robertson, Mrs S O, MCLIP, Customer Serv. Mgr., Kingston Univ. L., Surrey. [25808] 14/02/1976 **CM01/02/1979**

Robertson, Mr S O, MA MEd DipLib MCLIP, H. of L. Serv., Univ. of Chichester, W. Sussex. [23243] 08/11/1974 **CM01/01/1976**

Robertson, Ms S, BA(Hons) MA, Stud. (MA Lib.),Univ. of Sheffield, Sheffield. [10001475] 26/02/2007 **ME**

Robertson, Mrs V A A, BA MCLIP, Site Serv. Mgr., Kings Coll. London. Maughan L. & Inf. Serv. Cent. [5007] 03/11/1971 **CM02/08/1976**

Robertson, Mrs V R, MCLIP, P/t. Sen. L. Asst., Napier Univ., Edinburgh. [22859] 03/10/1974 **CM04/07/1977**

Robertson, Miss V, BA(Hons) MCLIP, Reader Serv. Lib., Univ. of London, Sch. of Pharmacy L. [48299] 25/11/1992 **RV04/03/2009** **CM22/07/1998**

Robin, Mrs C R W, MCLIP, Retired. [6298] 18/08/1971 **CM17/06/1975**

Robin, Ms S C, BA(Hons), Stud., Aberystwyth Univ. [10014423] 12/08/2009 **ME**

Robins, Mrs E M, MCLIP, Partner-Eng. Consultancy, Dove Thermal Eng. Ltd., Uttoxeter, Staffs. [12548] 01/01/1959 **CM01/01/1964**

Robins, Miss J, BA(Hons), Nat. Gallery of Scotland, Edinburgh. [10015772] 26/02/1991 **ME**

Robins, Ms P H, BA MCLIP, Ch. Catr. /S. E. Europe Specialist, UCL SSEES L., London. [24265] 06/05/1975 **CM04/10/1978**

Robins, Miss S E, BA(Hons) MCLIP, Lib., CWMTAF Health Board, Royal Glamorgan Hos. [62882] 18/11/2003 **CM11/06/2010**

Robinson, Ms A L, BA(Hons) MLib MCLIP, Academic Liaison Lib., Univ. of Bedfordshire [47949] 27/10/1992 **CM13/03/2002**

Robinson, Miss A M, BA(Hons) DipILM MCLIP, Literary Dev. Offr., Darwen Libs., Blackburn. [56675] 01/10/1998 **CM20/11/2002**

Robinson, Mrs A, MCLIP, Comm. Lib., N. Lanarkshire Council, Lanarkshire. [21293] 01/10/1973 **CM12/07/1976**

Robinson, Miss A, BA(Hons), L. Acquisitions, Slaughter & May, London. [50977] 04/11/1994 **ME**

Robinson, Ms A, BA(Hons) MA, Reader Devel. Mgr. – Hackney [65018] 11/10/2005 **ME**

Robinson, Miss A, MCLIP, Systems & Resources Lib., City of Sunderland Coll. [22013] 07/01/1974 **CM05/01/1977**

Robinson, Miss B E, MCLIP, Retired. [12554] 08/10/1941 **CM01/01/1952**

Robinson, Mrs B, Info. Serv. Offr., Redcar & Cleveland Bor. Council, Redcar. [21381] 31/10/1973 **ME**

Robinson, Miss C E, MCLIP, Inf. Lib., Midirs, Bristol [62869] 17/11/2003 **CM21/03/2008**

Robinson, Miss C I M, BA, Inf. Offr., Osborne Clarke, Bristol [63523] 16/06/2004 **ME**

Robinson, Mr D R, MCLIP, Comm. L. Mgr., Beaumont Leys L., Leicester City Council. [19154] 17/08/1972 **CM13/05/1977**

Robinson, Mrs D, BA DipLib MCLIP, Lib., Dallam Sch., Cumbria. [38867] 16/10/1985 **CM19/06/1991**

Robinson, Mrs E C, BA MCLIP, Sales & Operations Mgr., OCLC UK Ltd [41704] 03/02/1988 **CM18/11/1992**

Robinson, Mr E D G, JP DL MA FRSA MCLIP, Life Member. [12562] 28/09/1950 **CM01/01/1958**

Robinson, Ms E J, BSc MCLIP PhD, Freelance Res./Consultant. [30523] 01/02/1979 **CM16/09/1981**

Robinson, Mrs F, MA, Unwaged. [58823] 15/08/2000 **ME**

Robinson, Mr G A, BA(Hons) DipLIS MCLIP, L. Mgr., Barnet & Chase Farm Hosp. NHS Trust, London. [41260] 25/10/1987 **CM17/03/1999**

Robinson, Mrs G, BA DipLib MCLIP, Sen. Lib., Warwickshire L. [35308] 10/10/1982 **CM13/05/1986**

Robinson, Mrs H J, BA(Hons) PGDipLib, Head of Inf. Serv., Bevan Brittan, Bristol. [41289] 30/10/1987 **ME**

Robinson, Mrs H M, BA(Hons), Unknown. [10014375] 21/11/2000 **ME**

Robinson, Ms H, LLB(Hons) DipILS MCLIP, Reader Serv. Lib., Advocates L., Edinburgh [53614] 12/08/1996 **CM21/05/2003**

Robinson, Mr J A, KM Resources Offr., DLA Piper UK LLP, Manchester [62465] 08/07/2003 **ME**

Robinson, Mrs J L, CD MBE FCLIP LLD, Gen. Mgr., Jamaica Broadcasting Corp., Kingston, Jamaica. [17659] 07/07/1950 **FE01/01/1959**

Robinson, Mrs J L, MSc BA MCLIP RLIANZA, L. Mgr., Gore L, New Zealand [40341] 21/01/1987 **CM18/07/1991**

Robinson, Mrs J L, MCLIP, Retired. [20365] 15/02/1973 **CM10/08/1976**

Robinson, Ms J, BA(Hons) DipIS MCLIP, Inf. Offr. [57716] 02/04/1960 **CM02/04/1960**

Robinson, Mrs J, Stud. [65931] 10/07/2006 **ME**

Robinson, Miss K A, BA MCLIP, People's Ntwk. Dev Mgr., Hants. L. & Inf. Serv. Hampshire [38176] 04/02/1985 **CM27/05/1992**

Robinson, Mrs K M, JP MA MCLIP, Head of Academic Serv., Univ. of Bath. [44072] 30/04/1990 **CM24/06/1992**

Robinson, Ms K, BA(Hons) MA, Learning Resource Lib., City of London Academy, Islington. [61586] 02/10/2002 **ME**

Robinson, Ms L J, BA, L. Asst., Univ. of Oxford. [10001763] 21/02/2007 **ME**

Robinson, Mrs L, ACLIP, Asst. Access to Serv. Mgr., H.Q. [64644] 03/05/2005 **ACL24/11/2006**

Robinson, Mrs L, BSc (Hons), Asst. Lib., Univ. Sunderland, St. Peter's L. [61460] 14/08/2002 **ME**

Robinson, Mrs L, BSc, Sen. L. Asst., Hmp Holme House., Stockton On Tees. [10013632] 18/05/2009 **AF**

Robinson, Ms M M, MCLIP, Asst. Area Mgr., Suffolk C.C., Cent. L.
[12579] 24/02/1971 **CM06/08/1974**
Robinson, Ms M, BA DipLib MCLIP, Circ. Serv. Coordinator and ISS
Disability Adviser, Kings Coll. London, Maughan, L. [36940]
20/01/1984 **CM09/08/1988**
Robinson, Dr M, BA DipLib PhD, Faculty Lib., Crewe & Alsager Faculty,
Manchester Metro. Univ. [34849] 16/03/1982 **ME**
Robinson, Ms M, BSc MSc MLIS MCLIP, Inf. Specialist, R&RNAV
[10002939] 09/05/2007 **CM10/03/2010**
Robinson, Mr M, BA MCLIP, Programme Co-ordinator Lib., Northants.
C.C. [28888] 08/02/1978 **CM29/01/1981**
Robinson, Mr N K, DipLib, Support Asst., Nottingham [43085]
24/07/1989 **ME**
Robinson, Mr N, Res. Offr., Marylebone Cricket Club [63334]
16/04/2004 **ME**
Robinson, Mrs P M, Lib., NHS Direct, Southampton. [45195]
08/08/1990 **ME**
Robinson, Mrs R A M, BA PGCE MA MCLIP, Child. & Young People's
Lib., Reader Devel., Northants C.C. [44701] 29/11/1990
CM23/03/1993
Robinson, Ms R E, Sen. Stock Mgr. /Affiliated, Blackburn Cent. L.
[10011881] 25/11/2008 **AF**
Robinson, Miss R H, MSc BA(Hons) MCLIP, Lib. Scvs. Mgr. NHS, Gtr.
Glasgow & Clyde [43343] 24/10/1989 **CM25/05/1994**
Robinson, Mrs S F, BA(Hons) MCLIP, Asst. Lib., Hull Coll., Hull. [49505]
08/11/1993 **CM12/03/2003**
Robinson, Mrs S J, Unknown [10012511] 19/05/2009 **ME**
Robinson, Mr S L, BA DipLib MCLIP, Lib. & Arch., MOD, Aldershot.
[38684] 01/10/1985 **CM16/05/1990**
Robinson, Ms S M, BA MCLIP, Weekend site Mgr., Health Sciences L.,
Univ. of Leeds [28262] 26/10/1977 **CM27/11/1979**
Robinson, Ms S R, BA(Hons) MA MCLIP, Sen. Inf. Specialist, NICE.
[49167] 08/10/1993 **CM18/09/2002**
Robinson, Mrs S V, BA(Hons) DipIS MCLIP, Subj. Liaison Lib., Univ.
Campus Suffolk, Ipswich. [48088] 02/11/1992 **CM12/09/2001**
Robinson, Mrs T, BA DipLib MCLIP, Retired. [31361] 03/10/1979
CM09/12/1982
Robinson, Mrs V A, Lib., N. Lincs. Council. [47297] 06/07/1992 **ME**
Robisson, Mme J, DipLib MCLIP, Unknown [39066] 02/11/1985
CM18/04/1990
Roblin, Ms C, Web Content Mgr., Oxfordshire C.C. [40531] 01/03/1987
ME
Robson, Mr A C W, Stud., Univ. Coll. Wales. [49363] 22/10/1993 **ME**
Robson, Mr A J, MCLIP, Lib., Lasswade High Sch. Cent., Bonnyrigg,
Midlothian. [21450] 15/10/1973 **CM10/02/1977**
Robson, Mr G I, BSc (Hons), PG Dip RM, Arch. & Inf. Mgr., Hackney
Arch., London. [10011287] 09/10/2008 **ME**
Robson, Ms J M, MCLIP, Essex Co. L., Chelmsford [20637] 17/05/1973
CM09/12/1976
Robson, Miss L S, Asst. Lib., Gateshead Cent. L., Gateshead. [54877]
28/04/1997 **ME**
Robson, Mrs L T, Principal Lib.:Community Devel. & Access., Dudley
M.B.C. [49419] 21/10/1993 **ME**
Robson, Mr M S, BA MCLIP, Retired. [12599] 12/01/1965**CM01/01/1969**
Robson, Mr M, BSc(Hons), Inf. Offr, Linklaters. London. [10006331]
10/10/2007 **ME**
Roby, Mrs T A, BA(Hons) MCLIP, Retired [10006646] 06/10/1987
CM21/07/1993
Roche, Mrs C M L, BA(Hons) MCLIP, Res. Cent. Mgr., Holmesdale
Tech. Coll., Kent. [56636] 24/09/1998 **CM31/01/2007**
Roche, Ms K C, BA MLib MCLIP, LRC Mgr., W. Thames Coll.,
Middlesex. [41129] 11/10/1987 **CM12/12/1990**
Roche, Ms M N, BA MA, Sen. Lib., Royal Bor. of Kensington & Chelsea
L. [43337] 23/10/1989 **ME**

Rochelle, Miss S F, BA MCLIP, Lib., Telford & Wrekin Auth., Shropshire.
[39509] 11/02/1986 **CM14/03/1990**
Rochester, Ms E, BSc(Hons) MSc MCLIP, Cont. Mgmnt. Lib. [47027]
02/04/1992 **CM07/11/1996**
Rochester, Mrs W M, Lib., [55869] 02/12/1997 **ME**
Rock, Ms C J W, BA MA MCLIP, Univ. Lib., Coventry Univ. [40929]
05/08/1987 **CM24/04/1991**
Rockliff, Ms J A, BSc Pgd, Dep. Inf. Mgr., TUC. London. [46237]
18/10/1991 **ME**
Rodda, Mrs S J M, BA MSc (Econ), Asst. Lib., Bishop Grosseteste Coll.,
Lincoln. [61440] 29/07/2002 **ME**
Roddham, Mr M L, BA(Hons) MLib MCLIP, Head of L. Serv., W. Sussex
Health L., Chichester. [10000672] 14/01/1981 **CM08/07/1983**
Roddy, Ms K M, BA, Consultant, K. Roddy Res. & Consultancy, London.
[46076] 26/09/1991 **ME**
Rodenhurst, Mrs F H, BLib MCLIP, Lib., Oswestry L., Shropshire.
[41545] 20/01/1988 **CM14/11/1991**
Roderick, Mr G L, BA(Hons), Stud., Univ. of W. of England. [10015217]
27/10/2009 **ME**
Rodger, Mrs E A, MA MSc MCLIP, Lib. -IT & Systems (Educ.
Resources), S. Lanarkshire Council, Hamilton. [57455] 01/04/1999
CM23/01/2002
Rodger, Miss E M, BSc MCLIP, Life Member. [12608] 12/07/1965
CM01/01/1967
Rodger, Mrs J H, MA DipLib MCLIP, Unwaged. [21318] 26/09/1973
CM07/02/1978
Rodger, Mrs J, MCLIP, Retired. [9473] 10/10/1963 **CM01/01/1967**
Rodgers, Mrs E G, BA DipLib MCLIP, p. /t. Lib. Asst., S. Tyneside Coll.
[30582] 15/02/1979 **CM19/01/1983**
Rodgers, Mrs M P, BA MCLIP, Stock Mgr., Blackpool Bor. Council.
[8502] 14/01/1971 **CM30/10/1975**
Rodrick, Mrs S E, BA DipLib MCLIP, Sch. Lib., Royal Grammar Sch.,
High Wycombe, Bucks. [32783] 27/08/1980 **CM18/07/1985**
Rodriguez, Miss G M, Researcher, Medellin, Colombia. [41631]
05/02/1988 **ME**
Rodwell, Mr I G, BA(Hons) MBA, Inf. Mgr., Linklaters, London. [40271]
02/12/1986 **ME**
Roe, Miss A, BA, LRC Mgr., Belmont Sch. Community Arts Coll.,
Durham. [63643] 09/08/2004 **ME**
Roe, Mr G D, BA, Editor – Printed Indexes, Indexing and Data Mgmnt.,
House of Commons L. [10001596] 19/02/2007 **ME**
Roe, Mr J, BA MA FCLIP, Retired. [12621] 05/09/1949 **FE01/01/1958**
Roe, Mr N W, BA MCLIP, Bibl. Serv. Offr., N. E. Wales Inst. of H. E.,
Wrexham. [12625] 27/02/1972 **CM31/10/1974**
Roe, Mrs S, BA DipLib MCLIP, Child. Lib., Bebington Cent. L., Met. Bor.
of Wirral. [31336] 15/10/1979 **CM16/02/1983**
Rogan, Ms J T F, BA(Hons) MSc, Inf. Specilaist, Peavson, London.
[56852] 27/10/1998 **ME**
Rogan, Mr J, DipHE, Asst. Lib., Morecambe L., Lancashire. [63466]
14/05/2004 **ME**
Rogers, Mrs A D, MCLIP, Retired. [6713] 10/03/1962 **CM01/01/1969**
Rogers, Miss A M, MCLIP, Retired. [12633] 07/03/1933 **CM01/01/1945**
Rogers, Mrs B, BA MCLIP, Sch. Lib., Notts. C.C., Notts. [31835]
18/01/1980 **CM15/08/1984**
Rogers, Mr C E, MCLIP, Life Member. [12636] 16/07/1949
CM01/01/1955
Rogers, Mr C, BA(Hons) DipLib MCLIP, Multimedia Res. Cent. Mgr., N.
Glasgow Coll. [35034] 12/07/1982 **CM20/09/1995**
Rogers, Mrs D C, BA MCLIP, Retired. [12638] 04/08/1960
CM01/01/1963
Rogers, Mr F R, BA M PHIL FCLIP, Life Member [12641] 12/09/1952
FE01/01/1968
Rogers, Ms H M A, BA(Hons) MCLIP, L. Mgr., Charing Cross L.,
London. [38268] 18/02/1985 **CM21/07/1993**

Rogers, Mrs J A, BA MA MCLIP, Employment not known. [37814]
29/10/1984   **CM05/07/1988**
Rogers, Mr J D, BA FCLIP, Life Member. [12646] 21/03/1949
                                                                FE01/01/1963
Rogers, Mrs J, BSc MCLIP, Sch. Lib., The King's Sch., Peterborough.
[9072] 09/11/1971   **CM31/08/1974**
Rogers, Mrs L A, MCLIP, Elect. Journals Asst., UCL, London. [10935]
21/01/1972   **CM21/04/1975**
Rogers, Mrs L E, FCLIP, Retired. [7327] 17/02/1936   **FE01/01/1949**
Rogers, Mrs M, BSc MSc, Unwaged [60434] 01/04/1998   **ME**
Rogers, Mrs N B, BA(Hons) MCLIP, Dist. Mgr., Lincoln 1, Lincolnshire
CC. [49361] 28/10/1993   **CM19/03/1997**
Rogers, Mrs P, BA(Hons) MCLIP, Asst. Lib., Univ. of Bristol. [43499]
31/10/1989   **CM21/08/2009**
Rogers, Mr P, BA(Hons), Stud., Northumbria Univ. [10011899]
26/11/2008   **ME**
Rogers, Mrs S J, BA(Hons) MA MCLIP, Head of L. Serv., Inst. of Mech.
Engineers, London. [52902] 22/01/1996   **CM18/09/2002**
Rogers, Mrs S, BSc Econ, L. Mgr. & Post16 Study Skills Co-ordintor
Helston Comm. Coll., Cornwall. [10014088] 01/07/2009   **ME**
Rogerson, Prof I, MLS PhD DLitt FCLIP, Hon. Res. F., John Rylands
Inst., Univ. of Manchester. [12658] 13/03/1948   **FE12/03/1982**
Rogerson, Mrs L D, MCLIP, Life Member. [12659] 01/01/1945
                                                                CM01/01/1950
Rogula, Mrs E J, BA MCLIP, Inf. Asst., Careers Advisory Serv., Reading
Univ. [32667] 01/07/1980   **CM10/03/1983**
Roker, Mrs B, DipIM MCLIP, Acquisitions Lib., Buckinghamshire New
Univ., Bucks. [55909] 11/12/1997   **CM16/05/2001**
Roland, Mr J B, BA DipLib MCLIP, Learning Cent. Mgr., Lewisham Coll.,
London. [39136] 12/11/1985   **CM14/11/1990**
Rolf, Mrs D C, BA MCLIP, Retired. [22871] 14/10/1974   **CM19/01/1989**
Rolfe, Mrs K J E, BSc(Hons) DipIM MCLIP, Asst. Lib. - User Serv., Nat.
Oceanographic L., Univ. of Southampton. [52656] 16/11/1995
                                                                CM21/03/2001
Rolfe, Ms K, BA(Hons), Young People's Offr., Bristol L. [10014079]
01/07/2009   **AF**
Roll, Mrs M J, BA MCLIP MCMI, Lib., Johnson&Johnson, High
Wycombe. [14298] 07/01/1971   **CM05/12/1974**
Rollo, Mr D A T, MCLIP, Retired. [12667] 19/10/1971   **CM03/10/1973**
Rolls, Dr J J, BA MA MA(LIS) PhD, L. Administrator, The Warburg Inst.,
The Univ. of London. [58408] 07/02/2000   **ME**
Roncero, Mr J, MA, Sen. L. Asst., ESCP Europe Business Sch.,
London. [10015003] 08/10/2009   **AF**
Rone-Clarke, Mr D, MRSC MCLIP, General Asst., Tesco Supermarkets,
Basingstoke. [12672] 01/04/1971   **CM08/07/1974**
Ronson, Mrs A R, BA PgDip, Lifelong Learning Asst., Crosby L.,
Liverpool. [61774] 06/11/2002   **ME**
Rook, Ms R A, BSc(Hons) DipIS MCLIP, Voluntary Serv. & Operational
Mgr. Guy's & St. Thomas' NHS Foundation Trust, London. [50963]
03/11/1994   **CM20/05/1998**
Rooke, Mrs E A, BA DipLib MCLIP, Princ. Lib., Reading & Lend.,
Oxfordshire Co. L. [31969] 04/01/1980   **CM16/07/1982**
Roome, Mrs N, BA MCLIP, Info. Resource Mgmmt. Team Leader,
DEFRA, London. [22870] 04/10/1974   **CM03/02/1978**
Rooney, Ms C M, BA, Lib., AN Board Altranais, Dublin [39598]
09/03/1986   **ME**
Rooney, Ms E, MA MSc Econ, Lib., Westminster Ref. L., London.
[10014806] 18/09/2009   **ME**
Rooney-Browne, Ms C, BA(Hons) MSc, Stud [10006812] 10/12/2007
                                                                ME
Roos, Mrs J, BA(Hons) ACLIP, Sen. L. Asst., Newnham Coll. L.,
Cambridge. [58330] 11/01/2000   **ACL29/08/2008**
Roos, Ms M, BA, Stud., Aberystwyth Univ. [10014786] 16/09/2009 **ME**

Rooza, Mrs J, BA(Hons) DipILM MCLIP, Matrenity Leave [55441]
13/10/1997   **CM15/01/2003**
Roper, Miss A L, MA BMus MMus AKC MCLIP, Asst. Lib., Royal Coll. of
Music [59785] 02/10/2001   **CM03/10/2007**
Roper, Mr C T, BA DipLib MCLIP, Head of Learning Res., S. Thames
Coll. [31433] 15/10/1979   **CM24/05/1995**
Roper, Mr V D P, BSc MA FCLIP, Life Member. [12680] 25/09/1951
                                                                FE01/01/1965
Ropra, Ms S K S, BA, Asst. Lib., King Edward's Sch., Birmingham.
[37086] 16/01/1984   **ME**
Rosbottom, Ms L, MA BA, Subject Lib., Moorgate L., London. [66061]
18/09/2006   **ME**
Rose, Mr A D, MSc BA(Hons) MCLIP, Asst. Lib., Guildford Coll. [65508]
13/02/2006   **CM21/08/2009**
Rose, Mr D A, BA(Hons) DipLib MCLIP, Sen. Lib., City of London Sch.
[31435] 13/02/2003   **CM13/02/2003**
Rose, Miss E H, BA(Hons) MA MCLIP, Child. Lib., Selsdon L. [55706]
05/11/1997   **CM23/01/2002**
Rose, Mr G B K, BLib MCLIP, Inf. Offr., CMS Cameron McKenna,
London. [41615] 05/02/1988   **CM27/07/1994**
Rose, Mrs G, MCLIP, Site Lib., Stoke Mandeville, Aylesbury Hosp.,
Bucks. [53671] 28/08/1996   **CM29/11/2006**
Rose, Miss H L, BA MA, Academic Lib., Univ. of Northampton [63775]
06/10/2004   **ME**
Rose, Mrs J E, MCLIP, L. Mgr., Random House Grp.,
Rushden,Northants. [15232] 06/11/1971   **CM13/08/1975**
Rose, Mrs J P, BSc(Hons) DipLIS MCLIP, Customer Serv. Lib., L. & Inf.,
Gloucestershire C.C., Dursley L. [44026] 02/04/1990 **CM22/01/1997**
Rose, Mrs J, BA DipLib MCLIP, p. /t. Ref. Lib., Huddersfield L., Kirklees
M.B.C. [35761] 18/01/1983   **CM14/04/1987**
Rose, Mr K W, BSc MSc MCLIP, Sen. Inf. & Records Mgmnt. Analyst,
Dept. for Business, Innovation & Skills, London. [42368] 25/10/1988
                                                                CM24/03/1992
Rose, Miss K, BA, Stud. [10011150] 29/09/2008   **ME**
Rose, Mrs L M, BA(Hons) MSc(Econ) MCLIP, Lib. -Performing Arts,
Cent. L., Hatfield. [55988] 13/01/1998   **CM12/09/2001**
Rose, Mr S E, BA(Hons) DipLib MSc, Dep. Univ. Lib. (Learning
Resources & Academic Skills), Mountbatten L., Southampton Solent
Univ. [10002913] 29/04/1988   **ME**
Rose, Miss S L, BA(Hons), Stud., Univ. of Cent. England. [61658]
14/10/2002   **ME**
Rose, Mr T J, BA MCLIP, Asst. Lib. (Saturdays), Evesham L., Evesham,
Worcester. [40178] 05/11/1986   **CM13/03/2002**
Rosen, Miss J A, BA(Hons) DipLib MCLIP, Lib., Imperial War Mus.,
Dept. of Printed Books. [59900] 30/10/2001   **CM08/12/2004**
Rosenberg, Ms D B, MBE MA HonFLA FCLIP, Life Member. [12688]
06/10/1964   **FE16/01/1986**
Rosenberg, Mr S, MCLIP, E-Resources L., Francis Costello L., Rjah
[59368] 20/02/2001   **CM28/01/2009**
Rosenvinge, Mr P J L, MA DipLib MCLIP, Knowledge & Info DSTL,
Porton Down [34073] 02/09/1981   **CM09/07/2008**
Rosie, Miss A S, MCLIP, Team Lib. Inf., Aberdeen City L. [21313]
03/10/1973   **CM27/07/1976**
Ross, Mr C, MCLIP, Unknown. [10000089] 06/10/1978 **CM23/02/1982**
Ross, Miss J M, Subsurface Data Technician, Total E & P UK,
Aberdeen. [33133] 02/10/1980   **ME**
Ross, Mr J M, BSc MSc MILog MCLIP, Unknown, Brokbourne Solution,
Hoddesdon. [60633] 17/05/1977   **CM01/12/1979**
Ross, Mrs K A, BA MBA MA (Ed) MCLIP TEFL, Unwaged [35646]
18/11/1982   **CM16/02/1988**
Ross, Mrs K N, PG Dip MBA, Lect., BPP, Southampton. [10016861]
27/05/2010   **ME**
Ross, Miss K, BA(Hons) PG Dip, Stud., Robert Gordon Univ.
[10013583] 08/05/2009   **ME**

Ross, Mr N J, BA(Hons) DipIS MCLIP Msc, Planning,Communications Mgr., Univ. for the Creative Arts, Maidstone. [52760] 07/12/1995 **CM19/07/2000**

Ross, Mrs N, Mgr., Learning Resource Cent., Queen's Coll., Taunton. [59815] 10/10/2001 **AF**

Ross, Dr P C, BA MA DipLib PhD MCLIP, Asst. Lib., Guildhall L., London. [10009792] 27/11/1987 **CM15/08/1989**

Ross, Mr P D S, BA(Hons), Unknown. [10014618] 20/08/2009 **ME**

Ross, Ms R, BSc PGDipLib, Sch. Lib., King Edward VI Aston Sch., Birmingham [10000749] 01/08/2008 **ME**

Ross, Mrs S H, BA MCLIP, N. Area Sales Mgr., BBC Audiobooks, Bath. [175] 01/01/1972 **CM11/07/1975**

Rossall, Mr D K, BSc(Hons) MCLIP, Mgr. (Internet Serv. Grp.), The Inst. of Eng. & Tech., Stevenage. [10005268] 12/03/1982 **CM24/03/1988**

Rossell, Mrs D J, BA(Hons) MA MCLIP, Learning Resources. Mgr., Stephenson Coll. L., Coalville. [49102] 01/10/1993 **CM27/11/1996**

Rosset, Mr R W, BA DipLib MCLIP, Lib. Offr., L.B. Ealing. [37687] 17/10/1984 **CM14/09/1994**

Rossi, Ms M S, BA(Hons), Lib., CMH L., ACAD Cent., Cent. Middlesex Hosp., London. [57915] 01/10/1999 **ME**

Rossiter, Mrs S M, BA MCLIP, Lend. Lib., N. Somerset Council, Nailsea. [12711] 23/03/1965 **CM01/01/1969**

Ross-Parker, Mrs M M, BA MCLIP, Resource Tech. [30697] 09/03/1979 **CM31/08/1983**

Roth, Mrs K M, BA MCLIP, Lib., St. Aidan's C of E High Sch., Harrogate. [27263] 15/02/1977 **CM24/09/1981**

Rothera, Ms H M, BA(Hons) MA MCLIP, Sen. Subject Lib. (Educ.), Oxford Brookes Univ. [52424] 30/10/1995 **CM17/03/1999**

Rothman, Mrs C, BA, L. Mgr., Southbourne L., Bournemouth. [10016137] 05/09/2003 **ME**

Rothwell, Mrs J, BA DipLib MCLIP, LRC Mgr., Langley Grammar Sch. [32135] 21/01/1980 **CM24/06/1983**

Roulstone, L H, MCLIP, Fed. Lib., St. Cecilia's, Wandsworth & Blackheath Bluecoat Sch. [20169] 29/01/1973 **CM11/11/1975**

Round, Mrs U M, CertEd BA(Hons) MCLIP, p. /t. Catr., Roehampton Univ., London [29028] 26/03/1978 **CM15/04/1982**

Rounsevell, Mrs H J, L. Asst., Truro L., Truro. [64465] 31/03/2005 **AF**

Rouse, Ms K A, BSc(Hons) MSc, Princ. L. Mgr., Inf. Serv. & E-Gov., Brighton & Hove City L. & Mus. [65790] 01/05/2006 **ME**

Rouse, Ms R C, BA MCLIP, RADAR, Repository Serv. Devel. Mgr., Oxford Brookes Univ. [27624] 30/05/1977 **CM04/02/1987**

Rowan, Ms B, BA DipLib MCLIP, Princ. L. Offr. - Yth. Serv., Edinburgh City L. [29345] 05/06/1978 **CM03/10/1980**

Rowan, Miss E I S, MCLIP, Retired. [12729] 28/08/1953 **CM01/01/1963**

Rowan, Ms E S, MSc, Acquisitions & Metadata Serv. Mgr., Edinburgh Univ. L., Edinburgh. [40671] 30/04/1987 **ME**

Rowe, Miss H P, BA DIP LIB MCLIP, Employment not known. [35291] 06/10/1982 **CM01/07/1988**

Rowe, Mrs I, BSc, Freelance Inf. Specialist. [46099] 02/10/1991 **ME**

Rowe, Mrs J P, BA(Hons) PgDip ILM, Lib. Outreach Servs.,Wirral Univ. Teaching Hosp. NHS Trust, Wirral. [10001008] 15/10/1997 **ME**

Rowe, Miss L D, BA, Unemployed. [41703] 24/02/1988 **ME**

Rowe, Mr M W, BA(Hons), Military Med. Lib., DMLS Cent. L., Gosport, Hants. [26242] 06/09/1976 **ME**

Rowe, Mr N R, Systems Lib. m Cheshire W. and Chester Council. [58982] 16/10/2000 **ME**

Rowe, Mrs O F, FCLIP, Retired, Jamaica. [16605] 01/01/1956 **FE01/01/1966**

Rowe, Miss R M, MA MCLIP, Smuts Lib., S. Asian & Comm. Studies, Univ. of Cambridge. [37628] 09/10/1984 **CM06/09/1988**

Rowell, Mrs R, BA MCLIP, Account Mgr., Axiell, Newcastle upon Tyne. [38128] 23/01/1985 **CM07/06/1988**

Rowing, Ms E J, BA(Hons) MA, p. /t. Sch. Lib., Dulwich Coll. [62667] 01/10/2003 **ME**

Rowland, Mr A P, MCLIP, Learning Cent. Co-ordinator, Solihull Sixth Form Coll., Solihull. [60962] 18/01/2002 **CM11/03/2009**

Rowland, Ms D E, BLib MSc MCLIP, Inf. Serv. Mgr., Dept. for Business, Innovation & Skills. [25101] 01/11/1975 **CM28/01/1980**

Rowland, Miss H L, BA MCLIP, Head of L. & Collections., Soc. of Antiquaties of London [34102] 01/10/1981 **CM11/08/1986**

Rowland, Mrs H, BA MCLIP, Life Member. [12740] 22/02/1952 **CM01/01/1958**

Rowland, Ms J A B, BSc(Hons) MA, Subj. Lib. Informatics and Optometry, J. B. Priestley L., Univ. of Bradford. [55391] 07/10/1997 **ME**

Rowland, Mr J S, BSc MCLIP, Inf. and IP Specialist, Monier Tech. Cent., Crawley. [52379] 30/10/1995 **CM12/07/2000**

Rowland, Mr N H, Comm. Lib., Luton Cent. L. [10001562] 28/02/2007 **AF**

Rowland, Mrs S, BA DipLib MCLIP, Retired, Bor. Cllr., Basingstoke & Deane Bor. Council. [36289] 01/10/1983 **CM14/11/1989**

Rowlands, Mrs A M, DipInfMan, Learning Resources Mgr., Barnet Coll. [50473] 11/08/1994 **ME**

Rowlands, Miss C, Sen. Learning Res. Asst., Sir John Deane's Coll., Cheshire. [65057] 24/10/2005 **AF**

Rowlands, Mrs D L, BA MCLIP, Unemployed. [36353] 06/10/1983 **CM08/03/1988**

Rowlatt, Mrs E J, MCLIP, Teaching Asst., All Saints Montacute Sch., Somerset. [3078] 19/01/1971 **CM31/10/1973**

Rowlatt, Ms M E, BA MSc MCLIP, Freelance [23708] 08/01/1975 **CM30/07/1979**

Rowles, Mr J, MA, Stud., Univ. Coll. London, London. [65639] 15/02/2006 **ME**

Rowlett, Ms E J, BA MSc, Sen. Policy, Inf. & Parliamentary Offr., Stirling. [59549] 10/05/2001 **ME**

Rowley, Mrs A M, BSc MA MCLIP, Head of Knowledge Mgmt., Worcs. Health ICT Serv., Rowlands L. [12750] 01/01/1968 **CM01/01/1971**

Rowley, Ms B M, BA DipLIS MCLIP, Area Sch. Lib., Hants. C.C., Winchester. [44733] 27/11/1990 **CM25/01/1995**

Rowley, Prof J E, BA MSc FCLIP CEng MInstM, Prof. of Info. & Comms., Manchester Met. Univ. [32458] 01/04/1980 **FE18/01/1989**

Rowley, Mrs J, BA(Hons) MSc MCLIP, Head of Lib. Serv., Queen Margaret Univ., Edinburgh [47105] 30/04/1992 **CM12/09/2001**

Rowley, Mr T D, BA(Hons), Lib. Assist., Sandbach L., Cheshire. [10015392] 10/11/2009 **ME**

Rowley, Miss V, BA MA, L. Asst. & PA, Heythrop Coll. L., London. [66127] 29/09/2006 **ME**

Rowney, Mrs C L, BSc(Hons) MSc MA, Staffs. Univ. [65433] 23/02/2006 **ME**

Rowntree, Mr M E, BA(Hons) MA MCLIP, Team Lib., Inf., Northamptonshire C.C. [49014] 31/08/1993 **CM26/11/1997**

Rowntree, Mr M, BA MSc MCLIP, Operations Mgr., N. Tyneside Cent. L., N. Shields. [64853] 22/07/2005 **CM19/03/2008**

Roy, Mr J V, BA DipEdTech MCLIP, Dir., J. V Roy Ltd. [32165] 17/01/1980 **CM19/08/1988**

Royan, Prof B, BA MBA FSA(Scot) HonFCLIP, Retired. [29808] 02/10/1978 **FE22/05/1996**

Royce, Mr J R, BA MLib MCLIP, L. Dir., Robert Coll., Istanbul, Turkey. [29216] 13/04/1978 **CM31/10/1984**

Royds, Mr J, BA MCLIP, Llb., Southwark P. L. [27290] 14/02/1977 **CM15/06/1979**

Rozo Higuera, Miss C, MSc It, IT home visitor, RNIB [10014428] 30/07/2009 **AF**

Ruberry, Ms C S, BA MA, Lib., Covington & Burling (Solicitors), London. [47682] 13/10/1992 **ME**

Rubidge, Mr H E, MCLIP, Retired. [12761] 20/09/1949 **CM01/01/1955**

Rubra, Mrs E V, FCLIP, Life Member. [12762] 09/09/1948 **FE01/01/1964**

Ruck, Mrs R A, MA BEd MCLIP, P/T. Hosp. Lib. [2559] 01/01/1966
CM01/01/1970

Rudd, Mrs J, MCLIP, Lifelong Learning & Inf. Mgr., Bolton Met. Bor.
[8983] 13/01/1972
CM08/11/1974

Rudd, Miss J, CIB, Dip, Team Lib., Bolton Cent. L. [10011290]
10/10/2008
ME

Rudd, Mr P C, Lib, Azad Univ., Oxfordshire. [10006049] 24/08/2007 ME

Rudd, Mrs S, BA MCLIP, Lib. Advisor, Katoke Teacher's Coll., Bukoba,
Kagera, Tanzania [19167] 07/02/1964
CM01/01/1967

Ruddock, Ms B A, BA(Hons) MA MCLIP, Content Devel. Offr. L. &
Archive Servs., Mimas, Univ. of Manchester [10010589] 07/08/2008
CM05/05/2010

Ruddock, Mrs M S, BA PgDip, Stud. [66078] 01/10/2006
ME

Ruddom, Mr D A, MCLIP, Life Member. [12767] 20/09/1955
CM01/01/1962

Rudjord, Ms A, Dep. Lib., Literary & Philosophical Soc., Newcastle
upon Tyne. [48852] 02/07/1993
ME

Rudkin, Miss A, BA(Hons), Inf. & Estates Administrator, HJ Banks &
Co. Ltd., Durham. [54150] 07/11/1996
ME

Rudolph, Mrs J, MCLIP, Retired. [12769] 11/11/1968
CM18/01/1972

Ruehlmann, Ms A, MA, Lib., Inst. of Civil Engineers, London. [61750]
01/11/2002
ME

Ruff, Mrs B, HonFLA MCLIP, Retired. [17678] 22/02/1944 FE11/10/1988

Rugg, Miss S M, BA DipLib MCLIP, Asst. Lib., Inst. of Eng. & Tech.,
London [21883] 05/02/1974
CM07/09/1976

Rughoo, Mrs S D, BLib MCLIP, Sen. Lib., Municipality of Vacoas-
Phoenix, Mauritius. [32103] 22/01/1980
CM26/08/1987

Ruhlmann, Miss D E, MA, Dir. of L. Serv., Trintity Hall, Cambridge.
[46137] 07/10/1991
ME

Rule, Mrs R M, BA MCLIP, Faculty Liaison Lib., Anglia Ruskin Univ.,
Cambridge. [10716] 08/05/1970
CM13/11/1974

Rumsey, Mr D J, BA MCLIP, Head of L. Serv., Royal United Hosp. NHS
Trust, Bath, Banes. [22779] 15/10/1974
CM08/12/1976

Runciman, Miss R J, MCLIP, Arch., Cameron Mackintosh, London.
[28994] 22/02/1978
CM17/11/1983

Rundell, Mr K J, MCLIP, Retired [20021] 01/01/1969
CM01/01/1972

Ruse, Mr D J, MILAM MCLIP, Dir. of Lib. & Culture, Westminster City
Council, London. [12780] 01/01/1970
CM04/07/1973

Rush, Mrs C S, BSc DipLib MCLIP, Website Co-ordinator, St. Peters
High Sch., Gloucester. [27927] 10/10/1977
CM05/07/1985

Rush, Mrs J L, BA(Hons) CertEd MA, Learning Res. Mgr., Herne Bay
High Sch., Kent. [53755] 01/10/1996
ME

Rush, Mr N P, LLB(Hons) MA MCLIP, Asst. Lib., De Montfort Univ.,
Leicester [59410] 06/03/2001
CM29/03/2004

Rushbrook, Mrs A J, BA(Hons) MA, Acquisitions Mngr., House of
Commons L., Lib. Resources Sect., London [58390] 28/01/2000 ME

Rushton, Mrs D S, MCLIP, Lib. Community Hist., Blackburn with
Darwen Bor. Council, Cent. L. [28612] 17/01/1978
CM12/12/1980

Rushton, Mr I P, Learning & Inf. Offr., West L., LB of Islington.
[10011610] 29/10/2008
AF

Rushton, Mr J D, BA DipLib MCLIP, L. Operations Team Leader,
Inverclyde L. [29810] 05/10/1978
CM31/12/1981

Rushton, Mrs N J, BA(Hons) MA MCLIP, Sure Start Lib., Derbys. C.C.,
Matlock. [52337] 30/10/1995
CM19/11/2008

Rushton, Mr R J, MCLIP, Community Hist. Mgr., S. Ribble Dist., L. C.C.
[27018] 18/01/1977
CM27/11/1979

Russell, Miss A, Pg Dip, Lib., Halton Lea L. [10011285] 09/10/2008 ME

Russell, Mrs E M, MA MCLIP, Retired. [12790] 12/10/1964
CM01/01/1967

Russell, Mrs J A, MA DipLib MCLIP, Community Serv. Unit Mgr., L. N1,
Ballymena. [29812] 10/10/1978
CM11/02/1981

Russell, Mr M D, BA MCLIP, Devel. Mgr., Dumfries & Galloway Libs.,
Dumfries. [38336] 11/03/1985
CM06/09/1988

Russell, Mr M R, BA(Hons) DipILS MCLIP, Sch. Lib., Kirkland High Sch.
& Comm. Coll., Methil. [55887] 16/12/1997
CM16/05/2001

Russell, Ms R M, BA MA, Stud., UCL., London. [65665] 20/03/2006 ME

Russell, Ms S, BA(Hons) DipLib MCLIP, Lib., UCL Human Comm. Sci.
L., London. [52658] 16/11/1995
CM21/08/2009

Russell-Smith, Ms M, BA MA, Frontline Servs. Mgr., Gedling
Community & Vol. Servs. [65611] 28/02/2006
ME

Russon, Mr D, BSc FCLIP, Retired. [44350] 01/10/1990 FE09/04/1991

Ruston, Miss L, BA(Hons) PgDip, English Language Editor, CB Richard
Ellis, Bangkok. [10015288] 12/10/1994
ME

Ruthven, Miss J C, BA(Hons) MA, Asst. Lib., Hartley L., Univ. of
Southampton. [33736] 04/02/1981
ME

Ruthven, Ms L, MA, L Asst. [10006744] 10/12/2007
ME

Ruthven, Mr R A, MA DipLIS MCLIP, Sect. Head ICT & Learning, W.
Dunbartonshire Council, Dumbarton. [44069] 01/05/1990
CM21/05/1997

Rutland, Mrs C, BA(Hons), Lib., Halton L. [65126] 01/11/2005 ME

Rutland, Ms D, Elementary Sch. Lib., Belgium [10017023] 21/06/2010
ME

Rutland, Mrs J D, BSc DipLib MCLIP, Knowledge Mgr., Eastern Coast
Kent PCT, Aylesford. [32885] 17/10/1980
CM09/12/1982

Rutledge, Dr H R, BA(Hons) DipLib MCLIP MA PhD, Retired [40668]
14/04/1987
CM18/09/1991

Rutt, Ms J C, BA MCLIP Msc, L. Mgr., Sheffield Primary Care Trust.
[36879] 12/01/1984
CM22/05/1996

Rutt, Mrs J M, BA DipLib MCLIP, Coll. Lib., Queen Mary's Coll.,
Basingstoke. [31017] 04/07/1979
CM26/08/1982

Rutt, Miss S E, MCLIP, Unemployed. [12812] 18/02/1972 CM01/04/1975

Rutter, Mrs M R J, BSc, Learning Resource Mgr., E. Sussex C.C.
[53355] 23/05/1996
ME

Ryan, Mrs A M, p. /t. Stud., UWE, Aberconway L., Cardiff Univ.
[10000704] 23/10/2006
ME

Ryan, Ms B M, BA(Hons) MSc MCLIP, Electronic Serv. Support Mgr.,
LRC., Univ. of Glamorgan. [49421] 21/10/1993
CM21/11/2001

Ryan, Mr C W, Assoc. -Strategy & Planning, Barclays Capital, London
[10014991] 08/01/1996
ME

Ryan, Ms D C, BA MCLIP, Lib., Sen. Reader Serv., RNIB, NLS [35560]
26/10/1982
CM22/06/1987

Ryan, Dr F J, BSc, PhD, Unknown. [10011380] 15/10/2008 ME

Ryan, Mr G M, MA(Hons) DipILS MCLIP, Law Lib., Andersonian L., Univ.
of Strathclyde, Glasgow. [58092] 27/10/1999
CM15/09/2004

Ryan, Mrs J H, BA DipLib MCLIP, L. Mgr., Royal Australian Coll. of G. P.
s, Melbourne, Australia. [32213] 08/02/1980
CM17/02/1982

Ryan, Ms K A, BA DipLIS MSc, Sch. Lib.,St. Andrew's Coll., Dublin,
Ireland [42065] 21/09/1988
ME

Ryan, Mrs K C, BA MBA FCLIP, Retired. [12820] 14/02/1963
FE26/01/1994

Ryan, Miss L, BA(Hons) Pg Dip, L. Asst., Meadowbank L., Polmont.
[10006623] 15/03/2000
ME

Ryan, Mr M A, BA MCLIP, Retired. [12821] 13/10/1970 CM01/01/1976

Ryan, Mr P A, MBA BA MCLIP, Ch. Lib., MOD, London [30670]
19/01/1979
CM21/12/1981

Ryan, Mr P J, BA(Hons) MCLIP, Head of Lib. Serv., Canterbury Christ
Church Univ. [38410] 20/04/1985
CM07/06/1988

Ryan, Ms R, BA(Hons), Fiction and Reader Devel. Coordinator,
Manchester L. [62195] 13/03/2003
ME

Ryan, Mrs S A, BA DipLib MCLIP, Inf. Mgr., Women Like Us, London.
[10000935] 07/12/1978
CM12/01/1982

Ryan, Mrs S E, MCLIP, Med. Sec., Horton Hosp., Banbury. [10006532]
01/10/1972
CM03/10/1975

Ryder, Miss E, Unknown. [10006178] 18/09/2007
ME

Ryder, Mrs J A, MCLIP, L. Offr., Hants C.C. [12872] 06/03/1971
CM01/01/1975

Ryder, Mrs J C, BA MCLIP, L. & Inf. Sector Consultant, Julie Ryder Associates, Witley. [12830] 01/10/1965 **CM01/01/1969**

Rydzynski, Mrs M A, BA, MLIS, Team Lib – Child. & Young People, Northamptonshire L. & Info. Serv. [10011758] 11/11/2008 **ME**

S

Sabbage, Ms L, BA MSc, Inf. Specialist (Electronic Serv.), Charles Russell, LLP. [10001503] 11/10/2004 **ME**

Sabin, Mr J H, BA DipLib Dip MCLIP, Retired. [26005] 25/04/1976 **CM19/01/1982**

Sabovic, Ms Z, BA, H. of Coll. Mgmt., The Wellcome L., London. [46640] 02/12/1991 **ME**

Sach, Mrs V W, MA MCLIP, Life Member. [12836] 24/01/1954 **CM01/01/1959**

Sachs, Miss M A P, BA MCLIP, Team Lib., Oxford Cent., Oxon. C.C. [22934] 19/09/1974 **CM21/09/1978**

Sack, Mr T, Lib., Szilard L., Heidelberg. [64321] 02/03/2005 **ME**

Sackett, Mr E J C, MA MCLIP, Retired. [12840] 17/09/1955 **CM01/01/1959**

Sacre, Mr J F, MCMI MCLIP, L. Liaison Offr., Ulverscroft MagnaLarge Print Bks. [12842] 19/03/1968 **CM06/07/1972**

Saddington, Mr G H, DMA FCLIP ACIS MIMgt, Retired. [12843] 28/02/1958 **FE09/03/1982**

Saddleton, Mrs H A, ACLIP, Freelance. [45038] 01/07/1990 **ACL10/01/2006**

Sadeghi, Mrs S, MA, L. Asst., Univ. of Nottingham [62454] 03/07/2003 **ME**

Sage, Mr P, MCLIP, Lib. -Stock Serv., E. Sussex Co., Eastbourne. [12855] 01/01/1964 **CM01/01/1969**

Saich, Mrs B P, BA MCLIP, Life Member. [12861] 01/01/1954 **CM01/01/1958**

Saich, Mr M J, FCLIP, Life Member. [12862] 18/03/1950 **FE01/01/1964**

Sainsbury, Mrs A C, BA MCLIP, Collections Mgr., Univ. of Westminster, Marylebone. [12865] 01/01/1966 **CM01/01/1970**

Sainsbury, Mr I M, BA MCLIP, Liaison Lib., Univ. of Reading L. [12868] 04/12/1967 **CM01/01/1970**

Sainsbury, Mrs W V, BLib MCLIP, Unwaged [20065] 18/01/1973 **CM21/04/1980**

Saker, Miss J E, BA MCLIP, Retired. [12869] 13/07/1965 **CM01/01/1971**

Saksida, Mr M, HonFCLIP, Hon Fellow. [60751] 20/03/1986 **HFE01/03/1986**

Salem, Dr S M A, BA MA FCLIP, Chairman, Alex Cent. for Multimedia & L., Egypt. [60078] 01/10/1976 **FE24/03/1988**

Saletes, Mrs D L, BA DipLib MCLIP, Customer Serv. Lib., Watford Cent. L., Herts. C.C. [32471] 01/04/1980 **CM11/01/1985**

Salinie, Mrs F, MBE HonFLA, Asst. Dir. -France, Global Business Mgr., Brit. L. Serv., Paris. [41993] 01/07/1988 **HFE01/01/1993**

Salisbury, Mrs R M, DipLib MCLIP, Life Member. [29876] 16/10/1978 **CM14/12/1981**

Salkeld, Mrs D A, BA(Hons)DipLib MCLIP, Retired. [28765] 28/09/1957 **CM01/05/1978**

Salmon, Mrs B, BA DipLib MCLIP, Head of L. & Inf. Serv., C. I. P. D., London. [31151] 30/08/1979 **CM30/08/1981**

Salmon, Mrs C A, BA(Econ) PGCE, Sch. Lib., St Margarets Sch., Watford, Herts. [56838] 27/10/1998 **AF**

Salmon, Mrs C E, BA MCLIP, L. Devel. Mgr., Holy Cross Coll., Bury. [12878] 22/02/1972 **CM20/12/1974**

Salo-Oja, Miss M E, Unknown. [10014746] 09/09/2009 **ME**

Salt, Mr D P, BSc FCLIP, Retired. [12885] 03/05/1967 **FE25/01/1995**

Salt, Mrs F J, BA(Hons) MCLIP, Inf. Offr., Norton Rose, London. [55509] 16/10/1997 **CM15/11/2000**

Salt, Miss J A, Lib. Asst., Northcroft Lib., Erdington. [10017166] 12/07/2010 **AF**

Salter, Miss A J, BA MCLIP, Faculty Lib., St. Matthias Campus, Univ. of the W. of England, Bristol. [31694] 02/10/1979 **CM10/10/1983**

Salter, Mrs D J, BA(Hons) MA, Unwaged. [54986] 03/06/1997 **ME**

Salter, Ms E, BA DipLib MLib FCLIP, Lib. Mgr., Univ. of Westminster. [35225] 07/10/1982 **FE29/03/2006**

Salter, Mrs H M, MA MCLIP, Learning Res. Mgr., Aldercar Comm. Language Coll., Derbys. [22562] 30/06/1974 **CM01/04/1977**

Salter, Ms L A, BA(Hons), Young People's Lib., Devon Ls., Exeter. [10013717] 22/05/2009 **ME**

Salter, Ms L I, Lib., Harbor View Sch., Tianjin, China. [65710] 31/03/2006 **ME**

Salter, Mrs N E, BSc PGCE DipILM MCLIP, B. Sc., P. G. C. E., P. G. Dip. ILM., MCILIP [53903] 09/10/1996 **CM16/07/2003**

Sambrook, Miss C J, BA(Hons) MA MA MCLIP, Special Collections Lib., Kings Coll. London. [47042] 06/04/1992 **CM14/09/1994**

Samman, Miss M J, BA MCLIP, Retired. [12898] 10/10/1966 **CM01/01/1969**

Sammut, Mr H J, MBA MSc(Hons), Ass. Dir., KPMG, Pieta, Malta. [10016576] 16/04/2010 **ME**

Sampson, Mr A A, NDD ATD ACP FRSA MCLIP, Life Member. [12899] 02/01/1965 **CM01/01/1968**

Sampson, Ms J, BA MCLIP MInstLM, Knowledge & Res. Lib., Knowledge & L. Inf. Serv. for Health, Doncaster Royal Infirmary. [50354] 04/07/1994 **CM18/03/1998**

Sampson, Miss L, BA(Hons), Stud., Inf. &L. Studies, Univ. of Strathclyde. [10015452] 19/11/2009 **ME**

Sams, Mrs S, MCLIP, Inf. Resources Lib., The Royal Coll. of Surgeons of England. [65119] 01/11/2005 **CM11/03/2009**

Samson, Ms C, BTS DipTrans IoL, Inf. Asst., King's Coll. London, Guy's Campus, London. [10015265] 30/10/2009 **AF**

Samson, Mrs J M, BA MCLIP, Lib. Asst., Fife Council (P/T. Temp.) [31642] 22/10/1979 **CM07/09/1984**

Samson-Bunce, Mrs S, Serv. Mgr., Cassettes for Blind People. [10016863] 27/05/2010 **AF**

Samuels, Mr A R, BSc Dip Lib CMC MCLIP, Unwaged, seeking work. [10015014] 06/10/2009 **CM31/10/1990**

Sanati Nia, Mrs A, Stud., Univ. of Birmingham [10009324] 15/05/2008 **ME**

Sanchez-Gonzalez, Miss S, BA MA, L. Asst., The Heatons L., Stockport. [10010194] 10/07/2008 **AF**

Sanchez-Penas, Ms C, BA MSc MCLIP, Asst. Lib., DWP, Sheffield. [65816] 12/05/2006 **CM09/09/2009**

Sandell, Ms J E, MA DipLib MCLIP, Young People's Lib., Stirling Council [43338] 23/10/1989 **CM19/08/1992**

Sanders, Mr K J, BA(Hons), Stud., Univ. of Aberystwyth. [10015565] 15/12/2009 **ME**

Sandersfield, Miss K, BA, Lib. Asst., Sunderland [10015123] 15/10/2009 **ME**

Sanderson, Mrs G A, BSc(Hons) MSc, Info. Team Leader, Business Link E. Mildands. [51002] 08/11/1994 **ME**

Sanderson, Miss J B, BA MCLIP, Lib., Scottish Borders Council, Duns. [29282] 25/04/1978 **CM31/07/1980**

Sanderson, Mrs J, BA DipLib MCLIP, Dist. Mgr., Lichfield L., Staffs C.C. [34500] 18/11/1981 **CM18/06/1985**

Sanderson, Miss S, BSc (Hons), Stud., Northumbria Univ. [10010110] 03/07/2008 **ME**

Sandford, Mr A M, MCLIP, Catg., Bury P. L., Lancashire. [23869] 10/02/1975 **CM30/07/1980**

Sandhu, Mrs G K, BSc MSc MBA MCLIP, Assoc. Dir. (Systems), Univ. of E. London [47994] 30/10/1992 **CM22/11/1995**

Sandison, Mr P E C, MA DipLib MCLIP, Mgr. L. Serv. & Inf. Systems, Scottish Borders Campus, Heriot-Watt Univ., Galashiels. [35317] 01/10/1982 **CM20/11/1986**

Sandison, Mrs S M I, MA MCLIP, Sch. Lib. (Job Share), Galashiels Academy, Selkirkshire. [35756] 10/01/1983 **CM21/08/1986**

Sandles, Mr P M, BSc, Asst. Lib., Dept. for Work & Pension, London. [65049] 20/10/2005 **ME**

Sands, Mrs A, BA(Hons), Unwaged. [54847] 17/04/1997 **ME**

Sands, Mrs P, BA(Hons), Acc Lia. Lib., Nursing & Midwf., Univ. of Southampton, Hartley L. [47924] 26/10/1992 **ME**

Sandys, Mrs J, HonFLA, Life Member. [13272] 31/01/1952 **CM01/01/1958**

Sanford, Mr J D, MA MLIS, Lib., Dartington Coll. of Arts, Devon. [65896] 07/06/2006 **ME**

Sanger, Mrs S A C, MCLIP, Asst. Lib., Dept. for Business Innovation & Skills. [11577] 19/08/1969 **CM20/08/1973**

Sangha, Mrs H, BA(Hons) DipLIS MCLIP, Asst. Ref. Lib., Birmingham L. Serv., Sutton Coldfield L. [47650] 09/10/1992 **CM19/03/1997**

Sankalia, Ms U, Unknown. [10015183] 23/10/2009 **ME**

Sansby, Miss E J, BA(Hons) MA MCLIP, Dir. of L. & Knowledge Serv., Bishop Grosseteste Coll., Lincoln. [50268] 26/05/1994 **CM27/11/1996**

Sansom, Miss A J C, BA FCLIP, Retired. [12935] 07/03/1950 **FE01/01/1966**

Sansom, Mrs S E, BA MCLIP, Lib., Edgbaston High Sch., Birmingham. [39508] 30/01/1986 **RV19/10/2006** **CM10/05/1988**

Sansom, Mrs S, BA(Hons) MA MCLIP, Lib., Nottingham C.C. [55356] 03/10/1997 **CM08/12/2004**

Sansome, Mr B J, BA(Hons) PgCert, Asst. Lib., Dept. of Enterprise, Belfast. [65462] 23/02/2006 **ME**

Sant, Mr D, BA DipLib MCLIP, Unspecified [30248] 07/12/1978 **CM06/01/1982**

Santer, Mrs M A, MCLIP, P. /t. L. Asst., Devon C.C. [24200] 23/04/1975 **CM06/12/1977**

Sard, Mr D K, ACIM, Inf. Mgr, Clear Intelligence Limited, Coventry. [10011144] 26/09/2008 **AF**

Sarfo-Adu Amankwah, Mr K, MA, Unknown. [10007957] 20/03/2008 **ME**

Sarfraz, Mr M, Stud. [64043] 06/12/2004 **ME**

Sargant, Mr M J, MA DipLib MCLIP, Sen. Devel. Mgr., Crosby L., Sefton M.B.C. [27709] 06/07/1977 **CM20/07/1979**

Sargeant, Mr B, MCLIP, Retired. [17691] 01/01/1955 **CM01/01/1958**

Sargeant, Mrs R, BLib DMS MCLIP, Unknown. [38559] 01/07/1985 **CM04/10/1988**

Sargent, Mrs C D, MA MCLIP, Head of L., & Arch., Radley Coll., Abingdon. [40507] 26/02/1987 **CM18/11/1993**

Sargent, Miss J F, BA, Unknown [64982] 06/10/2005 **ME**

Sari, Mr B, Unknown. [10014368] 20/07/2009 **AF**

Saridakis, Mr A, unwaged [10010576] 07/08/2008 **ME**

Sarif, Mrs E B, Lib., Sydney. [31123] 14/09/1979 **ME**

Sarre, Ms N, BA MA MInstF MCLIP, Sch. Lib. Charles Edward Brooke Sch. [63858] 04/10/2004 **CM09/07/2008**

Sartin, Mrs C I, MCLIP, Hon. Lib., Kennedy-Grant Memorial L., Taunton. [6194] 01/01/1964 **CM01/01/1967**

Sarvilahti, Miss M, BA(Hons) MA, Lib., Univ. of Art & Design, Helsinki, Finland [57664] 01/07/1999 **ME**

Satchwell, Mrs C E, BA MCLIP, L. Mgr., Univ. of Westminster. [30548] 28/01/1979 **CM14/06/1982**

Saudi, Mr K, BA, Inf. Access Mngr., Burnley Coll., Burnley [10013361] 16/04/2009 **ME**

Sauer, Mr R, APMI MCLIP, Relationship Team Member, Pension Protection Fund, Croydon. [12958] 05/12/1967 **CM01/01/1971**

Saunders, Mrs A, Learning Resources Mgr., Turnford Sch., Cheshunt. [10014898] 01/10/2009 **AF**

Saunders, Miss C R, BA(Hons) MCLIP, Inf. Specialist., GCHQ., Cheltenham [62586] 03/09/2003 **CM21/03/2007**

Saunders, Mrs D L, BA MCLIP, Sen. Local Studies Lib., Cent. for Kentish Studies, Kent C.C. Edu. & Lib. [33984] 23/06/1981 **CM07/03/1985**

Saunders, Mr G, MSc MCLIP, Unknown. [10016670] 23/04/2010 **CM24/03/1988**

Saunders, Mrs H C, MA DipLib MCLIP, Asst. Lib. Cardiff Univ. [36405] 05/10/1983 **CM15/02/1989**

Saunders, Mr J C, BA MBA MCLIP, Head of Serv., Educ. L. Serv., Reading, Berkshire [21975] 17/01/1974 **CM01/07/1976**

Saunders, Miss K A, BA, Trainee Lib.,Kings Road L., Plymouth. [10015777] 25/01/2010 **ME**

Saunders, Mr M D, BSc DipLib MCLIP, Lib., Pinderfields Gen. Hosp., Wakefield [32817] 16/09/1980 **CM27/09/1982**

Saunders, Mr S C, BA, L. Customer Serv. Mgr., Barnet L. [10007692] 21/02/2008 **ME**

Savage, Mrs C L, BA(Hons) MA DipILM MCLIP, Community Events Devel. Mgr., Macmillan Cancer Support [54220] 05/11/1996 **CM07/09/2005**

Savage, Mrs D R L, Unknown. [39368] 16/01/1986 **ME**

Savage, Miss E M, MLS MCLIP, Life Member. [12978] 24/08/1957 **CM01/01/1964**

Savage, Mr J G, BA MCLIP, Ref. & Local Hist. Lib., Upper Norwood, London. [25811] 14/03/1976 **CM18/01/1978**

Savage, Mr P J, MSc, Unknown. [10005998] 24/08/2007 **ME**

Savage-Jones, Ms M, BSc MSc MAPM MCLIP, L. Systems Administrator, Wellcome Trust, London. [41990] 08/07/1988 **CM12/06/1979**

Savidge, Ms J C, MA MCLIP, Dir. of L. & Learning Support Serv., Surrey Univ. [34156] 06/10/1981 **CM18/07/1985**

Saville, Miss A J, MA MCLIP, Lib., The Queens Coll., Oxford. [38907] 18/10/1985 **CM15/11/1988**

Savin, Mr J A, MA(Oxon) DipLib, Tax Know How Professional, Slaughter & May, London. [40950] 01/10/1987 **ME**

Sawalhi, Mrs A L, BA MCLIP, Test Analyst, CAMSIS Project, Univ. of Cambridge. [33336] 25/11/1980 **CM13/11/1984**

Sawbridge, Mrs J A, BA MSc MCLIP, Inf. Communication Mgr., Nat. Probation Serv., W. Midlands, Birmingham. [31013] 02/07/1979 **CM30/11/1981**

Sawbridge, Mrs L, BA MCLIP, Unwaged [5358] 09/11/1971 **CM05/08/1975**

Sawdon, Mrs J, Inf. Cent. Asst., Unilever R. & D. Port Sunlight, Bebington. [62013] 08/01/2003 **AF**

Sawers, Mrs C G L, MSc FCLIP, Retired. [12986] 07/01/1955 **FE26/05/1993**

Sawers, Mr C J, BA(Hons) DPS MCLIP, Team Leader – Learning Resources, W. Nottinghamshire Coll. [53551] 16/07/1996 **CM04/10/2006**

Sawhney, Mr S C, MA MCLIP, Life Member. [12987] 14/02/1968 **CM01/01/1972**

Sawyer, Mrs I A, MA(Hons) MSc MCLIP, Unspecified [61014] 01/02/2002 **CM29/08/2007**

Sawyer, Mrs V B, BLS MCLIP, Sen. Lib., Educ. Lib. Serv., Notts. C.C. [33464] 01/01/1981 **CM06/05/1986**

Sawyerr, Jr., Mr W, MSc, Admin. & Serv. Asst., Brit. Red Cross, Sheffield. [10015785] 26/01/2010 **ME**

Saxby, Ms D, BSocSc(Hons) PGDip MCLIP, L. Coordinator, Internat. Sch. of Amsterdam, Netherlands. [50786] 18/10/1994 **CM07/09/2005**

Saxby, Miss H J, BLS MCLIP, Relief Staff, Glos. C.C., Co. L.,Arts, & Mus., Glos. [30250] 05/12/1978 **CM05/04/1983**

Saxby, Mrs J M, BA MA MCLIP, Stem Cent. Asst., Nat. Sci. Learning Cent., Univ. of York. [65999] 11/08/2006 **CM05/05/2010**

Saxon, Miss D G, MCLIP, Life Member. [12990] 07/10/1971
CM10/10/1974
Sayed, Mrs S, FCLIP, Life Member. [12993] 17/03/1950 **FE01/01/1958**
Sayer, Mr A M, BA(Hons), Serials Lib., Univ. of Cent. England,
Birmingham. [52423] 30/10/1995 **ME**
Sayers, Miss K A, BA(Hons) MA MSc MCLIP, Archive Asst., Unknown
[54138] 01/11/1996 **CM21/11/2001**
Sayers, Mrs S J, BSc MCLIP, Unwaged. [44441] 08/10/1990
CM26/05/1993
Scaife, Mr A M, BA MEd MCLIP, Retired [13001] 11/01/1968
CM01/01/1970
Scaife, Ms E P, BA MSc, Asst. Lib., Univ. of Brighton [43836]
29/01/1990 **ME**
Scales, Mr R P, BA DipLib MCLIP CLTHE, Academic Liaison Lib.,
Bucks. Chilterns Univ. Coll., Chalfont St. Giles. [32725] 23/07/1980
CM16/09/1985
Scallon, Miss R, BA, Stud., Univ. of the W. of England, Bristol.
[10015764] 22/01/2010 **ME**
Scally, Miss L, MA, Unknown. [10015177] 23/10/2009 **ME**
Scalpello, Mrs M, DipLib MA MCLIP, Lib., Glasgow Coll. of Nautical
Studies. [38726] 01/10/1985 **CM21/12/1988**
Scanlon, Mrs A J, BA(Hons) MCLIP, Dep. Head of L. & Learning
Resources., Swansea Met. Univ. [51824] 07/07/1995 **CM17/03/1999**
Scanlon, Mr M J, BA MCLIP, Ref. Lib., DEFRA, London. [34052]
13/08/1981 **CM13/08/1985**
Scarborough, Mrs D M, BA MCLIP MBA, Dist. Mgr., Chorley, Lancs.
[38125] 12/01/1985 **CM15/08/1989**
Scarce, Mrs M, BScEcon, Lib. [63915] 26/10/2004 **ME**
Scarlett, Mrs C A E, BA FCLIP, Life Member. [10828] 17/01/1960
FE01/01/1964
Scarpa, Mrs G J M, BA MLS MCLIP, Housewife. [25048] 10/11/1975
CM12/01/1979
Scarrott, Mr M, BA DipLib MCLIP ILTM, Asst. Dir. – L. Serv., St. Mary's
Coll., Twickenham. [41238] 13/10/1987 **CM12/12/1991**
Schaeper, Ms S D E, Dipl. Libr MLS, Retrospective Catr., St. John's
Coll., The L. St Giles. [10015984] 03/02/2010 **ME**
Schaff, Dr O, BA MA MA PhD, Asst. Lib., ERC L., Manchester. [65815]
15/05/2006 **ME**
Scharlau, Mrs F, MA MCLIP, Local Studies Lib. /Arch., Angus Council-
Cultural Serv., Angus Arch. [37681] 15/10/1984 **CM15/11/1988**
Scherr, Miss J M S, BA MCLIP, Head of Membership Serv., Univ.
Bristol, Bristol [13008] 25/09/1968 **CM01/01/1971**
Schlackman, Mrs E, BA MSc, Stud. [10006402] 17/10/2007 **ME**
Schleihagen, Ms B R, Exec. Dir., German L. Assoc., Berlin. [65652]
02/03/2006 **ME**
Schlenther, Mrs E C, BA DipLib MCLIP, Ret. [35852] 01/02/1983
CM05/04/1988
Schlesinger, Mr J T, BA(Hons) DipLIS MCLIP, Sen. L. Asst.,
Birmingham City Univ. [44815] 03/12/1990 **CM27/11/1996**
Schofield, Ms C, Seeking work. [10016869] 05/01/1989 **ME**
Schofield, Ms D T, BA(Hons) PGDipLIS MCLIP, Trust L. Serv. Mgr., S.
Manchester Univ. Hosp. NHS Trust, Manchester. [41074] 05/10/1987
CM17/09/2003
Schofield, Mrs D, Info. Lib. Offr., Ref. & Info. L., Truro [10013164]
27/03/2009 **AF**
Schofield, Mrs F A, BSc MCLIP, Retired [18157] 10/10/1972
CM17/01/1975
Scholes, Mr B, MCLIP, Retired [13016] 15/10/1967 **CM01/01/1971**
Scholey, Mrs E L, Access & Inclusion Lib., Bolsover L., Derbyshire C.C.
[10006682] 21/11/2007 **ME**
Schopflin, Ms K, MA(Hons) MA MCLIP, Head of Inf. Mgmnt., House of
Commons, London. [56760] 09/10/1998 **CM18/09/2002**
Schots, Mrs S, L. &Info. Mgr., Herbert Smith LLP, London. [10001501]
01/07/1995 **ME**

Schroeder, Miss A, MA, Inf. Exec., Web Serv., ICAEW, London. [64390]
14/03/2005 **ME**
Schulkins, Mr J A, BA MA MCLIP, Systems Lib. Univ. of Liverpool
[63126] 11/02/2004 **CM19/11/2008**
Schulte-Nahring, Mr S, DipLib DipCompMCLIP, Unknown. [50034]
23/02/1994 **CM20/09/2000**
Schulz, Mrs N G, BA DipLib, Project Off., Univ. Oxford [62037]
28/01/2003 **ME**
Schwedop-Hicks, Mrs L, Asst. to the Elementary Sch. Lib., Belgioum
[10017024] 18/06/2010 **ME**
Schwenk, Ms K, BSc, Unknown. [10013912] 15/06/2009 **ME**
Sciberras, Dr L, PhD MA AIL FCLIP, Retired. [17701] 21/09/1967
FE23/07/1997
Scolari, Mr A, PhD, Dir., Univ. of Pavia, Italy. [45938] 26/07/1991 **ME**
Scoones, Miss J, BA DipLib MCLIP, Dir. of Info. & KM., Trowers &
Hamlins, London. [36451] 06/10/1983 **CM08/08/1986**
Scoones, Mr M A, BSc MPhil FCLIP, Life Member. [13031] 28/08/1952
FE01/01/1957
Scorey, Ms S A, BA(Hons) PGCE MCLIP, Dir., Knowledge Svcs., Coll.
of Law, London. [40953] 01/10/1987 **CM26/05/1993**
Scothern, Ms E M, BA MCLIP, Employment not known. [30251]
08/01/1979 **CM13/01/1981**
Scotland, Mrs C J, MLib MCLIP, Lib., Featherstone High Sch., Middx.
[38531] 31/05/1985 **CM10/05/1988**
Scotney, Miss L H, MSc MCLIP, Inf. Operations, HQ DETS(A) Upavon.
[31939] 01/01/1980 **CM27/07/1983**
Scott Cree, Mr J A, MA FCLIP, Retired. [35101] 03/09/1982
FE23/09/1998
Scott Halls, Miss R, MSc MCLIP, Sen. Inf. Advisor (Business & Law),
Kingston Univ. [62268] 07/04/2003 **CM21/08/2009**
Scott, Dr A D, MA FSAILIS, Retired. [13032] 02/04/1963 **ME**
Scott, Ms B M, MCLIP, Inf. Serv. Mgr., Dept. for Business, Innovation &
Skills, London. [22691] 14/08/1974 **CM01/07/1992**
Scott, Mrs B, BLib MCLIP, Lib., Cheshire C.C., Chester. L. [29529]
22/09/1978 **CM15/03/1984**
Scott, Dr C F, MA MCLIP, Life Member. [13040] 05/01/1961
CM01/01/1965
Scott, Mrs C L, BA(Hons) MA MCLIP, Faculty Lib. for the Arts &
Humanities, Univ. of Sheffield. [46582] 20/11/1991 **CM18/11/1998**
Scott, Mrs C S, BA MCLIP, Freelance Indexer. [22483] 12/06/1974
CM20/08/1976
Scott, Mr C, BA(Hons) DipLib, Asst. Head. Lib. & Info Serv., Coventry
MDC [10017180] 30/09/1978 **CM19/09/1980**
Scott, Mrs C, BA MCLIP, Lib., Princethorpe Coll., Rugby, Warwickshire
[38407] 21/04/1985 **CM14/03/1990**
Scott, Mrs C, MSc, Sen. L. Asst., Cowbridge L., Vale of Glamorgan
C.C., Cowbridge L. [61018] 01/02/2002 **ME**
Scott, Mrs D K P, BFA, Asst. Lib, Falklands Island Community Sch.
[10012359] 05/02/2009 **ME**
Scott, Miss E L, BA ACLIP, Asst. Lib. Mgr., Watford Cent. L. [63738]
03/09/2004 **ACL09/08/2006**
Scott, Miss E S, BA FCLIP, Learning Resources Cent. Coordinator,
Menzies Hill Sch., Dundee. [13047] 04/01/1972 **FE15/10/2002**
Scott, Miss E W, MCLIP, Unknown. [28673] 17/01/1978 **CM07/07/1980**
Scott, Mrs E, Sch. Lib., Queen's Gate Sch., London [10006393]
23/10/2007 **ME**
Scott, Mr E, MA(Hons), Stud., Robert Gordon Univ., Aberdeenshire
[10012891] 19/03/2009 **ME**
Scott, Miss F A, MCLIP, Life Member. [13048] 12/02/1951
CM16/02/1979
Scott, Mrs F J, BA MCLIP, L. & ICT Offr., Arthurstone L., Dundee.
[27916] 09/10/1977 **CM18/12/1981**
Scott, Ms H V, BA(Hons) MSc MCLIP, Film Studies Subject Con.,
Oxford Univ. L. Serv. [51415] 10/02/1995 **CM22/07/1998**

Scott, Ms I M M, MA(Hons) MSc DipEd DipLib MCLIP, Cirriculum Lib., Curriculum Res. & Inf. Serv., Aberdeen. [32818] 02/09/1980
CM10/11/1983

Scott, Miss J A, BA(Hons) DipLib MCLIP, Lib., The Upper Bann Inst. of F. & H. E., Portadown Campus. [33145] 02/10/1980 **CM07/02/1986**

Scott, Mrs J, BA MA MCLIP, Sr. Lib., Chesterfield Lib., Derbyshire C.C. [46786] 23/01/1992 **CM25/09/1996**

Scott, Mrs J, Support Asst., FDI Solutions, Sheffield. [44273] 07/08/1990 **ME**

Scott, Ms K J, Inf. Offr., Simmons&Simmons, London. [10016231] 26/05/2010 **AF**

Scott, Ms K L, L. Asst., St. Marys Catholic Coll., Wallasey, Wirral. [10007440] 13/02/2008 **ME**

Scott, Mrs K M, MCLIP, Legal L. Consultant, Self-Employed, Kingston, Surrey. [13882] 18/02/1972 **CM26/09/1975**

Scott, Miss L B, BA(Hons), Arch., Univ. of Glos., Cheltenham. [41569] 21/01/1988 **ME**

Scott, Mrs M, L. Asst., The Olympia Cent., E. Kilbride. [10013730] 04/06/2009 **AF**

Scott, Ms N R, BA DipLib MCLIP, Learning Res. Mgr., Hackney Comm. Coll., Shoreditch Campus Learning Cent. [31696] 02/11/1979
CM08/02/1983

Scott, Miss O D, FCLIP, Life Member. [13066] 11/10/1944**FE01/01/1961**

Scott, Mr P J, BLS(Hons) MCLIP, Community, Learning, & Inf. Lib., Chesterfield L. [36795] 01/01/1984 **CM20/09/2000**

Scott, Miss P K, BA MCLIP, Head of L. & Inf. Serv., Min. of Justice [33558] 19/01/1981 **CM09/10/1986**

Scott, Mr P R, BA MA PGCE MCLIP, Campus Lib., Schiller Internat. Univ., London. [23828] 18/12/1963 **CM01/01/1972**

Scott, Mr P, BA DipLib MCLIP, I. T. Mgr., Wirral P. L. [31772] 12/12/1979
CM17/12/1981

Scott, Ms R J, L. Asst. - Serials, Oxford Univ. Sackler L. [10016096] 16/02/2010 **ME**

Scott, Mrs S M, BA MCLIP, Sen. L. Asst. Hampshire Partnership NHS Trust [37456] 03/10/1984 **CM19/01/1988**

Scott, Mrs S, MA MCLIP, Asst. Lib., Robert Gordon Univ. [18262] 03/10/1972 **CM12/02/1975**

Scott, Ms S, MSc, L. Asst., Andersonian L., Strathclyde. [10010887] 05/09/2008 **ME**

Scott, Mrs V P, ACLIP, Info. Co-ordinator, Aston Univ., Birmingham. [65028] 13/10/2005 **ACL19/10/2006**

Scott, Miss V, BA(Hons) MA, Learning Res. Cent. Mgr., Highlands Automotive & Eng. Training Cent. [57547] 28/04/1999 **ME**

Scott, Dr V, BSc PhD, Stud., Liverpool John Moores Univ. [10015082] 12/10/2009 **ME**

Scott-Denness, Miss H, BSc(Hons) MCLIP, Head of Inf. Cent., Knight Frank LLP, London. [48872] 07/07/1993 **CM18/11/1998**

Scotting, Mrs R, BLib MCLIP, Lib. :Child & Young Peoples Serv., N. Lincs. Council, Riddings L. [34694] 30/01/1982 **CM16/02/1988**

Scott-Picton, Miss L S, BA(Hons) MLib MCLIP, Lib., Downe House Sch., Thatcham, Berks. [44404] 05/10/1990 **CM24/05/1995**

Scourfield, Mrs K J, BA(Hons) MCLIP, Unknown. [40207] 08/11/1986
CM24/05/1995

Scown, Mr J M, BA MCLIP, Foursite Project Offr., Somerset C.C., Bridgwater. [37566] 02/10/1984 **CM16/10/1991**

Scragg, Mr A D R, MA LLB DipHE MCLIP, Liaison Lib., Collection Devel., Birmingham City Univ. [30255] 06/12/1978 **CM06/07/1981**

Scragg, Mrs B, MCLIP, Retired. [8504] 11/01/1957 **CM01/01/1967**

Screech, Mrs M, BA(Hons) MSc(Econ) MCLIP, Inf. Specialist, GCHQ. [61299] 16/05/2002 **CM21/05/2008**

Screene, Mrs H J, DipLib, Sch. Lib. & Curriculum Resource Mngr., Loddon Primary Sch., Reading [10017108] 23/06/2010 **ME**

Scrimshaw, Mr N, PGdip, Faculty Lib., Univ. of Creative Arts, Farnham. [10012417] 23/03/2010 **ME**

Scriven, Miss A J, BSc EC MCLIP, Team Lib., Weston Favell L., Northamptonshire. [10008658] 07/12/2000 **CM29/03/2004**

Scriven, Mrs D A, BLib MCLIP, Lib. :Local Stud., Wakefield Met. Dist. L. [6693] 02/02/1972 **CM23/11/1976**

Scrivener, Miss H L, BA MA, MA Graduate [10000805] 08/11/2006 **ME**

Scrogham, Mr M A, BA(Hons) MA MCLIP, Serv. Mgr., Inf. & Digital. [61687] 21/10/2002 **CM24/10/2008**

Scruby, Mr J D, FCLIP, Life Member. [13076] 18/01/1939 **FE01/01/1955**

Scruton, Miss C K, BA MCLIP, Team Lib., Mitchell L., Glasgow Dist. L. [28675] 08/01/1978 **CM09/12/1980**

Scull, Mrs N, BSc(Hons), Mgr. -IFS Knowledge Bank, IFS, Sch. of Finance [53431] 19/06/1996 **ME**

Scully, Mr E R, BA MCLIP, Head of Lib. and Pub. Serv., Medi. & Heathc. Prod. Reg. Agency, London. [35628] 09/11/1982 **CM10/05/1988**

Scurfield, Miss J G, FCLIP, Retired. [13077] 20/01/1936 **FE01/01/1943**

Scutchings, Ms L, BA(Hons) MSc MCLIP, Asst. Site Mgr., Edward Boyle L., Univ. of Leeds. [53959] 16/10/1996 **CM01/02/2006**

Scutt, Mrs C E, BA MCLIP, Inf. Consultant/Freelance Lib., Self-employed, Loughborough,Leics. [25185] 23/11/1975 **CM19/10/1979**

Scutt, Ms C S, BA(Hons) MSc MCLIP, Faculty Lib. (Educ.), Liverpool Hope Univ. [58314] 10/01/2000 **CM19/11/2008**

Scutt, Ms E M, BA DipLib CertEd CMS MCLIP, Head of Learning Res., W. Kent Coll., Tonbridge. [25208] 05/01/1976 **CM05/01/1978**

Seabourne, Miss J, BA(Hons) DipLIS MCLIP, Admin., Darwin Press, Feltham. [43240] 12/10/1989 **CM15/03/2000**

Seale, Miss L J, MA, Unknown. [61458] 02/08/2002 **ME**

Sealey, Miss M M T, MCLIP, Life Member. [13087] 13/01/1947
CM01/01/1953

Sealy, Miss A M, MCLIP, L. Asst., L.B. of Greenwich. [20127] 14/02/1973 **CM01/08/1976**

Sealy, Mr C P, BSc, L. Asst., The kennel Club, London. [10010424] 24/07/2008 **AF**

Seaman, Ms J A, 6th Form Lib., Capital City Academy [66105] 25/09/2006 **ME**

Seaman, Miss J M, BA MCLIP, Unknown. [13090] 03/01/1970
CM12/03/1973

Seamark, Mrs S J, BA(Hons) MA MCLIP, Sen. Lib., Medway Council, Strood L. [55489] 15/10/1997 **CM29/03/2004**

Seamens, Mrs M M, MCLIP, Lib. (Job Share), Bannockburn Community L., Stirling Council. [12276] 10/10/1971 **CM15/12/1975**

Searle, Mrs C, MA, Sen. Indexer, Indexing & Data Mgmnt. Sect., House of Commons L., London [62213] 17/03/2003 **ME**

Searle, Mr M, MA MCLIP, H. of Collection Serv., Radcliffe Sci. L., Oxford. [28902] 31/01/1978 **CM31/12/1989**

Searson, Mrs K P, B LIB MCLIP, Lib., The Brunts Sch., Mansfield Notts. [27977] 07/10/1977 **CM10/11/1981**

Seaton, Miss J G, BA DipLib MCLIP, Retired [13097] 01/10/1969
CM17/10/1972

Seaton, Mrs S M, BA DipLib MCLIP, p. /t. Serv. Devel. Lib., Gosport Discovery Cent. [32169] 12/02/1980 **CM11/03/1982**

Sebire, Mr L, MCLIP, Lib., UWE, Bristol. [10001557] 07/02/2007
CM27/01/2010

Sebury, Mr P L, BA(Hons) Dip Lib, Unknown. [10012589] 26/10/1988
ME

Secker, Dr J L, BA(Hons) PhD, Learning Tech. Lib., London Sch. of Economics. [54369] 25/11/1996 **ME**

Seddon, Ms J A, MCLIP DipLib, Tech. Author, OCLC(UK) Sheffield. [37101] 21/02/1984 **CM18/01/1989**

Seddon, Mrs L, BA(Hons) DipLib MCLIP, Reports Lib., Royal Military Coll. of Sci., Shrivenham,Wilts. [39985] 13/10/1986 **CM18/11/1993**

Seedhouse, Mrs E P, MCLIP, Dep. Head of Serv. [6466] 01/11/1970
CM27/07/1973

Seeley, Ms M A, BA MA, Asst. Lib., S. O. A. S, London. [63865] 11/10/2004 **ME**

367

Seelhoff, Ms K A, MSc MCLIP, Saturday Sup., Univ. Coll. for the Creative Arts, Epsom (On a career break) [10000685] 25/10/2006 **CM27/07/1994**

Sefton, Ms A M, BA(Hons) MCLIP, Unwaged [46398] 01/11/1991 **CM17/09/2003**

Segal, Mr K, BA, Sr. Systems Offr., Middlesex Univ., Hendon Campus. [38072] 17/01/1985 **ME**

Segall, Mr P H, BA, Stud. [10006395] 23/10/2007 **ME**

Segbert, Mrs M, DipBibl MBE HonFLA, Head,Inf. & Books, The Brit. Council, Germany. [44286] 13/08/1990 **HFE10/10/1995**

Segel, Mrs S E, BA(Hons), Sen. Lib-Br. Serv. L.B. of Haringey, Hornsey L. [61713] 24/10/2002 **ME**

Sekiete, Mr S S, MA BILS, Unknown. [10006743] 10/12/2007 **ME**

Selby, Mrs C G, MSc(Econ) MCLIP, Sch. L. Serv. Mgr., Sch. L. Serv., Caerphilly Bor. [20514] 01/03/1973 **CM01/07/1976**

Selby, Mr G A, FCLIP, Life Member. [13106] 10/04/1930 **FE01/01/1940**

Selby, Miss J F, MCLIP, Grp. Mgr., Hants C.C., Rumsey L. [22496] 04/06/1974 **CM03/08/1977**

Selby, Miss J R, FCLIP, Retired. [13107] 12/11/1943 **FE01/01/1955**

Self, Mrs D, MCLIP, Retired. [13108] 08/02/1957 **CM01/01/1959**

Selhorst, Miss K, Digitial L./knowledge Mgr. L. of Vlissingen [64586] 10/03/2005 **ME**

Sellah, Mr A, MSc, unknown [10015018] 07/10/2009 **ME**

Sellar, Mrs L D, BA DipLib MCLIP, Subject Lib., Oxford Brookes Univ. [22851] 03/10/1974 **CM12/01/1977**

Sellars, Mr J P, B LIB MCLIP, Serv. Devel. Lib., Nottm. C.C. [24805] 05/10/1975 **CM07/07/1980**

Seller, Ms M L, BSc(Hons) PgDip, Unknown. [65976] 07/08/2006 **ME**

Sellers, Rev J M, BA MCLIP, Methodist Minister. [13112] 24/08/1968 **CM05/02/1973**

Sellwood, Mrs K J, Lib., Merthyr Tydfil P. L. [61370] 01/07/2002 **ME**

Sellwood, Ms R, Unknown. [10008735] 10/12/2008 **ME**

Selman, Mr D, BA(Hons) MA, Info. Handling & Assurance Team., MOD, London. [54057] 24/10/1996 **ME**

Selvidge, Miss E C, BA(Hons) MA, Academic Lib., Roehampton Univ., London. [63939] 18/11/2004 **ME**

Selwood, Miss A M, BA MPhil MCLIP, Head of Standards Unit, NLW, Aberystwyth [19185] 07/08/1972 **CM10/10/1974**

Selwyn, Mrs P M, BA MCLIP, Retired. [1332] 24/07/1961 **CM01/01/1964**

Semogerere Nakiganda, Miss C C, BA, Lib., Electricity Regulatory Auth., Kampala, Uganda. [65953] 20/07/2006 **ME**

Semple, Mrs G, Retired. [22894] 01/10/1974 **ME**

Semple, Mrs H, BLib MCLIP, Head of L. and Inf. Serv., Law Soc. of N. Ireland, Belfast. [43638] 13/11/1989 **CM19/08/1992**

Semple, Miss M E, MCLIP, Retired. [17712] 11/07/1946 **CM01/01/1951**

Sen Gupta, Miss B D, MA(Hons), Sch. of Informatics, City Univ., Northampton. [10016200] 23/02/2010 **ME**

Sen, Mrs B A, BA(Hons) MA MCLIP, Lect., Dept. of Inf Studies, Univ. of Sheffield. [46578] 19/11/1991 **CM21/05/1997**

Sen, Mrs J C, BA MCLIP, Retired. [13123] 18/09/1967 **CM19/09/1972**

Sen, Miss L, MA(Hons) MSc, Inf. Off., Enable Scotland [10007237] 26/06/2002 **ME**

Senadhira, Dr M A P, FCLIP PhD, Life Member. [17714] 04/10/1963 **FE01/01/1974**

Senior, Mr C M, BA DipLib MCLIP FHEA, Project Mgr., Brotherton L., Univ. of Leeds. [41974] 01/07/1988 **CM16/12/1992**

Senior, Mr I E, MSc MSc, Stud. [65961] 24/07/2006 **ME**

Senior, Mrs K W, BA MCLIP MLib, Head of Internat. Campus, Learning Experience, Univ. of Bolton. [13129] 03/10/1968 **CM02/07/1972**

Sennitt, Ms J C, BA(Hons) MA MCLIP, Inf. & Learning Resources Mgr., Groby Community Coll., Leicester. [54172] 04/11/1996 **CM22/09/1999**

Sentongo, Miss D N M, DipLib, Asst. Lib., Lubiri Sch., Uganda. [35383] 04/10/1982 **ME**

Seok Kwan, Ms Y, MLib BA, Head, L. &Inf. Cent., NIE, Singapore. [46385] 01/11/1991 **ME**

Sephton, Mr R S, BA FCLIP LTCL CertEd, Life Member. [13133] 03/04/1945 **FE01/01/1965**

Seraphina, Mrs C, L. Advisor, Perth Coll. [10016039] 10/02/2010 **AF**

Serebriakoff, Ms E M, BSc, Sen. Devel. Asst., Kings Coll.,London. [58994] 17/10/2000 **ME**

Sergeant, Mrs C A, BA MCLIP, Sch. Lib., Falkirk Council, Falkirk. [28571] 10/01/1978 **CM10/08/1982**

Serjeant, Mr F P, BA DipLib, Ref. Lib., L.B. Hammersmith & Fulham. [33880] 05/04/1981 **ME**

Serjeant, Mrs M E, BA DipLib MCLIP, Lib., Kingston Grammar Sch., Surrey. [23757] 22/01/1975 **CM01/03/1978**

Serjeantson, Mr M, BA DipLib MCLIP, I. T. Consultant, Self-Employed. [23749] 02/02/1975 **CM22/05/1985**

Sermon, Mrs K M, BA MSc MCLIP, Mother & p. /t. Database Mgr. [42980] 15/05/1989 **CM21/07/1993**

Service, Mr D J, MA(Hons) DipLIS MCLIP, Sen. Inf. Offr., NHS Quality Improvement, Scotland. [49190] 12/10/1993 **CM19/03/1997**

Sevier, Miss A H, BA MCLIP, Asst. Lib., RAF Trenchard Hall L., Lincs. [43894] 12/02/1990 **CM07/09/2005**

Sewell, Mrs A M, MA FCLIP, Retired. [7070] 25/09/1953 **FE01/01/1966**

Sewell, Miss C E, BA, Stud. [10017088] 22/06/2010 **ME**

Sewerniak, Ms A T, BSc(Hons) DipLIS MCLIP, Unwaged. [43321] 19/10/1989 **CM19/01/2000**

Sexton, Mrs A, BA(Hons) PGDip MCLIP, Principal Leon Sch. Community L., MILTON KEYNES. [10004161] 23/05/2007 **CM18/12/2009**

Sexton, Ms C T, BA DipLib, Collections Lib., Royal Coll. of Physicians, London. [10015682] 13/01/2010 **ME**

Sexton, Ms T J, PGDipLib, Lib., Geldards LLP, Nottingham [44308] 23/08/1990 **ME**

Seyfert, Mrs R, Head Lib., Haynes L., Bahamas. [63593] 08/07/2004 **ME**

Seymour, Mr A J, BA(Hons) MA MCLIP, L. &Inf. Off., The Nat. Autistic Soc., London. [59693] 08/08/2001 **CM09/11/2005**

Seymour, Mrs C, Unknown [10017036] 18/06/2010 **AF**

Seymour, Mrs S M, BA DipLib MCLIP MPHIL, Lib., Piggott Sch., Wargrave. [27368] 20/02/1977 **CM29/03/1979**

Shackleton, Miss K E, BA MCLIP, Unknown. [35830] 28/01/1983 **CM24/04/1991**

Shackleton, Mrs S M, MCLIP, Life Member. [13158] 05/09/1951 **CM01/01/1957**

Shadbolt, Mrs J, BA MCLIP, Purchasing & Bibl. Mgr., Cent. L., Manchester City Council. [31942] 08/01/1980 **CM28/07/1983**

Shade, Mr J H, BA(Hons), Stud., Univ. of Brighton. [10015033] 07/10/2009 **ME**

Shafe, Mr M, BSc MCLIP, Life Member. [13160] 02/06/1959 **CM01/01/1963**

Shaffer, Mr D A, BA, Asst. Lib., Barlow, Lyde & Gilbert, London. [62237] 31/03/2003 **ME**

Shafi-Ullah, Mr F, Univ. L. Offr., Bahria Univ., Islamabad,Pakistan. [65620] 03/03/2006 **ME**

Shah, Ms A T, MA(Hons) DipLIS MCLIP, Sen. L & Inf. Offr., Dundee City C., Cent. L. [55791] 24/11/1997 **CM12/03/2003**

Shah, Mrs K D, Employment not known. [62544] 11/08/2003 **ME**

Shah, Mrs L, BA, Unknown. [10012476] 10/02/2009 **AF**

Shah, Miss M K, BA MCLIP, Lib., Edexcel, London [35606] 07/11/1982 **CM30/01/1991**

Shah, Mr P R, BSc MCLIP, Retired. [17719] 24/05/1954 **CM01/01/1958**

Shah, Mrs P, Asst. Lib., Sci. Mus., London. [10012120] 13/01/2010 **ME**

Shah, Mrs P, HND CELTA ACLIP, L. Asst., E. Barnet Sch., London. [10010191] 09/07/2008 **ACL23/09/2009**

Shah, Mr V, King's Coll. London [65682] 31/03/2006 **ME**

Shahtahmasebi, Dr B E, BA(Hons) PhD, Inf. E Design Team Mgr., Allan Bean Cent., NZ [37254] 14/05/1984 **ME**

Shahzad, Mr A, MLS, L. Super., Walthamstow L., London [64512] 26/04/2005 **ME**

Shaikh, Mrs L M, BA(Hons), Lib., Jones Day, London. [37562] 01/10/1984 **ME**

Shakeshaft, Miss G C, BA MA, Lower Coll. Lib., The Cheltenham Ladies Coll., Glos. [50647] 06/10/1994 **ME**

Shakespeare, Mr A D, BSc MCLIP, Academic Liaison, Univ. of Westminster. [55886] 09/12/1997 **CM01/02/2006**

Shakespeare, Mrs E J, Lib. /LRC Mgr., Thomas Alleyne's High Sch., Uttoxeter. [56374] 01/07/1998 **ME**

Shakespeare, Ms K, BA(Hons) MA MCLIP, Asst. Lib. (Loans), L., Univ. of Portsmouth. [48178] 11/11/1992 **CM20/03/1996**

Shallcross, Mrs E, BSc(Hons) MSc ILS, Inf. Colsultant, Queen Mother L., Univ. of Aberdeen. [53114] 13/03/1996 **ME**

Shamsuddin, Ms D, BA MSc MCLIP, Sen. Lib., Nat. L. Board, Singapore. [64057] 13/12/2004 **CM13/12/2004**

Shand, Ms A, Stud., Northumbria Univ. [10011070] 18/06/2009 **ME**

Shankar, Mrs K, MSc, Unwaged. [10016931] 10/06/2010 **ME**

Shanks, Mr J C, Unknown. [10008812] 21/04/2008 **ME**

Shannon, Ms J A, BA Hons, HDipEd, P. Grad Dip, Stud. [10013611] 13/05/2009 **ME**

Shannon, Mrs J, Prison Lib. & Info. Co-ordinator, Albany L., HMP Isle of Wight [10012977] 20/03/2009 **AF**

Shaper, Mrs S A, DipLib MA(Ed) FCLIP, Dir. of L. Res., The Broxbourne Sch., Herts. [23706] 01/01/1975 **FE31/01/2007**

Shapiro, Ms C M, MA, Lib. Asst., AIU, London [57939] 01/10/1999 **ME**

Share, Mrs L, Lib., Kellett Sch., Hong Kong. [10013708] 22/05/2009 **ME**

Sharif, Ms S, L. & Database Administrator, BSC. Geology. [10011950] 30/01/2009 **AF**

Sharma, Mr N D, BSc MCLIP, Dir. Global Documents & Record Mgmnt., Stiefel Labs. Ltd., Maidenhead. [60487] 07/11/2000 **CM07/11/2000**

Sharman, Miss A J, BSc MCLIP, Academic Lib., Univ. of Huddersfield. [42157] 06/10/1988 **CM19/06/1991**

Sharman, Mrs G S, BA MCLIP, Records Mgr., Surrey Heath Bor. Council. [34140] 05/10/1981 **CM01/07/1990**

Sharman, Miss J, MCLIP, Retired. [13175] 07/02/1953 **CM01/01/1964**

Sharp, Ms A, BLS(Hons) MCLIP, Local Studies Lib., Cent. L., S. Shields. [36113] 07/02/1983 **CM12/03/2003**

Sharp, Mrs C A, MSc MCLIP, Retired. [13179] 05/02/1968 **CM09/09/1974**

Sharp, Mrs C H, BA MCLIP, Lib., Montrose L., Angus Council. [27836] 30/08/1977 **CM01/07/1990**

Sharp, Ms C, BSc(Hons) MSc MCLIP, Early Years Lib., Falkirk Council. [56810] 23/10/1998 **CM10/07/2002**

Sharp, Mr D J, BSc(Hons) MSc, Info. Specialist, Brit. American Tobacco, Southampton [10000429] 10/10/2006 **ME**

Sharp, Mr D K, BA MCLIP, Head Lib., BFI Nat. L., London. [13180] 07/10/1968 **CM18/07/1972**

Sharp, Ms E M, Open Learning Offr., Wishaw L., N. Lanarkshire. [10005722] 25/07/2007 **ME**

Sharp, Ms H M, BA ALA, Unknown. [10012938] 20/03/1980 **ME**

Sharp, Ms J M, BA DipLib MCLIP, Child. Mgr., Manchester P. L. [34831] 01/03/1982 **CM18/06/1985**

Sharp, Mrs J, MCLIP, Br. Lib., Thameside M.B.C., Hyde. [57207] 15/01/1999 **CM11/03/2009**

Sharp, Miss L J, B LIB MCLIP, Team Lib., Greasby L., Met. Boro. of Wirral. [27710] 13/07/1977 **CM23/07/1980**

Sharp, Mrs R E A, BA MCLIP, Unknown. [41518] 11/01/1988 **CM18/09/1991**

Sharp, Mrs S J, BA MCLIP, IT Devel. Mgr., Leeds L. & Inf. Serv. [44931] 21/01/1991 **CM25/01/1995**

Sharp, Mrs Z, BA(Hons) MSc, Lib. Asst., Birmingham City Univ. [10000730] 30/10/2006 **ME**

Sharpe, Mrs R W, MCLIP, Inf. Lib., Derbys. C.C., Belper L. [10001132] 02/02/1987 **CM18/11/1998**

Sharples, Mr C, BA MA MCLIP, Inf. Specialist, Browne Jacobson Sols, Notts. [59983] 15/11/2001 **CM03/10/2007**

Sharples, Miss C, Unknown [10012085] 16/12/2008 **ME**

Sharpling, Mrs L, ACLIP, Lib., Oakgrove Sch., Milton Keynes, Bucks. [10001924] 22/03/2007 **ACL03/12/2008**

Sharrock, Mrs M I, BA MCLIP, Lib., Gateways Sch., Harewood Leeds. [38547] 18/06/1985 **CM15/08/1989**

Sharrocks, Miss H, MCLIP, Life Member. [13198] 18/03/1939 **CM01/01/1952**

Sharrocks, Mr M W, BA DipLib MCLIP, Learning Resources Mgr., Thames Valley Univ., Reading [36866] 09/01/1984 **CM01/07/1989**

Shaughnessy, Miss M, BA DipLib MCLIP, Unwaged. [33698] 12/01/1981 **CM31/01/1989**

Shaw, Mrs A E, MCLIP, Quality Admin., OCN N. N. W. Reg., Liverpool. [18082] 01/10/1972 **CM06/05/1976**

Shaw, Mrs C J, BA MCLIP, Retired [13206] 16/10/1967 **CM01/01/1971**

Shaw, Mrs C M, MA MCLIP, Freelance Editor & Indexer [13207] 09/01/1970 **CM01/01/1972**

Shaw, Mrs C, BA MCLIP, Acquisition Mgr., Bristol City Council. [18188] 10/10/1972 **CM11/03/1975**

Shaw, Ms C, BA(Hons) MA, Curator, Brit. L., London. [53861] 08/10/1996 **ME**

Shaw, Mrs D A, BA(Hons) PGCE MCLIP, Asst. Lib. (ext. hrs), Oxford Brooks Univ., Wheatley Campus. [36632] 30/10/1983 **CM26/07/1995**

Shaw, Mr D E, Inf. Skills, Career, Support to Head Profession [54746] 01/04/1997 **ME**

Shaw, Mr D N, BA DipEdTech MCLIP DMS, Inf. Offr., N. Lanarkshire Council. [13209] 14/02/1970 **CM01/01/1973**

Shaw, Mr D, MA MCLIP, Retired. [13208] 24/10/1966 **CM01/01/1969**

Shaw, Mrs D, Sen. L. Asst., Northumbria Univ. [62849] 17/11/2003 **ME**

Shaw, Miss H A, BA(Hons) DipILS, Liaison Lib., Sch. of Architecture, Design & Built Enviro., Trent Univ., Nottingham. [49440] 27/10/1993 **ME**

Shaw, Mrs I A, BSc MPhil MCLIP, Retired. [11914] 20/10/1967 **CM14/10/1969**

Shaw, Mrs I W, BSc MCLIP, Editor of 'Families London – Surrey Borders' Magazine. [60332] 30/06/1993 **CM30/06/1993**

Shaw, Miss J E, MA BEd MCLIP, H. of L. Systems Div., Univ. of Strathclyde, Glasgow. [24807] 01/10/1975 **CM18/10/1977**

Shaw, Mrs J G, BSc M PHIL, Retired. [33149] 01/10/1980 **ME**

Shaw, Mrs J R, BA(Hons), Stud., Leeds Met. Univ. [10015221] 27/10/2009 **ME**

Shaw, Mrs L E, MCLIP, Learning Res. Cent. Mgr., Nelson & Colne Coll., Lancs. [22305] 21/02/1974 **CM29/03/1977**

Shaw, Miss L F, MA, Stud. [10006524] 07/11/2007 **ME**

Shaw, Mr M A, BA DipLib MCLIP, Operations Mgr. -N., L. & Heritage Div., Derbys. C.C. [31943] 21/01/1980 **CM21/01/1982**

Shaw, Ms P A, MA BA(Hons), Asst. Lib., Univ. of the W. of England., Bristol. [61224] 15/04/2002 **ME**

Shaw, Mrs P S, BA PGCE, Unknown. [10014017] 18/06/2009 **ME**

Shaw, Miss S L, BA PGDip, Unknown. [10014214] 07/07/2009 **ME**

Shaw, Ms T M, BA(Hons) DipLib Dip T&D, Reader Serv. Lib., The Queen's Coll., Oxford [10017175] 11/07/2010 **ME**

Shaw, Mr T, BA(Hons) MSc, Lib. NHS Direct, Almondsbury, Bristol [64329] 04/03/2005 **ME**

Shawcross, Mrs R, BA(Hons), Asst. Lib., Walker Morris [59897] 30/10/2001 **ME**

Sheard, Mrs K, MCLIP, Independant Consultant. [13237] 25/03/1969 **CM15/12/1972**

369

Shearer, Mrs C M, BA MCLIP, Employment not known. [31672] 16/10/1979 **CM30/11/1984**

Shearer, Mr J R, MA DipLib MCLIP, Univ. Lect. & Inf. Consultant, Univ. of Westminster, Oxon. [13239] 12/10/1971 **CM31/12/1974**

Shearring, Mrs J A, BA MCLIP, Sen. Lib., Orpington L., L.B. of Bromley. [10762] 01/01/1970 **CM25/02/1974**

Shears, Mrs N M C, BA(Hons) RGNE, Sen. Lib., Trinity Sch., Teignmouth. [61357] 24/06/2002 **ME**

Sheasby, Mr A E, MCLIP, Retired. [13244] 06/02/1950 **CM01/01/1959**

Shedwick, Ms L A, BA(Hons) DipLib, Community Lib., Northfield Ls., Birmingham L. Serv. [31446] 01/10/1979 **ME**

Sheehan, Mr K J, BA Hons Cert Ed MCLIP, Learning Cent. Mgr., Offerton Sch., Stockport., Cheshire [10001387] 01/10/1998 **CM28/01/2009**

Sheerin, Mrs C E, BA DipLib MCLIP, Sch. Lib., MOD. [34272] 21/10/1981 **CM24/09/1985**

Sheffield, Mrs V C, BA MCLIP, Unwaged. [31250] 09/10/1979 **CM19/10/1982**

Shegog, Ms N J, BA MA PG Dip, Unknown. [10015464] 05/10/1993 **ME**

Sheikh, Mrs C, MCLIP, Child. Lib., Hampshire Co. Council, Winchester. [11775] 01/01/1970 **CM20/08/1973**

Sheikh, Mr J A, M Lib, Unknown. [10015677] 13/01/2010 **ME**

Sheldon, Mr M B, BA MCLIP, Br. Lib., Penylan L., Cardiff Co. L. Serv. [23528] 09/01/1975 **CM10/04/1979**

Shelley, Miss J, BSc(Hons) MA MCLIP, Asst. Lib. (Health & Soc. Care), Anglia Ruskin. Univ., Chelmsford. [48152] 11/11/1992 **CM20/09/1995**

Shelley, Mr K M, BA(Hons) MCLIP, Metadata, King's Coll., London. [55929] 11/12/1997 **CM16/07/2003**

Shelsher, Mr L J, CIB, Lib. Grp. Mgr., Brentwood [10007136] 18/01/2008 **ME**

Shelton, Ms A, BA(Hons) MA MCLIP, Dep. Public Serv. Mgr., St Mary's Univ. Coll., Twickenham [58766] 13/07/2000 **CM07/09/2005**

Shelton, Mrs M M, MCLIP, Area Mgr., W. Lothian Council. [15786] 01/01/1968 **CM01/01/1972**

Shenton, Dr A K, BA(Hons) MSc PhD PGCE, Study Cent. Asst., Monkseaton Comm. High Sch., Tyne and Wear. [43657] 20/11/1989 **ME**

Shenton, Mr D E, FCLIP, Retired. [13256] 10/02/1958 **FE06/10/1977**

Shenton, Miss S K, BA(Hons) MA MCLIP, Sen. Asst. Lib., Manchester Met. Univ. [56725] 07/10/1998 **CM15/09/2004**

Shepherd, Mr A, BA DMS MIMgt MCLIP, Freelance Lib. & Storyteller, London. [13262] 12/10/1965 **CM01/01/1969**

Shepherd, Miss B M, FCLIP, Life Member. [13266] 08/10/1940 **FE01/01/1952**

Shepherd, Miss D, BA PgDipIS, Inf. Lib., The Women's L., London Met. Univ. [64975] 05/10/2005 **ME**

Shepherd, Mrs H, MCLIP, Asst. Lib., Dept. for Communities & Local Government [19901] 01/01/1973 **CM16/09/1975**

Shepherd, Mrs H, BA MCLIP, Primary Advisory Lib., Learn. Resources for Educ., Northampton. [34512] 20/11/1981 **CM20/11/1985**

Shepherd, Ms J L, BA MCLIP, Lib., Wellington Coll., Crowthorne, Berks. [24963] 20/10/1975 **CM24/06/1980**

Shepherd, Miss M, MCLIP, Inf. Offr., N. Somerset Council [65113] 01/11/2005 **CM16/04/2010**

Shepherd, Mrs N M, BA MCLIP, Sen. Young Person's Devel. Lib., Reading Bor. Council. [13276] 12/10/1970 **CM16/10/1974**

Shepherd, Mr R C, BA DipLib MCLIP, Asst. Dir. of L. Serv., Anglia Ruskin Univ., Cambridge. [29822] 01/10/1978 **CM10/06/1982**

Sheppard, Mrs A, LLB MSc MCLIP, Dep. Head of Internal Online Resources, SJ Berwin LLP, London. [58272] 06/12/1999 **CM21/03/2007**

Sheppard, Mr G D, Sen. L. Asst., Cowbridge L., Vale of Glamorgan L. [65083] 01/11/2005 **ME**

Sheppard, Mrs J, BA(Hons) ACLIP, Sen. L. Asst., Mansfield Woodhouse L., Notts. [65674] 24/03/2006 **ACL29/03/2007**

Shercliff, Mrs C A, BA(Hons), Unknown. [10012305] 26/01/1973 **ME**

Sheridan, Rev D J, BA MCLIP, Chaplain, St Giles Hospice, Lichfield, Staffs. [18312] 01/10/1972 **CM30/10/1974**

Sheridan, Miss H, BA(Hons), Stud. [10016415] 22/03/2010 **ME**

Sheridan, Miss J, BA(Hons) MSc MCLIP, Asst. Learning Resources Mgr., Sparsholt Coll. [59103] 15/11/2000 **CM29/03/2004**

Sheridan, Mrs S A, BA MA MCLIP, Dist. Mgr., Canterbury Lib., Kent Lib. & Arch. [40248] 19/11/1986 **CM18/04/1990**

Sheriff, Mr I P, BSc(Hons) MSc, Inf. Sci., DNV Energy, London. [54529] 14/01/1997 **ME**

Sherington, Ms J O, MA DipLib MCLIP, Info. Serv. Lib., Clydebank Lib., W. Dunbartonshire [40243] 10/11/1986 **CM15/08/1989**

Sherlock, Mr C J A, BA(Hons), Sen. Researcher, Lovells, London. [49177] 08/10/1993 **ME**

Sherlock, Ms C, BA MLIS, Unknown. [10009025] 29/04/2008 **ME**

Sherman, Mrs E A, BA MA MCLIP, Arts and Health Offr., Cheshire E. Council [63900] 26/10/2004 **CM28/01/2009**

Sherman, Mrs G, BSc(Open) MCLIP, Relief Lib., Devizes L., Wilts. C.C. [13293] 25/03/1968 **CM01/01/1971**

Sherman, Mrs H, BSc MSc MCLIP, Serv. Devl. Mgr., Dawson Books, Rushden. [48643] 01/04/1993 **CM31/01/1996**

Sherratt, Miss A B, BA MCLIP, Life Member. [13294] 15/01/1951 **CM01/01/1953**

Sherriff, Miss E L, Outreach Support Offr., Cent. L., Plymouth. [66015] 31/08/2006 **ME**

Sherriffs, Mr G I F, MA(Hons) DipILS MCLIP, Acquisitions Lib., Royal Bot. Garden, Edinburgh. [53776] 01/10/1996 **CM15/03/2000**

Sherriffs, Mrs M B, Sen. LRC Asst., Pitlochry High Sch., Perthshire. [10013445] 27/04/2009 **AF**

Sherrin, Miss P A, MCLIP, Life Member. [13295] 29/02/1960 **CM01/01/1969**

Sherwell, Mr J R, MLib FCLIP MRSC, Info. Scientist, Birdlife Int., Cambridge. [18193] 02/10/1972 **FE18/04/1989**

Sherwin, Miss K, MCLIP, Lib., Sparke Helmore Lawyers [58792] 26/07/2000 **CM09/11/2005**

Sherwood, Miss A, BA, Inf. Asst., Northumbria Univ. [10015973] 03/02/2010 **ME**

Sherwood, Mrs D M, MSc(Econ) DipLib MCLIP, L. Serv. Devel. Mgr., L.B. Wandsworth. [10097] 23/01/1972 **CM24/12/1974**

Shewring, Mr P C, BA MCLIP, Inf. Lib., Univ. of Glamorgan, Pontypridd. [10014470] 14/01/1969 **CM01/01/1972**

Shieh, Miss L Y I, BA DipLib MA MCLIP, Sub-Lib., Univ. of Hong Kong Ls., Pokfulam, Hong Kong. [41006] 02/10/1987 **CM19/06/1991**

Shiel, Ms K A, BSc DipILM, CertEd, Records Mgr., Northumberland C.C. [10006149] 04/09/1991 **ME**

Shiell, Ms L M, BA(Hons) MCLIP, Indexer, Brit. Film Inst., London. [41899] 15/05/1988 **CM27/07/1994**

Shiels, Mrs E C, MCLIP, Retired [13302] 31/07/1962 **CM01/01/1967**

Shiels, Mr S M, BSc(Hons) PGDip MCLIP, L. Offr., Edinburgh C.C. [61304] 20/05/2002 **CM04/10/2006**

Shimmon, Mr R M, OBE HonFLA FCLIP, Unknown. [13305] 14/04/1961 **FE29/11/1972**

Shine, Mrs C R, BA DipLIS MCLIP, Sch. Lib., The Forest Sch., Winnersh. [40049] 08/10/1986 **CM15/09/2004**

Shipley, Mrs M, BA MCLIP, Bookstart and Early Yrs. Lib., Cent. L., Coventry. [42818] 01/03/1989 **CM15/09/1993**

Shippey, Miss I J, BA(Hons), Bibliographic Lib., RNIB Nat. L. Serv., Peterborough. [42579] 10/01/1989 **ME**

Shipsey, Ms F M, Unknown. [39937] 06/10/1961 **ME**

Shire, Mrs S A, MCLIP B SC, Lib., Bristol Baptist Coll., Bristol. [21248] 06/10/1973 **CM11/06/1976**

Shirt, Mr J L I, MCLIP, Life Member. [13315] 30/07/1947 **CM01/01/1957**

Shoemark, Mr H K, BSc MCLIP, Retired. [22685] 12/08/1974
CM01/07/1989
Shoemark, Mrs M L, BA MCLIP, Teaching Asst., City of York Council.
[23715] 17/01/1975 **CM16/05/1978**
Shoesmith, Miss C B, MCLIP, Retired. [19199] 01/10/1972
CM16/07/1975
Shone, Mr S A, BA(Hons) MA, Lib. Asst., Wigan Leisure & Culture Trust
[58407] 07/02/2000 **ME**
Shone, Mrs S E, MCLIP, Retired [3036] 16/01/1968 **CM14/08/1972**
Shoosmith, Mrs A, MLIS, Learning Serv. Lib., L.B. of Enfield L. [64843]
03/08/2005 **ME**
Shorley, Mrs D C, BA FCLIP, Dir. of Lib. Serv., Imperial Coll., London.
[27711] 01/07/1977 **FE15/09/2004**
Short, Miss A, BA(Hons) MSc, Asst. Lib., MOD [65032] 13/10/2005 **ME**
Short, Mrs B, MA DipLIS, L. Asst., Comm. Inf., Hertford L., Herts. C.C.
[64668] 17/05/2005 **ME**
Short, Mr P J, BA MCLIP, Retired. [13325] 26/07/1967 **CM13/08/1975**
Short, Mrs P M, ACLIP, Campus Lib., St Peter's Sixth Form Coll., City of
Sunderland Coll. [50181] 25/04/1994 **ACL06/02/2008**
Short, Miss T W, BA(Hons) Dip H. Ed, Resources/Reprographics
Technician, Outwood Academics Trust [10010369] 18/10/1994 **ME**
Shortreed, Ms J, BA MSc MCLIP, Sen. Inf. Offr., Univ. of Abertay
Dundee. [59469] 04/04/2001 **CM09/11/2005**
Shovlin, Mrs C L, BA DipLib, Sch. Lib., Barnard Castle Sch., Co.
Durham. [48236] 16/11/1992 **ME**
Showell, Mrs C, BA DipLib MCLIP, Lib., Brit. Trust for Ornithology,
Thetford. [30030] 13/11/1978 **CM29/01/1982**
Showunmi, Mrs J, BSc MCLIP, Lib., Phoenix High Sch., London.
[58952] 10/10/2000 **CM19/11/2008**
Shreef, Mrs R, L. Asst., Staff L., Barnsley Hosp. [66066] 18/09/2006 **AF**
Shreeve, Mrs S, BSc(Hons) MSc MCLIP, Legal Inf. Serv. Mgr., Integreon
Managed Solutions Ltd, Bristol. [61986] 07/01/2003 **CM21/06/2006**
Shrigley, Mr R M, BA MCLIP, Retired. [13330] 03/10/1966 **CM01/01/1970**
Shrive, Mr M A, BA MCLIP, Unknown. [45437] 06/02/1991
CM23/03/1994
Shub, Mrs I, MA MCLIP, Local Studies Lib., Medway Arch. Cent.,
Rochester. [62618] 18/09/2003 **CM21/11/2007**
Shute, Miss A J, BA MCLIP, Retired. [13336] 26/01/1961 **CM01/01/1964**
Shuttleworth, Mr D H, BLib MA MCLIP, Info. Servs. Mgr., Comm. Hist.,
Lancs. L. [20554] 03/04/1973 **CM21/06/1977**
Sibson, Mr M F D, LLB(Hons) BA(Hons) MCLIP, Med. Lib., Eastbourne
Dist. Gen. Hosp., E. Sussex. [36182] 04/07/1983 **CM14/11/1989**
Siddall, Mrs C L, PGDip MCLIP, Sch. & Comm. Lib., Warrington Boro.
Council. Cheshire. [61897] 27/11/2002 **CM01/02/2006**
Siddall, Miss G E, BA(Hons), Academic Lib, Univ. of Northampton.
[10006244] 26/09/2007 **ME**
Siddall, Miss M F, BA(Hons), Asst. Cent. Mgr., Sheffield Coll. [61912]
02/12/2002 **ME**
Siddall, Ms P M, MSc MCLIP, Independent Consultant. [13344]
16/03/1972 **CM29/10/1975**
Siddiqi, Mrs T, BA(Hons) DipLIS, Lib., Burntwood Sch., London. [40451]
25/01/1987 **ME**
Siddiqui, Mr A R, BA LLB MCLIP, Retired. [13345] 20/03/1964
CM01/01/1967
Siddiqui, Mr A, Unknown. [10012449] 11/02/2009 **ME**
Sidebottom, Miss M, MCLIP, Retired. [13348] 30/09/1942
CM01/01/1956
Sidera-Sideri, Mrs I, MSc, Stud., Northumbria Univ. [58051] 21/10/1999
ME
Sidgreaves, Mr I D, BA DipEd DipLib FCLIP, Retired. [13349]
03/10/1966 **FE23/07/1997**
Siegenthaler, Miss S, MA, Sunday Serv. Asst. /Stud. City Univ.,
London. [10012354] 05/02/2009 **ME**

Siemaszko, Ms A M, BA DipLib MCLIP, Unwaged. [34032] 25/07/1981
CM11/04/1985
Siemaszko, Mrs W M, MA DipLib MCLIP, Inf. Mgr., L.B. of Southwark.
[29341] 25/05/1978 **CM17/03/1981**
Siemsen, Ms A M A, BA DipLib MCLIP, Retired. [18152] 11/10/1972
CM04/05/1976
Sig, Ms H, BSc, Unemployed seeking work [61325] 22/05/2002 **ME**
Silburn, Mrs R E, BSc(Econ) MCLIP, Public Serv. Mgr., Suffolk L.,
Lowestoft. [59685] 31/07/2001 **CM29/08/2007**
Silcocks, Mrs S J, BA DipLib MCLIP, Inf. Offr., Scott Wilson,
Chesterfield. [31307] 29/09/1979 **CM03/09/1982**
Sillitto, Mr D W, MA MCLIP, Sen. Lib.,Database Mgmnt., Holborn L.,
L.B. of Camden. [23201] 30/10/1974 **CM20/10/1977**
Silman, Mrs R G, Faculty Team Lib., John Rylands L., Manchester.
[33152] 01/10/1980 **ME**
Silver, Mrs H L, BLib MCLIP, Inf. Cent. Mgr., Interfleet Tech. Ltd., Derby.
[21337] 17/01/1973 **CM07/02/1978**
Silver, Mrs M V, BA(Hons) DipIM MCLIP, Prison Lib., Medway Council.
[52441] 31/10/1995 **CM17/11/1999**
Silverside, Mrs C E, BA(Hons) MSc MCLIP, MOD, London. [49196]
12/10/1993 **CM25/04/2000**
Silvester, Mrs S C, MA PGDipHist MCLIP, Self-Employed, Resource Lib
– Virtual Ref. Project, p/t, Wovlerhampton Univ. [13356] 27/10/1966
CM01/01/1970
Silvester, Mrs S M, BSc BA MCLIP, Young People & Sch. Offr.,
Scarborough Cent. L., N. Yorks. C.C. [33785] 02/03/1981
CM16/04/1984
Sim, Mrs J R, BSc MCLIP, Hd. Lib., Leeds City Coll., Leeds [21877]
15/01/1974 **CM12/01/1976**
Sim, Mrs L A, BA MCLIP, Acting Head of L., W. Sussex C.C. [27881]
05/10/1977 **CM01/01/1979**
Simcox, Mr J L, BSc(Hons) PGDipILM, Researcher, Baker Tilly [52113]
04/10/1995 **ME**
Sime, Mrs A J, BA MCLIP, Sch. Lib., Fife Reg. Council, Glenrothes.
[29531] 02/08/1978 **CM16/09/1980**
Sime, Mr W C, BSc(Econ) FCLIP, Dir. of L. Servs., Royal Soc. of
Medicine, London [53224] 04/04/1996 **FE09/09/2009**
Siminson, Ms N J, BA(Hons) MA MCLIP, Jorum Community
Enhancement Offr., Univ. of Manchester, Manchester [49067]
27/09/1993 **CM19/01/2000**
Simkin, Mrs H M, MCLIP, Asst. Lib., City Coll., Brighton & Hove. [23710]
15/01/1976 **CM12/07/1977**
Simm, Mrs J R, BA MCLIP, Asst. Lib. Early Years Lib., Sunderland City
L. [37339] 04/07/1984 **CM10/11/1987**
Simmonds, Mr A, BA(Hons) MA MCLIP, Dep. Dir., The Coll. of Law,
York. [51229] 30/11/1994 **CM20/01/1999**
Simmonds, Mr G, BSc(Hons) MA, Lib., Southend L., Essex. [59624]
03/07/2001 **ME**
Simmonds, Mrs J M, MCLIP, Life member. [13365] 18/03/1941
CM01/01/1943
Simmonds, Ms P A, BA DipLib AMIPD MCLIP, Head of Training &
Devel., CILIP London. [34897] 15/04/1982 **CM16/05/1985**
Simmons, Ms A L, BA(Hons) MSc MCLIP, Sen. Lib., Luton Cultural
Serv. Trust [58865] 18/09/2000 **CM04/10/2006**
Simmons, Mrs M M, MCLIP, Retired. [13374] 18/01/1961 **CM01/01/1965**
Simmons, Mr N A, MA MA(LIB) MCLIP DMS, Life Member. [13375]
02/04/1972 **CM03/01/1975**
Simmons, Ms S, BA DipSoc MCLIP, Inf. Mgmt. Consultant. [55004]
12/06/1997 **CM04/09/1989**
Simmons, Mrs S, MCLIP, P/T Cambridgeshire L., Sawtry L. Super.
[9706] 29/06/1970 **CM16/09/1974**
Simms, Miss J E, MA(Hons), Inf. Asst., Univ. of Strathclyde, Glasgow.
[62887] 18/11/2003 **ME**

Simon, Ms A, BA(Hons) MSc, Lect., Aberystwyth Univ. [55859]
04/12/1997   **ME**

Simon, Mrs C, BA(Hons) MSc(Econ) MCLIP, Child. & Sch. Lib., Llanelli
Area L., Carmarthenshire C.C. [55344] 02/10/1997   **CM21/11/2001**

Simon, Ms E, HonFLA, Hon. Fellow. [54738] 01/01/1997 **HFE01/01/1997**

Simon, Miss L H, BA(Hons) MA MCLIP, Unknown. [43230] 01/10/1989
CM20/09/1995

Simon-Norris, Mrs F M, BA MCLIP, Teaching Asst., Hornton Primary
Sch., Hornton. [27161] 30/01/1977   **CM22/09/1979**

Simons, Miss J C, BA, L. Asst., Worthing L., W. Sussex. [10015372]
09/11/2009   **AF**

Simons, Mr J C, MCLIP, Learning Support Offr., Herts. C.C. [13381]
11/08/1968   **CM03/01/1973**

Simons, Mrs L A, MCLIP, ELS Mgr., Cheshire E., Educ. L. Serv.,
[20038] 16/01/1973   **CM24/05/1976**

Simons, Ms P A, BA DipLib MCLIP, Collections Devel. Mgr.,
Roehampton Univ. [29477] 20/08/1978   **CM07/01/1982**

Simpkin, Ms L, BA, Lib., Chester L. [46654] 02/12/1991   **ME**

Simpson, Mr A G, Sch. Lib., Strood Academy, Strood. [53064]
21/02/1996   **ME**

Simpson, Mr A J, BSc(Hons) MSc(Econ) MCLIP, L. & Knowledge Serv.
Mgr., N. Hants. Hosp. NHS Trust, Basingstoke. [54146] 07/11/1996
CM15/11/2000

Simpson, Miss A M, BA MCLIP, Community & Inf. Offcr., N. Yorkshire
Co. L. [24236] 06/05/1975   **CM10/02/1978**

Simpson, Mrs C A, BA(Hons) MA, Catr., Sothebys, London. [52097]
03/10/1995   **ME**

Simpson, Mrs C E, BSc (Hons), Stud., Northumbria Univ. [10014907]
23/09/2009   **ME**

Simpson, Miss D E B, MCLIP, Life Member. [13391] 11/10/1944
CM01/01/1964

Simpson, Mr D J, BSc (ECON) FCLIP, Life Member. [13393]
22/03/1946   **FE01/01/1954**

Simpson, Mr D M, MCLIP, Retired. [13394] 05/04/1971 **CM05/08/1975**

Simpson, Ms E A, BA(Hons) DipLIS MCLIP, Royal Coll. of Physicans of
Edinburgh [50154] 13/04/1994   **CM22/05/1996**

Simpson, Mrs E J, MCLIP, Community Lib., Norfolk C.C., Norfolk &
Norwich Millennium L. [19982] 09/01/1973   **CM01/01/1976**

Simpson, Miss E M, BA(Hons), Unknown [10006493] 24/10/2007   **ME**

Simpson, Mrs E P, Official Publications Curator, Nat. L. of Scotland,
Edinburgh. [10015658] 08/01/2010   **AF**

Simpson, Mr E W M, DipEdTech MCLIP, Retired. [19205] 26/02/1964
CM01/01/1968

Simpson, Miss J M, BA GradDipInfLib MA, Rare Books Lib., Wellcome
L., London. [50102] 23/03/1994   **ME**

Simpson, Mrs J M, BA MCLIP, Unwaged. [23250] 13/11/1974
CM29/10/1979

Simpson, Mrs J, JP BA(Hons) MCLIP, Comm. Facilitator, Stoke on Trent
City Council. [42000] 14/07/1988   **CM18/07/1990**

Simpson, Mrs J, L. Mgr., Christchurch L., Christchurch. [65939]
07/07/2006   **AF**

Simpson, Mrs M E, MCLIP, Employment not known. [227] 01/01/1969
CM16/07/1973

Simpson, Mrs M I, MCLIP, Life Member. [13404] 01/01/1940
CM01/01/1946

Simpson, Mr N A, MA MCLIP, Life Member. [13406] 25/01/1963
CM01/01/1966

Simpson, Mrs N, BSc(Hons) MA MCLIP, Unwaged. [56886] 30/10/1998
CM31/01/2007

Simpson, Mrs P D, MA MCLIP, Unemployed [22317] 01/04/1974
CM28/12/1977

Simpson, Miss P H, MCLIP, Retired. [13408] 06/01/1968 **CM18/10/1973**

Simpson, Mrs P, BA MCLIP, Retired [13407] 28/03/1961 **CM01/01/1966**

Simpson, Mr R A, Asst. Lib., HM Treasury & Cabinet Off. L., London.
[65978] 09/08/2006   **AF**

Simpson, Mr S A, BA PGDipIT MCLIP, Info. Offr., Cultural Serv., E.
Renfrewshire. [44136] 29/05/1990   **CM22/11/1995**

Simpson, Mrs S H, BA DipLib MCLIP, Arch. Asst., Angus Council,
Montrose. [33154] 07/10/1980   **CM19/10/1982**

Simpson, Ms S J, PGCE BA(Hons) MSc, Unwaged. [10013716]
22/05/2009   **ME**

Sims, Mrs A M, BA MCLIP, Lib., Uxbridge High Sch., Middx. [1651]
12/01/1972   **CM01/09/1974**

Sims, Mrs D E, BSc DipInfSc MCLIP, Lib., English Heritage, Swindon.
[40549] 06/03/1987   **CM18/11/1992**

Sims, Mrs G D, BA MCLIP, p. /t. Inf. Lib., Kingston Univ. L., Surrey.
[22903] 07/10/1974   **CM08/10/1976**

Sims, Mrs G J, BA(Hons), Lib. Asst., Harpenden P.L., [10016986]
16/06/2010   **AF**

Sims, Mr P S, MCLIP, Patent Search Inf. Ltd., Chester. [60354]
13/07/1995   **CM13/07/1995**

Simsova, Mrs S, M PHIL FCLIP, Retired. [13418] 07/03/1952
FE01/01/1957

Simspon, Ms M, Community Devel. & Inf. Lib. [63910] 26/10/2004   **ME**

Sinagoga, Miss M C, BA(Hons) MA, Lib. Mgr., Chesham Br., Bucks.
C.C. [58741] 01/07/2000   **ME**

Sinai, Mr A, BA DLS MCLIP, Retired. [17735] 28/08/1963**CM01/01/1967**

Sinar, Mr G T, BLib MCLIP, Applications & Systems Sen. Mgr., Lancs.
Co. L. [22492] 10/06/1974   **CM01/09/1976**

Sinclair, Mr C A, BA MCLIP, Head of Bibl. Serv., Univ. of Stirling.
[38530] 05/06/1985   **CM18/04/1990**

Sinclair, Ms C, MA MCLIP, Inf. & Knowledge Mgr., BSRIA Ltd. [63525]
16/06/2004   **CM20/04/2009**

Sinclair, Mrs F, BA MCLIP, Sch. Lib., Orkney Islands Council,
Stromness Academy. [41102] 05/10/1987   **CM24/05/1995**

Sinclair, Miss H A, BA(Hons) MA MCLIP, Dist. L. Operations Mgr.,
Welwyn Hatfield & Hertsmere. [53809] 02/10/1996   **CM17/05/2000**

Sinclair, Miss H, BA PGDip, Inf. Offr., Glasgow. [10001725] 03/10/2003
ME

Sinclair, Mrs J M, ACLIP, L. Asst., Highbury Coll., Portsmouth. [62455]
01/07/2003   **ACL14/06/2005**

Sinclair, Mrs K, MSc, Info. Off., NHS Grampian Knowledge Serv.,
Aberdeen [10014859] 16/04/2004   **ME**

Sinclair, Mrs M C, MA MSc MCLIP, Subject Lib. / Marketing Offr.,
Glasgow Univ. [41307] 02/11/1987   **CM12/12/1990**

Sinclair, Ms S C, Learning Res. Cent. Mgr. [10011405] 16/10/2008 **ME**

Sinclair, Mrs S J, MA DipLib MCLIP, LRC Co-ordinator, Dunblane High
Sch. [29854] 09/10/1978   **CM10/11/1981**

Sinclair, Miss S K, ACLIP, Sch. Lib. Consultant. [59719] 05/09/2001
ACL01/10/2006

Sinclair, Miss V M, BA DipInf, Asst. Lib., Wellcome L., London. [56950]
13/11/1998   **ME**

Sinden, Mrs M A, BSc MCLIP, Asst. Lib., Minstry of Defence [25591]
28/01/1976   **CM16/08/1978**

Sinden-Evans, Ms R, BA MA BMus MMus MCLIP, Sr. Liaison Lib., Arts
and Educ., Middlesex Univ. [35660] 13/11/1982   **CM14/04/1987**

Singer, Ms H J, BA(Hons) MA MCLIP, Knowledge Consultant, Univ. of
Herts., Hatfield [52818] 19/12/1995   **CM12/09/2001**

Singh Athwal, Mrs J, BSc, Unknown. [10015653] 12/01/2010   **ME**

Singh, Miss M, BA(Hons) MCLIP, Electronic Serv. Co-ordinator,
Electronic Knowledge Access Team, London. [61517] 29/08/2002
CM07/09/2005

Singleton, Mrs A L, MCLIP, L. Serv. for Sch. Mgr., Cumbria C.C.
[14373] 04/10/1970   **CM12/07/1973**

Singleton, Mrs J R, MCLIP, Sen. Lib., Bromley L., Cent. L. [13426]
25/08/1967   **CM01/01/1971**

Sinha, Mrs B, BA, Child. & Young Ppl. Lib., Chelsea Lib., London [10012777] 03/03/2009　**ME**

Sinkinson, Mr J V, BA MCLIP, Civil Servant. [24139] 04/04/1975　**CM19/09/1978**

Sippings, Mrs G M, MLib FCLIP, Head of Inf., Linklaters LLP. [24895] 14/10/1975　**FE24/02/1997**

Sisson, Miss F, BA(Hons) MA MCLIP, Sen. Inf. Advisor, Kingston Univ., Kingston-upon-Thames. [51461] 24/02/1995　**CM19/11/2003**

Sisson, Ms M, Temp. Sen. Asst. Lib. -Br. Mgr., Haslingden L., [10009711] 03/06/2008　**AF**

Sissons, Miss J T, BA(Hons) MA MCLIP, Study Cent. Team Leader, Worcester Coll. of Tech. [53559] 22/07/1996 **RV23/09/2009**　**CM20/09/2000**

Sissons, Miss S E, BA(Hons) PG Dip, Stud., Northumbria Univ., Newcastle-upon-Tyne. [10002962] 10/05/2007　**ME**

Siswell, Miss A, BA DipLib MCLIP, Dep. Lib., Bath Spa Univ., Bath [28162] 11/10/1977　**CM06/12/1979**

Sithamparanathan, Miss S P, MA MSc, Unwaged. [10015711] 19/01/2010　**ME**

Siviter, Ms D J, BA MSc MCLIP, Mgr., L. Serv. for Educ., Leics. [40423] 22/01/1987　**CM12/09/1990**

Siwek, Mrs G R, MA DipLib MCLIP, Community Lib., Portree Community L., Isle of Skye [32918] 08/10/1980　**CM18/07/1983**

Skakle, Mrs S M, MA(Hons) MLib MCLIP, Enquiries Team Leader., Scottish Parliament Inf. Cent., Edinburgh. [47746] 16/10/1992　**CM06/04/2005**

Skander, Mrs J R, Sen. L. Asst., Cheshire E. Council, Hurdsfield & Prestbury L. [21674] 03/01/1974　**ME**

Skea, Mrs J R, MCLIP, Retired. [13437] 07/03/1934　**CM01/01/1937**

Skeates, Mrs C A, BA DipLib MCLIP MBA, Performance Mgr., Audit Commission. [40334] 09/01/1987　**CM21/07/1989**

Skeen, Miss N K, MA, Acting Inf. Offr., The Coll. of Law, Birmingham [10011446] 08/07/1999　**ME**

Skelly, Rev O D G, BA MCLIP STB, Parish Priest, Diocese of Meath, Ireland. [26557] 12/10/1976　**CM15/10/1980**

Skelton, Ms H C, Inf. Mgr, DWP [41498] 04/01/1988　**ME**

Skelton, Miss J, BA, Unknown. [10015469] 25/11/2009　**ME**

Skelton, Ms S A, BA(Hons), Businnes Inf. Specialist, D. F. I. D., London. [49622] 18/11/1993　**ME**

Skene, Mrs S P, BA MCLIP, L. Asst., Robinson Coll., Cambridge [30461] 02/02/1979　**CM19/10/1982**

Skerrow, Mr C J D, MA(Hons) DipLib MCLIP, E-Resources Lib., Hull Coll. [48055] 03/11/1992　**CM13/06/2007**

Skiffington, Mrs M, BA MCLIP, Life Member. [17739] 01/01/1954　**CM01/01/1956**

Skilbeck, Mrs H L, BA(Hons), p. /t. Stud., Leeds Met. Univ. [64845] 02/08/2005　**ME**

Skillen, Mr B S, MLITT BA DipLib MCLIP, Catr., The Mitchell L., Glasgow. [31451] 01/10/1979　**CM16/07/1982**

Skillern, Mrs I H, FCLIP, Retired. [13452] 06/06/1932　**FE01/01/1936**

Skimming, Mrs J, MCLIP, Retired. [998] 22/01/1972　**CM04/11/1974**

Skinn, Mr E H, MCLIP, Retired. [13456] 01/01/1940　**CM01/01/1948**

Skinner, Miss A M, MA(Hons) MCLIP, Unknown. [64008] 02/12/2004　**CM11/03/2009**

Skinner, Mrs A P M, BSc(Hons) MCLIP, Inf. Specialist [13459] 01/01/1969　**CM01/11/1972**

Skinner, Mrs A R, BA MCLIP, L. Mgr. - Dept. of Culture, Callington L., Cornwall Council. [24929] 20/10/1975　**CM06/12/1979**

Skinner, Mr B J, BSc(Hons) MA MCLIP, Knowledge Mgmt. Lib., Brighton & Sussex Univ. Hosp. NHS, Brighton Gen. Hosp. [56486] 21/07/1998　**CM28/01/2009**

Skinner, Mrs H N, BLS MCLIP, Child. & Young Peopple's Serv. Mgr., Devon L., Inf. Serv. [27959] 20/10/1977　**CM11/11/1983**

Skinner, Miss J B, BLib MCLIP, Lib., Rating Directorate:Tech. Support Serv. L. Wingate House, London [21406] 06/11/1973 **CM01/10/1979**

Skinner, Ms J, L. Asst., Politics Psychology Sociology & Inter. Studies L., Univ. of Cambridge. [10010981] 12/09/2008　**AF**

Skinner, Mr N W, MCLIP, Asst. Lib., Kimberlin L., Leicester. [65008] 06/10/2005　**CM08/08/2008**

Skinner, Mrs P A, BA MCLIP, Sch. Resource Offr., W. Lothian Council, W. Lothian. [40111] 21/10/1986　**CM27/05/1992**

Skinner, Mrs S M, BA MCLIP, Network Lib., Aberdeenshire L. & Inf. Serv. [38981] 24/10/1985　**CM18/11/1992**

Skipp, Miss M, MCLIP, Life Member. [13468] 16/02/1956**CM01/01/1964**

Skipworth, Mrs J A P, BA MA MCLIP, Sch. Lib., St. Nicholas Sch., London [10006976] 21/08/1981　**CM01/07/1988**

Skirrow, Mrs I H, Cert Ed. MA MSc Econ ILS, Sch. L. Consultant; IASL Reg. Dir. Internat. Schs.; Sec. IBAEM LIS. [59569] 26/06/2001　**ME**

Skoyles, Miss R, BSc, Info. Asst., L. & Learning Serv., Northumbria Univ., Newcastle upon Tyne [10012101] 17/12/2008　**ME**

Slack, Miss E M, BA MCLIP, Life Member. [13471] 28/01/1960　**CM01/01/1964**

Sladowsky, Mrs Q, MSc BA, Chinese Lib., Westminster L. 's. [10010262] 16/07/2008　**ME**

Slaney, Mrs L, ACLIP, L. Support Asst. [10007020] 17/12/2007　**ACL04/03/2009**

Slaney, Mr R W, MCLIP, Tech. Leader, QinetiQ Ltd., Farnborough. [27299] 16/11/1965　**CM01/01/1974**

Slark, Mrs A M, MCLIP, Adult Serv. Mgr., Bedford Cent. L. [13480] 03/07/1965　**CM01/01/1970**

Slark, Mrs S L, MCLIP, Lib.,Unwaged member. [5800] 26/05/1971　**CM15/12/1974**

Slasor, Miss A, BA MA MCLIP, Unknown. [27022] 12/01/1977　**CM17/06/1980**

Slater, Mrs B G, MCLIP, Area., Principal Lib. Operations., W. Sussex C.C. [20156] 27/01/1973　**CM11/09/1975**

Slater, Mrs J A, BA MCLIP, Advisor, M&S, Perth. [20620] 03/05/1973　**CM21/07/1977**

Slater, Mrs J A, MA(Hons), Lib., Cyberskills & Open Learning Serv. [51971] 24/08/1995　**ME**

Slater, Ms J, MA MCLIP, Soc. of Analytical Psychology L. Lib. [13481] 31/01/1964　**CM01/01/1971**

Slater, Mrs J, BSc(Hons) DipIS MCLIP, Subject Enquiries Off., Winchester Discovery Cent. [52263] 19/10/1995　**CM17/01/2001**

Slater, Miss K, BA MCLIP, Sen. Lib. Primary, Cheshire Educ. L. Serv., Cheshire [34642] 20/01/1982　**CM05/05/1987**

Slater, Mr M K, BA MCLIP, Support Serv. Super., Shadwell Cent., L.B. of Tower Hamlets. [35384] 19/10/1982　**CM07/06/1988**

Slater, Mrs M, BEd(Hons) PGC, Learning Res. Co-ordinator, Perth Academy, Perth. [61446] 18/07/2002　**ME**

Slaughter, Mr R M, BA DipLib MCLIP, Local Studies Lib., Sandwell Met. Bo. C. [34508] 19/11/1981　**CM18/01/1985**

Slavic, Dr A, Unknown. [57683] 01/07/1999　**ME**

Sleap, Miss S E, BA DipLib MCLIP, Life Member. [31155] 07/09/1979　**CM07/09/1981**

Sleat, Mr A J F, BA(Hons) DipLib MCLIP, Subject Lib., Bristol Inst. of Tech., Univ. of the W. of England, Bristol. [36821] 01/01/1984　**CM26/07/1995**

Sleeman, Miss R A, Graduate Trainee, Nat. Met L., Exeter [10014849] 21/09/2009　**ME**

Sleith, Dr C J, BSc PhD, Stud. [10006381] 15/10/2007　**ME**

Slevin, Ms Z, BA(Hons), Dep. Customer Serv. Mngr., Royal Soc. of Medicine, London [62990] 04/12/2003　**ME**

Sliney, Miss M T, MSocSc DipLib MCLIP ALAI, Sen. Lib., Fingal C.C., Ireland. [33347] 16/11/1980　**CM08/06/1987**

Sliwinska, Miss K E, MSc, Unknown. [10014048] 23/06/2009　**ME**

Sloan, Mrs M G, BA MCLIP, Principal Educ. Lib., BA & SEELB Educ. Lib. Serv. [23506] 20/11/1974 **CM22/11/1977**
Slough, Mr N S J, BA(Hons) MA MCLIP, Asst. Lib., Corp. of London, Guildhall L. [44467] 10/10/1990 **CM23/09/1998**
Smales, Mrs J, BA(Hons) PGCE, Knowledge Serv. Mgr., Hull & E. Yorks. Hosp. NHS. Trust, ERMEC. [59423] 12/03/2001 **ME**
Smales, Mrs L A, MA(Hons) PGDipILS MCLIP, Sch. Lib., Queen Anne High Sch., Dunfermline, Fife. [56966] 11/11/1998 **CM23/06/2004**
Small, Mr G S, BA(Hons) DipLib MCLIP, LRC Mgr., Churchfields Sch., Swindon. [36830] 01/01/1984 **CM21/07/1989**
Smallwood, Ms L A, MSc, Unknown. [10012188] 09/01/2009 **ME**
Smart, Dr D, BSc(Hons) PhD, Grp. Mgr. & Mob. L. Serv. Coordinator, Harlow L., Essex. [10013745] 27/05/2009 **ME**
Smart, Mrs E, MA FCLIP PGCE, Lib., Rhondda Cynon Taf, Pontypridd. [27593] 18/05/1977 **FE11/11/2009**
Smart, Mrs T, BA(Hons) MA, Rare Books Catg., Trinity Coll., Cambridge. [58121] 03/11/1999 **ME**
Smeaton, Miss M, Life Member. [20529] 22/01/1973 **ME**
Smedley, Miss A, BA(Hons) MA MCLIP, Asst. Lib., Lancs. C.C., Ansdell L. [56804] 19/10/1998 **CM21/05/2008**
Smit, Mr D R, Stud. [10016687] 27/04/2010 **ME**
Smith, Mrs A H, BA MCLIP, LRC Coordinator, Aberdeen City Council, Aberdeen. [35772] 10/01/1983 **CM07/07/1987**
Smith, Dr A J M, PhD, Stud., Aberystwyth Univ. [10013504] 08/05/2009 **ME**
Smith, Miss A K, BA(Hons) MCLIP, Asst. Comm. L. Mgr., Worcester L., Worcs. C.C. [30043] 14/11/1978 **CM04/01/1985**
Smith, Mrs A L J, BA(Hons) MA MCLIP, Lib., L. Policy Team., London [52359] 26/10/1995 **CM15/03/2000**
Smith, Ms A M H, BA(Hons) MSc MCLIP, Academic Lib., Vaughan Memorial L., Canada. [48781] 21/05/1993 **CM17/11/1999**
Smith, Mrs A M, BTh MSc MCLIP, Grp. Inf. & Res. Analyst, ACERGY Grp., Aberdeen. [60251] 10/12/2001 **CM01/04/2002**
Smith, Mrs A M, BA MCLIP, TEFL Teacher, Self Employed. [36191] 01/07/1983 **CM20/01/1987**
Smith, Mr A P, BSc(Hons) PGCE DipIM MCLIP, Lib., Cent. Ecology and Hydrology, Oxon. [52197] 12/10/1995 **CM20/01/1999**
Smith, Mr A R, MCLIP, Life Member. [13530] 29/06/1948 **CM01/01/1951**
Smith, Mrs A V, MCLIP, Ret. [13532] 26/11/1964 **CM01/01/1971**
Smith, Mr A W, BLib MCLIP ARCM, Inf. Offr., Coll. of Law, York. [13533] 20/10/1971 **CM08/10/1976**
Smith, Mr A, BSc DipLib MCLIP, Knowledge Mgr., Dept. for Business, Innovation & Skills. [23159] 11/11/1974 **CM11/11/1985**
Smith, Mr A, BSc AIMgt MCLIP, Retired [13522] 19/10/1966 **CM01/01/1970**
Smith, Mrs A, Stud. [10016586] 14/04/2010 **ME**
Smith, Mr B B, DMS MIMgt MCLIP, Retired. [13537] 13/01/1954 **CM01/01/1960**
Smith, Mrs B G, BA MCLIP, Retired. [13538] 09/08/1968 **CM01/01/1971**
Smith, Mr B J, MA MCLIP, Unwaged. [10000690] 27/10/2006 **CM09/12/1975**
Smith, Mrs B M, BA MCLIP, Learning Resource Cent. Mgr., Esher Coe Hi. Sch., Surrey. [31681] 25/10/1979 **CM15/09/1983**
Smith, Mr C A, BA MCLIP, Learning Resource Advisor, City Coll., Norwich [35367] 11/10/1982 **CM16/02/1988**
Smith, Ms C A, MSc, Sen. Mgr., Stragic Collection Devel. at The Nat. Arch. [53971] 15/10/1996 **ME**
Smith, Mrs C A, MA DipLib MCLIP, Stud., Strathclyde Univ., Glasgow. [43534] 06/11/1989 **CM18/11/1993**
Smith, Ms C A, BSc DipLib MCLIP, Unwaged. [10005448] 19/03/1979 **CM22/12/1982**
Smith, Mrs C E, DipLib MA MCLIP, Housewife. [36453] 05/10/1983 **CM10/05/1988**

Smith, Mr C J, BSc PGDipLib MCLIP, Retired. [26217] 24/08/1976 **CM17/01/1980**
Smith, Mr C J, MCLIP, Retired. [13548] 08/01/1958 **CM01/01/1967**
Smith, Miss C L, Sch. Lib. [65121] 01/11/2005 **ME**
Smith, Miss C L, BA, Stud. [10000465] 09/10/2006 **ME**
Smith, Mrs C L, MCLIP, Unwaged. [20253] 27/01/1973 **CM16/09/1976**
Smith, Mrs C M, MA DipLib MCLIP, Inf. Mgr., RTC North Ltd. Sunderland. [27918] 01/10/1977 **CM22/12/1979**
Smith, Mrs C M, BA MCLIP, Lib., HMP Dovegate, Uttoxeter. [3384] 26/09/1969 **CM01/02/1977**
Smith, Ms C M, BA(Hons), Sen. L. Asst., Univ. of Glamorgan, Pontypridd. [64419] 16/03/2005 **ME**
Smith, Mrs C P, BLib MCLIP, Unwaged [39472] 30/01/1986 **CM21/10/1992**
Smith, Mrs C R H, BA DipLib MCLIP, Employment not known. [26775] 22/11/1976 **CM28/09/1979**
Smith, Miss C R, BA MCLIP, Unwaged [24814] 02/10/1975 **CM05/10/1979**
Smith, Mrs C, MCLIP, Asst. Lib., Univ. of Durham. [31183] 20/10/1979 **CM20/10/1981**
Smith, Miss C, BLib MCLIP, Collection Devel. Mgr., Univ. Bolton. [30792] 08/04/1979 **CM26/07/1982**
Smith, Mrs C, BA, Stud/Univ. of Wales Aberystwyth(Distant Learning)/Asst. Lib., Univ. of Cambridge. [10002616] 01/05/2007 **ME**
Smith, Mr D A, DipLib MCLIP, Asst. Inf. & Local Stud. Lib., William Patrick L., E. Dunbartonshire. [38937] 16/10/1985 **CM21/07/1993**
Smith, Mr D A, MA MCLIP, Head of Knowledge Communities & Local Govt., London [34206] 13/10/1981 **CM20/01/1986**
Smith, Dr D F, MA DPhil MCLIP, Lib., St Annes Coll. L., Oxford. [33427] 30/11/1980 **CM16/12/1986**
Smith, Mr D J, BA(Hons) DMS MCLIP FInstLM, Corp. Inf. & Complaints Mgr., Conwy Co. Bor. Council. [41578] 20/01/1988 **CM27/01/1993**
Smith, Mr D P, MLS, Unwaged [57805] 10/08/1999 **ME**
Smith, Ms D, BA MCLIP, Independent Inf. Professional, Wychford Inf. Serv., Sawbridgeworth. [60335] 01/10/1993 **CM01/10/1993**
Smith, Mr D, BA(Hons) MScEcon MCLIP, Sen. Local Studies Lib., Cent. L., Hull. [10000538] 16/10/2006 **CM17/09/2008**
Smith, Mr D, BA MCLIP, Team Lib., The Mitchell L., Glasgow. [33156] 01/10/1980 **CM01/07/1994**
Smith, Ms D, Unknown. [61233] 17/04/2002 **ME**
Smith, Mrs E A, BA(Hons) DipILM MCLIP, Sch. Lib., Pembroke Sch., Wales. [43633] 13/11/1989 **CM18/11/1993**
Smith, Miss E A, BA(Hons) MCLIP, Seeking employment. [39404] 27/01/1986 **CM22/07/1998**
Smith, Mrs E B, MCLIP, Retired. [754] 18/01/1972 **CM10/02/1975**
Smith, Mrs E L M, BA MCLIP, Lib., Angus Council. [33079] 09/10/1980 **CM27/10/1983**
Smith, Mrs E M A, BA(Hons), Lib., Franconian Inter. Sch., Erlangen, Germany. [10006336] 10/10/2007 **ME**
Smith, Mr E, MCLIP MCMI ABCS BA(Hons), Unwaged. [45495] 20/02/1991 **CM23/07/1997**
Smith, Mr E, MCLIP, Unwaged. [13563] 08/01/1967 **CM01/01/1970**
Smith, Ms E, Unknown. [10012184] 09/01/2009 **ME**
Smith, Ms F M M, BEd DipLIS MCLIP, Sch. Lib., Loudoun Academy, E. Ayrshire Council. [51573] 03/04/1995 **CM21/01/1998**
Smith, Miss G D, BA(Hons) PG Dip, Unknown. [10013973] 18/06/2009 **AF**
Smith, Mr G E, OBE FCLIP, Consultant/Life Member. [13579] 11/01/1948 **FE01/01/1956**
Smith, Miss G F, BA(Hons) MSc(Econ) MCLIP, Learning & Teaching Lib., The Open Univ. L., Milton Keynes. [52531] 06/11/1995 **CM20/09/2000**
Smith, Mr G H R, BA MCLIP, Retired. [13581] 23/02/1966 **CM01/01/1969**

Smith, Mrs G M, MCLIP, Greeting Cards Website Proprietor [8679]
25/01/1970   **CM05/07/1988**
Smith, Mrs G M, BEd DipLib, Lib., Kings Norton Girls'Sch., Birmingham.
[46040] 09/09/1991   **ME**
Smith, Ms G, BA MCLIP, Career Break. [36684] 03/11/1983
                                                                     CM19/08/1992
Smith, Mrs G, MA MA, Lib., Equality & Human Rights Commission,
Manchester. [59976] 14/11/2001   **ME**
Smith, Mr G, BA DipLib FCLIP, Retired. [26560] 03/10/1976
                                                                     FE20/09/2000
Smith, Mrs H E, BEd(Hons), Sch. Lib. Mgr., Rawmarsh Community
Sch., Rotherham. [62755] 13/10/2003   **ME**
Smith, Miss H E, BA MCLIP, Team Lib., Bor. of Poole. [37882]
01/11/1984   **CM18/04/1989**
Smith, Mrs H M, BA DipLib MCLIP, Dep. Grp. Leader, Neath Port Talbot
CBC., Port Talbot L. [23353] 20/11/1974   **CM11/01/1978**
Smith, Mrs H M, BA MCLIP, L. Asst., Northants. C.C. [24516]
11/09/1975   **CM28/06/1979**
Smith, Miss H R, MSc MCLIP, Inf. Mgr., Kennedys, London. [39825]
09/08/1986   **CM14/11/1989**
Smith, Miss H R, Postgrad Dip Inf. & Lib Studies, Knowledge Off.,
Oxford Univ. Careers Serv. [10015951] 28/01/2010   **ME**
Smith, Ms H S, Head Lib., Ashurst, London. [49581] 19/11/1993   **ME**
Smith, Mrs H, BA DMS MCLIP, Career break [39617] 01/04/1986
                                                                     CM24/06/1992
Smith, Miss H, BA(Hons), L. Asst. [10011611] 30/10/2008   **ME**
Smith, Mrs H, BA MCLIP, Team Leader, N. Yorks. C.C., Skipton. [40512]
24/02/1987   **CM12/12/1991**
Smith, Mrs I A, BA MA FCLIP, Lect., Dept. of Inf. Sci., Loughborough
Univ. [30718] 01/01/1971   **FE22/03/1995**
Smith, Mr I M, BA MSc DipLib MCLIP, Lib. (Part-Time) [35204]
05/10/1982   **CM16/05/1990**
Smith, Mrs J A, MA MCLIP, Freelance trainer/consultant/cataloguer.
[25665] 21/01/1976   **CM17/01/1978**
Smith, Ms J B, BA(Hons) MCLIP, Systems Lib., Newman Univ. Coll.,
Birmingham. [33158] 20/10/1980   **CM01/07/1989**
Smith, Mrs J B, Unknown. [10000646] 24/10/2006   **AF**
Smith, Miss J C, BSc MSc MCLIP, Learning Res. Serv. Mgr., UBHT,
Learning Res. Cent., Bristol. [47472] 26/08/1992   **CM23/03/1994**
Smith, Ms J E, BA MCLIP, Casual L. Work at Derbyshire Sch. L. Serv.
[31156] 16/09/1979   **CM21/06/1984**
Smith, Ms J E, Head of L. Collection & Serv., Natural Hist. Mus.,
London. [39592] 14/03/1986   **ME**
Smith, Miss J H, BLS(Hons) MCLIP, Inf. and Arch. Offr., Barnabas
Fund. [33462] 01/01/1981   **CM17/09/2003**
Smith, Miss J H, BSc(Hons) MSc MCLIP, SHERPA Serv. Devel. Offr.
Cent. for Res. Devel. (CRC), Univ. of Nottingham. [59090]
13/11/2000   **CM17/09/2008**
Smith, Miss J M, MCLIP, Retired. [13611] 01/01/1965   **CM01/01/1970**
Smith, Ms J M, BA(Hons) MCLIP, Snr. Inf. Offr., Hammonds, Leeds.
[43593] 09/11/1989 **RV27/11/2007**   **CM24/07/1996**
Smith, Ms J S, BA DMS MCLIP, Account Mgr., Axiell Notts. [40289]
07/01/1987   **CM16/09/1992**
Smith, Rev J S, MA FCLIP, Retired. [13619] 12/03/1954 **FE01/01/1968**
Smith, Ms J, BA(Hons) MA, Asst. Lib., Guildhall L., London. [10016644]
27/10/1998   **ME**
Smith, Mr J, MA MCLIP, Cent. Lend. Lib., Cent. L., Aberdeen. [30262]
06/12/1978   **CM02/04/1981**
Smith, Ms J, MCLIP, Customer Serv. Lib. Dacorum/St Albans Dist.,
Hertfordshire Co. Council., Hemel Hempstead L. [64440] 30/03/2005
                                                                     CM28/01/2009
Smith, Ms J, BA(Hons) MA MCLIP, Freelance Lib. [58452] 11/02/2000
                                                                     CM29/03/2004

Smith, Mrs J, MCLIP, Lib., Sixth Form Coll., Colchester. [64340]
07/03/2005   **CM11/11/2009**
Smith, Mrs J, LRC Inf. Asst., Guilford Coll., Worplesdon. [10016794]
18/05/2010   **ME**
Smith, Mr J, FCLIP, Retired. [13600] 05/10/1948   **FE01/01/1956**
Smith, Mrs J, ACLIP, Team Leader, Halfway L., S. Lanarkshire
[10012527] 24/02/2009   **ACL16/06/2010**
Smith, Mrs K A E, BA(Hons) MA MCLIP, Team Lib., Stock & Inf. [61246]
22/04/2002   **CM09/11/2005**
Smith, Ms K A M, MCLIP, Lib. Res. Cent. Co-ord. St Augustine`s H. S.
Edinburgh. [62044] 28/01/2003   **CM11/03/2009**
Smith, Mrs K B, BA MCLIP, Resources Lib., Cheshire W. and Chester
[33962] 18/06/1981   **CM31/10/1984**
Smith, Mr K C, Libr., OFGEM, London. [50122] 05/04/1994   **ME**
Smith, Mrs K L, BA MCLIP, Retired. [18275] 10/10/1972 **CM31/10/1975**
Smith, Dr K, BAppSc(LS) MA PhD, Sen. Lect., Curtin Univ. of Tech.,
Australia. [62190] 13/03/2003   **ME**
Smith, Miss L A, MCLIP, IT Support Mgr., City Business L., City of
London. [23094] 28/10/1974   **CM22/05/1979**
Smith, Miss L H, Unknown. [10006644] 11/09/2007   **ME**
Smith, Ms L J, MA MA, Asst. Lib., Essex Public Health Resource Unit
[43039] 10/07/1989   **ME**
Smith, Ms L L, BA, Unknown. [10006657] 15/11/2007   **ME**
Smith, Miss L M R, MCLIP, Life Member. [13632] 01/01/1955
                                                                     CM01/01/1963
Smith, Miss L M, MCLIP, Marketing and Communications Mgr.,
Nottingham Trent Univ. L. and Learning Resources [13631]
01/10/1971   **CM19/09/1974**
Smith, Mrs L M, MCLIP, Sch. Lib., Ecclesbourne Sch., Derbys. [8049]
02/01/1970   **CM24/07/1973**
Smith, Mrs L M, BA MA, Teacher Aide, Internat. Sch. of Aberdeen,
Aberdeen. [10006647] 11/09/2007   **ME**
Smith, Ms L N, BA(Hons) MSc, Unknown [10001064] 12/01/2007   **ME**
Smith, Mrs L, MCLIP, Head of L., Warks L., Warwick. [28605]
20/01/1978   **CM12/08/1981**
Smith, Mrs L, BSc DipLib MCLIP, Inf. Offr., SIGN, NHS QIS, Glasgow
[60302] 14/03/2000   **CM14/03/2000**
Smith, Miss L, BA Hons, L. Asst. & MA Stud., Univ. Sheffield.
[10015786] 25/01/2010   **ME**
Smith, Ms L, BA, Stud., Manchester Met. Univ. [10015812] 29/01/2010
                                                                                 ME
Smith, Mrs M A, MCLIP, Lib. in Charge, Tranent Br. L., E. Lothian.
[18386] 20/10/1972   **CM21/07/1976**
Smith, Mrs M A, MCLIP, Retired [5385] 09/09/1965   **CM01/01/1970**
Smith, Ms M C, BA(Hons), Inf. Mgr., Linklaters, London. [28367]
07/11/1977   **ME**
Smith, Mrs M E, BA PG DipLIS, p/t Devel. Mgr., Jumpstart Kidz
[10006463] 26/03/1996   **ME**
Smith, Dr M J, BSc(Hons) MSc MCLIP, Collection Mgmt. Lib., Natural
Hist. Mus. [47968] 28/10/1992   **CM20/05/1998**
Smith, Mr M J, BA(Hons) MSc MCLIP, Inf. Specialist, NBS., Newcastle
upon Tyne. [54683] 19/02/1997 **RV10/07/2009**   **CM20/11/2002**
Smith, Ms M J, MCLIP, Sen. Lib., Cambs. C.C., Cambridge. [26195]
18/08/1976   **CM01/01/1978**
Smith, Mrs M N E, BA, Unknown. [10010957] 15/09/2008   **ME**
Smith, Mrs M R, BA MCLIP, Med. Lib., Royal Devon & Exeter
Foundation NHS Trust, Exeter. [34554] 01/01/1982   **CM16/01/1986**
Smith, Mr M S, BA(Hons) MSc, Inf. Specialist, GCHQ, Glos. [10005052]
09/11/2001   **ME**
Smith, Mr M S, FCLIP, Retired. [13656] 15/09/1950   **FE01/01/1968**
Smith, Mr M T, BA(Hons) DipILM MCLIP, Stock Specialist, Cheshire
C.C., Chester. [58266] 03/12/1999   **CM20/11/2002**
Smith, Ms M, MCLIP, Coll. Lib., Royal Coll. of Surgeons, Edinburgh.
[13642] 21/09/1967   **CM05/11/1985**

Smith, Mrs M, BSc(Hons) MCLIP MSc, LRC Mgr., Inst. of Applied Tech., Dubai. [46940] 04/03/1992   **CM17/03/1999**

Smith, Mrs M, BA(Hons) PGCE MA, Res. Stud., Loughborough Univ., Res. Sch. of Informatics. [62740] 14/10/2003   **ME**

Smith, Miss M, BSc, Sen. L. Asst., N. Tees and Hartlepool NHS Foundation Trust. [10011804] 14/11/2008   **AF**

Smith, Ms M, Stud. [10006453] 19/10/2007   **ME**

Smith, Mrs M, MCLIP, Team Lib., Aberdeen City Council. [15241] 01/10/1971   **CM18/10/1976**

Smith, Mr N A, MA MCLIP, Under-Lib., Cambridge Univ. L. [13658] 06/11/1965   **CM01/01/1969**

Smith, Miss N E, MA MCLIP, Life Member. [13661] 31/05/1946   **CM01/01/1950**

Smith, Mr N G, BA(Hons) MA MCLIP, Consultant.,Hewitt New Bridge Street, London [55638] 30/10/1997   **CM04/02/2004**

Smith, Mr N J, BA(Hons) MPhil MSc, Unknown. [10013988] 27/09/1999   **ME**

Smith, Mrs N N, MA DipLib MCLIP, Dir. of Res., Right Mgmnt., London. [29437] 18/08/1978   **CM26/10/1981**

Smith, Dr N R, MSc MCLIP, Dir. -L. & Inf. Serv., Aston Univ., Birmingham. [60644] 20/11/1981   **CM20/11/1981**

Smith, Miss P L, BA MLS MCLIP, Retired. [17747] 16/01/1950   **CM01/01/1954**

Smith, Mr P M, BA(Hons) MSc(Econ) MCLIP, Lib., Bispham High Sch., Blackpool. [59573] 04/06/2001   **CM15/01/2003**

Smith, Mrs P M, BA MCLIP, Sch. Lib., Runcorn St. Chads High Sch., Cheshire. [22221] 25/02/1974   **CM31/03/1977**

Smith, Mrs P M, BA(Hons) DipILM MCLIP, Subject Inf. Offr., Liverpool John Moores Univ., Liverpool. [53988] 14/10/1996   **CM10/07/2002**

Smith, Mr P, MSc MCLIP, Inf. Adviser, Sheffield Hallam Univ. [61608] 03/10/2002   **CM19/03/2008**

Smith, Mr P, BA DipLib MCLIP DMS, Res., Projects & Mktg. Offr., Somerset C.C. [26806] 05/11/1976   **CM02/02/1979**

Smith, Mr R A, BA MCLIP, Head of Systems, Linda Hall L, Kanasas City [32180] 28/01/1980   **CM17/05/1983**

Smith, Mr R C, MCLIP, Sen. L. Asst., Arran L. Isle of Arran, Scotland. [13677] 24/06/1969   **CM01/02/1973**

Smith, Mr R F, MCLIP, Life Member [13680] 03/05/1937 **CM01/01/1947**

Smith, Mr R G, MCLIP, Retired. [13682] 10/01/1964   **CM01/07/1994**

Smith, Ms R J, BA(Hons) DipIS MCLIP, Academic Liaison Lib., Univ. of Westminster, London. [52196] 12/10/1995   **CM20/11/2002**

Smith, Miss R L, BA(Hons), L. Asst., Durham Univ. L., Durham. [10016633] 01/05/2010   **AF**

Smith, Dr R, MCLIP, Lect., Dept. of Info. Mgmnt., The Robert Gordon Univ., Aberdeen [10008073] 23/10/1985   **CM12/12/1990**

Smith, Ms R, MSc DIC MCLIP, Retired. [6498] 25/09/1964   **CM01/01/1968**

Smith, Miss S A L, BA, Asst. Lib., Featherstone High Sch., Ealing. [10010694] 26/08/2008   **ME**

Smith, Mrs S A, Lib. & Resource Cent. Mngr., Mottingham Bluecoat Sch., Nottingham [10015255] 29/10/2009   **AF**

Smith, Miss S E, BA MLS MCLIP, Learning Support Coordinator/Liason Lib., Reading Univ. [33160] 04/10/1980   **CM24/06/1983**

Smith, Mrs S E, BA(Hons) DipILM MCLIP, Lib., Queen Elizabeth High Sch., Northumberland [47822] 14/10/1992   **CM18/03/1998**

Smith, Mr S G, MSc BA(Hons) PGDip, Inf. Asst., Aberdeen Coll. L., Aberdeen. [61054] 19/02/2002   **ME**

Smith, Mr S J, BA(Hons) MCLIP, Br. Lib., Kenton L., Harrow L. [53720] 16/09/1996   **CM12/09/2001**

Smith, Mrs S J, BA MCLIP, Lifelong Learning & Local Studies Lib., Herts C.C. [41725] 22/02/1988   **CM26/05/1993**

Smith, Mr S K, BA(Hons) MCLIP, Grp. L. Mgr., N. Swindon L. [37351] 09/07/1984   **CM09/06/1988**

Smith, Mrs S L, BA MCLIP, Bor. Lib., Telford L., Shropshire. [25579] 22/01/1976   **CM01/07/1994**

Smith, Mr S P, BSc DipLib MCLIP, Site LIb., Inst. of Biological, Enviro. & Rural Sciences, Gogerddan Campus, Aberystwyth Univ. [30266] 30/12/1978   **CM08/02/1982**

Smith, Miss S R R, BSc MA MCLIP, L. Devel. Mgr., L.B. of Brent,L. Arts & Heritage [42989] 26/05/1989   **CM27/01/1993**

Smith, Ms S W, MCLIP, Sen. Lib., Jet L. Leighton Hosp., Crewe [64961] 04/10/2005   **CM19/11/2008**

Smith, Mrs S, Lib., Brit. Inst. of Radiology [10000697] 15/11/2006   **ME**

Smith, Mrs S, BA PGCE MCLIP, Retired [13690] 08/10/1969   **CM01/01/1972**

Smith, Mrs V E, p. /t. Stud., Leicester City L., Univ. of Wales, Aberystwyth. [64751] 28/06/2005   **ME**

Smith, Mrs V, BSc(Econ) MCLIP, L. Mgr., Napier Univ., Edinburgh. [50983] 07/11/1994   **CM17/05/2000**

Smith, Mrs W J, BA(Hons) MA MCLIP, Inf. Adviser, Univ. of Wales Inst., Cardiff. [46382] 30/10/1991   **CM21/05/1997**

Smith, Mrs W J, FCLIP, Life Member. [1149] 22/02/1937 **FE01/01/1948**

Smith, Miss Y M, MA MCLIP, Info. Advisor (Res.), Edge Hill Univ. [62884] 18/11/2003   **CM29/08/2007**

Smith, Mrs Y, BSc MCLIP, Unknown. [10012036] 05/11/1970   **CM26/10/1973**

Smith-Haye, Mrs M G, MCLIP, Consultant., ProBiblio, Netherlands. [20129] 16/02/1973   **CM10/01/1975**

Smithson, Mr D P R, BA(Hons) MSc MCLIP, Sen. Inf. Advisor – E learning, Kingston Coll., Kingston-upon-Thames. [56627] 23/09/1998   **CM15/01/2003**

Smithson, Mrs D, MCLIP, Retired. [13711] 23/08/1968 **CM01/01/1972**

Smithson, Mrs E, BA MA MALIS, Lib. Asst., Queen Mary Univ., London [10007998] 03/03/2008   **ME**

Smithson, Ms H, MA, Business Inf. Offr., Inst. of Dir., London. [59606] 27/06/2001   **ME**

Smithson, Mrs L E, BA MA MCLIP, Team Leader Acquisitons., Univ. of Surrey L. [59255] 19/01/2001   **CM21/06/2006**

Smithurst, Dr D L S, BSc MSc PhD MCLIP, Employment not known. [60523] 02/03/1976   **CM27/04/1981**

Smitton, Mr S, MCLIP, Mob. & Support Serv. Mgr., Walsal M.B.C., Mob. L. Unit, Bloxwich. [28895] 14/02/1978   **CM14/02/1980**

Smout, Mrs A M, MA DipIT MCLIP, Retired. [28168] 01/10/1977   **CM27/11/1980**

Smyth, Mr A L, MBE FCLIP, Life Member. [13719] 24/03/1936   **FE01/01/1946**

Smyth, Mrs A V, BA MLS MCLIP, Life Member. [13720] 01/01/1970   **CM26/09/1977**

Smyth, Ms D M, BA MCLIP CMS CertEd, Retired. [13721] 03/10/1967   **CM01/01/1971**

Smyth, Mrs J E, BSc PhD MSc MCLIP, Asst. lib., Scottish Government [39782] 17/07/1986   **CM29/03/2004**

Smyth, Ms L M, BA Business Enterprise, Stud., Manchester Met. Univ. [10009317] 15/05/2008   **ME**

Smyth, Mr N T, BA MSc(Econ) MCLIP, Arts Faculty Team Leader, Hallward L., Nottingham [56472] 23/07/1998   **CM06/04/2005**

Smythe, Mrs S D, BA(Hons), Inf. Offr., Mishcon de Reya, London. [63453] 12/05/2004   **ME**

Snape, Mr C H, BA(Hons) MA, L. Asst., Univ. Coll. London. [58873] 20/09/2000   **ME**

Snape, Mr W H, DPA FCLIP, Retired. [13731] 03/10/1933 **FE24/09/1948**

Sneath, Mrs L T, ACLIP, L. Mgr., Calverton L., Nottingham. [65436] 24/02/2006   **ACL29/03/2007**

Sneddon, Mrs L J, BA(Hons) PGCE ACLIP, Child. L. Serv., Parkstone L., Poole. [10003004] 10/05/2007   **ACL16/07/2008**

Sneesby, Miss M A, BA MCLIP, Stock Devel. Lib., Cent. Div., Hants. C.C. [20699] 29/05/1973   **CM04/10/1975**

Snell, Mrs C, BSc, Employment not known. [40701] 05/05/1987 **ME**

Snell, Miss H L, BA MCLIP, Training & Inf. Offr., S. Devon Healthcare Trust, Torquay [63908] 26/10/2004 **CM20/04/2009**

Snelling, Mrs C A, BA DMS MSc MCLIP, Sen. Lib.: Cent. L., Blackburn with Darwen B. C., Lancs. [34629] 19/01/1982 **CM24/03/1986**

Snelling, Mrs H R, BSc MCLIP, Asst. Lib., Pendlebury L. of Music, Univ. of Cambridge. [31479] 12/10/1979 **CM13/09/1984**

Snelling, Ms J R, BA(Hons) MA MCLIP, Lib., Corpus Christi Coll., Oxford. [50138] 08/04/1994 **CM21/03/2001**

Snelling, Mr M W, BA DMS MCLIP, E-Learning Support Mgr., John Rylands Univ. L., Univ. Manchester. [34563] 13/01/1982 **CM19/09/1984**

Snelling, Mrs P, Dep. Mgr., High Wycombe L. [62530] 06/08/2003 **ME**

Snelling, Mrs S M, BSc DipLib MCLIP, Sen. Inf. Advisor, Kingston Univ., Kingston. [25210] 02/01/1976 **CM01/12/1977**

Sng, Mrs S, BA, Unknown [13740] 06/10/1970 **ME**

Snoad, Mrs N J, BA Hist., Inf. Res. Asst., Watson, Farley & Williams [10001389] 14/02/2007 **ME**

Snook, Mrs C E, BSc DipIM, Seeking work. [49076] 01/10/1993 **ME**

Snook, Miss L M, LLB MSc MCLIP, Law Lib., Univ. of Exeter, Devon. [52227] 16/10/1995 **CM15/10/2002**

Snook, Mrs L M, BA(Hons), Unknown. [10014279] 21/10/1997 **ME**

Snow, Mrs D L, BA(Hons) MSc MCLIP, Unwaged. [54870] 24/04/1997 **CM19/01/2000**

Snow, Mrs J A, BA DipLib MCLIP, Reader Devel. Lib., Wellingborough L., Northants C.C. [36285] 03/10/1983 **CM05/05/1987**

Snow, Miss K, BA MSc MCLIP, Preservation Res. . Hatii, Univ. of Glasgow. [58810] 04/08/2000 **CM11/03/2009**

Snowden, Mr A, BSc MSc MCLIP, Consultant, Fujitsu Serv., Bracknell. [60647] 11/12/2001 **CM01/04/2002**

Snowden, Mr C W, MCLIP, Life Member. [13746] 18/03/1946 **CM01/01/1955**

Snowley, Mr I R, BA MBA FCLIP, Unknown. [35753] 11/01/1983 **FE15/09/2004**

Soar, Mr G D E, BA MCLIP, Retired. [13750] 04/06/1955 **CM01/01/1958**

Socha, Miss L A, BA(Hons) MSc MCLIP, Sen. Inf. Offr., Trowers & Hamlins, London [62442] 25/06/2003 **CM29/11/2006**

Softley, Ms K, BA MCLIP, Lib. Dev. Offr., N. Neighbourhood, Edinburgh City L. [33838] 14/03/1981 **CM27/09/1984**

Soley Barton, Mrs C F, MSc, Shiping Policy Team Member, Dept. for Transport, London. [37319] 02/07/1984 **ME**

Sollis, Mrs H, BSc MSc MCLIP, Intranet Site Mgr., Tower Watson Surrey. [56859] 02/11/1998 **CM21/06/2006**

Solomonsz, Ms F T, BA MCLIP, Retired. [13755] 28/08/1961 **CM01/01/1968**

Somerville, Ms A, MA, Unknown [65175] 09/11/2005 **ME**

Somerville, Mrs C J, BA BD, Asst. Lib., Belfast Bible Coll. [10009773] 11/06/2008 **ME**

Somerville, Mr J H B, BA MA MCLIP, Unemployed. [40051] 16/10/1986 **CM18/07/1990**

Somovilla, Miss C L, MA, Records & Inf. Mgr., Financial Ombudsman Serv., London. [56756] 08/10/1998 **ME**

Sonley, Mrs V, BA MCLIP, Sen. Asst. Subj. Lib., Teeside Univ., Tees Valley. [10014950] 16/10/1977 **CM18/09/1981**

Sooparlie, Mr A, LLB LEC, Unknown. [10007568] 21/05/2008 **ME**

Soprano Pellegrino, Mrs M, BA DipLib MCLIP, Unknown. [39886] 06/10/1986 **CM22/05/1991**

Sorby, Mrs B J, MCLIP MEd BA, Unwaged Area Lib. [10012780] 24/01/1964 **CM22/04/1985**

Sore, Mrs L A, BA DipLib MCLIP, Learning Resources for Ed., Northants. C.C. [28170] 17/10/1977 **CM29/10/1979**

Soto Rueda, Mr A, Unwaged. [10010316] 17/07/2008 **ME**

Soukup, Mrs D, ACLIP, Inf. Asst., Kings Coll. London. [59525] 25/04/2001 **ACL17/05/2009**

Souter, Ms L J, BA(Hons) MA, Inf. Offr., Nat. Yth. Agency, Leicester. [10012812] 16/10/1997 **ME**

South, Mrs A J, BSc DipLib, Young People's Serv. Lib., Herts. C.C., Watford & Three Rivers Dist. [42373] 24/10/1988 **ME**

South, Ms H L, BSc DipLib MCLIP, Faculty Lib., Univ. of Bath. [47594] 05/10/1992 **CM27/11/1996**

South, Mrs S, BA DipLib MCLIP, Head of L., Bradford Grammar Sch. [40796] 15/06/1987 **CM06/04/2005**

Southall, Mrs H V, BA MCLIP, Sch. Lib., The Red Maids Sch., Bristol. [32212] 25/01/1980 **CM27/01/1993**

Southern, Miss K, Lib., Herbert Smith, London. [10007886] 26/02/2008 **ME**

Southgate, Mrs D, DipHE BA MCLIP, Head of Inf. Servs., Chartered Inst. of Marketing, Maidenhead. [39247] 01/01/1986 **CM23/03/1993**

Southwell, Ms J, BA(Hons) Dip Lib MCLIP, Asst. Co. Lib., Oxfordshire L., Holton. [10014855] 03/11/1977 **CM26/10/1981**

Soutter, Mrs P, MCLIP, Life Member. [13778] 06/03/1957 **CM01/01/1961**

Sowerbutts, Mr D L, BA MCLIP, Retired. [13780] 14/01/1963 **CM01/01/1966**

Sowman, Ms S, BA MCLIP, Catr., Chartered Inst. of Personnel & Devel, London. [28573] 13/01/1978 **CM17/02/1983**

Sowood, Ms Y, ACLIP, Asst. Lib., Skelmersdale L. [10010716] 18/09/2008 **ACL17/06/2009**

Spacey, Dr R E, BA(Hons) MA PhD MCLIP, Self-employed Reseracher. [59230] 09/01/2001 **CM21/03/2007**

Spackman, Mrs K M, BLib MCLIP, Principal Lib. Inf. Serv., Oxon. C.C. Community Serv. [37187] 22/02/1984 **CM13/06/1989**

Spalding, Mr C A, MA(Hons), Stud., Strathclyde Univ. [10015227] 29/10/2009 **ME**

Spalding, Mrs C J, BA(Hons) MCLIP, Lib., Redland High Sch., Bristol. [28119] 04/10/1977 **CM20/09/1995**

Spalding, Mrs M A, BSc MCLIP, Unknown. [38224] 04/02/1985 **CM15/03/1989**

Spalding, Ms M P, BA(Hons) DipLib, Web Content Offr. (Asst. Lib.)., Dept. of Health., Skipton House., London [44409] 05/10/1990 **ME**

Spall, Miss J, Sch. L. Asst., Aith Jnr. Sch., Shetland. [64422] 16/03/2005 **AF**

Sparham, Mrs S E, BA(Hons) MCLIP, Lib., Sch. Lib. Serv., Northumberland [50148] 11/04/1994 **CM23/09/1998**

Sparkes, Mrs M, ACLIP, L. Mgr., Ixworth Middle Sch., Bury St. Edmunds. [10011233] 03/10/2008 **ACL07/08/2009**

Sparks, Miss H T, BA MCLIP, Retired [33162] 08/10/1980 **CM30/08/1985**

Sparks, Mrs J, BA DipLib MCLIP, Inf. Specialist, Cardiff Univ. [23305] 12/11/1974 **CM15/06/1981**

Sparks, Mr M D, BSc MSc DipLib MCLIP, Asst. Head (Compliance & Media Serv.), Univ. of Glamorgan, Pontypridd [23351] 11/11/1974 **CM07/12/1977**

Sparrow, Mr D A, MA MCLIP, L. & Inf. Cent. Mgr., Equality & Human Rights Comm., Manchester. [38924] 18/10/1985 **CM15/03/1989**

Sparrow, Mrs G M, BA MCLIP, Retired. [37939] 16/11/1984 **CM15/11/1988**

Sparrow, Mr K T, BA DipLib MCLIP, L. Asst., Sch. of Oriental & African Studies, Univ. of London. [34788] 16/02/1982 **CM13/12/1988**

Sparrowhawk, Mrs D, BA(Hons) DipLib, Stock & Reader Devel. Offr., Hartlepool Bor. L. [41607] 26/01/1988 **ME**

Speak, Ms M A, BA(Hons) MCLIP, Asst. Lib., Hull Univ., Scarborough Campus [27466] 19/04/1977 **CM17/11/1980**

Speake, Mrs A, BSc (Hons) MSc MCLIP, Programme Mgr. - Public Health and Social Care, NICE, Manchester. [61336] 29/05/2002 **CM29/03/2006**

Speake, Ms R A, BA(Hons) DipLIS MCLIP, Operational Mgr. Cent. Area., Coventry C.C. [49560] 12/11/1993 **CM19/05/1999**

Speakman, Mrs H C, MCLIP, Semi Retired. [25741] 22/03/1976 **CM30/10/1979**

Speare, Mrs C D, BA DipLib DHSA MCLIP, Subject Lib., Bradford Coll., W. Yorks. [41709] 19/02/1988 **CM31/01/1996**

Spears, Mr K G, OBE BSc MBA MCLIP, Lib., Wells Cathedral [13790] 08/05/1965 **CM01/01/1968**

Speed, Ms J L, BA MCLIP, Systems Lib., Cheshire Shared Serv. [38147] 23/01/1985 **CM16/11/1994**

Speedie, Ms C, MA(Hons), Admin. Asst., KSB, Stirling. [63550] 06/05/2004 **ME**

Speeding, Mrs T, BA(Hons), Inf. Mgr., Northumbria Univ., Newcastle. [50091] 14/03/1994 **ME**

Speight, Mr T D, MA(Oxon) MSc(Econ) MCLIP, L. Mgr., Berwin Leighton Paisner, London. [52497] 02/11/1995 **CM18/03/1998**

Speller, E A, BA(Hons), Lib., Trinity Coll. of Music, London. [63686] 24/08/2004 **ME**

Speller, Miss M J, Unknown. [10014004] 17/06/2009 **AF**

Spellman, Miss J F, BA MCLIP, Lib., Queen Elizabeth Sixth Form Coll., Darlington. [35032] 02/07/1982 **CM08/03/1988**

Spence, Mrs D A, BA(Hons) MSc PGDip, Healthcare Knowledge Specialist, Bupa Grp., London [64263] 22/02/2005 **ME**

Spence, Mrs G M, BA DipLib, L. Mgr., Sidmouth, Devon [44593] 01/11/1990 **ME**

Spence, Ms H P, BEd(Hons) MA MCLIP, Knowledge Mgr., Enfield P. C. T. [47578] 02/10/1992 **CM22/11/1995**

Spence, Mr I, BA DMS MCLIP, Consultant [30542] 17/01/1979 **CM10/11/1983**

Spence, Miss J B, MCLIP, Lib., Aloha Coll., Spain. [25424] 16/01/1976 **CM17/08/1978**

Spence, Mrs K, BA(Hons) MSc MCLIP, Lib., Geldards LLP, Cardiff. [54425] 09/12/1996 **CM06/04/2005**

Spence, Ms R, BA(Hons), Unknown. [10014281] 13/07/2009 **AF**

Spence, Mrs S A, BA(Hons) MCLIP, L. &Inf. Serv. Mgr., Swinton L. [29083] 06/03/1978 **CM01/07/1988**

Spencer, Mrs J, MBE BA MBA MCLIP, Head. of Serv., Bolton Libs., Bolton C.C. [28237] 03/10/1977 **CM09/07/1981**

Spencer, Ms K E, DipIS MA MCLIP, Site Lib., Univ. of Chester Wirral Campus. [50749] 17/10/1994 RV29/03/2007 **CM25/07/2001**

Spencer, Miss L A, BA DipLib MCLIP DMS MIMgt, Strategic Mgr., Kent Co. Council L. & Arch. [28174] 18/10/1977 **CM17/12/1980**

Spencer, Ms L O, MCLIP, Mgmt Consultant, Stafford. [16038] 19/02/1970 **CM29/07/1974**

Spencer, Mrs M M, MCLIP, Retired [26026] 04/10/1966 **CM31/12/1989**

Spencer, Ms T A, BA(Hons) MCLIP PGCE, NHS Lib. [41477] 07/01/1988 **CM23/03/1994**

Spendlove, Mrs L R, Lib. Mngr., Gisleham Middle Sch. Carlton Colville [10015539] 11/02/2000 **AF**

Spenser, Mrs E J, BA(Hons) MCLIP, Lib., Bridgnorth L., Shropshire. [52686] 21/11/1995 **CM25/07/2001**

Sperling, Mrs S V D, BA MA MCLIP, Consultant. [23063] 26/10/1974 **CM14/09/1979**

Sperring, Mr D, BSc, Asst. Lib. Wyggeston and Queen Elizabeth 1st Coll. [64964] 05/10/2005 **ME**

Spiby, Mr D R, MA FCLIP, Life Member. [17763] 11/07/1951 **FE01/01/1960**

Spiby, Mrs J N, MA DipLib MCLIP, Lib., Stuartholme Sch., Australia. [29462] 14/07/1978 **CM13/08/1981**

Spice, Mr C G, MBCS MCLIP CITP, Comp. Dev. Mgr., Ulster Univ., Co. Antrim. [60412] 25/03/1996 **CM25/03/1996**

Spicer, Mrs L, BLib MCLIP, Learning Resources Team Leader, Loughborough Coll. [22004] 16/01/1974 **CM28/11/1988**

Spickernell, Mrs M P, MCLIP, Retired. [16235] 05/02/1949 **CM01/01/1954**

Spiers, Mr D L, Adv. Dip. Ed MCLIP, LRC Co-ordinator, Craigroyston Comm. High Sch., Edinburgh. [23161] 07/11/1974 **CM17/11/1977**

Spillane, Ms S, Inf. Specialist/Administrator, Tipperary Inst., Ireland. [10016462] 26/03/2010 **AF**

Spiller, Miss D H, BA MCLIP, Sen. L. Asst., Univ. of Strathclyde Law L., Glasgow. [54675] 21/02/1997 **CM01/02/2006**

Spiller, Miss L, BA(Hons), Record Mgmnt. Asst., EBRD, London [10007883] 08/04/2004 **AF**

Spillman, Miss G A, BMus, Yth. Serv. Lib., Gateshead L. [62107] 19/02/2003 **ME**

Spina, Mrs R B, BA MA DipLib MCLIP, Hd. of Teaching & Res. Support, Sch. of Oriental & African Studies, Univ. of London [26424] 01/01/1976 **CM25/03/1985**

Spink, Mr H C, BA, Learning Res. Asst., Hugh Baird Coll., Bootle. [10006222] 26/09/2007 **ME**

Spink, Mr P J, BA MCLIP, Unknown. [21958] 22/01/1974 **CM22/09/1980**

Spink, Ms R E, MLS, Customer Serv. Bibl., YBP L. Servs. [10006255] 28/09/2007 **ME**

Spink, Mrs S, MSc BA MCLIP, Unwaged. [3746] 23/01/1968 **CM01/01/1973**

Spink, Mrs W T, BA MCLIP, Res. Offr. - Resources (Job Share), Age Concern and Help the Aged, London. [13829] 06/10/1971 **CM29/09/1980**

Spires-Lane, Mrs V M C, BSc(Hons) MCLIP, Med. Inf. Specialist, Inf. Inspires, Chalfont St. Peter. [24451] 05/07/1975 **CM01/11/1979**

Spittal, Mr C J, MCLIP, Life Member. [13831] 02/07/1945 **CM01/01/1948**

Splaine, Mrs J, MCLIP, Acting Arts Co-Ordinator, Manchester City Council, Manchester Cent. L. [55534] 20/10/1997 **CM08/08/2008**

Spokes, Mr N J, BA DipLib MCLIP, Community Lib., Ilford Cent. L. [10009362] 05/01/1979 **CM01/07/1993**

Spong, Miss A, BA, Grad. Trainee Lib., E. Surrey Coll., Surrey. [10015134] 14/10/2009 **ME**

Spong, Miss T M, PgDipIM, Comm. Mgr., Nat. Audit Off., London. [53166] 01/04/1996 **ME**

Spooner, Mrs D L, ACLIP, Sr. Lib. Asst., Thornton L., Lancs. [10013139] 02/04/2009 **ACL11/12/2009**

Spowage, Miss M, BA MA MCLIP, Inf. Researcher., Chartered Mgmnt. Inst., Corby, Northants [63111] 10/02/2004 **CM03/10/2007**

Spragg, Mr L R, MA, Asst. Lib., McDermott Will & Emery UK LLP, London. [58499] 14/03/2000 **ME**

Sprawling, Mrs J E, BA MCLIP, Sch. Lib., Bolton M.B.C., Turton Media Arts Coll. [35007] 15/06/1982 **CM21/08/1986**

Spreadbury, Ms H E, BSc(Hons) MA MCLIP, Unwaged. [54154] 07/11/1996 **CM29/03/2004**

Spreull, Mrs G S, ACLIP, Sch. Lib., Blackbourne Middle Sch., Bury St Edmunds. [10010827] 28/08/2008 **ACL23/09/2009**

Sprevak, Mrs M Y, BA DipLib MCLIP, Asst. Lib., Queens Univ. of Belfast. [13835] 05/10/1967 **CM01/01/1972**

Spriggs, Mrs K A, BA MCLIP, Stock Serv. Mgr., Cultural & Community Serv. Dept, Derbyshire C. C (job share) [11545] 08/09/1966 **CM01/01/1971**

Spring, Ms H C, BA(Hons) MCLIP, Sen. Lect./Clinical Lib., York St John Univ., York [52307] 25/10/1995 **CM16/05/2001**

Spring, Mr P N, MSc BA DipLib FCLIP, Metadata Lib., London Sch. of Economics L. [28175] 12/10/1977 **FE25/05/1994**

Springer, Mrs A, ACLIP, Lib., Balcarras Sch., Cheltenham. [65289] 28/11/2005 **ACL01/10/2008**

Springer, Mrs J M, BA DipLib MCLIP, Acquisitions/Periodicals L., Univ. of Southampton. [27914] 12/10/1977 **CM30/04/1981**

Springer, Mrs J, BA(Hons) MA, Career Break. [56232] 14/04/1998 **ME**

Springham, Miss S A, BLib MCLIP, Dep. H. of L. Serv., Brighton & Sussex Univ. Hosp., NHS Trust, E. Sussex. [41603] 26/01/1988 **CM29/01/1992**

Sproat, Miss A E, BA(Hons) MA DipLib MCLIP, Lib., Henry Moore Inst., Leeds. [47995] 30/10/1992 **CM18/03/1998**

Sproston, Mr G F, BA MCLIP, Retired. [13839] 14/02/1967
CM01/01/1970

Sproston, Miss S V, BA(Hons) MCLIP, Learning Resources Mgr., W. Notts. Coll., Mansfield [46469] 08/11/1991 **CM03/10/2007**

Spruce, Mrs W J, BA MCLIP, Retired. [13842] 28/01/1957
CM01/01/1961

Spry-Leverton, Capt H H S, Lib., Uppingham Sch. [37326] 01/07/1984 **ME**

Spurgin, Miss C B, MA(Hons), Sch. Lib., Kilgraston Sch., Bridge of Earn, Perth. [52050] 02/10/1995 **ME**

Squire, Mrs S C, BA MA, L. & Inf. Mgr., St Crispin's Sch., Berkshire [59795] 03/10/2001 **ME**

Squirrell, Ms A, BA(Hons) PGCE MSc, Learning Resource Mgr. [61262] 10/05/2002 **ME**

St Aubyn, Miss P, MSc Econ MCLIP, Lib., SPSA Scottish Police Coll., Kincardine, Fife. [29832] 02/10/1978 **CM22/10/1982**

St John, Ms S A, BA MA MCLIP, relief L. asst., Cambridgeshire C.C. [44941] 23/01/1991 **CM23/03/1994**

St. Cyr, Mrs D, Unknown. [10014052] 23/06/2009 **ME**

St. John-Coleman, Mrs M A, BSc MCLIP, Retired. [14285] 14/10/1971
CM11/10/1973

Stables, Mrs L, BA(Hons), Sen. Inf. Lib., Barnsley L., Cent. L. [10013613] 15/05/2009 **ME**

Stacey, Ms A, BA DipLib MCLIP, Business Analyst, Talis Inf. Ltd., Birmingham. [38129] 21/01/1985 **CM06/10/1987**

Stacey, Mr D J, BA(Hons) MA MCLIP, Subject Lib., Univ. of Bath. [64803] 15/07/2005 **CM17/09/2008**

Stacey, Miss K D, DipLIS, Sen. Lib. Asst., Inst. of Educ., Univ. of London. [41540] 19/01/1988 **ME**

Stacey, Mrs M C, BA MCLIP, Retired [13854] 02/10/1964 **CM01/01/1967**

Stacey, Mr M J, MA MCLIP, Lib., Business L., Nottingham City L. [13855] 22/04/1964 **CM01/01/1967**

Stacey, Mr R W, FCLIP, Life Member. [17771] 12/02/1952 **FE01/01/1959**

Stack, Mrs A, MCLIP, p. /t. Child. Lib., N. Finchley L., L.B. of Barnet. [5645] 01/01/1971 **CM18/12/1973**

Stack, Mrs G A, Sch. Lib., Northgate High Sch., Dereham, Norfolk. [65992] 11/07/2006 **ME**

Stack, Ms J, BA(Hons) Lit, L. Mgr., St John Fisher Sch., Peterborough. [10006521] 31/10/2007 **ME**

Stadler, Mrs D E, MCLIP, Life Member. [10007087] 16/03/1941
CM01/01/1947

Staffer, Mrs H B, BA(Hons) MA MCLIP, Head Assembley Goverment L., Welsh Assembly Govt., Cardiff. [41343] 06/11/1987 **CM18/11/1998**

Stafford, Mr C J, MCLIP, Retired. [13858] 04/11/1965 **CM01/01/1970**

Stafford, Mr G A, MA ALAA FCLIP, Life Member. [17772] 10/03/1953
FE01/01/1960

Stafford, Mrs J C, BA MCLIP, Sen. Mgr., Serving Communities Delivery Team N. Tyneside Bor. Council. [29348] 09/06/1978 **CM08/08/1980**

Stagg, Ms E J, L. Arch. & Info Serv. Sector Mgr., Lifelong Learning UK. [10011893] 26/11/2008 **ME**

Staines, Mrs E, Lib. Super., Bradford on Avon. [10012325] 27/01/2009 **AF**

Stainthorp, Mr J C, BSc (Hons) MSc Dip Info Sci, Mngr., Lib. & Inf. Serv., AWE, Aldermaston [10011056] 16/10/1989 **ME**

Stairmand-Jackson, Mrs A C, BSc(Hons) DipLib, Asst. Liaison Lib., Mary Seacole L., Birmingham City Univ. [10013724] 22/05/2009 **ME**

Stallard, Ms V M, BMus(Hons) MA MCLIP, Asst. Lib., Cardiff Univ. Cardiff [59082] 09/11/2000 **CM04/02/2004**

Stamford, Mrs S A, BA(Hons) MA, Lib., Selwyn Coll., Cambridge. [53214] 02/04/1996 **ME**

Stamp, Mr A D, MCLIP, Local Studies Lib., Wolverhampton City Council, Arch. & Loc. Studies. [25426] 08/01/1976 **CM22/12/1979**

Stanbury, Mrs F E D, MCLIP, Unwaged. [10780] 29/09/1970
CM03/01/1975

Stanbury, Mrs K S, MSc MCLIP JP, Asst.-In-Charge., S. molton L., Devon Co. Council L., Exeter [62421] 16/06/2003 **CM08/08/2008**

Stanbury, Mrs S C, BA MA MCLIP, Lib. [35088] 26/07/1982
CM13/09/1984

Stancombe, Mrs S, BA MCLIP, Sch. Lib. La Sante Union Secondary Sch., Highgate Road, London. [35928] 14/02/1983 **CM25/10/1984**

Standen, Mrs A J, BA(Hons), Sen. Lib., Moira House Girls Sch., Eastbourne. [63187] 03/03/2004 **ME**

Standen, Miss K L, BA, Unknown. [10011998] 09/12/2008 **ME**

Standen, Miss P M, MCLIP, Educ. Liaison Offr., E. Ayrshire Council. [22611] 01/07/1974 **CM07/02/1979**

Standfield, Mr S P, BSc, Cent. L. Mgr., Plymouth [10008551] 02/04/2008 **ME**

Standring, Miss M, BA(Hons), Unknown. [10014286] 14/07/2009 **ME**

Stanfield, Ms K B, BSc MCLIP, Head of Knowledge Mgmnt., CMS Cameron McKenna, London. [38646] 26/08/1985 **CM16/02/1988**

Stanford, Mrs A M, BA DipLib MCLIP, Head of Bibliographical Ser., Birmingham L. [33628] 26/01/1981 **CM10/11/1987**

Stanforth, Miss J M, MCLIP, Area Young People's Mgr., N. Area, Lancs C.C. [20302] 05/02/1973 **CM01/01/1977**

Staniforth, Mrs S C, BA MCLIP, Mgr., L. Serv. for Educ., Glos. C.C. [27431] 02/04/1977 **CM09/10/1980**

Stanistreet, Mrs J E, MA MCLIP, Retired. [13885] 25/11/1968
CM01/01/1972

Stanley, Mr A, BA, Stud., Univ. of Strathclyde. [10000461] 05/10/2006 **ME**

Stanley, Mrs S A, MCLIP, Consultant, Todays Off., Bishops Stortford, Herts. [10031] 14/10/1970 **CM29/05/1975**

Stanley, Ms T S, BA(Hons) MSc, Asst. Dir., UKCRN [50481] 18/08/1994 **ME**

Stanley, Mrs W, BA DipEd, Sch. Lib., Marlborough Sch., St. Albans. [43237] 13/10/1989 **ME**

Stannard, Mrs P, BA(Hons) MCLIP, Unwaged [54510] 09/01/1997
CM15/10/2002

Stannard, Miss T D, BA MA, Lib., Wiltshire Council. [10006543] 30/10/2007 **ME**

Stansbury, Ms C T, BLib MCLIP, Sec. [38554] 01/07/1985
CM21/12/1988

Stansfield, Mrs C A, BA MCLIP, Indexer, Self Employed. [31244] 11/10/1979 **CM17/10/1985**

Stansfield, Mrs E F, BA MCLIP, Inf. Specialist, GCHQ, Cheltenham. [32282] 25/02/1980 **CM19/01/1984**

Stanton, Mrs J R, MCLIP, Housewife, [20552] 04/04/1973
CM06/09/1978

Stanton, Mrs K A, BA DipLib, Chef Inf. Offr., & Coll. Lib., King's Coll. London [37091] 07/02/1984 **ME**

Stanton, Mr T M, BA(Hons) MA MCLIP, Inf. Lib., W. Sussex L. Serv., Crawley L. [55268] 11/09/1997 **CM15/01/2003**

Stanton, Mrs W J, BA MCLIP, Med. Lib., Univ. of Nottingham, Queens Med. Cent., Notts. [23718] 01/01/1975 **CM29/01/1979**

Staples, Mr F D, MCLIP, Retired. [13900] 09/02/1954 **CM01/01/1958**

Staples, Mrs K J, BMus MSc MCLIP, Subj. Lib., Health & Social Care, Oxford Brookes Univ. Lib., Oxford [58162] 10/11/1999 **CM19/11/2003**

Staples, Mrs L M, MCLIP, Life Member. [13902] 26/09/1949
CM01/01/1961

Starbuck, Mrs F A, BA DipLib MCLIP, Sen. Inf. Offr., Leeds Met. Univ. L., Leeds. [40447] 31/01/1987 **CM30/01/1991**

Starbuck, Mrs S R, LLB DipLib MA MCLIP, Inf. Offr., Faculty of Arts & Human Sciences., Univ. of Surrey [39912] 01/10/1986 **CM01/07/1991**

Stark, Miss C A, MA, Unknown. [10012078] 27/10/1982 **ME**

Stark, Miss K L, BA(Hons) MA MCLIP, Lib., Burton Coll., Staffs. [59974] 14/11/2001 **CM09/11/2005**

Stark, Mrs L A, BA DipLib MCLIP, Br. Lib., Harrow Pub. L., Middlesex. [25518] 21/01/1976 **CM07/09/1979**

Stark, Mrs N C, BA DipLib MCLIP, Inf. Mgr., Shropshire Council. [41421] 09/12/1987 **CM14/11/1990**

Starkey, Miss G M, BA MCLIP, Team Leader: Operations, Northumberland Co. L., Morpeth. [26565] 01/10/1976 **CM05/02/1981**

Starling, Miss L, BA(Hons), Team Lib., Inf. & Enquiry Cent., Taunton L. [56483] 21/07/1998 **ME**

Starr, Mr S R, Driver/Asst., Sch. L. Serv., Hants. C.C. [62388] 21/05/2003 **ME**

Statham, Mr M H W, MA FCLIP, Life Member. [13912] 01/01/1953 **FE01/01/1959**

Statham, Mr M S, BA(Hons) MA MCLIP, Coll. Lib., Gonville & Caius Coll., Cambridge. [49164] 08/10/1993 **CM27/11/1996**

Stauch, Mrs J P, BA MCLIP, P. /T. Coordinator ILS NVQ Cent. Richmond-Upon-Thames Coll. [13914] 01/01/1972 **CM14/05/1975**

Staunton, Ms M T, BA DipLib MCLIP, Dist. Lib., Watford. [39605] 01/04/1986 **CM15/05/1989**

Stead, Mrs C E, BA(Hons) MA MCLIP, Sheffield Univ., Sheffield [59672] 25/07/2001 **CM15/10/2002**

Stead, M, BA(Hons) MA, Transformation Offr., Wigan Lib. [59776] 02/10/2001 **ME**

Stead, Ms M, BA(Hons) DipLIS, Unknown. [50624] 01/10/1994 **ME**

Stearn, Mrs C G, BA, Lib., Dewsbury L., Kirklees M. C. [40613] 03/04/1987 **ME**

Stearn, Mr R R, BA MCLIP, Child. Serv. Lib. -Special Serv., Wheatsheaf L., Rochdale M.B.C. [30878] 22/05/1979 **CM13/07/1981**

Stebbing, Ms D J, BLib MCLIP, Subject Lib., Anglia Ruskin Univ., Chelmsford. [26137] 01/07/1976 **CM20/09/1979**

Stebbings, Mrs A C, BA MLib MCLIP, Sen. Lib., L.B. of Barnet. [45445] 06/02/1991 **CM16/12/1992**

Stedman, Mr R, FCLIP, Life Member, [13923] 05/02/1956 **FE01/01/1971**

Steel, Mrs C J, Asst. Lib., English Heritage L., Wilts. [10016023] 10/02/2010 **AF**

Steel, Miss L, BA, Stud. Univ of Sheffield [10010831] 28/08/2008 **ME**

Steel, Mrs M, MCLIP, Team Lib., Norfolk Sch. L. Serv., Norwich. [10015966] 02/10/1973 **CM01/08/1977**

Steele, Mr C R, MA FALIA FCLIP, Retired. [13925] 14/01/1966 **FE22/07/1998**

Steele, Mr G, BA(Hons) MA, Electronic Serv. & Systems Lib., Cent. for Anthropology, the Brit. Mus. [66158] 04/10/2006 **ME**

Steele, Mr H F, BA FCLIP, Life Member. [17777] 21/10/1944 **FE01/01/1951**

Steele, Ms M E, BA MCLIP, Sch. Serv. Lib., L.B. of Harrow. [21074] 03/10/1973 **CM22/12/1976**

Steele, Mr P R, BSc Dipl Inf Sci MCLIP, Dir. Current Awareness, Thomson Sci. London. [10007261] 16/04/1974 **CM16/04/1974**

Steele, Miss R E, BA MA, Unknown. [10006613] 11/09/2007 **ME**

Steele-Morgan, Miss S, B Ed DipLib MCLIP, Sen. Asst. Lib., Neath Port Talbot Co. Bor., Port Talbot. [36491] 17/10/1983 **CM19/01/1988**

Steemson, Mr M J, Princ., The Caldeson Consultancy, Wellington, New Zealand. [60100] 21/07/1998 **ME**

Steer, Miss C M, BA MCLIP, Life Member. [13932] 07/01/1952 **CM01/01/1955**

Steer, Mrs M J, BA(Hons) DipLIS MCLIP, Subject Lib., Univ. of Bristol, Bristol. [46498] 12/11/1991 **CM16/11/1994**

Steer, Mrs R A, BA(Hons) MBA Dip, Unknown. [10014981] 01/10/2009 **ME**

Steere, Mrs A M, BA(Hons) MCLIP, L. Offr., Hants. C.C., Winchester [26625] 27/10/1976 **CM01/10/1979**

Stein, Mrs H, BA(Hons), Stud. [10006256] 26/09/2007 **ME**

Stein, Mr J, BSc DipLib MSc, Sen. Inf. Specialist, Cent. Sci. Lab., York. [46726] 02/01/1992 **ME**

Stein, Mrs L, BA(Hons) PgDipLS MCLIP, Sch. Lib., Alness Academy, Ross-Shire. [65166] 01/11/2005 **CM11/03/2009**

Steinhaus, Mrs E R, BA DipLib MCLIP, p. /t. Sch. Lib., Menorah Primary Sch., London. [28055] 06/10/1977 **CM14/01/1980**

Steinke, Mrs E, MA, Stud., London Met. Univ. [10013859] 04/06/2009 **ME**

Stekis, Miss S J, MCLIP, Life Member. [17781] 22/02/1954 **CM01/01/1958**

Stelling, Mrs C R, BA MCLIP, Serv. Dev. Lib., Hampshire L. Serv., Hants C.C. [28364] 04/11/1977 **CM26/08/1981**

Stelling, Mr D E, BA MCLIP, L. Offr., Basingstoke L. [25427] 06/01/1976 **CM02/08/1978**

Stemp, Miss A J, BA, Unwaged [27467] 04/04/1977 **ME**

Stemp, Ms J, BA(Hons) PgDipILM MCLIP, Lib., Trust L., Clinical Skills, Queen Elizabeth Hosp., Gateshead. [51753] 21/06/1995 **CM19/03/2008**

Stemp, Miss L M, Legal Advisers Br. Lib., Home Off., London. [52388] 26/10/1995 **ME**

Stennett, Ms R E, MA DipInf, Bibl. Serv. Asst. Lib., Canterbury Christ Church Univ. [47600] 05/10/1992 **ME**

Stenning, Mr C M, BA DipLib MCLIP, Web Serv. Mgr., Bracknell Forest Council. [36590] 16/10/1983 **CM06/10/1987**

Stepan, Mrs S M, BA, Content Creation Offr., Leeds City Council. [41738] 28/02/1988 **ME**

Stephan, Ms K, BS(Hist.) MA MCLIP, Community Lib., Norfolk Co. Council, Norwich. [65754] 04/05/2006 **CM03/10/2007**

Stephen, Miss A E, B ED MCLIP, Child. Servs. Lib., Aberdeen City L. [25114] 17/10/1975 **CM17/11/1978**

Stephen, Ms H E, MSc MCLIP, Sunday Super. & PACE Sub. Lib., Goldsmiths Univ., London. [44030] 03/04/1990 **CM25/07/2001**

Stephen, Ms M E, BA(Hons), Res. Mgr., Hlth. Promotion L. (CRIS), Belfast. [64618] 27/04/2005 **AF**

Stephen, Mrs R A R, MA DipLib MCLIP, Systems & Support Lib.,The Moray Council [36357] 01/10/1983 **CM14/02/1990**

Stephens, Mrs A J, MCLIP, Lib., Thomas Knyvett Coll., Middx. [13948] 25/02/1965 **CM01/01/1970**

Stephens, Mr A R C, BSc, Board Sec., Brit. L., London [10007773] 20/11/1977 **ME**

Stephens, Ms D, BSc (Hons), Unknown. [10012743] 01/06/2010 **ME**

Stephens, Mrs E R, BScEcon MCLIP, User Serv. Super., Univ. of London. [62435] 25/06/2003 **CM17/09/2008**

Stephens, Ms K A, BA(Hons) MA, Unwaged. [10001108] 12/01/2007 **ME**

Stephens, Mrs K D, B. Ed (Hons), L. Asst., Hatfield L., Herts. [10015954] 03/02/2010 **AF**

Stephens, Mrs L B, Resource Lib., Telford Learning Cent., Telford. [48438] 08/01/1993 **ME**

Stephens, Mr P A, BA(Hons) MA, Unknown. [10012475] 10/02/2009 **ME**

Stephens, Miss S V, BA, Lib., Bird & Bird LLP, London. [37404] 20/08/1984 **ME**

Stephenson, Ms A, MCLIP, Child. Serv. & Reader Devel. Mgr., N. Tyneside L. & Mus., Wallsend L. [53299] 26/04/1996 **CM21/11/2007**

Stephenson, Mrs D, Career Break [62682] 02/10/2003 **ME**

Stephenson, Mrs J T, BA(Hons) MCLIP, Inf. & Comm. Devel. Mgr., Durham C.C., Culture & Leisure. [51346] 25/01/1995 **CM23/07/1997**

Stephenson, Mrs J, BLib MCLIP, Head of Health Serv. L., Univ. of Southampton, Southampton. [29769] 09/10/1978 **CM30/06/1983**

Stephenson, Mrs M A, ACLIP, L. Asst., Oakmere L., Potters Bar. [10013739] 27/05/2009 **ACL16/06/2010**

Sterling, Mrs L J, BA MCLIP, Bibl. Serv. Mgr., Met. Boro. of Wirral, Cent. L. [4321] 05/03/1969 **CM09/09/1974**

Steven, Mrs E J, BEng, Unwaged. [61609] 03/10/2002 **ME**

Stevens, Mrs A E, BA MCLIP, Cent. L. Mgr., Blackpool Cent. L., Blackpool Bor. Council. [38544] 25/06/1985 **CM15/08/1990**

Stevens, Ms A H, BA MCLIP, Sch. Lib. Serv., Hants C.C. [34125] 26/09/1981 **CM21/12/1984**

Stevens, Mr A J, BA MCLIP, Asst. Dir., Learning & Culture, Slough Bor. C. [36565] 04/10/1983 **CM19/01/1988**

Stevens, Ms A J, BA MCLIP, Resources Team Leader. [35771] 19/01/1983 **CM15/02/1989**

Stevens, Dr B E S, BA PhD MCLIP, Retired. [13980] 01/04/1957 **CM01/01/1963**

Stevens, Miss C, BSc (Hons), Asst. Lib., The Coll. of St. Mark & St. John, Plymouth [10001778] 06/07/2004 **ME**

Stevens, Mrs D L, BLib MCLIP, Team Lib. Stock and Community, Somerset Cultural Serv. [36948] 18/01/1984 **CM04/08/1987**

Stevens, Miss E A, MCLIP, Inf. Res. Exec., Bristol-Myers Squibb Pharmaceutical, Uxbridge. [43014] 12/06/1989 **CM01/04/2002**

Stevens, Miss E, BA(Hons) PGCE MCLIP, Lib., P.L., Herefordshire. [56445] 10/07/1998 **RV02/03/2010** **CM29/03/2004**

Stevens, Mrs H, Casual Customer Serv. Lib., Vancouver Island Reg. L., Canada [10017091] 13/10/1988 **CM27/05/1992**

Stevens, Ms I F, BA MCLIP, L. Mgr., Cornwall C.C. [30682] 24/01/1979 **CM21/11/1983**

Stevens, Mr J F, BA MCLIP, Lib. -Stock Serv., Warwickshire L., Warwick. [26567] 07/10/1976 **CM17/01/1980**

Stevens, Mrs J L, BSc(Hons) MCLIP, Unwaged [47137] 06/05/1992 **CM19/03/1997**

Stevens, Mrs J, L. Systems Admin., W. Berks. Council Ls., Cultural Serv., Newbury [58292] 15/12/1999 **AF**

Stevens, Ms J, BA MCLIP, Mob. & Home L. Serv. Lib., Solihull M.B.C. [32184] 13/02/1980 **CM05/08/1983**

Stevens, Mrs J, BA(Hons) MCLIP, Site Lib., Manchester L. & Inf. Serv., Jobshare [49686] 25/11/1993 **CM09/11/2005**

Stevens, Miss K E, BA(Hons), Child. Lib., Northcote L. L.B. of Wandsworth [44228] 18/07/1990 **ME**

Stevens, Miss L A, Site Lib., Shrewsbury & Telford Hosp. NHS Trust – Princess Royal Hosp., Telford. [58383] 24/01/2000 **ME**

Stevens, Mrs M E, MCLIP, L. IT Mgr., Cent. L., Swindon Bor. Council. [4686] 30/10/1969 **CM10/09/1973**

Stevens, Miss P M, MCLIP, Retired. [13991] 04/09/1964 **CM01/01/1971**

Stevens, Miss S C, L. Asst., Sutton Cent. L. [10015908] 01/02/2010 **AF**

Stevens, Miss S R, MCLIP, Knowledge Servs. Project Mgr., NHS Westmidlands, Birmingham. [62669] 02/10/2003 **CM28/01/2009**

Stevens, Miss W D, FCLIP, Retired. [13996] 29/09/1944 **FE01/01/1957**

Stevenson, Mr B G, BA DMS MCLIP, Retired. [14001] 02/04/1966 **CM01/01/1971**

Stevenson, Mrs C A, BA(Hons), Stud., Univ. Teesside. [10016181] 05/03/2010 **ME**

Stevenson, Mr C C, MCLIP, Retired. [14004] 01/01/1958 **CM01/01/1965**

Stevenson, Mr D J, BA MCLIP, Sen. Area Lib. (W.), Midlothian Dist. L., Bonnyrigg L. [30546] 09/02/1979 **CM08/07/1982**

Stevenson, Mrs E J, BA MCLIP LLB, Lib., Edinburgh Univ. L., Law & Europa L. [32185] 11/01/1980 **CM27/07/1983**

Stevenson, Miss E P, BSc MCLIP, Unknown. [35105] 03/09/1982 **CM10/05/1988**

Stevenson, Miss F M J, BA MCLIP, Sch. Lib., Bannerman High Sch., Baillieston. [23693] 13/01/1975 **CM02/07/1979**

Stevenson, Ms H A, BLib MCLIP, Asst. Lib., Lancing Coll. [21925] 01/02/1974 **CM18/12/1978**

Stevenson, Mrs K L, MA, Stud., Nothumbria Univ. [10015541] 11/12/2009 **ME**

Stevenson, Ms K, Unemployed. [57559] 04/05/1999 **ME**

Stevenson, Mr M A, BA MCLIP, Life Member. [14009] 09/09/1957 **CM01/01/1961**

Stevenson, Mr M A, Unknown. [10016898] 01/06/2010 **AF**

Stevenson, Dr M B, BSc PhD MA, Retired. [45871] 01/07/1991 **ME**

Stevenson, Mrs P, BA(Hons) MCLIP RLIANZA, Learning Resources Mgr., Rangitoto Coll., New Zealand. [55569] 21/10/1997 **CM15/05/2002**

Stevenson, Mrs S V, BA MCLIP, Asst. Faculty. Lib., Univ. of Portsmouth [26641] 26/10/1976 **CM30/01/1979**

Stevenson, Ms V E, BA(Hons), Academic Serv. Mgr., Liverpool John Moores Univ. [33165] 14/10/1980 **ME**

Steventon, Ms L A, BA(Hons), Sch. Libr., Wolverhampton Girls High Sch. [63659] 09/08/2004 **ME**

Steward, Mr R D, BA DAA MCLIP, Retired. [14015] 16/10/1965 **CM29/04/1974**

Steward, Ms Y F, BA(Hons) MSc MCLIP, Lib., Merchant Taylor's Sch., Northwood. [43013] 12/06/1989 **CM02/02/2005**

Steward-Conn, Ms A K, Lib. Asst., Sheringham high Sch., Sheringham [10015555] 14/12/2009 **ME**

Stewart, Mrs A, BSc, L. Super., Reaseheath Coll., Cheshire. [10013182] 31/03/2009 **AF**

Stewart, Ms C H, BA(Hons) MA MCLIP, Systems Lib., NHS Greater Glasgow & Clyde [53833] 03/10/1996 **RV29/03/2007 CM17/03/1999**

Stewart, Miss C L, BSc, Stud., Aberystwyth Univ. [10011309] 13/10/2008 **ME**

Stewart, Mrs C, ACLIP, Lib. Super., Pollok L., Glasgow. [10015107] 13/10/2009 **ACL16/06/2010**

Stewart, Mr D C, BA DipLib MCLIP, Dir. of Health L. N. W., NHS Reg. [33528] 14/01/1981 **CM01/04/1986**

Stewart, Miss H M, MA DipLib, F/T, Ayr Academy, Ayrshire. [10001956] 03/11/1992 **ME**

Stewart, Miss H R, BSc(Hons) MSc MCLIP, Liason Lib., Univ. Edinburgh L. [54418] 05/12/1996 **CM12/03/2003**

Stewart, Mrs J A, BLib MLib MCLIP, Faculty Lib., Univ. of W. England, Frenchay Bolland L. [23770] 04/02/1975 **CM26/09/1977**

Stewart, Mrs J A, BA MCLIP, Serv. Devel. Lib., Fife Council [39419] 19/01/1986 **CM18/09/1991**

Stewart, Ms J E D, BLib MA MCLIP, Learning Res. Cent. Mgr., Yale Coll. of Wrexham. [42997] 31/05/1989 **CM19/11/2003**

Stewart, Mr J M, BA(Hons) DipIS, Asst. Lib., Min. of Justice, London. [46317] 24/10/1991 **ME**

Stewart, Ms L A, MCLIP, Customer Serv. Dir., Axiell, Nottingham. [23146] 04/11/1974 **CM28/06/1979**

Stewart, Miss M A, MA, Sub Lib., Univ. of the W. of Scotland., Ayr Campus [44238] 23/07/1990 **ME**

Stewart, Mrs M C, BA AKC MCLIP, Lib., Rydens Sch., Surrey [24715] 03/10/1975 **CM03/10/1977**

Stewart, Miss M J, BA MCLIP, Sch. Lib., Gourock High Sch., Strathclyde Reg. [28686] 27/11/1977 **CM30/04/1982**

Stewart, Mrs M, BSc(Hons)Econ MCLIP, Subject Lib., Exeter Coll. [49195] 11/10/1993 **CM01/06/2005**

Stewart, Miss O J, MA DipLib, unwaged. [10013639] 25/10/1984 **ME**

Stewart, Mrs O, MCLIP, Life Member. [14036] 22/02/1962 **CM01/01/1968**

Stewart, Dr R M, BA MCLIP, Comm. Lib., Wishaw L., N. Lanarks. [31160] 28/08/1979 **CM22/11/1995**

Stewart, Dr S M, MA(Hons) PhD MCLIP, Lib., Broxburn Academy, W. Lothian. [60866] 13/12/2001 **CM15/09/2004**

Stewart, Mr W J, BA(Hons) MA, (P/T) Essex Co. L. Serv. [56353] 08/06/1998 **ME**

Stewart-Macdonald, Dr R H, Dip ABRSM LRSM MA MPHIL PhD, Stud. [10013656] 15/05/2009 **ME**

Stidworthy, Mrs S E, BA MCLIP, Retired. [60651] 27/05/1969 **CM01/04/1984**

Stiemens, Ms V M, BA DipLib MSc MCLIP, Lib., Policy Studies Inst., London. [32228] 15/02/1980 **CM10/05/1988**

Stiles, Mr D E, MCLIP, Retired. [17790] 19/10/1942 **CM01/01/1949**

Still, Miss B M, FCLIP, Retired. [14049] 15/01/1941 **FE01/01/1956**

Still, Mr J G, MA FCLIP, Life Member. [14050] 16/10/1947 **FE01/01/1965**

Stillone, Ms P, BA(Hons) DipInfSc, Sen. Lib. . Asst., Univ. Coll. London. [52987] 13/02/1996 **ME**

Stimpson, Mrs F H, BA MA DipLib MCLIP, Freelance Lib/Researcher. [24730] 10/10/1975 **CM12/09/1977**

Stirland, Mrs J, Sen. L. Mgr., Derbyshire C.C. [10016095] 16/02/2010 **ME**

Stirling, Miss C S, BA(Hons) PgDip, Sen. L. Asst., Edinburgh Univ. Main L. [59292] 31/01/2001 **ME**

Stirling, Ms I E, BA MCLIP FHEA, Inf. Serv. Lib., Strathclyde Univ., Faculty of Educ., Glasgow. [19554] 20/11/1972 **CM29/12/1978**

Stirrat, Mrs E G, Stud., Aberystwyth Univ. [10013945] 18/06/2009 **ME**

Stirrup, Mrs A C, MCLIP, Employment not known. [14054] 23/03/1966 **CM01/01/1972**

Stirrup, Ms A J, BA(Hons) MCLIP, Ops. Mgr., Richmond upon Thames Lib. [34952] 14/05/1982 **CM14/12/1984**

Stirton, Mrs B J, BA MCLIP, Full Time Mother [10000556] 24/01/1986 **CM22/03/1993**

Stitson, Miss C A, BA DipLib MCLIP, Principal Lib., Child. & Young People, Oxfordshire L. [38891] 15/10/1985 **CM27/05/1992**

Stitt, Ms D E, BA, Sr. Researcher, Lovells LLP, London. [61117] 21/02/2002 **ME**

Stock, Ms E J, Sch. L. Serv. Co-ordinator, Salford City Council, Salford. [47567] 02/10/1992 **ME**

Stock, Ms E R, Liaison Lib., Univ. of Sheffield. [65071] 24/10/2005 **ME**

Stock, Miss K M, BA(Hons) MSc(Econ), Policy Support Lib., Welsh Assembly Govt., Cardiff. [51156] 23/11/1994 **ME**

Stock, Mr N M, Dip. Lib. MCLIP, Asst. Lib., Min. of Justice., London [40005] 09/10/1986 **CM16/10/1989**

Stockbridge Bland, Mrs S C, BA MA MCLIP, Stock Serv, Mgr., LB of Lambeth, Carnegie L. [14063] 01/01/1970 **CM28/09/1973**

Stockbridge, Mrs H D, MCLIP, Unknown. [20130] 23/01/1973 **CM01/09/1976**

Stockdale, Miss J H, MCLIP, Customer Serv. Offr., Kirklees Council., Huddersfield [14064] 24/01/1969 **CM24/09/1973**

Stockden, Mr D, L. R. C Coordinator, Lawnswood Sch., Leeds. [14065] 15/12/2004 **ME**

Stocken, Mrs J M, BA(Hons) MBA MCLIP, Head of Res. and Inf., WhiteHead Mann LLP, London. [21823] 07/02/1974 **CM05/07/1979**

Stocker, Mrs F M, BA DipLib MCLIP, Principal, Kestel Info. Servs. [31185] 03/10/1979 **CM09/09/1982**

Stockley, Ms L J, BA(Hons) MA, Sen. Lib., Inst. Elect. Engineers, London. [53854] 07/10/1996 **ME**

Stocks, Miss M Y, MCLIP CertEd, Life Member. [14071] 17/03/1941 **CM01/01/1946**

Stocks, Mr P J, Stud., Univ. of the W. of England. [10014589] 18/08/2009 **ME**

Stocks, Miss R, PgDip, Assit lib., City of London Sch., London [10004948] 06/06/2007 **ME**

Stockton, Earl Hon. Vice President. [46051] 11/09/1991 **ME**

Stockwell, Mrs A P, MCLIP, Sch. Lib., St. Augustines Catholic High Sch., Redditch. [32742] 01/08/1980 **CM02/08/1982**

Stockwell, Mrs C A, BA MCLIP, Gap Year. [37556] 07/10/1984 **CM18/07/1991**

Stoddard, Mrs K, BA(Hons) MSc, Researcher, Guardian News & Media, London. [10016626] 01/05/2010 **ME**

Stoddart, Miss A, BA DipLib MCLIP, Employment not known. [36564] 21/10/1983 **CM10/11/1987**

Stoffel, Ms C, ACLIP, Unknown. [10009308] 01/06/2008 **ACL03/12/2008**

Stoker, Mrs A H, BA MCLIP, Unwaged [18325] 07/10/1972 **CM20/07/1976**

Stokes, Mr D, BA DLIS MSc(ECON), Liaison Lib., Univ. Coll. Dublin, ROI. [65842] 01/06/2006 **ME**

Stokes, Mrs G B, MCLIP, Lib., Nottingham C.C., Cent. L. [23780] 27/01/1975 **CM01/10/1978**

Stokes, Mrs K, BA(Hons) MSc MCLIP, Business Inf. Specialist, Cranfield Sch. of Mgmnt., Cranfield Univ., Bedfordshire. [55792] 24/11/1997 **CM12/03/2003**

Stokes, Mrs L R, FCLIP, Life Member. [17793] 12/04/1937 **FE01/01/1951**

Stone, Mrs A F, MCLIP, Unemployed. [19575] 14/11/1972 **CM08/07/1976**

Stone, Mrs A L, BA, Stud. [10006262] 26/09/2007 **ME**

Stone, Mr G, BSc DipILS MCLIP, Electronic Resources Mgr., Univ. of Huddersfield [49528] 10/11/1993 **CM31/01/1996**

Stone, Ms G, BA MLS, L. S. A., Western Primary Sch., Winchester. [38652] 02/09/1985 **ME**

Stone, Mr H L, BA MCLIP, Learning Cent. Co-ordinator, E. Berkshire Coll., Berkshire. [37594] 03/10/1984 **CM19/07/2000**

Stone, Mrs L R, FCLIP, Retired. [17798] 20/08/1931 **FE01/01/1931**

Stone, Mr M B, DipLib MCLIP, Grp. L. Mgr., L.B. of Greenwich. [30549] 31/01/1979 **CM16/02/1981**

Stone, Mrs M I, BA MA MCLIP, Asst. Lib., Univ. Coll. London. [55798] 26/11/1997 **CM21/03/2001**

Stone, Mr M L, BA(Hons), Asst. Lib., Bradford Teaching Hos. NHS, Bradford. [65872] 12/06/2006 **ME**

Stone, Mr M P, BA MCLIP HonFCLIP, Co. Sec., Guinevere Hotels Ltd. [27371] 18/03/1977 **CM17/07/1981**

Stone, Mr N H F, MCLIP, Retired. [14091] 24/01/1952 **CM01/01/1961**

Stone, Mrs P A, Teaching Asst. [10010169] 09/07/2008 **ME**

Stone, Ms R G, BA(Hons), Stud., Sheffield Univ. [63990] 22/11/2004 **ME**

Stone, Mr R N, BA MArAd MCLIP, Sen. Records Mgr., ABN AMRO Bank, London. [60430] 07/10/1997 **CM07/10/1997**

Stone, Dr R S, PhD MLib MCLIP, Dep. Lib. Catr., Fitzwilliam Mus., Cambridge [41728] 24/02/1988 **CM18/04/1990**

Stone, Mr R W, MCLIP, Life Member. [14094] 01/01/1933 **CM01/01/1951**

Stone, Miss S, BA DipLib MCLIP, Reader Devel., Knowsley L. Serv. [10008856] 18/10/1977 **CM30/11/1979**

Stonebanks, Mrs J, BA(Hons) MCLIP, Neigbourhood L. Mgr., Pendleton. [28685] 06/01/1978 **CM06/11/1981**

Stones, Miss B J, BA(Hons) DipInfMgmt, Unwaged. [10000571] 16/10/2006 **ME**

Stones, Mrs S J, BA(Hons) MCLIP, Lib., Nottingham Univ., Sch. of Nursing, Midwifery & Physiotherapy, Mansfield. [40411] 03/02/1987 **CM24/09/1997**

Stoney, Ms L, BA MCLIP, Unknown. [22226] 17/02/1974 **CM11/10/1976**

Stopforth, Mr N P, ACLIP, L. & Info. Offr., City L., Newcastle Upon Tyne [65787] 24/04/2006 **ACL16/04/2008**

Stoppani, Miss J M, BA(Hon) MCLIP, Dep. L. Mgr., Medway NHS Trust., Kent. [50124] 05/03/1994 **CM23/01/2008**

Stopper, Miss J, BA(Hons) MCLIP, Asst. L. and Inf. Serv. Mgr., N. Lincs. Council, Scunthorpe. [32613] 29/05/1980 **CM04/10/1983**

Storey, Mrs A V, BA MCLIP, Res. Lib., Baker & Mckenzie, London. [18316] 13/10/1972 **CM20/08/1975**

Storey, Dr C, BA MPhil PhD FCLIP, Univ. Lib., The Chinese Univ. of Hong Kong, Shatin. [14105] 29/09/1971 **FE25/09/1996**

Storey, Ms I N J, BSc MSc MCLIP, Career Break. [32705] 01/07/1980 **CM25/01/1983**

Storey, Mrs J, BA MCLIP ACIM DipMkt, Subject & Liasion Mgr., Northumbria Univ., Newcastle. [25581] 28/01/1976 **CM19/12/1978**

Storey, Ms K M, Customer Serv., parsons L., Newcastle Coll. [10000532] 13/10/2006 **AF**

Storey, Mrs M, BA, Career Break [60982] 23/01/2002 **ME**

Storey, Mrs S C, MSc MCLIP, Head of L. Customer Serv., Univ. of Nottingham. [49901] 10/01/1994 **CM10/01/1994**

Storey, Mr S M, BSc DipLib, Lib., Univ. of Wales, Swansea, Swansea. [33654] 03/02/1981 **ME**

Storey, Mrs T, BA(Hons) MCLIP, Indexer, Brotherton L., Univ. of Leeds. [48423] 14/05/1993 **CM20/11/2002**

Storie, Ms C, BA MCLIP, Comm. Lib., Foxbar, Comm. Lib., Renfrewshire. [32191] 06/02/1980 **CM30/04/1985**

Storms, Ms K M, BA MSc, Learning Cent. Co-ord., W. Herts Coll., Cassio Campus, Watford. [61959] 17/12/2002 **ME**

Story, Mrs B A, BSc MCLIP, Lib., Maidenhead L., Royal Bor. of Windsor & Maidenhead [20931] 17/09/1973 **CM01/11/1976**

Stoter, Mr A P, BSc, Learning Support Lib., Victoria L., London. [64444] 30/03/2005 **ME**

Stott, Mrs F, MA BA MCLIP, Retired. [8749] 01/01/1971 **CM04/07/1974**

Stout, Mr R W, MA MCLIP, Retired. [17800] 23/10/1963 **CM01/01/1967**

Stovin, Mrs K A, BA DipLib MCLIP, Learning Resource Cent. Mgr., Priory Sch., Hitchin. [33609] 22/01/1981 **CM16/05/1985**

Stow, Miss E A, MA MCLIP, Retired. [10484] 27/09/1954 **CM01/01/1957**

Stowe, Ms K, Sen. Learning Support Coordinator/Lib., Waltham Forest Coll, London. [62532] 06/08/2003 **AF**

Strachan, Mr A D, MA(Hons) DipLib, Dir. IT, UK Trade & Investment, London. [42219] 11/10/1988 **ME**

Strachan, Mrs E, MA MCLIP, Lib., William Harvey Hosp., Ashford. [58819] 09/08/2000 **CM06/05/2009**

Strachan, Mrs M E, FCLIP, Lib., Supreme Courts, Edinburgh. [26808] 04/11/1976 **FE07/04/1986**

Strachan, Mrs M, BA MCLIP, Writer. [28459] 15/01/1969 **CM14/06/1978**

Stradling, Mr B, MBE FCLIP LRPS FRSA, Life Member. [14129] 17/02/1947 **FE01/01/1966**

Stradling, Ms J, BA(Hons) DipLib MCLIP, Lend. Lib., Southampton Cent. L. [49329] 22/10/1993 **CM21/11/2001**

Strafford, Mrs L, BA(Hons) MCLIP, L. & Knowledge Serv. Mgr., Ashford & St. Peter's NHS Trust Chertsey [60471] 11/12/2001 **CM31/01/2007**

Strain, Mrs M H, BA MA MCLIP, Life Member. [39541] 29/09/1954 **CM14/10/1960**

Strain, Mr W M, MA FCLIP, Life Member. [14131] 22/03/1958 **FE01/01/1968**

Straker, Miss A C, BA(Hons), Learning Resources Asst., City Coll., Norwich [10012655] 05/03/2009 **ME**

Stranders, Mrs A E, BA(Hons) MA MCLIP, Astrande@havering-college. ac. uk [43668] 21/11/1989 **CM16/11/1994**

Strange, Miss A L, Unknown. [62453] 03/07/2003 **ME**

Strasburger, Mrs H A, BA DipLib MCLIP, Rushcliffe Dustrict L. Mgr., Notts. C.C. [36495] 12/10/1983 **CM20/01/1987**

Stratton, Ms B, BA DipLib MSc MCLIP, Copyright & Inf. Soc. Consultant [30274] 17/01/1979 **CM12/05/1981**

Stratton, Ms N L, MA(Hons), Asst. Curator, Nat. L. of Scotland, Edinburgh [10012885] 17/03/2009 **ME**

Strauss, Mrs S M, BA FCLIP, Life Member. [14140] 09/03/1965 **FE01/01/1966**

Streatfield, Mr D, MA MCLIP, Principal, Inf. Mgmnt. Assoc., Twickenham. [14142] 06/02/1962 **CM01/01/1966**

Streather, Miss S K, BA DipLib MCLIP, Res. & Learner Support Off. [29840] 09/10/1978 **CM20/10/1981**

Street, Mrs E N, MCLIP, Retired. [14143] 17/01/1970 **CM24/09/1973**

Street, Mrs H, Bsc, Head of Inf. Serv., MHRA, London. [10007558] 15/01/2010 **AF**

Street, Mrs M S, BSc MA MCLIP, Bookstart Devel. Off. for Hertfordshire C.C. (jobshare) [43196] 02/10/1989 **CM18/11/1993**

Street, Mrs R I, MCLIP, Stud., Northumbria Univ., Newcastle. [64430] 14/09/1967 **CM01/07/1976**

Streeter, Miss H J, BLS, Team Lib., Local Stud., Cent. for Kentish Stud., Maidstone. [36793] 01/01/1984 **ME**

Streets, Mr C J, BA(Hons) MSc MCLIP, Inf. Offr., SCIE, London. [57481] 06/04/1999 **CM17/08/2008**

Stretton, Mrs E M, BA Dip MCLIP, Inf. Advisor, Sheffield Hallam Univ. [65733] 19/04/2006 **CM19/03/2008**

Strickland, Mrs S A, Stud. [10016564] 16/04/2010 **ME**

Stringer, Mrs G R, BA(Hons) DipLIS MCLIP, Asst. Lib., City Business L., London. [39827] 10/08/1986 **CM19/05/1999**

Stringer, Mr I M, MCLIP HonFCLIP, Retired [14150] 01/02/1968 **CM27/07/1972**

Stringer, Miss J E, MSc BA MCLIP, Inf. Specialist, GCHQ, Cheltenham. [10013638] 01/04/1997 **CM15/11/2000**

Stringer, Ms K, MSc BA(Hons), Knowledge and Inf. Asst., Lupton Fawcett, York. [10006086] 11/09/2007 **ME**

Stringer, Mrs L H, BA MCLIP, Business Info., Audience Dev. Offr., Essex Lib. [39265] 07/01/1986 **CM12/12/1991**

Stringer, Mr R D, BA DipLib MBA MCLIP, Self-Employed Publishing/Book Consultant, Textpertise Ltd., Zimbabwe. [19094] 24/09/1972 **CM12/02/1976**

Stringwell, Miss S, Stud., Northumbria Univ., Newcastle [10012653] 02/03/2009 **ME**

Stromberg, Mrs D, MCLIP, Sch. Lib., Beds. C.C., Kempston. [7169] 13/01/1966 **CM01/01/1970**

Stroud, Mr W T, MLib ALA MCLIP, Sr. Admin. Asst., CRT, Alton [14160] 05/03/1972 **CM13/11/1974**

Strudwick, Mrs N J, BA(Hons) MCLIP, Career Break. [52674] 17/11/1995 **CM20/11/2002**

Strugnell, Mr M, BA DipLib, L. Mgr., Thames Valley Univ., Reading [33801] 30/01/1981 **ME**

Strutt, Miss K A, BA MCLIP, Bibl. Servs. Lib., Argyll & Bute Council, Dunoon, Argyll. [23252] 14/11/1974 **CM27/10/1978**

Strutt, Mrs S E, MA, Estate Historian [36439] 10/10/1983 **ME**

Stuart Edwards, Mrs E L, BA(Hons), Lib., Univ. of Bath. [10015950] 29/01/2010 **ME**

Stuart, Mrs C A, MCLIP, Dir. /Co. Sec., CARISS, Kent. [30018] 01/11/1978 **CM02/08/1982**

Stuart, Mr D W K, Unknown. [10012100] 17/12/2008 **ME**

Stuart, Mrs E E J, MVO MA MA, Asst. Bibl., Royal Collection Trust, Windsor. [46140] 07/10/1991 **ME**

Stuart-Jones, Mr E A L, MCLIP MA, Retired. [14169] 29/07/1966 **CM01/01/1969**

Stubbings, Ms R E, BA, Head of Acad. Serv. Mgr., Loughborough Univ. [40462] 12/02/1987 **ME**

Stubbington, Miss Y, BA(Hons) MCLIP, Team Lib., Weston Favell L., Northampton. [10000751] 20/10/1993 **CM10/07/2002**

Stubbs, Mr E A, Lib., UNLP Facultnd & Bellas Artes Bibliotecs. [58638] 25/04/2000 **ME**

Stubbs, Mrs J K, ACLIP, Principle L. Asst., Manchester Met. Univ. [10009345] 01/06/2008 **ACL03/12/2008**

Stubbs, Mrs L J H, BA(Hons), Inf. Lib., Cambridgeshire Co. Council L. [52360] 26/10/1995 **ME**

Stubbs, Mr M F, BTH DipLib MCLIP, Community L., Cent. L., Luton. [41480] 11/01/1988 **CM17/10/1990**

Stuckey, Mrs G V, MCLIP, Interlending Lib., Wiltshire Council. [14181] 25/03/1971 **CM24/05/1977**

Studd, Miss J L, BA(Hons), Unemployed. [46027] 28/08/1991 **ME**

Studinska, Ms O, Stud., Univ. of Aberystwith. [10015097] 23/10/2009 **ME**

Sturdy, Miss G M, MCLIP, Retired. [14184] 24/02/1969 **CM17/03/1975**

Sturdy, Mr W, CChem MRSC MCLIP, Semi-Retired [60604] 25/03/1971 **CM01/04/1984**

Sturges, Prof R P, MA PhD FCLIP, Retired [14191] 24/11/1966 **FE27/03/1991**

Sturgess, Mrs S A, MCLIP, Housebound Serv. Lib., L.B. of Harrow. [15573] 11/03/1969 **CM30/07/1972**

Sturt, Mrs F, FCLIP, Life Member. [14193] 16/01/1952 **FE01/01/1960**

Sturt, Mr N F, BA(Hons) MCLIP, Coll. Lib., Highbury Coll., Portsmouth. [41254] 24/10/1987 **CM21/03/2001**

Stuttard, Mrs B, MCLIP, Learning Res. Mgr., Wolsingham Sch. & Comm. Coll., Bishop Auckland. [21211] 29/09/1973 **CM04/08/1976**

Styant, Mrs S E, Lib. Mngr., Houghton Regis L., Bedfordshire [10017061] 21/06/2010 **AF**

Stych, Mr F S, PH D MA FCLIP, Bagno Alla Villa, Bagni Di Lucca Villa, Italy. [14195] 08/08/1933 **FE01/01/1960**

Styles, Miss C, BA(Hons) MSc(Econ) MCLIP, Arts and L. Consultant. [51152] 23/11/1994 **CM17/03/1999**

Styles, Mrs S A, BLib MCLIP, Support Serv. Lib., Oxfordshire C.C., Cultural Serv. [10417] 12/06/1972 **CM20/10/1975**

Suckle, Mr Z, BA, MA, Lib., Capital City Academy, London. [10010983] 25/09/2008 **ME**

Suckley, Ms J B, BLib, Learning Res. Cent. Asst., Yale Coll. of Wrexham. [28180] 01/10/1977 **ME**

Suddaby, Miss K M, MCLIP, Life Member. [14200] 25/02/1955 **CM01/01/1959**

Suddards, Mrs P, Unknown. [10013986] 15/06/2009 **AF**

Suddell, Mrs G, MSc, Inf. Serv. Lib., S. Glos. Council, Winterbourne L. [61151] 15/03/2002 **ME**

Sudworth, Mrs R A, BA MCLIP, Asst. Div. Lib., Lancashire C.C. [31845] 10/01/1980 **CM15/09/1983**

Suga, Ms C, BA MLIS, Lect., Keio Univ. [61478] 14/08/2002 **ME**

Sugden, Mrs C, BA MCLIP, Unwaged [29673] 17/10/1978 **CM17/10/1980**

Sugden, Mr P V, MA DipLib MCLIP, Area Lib., Cent. Area L., W. Sussex C.C. [32467] 17/04/1980 **CM22/06/1982**

Sukal, Mrs R, BA MA DipIM MCLIP, Tech. Serv. Lib., Richmond-upon-Thames Coll. L., Surrey. [55352] 03/10/1997 **CM15/05/2002**

Sulch, Mrs K J, MCLIP, Sch. Lib., Thomas Alleyne Sch., Stevenage, Herts. [21807] 04/02/1974 **CM16/01/1976**

Sulistyo-Basuki, Mr L, PhD, Prof., Univ. of Indonesia [49213] 13/10/1993 **ME**

Sullivan, Mrs C R, LRC Mgr., Heston Comm. Sch., Hounslow. [10013695] 21/05/2009 **ME**

Sullivan, Mrs F D E, BA DipLib MCLIP, Faculty Team Lib., John Rylands L., Univ. Manchester. [37212] 10/04/1984 **CM21/12/1988**

Sullivan, Ms J, Beaverwood Sch. for Girls. [10012870] 19/03/2009 **ME**

Sullivan, Ms J, BA(Hons) MCLIP, p. /t. Arch., Roedean Sch., Brighton. [46950] 09/03/1992 **CM22/03/1995**

Sullivan, Miss R C, BFA MA, L. & Academic Affairs Asst., Boston Univ. Brit. Prog., London. [10014477] 04/08/2009 **AF**

Sulston, Mrs D E, MA, Retired. [50288] 01/06/1994 **ME**

Summerfield, Mrs S A, BA MCLIP, Inf. Res. Mgr., Min. of Defence, Cambs. [19984] 12/01/1973 **CM03/10/1975**

Summers, Mr D, BA(Hons) MA MCLIP, Dep. Lib., Lancaster Univ. L. [34123] 06/10/1981 **CM07/02/1985**

Summers, Miss P A, BA DipLIS MCLIP, Lib., Invergordon Academy [53324] 07/05/1996 **CM19/05/1999**

Summers, Ms S, BA, I. C. T. Coordinator, Welshpool L., Powys C.C. [43800] 16/01/1990 **ME**

Summerscales, Mrs J, BA ILS, Learning Res. Cent. Administrator, St. John Fisher Catholic High Sch., Dewsbury. [27221] 08/02/1977 **ME**

Summit, Dr R K, HonFCLIP, Hon Fellow. [60083] 07/12/2001 **HFE09/08/1999**

Sumner, Mrs J, BA DipLib MCLIP, Lib., Gravesend Grammar Sch. for Girls, Kent. [31574] 25/10/1979 **CM27/07/1983**

Sumpter, Mrs S L, BA(Hons) MCLIP, Independent Consultant. [46480] 12/11/1991 **CM31/01/1996**

Sunderland, Mr D, BA FRSA MCLIP, Med. Lib., Sheffield Teaching Hosp. Trust, Weston Park Hosp. [14223] 18/01/1963 **CM01/01/1969**

Sunderland, Mrs J C, BSc(Hons) MA MCLIP, Inf. Mgr., Connexions Thames Valley. [58911] 03/10/2000 **CM12/03/2003**

Sung, Miss H Y, MA, Res. Stud., Loghborough Univ. [10014543] 14/08/2009 **ME**

Sunley, Mr J W, MCLIP, Life Member. [14226] 10/08/1950 **CM01/01/1959**

Sunmonu, Ms Y, BA(Hons) MA, Sen. Inf. Offr., London [10008079] 12/08/2009 **ME**

Surman, Miss R E, Stud. [10011054] 17/09/2008 **ME**

Surmiak, Ms A E, MA, Unknown [10006582] 23/10/2007 **ME**

Surrey, Mrs S E, MCLIP, Retired. [16380] 30/01/1970 **CM13/10/1972**

Surridge, Dr C, BSc PhD, Asst. Registrar, Brunel Univ. [64041] 06/12/2004 **ME**

Surridge, Mr R G, MA FRSA HonFLA FCLIP, Freelance Consultant, Surrey. [14232] 10/03/1947 **FE01/01/1953**

Surtees, Ms J, BA(Hons), Clinical Lib., L. &Knowledge Serv., Royal Derby Hosp. [10014654] 14/11/2002 **ME**

Surzyn, Miss A J M, BLS MCLIP, Ret. [30275] 08/12/1978 **CM12/02/1981**

Sutcliffe, Mr G S, MPhil MCLIP, Freelance Indexer. [14238] 19/07/1972 **CM18/09/1976**

Suter, Mrs A J, BA DipLib MCLIP, Lib., CEB Sch., London. [41557] 21/01/1988 **CM18/09/1991**

Suter, Mr M, BA, Asst. Lib., Kingston Coll., Kingston. [35641] 25/11/1982 **ME**

Sutherland, Miss A M, MA DipLib MCLIP, Career break [34328] 23/10/1981 **CM09/11/2005**

Sutherland, Mr A M, BA MCLIP, Lib., Carnoustie L. [14254] 01/01/1969 **CM01/12/1972**

Sutherland, Miss A M, MCLIP, Life Member. [26076] 23/01/1962 **CM01/01/1964**

Sutherland, Mr A P, BA MCLIP, Asst. Lib., City of Sunderland Educ. & Community Serv., Sunderland, Tyne & Wear. [25119] 13/10/1975 **CM30/01/1978**

Sutherland, Mr A, FCLIP, Life Member. [14244] 31/01/1941 **FE01/01/1949**

Sutherland, Mr J G, BA MCLIP, Unemployed. [28692] 13/01/1978 **CM08/12/1987**

Sutherland, Miss J, BA(Hons) MCLIP, L. Res. Cent. Coordinator, City of Edinburgh Council, Forrester High Sch. [61383] 08/07/2002 **CM09/11/2005**

Sutherland, Miss K A, MA(Hons), Asst. Lib., Sherborne Sch. [10011347] 09/10/2008 **ME**

Sutherland, Miss L M, MA DipLib MCLIP Msoc Ind, Freelance Lib. & Indexer. [26247] 02/09/1976 **CM25/01/1979**

Sutherland, Mrs M R, BA MCLIP, Retired. [14255] 04/10/1947 **CM01/01/1950**

Sutherland, Ms N M, BA(Hons) DipInf, Reader's Adviser, House of Commons L., London. [58387] 31/01/2000 **ME**

Sutherland, Mrs R, Stud. [66091] 21/09/2006 **ME**

Sutherland, Ms S, MLIS, Unwaged. [10016770] 10/05/2010 **ME**

Sutlieff, Miss L C, BA(Hons) MSc, Inf. Mgr., Laser Learning Ltd. [65223] 18/11/2005 **ME**

Suto, Mrs J C, MCLIP ALAA, Retired. [17848] 29/09/1943 **CM01/04/1949**

Sutton, Miss A J, BA(Hons) MA MCLIP, Inf. Offr., Univ. of Sheffield, ScHARR. [59010] 24/10/2000 **CM19/11/2008**

Sutton, Mrs A M, BA MA DipLib MCLIP, Repository Mgr., Planning Off., Univ. Reading [41140] 13/10/1987 **CM18/09/1991**

Sutton, Dr A M, MA(Hons) DipLib PhD MCLIP, Unknown. [10013966] 17/10/1983 **CM01/07/1987**

Sutton, Mrs D E, BSc(Hons) MA, Unemployed. [55103] 14/07/1997 **ME**

Sutton, Miss E, FCLIP, Life Member. [14257] 21/03/1941 **FE01/01/1951**

Sutton, Mr G W, BA MCLIP, Knowledge Servs. Outreach Co-ordinator, Warrington & Halton Hosps. NHS Foundation Trust. [50695] 12/10/1994 **CM16/10/2009**

Sutton, Mr I W, BA MCLIP, Learning & Inf. Mgr., Rochdale Met. Bor. Council. [29097] 16/01/1978 **CM09/07/1981**

Sutton, Mr J H, Ref. Team Leader, Brit. L., Oriental & Ind. Off. Collection, London. [31709] 13/11/1979 **ME**

Sutton, Mrs J P, MCLIP, p./t. Asst. Sch. Lib., Haberdashers Aske's Boys Sch., Borehamwood, Herts. [6613] 11/09/1971 **CM09/09/1974**

Sutton, Mrs K, BA MCLIP, Head of L. & Inf. Serv. [28813] 18/01/1978 **CM25/06/1982**

Sutton, Mr L, BA MCLIP, Grp. Mgr., Bexley Lib. Serv. [22877] 01/10/1974 **CM07/07/1977**

Sutton, Mrs L, MSc, Inf. Offr., Coll. of Law, Guildford. [10003975] 23/05/2007 **ME**

Sutton, Ms S A, BA MBA MCLIP, Clinical Lib., Univ. of Leicester. [26577] 05/10/1976 **CM16/10/1979**

Suzuki, Mr H, Life Member. [17849] 01/01/1970 **ME**

Svoboda, Mr E, BA MA DLIS MCLIP, Lib., Internat. Study Cent., Queen's Univ. Canada, Herstmonceux Castle, E. Sussex. [32348] 26/02/1980 **CM26/06/1985**

Swain, Ms B, BSc DipInfSc MCLIP, Self Employed. [60654] 11/12/2001 **CM11/12/2001**

Swain, Miss C O M, Stud., Univ. of Sheffield. [65326] 15/12/2005 **ME**

Swain, Ms D C, BA MA PGDip ILS, Unemployed [10006282] 10/10/2007 **ME**

Swain, Ms E, MA(Hons) MSc MCLIP, Inf. Specialist, Cardiff Univ. [58680] 18/05/2000 **CM29/03/2004**

Swain, Mrs H J, Lib. E. I., MDPGA Wethersfield, Braintree. [61319] 17/05/2002 **AF**

Swain, Ms M, MA MCLIP, Contract Catr. [19217] 01/10/1972 **CM10/10/1974**

Swain, Miss M, BA, Retired. [14262] 04/02/1952 **ME**

Swainson, Miss N J, BA DipLib MCLIP, Learning Resources Mgr, Barton Peveril Coll. [33168] 11/10/1980 **CM16/05/1985**

Swaisland, Mrs C A, MCLIP BSc(Hons) MSc, Quality Support Inf. Co-ord., Liverpool John Moores Univ. [56948] 09/11/1998 **CM21/05/2003**

Swaisland, Mr M, BSc, Asst. Lib., Chaowick Lib., Warrington. [10015737] 19/01/2010 **ME**

Swales, Mrs B J, BA MCLIP MSc, Career Break [34891] 15/04/1982 **CM03/02/1986**

Swales, Mrs D G, ACLIP, L. Serv. Advisor, Southwell L., Southwell. [10012654] 02/03/2009 **ACL02/03/2010**

Swales, Ms G E, BA DipLib MCLIP, YP Serv. Co-ord., Scot. Borders Council Scot. Borders L., [29287] 23/04/1978 **CM23/04/1980**

Swamy-Russell, Mrs J A, MLib, Learning Serv. Co-ordinator, City of Westminster F.E. Coll., London. [45893] 10/07/1991 **ME**

Swan, Ms J, BSc(Hons) MA DipILS MCLIP, Dir., A Good Read Ltd, Burnley. [52985] 12/02/1996 **CM18/11/1998**

Swan, Mrs P, BA, Stud., City Univ. [10011898] 26/11/2008 **ME**

Swanick, Mrs V P, MCLIP, Retired. [20861] 26/02/1959 **CM06/09/1973**

Swann, Miss K L, BA(Hons) MA MCLIP, L. Offr., City of Edinburgh Council, Cent. L. [54634] 27/01/1997 **CM18/09/2002**

Swann, Mrs M J, BA MCLIP, Retired [590] 16/03/1965 **CM01/01/1969**

Swann, Ms S E, BA(Hons) MCLIP, Lib., Bloxham Sch., Banbury. [33170] 26/09/1980 **CM26/09/1983**

Swann-Price, Mrs J M B, BA(Hons) MSc MCLIP, p/t Peripatetic Lib., Wilts. C.C. [55994] 13/01/1998 **CM23/06/2004**

Swanson, Mrs C A, BA(Hons) MA MCLIP, Unwaged/Career break. [52713] 24/11/1995 **CM21/11/2001**

Swanson, Mr E, MA, Retired. [45568] 18/03/1991 **ME**

Swarbrick, Miss M J, BA MCLIP, Life Member. [14280] 09/10/1958 **CM01/01/1961**

Swart, Ms M A, MA BA, KM Resources Offr., DLA Piper UK LLP, Sheffield [10015792] 20/01/2010 **ME**

Swash, Mrs G D, MCLIP, Knowledge & L. Project Mgr., Cheshire W. P. C. T., Chester. [23070] 30/10/1974 **CM02/08/1978**

Sweek, Mrs C, BA(Hons) MA, Inf. Analyst, Cushman & Wakefield, London. [10002675] 13/10/1994 **ME**

Sweeney, Mr J M, MSc MCLIP, Retired. [60653] 05/06/1975 **CM27/04/1981**

Sweeney, Mr R, BA FCLIP, Retired. [14284] 01/01/1950 **FE01/01/1964**

Sweet, Mrs K L, BSc MCLIP, Inf. Resources Exec., Contractor. [60800] 01/10/1979 **CM10/07/1985**

Sweetland, Ms J M, BA(Hons) MSc MCLIP, Neurosciences Lib., N. Bristol NHS Trust, Frenchay Hosp. [29323] 17/06/1978 **CM16/07/1980**

Sweetman, Mr P B, BA MCLIP, Part Time Archival Work., Horsham [22970] 24/09/1974 **CM01/11/1976**

Sweetman, Mrs S, MCLIP, Lib., Preston Coll. [23416] 06/01/1975 **CM14/02/1977**

Swepstone, Mrs J, ACLIP, Asst. in Charge, Ilkeston Lib. (Jobshare) [10007033] 04/01/2008 **ACL28/01/2009**

Swift, Ms A J, BA(Hons) MCLIP, Sch. Lib., Welshpool High Sch., Powys. [37251] 11/05/1984 **CM17/11/1999**

Swift, Mr M J, Life Member. [14293] 01/01/1947 **ME**

Swift, Mr R A, BA DipLib MCLIP, Faculty Support Team Mgr., Univ. of Derby [34678] 01/02/1982 **CM22/04/1992**

Swindells, Mr R J, MSc MCLIP, Retired. [14295] 24/05/1965 **CM01/01/1969**

Swinyard, Miss J K F, MCLIP, Area Lib., Wells Area, Somerset Co. L. [14296] 25/03/1958 **CM01/01/1963**

Swyny, Ms L F, BA(Hons) MA MCLIP, Lib., Dept. of Health [55408] 08/10/1997 **CM29/08/2007**

Sydenham, Mrs R E, MCLIP, Unemployed – bringing up family. [37610] 09/10/1984 **CM19/01/1988**

Syder, Mrs C H M, BA DipLib MCLIP, Lib., Halton Bor. Council. [29789] 05/10/1978 **CM12/11/1981**

Syed, Mr M, Unknown. [10007570] 18/02/2008 **ME**

Sykes, Mrs E, Lib., The Hulme Grammar Schs., Oldham. [46775] 22/01/1992 **ME**

Sykes, Mr H G, BA MCLIP, Stock Lib., Bristol Cent. L., Ref. L. [27373] 07/03/1977 **CM24/05/1984**

Sykes, Mrs J M, MA DipLib MCLIP, Lib. & Dir. (Inf. Serv.), L., London Sch. of Econ. [21020] 03/10/1973 **CM12/04/1983**

Sykes, Miss J, BSc (Hons) PG CE, Trainee Lib., Nottingham Cent. Lib. [10012778] 03/03/2009 **ME**

Sykes, Mrs P A, BA(Hons) MCLIP, Inf. Specialist, GCHQ, Cheltenham. [49577] 19/11/1993 **CM19/03/1997**

Sykes, Mr P, BA DipLib MCLIP, Lib., Univ. of Liverpool, Sydney Jones L. [40628] 06/04/1987 **CM18/04/1990**

Sykes, Miss R A, BA(Hons) DipILM MCLIP, LRC Team Leader, Canterbury Coll. [47788] 14/10/1992 **CM15/01/2003**

Sykes-Little, Ms S, BA(Hons), Unknown. [65167] 01/11/2005 **ME**

Sylph, Ms E A, BSc MSc MCLIP, p. /t. Lib., Zoological Soc. of London. [60691] 01/12/1982 **CM10/03/1987**

Syme, Mrs J, BA MA MCLIP, Sch. Lib., Simon Balle Sch. Hertford [41304] 01/11/1987 **CM22/07/1992**

Symes, Mrs M R, BA MCLIP, p. /t. Asst. Lib., Univ. of Brighton. [42663] 07/02/1989 **CM27/07/1994**

Symmons, Mrs B, MCLIP, Retired, Australia. [17851] 17/09/1931 **CM01/01/1938**

Symonds, Mr K M, Lib. & Info. Serv. Mgr., MRC Cognition & Brain Sci. Unit, Cambridge. [51198] 23/11/1994 **ME**

Symons, Mrs A C, DipLIS MCLIP, Res. Cent. Mgr., Sch. L., Shaftesbury Sch., Dorset. [45347] 19/10/1990 **CM19/07/2000**

Sytsema, Dr J, PhD MCLIP, Linguistics Sub. Consultant, Oxford Univ. L. Serv., Taylor Inst. L. [60987] 25/01/2002 **CM21/05/2008**

Szczepanska, Ms M J, MSc, Knowledge Support Lib., NHS Hampshire Partnership Trust Fundation. [10010211] 10/07/2008 **AF**

Szczyglowski, Mr W L, BSc MSc, Lib., Wyeth Res. (UK) Ltd, Berks. [34172] 08/10/1981 **ME**

Szpera, Miss J, MCLIP, L. Offr., City of Edinburgh Council. [22050] 16/01/1974 **CM16/01/1977**

Szpytman, Miss T M, BSc MSc MCLIP, Unknown. [41397] 20/11/1987 **CM18/04/1990**

Szurko, Mrs M M, BA DipLib MRes MCLIP, Lib., Oriel Coll., Oxford Univ. [31955] 21/01/1980 **CM21/01/1982**

Szwann, Ms A J, BA MA MCLIP, Asst. Lib., Tavistock & Portman NHS Foundation Trust L., London. [59526] 25/04/2001 **CM28/10/2004**

T

Taberner, Mrs L K, BA(Hons) MCLIP, Asst. Lib., Lancs. Co. L. Serv., Preston. [48225] 16/11/1992 **CM22/09/1999**

Tacey, Miss H C, MA,MSc, Inf. Lib. [65139] 03/11/2005 **ME**

Tagg, Mrs E J, MA(Hons) FCLIP, Life Member. [14321] 01/01/1941 **FE01/01/1951**

Taggart, Mrs C, MCLIP, Unknown. [14323] 22/08/1967 **CM01/01/1970**

Tahan, Mrs I A, MPhil, Curator, Brit. L., APAC, London. [39440] 28/01/1986 **ME**

Tailby, Mrs A P, BA(Hons), Arch., Dept. for Work & Pensions, London. [41301] 01/11/1987 **ME**

Tailby, Miss S J, BA, Asst. Lib., Eastleigh Coll. [57206] 15/01/1999 **ME**

Tait, Mr D R, MA DipLib MCLIP, Subject Lib., Univ. of Glasgow. [32564] 06/05/1980 **CM06/10/1982**

Tait, Ms D, BA(Hons), L. and Inf. Asst., Newcastle L. and Inf. Serv. [64129] 18/01/2005 **AF**

Tait, Mrs J M, MA MCLIP, Head of Arch. and L., The Tank Mus., Dorset. [28697] 12/01/1978 **CM16/01/1980**

Tait, Mrs L, BA(Hons) MCLIP, Lib., Scottish Water, Edinburgh. [54374] 28/11/1996 **CM15/05/2002**

Takawashi, Mr T, B ED, Prof., Yashima Gakuen Univ., Japan. [24452] 24/07/1975 **ME**

Talbi, Mr H, BA MA LIS, Dir. of L., Univ. of Bahrain. [42012] 14/07/1988 **ME**

Talbot, Mrs A L, BA(Hons) MA MCLIP, Head of L. Serv., Newcastle Coll., Rye Hill Campus. [56765] 08/10/1998 **CM13/03/2002**

Talbot, Miss B, BLib MCLIP, Sch. Lib., Queen Elizabeths Sch., Mansfield, Notts. [26809] 23/10/1976 **CM06/11/1980**

Talbot, Mrs H D, MCLIP, Life Member. [14333] 01/01/1957 **CM01/01/1962**

Talbot, Mr R G, Data Protection Offr., Dorset [54585] 11/02/1997 **AF**

Tales, Mrs A, BA MCLIP, Lib., Princess Marina L., Northampton Teaching PCT. [20410] 03/03/1973 **CM15/09/1977**

Tallentire, Mr P, BSc (Econ), Stud. [10017177] 11/07/2010 **ME**

Tam, Miss W, Unwaged. [10009538] 02/06/2008 **ME**

Tamblyn, Mrs K L, BA DipLib MCLIP, Med. Records Clerk, Maidstone & Tunbridge Wells Hlth. Tr Pembury Hosp. [44440] 08/10/1990 **CM18/11/1993**

Tamby, Miss Z, B EC MCLIP, Sen. Asst. Lib., Inst. of S. E. Asian Studies, Singapore. [22156] 30/01/1974 **CM12/02/1980**

Tan, Miss C H, MCLIP, Mngr. Catg., Lien Ying Chow Lib., Singapore. [22462] 09/05/1974 **CM21/07/1977**

Tancock, Miss J A, MCLIP, Lib., Morecambe Bay Hosp. NHS Trust, Barrow-in-Furness. [27223] 14/02/1977 **CM07/07/1980**

Tandy-Rackham, Miss H L, BA PostGrad Dip, Unknown. [10001820] 15/03/2007 **ME**

Tang, Ms A, MSc, Intranet Editor, Min. of Defence. [64106] 17/01/2005 **ME**

Tanker, Mrs A C, BA(Hons), Lib., Sheffield Primary Care Trust. [10009977] 30/06/2008 **ME**

Tanna, Mrs A M, BA DipLib MCLIP, Lib., Westfield Comm. Tech. Coll., Watford. [28805] 07/02/1978 **CM01/07/1993**

Tanner, Mr M E, BA DipLib MCLIP, Sen. Lib., Torfaen Ls., Pontypool. [39168] 04/11/1985 **CM09/08/1988**

Tanner, Mr S G, BA MCLIP, Dir., Kings Digital Consultancy Serv., Kings Coll. London. [39395] 13/01/1986 **CM15/09/1993**

Tansley, Mr I P, MCLIP, Retired Grp. Lib., N. W. Devon, Devon L. & Inf. Serv. [14343] 11/03/1968 **CM01/01/1971**

Tansley, Mrs U M, MA MCLIP, Asst. Lib., De Montfort Univ., Leicester [66117] 01/10/2006 **CM11/11/2009**

Tanti, Mrs C, BA(Hons) DipLib, Asst. Lib., Northants. Cent. L., Northampton. [41920] 20/05/1988 **ME**

Taplin, Mr B K, BA(Hons) DipIM MCLIP, Collections Mgr., JISC Collections, London. [51013] 09/11/1994 **CM17/05/2000**

Taplin, Mrs M S, MCLIP, Unwaged. [3631] 01/01/1972 **CM13/06/1975**

Taplin, Mrs S V, Inf. Serv. Asst., Hugh James Solicitors, Cardiff [10007552] 13/02/2008 **AF**

Tarling, Mr M R, MCLIP, Retired [14348] 01/08/1971 **CM02/07/1974**

Tarn, Miss F J, BSc DipInf MCLIP, Info. Servs. & Adult Learning Mgr. [46142] 07/10/1991 **CM14/09/1994**

Tarrant, Miss G A, MSc, Inf. Mngr., Yell Grp. Ltd [62719] 08/10/2003 **ME**

Tarrant, Mrs S C, BA(Hons), Lib., Milton Abbey Sch., Blandford,Dorset. [65916] 04/07/2006 **ME**

Tarrant, Mrs S E, BA MCLIP, Retired [14352] 12/01/1967 **CM01/01/1970**

Tarron, Mrs M P, BA DipIS, Academic Liaison Lib., Univ. of Surrey, Guildford. [55472] 14/10/1997 **ME**

Tarter, Mrs A M, BA MS MCLIP, Sch. Lib., Ripon Grammar Sch., N. Yorks. [44316] 29/08/1990 **CM16/11/1994**

Tasker, Miss M J, Employment not known. [41716] 17/02/1988 **ME**

Tate, Mrs J M, BA(Hons) MSc(Econ) MCLIP, Unwaged. [58318] 07/01/2000 **CM16/07/2003**

Tate, Mr S, Learning Resource Mngr., Graham sch., Scarborough [10014449] 31/07/2009 **AF**

Tatem, Ms S, MCLIP, Retired. [14359] 01/10/1971 **CM26/02/1982**

Tatham, Mrs S, BScEcon MA, Asst. Info. Adviser, Brighton Univ. [58533] 22/03/2000 **ME**

Tatham, Ms V J, LLB(Hons) MA MCLIP, Sen. Data Mgmnt. Off. Bolton Council Childrens Serv. [44048] 10/04/1990 **CM19/11/2003**

Tattersall, Mr S, MSc MCLIP, ICT Devel. Mgr., Bristol City Council. [29536] 18/09/1978 **CM05/09/1980**

Tatton, Mrs H D, PGDipLib, Sch. Lib., Ilford Ursuline High Sch., Ilford. [36832] 01/01/1984 **ME**

Taubinger, Mrs S L, BA(Hons) MCLIP, L. Mgr., Cheshire C.C., Northwich L. [46525] 18/11/1991 **CM26/07/1995**

Taverner, Mrs H F, BA DipLib MCLIP, Unknown. [36325] 01/10/1983 **CM17/10/1990**

Tavner, Mrs E H, MA MCLIP, Grp. Mgr., Consett Lib., Co. Durham [14364] 06/10/1969 **CM19/12/1972**

Tawfik, Mrs N, Unknown. [62895] 18/11/2003 **ME**

Tawn, Mrs H V, BA(Hons) DipLib MCLIP, Unemployed. [44343] 01/10/1990 **CM25/01/1995**

Tayler, Mrs J, BA DipLib MCLIP, Community Tutor, Worcester Coll. Tech., Worcester. [44611] 06/11/1990 **CM23/03/1994**

Taylerson, Mrs J M, MPhil MALIM MCLIP, Faculty Lib., Univ. of Turku, Finland. [62567] 03/09/2003 **CM11/03/2009**

Taylor, Ms A C, MA, Lib., King Fahad Academy, London. [10014875] 18/09/2009 **ME**

Taylor, Ms A E, BSc MCLIP, Carers Support Worker, Vol. Serv. Aberdeen, Aberdeen. [30868] 29/04/1979 **CM26/02/1982**

Taylor, Mrs A M, BA, Acquisitions Team Leader, Univ. of Reading L. [62910] 18/11/2003 **ME**

Taylor, Mrs A M, MCLIP, Retired. [4304] 11/02/1963 **CM01/01/1970**

Taylor, Miss A P, BA MA MCLIP, Inf. Lib., Somerset C.C. [43653] 16/11/1989 **CM21/10/1992**

Taylor, Mrs B J, MA MCLIP PGCE, Learning Res. Mgr., Macclesfield Coll., Cheshire. [20959] 06/09/1973 **CM04/08/1975**

Taylor, Mrs B M, MA, Career Break [62292] 17/04/2003 **ME**

Taylor, Mrs C A, MCLIP, Lib., The L., Forest Sch., London. [32765] 12/08/1980 **CM27/07/1983**

Taylor, Miss C C A, BA(Hons) MA, Stud. [10000437] 10/10/2006 **ME**

Taylor, Ms C J, BA DipLib MCLIP, Co. Lib., Oxon. C.C., L. Serv. H.Q. [34727] 05/02/1982 **CM29/07/1986**

Taylor, Miss C M, BA, Stud., Northumbria Univ. [10013634] 18/05/2009
ME

Taylor, Miss C M, MA MCLIP, Team Lib. Local Studies, Aberdeen City. L. [21038] 02/10/1973
CM06/10/1975

Taylor, Mr C V, BA(Hons) MA MCLIP, Curator-Collection Devel., Nat. L. of Scotland, Edinburgh. [47731] 15/10/1992
CM25/09/1996

Taylor, Miss C, BSc(Hons) MA MCLIP, Inf. Offr., Field Fisher Waterhouse, London. [52951] 26/01/1996
CM18/09/2002

Taylor, Mr D A, BA MLS MCLIP, Application Serv. Mgr., OCLC (UK) Ltd., Sheffield. [14387] 14/08/1970
CM26/10/1972

Taylor, Mrs D A, BA(Hons), Serv. Dev. Lib., Teen & Engagement, Dudley, MBC [40781] 06/06/1987
ME

Taylor, Miss D E, MSc MCLIP M I BIOL, Storyteller [25120] 15/11/1975
CM07/06/1978

Taylor, Mr D N, BA MCLIP, Unwaged. [34643] 30/01/1982 **CM14/11/1989**

Taylor, Mr D, BA(Hons), MSc, Lib. Systems Mngr, Univ. of Worcester [10011085] 02/10/1995
ME

Taylor, Mrs D, BA MCLIP, Sch. Lib., Strathclyde Reg. Council, Dunbarton. [14383] 17/01/1970
CM13/06/1988

Taylor, Mrs E E, MCLIP, Life Member. [14392] 01/01/1936
CM01/01/1946

Taylor, Mrs E G, BSc DipLib MCLIP, Sch. Lib., Exeter Sch. [32081] 06/02/1980
CM08/12/1982

Taylor, Miss E J, BA MA MCLIP, Lib. -Support Serv., Lincs. C.C. [43392] 19/10/1989
CM18/11/1992

Taylor, Miss E, BLib MCLIP, L. Offr. -Cent. Lend. Serv., Edinburgh Cent. L. [27026] 11/01/1977
CM26/09/1980

Taylor, Ms E, MA, Learning & Inf. Specialist, RCN Scotland Learning Hub, Edinburgh [59587] 11/06/2001
ME

Taylor, Mrs F M, Young People's Area Lib., Kendal L., Cumbria. [35160] 24/09/1982
ME

Taylor, Mr G A, BA(Hons) MA MCLIP, Public Relations Offr., Metro(W. Yorks. PTE), Leeds. [58321] 05/01/2000
CM29/03/2004

Taylor, Mrs G S, MCLIP, Lib., Trenchyard L., Wolverhampton [10002908] 14/01/1971
CM06/11/1974

Taylor, Mrs G, BSc(Hons) MCLIP, Area Mgr., S. E. [59671] 25/07/2001
CM29/03/2004

Taylor, Mrs G, BA MCLIP, Stock & Resources Unit Mgr., Stoke-on-Trent City C. [28248] 25/10/1977
CM04/09/1980

Taylor, Miss H L, BA(Hons) MA, Inf. Specialist, GCHQ. [63592] 08/07/2004
ME

Taylor, Mrs H M, MA MCLIP, Unknown. [26700] 27/10/1976
CM01/07/1981

Taylor, Ms H, BA MLS MCLIP, Adviser: Qualifications & Professional Devel., CILIP, London. [28184] 14/10/1977
CM01/10/1979

Taylor, Mrs H, MCLIP, Coll. Lib., Bourne Community Coll., Emsworth. [8814] 06/11/1971
CM20/10/1975

Taylor, Mrs J A, MLS MCLIP, Retired. [3440] 16/10/1969 **CM17/07/1972**

Taylor, Miss J A, Stud., Leeds Met. Univ. / P/T L. Asst., BPP Law Coll. [10011706] 06/11/2008
ME

Taylor, Mrs J C, BSc(Hons) MA MCLIP, L. Asst., Lancashire Co. L. Serv., Preston. [55587] 22/10/1997
CM01/02/2006

Taylor, Mrs J K K, BA BSc MCLIP, Customer Serv. Lib., Loughborough L. [20317] 05/02/1973
CM29/09/1976

Taylor, Miss J M, MCLIP, Retired. [14418] 26/04/1967 **CM01/01/1971**

Taylor, Mr J R H, MA, Head,Collection Dev. The L., Cambridge Univ. [63311] 08/04/2004
ME

Taylor, Mr J R, BA(Hons), Inf. Sci., DSTL, Knowledge Serv., Salisbury. [65393] 30/01/2006
ME

Taylor, Mr J W, BA MCLIP, Retired. [19110] 20/03/1957 **CM01/01/1961**

Taylor, Mrs J, BLib MCLIP, Asst. Lib., Stockport M.B.C. [28136] 12/10/1977
CM08/08/1980

Taylor, Ms J, BA MA, Clinical Lib., NHS Foundation Trust, Lancashire [10009445] 01/12/2004
ME

Taylor, Ms J, MA BA DipLib MCLIP, Proj. Lib., Working Class Movement Lib., Salford [39363] 16/01/1986
CM15/02/1989

Taylor, Mrs J, Snr. L. Asst., Rampton Hosp., Notts. [64473] 31/03/2005
AF

Taylor, Mrs K E, MA DipM MCLIP, Sen. Lib. Mgr., Woolwich L., L.B. Greenwich [10344] 07/01/1971
CM22/04/1974

Taylor, Ms K J, MSc, Asst. Subject Lib., Coventry Univ. [64030] 02/12/2004
ME

Taylor, Miss K J, BA DipLib MCLIP DipMgmt (Open), Home Off. [38956] 24/10/1985
CM11/12/1989

Taylor, Miss K J, BA(Hons) MCLIP, Inf. Specialist, GCHQ, Cheltenham. [45458] 11/02/1991 **RV16/07/2008**
CM31/01/1996

Taylor, Mrs K, BA(Hons) MSc, Dep. Lib., Judge Business Sch. L., Cambridge. [58435] 11/02/2000
ME

Taylor, Miss K, BSc(Hons), Inf. Offr, Bell & Scott LLP, Edinburgh [10006721] 03/12/2007
ME

Taylor, Mrs K, Unknown. [10015609] 17/12/2009
ME

Taylor, Mr L H, BA(Hons) MA MCLIP, Mgmt. Co-Ordinator – E., Scarborough L., N. Yorks. [46636] 29/11/1991
CM24/09/1997

Taylor, Mrs L J, MEd BA ILTM MCLIP, Dir. of Learning Res., Liverpool Hope Univ. Coll. [29145] 16/04/1978
CM07/12/1981

Taylor, Mr L J, BA FCLIP, Retired, Tamarisk Books, Hastings, E. Sussex. [14426] 28/08/1958
FE14/11/1991

Taylor, Mr L S, BA(Hons) MA, Lib., Brit. L., London. [55801] 24/11/1997
ME

Taylor, Mrs L, BLib MCLIP MSc(Econ), Learning Res. Mgr., City of London Academy. [26434] 06/10/1976
CM01/11/1979

Taylor, Ms L, MA, Unknown. [40947] 25/09/1987
ME

Taylor, Mr M H, Lib., English Folk Dance & Song Soc., London. [64364] 14/03/2005
ME

Taylor, Mr M J, BA MCLIP, Retired. [14435] 07/08/1957 **CM01/01/1960**

Taylor, Miss M J, MCLIP, Retired. [14436] 01/01/1941 **CM01/01/1945**

Taylor, Mr M R, BA MCLIP, Res. Asst., Cent. & N. W. London Mental Hlth. NHS Trust. [39246] 01/01/1986
CM09/08/1988

Taylor, Mr M S, BEd CertEd MA, Transportation Lib., AECOM, Birmingham. [52329] 30/10/1995
ME

Taylor, Ms M T, MA(Hons) DipILS MCLIP, Unknown. [52947] 26/01/1996
CM20/09/2000

Taylor, Mr M, BA MCLIP, Head of L., Inf., Heritage & Arts Serv., Royal Bor. of Windsor & Maidenhead, Maidenhead. [29842] 03/10/1978
CM22/08/1984

Taylor, Mrs N M E, Inf. Offr., Liverpool John Moores Univ. [59737] 10/09/2001
ME

Taylor, Mrs N R, MCLIP, Asst. Area Sch. Lib., Hants. C.C., Farnborough. [14442] 01/01/1967
CM01/01/1971

Taylor, Miss P A, BA MCLIP, Lib. Asst., Cambridgeshire CC. [30554] 08/02/1979
CM15/07/1985

Taylor, Mrs P J, Asst. Lib., Cardigan L., Cardigan [10014532] 12/08/2009
ME

Taylor, Mr P, BSc(Hons) MCLIP, Lib., The Area L., Peebles. [10001730] 10/03/1971
CM01/03/1974

Taylor, Ms R C, BA MA, L. Consultant. [42263] 13/10/1988 **ME**

Taylor, Mrs R G, MCLIP, Sch. Lib. Lea Manor High Sch. Northwell Drive, Luton Beds. [22035] 21/02/1974
CM04/08/1976

Taylor, Miss R L, MA(Hons), p. /t. Stud. /L. Asst., Univ. of Aberystwyth, Fintry L. [65316] 08/12/2005
ME

Taylor, Mr R S, BA(Hons) DipILM MCLIP, Inf. Mgr., Bath Spa Univ., Bath. [46820] 11/02/1992
CM24/09/1997

Taylor, Miss R, MA MPHIL MCLIP, Life Member. [14451] 09/01/1958
CM01/01/1962

Taylor, Mr S C, BA, Bookshop Asst. (p./t.), Wells,Somerset. [24966] 13/10/1975
ME

Taylor, Mrs S C, BSc(Hons) DipMan, Learning Resources Mgr., Sparsholt Coll., Winchester. [59855] 17/10/2001
ME

Taylor, Miss S E C, MA(Hons) DipILS MCLIP, Lib., Access Serv., Culture & Sport, Glasgow [53974] 15/10/1996   **CM20/09/2000**

Taylor, Mrs S E, BA(Hons) MPhil PgDip MCLIP, Electronic Resources Lib., Univ. of Bolton [62922] 20/11/2003   **CM21/11/2007**

Taylor, S H, BA(Hons) MA MCLIP, Records Mgr., New Coll. Durham. [56311] 01/05/1998 **RV06/02/2008**   **CM18/09/2002**

Taylor, Mr S J, BA MCLIP, Adult Serv. Mgr., Suffolk C.C. [41577] 28/01/1988   **CM27/05/1992**

Taylor, Miss S L, Info. Advisor, Health & Safety Lab., Debrbyshire [10017022] 18/06/2010   **AF**

Taylor, Miss S L, BA(Hons) MSc, Unwaged [10014572] 19/01/2005 **ME**

Taylor, Mrs S M, BA(Hons) MA MCLIP, Inf. Offr., The Nat. Autistic Soc., London. [59923] 02/11/2001   **CM01/02/2006**

Taylor, Miss S M, BSc(Hons) DipLIM MCLIP, Leraning Res. Cent. Co-ordinator, Bicton Coll., Devon [51376] 01/02/1995   **CM29/03/2006**

Taylor, Ms S, BA(Hons) MCLIP, Administrator Admissions, Univ. of Cumbria, Lancaster. [44756] 15/11/1990 **RV27/11/2007**   **CM20/03/1996**

Taylor, Miss S, BA(Hons), Co. Dir., Critical Eye Comm. Ltd., High Peak. [10000741] 07/11/2006   **ME**

Taylor, Mrs S, MCLIP, Life Member. [14461] 01/02/1955 **CM01/01/1959**

Taylor, Mrs S, ACLIP, Study Ctr. Mgr., Jubilee High Sch., Addlestone. [10006489] 24/10/2007   **ACL04/03/2009**

Taylor, Miss S, MA DipLib DMS MCLIP, Unemployed. [25672] 28/01/1976   **CM03/07/1978**

Taylor, Ms S, BA(Hons) MSc, Unwaged. [47569] 02/10/1992   **ME**

Taylor, Miss S, BA(Hons) PgDip, Unknown. [64516] 22/04/2005   **ME**

Taylor, Miss T P, Campus Lib. [10005036] 06/06/2007   **ME**

Taylor, Mr T, BA(Hons) DipILS MCLIP, Unknown. [48125] 10/11/1992   **CM25/09/1996**

Taylor, Mrs V L, MSc BA MILAM MCLIP, Retired. [1229] 07/10/1965   **CM01/01/1970**

Taylor, Mrs W M, PGDip, Lib., RNIB Nat. L. Serv. [10002991] 24/04/1997   **ME**

Taylor-Bradshaw, Mrs L, Lib., Clarence Fitzroy Bryant Coll., St. Kitts. [10015456] 25/11/2009   **ME**

Taylor-Reid, Mrs J P, Sen. Inf. Off., Inf. Serv., Kennedys, London. [44788] 15/11/1990   **ME**

Taylor-Roe, Mrs J L, MA MCLIP, Head of Liaison, Acad. Serv. &Special Coll., Newcastle Univ. L. [35137] 13/09/1982   **CM20/01/1986**

Taylor-Roome, Mrs D, BSc MCLIP AdvDipEd, Retired – Literacy Volunteer,Tuxford Primary Sch, Nottinghamshire [14470] 24/01/1962   **CM01/01/1968**

Taylor-Williams, Mrs D M, BA(Hons) MCLIP, Sen. Inf. Offr., Olswang, London. [54265] 11/11/1996   **CM21/11/2001**

Teague, Mrs K, MLIS MCLIP, Catg. & Tech. Support Lib., RNIB, Peterborough. [64113] 17/01/2005   **CM21/08/2009**

Teague, Mr S J, BSc(Econ) FCLIP FRSA, Retired. [14474] 02/01/1940   **FE01/01/1950**

Tearle, Miss B M, LLB MSt MCLIP, Retired. [15583] 18/02/1967   **CM01/01/1970**

Teasdale, Mrs F S, BSc(Hons) DipIS MCLIP, LLS Cent. Serv. Mgr. & Head of Collections, Univ. for the Creative Arts, Farnham. [51892] 31/07/1995   **CM01/04/2002**

Teather, Miss J K, BA MCLIP, Career Break. [35872] 31/01/1983   **CM11/12/1989**

Tedeschi, Mr A M, BA MLS, Rare Books Lib., Dunedin P.L., Dunedin, New Zealand [64574] 05/05/2005   **ME**

Teeger, Mrs B S, BA MCLIP, Communications Mgr., Communities & Local Government., London [30048] 10/11/1978   **CM19/10/1983**

Teijken, Ms A, BA(Hons), Retired [45914] 19/07/1991   **ME**

Telfer, Mrs J E, BA MCLIP, Asst. Lib., Barnsley M.B.C., Cent. L. [21847] 03/02/1974   **CM25/02/1977**

Telford, Ms N T, MA DipLib MCLIP, Retired. [23641] 06/01/1975   **CM01/10/1977**

Templar, Mrs A, BA(Hons), Locality Lib., Dudley M. B. C [61545] 10/09/2002   **ME**

Temple, Ms E, MSc MCLIP, Inf. Mgr., W. Sussex C.C., Chichester. [60856] 07/08/1998   **CM07/08/1998**

Temple, Mr J, BA(Hons) Pg Dip LIB, Unemployed. [10015967] 08/04/1991   **ME**

Templeton, Ms J, BA(Hons) MSc, Inf. Assist., Edinburgh Napier Univ., Edinburgh. [10015293] 30/10/2009   **ME**

Terrell, Mrs J M, BSc DipLib MCLIP, Serv. Devel. Lilbrarian., Suffolk Co. Council [41649] 01/02/1988   **CM15/05/2002**

Terrell, Miss R J, Sen. Lib. Asst., Lostwithiel I., Cornwall. [10016989] 16/06/2010   **AF**

Terris, Mr G K, BSc MCLIP, Retired. [21611] 24/11/1973 **CM31/10/1975**

Terry, Mrs C P, MCLIP, Inf. Offr., Element Six Ltd., Berks. [60655] 13/04/1976   **CM01/04/1984**

Terry, Ms J V, BA DipLib MCLIP, Retired. [21301] 11/10/1973   **CM11/12/1975**

Terry, Mrs P M, L. Mgr., Cornwall L. Serv. [64417] 15/03/2005   **AF**

Tester, Miss C J, ACLIP, Sen. L. Super., Burgess Hill P. L [65380] 04/01/2006   **ACL27/09/2006**

Tew, Mr C S, B ED, Childrens Lib., John Laing Ltd. for Hounslow Bor. Council. [41454] 01/01/1988   **ME**

Tew, Mrs K A, p. /t. Stud., Univ. of Wales, Aberystwyth, Coventry City Council. [10000709] 26/10/2006   **ME**

Thacker, Mrs P, MSc ILS BA(Hons) PGCE, Lib., S. Essex Coll. of Further & Higher Educ. [61663] 14/10/2002   **ME**

Thacker, Mrs S E, BA MCLIP, Life Member. [14503] 16/07/1941   **CM01/01/1958**

Thacker, Mrs S J, BA(Hons) MCLIP, Inf. Co-ordinator, Prospects Black Country, Tipton. [52632] 16/11/1995   **CM23/01/2008**

Thackeray, Mrs E, Asst. Clinical Lib., Royal Preston Hosp. [64394] 14/03/2005   **ME**

Thain, Ms A E, BA MCLIP, Cancer Knowledge Serv. Adviser, NHS Educ. fo Scotland, Glasgow. [25431] 18/12/1975   **CM26/01/1983**

Thain, Miss E, MA, Inf. Specialist, GCHQ [10008734] 14/04/2008   **ME**

Thantrey, Miss A, BA, Unknown. [10012286] 21/06/2010   **ME**

Theakston, Mr C, BA DipLib PGCE MPhil MCLIP, Departmental Lib., Business Sch., Univ. of Durham. [42852] 01/04/1989 **CM26/11/1997**

Thebridge, Mrs S W, BA DipLib MCLIP, p. /t. Serv. Devel. Offr. /children, young people & families, Warwickshire L., Warwick L. [29788] 02/10/1978   **CM26/02/1982**

Thickins, Mr J O T, BA(Hons) MA MCLIP, Academic Liaison Lib., Univ. of Westminster [57966] 06/10/1999   **CM23/06/2004**

Thies, Ms A M, BA MLib MCLIP MCIPD, Serv. dev. Mgr., Co. L. H.Q., Lancs. C.C. [39981] 03/10/1986   **CM16/10/1989**

Thimann, Ms C F, MCLIP, Retired. [28933] 29/08/1967 **CM01/01/1970**

Thirsk, Mr J W, FCLIP, Life Member. [14515] 20/06/1933 **FE01/01/1947**

Thistlethwaite, Ms L E, MCLIP, Team Lib., Resources, Bolton Cent. L., Lancs. [11558] 11/09/1971   **CM02/07/1975**

Thoburn, Ms J, BA DipLib MCLIP DMS, Asst. Dir., Northumbia Univ., Newcastle. [31711] 05/11/1979   **CM29/09/1985**

Thom, Mrs T L, BA MA MCLIP, Lib., The Hon. Soc. of Grays Inn L., London. [26576] 07/10/1976   **CM08/10/1979**

Thomas, Mrs A A, BA DipLib MCLIP, Lib., Harrow High Sch., Middx. [25632] 17/01/1976   **CM26/01/1979**

Thomas, Mrs A E, BA MA MCLIP, Sen. Team Leader, Warks. C.C. [41179] 14/10/1987   **CM27/01/1993**

Thomas, Miss A M J, BA(Hons), Asst. Lib., Birmingham Post & Mail. [58403] 26/01/2000   **ME**

Thomas, Mr A R, MA FCLIP, Life Member. [14525] 01/07/1947   **FE01/01/1958**

Thomas, Miss A, BA(Hons), L. Asst., Brit. Mus., London. [10006758]
17/12/2007   **AF**

Thomas, Ms A, BA(Hons) MCLIP, Lib., Conwy Co. Bor. Council. [29099]
27/02/1978   **CM18/09/2002**

Thomas, Miss A, BA(Hons), Res. Lib. [65696] 03/01/2006   **ME**

Thomas, Mr B, BA(Hons), Inf. & Marketing Offr., Reddie & Grose,
London. [47895] 22/10/1992   **ME**

Thomas, Mrs C E, BSc MRPharmS PgDip, BNI Indexer, Bournemouth
Univ. L. [61740] 01/11/2002   **ME**

Thomas, Mrs C E, BA(Hons) MA MCLIP FHEA, Head of Learning
Support Serv., Univ. of Chester, Cheshire. [10004060] 07/03/1986
CM26/01/1994

Thomas, Mr C J, BA, Sen. Inf. Offr., Bank of England Inf. Cent., London.
[39303] 09/01/1986   **ME**

Thomas, Mrs C K, BLib MCLIP, p. /t. Curriculum Support Lib., Powys
Co. L. Serv., Llandrindod Wells. [31248] 07/10/1979 **CM08/03/1985**

Thomas, Miss C M, BA(Hons) DipLib MCLIP, Inf. Offr., Linklaters,
London. [31163] 12/09/1979   **CM28/09/1983**

Thomas, Miss C M, MCLIP, Sch. Lib., Southampton City Council.
[14532] 05/10/1971   **CM22/09/1975**

Thomas, Ms C R, Unknown [10005598] 25/07/2007   **ME**

Thomas, Ms D G, BSc(Hons) MCLIP MSc, Sr. L. Exec., Nat. Assembly
for Wales, Cardiff. [54088] 25/10/1996   **CM17/01/2001**

Thomas, Miss D N, BSc BA, Stud., Liverpool John Moores Univ.
[10014787] 18/09/2009   **ME**

Thomas, Mr D P, BA DipLib MCLIP, Lib. & Heritage Mgr., Carms C.C.
[30938] 08/06/1979   **CM23/09/1981**

Thomas, Mr D R, MA DipLib MCLIP, Product Mgr., SIRSI Dynix, Potters
Bar. [24831] 01/10/1975   **CM18/10/1978**

Thomas, Miss E J, BA MCLIP, Loc. Stud. Lib., Wrexham Co. Bor.
Council. [25124] 14/11/1975   **CM09/07/1980**

Thomas, Miss E L, BA MCLIP, Project Offr., Hants. L. & Inf. Serv.,
Winchester. [26810] 24/11/1976   **CM13/08/1979**

Thomas, Mrs E, MCLIP, Community Lib., Gwynedd Council, Caernarfon
L. [29234] 10/04/1978   **CM17/06/1982**

Thomas, Mrs E, MCLIP, Life Member. [14541] 28/02/1939
CM01/01/1942

Thomas, Mrs F, MCLIP, Retired. [14547] 01/01/1939   **CM01/01/1946**

Thomas, Miss F, BA(Hons) MA ODE DipLib MCLIP, Ships L. Offr., Min.
of Defence, Portsmouth. [40633] 03/04/1987   **CM15/12/1992**

Thomas, Mr G C G, BA MA MCLIP, Retired. [14551] 05/04/1971
CM15/05/1979

Thomas, Mrs G N, BA DipIS MCLIP, Sen. Lib. -Community Outreach,
L.B. of Barking & Dagenham, Cent. L. [44109] 16/05/1990
CM21/07/1999

Thomas, Mr G, BA FCLIP, Life Member. [14548] 21/09/1951
FE01/01/1961

Thomas, Miss G, MLib BA DipLib PGC MCLIP, Unwaged. [33941]
01/06/1981   **CM09/03/1989**

Thomas, Ms H C, BSc DipLib MCLIP, Retired. [24146] 01/04/1975
CM18/01/1983

Thomas, Miss H I, MA MCLIP, Lend. Serv. Lib., Royal Coll. of Nursing,
London. [32196] 11/02/1980   **CM16/05/1984**

Thomas, Miss H J, BA(Hons), Rare Books Catr., Nat. Trust [10000876]
16/11/2006   **ME**

Thomas, Mrs H J, BA(Hons) PGDipILM, Subject Lib., Univ. of Chester
[58684] 25/05/2000   **ME**

Thomas, Ms H, BA MSc MCLIP, Cent. Serv. Lib., Univ. of Wales Inst.
Cardiff [59954] 09/11/2001   **CM07/09/2005**

Thomas, Mr H, BMus DipRCM DipLIS, L. Mgr., City of Westminster.
[49366] 29/10/1993   **ME**

Thomas, Ms I J, BA(Hons), Inf. Offr., Linklaters, London. [49407]
21/10/1993   **ME**

Thomas, Dr J A, MA DipLib DipLA MCLIP PhD, Res. Lib., Univ. of
Wolverhampton [22938] 01/10/1974   **CM09/11/1976**

Thomas, Mrs J E, BA(Hons) MLitt MSc(Econ), Community Lib., Moray
Council. [57900] 01/10/1999   **ME**

Thomas, Mr J E, BA MCLIP, Sen. Asst. Lib., Wrexham Co. Bor. C.
[29423] 10/07/1978   **CM24/10/1980**

Thomas, Mrs J H, BA MCLIP, Sch. Lib., St. Bartholomews Sch.,
Newbury. [14562] 29/04/1972   **CM31/08/1974**

Thomas, Miss J L, BA MCLIP, Stock Devel. Lib., Bexley Council.
[29846] 02/10/1978   **CM19/01/1983**

Thomas, Mrs J M, ACLIP, Sen. L. Asst., Garstang L., Preston.
[10009346] 01/06/2008   **ACL01/10/2008**

Thomas, Mr J R, BSc DipLib MCLIP, Head of Serv., Leisure & Heritage,
Ynys Mon. [37926] 21/11/1984   **CM16/10/1989**

Thomas, Ms J, BA MCLIP, Prog. Mgr., Woking L., Surrey C.C. [33173]
08/10/1980   **CM30/11/1984**

Thomas, Mrs K M, BA MCLIP, Sch. Lib., Bishopbriggs Academy,
Bishopbriggs, Glasgow [36860] 10/01/1984   **CM03/03/1987**

Thomas, Ms L C, Lib. Asst. (IT), LAW SOC, London. [64996]
06/10/2005   **ME**

Thomas, Miss L G, LLB(Hons) MSc(Econ) MCLIP, Info. & Computer
Serv. Mgr., L., Caerphilly CBC, Penallta [61975] 08/01/2003
CM29/03/2006

Thomas, Miss L, BA(Hons) DipLIS MCLIP, Asst. Lib., Learning Res.
Cent., Univ. of Glamorgan. [44321] 07/09/1990   **CM17/11/1999**

Thomas, Mrs M G, BA MA MCLIP, Retired. [14570] 10/08/1954
CM01/01/1957

Thomas, Mr M H, BA DipLib MCLIP, Retired. [14571] 10/09/1971
CM21/10/1974

Thomas, Mrs M J, BA(Hons) DipLIS, Asst. Area Sch. Lib., S. Ham L.,
Hants. C.C. [46727] 03/01/1992   **ME**

Thomas, Mrs M, MCLIP, Community Lib., Wrexham Co. Bor. Council.
[21536] 11/10/1973   **CM13/09/1977**

Thomas, Miss M, BA MCLIP, Hosp. Lib., Rampton Hosp., Notts. [24832]
06/10/1975   **CM02/03/1978**

Thomas, Mrs M, BA DipLib MCLIP, L. Mgr., Community L. Serv.,Milton
Keynes [44229] 18/07/1990   **CM26/01/1994**

Thomas, Mrs M, BA(Hons) DipLis, Sch. Lib., Hextable Sch., Kent
[63280] 24/03/2004   **ME**

Thomas, Miss N J, BA(Hons) MA MCLIP, Asst. Lib., Solihull M.B.C.
[50921] 01/11/1994   **CM21/07/1999**

Thomas, Mr N R, BLib(Hons) DPLM MCLIP, Serv. Delivery Mgr., Leics.
C.C., Leicester. [30689] 28/02/1979   **CM30/12/1983**

Thomas, Mr O C, BA(Hons) DipIS MCLIP, Asst. Lib., De Montfort Univ.,
Leicester. [50214] 05/04/1994   **CM16/07/2003**

Thomas, Mrs P A, ACLIP, Learning Cent. Coordinator, Ystrad Mynach
Coll., Hengoed [10006765] 17/12/2007   **ACL29/08/2008**

Thomas, Mr P D, ACIB MCLIP, Life Member. [23968] 25/02/1975
CM25/09/1978

Thomas, Mrs P, MCLIP, Lib., Notre Dame Sch., Cobham. [15385]
21/09/1969   **CM01/01/1973**

Thomas, Miss P, Stud. [10016927] 16/06/2010   **ME**

Thomas, Mr R E, BA MCLIP, L. Mgr., Inst. of Structural Engineers,
London. [39500] 07/02/1986   **CM22/07/1992**

Thomas, Mr R H, BA DipLib MCLIP, General Mgr. Town Hall, Reading
Bor. Council, [41357] 11/11/1987   **CM13/06/1990**

Thomas, Mrs S A, BA MCLIP, p. /t. Lib., Leeds Coll. of Building. [25746]
23/02/1976   **CM30/10/1979**

Thomas, Mrs S G, BA(Hons) MA MCLIP, LR. Mgr., Sir John Deane's
Coll. [62829] 05/11/2003   **CM31/01/2007**

Thomas, Ms S J, BA DipLib MCLIP, Health Promotion L. Nat. Assembly
for Wales, Cardiff. [33845] 01/04/1981   **CM07/03/1985**

Thomas, Mrs S J, Sch. Lib., Sir William Romney Sch., Tetbury,Glos.
[48930] 26/07/1993   **ME**

Thomas, Mrs S M, BA Space MWeldl MCLIP, Weldasearch Mgr., TWI Ltd, Cambridge. [60657] 29/11/1979 **RV16/04/2008   CM29/11/1979**

Thomas, Mrs S R, BA MCLIP, Inf. Consultant, Univ. of Herts., Hatfield de Havilland Campus. [5404] 19/10/1971   **CM10/10/1974**

Thomas, Mrs S, BA(Hons) MA MCLIP, Learning & Teaching Lib., The Open Univ. [56864] 29/10/1998   **CM15/10/2002**

Thomas, Mrs S, BA MCLIP, Lib., City of Salford, Cultural Serv. [33685] 05/02/1981   **CM10/12/1985**

Thomas, Mrs S, BA, Lib., Westminster Sch., London. [43782] 11/01/1990   **ME**

Thomas, Mrs T C, BA(Hons) MA, Unwaged. [58976] 13/10/2000   **ME**

Thomas, Mrs V, MCLIP, Outreach and Rural Serv. Lib., Monmouthshire C.C. [8597] 01/01/1970   **CM01/01/1975**

Thomas, Dr W T, MSc PhD, Sen. Lib., The Regents Sch., Thailand. [61384] 05/07/2002   **ME**

Thomas, Miss Z, BA(Hons), Unknown. [64277] 23/02/2005   **ME**

Thompson, Mrs A E, BSc (Hons) PgDip, Lib., Royal Lpool&Broadgreen Univ. Hosp., Staff Lib. [59426] 12/03/2001   **ME**

Thompson, Dr A H, MA FCLIP HonFCLIP, Retired;Chairman CILIP Multimedia Inf. & Tech Grp. [14593] 26/02/1957   **FE01/01/1962**

Thompson, Mrs A M, BSc, Lib., Notre Dame Prep. Sch., Cobham. [59906] 01/11/2001   **ME**

Thompson, Ms A, Community Lib., Medway L. [66032] 04/09/2006 **ME**

Thompson, Mrs A, MCLIP, Life Member. [19177] 01/01/1958   **CM01/01/1967**

Thompson, Mrs B A, BSc DipLib MCLIP MA, Retired. [14595] 01/01/1969   **CM01/01/1972**

Thompson, Mrs C A P, BA MCLIP, Coll. Lib., Coombeshead Coll., Newton Abbot. [28188] 12/10/1977   **CM18/07/1991**

Thompson, Mrs C A, MCLIP, Team Leader-Child. Lib., Hounslow L., L.B. of Hounslow. [18282] 03/10/1972   **CM06/10/1976**

Thompson, Mr D G, BA MCLIP, Asst. Lib., De Montfort Univ., Leicester. [22503] 04/06/1974   **CM18/02/1977**

Thompson, Mr D J, BA(Hons) MA MCLIP, Academic Subject Lib., Univ. of Gloucestershire. [53678] 04/09/1996   **CM17/01/2001**

Thompson, Ms D M, MCLIP, Sch. Serv. Offr., Cumbria CC., Carlisle. [15344] 27/10/1971   **CM25/07/1975**

Thompson, Mr D W, Unknown [63165] 02/03/2004   **ME**

Thompson, Mr D, Digital Curator, Wellcome L., London. [62971] 01/12/2003   **ME**

Thompson, Mrs G M, MCLIP, Unknown. [10891] 10/02/1972   **CM19/01/1976**

Thompson, Mrs G, BA MCLIP, Casual Data Mgr., RM Data Solutions. [18406] 25/10/1972   **CM04/02/1976**

Thompson, Miss H J, BA(Hons) MSc MCLIP, Lib., Leeds P. C. T. (maternity leave) [49746] 29/11/1993   **CM22/05/1996**

Thompson, Dr H M A, MPhys PhD, Unknown. [10014377] 21/07/2009 **AF**

Thompson, Mrs H M, MSc MCLIP, Lib., Tring Sch., Herts. [44416] 05/10/1990   **CM23/03/1994**

Thompson, Ms H S, MA(Hons) PG Dip MCLIP, Inf. Offr., Idox Inf. Serv. [64924] 12/09/2005   **CM11/11/2009**

Thompson, Mrs H, BA(Hons), Grp. Mgr., Durham C.C. [46310] 28/10/1991   **ME**

Thompson, Mrs H, Lib. Asst., Forest Town L., Mansfield [10014811] 16/09/2009   **AF**

Thompson, Mr H, FCLIP, Retired. [14616] 05/10/1936   **FE01/01/1951**

Thompson, Ms I J R, MA DipLib MCLIP, Career Break [25433] 05/01/1976   **CM26/09/1978**

Thompson, Mr J E, BA DipLib MCLIP, S. L. O., Edinburgh City L. [33383] 21/11/1980   **CM27/07/1983**

Thompson, Mrs J M, MCLIP, Sch. Lib., Haygrove Sch., Bridgwater,Somerset. [41505] 01/01/1966   **CM05/04/1989**

Thompson, Mr J, BA FCLIP, Life Member. [14618] 18/02/1949   **FE01/01/1963**

Thompson, Miss J, MA(Hons), PGDE, Stud., Univ. Strathclyde, Glasgow. [10016004] 10/02/2010   **ME**

Thompson, Ms K E, BA(Hons) PGDipLIS MCLIP, Academic Liason Lib., Univ. Westminster, London. [55907] 12/12/1997   **CM19/11/2003**

Thompson, Miss K, BSc MA, Unemployed. [57208] 18/01/1999   **ME**

Thompson, Mrs L M, BA(Hons) MCLIP, Academic Subject Lib., Univ. of Lincoln. [52652] 16/11/1995   **CM19/11/2003**

Thompson, Mr M J, MSc, Inf. Asst., Univ. of Birmingham. [62965] 25/11/2003   **ME**

Thompson, Mrs M K N, MCLIP, Life Member. [14626] 01/01/1940   **CM01/01/1943**

Thompson, Mrs M, Business Res., London. [52427] 26/10/1995   **AF**

Thompson, Miss M, BA MSc, Seeking work. [40709] 09/05/1987 **ME**

Thompson, Mr P S, BA(Hons) MCLIP, Child. & Sch. L. Serv. Mgr., Walsall M.B.C., Educ. Devel. Cent. [20218] 26/01/1973   **CM03/10/1975**

Thompson, Mrs R C, ACLIP, P/T Lib. (Resources), Kirkby in Ashfield Lib. (Nottinghamshire C.C.) [65480] 24/02/2006   **ACL29/03/2007**

Thompson, Ms R E A, BA(Hons), Inf. Mgr., Univ. of Strathclyde, Careers Serv. [39132] 10/11/1985   **ME**

Thompson, Mr R H, FSA MCLIP, Retired. [14630] 03/02/1963   **CM06/11/1972**

Thompson, Mr R M, BA MA DipLib MCLIP, Retired. [28381] 08/11/1977   **CM22/07/1980**

Thompson, Mrs S L, BA(Hons) MSc MCLIP, L. Serv. Mgr., Frimley Park Hosp., Surrey. [49617] 19/11/1993   **CM22/01/1997**

Thompson, Mrs S M, BA MCLIP, Retired. [32386] 01/01/1956   **CM24/07/1980**

Thompson, Mrs V E, BA MCLIP, Head of Learning Res. Cent., Univ. of Sohar, Oman. [14640] 17/03/1967   **CM19/07/2000**

Thompson, Mrs W J, BA DipLib MCLIP, Sen. Res., UBS Investment Bank, London. [43557] 07/11/1989   **CM29/01/1992**

Thomson, Ms A J, BA MCLIP, p. /t. Catr., Soc. of Genealogists, London. [18212] 05/10/1972   **CM13/07/1976**

Thomson, Ms A, LLB MA, Dep. Lib., Ashurst, London. [52033] 02/10/1995   **ME**

Thomson, Mrs D M, MCLIP, Adult Non-fiction Lib., Aberdeenshire L. & Inf. Serv., Aberdeenshire. [21016] 01/10/1973   **CM15/09/1976**

Thomson, Ms E H, BSc MSc MCLIP, Head of Inf. Mgmnt., Surrey Police, Guildford. [60702] 07/03/1983   **CM25/04/1989**

Thomson, Mrs E S, BA(Hons) MCLIP, Unknown. [63665] 12/08/2004 **CM28/01/2009**

Thomson, Miss E, Lib. Super., L. @ The Bridge (Easterhouse), Glasgow [10017056] 21/06/2010   **AF**

Thomson, Mr G, L. Systems Mgr., Royal Coll. of Surgeons of England, London. [10015323] 16/11/2009   **ME**

Thomson, Mrs J E, MA DipLib MCLIP, Customer Serv. Co-ordinator, Lib. & Museums HQ, Fife Council. [24800] 08/10/1975 **CM30/11/1977**

Thomson, Miss K S, BSc(Hons) MSc MCLIP, Subject Lib., Univ. of the W. of Scotland. [58925] 05/10/2000   **CM21/11/2007**

Thomson, Miss L, MA(Hons), Unknown [59110] 16/11/2000   **ME**

Thomson, Mrs M M, BA MCLIP, Vol. Lib. & Counselling Co-ordinator, Grampian Racial Equality Council, Aberdeen. [30050] 26/10/1978   **CM07/08/1981**

Thomson, Mr R E, BA(Hons) DipLis, Asst. Lib., St Hugh's Coll., Oxford. [10006246] 19/10/1992   **ME**

Thomson, Mr R J, MA(Hons) DipLIS MCLIP, Unwaged. [50290] 31/05/1994   **CM15/05/2002**

Thomson, Ms S, ACLIP, Inf. Offr., NHS Grampian, Aberdeen. [64875] 22/08/2005   **ACL27/06/2006**

Thorbinson, Mrs A E, BA(Hons) MCLIP, Res. Lib., City of Ely Comm. Coll., Cambs. [35624] 16/11/1982   **CM21/07/1999**

Thorburn, Mr D, BA(Hons) MA PG DipIS MCLIP, Inf. Exec., Royal Inst. of Chartered Surveyors, London. [51460] 27/02/1995 CM01/02/2006

Thorn, Mrs L, BSc PGDip MCLIP, Archive/L. Coordinator, Fugro GeoConsulting Ltd, Wallingford, Oxfordshire. [60474] 02/02/2000 CM02/02/2000

Thornborow, Mr P, MSc MA BA DipLib MCLIP, Collections & Learning Resources Mgr., Univ. of Northampton [29851] 02/10/1978 CM04/06/1981

Thorne, Mrs A A, MSc BA(Hons) MCLIP, Inf. Mgr., Soc. of Motor Manufacturers & Traders Ltd., London. [43999] 01/04/1990 CM19/11/2003

Thorne, Miss A M, BLib MCLIP, Comm. Lib., Norfolk C.C., Dersingham L. [41604] 26/01/1988 CM24/03/1992

Thorne, Mr J D, BSc MSc MCLIP, Lib. Ecec., House of Commons, London [57539] 21/04/1999 CM15/05/2002

Thorne, Mrs M F, ACLIP, L. S. A., Cent. L., Sutton in Ashfield. [65203] 17/11/2005 ACL05/10/2007

Thorne, Ms M L, BA, Lib., Bearwood Coll., Wokingham [10006820] 17/12/2007 ME

Thorne, Mr R G, BA(Hons), Lib. & Inf. Asst., Taunton L., Taunton [10017034] 18/06/2010 ME

Thorne, Mrs S M, BA MA MCLIP, Accounts Asst., AWM Intl., Worthing [33178] 06/10/1980 CM20/12/1982

Thorne, Miss V M, BA MCLIP, Customer Serv. Mgr., L.B. of Barking & Dagenham. [40350] 21/01/1987 CM18/11/1992

Thorner, Miss J, BA MA MCLIP, Job Seeking [29852] 11/10/1978 CM14/10/1981

Thornes, Miss S L, BSc(Hons) MSc MCLIP, Faculty Team Lib., Univ. of Leeds [59801] 03/10/2001 CM04/10/2006

Thornhill, Ms B J, JP DipSoc DipPsych MCLIP, Life Member. [14670] 27/09/1952 CM01/01/1967

Thornhill, Mrs M A, MPhil FCLIP, Life Member. [17859] 12/02/1941 FE01/01/1954

Thornley, Miss L, BA(Hons) MCLIP, Learning Advisor, Univ. of Cumbria. [43863] 05/02/1990 CM24/07/1996

Thornley, Ms V, Lib. Asst., MKC L., Milton Keynes. [10016933] 10/06/2010 AF

Thornton, Mrs C A, BA MCLIP, Team Leader., Shrewsbury Coll. of Arts & Tech [34674] 01/02/1982 CM06/10/1987

Thornton, Mrs C S, BEd(Hons) MA MCLIP, Head of L. Serv., Cent. Manchester & Manchester Child. Univ. Hosp. NHS Trust. [46055] 17/09/1991 CM18/03/1998

Thornton, Mrs C V S L, BA DipILS MCLIP, L. and Inf. Mgr., NDA, Harwell. [55775] 18/11/1997 CM21/11/2001

Thornton, Ms D K, BA(Hons) MCLIP, Community Inf. Offr, Knaresborough L., Yorks. [34737] 03/02/1982 CM21/02/1984

Thornton, Mrs D, Knowledge and L. Serv. Mngr, Blackpool Victoria Hosp. [33702] 06/02/1981 ME

Thornton, Mr D, BA, Unwaged. [10010834] 04/09/2008 AF

Thornton, Ms I, BA, Comm. Lib., Aston L., Birmingham. [38053] 17/01/1985 ME

Thornton, Miss K I M, MCLIP, Life Member. [14686] 27/01/1949 CM01/01/1969

Thornton, Mrs K S, BA(Hons) MCLIP, Team Leader, Ripon L. & Inf. Cent., N. Y. C.C. [47847] 20/10/1992 CM21/05/1997

Thornton, Miss L H, MSc MSc(Hons), Sen. Inf. Analyst, The NHS Info. Cent. for Health & Social Care, Leeds. [10002031] 26/03/2007 ME

Thornton, Mr S A, MCLIP, Retired [14688] 02/02/1971 CM01/12/1975

Thornton, Mrs T J, BA(Hons) MCLIP, LRC Mgr., Hazelwick Sch. W. Sussex. [48251] 18/11/1992 CM23/09/1998

Thorp, Dr R G, MA MSc DPhil CChem MRSC MCIL MCLIP, Retired. [60616] 09/11/1984 CM02/12/1986

Thorp, Mr R J S, MSc BSc, Consultant. [10015137] 14/10/2009 ME

Thorpe, Ms C M, BSc(Hons) MSc MCLIP, Sen. Inf. Adviser (Web Serv.), Sheffield Hallam Univ. LITS [33424] 27/11/1980 CM22/07/1998

Thorpe, Ms D, BA(Hons) MCLIP, Sch. Lib., New Charter Academy, Tameside. [52567] 06/11/1995 CM13/03/2002

Thorpe, Ms H M, PGCE MA MCLIP, Supply Teacher, Nottinghamshire. [30723] 01/01/1973 CM01/01/1977

Thorpe, Mrs J M, MCLIP, Retired. [14692] 16/01/1961 CM01/01/1965

Thorpe, Mrs M M M, MCLIP, Learning Resources Admin., Loughborough Coll. [177] 01/01/1967 CM01/01/1970

Thorpe, Mr P, BSc FCLIP, Ret. [14694] 12/03/1971 FE01/04/2002

Thorpe, Mr P, Search Engine Visitor Serv. Asst., Nat. Railway Mus., York. [10015394] 12/11/2009 AF

Thow, Mrs J A, MCLIP, Retired. [22392] 12/03/1951 CM01/01/1957

Thow, Miss L R, BA Hons Pg DIP/CPE, Sen. L. Asst., Whitley Bay High Sch., Tyne & Wear. [10016169] 18/02/2010 ME

Thresh, Mrs P A, BA(Hons) MCLIP, Community Devel. Lib., Leeds [30061] 06/11/1978 CM18/11/1980

Thrift, Mrs H, BMus MA MCLIP, Assoc. Dir. of L. Serv., Univ. of Sheffield. [39021] 28/10/1985 CM09/08/1988

Throssell, Mrs M, MCLIP, Retired. [14704] 23/10/1942 CM01/01/1946

Throwgood, Mrs H, Unknown. [10013969] 17/06/2009 ME

Thurley, Miss M J, MCLIP, Retired. [17860] 26/10/1942 CM01/01/1948

Thurley, Mr N M, BA(Hons) MA MCLIP, Outreach Lib., Univ. of Oxford. [54461] 16/12/1996 CM29/03/2004

Thursfield, Mrs J, MCLIP, Prin. Lib. ; Serv. Delivery, Stoke on Trent L. I. A. [22980] 01/10/1974 CM24/02/1978

Thurston, Mrs T, Systems Lib., Law Soc., London. [58139] 08/11/1999 ME

Thwaite, Ms N, MA, Asst. Lib. Curator, N. Trust [42136] 07/10/1988 ME

Thwaites, Ms M E, BA(Hons) DipILS MCLIP, Lib., Nottinghamshire C.C., Arnold L. [46584] 20/11/1991 CM27/11/1996

Tibbetts, Mrs W A, MCLIP, Asst. Locality Lib., Stourbridge [20671] 01/01/1973 CM01/08/1975

Tibbitts, Mrs G M, MCLIP, P. /t. Team Lib., L.B. Tower Hamlets, Lansbury L. [31118] 20/08/1979 CM16/07/1982

Tidswell, Miss J, BA(Hons) BA(Hons), Grad. Trainee, Univ. for the Creative Arts, Sidney Cooper L., Canterbury. [10006595] 06/02/2007 ME

Tiernan, Mr J J, MA FCLIP FRSA, Retired. [19810] 01/12/1972 FE14/08/1991

Tighe, Mrs E A, ACLIP, Sen. Lib. Asst., Wolverton L., Milton Keynes. [10006063] 24/08/2007 ACL16/06/2010

Tighe, Ms J A R, BA(Hons) MA, Unknown. [37749] 15/10/1984 ME

Tighe, Mr P A, BA(Hons), Sen. Res. Lib., Berwin Leighton Paisner., LLP [50379] 12/07/1994 ME

Tiley, Mr S D, BA(Hons) MA DipLIM MCLIP, Lib., Sidney Sussex Coll., Cambridge. [55578] 21/10/1997 CM16/05/2001

Tilke, Dr A, BA MEd FRSA FCLIP ATCL, Head of Lib., Bangkok Patana Sch., Thailand [26582] 23/10/1979 FE24/09/1997

Tillett, Mrs V J, BSc(Hons) MSc, Asst. L. Serv. Mngr. Health Sciences L., Frimley Park Hosp. NHS Foundation Trust [55714] 06/11/1997 ME

Tilley, Mrs B J, MCLIP, Life Member. [14721] 01/01/1948 CM18/02/1974

Tilley, Mr D, Unwaged. [64662] 12/05/2005 ME

Tilley, Mrs E A, BA(Hons) MSc(Econ) MCLIP, Eng. Faculty Lib., Univ. of Cambridge [58942] 05/10/2000 CM01/06/2005

Tilley, Mrs E F, MA DipLib CertEd MCLIP, User Support Lib., Univ. of Wales, Bangor [10001774] 07/10/1976 CM14/12/1978

Tilley, Ms J E, BA MA DipLaw, Sr. Info. Advr., Kingston Univ. [41076] 02/10/1987 ME

Tilley, Ms J, BSc, Sen. Asst. Subject Lib., Teeside Univ. L., Tees Valley [10017043] 21/06/2010 AF

Tilley, Mr N V, MCLIP, Retired. [19117] 10/03/1951 CM01/01/1958

Tillotson, Miss F E, Sch. Lib., Lancs. C.C. [63089] 27/01/2004 ME

Tillson, Miss S, BSc (Hons), Customer Suport Offr., Salisbury L. & Galeries. [10014678] 27/08/2009 **AF**

Tilly, Mr N J, MCLIP, Life Member. [14726] 14/03/1954 **CM01/01/1960**

Timmons, Mr A, BA(Hons) DipLIS MCLIP, Inf. Serv. Mgr., Food Standards Agency, London. [49995] 07/02/1994 **CM22/09/1999**

Timms, Mr D B, MCLIP, Retired. [14730] 17/03/1953 **CM01/01/1962**

Timms, Mrs J A, BA MCLIP, Catr., Derbys. L. & Heritage, Matlock. [28908] 18/01/1978 **CM15/09/1983**

Timms, Mr M G, BA MCLIP, Retired. [18448] 23/10/1972 **CM26/09/1975**

Timms, Mrs M J, BA MCLIP, Br. Lib., Hatch End L., L.B. of Harrow [22006] 12/12/1973 **CM01/10/1976**

Timoney, Mrs E, BA, Unknown. [10011575] 27/10/2008 **AF**

Timothy, Mrs W, BA MLib MCLIP, Sen. Lib., Mgmnt Inf., Staffs. C.C. [43896] 13/02/1990 **CM22/07/1992**

Timson, Ms J, Unknown. [10011483] 12/01/1995 **ME**

Tindale, Mr J W, BA(Hons) MA MCLIP, Inf. Mgr., Dept. for Work & Pensions, London. [54990] 12/06/1997 **CM13/03/2002**

Tiney, Mrs P C, DipLib MCLIP, Catr., The Brit. L., Boston Spa. [29955] 23/11/1978 **CM24/01/1984**

Tinker, Dr A J, MSc PhD MCLIP, p. /t. Academic Skills Tutor, p. /t. Sen. Asst. Lib., Univ. of Huddersfield. [53582] 01/08/1996 **CM08/11/1999**

Tinker, Mr M E, BA(Hons) MCLIP, Local Hist. Lib., Sefton L., Southport L. [41440] 05/12/1987 **CM18/11/1998**

Tinkler, Mrs F E, MA(Hons), Edin, MSc Brist., Learning Resource Cent. Mgr., Beechen Cliff Sch., Bath. [64242] 22/02/2005 **ME**

Tinson, Miss S L, BA(Hons) MCLIP, Cent. Mgr., Plymouth Sch. L. Serv. [49420] 21/10/1993 **CM20/05/1998**

Tinworth, Mrs R S, BA MA MCLIP, Career Break [52603] 13/11/1995 **CM19/01/2000**

Tipler, Mrs L J, MCLIP, Res. Asst. (p. /t.) Queenwood L., Eastbourne, Sussex. [19173] 05/08/1972 **CM01/11/1975**

Tipple, Mr A, ACLIP, Inf. & ICT Offr., Church End L., London. [10003948] 23/05/2007 **ACL04/03/2009**

Tirimanne, Mrs G S, DipLib MCLIP, Tech. Serv. Lib., Kangan Inst. of TAFE, Broadmeadows, Australia. [27010] 10/01/1977 **CM25/05/1988**

Titchmarsh, Mrs J E, BA PGCE MCLIP, Lib., Gtr. Manchester Police, Training Sch., Prestwich. [40773] 02/06/1987 **CM29/01/1992**

Titcombe, Mrs J M, MPhil FCLIP, Retired [3367] 25/09/1968 **FE18/07/1990**

Tither, Mrs J M, BA MCLIP, Lib., RAF Menwith Hill [5810] 05/01/1971 **CM03/08/1973**

Titley, Mr G D C, BA MCLIP, Subject Lib. & Copyright Advisor., Plymouth Univ. [34141] 05/10/1981 **CM17/09/1986**

Tito, Miss M, BA, Unknown. [10013570] 07/05/2009 **ME**

Titterington, Mrs S F, MCLIP, Community Devel. Mgr., Leeds City Council. [36619] 24/10/1983 **CM19/01/1988**

Titterton, Miss G R, BEd(Hons) DipLib MSc MCLIP, Res. Offr., Manchester Cent. L. [31964] 06/01/1980 **CM16/05/1985**

Tivey, Ms G P, BA MA MCLIP, Lib. & Inf. Mgr, Sci. & Advice for Scottish Agriculture (SASA), Edinburgh [36723] 04/11/1983 **CM15/08/1989**

Toal, Miss E S, BA(Hons.) French Studies, Lib., Renfrew High Sch., Glasgow. [10001269] 14/02/2007 **ME**

Toase, Mr C A, HonFLA, Ref. Bks. Consultant, London . [14747] 09/02/1946 **CM01/01/1955**

Toase, Mrs S A, BA MCLIP, Cust. Serv. Mgr., Cent. L., Oxfordshire C.C. [33779] 06/02/1981 **CM07/10/1986**

Tobin, Mrs C M, MA MCLIP, Area Co-ordinator, Worksop L., Notts. C.C. [52078] 02/10/1995 **CM20/11/2002**

Tobin, Mrs P V, Community Lib., Luton Bor. Council [10006906] 02/07/1996 **ME**

Tocock, Mr A, BA(Hons), Graduate Trainee L. Asst., Archway Healthcare L. [10016036] 11/02/2010 **ME**

Tod, Mrs J L, BSc(Hons) MCLIP, Interim L. Mgr., Rochdale MBC, Rochdale [4240] 12/01/1971 **CM08/01/1975**

Todd, Mr C P, A. V. Co-ordinator, Sutton Cent. L., Sutton. [65453] 24/02/2006 **AF**

Todd, Mrs M E, BSc(Econ) MCLIP, Principal Lib., Belfast Educ. & L. Board. [54494] 02/01/1997 **CM15/10/2002**

Todd, Miss R E, BA(Hons) MA, L. Serv. Offr., Ravensbourne Coll. of Design & Comm. Kent. [57482] 06/04/1999 **ME**

Todd, Mrs S C, BSc MCLIP, Asst. Lib. (catg), Oxford Brookes Univ. [36444] 13/10/1983 **CM10/11/1987**

Todd, Mrs S, BA MA(Ed) MCLIP, Lib., St. Johns Sch., Leatherhead. [1310] 21/09/1970 **CM01/11/1972**

Todd, Mr W G, MA BA, Unknown. [10014983] 01/10/2009 **ME**

Todd-Jones, Mr M J, MCLIP, Asst. Lib., Univ. of Cambridge, Dept. of Chemis. [28705] 17/01/1978 **CM07/04/1981**

Toerien, Mr D, BA(Hons) MA PDC, Head of L. and Inf. Serv., Oakham Sch. [63772] 06/10/2004 **ME**

Toft, Miss S D, BA PgDip, Asst. Lib., Royal Derby Hosp. [10009978] 27/06/2008 **ME**

Tokwe, Mr H, HND, Sen. L. Asst., Midlands State Univ., Zimbabwe. [61664] 14/10/2002 **ME**

Tollington, Ms J, MCLIP, Team Lib – Serv. Devel.,Taunton L.,Taunton Somerset [10001490] 01/07/1972 **CM07/08/1975**

Tomalin, Ms A L, MA BA MCLIP, Customer Serv. L. [34145] 05/10/1981 **CM11/04/1985**

Tomblin, Mrs J M, MA MCLIP, Life Member. [17865] 22/03/1966 **CM01/01/1971**

Tomes, Mrs J, FCLIP, Life Member. [14768] 10/04/1953 **FE01/01/1964**

Tomes, Mr P C, BLib MCLIP, Lib., Salisbury L. [42463] 14/11/1988 **CM22/05/1996**

Tomkinson, Ms G M, MA MCLIP, Catr., Inf. Resources, L. and Learning Resources, Nottingham Trent Univ. [38659] 17/09/1985 **CM16/07/2003**

Tomlin, Ms C M, BA DipLib MCLIP, Asst. Head of L. (Job Share), City & Co. of Swansea. [39566] 06/03/1986 **CM30/01/1991**

Tomlinson, Miss J A, BA MA MCLIP, Catg. and Metadata Servs. Mgr., Wellcome L., London. [34485] 12/11/1981 **CM18/06/1985**

Tomlinson, Mrs J H, BA, Unwaged [10014438] 31/07/2009 **ME**

Tomlinson, Ms J, Dep. Head of Inf. & Learning Serv., Exeter Coll. [10001337] 03/10/2000 **ME**

Tomlinson, Miss K E, BSc MSc MCLIP, Inf. Offr., Careers Advisory Serv., Univ. of Bath. [10007791] 11/02/2004 **CM18/12/2009**

Tomlinson, Ms K S, BA MLS MCLIP, Unwaged. [43194] 02/10/1989 **CM27/07/1994**

Tomos, Mrs E L, BLib MCLIP, Dir. Cymal Welsh Assembly Govt., Aberystwyth. [20863] 01/01/1973 **CM01/07/1987**

Tomos, Mr M W, BA PGCE DAA MCLIP, Meirionnydd Arch., Gwynedd Council. [14572] 01/01/1971 **CM01/07/1987**

Toms, Miss A L, BA(Hons) DipILM MCLIP, Reader Serv. Offr., RNIB Nat. Lib. Serv., [58874] 20/09/2000 **CM23/06/2004**

Toner, Mrs L J, BA MCLIP, Site L. Mgr., St. Martins Coll., Lancaster. [39203] 02/01/1986 **CM06/09/1988**

Tong, Mrs C G, BA(Hons) MA MCLIP, KnowledgeConsultant, Univ. of Herts., Dehavilland. [55033] 01/07/1997 **CM13/06/2007**

Tong, Miss L, MA MCLIP, Unknown. [42283] 19/10/1988 **CM27/07/1994**

Tong, Mr R K L, L. Asst., European Sch. of Osteopathy, Maidstone. [62977] 02/12/2003 **AF**

Tongue, Mrs S, Principal. L. Asst. -Inf. & Local Studies, Solihull L. & Arts, Solihull Cent. L. [57790] 06/08/1999 **ME**

Tonkiss Cameron, Mrs R, BA(Hons) MA MCLIP, Arch., Union Theological Seminary, New York. [22081] 01/01/1974 **CM12/06/1979**

Tonkiss, Mr M F, BA, Systems Lib., Carshalton Coll., Surrey. [53799] 01/10/1996 **ME**

Tonks, Mrs G, BA(Hons), Stud. [10017138] 14/07/2010 **ME**

Tonks, Mr J D M, BA DipLib MCLIP, Inf. Lib., Northants. L. & Inf. Serv., Wellingborough L. [38333] 15/03/1985 **CM14/11/1989**

Tonner, Mrs N C, BA(Hons) PgDipLib MCLIP, Team Leader, Edinburgh Council, Edinburgh. [48976] 12/08/1993 **CM20/03/1996**

Tooke, Miss J, MCLIP, Lib., Shropshire C.C., Bridgnorth. [24837] 06/10/1975 **CM29/12/1978**

Tooley, Mrs K, BA(Hons) MA MCLIP, Devel. & Support Mgr., Hants. Sch. L. Serv., Winchester. [62038] 28/01/2003 **CM29/03/2006**

Toomey, Miss M C, MCLIP, Career break [30693] 15/01/1979 **CM28/10/1986**

Toon, Mr J E, MCLIP MA, Life Member. [14797] 29/08/1957 **CM01/01/1960**

Toop, Mr S, BSc MCLIP, Communications Offr., Connexions Shropshire, Shrewsbury. [10006660] 05/05/1992 **CM17/01/2001**

Tooth, Mrs G M, MCLIP, Retired. [14802] 06/02/1961 **CM01/01/1967**

Tootill, Dr C E, BA MCLIP MCMI, Unwaged. [31026] 02/07/1979 **CM21/09/1984**

Topham, Miss E M, MCLIP, Retired. [17871] 14/10/1937 **CM01/01/1941**

Topping, Mrs D, BLib MCLIP, Asst. Lib. (p. /t.), De Montfort Univ., Leicester. [34995] 08/06/1982 **CM09/04/1987**

Topping, Mrs K J, BA DipLib MCLIP, Inf. Offr., Neurosupport, Liverpool. [39676] 07/05/1986 **CM14/03/1990**

Topping, Mrs P R, BA(Hons) BEd MEd, Lib., Kingussie High Sch., Highland Council. [57761] 28/07/1999 **ME**

Torley, Mr G, BA MSc MCLIP, Supply and Acquisitions Offr., Mitchell L., Glasgow. [34815] 12/03/1982 **CM11/11/1986**

Torpey, Mrs S L, BA(Hons), Career Break [56071] 06/02/1998 **ME**

Torrero, Mr C L, BA MCLIP, Sen. Inf. Offr., LGC Limited, Teddington. [53600] 06/08/1996 **CM04/05/1993**

Toscani, Mrs D, BA MA, Grp. Mgr., Canzey L., Essex CC. [10007758] 22/04/2002 **ME**

Toth, Mr G, Inf. Asst., Nat. Maritime Mus., London. [10016566] 16/04/2010 **AF**

Totham, Mrs P, BA(Hons) MCLIP, Self-employed, Snodland, Kent. [26554] 01/10/1976 **CM16/07/1981**

Totten, Mrs J, L. Asst., L. NI. [61741] 31/10/2002 **ME**

Totterdell, Mrs A C, BA(Hons) MCLIP, Retired [42935] 01/01/1954 **CM01/01/1959**

Totty, Miss J T, MA BA(Hons) PGCE, Lib. Servs. Mgr., Middlesbrough Coll. [56081] 12/02/1998 **ME**

Tough, Mrs B, MA(Hons) MCLIP, Lib.,Garden Court Chambers, London [10014450] 05/10/1995 **CM19/05/1999**

Tough, Miss D S, MA MCLIP FLS, Head of Catg., Natural Hist. Mus. London. [14814] 18/01/1972 **CM14/07/1976**

Touhey, Ms J, Unknown. [10008575] 14/05/1991 **ME**

Tout, Ms F, ACLIP, Learning Resource Cent. Mgr., Broadoak Maths & Computing Coll., Weston-super-Mare. [10008377] 19/03/2008 **ACL03/12/2008**

Tovell, Mr P J, BA(Hons) MA MCLIP, Team Leader: Books, Reading and Learning Staffordshire Co. Council [63065] 27/01/2004 **CM29/11/2006**

Tovey, Mrs H G, MCLIP, Retired. [6544] 13/01/1950 **CM01/01/1963**

Towers, Mrs G M, BA MCLIP, Housewife. [15147] 05/09/1968 **CM27/03/1975**

Towers, Miss H S, BA MA MCLIP, Young Peoples Serv. Lib., St. Albans Cent. L., Herts. [58439] 14/02/2000 **CM29/03/2004**

Towers, Mrs H, BA DipLib MCLIP, Reader Devel. Offr., Cumbria C.C. [36334] 04/10/1983 **CM21/07/1989**

Towle, Ms D, BA(Hons) MLib MCLIP, Res. Offr., Birmingham City Council. [43447] 26/10/1989 **CM26/02/1992**

Towle, Dr G, BA Phd PGCert, Unknown. [10015108] 14/10/2009 **ME**

Towler, Mr J W, MA MCLIP, Retired, (Member, Sydenham Soc.). [14820] 07/09/1964 **CM01/01/1968**

Towler, Mrs S, BA(Hons) MA, Lib., Acle High Sch., Norfolk. [62726] 13/10/2003 **ME**

Towlson, Ms K B, BSc(Hons) MA FHEA MCLIP, Sen. Asst. Lib., DeMontfort Univ., Leicester. [41078] 08/10/1987 **CM12/12/1990**

Town, Mr J S, MA DipLib FCLIP, Dir. of Inf., Univ. of York. [29350] 02/06/1978 **FE22/05/1991**

Towner, Mr S, MCLIP, Retired. [14821] 01/01/1949 **CM01/01/1966**

Townsend, Miss A C, BA MA MCLIP, Reading Resources Mgr., Kingston L. [44112] 18/05/1990 **CM21/07/1993**

Townsend, Mrs A L, MCLIP, p. /t. Sch. Lib., Wisbech Grammar Sch., Cambs. [18175] 08/10/1972 **CM16/07/1975**

Townsend, Miss C, BA MScEcon, Stud. [10000473] 09/10/2006 **ME**

Townsend, Mrs W A, BA(Hons) MSc MCLIP, L. Serv. Mgr., Coventry & Warwickshire Partnership Trust [63666] 12/08/2004 **CM29/11/2006**

Townson, Mrs A, MA MCLIP, Unwaged. [55161] 28/07/1997 **CM25/07/2001**

Towsey, Mr M A, MA MCLIP, Princ. Lib., L.B. of Lambeth. [23652] 20/01/1975 **CM04/02/1977**

Toy, Mrs L, BA MCLIP, L. & Inf. Offr., Newcastle upon Tyne City Council, City L. [35738] 21/01/1983 **CM15/02/1989**

Toyne, Miss J, BSc(Econ) MCLIP, Lifelong Learning and Local Studies Lib., Hoddesdon L., Hertfordshire [54393] 02/12/1996 **CM07/09/2005**

Tozer, Mrs A E, BSc DipLib MCLIP, Specialist . Lib., Hampshire C.C., Winchester [27938] 01/10/1977 **CM22/12/1980**

Tozer, Miss C J, BA(Hons), Unknown. [10012843] 13/03/2009 **ME**

Tozer-Hotchkiss, Dr G, MA PhD, Part-Time Stud. & Freelance Chemical Inf. Specialist [60717] 25/08/1984 **ME**

Tracey, Ms C C, BA(Hons) DipInf, Inf. Mgr., Mercer Oliver Wyman, London. [49130] 07/10/1993 **ME**

Trafford, Mrs D M, BA(Hons) PGCE, Sch. Lib., St. Peters Sch., Cambs. [62379] 19/05/2003 **AF**

Trafford-Smith, Mr P C, DipBus IFA AAT, LRC. Mgr., The Langley Academy, Berks. [65500] 08/02/2006 **AF**

Train, Mrs J P, BSc PhD, Lib., Dorridge Junior Sch., Solihull, W. Mids. [10004922] 06/06/2007 **AF**

Tramantza, Mrs E, BA MSc MCLIP, Academic Liason Lib., Faculty of Eng. & Physical Sci., Univ. of Surrey, Guildford [10001713] 15/03/2007 **CM05/05/2010**

Tran, Ms A B, BA(Hons) MSc MCLIP, Policy Res., & KM Offr., Dept. of Health S. E., Guildford, Surrey [10001784] 22/11/1999 **CM30/11/2009**

Tranmer, Ms C, MLS MCLIP, p. /t. Inf. Consultant, (Built Environment), Oxford. [14836] 01/01/1967 **CM01/01/1970**

Traue, Miss S I, Lib. Serv. Mngr., Treasury Solicitors Dept., London London. [64038] 06/12/2004 **ME**

Travers, Mr J, BA(Hons) MA, Dep. Br. Lib., Balham L., L.B. of Wandsworth. [58540] 01/04/2000 **ME**

Travers, Miss K S, BA(Hons) MA, Asst. Lib., Univ. of E. London [59537] 01/05/2001 **ME**

Travers, Mr O M, B ED(Hons), Unknown. [10014063] 23/06/2009 **AF**

Travers, Mrs S A, BA(Hons) MSc(Econ) MCLIP, Web Editor, BIS, London. [55424] 13/10/1997 **CM13/03/2002**

Traves, Mrs C J, MA DipTefla, Sen. Lib. -IT, Bournemouth L. [59940] 08/11/2001 **ME**

Travis, Mrs K L, BA(Hons) MCLIP, Unwaged. [55414] 08/10/1997 **CM25/07/2001**

Trayhurn, Mr R J, MCLIP, Lib., Inf. Serv., Swindon Bor. L. [14846] 01/01/1965 **CM01/01/1968**

Traynor, Miss E M, BA DipLib MCLIP, Asst. Dir. (L. Serv. & Res. Support), Queens Univ. Belfast [37494] 01/10/1984 **CM07/07/1987**

Treacy, Mr N, BSc DipLib MCLIP, L. Inf. Offr., Amnesty Internat., London. [24838] 06/10/1975 **CM01/01/1980**

Treadwell, Mrs H M, BA(Hons) MSc MCLIP, Unwaged. [58975] 13/10/2000 **CM21/06/2006**

Treadwell, Mr M R, BSc(Hons) MA MA MCLIP, Inf. Specialist. [57435] 01/04/1999 **RV24/04/2009** **CM07/09/2005**

Tredinnick, Mr L M, Sen. Lect., London Met. Univ. [58432] 11/02/2000
ME
Tree, Mr K S, Lib., The Law Comm., London. [35988] 17/03/1983　**ME**
Tree, Mrs L, BA MCLIP, Community Lib., Cent. Inf. Team, Norfolk L. &
Inf. Serv. [25160] 11/12/1975　**CM19/11/1979**
Tregear, Mrs M E, FCLIP, Retired. [3203] 28/02/1940　**FE01/01/1950**
Tregellas, Miss M, BA, Stud., Aberystwyth Univ. [10011358] 14/10/2008
ME
Tregellas, Miss N C, BSc (Honours), Stud. [10006337] 15/10/2007　**ME**
Trela, Ms A, MA, Configuration Lib., EUROPOL, Netherlands
[10017038] 18/06/2010　**ME**
Trenbath, Ms K E, Unknown. [10014082] 25/06/2009　**ME**
Trenchard, Mrs S M, MCLIP, Retired. [491] 04/10/1967　**CM01/01/1971**
Trestain, Mrs J, BA(Hons) MA PGDip, Knowledge Mgmnt. Offr., FCO
Serv., Hanslope Park [55981] 08/01/1998　**ME**
Trevett, Ms P A, BA FCLIP, Retired. [14861] 01/01/1956　**FE01/01/1964**
Trevor, Mrs R W, BA(Hons) MCLIP, Sch. Lib. Sir John Lawes Sch.,
Herts [32101] 05/02/1980　**CM06/06/1984**
Trickey, Mrs H F, BA(Hons) MA, Inf. Cent. Mgr., Wilsthorpe B & E Coll.,
Derbs. C.C. [63489] 15/06/2004　**ME**
Trickey, Mr K V, BA MA FCLIP, Trainer, Consultant, & p. /t. Lect.,
Sherrington Sanders & Liverpool John Moores Univ. [21882]
28/01/1974　**FE23/09/1998**
Trifilo, Ms D E, MLS, Lib., San Francisco P.L., USA [10015292]
30/10/2009　**ME**
Trimming, Mrs F J, BA(Hons) MCLIP, Child. Serv. Lib., Bognor Regis L.,
London [47883] 23/10/1992　**CM21/07/1999**
Trinder, Miss V M, BEd FCLIP LTCL, Retired. [31100] 13/08/1979
FE20/05/1998
Tring, Mr T J, BA MSc MCLIP, Lib., Castle Coll., Nottingham. [61015]
01/02/2002　**CM23/06/2004**
Tringham, Mrs C, L. Co-ordinator, Rutland Coll., Rutland. [10016630]
01/05/2010　**ME**
Tripathi, Mrs U, MA MCLIP, Life Member. [14870] 11/09/1962
CM01/01/1965
Troake, Miss A, Bsc(Hons) PGCE, L. Asst., Carlton L., Nottingham
[10014478] 04/08/2009　**AF**
Troake, Mr J, MCLIP, Retired. [14876] 01/01/1948　**CM01/01/1960**
Trodd, Miss J E, MA, Acting Mgr., IME, London [10008657] 24/01/1994
ME
Trollope, Miss H L, BA(Hons), Inf. Asst., Univ. Wales, Newport [63755]
29/09/2004　**ME**
Tromans, Ms E H C, BA(Hons) MCLIP, L. & Learning Res. Mgr,
Halesowen Coll. [49694] 25/11/1993 **RV01/10/2008 CM12/03/2003**
Troon, Mr M, Judicial & Court Inf. Srvc., Min. of Justice L., Birmingham
[59023] 27/10/2000　**AF**
Trotman, Ms S E D, PgD BA DipCert, Info. Educ. & Comm. Specialist.,
OECS, HIV/AIDS Project Unit (HAPU) (Internat. Organisation)
[43956] 01/03/1990　**ME**
Trott, Mrs A, BA DipLib MCLIP, Inf. Spec. (L.), Kings Coll., Univ. of
London. [34660] 18/01/1982　**CM21/01/1986**
Trott, Mrs F J, BA MCLIP, Inf. Consultant, BCIS Associates, E. Bergholt.
[27078] 26/01/1977　**CM01/10/1982**
Trotter, Mr R R, BA FCLIP, Retired. [14882] 01/01/1966　**FE24/09/1997**
Trout, Mr E A R, BA DipLib MCLIP, Mgr. Inf. Serv., The Concrete Soc.,
Camberley. [38385] 03/04/1985　**CM15/05/2002**
Trowsdale, Mrs J M, B Ed(Hons) MCLIP, SLS Co-ordinator, Sch. L.
Serv., Lincoln. [65830] 22/05/2006　**CM09/09/2009**
Truebridge, Ms J E, Ret. [39645] 21/04/1986　**ME**
Truelove, Ms M, MCLIP, Unwaged. [28707] 13/01/1978 **CM02/04/1982**
Trueman, Mrs G R, MA MCLIP, Lib., Peasedown St. John Primary Sch.
[41939] 22/05/1988　**CM27/11/1996**
Truman, Miss E, BA(Hons), L. Asst., Worthing L., W. Sussex.
[10016044] 10/02/2010　**AF**

Trumper, Miss M C, BLS MCLIP, Community Devel. Lib.,
Maidstone/Tunbridge Wells, Kent. [31966] 10/01/1980**CM03/11/1983**
Truran, Mrs J E, BA ACLIP, Sch. Lib., Francis Coombes Sch., Watford.
[59051] 06/11/2000　**ACL29/03/2006**
Truslove, Mrs E J, BSc(Hons) MA MCLIP, Child. Lib., Daventry L.,
Northamptonshire. [57040] 27/11/1998　**CM17/09/2003**
Tsang, Ms P K Y, MCLIP, Sen. Tech., Map L., Dept. of Geography, Univ.
of Hong Kong. [52782] 12/12/1995　**CM20/11/2002**
Tsang, Miss S S Y, BA MLib MCLIP, Sect. Head-Inf. Serv., Hong Kong
Poly. Univ. L [39932] 03/10/1986　**CM30/01/1991**
Tsang, Miss T K L, BA(Hons) MA MA MCLIP, Access Team Leader,
Kings Coll. London. [61575] 02/10/2002　**CM01/02/2006**
Tse, Miss T L P, BA(Hons) MA, Sen. Lib., Herbert Smith, London.
[52950] 26/01/1996　**ME**
Tseng, Mrs G M, MSc MCLIP, Unwaged. [25017] 31/10/1975
CM11/11/1985
Tubb, Mrs T C, BA(Hons) MA MCLIP, Dep. Lib., Nuffield Coll. L., Oxford.
[53837] 03/10/1996　**CM15/01/2003**
Tuck, Mr J P, MA MCLIP, Dir. of Lib., Royal Holloway, London. [30799]
10/04/1979　**CM11/12/1981**
Tuck, Mrs J, LLB(Hons), Lib. Asst., St. Catherine's Hospice, Crawley.
[64200] 03/02/2005　**ME**
Tuck, Miss N, MCLIP, Retired. [14897] 01/01/1948　**CM01/01/1958**
Tucker, Mrs C L, BA DLS, Lib., Leicester Coll. [34386] 21/10/1981　**ME**
Tucker, Ms K F, BA(Hons) MSc MCLIP, Child. Serv. Lib., W. Sussex
[63124] 11/02/2004　**CM19/11/2008**
Tucker, Miss L K, BA(Hons) MSc MCLIP, Subject Support Lib., The Sir
Michael Cobham L., Bournemouth Univ. [10010856] 01/07/2002
CM27/01/2010
Tucker, Mrs M E, BA MLib MCLIP, Area Mgr., Stroud & Cotswold, Glos.
Co. L. [6753] 10/01/1968　**CM02/08/1973**
Tucker, Mr M R, MA, Inf. Mgr., Min. of Defence, Whitehall L.,London.
[10000917] 12/03/1986　**ME**
Tucker, Miss S J F, MCLIP, Retired. [14906] 01/01/1964 **CM01/01/1969**
Tucker, Ms S, MA BBS DipLib MCLIP, Asst. Lib., Trinity Coll. [27033]
12/01/1977　**CM12/01/1979**
Tuckwell, Mr G C, BA MCLIP, Not Working [28709] 11/01/1978
CM07/07/1980
Tudge, Miss I M, BSc MSc, Tech. Mgr., MOD. [10008229] 25/03/2004
ME
Tudor, Mrs B, PA & Admin. Co-ordinator, Mostyn House Sch., Neston
[10014430] 30/07/2009　**ME**
Tudor, Mr J A, MBA MCLIP FHEA, Subject Lib., Bournemouth Univ.,
Poole. [14909] 01/01/1965　**CM01/01/1969**
Tugwell, Mr A C, BPharm MSc MPS MCLIP, Sr. Dir. Pharm., Barts. &
the London NHS Trust, The Royal London Hosp. [60736] 22/10/1985
CM22/10/1985
Tulasiewicz, Mr E, MA, Communication Offr., Westminster, London.
[61193] 08/04/2002　**ME**
Tull, Mrs J, ACLIP, Lib., Highdown Sch, Reading. [62304] 23/04/2003
ACL01/06/2005
Tull, Mrs V M, BA(Hons) PGDipIM MCLIP, Br. Lib., Moreton Bay Reg.
C., Australia [51497] 16/03/1995　**CM21/05/2003**
Tulloch, Ms M K, Post-16 Lib., Cotham Sch., Bristol. [64383]
14/03/2005　**ME**
Tulloch, Ms P, MA MBA DipLib MCLIP, Inf. Serv. mgr., Culture & Sport
Glasgow [37670] 17/10/1984　**CM16/02/1988**
Tully, Miss N, BSc(Hons), LRC Mgr., Wilmslow High Sch., Wilmslow,
Sheshire. [10013718] 22/05/2009　**AF**
Tumelty, Ms N, BA, Unknown. [10011527] 17/10/2008　**ME**
Tumilty, Miss A M, MCLIP, Retired. [14917] 01/01/1964 **CM01/01/1968**
Tunesi of Liongam, Mrs J E M, MSc MCLIP, Specialist Administrator.
[38329] 20/03/1985　**CM16/05/1990**

Tunks, Mrs D C, BA DipLib MCLIP, Unemployed. [42365] 24/10/1988
CM14/08/1991

Tunley, Mr M F, MA FCLIP, Life Member. [14920] 01/01/1954
FE01/01/1963

Tunley, Mrs S A V, FCLIP, Retired. [14921] 26/03/1957   FE01/01/1965

Tunnicliffe, Mr N W, BSc MCLIP, Retired. [14923] 01/01/1967
CM01/01/1969

Tupling, Mr A M, MA FCLIP, Life Member. [14924] 01/01/1951
FE01/01/1959

Turk, Miss S C, Asst., Collection Devel. Lib., Univ. of the Arts, London.
[65210] 17/11/2005   ME

Turkington, Mrs S, MSc BA(Hons) MCLIP, Lib., Scottish Goverment
[62617] 18/09/2003   CM10/07/2009

Turley, Mrs P J, BSc(Econ)(Hons), Head of Inf. Resources, House of
Commons L., London. [45157] 27/07/1990   ME

Turnbull, Mrs B, BSc, Unknown. [65775] 01/05/2006   ME

Turnbull, Mr G T, BA MCLIP, Heritage Inf. Coordinator, Cent. L.,
Manchester. [14932] 01/01/1968   CM27/07/1972

Turnbull, Mrs J A, BA DipLib MCLIP, Retired. [44952] 22/01/1991
CM15/09/1993

Turnbull, Mrs L, BA, Unknown. [10015599] 28/10/1994   ME

Turnbull, Ms S E, BLib MCLIP MSc, Internat. Tax Inf. Mgr.,
PricewaterhouseCoopers, London. [24840] 01/10/1975
CM10/04/1981

Turnbull, Mrs V, BA PGDip, Sch. Lib., Trinity Sch., Carlisle. [58749]
05/07/2000   ME

Turner, Mrs A F, BA MCLIP, Family Inf., L.B. of Hammersmith &
Fulham., London. [27889] 04/10/1977   CM10/10/1982

Turner, Mrs A H, BA MCLIP, Young Peoples Serv. Mgr., Lancashire Co.
Libs. [37867] 08/11/1984   CM15/11/1988

Turner, Mrs A J, BA(Hons) MLib MCLIP, Ch. Knowledge Offr.,
Wolverhampton City PCT, [10009803] 16/10/1992 RV10/01/2006
CM26/11/1997

Turner, Mr A J, Subject Lib., Bournemouth Arts Inst. [66017] 24/08/2006
ME

Turner, Mr A R, BA MCLIP, Online Systems Mgr., Thames Valley Univ.,
Reading. [35987] 17/03/1983   CM07/07/1987

Turner, Mrs B, Stud., Aberystwyth Univ. [10009215] 07/05/2008   ME

Turner, Ms C A, MSc, Applications Support Consultant, Axiell,
Ferndown, Dorset. [29899] 19/10/1978   ME

Turner, Mrs C A, BA, Sen. L. Asst., Newbold Coll., Binfield, Berks.
[56335] 26/05/1998   ME

Turner, Mr C M, BA MA DipLib MCLIP, Freelance IT Consultant, L.,
Museums and Arch.,London. [22414] 07/05/1974   CM06/07/1977

Turner, Mrs D F, BA MCLIP, Retired. [14943] 01/01/1956 CM01/01/1963

Turner, Mrs D, BA(Hons) MSc PgCLTHE MCLIP, Subject Lib., Teesside
Univ. L. [10013148] 06/02/1981   CM30/08/1985

Turner, Ms G C, MA MCLIP, Head of Acquisitions &, Spanish Acq. L.,
The London L. [49957] 31/01/1994   CM21/01/1998

Turner, Mrs I, MA DipLib MCLIP, Network Lib., Aberdeenshire Council,
Banff Academy. [22653] 01/06/1974   CM23/03/1993

Turner, Ms J A, BA MCLIP, Project Mgr., CCRA, Winchester. [26149]
08/07/1976   CM22/09/1978

Turner, Ms J F, BA(Hons) DipLIS MCLIP, Trust Lib., E. Sussex Hosp.
NHS Trust, St. Leonards on Sea. [41780] 08/04/1988 CM17/03/1999

Turner, Mr J P, BA MCLIP, Team Leader, Lend. & Inter L. Loans, Univ. of
Nottingham. [14960] 01/01/1970   CM01/01/1972

Turner, Mrs J R, BA(Hons) MCLIP, Bookseller/Floor Mgr., Ottakars plc,
Lincoln. [50370] 07/07/1994   CM22/07/1998

Turner, Miss J S, MCLIP, Asst. Lib., Oxford Brookes Univ., Oxford.
[14961] 01/01/1969   CM18/09/1972

Turner, Mr J W S, MA MCLIP, Life Member. [14962] 01/01/1960
CM01/01/1965

Turner, Mrs J, MA BA MCLIP, Reader Devl. Mgr., Essex C.C.,
Chelmsford. [28347] 01/11/1977   CM03/10/1979

Turner, Mrs J, MCLIP, Retired. [2968] 01/01/1968   CM01/01/1972

Turner, Mrs K E, BEng, Inf. Serv. Lib., Leeds Met. Univ. Leeds [58979]
16/10/2000   ME

Turner, Mr K F, BSc(Hons) MCLIP, Info. Mgmt Offr., Leicestershire Co.
Council [10001760] 19/02/1983   CM14/11/1991

Turner, Mr K G, MCLIP, Retired. [14963] 01/01/1954   CM01/01/1957

Turner, Mrs K J, BA DipLib MCLIP, Info. Devel. Lib., Suffolk C.C.
[41441] 06/01/1988   CM15/08/1990

Turner, Miss K L, BSc MSc MCLIP, Dep. Lib., Min. of Justice, London.
[61728] 29/10/2002   CM23/01/2008

Turner, Ms K, MA(Hons) MA MCLIP, Consortium & Performance Mgr.,
Somerset C.C. [55409] 08/10/1997   CM23/01/2002

Turner, Mrs L J, BSc MCLIP, Area Co-ordinator, Notts. Co., W. Bridgford
L. [36702] 07/11/1983   CM16/10/1989

Turner, Mrs L J, MCLIP, Learner Serv. Mgr., Stafford Coll. [15881]
01/01/1971   CM01/01/1974

Turner, Mrs L M, BA MCLIP, Serv. Mgr., [20983] 22/07/1973
CM01/10/1976

Turner, Miss M P, ACLIP, Sen. L. Asst., Univ. of E. Anglia L., Norwich.
[64762] 28/06/2005   ACL29/01/2007

Turner, Mrs M, BA(Hons) MCLIP, Retired. [35581] 06/10/1982
CM25/01/1995

Turner, Mr N D W, BA(Hons) MA MCLIP, Faculty Lib., Univ. for the
Creative Arts, Maidstone. [54580] 27/01/1997   CM19/07/2000

Turner, Mr N W, LLB FCMI MCLIP FSA Scot, Dir., Turnaround
Associates Ltd. [14969] 01/01/1968   CM01/01/1971

Turner, Mrs P M, MCLIP, Retired. [14974] 01/01/1969   CM21/08/1972

Turner, Mr P N, FCLIP, Life Member. [14975] 01/01/1952 FE01/01/1961

Turner, Mr R J, BA DipLib MA MCLIP, unwaged [41947] 08/06/1988
CM26/02/1992

Turner, Mr R, Unknown. [10006180] 18/09/2007   ME

Turner, Miss S, BLib MCLIP, Sen. Inf. Adviser, Univ. of Gloucestershire.
[44597] 02/11/1990   CM27/07/1994

Turpin, Ms C M, MA(Oxon) MA MCLIP, Self-Employed, Ranociel
Publishing Serv., Perthshire. [41121] 02/10/1987   CM21/11/2001

Turrell, Mrs K H, BA, p. /t. Sch. Lib., Westbrook Hay Prep Sch., Herts.
[60760] 02/03/1987   ME

Turrell, Mrs N, BA(Hons), Inf. Off., Kennedys, London. [10007888]
26/02/2008   ME

Turrell, Mrs S A, BA DipLib MCLIP, Resource Ctr. Mgr., Sir Roger
Manwoods Sch., Sandwich [35497] 25/10/1982   CM04/08/1987

Turriff, Dr A, BA MEd PhD FCLIP, Unwaged. [24388] 04/07/1975
FE22/05/1996

Turtle, Mrs K M, BA MSc MCLIP, Retired [22132] 15/02/1974
CM06/05/1976

Turton, Mrs M, MCLIP, Asst. Lib. (Catg.), Shakespeare Birthplace Trust,
Stratford upon Avon. [14988] 01/01/1968   CM01/01/1968

Tutill, Mrs A, Community Inf. Offr., Sherburn L. [10016934] 10/06/2010
AF

Tutin, Miss P D, BA MCLIP, Life Member. [14991] 01/01/1954
CM01/01/1962

Tuttiett, Ms P J, BA MCLIP, Community Lib. Proj. Offr., L.B. of Enfield.
[28973] 17/01/1978   CM10/12/1981

Tweed, Mrs J E, BLib MCLIP, p. /t. L. Asst., NILA. [25953] 09/05/1976
CM03/03/1980

Tweedy, Miss J A, BA MCLIP, L. Mgr., ICT/Devel., Middlesborough
Council. [38228] 09/02/1985   CM14/11/1991

Twelves, Mrs S, Retired. [14999] 01/01/1945   ME

Twiddy, Mr P, BA DipLib MCLIP, Lib. &Inf. Serv. Mgr., Leeds Teaching
Hosp. NHS Trust. [34706] 02/02/1982   CM18/06/1985

Twinberrow, Mr P K, Unknown. [64099] 14/01/2005   ME

Twine, Mr T J, BA DipLib, Managing Dir., EOS Internat., London. [38929] 21/10/1985 **ME**

Twinn, Ms R D T, BA, Dip Lib, P/t. Lib., BBC Television L., Plymouth. [39335] 16/01/1986 **ME**

Twist, Mrs M, BA MCLIP, Retired. [8534] 01/04/1967 **CM01/01/1969**

Twite, Mrs V J, MCLIP, Retired. [15007] 29/08/1964 **CM01/01/1968**

Twomey, Mrs C E J, BSc(Hons) MA PhD MCLIP, Head of EKAT, Electronic Knowledge Access Team, London. Health Lib. [55171] 29/07/1997 **CM12/09/2001**

Twomey, Miss R E, MA MCLIP, Patient Inf. Lead, St. Thomas Hosp., London. [10013725] 07/11/2002 **CM07/07/2010**

Twose, Mrs M J, MCLIP, L. Serv. Outreach Offr., Redruth L., Cornwall C.C. [29103] 15/03/1978 **CM16/09/1980**

Tyas, Mrs D A, BA(Hons), Sen. L. Mgr., Bakersfield L., Nottingham City Council. [36924] 01/01/1984 **AF**

Tye, Miss M M, MCLIP BA, Life Member. [15008] 01/01/1951 **CM01/01/1956**

Tyers, Mrs M K, BA, p. /t. Stud. /L. Asst., Harold Bridges L., Lancaster. [59570] 04/06/2001 **ME**

Tylee, Ms C, BA(Hons) MA MCLIP, Bibl. Serv. Lib., Univ. Bath. [50793] 18/10/1994 **CM17/03/1999**

Tyler, A, MCLIP, Retired. [15012] 07/08/1963 **CM26/10/1981**

Tyler, Ms D F, BA(Hons) MA, Asst. Curator, Ruskin L., Lancaster Univ. [64147] 19/01/2005 **ME**

Tyler, Mrs L J, MSc BSc, Lib. Super. - Young People's Serv., E. Dunbartonshire L. [10015534] 20/11/1991 **ME**

Tyler, Mr S C, BA MSc MCLIP, Systems Admin., Univ. Reading. [61708] 23/10/2002 **CM19/03/2008**

Tyler, Prof W E, MA FCLIP, Retired. [15018] 01/01/1938 **FE01/01/1950**

Tyne, Mrs K M, BA(Hons) MSocSc, Princ. L. Asst., Bodleian Law L., Oxford. [64606] 12/04/2005 **ME**

Tyrell, Ms A, BA(Hons) PGDipLIS MCLIP, Lib., Univ. of Notre Dame, London. [55845] 25/11/1997 **CM19/11/2003**

Tyrer, Mrs J A, BA DipLib MCLIP, Bibl. Serv. Offr., N. Yorks. C.C. [42836] 28/03/1989 **CM19/08/1992**

Tyrka, Ms M B, MA, Stud., Stanmore Coll., Harrow, London. [10009227] 07/05/2008 **ME**

Tyrrell, Ms E V, Sch. Lib., Park House Sch., Newbury. [65636] 22/03/2006 **AF**

Tyrrell, Ms F, BA(Hons) MCLIP, Asst. Lib. [43799] 15/01/1990 **CM23/07/1997**

Tyrrell, Mrs S, BA MA LIS MCLIP, Inf. & Records Mgr., Government Off. for the S. E. [63848] 01/10/2004 **CM19/03/2008**

Tyson, Mrs K E, BA MA MCLIP, LRC Mgr., The Blandford Sch., Dorset. [28196] 29/09/1977 **CM16/11/1979**

Tytler, Mrs S, DipLib, Asst. Lib., London Met. Univ., [39583] 03/03/1986 **ME**

Tzogas, Mr I, Unwaged. [10014610] 19/08/2009 **ME**

U

Udogaranya, Mrs I O, BA, Learning Cent. Facilitator, LRC Southwark Coll., London [10004845] 22/01/1996 **ME**

Ulargiu, Ms B, MA, Seeking work. [10012545] 28/07/1998 **ME**

Ulas, Ms E, MCLIP, Head of Reader Serv., Univ. of Strathclyde, Glasgow. [10008259] 01/01/1953 **CM20/07/1982**

Ule, Ms S, MCLIP, Sen. L. Asst., Seeley Hist. L., Cambridge Univ. [65564] 28/02/2006 **CM27/01/2010**

Ullersperger, Miss K A, BA(Hons) DipLIS MCLIP, Sen. Lib., Kensington Ref. L., Royal Bor. of Kensington & Chelsea. [47956] 27/10/1992 **CM19/03/1997**

Ulloa, Mr G, MA, Unwaged [10009513] 06/06/2008 **AF**

Umansky, Miss G, MA, Unknown. [10015925] 03/02/2010 **ME**

Umbima, Mrs P, CertEd MCLIP, Life Member. [17889] 15/03/1948 **CM01/01/1955**

Umendi, Mr C U, Asst. Lib., Concordia Coll., Nigeria [10014567] 17/08/2009 **ME**

Unamboowe, Ms S, MCLIP, Sen. Lib. Asst., Harefield Hosp. Med. Lib. [64045] 06/12/2004 **CM11/11/2009**

Underwood, Mrs A F, MA DipLib MCLIP, Lib., St. Gregorys High Sch., L.B. of Brent. [27036] 26/01/1977 **CM31/01/1979**

Underwood, Mrs A M, CertEd BA DipLib MCLIP, Unwaged. [47745] 16/10/1992 **CM20/01/1999**

Underwood, Mr G M, BA MCLIP, Retired. [15037] 21/08/1958 **CM01/01/1964**

Underwood, Mr J, BSc, Asst. Lib., Sci. Mus., Wroughton. [10012121] 11/11/2009 **ME**

Underwood, Mrs J, BA(Hons), Inf. Asst., Univ. of Westminster, London. [10011122] 02/10/2008 **AF**

Underwood, Ms J, Stud. /Asst. Map Lib. [10013693] 22/05/2009 **ME**

Underwood, Mr K, ACLIP, L. Asst., Weston Favell L., Northampton. [10001786] 01/04/2006 **ACL05/10/2007**

Underwood, Miss L, BA DipLib MCLIP, Retired. [26592] 14/10/1976 **CM14/10/1978**

Underwood, Prof P G, MBA MIIS FCLIP, Prof. of Lib., Univ. of Cape Town, R. S. A., [19134] 15/10/1966 **FE11/07/1977**

Uniechowski, Mrs K J, FCLIP, Retired. [17893] 01/01/1930 **FE01/01/1945**

Unwin, Mrs K E, BA MCLIP, Sch. Lib., Mark Rutherford Upper Sch., Bedford. [30304] 15/01/1979 **CM17/07/1984**

Unwin, Mrs R C, BA(Hons) MA MCLIP, Careers Serv. Asst., Univ. of Cambridge [58371] 31/01/2000 **CM08/12/2004**

Upson, Mrs J S, Study Cent. Mgr., Longdean Sch., Hemel Hempstead. [62461] 30/06/2003 **AF**

Upton, Ms A H, BA DipLib MCLIP, Info. Mgr., SCIE., London. [36985] 23/01/1984 **CM01/07/1990**

Upton, Dr D, BSc(Hons) PhD MSc, Lib., Millfield Sch. L., Somerset. [36181] 05/07/1983 **ME**

Upton, Mr J C, Dep. Dir. of L. Serv., Univ. of St. Andrews, Main L. [39888] 03/10/1986 **ME**

Urch, Miss M E, MCLIP, Life Member. [15044] 04/11/1932 **CM01/01/1947**

Ure, Mr A M, BA MA DipLib MCLIP, Audience Devel. Offr., Essex C.C., Chelmsford [38238] 04/02/1985 **CM18/04/1990**

Uren, Dr V S, MSc MCLIP, Res. Fellow, Open Univ., Milton Keynes. [60794] 09/01/1989 **CM11/08/1994**

Urrestarazu, Mrs F, BSc, p. /t. Stud.,Lib., City Univ.,Internat. Sch. of London. [62231] 24/03/2003 **ME**

Urwin, Ms J P, MEd BA(Hons), Sen. Lect., Northumbria Univ., Newcastle. [34928] 19/04/1982 **ME**

Usher, Mr J A, BSc DipLib, ICT Devel. Mgr., Islington Council L. & Inf. Serv., London. [39462] 01/02/1986 **ME**

Usher, Mrs J M, BA MCLIP, Co. Inf. Lib., Worthing L., W. Sussex [40543] 03/03/1987 **CM16/10/1991**

Usher, Mrs K P H, MCLIP HonFCLIP, Lib., S. Hunsley Sch., N. Ferriby. [13628] 12/10/1971 **CM09/07/1975**

Usher, Mrs P J, BA DMS MCLIP, L. Serv. Mgr., Southwark. [31450] 12/10/1979 **CM06/11/1981**

Usher, Ms S E, BA(Hons)DipLib MCLIP, Subject Lib. for English, English Faculty L., Oxford Univ. L. Serv. [24383] 01/07/1975 **CM01/01/1978**

Usherwood, Prof R C, BA PhD HonFLA FRSA FCLIP, Prof. of Lib, Dept. of Inf. Studies, Univ. of Sheffield. [15049] 19/02/1962 **FE01/01/1968**

Ustun, Mrs A J, MA(Hons) PGCE, Stud., Robert Gordon Univ. [10015271] 29/10/2009 **ME**

Uta, Dr J J, MLS PhD FCLIP, Univ. Lib., Mzuzu Univ., Mzuzu, Malawi. [17894] 24/08/1967 **FE17/11/1999**

Utting, Mrs S J, MCLIP, Life Member. [16665] 06/03/1953 **CM01/01/1957**
Uttley, Mr P D, BA(Hons), Sen. Inf. Offr., Hammonds, Birmingham.
[59077] 08/11/2000 **AF**

V

Vaananen, Mrs R J, BA(Hons) MCLIP, Knowledge & Resource
Specialist, Leeds [56105] 17/02/1998 **CM21/03/2001**
Vaisey, Mr C R, BSc DipLib MCLIP, Freelance Consultant, Self-
employed. [26593] 07/10/1976 **CM01/05/1979**
Vale, Mr P, Info. Systems Mgr., Arup, London. [10013398] 23/04/2009
ME
Valencia, Ms M A, MA(Hons) MA MCLIP, Joint Lib., Poetry L., Royal
Festival Hall. [58213] 18/11/1999 **RV04/03/2009** **CM19/11/2003**
Valentine, Ms A B, BA MCLIP, Lib., N. Lanarkshire Council. [23199]
19/10/1974 **CM22/05/1978**
Valentine, Mrs M, MCLIP, Trust Lib., Freeman Hosp., Newcastle-upon-
Tyne Hosp. NHS Foundation Trust. [9413] 09/01/1968 **CM01/01/1972**
Valentine, Mr P, BA MCLIP, L. Serv. Mgr., W. London Mental Health
NHS Trust, Southall, Middx. [15055] 25/09/1970 **CM11/01/1974**
Valentine, Mrs S A, BA MCLIP, Head of Stock Reader Devel. &
Customer Serv., Hertfordshire L. [27840] 15/09/1977 **CM17/07/1981**
Vallance, Miss D M, BA(Hons) DipLIS MCLIP, Inf. Offr., The Dick Inst.,
Kilmarnock. [50457] 04/08/1994 **CM31/01/1996**
Valouchova, Miss I, BA, Denton Wilde Sapte LLP. [64065] 15/12/2004
ME
Valpereiro, Miss R S C, Stud., MMU. [62553] 20/08/2003 **ME**
Van Den Born, Mrs P, Head, Refence & User Serv., UNESCO L.,
France. [64020] 02/12/2004 **ME**
Van Der Hulks, Ms J L, BSc (Hons), Asst. Lib. (Cust. Serv.), Anglia
Ruskin Univ. [10016444] 24/04/2001 **ME**
Van Der Laan, Mrs P A, BSc, Sen. Inf. Asst., Aberdeen Univ. [61434]
24/07/2002 **ME**
Van Der Meer, Dr K, PhD MCLIP, Reader, Delft Univ. of Tech.,
Netherlands. [60057] 06/10/1980 **CM21/10/1982**
Van Der Schaar, Mrs F, DipInfSc, p/t Sch. Lib. [63859] 04/10/2004 **ME**
Van Der Wateren, Mr J F, MA FCLIP, Retired. [15064] 25/04/1967
FE22/11/1995
Van Dort, Mr C, BSc(Hons) MSc, Lib. /Team Leader, Defra, London.
[57263] 02/02/1999 **ME**
Van Dort, Mrs K L, MA BA(Hons), High sch. Lib., ACS Cobham
international Sch., Cobham [10001946] 10/11/1998 **ME**
Van Loo, Mrs N S, MA BA MCLIP, Lib., New Coll., Oxford. [20738]
15/06/1973 **CM29/03/1976**
Van Mellaerts, Mrs M H, MA MCLIP, Interlend. Mgr., Essex C.C., Co. L.
H.Q., Chelmsford. [21608] 27/11/1973 **CM01/08/1976**
Van Niekerk, Mrs J M, BA(Hons) MA, Head of L. and Media Cent.
[55315] 01/10/1997 **ME**
Van Noorden, Mr A, BSc(ECON) MA MCLIP, Life Member. [15068]
29/03/1962 **CM01/01/1965**
Van Ochten, Miss J, BA(Hons) MSc(Econ), KM Team Leader., Inst. of
Directors, London. [55817] 28/11/1997 **ME**
Van Riel, Ms R, Unknown. [10000716] 19/10/2006 **ME**
Van Tol, Mrs L, BA MCLIP, Co-ordinator Bus. Inf. Cent., Haskoning UK
Ltd, Peterborough. [23240] 08/11/1974 **CM05/10/1978**
Van Zetten, Mrs F S, MCLIP, Asst. Lib., Guildford Coll. of F. E., Surrey.
[30894] 11/06/1979 **CM26/08/1982**
Vane, Mrs G M, MCLIP, Lib. Offr., Chandler's Ford L., Hampshire. [7461]
16/10/1968 **CM20/10/1972**
Vanes, Ms A, BA MCLIP, Learning Resource Cent. Mngr. David Young
Comm. Academy, Leeds [10015026] 01/10/1977 **CM19/11/1979**
Varfis, Mr E, Stud., Robert Gordon Univ. [10016881] 01/06/2010 **ME**

Vargues, Miss M M, Lib., Universidade do Algarve, Faro, Portugal.
[40811] 30/06/1987 **ME**
Varilly, Mrs S, MCLIP, Lib., Havant Coll., Hants. [516] 17/01/1968
CM01/01/1972
Varley, Mr A, FCLIP, Life Member. [15071] 18/02/1950 **FE01/01/1968**
Varley, Mrs D L, DipRSA MCLIP, Head of Learning Res. Cent., Sponne
Sch., Towcester. [59924] 01/01/1967 **CM21/03/2007**
Varley, Mrs V, Ref. Lib., Oldham L. [10000698] 12/01/2007 **ME**
Varney, Ms N A, BSc(Hons) MCLIP, Inf. Offr., AIG, London. [46996]
23/03/1992 **CM22/11/1995**
Varney-Bowers, Mrs C, B'Ed Hons, Community Lib., Norfolk & Norwich
Millenium L., Norwich. [10005430] 12/07/2007 **ME**
Varty, Miss E J, BA DipLib MCLIP, Asst. Lib., Dept. for Work & Pension,
London. [34601] 17/01/1982 **CM01/04/1986**
Varty, Miss J, MCLIP, Life Member. [15078] 15/03/1956 **CM01/01/1965**
Vass, Ms J, MA, Lib., Freshfields Bruckhaus Deringer, London.
[10012093] 17/12/2008 **ME**
Vassar, Ms M, BA(Hons) PGDip DipILM MCLIP, Prison Lib., YO1 HMP
Portland, Dorset [51684] 11/05/1995 **CM12/09/2001**
Vaughan, Mr A, DipLIS, Ch. Lib., Mayo Co. L., Eire. [55013] 25/06/1997
ME
Vaughan, Mr G A, BA, Catr., The Stationery Off., London. [41729]
26/02/1988 **ME**
Vaughan, Miss N J, BA MA MCLIP, Unknown [65854] 06/06/2006
CM05/05/2010
Veal, Dr D C, BSc PhD FRSC FCLIP, Hon Fellow. [60660] 19/11/1981
FE25/03/1993
Veale, Mr T, BA MSc H Dip, Asst. Lib., Peterborough and Stamford
Hosp., Peterborough. [10012369] 29/01/2009 **ME**
Veasey, Mr B T, LLB MA, Picture Researcher/News Lib., Sky News L.,
Isleworth. [10017141] 14/07/2010 **ME**
Veitch, Mrs R, BA(Hons) MCLIP, Early Years Lib., March L. [10007744]
08/10/1980 **CM01/07/1989**
Velluet, Mrs E, BA MCLIP, Unknown. [842] 08/10/1966 **CM01/01/1970**
Venables, Mrs S P, ACLIP, Property & Supplies Admin., Nat. Probation
Serv., Liverpool. [45391] 21/11/1990 **ACL27/11/2007**
Veness, Mrs V M, BSc MA, Dep. L. Serv. Mgr., Royal Surrey Co. Hosp.
NHS Trust, Guildford. [10001026] 12/10/1999 **ME**
Verlander, Mrs S, MA MCLIP, Inf. Offr., Coll. of Law, Chester. [62326]
29/04/2003 **CM13/06/2007**
Vernall, Mr G S, Unknown. [10006376] 15/10/2007 **ME**
Vernon, Miss E A, MA DipLib MCLIP, Area Lib., N. Ayrshire Council.
[56716] 07/10/1998 **CM02/02/2005**
Vernon, Ms J T M, BA MA, Curator, The Brit. L., London. [41122]
08/10/1987 **ME**
Versteeg, Mr J H J, BA, Acting Coll. Lib. at the Oxford Univ Coll. Lib.
[62290] 17/04/2003 **AF**
Verth, Ms M, BA MCLIP, EMEA KM CRM Mgr., IBM Business Con.
Serv., Edinburgh. [39255] 13/01/1986 **CM25/01/1995**
Veryard, Mrs C M, BA MCLIP, L. Operations Mgr., Yeovil L., Somerset
Co. [13476] 05/01/1970 **CM01/08/1972**
Vicente, Ms G, MA, Inf. Mgr., Amnesty Internat. UK, London [10013604]
12/05/2009 **ME**
Vickerman, Mrs H J, BA MCLIP, Princ. L. Offr. (Learning and Info.),
Sandwell M.B.C., W. Bromwich,W. Mids. [30694] 22/02/1979
CM26/08/1982
Vickers, Mr P H, FCLIP, Lib., Prince Consort's L., Aldershot. [20555]
03/04/1973 **FE03/10/2007**
Vickers, Dr R W, Enquiry Serv. Specialist, Univ. of Salford, Greater
Manchester. [10001096] 12/01/2007 **ME**
Vickery, Mr J E, MA FCLIP, Retired [15118] 01/03/1972 **FE20/05/1998**
Vickery, Miss S J, BA(Hons) MSc(Econ) MCLIP, Unknown. [58458]
22/02/2000 **CM17/09/2003**

Victor, Mr L M, BA, Sch. Lib., Hatch End High Sch., Harrow, Middx. [34598] 01/01/1982 **ME**

Victory, Dr I, BA, PhD, DipLIS, Dep. Lib., House of Lords. [10011630] 11/11/2008 **ME**

Vidgen, Mr G A, BLib MCLIP, Business Consultant, Capita Business Serv., Cardiff. [40917] 20/08/1987 **CM01/12/1995**

Vignoli, Ms N A, Legal Researcher, Bond Pearce LLP, Bristol. [57747] 16/07/1999 **ME**

Vijayakumar, Dr J K, BSc MLIS PhD, King Abdullah Univ. of Sci. & Tech., Saudi Arabia. [65969] 01/08/2006 **ME**

Vila-Bosch, Mrs N, Bsc Hons, Eli Lilly & Co, Surrey. [10015968] 03/02/2010 **ME**

Viles, Mr J F, MCLIP, Independent Consultant, Norfolk. [15122] 16/02/1951 **CM01/01/1957**

Villa, Mrs D J, BA MCLIP, Frenchay L. Mgr., N. Bristol NHS Trust, Bristol. [3767] 27/10/1970 **CM20/07/1976**

Villa, Mrs L, MA, Know How Content Developer, Lovells, London [10007129] 25/01/2008 **ME**

Villa, Mr P, MLib MCLIP, Off. Mgr., Hospice Care Kenya. [15125] 15/10/1965 **CM12/12/1973**

Vincent, Mr G D, BSc MCLIP, Applications Consultant, Accent on Systems Ltd., Burnham. [60659] 21/03/1972 **CM01/07/1979**

Vincent, Mrs H F, BA(Hons) DipILM MCLIP, IT Mgr., L.B. of Hillingdon. [50645] 06/10/1994 **CM17/05/2000**

Vincent, Mr I W, BA MCLIP, Retired. [15130] 17/03/1963 **CM01/01/1966**

Vincent, Mr J C, MCLIP, Networker, The Network-Tackling Soc. Exclusion [15131] 10/10/1966 **CM01/01/1971**

Vine, Miss A L, BA(Hons) DipLib, Administrator, My Travel, Mallorca. [46518] 15/11/1991 **ME**

Viner, Mr D, BA(Hons) PgDipILM MSc, Asst. Lib., Solihull MBC, Birmingham. [61284] 08/05/2002 **ME**

Vinnicombe, Mr R A J, DMA MCLIP, Retired. [15139] 10/09/1964 **CM01/01/1969**

Violet, Mr R J C, MCLIP, Community Lib., Wiltshire C.C., Warminster L. [20212] 15/01/1973 **CM29/12/1975**

Virdi, Mrs S K, Sen. Multicultural Lib. Asst., Coventry CC [10017185] 11/07/2010 **AF**

Virgo, Mrs A J, BA PGCE MCLIP, Sch. Lib. & Arch., Stamford High Sch. [10007029] 13/12/1979 **CM24/10/1984**

Virgo, Mrs P J, BA MCLIP, Project Devel. Offr., Lancashire Lib., Lancs. [1827] 01/10/1971 **CM29/01/1992**

Virnes, Mrs H, MSc, Career Break. [58363] 26/01/2000 **ME**

Virone, Mrs J A, BSc(Hons) MCLIP, Unwaged. [58968] 11/10/2000 **CM15/01/2003**

Visram, Mrs T A, MCLIP, Asst. Lib., Newham Univ. Hosp., London [15381] 01/01/1968 **CM24/08/1972**

Visser, Mrs C, L. Mgr., Accrington & Rossendale Coll., Accrington. [10005111] 06/06/2007 **AF**

Vitai, Mrs J G T, FCLIP, Life Member. [17911] 26/05/1952 **FE01/01/1963**

Vodden, Ms G J, BSc(Hons) DipIS MCLIP, Knowledge Offr., Nabarro., London [46334] 28/10/1991 **CM21/05/2003**

Vogtherr, Mr G A, MSc, Unknown. [10017153] 11/07/2010 **ME**

Voisey, Ms J, ACLIP, Lend. L. Super., Bristol Cent. L., Bristol. [65770] 24/04/2006 **ACL06/02/2008**

Voisey, Mr P G, BA(Hons), Unknown. [10017066] 21/06/2010 **ME**

Vollmer, Miss S, BA(Hons), DipLib, MSc, Unknown. [10007951] 09/09/2005 **ME**

Von Bulow, Miss B K, Video Lib., CNN London. [61400] 04/07/2002 **ME**

Voy, Mr E, MCLIP, Life Member. [15150] 01/01/1954 **CM01/01/1963**

Voyce, Mr P D, BA MCLIP, Comm. L. Mgr., Wednesbury Town, Sandwell M.B.C. [35649] 01/12/1982 **CM13/12/1984**

Voysey, Miss J P, MCLIP, Life Member. [15152] 02/09/1949 **CM01/01/1959**

Vraca, Mrs M, Unknown. [10013352] 16/04/2009 **ME**

Vuolo, Ms D, BA MA MCLIP, Sen. Lib. : Inf. Serv., Cent. Bedfordshire Council. [31480] 01/10/1979 **CM17/11/1981**

Vyas, Mrs M, BA(Hons) MCLIP, Learning Res. Cent. Mgr., Sir Jonathan N. Comm. Coll., Leicester. [10000809] 10/01/1985 **CM04/10/1988**

Vyas, Mrs S, B. Ed, Dip Info, Unknown. [10012600] 19/02/2009 **ME**

W

Waddell, Mrs C, BA(Hons) MCLIP, Tell. Mgr., N. Lanarkshire Council, Toy & Equipment Lend. L. [53066] 09/02/1996 **CM23/09/1998**

Waddilove, Ms K, MA MCLIP, Head of Learning Res., JFS Sch., Harrow. [15155] 13/02/1970 **CM16/10/1972**

Waddington, Mrs A E F, BA(CNAA) MCLIP, Lib., HMP Ranby [65673] 23/03/2006 **CM11/11/2009**

Waddington, Mrs M A, BA(Hons) DipIM MCLIP, Clinical Effectiveness Lib., Royal Free Hosp., UCL, London. [53856] 07/10/1996 **CM12/09/2001**

Wade, Mr A J, MA FCLIP, Retired. [15159] 24/06/1951 **FE01/01/1962**

Wade, Ms E C, BA(Hons) MA MCLIP, Asst. Lib., UWE, Bristol. [49598] 19/11/1993 **CM23/07/1997**

Wade, Ms L, BA(Hons) MSc, Buisness Intelligence Inf. Offr., Osborne Clarke, Bristol. [58953] 10/10/2000 **ME**

Wade, Mr M J, BA MLib MCLIP, Nat. Lib., Nat. L. of Scotland. [23782] 22/01/1975 **CM10/11/1978**

Wadey, Mrs C A, BA MCLIP, Unwaged. [31666] 01/11/1979 **CM09/09/1985**

Wadsworth, Mrs C J, BLib MCLIP, Sch. Lib., Retford Oaks High Sch., Notts. [26354] 06/10/1976 **CM02/11/1984**

Wadsworth, Ms C L, MA, Learning Support Lib., Kirkby-in-Ashfield L., Nottinghamshire Co. Council [10001299] 03/09/2004 **ME**

Wafer, Mr R A, MCLIP, Life Member. [19374] 10/03/1947 **CM01/01/1950**

Wagstaff, Mrs D A, p. /t. Asst. Community Lib., Birmingham City Council [63178] 03/03/2004 **ME**

Wagstaff, Mr D J, BA MMus FCLIP, Resident in USA. [44195] 04/07/1990 **FE21/05/2003**

Wainwright, Mrs J M, OBE BA FCLIP, Retired. [60661] 01/01/1979 **FE01/03/1986**

Waiswa, Mr R, MSc, Asst. Lect., Kyambogo Univ. – Kamuli, Uganda [10016409] 22/03/2010 **ME**

Wait, Mrs C, MCLIP, Retired. [12874] 01/10/1970 **CM10/01/1975**

Waite, Mr A T, BSc, Unwaged -seeking work [10015020] 07/10/2009 **AF**

Waite, Miss C G, BA(Hons), PGDipLib, Sen. Inf. Serv. Mgr., Lancashire Co. & Inf. Serv., Preston. [10008284] 26/10/1989 **ME**

Waite, Mrs J A, MCLIP, Inst. Lib., Arts Inst. at Bournemouth, Dorset. [15178] 18/06/1969 **CM20/11/1972**

Waite, Mrs J A, BA BSc(Hons), Retired. [57228] 25/01/1999 **ME**

Waite, Mrs M H, BA MCLIP, Prison Lib., Leeds L. & Inf. Serv., HMP Wealstun. [15458] 21/01/1969 **CM01/01/1973**

Wake, Mrs M C, BA(Hons) MA MCLIP, Head L. and Inf. Serv., The Sch. of Pharmacy, Univ. of London. [46254] 21/10/1991 **CM19/03/1997**

Wake, Mr R L, MA MA MCLIP, Dep. Lib., Univ. of Southampton. [32353] 20/02/1980 **CM25/11/1982**

Wakefield, Miss J D, BA MCLIP, Inf. & Learning Co-ordinator, Lincoln Coll. [33181] 21/10/1980 **CM09/01/1986**

Wakefield, Mr P W, LLB LLM DipLib MCLIP, Form. Divisonal Head: L., Castle Coll., Notingham. [30564] 12/01/1979 **CM09/02/1982**

Wakeham, Mr M W, MA DipLib FCLIP, Faculty Liaison Lib., Health & Soc. Care, Anglia Ruskin Univ. [39820] 30/07/1986 **FE09/09/2009**

Wakeling, Mrs M, BA(Hons) DipLib MCLIP, Project Co-ordinator, Cent. for Rural Health, Inverness [29829] 23/10/1978 **RV23/01/2007** **CM31/10/1980**

Wakeman, Mrs I J, BA MCLIP, Retired. [15190] 17/01/1969 **CM01/01/1971**

Walaitis, Miss C J, B LIB MCLIP, Lib., Cathkin L., Glasgow. [30289]
09/01/1979 **CM09/01/1981**
Waldhelm, Mr R J, BA DipLib MCLIP, Head of Solicitors Legal Inf. Cent.,
Scottish Government, Edinburgh. [29859] 10/10/1978**CM17/07/1984**
Waldron, Miss H J, BA, Inf. Asst., Univ. of Chichester, W. Sussex.
[10002483] 20/04/2007 **ME**
Wale, Ms D A, BA MCLIP, Reader Devel. Lib., L.B. of Hammersmith &
Fulham. [33182] 06/10/1980 **CM17/07/1984**
Wales, Mrs C M, BA MCLIP, Lend. Serv. Mgr., N. Lanarkshire Council.
[31472] 16/10/1979 **CM25/10/1983**
Wales, Mr J G, MCLIP, I. . Serv. Devel. Mgr. Putney L. L.B. of
Wandsworth [15197] 06/10/1970 **CM05/10/1973**
Wales, Mrs J, MCLIP, Sch. Lib., Glasgow City Council. [14416]
06/06/1972 **CM15/12/1976**
Wales, Mr T B, BA(Hons) MSc MCLIP FHA, Assoc. Dir., Royal Holloway,
Egham [55082] 09/07/1997 **CM12/09/2001**
Walford, Mrs J E, FCLIP, Retired. [15199] 19/11/1942 **FE01/01/1954**
Walke, Ms P, BSc, Dep. L. Serv. Mgr., Health Sci. L.,Frimley Park Hosp.
NHS Trust. [10009923] 02/07/1998 **ME**
Walke, Mrs V, BA MCLIP, Unwaged. [43326] 19/10/1989 **CM26/01/1994**
Walker, Miss A C, BSc(Hons), Sen. L. Asst., Wellcome Trust, London.
[54800] 03/03/1997 **AF**
Walker, Mrs A D, BA(Hons) MCLIP, Digital Devel. and Systems Team
Leader, Univ. of Salford. [48442] 11/01/1993 **CM22/07/1998**
Walker, Mrs A F, BA MCLIP, Resource Cent. Coordinator, Lossiemouth
High Sch. [26010] 04/05/1976 **CM18/07/1979**
Walker, Mr A J, BA MCLIP, Devel. Lib.,Operations, Isle of Wight L. Serv.
[36587] 21/10/1983 **CM11/11/1986**
Walker, Miss A M, MA DipLib MCLIP, Lifelong Learning Lib., L.B. of
Havering L. Serv., Romford. [38723] 01/10/1985 **CM21/07/1989**
Walker, Ms A R, BA MCLIP, Lib., Turcan Connell, Solicitors, Edinburgh.
[38057] 10/01/1985 **CM18/09/1991**
Walker, Miss A, BSc (Hons), Stud., Strathclyde Univ. [10015076]
12/10/2009 **ME**
Walker, Mrs A, MCLIP, Unemployed. [15204] 25/02/1960**CM01/01/1966**
Walker, Mrs A, BA(Hons) MCLIP, Unknown. [43389] 06/10/1989
CM23/07/1997
Walker, Mr C G, BA(Hons) PGCE MA MCLIP, PhD Researcher/Ass.
Lect., Leeds Met. Univ. [47929] 26/10/1992 **CM31/01/1996**
Walker, Mrs C M, BA(Hons) MSc MCLIP, Resource Asst., Halesowen
Coll., Halesowen. [62273] 07/04/2003 **CM09/07/2008**
Walker, Mrs C, BA MA MCLIP, Campus L. Mgr., Edinburgh Napier Univ.,
Edinburgh. [45875] 03/07/1991 **CM21/01/1998**
Walker, Mrs C, ACLIP, Learing Resourse Cent. Mgr., Aylsham High
Sch., Norfolk. [65625] 13/03/2006 **ACL28/01/2009**
Walker, Mr D, BSc MCLIP, Local Studies and Arch. Mgr., London.
[38649] 23/08/1985 **CM29/01/1992**
Walker, Mrs E Y, BSc(Hons), Self Employed Inf. Consulting [41265]
23/10/1987 **ME**
Walker, Miss F E M, Trainee Lib., All Nations Christian Coll., Ware
[10016424] 24/03/2010 **AF**
Walker, Mrs F M, MEd FSA(S) MCLIP, Retired [6538] 17/03/1969
CM17/07/1972
Walker, Dr G P M, MA PhD FCLIP, Retired. [15220] 30/06/1964
FE24/12/1980
Walker, Mrs H S, Retired. [15221] 01/09/1950 **ME**
Walker, Mr I C, BA MCLIP, Lib. Stock Procurement Mgr., Doncaster
[15222] 26/08/1969 **CM10/10/1983**
Walker, Mr I J, Brit. Lib., London [65547] 03/03/2006 **ME**
Walker, Miss I R Y, MCLIP, Retired [15224] 04/04/1965 **CM01/01/1968**
Walker, Miss J A, BSc MCLIP, Dir. of Operations, S. of England, The
Stroke Assoc. [60715] 29/06/1984 **CM29/06/1984**
Walker, Mrs J E, LRC Mgr., Sandbach High Sch., Sandbach.
[10000872] 17/11/2006 **AF**

Walker, Mr J R A, FCLIP, Life Member. [15235] 25/10/1946
FE04/06/1965
Walker, Ms J, BA MCLIP, Retired. [3181] 01/01/1962 **CM26/10/1978**
Walker, Miss J, BA(Hons) PG Cert, Stud., Liverpool John Moores Univ.
[10010958] 10/09/2008 **ME**
Walker, Miss J, Unknown. [10013576] 07/05/2009 **ME**
Walker, Mr K C, BA FCLIP, Life Member. [15237] 06/10/1949
FE01/01/1962
Walker, Mrs K E, BA DipLib MCLIP, Sen. Analyst, Infor, Bristol. [39107]
04/11/1985 **CM18/04/1989**
Walker, Mrs K J, BA MCLIP, Sen. Inf. & Res. Offr., Evangelical Alliance
[33564] 17/01/1981 **CM16/02/1988**
Walker, Miss K M B, BA MA MCLIP, Retired. [15238] 15/01/1968
CM01/01/1970
Walker, Mr K, MA(Hons) PGDipILS MCLIP, Inf. Serv. Advisor, Napier
Univ., Edinburgh. [57033] 27/11/1998 **CM07/09/2005**
Walker, Ms L E, MA BA BSc, Lib., Pembroke Coll., Oxford. [58072]
25/10/1999 **ME**
Walker, Mrs M E, BA MCLIP, Retired. [10297] 29/03/1956**CM01/01/1963**
Walker, Mrs M L, Liaison Adv., Northumbria Univ., Newcastle. [59012]
24/10/2000 **ME**
Walker, Mr M, BA(Hons) LLB (Hons) MSc, Div. Knowledge Mgr.,
Linklaters, London. [52937] 29/01/1996 **ME**
Walker, Mrs P V, MCLIP, Retired. [15253] 19/01/1948 **CM01/01/1953**
Walker, Mrs P, BA(Hons) ACLIP, Lib. Asst., Mansfield L., Notts.
[10002966] 10/05/2007 **ACL16/04/2008**
Walker, Mrs P, BA(Hons) MA MCLIP, Prison Lib., Northallerton Young
Offenders Inst. [58211] 17/11/1999 **CM11/03/2009**
Walker, Miss P, BA MCLIP, Unwaged. [29861] 10/10/1978
CM23/09/1985
Walker, Mrs R F M, BA(Hons), Inf. Asst., Univ. of Exeter [65019]
07/10/2005 **ME**
Walker, Mrs R M, BSc(Hons) MCLIP, Unwaged [48147] 11/11/1992
CM24/09/1997
Walker, Mr R P, MA(Oxon) DipLib MCLIP, Customer Support Serv. Mgr.,
Eastleigh Coll., Hampshire [42795] 06/03/1989 **CM24/03/1992**
Walker, Mr S B, BA(Hons) MA MCLIP, Med. Lib., Med. L., Brit. Forces
Germany. [55838] 21/11/1997 **CM15/09/2004**
Walker, Mr S J, BA BSc MSc, Bor. Liaison Offr., TFL, London. [60457]
31/03/1999 **ME**
Walker, Mrs S L, BA(Hons) MCLIP, Sen. Asst. Lib., Univ. of
Huddersfield. [46459] 07/11/1991 **CM21/01/1998**
Walker, Mrs S M, BSc MCLIP, Legal Lib. &Copyright Mgr., Home Off.,
London. [13260] 09/10/1968 **CM24/08/1972**
Walker, Mrs S M, HNC MCLIP, Med. Inf. Sci., Sharon Walker Med. Inf.
Serv., Newmarket. [60831] 01/03/1990 **CM01/03/1990**
Walker, Mrs S M, MLitt MA MCLIP, Retired. [29340] 06/06/1978
CM12/09/1980
Walker, Mrs S, Inf. Serv. Mgr., CEFAS, Weymouth, Dorset. [52102]
02/10/1995 **ME**
Walker, Mrs V L, MCLIP, Lib., Maidenhill Sch., Stonehouse,Glos.
[19967] 09/01/1973 **CM01/01/1975**
Walker, Ms V M, MCLIP, Educ. Res. Devel. Offr., City of Edinburgh
Council, Educ. Res. [10583] 01/01/1967 **CM01/01/1971**
Walker, Miss V, MTheol(Hons) MSc MCLIP, Head of Info. &Res.,
Watson, Farley & Williams, London. [50600] 29/09/1994
CM21/05/1997
Walker, Mrs W E, BA MCLIP, Resource Area Mgr., Glyn Tech. Sch.,
Surrey. [31767] 10/12/1979 **CM23/01/2008**
Walkington, Ms E, BA DipLib MCLIP, L. & Resource Cent. Asst.,
Halesowen Coll. [44435] 08/10/1990 **CM21/07/1993**
Walkinshaw, Mr B R, BA MCLIP, Retired. [15263] 10/02/1965
CM01/01/1968

Walkley, Mrs R J, Inf. Scientist., Unilever R&D Port Sunlight, Wirral. [61716] 25/10/2002 **ME**

Wall, Mr C J, MCLIP, Knowledge Mgr., Accenture, London. [42387] 27/10/1988 **CM15/09/1999**

Wall, Mr M D, BSc DipLib MCLIP, Head of Inf. Mgmnt & Lib. Devel., Univ. Bristol [39970] 07/10/1986 **CM21/07/1989**

Wall, Dr R A, PhD FCLIP HonFCLIP HonMAslib, Life Member. [15266] 24/01/1942 **FE01/01/1950**

Wallace, Miss A, BA MCLIP, Learning Res. Offr., Buxton Comm. Sch., Derbys. C.C. [36588] 26/10/1983 **CM15/11/1988**

Wallace, Mr A, FCLIP DMA, Life Member. [15269] 11/03/1936 **FE01/01/1951**

Wallace, Mrs C A, MCLIP, Team Leader., Business Insight, Birmingham Cent. L. [31370] 19/10/1979 **CM07/09/1982**

Wallace, Mr D A, MCLIP, Life Member. [15270] 17/03/1950 **CM01/01/1962**

Wallace, Miss E J, BA(Hons) MCLIP, Unknown [62663] 01/10/2003 **CM21/11/2007**

Wallace, Mrs J M, BA, Sen. Researcher, BBC Monitoring, Reading. [62812] 24/10/2003 **ME**

Wallace, Mr J, Stud., Northumbria Univ. [10012973] 17/03/2009 **ME**

Wallace, Mrs K M, BA MCLIP, Area Lib. - Western Area, L. Serv., W. Sussex Co. Council, Chichester L. [35316] 11/10/1982 **CM11/06/1986**

Wallace, Ms L G, BSc MSc CPsychol, Learning Res. Mgr, Mid-Cheshire Coll. [62767] 20/10/2003 **ME**

Wallace, Mrs M G, BA MCLIP DPA, p. /t. Lib., Falkirk Council L. [23590] 21/01/1975 **CM12/03/1980**

Wallace, Miss M, MCLIP, Lib., Warrington P. L. [15274] 04/02/1971 **CM01/05/1975**

Wallace, Miss M, MCLIP, Retired. [15275] 08/03/1964 **CM01/01/1970**

Wallace, Mr P R, BA MCLIP, Reader Devel. Offr., Kensington Comm. L., Liverpool L. & Inf. Serv. [15277] 20/01/1972 **CM21/02/1974**

Wallace, Miss S A, BSc MCLIP, LRC Mgr., Brannock High. Sch., Motherwell. [22840] 01/10/1974 **CM01/10/1976**

Wallace, Mrs S M, BLib PGCE MCLIP, Casual Lib., Norfolk Co. Council. [37194] 01/04/1984 **CM16/02/1988**

Wallace, Mrs T R, DipLib MA MCLIP, Communications and Inf. Offr., Learning & Teaching Scotland, Dundee. [32956] 03/10/1980 **CM18/08/1983**

Wallace, Mr W, MA MCLIP, Retired [21896] 17/02/1974 **CM01/01/1976**

Wallbank, Mrs M M, MCLIP, p. /t. Community Lib., Flintshire C.C., Holywell. [4369] 19/09/1970 **CM04/10/1973**

Waller, Miss A V, MCLIP, Life Member. [15280] 12/09/1951 **CM01/01/1962**

Waller, Mr R M, BD MCLIP, Res. and Dev. Offr., Wigan Leisure and Culture Trust. [22509] 01/04/1974 **CM11/02/1977**

Waller, Mrs S, MCLIP, L. Res. Mgr., Kent Coll., Pembury, Kent. [22196] 18/02/1974 **CM01/01/1977**

Wallis, Mrs D V, L. Asst., St. Austell L., Cornwall. [64238] 22/02/2005 **AF**

Wallis, Mrs J M, BA DipLib MCLIP, Retired. [14185] 08/10/1968 **CM01/01/1971**

Wallis, Mrs K M, BA(Hons) MA MCLIP, Learning Res. Co-ordinator, Peterborough Reg. Coll. [59043] 07/11/2000 **CM04/10/2006**

Wallis, Ms K, BA MCLIP, Cust. Serv. Lib., Oadby L., Leics. C.C. [37358] 10/07/1984 **CM16/10/1991**

Wallis, Ms M K, BA DipLib MCLIP, Cent. Dir., Univ. Cent. Haskings [20602] 24/04/1973 **CM11/11/1975**

Wallner, Mr R J G, BA BA MCLIP, Unknown. [24191] 15/02/1975 **CM18/01/1978**

Walls, Mr R, MA DipLib MCLIP, StockOffr., L. HQ, N. Yorks. C.C. [32210] 28/01/1980 **CM26/10/1982**

Walmsley, Mr A J, BA MA DipLib MCLIP, Community Hist. Mgr. – Fylde. [42197] 10/10/1988 **CM27/07/1994**

Walne, Mrs L R, BA(Hons) MA MCLIP, Retired. [15300] 08/02/1952 **CM01/01/1958**

Walne, Mr M J, BA(Hons) MCLIP, Asst. Lib., W. Middx. Univ. Hosp. NHS Trust, Isleworth. [58872] 20/09/2000 **CM23/06/2004**

Walpole, Mr J M, BA MCLIP AIL, Life Member. [17926] 29/10/1948 **CM01/01/1953**

Walsgrove, Ms S M, Sen. Learning Cent. Coordinator, City of Wolverhampton Coll., W. Midlands. [45417] 21/01/1991 **AF**

Walsh, Mrs A C, MA(Hons) DipILS MCLIP, Sen. Resc. Dev. Offr., N. Lanarkshire C.C. [56872] 27/10/1998 **CM15/11/2000**

Walsh, Mr A, BSc MSc MCLIP, Academic Lib., Huddersfield Univ. [62927] 20/11/2003 **CM31/01/2007**

Walsh, Ms C J, BA MA PG DIP LIB, Assoc. Dir., L. & Learning Serv., Univ. E. London. [10015771] 19/02/1986 **ME**

Walsh, Miss C, MA, Princ. Bib. Asst., Robert Gordon Univ., Aberdeen [10012826] 13/03/2009 **ME**

Walsh, Mrs D C, BA DipLib, Lib., City of Birmingham Educ. Dept. [35014] 29/06/1982 **ME**

Walsh, Mrs E K, MA(Hons) MSc(Econ) MCLIP, Site Lib., Warrington Campus, Univ. of Chester. [51197] 23/11/1994 **CM06/04/2005**

Walsh, Miss H M, MCLIP, Retired. [15305] 19/10/1945 **CM01/01/1951**

Walsh, Mrs J A, BA(Hons) MA MCLIP, Sen. L. Asst., Univ. of Nottingham. [54392] 02/12/1996 **CM16/07/2003**

Walsh, Mrs J A, BA MCLIP, Team Leader, N. Yorks. C.C., Northallerton Area. [29396] 18/06/1978 **CM17/07/1981**

Walsh, Miss K M, PT Lib. Asst., Accrington L., Accrington. [10014852] 18/09/2009 **AF**

Walsh, Mr P A, Stud., LJMU. [64300] 23/02/2005 **ME**

Walsh, Miss R L, MSc, Inf. Offr., Linklaters, London. [49199] 12/10/1993 **ME**

Walsh, Ms R M, Sen. Lib., Cumbria Lib. Serv. [61358] 24/06/2002 **ME**

Walsh, Mrs S A, BSc HDLS MCLIP, Inf. Serv. Mgr., Burgoyne Mgmnt. Ltd., London. [48350] 01/12/1992 **CM03/07/1996**

Walsh, Mrs S, BA DipLib MCLIP, Mgr. Sch. L. Serv., Plymouth C.C. [35454] 18/10/1982 **CM15/02/1989**

Walsh, Mrs T, BA MA, Unknown. [10014292] 14/07/2009 **AF**

Walter, Mr M A, BA MCLIP, L. Project Offr., [18273] 03/10/1972 **CM04/11/1974**

Walters, Mr J, BA MCLIP, Retired. [15322] 23/02/1954 **CM01/01/1962**

Walters, Mrs K O, BA DipLib MCLIP, Lib., The Athenaeum, London. [33678] 09/02/1981 **CM17/02/1987**

Walters, Miss M G, BA(Hons), Lib., Univ. of W. of England, Bristol. [64589] 11/04/2005 **ME**

Walters, Mr R J, MBE MA B PHIL MCLIP, Retired. [18228] 06/10/1972 **CM25/10/1974**

Walters, Dr W H, PhD FCLIP, Dean of Lib. Serv., Menlo Coll., California, USA. [62143] 28/02/2003 **FE13/06/2007**

Walter-Smith, Ms L L E, BA(Hons) MA, Lib., Glenside Campus L., U. W. E, Bristol [10008005] 20/03/2008 **ME**

Walton, Mr A D, MCLIP, Life Member. [15326] 01/01/1939 **CM01/01/1948**

Walton, Miss E A, BSc, Snr. Res. Offr., E. Lancs. Public Health Network, Accrington. [41602] 25/01/1988 **ME**

Walton, Ms E L, BA(Hons) MA, Learning and Teaching Support Mgr., Brighton [10007746] 01/11/1996 **ME**

Walton, Mr G L, BA(Hons), MA, PGCHPE, PhD, MCLIP, FHEA, p. /t. Subject & Learning Supp. Lib., Staffs. Univ., Thompson L., Stoke-on-Trent. [47672] 13/10/1992 **CM25/09/1996**

Walton, Ms H L, BLS MCLIP, Lib. & Cust. Servs. Mgr., Cent. L., Broadway, Peterborough [10012842] 08/06/1992 **CM25/05/1994**

Walton, Mrs H M, BA MCLIP, Area Sch. Lib., Sch. L. Serv., Hants. C.C. [38037] 08/01/1985 **CM18/04/1990**

Walton, Mrs I C, BA(Hon)MA DipINF, Unwaged [49996] 07/02/1994 **ME**

Walton, Dr J G, BSc MA MBA FETC MCLIP, Head of Planning & Res., Loughborough Univ. [26599] 01/10/1976 **CM31/10/1978**

Walton, Miss J, BA MCLIP FCIPD, Campaign Leader, Enterprise Insight, Wakefield Coll, Wakefield. [34683] 26/01/1982 **RV04/04/2006** **CM14/11/1985**

Walton, Miss N, MA ILM, Learning Resources Cent. Mgr., Pynton High Sch., Stockport. [10014853] 04/03/2003 **ME**

Walton, Mrs R, BA(Hons) MA MCLIP, Lib., N. Tyneside Council Cent. L., N. Shields. [58772] 17/07/2000 **CM09/07/2008**

Walton, Miss V A, Stud. [10006307] 10/10/2007 **ME**

Walworth, Dr J C, MA PhD, Fellow Lib., Merton Coll., Oxford. [47108] 01/05/1992 **ME**

Walwyn, Miss O, MA, Stud. [10012728] 25/02/2009 **ME**

Wan Cheung, Mrs M Y A, Sen. Lib., Hong Kong P. L. [41865] 26/04/1988 **ME**

Wan, Miss L T, BSc MCLIP, Dep. Dir. Tech. Serv., Singapore Poly. [22159] 25/01/1974 **CM05/09/1977**

Wan, Ms V, MA BSc, Subject Classifier, Nielsen Bookdata, Herts. [10012974] 19/03/2009 **ME**

Wan, Dr Y C, BA MPhil PhD MCLIP FHKLA, Sen. Sub. Lib., Univ. of Hong Kong L. [41864] 26/04/1988 **CM19/08/1992**

Wang, Ms M L, Prof., Nat. Cheng-Chi Univ., Taiwan. [52083] 22/09/1995 **ME**

Wann, Miss L S, BA(Hons) MCLIP, Asst. Lib., W. Middx. Univ. Hosp. NHS Trust, Isleworth. [56744] 08/10/1998 **CM23/01/2002**

Wannop, Miss S, BA DipLib MCLIP, User Support Mgr., EUMETSAT Germany [42601] 17/01/1989 **CM12/12/1991**

Want, Miss P C, MCLIP, Retired. [15338] 10/11/1966 **CM15/12/1969**

Warburton, Mr J, BA MSc, Sen. L. Asst., HMPS Young Offenders Inst., Littlehey Cambridgeshire [63732] 09/09/2004 **ME**

Warburton, Ms L L, BA(Hons) MCLIP, Copyright Advisor, Nottingham Trent Univ. [26816] 27/10/1976 **CM11/09/1980**

Warburton, Mr S R, PGDipIS, Asst. Lib., Wellcome Trust, London. [48767] 17/05/1993 **ME**

Ward, Ms A D, BA(Hons) MA, Audience Devel. Offr., Chelmsford L., Essex [57769] 29/07/1999 **ME**

Ward, Mr A J, BA MCLIP, Info. & Stock Lib., Northampton Cent. L. [19934] 16/01/1973 **CM27/09/1976**

Ward, Mrs A, BA MA MCLIP, Academic Serv. Mgr., Sheffield Hallam Univ., Sheffield. [29675] 02/10/1978 **CM14/05/1981**

Ward, Miss C D, Inf. Res. Mgr., AECOM, St. Albans [54005] 17/10/1996 **AF**

Ward, Miss C E, BA(Hons) BA(Hons) DipMS, Lib., Luton Cent. L., Beds. [35486] 19/10/1982 **ME**

Ward, Mrs D J, BA(Hons), Sch. Lib., Grange Sch., Shropshire. [38146] 25/01/1985 **ME**

Ward, Mrs D M, MCLIP, Retired. [11858] 26/09/1969 **CM15/07/1972**

Ward, Mr G B J, BA(Hons) PGCE MEd MSc MCLIP, Sen. L. Asst., Univ. of Sheffield. [57644] 09/06/1999 **CM20/11/2002**

Ward, Mrs G, p. /t. Br. Lib., Lancs. C.C., E. Lancs. Div. [39420] 23/01/1986 **ME**

Ward, Mrs G, BA, Sen. Lib. & Independent Studies Mgr., Fortismere Sch., London. [10009294] 13/05/2008 **ME**

Ward, Mrs H J, BA MSc MCLIP, Unknown. [53989] 14/10/1996 **CM08/12/2004**

Ward, Ms H, BA DIP LIB MCLIP, Collections Mgr., Kingston Univ., Kingston Upon Thames. [35809] 17/01/1983 **CM18/02/1992**

Ward, Ms J L, BA MSc, Learning Zone Team Leader, Transport for London. [56696] 05/10/1998 **ME**

Ward, Mrs J M, FCLIP, Retired. [15353] 18/09/1940 **FE01/01/1946**

Ward, Mrs K M, BA MCLIP, Lib., Thompsons Solicitors, Manchester. [16205] 25/04/1969 **CM09/09/1974**

Ward, Mrs L J, BA MCLIP, Inf. Offr. [41819] 21/04/1988 **CM26/01/1994**

Ward, Mrs L M, BSc(Hons) MSc MScHSR MCLIP, L. Serv. Mgr., Univ. Hosp. of Leicester NHS Trust. [52672] 17/11/1995 **CM15/03/2000**

Ward, Mr M S, Serials Lib., Nat. Art L., V&A Mus., London. [47313] 10/07/1992 **ME**

Ward, Mr N J, BA MA DMS MCLIP, Retired. [28201] 04/10/1977 **CM25/02/1981**

Ward, Ms N R, BA MCLIP, Sr. Asst. Lib., Manchester Met. Univ., All Saints L. [61261] 10/05/2002 **CM11/03/2009**

Ward, Miss P L, BA DipLib MCLIP, Snr. Asst. L., House of Lords [36545] 21/10/1983 **CM15/11/1988**

Ward, Mrs P M, BA ATCL MCLIP MLib, Sr. Mngr., Collection Dev., Lancashire [18203] 05/10/1972 **CM01/08/1976**

Ward, Mrs P, BLS MBA MCLIP, Asst. Ch. Lib., Western Educ. & L. Board, Cent. L. [34740] 20/01/1982 **CM03/05/1989**

Ward, Mrs R H, BA MCLIP, Area Community Mgr., Leicestershire C.C. [26491] 06/10/1976 **CM12/03/1979**

Ward, Mr R M, Stud. Supp. Off. Asst., Sch. of Computer Sci., Univ. of Manchester. [49599] 19/11/1993 **ME**

Ward, Mr R, BA MCLIP FBIS, Asst. Lib., Univ. of Brighton. [15363] 01/01/1965 **CM01/01/1970**

Ward, Miss S A, MA, Inf. Lib., Southampton Solent Univ. [59565] 30/05/2001 **ME**

Ward, Dr S E, BSc PhD CertEd FCLIP HonFCLIP, Sen. Consultant, Beaworthy Consulting, Devon. Sen. Assoc. Consultant, TFPL Ltd., London. [60663] 06/12/1973 **FE02/04/1987**

Ward, Mrs S M, BA MA MCLIP, Child. Lib., Chesterfield L., Derbys. C.C. [29898] 23/10/1978 **CM23/10/1980**

Ward, Mr S, MA(Hons) MSc MSc, Res. Assoc., Scottish Cent. for the Book., Napier Univ. [65612] 28/02/2006 **ME**

Ward, S, MA CertEd MCLIP, Subject Specialist, Learning & Teaching Fellow, Univ. of Bolton. [21938] 01/02/1974 **CM06/10/1979**

Ward, Mr T, BLib MCLIP, Head of L. Serv., Prince Consort's L., Aldershot. [24306] 07/06/1975 **CM19/09/1980**

Ward, Ms T, BA(Hons) PgCE, Lib. Serv. Offr., Wiltshire L. [10014971] 01/10/2009 **ME**

Warden, Mrs J A, MCLIP, Lib. Asst., Univ. Oxford [2145] 14/10/1971 **CM25/03/1975**

Wardlaw, Ms J E, BA(Hons) MA MCLIP, Unknown. [51301] 01/01/1995 **CM23/01/2002**

Wardle, Mr R J, BA DipLib MCLIP, Corps Lib., CTCRM [36364] 05/10/1983 **CM01/01/1987**

Wardley, Mrs G, Stud., Aberystwyth Univ. [10014680] 27/08/2009 **ME**

Wardrope, Miss A, L. & Study Cent. Mgr., Stevenson Coll., Edinburgh. [35750] 14/01/1983 **ME**

Ware, Ms C H, BA BLS MIIS, Inf. Mgr. -Policy & Res. Dept., Heritage Lottery Fund, London. [42007] 18/07/1988 **ME**

Ware, Mrs F, BA(Hons) MCLIP, p. /t. Academic Support Lib., Fountains Learning Cent., York St. John Coll. [46931] 28/02/1992 **CM20/03/1996**

Ware, Mr P T, BA MCLIP, Sen. Grp. Mgr., Bexley L. Serv, London. [23105] 08/10/1974 **CM02/10/1978**

Wareham, Mrs A, BA(Hons) FCLIP, Lib. & H. of Inf. Servs., NMRN, Portsmouth. [37825] 06/11/1984 **FE18/09/2003**

Wares, Mr C, BA(Hons) MA MCLIP, Dir. of Knowledge Serv., BPP Prof. Edu., London. [52029] 02/10/1995 **CM20/01/1999**

Warhurst, Mrs C M, BA MCLIP, L. & Inf. Serv. Mgr., London's Transport Mus., Transport for London. [25276] 05/01/1976 **CM04/02/1980**

Waring, Mrs K, Unwaged. [10007045] 17/12/2007 **ME**

Wark, Mr A, MA(Hons) PGDip MCLIP, InterL. Serv. Asst., Nat. L. of Scotland, Edinburgh. [62184] 10/03/2003 **CM21/03/2007**

Wark, Mr P P, MCLIP, Princ. Lib., Midlothian Council, Loanhead. [21511] 22/10/1973 **CM01/12/1976**

Warman, Ms T, Learning Resources Asst., City Coll., Norfolk. [10015010] 01/10/2009 **AF**

Warmington, Mr J, MA DipLib MCLIP, Retired. [15379] 07/09/1966 **CM01/01/1969**

Warmoth, Mrs K M, BA DipLib, Lib., Fladgate LLP., London. [41141] 08/10/1987 **ME**

Warne, Mr P, MA MCLIP, Life Member. [15380] 13/02/1960 **CM01/01/1962**

Warner, Mr A M, BA, Metadata & Taxonomy Adviser, Civil Serv., Swindon. [33442] 05/01/1981 **ME**

Warner, Miss A R, BA MCLIP, Asst. Lib., CLG L., London. [23535] 05/01/1975 **CM25/04/1979**

Warner, Mrs F M, BA DipLib MCLIP, Comm. Lib., Bishopbriggs L., E. Dunbartonshire Council. [35307] 10/10/1982 **CM22/05/1996**

Warner, Mrs J M, BSc(Hons) MA MCLIP, Sect. Head – Resources Kingston Coll., Surrey. [58392] 20/01/2000 **CM07/09/2005**

Warner, Mrs J, MCLIP, Head of Learning Res. Leeds City Coll., Leeds. [1481] 03/10/1969 **CM19/02/1974**

Warner, Ms S L, MCLIP, Sch. Lib., The Ravenscroft Sch., L.B. of Barnet. [60490] 11/12/2001 **CM11/12/2001**

Warner, Miss S, BA(Hons) MSc MCLIP, Ch. Editor., Mod Corporate Internet., London [49202] 12/10/1993 **CM19/05/1999**

Warner, Mr T, BA MA MCLIP, Lib., Notts. C.C. [40326] 21/01/1987 **CM21/10/1992**

Warnock, Mr A P, MA DipLib, Acquisitions Lib., Dept. for Work & Pensions. [29865] 19/10/1978 **ME**

Warr, Dr W A, MA DPhilCChem FRSC FCLIP, Retired. [60615] 25/09/1984 **FE09/04/1991**

Warren, Miss B M, MCLIP, Life Member. [15392] 14/03/1952 **CM01/01/1958**

Warren, Miss C E, MA, Unknown. [10012557] 23/02/2009 **ME**

Warren, Miss D, BA(Hons) PgDipLib, Inf. Mgr., Bevan Brittan, Bristol. [41779] 08/04/1988 **ME**

Warren, Mrs D, MCLIP, Sch. Lib., Biddenham Upper Sch., Beds. C.C. [2760] 25/01/1969 **CM01/01/1973**

Warren, Mrs G E, BA(Hons) MScEcon MA MCLIP, Lib., Norwich Cathedral. [54098] 28/10/1996 **CM20/01/1999**

Warren, Mrs H, BA MCLIP, Sch. Lib., Amberfield Sch., Ipswich. [5599] 29/09/1971 **CM16/08/1976**

Warren, Miss J, BSc, Graduate Trainee, Univ. Chester, Seaborne L., Chester. [10016040] 10/02/2010 **ME**

Warren, Mrs J, BA MCLIP, L. Asst., Hillel Day Sch., Farmington Hills, U. S. A. [15088] 17/11/1971 **CM16/10/1974**

Warren, Mr P J R, BA MCLIP, Life Member. [15396] 19/09/1952 **CM01/01/1959**

Warren, Mrs S A, ACLIP, Advisory Co-ordinator, Hertfordshire Co. Council, Sch. L. Serv., New Barnfield [10007915] 28/02/2008 **ACL01/10/2008**

Warren, Mrs S P, BA DipLib MCLIP, Casual L. Asst., Cheshire CC. [22997] 02/10/1974 **CM01/12/1977**

Warren, Ms S, BA MCLIP, Dir. of Inf. Serv., Halliwell LLP, Manchester. [41531] 14/01/1988 **CM12/12/1991**

Warren, Mrs V M, Retired. [15398] 04/08/2004 **ME**

Warren, Mrs Y E, BA MCLIP, Area Cust. Contact Mgr., DMBC, Armthorpe L. [29288] 15/05/1978 **CM03/11/1981**

Warren-Jones, Mrs A S, MA MCLIP, Asst. Lib., Milton Keynes L., Bucks. Co. Council. [15391] 27/11/1967 **CM01/01/1971**

Warriner, Ms K P, MSc, Asst. Ref. Lib., Calderdale Met. Bor. Council, Northgate. [58396] 01/02/2000 **ME**

Warwick, Mrs J, MCLIP, Sch. Lib., Luckley-Oakfield Sch., Wokingham. [10818] 15/10/1966 **CM01/01/1970**

Warwicker, Mrs S M, Lib. Asst., SAltash L., Cornwall [10017098] 23/06/2010 **AF**

Warwood, Mrs A H, MSc, L. Asst., Ulverston P.L. [62070] 07/02/2003 **ME**

Warzelova, Miss M, MA, Unknown. [10013972] 17/06/2009 **ME**

Washford, Miss S J, BA, Unknown [59555] 16/05/2001 **AF**

Washington, Mrs J K, BSc(Hons) MSc(Econ) MCLIP, Info. Scientist., Unilever Res. &Devel. Port Sunlight, Wirral. [55466] 13/10/1997 **CM20/11/2002**

Washington, Dr L, BA MA MCLIP, Lib., Univ. of Cambridge. [42571] 03/01/1989 **CM27/05/1992**

Wason, Mrs G A, AIPM ACLIP, Sen. L. Asst., Holmes Chapel L., Cheshire. [65528] 07/02/2006 **ACL08/02/2007**

Wassell, Mrs R, L. Asst., Bond Pearce, Devon. [64671] 24/05/2005 **AF**

Waswa, Miss M, Unknown [10005105] 06/06/2007 **ME**

Waterfield, Miss Z A, Idea Store Sup., Towerhamlets CC, London [10017011] 17/06/2010 **AF**

Waterhouse, Mrs A, BA, Unknown. [64205] 09/02/2005 **ME**

Waterhouse, Mr B W C, BA, L. Resource Mgr., Medina High Sch., Newport [10011288] 02/04/1990 **ME**

Waterhouse, Ms J, BA(Hons) MSc, Sen. Asst. Lib., Univ. of Huddersfield, W. Yorks. [54267] 11/11/1996 **ME**

Waterhouse, Mr N, BA(Hons) MA, Nat. Inf. Serv. Asst. Mgr., Baker Tilly Mgmnt. Ltd., Bromley. [59838] 16/10/2001 **ME**

Waterman, Mr P J, MSc MCLIP, Community Lib., Wilts Council, Wilts. [62565] 03/09/2003 **CM21/11/2007**

Waters, Mr B J, Unwaged. [64816] 13/07/2005 **ME**

Waters, Miss C J, BA MA MCLIP, Head of L. &Inf. Serv. (4 Div.), Army L. & Inf. Serv. [46649] 02/12/1991 **RV27/11/2007** **CM23/06/2004**

Waters, Miss E, Stud., Brighton Univ. [65366] 16/01/2006 **ME**

Waters, Mrs J A, DipLib MCLIP MA(Ed), Retired. [44305] 22/08/1990 **CM22/03/1995**

Waters, Mrs J S, BA DipLS MCLIP, LRC Mgr., Totton Coll., Southampton. [36049] 01/05/1983 **CM04/02/2004**

Waterson, Mr E S, MA FCLIP, Life Member. [15424] 06/10/1949 **FE01/01/1958**

Waterson, Ms S, BA MCLIP, Lib., Dept. of Consumer & Employment Protection., Western Australia [21258] 14/10/1973 **CM05/12/1977**

Waterton-Duly, Mrs T C, BA(Hons) MA MCLIP, P/T Inf. Serv., Suffolk C.C. [55516] 16/10/1997 **CM23/03/2007**

Wathen, Dr B, BA(Hons) MA PHd, Unknown. [10016947] 10/06/2010 **AF**

Wathern, Ms A K, BA(Hons) DipLib MCLIP, p. /t. Asst., St. Georges Med. Sch. [46957] 11/03/1992 **CM29/03/2006**

Watkin, Mr A, BA DipLib FCLIP MIMgt FRSA, Ch. Offr. -L.,Leisure & Culture. Co. Bor. of Wrexham, Wrexham. [23110] 24/10/1974 **FE19/08/1992**

Watkin, Miss V L, BA(Hons) DipILS MCLIP, Learning Support Lib., Staffs. Univ. [52489] 02/11/1995 **CM19/05/1999**

Watkins, Mrs A E, MA MCLIP, Retired. [15427] 19/09/1967 **CM01/01/1972**

Watkins, Ms C A, BA MCLIP, Internat. Conflicts and Records Mgr., Simmons & Simmons, London. [15431] 21/01/1971 **CM16/03/1976**

Watkins, Mrs C J H, BA(Hons) MCLIP, Sixth Form Lib., St. Peter's High Sch., Gloucester [10011880] 13/11/1991 **CM16/05/2001**

Watkins, Mr D T, BA(Hons) DipLib, Skills for Life Mgr., L.B. Southwark [36136] 13/06/1983 **ME**

Watkins, Mrs F R, MCLIP, Volunteer Lib., RHS Wisley, Surrey. [24120] 08/04/1975 **CM19/09/1978**

Watkins, Mrs J, LRC Facilitator., Herefordshire Coll. of tech., Hereford. [10001568] 22/02/2007 **AF**

Watkins, Miss T J, BA DipLib MCLIP, Unwaged. [41224] 16/10/1987 **CM18/07/1990**

Watkinson, Mrs J, BA MCLIP, Area Mgr., Brighouse L., E. Calderdale, Calderdale L., Halifax. [35539] 29/10/1982 **CM23/09/1985**

Watkinson, Ms N J, BSc MCLIP, Academic Liaison Co-ordinator, Glyndwr Univ., Wrexham. [58588] 06/04/2000 **CM15/05/2002**

Watkinson, Mrs P M, BA MCLIP, Asst. Lib., Wiltshire C.C. [20004] 08/01/1973 **CM24/05/1976**

Watkis, Mrs M J, MCLIP, Lib., Glos. Co. L. [19116] 31/08/1972
CM19/01/1976
Watling, Mrs P C, MCLIP, Retired. [31043] 01/01/1957 **CM01/01/1963**
Watmough, Miss D J, MCLIP, Dep. Site Mgr. /Inf. Advisor, S. Bank
Univ., London. [21609] 27/11/1973 **CM15/08/1977**
Watson, Mrs A J, MSc MCLIP, p. /t. Home Literature Searcher, Royal
Coll. of Nursing, London. [37755] 23/10/1984 **CM14/11/1991**
Watson, Mr A M, MA, Head of Retrospective Catg., UCL [62067]
07/02/2003 **ME**
Watson, Mrs A, LRC Mgr., The St. Lawrence Academy, Scunthorpe.
[10015436] 18/11/2009 **ME**
Watson, Mr B, BA(Hons) MA MCLIP, Academic Liaison Lib., Univ. at
Medway [62633] 01/10/2003 **CM19/03/2008**
Watson, Mr C C W, BA MCLIP, Sen. Lib., Defence Equipment &
Support, Bristol. [24844] 01/10/1975 **CM17/08/1978**
Watson, Mrs C, BA MCLIP, Retired. [15459] 01/01/1969 **CM01/12/1972**
Watson, Mrs D A H, MCLIP, L. Asst., Chandlers Ford L., Hampshire.
[5852] 04/01/1971 **CM05/03/1974**
Watson, Mrs D E, PGDip, Lib., NHS Fife, Kirkcaldy. [10013679]
18/05/2009 **ME**
Watson, Mr D I, BA(Hons) MPhil, Unknown. [10015184] 23/10/2009 **ME**
Watson, Mr D J, BA MCLIP, Knowledge Mgr, Knowledge Servs.,
Derbyshire C. PCT [40937] 05/09/1987 **CM30/01/1991**
Watson, Mr D T, MA DipLib MCLIP, Network Lib., The Gordon Sch.,
Aberdeenshire. [41761] 07/03/1988 **CM14/08/1991**
Watson, Mr D, MA(Hons), Stud., City Univ. [10015736] 19/01/2010 **ME**
Watson, Mrs E, BA(Hons) MA MCLIP, Learning Res. Cent. Mgr., E.
Surrey Coll., Redhill. [58935] 09/10/2000 **CM23/01/2008**
Watson, Mr G L, PGDip MCLIP, Knowledge Mgr., Darlington. [63630]
02/08/2004 **CM04/10/2006**
Watson, Mrs H M, MCLIP, Retired. [15450] 19/01/1940 **CM01/01/1943**
Watson, Ms H, BA(Hons) MA MCLIP, Lib., Michelmores, Exeter. [48829]
16/06/1993 **CM24/01/1995**
Watson, Mr I, BA(Hons) MCLIP, Head of Cultural Serv., Lancashire C.C.
[35028] 04/07/1982 **CM15/08/1989**
Watson, Mr I, MA MCLIP, Knowledge and Inf. Mgr., Inst. for Res. &
Innovation in Social Serv. [61328] 29/05/2002 **CM29/05/2002**
Watson, Ms J A, BA MCLIP, L. & Inf. Serv. Co-ordinator, Highland
Council, Inverness. [32355] 13/02/1980 **CM13/06/1990**
Watson, Mrs J E, BA(Hons), Stud., Robert Gordan Univ., Aberdeen.
[50899] 28/10/1994 **ME**
Watson, Miss J, BLib MCLIP, Cust. Servs. Lib., Fife Council, Kirkcaldy
Cent. L. [23074] 21/10/1974 **CM30/09/1977**
Watson, Mr J, DMS MCLIP, Retired. [15451] 28/04/1967 **CM01/01/1970**
Watson, Ms L J, BA(Hons) DipILM MCLIP, Customer Servs. Lib., Leics
C.C. [52015] 12/09/1995 **CM21/01/1998**
Watson, Mrs L S, MCLIP, L. Asst., Herts. C.C., St. Albans. [18110]
04/10/1972 **CM15/03/1978**
Watson, Mrs M A, BA MA FCLIP HonFCLIP, Retired. [15456]
21/09/1966 **FE15/09/2004**
Watson, Miss M C, MCLIP, Team Lib., Prudhoe L., Northumberland
[65588] 23/02/2006 **CM20/04/2009**
Watson, Mr M J, BA(Hons) DipILM MCLIP, Team Lib., Bolton L. [57428]
12/05/1998 **CM12/05/1998**
Watson, M, MA DipLib MCLIP, Academic Serv. Lib., Bodleian Law L.,
Oxford. [35181] 06/10/1982 **CM07/06/1988**
Watson, Mrs M, BSc MCLIP, Principal Lib. Asst., Univ. of Liverpool
[9616] 01/01/1964 **CM01/01/1969**
Watson, Miss N A, BA(Hons), Unknown. [61871] 25/11/2002 **ME**
Watson, Miss R K, BA DipLib MCLIP, Lib., Jesus Coll., Cambridge.
[42064] 18/09/1988 **CM15/09/1993**
Watson, Mr R P, BSc MCLIP, Inf. Serv. Agent, Exeter Internat. Airport
[15463] 15/02/1971 **CM12/04/1976**
Watson, Miss S D, Retired. [15465] 03/02/1956 **ME**

Watson, Mrs S E, MCLIP, Customer Serv. Mgr., Cent. L., Nottingham.
[22583] 11/07/1974 **CM16/05/1978**
Watson, Mrs S J, BA MCLIP, Lib., Derbyshire C.C. [34774] 12/02/1982
CM30/08/1985
Watson, Miss S J, BA(Hons), Stud. [10015937] 28/01/2010 **ME**
Watson, Miss S M, BA MCLIP, Reader & Learning Devel. Lib., Trafford
[28717] 09/01/1978 **CM25/02/1980**
Watson, Miss S, BA(Hons) MA MCLIP, Sen. Mgr., Data Analysis &
Integration, Nielsen Bookdata Stevenage, Herts. [50625] 01/10/1994
CM19/05/1999
Watson, Mr W H, BA MCLIP, Lib. Culture & Sport Glasgow. [26655]
27/10/1976 **CM17/07/1980**
Watson, Mr W M, DAES FCLIP, Life Member. [15468] 09/08/1950
FE01/01/1958
Watson-Bore, Mrs J, BA CertEd MCLIP, Dir. of L., Ashford Sch., Kent.
[27230] 04/02/1977 **CM05/02/1979**
Watt, Mrs A J, BA MCLIP, Young Person's Offr., Halton Bor. Council,
Runcorn, Cheshire. [39597] 14/03/1986 **CM26/02/1992**
Watt, Mr A, Catr., Met Off., Exeter. [63184] 03/03/2004 **ME**
Watt, Ms D M, BSc MA MCLIP, Collections & Servs. Mgr., Cent. Sch. of
Speech & Drama, London [61629] 09/10/2002 **CM13/06/2007**
Watt, Ms G K, MCLIP, Inf. Serv. Mgr., Morgan Cole, Cardiff. [49522]
10/11/1993 **CM25/09/1996**
Watt, Mr I, MCLIP, Head of Strategy, The L., European Parliament,
Bruxelles. [35873] 04/02/1983 **CM11/11/1986**
Watt, Mrs S J, BA MCLIP, Asst. Libr., Queen Margaret Univ. Coll.
[42671] 07/02/1989 **CM26/01/1994**
Watt, Mrs S M, BA MCLIP, L. & Inf. Offr., Newcastle City L. [33295]
16/10/1980 **CM14/10/1985**
Watt, Mrs V A, MA(Hons) MA, Unknown. [54711] 06/03/1997 **ME**
Watt, Mr W J, MCLIP, Position unknown, Glasgow City Council. [22085]
25/01/1974 **CM22/06/1976**
Wattam, Mrs Y J, BA MSc, Asst. Lib., Record Off. (Arch.), Leicester.
[56917] 04/11/1998 **ME**
Watters, Mr J W H, MCLIP, Life Member. [15472] 27/01/1952
CM01/01/1961
Watters, Mrs S J, BA(Hons) MCLIP, Asst. Lib., W. Sussex Co. Council
[60015] 26/11/2001 **CM19/12/2008**
Watthews, Miss E M, BA MCLIP, Life Member. [15474] 12/01/1954
CM01/01/1957
Wattis, Mrs L L, BA MCLIP, Unknown. [10012895] 13/01/1981
CM01/07/1989
Watts, Ms A E, BSc MSc MCLIP, Inf. Scientist, Unilever Res. & Devel.,
Wirral. [33186] 15/09/1980 **CM06/10/1987**
Watts, Miss G, MCLIP, Retired. [15481] 04/02/1935 **CM01/01/1942**
Watts, Mrs L J, B. Lib., MCLIP, Lib., King Edward VI Sch., Stratford
Upon Avon. [10011226] 19/03/1975 **CM10/12/1979**
Watts, Miss N J, BSc MSc MCLIP, Med. Inf. Team Leader, Sanofi-
Aventis, Guildford. [60706] 12/12/2001 **CM12/12/2001**
Watts, Mr S D, MCLIP, Retired. [15484] 01/10/1966 **CM01/01/1970**
Watts, Mr S G, BA CSci MRSC MCLIP, Inf. Offr., Brit. L., Sci. Tech. &
Innovation, London. [60744] 16/04/1986 **CM01/03/1989**
Watts, Mr S L, BA DipLib, Retired. [30060] 26/10/1978 **ME**
Waudby, Mr A D, MCLIP, Life Member. [17938] 01/01/1939
CM01/01/1948
Waugh, Mrs J D, BA DipLib MCLIP, Workforce and Audience Devel.
Mgr., Essex C.C. L., Chelmsford. [33502] 12/01/1981 **CM24/09/1985**
Wawa, Mr J N O, Stud., UCL. [64074] 15/12/2004 **ME**
Way, Mr D J, MA FCLIP, Life Member. [15492] 24/01/1951 **FE01/01/1958**
Wayne, Mrs L, BA MCLIP, Info. Servs. Mgr., Dixon City Academy,
Bradford. [21931] 24/01/1974 **CM01/11/1976**
Wayte, Miss A C, MCLIP, L. Mgr., Southwark P. L. [15494] 12/01/1965
CM01/01/1968

403

Weare, Mrs J, MA BA MCLIP, Hist. Researcher. [15496] 13/03/1964 **CM01/01/1968**

Wearing, Mrs C, BA MCLIP, Lib. Serv. Mgr., Medway Hosp. NHS Trust, Gillingham. [35001] 08/06/1982 **CM12/09/2001**

Weatherall, Mrs J, MA Dip Lib, Sch. Lib., The Perse Sch., Cambridge. [10014185] 14/05/1982 **ME**

Weatherall, Mr P, MA MCLIP, L. & Arch. Serv. offr., Manx Nat. Heritage. [15498] 01/01/1970 **CM23/06/1975**

Weatherhead, Mrs A F, BSc(Hons) MA MSc, Br. Lib., Brixham L.,Torbay Council [60887] 20/12/2001 **ME**

Weatherly, Miss K, MCLIP, Retired. [15501] 13/01/1967 **CM01/01/1970**

Weatley, Mrs C E, BA(Hons) MCLIP, Unemployed [51473] 20/02/1995 **CM16/07/2003**

Weaver, Mrs E A, BA MCLIP MSc, Lib., Alexandra House Sch., Mauritius. [38058] 08/01/1985 **CM18/07/1990**

Weaver, Mrs M L, BA MCLIP MSc, Head of Learning & Inf. Serv., Univ. of Cumbria [44022] 05/04/1990 **CM14/11/1991**

Weaver, Mrs M, BA, Shaftesbury Assoc., Toronto. [54996] 12/06/1997 **ME**

Webb, Ms A E, MBA DipIM, L. Operations Mgr., The Christie NHS Foundation Trust, Withington. [59704] 14/08/2001 **ME**

Webb, Miss C J M, BA MA FCLIP, Sch. Lib., Forest Hill Sch., London. [37905] 07/11/1984 **FE21/03/2007**

Webb, Mr D R, BA FCLIP, Life Member. [15513] 10/03/1962 **FE28/01/1975**

Webb, Dr E R, BA(Hons) MA MCLIP, Periodicals Lib., Univ. of Sunderland., Tyne & Wear. [31491] 08/10/1979 **CM24/09/1997**

Webb, Mrs G L, BA(Hons) DipILM, Project Mngr., House of Commons L., London [55598] 24/10/1997 **ME**

Webb, Miss H J, BA(Hons), Stud., Brighton Univ. [10000715] 19/10/2006 **ME**

Webb, Miss H S, MA, Inf. Serv. Lib., Royal Coll. of Surgeons, London. [55897] 15/12/1997 **ME**

Webb, Ms J M, MA MLib MBA FCLIP FHEA FRSA, Head of Academic Serv., De Montfort Unv., Leics. [42399] 27/10/1988 **FE03/10/2007**

Webb, Mrs K J W, BA(Hons) MA MCLIP, Dep. Lib., English Faculty L., Oxford Univ. [60867] 13/12/2001 **RV23/11/2009** **CM09/11/2005**

Webb, Ms K, BSc(Hons), Lib. [65647] 11/01/2006 **AF**

Webb, Mrs M I, MCLIP, Life Member. [15525] 01/01/1939 **CM01/01/1942**

Webb, Mrs M, BA(Hons) DipILM MCLIP, Web Administrator [54084] 24/10/1996 **CM20/11/2002**

Webb, Mrs S P, BA(Hons) FCLIP, Life Member. [9175] 30/01/1957 **FE22/05/1987**

Webb, Miss S, Enquiry Off., Northumbria Univ., Newcastle Upon Tyne. [10015952] 28/01/2010 **ME**

Webb, Ms S, Sen. L. Asst., Manchester Met. Univ. [65079] 01/11/2005 **AF**

Webb, Ms Y, BSc(Hons), Local Studies Collections Mgr., L.B. of Barnet. [55209] 15/08/1997 **ME**

Webber, Mrs E, MCLIP, Dep. Lib., Harrow Sch., Middlesex. [12158] 01/10/1967 **CM01/01/1971**

Webber, Dr N A, MA PhD FCLIP, Life Member. [15535] 27/07/1950 **FE01/01/1962**

Webber, Mr P N, MCLIP, Retired. [15537] 21/01/1970 **CM12/07/1973**

Webber, Mrs S A E, BA FCLIP, Sen. Lect., Dept. of Inf. Studies., Univ. of Sheffield [28718] 16/01/1978 **FE01/04/2002**

Weber, Ms G, BA(Hons), Lib. Asst., UCL Lib. Serv., London. [10011159] 29/09/2008 **ME**

Weber, Mrs L D R, BA MLS MCLIP, Contract Catr., Self-employed. [42141] 06/10/1988 **CM18/07/1990**

Webster, Ms D C F, MA MCLIP, Retired. [19068] 19/09/1972 **CM04/11/1974**

Webster, Mr G J, BSc DipLib FCLIP, Inf. Coordinator, FCO, London. [27039] 17/12/1976 **FE22/05/1987**

Webster, Mrs H F, Stud., Aberystwyth Univ. [10016483] 01/04/2010 **ME**

Webster, Mrs H L, Self Employed. [15540] 01/07/1971 **ME**

Webster, Mr H T I, Life Member. [15541] 23/02/1953 **ME**

Webster, Mr J N G, BA MCLIP, Info. Servs. Team Leader, Bucks C.C. [10013150] 15/10/1982 **CM21/10/1992**

Webster, Mr K G, BSc(Hons) MLib AALIA FCLIP Ho, Univ. Lib. &Dir. of Learning Serv., Universtiy of Queensland, Australia. [36428] 06/10/1983 **FE01/04/2002**

Webster, Mrs M, LLB MA MCLIP, L. & Inf. Serv. Mgr., Browne Jacobson, Nottingham. [49750] 01/12/1993 **CM12/02/2001**

Webster, Mrs M, BA MCLIP, Leader of the Learning Resource Cent., The Becket Sch., Nottingham [36637] 27/10/1983 **CM16/02/1988**

Webster, Mr P, MA MCLIP, Force Lib., Thames Valley Police, Reading. [37008] 31/01/1984 **CM15/10/2002**

Webster, Mr S A H, MA MCLIP MSc, Inf. Offr., MS Trust, Letchworth. [10001036] 01/10/1987 **CM14/11/1991**

Webster, Miss S C M, BSc(Hons) MA, Unknown. [54038] 22/10/1996 **ME**

Webster, Miss W A, Sen. Lib. Asst., Law L. Univ. of W. Indies, Barbados [10017021] 18/06/2010 **ME**

Wedlake, Mrs C K, BSc MA, Team Lib., Oxfordshire Co. Council [59891] 29/01/2001 **ME**

Weech, Mr E J P, BA MPHIL, Unknown. [10007748] 21/02/2008 **AF**

Weedon, Mr P D, BSc Econ, Unwaged [10014539] 12/08/2009 **ME**

Weedon, Mr R L, BA MA, Complliance Offr., Univ. of Strathclyde, Glasgow. [60305] 15/11/2000 **AF**

Weeks, Mrs H, MCLIP, Cultural Serv. Team Leader, Aberdeenshire Council. [11958] 01/01/1971 **CM01/12/1973**

Weeks, Mr J B, MCLIP, Br. Libr., Gants Hill L., L.B. of Redbridge. [25823] 17/02/1976 **CM11/11/1985**

Weetman Dacosta, Ms J D, BA DipLib MBA MCLIP, Inf. Literacy Lib., Coll. of New Jersey, USA. [37022] 30/01/1984 **CM09/08/1988**

Weglarz, Mrs J, MA, Catr., Polish Social & Cultural Assoc. [10012829] 13/03/2009 **AF**

Weighell, Mrs E A, BA MCLIP, L. Mgr., Hampshire C.C. [39163] 25/11/1985 **CM21/12/1988**

Weightman, Dr A L, BSc PhD DipLib, Head of L. Serv. Devel., Inf. Serv., Cardiff Univ. [48543] 11/02/1993 **ME**

Weintraub, Miss S M, Inf. Serv. Asst., BPP Coll. of Professional Studies, Holborn [64707] 01/06/2005 **ME**

Weir, Ms A L C, MA MA, L. Offr., Edinburgh City L. & Inf. Serv. [60977] 23/01/2002 **ME**

Weir, Mrs H E, BSc PGDipLib MCLIP, Dep. Serv. Mgr., Harrogate Dist. Hosp. L. & Inf. Serv. [43754] 01/01/1990 **CM17/09/2003**

Weir, Mrs H W, BA MCLIP, Life member. [33428] 17/10/1980 **CM03/05/1988**

Weir, Mrs J H, BA MCLIP, Learning Serv. Mgr., E. Renfrewshire Council. [29764] 10/10/1978 **CM21/04/1982**

Weir, Miss L J, BSc(Hons) MSc MCLIP, Content Mgr., MWH Ltd., Edinburgh. [56350] 04/06/1998 **CM15/10/2002**

Weir, Mrs S D, MSc BEd(Hons), Academic Liaison Lib., Univ. of Bedfordshire. [10006249] 28/09/2007 **ME**

Weir, Miss S M, Volunteer. [10015783] 26/01/2010 **AF**

Weir, Mrs S, Unknown. [10014542] 01/10/1982 **ME**

Weist, Ms A H, BA(Hons) MSc MCLIP, Educ. Mgr., NHS Evidence, Nice [42214] 10/10/1988 **CM20/09/1995**

Weisz, Ms G, Stud., London Met. Univ. [65106] 01/11/2005 **ME**

Welburn, Mrs D, p. t. /Lib., Cheshire L., Chesher C.C. [64443] 30/03/2005 **ME**

Welby, Mrs J P, MCLIP, Lib., Shebbear Coll., Devon. [22749] 04/09/1974 **CM01/10/1977**

Welch, Ms C A, MCLIP, Chartered Lib., Bramcote Park Sch., Nottingham. [38274] 03/02/1985 **CM20/01/1987**

Welch, Mr D H, FCLIP, Life Member. [15571] 22/03/1956 **FE01/01/1964**

Wella, Mr K, Lib., Kamuzu Coll. of Nursing, Lilongwe, Malawi. [10013692] 22/05/2009 **ME**

Wellard, Ms E K, BA(Hons) DipILS MCLIP, Sen. Lib. - Inf., Somerset Council. [10010616] 07/11/1995 **CM21/03/2001**

Wellburn, Mr P, BA MCLIP, Retired. [17942] 21/09/1965 **CM01/01/1969**

Weller, Miss A L, MCLIP, Child. L. Co-ordinator, L.B. of Sutton. [22710] 16/09/1974 **CM12/08/1977**

Weller, Ms J C, BA(Hons) DipLib MCLIP, Princ. Lib. -Inf. Serv., Hampshire Co. L., H.Q. L., Winchester. [23340] 20/11/1974 **CM28/02/1977**

Wellings, Mrs K M, MCLIP, Application Support Consultant, Axiell, Nottingham. [30032] 24/11/1978 **CM25/11/1982**

Wells, Mrs A M, BA MCLIP, Lib., Withington Girls Sch., Fallowfield,Manchester. [21678] 03/01/1974 **CM24/08/1976**

Wells, Miss C E, BA, Grad. Trainee Lib., St Deiniol's L., Hawarden. [10015359] 12/11/2009 **ME**

Wells, Ms E A, BSc DipLIS MCLIP, Head of L. & Inf. Serv., Freshfields Bruckhaus Deringer, London. [40344] 23/01/1987 **CM12/03/2003**

Wells, Ms E A, BA DipLib MCLIP, Lib., Barbican L., London. [33879] 22/04/1981 **CM21/05/2008**

Wells, Ms G, L. Asst., Sydney Jones L., Univ. Liverpool. [64770] 16/06/2005 **ME**

Wells, Mrs H J, BSc MSc MCLIP, Head of User Servs., Univ. of E. Anglia, Norfolk. [29367] 10/07/1978 **CM17/11/1980**

Wells, Miss J M, MBA MCLIP, Customer Serv. Mgr., Anglia Ruskin Univ., Cambridge. [42126] 03/10/1988 **CM14/08/1991**

Wells, Miss J M, MCLIP, Life Member. [15588] 25/07/1949 **CM03/09/1954**

Wells, Miss J T, BA DipLib MCLIP, Lib., London Bor. of Bexley [33606] 24/01/1981 **CM18/04/1989**

Wells, Mr P, BSc(Hons) MSc, Asst. Lib. (Trainee), Anglia Ruskin Univ., Cambridge [10000949] 04/12/2006 **ME**

Wells, Mrs R E, BA(Hons) MCLIP, Career Break. [56890] 02/11/1998 **CM19/11/2003**

Wells, Mrs S E, BSc MCLIP, Sch. Lib., St. John Houghton Sch., Derbys. [15592] 22/04/1971 **CM01/09/1973**

Wells, Mr S L M, BA MCLIP, Head of Inf. Mgmnt., Dept. of Health, London. [60423] 15/05/1997 **CM15/05/1997**

Wells, Mrs S L, ACLIP, Snr. L. Asst., Hucknall L., Notts. [64686] 25/05/2005 **ACL29/03/2007**

Wellsted, Mrs J L, BA DipLib MCLIP, Legal Lib., Esso Petroleum Co. Ltd., Leatherhead. [34938] 22/04/1982 **CM07/07/1987**

Welsh, Ms A, MA(Hons) MSc(Econ), Inf. Specialist., NHS Educ. for Scotland [49026] 03/09/1993 **ME**

Welsh, Rev J A, BA(Hons) DipLib MCLIP, Campus Lib., Univ. of Wales Inst., Cardiff, Llandaff Learning Cent. [15601] 19/01/1967 **CM01/07/1972**

Welsh, Mrs L J, Sch. Lib., Boswells. [63578] 08/07/2004 **ME**

Welsh, Ms S B, BSc(Open) ACLIP, Asst Lib., Bournmouth Univ., Poole [66021] 25/08/2006 **ACL06/02/2008**

Welsh, Miss S M, PhD DipLib MCLIP, Business & Inf. Systems Team Leader (Meta Data), Liverpool John Moores Univ. L. Serv. [30293] 12/01/1979 **CM10/12/1981**

Welsher, Miss A D, MCLIP, Retired. [15602] 15/09/1967 **CM01/01/1971**

Wemyss, Mrs E M, BSc DipLib MCLIP, Team Lib., Local Studies, Aberdeen L. &Inf. Serv. [28137] 08/10/1977 **CM19/11/1979**

Wenham, Mrs J M M, FCLIP, P/t Lib., Bournemouth Sch. for Girls. [15606] 01/01/1952 **FE01/01/1959**

Wentworth, Ms S F, BA DipLib MCLIP, Sen. Lib., Info. Servs., Oxon C.C. [32767] 12/08/1980 **CM03/09/1982**

Wentzell, Mr C, BA, Inf. Lib., Univ. of Bath. [65653] 02/03/2006 **ME**

Werb, Mrs S L, Lib. Asst., Sidmouth L. [10016563] 14/04/2010 **ME**

Werndly, Mrs H, BA MCLIP, Unwaged. [33190] 30/09/1980 **CM14/10/1982**

West, Ms A, BA DipLib MCLIP, Lib., Royal Coll. of Nursing, Inf. & Advice Serv., Cardiff. [42819] 08/03/1989 **CM31/01/1996**

West, Mrs C A, BA(Hons) MA MCLIP, Learning Res. Mgr., City Coll., Birmingham. [41218] 12/10/1987 **CM16/11/1994**

West, Mr C B, BA DipLib MCLIP, Retired. [15612] 04/10/1962 **CM01/01/1972**

West, Mr C M, MA BA DipLib MCLIP, Dir. of L. & Inf. Serv., Univ. of Wales, Swansea. [25132] 27/10/1975 **CM26/01/1979**

West, Ms C, BA MSc, Lib., The Pensions Regulator, Brighton. [10001106] 12/01/2007 **ME**

West, Ms E, BA MCLIP, Online and Web Serv. Mgr., Northumbria Univ., Newcastle-upon-Tyne. [39948] 06/10/1986 **CM12/12/1991**

West, Miss H, BA/MA/MSc, Know. Serv. Co-ordinator, Chartered Ins. Inst. [10006383] 23/10/2007 **ME**

West, Mr J, BA DipLib MCLIP, Area Lib., N. Ayrshire Council. [44166] 18/06/1990 **CM16/10/1991**

West, Ms K, BSc(Hons) MSc MCLIP, Head of L. The Operations Cent. L., Norwich Bioscience Inst., Norfolk [56977] 17/11/1998 **CM02/02/2005**

West, Mrs L E, Desk and Facilities Serv. Mgr., York St John Univ. [10006341] 10/10/2007 **ME**

West, Mr L E, BSc MCLIP, p. /t. Catr., Kingston Hosp., Kingston upon Thames. [60666] 21/03/1972 **CM04/07/1977**

West, Mrs L M, Sen. L. Asst., Univ. Coll. for the Creative Arts, Maidstone [47247] 01/07/1992 **AF**

West, Mrs L S, ACLIP, Assist-in-charge, Buckfastleigh Lib., Devon Co. Council. [10013400] 23/04/2009 **ACL16/06/2010**

West, Mrs M J, BA DipLib MCLIP, Position unknown, N. Ayrshire Council. [41582] 21/01/1988 **CM11/12/1989**

West, Mr M L, BA DipLib MCLIP, Child. Lib., Devon L. & Inf. Servs., Exeter. [40742] 23/05/1987 **CM14/08/1991**

West, Ms M, MSc, Lib. Asst., Sandwick Junior High Sch. [10007942] 03/11/2005 **ME**

West, Miss N H, BA(Hons) MCLIP, Knowledge & Records Mgr., Brit. Dental Assoc., London. [56892] 02/11/1998 **CM08/12/2004**

West, Mr N J M, BA(Hons) DipLIS MCLIP, L. Training Offr., L.B. of Camden. [43018] 23/06/1989 **CM20/03/1996**

West, Mrs N L, MSc Econ BA(Hons), Catr., The London L. [56492] 21/07/1998 **ME**

West, Mr R W C, BA MCLIP, Life Member. [15618] 14/01/1963 **CM01/01/1965**

West, Miss S I, MSc ECON MCLIP, Lib. /Info. Specialist, Countess Chester Hosp. [10013008] 02/11/1995 **CM10/03/2010**

West, Mrs S, BA AKC DipLib MCLIP, Community Devel. Lib., Tonbridge L., Kent [8454] 27/07/1972 **CM17/12/1974**

Westaway, Mr J, PhD, Law Lib., Univ. of Cent. Lancashire [10010173] 05/10/1998 **ME**

Westbrook, Mrs K B, BA MA(Hons) TQFE MCLIP, Postgrad. Stud., Univ. of Edinburgh. [27794] 05/11/1965 **CM01/01/1970**

Westcott, Mrs D M, BA DipLib MCLIP, Unknown [33076] 03/10/1980 **CM02/07/1985**

Westcott, Miss E L, BA MCLIP, Life Member. [15624] 11/01/1958 **CM01/01/1960**

Westcott, Ms J, BLib MCLIP, Lib., Poole Cent. L. [38999] 24/10/1985 **CM27/03/1991**

Westcott, Miss M R, MA MCLIP, Life Member. [15625] 19/09/1958 **CM01/01/1962**

Westcott, Ms S A, BA(Hons) ACLIP, Learning Cent. Co-ordinator, Exeter Coll. [56121] 03/03/1998 **ACL03/12/2008**

Westcott, Ms S R, MA DipLib FCLIP, Br. Head., Inf. & Communications Communities., Local Government [43264] 10/10/1989 **FE29/03/2004**

Westerhof, Dr D, MA PhD, Stud., Univ. of Aberystwyth. [10011117] 25/09/2008 **ME**

Western, Miss R, BA(Hons), Unknown. [10015470] 25/11/2009 **ME**

Westgate, Mrs S, BEcon MCLIP, Lib. & Inf. Offr., Dundee C.C. [57509] 14/04/1999 **CM21/06/2006**

Westland, Mrs A C, MScLIS, Lib., Surbiton High Sch., Kingston. [47734] 16/10/1992 **ME**

Westmancoat, Mrs H T, MCLIP, Dep. Univ. Lib., York St. John Univ. [9719] 19/10/1971 **CM07/10/1976**

Westmorland, Ms L, BA(Hons) MA MCLIP, L. Serv. Mgr. - Child. and Young People, Shropshire Council. [49012] 31/08/1993 **CM15/05/2002**

Weston, Mr C G H, B ENG MIET MCLIP, Retired. [15630] 05/10/1969 **CM22/10/1974**

Weston, Mr M K, BA MCLIP, Knowledge & Inf. Mgr., URS Corp. Ltd., Bedford. [24851] 17/10/1975 **CM12/01/1982**

Weston, Mr N, BA MA MCLIP, Lib. i/c., S. Glos. Council, Yate,nr. Bristol. [43849] 31/01/1990 **CM18/11/1993**

Weston, Mrs R E, BLib MCLIP, Volunteer Lib., ETP UK, High Wycombe. [26685] 26/10/1976 **CM14/10/1981**

Weston, Ms S A, BA(Hons) PGCE MSc, Unknown. [66072] 20/09/2006 **ME**

Weston-Smith, Ms S J, BA(Hons) MA, Unwaged. [56853] 27/10/1998 **ME**

Westwood, Miss C A, BA, Stud., Manchester Met. Univ. [10015081] 12/10/2009 **ME**

Westwood, Mr D G, L. Asst., Hackney L. Serv., CLR James L. [45467] 14/02/1991 **ME**

Westwood, Miss H M, BA(Hons), Unknown. [10012371] 09/04/2001**ME**

Westwood, Miss J, BSc(Econ) MSc MCLIP, Inf. Asst., Univ. of Wales, Aberystwyth. [55636] 30/10/1997 **CM21/11/2001**

Westwood, Miss R, BA(Hons) MSc MCLIP, Liaison Lib., Newman Univ. Coll. [61303] 16/05/2002 **CM17/09/2008**

Westworth, Miss R, BA, Stud., Univ. of Brighton. [10015224] 27/10/2009 **ME**

Wetenhall, Mrs M C, MLib BA DipLib MCLIP, Retired. [36776] 08/09/1967 **CM23/08/1985**

Wetherell, Mrs F D, BA(Hons) MCLIP, Catr., Trinity Coll. L., Cambridge. [10005273] 26/10/1971 **CM04/04/1975**

Wetherell, Ms S D, MSc BENG(Hons), PHIR Mgr., PHIR L., Bedford. [10015326] 10/11/2009 **ME**

Wetherill, Mrs H C, BA(Hons) MA MCLIP, Inf. Serv. Offr., DPPLLP, Bedford. [42670] 07/02/1989 **CM19/03/1997**

Wetherill, Mr J, BA MA MCLIP, Res. Cons., Futuresource Consulting, Dunstable. [42495] 23/11/1988 **CM19/06/1991**

Weyman, Miss M, BA MCLIP, Life Member. [15645] 26/09/1957 **CM01/01/1963**

Whaite, Mrs K C, BA, Graduate Trainee, Gray's Inn L., London [10012530] 19/02/2009 **ME**

Whale, Mrs H A, MCLIP, Inf. & Educ. Co-ordinator, S. Tyneside M.B.C. [2373] 08/02/1966 **CM01/01/1970**

Whaley, Miss G A, BA(Hons), Sen. Inf. Offr., Hill Dickinson LLP, London. [10016798] 03/03/2003 **ME**

Whalley, Mr J H, BLib MCLIP, Sen. Asst. Lib., Manchester Metro. Univ., Cheshire. [30570] 28/01/1979 **CM31/12/1989**

Whalley, Ms J, BA(Hons) PG Dip, Catr., Natural England, KMIS, Cambs. [10015936] 01/02/2010 **ME**

Whapham, Miss E B G, MCLIP, Life Member. [15650] 27/02/1940 **CM01/01/1944**

Wharam, Ms H M, BSc MSc MCLIP, Trust Lib., NHS, Torbay Hosp. [60348] 11/08/1994 **CM11/08/1994**

Wharrad, Mr A J, MSc PGDip MCLIP, Data Architect, DEFRA., London [54270] 12/11/1996 **CM01/04/2002**

Wharton, Miss J C, BA DipLib PhD MCLIP, Catg. & Metadata Lib., Univ. of Nottingham. [40010] 14/10/1986 **CM24/07/1996**

Wharton, Miss L, Sch. L. &Inf. Cent. Mgr., Colton Hills Community Sch., Wolverhampton. [55292] 17/09/1997 **ME**

Wharton, Mrs S B, BA MCLIP, Retired. [10695] 02/12/1968 **CM01/01/1972**

Whatley, Mr H A, MA FCLIP, Life Member. [15654] 02/03/1931 **FE01/01/1937**

Whatmore, Mrs I A, BLib MCLIP, LRC Mgr., Farnham Coll., Surrey. [25035] 31/10/1975 **CM30/01/1981**

Wheadon, Miss K L, BA(Hons) MSc, Unknown. [62048] 29/01/2003**ME**

Wheatcroft, Mrs A V, BSc MA DMS MCLIP, Freelance. [47560] 01/10/1992 **CM19/07/2000**

Wheatcroft, Miss L E M, BA MA MCLIP, Team L., Child. & Young People, Northamptonshire C.C. [64833] 02/08/2005 **CM17/09/2008**

Wheater, Mrs E A, BEd DipLib MCLIP, Retired. [42290] 12/10/1988 **CM21/07/1993**

Wheatley, Mrs G F M, BA(Hons) MCLIP, Lib. Mgr., Wimborne L., Dorset [50816] 19/10/1994 **CM16/05/2001**

Wheatley, Mr G W J, FCLIP DipFE, Life Member. [15661] 22/03/1943 **FE01/01/1966**

Wheatley, Mrs J F, FCLIP, Life Member. [15662] 10/03/1941 **FE01/01/1950**

Wheatman, Mrs H E, MCLIP, Learning Resource Ctr. Mgr., The Samworth Church Academy, Mansfield [11097] 12/03/1971 **CM01/07/1988**

Wheeldon, Mrs C, MCLIP, Co. Sec., ERW Consulting Ltd., Bedfordshire. [15486] 06/02/1969 **CM20/12/1972**

Wheeler, Mrs A R, PG Celt Mgnet MCLIP, Hd. of Serv. Devel., Suffolk C.C. [28393] 25/10/1977 **CM24/08/1981**

Wheeler, Mr A T F, Unknown. [65614] 17/03/2006 **ME**

Wheeler, Ms A, BA(Hons) MCLIP, User Serv. Lib., (Jobshare), Univ. of Brighton. [49160] 08/10/1993 **CM24/07/1996**

Wheeler, Mrs E L, BSc(Hons) MSc(Econ) MCLIP, Community Lib., Wiltshire Council. [57521] 15/04/1999 **CM20/11/2002**

Wheeler, Miss E, Unknown. [10011532] 06/11/2008 **ME**

Wheeler, Miss H A, BA(Hons) MCLIP MA, Dep. Learning Resources Mgr., Vauxhall Cent., Lambeth Coll. [15666] 01/01/1971 **CM31/08/1974**

Wheeler, Mr M, BA(Hons), Stud. [10006312] 05/10/2007 **ME**

Wheeler, Miss P C, MCLIP BA, Retired. [15668] 29/01/1962 **CM01/01/1964**

Wheeler, Mr W G, MA DipLib FCLIP ALAI, Life Member, [15669] 29/10/1954 **FE01/01/1960**

Wheelton, Mrs J H, MCLIP, Sen. Lib., Banbury L., Oxon. [13472] 03/01/1970 **CM22/06/1978**

Whelan, Mr D A, BA(Hons), E-Learning Cent. Mgr., St. Philip Howard Catholic Sch., Derbys. [58197] 16/11/1999 **ME**

Whelehan, Mr B M, BA(Hons) MCLIP, Sen. L. Asst., Help Desk, Public Serv., Cent. L., Imperial Coll., London. [46450] 07/11/1991 **CM23/07/1997**

Whibley, Mr V, MA FRSA MCMI FCLIP, Retired. [15672] 21/09/1959 **FE01/07/1972**

Whincup, Mrs P E, MCLIP, Retired. [15677] 08/09/1955 **CM01/01/1961**

Whitaker, Mr D H, OBE BA, Chairman, J. Whitaker & Sons, London. [40257] 11/11/1986 **ME**

Whitaker, Ms G L, Unwaged. [65179] 07/11/2005 **AF**

Whitaker, Mr R, BA MA, Town Planning Offr., Civic Cent., L.B. Hounslow. [52599] 10/11/1995 **ME**

Whitby, Mrs J, Dip ILS, Tech. L. Team Leader, Thomas Cook Tech. L., Manchester. [10009358] 12/05/1994 **ME**

Whitcombe, Mrs A C, MSc MCLIP, Inf. Mgr., NHS Grampian, Aberdeen. [60231] 29/01/1983 **CM29/01/1983**

Whitcombe, Mrs J M, RN (Dip), Stud.,Manchester Met. Univ [10014808] 16/09/2009 **ME**

Whitcombe, Ms N E, Sen. L. Asst., Univ. of Wales, Swansea. [52908] 22/01/1996 **AF**

White, Mr A J, BSc DipLib MCLIP, Sen. Consultant, Serco Assurance, Risley. [46361] 30/10/1991 **CM01/04/2002**

White, Miss A M, L. Asst., Calne L. Wiltshire. [10010495] 30/07/2008**AF**

White, Miss A M, BEd(Hons) DipLIS MCLIP, Team Lib., Oxon. C.C. [45730] 03/05/1991 **CM20/05/1998**

White, Ms A, MLS, Off. Asst., Cheltenham Township L. System, Glenside, USA. [10011886] 26/11/2008 **ME**

White, Mrs B, HonFCLIP FCLIP, Retired. [15691] 29/08/1955 **FE19/01/1982**

White, Miss C E, BA MCLIP, Sch. L. Consultant, Sch. L. Support Serv., Walsall. [22301] 21/02/1974 **CM31/10/1978**

White, Mrs C J, BA(Hons) MSc MCLIP, Inf. Offr., MOD, London [59140] 28/11/2000 **CM31/01/2007**

White, Miss E R, BA MA, Inf. Offr., Internat. Inf. Unit, NFER. [63105] 30/01/2004 **ME**

White, Miss E, BA(Hons), Systems Lib., TRL Ltd, Wokingham. [64342] 07/03/2005 **ME**

White, Mrs G L W, BA Dip Ed, Mgr. Learning Resource Cent., Crossways 6th Form, London. [10014679] 27/08/2009 **ME**

White, Ms G M, BA(Hons)PG DipLib, Head of Remote Serv., Nat. Art L., Word & Image Dept., Victoria & Albert Mus. [34653] 19/01/1982 **ME**

White, Mrs G, BA MCLIP, Self Employed. [27515] 13/05/1977 **CM29/12/1980**

White, Miss H, BA(Hons), L. Asst., Dudley L., W. Midlands. [10016622] 01/05/2010 **AF**

White, Mr H, MCLIP, Retired. [15703] 20/02/1950 **CM01/01/1955**

White, Mrs J A, BA(Hons) MA, Asst. Lib., Prince Consorts Lib., Aldershot. [57615] 28/05/1999 **ME**

White, Mrs J A, MA MCLIP, Unknown. [28848] 23/01/1978 **CM30/06/1982**

White, Mrs J C, BA MCLIP, Team Lib., Child. & Young People, Northumb. Co. L. [35754] 10/01/1983 **CM15/11/1988**

White, Mrs J M E, MSc MCLIP, Retired. [10612] 02/10/1968 **CM01/01/1972**

White, Mrs J M O, MLib AMus TCL MCLIP, Unwaged. [25824] 01/03/1976 **CM07/03/1980**

White, Mr J M, BA MA, Learning Facilitator., Walsall Coll. [57476] 01/04/1999 **ME**

White, Mr J P, BA MA, Curriculum Learning Resource Specialist, Rotherham Coll. of Arts & Tech. [65029] 13/10/2005 **ME**

White, Mrs J S, Met. Police Serv. [64393] 14/03/2005 **ME**

White, Mr J T, FCLIP, Unknown. [15710] 17/10/1935 **FE01/01/1951**

White, Mrs J, MCLIP, LRC Mgr., The Winton Sch., Andover. [471] 01/01/1971 **CM01/01/1975**

White, Mrs L A, Stud (PT)., Univ. of Brighton. [10010838] 28/08/2008**AF**

White, Mr L, FCLIP, Life Member. [15714] 28/09/1950 **FE01/01/1968**

White, Mrs M A, MLIS, Inf. Professional, Search Engine, York [10008411] 19/03/2008 **ME**

White, Mr M S, BA(Hons), L. Admin., BLP, London/Stud. [10007943] 28/02/2008 **ME**

White, Mr M S, BSc FCLIP HonFIInfSci FRSA, Managing Dir., Intranet Focus Ltd, Horsham. [60667] 11/12/2001 **FE01/04/2002**

White, Mrs R K, BA MA MCLIP, Child. & Yth. & Community Learning Lib., Bexley Council, Kent. [31388] 08/10/1979 **CM14/12/1981**

White, Miss R K, BSc(Hons) MSc, Sen. L. Asst., Imperial Coll., royal Brompton Campus Lib. [56879] 29/10/1998 **ME**

White, Mrs R O, BA DIP HE MCLIP, Resource Cent. Mgr., City of York Council, York. [26297] 21/10/1976 **CM10/09/1981**

White, Mr R, Unknown [10006815] 10/12/2007 **ME**

White, Mrs S A, BA DipLib MCLIP, Head of L. Serv., Univ. of Huddersfield. [32693] 11/07/1980 **CM01/07/1984**

White, Mrs S A, MSc MCLIP, Res. Co-ordinator, Queen Mary, Univ. of London. [24384] 02/07/1975 **CM30/03/1981**

White, Mrs S E, BA MLib MCLIP, Retired [41284] 15/10/1987 **CM27/03/1991**

White, Ms S J, BA, PA, Oxford Univ. Press [10011124] 02/10/2008 **AF**

White, Mrs S K, BLib MCLIP, Subject Lib., Univ. of Bath [42745] 21/02/1989 **CM21/10/1992**

White, Mrs S M, MCLIP, Principal Lib., Co. Bor. of Blaenau, Gwent. [22224] 01/03/1974 **CM13/07/1974**

White, Ms W H, BA(Hons) MA DipLib MCLIP, Asst. Lib., Univ. of Southampton. [51201] 23/11/1994 **CM18/11/1998**

White, Mrs W J, BA DipLib MCLIP, Lib. Clark Smith Partnership [39489] 08/02/1986 **CM15/05/1989**

Whitehead, Ms C J, BA, Lect., Robert Gordon Univ., Aberdeen. [57096] 08/12/1998 **ME**

Whitehead, Mr D, MSc, Inf. Serv. Mgr., leicestershire Chamber of Commerce [65427] 24/02/2006 **ME**

Whitehead, Ms P, BA DipLib MCLIP, Equalities Devel. Lib., Herts L. [28390] 24/10/1977 **CM23/03/1981**

Whitehead, Mrs P, FCLIP, Life Member. [15741] 02/09/1942 **FE01/01/1949**

Whitehead, Mrs V E, BA MCLIP, Learning Resource Mgr. & ICT Trainer, Gordon's Sch., Woking. [27636] 27/06/1977 **CM23/07/1979**

Whitehouse, Mrs H D, BSc DipInfSc, Head of Inf. Resources, Aston Univ., Birmingham. [40940] 08/09/1987 **ME**

Whitehouse, Miss J C, Learning Resources Mgr., Eckington Sch., Derbyshire. [65238] 25/11/2005 **ME**

Whitehouse, Mrs S A, BA MSc MCLIP, Buisness Intelligence Serv. Mgr., Edwards Angell Palmer & Dodge, London [57766] 29/07/1999 **CM21/03/2007**

Whitehouse, Mrs S E, BA MCLIP, Locality Lib., Dudley P. L. [33196] 02/10/1980 **CM28/01/1985**

White-Hunt, Prof K, BAHons MSc DSc(Econ) CertEd MCLIP, Prof. /Vice-President, Univ. Coll. of Bahrain [10005401] 25/07/2007 **CM01/01/1986**

Whitelaw, Mrs J L, MSc, Sch. Lib., Heckmondwike Grammar Sch., W. Yorkshire. [63077] 27/01/2004 **ME**

Whitelegg, Ms K L, ACLIP, LRC Mngr. Dronfield Henry Fanshawe Sch., Derbyshire [62468] 08/07/2003 **ACL27/06/2006**

Whiteley, Mrs A J, BA(Hons), Stud., Northumbria Univ. [10015270] 29/10/2009 **ME**

Whitelock, Dr J, MA MPhil PhD MA MCLIP, Head of Special Collections, Cambridge Univ. L. [55976] 07/01/1998 **CM17/01/2001**

Whiten, Ms B H, MA, Unknown. [61888] 20/11/2002 **ME**

Whiteside, Miss J M, MA MCLIP, Retired [21898] 24/01/1974 **CM07/07/1976**

Whitethread, Mrs E A, BSc(Hons) MA MCLIP, Sen. Researcher, Lovells, London. [51217] 28/11/1994 **CM22/07/1998**

Whitfield, Mr C, MA, Stud., Thames Valley Univ., London [10008393] 19/03/2008 **ME**

Whitfield, Mrs R, BA MA, Dep. Subject Lib., Swansea Univ. [10003069] 08/12/1998 **ME**

Whiting, Mr A D, BA MCLIP, Life Member. [19412] 06/01/1958 **CM01/01/1961**

Whiting, Mrs J P, MCLIP, Freelance Lib., London [10001522] 04/10/1971 **CM07/07/1976**

Whitlock, Mrs C R, BSc MRPharmS MCLIP, Freelance Med. Inf. Consultant [60750] 05/08/1986 **CM11/05/1988**

Whitmill, Mrs H J, BA DipLib MCLIP, Sch. Lib. p. /t.,Beds. C.C., Arlesey. [34704] 11/01/1982 **CM24/04/1986**

Whitmore, Miss J M, BA MCLIP, Life Member. [15771] 26/09/1962 **CM01/01/1965**

Whitmore, Miss K B, MCLIP, Retired. [15773] 06/02/1953 **CM01/01/1959**

Whitrow, Mrs A M, BA MCLIP, Retired. [15776] 27/08/1945 **CM01/01/1947**

Whitsed, Mrs N J, MSc FCLIP, Dir., L. Serv., Open Univ., Milton Keynes. [786] 14/09/1970   **FE16/09/1992**

Whittaker, Miss B A, BA(Hons) MA MCLIP, Cultural Serv. Adviser., Lincoln Cent. L., Lincoln [43398] 19/10/1989   **CM02/02/2005**

Whittaker, Mrs D B, MCLIP, Retired, Resident France. [17955] 19/03/1945   **CM01/01/1953**

Whittaker, Ms H K, BA DipLib MCLIP, Sub. Team Leader, Oxford Brookes Univ. [43654] 16/11/1989   **CM26/02/1992**

Whittaker, Ms J C, MA MCLIP, Contracts Offr., Univ. of Edinburgh. [44486] 12/10/1990   **CM26/11/2001**

Whittaker, Mr K A, MA FCLIP, Life Member. [15779] 20/02/1950   **FE01/01/1957**

Whittaker, Ms S R, BMus(Hons) MA, Sen. Inf. Asst., Leicester Royal Infirmary, Clinical Sci. L. [56715] 07/10/1998   **ME**

Whittaker, Mrs V I, BA MCLIP, Inf. Offr. -Young People and Schs., Sherburn L., N. Yorks. [39556] 28/02/1986   **CM25/05/1994**

Whittall, Mr G K, Subject Lib., Univ. Cent. at Doncaster Coll. [62023] 20/01/2003   **ME**

Whittingham, Miss C F, BA DipLib MCLIP, Lib. /Learning Res. Mgr., Walford & N. Shropshire Coll., Oswestry. [38569] 05/07/1985   **CM14/02/1990**

Whittingham, Mrs C M, BSc MCLIP, Retired [15784] 08/10/1968   **CM06/11/1972**

Whittingham, K, L. Asst. [66132] 02/10/2006   **ME**

Whittle, Ms V E, BHort MLIS, Systems Admin. Lib., DWP, London [62358] 09/05/2003   **ME**

Whittock, Mrs S R, Yth. Serv. Lib., Gateshead M.B.C. [38444] 18/04/1985   **ME**

Whitton, Mr J B, MA MCLIP, Retired. [15789] 16/08/1967 **CM19/03/1971**

Whitton, Mr M J, MA MChem MCLIP, Academic Liaison Lib., Univ. of Southampton, Hartley L. [59148] 28/11/2000   **CM04/10/2006**

Whitty, Mrs R M, BA MSc Econ, Unknown [65738] 19/04/2006   **ME**

Whitworth, Mrs J M, BA MCLIP, Dep. Head of L. & Study Cent., Worcester Coll. of Tech. [20160] 24/01/1973   **CM18/09/1978**

Whybrow, Mrs K M, MCLIP, Life Member. [15790] 01/01/1948   **CM09/10/1959**

Whyte, Ms L C, BA DipLib, Managing Dir., Bibliographic Data Serv. Ltd., Dumfries. [34150] 08/10/1981   **ME**

Whyte, Ms S M, MA DipLis, Inf. Specialist, Univ. Abertay, Dundee. [63354] 20/04/2004   **ME**

Wickenden, Mr J A, FCLIP, Biomedical Inf. Sci., Eli Lilly & Co. Ltd., Windlesham, Surrey. [15795] 01/10/1971   **FE28/01/2009**

Wickenden, Mrs J V S, MA(Oxon) DipLib, Historic Collections Lib., Inst. of Naval Medicine., Gosport. [60886] 19/12/2001   **ME**

Wickens, Mr S C, BA(Hons) PGDip MA MCLIP, Learning Cent. Mgr., London. [60872] 18/12/2001   **CM29/03/2006**

Wickham, Mrs J G, BA MA, Open Access Advisor, Cent. for res. Communications Univ. of Nottingham [37001] 26/01/1984   **ME**

Wickramasinghe, Miss B C, BA MCLIP, L. Offr., Nadesan Cent. L., Colombo, Sri Lanka. [17959] 06/11/1969   **CM01/11/1974**

Wickremasinghe, Ms D, MA, Inf. & Knowledge Mgr., Healthline Worldwide [63960] 22/11/2004   **ME**

Wicks, Mr J D, BEd(Hons) MA MCLIP, Audience Devel. Offr., Essex C.C., Chelmsford, Essex. [47830] 15/10/1992   **CM22/05/1996**

Widdicombe, Ms K, BA(Hons) MA MSc MCLIP, Academic Liaison Lib., Univ. for the Creative Arts at Canterbury, Epsom (Fashion, FPI, Fashion Journalism, Fashion Mgmnt. & Marketing, Music & Lifestyle Journalism) [63717] 08/09/2004   **CM19/11/2008**

Widdows Doughty, Mrs C D, PGCE BSc(Hons) MSc, L. Asst., Berkhamsted L., Herts. [48584] 22/02/1993   **ME**

Widdows, Miss K, BSc(Hons) MCLIP, Enquiry Support Offr., Univ. of Warwick L. [64631] 29/04/2005   **CM06/05/2009**

Wieczorek, Mrs J A, MCLIP, Casual Lib. /Relief, Cambs. Co. L., Cambridge & Huntingdon. [19079] 02/10/1972   **CM04/08/1976**

Wielgosz, Mr D, Msc, Stud., Strathclyde Univ., Glasgow. [10016182] 19/02/2010   **ME**

Wiener, Miss S J, Unknown. [10011806] 14/11/2008   **AF**

Wiggans, Mrs E L, MCLIP, Life Member. [22599] 03/07/1974   **CM30/12/1977**

Wiggins, Mr S H, BA Hons (CANTAB), Graduate Trainee, Norton Rose LLP, London. [10016197] 23/02/2010   **ME**

Wigglesworth, Ms G S S, BA MCLIP, Lib., Immanuel Coll. [31979] 04/01/1980   **CM23/09/1998**

Wigglesworth, Ms J S, BA(Hons) DipILS, Unwaged. [58773] 17/07/2000   **ME**

Wiggs, Ms H B Z, BA, Team Lib., Northumbria Univ., Newcastle-Upon-Tyne. [10015808] 27/01/2010   **ME**

Wight, Mrs K, BA(Hons) MCLIP, Outreach & e-Resources Lib., Birmingham & Solihull Mental Health Trust [60460] 24/05/1999   **CM24/05/1999**

Wigley, Mrs J E, BLib MCLIP, Teaching Asst., Holbrook Primary Sch., Wiltshire. [39145] 12/11/1985   **CM21/07/1989**

Wigley, Mr S J, BA(Hons) MA, Stud., Univ. Coll. London. [64977] 04/10/2005   **ME**

Wignall, Mr J R, BA MCLIP MSc, Lib., Swindon Cent. L. [21345] 15/10/1973   **CM24/11/1975**

Wignall, Mrs J, MCLIP, Sen. Lib., Strouden Lib., Bournemouth BC. (On Maternity Leave) [60018] 26/11/2001   **CM28/01/2009**

Wijnstroom, Ms M, FCLIP, Retired. [41389] 06/01/1987 **FE06/01/1987**

Wilcock, Mrs J, BSc MSc MCLIP, Employment not known. [60703] 12/12/2001   **CM12/12/2001**

Wilcockson, Miss J, BA, Stud. [10006363] 17/10/2007   **ME**

Wilcox, Mrs C A, BA MCLIP, Keeper of the L., S. S. C. Soc., Edinburgh. [34699] 18/01/1982   **CM30/01/1991**

Wild, Mrs D M, MA MCLIP, Lib. /Field Offr., City of Edinburgh Council (Educ.), Edinburgh. [32215] 21/01/1980   **CM10/09/1984**

Wilde, Mrs L J, Learn. Cent. Mgr., Ealing,Hammersmith & W. London Coll. [26817] 02/11/1976   **AF**

Wilde, Mr N C, BA MCLIP, Retired. [15822] 28/09/1962 **CM01/01/1967**

Wildgoose, Ms E, BA(Hons) MA, Lib. Asst., Portsmouth Univ. [57754] 23/07/1999   **ME**

Wilding, Miss J M, BA DipLib MCLIP, User Serv. Lib., Shakespeare Birthplace Trust, Stratford-Upon-Avon. [25682] 28/01/1976   **CM20/09/1979**

Wildman, Mrs A R, BA MA, Asst. Lib., Peterborough Reg. Coll. [62997] 25/11/2003   **ME**

Wildridge, Ms V K, BA MCLIP, Unknown. [10009033] 25/01/1979   **CM21/09/1983**

Wildsmith, Ms S M, MCLIP Dip MLIS, Ret. [4149] 14/02/1969   **CM01/01/1972**

Wileman, Mr D, MA MCLIP, Retired. [15829] 05/11/1966 **CM01/01/1971**

Wiley, Ms M E, BA, MA, Stud., Univ. of W. of England, Bristol. [10011319] 13/10/2008   **ME**

Wilhelm, Mr P, MA, Document Mgmnt. Offr., EEA, Copenhagen [10007802] 03/03/2008   **ME**

Wilkes, Mrs F E, BA(Hons) MA DipLib MCLIP, Lib., Wolfson Coll. Oxford. [44967] 28/01/1991   **CM16/11/1994**

Wilkes, Mrs L D, MCLIP, Trust lib., W. Suffolk NHS Trust [65292] 14/12/2005   **CM17/09/2008**

Wilkes, Mrs R J, BSc MA MCLIP, Br. Mgr., Orange Co. P. L., U. S. A. [46594] 21/11/1991   **CM26/07/1995**

Wilkie, Miss C M, Stud., Univ. of Aberystwyth Wales. [10005567] 25/07/2007   **ME**

Wilkie, Mrs E A, BSc(Hons) DipGeog MCLIP DipRS, L. Super., Hampshire C.C. [56371] 22/06/1998   **CM19/11/2008**

Wilkie, Mr G A, PGDip, Unknown [10001738] 15/03/2007   **ME**

Wilkie, Mrs S J, BLib MCLIP, Freelance Consultant. [26263] 24/09/1976   **CM24/09/1979**

Wilkins, Mrs F M, BA MCLIP, L. Res. Mgr., Swanmore Coll. of Tech. Sch., Hants. [21210] 29/09/1973 **CM15/09/1975**

Wilkins, Miss J A, BA MCLIP, Stud. Serv. Mgr., Wakefield Coll., W. Yorks. [33623] 30/01/1981 **CM25/10/1983**

Wilkins, Mrs J A, BA MCLIP, Unknown. [28210] 01/10/1977 **CM24/06/1981**

Wilkins, Mrs J I, BA MCLIP BA(Hons) MCLIP, Head of Serv. (Strategy), Dudley L. [33529] 13/01/1981 **CM31/07/1984**

Wilkins, Mrs J, BSc Econ ILS MCLIP, Lib., Dartington Coll. of Arts, Devon. [65897] 07/06/2006 **CM17/09/2008**

Wilkins, Ms L A, BA MCLIP, L. Mgr., Croydon L., Surrey. [41560] 28/01/1988 **CM20/03/1996**

Wilkins-Jones, Dr C, BA MCLIP, Team Lib., Norfolk & Norwich Millennium L. [7971] 01/01/1970 **CM01/01/1972**

Wilkinson, Ms A M, MCLIP, Lib., Buxton L., Derbyshire C.C. [20322] 07/03/1973 **CM23/08/1976**

Wilkinson, Mrs D K, BA(Hons) PgD, Unknown. [52524] 03/11/1995 **ME**

Wilkinson, Miss D L, MA(Hons) MSc MCLIP, Inf. Specialist, Univ. Abertay, Dundee. [58531] 21/03/2000 **CM23/06/2004**

Wilkinson, Mrs D, BA MCLIP, Life Member. [10940] 12/03/1963 **CM01/01/1966**

Wilkinson, Mrs E C, BA MCLIP, Reading Promotion Lib. :Adults, Cent. L., Peterborough L. [46187] 14/10/1991 **CM21/05/1997**

Wilkinson, Miss E E, BA MA, Asst. Lib. (Humanities), Univ. of Essex. [58837] 25/08/2000 **ME**

Wilkinson, Mrs E M H, MCLIP, Teaching Asst., p/t. [29501] 10/01/1974 **CM30/10/1979**

Wilkinson, Ms H, BA(Hons) MA, Knowledge Mgr., Nat. Diabetes Support Team, Leicester [10007937] 23/05/1995 **ME**

Wilkinson, Mrs J, BA MCLIP, Unknown. [9734] 07/10/1971 **CM23/07/1974**

Wilkinson, Mrs K, ACLIP, Asst. Lib., St. John's Intl. Sch., Waterloo, Belgium [10001649] 06/03/2007 **ACL17/06/2009**

Wilkinson, Miss M E, FCLIP, Life Member. [15863] 14/09/1943 **FE01/01/1957**

Wilkinson, Ms N A J, BA MCLIP MLib, Lib., RAF Cent. of Aviation, Henlow. [15868] 06/10/1970 **CM01/01/1973**

Wilkinson, Ms R E, BA MCLIP, Site Serv. Lib., Oxford Brookes Univ., Oxford. [28479] 18/01/1978 **CM06/10/1980**

Wilkinson, Mrs R, BSc(Hons) MCLIP, Inf. Servs. Coordinator, NBS, Newcastle-upon-Tyne. [64653] 22/04/2005 **CM21/03/2007**

Wilkinson, Ms S A, BA DipLib MCLIP AIL, Dir. of Learning Res., Trinity Coll., Carmarthen. [39059] 28/10/1985 **CM16/12/1992**

Wilkinson, Mrs S J, Inf. Offr., Isaac Newton Inst. for Math. Sci., Univ. of Cambridge. [51650] 27/04/1995 **AF**

Wilkinson, Mrs S M, MCLIP, Enquiry Team Lib., Off. Publications, Cent. Resources Lib., New Barnfield, Herts [7844] 08/06/1968 **CM01/01/1972**

Wilkinson, Mrs S M, FCLIP MBE FRSA, Reader Dev. Offr., Birmingham Lib. & Arch. [20273] 22/02/1973 **FE13/06/2007**

Wilkinson, Mrs S, OBE BA MCLIP, L. Serv. Mgr., Cheshire W. & Chester Elleswere Port L. [9005] 01/01/1970 **CM01/10/1972**

Wilkinson, Mr T, BSc MCLIP, Unemployed. [60672] 11/12/2001 **CM01/04/2002**

Wilkinson, Mrs Z A, BSc(Hons), L. Devel. Worker, Leics. C.C. [52389] 26/10/1995 **ME**

Wilkinson-Graham, Mrs V L, MA, Head of L. & R. Cent., Lewis Silkin, London. [56451] 14/07/1998 **ME**

Wilks, Mrs J, L. Asst., Winchester Coll., Winchester. [10016792] 18/05/2010 **AF**

Wilks, Dr L J, BA MA MSc MCLIP ACIM, Res. Assoc. – Digital Humanities, Open Univ., Milton Keynes. [34220] 11/10/1981 **CM13/12/1984**

Will, Dr C D, PhD BA MCLIP, Retired. [15873] 16/10/1964 **CM01/01/1971**

Will, Dr L, BSc PhD MCLIP, Inf. Mgmt. Consultant, Willpower Inf., Enfield,Middx. [24855] 26/09/1975 **CM28/11/1977**

Willans, Mrs S J, MCLIP, Asst. Grp. Mgr., Cent. L., L.B. of Bromley. [14585] 01/01/1972 **CM24/11/1975**

Willars, Mrs G, MA MCLIP, Lib. Serv. Dev. Mgr., Leics C.C. [6788] 01/01/1971 **CM26/11/1973**

Willatts, Ms E M, MCLIP BA, Lib., Watson Farley & Williams, London. [21995] 19/01/1974 **CM29/01/1976**

Willatts, Miss N M, BSc MA, L. Technician, Stenhouse L., Kingston Hosp., London. [66144] 03/10/2006 **ME**

Willett, Ms M F, Weekend Lib., Birkbeck Coll., London [46157] 02/10/1991 **ME**

Willett, Mrs M T, BSc(Hons) MSc MCLIP, Site Lib., Univ. of Sheffield. [59860] 18/10/2001 **CM06/04/2005**

Willetts, Mr A J, BSc, Stud. [10015336] 10/11/2009 **ME**

Willetts, Mrs L, BA DipLib MCLIP, General Mgr., L. & Community Serv. [31415] 01/10/1979 **CM07/09/1982**

Willetts, Ms S J, MA MSc BA DipLib MCLIP, Sen. L. Asst., Inst. of Classical Studies, Hellenic & Roman Soc., London. [33371] 27/11/1980 **CM16/05/1984**

Williams, Ms A E, Unknown [42352] 26/10/1988 **ME**

Williams, Mr A F, BA, Unwaged [55990] 12/01/1998 **ME**

Williams, Mr A H, BA DipLib MCLIP, Inf. Serv. Mgr., Gwynedd L. Serv., Caernarfon L. [27379] 09/03/1977 **CM12/06/1980**

Williams, Mr A J A, BA MCLIP, Freelance. [15885] 20/10/1967 **CM01/01/1972**

Williams, Miss A J, BEd DipLib MCLIP, Br. L., Putney Lib., London. [38731] 01/10/1985 **CM18/11/1993**

Williams, Ms A J, BA(Hons), Curriculum Cent. Co-ordinator, Univ. of Brighton. [10015487] 09/12/2009 **AF**

Williams, Mr A J, BA DipLib MCLIP, Strategic Lib. Serv. Mngr., Bridgnorth L., Shropshire. [26609] 11/10/1976 **CM25/10/1978**

Williams, Mrs A J, BA DipLib MCLIP, Subject Lib. /Aquisitions Mgr., Univ. of Chester. [37631] 09/10/1984 **CM15/11/1988**

Williams, Miss A K, Asst. Lib., Royal Glamorgan Hosp., Cwm Taf Health. [64463] 31/03/2005 **ME**

Williams, Mrs A M, MSc(Econ), Inf. Offr., St. Michael's Coll., Cardiff. [59629] 05/07/2001 **ME**

Williams, Ms A, BA(Hons) MA, L. Mgr., Bromsgrove L., Worcester CC [59251] 17/01/2001 **ME**

Williams, Miss A, Unknown. [10006382] 23/10/2007 **ME**

Williams, Miss A, BA MRS, Unknown. [10013198] 03/04/2009 **ME**

Williams, Mr B J S, MA HonFLA FCLIP, Life Member. [15891] 10/10/1991 **FE01/01/1969**

Williams, Mrs C A, BA(Hons) MSc(Econ) MCLIP, Aquisitions Lib., Buckinghamshire New Univ., High Wycombe. [51206] 23/11/1994 **CM17/01/2001**

Williams, Ms C A, BA DipLib MCLIP, Sch. Lib., Fernwood Comp. Sch., Nottingham. [29869] 02/10/1978 **CM15/12/1980**

Williams, Mr C C, DMA MCLIP, Retired. [15896] 03/06/1961 **CM01/01/1964**

Williams, Mrs C D, BSc(Econ) MCLIP, Br. Lib., Porthcawl L. [65088] 31/10/2005 **CM19/11/2008**

Williams, Miss C E, BA MA, Sen. Inf. Asst., KCL, Inf. Serv. Cent., London. [10014369] 24/11/1998 **ME**

Williams, Miss C F H, BA MLib MCLIP, Professional Stream Leader: Learning Resources, Leeds Met. Univ., Leeds [42342] 10/10/1988 **CM16/09/1992**

Williams, Mr C R G, Lib. /Researcher, CS Associates, London. [48924] 23/07/1993 **ME**

Williams, Miss C R, BA FCLIP, Life Member. [15899] 24/09/1958 **FE01/01/1965**

Williams, Mrs C S, BA(Hons) MA MCLIP, Catr., Bor. of Lewisham, London. [59099] 14/11/2000 **CM08/12/2004**

Williams, Mrs D E, BA MCLIP, Lib., Kirklees Educ. Dept., Salendine Nook High Sch. [41211] 15/10/1987 **CM15/09/1993**

Williams, Mr D G, BA(Hons) PGDipIM, Public Health Knowledge Mgr., NHS Portsmouth. [10002531] 03/10/1994 **ME**

Williams, Miss E A, BSc, Info. Lib., Sandwell Cent. Lib. [62196] 13/03/2003 **ME**

Williams, Miss E M, BA MLIS, Dep. Lib., Royal Agricultural Coll., Cirencester. [10002965] 10/05/2007 **ME**

Williams, Miss E M, BA MCLIP, Unwaged. [34804] 18/02/1982 **CM02/02/1987**

Williams, Ms E P, L. Mgr., City of Westminster, London. [64743] 14/06/2005 **AF**

Williams, Mrs E, BChD DipLib ILTM MCLIP, Faculty Lib., Bristol Business Sch., Univ. W. England. [45196] 08/08/1990 **CM25/01/1995**

Williams, Dr E, BA MA PhD, Unknown. [10014354] 17/07/2009 **ME**

Williams, Ms F C, BA(Hons) DipLib MCLIP, Head of L. & Heritage, City of York Council. [10001560] 15/02/1988 **CM27/05/1992**

Williams, Miss F H B, MA DipLib MCLIP, Retired. [24178] 04/10/1950 **CM01/01/1959**

Williams, Mrs F H M, BA(Hons), Lib., Bishops Stortford Coll., Herts. [56086] 04/02/1998 **ME**

Williams, Mrs G A, BA(Hons), Child. & Young Peoples Serv. Mgr., Knowsley Lib. Serv. [38071] 11/01/1985 **ME**

Williams, Mr G A, BA(Hons), Inf. Offr., Simmons & Simmons, London [59482] 09/04/2001 **ME**

Williams, Mr G D, MCLIP, Retired. [15930] 08/11/1940 **CM01/01/1948**

Williams, Mrs G, BA DipLib MCLIP, Child. & Young Peoples Lib., Llyfrgell Llangefni, Ynys Mon. [26763] 10/11/1976 **CM15/11/1979**

Williams, Ms H A K, MSc MCLIP, Lib., Bindmans LLP, London. [31497] 07/10/1979 **CM22/06/1982**

Williams, Mr H A, MA, Lib., Oxford & Cambridge Club, London. [58991] 12/10/2000 **ME**

Williams, Mrs H E M, BA MCLIP, p. /t. Serv. Devel. Lib., Hants. C.,C., New Milton Br. [29631] 17/10/1978 **CM15/03/1988**

Williams, Mrs H F, BA(Hons) MCLIP, Electronic Serv. Lib., Winchester & Eastleigh Hlthcare. NHS Royal Hants. Co. Hosp. [52355] 26/10/1995 **CM21/11/2001**

Williams, Miss H K R, MA MCLIP, Asst. Lib., Bibl. Serv., LSE, London. [59494] 09/04/2001 **CM01/02/2006**

Williams, Mrs H M J, MSc. Econ. ILS, Trainee Asst. Lib., Bolland L., Bristol [37184] 28/03/1984 **ME**

Williams, Mrs H M, BA MCLIP, Housewife. [23977] 27/02/1975 **CM26/09/1979**

Williams, Mrs H S, MA MPhil MCLIP, Freelancer. [34110] 30/09/1981 **CM13/05/1986**

Williams, Dr I A, MA PhD CChem FRSC MCLIP, Retired. [60676] 12/12/2001 **CM12/12/2001**

Williams, Mrs J E, BA DipLib MCLIP, Lib., Shropshire C.C., Shrewsbury. [27265] 12/02/1977 **CM20/09/1979**

Williams, Ms J L, MA MCLIP, Retired. [15941] 01/02/1965 **CM01/01/1969**

Williams, Mrs J M, BA MCLIP, L. Serv. Mgr., Royal Bolton NHS Trust, Bolton. [45500] 21/02/1991 **CM15/11/2000**

Williams, Mr J T, MIPP BA MCLIP, Tech. Serv. Lib., Johns Hopkins Univ., Bologna, Italy. [30874] 03/05/1979 **CM07/12/1981**

Williams, Mrs J V, BSc(Hons) MSc, Asst. Lib., Univ. of Glamorgan, Pontypridd. [53038] 16/02/1996 **ME**

Williams, Miss J, BA MPhil MCLIP, Asst. Lib., Durham Cathedral L. [18187] 04/10/1972 **CM14/07/1975**

Williams, Mrs J, ACLIP, Customer Servs. Lib., Stevenage & N. Herts. Dist. [54901] 06/05/1997 **ACL16/04/2008**

Williams, Mr J, Inf. Asst. (ILL), Scottish Government., Edinburgh. [63478] 14/05/2004 **AF**

Williams, Ms J, BA(Hons) DipLib MCLIP, L. Mgr., Croydon Health L. & Resource Serv., Croydon. [10008466] 01/01/1969 **CM29/04/1975**

Williams, Ms J, LRC Mgr., Caerphilly Co. Bor. Council, Blackwood. [63930] 03/11/2004 **ME**

Williams, Mrs J, MCLIP, Retired. [17967] 28/01/1961 **CM01/01/1966**

Williams, Ms J, BA DipLib MCLIP, Stock Devel. Offr., L.B. of Ealing, L. Support Cent. [35358] 11/10/1982 **CM16/10/1989**

Williams, Ms K C, BA(Hons) MA, CASH Serv. Offr, NHS Derbyshire Co. PCT, Chesterfield. [10006810] 10/12/2007 **ME**

Williams, Miss K M, ACLIP, Child. L. Super., Birkenhead Cent. L. [10010996] 12/09/2008 **ACL11/12/2009**

Williams, Miss K R, Lib. Asst., Aberyswyth Univ., Ceredigion [10012666] 05/03/2009 **ME**

Williams, Mrs K, PgDip, L. Asst., Swansea Univ. [10010116] 04/07/2008 **AF**

Williams, Ms K, BA(Hons) MSc, Unknown. [10014278] 18/11/2003 **ME**

Williams, Miss L A, Asst. Lib., Univ. of Glamorgan [65066] 24/10/2005 **ME**

Williams, Mrs L M, MCLIP, Stock Mgr., Cardiff C.C., Cardiff. [4681] 10/03/1970 **CM02/07/1973**

Williams, Ms L, Unknown. [10007947] 27/06/2009 **ME**

Williams, Mrs M A M, BA DipLib MCLIP, Learning Resources Asst., Univ. of Glamorgan, Pontypridd. [34594] 01/01/1982 **CM20/01/1986**

Williams, Mr M A, BSc MSc, Inventory Control Mgr., Univ. of Oxford. [59072] 07/11/2000 **ME**

Williams, Miss M E, Comm. Lib., Caerphilly Co. Bor. [35647] 18/11/1982 **ME**

Williams, Miss M G, BA FCLIP, Retired. [15958] 17/09/1953 **FE01/01/1963**

Williams, Mrs M H M, MA DipLib MCLIP, Serv. Devel. Offr., Stafford. [29419] 12/08/1978 **CM29/12/1981**

Williams, Mrs M M M, MCLIP, Circulations Lib., Ammanford L., Carmarthenshire. [13958] 10/04/1969 **CM25/01/1973**

Williams, Mr M, Asst. Lib., MOD, London [60042] 03/12/2001 **ME**

Williams, Mr M, BLib MCLIP MA, Electronic Res. Lib., Univ. of Wolverhampton. [38510] 30/05/1985 **CM07/06/1988**

Williams, Mrs M, BA(Hons)Econ, Family Link L. Worker., LCYP Team., Longsight L., Manchester [10001573] 14/02/2007 **ME**

Williams, Prof M, BA MA HonFCLIP, Hon Fellow. [60087] 07/12/2001 **HFE08/11/1999**

Williams, Mrs M, BA MCLIP, Retired [15955] 01/01/1965 **CM01/01/1968**

Williams, Mrs N M J, BA DipLib MCLIP, Sen. Inf. Adviser, Univ. of Gloucestershire. [41675] 10/02/1988 **CM16/12/1992**

Williams, Miss N M, BA, Higher Offr. of Newspapers & Periodicals digitisation Proj, SCIF, LIGC [10011555] 27/10/2008 **ME**

Williams, Ms N P, BA DipLib MCLIP, Local Hist. Asst., L.B. of Ealing. [43786] 11/01/1990 **CM20/11/2002**

Williams, Mr N P, MA, Res. Offr. Procurement Reading Lists, Univ. of Warwick L., Conventry. [10016706] 28/04/2010 **ME**

Williams, Mr N R, BA MCLIP, Business Process Mgr., Inst. of Chartered Accountants in England & Wales,London. [21571] 30/10/1973 **CM19/11/1979**

Williams, Mrs N T, BSc DipLib, Self Employed [40615] 01/04/1987 **ME**

Williams, Mrs N, Stud., Univ. of Aberystwyth. [10009335] 01/06/2008 **ME**

Williams, Mrs P C, BA MCLIP, Lib., Birmingham P. L. [5205] 07/08/1967 **CM03/03/1975**

Williams, Miss P C, MCLIP, Retired. [15970] 08/03/1961 **CM01/01/1964**

Williams, Miss P J, BA, Lib., St Deiniols L., Flintshire. [39987] 08/10/1986 **ME**

Williams, Mrs P L, BA(Hons) MA MCLIP, Res. Consultant. [52168] 11/10/1995 **CM19/01/2000**

Williams, Mrs P M, BLib MCLIP, Lib., Morgan Cole, Cardiff. [2414] 18/01/1972 **CM14/10/1975**

Williams, Mrs P, BA(Hons) MCLIP, Acq. Lib., Liverpool Hope Univ. [49434] 27/10/1993 **CM18/09/2002**

Williams, Mrs P, BSc DipLib MCLIP, Map Curator/Catr., Nat. L. of Scotland, Edinburgh. [43642] 15/11/1989 **CM23/03/1993**

Williams, Dr R G, MA MPhil PhD MCLIP, Inf. Tech. Trainer/Lib. /Arch., London & Quadrant Housing Trust, Mapledurham & Hendred House. [15978] 27/01/1968 **CM01/01/1971**

Williams, Ms R G, BA DipLib MCLIP, Princ. Lib., Conwy Co. Bor. Council, Conwy L.,Community Dev. Serv. [28211] 26/09/1977 **CM07/11/1980**

Williams, Mr R G, BA(Hons) MCLIP, Retired. [15977] 22/02/1962 **CM01/01/1967**

Williams, Mrs R L, BA(Hons) MA MCLIP, L. and Inf. resources Mgr., Bradford Dist. Caretrust [58833] 23/08/2000 **CM08/12/2004**

Williams, Mr R N, BA(Hons) MA MCLIP, Head of L. and Arch., The Sci. Mus., London and Swindon. [52077] 02/10/1995 **CM20/05/1998**

Williams, Mr R P, Unknown. [10006358] 23/10/2007 **AF**

Williams, Mrs R, MSc MCLIP, Area Lib., N., Rhondda Cynon Taff Co. Bor. L., Aberdare. [24034] 07/03/1975 **CM29/10/1979**

Williams, Ms R, BA(Hons) MA MCLIP, Devel. Lib., Nottingham C.C. [64175] 07/01/2005 **CM23/01/2008**

Williams, Ms R, BA, Grqad. Trainee, RACC, Richmond [10015272] 29/10/2009 **ME**

Williams, Mr R, BA MCLIP, Sen. Br. Lib., Cardiff C.C. [33974] 30/06/1981 **CM05/12/1985**

Williams, Miss R, BSc(Hons) MCLIP, UCH Learning Resources Co-ordinator, Univ. Cent. Hastings [58120] 03/11/1999 **CM02/02/2005**

Williams, Mrs S A, BSc(Hons) ACRS Mont. Cert., Unknown. [10016883] 01/06/2010 **AF**

Williams, Ms S F, BSc(Hons) MCLIP, Lib., S. Wales Miners' L., Univ. of Wales, Swansea, Swansea. [45623] 04/04/1991 **CM27/07/1994**

Williams, Mrs S M, BA MCLIP, Lib. Pipers Corner Sch. [26607] 17/10/1976 **CM07/11/1978**

Williams, Dr S P, BSc PGCE PgDip MSc MEd PhD, Prof., Univ. Sydney, Australia. [64735] 08/06/2005 **ME**

Williams, Miss S, BA(Hons) MSc MCLIP, Asst. Lib. [58711] 01/07/2000 **CM21/05/2003**

Williams, Mrs S, BA MCLIP, Retired. [4545] 06/10/1961 **CM01/01/1962**

Williams, Mr T D, B. th(Hons) DipLib, Inf. Offr., McGrigors LLP, London [59480] 09/04/2001 **ME**

Williams, Ms T D, BA MCLIP, Local Studies Lib., Solihull M.B.C., Cent. L. [36567] 20/10/1983 **CM11/12/1989**

Williams, Mr T G, PGDipLib, Lib. /Inf. Offr., Roskill Inf. Serv., London. [37900] 20/10/1984 **ME**

Williams, Ms T L, BA(Hons) MSc(Econ) MCLIP, Inf. Offr., Halliwells LLP, Manchester. [59205] 08/01/2001 **CM31/01/2007**

Williams, Mrs V K, BSc(Hons) CertEd MSc MCLIP, Lib., The Leeds Teaching Hosp. NHS Trust, Otley. [50127] 17/03/1994 **CM15/03/2000**

Williams, Mrs V, Unknown. [64670] 13/05/2005 **ME**

Williams, Mr W G, OBE HonFLA MInstAM FRSA, Head of Cultural Serv., Denbighshire C.C. [15993] 12/06/1964 **CM01/01/1967**

Williamson, Mr A R, BA MA, Multimedia Lib., Bor. of S. Tyneside, Cent. L. [42185] 11/10/1988 **ME**

Williamson, Mrs J B, MLib MCLIP, Retired. [17969] 25/02/1962 **CM01/01/1966**

Williamson, Mr M C, MCLIP, Unknown. [10014086] 19/03/1985 **CM08/12/1987**

Williamson, Mr M G, JP BA MCLIP MCMI LCGI DL, Inf. Dir. /Consultant, Cambs. Arts & Training Serv. [15999] 03/02/1962 **CM01/01/1966**

Williamson, Mrs M J, BA MCLIP, Asst. Lib., Rutherford Appleton Lab., Oxon. [20652] 20/05/1973 **CM23/11/1976**

Williamson, Ms S A, BA(Hons) MCLIP, Editorial Mgr., NBS., Newcastle-upon-Tyne. [44752] 19/11/1990 **CM01/04/2002**

Williamson, Mrs S L, MCLIP, Customer Serv. Mgr., Cambridgeshire L. [63408] 05/05/2004 **CM17/09/2008**

Williamson, Mrs T H, BA(Hons), Sen. Asst. Lib., Univ. Huddersfield, Queensgate [65432] 23/02/2006 **ME**

Willimott, Mrs P M, BA(Hons) MCLIP, Learning Resource Cent. site Mgr., Park Lane Coll., Leeds, N-Yorkshire [20467] 01/01/1969 **CM25/05/1994**

Willing, Ms J A, BA MCLIP, Sen. Lib., Glasgow L, Mitchell L. [16004] 24/10/1969 **CM05/08/1974**

Willis, Mrs A J, BA(Hons) MCLIP, Asst. Site Mgr., Brotherton L., Leeds. [52687] 20/11/1995 **CM20/01/1999**

Willis, Miss A L, MCLIP, Unemployed. [16007] 10/09/1968 **CM09/01/1973**

Willis, Mrs C A, BA DipLib MA, Gaelic Programme Mgr., FOTIM, Johannesburg. [59320] 07/02/2001 **ME**

Willis, Mrs G, BA, Sen. Learning Cent. Asst., Sandwell Coll., Wednesbury. [35292] 12/10/1982 **ME**

Willis, Miss H G, MCLIP, Retired. [17971] 29/01/1957 **CM01/01/1961**

Willis, Mrs J, Lib., Havering Coll. of F&HE, Hornchurch. [10016451] 24/03/2010 **ME**

Willis, Mrs M A, Lib., Walter Scott & Partners Ltd., Edinburgh [62999] 27/11/2003 **ME**

Willis, Mr M, ACLIP, Sen. L. Mgr., Nottingham Cent. L. [64124] 17/01/2005 **ACL22/06/2007**

Willis, Mr P J, MCLIP, Life Member. [16013] 01/01/1957 **CM01/01/1964**

Willis, Mr R, BSc(hons) MPhil, Sen. Res. Fellow, Sch. of Educ., Roehampton Univ. [10006165] 18/09/2007 **ME**

Willis, Mrs S, MCLIP, Sen. Res. Admin., Univ. of Brighton [56132] 03/03/1998 **CM03/03/1998**

Willis-Fear, Mrs R M, BA MCLIP, Principal Lib. Customer Serv. and Staff Devel., Cent. L., Ilford. [33818] 21/02/1981 **CM14/02/1985**

Willison, Mr I R, CBE HonFLA, Hon. Fellow. [44039] 30/09/1988 **HFE30/09/1988**

Willmot, Mrs D M, MCLIP, Unemployed. [12788] 08/02/1972 **CM20/10/1975**

Willmott, Miss E M, MA MCLIP, Life Member. [16018] 14/03/1959 **CM01/01/1961**

Willoughby, Mrs C B, BA DipLib DMS MCLIP, Dep. Dir., Northumbria Univ., Newcastle. [23387] 01/01/1975 **CM12/09/1977**

Willox, Miss N P, MA MCLIP, Life Member. [16024] 27/09/1953 **CM01/01/1958**

Wills, Mr A L, MCLIP, Hon. Ed. Northern Lib., Kendal. [16025] 03/03/1951 **CM01/01/1957**

Wills, Mr A, BA MCLIP, Head of L. & Inf. Serv., Leicester L. [19926] 16/01/1973 **CM15/08/1978**

Wills, Ms H J, BLib MBA MCLIP, Head of Community Cohesion & Equalities, L.B. of Barking & Dagenham. [40832] 01/07/1987 **CM18/11/1992**

Wills, Mrs J J, BA DipLib MCLIP, Catr., Warwickshire Coll., Leamington Spa. [39737] 02/06/1986 **CM24/04/1991**

Wills, Mrs S E, BA MCLIP, Sen. Lib., Salisbury. [31769] 05/12/1979 **CM02/03/1983**

Willsher, Mr M J D, BSc DipLib MCLIP, Retired [16033] 20/10/1964 **CM01/01/1971**

Willson, Miss J L, BA MA MCLIP, Lib., Richmond L. Teaching PCT, Northants. [63456] 12/05/2004 **CM21/03/2007**

Wilman, Mrs L, MCLIP, Ret. [24458] 21/07/1975 **CM28/08/1981**

Wilmot, Ms C, MA(Hons) MA MCLIP, Subject Lib., Arts Univ. Coll., Bournemouth. [59083] 10/11/2000 **CM09/11/2005**

Wilmot, Mr R S, BA DipLib, Lib., King Edward VI Five Ways Sch., Birmingham. [42165] 11/10/1988 **ME**

Wilsher, Mr R F, MA DipLib, Retired Inf. Specialist [37074] 23/01/1984 **ME**

Wilshere, Mrs J P, BA, Lib., Notts. Sci. & Bus. L. [41409] 26/11/1987 **ME**

Wilson, Mrs A C, MA Cert. Ed MCLIP, Learning Serv. Devel. Mgr., Lancaster and Morecambe Coll., Lancs. [10015138] 10/10/1978 CM30/07/1981

Wilson, Mrs A E, BSc(Hons) MCLIP, Unknown. [58573] 03/04/2000 CM20/11/2002

Wilson, Mrs A M, MA MCLIP, Dep. Lib., Bromley Coll. of F. & H. E., Kent. [23595] 22/01/1975 CM12/03/2003

Wilson, Ms A M, MA MSc DipLib MCLIP, Life Member. [35682] 26/09/1966 CM30/06/1983

Wilson, Miss C A, MA MCLIP, Retired. [16050] 20/02/1959 CM01/01/1965

Wilson, Miss C E, BA(Hons) PGCE MA MCLIP, Dep. L. Serv. Mgr., Manchester Metro. Univ. L [48881] 09/07/1993 CM22/09/1999

Wilson, Mrs C H, BA(Hons) MA MCLIP, Extended Hours Super. Durham Univ. Lib. [55949] 23/12/1997 CM25/07/2001

Wilson, Mr C J, BA(Hons) DipLib MA MCLIP, Sen. Asst. Lib. -Inf. Servs., London Sch. of Economics. [48289] 24/11/1992 CM22/11/1995

Wilson, Miss C S, BA(Hons) MCLIP, Lib., Bromsgrove L., Worcs. C.C. [43387] 13/10/1989 CM20/05/1998

Wilson, Mr C W J, FCLIP, Life member. [16055] 01/01/1941 FE01/01/1950

Wilson, Mr C, Lib., Sup. / Stud., Whifflet L., Coatbridge. [65906] 01/07/2006 ME

Wilson, Mr D A G, MA MCLIP, Life Member. [16056] 15/09/1948 CM01/01/1951

Wilson, Miss D A, BA(Hons), Asst. Lib., Thompsons Solicitors, Manchester [59238] 12/01/2001 ME

Wilson, Miss D A, MA(Hons) MLitt MCLIP, Devel. Co-ordinator, Fife Employability Network, Fife Council. [55959] 22/12/1997 CM21/03/2001

Wilson, Mr D V, FCLIP, Retired. [16058] 04/09/1952 FE01/01/1964

Wilson, Mrs D, BA MSc HS MCLIP, Co. Lib., Roche Products Ltd. [60205] 10/12/2001 CM10/12/2001

Wilson, Ms D, BSc(Hons), LRC ILT Advisor, Middlesbrough Coll. [10001316] 16/01/2007 AF

Wilson, Mrs D, MCLIP, Young People Servs. Lib., Borehamwood L., Herts. [12845] 01/10/1971 CM30/01/1985

Wilson, Miss E F, MCLIP, Sen. L. Asst., Sheffield Univ., Main L. [30300] 02/01/1979 CM23/02/1983

Wilson, Mrs E M, MCLIP, Retired. [16063] 30/01/1964 CM01/01/1968

Wilson, Mrs E, BA(Hons), Stud., Liverpool John Moores Univ. [65719] 15/03/2006 ME

Wilson, Ms F C, MA MSc, Subject Liaison Lib., Brunel Univ., Uxbridge. [59308] 01/02/2001 ME

Wilson, Miss F M, BSc(Hons) MSc MCLIP, Lib., Bournemouth Univ., Bournemouth. [57219] 20/01/1999 CM16/07/2003

Wilson, Miss F, Co. Dir. [10007938] 28/02/2008 ME

Wilson, Mrs G M, BA DipLib MCLIP, Sen. Lib. Literacy Devel., Blackburn with Darwen B. C., Blackburn Cent. L. [24237] 01/05/1975 CM13/07/1977

Wilson, Miss G S, BA(Hons) PGCE, L. Asst., Univ. Hosp. of Hartlepool, Hartlepool. [10016724] 30/04/2010 AF

Wilson, Ms G, NWLIP Mgr., Lancs. C.C. [62730] 20/10/2003 AF

Wilson, Mrs H V, BSc MA MCLIP, Info. Mngr., Lloyds TSB, Bristol [10014089] 06/04/1990 CM24/07/1996

Wilson, Mr I L, BA MCLIP, Retired [16072] 04/01/1971 CM21/01/1974

Wilson, Mrs J E S, BA MCLIP, Sch. Lib. /Webmaster [25105] 28/10/1975 CM20/07/1979

Wilson, Mrs J E, BA MCLIP, Upper Elementary Lib., Parish Episcopal Sch., Dallas, USA. [40866] 23/07/1987 CM16/10/1991

Wilson, Ms J M, MCLIP, Liaison & Planning Mgr., ISD, Univ. of Salford. [10001312] 15/08/1988 CM30/01/1991

Wilson, Mr J, BA(Hons) MSc, Asst. Lib., Health Mgmnt. L., Scottish Health Serv. Cent., Edinburgh. [66131] 02/10/2006 ME

Wilson, Ms J, BSc MSc, Info. Scientist, Depuy Intl., Leeds [10002316] 11/12/2001 ME

Wilson, Ms J, Lib. Mngr., BPP Coll. of Professional Studies, London [10005844] 10/12/2007 ME

Wilson, Mrs J, BA MCLIP, SHEQ Mgr., DNV, Aberdeen. [39859] 19/09/1986 CM21/07/1993

Wilson, Miss J, Stud. [10006789] 13/12/2007 ME

Wilson, Mr J, BA, Warehouse Operations Mgr., Strathearn Stone & Timber, Forteviot [10016473] 01/04/2010 ME

Wilson, Miss K J, BA(Hons), Learning Res. Asst., Middlesex Univ. [62650] 01/10/2003 ME

Wilson, Miss K, BSc(Hons) MSc DipLIS MCLIP, Inf. Offr., BAAF Adoption & Fostering, London. [53796] 01/10/1996 CM19/05/1999

Wilson, Mr K, BA FCLIP, Tech. Inf. Dir., RIBA Enterprises Ltd, Newcastle upon Tyne. [16078] 19/01/1972 FE04/10/2006

Wilson, Mrs L, MA(Hons), MSc, Knowledge Offr., Young Scot [63284] 26/03/2004 ME

Wilson, Mrs L, BA DipLib MCLIP, p. /t. Team Lib., Northumbria Univ., Newcastle. [28088] 13/10/1977 CM05/12/1979

Wilson, Mrs M A, DipLib, Child. Lib., Glossop L., Derbys. [9801] 15/01/1969 ME

Wilson, Ms M A, MCLIP, Lib., Nuneaton L., Warks. [18063] 04/10/1972 CM06/03/1978

Wilson, Mrs M B, MCLIP, Retired. [12082] 26/09/1958 CM01/01/1963

Wilson, Mrs M E, MA(Hons) DipILS MCLIP, Sch. Lib., Northfield Academy, Aberdeen [54320] 18/11/1996 CM21/03/2001

Wilson, Miss M E, MA(Hons) PgDip, Trainee Lib., Falkirk Council L. Serv. [61526] 13/09/2002 ME

Wilson, Miss M H, OBE MSc MCLIP, Life Member. [16086] 08/03/1963 CM01/01/1968

Wilson, Dr M I, BA PhD MCLIP, Ret. [39627] 16/04/1986 CM19/01/1988

Wilson, Mr M P, BA(Hons) MA, Asst. Lib., Selwyn Coll., Cambridge. [54332] 21/11/1996 ME

Wilson, Mrs P A, MCLIP, Bibl. Serv. Offr., Cent. L, L.B. of Kensington & Chelsea. [29308] 01/01/1967 CM01/01/1970

Wilson, Mr P R, BA MA, Coll. Lib., Fakenham Coll., Norfolk. [10015438] 01/08/2002 ME

Wilson, Mr P, MA DLIS MCLIP, Curriculum Support Mgr., S. Nottingham Coll., W. Bridgford. [20968] 24/08/1973 CM08/09/1976

Wilson, Mrs R A, BA, Unknown. [10011462] 21/10/2008 AF

Wilson, Miss R J, BA MCLIP, Dep. Parliamentary Clerk, Min. of Justice, London. [32360] 02/02/1980 CM20/09/1984

Wilson, Mrs R S, BA DipLib MCLIP, (Job Share) Young People's L. Mgr., Middlebrough Bor. C. [33742] 08/02/1981 CM01/07/1984

Wilson, Miss S A, MCLIP, Life Member. [16098] 28/02/1950 CM01/01/1956

Wilson, Mrs S J, Head of Member's L. Nat. Assembly for Wales, Cardiff. [39763] 01/07/1986 ME

Wilson, Mrs S J, BA DipLib MCLIP, Seeking employment. [32973] 01/10/1980 CM08/12/1983

Wilson, Mr S J, BA(Hons) MSc MCLIP, Sen. Inf. Sci., DePuy Internat. Ltd., Leeds. [53783] 01/10/1996 CM22/09/1999

Wilson, Mrs S L, BA(Hons) MSc MCLIP, Trainee Indexer [45690] 24/04/1991 CM08/12/2004

Wilson, Ms S M, DipInf, Comm. Mgr., The Low Pay Commission, London. [52934] 30/01/1996 ME

Wilson, Mrs S M, BA DipLib MCLIP, Med. Summariser, Southernhay House Surgery, Exeter. [27009] 07/01/1977 CM13/03/1980

Wilson, Mrs S, Cust. Support Asst., Kent C.C. [62437] 18/06/2003 ME

Wilson, Miss S, MSc(Hons) MCLIP, Inf. Scientist, NHS Quality Improvement, Scotland. [63942] 18/11/2004 CM19/03/2008

Wilson, Mr S, BA(Hons) DipLib MCLIP, Info. Offr., Traffic Penalty
Tribunal, Manchester [43885] 08/02/1990 **CM20/01/1999**
Wilson, Prof T D, BSc FCLIP HonFCLIP, Retired. [16101] 24/01/1952
FE01/01/1961
Wilson, Mr W P, BA(CNAA) MRI, Admin. Offr., Dept. for Work and
Pensions, Jobcentre Plus, Sheffield. [54849] 17/04/1997 **ME**
Wilson-Whalley, Mrs K C, MA(Hons) MLitt MSc MCLIP, Lib., James
Young High Sch., W. Lothian. [61761] 06/11/2002 **CM21/06/2006**
Wilton, Mrs S E, MA MCLIP, Devel. Team Lib., Redhill L., Surrey C.C.
[59212] 08/01/2001 **CM11/03/2009**
Wimpenny, Miss M, Info. Skills Offr., Oldham Coll. [62502] 29/07/2003
ME
Winchester, Ms J, Trainee Lib., Worthing L., W. Sussex Co. Council
[64270] 22/02/2005 **ME**
Winchester, Ms K, BA DipLib, Inf. Mgr., Social Care Inst. for Excellence,
London. [44219] 12/07/1990 **ME**
Winchester, Miss S J, MCLIP AALIA, Retired [16114] 10/01/1972
CM29/12/1976
Winfield, Mrs J A, BA MCLIP, Early Years Mgr., Derby City L. [33670]
04/02/1981 **CM24/04/1986**
Wing, Mrs B, L. Asst., St. Georges Coll., Surrey. [65557] 24/02/2006 **ME**
Wing, Mr H J R, MA MCLIP, Retired. [16125] 01/01/1957 **CM01/01/1970**
Wingate Gray, Ms S, BA MA, Stud. [10016646] 23/04/2010 **ME**
Wingate-Martin, Prof D E, BA MCLIP MCIPD, Ch. Inf. Offr., Univ. of
Hertfordshire. [15214] 09/10/1970 **CM28/09/1973**
Winkworth, Mrs L T, MCLIP, Sch. Lib., Headington Sch., Oxford.
[45405] 03/01/1991 **CM03/10/2007**
Winkworth, Miss R A, BA MCLIP, Unknown. [22561] 06/06/1974
CM13/03/1980
Winlo, Mrs R E M, MA MCLIP, Freelance Translator. [28871] 01/02/1978
CM03/11/1980
Winning, Miss M A, BSc(Hons) MSc MCLIP, Sen. Health Info. Scientist,
NHS Quality Improvement Scotland. [57058] 02/12/1998
CM16/07/2003
Winser, Miss A J, BA MCLIP, Retired/L. Volunteer, Sussex
Archaelogical Soc., Lewes. [16134] 21/03/1958 **CM01/01/1960**
Winship, Mr I R, BA MA MCLIP, Consultant, Newcastle upon Tyne
[16135] 03/04/1968 **CM01/01/1971**
Winsor, Mrs A N, MCLIP, Child. Cent. Coordinator, Bucks CC. [28343]
18/10/1977 **CM12/08/1981**
Winstanley, Mrs J V, BA MCLIP, L. Asst., Beech Green Primary Sch.,
Gloucester. [23563] 21/01/1975 **CM13/12/1978**
Winstanley, Mr L A, Unknown. [65800] 03/05/2006 **ME**
Winter, Mrs D, BA(Hons), Principal Lib. Offr., Cent. L., W. Bromwich
[10012874] 21/10/1993 **ME**
Winter, Mr E C, MA FCLIP HonFLA, Sec., CILIP Benevolent Fund,
London. [19435] 10/03/1953 **FE01/01/1957**
Winter, Mrs S E, BA(Hons) PGCE MA, L. I. C. Mgr., Baker & McKenzie,
London. [53887] 09/10/1996 **ME**
Winter, Ms S J, BSc(Hons) PgDip MSc MCLIP, Managing Dir. [60669]
23/06/2000 **CM23/06/2000**
Winterbotham, Miss D, MBE FCLIP, Life Member. [19436] 23/03/1953
FE01/01/1963
Winterbottom, Mr W, DMS, Computing & L. Serv. Mgr., Huddersfield
Univ., Oldham. [10016405] 22/03/2010 **ME**
Winterman, Dr V, BSc MSc PhD MCLIP, Snr. Consultant, TFPL Ltd.,
London. [40330] 08/01/1987 **CM01/04/2002**
Winters, Mrs M R, BA MCLIP, Lifelong Learning Lib. (Job Share),
Renfrewshire Council. [32751] 12/08/1980 **CM17/08/1982**
Winters, Mr M, BA MSc(Econ), LIS Mgr., Freshfields Bruckhaus
Deringer, London. [56103] 17/02/1998 **ME**
Wintersgill, Mr I, BA DipLib MCLIP, Retired [16140] 25/01/1972
CM21/06/1974

Wintle, Mrs E M, LLB DipLib MCLIP, Lib., Blackstone Chambers,
London. [27376] 24/02/1977 **CM16/07/1979**
Wintle, Miss K E, BA DipLib, Unwaged. [43791] 09/01/1990 **ME**
Winton, Mr S R, BA DipLib MCLIP, Sen. Lib. -Inf. & Systems Support,
Midlothian Council L. [33430] 29/11/1980 **CM16/08/1985**
Wintour, Mr B J C, MA MCLIP, Life Member. [16142] 28/04/1954
CM01/01/1958
Wintrip, Mr J A, BA MSc MCLIP, Freelance indexer [22919] 05/10/1974
CM28/01/1977
Wiper, Mr C K, BA(Hons) DipLib MCLIP LLM, Corporate Inf. Mgr.,
Bolton MBC. [31984] 07/01/1980 **CM30/04/1982**
Wisdom, Mr J J, MA MCLIP, Asst. Lib. /Lib., Guildhall L. /St. Paul's
Cathedral. [30302] 11/12/1978 **CM19/06/1981**
Wisdom, Miss S, BA(Hons) MA MCLIP, Head of Collection Storage N.,
The Brit. L., Boston Spa. [54489] 08/01/1997 **CM29/03/2006**
Wise, Miss C C, BA(Hons), Asst. Lib., News Internat., London.
[10005251] 11/11/1992 **ME**
Wise, Mrs C M, BA MA Dip Lib MCMI MCLIP, Head Special Collections,
Senate House L., Univ. of London. [36234] 09/08/1983
CM24/04/1991
Wise, Ms F, MSc, Inf. Offr., Amnesty Internat. [10008664] 13/03/2003 **ME**
Wiseman, Miss H, BSc MSc, Clinical Sci., Guys & St. Thomas NHS
Trust, Med. Toxicology Unit, London. [60682] 12/12/2001 **ME**
Wiseman, Mrs L K, BA MLib MCLIP, Lib., All Nat. Christian Coll.,
Hertfordshire. [39956] 09/10/1986 **CM14/03/1990**
Wishart, Mrs L, BSc MA DipLib MCLIP, Head of Knowledge & Inf.
Mgmt., Dept. of Health, London. [8553] 02/01/1972 **CM24/12/1974**
Wisher, Mrs E L, BA(Hons) MA MCLIP, Asst. Lib. (Humanities), Albert
Sloman L., Univ. of Essex, Colchester. [58235] 23/11/1999
CM15/10/2002
Witherden, Miss D M, BA(Hons) MCLIP, Knowledge & Inf. Specialist,
Audit Commission, Bristol. [44912] 14/01/1991 **CM23/01/2002**
Witherick, Mrs T K, BSc(Hons) MSc MCLIP, Sen. Lib. Inf. N. Somerset
C., Weston L. [61135] 07/03/2002 **CM13/06/2007**
Withers, Mrs L K, BA(Hons), Skills Co-ordinator, CTC Kingshurst
Academy, Birmingham. [10009949] 24/06/2008 **ME**
Withington, Miss L M, BA MCLIP, Unwaged. [29873] 12/10/1978
CM07/12/1981
Withnall, Miss J C, BA(Hons) MA MCLIP, Info. Consultant, Integreon
Managed Solutions Ltd, Bristol. [53894] 09/10/1996 **CM17/01/2001**
Witkowski, Mr S F, BA MCLIP, Lib. /Inf. Offr., Housing Tec. L.,
Manchester City Council. [36700] 14/11/1983 **CM24/04/1991**
Wodezki, Ms K, Not known, Corus RD&T, Rotherham. [10014459]
31/07/2009 **ME**
Wojnar, Miss M, MA, Resources Asst., Jewel and Esk Valley Coll.,
Dalkeith. [10006343] 10/10/2007 **ME**
Wolf, Ms C A, MA(Hons) MA, Unknown [53780] 01/10/1996 **ME**
Wolf, Ms D C, BA MLS, Unwaged. [54785] 01/04/1997 **ME**
Wolf, Mr M J, BA(Hons) MA MCLIP, Art Faculty Lib., Sydney Jones L.,
Liverpool Univ. [58442] 16/02/2000 **RV11/12/2009 CM19/11/2003**
Wolfe, Mrs R J, Inf. Mgr., Careers Cent., Univ. of Leeds. [56741]
12/10/1998 **AF**
Wolfenden, Mrs S, Stud., [65958] 21/07/2006 **ME**
Wolff, Miss M E, DipLib MCLIP, Community Lib., Selly Oak & Stirchley
L., Birmingham. [28725] 07/01/1978 **CM04/09/1981**
Wolffsohn, Miss P J, BA(Hons) MCLIP, Knowledge Serv. Mgr.,
Nabarro., London [46520] 15/11/1991 **CM17/05/2000**
Wolfisz, Ms L S, BA, L. &Off. Mgr., SOAS, London. [10014473]
04/08/2009 **AF**
Wollerton, Ms V C, BA MA, Inf. Advisor, Health & Safety Exec., Bootle
[10006609] 15/11/2007 **ME**
Wolniczak MacDonald, Mrs S, BA, Unknown. [10009786] 09/06/2008
AF

Wolpert, Prof L, DIC PhD FRS HonFCLIP, Hon Fellow. [60743]
12/12/2001　　　　　　　　　　　　　　**HFE29/03/1999**

Wolstenholme, Mrs C J, Special Needs/Access Mgr., Burnley Cent. L., Burnley. [65918] 03/07/2006　　　　　　**ME**

Wolton, Mrs M C, BA(Hons), Inf. Offr. (website), TPAS, Manchester. [53629] 19/08/1996　　　　　　　　　**ME**

Womersley, Miss P A, BA MCLIP, Team Coordinator Property, Environment & Stock team Cultural Serv., Surrey CC [25456]
12/01/1976　　　　　　　　　　　　　　**CM12/01/1978**

Wong, Miss L, Bsc, Stud., City Univ., London. [10011340] 09/10/2008　　　　　　　　　　　　　　　**ME**

Wong, Mrs R, BA MCLIP, Resources Lib., Bedford Bor. Council. [22802]
11/10/1974　　　　　　　　　　　　　　**CM11/10/1976**

Wong, Ms W M, FCLIP, Lib., The Open Univ. of Hong Kong. [36446]
10/10/1983　　　　　　　　　　　　　　**FE12/03/2003**

Wontner Osborne, Mrs E M J, BA(Hons) MSc MCLIP, Inf. Mgr. - Export Control Org., BIS, London. [56723] 07/10/1998　　**CM02/02/2005**

Woo, Mr T Y L, BSocSc DipLib MCLIP, Lib., Theological Coll. of Cent. Africa, Ndola, Zambia. [31725] 02/11/1979　　**CM23/02/1983**

Wood, Mr A F, BA MCLIP, Life Member. [16172] 21/08/1960
　　　　　　　　　　　　　　　　　　CM01/01/1963

Wood, Dr A J, PhD MA BA FCLIP MITOL AssocCIP, Training & Devel. Facilitator. [21783] 04/02/1974　　　　　**FE21/06/2006**

Wood, Mrs A K A, MSc BSc(Hons), Unwaged. [45714] 01/05/1991 **ME**

Wood, Miss A M, BA, Lib., Campden BRI, Chipping Campden. [35823]
21/01/1983　　　　　　　　　　　　　　**ME**

Wood, Miss A, BA MCLIP, Asst. Lib., Dept. for Child., Sch. and Families, London [16171] 02/01/1969　　　**CM03/04/1973**

Wood, Mrs A, L. Mgr. Lend. Serv., L's. & Heritage, Walsall M.B.C. [56035] 28/01/1998　　　　　　　　　　**ME**

Wood, Miss A, BA, Stud. [10011059] 13/05/2009　　　**ME**

Wood, Mrs C A, BA MCLIP, Lib., Norwich Sch., Norfolk [58671]
16/05/2000　　　　　　　　　　　　　　**CM23/01/2002**

Wood, Mrs D, BA MA, Currently Unemployed. [10016082] 21/10/1998
　　　　　　　　　　　　　　　　　　ME

Wood, Mrs D, MCLIP, Retired. [16178] 01/01/1959　　**CM01/01/1963**

Wood, Miss D, MA Cert GSMD (P), Stud., Aberystwyth Univ. [10009214] 07/05/2008　　　　　　　　　　**ME**

Wood, Mrs E M, MCLIP, Sch. Lib., S. Wilts. Grammar Sch., Salisbury. [13802] 01/01/1969　　　　　　　　**CM09/01/1974**

Wood, Miss F C, Issue Desk Super., Sci. Lib., DMS Watson Building, UCL. [10001317] 16/01/2007　　　　　　**AF**

Wood, Mrs G, LRC. Mgr., Bramhall High Sch., Stockport. [65221]
18/11/2005　　　　　　　　　　　　　　**AF**

Wood, Miss H J, BA(Hons) MCLIP, Lib., Lamport Bassitt, Southampton. [46609] 25/11/1991　　　　　　　　**CM22/01/1997**

Wood, Mr I J, L. Asst., Durham Univ. L., Durham. [59958] 12/11/2001
　　　　　　　　　　　　　　　　　　ME

Wood, Mrs J H, MA(Cantab) DipLIS, Lib. & Resource Cent. Mgr., Farnborough Hill Farnborough [40001] 06/10/1986　　**ME**

Wood, Mr J M, MA FCLIP, Life Member. [16199] 07/08/1957
　　　　　　　　　　　　　　　　　　FE01/01/1961

Wood, Mrs J M, MCLIP, Retired. [17997] 01/01/1946　**CM01/01/1952**

Wood, Mrs J O, BSc MCLIP, Performance & Res. Mgr., Stockport M.B.C., Stockport. [46687] 11/12/1991　　　**CM15/09/1993**

Wood, Mr J R, FCLIP, Life Member. [16201] 01/01/1945 **FE01/01/1965**

Wood, Mrs J, MA PgDip ILS MCLIP, L., Cafcass, London. [62885]
18/11/2003　　　　　　　　　　　　　　**CM23/01/2008**

Wood, Mrs J, Lib., Toynbee Sch., Hampshire [61580] 02/10/2002　**ME**

Wood, Ms K, MA HonFIInfSc HonFLA FCLIP, Retired. [16217]
01/01/1959　　　　　　　　　　　　　　**FE21/03/2001**

Wood, Miss L G C, BA MCLIP, Operational Support Asst., Devon L. Serv. H.Q., Exeter. [16208] 05/10/1970　　**CM31/12/1973**

Wood, Mrs L, MCLIP, Sen. Lib., E. Lancs. Div., Lancs. C.C. [16223]
08/10/1971　　　　　　　　　　　　　　**CM13/11/1975**

Wood, Mrs M E, MCLIP, Employment Unknown [9236] 01/01/1969
　　　　　　　　　　　　　　　　　　CM11/01/1973

Wood, Mrs M E, Info. Researcher, Chartered Mgmnt. Inst., Corby [10001535] 13/12/1993　　　　　　　　**ME**

Wood, Mr M, MCLIP, Retired. [16212] 28/09/1971　　**CM22/07/1974**

Wood, Dr M, MA, Special Collections & Arch. Lib., Univ. of Newcastle upon Tyne, Robinson L. [59798] 03/10/2001　　**ME**

Wood, Mr N V, ACIL MCLIP, Retired. [16215] 08/02/1964**CM01/01/1968**

Wood, Miss N, BA(Hons) MCLIP, L. Coll. Mgmnt., Royal Soc. of Med. L., London. [41506] 13/01/1988　　　　**CM22/07/1998**

Wood, Ms P, LRC Mgr., Ashington High Sch., Northumberland. [65409]
24/02/2006　　　　　　　　　　　　　　**AF**

Wood, Mr R J M, BPHIL MA DipLib ILTM, Head of Collections, Reading Univ. L. [28215] 11/10/1977　　　　　**ME**

Wood, Mrs S D, L. Asst., Regent's Pk. Coll., Oxford. [54955] 28/05/1997
　　　　　　　　　　　　　　　　　　AF

Wood, Ms S E, MCLIP, Unknown . [10006519] 31/10/2007
　　　　　　　　　　　　　　　　　　CM19/12/2008

Wood, Mrs S M, BA MCLIP, Product Mgr. [24297] 20/05/1975
　　　　　　　　　　　　　　　　　　CM17/01/1979

Wood, Ms S P, BA MCLIP, Electronic Inf. Mgr., Thames Valley Univ., Ealing. [32769] 08/08/1980　　　　　**CM24/08/1982**

Wood, Miss S S, BA DipLib MCLIP, Metadata Co-ordinator/Liaison Lib., Univ. of Reading. [38934] 15/10/1985　　**CM07/06/1988**

Wood, Mr S, Lib. Assist., Univ. of Sussex, Brighton. [10015307]
30/10/2009　　　　　　　　　　　　　　**AF**

Wood, Ms S, Sch. Lib., Holy Cross Preparatory Sch. [33819] 10/03/1981
　　　　　　　　　　　　　　　　　　ME

Woodacre, Mrs C R, B. Ed(Hons) ACLIP, Lib., Arnewood Sch., Hampshire [63472] 14/05/2004　　　　**ACL29/03/2007**

Woodall, Mr A S, BA(Hons), Sen. Lib. Asst., Dudley L., Dudley [10017042] 21/06/2010　　　　　　　　**ME**

Woodbridge, Ms S, MA MCLIP, Employment not known. [44420]
08/10/1990　　　　　　　　　　　　　　**CM31/01/1996**

Woodburn, Mrs S, MCLIP, Distric Mgr., Lancashire L. & Inf. Serv. [63169] 02/03/2004　　　　　　　　**CM21/11/2007**

Woodcock, Ms L, BA(Hons) MA MCLIP, Asst. Registrar Learning, Univ. Sheffield. [55785] 17/11/1997　　　　**CM19/01/2000**

Woodcock, Mrs R E, BSc(Hons) DipLib, Catr., Doncaster M.B.C., Carcroft L. H.Q. [28004] 11/10/1977　　　　**ME**

Wood-Fisher, Mrs C, BSc, Stud., Aberystwyth Univ. [10015554]
14/12/2009　　　　　　　　　　　　　　**ME**

Woodforde, Mrs S E, MCLIP, Sen. Lib., Grangemouth L., Stirlingshire. [23211] 14/11/1974　　　　　　　**CM01/01/1977**

Woodhams, Mrs G C, BA DipLib MCLIP, Head of Planning and Admin., Inf. Serv., Univ. of Kent [34415] 05/11/1981　　**CM01/02/1986**

Woodhead, Mr P A, MCLIP BA MLS, Retired. [16238] 22/02/1968
　　　　　　　　　　　　　　　　　　CM01/01/1971

Woodhouse, Mr B W, MA DipLib MCLIP, Sch. Lib., Smithycroft Sch., Glasgow C. Co. Educ. Dept. [43134] 10/08/1989　**CM23/03/1994**

Woodhouse, Mrs C A, BA(Hons), Resource Mgr., Sharnbrook Upper Sch., Beds. [10000782] 09/11/2006　　　**AF**

Woodhouse, Mrs D E, MCLIP, Retired. [7988] 18/03/1948
　　　　　　　　　　　　　　　　　　CM01/01/1953

Woodhouse, Mrs J M, DipLib MCLIP, Dist. L. Mgr., Mansfield Dist., Notts C.C. [34242] 10/10/1981　　　　**CM23/06/1986**

Woodhouse, Mr R G, BA MA PGCE MCLIP, Life Member. [16245]
20/07/1959　　　　　　　　　　　　　　**CM01/01/1964**

Woodhouse, Mrs S, MA DipLib MCLIP, Inf. Mgmnt. Consultant. [22830]
09/10/1974　　　　　　　　　　　　　　**CM20/10/1977**

Woodhouse, Mrs S, MA, Lib., The Brit. Mus., Dept. of Ancient Egypt & Sudan, London. [63227] 01/03/2004　　　**ME**

Wood-Lamont, Mrs S M, MBE FCLIP, L. Consultant, Univ. Med. & Pharmacy, Cluj-Napoca, Romania. [21777] 04/01/1974 **FE25/09/1996**

Woodland, Mr A N, MCLIP, Unknown. [18000] 23/01/1948 **CM01/01/1961**

Woodland, Mrs J K, BA(Hons) MCLIP, Sunday Lib., Bishop's Stortford P.L. [49572] 19/11/1993 **CM18/03/1998**

Woodland, Miss R E, BA(Hons) MSc MCLIP, Subject Liaison Lib., Brunel Univ., Uxbridge. [57110] 11/12/1998 **CM09/11/2005**

Woodley, Ms Z, BA(Hons) MCLIP, L. Res. Mgr., Mid-Essex Hosp. Trust, Warner L., Broomfield Hosp. [52809] 01/12/1995 **CM01/04/2002**

Woodman, Mr G D, BA DipLib MCLIP, Res. Team Lib., N. Ireland Assembly L., Belfast. [24861] 07/10/1975 **CM15/01/1979**

Woodman, Ms G, BA(Hons) MCLIP, Customer Serv. Mgr., Leeds Univ. [46275] 22/10/1991 **CM23/07/1997**

Woodman, Mrs M C, BSc ACLIP, Lib., Gorseland Primary Sch., Martlesham Heath. [10011001] 12/09/2008 **ACL23/09/2009**

Woodman, Ms R M, BA MLS, Sen. Lib., Educ. L. Res. Cent., Reading. [33431] 01/11/1980 **ME**

Woodman, Miss S M, BA MCLIP, Lib., Building Res. Estab., Watford. [36012] 08/04/1983 **CM15/11/1988**

Woodman, Ms Z, Sch. Lib., ISCA Coll. of Media Arts, Exeter [10007544] 13/02/2008 **ME**

Woodmansey, Mrs J, BA(Hons), Lib., HMP Wolds, Everthorpe. [10011621] 30/10/2008 **ME**

Woodroffe, Ms J E, BA MCLIP, Retired. [35996] 01/01/1964 **CM27/03/1985**

Woodroofe, Mr S R, BA(Hons) PGDipInfMgt, Asst. Prison Lib., HM Prison Pentonville, London. [49380] 01/11/1993 **ME**

Woodrow, Mrs E M, BA MCLIP, Retired. [16251] 08/01/1969 **CM21/09/1973**

Woodrow, Miss G L, BA(Hons) MCLIP, Inf. Offr., Thomas Eggar, Chichester. [42666] 06/02/1989 **CM19/07/2000**

Woodruff, Mrs E T C, BSc MCLIP, Retired. [33802] 11/03/1981 **CM15/02/1989**

Woods, Mr A D, BSc MCLIP, Electronic Sers. Dev. Offr., Nat. Museums Scotland, Edinburgh [62066] 07/02/2003 **CM09/07/2008**

Woods, Mr B M, Sr. Lib Asst., UCL Lib., London [64640] 13/05/2005 **AF**

Woods, Miss D M, FCLIP, Life Member. [16257] 28/01/1951 **FE01/01/1963**

Woods, Mr D N, BA MCLIP, Retired. [20035] 15/01/1973 **CM21/07/1976**

Woods, Mrs D, BA MCLIP, Mgr. :SLS, Sch. L. Serv., Worcs. C.C. [31947] 05/01/1980 **CM29/01/1985**

Woods, Miss E D, BA(Hons), Sale Asst. [10014373] 26/01/1989 **ME**

Woods, Miss E L, BA, Lib. CILT [63991] 22/11/2004 **ME**

Woods, Mrs G A, BA, Dep. Lib., L. of the European Court of Human Rights, Council of Europe, Strasbourg. France [35174] 06/10/1982 **ME**

Woods, Ms H B, BA(Hons) MSc MCLIP, Inf. Adviser, Sheffield Hallam Univ. [56481] 22/07/1998 **CM15/09/2004**

Woods, Miss L E, BA(Hons) MSc, L. Asst. /Periodicals, Inst. of Classical Studies L., London. [57226] 22/01/1999 **ME**

Woods, Mr L, BSc GDipLIM, Electronic Systems & Serv. Mgr., Univ. Coll. for the Creative Arts, Surrey. [56595] 07/09/1998 **ME**

Woods, L, Inf. Asst., Davies Arnold Cooper LLP, London. [10008139] 11/03/2008 **ME**

Woods, Mrs N, MCLIP, Sen. Lib., Lancs. Co. L.,Sch. L. Serv., Preston. [1119] 01/07/1971 **CM29/01/1975**

Woods, Mr P G, MA DipLib MCLIP, Head L. Inf. Cent., Treasury Solicitors Dept., London. [41938] 31/05/1988 **CM12/12/1991**

Woods, Mr R G, MA DipLib MCLIP, Life Member. [16264] 10/10/1951 **CM01/01/1957**

Woods, Ms R, BA DipLib, Lib., N. Lanarkshire Council, Motherwell. [44134] 25/05/1990 **ME**

Woods, Mr S R, MCLIP, Grp. L. Mgr., L.B. of Greenwich. [22704] 17/09/1974 **CM03/08/1977**

Woods, Mr S, BA(Hons), Unknown. [10012477] 10/02/2009 **ME**

Woods, Mrs V L, BA MCLIP, Housewife. [33682] 16/01/1981 **CM06/12/1983**

Woodward, Mrs A, Inf. Adviser., Univ. of Goucestershire [62063] 07/02/2003 **ME**

Woodward, Mrs C A, BA MCLIP, Asst. Lib., Nat. Aerospace L., Farnborough. [21792] 18/01/1974 **CM12/09/1977**

Woodward, Dr H M, BA PhD MCLIP, Univ. Lib., Cranfield Univ. [7765] 10/11/1969 **CM15/10/1974**

Woodward, Ms J, BA(Hons) DipInf MSc MCLIP, Resource Cent. Mgr., Shipley Coll., Shipley. [57655] 17/06/1999 **CM25/07/2001**

Woodward, Mrs K S, BA MCLIP, Sen. Lib., Market Drayton L., Shropshire C.C. [32860] 06/10/1980 **CM05/03/1984**

Woodward, Mr R J, BA MCLIP, Acquisitions Lib., Shropshire L. H.Q., Shrewsbury. [40526] 20/02/1987 **CM15/05/1989**

Woodward, Mr R J, MA, Unknown. [65982] 07/08/2006 **ME**

Woodworth, Mrs A, BSc MCLIP, ILC Mgr., Baines Sch., Poulton-le-Fylde. [64274] 22/02/2005 **CM28/01/2009**

Woolcock, Miss K, Stud., Aberystwyth Univ. [10015780] 26/01/2010 **ME**

Woolcombe, Mr K I, BSc PGCE, L. Asst., Oakmere L., Potters Bar, Herts. [10013790] 29/05/2009 **AF**

Woolf, Miss J L A, BA Hons, Stud., Aberystwyth Univ., Wales. [10015942] 29/01/2010 **ME**

Woolf, Mr J, MA BA MCLIP, Asst. Lib., Wanstead L. London [39890] 06/10/1986 **CM21/05/2008**

Woolf, Mrs K, Knowledge Mgr., DEFRA, London [10016411] 22/03/2010 **ME**

Woolfrey, Miss C G, BA MCLIP, Unemployed. [37052] 03/02/1984 **CM14/09/1994**

Woolgar, Mr T, MCLIP, Customer Serv. Mgr., L.B. of Bromley Asst. Head of L., Archive & Mus. Serv., L.B. of Bromley [32476] 01/04/1980 **CM10/09/1984**

Woollard, Mrs C J, BA(Hons) MSc MCLIP, Career Break [50352] 04/07/1994 **CM21/05/1997**

Woollatt, Miss J, MCLIP, Life Member [16285] 11/07/1961 **CM01/01/1970**

Woolley, Mrs D, BSc MSc MCLIP, Lib. in the NHS Fife Public Health L., Cameron Bridge [26219] 14/08/1976 **CM31/08/1979**

Woolley, Mr M, BA MCLIP, Dep. Dir. Univ. of Beds. [35837] 14/01/1983 **CM04/08/1987**

Woolley, Mrs S E, BA(Hons) DipLIS MCLIP, Sen. Asst. Subject Lib. Teeside Univ. Middlesbrough. [49415] 21/10/1993 **CM23/07/1997**

Woolley, Mr W N L, BSc(Hons) MSc, Inf. Specialist, King's Coll. London, Strand,London. [64554] 10/05/2005 **ME**

Woolridge, Mrs E A, BA MCLIP, Sen. Lib., Carlisle L., Cumbria L. Serv. [21771] 07/01/1974 **CM05/01/1977**

Woolven, Ms G B, BA MCLIP, Retired from post at Assoc. of Commonwealth Univ., London. [16290] 01/01/1959 **CM01/01/1967**

Woolven, Mrs J, Grp. Mgr., Braintree L., Essex C.C. [62152] 03/03/2003 **AF**

Wootton, Ms A M, BA(Hons) DipLib MCLIP, Sen. Lib., Dept. of Printed Books, Imperial War Mus. [16295] 08/01/1971 **CM11/01/1974**

Wootton, Mrs C B, MSc BEd, Lib., Doncaster Coll., Doncaster [59065] 01/11/2000 **ME**

Worden, Ms A E, MA MCLIP, Faculty Lib. Humanities and Social Sciences, Univ. of Portsmouth. [42203] 11/10/1988 **CM17/10/1990**

Worden, Miss K E, BA(Hons) MA MCLIP, Academic Support Lib., Univ. of Greenwich. [43353] 25/10/1989 **CM22/03/1995**

Workman, Dr H M, BSc MA MBA PhD MCLIP, Dir. of Learning Res. /Univ. Lib., Oxford Brookes Univ. [28216] 12/10/1977 **CM30/09/1980**

Workman, Miss H, BA MA, Stud. [10010900] 04/09/2008 **ME**

Workman, Mrs M J, MCLIP, Off. Mgr. /Lib., Birkett Stevens Colman Ptnr. LTD., Leeds. [12503] 17/01/1970 **CM22/08/1973**

Workman, Mrs M, MCLIP, Lib. [61531] 16/09/2002 **CM23/01/2008**

Workman, Ms V, Grp. Lib. [61196] 08/04/2002 **ME**

Worley, Ms L M, BA MCLIP, Sen. Mgr. EME L. Operations, Reed Smith Richards Butler LLP, London [27100] 24/01/1977 **CM25/04/1979**

Wormald, Mr J H, ISO BSc(Econ) MCLIP, Life Member. [16305] 12/09/1951 **CM01/01/1962**

Worrall, Mrs C B E, BA MCLIP, Asst. Lib, Hunter Street L., Univ. of Buckingham [35433] 01/10/1982 **CM15/05/1989**

Worrall, Miss S, BA(Hons) MCLIP, Inf. Lib., W. Sussex C.C., Horsham P. L. [54169] 04/11/1996 **CM15/05/2002**

Worrell, Ms H, MA, Stud. [10016875] 27/05/2010 **ME**

Worron, Mr A J, DIP LIS, Unknown. [10016755] 15/05/2010 **ME**

Worster, Ms D M, BA MLIS, Info. Offr., Brit. Heart Found., London [65761] 05/05/2006 **ME**

Worthington, Mrs G R A, BSc(Econ) MCLIP, Lib., Child. Team Cambs. Ls. & Inf. Serv., Cambridge. [54692] 05/03/1997 **CM08/12/2004**

Worthington, Ms S, L. Super., E. Grinstead L. [10010377] 04/09/2008 **AF**

Worthy, Miss A M, BA(Hons) MSc MCLIP, Sen. Metadat Lib., Univ. of Westminster., Harrow. [54244] 14/11/1996 **CM21/07/1999**

Wotherspoon, Ms G C, BA(Hons) MSc MCLIP, Retired [49250] 18/10/1993 **CM10/07/2002**

Wragge-Morley, Miss J C, BLib MA MCLIP, Web Mgr., Booktrust [31988] 22/01/1980 **CM15/05/1985**

Wraith, Mrs E, MCLIP, Lib., Norwich High Sch. For Girls, Norwich [56080] 12/02/1998 **CM23/01/2008**

Wrathall, Mrs C, BA(Hons), Proj. Mgr. [52486] 02/11/1995 **ME**

Wray, Mrs B, MCLIP, Retired. [16323] 01/01/1957 **CM01/01/1964**

Wray, Miss D C, BA MCLIP, Off. manager., IWAC., London [30305] 02/01/1979 **CM19/03/1985**

Wray, Miss J L, BA(Hons), Sen. L. Asst., English Faculty L., Oxford Univ. [62777] 22/10/2003 **ME**

Wray, Mrs S J, BA MCLIP, Asst. Lib., Royal United Hosp. NHS Trust, Bath. [32106] 28/01/1980 **CM20/02/1987**

Wray, Mrs S J, BA MCLIP, Sch. Lib., Dame Alice Harpur Sch., Bedford [34215] 07/10/1981 **CM10/05/1986**

Wreghitt, Ms V, PgDip, Electronic Res. Offr., Careers Cent., Univ. of Warwick, Coventry. [10013722] 22/05/2009 **ME**

Wren, Mrs D J, BA MCLIP, Sch. Lib., Beeslack High Sch., MidLothian. [38664] 14/09/1985 **CM18/07/1991**

Wren, Miss L A, BSc, Unwaged [62476] 07/07/2003 **ME**

Wride, Mrs P L, BA MCLIP, Collection Offr., Seven Stories, Newcastle-upon-Tyne. [31609] 17/10/1979 **CM28/07/1983**

Wright, Mr A B, BA MSc MCLIP, Lib., Meadow Bank Lib. [56339] 27/05/1998 **CM29/03/2004**

Wright, Ms A C, BA(Hons) MCLIP, Lib. Mngr, Redditch L., Worcestershire [42303] 07/10/1988 **CM04/10/2006**

Wright, Mrs A C, BSc(Hons) MCLIP, Lib., Cadbury Health Lib., Bristol. [46352] 30/10/1991 **CM24/09/1997**

Wright, Mrs A E, BA MA MCLIP, Lib., Royal Northern Coll. of Music, Manchester. [31452] 07/10/1979 **CM28/10/1981**

Wright, Mrs A M, BA(Hons) PGCE, Learning Ctre. Asst., Saffron Walden Co. H. S. [61267] 13/05/2002 **ME**

Wright, Miss A, B LIB MCLIP, Team Leader, Edinburgh City L. [29542] 24/08/1978 **CM14/08/1985**

Wright, Miss B A, LVO MA DipLib MCLIP, Bibl., Royal L., Windsor Castle, Berks. [26619] 11/10/1976 **CM03/03/1982**

Wright, Mrs C M, BA(Hons) MCLIP, Sch. Lib. & Learning Res. Mgr., RNIB New Coll., Worcester. [33955] 17/06/1981 **CM18/11/1993**

Wright, Mrs D J, BA DipLib MCLIP, Child. Lib., Rutland C.C., Oakham. [36242] 01/08/1983 **CM27/11/1996**

Wright, Miss D J, BA(Hons) MA, L. Asst., Literary & Philosphical Soc., Newcastle upon Tyne. [59349] 13/02/2001 **ME**

Wright, Mrs D J, BA MCLIP, Unwaged. [6274] 04/10/1971 **CM03/06/1975**

Wright, Ms D W, BA MCLIP, Lib., Berwick L., Walkergate. [38438] 16/04/1985 **CM14/02/1990**

Wright, Mrs E A, BA MA MCLIP, Sub. Lib., Doncaster Coll. [59350] 13/02/2001 **CM10/07/2009**

Wright, Mr E W, MA B SOC B PHIL MCLIP, Retired [25191] 15/12/1975 **CM05/01/1978**

Wright, Mrs F J, MCLIP, Life Member. [16342] 01/01/1945 **CM01/01/1951**

Wright, Mr G H, FIRT MCLIP, Retired. [18005] 02/01/1940 **CM01/01/1950**

Wright, Mrs G J, BA(Hons), Lib., Mus. of The Hist. of Sci., Oxford. [63388] 27/04/2004 **ME**

Wright, Ms G J, MCLIP MA, Retired [6819] 10/01/1966 **CM01/01/1969**

Wright, Mr G W, BA DipLib DMS MCLIP, Career break [35263] 07/10/1982 **CM09/08/1988**

Wright, Mr G, Inf. Offr., Linklaters LLP. [64562] 11/05/2005 **ME**

Wright, Mrs H C, BA(Hons) DipILM MCLIP, E-Serv. Lib., Trafford M.B.C., Manchester. [50759] 18/10/1994 **CM21/01/1998**

Wright, Ms H C, MA(Hons), Website Mgr., VLA., Surrey. [57080] 04/12/1998 **ME**

Wright, Miss H L, BA(Hons) MSc MCLIP, Asst., L. NSPCC, London [65381] 03/01/2006 **CM11/06/2010**

Wright, Miss H L, BSc, Unknown. [64774] 22/06/2005 **ME**

Wright, Miss H M, BA DipLib MCLIP, L. and Knowledge Mgr., NPHS for Wales, Carmarthen. [31727] 22/11/1979 **CM22/02/1982**

Wright, Miss H M, MA MCLIP, Retired. [16346] 24/11/1965 **CM01/01/1968**

Wright, Mr J C, ALA, Unknown. [10012308] 01/01/1969 **ME**

Wright, Ms J S, MA(Hons) PG DipLib, Catr., Bibliographic Data Serv. Ltd, Dumfries. [10008962] 06/11/1992 **ME**

Wright, Mr J, BA(Hons) DipILM MCLIP, Inf & L. Serv. Team Leader. [56752] 08/10/1998 **CM21/05/2003**

Wright, Miss J, BA(Hons) MCLIP, Liaison Lib. (Learning and Teaching), Birmingham City Univ. [46977] 17/03/1992 **CM20/03/1996**

Wright, Ms K E, BA MA MCLIP, Inf. Serv. Mgr., Cent. for Reviews & Dissemination. [10006728] 03/10/1977 **CM01/10/1979**

Wright, Miss L A, BA(Hons) DipIS, Sen. Inf. Asst., Kings Coll. London, Guys Campus. [55265] 28/08/1997 **ME**

Wright, Miss L D, ACLIP, Career Break [65599] 27/02/2006 **ACL17/10/2006**

Wright, Ms L J, MA(Hons) MSc, Stud. [10006481] 24/10/2007 **ME**

Wright, Mr M A, DipSAM ACLIP, Asst. Stock Devel. Lib., Cent. L., Romford. [64971] 05/10/2005 **ACL16/07/2008**

Wright, Mrs M C, FCLIP, Retired. [16362] 03/04/1929 **FE01/01/1932**

Wright, Mr M G H, MA FCLIP, Life Member. [16365] 23/03/1953 **FE01/01/1967**

Wright, Mr M M B, BSocSc, Stud., UCD, Dublin. [10016164] 16/02/2010 **ME**

Wright, Miss N, MCLIP, Life Member. [16367] 17/09/1948 **CM01/01/1953**

Wright, Mr P K J, BA FCLIP, Life Member. [16372] 10/06/1949 **FE01/01/1958**

Wright, Mr P P, BA(Hons) DipLib MCLIP, Lib., City Coll., Plymouth. [10011627] 28/01/1991 **CM19/03/1997**

Wright, Mrs P, BA(Hons) MA MCLIP, Internet Mgr., MOD, London [55651] 31/10/1997 **CM23/01/2002**

Wright, Mr P, BA(Hons) MA PGCE, Lib., Foyle and Londonderry Coll., N Ireland [10016445] 26/03/2010 **ME**

Wright, Ms R E, BA MCLIP, Asst. Lib., House of Lords, Westminster. [16376] 28/08/1970 **CM05/03/1973**

Wright, Mrs R J, BA MCLIP, Career Break. [40578] 02/04/1987
CM22/04/1992

Wright, Mrs S E, Application Support Consultant, OCLC. [38748]
02/10/1985 **ME**

Wright, Miss S, Relationship Mgr., Business Link, Co Durham. [39424]
25/01/1986 **ME**

Wright, Ms S, BA(Hons), Unknown. [10007031] 09/12/2004 **ME**

Wright, Mr T C, BA(Hons) DipLIS MCLIP, Head of KM and ICT, ITI
Scotland, Glasgow. [46577] 13/11/1991 **CM25/05/1994**

Wright, Mrs V, BA DipLib, Asst. Head of L., Customer Serv., E. Sussex
C.C. [35076] 08/07/1982 **ME**

Wright, Mrs V, MA, Unwaged. [10016923] 10/06/2010 **ME**

Wright, Ms Z, MA, KM Mgr., DLA Piper, Manchester. [53928]
11/10/1996 **ME**

Wrighting, Mr A M, BA MCLIP, Employment not known. [35345]
14/10/1982 **CM02/06/1987**

Wrightson, Mrs C, BA FHEA MCLIP, Learning Cent. Mgr., Univ. of
Gloucestershire, Cheltenham. [25874] 26/03/1976 **CM08/07/1980**

Wrigley, Mrs G J, Lib., Thompsons Solicitors, Newcastle upon Tyne.
[44966] 28/01/1991 **ME**

Wrigley, Mrs S M, BA MCLIP, Inf. Res. Lib., Dudley Grp. of Hosp. NHS
Foundation Trust. [23534] 02/01/1975 **CM13/10/1977**

Wyatt, Miss A M E, BA(Hons) MA, Sen. L. & Inf. Asst., Jubilee Cres. L.,
Coventry. [62956] 25/11/2003 **ME**

Wyatt, Ms C A, BA DipLib MCLIP, Dep. Head, FOL Team, Dept. of
Health, London. [28729] 16/01/1978 **CM16/02/1981**

Wyatt, Mrs L M, L. External Serv. Lead, SCC Cultural Serv., Dorking L.
[53790] 01/10/1996 **AF**

Wyatt, Mr M A, BA DipLib MCLIP, Unemployed. [39824] 10/08/1986
CM21/07/1993

Wyatt, Miss M, BA DipHE MCLIP, Lib. & Inf. Mgr., Roy. Town Planning
Inst., London. [58715] 01/07/2000 **CM03/10/2007**

Wyatt, Mr N J, BA, L. Mgr., Sci. Mus., London. [34978] 24/05/1982 **ME**

Wyatt, Miss P M, MCLIP, Retired. [16394] 04/02/1952 **CM01/01/1952**

Wyburn, Mr R M, BSc DipLib MCLIP, Asst. Lib., The Wellcome L.,
London. [10003015] 01/04/1976 **CM08/09/1978**

Wylie, Miss K, RGN, Sen. Inf. Offr., Manchester Royal Infirmary. [44764]
14/11/1990 **ME**

Wylie, Ms S J, BTh(Oxon), Unemployed. [51707] 23/05/1995 **ME**

Wyman, Mrs R E, MCLIP, Advisory Lib., Northamptonshire C.C. [18126]
03/10/1972 **CM06/08/1975**

Wymer, Mrs C J, MCLIP, Locality Mgr., Norfolk Co. L. [19088]
02/10/1972 **CM31/10/1975**

Wyn, Mr D, Unknown. [10015651] 07/01/2010 **AF**

Wyness, Mrs E A, MA MCLIP, Asst. Lib. p. /t., De Montfort Univ.,
Leicester. [57083] 04/12/1998 **CM21/05/2003**

Wynne, Mr B B L, BA DipLib MCLIP DMS, Programme Mgr., JISC
Exec., London. [39475] 01/02/1986 **CM13/06/1990**

Wynne, Mr P, BA MLiH DipLib FRSA MCLIP, Nowal Exec. Sec.,
Manchester Met. Univ. [10013055] 21/01/1985 **CM06/09/1988**

Wynn-Jones, Mrs J B, BEd(Hons) MA, Resources Cent. Mgr.,
Hounsdown Sch., Southampton. [62712] 03/10/2003 **ME**

Wynton-Doig, Mrs S T, BA MCLIP, Unwaged. [32718] 01/07/1980
CM23/12/1983

Wythers, Ms H M, BA(Hons) MSc (Econ) MCLIP, Learning Resources
Mgr., Linden Lodge Sch., London. [61271] 09/05/2002 **CM03/10/2007**

Wyver, Mrs G K L, BA(Hons) MA MCLIP, Academic Liaison Lib. -
Fashion & Clothing, Univ. for the Creative Arts, Rochester. [43060]
01/07/1989 **CM20/05/1998**

X

Xavier, Ms A C, BA MA DipEd Tech Dip Inf MCLIP, L. Project Offr., Queen
Mary Univ. of London. [10010572] 21/10/1991 **CM18/11/1993**

Y

Yam, Mr J K C, BA MSc, Lib., TAFE, NSW, Australia. [40104]
16/10/1986 **ME**

Yam, Miss T, MA, Info. Mgr., Amnesty Intl. UK, London [10008679]
13/10/1997 **ME**

Yandle, Miss A C, BA(Hons) PGDipPhil, Head of Faculty, Westfield
Comm. Sch., Yeovil. [49126] 06/10/1993 **ME**

Yarde, Ms M, BA DipLib MCLIP, Neighbourhood Lib., Lewisham L.
[33673] 05/02/1981 **CM06/04/1984**

Yardley Jones, Miss A, BLib MCLIP, Community Lib., Gwynedd.
[39879] 01/10/1986 **CM16/10/1991**

Yardley, Mr A K, BA MCLIP, Music Lib., Guildhall Sch. of Music &
Drama, London. [22795] 15/10/1974 **CM01/11/1976**

Yardley, Ms C A, BA(Hons) DipILS MCLIP, Sen. Lib. -Systems & Catg.,
Stoke-on-Trent Ls., Inf. & Arch. [49678] 25/11/1993 **CM17/11/1999**

Yardley, Mr R J E, MA MSc MCLIP, Lib., Inf. Team, Cambs. C.C.
[22847] 02/10/1974 **CM07/10/1976**

Yarwood, Mrs K J, BA MCLIP, Reader Serv. Lib., Salford City L. [1788]
06/10/1969 **CM30/04/1973**

Yates, Mrs C A, BA(Hons) MCLIP, Head of Lib. Serv., M. O. D. [53628]
19/08/1996 **CM15/03/2000**

Yates, Miss C J, BLib MCLIP, Local Studies Lib., Walsall M.B.C. [36179]
05/07/1983 **CM17/03/1999**

Yates, Mrs J M, DipIM BEd (Hons) MCLIP, Resources Mgr., EMTAS
Hampshire C.C. [56004] 19/01/1998 **CM06/04/2005**

Yates, Mrs J, MA MCLIP, Asst. Sch. Lib., Highlands Sch., London.
[8249] 04/01/1971 **CM30/01/1973**

Yates, Mrs K, BA(Hons) MA MCLIP, Lib., Macclesfield L., Cheshire C.C.
[59825] 10/10/2001 **CM21/06/2006**

Yates, Miss N, Trials Search Co-ordinator, Univ. of Liverpool. [61854]
20/11/2002 **ME**

Yates, Mrs P J, BA MCLIP, Lib., Van Dyke Upper Sch., Leighton
Buzzard. [32040] 07/02/1980 **CM12/10/1984**

Yates, Mr S G, BA(Hons), L. & Inf. Offr., Sandwell Clinical L., W.
Bromwich. [57120] 15/12/1998 **ME**

Yates, Mrs S J, BA MCLIP, Life Member. [16419] 01/01/1951
CM01/01/1954

Yates-Mercer, Dr P A, BSc MSc PhD FCLIP, Retired/Hon. Visiting
Fellow, City Univ., London. [60806] 12/12/2001 **FE01/04/2002**

Yeadon, Mrs J E, MSc MCLIP, Retired. [16422] 02/11/1963
CM03/11/1970

Yeates, Mr A R, BA MA MCLIP, E-L. Systems Offr., L.B. Barnet. [26657]
25/10/1976 **CM09/10/1979**

Yeats, Mrs F J, BA MCLIP, Unwaged [23679] 13/01/1975**CM22/02/1977**

Yelland, Mr M, BA MCLIP, Life Member. [16429] 27/09/1951
CM01/01/1956

Yeoh, Dr J M, BA MEd PhD FCLIP, Unknown. [19089] 01/01/1972
FE29/03/1904

Yeoman, Mrs F A, MA MCLIP, Site Lib., Merrist Wood Campus.,
Guildford Coll. [42252] 13/10/1988 **CM14/08/1991**

Yeoman, Ms K R, MA DipLib MCLIP, Sch. Lib., Aberdeen City Council,
Dyce Academy. [42236] 18/10/1988 **CM24/06/1992**

Yeomans, Mrs J J, Unknown. [10016935] 10/06/2010 **AF**

Yeomans, Miss J, BSc MA, Dir., EBLIDA, Netherlands. [10014164]
07/07/2009 **ME**

Yeomans, Mrs K H, BA(Hons) MCLIP, Dist. Mgr., Staffordshire C.C.,
Cannock/Stafford. [44748] 15/11/1990 **CM25/01/1995**

Yeomans, Mrs T I, MCLIP, Retired. [16434] 23/01/1935 **CM01/01/1940**
Yescombe, Mr E R, MBE FIM FCLIP, Life Member. [16435] 06/01/1933
FE01/01/1950
Yewdall, Mrs A J, BA(Hons) MA MCLIP, Asst. Lib., DCSF [47576]
02/10/1992 **CM17/11/1999**
Yiend, Mrs P, BA ACLIP, Team Offr., Property Environment & Stock
Team [65769] 24/04/2006 **ACL01/12/2006**
Yip, Ms S Y, BA(Hons), Tech. Serv. Lib., Univ. of the Arts London.
[61781] 05/11/2002 **ME**
Yockney, Mrs S A J, BA DipLib MCLIP, Sch. Lib., Educ. Resource
Cent., Dorset C.C. [27102] 26/01/1977 **CM15/05/1981**
York, Miss C A, BA(Hons) PGCE, L. Mgr., Canon Lee Sch., York.
[64068] 15/12/2004 **ME**
York, Mrs J A, MCLIP, Dist. Lib., Birmingham City Council. [6534]
01/01/1971 **CM01/01/1975**
York, Ms J M, BA MCLIP, Building Devel. Mgr., Bristol City Council,
Cent. L., Bristol City Council Leisure Serv. [35178] 05/10/1982
CM02/07/1986
Youd, Mrs A M, BSSc MCLIP, Unemployed. [26675] 05/10/1976
CM19/11/1979
Young, Mrs A C, MA(Hons) MA MCLIP, Inf. Skills Trainer, Royal Free
Hosp. Med. L. UCL, London [56018] 05/01/1998 **CM16/05/2001**
Young, Mrs A P M, MCLIP, Retired. [16440] 30/09/1951 **CM30/04/1994**
Young, Mrs B P, Academic Liason Lib. [10007008] 26/01/1984 **ME**
Young, Mrs D, MCLIP, Life Member. [9443] 01/03/1964 **CM01/01/1969**
Young, Ms E, DipILS MCLIP, L. & Info. Offr., Ardler L., Dundee [42344]
23/10/1988 **CM12/03/2003**
Young, Mrs G R, BA(Hons) PgDipLIS MCLIP, NOWAL Support Offr., N.
W. Academic L., Manchester. [50008] 18/02/1994 **CM20/05/1998**
Young, Mrs G, Lib. Resource Asst., Stafford Coll. [62952] 25/11/2003
ME
Young, Mr G, FCLIP, Retired. [16452] 23/04/1949 **FE01/01/1957**
Young, Mrs H B, BA(Hons) DipIM MCLIP, L. Offr. :Child. & Learning,
The Bournemouth L., Bournemouth Bor. Council, [51318] 10/01/1995
CM20/11/1999
Young, Mrs H M, BA(Hons) MA MCLIP, Academic Lib., Social Sciences
& Humanities, Univ. of Loughborough [50771] 18/10/1994
CM18/09/2002
Young, Mrs H, BA(Hons), Info. Lib., Aberyswyth. [64997] 06/10/2005**ME**
Young, Mr I A, BA DipLib MCLIP, Faculty Team Leader, Edward Boyle
L., Univ. of Leeds. [41791] 05/04/1988 **CM24/06/1992**
Young, Mr I W, MA(Hons) PGDip ILS MCLIP, Lib., Heriot-Watt Univ. L.,
Edinburgh. [54668] 17/02/1997 **CM07/09/2005**
Young, Miss J E, MCLIP, Life Member. [16461] 05/09/1942
CM01/01/1946
Young, Mrs J, MCLIP, L. Mgr., Cheshire C.C., Macclesfield L. [22953]
22/09/1974 **CM16/08/1977**
Young, Mrs J, BA(Hons) MA, Lib. (Business Inf.), Freshfields
Bruckhaus Deringer, London. [62202] 13/03/2003 **ME**
Young, Ms J, BA MCLIP, Retired [22557] 01/07/1974 **CM22/09/1980**
Young, Ms L A, BA DipLib MCLIP, Info. Res. Mgr., Inst. of Advanced
Legal Studies. [36171] 11/07/1983 **CM20/03/1985**
Young, Mrs L C, BA(Hons), Sen. Researcher, Irwin Mitchell Solicitors,
Birmingham. [58974] 13/10/2000 **ME**
Young, Ms L, BA(Hons) MA, Distance Serv. Co-ordinator, St. Peter's L.,
Univ. of Sunderland [10001816] 22/06/2005 **ME**
Young, Mr M R, BA(Hons) PGDipLib MCLIP, Inf. Unit Mgr., Hewitsons,
Cambridge. [25139] 25/10/1975 **CM01/01/1978**
Young, Mrs P M, BA MCLIP, Serv. Devel. Lib., Bromley L [42353]
25/10/1988 **CM22/07/1992**
Young, Mrs P O, MCLIP, Retired. [16472] 17/10/1944 **CM06/06/1952**
Young, Mr R J, MCLIP, Br. Lib., Stanmore, L.B. of Harrow. [16474]
17/08/1971 **CM15/07/1975**

Young, Mrs R S, MCLIP, Res. & Info. Mgr., NZDF Command & Staff
Coll., NZ [36732] 16/11/1983 **CM02/06/1987**
Young, Mrs R, L. Asst., Strathaven L., Strathaven. [10013468]
28/04/2009 **AF**
Young, Mr S, ICT Support Offr., Leamington L. [10010980] 12/09/2008
AF
Young, Miss S, Legal Registration Offr., Registers of Scotland,
Edinburgh. [57125] 14/12/1998 **ME**
Young, Ms Z L, BSc(Hons) MSc(Econ), Subject Lib., Cardiff Univ.
[58912] 03/10/2000 **ME**
Younger, Mrs L, BA MCLIP, Serv. Mgr., Bibliographic Serv., Northumbria
Univ. [16476] 18/01/1972 **CM15/11/1974**
Younger, Miss M C, BLib MCLIP, Lib. Supreme Court of the UK, London
[10002026] 01/07/1976 **CM24/11/1980**
Younger, Ms P M, PGCE MA MCLIP, Lib. Mgr., N. Somerset Healthcare
L. [52680] 20/11/1995 **CM10/07/2002**
Youngman, Dr F, BSc MSc DPhil MCLIP, Stud., Oxford Univ. [60728]
12/12/2001 **CM12/12/2001**
Youngman, Mrs G, BA DipLib MCLIP, Team Co-ordinator, Virtual
Content Servs., Surrey C.C. [35071] 02/07/1982 **CM09/08/1988**
Yu, Miss Y N R, BEd(Hons) MA MCLIP, Asst. Lib., Bibl. Control Sect.,
Hong Kong. Poly. Univ. [54577] 14/01/1997 **CM23/09/1998**
Yuen, Miss L W, BSc MLib MCLIP, Lib., Hong Kong Govt. [58537]
01/04/2000 **CM16/07/2003**
Yuen, Miss S W R, Unknown [64642] 03/05/2005 **ME**
Yuen, Mr T K, MCLIP, Retired [19867] 01/01/1973 **CM12/01/1982**
Yuile, Mr D M, BA MCLIP, Stragic L. Serv Mgr., Shropshire Council.
[16478] 04/10/1971 **CM22/07/1974**

Z

Zado, Dr V Y, BSc MSc MPhil PhD, Employment not known. [36000]
15/04/1983 **AF**
Zaghini, Mr E O, PGDipLib MCLIP, Customer Serv. Lib., L.B. Bromley.
[45983] 08/08/1991 **CM31/01/1996**
Zahnhausen, Ms P M, MA, Graduate Trainee, Inst. of Advanced Legal
Studies, London. [10007036] 04/01/2008 **AF**
Zain, Ms Z, Inf. Advisor, Geldards LLP, Cardiff [10007606] 28/02/2008
AF
Zalin, Mrs R A, BA MCLIP, Retired. [17414] 08/01/1968 **CM01/01/1970**
Zandonade, Mr T, MA DIS, Adjunct. Prof., Univ. of Brasilia, Brasilia, DF
(Brazil). [24308] 30/05/1975 **ME**
Zanelli, Mr P, BA(Hons), Sen. Lib., Digital Citizenship Team, Enfield
Town Lib. [10001694] 26/02/1999 **ME**
Zaremba, Miss A K, MA Dip, Info. Lib., Somerset [10013169]
03/04/2009 **ME**
Zarywacz, Mrs S G, BA MCLIP, Archive Clerk, RGP Architects,
Barnstaple. [38876] 14/10/1985 **CM15/03/1989**
Zazani, Ms E, BA (Lib. Sci.), Learning Support Adv., Birkbeck Coll.,
London. [10012832] 13/03/2009 **ME**
Zeb, Mr A, MA, Stud [10007262] 01/02/2008 **ME**
Zebian, Mrs S, BA, Inf. Asst., Royal Inst. of Chartered Surveyors,
Parliament Square, London. [10015988] 03/02/2010 **ME**
Zehtabi, Mr A F, PGDip, Career Break [58958] 10/10/2000 **ME**
Zelinger, Mr A J, BA(Hons) DipIM, Sen. Asst. Lib., House of Lords,
London. [55928] 11/12/1997 **ME**
Zenobi-Bird, Mrs L, BA MA MA MCLIP, Sen. Support Consultant,
Sirsidynix [53853] 07/10/1996 **CM20/09/2000**
Zerafa, Mr L, Overseas., [49895] 07/01/1994 **ME**
Zessimedes, Ms J A, BSc(Hons) MCLIP, L. Serv. Mgr., E. Cornwall.
[57542] 28/04/1999 **CM28/10/2004**
Zhang, Mrs H, MSc, Unknown. [10005999] 24/08/2007 **ME**

Zhang, Mrs S Z, BSc, Asst. Lib., American Intercontinental, London.
[53170] 01/04/1996   **ME**
Zhang, Mrs Y, MA, Inf. /E-Learning Offr., Inf. Serv., Univ. of Nottingham,
Ningbo, China. [55711] 06/11/1997   **ME**
Zhaodong, Mr L I U, HonFCLIP, Hon Fellow. [60088] 07/12/2001
                                                          HFE01/04/1987
Zimmerman, Ms K, BA MA PhD, Unwaged. [62443] 23/06/2003   **ME**
Zinn, Dr K, PhD MA Diploma, Sen. L. & Inf. Asst., Judge Business Sch.
L., Cambridge Univ. [10007676] 29/08/2008   **ME**
Zissimos, Mr D, BA, Lib., Berwin Leighton Paisner, London. [58701]
09/06/2000   **ME**

Zolynski, Ms B A, BA DipECLaw DipLib MCLIP, Head of L. & Inf.,
Herbert Smith, London. [28731] 01/01/1978   **CM17/03/1980**
Zolynski, Miss R H, BA DipLib MCLIP, Inf. & Records Strategy Mgr.,
BIS., London. [33205] 03/10/1980   **CM29/10/1982**
Zorba, Miss I, BA, Manchester Met. Univ., Dept. of Info. & Comm., PhD
Stud. [58621] 19/04/2000   **ME**
Zulu, Mrs N, BiBibl, Unknown. [10014101] 25/06/2009   **ME**
Zumpe, Mr M, BA MA MCLIP, Inf. & Stock Lib., Portsmouth City L. Serv.
[59665] 24/07/2001   **CM02/02/2005**

Organisation
Members

UK Organisation Members

Aberystwyth University, Aberystwyth	01/01/1965	8000007
Academy 360, Sunderland	21/05/2009	10013564
Amnesty International UK, London	18/05/1995	8001235
Angus Council, Forfar	01/01/1930	8000014
Aquinas College, Stockport	15/11/2002	8001447
Ashcroft Technology Academy, London	13/08/2001	8001419
Aston University, Birmingham	03/12/2002	8001449
Bangor University, Bangor	01/01/1937	8000029
Barnsley MBC, Barnsley	01/01/1909	8000035
Barry College, Barry	14/07/2004	10001293
BBC, London	21/06/1985	8001021
Belvoir High School and Community Centre, Bottesford	07/11/2008	10011727
Birkbeck College, London	09/08/1996	8001277
Birkenhead Sixth Form College, Birkenhead	13/03/2008	10008080
Birmingham City Council, Birmingham	01/01/1887	8000067
Birmingham City University, Birmingham	30/11/1976	8000065
Bishopsgate Institute, London	01/01/1952	8000432
Blackburn College, Blackburn	31/01/2007	10001294
BMJ Publishing Group, London	29/10/2009	10000905
Bolton MBC, Bolton	01/01/1986	8000081
Bridgend County Borough Council, Bridgend	01/01/1929	8000286
British Council, Manchester	06/06/2007	10002593
British Library, London	18/09/2000	8001386
British Library, London	01/01/1966	8001103
British Museum, London	23/05/2001	8001412
Britten-Pears Library, Aldeburgh	03/03/1999	8001348
Brunel University, Uxbridge	01/01/1961	8000759
BSix Brooke House Sixth Form College, London	16/03/2005	8001489
Burnley College, Burnley	25/05/1995	8001239
Bury MBC, Bury	01/01/1901	8000121
Cadbury Sixth Form College, Birmingham	04/01/1993	8001164
Calderdale MBC, Halifax	25/07/2007	10005483
Cardiff Council, Cardiff	18/03/2008	10005725
Cardiff University, Cardiff	06/05/2003	8001456
Carlisle College, Carlisle	01/01/1959	8000147
Caterham School, Caterham	05/07/2000	8001382
Ceredigion CC, Aberystwyth	01/01/1925	8000146
Cirencester College Library, Cirencester	31/08/2006	8001517
City of Bath College, Bath	18/11/1987	8001049
City of Bradford MDC, Bradford	01/01/1964	8000092
City of London, London	01/01/1878	8000453
City University, London	01/01/1966	8000444
Coleg Meirion-Dwyfor, Gwynedd	01/03/2009	10012961
Courtauld Institute of Art, London	01/12/1996	8001290
Cranford Community College, Cranford	12/03/2008	10008230
Croydon College, Croydon	08/06/2005	8001502

Darent Valley Hospital, Dartford	17/08/1990	8001106
Darlington College of Technology, Darlington	03/12/2002	8001448
Darwen Vale High School, Darwen	14/07/2009	10014293
De Montfort University, Leicester	01/01/1970	8000400
Department of Culture Media and Sport, London	22/06/2010	10012175
Derby City Council, Derby	18/07/1997	8001310
Derbyshire CC, Matlock	01/01/1898	8000204
Derwentside College, Consett	09/12/2004	8001486
Devon CC, Exeter	01/01/1927	8000205
Doncaster MBC, Doncaster	01/01/1907	8000210
Dr Williams's Library, London	01/01/1897	8000448
Drayton Manor High School, London	16/12/2003	8001464
Dumfries and Galloway Council, Dumfries	02/05/1979	8000977
Dundee City Council, Dundee	01/01/1883	8000223
Durham CC, Spennymoor	01/01/1930	8000226
Durrants, London	16/04/2007	10002452
East Ayrshire Council, Kilmarnock	01/01/1968	8000963
East Riding College, Beverley	16/04/2007	10002454
East Riding of Yorkshire Council, Skirlaugh	01/01/1926	8000235
Edge Hill University, Ormskirk	16/03/1998	8001328
Edinburgh College of Art, Ebinburgh	14/04/1993	8001174
Edinburgh Napier University, Edinburgh	01/03/1976	8000930
Education For Change Ltd, London	10/12/1990	8001112
Eton College, Windsor	14/01/1993	8001165
European Medicines Agency (EMA), London	15/07/2010	10009382
European School of Osteopathy, Boxley	25/04/1985	8001016
Farnham Heath End School, Farnham	18/11/1992	8001162
Fashion Retail Academy, London	15/05/2006	8001512
Filsham Valley Secondary School, St. Leonards-on-Sea	17/06/2010	10017000
Filton College, Bristol	12/02/2004	8001468
Forestry Commission Library, Farnham	10/11/2005	8001508
Gateshead College, Gateshead	27/03/1995	8001231
Gateshead Council, Gateshead	19/03/1975	8000899
Godalming College, Godalming	20/02/2001	8001404
Goethe-Institut London, London	19/02/1973	8000829
Great North Museum: Hancock, Newcastle upon Tyne	14/04/2010	10016597
Greenwich Community College, London	18/05/2006	8001514
Guille-Allès Library, St Peter Port	22/04/1987	8001043
Harrogate Grammar School, Harrogate	15/03/2006	8001509
Hartlepool Borough Council, Hartlepool	28/05/1996	8001268
Hereford Cathedral School, Hereford	17/02/2003	8001450
Highlands & Islands Enterprise, Dingwall	30/09/2009	10014955
Highlands College, St Saviour	21/10/2008	10011489
House of Commons, London	01/01/1963	8000455
House of Lords, London	29/02/1996	8001263

Imperial College London, London	14/12/2000	8001401
Imperial War Museum, London	01/01/1949	8000458
Inner Temple Library, London	19/02/1996	8001261
Institut Francais, London	31/05/1996	8001269
Institute of Development Studies, Brighton	09/05/1995	8001232
Institute of Education, London	01/01/1960	10006865
International Business School, Douglas	16/04/2007	10002456
John Laing Integrated Services, London	29/01/2010	10014528
Kent CC, West Malling	01/01/1926	8000371
Key Note LTD, Teddington	15/05/2009	10013431
King Edward VI College, Nuneaton	16/11/2004	8001485
King Edward VI High School for Girls, Birmingham	15/01/2001	8001403
King Edward's School, Birmingham	30/05/2002	8001438
King's College London, London	27/07/1992	8001151
King's Fund, London	28/02/1991	8001116
Kingston College, Kingston upon Thames	17/02/1998	8001323
Kingston University, Kingston upon Thames	01/01/1962	8000377
Kirklees Metropolitan Council, Huddersfield	01/01/1898	8000346
Lanarkshire NHS Board, East Kilbride	07/03/2007	10001860
LB of Bexley, Sidcup	01/01/1959	8000056
LB of Brent, Wembley	01/01/1965	8000098
LB of Bromley, Bromley	01/01/1965	8000115
LB of Camden, London	01/01/1967	8000135
LB of Greenwich, London	01/01/1966	8000302
LB of Hackney, London	01/01/1929	8000306
LB of Harrow, Harrow	01/01/1965	8000321
LB of Havering, Romford	01/01/1969	10005540
LB of Islington, London	01/01/1905	8000363
LB of Lambeth, London	01/03/1994	8001190
LB of Redbridge, Ilford	01/01/1965	8000653
LB of Southwark, London	01/01/1972	8000715
Leeds Metropolitan University, Leeds	03/10/2008	10011241
Leeds Metropolitan University, Leeds	01/01/1947	8000396
Leeds Trinity & All Saints College, Leeds	01/01/1966	10002491
Lewisham College, London	08/06/1998	8001335
Libraries NI, Lisburn	10/09/2009	10002890
Lincoln's Inn Library, London	01/01/1974	8000849
Literary & Philosophical Society, Newcastle upon Tyne	01/01/1947	8000569
Liverpool City Council, Liverpool	01/01/1884	10005087
Liverpool Institute for Performing Arts, Liverpool	11/12/1995	8001253
Liverpool John Moores University, Liverpool	21/02/1977	8000955
London College of Fashion, London	27/11/2009	10015482
London Fire & Emergency Planning Authority, London	26/04/2005	8001501
London Metropolitan University, London	01/01/1961	8000870
London School of Economics, London	25/03/1999	8001349
London South Bank University, London	18/09/1989	8001075
Loughborough University, Loughborough	01/01/1965	8000524
Luton Cultural Services Trust, Luton	16/12/2009	10005561
Macmillan Cancer Support, London	24/01/2000	8001368
Manchester Metropolitan University, Manchester	01/01/1963	8000539
Marist Senior School, Ascot	01/07/2003	8001457
Marks and Clerk, Oxford	14/06/2007	10005121
Marlborough College, Marlborough	03/05/2007	10002925
Merseyside Maritime Museum, Liverpool	16/10/2000	8001389
Middlesbrough BC, Middlesbrough	26/06/1996	8001272

Middlesex University, London	01/01/1971	8000253
MLA, London	17/07/2008	10010296
National Acquistions Group, Wakefield	25/01/2010	10015916
National Institute for Biological Standards & Control (NIBSC), Potters Bar	20/03/1987	8001040
National Library of Scotland, Edinburgh	01/01/1930	8000248
National Library of Wales, Aberystwyth	01/01/1921	8000005
National Museum & Gallery Wales, Cardiff	14/07/2010	10017221
Newham College of F E, London	03/05/2007	10002902
Newham Sixth Form College, London	08/10/1992	8001157
Newport City Council, Newport	31/01/1990	8001090
Newquay Tretherras School, Newquay	29/01/1996	8001256
NHS24, Clydebank	20/03/2009	10013066
Norfolk & Waveney Mental Health NHS Foundation Trust, Norwich	09/04/2009	10013270
North East Lincolnshire Council, Grimsby	17/02/1975	8000894
North Hertfordshire College, Hitchin	19/03/1993	8001168
North Lindsey College, Scunthorpe	08/01/2004	8001466
North Yorkshire CC, Northallerton	24/06/1974	8000869
Northern Ireland Assembly Library, Belfast	20/09/2001	8001420
Northern Ireland Publications Resource (NIPR), Belfast	31/10/2005	8001507
Northumberland CC, Morpeth	01/01/1930	8000586
Northumbria University, Newcastle upon Tyne	01/01/1948	8000563
Norwich University College of the Arts (NUCA), Norwich	22/04/1986	8001030
Nottingham Trent University, Nottingham	16/02/1993	8001166
Oldham MDC, Oldham	01/01/1931	8000604
Oldham Sixth Form College, Oldham	11/01/2010	10012793
Onchan Public Library, Onchan	01/12/1997	8001320
Orkney Islands Council, Kirkwall	19/03/2008	10005690
Oxford Brookes University, Oxford	03/03/1995	8001229
Oxford High School, Oxford	19/03/1993	8001173
Oxford University Library Service, Oxford	03/04/2009	10011636
Oxford University Press, Oxford	18/06/2008	10002237
Oxfordshire CC, Oxford	01/01/1929	8000613
Pembrokeshire CC, Haverfordwest	01/01/1931	8000939
Pembrokeshire College, Haverfordwest	02/04/2004	8001475
Perth & Kinross Council, Perth	01/01/1926	8000621
PETROC, Barnstaple	01/07/1991	8001125
Pimlico Academy, London	16/03/2002	8001432
Portsmouth City Council, Portsmouth	01/01/1918	8001314
Queen Elizabeth Hospital Birmingham, Birmingham	13/04/2006	8001511
Redbridge College, Romford	23/01/1997	8001295
Redcar & Cleveland Borough Council, Redcar	24/05/1996	8001267
Regent's College, London	25/07/1986	8001036
Robert Gordon University, Aberdeen	01/01/1960	8000003
Roehampton University, London	17/07/2008	10001100
Rotherham MBC, Rotherham	01/01/1890	8000667
Royal Academy of Dance, London	08/06/1995	8001240
Royal College of Art, London	01/07/2005	8001505
Royal College of Psychiatrists, London	20/03/2009	10007231
Royal Society of Arts, London	30/06/2008	10001396
Royal Veterinary College, Hatfield	16/01/2007	10001295
Salford College, Manchester	09/02/2010	10016046
Sandwell MBC, West Bromwich	01/01/1937	8000781
School of Oriental & African Studies, London	05/02/1997	8001297

Science Museum, London	01/01/1971	8000506
Scottish Borders Council, Selkirk	01/05/1976	8000937
Sheffield Hallam University, Sheffield	01/10/1989	8001082
Shooters Hill Post 16 Campus, London	11/03/2008	10006269
Sir George Monoux College, London	09/06/2004	8001478
Sotheby's Institute of Art, London	13/03/2008	10003714
South Birmingham PCT, Birmingham	30/07/2003	8001461
South Place Ethical Society, London	25/01/2010	10015929
South Thames College, Morden	01/06/1993	8001175
Southbank Centre, London	17/08/1989	8001078
Southwark College, London	30/04/2001	8001410
St Francis Xavier 6th Form College, London	18/03/1999	8001350
St George's, University of London, London	17/07/2002	8001440
St Helens Council, St Helens	01/01/1950	8000679
St Mary's College, Blackburn	10/10/2007	10006315
Stockport MBC, Stockport	01/01/1909	8000727
Stockton on Tees BC, Stockton-On-Tees	01/01/1914	8000746
Surrey CC, Kingston upon Thames	01/01/1965	10001616
Surrey History Centre, Woking	01/01/1999	8001346
TASMAC London – School of Business, London	17/06/2010	10016991
Tate Britain, London	18/05/2010	10006737
Teesside University, Middlesbrough	21/01/2009	10002872
Thames Valley University, London	01/01/1955	8000233
The Blue Coat School, Oldham	12/03/2004	8001472
The Charter School, London	19/12/2008	10007283
The English Speaking Union, London	19/03/1993	8001171
The Goldsmiths' Company, London	01/01/1948	8000518
The National Archives, Richmond	16/02/1977	8000952
The National Maritime Museum, London	21/01/2009	10002910
The Open University, Milton Keynes	01/01/1970	8000077
Trinity College, Bristol	30/06/1980	8000989
Tyne Metropolitan College, Wallsend	27/09/1991	8001131
UHI Millennium Institute, Inverness	21/10/2005	8001506
University College Falmouth, Penryn	19/02/2009	10008030
University College London, London	01/01/1930	8000513
University College School, London	21/07/2008	10007168
University of Aberdeen, Aberdeen	01/01/1928	8000004
University of Bath, Bath	01/01/1956	8000042
University of Birmingham, Birmingham	25/06/2008	10001764
University of Brighton, Brighton	01/01/1862	8000104
University of Cambridge, Cambridge	01/01/1968	8000132
University of Dundee, Dundee	01/01/1946	8000224
University of East Anglia, Norwich	01/01/1963	8000591

University of Edinburgh, Edinburgh	01/01/1947	8000249
University of Evansville, Grantham	27/06/1989	8001073
University of Exeter, Exeter	01/01/1929	8000262
University of Greenwich, London	27/05/2009	10002164
University of Huddersfield, Huddersfield	01/01/1952	8000345
University of Kent, Canterbury	24/11/2003	8001463
University of Liverpool, Liverpool	01/01/1929	10001857
University of Manchester, Manchester	01/01/1917	8000543
University of Plymouth, Plymouth	01/01/1972	8000626
University of Portsmouth, Portsmouth	01/01/1956	8000639
University of Reading, Reading	01/01/1929	8000652
University of Salford, Greater Manchester	01/01/1957	8000686
University of Sheffield, Sheffield	01/01/1939	10000438
University of Stirling, Stirling	01/01/1967	8000725
University of Strathclyde, Glasgow	01/01/1953	8000287
University of Surrey, Guildford	01/01/1963	8000305
University of Sussex, Brighton	01/01/1961	8001352
University of the Arts London, London	24/07/2000	8001384
University of the West of England, Bristol	03/04/1987	8001042
University of the West of Scotland, Paisley	25/03/1976	8000933
University of Ulster, Coleraine	01/01/1968	8000830
University of Wales Institute, Cardiff, Cardiff	24/04/1996	8001265
University of Warwick, Coventry	19/05/2005	8001499
University of Wolverhampton, Wolverhampton	01/01/1971	8001374
University of Worcester, Worcester	30/03/1994	8001194
University of York, York	01/01/1962	8000823
Victoria & Albert Museum, London	31/07/1986	8001035
Wakefield MDC, Wakefield	02/08/1974	8000877
Walsall Council, Walsall	01/01/1893	8000766
Warwickshire CC, Warwick	15/07/2010	10002900
Warwickshire College, Leamington Spa	03/03/2006	8001510
Wellingborough School, Wellingborough	17/06/2008	10008785
Welsh Assembly Government, Cardiff	21/05/2003	8001458
Welsh Health CWM TAF NHS Trust, Cardiff	16/03/2005	8001488
West Dunbartonshire Council, Dumbarton	01/01/1944	8000220
Westminster Kingsway College, London	18/01/2007	10007714
Weston College, Weston Super Mare	17/02/1983	8000999
Wigan & Leigh College, Wigan	30/04/2000	8001379
Wigan Leisure & Culture Trust, Wigan	01/01/1919	8000802
Wimbledon College of Art, London	13/03/2003	8001453
Winstanley College, Wigan	05/05/2006	8001513
Wirral MBC, Birkenhead	01/01/1898	8000060
Wolverhampton City Council, Wolverhampton	01/01/1888	8000810

Overseas Organisation Members

Australia

City of Armadale Libraries, Armadale	05/11/2001	9000751
City of Perth Library, Perth	24/06/2004	9000765
Macquarie University, Sydney	01/01/1966	9000028
National Library of Australia, Canberra	01/01/1965	9000439
RMIT Libraries, Melbourne	30/05/1977	9000562
RMIT University, Melbourne	16/10/2009	10015122
State Library of South Australia, Adelaide	01/01/1969	9000000

Bangladesh

International Centre For Diarrhoeal Disease Research, Bangladesh, Dhaka	11/06/2009	10013762

Belgium

Gem Openb Bib, Ichtegem	29/07/2003	9000758
Universiteitsbibliotheek K U L, Leuven	29/04/1974	9000484

Canada

McGill University Library, Montreal	01/01/1956	9000061
Memorial University of Newfoundland, St Johns	01/01/2010	10016400
University of Alberta, Edmonton	01/01/1967	9000053
University of British Columbia, Vancouver	01/01/1962	9000082
University of Toronto, Toronto	01/01/1972	9000078

Cayman Islands

Cayman Islands National Archives, Grand Cayman	31/01/1990	9000695

China

Dulwich College Beijing, Beijing	19/06/2008	10009830
The Chinese University of Hong Kong, Shatin	17/06/2008	10008424

Denmark

Statsbiblioteket, Arhus	01/01/1970	9000098

Fiji Islands

The University of the South Pacific, Suva	01/01/1969	9000123

Germany

Bucerius Law School, Hamburg	30/03/2006	9000771
Universitätsbibliothek Giessen, Giessen	01/02/1973	9000448

Guyana

National Library, Georgetown	01/01/1947	9000138
University of Guyana Library, Georgetown	17/06/2008	10009839

Hong Kong

Hong Kong Public Libraries, Central	01/01/1960	9000140
The Hong Kong Polytechnic University, Kowloon	01/08/1973	9000465

Ireland

Cork CC, Cork	31/05/1983	9000623
Donegal County Council, Letterkenny	16/02/1996	9000701
Dublin City Council, Dublin	01/01/1935	9000112
Dublin City Public Libraries, Dublin	01/01/1935	10011257
Dublin City University, Dublin	16/10/2000	9000744
Houses of the Oireachtas, Dublin	12/05/2006	9000772
Institute of Technology Carlow, Carlow	11/03/1998	9000733
Institute of Technology Tallaght, Dublin	23/04/2004	9000763
Irish Management Institute, Dublin	18/06/2008	10009919
Law Library, Dublin	23/04/2004	9000762
Longford CC, Longford	17/02/1989	9000683
National Library of Ireland, Dublin	01/01/1958	9000111
National University of Ireland, Galway, Galway	01/01/1971	9000117
Royal Dublin Society Library, Dublin	13/01/2007	10001297
South Dublin CC, Dublin	01/01/1964	9000108
The Library Council Ireland (An Chomhairle Leabharlanna), Dublin	01/01/1968	9000109
Trinity College Dublin, Dublin	01/01/1959	9000115
University College Dublin, Dublin	17/01/1977	9000556
University of Limerick, Limerick	01/01/1978	9000588
Wicklow CC, Bray	21/11/2007	10005805

Israel

Bar-Ilan University, Ramat Gan	23/03/1981	9000635
Hebrew University of Jerusalem, Jerusalem	11/06/2009	10013927

Jamaica

Jamaica Library Service, Kingston	01/01/1950	9000416
University of the West Indies – Jamaica, Kingston	21/02/1975	9000504

Japan

Keio University, Tokyo	01/01/1986	9000668

Malta

University of Malta, Msida	10/08/2009	10000927

Netherlands

Ingressus BV, Rotterdam	04/08/2008	10010533

New Zealand

Auckland City Libraries, Auckland	01/01/1922	9000213
Christchurch City Libraries, Christchurch	01/01/1935	9000215
Dunedin Public Library, Dunedin	01/01/1934	9000218
Massey University, Palmerston North	31/01/1990	9000696
Rodney Libraries, Auckland	17/12/2003	9000759
University of Auckland, Auckland	01/01/1971	9000214
Wellington Library, Wellington	01/01/1930	9000226

Qatar

Qatar Foundation, Doha	16/10/2009	10015126

Singapore

Temasek Polytechnic, Singapore	19/03/1993	9000720

South Africa

Kwazulu Natal Province Library Service, Pietermaritzburg	09/07/2010	10017198
North West University, Potchefstroom	25/11/1974	9000498

Spain

Universitat De Barcelona, Barcelona	30/07/1987	9000673

Sweden

Lund University, Lund	01/01/1931	9000287
Uppsala University, Uppsala	01/01/1931	9000291

Switzerland

International Labour Office, Geneva	02/09/1992	9000715

Turkey

Bilkent University, Ankara	30/04/1991	9000705
Sabanci University, Istanbul	25/08/2009	10014649

United Arab Emirates

University of Bolton, Nakheel	24/11/2009	10002883

USA

East Carolina University, Greenville	14/02/2002	9000753
EBSCO Publishing Ipswich, Ipswich	01/05/2010	10016764
Harvard College Library, Cambridge	01/01/2010	10015732
Northwestern University, Evanston	01/01/1929	9000339
OCLC, Dublin	17/10/2001	9000752
State Library of Ohio, Columbus	01/11/1999	9000738
State University of NY at Binghamton, Binghamton	01/01/1971	9000308
University of Georgia, Athens	01/01/1951	9000301
University of Hawaii, Honolulu	01/01/1965	9000345
University of Maryland, Maryland	01/01/1968	9000327
University of Michigan, Ann Arbor	01/01/1935	9000299
University of Pittsburgh, Pittsburgh	01/01/1968	10014957
University of South Carolina, Columbia	01/01/1995	9000729
University of Texas at Austin, Austin	01/01/1935	9000303
Yale University, New Haven	11/08/1976	9000534

Part 5
HISTORICAL INFORMATION

A short history of the Institute of Information Scientists

The Institute of Information Scientists (IIS) was born in response to rapid advances in science and technology. Fittingly, it was thanks to convergence in technology, and increasingly generalised access to the applications of some of the technology, that IIS has joined forces with the library community once more, after a schism lasting more than 40 years.

Although it was not set up until 1958, the IIS can trace its history back to 1923. In that year a meeting was organised by Professor Hutton of Oxford University and Ben Fullman of the British Non-Ferrous Metals Research Association to discuss issues arising from the rapid growth of scientific research and publication after WW1. The Library Association declined to take part in that meeting, and as a result the Association of Special Libraries and Information Bureaux was set up in 1924. Jumping forward to 1948 Fullman presented proposals to the Aslib Annual Conference for a syllabus for the education of information professionals to cope with the even more rapid growth of science after the Second World War. This visionary approach was not adopted, and for the next few years progress towards professional education and standards for information work (rather than librarianship) was minimal.

The final straw for scientific information officers was the defeat of some revised proposals at the Aslib Conference in 1957 and on 23 January 1958 a meeting was held at the IEE to discuss proposals for a new professional association. The meeting was chaired by Dr G. Malcolm Dyson. Jason Farradane and Chris Hanson made the opening speeches to a motion: 'that a professional body be, and is hereby set up, to promote and maintain high standards in scientific and technical information work and to establish qualifications for those engaged in the profession'. There were 125 people at this first meeting. At a subsequent meeting on 23 May 1958 at the Royal Society of Arts the Constitution of the Institute of Information Scientists was approved. Dr Dyson was elected as President, Chris Hanson as Vice President, Gordon Foster as Hon. Treasurer and Jason Farradane as Hon. Secretary. By the end of the year around 100 Members had joined the Institute.

The first issue of the *Bulletin* was written by Farradane and published in April 1959. Although slightly outside the scope of a history of the IIS it is important to record the establishment in 1963 of the first full-time post-graduate course in information science at what was then the Northampton College of Advanced Technology (now City University). In 1964 the IIS held its first conference at Merton College, Oxford, at which there were 60 delegates. A notable event in 1965 was the first Salary Survey, developed by Dr Malcolm Campbell.

The first issue of *The Information Scientist*, the direct forerunner of the *Journal of Information Science*, was published in 1967. Peter Vickers and John Williams were the initial Editors, until Alan Gilchrist took over in the mid-1970s, continuing as Editor of JIS until 2002.

Widening the scope

As the Institute grew in size in the late 1960s and early 1970s it became clear that the use of the phrase 'scientific and technical information work' was too limiting. At the 1972 AGM there was a motion to widen the scope, but there was also concern that this would mean rewriting the Memorandum of Association, so the proposals were withdrawn. Subsequently Council found that there was no need to change the Memorandum, and they could construe the phrase as they wished, which they then proceeded to do.

Inform was launched in 1975 to complement *The Information Scientist*. Also in 1975 another major change in the structure of the IIS took place. At the AGM Martin White, together with Charles Oppenheim, decided that it was time that Associate Members were represented on Council, rather than just Members and Fellows. To the surprise of Council the motion was passed.

In 1978 the publishing activities of the Institute expanded further with the publication of the first of the celebrated Monograph series of books on information science, managed by John Campbell. The year was also notable for a very lively discussion at the Annual Conference about the future of the Institute as it neared its 21st Anniversary with around 1400 Members. This was to a significant extent the result of an informal meeting of the STIR group of younger members (the Steering Team for Institute Reform). That year had already marked the creation of Special Interest Groups which could accept non-Members of the IIS. The first to be set up was the Online User Group (now Ukolug), followed soon after by the Patent and Trade Marks Group.

1979 was quite a year, and not only because the IIS office moved out to Reading. For the first time the Annual Conference was held at a hotel, the Imperial Hotel, Torquay, and ended up making a very substantial profit for the Institute in its 21st year. Discussions were also taking place to heal the differences between the IIS, The Library Association and Aslib through the creation of the first Tripartite Conference, to be held in Sheffield in 1980. Further cooperation with The Library Association resulted in the first combined Salary Survey.

By 1980 Council had approved a radical reshaping of the membership and committee decision-making structures of the Institute. This made it much more welcoming and open to younger people and to those from outside traditional scientific and technical information backgrounds. New entrants to the profession could now participate fully in the activities and governance of the Institute, and make their voices heard.

A sign that the Institute had become much more open and informal was its launch of the Infotainers. There were four major shows in 1980, 1983, 1985 and 1990, and several smaller ones, all in the best tradition of satirical review.

Acquiring a secretariat

The Silver Jubilee Conference took place in 1983 at St Catherine's College, Oxford, though Council were not exactly concentrating on the papers as there was a very real chance that the IIS had fallen foul of VAT legislation over its charitable/educational status. Luckily the danger passed. The problems did highlight the need for a full-time employee running the IIS office, and the IIS was very fortunate to be able to appoint Sarah Carter, a Member of the Institute, to the post of Executive Secretary in 1984, by which time the membership had reached almost 2000.

From 1985 the IIS had a central focus for its activities with a central London base. Its administrative structure was developed, but it continued to be very dependent on its Members for organising events and conferences, drafting and agreeing professional standards, and accreditation activities in universities and colleges offering courses in information science. Lobbying and advocacy, and all the Branch and Special Interest Group activities, also depended on volunteers from the membership. In addition to Ukolug and PATMG, the IIS set up the City Information Group, the Computerised Information Management Special Interest Group (it was later disbanded), the Small Business Group for consultants et al. (which lasted into the early 1990s), and ALGIS (the Affiliation of Local Government Information Specialists). At least three of these groups became significant organisations within their own specialisations, due entirely to the hard work and enthusiasm of their members.

During this period the Branch structure was revised, and the Midlands Branch disappeared, mainly because the road and public transport links did not make it easy for members from both East and West Midlands to attend any meeting. There were also Local Groups in Reading, Oxford and elsewhere that thrived for a time. The number of branches was a tribute to the energy of Members, given the comparatively small size of the IIS as a whole.

Significant activities organised and developed by members for members included the very successful series of annual Text Retrieval Conferences, and the IIS Evening Events. These were short, affordable professional development workshops and seminars conceived by Martin White when he was IIS President. They attracted many younger members. They came to learn from eminent senior members who were generous in offering their time for professional development opportunities.

The second tripartite conference was held in 1985, as a five-way multipartite event in Bournemouth. The third and final multipartite conference was held in 1990, also in Bournemouth.

1990 was a momentous year for the Institute. After a series of exploratory discussions with the Charity Commissioners, the Institute was granted charitable status. This conferred considerable tax advantages, and enabled the IIS to make the best use of a generous bequest from an early member, John Campbell. Part of the bequest was used to set up the John Campbell Trust, which was to be used for the provision of scholarships, prizes, travel grants or research fellowships. Its work continues today.

1990 also marked the first serious effort by The Library Association, Aslib and the IIS to move closer together with a view to merger. Although support for the merger was not strong enough for formal moves to be made, the discussions (marked by the Saunders Report), and a second series of discussions (the Tripartite discussions) did result in some fundamental reviews of the similarities and differences between the organisations.

For the Institute, the 1990s were dominated by two significant factors:

- Changes in work, cultures and attitudes, that resulted in members having much less time to devote to running the Institute and its activities.
- Increasing use of electronic sources of information, increased availability and ease of use of information resources by non-specialists, and from 1995 onwards, the development of the world wide web and its prospects of freely available information.

These developments led to uncertainties about the long-term future of the Institute, its role, its name and who should form its core membership – their background, qualifications, and what the criteria for Information Science should be. Until then, the IIS had been a group of specialists with fairly clearly defined skills. Once the specialist focus had been lost, it became harder to sustain the IIS network. It was at this point that I succeeded Sarah Carter with a much wider brief: to represent and promote the IIS externally.

By this time, the opportunities for information professionals to attract publicity were enormous. But so was the logic of increased collaboration. The IIS, working with The Library Association and supported by the Association for Geographic Information, launched the Coalition for Public Information. This was a broad-based, cross-sectoral body of organisations with an interest in 'public information' – information generated by government in the course of conducting its business. With some success, CoPI lobbied the government on issues associated with 'the information society' – a term then only beginning to find common currency.

It was not only on grounds of a shared platform for advocacy that the IIS was moving closer to The Library Association. Advances in technology and much more generalised use of electronic resources, together with much more widespread adoption of information management techniques in industry and the public sector, was making it increasingly difficult to distinguish between those who were clearly information scientists, and librarians who used the techniques of information science.

Informal talks on greater collaboration, and a proposal by Dr Ray Lester at the IIS's AGM in 1996 suggesting more of the same, led to more formal talks, and, eventually to unification in April 2002.

In the meantime, and without prejudice to attempts at unification, a joint working party of senior Library Association and IIS members (led by Kate Wood, and Professor Peter Enser) aligned the criteria of both organisations for accrediting academic courses in information science and library management. And IIS celebrated its 40th anniversary with its Ruby Conference in Sheffield in 1998.

In its heyday the IIS's membership reached nearly 2750 members. In proportion to its size, its profile was high, thanks to the personal commitment and direct involvement of many eminent senior members. In the end, the logic of convergence (in academic criteria and technologies and the practice of both professional bodies) on the one hand, and of the need for advocacy from a shared platform on the other, made unification the only logical option.

Compiled with information from and the generous help of a number of IIS members, including most notably Martin White, Sarah Carter, Diana Clegg and Charles Oppenheim.

Elspeth Hyams
Editor, *Library & Information Update*

The Library Association 1877–2002

'We have only to hope that the Library Association of the United Kingdom will flourish and that it will justify itself in public estimation by assisting libraries to become what they ought to be, efficient instruments of national education.' With these words, The Athenaeum welcomed the newly established association in 1877.

Foundation

The Association was founded at an international conference held at the London Institution, attended by over 200 delegates from Australia, Belgium, Denmark, France, Germany, Greece, Italy and the USA, in addition to those from the UK. Melvil Dewey, later to become famous as the author of the Decimal Classification, was there as Secretary of the American Library Association, founded the previous year. Some of the topics discussed at the conference sound familiar 125 years later: Sunday opening, the application of the latest technology (in the shape of the telephone) and salaries of librarians were among them. The organiser of the conference, Edward Nicholson, librarian of the host institution, was moved to describe the salaries then on offer as an 'insult to the liberality and intelligence of our great towns.'

Purpose

The Association was born in the great Victorian tradition of mutual self-improvement, with the intention of promoting the role of libraries and librarians by the exchange of information on good practice, visits to interesting libraries, publishing a journal and manuals, the holding of conferences and, in due course, the running of training courses and holding examinations. Its original object was to 'unite all persons engaged or interested in library work, for the purpose of promoting the best possible administration of existing libraries and the formation of new ones...'

Advocacy

The first President was John Winter Jones, Principal Librarian of the British Museum. Most of those closely involved in the early development of the association were librarians of university and research libraries. However, the fledgling Association devoted a great deal of time and effort in campaigning for the abolition of the restrictions on the amount local councils could spend on their public libraries (they were prevented at that time from spending more than the product of a penny rate on the value of property in their areas) and in persuading councils to establish such libraries under the legislation, which was enabling rather than compulsory. Thus began a long tradition of working to influence public policy, which would be described these days as advocacy and lobbying. Because so much of this has to be conducted behind closed doors and because the final decisions cannot usually be firmly attributed to the Association's efforts, its Members have probably given it less credit for success in this activity than it has deserved. The Association continued its interest in the relationship between local government and public libraries until the present day. After the First World War, the association worked with the Carnegie United Kingdom Trust (CUKT) to persuade the Government finally to lift the restrictions on the amount councils were permitted to spend on public libraries. This resulted in legislation in 1919, which not only did that, but also allowed county councils to provide public libraries for the first time. A large network in rural areas of branch and mobile libraries and collections in village halls and similar locations gradually emerged as a result. At about same time, the Association proposed the establishment of a national library of science and technology, as part of a plan to establish technical and commercial services in public libraries, and pleaded for greater cooperation between public libraries and specialised libraries. After the Second World War, the Association also actively encouraged the development of regional technical and commercial library services by cooperation between different kinds of libraries and Government agencies. It was not until the successful Russian space shot in the sixties prompted greater investment in scientific research that the Government set up the National Lending Library of Science and Technology (NLLST) in Boston Spa, Yorkshire, which eventually became the Document Supply Centre of the British Library.

Public policy

The Association gave firm evidence to the Dainton Committee in 1968, stressing the need for a UK national library. The Committee's findings led directly to the formation of the British Library, by bringing together the National Central Library, the NLLST, the British Museum Library, the National Reference Library of Science and Invention and the British National Bibliography (BNB). The latter had been established by cooperation between a number of groups representing libraries and the book trade, with an initial financial guarantee by the Association.

Another area of public policy that the Association can be fairly said to have influenced is the allocation of public library responsibilities to local councils. Since the publication in 1942 of its own radical report on the subject, prepared by Lionel McColvin, it fairly consistently supported larger authorities, as more able to provide comprehensive services. This approach inevitably led to great controversy within the profession and the establishment from time to time of breakaway groups representing those working in smaller councils.

The Association also took a great interest in copyright legislation, both within the UK and the European Union, undoubtedly influencing the 1988 Copyright, Designs and Patents Act, especially the inclusion of the concept of fair dealing exceptions for libraries and for the purposes of research and private study. The fight still goes on to ensure that the implementation of the European Directive does not abolish this provision in the UK.

Among the many areas of public policy which have engaged the attention of the Association were postage rates for materials for the visually impaired, public lending right, taxes on publications, the national school curricula, freedom of information legislation, and the provision of libraries in prisons, hospitals and other institutions.

A recent success story, which the Association initiated, is the People's Network, linking every public library to the internet and providing electronic content and training for public library staff. Although it was a report by the former Library and Information Commission (LIC) that persuaded the government to adopt the idea, it was the Association's earlier bid for National Lottery funding which established the desirability of such a project. The Library Association campaigned, with several other organisations, for a government advisory body on library and information matters, which finally came into existence as the LIC. The Commission recently merged with a similar body for museums to become Resource: the Council for Museums, Archives and Libraries.

The Association developed its contacts with politicians and civil servants over the years and was instrumental in the establishment of the All-Party Parliamentary Group on Libraries, which ensures that a wide range of library and information issues are drawn to the attention of MPs and peers.

Education and training

The education and training of library staff was a constant concern of the Association. Its first move, in 1885, was to hold examinations leading to certificates in English and European literature, classification and cataloguing and library administration. Few sat these tests and fewer passed. But summer schools began in 1894. The first lasted three days attracting 45 students. The summer schools increased in length and attendance, the examinations broadened in scope, eventually leading to formal qualifications and Fellowship of the Association. Correspondence courses were set up, to be handed over later to the once independent Association of Assistant Librarians (AAL), after it came within The Library Association's fold as a specialist section. The first full-time library school was established in 1919, at University College London, with the help of the CUKT. In the inter-war period many part-time day and evening classes developed to prepare candidates for the Association's examinations held at several centres around the country. After World War Two, education and training of returning servicemen became a priority for the Government. A number of full-time library schools were set up in colleges of technology under this programme, as the result of negotiations by The Library Association. They were intended to be temporary arrangements, but demand was such that the schools developed along with their institutions, which later became polytechnics and eventually universities. New schools were also set up in the 1960s in a few universities and one, the College of Librarianship Wales, Aberystwyth, was established as a separate institution, only becoming a part of the University of Wales much later. These schools gradually developed systems of internal examining, followed by their own syllabuses, recognised by the Association and, in the case of those in polytechnics, validated by the former Council for National and Academic Awards (CNAA). These developments, not without controversy, eventually led to an all-graduate entry to the profession, and a great variety of courses at undergraduate, post-graduate and master's levels. The Association gave up its own examinations in the 1970s, in favour of accrediting courses, latterly often as a joint exercise with the Institute of information Scientists (IIS).

The Royal Charter

The Association acquired a Royal Charter in 1898, with revised objects. At the same time, its name became simply The Library Association, which it retained, despite some attempts in the 1980s to change it to include 'information', until unification with the IIS under the title Chartered Institute of Library and Information Professionals (CILIP). The professional register was introduced after the Second World War. Those who completed the newly introduced registration examination, followed by a period of approved employment in a library, could describe themselves as 'Chartered Librarians'. They were also entitled to use the post nominal letters 'ALA' (Associate of the Library Association). After a further period of employment, they could progress, by means of a final examination, to become Fellows (FLA). When the undergraduate and postgraduate courses replaced the registration examination, Fellowship could be obtained by means of a thesis, later replaced by a variety of routes, leading to proof of attainment of a high standard of professional achievement. Discussions took place over a long period on the possibilities for introducing a system of validating continuing professional development. A voluntary scheme was introduced in the 1990s. The possibility of developing in due course a compulsory 're-licensing' requirement, similar to those coming into vogue in other professions was discussed, but never agreed. The possession of the Royal Charter gave the Association status comparable to professional bodies in other spheres, and was the source of much pride. The centenary of the granting of the Charter by Queen Victoria was celebrated in style at the new British

Library building at St Pancras in 1998, in the presence of the Princess Royal and the Secretary of State for Culture, Chris Smith. The Princess presented centenary medals to one hundred Library Association Members representing the thousands who had worked for the profession over the century.

Awards

One way to encourage high standards in any field is to present awards. The Library Association's first initiative in this area was the Carnegie Medal for the best children's book. Awarded for the first time in 1937 to Arthur Ransome for *Pigeon Post* and occasionally not awarded at all for a lack, in the opinion of the judges, of a suitable winner, it has become established as a coveted honour. It was joined in 1955 by the Kate Greenaway Medal for the best illustrated children's book. The Youth Libraries Group judges the nominations for both medals, which have attracted significant sponsorship in recent years and increasing publicity in the national press, aided by a 'shadow' judging process organised in schools. Other awards introduced over the years recognise excellence in published indexes (jointly with the Society of Indexers), bibliographies and reference works, as well as best practice in publicity and public relations.

Publications

The publication of a journal is a basic function of most professional bodies. The Library Association's first initiative in this area was to decide at its inaugural meeting to adopt the *American Library Journal* as its official organ (without the first word in its title). This had obvious drawbacks, exacerbated when Melvil Dewey became its editor and introduced his simplified spelling. In 1880, *Monthly Notes of the Library Association of the United Kingdom*, published commercially on behalf of the Association, took

over the role. It was itself succeeded by *The Library Chronicle* in 1884 and *The Library* in 1888. The latter was the personal property of John MacAlister, at that time Honorary Secretary of the Association, an unsatisfactory arrangement. Ten years later *The Library Association Record* was established as the official organ of the Association, the property of the Association and 'under the control of Council'. It continued until 2002, celebrating its centenary in 1998. For most of that time it was edited by a series of Honorary Editors, until the appointment in 1976 of the first full-time professional Editor, Roger Walter. One of the first publications of the Association in book form was the *Yearbook*, first published in 1891, which, despite its title, did not become a regular annual, until 1932. For many years the financing of publications caused concern to the Association's Council. Various arrangements were made for the sale and distribution of a growing range of titles, including manuals, textbooks and guidelines to standards of service. At first contracts were made with commercial publishers, at other times the responsibilities were carried out in-house and, for a while in the 1970s and 80s, a wholly-owned company was responsible. Eventually all the business units of the Association (Library Association Publishing; INFOmatch, the recruitment agency; the *Record* and conferences and continuing education) were brought together under the title Library Association Enterprises. At the time of unification, approximately 30 new titles were published a year, with a backlist of over 200.

Branches

In common with many membership organisations in the UK, the Association exhibited tensions between those based in London and those elsewhere in the country. This tension was emphasised by the fact that, in the public library sphere at least, development was much slower in London in the early days than in other major cities. It was also not helped by the fact that most of the early meetings were held in London. Long working hours and poor salaries combined to prevent many from outside the capital taking part in the affairs of the Association. This led to the establishment of several independent regional Associations, for example the Birmingham and District and the North Midlands Library Associations. They amalgamated with The Library Association in 1928–9. The Scottish Library Association, formed in 1908, also affiliated under special conditions in 1931 and new Branches were formed to cover Wales and Monmouthshire and Northern Ireland. However, complete coverage of the UK by a network of Branches was not achieved until after the Second World War.

Sections and Groups

A characteristic of most professional bodies is the need to cater for specialisms within the overall discipline. It was gradually recognised that The Library Association had to cater for different types of library, or client groups, and specialist materials and skills. In 1932, two sections were established to reflect the interests of those working in county libraries and those in university and research libraries. The union with the independent AAL, which had taken place in 1930, provided a section designed to provide for those at an early stage in their careers. It was to prove a useful training ground for future leaders of the profession. Sections, later renamed 'Groups', were gradually added to reflect such diverse interests as prison libraries, information technology and library history.

Headquarters

As early as 1888, the Association identified the need for permanent premises. Its first home was in Hanover Square in London, which it rented from 1890 to 1898. This was followed by a series of other rented premises, one shared with the trade union NALGO, another with Association of Special Libraries and Information Bureaux (Aslib) and the

CUKT. Eventually the CUKT provided a more permanent solution with the offer of a derelict property in what was to become Malet Place. Opened in 1933 by Lord Irwin, deputising for the then Prime Minister, Stanley Baldwin, it was named Chaucer House. The refurbished building provided offices, a members' room and a council chamber, with spare floors which were rented to other organisations. One of the initial tenants was the Museums Association. Chaucer House served until 1965, when the present purpose-built headquarters in Ridgmount Street was completed. The Association was fortunate in that the University of London offered to build the Ridgmount Street building in exchange for the acquisition of Chaucer House, which it required to cater for the needs of the rapidly expanding institution. The new building was considerably larger and contained many highly desirable new facilities. From time to time there were discussions on the desirability of moving the headquarters to a location outside London. During the 1980s the most concrete proposal, to move to the University of Liverpool campus, was considered and rejected. The transport routes of the UK, which radiate from London, rendered such proposals unviable. The Ridgmount Street building was recently refurbished and extended.

International developments

Given that the Association was born at an international conference, it is not surprising that it has often been involved in international developments. At its fiftieth anniversary Conference, held in Edinburgh in 1927, a resolution, which led to the establishment of the International Federation of Library Associations and Institutions (IFLA), was adopted. K. C. Harrison was inaugurated as the first President of the Commonwealth Library Association (COMLA) at its formation in Lagos, Nigeria, in 1972. He became Library Association President in the same year. During the 1987 IFLA Conference in Brighton talks were started in London, which led to the formation of the European Bureau of Library, Information and Documentation Associations (EBLIDA) in The Hague in 1992. George Cunningham, Chief Executive of The Library Association from 1984 to 1992, played a leading role in identifying the need for such a body to ensure that the profession's views were heard the European Union's institutions. Ross Shimmon, Library Association Chief Executive from 1992 to 1999, was its founder President.

Unification

The Association was, at times with some justification, more recently with none, criticised for being primarily a public library association. Received wisdom suggests that it was this bias that led to the establishment of the Aslib to cater for those working in specialist libraries in industry. W. A. Munford, the Association's official historian for its first century, argued that the Library Association Council 'could hardly have done more to make [such a move] unnecessary.' Nevertheless, Aslib was established in 1926. After the Second World War, alleged lack of flexibility on the part of the Association is said to have led to the establishment of the Institute of Information Scientists in 1958. The existence of several bodies representing different elements of the profession was thought by many to be unhelpful in the task of influencing government and other decision makers. Various moves were made to try to bring the organisations together, including the organisation

of joint conferences. The Library Association Council, on behalf of all three organisations, commissioned Professor Wilfred Saunders, a former president of both the Association and the Institute, to write a pamphlet exploring the pros and cons of unification. In the pamphlet, published in 1989, he recommended the establishment of a new organisation, representing the broad spectrum of library and information professionals. The Association's Council approved the proposal in principle. But Aslib pulled out of the subsequent talks and the IIS soon followed suit. However, his efforts proved not to have been entirely in vain. Informal talks between representatives of the Association and the Institute began in 1998, which eventually led to the unification of the two bodies to form CILIP in 2002. This satisfactorily closed an era in professional history which had lasted exactly 125 years.

The main sources used in the preparation of this article were:

Munford, W. A. (1977) *A History of The Library Association 1877–1977*, London, The Library Association.
Plumb, Philip (1977) *Libraries by Association: The Library Association's first century*, London, The Library Association.

Ross Shimmon
Former Chief Executive,
The Library Association

Presidents of the Institute of Information Scientists

2001–02	P. Enser
2000–01	P. Enser
	Director, M. Shearer (started)
1999–2000	B. Clifford
1998–99	P. Brophy
1997–98	S. E. Ward
1996–97	B. Hatvany
1995–96	M.·F. Lynch
1994–95	C. Oppenheim
	Director, E. Hyams (started)
1993–94	B. A. Lang
1992–93	M. White
1991–92	M. Saksida
1990–91	B. White
1989–90	P. Laister
1988–89	K. Cooper
1987–88	T. Aitchison
1986–87	Prof. L. Wolpert

1985–86	Sir R. Clayton
1984–85	M. Aldrich
	Director, S. A. Carter (started)
1983–84	A. R. Haygarth Jackson
1982–83	J. Dukes
1981–82	R.·K. Appleyard
1980–81	C.·W. Cleverdon
1979–80	M. Hyams
1978–79	J. W. Barrett
1977–78	Dr J. W. Barrett
1975–76	H. T. Hookway
1974–75	H. T. Hookway
1973–74	H. T. Hookway
1972–73	Sir James Tait
1968–69	Prof. Sir H. Thompson
1960–61	Dr M. Dyson
1958–59	Dr M. Dyson

Presidents of The Library Association

2001	Mr B. Naylor	1962	Prof. W. B. Paton OBE
2000	Rev. G. P. Cornish	1961	Sir Charles Snow CBE
1999	Mrs V. Taylor	1960	Dr B. S. Page
1998	Prof. R. C. Usherwood	1959	The Rt Hon. The Earl Attlee KG PC OM CH
1997	Mr J. D. Hendry		
1996	Ms S. M. Parker	1958	Prof. Raymond Irwin
1995	Mr M. P. K. Barnes OBE	1957	Dr J. Bronowski
1994	Dr G. A. Burrington OBE	1956	Mr E. Sydney MC
1993	Mr R. G. Astbury	1955	Sir Philip Morris KCMG Kt CBE
1992	Mr P. W. Plumb	1954	Mr C. B. Oldman CB CVO
1991	Mr T. M. Featherstone	1953	Sir Sidney C. Roberts Kt
1990	Prof. M. B. Line	1952	Mr L. R. McColvin CBE
1989	Mr A. G. D. White	1951	Mr J. Wilkie MC
1988	Miss Jean M. Plaister OBE	1950	His Royal Highness The Prince Philip, Duke of Edinburgh Kg Kt Com GBE PC
1987	Mr E. M. Broome OBE		
1986	Mr A. Wilson CBE		
1985	Sir Harry Hookway Kt	1949	Sir Ronald Forbes Adam Bt KCE GCB CB DSO OBE
1984	Mr R. G. Surridge		
1983	Dr N. Higham OBE	1948	Mr C. Nowell
1982	Mr K. A. Stockham	1947	Mr R. J. Gordon
1981	Mr A. Longworth OBE	1946	Mr H. M. Cashmore MBE
1980	Prof. W. L. Saunders CBE	1939–45	Mr A. Esdaile CBE
1979	Mr W. A. G. Alison	1938	Mr W. C. Berwick Sayers
1978	Mr G. Thompson	1937	The Most Rev. & Hon. Wm. Temple
1977	The Lord Dainton	1936	Mr E. A. Savage
1976	Mr D. J. Foskett OBE	1935	Mr E. S. Davies CBE
1975	Mr E. V. Corbett	1934	Mr S. A. Pitt
1974	Mr E. A. Clough	1932–3	Sir Henry A. Miers Kt DSC
1973	Mr K. C. Harrison OBE	1931	Lt Col J. M. Mitchell OBE MC
1972	Dr Donald J. Urquhart	1930	Mr L. Stanley Jast
1971	Mr G. Chandler	1929	The Lord Balniel MP
1970	Mr D. T. Richnell CBE	1928	Mr A. D. Lindsay CBE
1969	Prof. W. Ashworth	1927	The Rt Hon. The Earl of Elgin and Kincardine Kt CMG
1968	Mr T. E. Callander		
1967	Mr F. G. B. Hutchings OBE	1926	Mr H. Guppy CBE
1966	Miss Lorna V. Paulin OBE	1925	Sir Charles Grant Robertson Kt CVO
1965	Sir Frank Francis KCB	1924	Sir Robert Sangster Rait Kt CBE
1964	Mr F. M. Gardner CBE	1923	The Most Honourable The Marquis of Hartington MP MBE
1963	Mr J. N. L. Myres OBE		

1922	Sir John Ballinger KBE
1921	Alderman T. C. Abbott JP
1920	The Rt Hon. Sir John H. Lewis PC GBE
1919	Mr G. F. Barwick
1915–18	Sir J. Y. W. MacAlister
1914	Mr F. Madan
1913	The Rt Hon. The Earl of Malmesbury
1912	Mr F. J. Leslie CC
1911	Sir John A. Dewar Bt MP
1910	Sir Frederic G. Kenyon
1909	Alderman W. H. Brittain JP Chairman, Sheffield Public Libraries Committee
1908	Sir C. Thomas-Standford
1907	Mr F. T. Barrett
1906	Sir William H. Bailey
1905	Mr F. J. Jenkinson
1904	Dr T. Hodgkin
1902–3	Prof. W. Macneile Dixon
1901	Mr G. K. Fortescue
1900	The Rt Hon. Sir Edward Fry PC
1899	Sir James W. Southern JP
1898	The Rt Hon. The Earl of Crawford Kt
1897	Mr H. R. Tedder
1896	Alderman H. Rawson
1895	The Lord Windsor
1894	The Most Honourable the Marquess of Dufferin and Ava KP GCB
1893	Mr R. Garnett
1892	Mr A. Beljame
1891	Mr R. Harrison
1890	Sir E. Maunde Thompson
1889	Mr R. Copley Christie
1888	Prof. W. P. Dickson
1887	Mr G. J. Johnson
1886	Sir Edward A. Bond KCB
1885	Mr E. James
1884	Prof. J. K. Ingram
1883	Sir James Picton
1882	Mr Henry Bradshaw
1881	His Honour Judge Russell
1879–80	Mr H. O. Coxe
1877–78	Mr J. Winter Jones

Honorary Secretaries of the Institute of Information Scientists

2001–02	K. G. Webster		1984–85	P. Brown
2000–01	K. G. Webster		1983–84	P. J. Brown
1999–2000	K. G. Webster		1982–83	J. M. Pope
1998–99	K. G. Webster		1981–82	J. M. Pope
1997–98	K. G. Webster		1980–81	J. M. Pope
1996–97	K. G. Webster		1979–80	Mrs S. A. Carter
1995–96	K. G. Webster		1978–79	Mrs S. A. Carter
1994–95	K. G. Webster		1977–78	M G. Howes,
1993–94	A. J. Wood		1975–76	Mrs M. Siddiqui,
1992–93	P. Griffiths		1974–75	Mrs M. Siddiqui
1991–92	D. Clegg		1973–74	Mrs M. Siddiqui
1990–91	D. Clegg		1972–73	S.•P.•Cooper
1989–90	D. Clegg		1970–71	R.•W.•Prior
1988–89	D. Edmonds		1968–69	J. Farradane
1987–88	D. Edmonds		1960–61	J. Farradane
1986–87	D. Edmonds		1958–59	J. Farradane
1985–86	P. Brown			

Secretaries of The Library Association

1999–2002	Dr R. McKee
1992–99	Mr R. Shimmon
1984–92	Mr G. Cunningham
1978–84	Mr K. Lawrey
1974–78	Mr R. P. Hilliard
1959–74	Mr H. D. Barry
1931–59	Mr P. S. J. Welsford
1928–31	Mr G. Keeling

Honorary Secretaries of The Library Association

1961	Honorary Secretary appointments discontinued
1955–61	Mr W. B. Paton
1952–55	Dr W. A. Munford
1934–51	Mr L. R. McColvin
1933–34	Mr E. A. Savage and Mr L. R. McColvin

1928–33	Mr E. Savage
1919–28	Mr F. Pacy
1918–19	Mr F. Pacy and Mr G. F. Barwick
1915–18	Mr F. Pacy (Acting Secretary)
1905–15	Mr L. S. Jast
1902–05	Mr L. Inkster (Mr L. S. Jast, Acting Secretary 1904–1905)
1902	Mr B. Soulsby
1898–1901	Mr F. Pacy
1892–98	Sir J. Y. W. MacAlister
1887–90	Sir J. Y. W. MacAlister and Mr T. Mason
1882–87	Mr E. C. Thomas and Mr J. Y. W. MacAlister
1880–82	Mr E. C. Thomas and Mr C. Welch
1878–80	Mr H. R. Tedder and Mr E. C. Thomas
1877–78	Mr E. B. Nicholson and Mr H. R. Tedder

Library Association honorary awards

Dates below apply to the year the award was made.

Honorary Vice-Presidents

1995	Prof. J. Meadows
1993	Dame E. Esteve-Coll
1991	Dr H.-P. Geh
1990	Baroness David of Romsey
	Mr D. Whitaker
1988	Alexander Macmillan, The Earl of Stockton
1987	Miss M. Wijnstroom
1973	Mr H. Liebaers
	Mrs J. L. Robinson
1969	Mr Bengt Hjelmqvist
1967	Miss M. O'Byrne

Honorary Fellows

2002	Ms M. J. Auckland
	Mr R. Craig
	Mr R. W. Kirk
	Mr M. P. Stone
	Ms K. Wood
2001	Dr M. Clanchy
2000	Miss M. E. Going
	Mr E. Moon
	Miss C. F. Pinion
	Mr R. Shimmon
1999	Mr R. Collis
	Mr C. Earl
	Mr M. Evans
	Mr G. Pau
1998	Mr C. Batt
	Mr B. C. Bloomfield
	Mr P. R. Craddock
	Ms M. Hoffman
	Dr N. Horrocks

1997	Sir Brian Follett
	Ms S. Hughes
	Dr B. Lang
	Ms E. Simon
1996	Ms L. A. Colaianni
	Cllr F. Emery-Wallis
	Mr D. Jones
	Miss J. Shepherd
1995	Mr E. M. Broome
	Mr P. A. Hoare
	Ms M. Segbert
	Mr E. C. Winter
1994	Mr P. Blunt
	Prof. R. Bowden
	Mr M. Bragg
	Miss A. M. Parker
	Mr B. Roberts
1993	Dame C. A. Cookson
	Dr I. Lovecy
	Ms F. Salinie
	Mr C. A. Toase
	Mr W. G. Williams
1992	Mr P. Bryant
	Mr G. Cunningham
	Mr J. Gattegno
	Mr W. D. Linton
	Dr R. C. Usherwood
1991	Mr T. Dickinson
	Mr P. H. Mann
	Ms D. B. Rosenberg
	Mr B. J. S. Williams
1990	Prof. G. W. A. Dick
	Prof. A. J. Evans
	Mrs S. G. Ray
	Mr J. W. Sumsion
	Mr A. L. van Wesemael

1989	Mr W. R. H. Carson		Dr W. A. Munford
	Mr E.Dudley		Mr P. H. Sewell
	Mr P. R. Lewis	1976	Prof J. D. Pearson
	Dr G. Pflug	1975	Mr E. A. Clough
1988	Mr D. Harrison		Mr S. W. Hockey
	Mrs B. Ruff	1974	Mr D. J. Foskett
	Mr R. G. Surridge		Mr F. W. Jessup
	Mr I. R. Willison		Mr T. Kelly
1987	Mr D. Mason		Mr B. I. Palmer
	Prof. M. B. Line	1973	Mr H. D. Barry
	Dr F. W. Ratcliffe		Mr A. D. Jones
1986	Prof. R. C. Alston		Mr W. B. Paton
	Mr C. H. Bingley	1972	Mr H. Coblans
	The Lord Dainton		Dr A. J. Walford
	Prof. P. Havard-Williams		Mr A. J. Wells
1985	Mrs H. Anuar	1971	Miss E. H. Colwell
	Mrs E. Granheim		Mr W. S. Haugh
	Dr H. Wallis		Mr S. H. Horrocks
1984	Mrs D. Anderson	1970	Mr A. H. Chaplin
	Mr D. K. Devnally		Miss A. S. Cooke
	Mr M. C. Fessey		Mr W. R. LeFanu
	Mr T. Kaung		Mr R. D. Macleod
	Mr A. Wilson		Mr W. Tynemouth
1983	Mr L. J. Anthony	1969	Mr T. Besterman
	Mr L. A. Gilbert		F. N. Withers
1982	Mr H. Faulkner Brown	1968	Mr S. W. Martin
	Sir Harry Hookway		Mr E. F. Patterson
	Mr P. E. Morris		Mr N. F. Sharp
	Mr C. L. J. O'Connell	1966	Mr E. Austin Hinton
1981	Mr R. Brown		Miss F. E. Cook
	Mr J. C. Downing		Mr F. M. Gardner
	Mr A. C. Jones	1965	Miss E. J. A. Evans
1980	Prof R. C. Benge		Mr W. J. Harris
	Miss L. V. Paulin	1964	Sir Sydney Roberts
	Mr K. W. Humphreys		Mr E. Sydney
	Mr P. A. Larkin	1963	Mr R. Irwin
1979	Mr R. Buchanan		Mr C. B. Oldman
	Mr E. Coates	1962	Mr E. J. Carter
	Mr R. P Hilliard		Sir Frank Francis
	Mr D. T Richnell	1961	Mr L. R. McColvin
1978	Mrs D. M. Palmer		Mr B. S. Page
	Mr H. Holdsworth	1959	Mr J. D. Stewart
1977	Mr P. Kirkegaard		Mr P. S. J. Welsford
	Sir Robin Mackworth Young		

1948	Mr R. J. Gordon
1947	Mr W. C. Berwick Sayers
	Mr H. M. Cashmore
1946	Mr Arundell Esdaile
	Mr Albert Mansbridge
1938	Mr Wilson Benson Thorne
1935	Mr H. Tapley-Soper
1933	Rt Hon. Stanley Baldwin
	Mr Ernest A. Savage
1932	Rt Hon. Earl of Elgin and Kincardine
	Mr J. M. Mitchell
1931	Mr W. W. Bishop
	Mr George H. Locke
1929	Sir John Ballinger
1924	Mr A. W. Pollard
	Mr W. E. Doubleday
1915	Mr L. S. Jast
1914	Mr J. Potter Briscoe
	Mr R. K. Dent
1913	Mr James Duff Brown
1909	Mr T. C. Abbott
	Mr H. W. Fovargue
1908	Mr J. J. Ogle
1907	Rt Hon. Earl of Plymouth
1906	Mr Henry D. Roberts
1905	Mr Lawrence Inkster
1903	Mr Henry Guppy
1902	Mr W. Macneile Dixon
	Mr Frank Pacy
1901	Mr Thomas Greenwood
1899	Rt Hon. Lord Avebury
	Marquess of Dufferin and Ava
	Mr Samuel Timmins
	Rt Hon. Lord Windsor
1898	Mr J. Y. W. MacAlister
1896	Mr James Bain
	Conte Ugo Balzani
	Prof. Alexander Beljame
	Mr J. S. Billings
	Mr R. R. Bowker
	Mr C. W. Bruun
	Mr Andrew Carnegie
	Mr C. A. Cutter
	Mr Leopold Delisle

	Mr Melvil Dewey
	Sir George Grey
	Mr Justin Winsor
	Mr C. Dziatzko
	Mr J. Passmore Edwards
	Mr S. S. Green
1896	Mr P. G. Horsen
	Rt Hon. Sir John Lubbock
	Sir Henry Tate
	Baron O. de Watteville

Certificates of Merit

2002	Mrs P. Bonnett
	Mr D. R. Butcher
	Ms D. Dixon
	Mr B. M. Hall
	Mr D. N. Rigglesford
2001	Mr R. S. Eagle
	Ms A. Edmunds
	Dr J. Harvey
2000	Mrs V. Nurcombe
1999	Mr M. Stacey
1998	none
1997	Mr I. M. Jamieson
	Mrs J. Machell
1996	Dr H. Fuchs
	Ms F. M. M. Redfern
1995	Miss V. A. Fea
	Mr R. Sweeney
1994	Mr F. Chambers
	Mrs L. Elliott
	Mrs S. Harrity
	Mr J. Pyle
	Mr J. Merriman
1993	Mr A. Chadwick
	Mr D. F. Keeling
1992	Mr P. Thomas
1991	Mr R. Phillips
1990	Mr T. C. Farries
1989	Mr E. Frow
	Mrs R. Frow
1985	Dr F. A. Thorpe

Institute of Information Scientists Award winners

Jason Farradane Award winners

2001 Professor Bruce Royan for SCRAN

2000 Jill Foster for her pioneering work in establishing the Mailbase discussion and distribution list

1999 Michael Keen for his Lifetime's Work in Information Retrieval

1998 Norman Wood and the EIRO Team of the European Foundation for the Improvement of Living and Working Conditions Dublin, for their outstanding and original work on the European Industrial Relations Observatory (EIRO)

1997 Newcastle University Library for the Development and Administration of the Newcastle Electronic Reference Desk – NERD

1996 The Higher Education Funding Council's Electronic Libraries Programme for innovation in the exploitation of IT in Higher Education Libraries

1995 Dennis Nicholson and the BUBL team for the development of the Bulletin Board for libraries

1994 Rita Marcella and colleagues at the School of Librarianship and Information Studies at Robert Gordon University for the development of their innovative Postgraduate Course in Information Analysis

1993 Peter Ingwersen in recognition of his services to Information Science

1992 European Foundation for the Improvement of Living and Working conditions, Dublin, for developing the series of European and Industrial Relations Glossaries

1991 Arnold Myers, Information Scientist, for contribution to information services with the international oil and gas industry

1990 Scottish Science Library, setting up of an important new library for Scotland

1989 Patricia Baird, Blaise Cronin, Noreen MacMarrow, academics, University of Strathclyde, work in the field of hypertext on producing an electronic conspectus on the life and times of the City of Glasgow

1988 No award – no nomination received before closing date

1987 Sandra Ward, Information Scientist, work in raising the profile of industrial information services

1986 Phil Williams, academic and businessman, contributions to making online searching more readily accessible to users

1985 Phil Holmes, achievements in applying technological advances to library development especially in the development of BLAISE (British Library), and PEARL (Blackwell Technical Services)

1984 Jacqueline Welch, librarian at Wessex Medical Library, contributed to promotion of information science particularly within the field of medical information

1983 Karen Sparck-Jones, academic, information science research, eg automation classification and indexing, methods of testing and evaluation, weighting and relevance feedback

1982 Monty Hyams, businessman, Derwent Publictaion Ltd. Developed Central Patents Index for patent searching

1981   William Wisswesser (USA), work with chemical notation, giving his name to Wisswesser line notation (WLN)

1980   Michael Lynch, academic, Sheffield University, expert in chemical structure handling

1979   Jason Farradane, founder of the IIS and a cornerstone of information science teaching and research

Tony Kent Strix Award winners

2002   Malcolm Jones

2001   Professor Peter Willett.

2000   Dr Martin Porter

1999   Dr Donna Harman

1998   Professor Stephen Robertson

These awards are now administered by UKeiG, see p.155

Library Association Medal and Award winners

Carnegie Medal winners

Please note that the year refers to when the book was published rather than when the medal was awarded i.e. the 1999 winner was announced and the medal presented in July 2000.

2000 Beverley Naidoo, *The Other Side of Truth*, Puffin

1999 Aidan Chambers, *Postcards From No Man's Land*, Bodley Head

1998 David Almond, *Skellig*, Hodder Children's Books

1997 Tim Bowler, *River Boy*, OUP

1996 Melvin Burgess, *Junk*, Andersen Press

1995 Philip Pullman, His Dark Materials: Book 1 *Northern Lights*, Scholastic

1994 Theresa Breslin, *Whispers in the Graveyard*, Methuen

1993 Robert Swindells, *Stone Cold*, H Hamilton

1992 Anne Fine, *Flour Babies*, H Hamilton

1991 Berlie Doherty, *Dear Nobody*, H Hamilton

1990 Gillian Cross, *Wolf*, OUP

1989 Anne Fine, *Goggle-eyes*, H Hamilton

1988 Geraldine McCaughrean, *A Pack of Lies*, OUP

1987 Susan Price, *The Ghost Drum*, Faber

1986 Berlie Doherty, *Granny was a Buffer Girl*, Methuen

1985 Kevin Crossley-Holland, *Storm*, Heinemann

1984 Margaret Mahy, *The Changeover*, Dent

1983 Jan Mark, *Handles*, Kestrel

1982 Margaret Mahy, *The Haunting*, Dent

1981 Robert Westall, *The Scarecrows*, Chatto & Windus

1980 Peter Dickinson, *City of Gold*, Gollancz

1979 Peter Dickinson, *Tulku*, Gollancz

1978 David Rees, *The Exeter Blitz*, H Hamilton

1977 Gene Kemp, *The Turbulent Term of Tyke Tiler*, Faber

1976 Jan Mark, *Thunder and Lightnings*, Kestrel

1975 Robert Westall, *The Machine Gunners*, Macmillan

1974 Mollie Hunter, *The Stronghold*, H Hamilton

1973 Penelope Lively, *The Ghost of Thomas Kempe*, Heinemann

1972 Richard Adams, *Watership Down*, Rex Collings

1971 Ivan Southall, *Josh*, Angus & Robertson

1970 Leon Garfield & Edward Blishen, *The God Beneath the Sea*, Longman

1969 Kathleen Peyton, *The Edge of the Cloud*, OUP

1968 Rosemary Harris, *The Moon in the Cloud*, Faber

1967 Alan Garner, *The Owl Service*, Collins

1966 Prize withheld as no book considered suitable

1965 Philip Turner, *The Grange at High Force*, OUP

1964 Sheena Porter, *Nordy Bank*, OUP

1963 Hester Burton, *Time of Trial*, OUP

1962 Pauline Clarke, *The Twelve and the Genii*, Faber

1961 Lucy M. Boston, *A Stranger at Green Knowe*, Faber

1960 Dr I. W. Cornwall, *The Making of Man*, Phoenix House

1959 Rosemary Sutcliff, *The Lantern Bearers*, OUP

1958 Philipa Pearce, *Tom's Midnight Garden*, OUP

1957 William Mayne, *A Grass Rope*, OUP

1956 C. S. Lewis, *The Last Battle*, Bodley Head

1955 Eleanor Farjeon, *The Little Bookroom*, OUP

1954 Ronald Welch (Felton Ronald Oliver), *Knight Crusader*, OUP

1953 Edward Osmond, *A Valley Grows Up*

1952 Mary Norton, *The Borrowers*, Dent

1951 Cynthia Harnett, *The Woolpack*, Methuen

1950 Elfrida Vipont Foulds, *The Lark on the Wing*, OUP

1949 Agnes Allen, *The Story of Your Home*, Faber

1948 Richard Armstrong, *Sea Change*, Dent

1947 Walter De La Mare, *Collected Stories for Children*

1946 Elizabeth Goudge, *The Little White Horse*, University of London Press

1945 Prize withheld as no book considered suitable

1944 Eric Linklater, *The Wind on the Moon*, Macmillan

1943 Prize withheld as no book considered suitable

1942 'BB' (D. J. Watkins-Pitchford), *The Little Grey Men*, Eyre & Spottiswoode

1941 Mary Treadgold, *We Couldn't Leave Dinah*, Cape

1940 Kitty Barne, *Visitors from London*, Dent

1939 Eleanor Doorly, *Radium Woman*, Heinemann

1938 Noel Streatfield, *The Circus is Coming*, Dent

1937 Eve Garnett, *The Family from One End Street*, Muller

1936 Arthur Ransome, *Pigeon Post*, Cape

Kate Greenaway Medal winners

Please note that the year refers to when the book was published rather than when the medal was awarded i.e. the 1999 winner was announced and the medal presented in July 2000.

2000 Lauren Child, *I Will Not Ever Never Eat a Tomato*, Orchard Books

1999 Helen Oxenbury, *Alice's Adventures in Wonderland*, Walker Books

1998 Helen Cooper, *Pumpkin Soup*, Doubleday

1997 P. J. Lynch, *When Jessie Came Across the Sea*, Walker Books

1996 Helen Cooper, *The Baby Who Wouldn't Go To Bed*, Doubleday

1995 P. J. Lynch, *The Christmas Miracle of Jonathan Toomey*, Walker Books

1994 Gregory Rogers, *Way Home*, Andersen Press

1993 Alan Lee, *Black Ships Before Troy*, Frances Lincoln

1992 Anthony Browne, *Zoo*, Julia MacRae

1991 Janet Ahlberg, *The Jolly Christmas Postman*, Heinemann

1990 Gary Blythe, *The Whales' Song*, Hutchinson

1989 Michael Foreman, *War Boy: a Country Childhood*, Pavilion

1988 Barbara Firth, *Can't You Sleep Little Bear?*, Walker Books

1987 Adrienne Kennaway, *Crafty Chameleon*, Hodder & Stoughton

1986 Fiona French, *Snow White in New York*, OUP

1985 Juan Wijngaard, *Sir Gawain and the Loathly Lady*, Walker Books

1984 Errol Le Cain, *Hiawatha's Childhood*, Faber

1983 Anthony Browne, *Gorilla*, Julia MacRae

1982 Michael Foreman, *Long Neck and Thunder Foot* and *Sleeping Beauty and*

Other Favourite Fairy Tales, Kestrel and Gollancz

1981 Charles Keeping, *The Highwayman*, OUP

1980 Quentin Blake, *Mr Magnolia*, Cape

1979 Jan Pienkowski, *The Haunted House*, Heinemann

1978 Janet Ahlberg, *Each Peach Pear Plum*, Kestrel

1977 Shirley Hughes, *Dogger*, Bodley Head

1976 Gail E. Haley, *The Post Office Cat*, Bodley Head

1975 Victor Ambrus, *Horses in Battle* and *Mishka*, OUP

1974 Pat Hutchins, *The Wind Blew*, Bodley head

1973 Raymond Briggs, *Father Christmas*, H Hamilton

1972 Krystyna Turska, *The Woodcutter's Duck*, H Hamilton

1971 Jan Pienkowski, *The Kingdom under the Sea*, Cape

1970 John Burningham, *Mr Gumpy's Outing*, Cape

1969 Helen Oxenbury, *The Quangle Wangle's hat* and *The Dragon of an Ordinary Family*, Heinemann

1968 Pauline Baynes, *Dictionary of Chivalry*, Longman

1967 Charles Keeping, *Charlotte and the Golden Canary*, OUP

1966 Raymond Briggs, *Mother Goose Treasury*, H Hamilton

1965 Victor Ambrus, *The Three Poor Tailors*, OUP

1964 C. W. Hodges, *Shakespeare's Theatre*, OUP

1963 John Burningham, *Borka: the Adventures of a Goose with No Feathers*, Cape

1962 Brian Wildsmith, *A.B.C.*, OUP

1961 Antony Maitland, *Mrs Cockle's Cat*, Constable

1960 Gerald Rose, *Old Winkle and the Seagulls*, Faber

1959 William Stobbs, *Kashtanka* and *A Bundle of Ballads*, OUP

1958 Prize withheld as no book considered suitable

1957 V. H. Drummond, *Mrs Easter and the Storks*, Faber

1956 Edward Ardizzone, *Tim All Alone*, OUP

1955 Prize withheld as no book considered suitable

Libraries Change Lives Award winners

2001 Merton Libraries Refugee Resources Collection and Service

2000 Kensal Library's Community Action Initiative

1999 The Ad Lib Project, Sheffield

1998 Pontefract's Readers Group

1997 Horley's Local History Centre

1996 Liverpool 8 Law Centre

1995 Sunderland Libraries Bookstart Project

1994 Petersburn Community Library and Teenage Drop in Centre

1993 Wandsworth Prison and Springfield Psychiatric Hospital

1992 Annex Community Centre, Hartlepool

Library Association/ESU Travelling Librarian Award Winners

2001 Robert Atkinson

2000 Paul Anderson

1999 Not awarded

1998 Fiona Hooper

1994–97 Not awarded

1993 Julie Scott (Cully)

1983–92 Not awarded

1982 Kirsten Bax

1981	Stephen Roberts
1980	Ian Johnson
1979	Joe Hendry
1978	David Ferro
1977	Peter Smith
1976	Carol Buxton
1975	Catherine Pinion
1974	Peter R. Brodnax Moore
1973	David Horn
1972	John Chapman
1971	Gillian Clegg
1970	Simon Francis
1969	Antonia Bunch
1968	David Bromley
1967	Janet Hunt
	Frances Anderson (Burgess)
1966	Not awarded
1965	Carol Ashcroft
	Kathleen Asbery (Smith)
	Ivan G. Sparkes
	Marion Wilden-Hart

Public Relations and Publicity Awards

Personal PR Achievement winners

2001	June Turner, Essex Libraries
2000	Jim Jackson, Library Association Affiliated Members National Committee
1999	Desmond Heaps, Warwickshire County Council Libraries and Heritage
1997	The Awards programme for 1997–8 did not run
1996	Dominic Bean, Southwark Library and Information Service
1995	Annie Everall, Centre for the Child, Birmingham City Library
1994	Maggie Goodbarn, Gateshead Libraries and Arts Service
1993	John Stafford, Northamptonshire Libraries and Information Service
1992	Gill Whitehead, Brent Department of

	Education, Arts and Libraries
1991	Ann-Marie Parker, Hertfordshire Libraries, Arts and Information Service
1990	Max Broome, Library Association President 1987
1989	Peter Grant, City Librarian, Aberdeen
1987	Sue Broughton, Hungerford Branch Library, Berkshire County Libraries
1986	Liz Weir, Belfast Education and Library Board
1985	Joe Hendry, Renfrew District Libraries
1984	Ron Surridge, Library Association President 1984

Reference Award winners

The Library Association Reference Awards comprised the Besterman/ McColvin Medals, the Walford Award and the Wheatley Medal.

Besterman/McColvin Medal winners

Electronic category

2001	*The World Shakespeare Bibliography Online* by James L. Harner. The Folger Shakespeare Library www-english.tamu.edu/wsb/
1999/2000	*The British 1881 Census Index on CDROM*. Church of Jesus Christ of the Latter Day Saints

Printed category

2001	*The Encyclopedia of Ephemera* by Maurice Rickards / Michael Twyman (Ed.). The British Library
1999/2000	*The Oxford Companion to Food* by Alan Davidson. OUP

Previously, a Besterman Medal was awarded for bibliography and a McColvin Medal for an outstanding reference work – hence the two lists below.

Besterman Medal winners

1998   *The Victoria and Albert Museum – a Bibliography and Exhibition Chronology 1852–1996* by Elizabeth James. Fitzroy Dearborn

1997   *Handbook for British and Irish Archaelogy* by Cherry Lavell. Edinburgh University Press

1996   *The World Shakespeare Bibliography 1990–1993 on CD/ROM* by Professor James L. Harner. Cambridge University Press

1995   *A Football Compendium: a comprehensive guide to the literature of Association Football* by Peter J. Seddon. The British Library

1994   *Bibliography of Printed Works on London History to 1939* by Heather Creaton. Library Association Publishing

1993   *Africa: A Guide to Reference Material* by John McIlwaine. Hans Zell

1992   Award witheld.

1991   *A Short-title Catalogue of Books Printed in England, Scotland, Ireland and English Books Printed Abroad 1475–1640...* volume 3 by Katherine Pantzer. Oxford University Press/The Bibliographical Society

1990   *British Architectural Books and Writers 1556–1785* by Eileen Harris and Nicholas Savage. Cambridge University Press

1989   *Bibliography and Index of English Verse Printed 1476–1558* by William Ringler Jnr. Mansell

1988   *T E Lawrence: a bibliography* by Philip O'Brien. St Paul's Bibliographies

1987   *Dickens Dramatized* by Philip H. Bolton. Mansell

1986   *English Poetry of the Second World War: a bibliography* by Catherine W. Reilly. Mansell

1985   *Employee Relations Bibliography and Abstracts* by Arthur Marsh. Employee relations bibliography and abstracts

1984   *A Bibliography of the Kelmscott Press* by William S. Peterson. Clarendon Press

1983   *London Illustrated, 1604–1851: a survey and index to topographical books and their plates* by Bernard Adams. Library Association Publishing and *Ted Hughes: a bibliography, 1946–1980* by Keith Sagar and Stephen Tabor. Mansell

1982   *Walford's Guide to Reference Material* 4th edition. Vol. 2: *Social and Historical Sciences, Philosophy and Religion* edited by A. J. Walford. Library Association Publishing

1981   *British and Irish Architectural History: a bibliography and guide to sources of information* by Ruth H. Kamen. Architectural Press

1980   *Alchemy: a bibliography of English-language writings,* by Alan Pritchard. Routledge and Kegan Paul jointly with The Library Association

1979   *Knowhow: a guide to information, training and campaigning materials for information and advice workers* compiled by G. Morby, edited by E. Kempson. Community Information project and *South Asian Bibliography: a handbook and guide* compiled by the South East Asia Library Group, general editor J. D. Pearson. Harvester Press

1978   Award withheld.

1997   *A Bibliography of Cricket* compiled by E. W. Padwick. Library Association Publishing for the Cricket Society

1976	*Guide to Official Statistics*, No 1, 1976 by Central Statistical Office. HMSO
1975	*Printed Maps of Victorian London* by Ralph Hyde. Dawson
1974	*Agriculture: a bibliographical guide* by E. A. R. Bush. Macdonald and Jane's
1973	Award withheld.
1972	*A Bibliography of British and Irish Municipal History* Vol. 1: *General Works.* by Dr G. H. Martin and Sylvia McIntyre. Leicester University Press
1971	*Sourcebook of Planning Information: a discussion of sources of information for use in urban and regional planning; and in allied fields* by Brenda White. Bingley
1970	*English Theatrical Literature 1559–1900* by J. F. Arnott and J. W. Robinson. Society for Theatre Research

McColvin Medal winners

1998	*Parrots* by Tony Juniper and Mike Par. Pica Press
1997	*Ancestral Trails* by Mark D. Herber. Sutton Publishing/ Society of Genealogists
1996	*Who's Who 1897–1996 on CD/ROM* by Christine Ruge-Cope and Roger Tritton. A & C Black and Oxford University Press.
1995	*The Tithe Maps of England and Wales* by Roger Kain and Richard Oliver. Cambridge University Press
1994	*Dictionary of British and Irish Botanists and Horticulturists* by Ray Desmond. Taylor and Francis
1993	*History of Canal and River Navigation* edited by Edward Paget-Tomlinson. Sheffield Academic Press
1992	*The New Grove Dictionary of Opera* edited by Stanley Sadie. Macmillan
1991	*The Cambridge Encyclopedia of Ornithology* by Michael Brooke and Tim Birkhead. Cambridge University Press
1990	*William Walton: a catalogue* by Stewart Craggs. 2nd edition. Oxford University Press.
1989	*The Oxford English Dictionary* 2nd edition edited by John Simpson and Edmund Weiner. Oxford University Press
1988	*The Encyclopaedia of Oxford* edited by Christopher Hibbert. Macmillan
1987	*Fermented Foods of the World: a dictionary and guide* by Geoffrey Campbell- Platt. Butterworths
1986	*The British Musical Theatre* by Kurt Ganzl. Vol 1: *1865–1914*; Vol 2: *1915–1984*. Macmillan
1985	*The Artist's Craft: a history of tools, techniques and material* by James Ayres. Phaidon
1984	*The History of Glass* general editors Dan Klein and Ward Lloyd. Orbis
1983	*Dictionary of British Book Illustrators: the twentieth century* by Brigid Peppin and Lucy Micklewait. Murray
1982	*The Dictionary of Blue and White Printed Pottery, 1780–1880* by A. W. Coysh and R. K. Henrywood. Antique Collectors' Club
1981	*The New Grove Dictionary of Music and Musicians* edited by Stanley Sadie. Macmillan
1980	*Guide to the Local Administrative Units of England*, Volume 1: *Southern England* by Frederic A. Youngs Jr. Royal Historical Society
1979	Award withheld.
1978	Award withheld.
1977	Award withheld.
1976	*A Manual of European Languages for Librarians* by C. G. Allen. Bowker
1975	*Folksongs of Britain and Ireland* by Peter Kennedy. Cassell

1974	*Reviews of United Kingdom Statistical Sources* Volumes 1 to 3. edited by W. F. Maunder, Heinemann Educational Books published for the Royal Statistical Society and the Social Science Research Council	1997	Ross, Jan, for the index to *Rheumatology*. Mosby International
1973	Award withheld.	1996	Levitt, Ruth and Northcott, Gillian, for the index to *Dictionary of Art*. Macmillan
1972	*Music Yearbook 1972/3* edited by Arthur Jacobs. Macmillan	1995	Richardson, Ruth and Thorne, Robert, *The Builder Illustrations Index*. Hutton and Rostron
1971	*Shepherd's Glossary of Graphic Signs and Symbols* by Walter Shepherd. Dent	1994	Matthew, Professor H G C, for the index to *The Gladstone Diaries*. Clarenden Press
1970	*Councils, Committees and Boards: a handbook of advisory, consultative, executive and similar bodies in British political life*. CBD	1993	Merrall Ross, Janine, for the index to *Encyclopedia of Food Science, Food Technology and Nutrition*. Academic Press

Walford Award winners

2001	Professor John McIlwaine	1992	Nash, Paul, for the index to *The World Environment 1972–1992*. London, Chapman and Hall (on behalf of the United Nations Environment Programme)
1999/2000	Charles Toase HonFLA		
1998	George Ottley FLA		
1997	Barry Bloomfield MA FLA HonFLA		
1996	Professor Ian Rogerson MLS PhD Dlitt FLA	1991	Moys, Elizabeth, for the index to *British Tax Encyclopedia*. Sweet and Maxell
1995	Magda Whitrow BA ALA		
1994	Professor S W Wells	1990	Award withheld as no index considered suitable.
1993	Professor D F McKenzie	1989	Raper, Richard, for the index to *The Works of Charles Darwin*. Pickering and Chatto
1992	Professor Robin C Alston OBE MA PhD FSA HonFLA FLA		
1991	Professor James Douglas Pearson MA HonFLA	1988	Burke, Bobby, for the index to *Halsbury's Laws of England*. 4th edition. Butterworths

Wheatley Medal winners

2001	Crystal, David and Crystal, Hilary for index to *Words on Words*. Penguin Books	1987	Fisk, Neil R., for the index to *A Short History of Wilson's School*. 3rd edition. Wilson's School Charitable Trust
1999/2000	Hird, Barbara for index to *The Cambridge History of Medieval English Literature*. Cambridge University Press	1986	Award withheld as no index considered suitable.
1998	Sheard, Caroline, for the index to *Textbook of Dermatology*. 6th ed. 4 vols. Blackwell Science	1985	Gibson, John, for the index to *Brain's Diseases of the Nervous System*. 9th edition. Oxford University Press
		1984	Award withheld as no index considered suitable.
		1983	Hewitt, A. R., for the index to *The Laws of Trinidad and Tobago*. Government of Trinidad and Tobago

and Latham, Robert, for the index to *The Diary of Samuel Pepys*. Bell and Hyman

1982 Blayney, Peter W. M., for the index to *The Texts of King Lear and their Origins*. Volume 1: *Nicholas Okes and the First Quarto*. Cambridge University Press

1981 Holmstrom, J. Edwin. *Analytical Index to the Publications of the Institution of Civil Engineers. January 1975–1979*. Institution of Civil Engineers

1980 Taylor, Laurie J., for the index to *The Librarian's Handbook*. Vol. 2. Library Association Publishing

1979 Bakewell, K. G. B., for the index to *Anglo-American Cataloguing Rules*. 2nd edition. Library Association Publishing
and
Surrey, A., for the index to *Circulation of the Blood*. Pitman Medical

1978 Prize withheld as no index considered suitable.

1977 Pavel, T. Rowland, for the index to *Archaeologia Cambrensis 1901–60*. Cambrian Archaeological Association

1976 Vickers, John A., for the index to Vol 11 of *The Works of John Wesley: the appeals to men of reason and religion and certain related open letter*. Oxford, Clarendon Press

1975 Anderson, M. D., for the index to *Copy-editing*. Cambridge University Press.

1974 Banwell, C. C., for the index to Encyclopaedia of Forms and Precedents. 4th ed. Butterworths

1973 Boodson, K., for the index to *Non-ferrous Metals*. Macdonald Technical and Scientific
and
Harrod, L. M. Index to *History of King's Works*. Vol. 6. HMSO

1972 Prize withheld as no index considered suitable.

1971 Prize withheld as no index considered suitable.

1970 Mullins, E.L.C., for the index to *A Guide to the Historical and Archaeological Publications of Societies in England and Wales, 1901–1933*. Athlone Press

1969 Thornton, James, for the index to *The Letters of Charles Dickens*. Vol 2. Oxford, Clarendon Press

1968 Blake, Doreen and Bowden, Ruth E. M. for the index to the *Journal of Anatomy, first 100 years, 1866–1966*. Cambridge University Press

1967 Knight, G. Norman, for the index to *Winston S. Churchill*. Vol. 2. Heinemann

1966 Prize withheld as no index considered suitable.

1965 Quinn, Alison, for the index to *The Principall Navigation Voyages and Discoveries of the English Nation* by R. Hakluyt. Cambridge University Press, for the Hakluyt Society and Peabody Museum of Salem

1964 Parsloe, Guy, the index to *The Warden's Accounts of the Worshipful Company of Founders of the City of London, 1497–1681*. Athlone Press

1963 Dickie, J. M. for the index to *How to Catch Trout*. 3rd ed. W & R Chambers

1962 Maclagan, Michael, for the index to *Clemency Canning*. Macmillan

Robinson Medal winners

1999 Margie Mason for Battling with books, a guide for new library staff.

1997 Janet Audain for the design, development and delivery of library services to users with disabilities.

1995 (Award re-launched) Beverley Britton for online submission of off-print database for a reading list database.

1994 Award withheld

1992 Award withheld

1990 JANET Users Group for Libraries for their work in promoting the Joint Academic Network, and plescon limited for the development of the DISCOSAFE and VIDEO TAG electronic security devices.

1988 Award withheld

1986 Prof Nick Moore for the production of guidelines for conducting library and information manpower surveys.

1984 Renfrew district libraries for the inauguration of the Johnstone Information and Leisure Library (JILL).

1982 Award withheld

1980 London Borough of Sutton for innovation in library marketing.

1978 Award withheld

1976 Award withheld

1974 Award withheld

1972 University of Lancaster library research for the development of simulation games in education for library management.

1970 Mr Frank Gurney, of Automated Library Systems Limited for book-charging.

1968 Mansell Information Publishing Limited, of London, for their development of an automatic abstracting camera for use in producing book catalogues from library cards or other sequential material.

Index